SACRAMENTO PUBLIC LIBRARY
828 "I" STREET
SACRAMENTO, CA 95814

11/2020

YO-BSR-018

America's Top-Rated Cities: A Statistical Handbook

Volume 3

REFERENCE USE ONLY

SACRAMENTO PUBLIC LIBRARY

2020
Twenty-seventh Edition

America's
Top-Rated Cities:
A Statistical Handbook

Volume 3: Central Region

A UNIVERSAL REFERENCE BOOK

Grey House
Publishing

Cover image – Chicago, Illinois

PRESIDENT: Richard Gottlieb
PUBLISHER: Leslie Mackenzie
EDITORIAL DIRECTOR: Laura Mars
SENIOR EDITOR: David Garoogian

RESEARCHER & WRITER: Jael Bridgemahon
PRODUCTION MANAGER: Kristen Hayes
MARKETING DIRECTOR: Jessica Moody

A Universal Reference Book
Grey House Publishing, Inc.
4919 Route 22
Amenia, NY 12501
518.789.8700 • Fax 845.373.6390
www.greyhouse.com
books@greyhouse.com

While every effort has been made to ensure the reliability of the information presented in this publication, Grey House Publishing neither guarantees the accuracy of the data contained herein nor assumes any responsibility for errors, omissions or discrepancies. Grey House accepts no payment for listing; inclusion in the publication of any organization, agency, institution, publication, service or individual does not imply endorsement of the editors or publisher.

Errors brought to the attention of the publisher and verified to the satisfaction of the publisher will be corrected in future editions.

Except by express prior written permission of the Copyright Proprietor no part of this work may be copied by any means of publication or communication now known or developed hereafter including, but not limited to, use in any directory or compilation or other print publication, in any information storage and retrieval system, in any other electronic device, or in any visual or audio-visual device or product.

This publication is an original and creative work, copyrighted by Grey House Publishing, Inc. and is fully protected by all applicable copyright laws, as well as by laws covering misappropriation, trade secrets and unfair competition.

Grey House has added value to the underlying factual material through one or more of the following efforts: unique and original selection; expression; arrangement; coordination; and classification.

Grey House Publishing, Inc. will defend its rights in this publication.

Copyright © 2020 Grey House Publishing, Inc.
All rights reserved

Twenty-seventh Edition
Printed in Canada

Publisher's Cataloging-in-Publication Data
(Prepared by The Donohue Group, Inc.)

America's top-rated cities. Vol. 3, Central region : a statistical handbook. — 1992-

    v. : ill. ; cm.
    Annual, 1995-
    Irregular, 1992-1993
    ISSN: 1082-7102

1. Cities and towns--Ratings--Central States--Statistics--Periodicals. 2. Cities and towns--Central States--Statistics--Periodicals. 3. Social indicators--Central States--Periodicals. 4. Quality of life--Central States--Statistics--Periodicals. 5. Central States--Social conditions--Statistics--Periodicals. I. Title: America's top rated cities. II. Title: Central region

HT123.5.S6 A44
307.76/0973/05
                                                 95644648

4-Volume Set	ISBN: 978-1-64265-453-0
Volume 1	ISBN: 978-1-64265-455-4
Volume 2	ISBN: 978-1-64265-456-1
Volume 3	**ISBN: 978-1-64265-457-8**
Volume 4	ISBN: 978-1-64265-458-5

Davenport, Iowa

Des Moines, Iowa

Fargo, North Dakota

Fort Wayne, Indiana

Lincoln, Nebraska

Little Rock, Arkansas

Madison, Wisconsin

Milwaukee, Wisconsin

Minneapolis, Minnesota

Oklahoma City, Oklahoma

Omaha, Nebraska

Peoria, Illinois

Tulsa, Oklahoma

Wichita, Kansas

Appendixes

Introduction

This twenty-seventh edition of *America's Top-Rated Cities* is a concise, statistical, 4-volume work identifying America's top-rated cities with estimated populations of approximately 100,000 or more. It profiles 100 cities that have received high marks for business and living from prominent sources such as *Forbes, Fortune, U.S. News & World Report, The Brookings Institution, U.S. Conference of Mayors, The Wall Street Journal,* and *CNNMoney.*

Each volume covers a different region of the country—Southern, Western, Central and Eastern—and includes a detailed Table of Contents, City Chapters, Appendices, and Maps. Each city chapter incorporates information from hundreds of resources to create the following major sections:

- **Background**—lively narrative of significant, up-to-date news for both businesses and residents. These combine historical facts with current developments, "known-for" annual events, and climate data.
- **Rankings**—fun-to-read, bulleted survey results from over 250 books, magazines, and online articles, ranging from general (Great Places to Live), to specific (Friendliest Cities), and everything in between.
- **Statistical Tables**—127 tables and detailed topics that offer an unparalleled view of each city's Business and Living Environments. They are carefully organized with data that is easy to read and understand.
- **Appendices**—five in all, appearing at the end of each volume. These range from listings of Metropolitan Statistical Areas to Comparative Statistics for all 100 cities.

This new edition of *America's Top-Rated Cities* includes cities that not only surveyed well, but ranked highest using our unique weighting system. We looked at violent crime, property crime, population growth, median household income, housing affordability, poverty, educational attainment, and unemployment. You'll find that a number of American cities remain "top-rated" despite less-than-stellar numbers. New York, Los Angeles, and Miami remain world-class cities despite challenges faced by many large urban centers. Part of the criteria, in most cases, is that it be the "primary" city in a given metropolitan area. For example, if the metro area is Raleigh-Cary, NC, we would consider Raleigh, not Cary. This allows for a more equitable core city comparison. In general, the core city of a metro area is defined as having substantial influence on neighboring cities. A final consideration is location—we strive to include as many states in the country as possible.

New to this edition are:
Volume 1 - Jackson, MS; Lakeland, FL; Tuscaloosa, AL
Volume 2 - Sacramento, CA; Tucson, AZ
Volume 3 - Davenport, IA; Milwaukee, WI; Tulsa, OK; Wichita, KS
Volume 4 - Cleveland, OH; New Haven, CT

Praise for previous editions:

> "...[ATRC] has...proven its worth to a wide audience...from businesspeople and corporations planning to launch, relocate, or expand their operations to market researchers, real estate professionals, urban planners, job-seekers, students...interested in...reliable, attractively presented statistical information about larger U.S. cities."
> —ARBA

> "...For individuals or businesses looking to relocate, this resource conveniently reports rankings from more than 300 sources for the top 100 US cities. Recommended..."
> —Choice

> "...While patrons are becoming increasingly comfortable locating statistical data online, there is still something to be said for the ease associated with such a compendium of otherwise scattered data. A well-organized and appropriate update...
> —Library Journal

BACKGROUND
Each city begins with an informative Background that combines history with current events. These narratives often reflect changes that have occurred during the past year, and touch on the city's environment, politics, employment, cultural offerings, and climate, and include interesting trivia. For example: Peregrine Falcons were rehabilitated and released into the wild from Boise City's World Center for Birds of Prey; Grand Rapids was the first city to introduce

fluoride into its drinking water in 1945; and Thomas Alva Edison discovered the phonograph and the light bulb in the city whose name was changed in 1954 from Raritan Township to Edison in his honor.

RANKINGS

This section has rankings from a possible 252 books, articles, and reports. For easy reference, these Rankings are categorized into 16 topics including Business/Finance, Dating/Romance, and Health/Fitness.

The Rankings are presented in an easy-to-read, bulleted format and include results from both annual surveys and one-shot studies. **Fastest-Growing Economies . . . Best Drivers . . . Most Well-Read . . . Most Wired . . . Healthiest for Women . . . Best for Minority Entrepreneurs . . . Safest . . . Best to Retire . . . Most Polite . . . Best for Moviemakers . . . Most Frugal . . . Best for Bikes . . . Most Cultured . . . Least Stressful . . . Best for Families . . . Most Romantic . . . Most Charitable . . . Best for Telecommuters . . . Best for Singles . . . Nerdiest . . . Fittest . . . Best for Dogs . . . Most Tattooed . . . Best for Wheelchair Users,** and more.

Sources for these Rankings include both well-known magazines and other media, including *Forbes, Fortune, USA Today, Condé Nast Traveler, Gallup, Kiplinger's Personal Finance, Men's Journal,* and *Travel + Leisure,* as well as *Asthma & Allergy Foundation of America, American Lung Association, League of American Bicyclists, The Advocate, National Civic League, National Alliance to End Homelessness, MovieMaker Magazine, National Insurance Crime Bureau, Center for Digital Government, National Association of Home Builders,* and the *Milken Institute.*

Rankings cover a variety of geographic areas; see Appendix B for full geographic definitions.

STATISTICAL TABLES

Each city chapter includes a possible 127 tables and detailed topics—70 in BUSINESS and 57 in LIVING. Over 94% of statistical data has been updated. In addition, a new table covering key congestion measures, has been added to the Transportation section. This table includes data on annual hours of delay and annual congestion costs.

Business Environment includes hard facts and figures on 10 major categories, including City Finances, Demographics, Income, Economy, Employment, and Taxes. *Living Environment* includes 11 major categories, such as Cost of Living, Housing, Health, Education, Safety, Recreation, and Climate.

To compile the Statistical Tables, editors have again turned to a wide range of sources, some well known, such as the *U.S. Census Bureau, U.S. Environmental Protection Agency, Bureau of Labor Statistics, Centers for Disease Control and Prevention,* and the *Federal Bureau of Investigation,* plus others like *The Council for Community and Economic Research, Texas A&M Transportation Institute,* and *Federation of Tax Administrators.*

APPENDICES: Data for all cities appear in all volumes.
- **Appendix A**—*Comparative Statistics*
- **Appendix B**—*Metropolitan Area Definitions*
- **Appendix C**—*Government Type and County*
- **Appendix D**—*Chambers of Commerce and Economic Development Organizations*
- **Appendix E**—*State Departments of Labor and Employment*

Material provided by public and private agencies and organizations was supplemented by original research, numerous library sources and Internet sites. *America's Top-Rated Cities, 2020,* is designed for a wide range of readers: private individuals considering relocating a residence or business; professionals considering expanding their businesses or changing careers; corporations considering relocating, opening up additional offices or creating new divisions; government agencies; general and market researchers; real estate consultants; human resource personnel; urban planners; investors; and urban government students.

Customers who purchase the four-volume set receive free online access to *America's Top-Rated Cities* allowing them to download city reports and sort and rank by 50-plus data points.

AMERICA'S TOP-RATED CITIES

CBSA: Core Based Statistical Area

STATE

○ Top Rated City

East Region
Central Region
West Region
South Region

©Larry Mandelin 2020

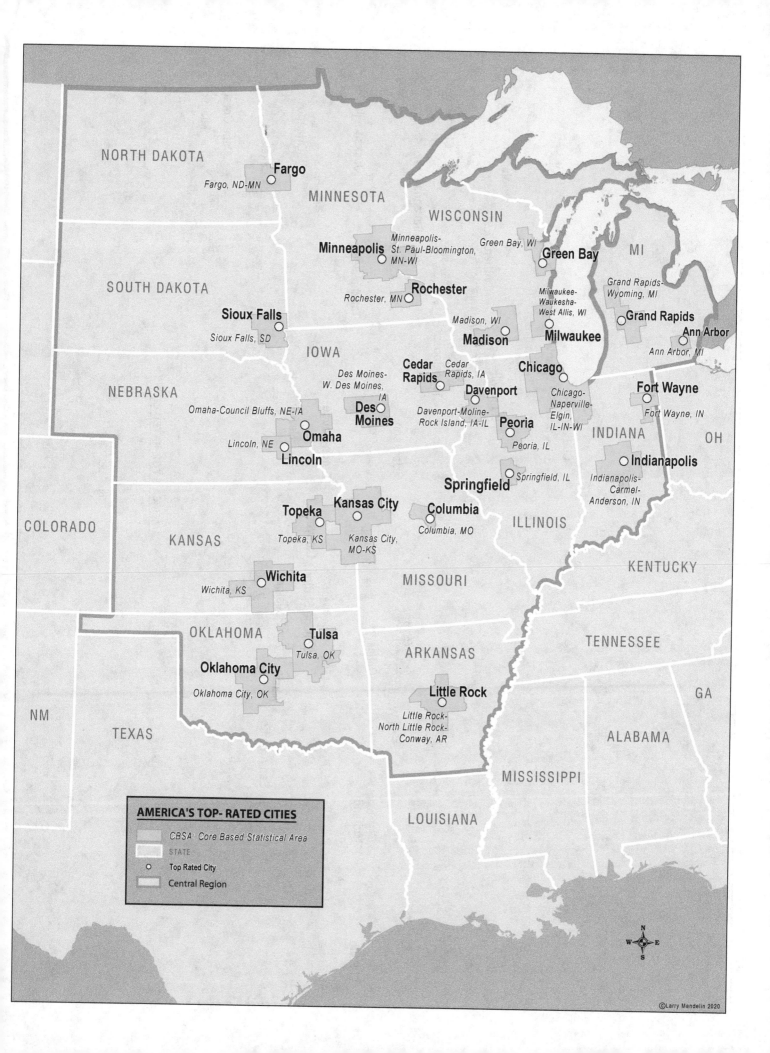

AMERICA'S TOP- RATED CITIES

CBSA: Core Based Statistical Area
STATE
○ Top Rated City
Central Region

NORTH DAKOTA

Fargo
Fargo, ND-MN

MINNESOTA

MINNEAPOLIS
Minneapolis-
St. Paul-Bloomington,
MN-WI

WISCONSIN

Green Bay, WI

Green Bay

MI

SOUTH DAKOTA

Rochester
Rochester, MN

Milwaukee-
Waukesha-
West Allis, WI

Grand Rapids-
Wyoming, MI

Sioux Falls
Sioux Falls, SD

IOWA

Madison, WI

Madison

Milwaukee

Grand Rapids

Ann Arbor
Ann Arbor, MI

NEBRASKA

Des Moines-
W. Des Moines,
IA

Cedar
Rapids

Cedar
Rapids, IA

Chicago

Fort Wayne
Fort Wayne, IN

Omaha-Council Bluffs, NE-IA

Des
Moines

Davenport

Chicago-
Naperville-
Elgin,
IL-IN-WI

Lincoln, NE

Omaha

Davenport-Moline-
Rock Island, IA-IL

Peoria

INDIANA

OH

Lincoln

Peoria, IL

Springfield, IL

Indianapolis

COLORADO

Topeka

Kansas City

Springfield

Columbia
Columbia, MO

Indianapolis-
Carmel-
Anderson, IN

KANSAS

Topeka, KS

Kansas City,
MO-KS

ILLINOIS

KENTUCKY

Wichita
Wichita, KS

MISSOURI

NM

OKLAHOMA

Tulsa
Tulsa, OK

TENNESSEE

Oklahoma City
Oklahoma City, OK

ARKANSAS

Little Rock
Little Rock-
North Little Rock-
Conway, AR

GA

TEXAS

ALABAMA

MISSISSIPPI

LOUISIANA

©Larry Mandelin 2020

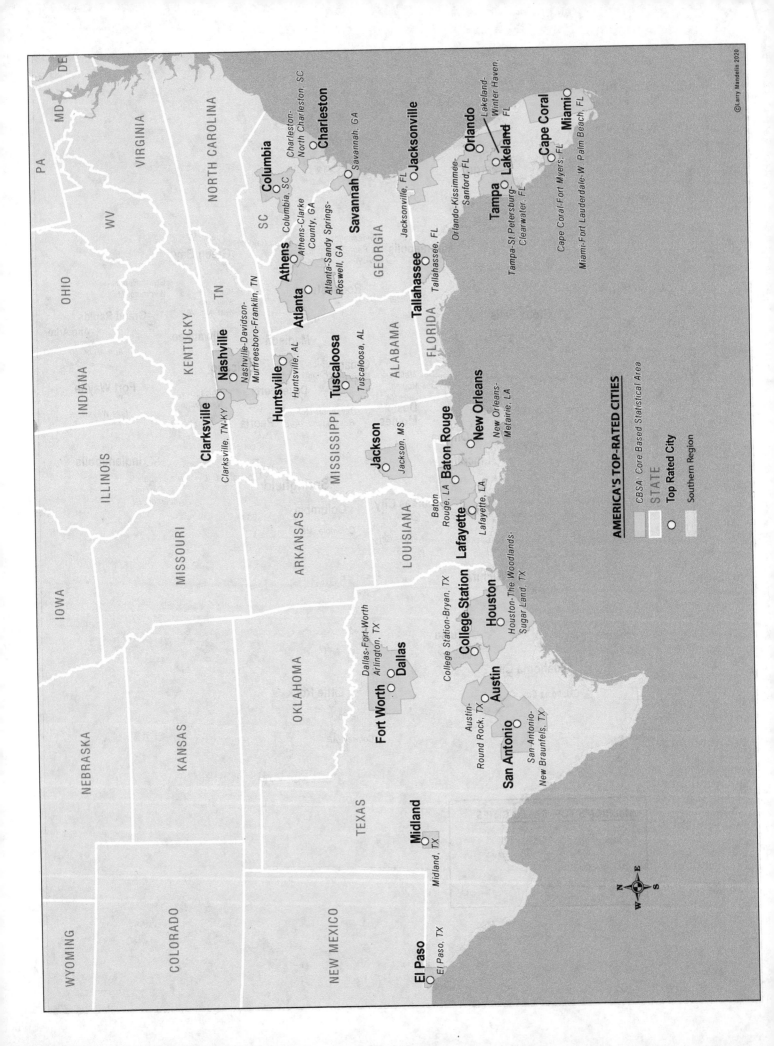

AMERICA'S TOP-RATED CITIES

CBSA: *Core Based Statistical Area*

STATE

○ Top Rated City

Southern Region

El Paso
El Paso, TX

Midland
Midland, TX

San Antonio
San Antonio-New Braunfels, TX

Austin
Austin-Round Rock, TX

Fort Worth

Dallas
Dallas-Fort-Worth Arlington, TX

College Station
College Station-Bryan, TX

Houston
Houston-The Woodlands-Sugar Land, TX

Lafayette
Lafayette, LA

Baton Rouge
Baton Rouge, LA

New Orleans
New Orleans-Metairie, LA

Jackson
Jackson, MS

Clarksville
Clarksville, TN-KY

Nashville
Nashville-Davidson-Murfreesboro-Franklin, TN

Huntsville
Huntsville, AL

Tuscaloosa
Tuscaloosa, AL

Atlanta
Atlanta-Sandy Springs-Roswell, GA

Athens
Athens-Clarke County, GA

Columbia
Columbia, SC

Charleston
Charleston-North Charleston, SC

Savannah
Savannah, GA

Jacksonville
Jacksonville, FL

Tallahassee
Tallahassee, FL

Tampa
Tampa-St. Petersburg-Clearwater, FL

Orlando
Orlando-Kissimmee-Sanford, FL

Lakeland
Lakeland-Winter Haven, FL

Cape Coral
Cape Coral-Fort Myers, FL

Miami
Miami-Fort Lauderdale-W. Palm Beach, FL

N E W S

©Larry Mandelin 2020

WYOMING · COLORADO · NEW MEXICO · NEBRASKA · KANSAS · OKLAHOMA · TEXAS · IOWA · MISSOURI · ARKANSAS · LOUISIANA · ILLINOIS · INDIANA · OHIO · KENTUCKY · TN · MISSISSIPPI · ALABAMA · GEORGIA · FLORIDA · SC · NORTH CAROLINA · VIRGINIA · WV · PA · MD · DE

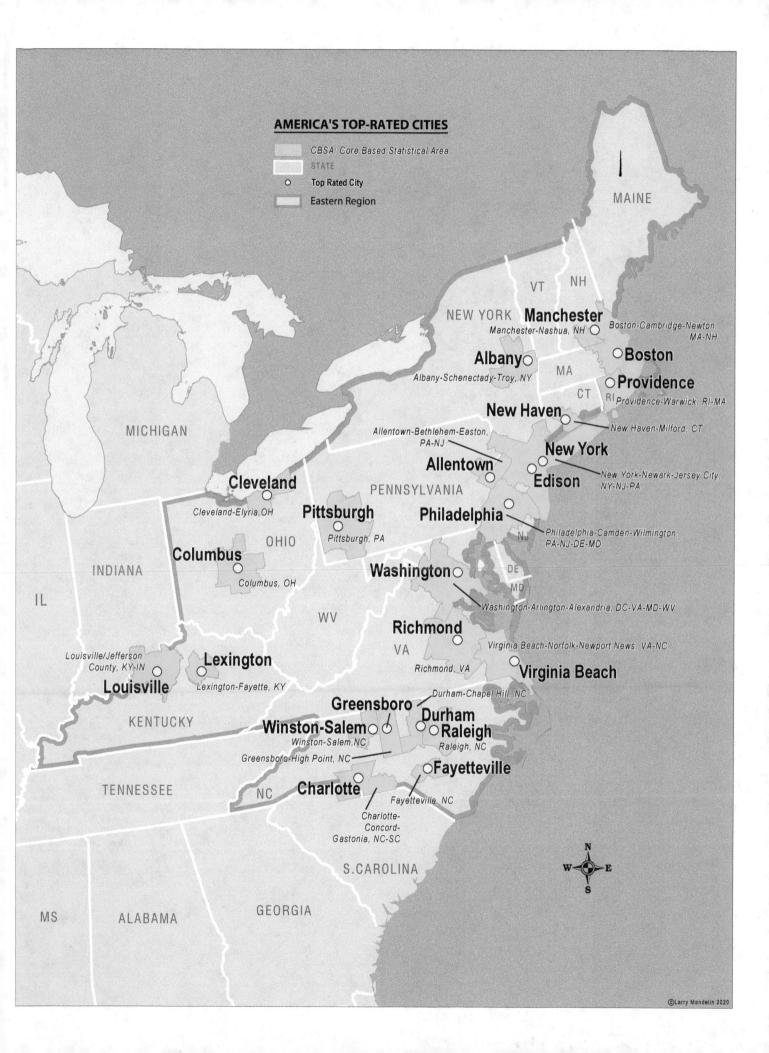

AMERICA'S TOP-RATED CITIES

CBSA: Core Based Statistical Area
STATE
○ Top Rated City
Eastern Region

MAINE

VT   NH

NEW YORK   **Manchester**
Manchester-Nashua, NH ○

Boston-Cambridge-Newton, MA-NH

○ **Boston**

Albany ○
Albany-Schenectady-Troy, NY

MA

○ **Providence**
CT
RI   Providence-Warwick, RI-MA

New Haven ○
New Haven-Milford, CT

Allentown-Bethlehem-Easton,
PA-NJ

New York

Cleveland
○
Cleveland-Elyria,OH

Allentown ○
Edison
New York-Newark-Jersey City,
NY-NJ-PA

PENNSYLVANIA

Pittsburgh
○
Pittsburgh, PA

Philadelphia ○
Philadelphia-Camden-Wilmington,
PA-NJ-DE-MD

NJ

OHIO

Columbus
○
Columbus, OH

MICHIGAN

INDIANA

IL

DE
MD

Washington ○
Washington-Arlington-Alexandria, DC-VA-MD-WV

WV

Richmond
○
VA
Richmond, VA

Virginia Beach-Norfolk-Newport News, VA-NC

○ **Virginia Beach**

Louisville/Jefferson
County, KY-IN
○
Louisville

Lexington
○
Lexington-Fayette, KY

Durham-Chapel Hill, NC

KENTUCKY

Greensboro
○ ○
Winston-Salem
Winston-Salem,NC

Durham
○ ○
Raleigh
Raleigh, NC

Greensboro-High Point, NC

○ **Fayetteville**

TENNESSEE

NC

Charlotte
○
Charlotte-
Concord-
Gastonia, NC-SC

Fayetteville, NC

S.CAROLINA

N
W   E
S

MS   ALABAMA   GEORGIA

©Larry Mandelin 2020

Ann Arbor, Michigan

Background

Ann Arbor is located on the Huron River, 36 miles west of Detroit. It was founded in 1824 by John Allen and Elisha W. Rumsey, two East Coast entrepreneurs who named the settlement for their wives—both Ann—and for the community's location within natural groves. In 1851, Ann Arbor was chartered as a city.

After the arrival of the Michigan Central Railroad in 1839, the settlement developed as an agricultural center, and it continues to be such for the rich agricultural area surrounding it.

Before the arrival of settlers, the Ojibwa tribe roamed the area, which they called Washtenaw—the land beyond—which now serves as the county for which Ann Arbor is the seat.

The city manufactures machinery, tools, steel ball bearings, scientific instruments, doors and blinds, cameras, and coil springs. Lasers, computers, hospital and laboratory equipment, automotive parts, and high-tech/software products are also vibrant industries. Major opportunities exist in health care, with the University of Michigan Medical Center and St. Joseph Mercy Hospital employing over 11,000. The region is also strong in book printing and manufacturing.

Ann Arbor's population is about one-third college or university students. The University of Michigan, the town's largest employer, played a prominent role in Ann Arbor's development as a major Midwest center for aeronautical, space, nuclear, chemical, and metallurgical research. The university also houses fascinating exhibits within its Museum of Natural History, known for an outstanding collection of dinosaur and mastodon skeletons and fossils, detailed dioramas of prehistoric life and Native American cultures, exhibits on Michigan wildlife, anthropology, and geology, and even its planetarium. Also located at the university is a 250-acre botanical garden with a conservatory featuring tropical, temperate, and arid houses, over six miles of nature trails, and a variety of outdoor display gardens. The University of Michigan Museum of Art (UMMA), with more than 18,000 works of art from all over the world, and the university's Detroit Observatory, a historic scientific laboratory built in 1854, make this a truly unique, world-class institution. UMMA expanded in 2009, more than doubling its space.

The university is also home to the Gerald R. Ford School of Policy, named in honor of the former President, who graduated from the university in 1935. The 85,000 square-foot Joan and Sanford Weill Hall, designed by the noted firm of Robert A. M. Stern Architects, opened in 2006. The University of Michigan is also the site of the Ford Presidential Library.

Other cultural attractions in the city include: the African-American Cultural and Historical Museum; the Ann Arbor Art Center, including two contemporary art galleries, and art classes for all ages; the Ann Arbor Hands-On Museum, offering interactive exhibits in physics, mathematics, biology, physiology, botany and geology; and Gallery Von Glahn, specializing in serigraphs, lithographs, and original bronze and porcelain art. The Detroit Institute of Arts displays Diego Rivera's spectacular "Detroit Industry" frescoes. In addition, Ann Arbor offers dozens more artists' guilds, museums, top-rated art fairs, music and film festivals, plus its share of fine restaurants with cuisine ranging from Italian to Ethiopian.

In nearby Dearborn are the Henry Ford Estate and Museum and the Automotive Hall of Fame. Historic Ypsilanti hosts the annual Orphan Car Show, which pays homage to elegant vehicles of a bygone era such as the Kaiser, Triumph and Packard.

With its high-tech industries and great university, Ann Arbor is an exceptionally livable city and full of cultural events, including an annual arts fair, and jazz, film, and summer festivals. The city boasts 157 city parks, seven golf courses and endless trails.

Located in the humid continental climate zone, Ann Arbor's summers are hot, winters are cold, and there is an above-average occurrence of snow and rain. Proximity to the Great Lakes causes extreme temperatures to be moderated, but also results in high humidity and cloud cover two-thirds of the year.

Rankings

Business/Finance Rankings

- 24/7 Wall Street used metro data from the Bureau of Labor Statistics' Occupational Employment database to identify the cities with the highest percentage of those employed in jobs requiring knowledge in the science, technology, engineering, and math (STEM) fields as well as average wages for STEM jobs. The Ann Arbor metro area was #13. *247wallst.com, "15 Cities with the Most High-Tech Jobs," January 11, 2020*

- The Ann Arbor metro area appeared on the Milken Institute "2020 Best Performing Cities" list. Rank: #81 out of 200 large metro areas. Criteria: job growth; wage and salary growth; high-tech output growth. *Milken Institute, "Best-Performing Cities 2020," February 26, 2020*

- *Forbes* ranked the 200 most populous metro areas to determine the nation's "Best Places for Business and Careers." The Ann Arbor metro area was ranked #71. Criteria: costs (business and living); job growth (past and projected); income growth; quality of life; educational attainment (college and high school); projected economic growth; cultural and leisure opportunities; workplace tolerance laws; net migration patterns. *Forbes, "The Best Places for Business and Careers 2019: Seattle Still On Top," October 30, 2019*

Dating/Romance Rankings

- Ann Arbor was selected as one of America's best cities for singles by the readers of *Travel + Leisure* in their annual "America's Favorite Cities" survey. Criteria included good-looking locals, cool shopping, an active bar scene and hipster-magnet coffee bars. *Travel + Leisure, "Best Cities in America for Singles," July 21, 2017*

- Ann Arbor was selected as one of the nation's most romantic cities with 100,000 or more residents by Amazon.com. The city ranked #10 of 20. Criteria: per capita sales of romance novels, relationship books, romantic comedy movies, romantic music, and sexual wellness products. *Amazon.com, "Top 20 Most Romantic Cities in the U.S.," February 1, 2017*

Education Rankings

- Personal finance website *WalletHub* analyzed the 150 largest U.S. metropolitan statistical areas to determine where the most educated Americans are choosing to settle. Criteria: education levels; percentage of workers with degrees; education quality and attainment gap; public school quality rankings; quality and size of each metro area's universities. Ann Arbor was ranked #1 (#1 = most educated city). *www.WalletHub.com, "2019's Most and Least Educated Cities in America," July 22, 2019*

Environmental Rankings

- Niche compiled a list of the nation's snowiest cities, based on the National Oceanic and Atmospheric Administration's 30-year average snowfall data. Among cities with a population of at least 50,000, Ann Arbor ranked #19. *Niche.com, Top 25 Snowiest Cities in America, December 10, 2018*

Health/Fitness Rankings

- The Ann Arbor metro area ranked #12 out of 189 in The Gallup-Sharecare Well-Being Index. Criteria: purpose; social well being; financial health; community and physical health. Results are based on telephone interviews with adults, aged 18 and older, living in metropolitan areas in the 50 U.S. states and the District of Columbia. *Gallup-Sharecare, "State of American Well-Being, 2017 Community Well-Being Rankings" March 2018*

Real Estate Rankings

- Ann Arbor was ranked #94 out of 238 metro areas in terms of housing affordability in 2019 by the National Association of Home Builders (#1 = most affordable). Criteria: the share of homes sold in that area affordable to a family earning the local median income, based on standard mortgage underwriting criteria. *National Association of Home Builders®, NAHB-Wells Fargo Housing Opportunity Index, 4th Quarter 2019*

Safety Rankings

- The National Insurance Crime Bureau ranked 382 metro areas in the U.S. in terms of per capita rates of vehicle theft. The Ann Arbor metro area ranked #322 (#1 = highest rate). Criteria: number of vehicle theft offenses per 100,000 inhabitants in 2018. *National Insurance Crime Bureau, "Hot Spots 2018," June 25, 2019*

Seniors/Retirement Rankings

- From its Best Cities for Successful Aging indexes, the Milken Institute generated rankings for metropolitan areas, weighing data in nine categories—health care, wellness, living arrangements, transportation and convenience, financial characteristics, education, employment, community engagement, and overall livability. The Ann Arbor metro area was ranked #6 overall in the small metro area category. *Milken Institute, "Best Cities for Successful Aging, 2017" March 14, 2017*

Women/Minorities Rankings

- NerdWallet examined data for 529 U.S. cities and ranked them based on the environment for working women. Ann Arbor ranked #7. Criteria: women's earnings; labor force participation rate; cost of living; unemployment rate. *www.nerdwallet.com, "Best Cities for Women in the Workforce 2016," April 4, 2016*

- *24/7 Wall St.* compared median annual earnings for men and women who worked full-time, year-round, female employment in management roles, bachelor's degree attainment among women, female life expectancy, uninsured rates, and preschool enrollment to identify the better cities for women. The U.S. metropolitan area, Ann Arbor was ranked #7 in pay disparity and other gender gaps. *24/7 Wall St., "Here's Where It's Easier (or Harder) For Working Women to Find Balanace, Pay Equity," October 5, 2019*

Business Environment

CITY FINANCES

City Government Finances

Component	2017 ($000)	2017 ($ per capita)
Total Revenues	349,154	2,982
Total Expenditures	312,269	2,667
Debt Outstanding	313,661	2,679
Cash and Securities[1]	728,499	6,223

Note: (1) Cash and security holdings of a government at the close of its fiscal year, including those of its dependent agencies, utilities, and liquor stores.
Source: U.S. Census Bureau, State & Local Government Finances 2017

City Government Revenue by Source

Source	2017 ($000)	2017 ($ per capita)	2017 (%)
General Revenue			
From Federal Government	34,881	298	10.0
From State Government	22,652	193	6.5
From Local Governments	3,433	29	1.0
Taxes			
Property	94,880	810	27.2
Sales and Gross Receipts	2,232	19	0.6
Personal Income	0	0	0.0
Corporate Income	0	0	0.0
Motor Vehicle License	0	0	0.0
Other Taxes	5,479	47	1.6
Current Charges	76,476	653	21.9
Liquor Store	0	0	0.0
Utility	26,602	227	7.6
Employee Retirement	64,030	547	18.3

Source: U.S. Census Bureau, State & Local Government Finances 2017

City Government Expenditures by Function

Function	2017 ($000)	2017 ($ per capita)	2017 (%)
General Direct Expenditures			
Air Transportation	697	6	0.2
Corrections	0	0	0.0
Education	0	0	0.0
Employment Security Administration	0	0	0.0
Financial Administration	3,578	30	1.1
Fire Protection	16,415	140	5.3
General Public Buildings	0	0	0.0
Governmental Administration, Other	2,334	19	0.7
Health	0	0	0.0
Highways	33,301	284	10.7
Hospitals	0	0	0.0
Housing and Community Development	21,971	187	7.0
Interest on General Debt	6,675	57	2.1
Judicial and Legal	6,587	56	2.1
Libraries	0	0	0.0
Parking	21,971	187	7.0
Parks and Recreation	15,097	129	4.8
Police Protection	27,267	232	8.7
Public Welfare	0	0	0.0
Sewerage	34,277	292	11.0
Solid Waste Management	15,498	132	5.0
Veterans' Services	0	0	0.0
Liquor Store	0	0	0.0
Utility	21,035	179	6.7
Employee Retirement	35,437	302	11.3

Source: U.S. Census Bureau, State & Local Government Finances 2017

DEMOGRAPHICS

Population Growth

Area	1990 Census	2000 Census	2010 Census	2018* Estimate	Population Growth (%)	
					1990-2018	2010-2018
City	111,018	114,024	113,934	120,641	8.7	5.9
MSA[1]	282,937	322,895	344,791	365,961	29.3	6.1
U.S.	248,709,873	281,421,906	308,745,538	322,903,030	29.8	4.6

Note: (1) Figures cover the Ann Arbor, MI Metropolitan Statistical Area—see Appendix B for areas included;
(*) 2014-2018 5-year estimated population
Source: U.S. Census Bureau, 1990 Census, Census 2000, Census 2010, 2014-2018 American Community Survey 5-Year Estimates

Household Size

Area	Persons in Household (%)							Average Household Size
	One	Two	Three	Four	Five	Six	Seven or More	
City	34.8	36.9	12.0	11.1	3.0	1.5	0.8	2.30
MSA[1]	29.6	36.3	14.0	12.6	4.7	1.8	1.0	2.50
U.S.	27.7	33.9	15.7	13.0	6.0	2.3	1.4	2.60

Note: (1) Figures cover the Ann Arbor, MI Metropolitan Statistical Area—see Appendix B for areas included
Source: U.S. Census Bureau, 2014-2018 American Community Survey 5-Year Estimates

Race

Area	White Alone[2] (%)	Black Alone[2] (%)	Asian Alone[2] (%)	AIAN[3] Alone[2] (%)	NHOPI[4] Alone[2] (%)	Other Race Alone[2] (%)	Two or More Races (%)
City	71.0	6.5	17.3	0.3	0.0	0.7	4.1
MSA[1]	73.7	11.8	9.1	0.3	0.1	0.7	4.3
U.S.	72.7	12.7	5.4	0.8	0.2	4.9	3.2

Note: (1) Figures cover the Ann Arbor, MI Metropolitan Statistical Area—see Appendix B for areas included;
(2) Alone is defined as not being in combination with one or more other races; (3) American Indian and Alaska Native; (4) Native Hawaiian and Other Pacific Islander
Source: U.S. Census Bureau, 2014-2018 American Community Survey 5-Year Estimates

Hispanic or Latino Origin

Area	Total (%)	Mexican (%)	Puerto Rican (%)	Cuban (%)	Other (%)
City	4.7	2.2	0.3	0.3	2.0
MSA[1]	4.6	2.5	0.3	0.2	1.7
U.S.	17.8	11.2	1.7	0.7	4.2

Note: Persons of Hispanic or Latino origin can be of any race; (1) Figures cover the Ann Arbor, MI Metropolitan Statistical Area—see Appendix B for areas included
Source: U.S. Census Bureau, 2014-2018 American Community Survey 5-Year Estimates

Segregation

Type	Segregation Indices[1]				Percent Change		
	1990	2000	2010	2010 Rank[2]	1990-2000	1990-2010	2000-2010
Black/White	n/a	n/a	n/a	n/a	n/a	n/a	n/a
Asian/White	n/a	n/a	n/a	n/a	n/a	n/a	n/a
Hispanic/White	n/a	n/a	n/a	n/a	n/a	n/a	n/a

Note: All figures cover the Metropolitan Statistical Area—see Appendix B for areas included; Figures are based on an analysis of 1990, 2000, and 2010 Census Decennial Census tract data by William H. Frey, Brookings Institution and the University of Michigan Social Science Data Analysis Network. In this analysis all racial groups (whites, blacks, and asians) are non-Hispanic members of those races. Hispanics are shown as a separate category; (1) Segregation Indices are Dissimilarity Indices that measure the degree to which the minority group is distributed differently than whites across census tracts. They range from 0 (complete integration) to 100 (complete segregation) where the value indicates the percentage of the minority group that needs to move to be distributed exactly like whites; (2) Ranges from 1 (most segregated) to 102 (least segregated); n/a not available.
Source: www.CensusScope.org

Ancestry

Area	German	Irish	English	American	Italian	Polish	French[2]	Scottish	Dutch
City	17.3	9.5	9.5	4.3	5.1	6.2	3.2	2.5	2.3
MSA[1]	19.3	10.5	10.0	6.8	4.9	6.6	3.3	2.6	2.2
U.S.	13.7	9.9	7.3	6.4	5.2	2.8	2.4	1.7	1.2

Note: Figures are the percentage of the total population reporting a particular ancestry. The nine most commonly reported ancestries in the U.S. are shown. Figures include multiple ancestries (e.g. if a person reported being Irish and Italian, they were included in both columns); (1) Figures cover the Ann Arbor, MI Metropolitan Statistical Area—see Appendix B for areas included; (2) Excludes Basque
Source: U.S. Census Bureau, 2014-2018 American Community Survey 5-Year Estimates

Foreign-born Population

Area	Percent of Population Born in								
	Any Foreign Country	Asia	Mexico	Europe	Caribbean	Central America[2]	South America	Africa	Canada
City	19.4	12.9	0.4	3.2	0.3	0.2	0.8	0.8	0.8
MSA[1]	12.4	7.3	0.4	2.2	0.2	0.3	0.5	0.8	0.6
U.S.	13.5	4.1	3.5	1.5	1.3	1.1	0.9	0.7	0.3

Note: (1) Figures cover the Ann Arbor, MI Metropolitan Statistical Area—see Appendix B for areas included; (2) Excludes Mexico.
Source: U.S. Census Bureau, 2014-2018 American Community Survey 5-Year Estimates

Marital Status

Area	Never Married	Now Married[2]	Separated	Widowed	Divorced
City	55.9	34.3	0.5	2.7	6.8
MSA[1]	42.8	44.1	0.8	3.8	8.6
U.S.	33.3	48.1	2.0	5.8	10.8

Note: Figures are percentages and cover the population 15 years of age and older; (1) Figures cover the Ann Arbor, MI Metropolitan Statistical Area—see Appendix B for areas included; (2) Excludes separated
Source: U.S. Census Bureau, 2014-2018 American Community Survey 5-Year Estimates

Disability by Age

Area	All Ages	Under 18 Years Old	18 to 64 Years Old	65 Years and Over
City	7.0	2.5	4.8	26.2
MSA[1]	9.1	3.2	7.0	28.6
U.S.	12.6	4.2	10.3	35.0

Note: Figures show percent of the civilian noninstitutionalized population that reported having a disability. Disability status is determined from six types of difficulty: vision, hearing, cognitive, ambulatory, self-care, and independent living. For children under 5 years old, hearing and vision difficulty are used to determine disability status. For children between the ages of 5 and 14, disability status is determined from hearing, vision, cognitive, ambulatory, and self-care difficulties. For people aged 15 years and older, they are considered to have a disability if they have difficulty with any one of the six difficulty types; Note: (1) Figures cover the Ann Arbor, MI Metropolitan Statistical Area—see Appendix B for areas included
Source: U.S. Census Bureau, 2014-2018 American Community Survey 5-Year Estimates

Age

Area	Percent of Population									Median Age
	Under Age 5	Age 5–19	Age 20–34	Age 35–44	Age 45–54	Age 55–64	Age 65–74	Age 75–84	Age 85+	
City	3.8	18.5	39.7	9.6	8.4	8.4	6.6	3.3	1.6	27.5
MSA[1]	5.0	19.6	27.5	11.4	12.0	11.4	7.9	3.5	1.6	33.4
U.S.	6.1	19.3	20.7	12.6	13.2	12.8	8.8	4.5	1.9	37.9

Note: (1) Figures cover the Ann Arbor, MI Metropolitan Statistical Area—see Appendix B for areas included
Source: U.S. Census Bureau, 2014-2018 American Community Survey 5-Year Estimates

Gender

Area	Males	Females	Males per 100 Females
City	59,813	60,828	98.3
MSA[1]	181,376	184,585	98.3
U.S.	158,984,190	163,918,840	97.0

Note: (1) Figures cover the Ann Arbor, MI Metropolitan Statistical Area—see Appendix B for areas included
Source: U.S. Census Bureau, 2014-2018 American Community Survey 5-Year Estimates

Religious Groups by Family

Area	Catholic	Baptist	Non-Den.	Methodist[2]	Lutheran	LDS[3]	Pentecostal	Presbyterian[4]	Muslim[5]	Judaism
MSA[1]	12.4	2.2	1.6	3.1	2.9	0.9	1.9	3.0	1.3	0.9
U.S.	19.1	9.3	4.0	4.0	2.3	2.0	1.9	1.6	0.8	0.7

Note: Figures are the number of adherents as a percentage of the total population; (1) Figures cover the Ann Arbor, MI Metropolitan Statistical Area—see Appendix B for areas included; (2) Methodist/Pietist; (3) Latter Day Saints; (4) Reformed; (5) Figures are estimates
Source: Association of Statisticians of American Religious Bodies, 2010 U.S. Religion Census: Religious Congregations & Membership Study

Religious Groups by Tradition

Area	Catholic	Evangelical Protestant	Mainline Protestant	Other Tradition	Black Protestant	Orthodox
MSA[1]	12.4	7.3	7.5	3.8	1.6	0.3
U.S.	19.1	16.2	7.3	4.3	1.6	0.3

Note: Figures are the number of adherents as a percentage of the total population; (1) Figures cover the Ann Arbor, MI Metropolitan Statistical Area—see Appendix B for areas included
Source: Association of Statisticians of American Religious Bodies, 2010 U.S. Religion Census: Religious Congregations & Membership Study

ECONOMY

Gross Metropolitan Product

Area	2017	2018	2019	2020	Rank[2]
MSA[1]	23.5	24.6	25.5	26.4	112

Note: Figures are in billions of dollars; (1) Figures cover the Ann Arbor, MI Metropolitan Statistical Area—see Appendix B for areas included; (2) Rank is based on 2018 data and ranges from 1 to 381
Source: U.S. Conference of Mayors, U.S. Metro Economies: GMP & Employment 2018-2020, September 2019

Economic Growth

Area	2015-17 (%)	2018 (%)	2019 (%)	2020 (%)	Rank[2]
MSA[1]	2.1	2.5	1.9	1.3	123
U.S.	1.9	2.9	2.3	2.1	–

Note: Figures are real gross metropolitan product (GMP) growth rates and represent average annual percent change; (1) Figures cover the Ann Arbor, MI Metropolitan Statistical Area—see Appendix B for areas included; (2) Rank is based on 2017 2-year average annual percent change and ranges from 1 to 381
Source: U.S. Conference of Mayors, U.S. Metro Economies: GMP & Employment 2018-2020, September 2019

Metropolitan Area Exports

Area	2013	2014	2015	2016	2017	2018	Rank[2]
MSA[1]	1,156.2	1,213.6	1,053.0	1,207.9	1,447.4	1,538.7	123

Note: Figures are in millions of dollars; (1) Figures cover the Ann Arbor, MI Metropolitan Statistical Area—see Appendix B for areas included; (2) Rank is based on 2018 data and ranges from 1 to 387
Source: U.S. Department of Commerce, International Trade Administration, Office of Trade and Economic Analysis, Industry and Analysis, Exports by Metropolitan Area, data extracted April 15, 2020

Building Permits

Area	Single-Family			Multi-Family			Total		
	2017	2018	Pct. Chg.	2017	2018	Pct. Chg.	2017	2018	Pct. Chg.
City	105	126	20.0	7	0	-100.0	112	126	12.5
MSA[1]	583	652	11.8	74	153	106.8	657	805	22.5
U.S.	820,000	855,300	4.3	462,000	473,500	2.5	1,282,000	1,328,800	3.7

Note: (1) Figures cover the Ann Arbor, MI Metropolitan Statistical Area—see Appendix B for areas included; Figures represent new, privately-owned housing units authorized (unadjusted data); All permit data are based on estimates with imputation
Source: U.S. Census Bureau, Manufacturing, Mining, and Construction Statistics, Building Permits, 2017, 2018

Bankruptcy Filings

Area	Business Filings			Nonbusiness Filings		
	2018	2019	% Chg.	2018	2019	% Chg.
Washtenaw County	12	10	-16.7	583	654	12.2
U.S.	22,232	22,780	2.5	751,186	752,160	0.1

Note: Business filings include Chapter 7, Chapter 9, Chapter 11, Chapter 12, Chapter 13, Chapter 15, and Section 304; Nonbusiness filings include Chapter 7, Chapter 11, and Chapter 13
Source: Administrative Office of the U.S. Courts, Business and Nonbusiness Bankruptcy, County Cases Commenced by Chapter of the Bankruptcy Code, During the 12-Month Period Ending December 31, 2018 and Business and Nonbusiness Bankruptcy, County Cases Commenced by Chapter of the Bankruptcy Code, During the 12-Month Period Ending December 31, 2019

Housing Vacancy Rates

Area	Gross Vacancy Rate[2] (%)			Year-Round Vacancy Rate[3] (%)			Rental Vacancy Rate[4] (%)			Homeowner Vacancy Rate[5] (%)		
	2017	2018	2019	2017	2018	2019	2017	2018	2019	2017	2018	2019
MSA[1]	n/a	n/a	n/a	n/a	n/a	n/a	n/a	n/a	n/a	n/a	n/a	n/a
U.S.	12.7	12.3	12.0	9.9	9.7	9.5	7.2	6.9	6.7	1.6	1.5	1.4

Note: (1) Figures cover the Ann Arbor, MI Metropolitan Statistical Area—see Appendix B for areas included; (2) The percentage of the total housing inventory that is vacant; (3) The percentage of the housing inventory (excluding seasonal units) that is year-round vacant; (4) The percentage of rental inventory that is vacant for rent; (5) The percentage of homeowner inventory that is vacant for sale; n/a not available
Source: U.S. Census Bureau, Housing Vacancies and Homeownership Annual Statistics: 2017, 2018, 2019

INCOME

Income

Area	Per Capita ($)	Median Household ($)	Average Household ($)
City	40,868	63,956	92,977
MSA[1]	39,486	69,434	97,553
U.S.	32,621	60,293	84,938

Note: (1) Figures cover the Ann Arbor, MI Metropolitan Statistical Area—see Appendix B for areas included
Source: U.S. Census Bureau, 2014-2018 American Community Survey 5-Year Estimates

Household Income Distribution

Area	Percent of Households Earning							
	Under $15,000	$15,000 -$24,999	$25,000 -$34,999	$35,000 -$49,999	$50,000 -$74,999	$75,000 -$99,999	$100,000 -$149,999	$150,000 and up
City	14.4	7.9	7.8	10.2	15.7	11.1	15.2	17.9
MSA[1]	10.6	7.5	7.4	11.3	16.5	11.8	16.7	18.2
U.S.	10.9	9.3	9.3	12.6	17.5	12.5	14.6	13.3

Note: (1) Figures cover the Ann Arbor, MI Metropolitan Statistical Area—see Appendix B for areas included
Source: U.S. Census Bureau, 2014-2018 American Community Survey 5-Year Estimates

Poverty Rate

Area	All Ages	Under 18 Years Old	18 to 64 Years Old	65 Years and Over
City	22.6	11.3	27.4	7.7
MSA[1]	14.2	12.2	16.3	6.4
U.S.	14.1	19.5	13.2	9.3

Note: Figures are percentage of people whose income during the past 12 months was below the poverty level; (1) Figures cover the Ann Arbor, MI Metropolitan Statistical Area—see Appendix B for areas included
Source: U.S. Census Bureau, 2014-2018 American Community Survey 5-Year Estimates

EMPLOYMENT

Labor Force and Employment

Area	Civilian Labor Force			Workers Employed		
	Dec. 2018	Dec. 2019	% Chg.	Dec. 2018	Dec. 2019	% Chg.
City	66,203	66,802	0.9	64,754	65,636	1.4
MSA[1]	198,749	200,349	0.8	193,447	196,082	1.4
U.S.	162,510,000	164,007,000	0.9	156,481,000	158,504,000	1.3

Note: Data is not seasonally adjusted and covers workers 16 years of age and older; (1) Figures cover the Ann Arbor, MI Metropolitan Statistical Area—see Appendix B for areas included
Source: Bureau of Labor Statistics, Local Area Unemployment Statistics

Unemployment Rate

Area	2019											
	Jan.	Feb.	Mar.	Apr.	May	Jun.	Jul.	Aug.	Sep.	Oct.	Nov.	Dec.
City	2.6	2.4	2.6	2.1	2.3	2.8	3.4	2.6	2.2	1.9	1.8	1.7
MSA[1]	3.1	3.0	3.1	2.6	2.8	3.4	4.2	3.2	2.7	2.4	2.2	2.1
U.S.	4.4	4.1	3.9	3.3	3.4	3.8	4.0	3.8	3.3	3.3	3.3	3.4

Note: Data is not seasonally adjusted and covers workers 16 years of age and older; (1) Figures cover the Ann Arbor, MI Metropolitan Statistical Area—see Appendix B for areas included
Source: Bureau of Labor Statistics, Local Area Unemployment Statistics

Average Wages

Occupation	$/Hr.	Occupation	$/Hr.
Accountants and Auditors	35.40	Maintenance and Repair Workers	18.10
Automotive Mechanics	30.10	Marketing Managers	63.70
Bookkeepers	20.20	Network and Computer Systems Admin.	37.40
Carpenters	30.70	Nurses, Licensed Practical	25.60
Cashiers	11.90	Nurses, Registered	38.10
Computer Programmers	33.80	Nursing Assistants	16.60
Computer Systems Analysts	39.30	Office Clerks, General	16.00
Computer User Support Specialists	23.20	Physical Therapists	42.10
Construction Laborers	21.70	Physicians	89.40
Cooks, Restaurant	14.50	Plumbers, Pipefitters and Steamfitters	34.50
Customer Service Representatives	17.90	Police and Sheriff's Patrol Officers	31.50
Dentists	86.10	Postal Service Mail Carriers	25.10
Electricians	32.80	Real Estate Sales Agents	25.30
Engineers, Electrical	42.00	Retail Salespersons	14.10
Fast Food and Counter Workers	11.60	Sales Representatives, Technical/Scientific	52.00
Financial Managers	63.70	Secretaries, Exc. Legal/Medical/Executive	21.20
First-Line Supervisors of Office Workers	29.10	Security Guards	13.90
General and Operations Managers	66.10	Surgeons	n/a
Hairdressers/Cosmetologists	12.60	Teacher Assistants, Exc. Postsecondary*	14.50
Home Health and Personal Care Aides	12.40	Teachers, Secondary School, Exc. Sp. Ed.*	28.80
Janitors and Cleaners	15.50	Telemarketers	n/a
Landscaping/Groundskeeping Workers	15.80	Truck Drivers, Heavy/Tractor-Trailer	23.00
Lawyers	63.20	Truck Drivers, Light/Delivery Services	19.10
Maids and Housekeeping Cleaners	12.60	Waiters and Waitresses	12.50

Note: Wage data covers the Ann Arbor, MI Metropolitan Statistical Area—see Appendix B for areas included; (*) Hourly wages were calculated from annual wage data based on a 40 hour work week; n/a not available.
Source: Bureau of Labor Statistics, Metro Area Occupational Employment & Wage Estimates, May 2019

Employment by Occupation

Occupation Classification	City (%)	MSA[1] (%)	U.S. (%)
Management, Business, Science, and Arts	66.0	53.2	37.9
Natural Resources, Construction, and Maintenance	1.8	4.2	8.9
Production, Transportation, and Material Moving	5.3	9.7	13.3
Sales and Office	14.0	17.0	22.1
Service	12.9	15.8	17.9

Note: Figures cover employed civilians 16 years of age and older; (1) Figures cover the Ann Arbor, MI Metropolitan Statistical Area—see Appendix B for areas included
Source: U.S. Census Bureau, 2014-2018 American Community Survey 5-Year Estimates

Employment by Industry

Sector	MSA[1]		U.S.
	Number of Employees	Percent of Total	Percent of Total
Construction, Mining, and Logging	4,900	2.1	5.4
Education and Health Services	30,100	12.9	16.1
Financial Activities	6,900	3.0	5.8
Government	89,000	38.1	15.0
Information	5,600	2.4	1.9
Leisure and Hospitality	17,900	7.7	10.8
Manufacturing	14,800	6.3	8.4
Other Services	6,300	2.7	3.9
Professional and Business Services	31,100	13.3	14.1
Retail Trade	16,300	7.0	10.6
Transportation, Warehousing, and Utilities	4,300	1.8	4.2
Wholesale Trade	6,600	2.8	3.9

Note: Figures are non-farm employment as of December 2019. Figures are not seasonally adjusted and include workers 16 years of age and older; (1) Figures cover the Ann Arbor, MI Metropolitan Statistical Area—see Appendix B for areas included
Source: Bureau of Labor Statistics, Current Employment Statistics, Employment, Hours, and Earnings

Occupations with Greatest Projected Employment Growth: 2019 – 2021

Occupation[1]	2019 Employment	2021 Projected Employment	Numeric Employment Change	Percent Employment Change
Combined Food Preparation and Serving Workers, Including Fast Food	126,900	131,480	4,580	3.6
Personal Care Aides	44,410	46,750	2,340	5.3
Registered Nurses	99,260	101,320	2,060	2.1
Laborers and Freight, Stock, and Material Movers, Hand	76,940	78,870	1,930	2.5
Cooks, Restaurant	37,590	39,390	1,800	4.8
Heavy and Tractor-Trailer Truck Drivers	61,220	62,880	1,660	2.7
Waiters and Waitresses	82,010	83,590	1,580	1.9
Software Developers, Applications	30,250	31,730	1,480	4.9
Home Health Aides	27,070	28,240	1,170	4.3
General and Operations Managers	61,080	62,190	1,110	1.8

Note: Projections cover Michigan; (1) Sorted by numeric employment change
Source: www.projectionscentral.com, State Occupational Projections, 2019–2021 Short-Term Projections

Fastest Growing Occupations: 2019 – 2021

Occupation[1]	2019 Employment	2021 Projected Employment	Numeric Employment Change	Percent Employment Change
Flight Attendants	3,640	3,980	340	9.3
Airline Pilots, Copilots, and Flight Engineers	3,210	3,480	270	8.4
Dental Laboratory Technicians	1,670	1,790	120	7.2
Veterinary Assistants and Laboratory Animal Caretakers	3,820	4,080	260	6.8
Commercial Pilots	1,350	1,440	90	6.7
Veterinarians	2,500	2,650	150	6.0
Veterinary Technologists and Technicians	2,630	2,780	150	5.7
Transportation Attendants, Except Flight Attendants	1,410	1,490	80	5.7
Statisticians	890	940	50	5.6
Personal Care Aides	44,410	46,750	2,340	5.3

Note: Projections cover Michigan; (1) Sorted by percent employment change and excludes occupations with numeric employment change less than 50
Source: www.projectionscentral.com, State Occupational Projections, 2019–2021 Short-Term Projections

TAXES

State Corporate Income Tax Rates

State	Tax Rate (%)	Income Brackets ($)	Num. of Brackets	Financial Institution Tax Rate (%)[a]	Federal Income Tax Ded.
Michigan	6.0	Flat rate	1	(a)	No

Note: Tax rates as of January 1, 2020; (a) Rates listed are the corporate income tax rate applied to financial institutions or excise taxes based on income.
Source: Federation of Tax Administrators, State Corporate Income Tax Rates, January 1, 2020

State Individual Income Tax Rates

State	Tax Rate (%)	Income Brackets ($)	Personal Exemptions ($)			Standard Ded. ($)	
			Single	Married	Depend.	Single	Married
Michigan (a)	4.25	Flat rate	4,400	8,800	4,050	–	–

Note: Tax rates as of January 1, 2020; Local- and county-level taxes are not included; Federal income tax is not deductible on state income tax returns; (a) 19 states have statutory provision for automatically adjusting to the rate of inflation the dollar values of the income tax brackets, standard deductions, and/or personal exemptions. Michigan indexes the personal exemption only. Oregon does not index the income brackets for $125,000 and over.
Source: Federation of Tax Administrators, State Individual Income Tax Rates, January 1, 2020

Various State Sales and Excise Tax Rates

State	State Sales Tax (%)	Gasoline[1] (¢/gal.)	Cigarette[2] ($/pack)	Spirits[3] ($/gal.)	Wine[4] ($/gal.)	Beer[5] ($/gal.)	Recreational Marijuana (%)
Michigan	6	41.98	2.00	11.95	0.51	0.20	10

Note: All tax rates as of January 1, 2020; (1) The American Petroleum Institute has developed a methodology for determining the average tax rate on a gallon of fuel. Rates may include any of the following: excise taxes, environmental fees, storage tank fees, other fees or taxes, general sales tax, and local taxes; (2) The federal excise tax of $1.0066 per pack and local taxes are not included; (3) Rates are those applicable to off-premise sales of 40% alcohol by volume (a.b.v.) distilled spirits in 750ml containers. Local excise taxes are excluded; (4) Rates are those applicable to off-premise sales of 11% a.b.v. non-carbonated wine in 750ml containers; (5) Rates are those applicable to off-premise sales of 4.7% a.b.v. beer in 12 ounce containers.
Source: Tax Foundation, 2020 Facts & Figures: How Does Your State Compare?

State Business Tax Climate Index Rankings

State	Overall Rank	Corporate Tax Rank	Individual Income Tax Rank	Sales Tax Rank	Property Tax Rank	Unemployment Insurance Tax Rank
Michigan	12	18	12	9	24	17

Note: The index is a measure of how each state's tax laws affect economic performance. The lower the rank, the more favorable a state's tax system is for business. States without a given tax are given a ranking of 1. The scores/rankings for the District of Columbia do not affect other states. The 2020 index represents the tax climate as of July 1, 2019.
Source: Tax Foundation, State Business Tax Climate Index 2020

COMMERCIAL UTILITIES

Typical Monthly Electric Bills

Area	Commercial Service ($/month)		Industrial Service ($/month)	
	1,500 kWh	40 kW demand 14,000 kWh	1,000 kW demand 200,000 kWh	50,000 kW demand 32,500,000 kWh
City	n/a	n/a	n/a	n/a
Average[1]	203	1,612	25,706	2,520,671

Note: Figures are based on annualized rates; (1) Average based on 187 utilities surveyed; n/a not available
Source: Edison Electric Institute, Typical Bills and Average Rates Report, Summer 2019

TRANSPORTATION

Means of Transportation to Work

Area	Car/Truck/Van		Public Transportation			Bicycle	Walked	Other Means	Worked at Home
	Drove Alone	Car-pooled	Bus	Subway	Railroad				
City	53.2	6.7	10.6	0.1	0.0	4.2	16.6	0.8	7.7
MSA[1]	71.7	7.9	5.1	0.0	0.0	1.6	7.1	0.7	5.9
U.S.	76.4	9.1	2.5	1.9	0.6	0.6	2.7	1.3	4.9

Note: Figures are percentages and cover workers 16 years of age and older; (1) Figures cover the Ann Arbor, MI Metropolitan Statistical Area—see Appendix B for areas included
Source: U.S. Census Bureau, 2014-2018 American Community Survey 5-Year Estimates

Travel Time to Work

Area	Less Than 10 Minutes	10 to 19 Minutes	20 to 29 Minutes	30 to 44 Minutes	45 to 59 Minutes	60 to 89 Minutes	90 Minutes or More
City	13.5	44.8	19.6	13.7	4.8	2.7	0.8
MSA[1]	11.0	32.9	24.0	19.5	7.1	4.3	1.3
U.S.	12.5	28.7	20.9	20.7	8.2	6.3	2.8

Note: Note: Figures are percentages and include workers 16 years old and over; (1) Figures cover the Ann Arbor, MI Metropolitan Statistical Area—see Appendix B for areas included
Source: U.S. Census Bureau, 2014-2018 American Community Survey 5-Year Estimates

Key Congestion Measures

Area	1982	1992	2002	2012	2017
Annual Hours of Delay, Total (000)	n/a	n/a	n/a	n/a	7,020
Annual Hours of Delay, Per Auto Commuter	n/a	n/a	n/a	n/a	22
Annual Congestion Cost, Total (million $)	n/a	n/a	n/a	n/a	146
Annual Congestion Cost, Per Auto Commuter ($)	n/a	n/a	n/a	n/a	466

Note: n/a not available
Source: Texas A&M Transportation Institute, 2019 Urban Mobility Report

Freeway Travel Time Index

Area	1982	1987	1992	1997	2002	2007	2012	2017
Urban Area Index[1]	n/a	n/a	n/a	n/a	n/a	n/a	n/a	1.11
Urban Area Rank[1,2]	n/a	n/a	n/a	n/a	n/a	n/a	n/a	n/a

Note: Freeway Travel Time Index—the ratio of travel time in the peak period to the travel time at free-flow conditions. For example, a value of 1.30 indicates a 20-minute free-flow trip takes 26 minutes in the peak (20 minutes x 1.30 = 26 minutes); (1) Covers the Ann Arbor MI urban area; (2) Rank is based on 101 larger urban areas (#1 = highest travel time index); n/a not available
Source: Texas A&M Transportation Institute, 2019 Urban Mobility Report

Public Transportation

Agency Name / Mode of Transportation	Vehicles Operated in Maximum Service[1]	Annual Unlinked Passenger Trips[2] (in thous.)	Annual Passenger Miles[3] (in thous.)
Ann Arbor Transportation Authority (AATA)			
Bus (directly operated)	85	6,617.8	23,275.9
Commuter Bus (directly operated)	2	26.1	442.8
Commuter Bus (purchased transportation)	2	91.3	2,421.5
Demand Response (purchased transportation)	58	166.6	1,123.6
Demand Response Taxi (purchased transportation)	9	30.6	305.2
Vanpool (purchased transportation)	109	234.4	7,463.8

Note: (1) Number of revenue vehicles operated by the given mode and type of service to meet the annual maximum service requirement. This is the revenue vehicle count during the peak season of the year; on the week and day that maximum service is provided. Vehicles operated in maximum service (VOMS) exclude atypical days and one-time special events; (2) Number of passengers who boarded public transportation vehicles. Passengers are counted each time they board a vehicle no matter how many vehicles they use to travel from their origin to their destination. (3) Sum of the distances ridden by all passengers during the entire fiscal year.
Source: Federal Transit Administration, National Transit Database, 2018

Air Transportation

Airport Name and Code / Type of Service	Passenger Airlines[1]	Passenger Enplanements	Freight Carriers[2]	Freight (lbs)
Detroit Metro Wayne County (25 miles) (DTW)				
Domestic service (U.S. carriers - 2019)	31	16,271,489	17	138,424,055
International service (U.S. carriers - 2018)	11	1,558,557	3	35,075,901

Note: (1) Includes all U.S.-based major, minor and commuter airlines that carried at least one passenger during the year; (2) Includes all U.S.-based airlines and freight carriers that transported at least one pound of freight during the year.
Source: Bureau of Transportation Statistics, The Intermodal Transportation Database, Air Carriers: T-100 Domestic Market (U.S. Carriers), 2019; Bureau of Transportation Statistics, The Intermodal Transportation Database, Air Carriers: T-100 International Market (U.S. Carriers), 2018

Other Transportation Statistics

Major Highways:	I-94
Amtrak Service:	Yes
Major Waterways/Ports:	None

Source: Amtrak.com; Google Maps

Major Business Headquarters

Company Name	Industry	Rankings	
		Fortune[1]	Forbes[2]
No companies listed	-	-	-

Note: (1) Companies that produce a 10-K are ranked 1 to 500 based on 2018 revenue; (2) All private companies with at least $2 billion in annual revenue through the end of their most current fiscal year are ranked 1 to 228; companies listed are headquartered in the city; dashes indicate no ranking
Source: Fortune, "Fortune 500," June 2019; Forbes, "America's Largest Private Companies," 2019 Rankings

Minority Business Opportunity

Ann Arbor is home to one company which is on the *Black Enterprise* Industrial/Service list (100 largest companies based on gross sales): **Arcade Travel** (#54). Criteria: operational in previous calendar year; at least 51% black-owned and manufactures/owns the product it sells or provides industrial or consumer services. Brokerages, real estate firms and firms that provide professional services are not eligible. *Black Enterprise, B.E. 100s, 2019*

Minority- and Women-Owned Businesses

Group	All Firms		Firms with Paid Employees			
	Firms	Sales ($000)	Firms	Sales ($000)	Employees	Payroll ($000)
AIAN[1]	86	1,866	6	528	17	315
Asian	709	234,063	153	220,708	2,000	83,027
Black	657	49,598	26	33,952	329	12,062
Hispanic	335	21,494	28	13,195	143	6,737
NHOPI[2]	n/a	n/a	n/a	n/a	n/a	n/a
Women	3,885	337,383	345	249,277	3,290	86,638
All Firms	11,982	9,905,332	2,455	8,098,875	48,259	2,231,617

Note: Figures cover firms located in the city; minority- and women-owned business are defined as firms in which the corresponding group own 51% or more of the stock or equity of the company; (1) American Indian and Alaska Native; (2) Native Hawaiian and Other Pacific Islander; n/a not available
Source: U.S. Census Bureau, 2012 Economic Census, Survey of Business Owners

Hotels, Motels and Vacation Rentals

Area	5 Star		4 Star		3 Star		2 Star		1 Star		Not Rated	
	Num.	Pct.[3]	Num.	Pct.[3]	Num.	Pct.[3]	Num.	Pct.[3]	Num.	Pct.[3]	Num.	Pct.[3]
City[1]	0	0.0	3	4.6	17	26.2	12	18.5	4	6.2	29	44.6
Total[2]	266	1.3	1,517	7.2	4,627	21.8	3,210	15.1	3,974	18.7	7,601	35.9

Note: (1) Figures cover Ann Arbor and vicinity; (2) Figures cover all 100 cities in this book; (3) Percentage of hotels which have a given star rating; Star ratings are determined by priceline.com and offer an indication of the general quality of a particular hotel.
Source: priceline.com, April 27, 2020

Major Convention Centers

Name	Overall Space (sq. ft.)	Exhibit Space (sq. ft.)	Meeting Space (sq. ft.)	Meeting Rooms

There are no major convention centers located in the metro area

Source: Original research

Living Environment

COST OF LIVING

Cost of Living Index

Composite Index	Groceries	Housing	Utilities	Trans-portation	Health Care	Misc. Goods/ Services
n/a	n/a	n/a	n/a	n/a	n/a	n/a

Note: The Cost of Living Index measures regional differences in the cost of consumer goods and services, excluding taxes and non-consumer expenditures, for professional and managerial households in the top income quintile. It is based on more than 50,000 prices covering almost 60 different items for which prices are collected three times a year by chambers of commerce, economic development organizations or university applied economic centers in each participating urban area. The numbers shown should be read as a percentage above or below the national average of 100. For example, a value of 115.4 in the groceries column indicates that grocery prices are 15.4% higher than the national average. Small differences in the index numbers should not be interpreted as significant; n/a not available.
Source: The Council for Community and Economic Research, ACCRA Cost of Living Index, 2019

Grocery Prices

Area[1]	T-Bone Steak ($/pound)	Frying Chicken ($/pound)	Whole Milk ($/half gal.)	Eggs ($/dozen)	Orange Juice ($/64 oz.)	Coffee ($/11.5 oz.)
City[2]	n/a	n/a	n/a	n/a	n/a	n/a
Avg.	11.40	1.41	1.93	1.54	3.51	4.30
Min.	7.40	0.92	0.85	0.58	2.67	2.90
Max.	15.58	2.68	4.09	4.18	5.57	8.10

Note: (1) Values for the local area are compared with the average, minimum and maximum values for all 290 areas in the Cost of Living Index; (2) Figures cover the Ann Arbor MI urban area; n/a not available; **T-Bone Steak** (price per pound); **Frying Chicken** (price per pound, whole fryer); **Whole Milk** (half gallon carton); **Eggs** (price per dozen, Grade A, large); **Orange Juice** (64 oz. Tropicana or Florida Natural); **Coffee** (11.5 oz. can, vacuum-packed, Maxwell House, Hills Bros, or Folgers).
Source: The Council for Community and Economic Research, ACCRA Cost of Living Index, 2019

Housing and Utility Costs

Area[1]	New Home Price ($)	Apartment Rent ($/month)	All Electric ($/month)	Part Electric ($/month)	Other Energy ($/month)	Telephone ($/month)
City[2]	n/a	n/a	n/a	n/a	n/a	n/a
Avg.	362,090	1,142	174.35	100.00	67.76	179.60
Min.	198,329	501	91.58	31.44	28.51	165.30
Max.	2,074,561	5,050	388.18	239.41	306.15	207.90

Note: (1) Values for the local area are compared with the average, minimum and maximum values for all 290 areas in the Cost of Living Index; (2) Figures cover the Ann Arbor MI urban area; n/a not available; **New Home Price** (2,400 sf living area, 8,000 sf lot, in urban area with full utilities); **Apartment Rent** (950 sf 2 bedroom/1.5 or 2 bath, unfurnished, excluding all utilities except water); **All Electric** (average monthly cost for an all-electric home); **Part Electric** (average monthly cost for a part-electric home); **Other Energy** (average monthly cost for natural gas, fuel oil, coal, wood, and any other forms of energy except electricity); **Telephone** (price includes the base monthly rate plus taxes and fees for three lines of mobile phone service).
Source: The Council for Community and Economic Research, ACCRA Cost of Living Index, 2019

Health Care, Transportation, and Other Costs

Area[1]	Doctor ($/visit)	Dentist ($/visit)	Optometrist ($/visit)	Gasoline ($/gallon)	Beauty Salon ($/visit)	Men's Shirt ($)
City[2]	n/a	n/a	n/a	n/a	n/a	n/a
Avg.	114.85	97.58	106.10	2.50	38.15	32.15
Min.	39.00	62.22	52.22	1.53	16.88	10.27
Max.	206.67	151.53	258.67	3.79	79.29	59.30

Note: (1) Values for the local area are compared with the average, minimum and maximum values for all 290 areas in the Cost of Living Index; (2) Figures cover the Ann Arbor MI urban area; n/a not available; **Doctor** (general practitioners routine exam of an established patient); **Dentist** (adult teeth cleaning and periodic oral examination); **Optometrist** (full vision eye exam for established adult patient); **Gasoline** (one gallon regular unleaded, national brand, including all taxes, cash price at self-service pump if available); **Beauty Salon** (woman's shampoo, trim, and blow-dry); **Men's Shirt** (cotton/polyester dress shirt, pinpoint weave, long sleeves).
Source: The Council for Community and Economic Research, ACCRA Cost of Living Index, 2019

HOUSING

House Price Index (HPI)

Area	National Ranking[2]	Quarterly Change (%)	One-Year Change (%)	Five-Year Change (%)
MSA[1]	173	0.04	3.92	36.45
U.S.[3]	–	1.26	5.09	32.88

Note: The HPI is a weighted repeat sales index. It measures average price changes in repeat sales or refinancings on the same properties. This information is obtained by reviewing repeat mortgage transactions on single-family properties whose mortgages have been purchased or securitized by Fannie Mae or Freddie Mac in January 1975; (1) Figures cover the Ann Arbor, MI Metropolitan Statistical Area—see Appendix B for areas included; (2) Rankings are based on annual percentage change for all metro areas containing at least 15,000 transactions over the last 10 years and ranges from 1 to 232; (3) figures based on a weighted average of Census Division estimates using a seasonally adjusted, purchase-only index; all figures are for the period ending December 31, 2019
Source: Federal Housing Finance Agency, House Price Index, February 25, 2020

Median Single-Family Home Prices

Area	2017	2018	2019[p]	Percent Change 2018 to 2019
MSA[1]	263.7	281.0	294.7	4.9
U.S. Average	248.8	261.6	274.6	5.0

Note: Figures are median sales prices of existing single-family homes in thousands of dollars; (p) preliminary; (1) Figures cover the Ann Arbor, MI Metropolitan Statistical Area—see Appendix B for areas included
Source: National Association of Realtors, Median Sales Price of Existing Single-Family Homes for Metropolitan Areas, 4th Quarter 2019

Qualifying Income Based on Median Sales Price of Existing Single-Family Homes

Area	With 5% Down ($)	With 10% Down ($)	With 20% Down ($)
MSA[1]	60,199	57,031	50,694
U.S. Average	58,663	55,575	49,400

Note: Figures are preliminary; Qualifying income is based on a mortgage rate of 3.76%. Monthly principal and interest payment is limited to 25% of income; (1) Figures cover the Ann Arbor, MI Metropolitan Statistical Area—see Appendix B for areas included
Source: National Association of Realtors, Qualifying Income Based on Median Sales Price of Existing Single-Family Homes for Metropolitan Areas, 4th Quarter 2019

Median Apartment Condo-Coop Home Prices

Area	2017	2018	2019[p]	Percent Change 2018 to 2019
MSA[1]	n/a	n/a	n/a	n/a
U.S. Average	234.3	241.0	249.5	3.5

Note: Figures are median sales prices of existing apartment condo-coop homes in thousands of dollars; (p) preliminary; n/a not available; (1) Figures cover the Ann Arbor, MI Metropolitan Statistical Area—see Appendix B for areas included
Source: National Association of Realtors, Median Sales Price of Existing Apartment Condo-Coop Homes for Metropolitan Areas, 4th Quarter 2019

Home Value Distribution

Area	Under $50,000	$50,000 -$99,999	$100,000 -$149,999	$150,000 -$199,999	$200,000 -$299,999	$300,000 -$499,999	$500,000 -$999,999	$1,000,000 or more
City	2.0	4.2	6.5	10.0	27.6	34.4	13.5	1.7
MSA[1]	6.5	6.9	9.1	15.2	24.6	26.1	9.9	1.6
U.S.	7.6	13.0	14.0	14.3	19.2	18.3	10.5	3.1

Note: Figures are percentages and cover owner-occupied housing units; (1) Figures cover the Ann Arbor, MI Metropolitan Statistical Area—see Appendix B for areas included
Source: U.S. Census Bureau, 2014-2018 American Community Survey 5-Year Estimates

Homeownership Rate

Area	2011 (%)	2012 (%)	2013 (%)	2014 (%)	2015 (%)	2016 (%)	2017 (%)	2018 (%)	2019 (%)
MSA[1]	n/a	n/a	n/a	n/a	n/a	n/a	n/a	n/a	n/a
U.S.	66.1	65.4	65.1	64.5	63.7	63.4	63.9	64.4	64.6

Note: (1) Figures cover the Ann Arbor, MI Metropolitan Statistical Area—see Appendix B for areas included; n/a not available
Source: U.S. Census Bureau, Housing Vacancies and Homeownership Annual Statistics: 2011-2019

Year Housing Structure Built

Area	2010 or Later	2000 -2009	1990 -1999	1980 -1989	1970 -1979	1960 -1969	1950 -1959	1940 -1949	Before 1940	Median Year
City	3.1	6.1	11.0	10.7	16.8	18.0	13.5	5.6	15.3	1969
MSA[1]	2.9	13.4	17.2	11.5	16.2	12.2	10.6	4.4	11.6	1977
U.S.	4.1	14.3	13.9	13.5	15.3	10.7	10.4	5.0	12.8	1977

Note: Figures are percentages except for Median Year; Note: (1) Figures cover the Ann Arbor, MI Metropolitan Statistical Area—see Appendix B for areas included
Source: U.S. Census Bureau, 2014-2018 American Community Survey 5-Year Estimates

Gross Monthly Rent

Area	Under $500	$500 -$999	$1,000 -$1,499	$1,500 -$1,999	$2,000 -$2,499	$2,500 -$2,999	$3,000 and up	Median ($)
City	4.4	26.8	39.2	17.5	7.4	2.3	2.4	1,213
MSA[1]	5.5	37.1	36.7	13.1	4.4	1.6	1.6	1,083
U.S.	9.8	38.5	29.6	12.9	5.1	2.1	2.0	1,023

Note: Figures are percentages except for Median; Gross rent is the contract rent plus the estimated average monthly cost of utilities (electricity, gas, and water and sewer) and fuels (oil, coal, kerosene, wood, etc.) if these are paid by the renter (or paid for the renter by someone else); (1) Figures cover the Ann Arbor, MI Metropolitan Statistical Area—see Appendix B for areas included
Source: U.S. Census Bureau, 2014-2018 American Community Survey 5-Year Estimates

HEALTH

Health Risk Factors

Category	MSA[1] (%)	U.S. (%)
Adults aged 18–64 who have any kind of health care coverage	n/a	87.3
Adults who reported being in good or better health	n/a	82.4
Adults who have been told they have high blood cholesterol	n/a	33.0
Adults who have been told they have high blood pressure	n/a	32.3
Adults who are current smokers	n/a	17.1
Adults who currently use E-cigarettes	n/a	4.6
Adults who currently use chewing tobacco, snuff, or snus	n/a	4.0
Adults who are heavy drinkers[2]	n/a	6.3
Adults who are binge drinkers[3]	n/a	17.4
Adults who are overweight (BMI 25.0 - 29.9)	n/a	35.3
Adults who are obese (BMI 30.0 - 99.8)	n/a	31.3
Adults who participated in any physical activities in the past month	n/a	74.4
Adults who always or nearly always wears a seat belt	n/a	94.3

Note: n/a not available; (1) Figures cover the Ann Arbor, MI Metropolitan Statistical Area—see Appendix B for areas included; (2) Heavy drinkers are classified as adult men having more than 14 drinks per week and adult women having more than 7 drinks per week; (3) Binge drinkers are classified as males having five or more drinks on one occasion or females having four or more drinks on one occasion
Source: Centers for Disease Control and Prevention, Behaviorial Risk Factor Surveillance System, SMART: Selected Metropolitan Area Risk Trends, 2017

Acute and Chronic Health Conditions

Category	MSA[1] (%)	U.S. (%)
Adults who have ever been told they had a heart attack	n/a	4.2
Adults who have ever been told they have angina or coronary heart disease	n/a	3.9
Adults who have ever been told they had a stroke	n/a	3.0
Adults who have ever been told they have asthma	n/a	14.2
Adults who have ever been told they have arthritis	n/a	24.9
Adults who have ever been told they have diabetes[2]	n/a	10.5
Adults who have ever been told they had skin cancer	n/a	6.2
Adults who have ever been told they had any other types of cancer	n/a	7.1
Adults who have ever been told they have COPD	n/a	6.5
Adults who have ever been told they have kidney disease	n/a	3.0
Adults who have ever been told they have a form of depression	n/a	20.5

Note: n/a not available; (1) Figures cover the Ann Arbor, MI Metropolitan Statistical Area—see Appendix B for areas included; (2) Figures do not include pregnancy-related, borderline, or pre-diabetes
Source: Centers for Disease Control and Prevention, Behaviorial Risk Factor Surveillance System, SMART: Selected Metropolitan Area Risk Trends, 2017

Health Screening and Vaccination Rates

Category	MSA[1] (%)	U.S. (%)
Adults aged 65+ who have had flu shot within the past year	n/a	60.7
Adults aged 65+ who have ever had a pneumonia vaccination	n/a	75.4
Adults who have ever been tested for HIV	n/a	36.1
Adults who have ever had the shingles or zoster vaccine?	n/a	28.9
Adults who have had their blood cholesterol checked within the last five years	n/a	85.9

Note: n/a not available; (1) Figures cover the Ann Arbor, MI Metropolitan Statistical Area—see Appendix B for areas included.
Source: Centers for Disease Control and Prevention, Behavioral Risk Factor Surveillance System, SMART: Selected Metropolitan Area Risk Trends, 2017

Disability Status

Category	MSA[1] (%)	U.S. (%)
Adults who reported being deaf	n/a	6.7
Are you blind or have serious difficulty seeing, even when wearing glasses?	n/a	4.5
Are you limited in any way in any of your usual activities due of arthritis?	n/a	12.9
Do you have difficulty doing errands alone?	n/a	6.8
Do you have difficulty dressing or bathing?	n/a	3.6
Do you have serious difficulty concentrating/remembering/making decisions?	n/a	10.7
Do you have serious difficulty walking or climbing stairs?	n/a	13.6

Note: n/a not available; (1) Figures cover the Ann Arbor, MI Metropolitan Statistical Area—see Appendix B for areas included.
Source: Centers for Disease Control and Prevention, Behavioral Risk Factor Surveillance System, SMART: Selected Metropolitan Area Risk Trends, 2017

Mortality Rates for the Top 10 Causes of Death in the U.S.

ICD-10[a] Sub-Chapter	ICD-10[a] Code	Age-Adjusted Mortality Rate[1] per 100,000 population	
		County[2]	U.S.
Malignant neoplasms	C00-C97	140.3	152.4
Ischaemic heart diseases	I20-I25	83.5	92.7
Other forms of heart disease	I30-I51	46.0	52.5
Chronic lower respiratory diseases	J40-J47	26.8	40.4
Cerebrovascular diseases	I60-I69	34.1	37.3
Other degenerative diseases of the nervous system	G30-G31	40.8	36.4
Other external causes of accidental injury	W00-X59	35.2	35.3
Organic, including symptomatic, mental disorders	F01-F09	21.6	30.0
Hypertensive diseases	I10-I15	28.4	22.9
Diabetes mellitus	E10-E14	11.5	21.3

Note: (a) ICD-10 = International Classification of Diseases 10th Revision; (1) Mortality rates are a three year average covering 2016-2018; (2) Figures cover Washtenaw County.
Source: Centers for Disease Control and Prevention, National Center for Health Statistics. Underlying Cause of Death 1999-2018 on CDC WONDER Online Database

Mortality Rates for Selected Causes of Death

ICD-10[a] Sub-Chapter	ICD-10[a] Code	Age-Adjusted Mortality Rate[1] per 100,000 population	
		County[2]	U.S.
Assault	X85-Y09	3.2	6.0
Diseases of the liver	K70-K76	8.6	14.2
Human immunodeficiency virus (HIV) disease	B20-B24	Suppressed	1.6
Influenza and pneumonia	J09-J18	8.6	14.2
Intentional self-harm	X60-X84	10.4	13.9
Malnutrition	E40-E46	Unreliable	1.9
Obesity and other hyperalimentation	E65-E68	Suppressed	2.1
Renal failure	N17-N19	9.0	12.8
Transport accidents	V01-V99	7.6	12.5
Viral hepatitis	B15-B19	Suppressed	1.4

Note: (a) ICD-10 = International Classification of Diseases 10th Revision; (1) Mortality rates are a three year average covering 2016-2018; (2) Figures cover Washtenaw County; Data are suppressed when the data meet the criteria for confidentiality constraints; Mortality rates are flagged as unreliable when the rate would be calculated with a numerator of 20 or less.
Source: Centers for Disease Control and Prevention, National Center for Health Statistics. Underlying Cause of Death 1999-2018 on CDC WONDER Online Database

Health Insurance Coverage

Area	With Health Insurance	With Private Health Insurance	With Public Health Insurance	Without Health Insurance	Population Under Age 19 Without Health Insurance
City	97.3	87.8	19.8	2.7	1.1
MSA[1]	96.1	83.5	25.1	3.9	1.9
U.S.	90.6	67.7	34.7	9.4	5.2

Note: Figures are percentages that cover the civilian noninstitutionalized population; (1) Figures cover the Ann Arbor, MI Metropolitan Statistical Area—see Appendix B for areas included
Source: U.S. Census Bureau, 2014-2018 American Community Survey 5-Year Estimates

Number of Medical Professionals

Area	MDs[3]	DOs[3,4]	Dentists	Podiatrists	Chiropractors	Optometrists
County[1] (number)	4,523	153	656	27	94	61
County[1] (rate[2])	1,230.3	41.6	176.8	7.3	25.3	16.4
U.S. (rate[2])	281.9	23.4	69.1	6.0	27.5	16.4

Note: Data as of 2018 unless noted; (1) Data covers Washtenaw County; (2) Rate per 100,000 population; (3) Data as of 2017 and includes all active, non-federal physicians; (4) Doctor of Osteopathic Medicine
Source: U.S. Department of Health and Human Services, Health Resources and Services Administration, Bureau of Health Professions, Area Resource File (ARF) 2018-2019

Best Hospitals

According to *U.S. News,* the Ann Arbor, MI metro area is home to two of the best hospitals in the U.S.: **Kellogg Eye Center-Michigan Medicine** (14 adult specialties and 10 pediatric specialties); **University of Michigan Hospitals-Michigan Medicine** (Honor Roll/14 adult specialties and 10 pediatric specialties). The hospitals listed were nationally ranked in at least one of 16 adult or 10 pediatric specialties. Only 206 hospitals nationwide were nationally ranked in one or more adult or pediatric specialty. Twenty hospitals in the U.S. made the Honor Roll. The Best Hospitals Honor Roll takes both the national rankings and the procedure and condition ratings into account. Hospitals received points if they were nationally ranked in one of the 16 adult specialties—the higher they ranked, the more points they got—and how many ratings of "high performing" they earned in the nine procedures and conditions. *U.S. News Online, "America's Best Hospitals 2019-20"*

According to *U.S. News,* the Ann Arbor, MI metro area is home to one of the best children's hospitals in the U.S.: **C.S. Mott Children's Hospital-Michigan Medicine** (10 pediatric specialties). The hospital listed was highly ranked in at least one of 10 pediatric specialties. Ninety-one children's hospitals in the U.S. were nationally ranked in at least one specialty. Hospitals received points for being ranked in a specialty, and the 10 hospitals with the most points across the 10 specialties make up the Honor Roll. *U.S. News Online, "America's Best Children's Hospitals 2019-20"*

EDUCATION

Public School District Statistics

District Name	Schls	Pupils	Pupil/ Teacher Ratio	Minority Pupils[1] (%)	Free Lunch Eligible[2] (%)	IEP[3] (%)
Ann Arbor Public Schools	33	18,054	15.3	48.6	22.2	11.9

Note: Table includes school districts with 2,000 or more students; (1) Percentage of students that are not non-Hispanic white; (2) Percentage of students that are eligible for the free lunch program; (3) Percentage of students that have an Individualized Education Program.
Source: U.S. Department of Education, National Center for Education Statistics, Common Core of Data, Local Education Agency (School District) Universe Survey: School Year 2018-2019; U.S. Department of Education, National Center for Education Statistics, Common Core of Data, Public Elementary/Secondary School Universe Survey: School Year 2018-2019

Highest Level of Education

Area	Less than H.S.	H.S. Diploma	Some College, No Deg.	Associate Degree	Bachelor's Degree	Master's Degree	Prof. School Degree	Doctorate Degree
City	2.9	7.3	10.4	3.8	30.5	26.9	7.3	10.8
MSA[1]	4.8	14.9	18.0	7.1	26.2	18.8	4.6	5.6
U.S.	12.3	27.1	20.6	8.4	19.4	8.6	2.1	1.4

Note: Figures cover persons age 25 and over; (1) Figures cover the Ann Arbor, MI Metropolitan Statistical Area—see Appendix B for areas included
Source: U.S. Census Bureau, 2014-2018 American Community Survey 5-Year Estimates

Educational Attainment by Race

Area	High School Graduate or Higher (%)					Bachelor's Degree or Higher (%)				
	Total	White	Black	Asian	Hisp.[2]	Total	White	Black	Asian	Hisp.[2]
City	97.1	98.3	87.8	96.6	91.8	75.5	78.0	36.6	84.2	69.2
MSA[1]	95.2	96.4	88.9	95.9	84.7	55.2	57.0	27.1	82.0	41.6
U.S.	87.7	89.6	85.4	86.8	67.7	31.5	32.9	21.1	53.5	15.8

Note: Figures shown cover persons 25 years old and over; (1) Figures cover the Ann Arbor, MI Metropolitan Statistical Area—see Appendix B for areas included; (2) People of Hispanic origin can be of any race
Source: U.S. Census Bureau, 2014-2018 American Community Survey 5-Year Estimates

School Enrollment by Grade and Control

Area	Preschool (%)		Kindergarten (%)		Grades 1 - 4 (%)		Grades 5 - 8 (%)		Grades 9 - 12 (%)	
	Public	Private	Public	Private	Public	Private	Public	Private	Public	Private
City	25.3	74.7	92.2	7.8	91.3	8.7	84.3	15.7	94.6	5.4
MSA[1]	44.1	55.9	86.4	13.6	87.3	12.7	86.9	13.1	92.0	8.0
U.S.	59.0	41.0	87.7	12.3	89.6	10.4	89.5	10.5	90.2	9.8

Note: Figures shown cover persons 3 years old and over; (1) Figures cover the Ann Arbor, MI Metropolitan Statistical Area—see Appendix B for areas included
Source: U.S. Census Bureau, 2014-2018 American Community Survey 5-Year Estimates

Average Salaries of Public School Teachers

Area	2016-17		2017-18		Change from 2016-17 to 2017-18	
	Dollars	Rank[1]	Dollars	Rank[1]	Percent	Rank[2]
Michigan	62,287	12	61,911	13	-0.6	49
U.S. Average	59,539	–	60,477	–	1.58	–

Note: (1) Rank ranges from 1 to 51 where 1 indicates highest salary; (2) Rank ranges from 1 to 51 where 1 indicates highest percent change.
Source: National Education Association, Rankings & Estimates: Rankings of the States 2018 and Estimates of School Statistics 2019

Higher Education

Four-Year Colleges			Two-Year Colleges			Medical Schools[1]	Law Schools[2]	Voc/ Tech[3]
Public	Private Non-profit	Private For-profit	Public	Private Non-profit	Private For-profit			
1	1	0	1	0	0	1	1	1

Note: Figures cover institutions located within the city limits and include main campuses only; (1) includes schools accredited by the Liaison Committee on Medical Education and the American Osteopathic Association's Commission on Osteopathic College Accreditation; (2) includes ABA-accredited schools, schools with provisional ABA accreditation, and state accredited schools; (3) includes all schools with programs that are less than 2 years.
Source: National Center for Education Statistics, Integrated Postsecondary Education System (IPEDS), 2018-19; Wikipedia, List of Medical Schools in the United States, accessed May 1, 2020; Wikipedia, List of Law Schools in the United States, accessed May 1, 2020

According to *U.S. News & World Report*, the Ann Arbor, MI metro area is home to one of the top 200 national universities in the U.S.: **University of Michigan—Ann Arbor** (#25 tie). The indicators used to capture academic quality fall into a number of categories: assessment by administrators at peer institutions; retention of students; faculty resources; student selectivity; financial resources; alumni giving; high school counselor ratings of colleges; and graduation rate. *U.S. News & World Report, "America's Best Colleges 2020"*

According to *U.S. News & World Report*, the Ann Arbor, MI metro area is home to one of the top 100 law schools in the U.S.: **University of Michigan—Ann Arbor** (#9 tie). The rankings are based on a weighted average of 12 measures of quality: peer assessment score; assessment score by lawyers/judges; median LSAT scores; median undergrad GPA; acceptance rate; employment rates for graduates; placement success; bar passage rate; faculty resources; expenditures per student; student/faculty ratio; and library resources. *U.S. News & World Report, "America's Best Graduate Schools, Law, 2021"*

According to *U.S. News & World Report*, the Ann Arbor, MI metro area is home to one of the top 75 medical schools for research in the U.S.: **University of Michigan—Ann Arbor** (#15 tie). The rankings are based on a weighted average of 11 measures of quality: quality assessment; peer assessment score; assessment score by residency directors; research activity; total research activity; average research activity per faculty member; student selectivity; median MCAT total score; median undergraduate GPA; acceptance rate; and faculty resources. *U.S. News & World Report, "America's Best Graduate Schools, Medical, 2021"*

According to *U.S. News & World Report,* the Ann Arbor, MI metro area is home to one of the top 75 business schools in the U.S.: **University of Michigan—Ann Arbor (Ross)** (#12 tie). The rankings are based on a weighted average of the following nine measures: quality assessment; peer assessment; recruiter assessment; placement success; mean starting salary and bonus; student selectivity; mean GMAT and GRE scores; mean undergraduate GPA; and acceptance rate. *U.S. News & World Report, "America's Best Graduate Schools, Business, 2021"*

PRESIDENTIAL ELECTION

2016 Presidential Election Results

Area	Clinton	Trump	Johnson	Stein	Other
Washtenaw County	67.6	26.6	3.1	1.3	1.4
U.S.	48.0	45.9	3.3	1.1	1.7

Note: Results are percentages and may not add to 100% due to rounding
Source: Dave Leip's Atlas of U.S. Presidential Elections

EMPLOYERS

Major Employers

Company Name	Industry
Ann Arbor Public Schools	Education
Citizens Insurance Company of America	FInance & insurance
City of Ann Arbor	Government
Domino's Pizza	Food services
Eastern Michigan University	Education
Faurecia Interior Systems	Automotive component mfg.
Ford Motor Company	Automotive component mfg.
General Motors Milford Proving Grounds	OEM research
Grupo Antolin	Automotive component mfg.
Integrated Health Associates (IHA)	Medical center
JAC Products	Auto component mfg.
ProQuest	Data & information
Terumo Carviocascular Systems	Medical device manufacturer
Thai Summit America	Automotive component mfg.
Thomson Reuters	Software/IT
Toyota Technical Center	Automotive research & development
Trinity Health	Medical center
Truven Health Analytics	Data & information
University of Michigan	Education
University of Michigan Medical Center	Medical center
VA Ann Arbor Healthcare System	Medical center
Washtenaw Community College	Education
Washtenaw County Government	Government
Ypsilanti Public Schools	Education
Zingerman's	Food processing

Note: Companies shown are located within the Ann Arbor, MI Metropolitan Statistical Area.
Source: Hoovers.com; Wikipedia

PUBLIC SAFETY

Crime Rate

Area	All Crimes	Violent Crimes				Property Crimes		
		Murder	Rape[3]	Robbery	Aggrav. Assault	Burglary	Larceny -Theft	Motor Vehicle Theft
City	1,796.5	1.6	44.9	36.7	137.1	175.4	1,346.2	54.7
Suburbs[1]	1,829.6	4.4	76.3	41.0	251.3	252.1	1,096.9	107.6
Metro[2]	1,818.7	3.5	65.9	39.6	213.6	226.8	1,179.1	90.1
U.S.	2,580.1	5.0	42.6	86.2	246.8	376.0	1,594.6	228.9

Note: Figures are crimes per 100,000 population; (1) All areas within the metro area that are located outside the city limits; (2) Figures cover the Ann Arbor, MI Metropolitan Statistical Area—see Appendix B for areas included; (3) The city and U.S. figures shown were reported using the revised Uniform Crime Reporting (UCR) definition of rape. The suburban and metro area figures shown are an aggregate total of the data submitted using both the revised and legacy UCR definitions.
Source: FBI Uniform Crime Reports, 2018

Hate Crimes

Area	Number of Quarters Reported	Number of Incidents per Bias Motivation					
		Race/Ethnicity/ Ancestry	Religion	Sexual Orientation	Disability	Gender	Gender Identity
City	4	3	5	1	0	0	0
U.S.	4	4,047	1,419	1,196	159	47	168

Source: Federal Bureau of Investigation, Hate Crime Statistics 2018

Identity Theft Consumer Reports

Area	Reports	Reports per 100,000 Population	Rank[2]
MSA[1]	512	138	110
U.S.	650,572	198	-

Note: (1) Figures cover the Ann Arbor, MI Metropolitan Statistical Area—see Appendix B for areas included; (2) Rank ranges from 1 to 386 where 1 indicates greatest number of identity theft reports per 100,000 population
Source: Federal Trade Commission, Consumer Sentinel Network Data Book for January–December 2019

Fraud and Other Consumer Reports

Area	Reports	Reports per 100,000 Population	Rank[2]
MSA[1]	1,953	526	216
U.S.	2,590,177	789	-

Note: (1) Figures cover the Ann Arbor, MI Metropolitan Statistical Area—see Appendix B for areas included; (2) Rank ranges from 1 to 386 where 1 indicates greatest number of fraud and other consumer reports per 100,000 population
Source: Federal Trade Commission, Consumer Sentinel Network Data Book for January–December 2019

SPORTS

Professional Sports Teams

Team Name	League	Year Established
No teams are located in the metro area		

Source: Wikipedia, Major Professional Sports Teams of the United States and Canada, May 4, 2020

CLIMATE

Average and Extreme Temperatures

Temperature	Jan	Feb	Mar	Apr	May	Jun	Jul	Aug	Sep	Oct	Nov	Dec	Yr.
Extreme High (°F)	62	65	81	89	93	104	102	100	98	91	77	68	104
Average High (°F)	30	33	44	58	70	79	83	81	74	61	48	35	58
Average Temp. (°F)	23	26	36	48	59	68	72	71	64	52	40	29	49
Average Low (°F)	16	18	27	37	47	56	61	60	53	41	32	21	39
Extreme Low (°F)	-21	-15	-4	10	25	36	41	38	29	17	9	-10	-21

Note: Figures cover the years 1958-1990
Source: National Climatic Data Center, International Station Meteorological Climate Summary, 9/96

Average Precipitation/Snowfall/Humidity

Precip./Humidity	Jan	Feb	Mar	Apr	May	Jun	Jul	Aug	Sep	Oct	Nov	Dec	Yr.
Avg. Precip. (in.)	1.8	1.8	2.5	3.0	2.9	3.6	3.1	3.4	2.8	2.2	2.6	2.7	32.4
Avg. Snowfall (in.)	10	9	7	2	Tr	0	0	0	0	Tr	3	11	41
Avg. Rel. Hum. 7am (%)	80	79	79	78	78	79	82	86	87	84	82	81	81
Avg. Rel. Hum. 4pm (%)	67	63	59	53	51	52	52	54	55	55	64	70	58

Note: Figures cover the years 1958-1990; Tr = Trace amounts (<0.05 in. of rain; <0.5 in. of snow)
Source: National Climatic Data Center, International Station Meteorological Climate Summary, 9/96

Weather Conditions

Temperature			Daytime Sky			Precipitation		
5°F & below	32°F & below	90°F & above	Clear	Partly cloudy	Cloudy	0.01 inch or more precip.	0.1 inch or more snow/ice	Thunder-storms
15	136	12	74	134	157	135	38	32

Note: Figures are average number of days per year and cover the years 1958-1990
Source: National Climatic Data Center, International Station Meteorological Climate Summary, 9/96

**HAZARDOUS
WASTE**

Superfund Sites

The Ann Arbor, MI metro area has no sites on the EPA's Superfund Final National Priorities List. There are a total of 1,387 Superfund sites with a status of proposed or final on the list in the U.S.
U.S. Environmental Protection Agency, National Priorities List, May 5, 2020

**AIR & WATER
QUALITY**

Air Quality Trends: Ozone

	1990	1995	2000	2005	2010	2012	2014	2016	2017	2018
MSA[1]	n/a	n/a	n/a	n/a	n/a	n/a	n/a	n/a	n/a	n/a
U.S.	0.088	0.089	0.082	0.080	0.073	0.075	0.067	0.069	0.068	0.069

*Note: (1) Data covers the Ann Arbor, MI Metropolitan Statistical Area—see Appendix B for areas included; n/a not available. The values shown are the composite ozone concentration averages among trend sites based on the highest fourth daily maximum 8-hour concentration in parts per million. These trends are based on sites having an adequate record of monitoring data during the trend period. Data from exceptional events are included.
Source: U.S. Environmental Protection Agency, Air Quality Monitoring Information, "Air Quality Trends by City, 1990-2018"*

Air Quality Index

Area	Percent of Days when Air Quality was...[2]					AQI Statistics[2]	
	Good	Moderate	Unhealthy for Sensitive Groups	Unhealthy	Very Unhealthy	Maximum	Median
MSA[1]	77.0	21.4	1.6	0.0	0.0	150	40

*Note: (1) Data covers the Ann Arbor, MI Metropolitan Statistical Area—see Appendix B for areas included; (2) Based on 365 days with AQI data in 2018. Air Quality Index (AQI) is an index for reporting daily air quality. EPA calculates the AQI for five major air pollutants regulated by the Clean Air Act: ground-level ozone, particle pollution (aka particulate matter), carbon monoxide, sulfur dioxide, and nitrogen dioxide. The AQI runs from 0 to 500. The higher the AQI value, the greater the level of air pollution and the greater the health concern. There are six AQI categories: "Good" AQI is between 0 and 50. Air quality is considered satisfactory; "Moderate" AQI is between 51 and 100. Air quality is acceptable; "Unhealthy for Sensitive Groups" When AQI values are between 101 and 150, members of sensitive groups may experience health effects; "Unhealthy" When AQI values are between 151 and 200 everyone may begin to experience health effects; "Very Unhealthy" AQI values between 201 and 300 trigger a health alert; "Hazardous" AQI values over 300 trigger warnings of emergency conditions (not shown).
Source: U.S. Environmental Protection Agency, Air Quality Index Report, 2018*

Air Quality Index Pollutants

Area	Percent of Days when AQI Pollutant was...[2]					
	Carbon Monoxide	Nitrogen Dioxide	Ozone	Sulfur Dioxide	Particulate Matter 2.5	Particulate Matter 10
MSA[1]	0.0	0.0	64.1	0.0	35.9	0.0

*Note: (1) Data covers the Ann Arbor, MI Metropolitan Statistical Area—see Appendix B for areas included; (2) Based on 365 days with AQI data in 2018. The Air Quality Index (AQI) is an index for reporting daily air quality. EPA calculates the AQI for five major air pollutants regulated by the Clean Air Act: ground-level ozone, particle pollution (also known as particulate matter), carbon monoxide, sulfur dioxide, and nitrogen dioxide. The AQI runs from 0 to 500. The higher the AQI value, the greater the level of air pollution and the greater the health concern.
Source: U.S. Environmental Protection Agency, Air Quality Index Report, 2018*

Maximum Air Pollutant Concentrations: Particulate Matter, Ozone, CO and Lead

	Particulate Matter 10 (ug/m³)	Particulate Matter 2.5 Wtd AM (ug/m³)	Particulate Matter 2.5 24-Hr (ug/m³)	Ozone (ppm)	Carbon Monoxide (ppm)	Lead (ug/m³)
MSA[1] Level	n/a	8.3	21	0.072	n/a	n/a
NAAQS[2]	150	15	35	0.075	9	0.15
Met NAAQS[2]	n/a	Yes	Yes	Yes	n/a	n/a

Note: (1) Data covers the Ann Arbor, MI Metropolitan Statistical Area—see Appendix B for areas included; Data from exceptional events are included; (2) National Ambient Air Quality Standards; ppm = parts per million; ug/m³ = micrograms per cubic meter; n/a not available.
Concentrations: Particulate Matter 10 (coarse particulate)—highest second maximum 24-hour concentration; Particulate Matter 2.5 Wtd AM (fine particulate)—highest weighted annual mean concentration; Particulate Matter 2.5 24-Hour (fine particulate)—highest 98th percentile 24-hour concentration; Ozone—highest fourth daily maximum 8-hour concentration; Carbon Monoxide—highest second maximum non-overlapping 8-hour concentration; Lead—maximum running 3-month average
Source: U.S. Environmental Protection Agency, Air Quality Monitoring Information, "Air Quality Statistics by City, 2018"

Maximum Air Pollutant Concentrations: Nitrogen Dioxide and Sulfur Dioxide

	Nitrogen Dioxide AM (ppb)	Nitrogen Dioxide 1-Hr (ppb)	Sulfur Dioxide AM (ppb)	Sulfur Dioxide 1-Hr (ppb)	Sulfur Dioxide 24-Hr (ppb)
MSA[1] Level	n/a	n/a	n/a	n/a	n/a
NAAQS[2]	53	100	30	75	140
Met NAAQS[2]	n/a	n/a	n/a	n/a	n/a

Note: (1) Data covers the Ann Arbor, MI Metropolitan Statistical Area—see Appendix B for areas included; Data from exceptional events are included; (2) National Ambient Air Quality Standards; ppm = parts per million; ug/m³ = micrograms per cubic meter; n/a not available.
Concentrations: Nitrogen Dioxide AM—highest arithmetic mean concentration; Nitrogen Dioxide 1-Hr—highest 98th percentile 1-hour daily maximum concentration; Sulfur Dioxide AM—highest annual mean concentration; Sulfur Dioxide 1-Hr—highest 99th percentile 1-hour daily maximum concentration; Sulfur Dioxide 24-Hr—highest second maximum 24-hour concentration
Source: U.S. Environmental Protection Agency, Air Quality Monitoring Information, "Air Quality Statistics by City, 2018"

Drinking Water

Water System Name	Pop. Served	Primary Water Source Type	Violations[1]
Ann Arbor	118,017	Surface	42

Note: (1) Total number of violations (both active and inactive) in the EPA database
Source: U.S. Environmental Protection Agency, Office of Ground Water and Drinking Water, Safe Drinking Water Information System (based on data extracted May 5, 2020)

Cedar Rapids, Iowa

Background

Cedar Rapids, on the Cedar River that gave it its name, is the principal city in eastern Iowa, located some 100 miles northeast of Des Moines. The Cedar Rapids of today is one of the Midwest's most diversified and modern cities.

Prior to European expansion, the site was intermittently home to nomadic bands of Fox, Meskwaki, and Winnebago Indians. Its first western settler was Osgood Shephard, a hunter, trapper, and horse trader who lived in a cabin on the river at the current corner of First Avenue and First Street SE. A stainless-steel sculpture, The Tree of Five Seasons, commemorates Shephard's first settlement, and is a common point of reference for the city's citizens.

Cedar Rapids, first called Rapids City, was incorporated as a town in 1849 and as a city in 1856. By 1858 the city boasted a population of 1,400. Both in the city itself and in the immediate environs, one is exposed to rich ethnic traditions and a pride in the preservation of local performing and visual arts.

Cedar Rapids, distinctively, was the first home of the North Star Oatmeal Mill, which eventually became Quaker Oats, long a giant in the cereal industry. The Cedar Rapids-based company still operates, under one roof, the largest cereal mill in the world.

The city has extensively diversified, however, from its original agricultural focus. Many industries, both locally and internationally owned, provide stability and dynamism to the local economy, which is increasingly tied into a larger global framework. Cedar Rapids also hosts industries specializing in food processing, construction machinery, pharmaceuticals, financial services, and biotechnology, and is one of the largest exporter per capita in the United States, with the nearby Eastern Iowa Airport designated as a foreign trade zone. The city has also become a major telecommunications hub.

Cedar Rapids is home to Coe College, founded in 1851, and Mount Mercy College, founded in 1928. The National Capital Language Resource Center (NCLRC) in Washington DC maintains 93 schools that teach Arabic, one of which is in Cedar Rapids. The town also benefits from the presence of the Cedar Rapids Museum of Art, the Cedar Rapids Symphony Orchestra, the Science Station, which boasts the first IMAX Theater in Iowa, the History Center, and the National Czech and Slovak Museum and Library. Other area attractions include Duffy's Collectible Cars, Brucemore Mansion, the Iowa Children's Museum, the Indian Creek Nature Center, and the Czech Village. Government buildings are located on Municipal Island in the main channel of the Cedar River. Within a half-hour's drive are 75 public parks and seven public golf courses.

Nearby are several points of historical interest, including the Herbert Hoover Birthplace and Library, and the Amana Colonies, founded in the 1850s as a utopian society by members of a German religious sect. At the Amana villages, visitors can still view the operations of working farms, wool mills, and bakeries. Cedar Rapids is also the home to a large number of American Muslims. The oldest exclusively Muslim cemetery in the United States is located in Cedar Rapids, along with the historic Mother Mosque of America.

Grant Wood—the famous painter of *American Gothic* and other icons of the Great Plains—was a resident of the city and taught there for many years. Many of his canvases are on display and others are owned by private citizens. The Cedar Rapids Museum houses 7,200 works of art, including the world's largest collections of works by Wood, Marvin D. Cone, and Mauricio Lasansky. The Museum also operates the Grant Wood Studio and Visitor Center.

In June 2008, the Cedar River flooded its banks, leaving 1,300 city blocks under water. The city was almost entirely evacuated and hundreds of homes were destroyed. Rebuilding efforts have been strong and a restored City Hall and Paramount Theater opened in 2012, with many other facilities opening in 2013, including fire stations, the library, and the ground transportation center. In September 2016, when Hurricane Paine threatened to flood Cedar Rapids again, the residents were prepared as hundreds of thousands of volunteers, as well as over 400 National Guard troops, filled more than 250,000 sand bags which effectively prevented major flooding of the city.

There are four distinct seasons in Cedar Rapids. Winters are cold and dry, with winds out of the northwest. Some summer days bring rain from the Gulf of Mexico, but on other days hot dry air from the southwest can cause unusually high temperatures. Fall and spring can be mild, tempered by air from the Pacific. Precipitation throughout the year is moderate.

Rankings

General Rankings

- Cedar Rapids was selected as one of the best places to live in the United States by *Money* magazine. The city ranked #83 out of 100. This year's list focused on cities with populations of 50,000 or greater. Beginning with a pool of 1,796 candidates, editors looked at 80 separate types of data, from local economy and housing market to education, diversity and ease of living—and then sent reporters to interview residents, search neighborhoods and look for other intangibles. *Money, "Best Places to Live, 2019" September 16, 2019*

- In their sixth annual survey, Livability.com looked at data for more than 1,000 U.S. cities to determine the rankings for Livability's "Top 100 Best Places to Live" in 2019. Cedar Rapids ranked #50. Criteria: median home value capped at $250,000; affordable living; vibrant economy; education, demographics, health care options, transportation & infrastructure; abundant lifestyle amenities. *Livability.com, "Top 100 Best Places to Live 2019" March 2019*

Business/Finance Rankings

- The Cedar Rapids metro area appeared on the Milken Institute "2020 Best Performing Cities" list. Rank: #164 out of 200 large metro areas. Criteria: job growth; wage and salary growth; high-tech output growth. *Milken Institute, "Best-Performing Cities 2020," February 26, 2020*

- *Forbes* ranked the 200 most populous metro areas to determine the nation's "Best Places for Business and Careers." The Cedar Rapids metro area was ranked #154. Criteria: costs (business and living); job growth (past and projected); income growth; quality of life; educational attainment (college and high school); projected economic growth; cultural and leisure opportunities; workplace tolerance laws; net migration patterns. *Forbes, "The Best Places for Business and Careers 2019: Seattle Still On Top," October 30, 2019*

Environmental Rankings

- Cedar Rapids was highlighted as one of the cleanest metro areas for ozone air pollution in the U.S. during 2015 through 2017. The list represents cities with no monitored ozone air pollution in unhealthful ranges. *American Lung Association, "State of the Air 2019," April 24, 2019*

Health/Fitness Rankings

- The Cedar Rapids metro area was identified as one of the worst cities for bed bugs in America by pest control company Orkin. The area ranked #41 out of 50 based on the number of bed bug treatments Orkin performed from December 2018 to November 2019. *Orkin, "Washington, D.C. Surpasses Baltimore to Secure Top Spot on Orkin's 2020 Bed Bug Cities List," January 13, 2020*

- The Cedar Rapids metro area ranked #135 out of 189 in The Gallup-Sharecare Well-Being Index. Criteria: purpose; social well being; financial health; community and physical health. Results are based on telephone interviews with adults, aged 18 and older, living in metropolitan areas in the 50 U.S. states and the District of Columbia. *Gallup-Sharecare, "State of American Well-Being, 2017 Community Well-Being Rankings" March 2018*

Real Estate Rankings

- *WalletHub* compared the most populated U.S. cities, as well as at least two of the most populated cities in each state, for a total of 179, to determine which had the best markets for real estate agents. Cedar Rapids ranked #141 where demand was high and pay was the best. Criteria: sales per agent; annual median wage for real-estate agents; monthly average starting salary for real estate agents; real estate job density and competition; unemployment rate; home turnover rate; housing-market health index; and other relevant metrics. *www.WalletHub.com, "2019's Best Places to Be a Real Estate Agent," April 24, 2019*

Safety Rankings

- The National Insurance Crime Bureau ranked 382 metro areas in the U.S. in terms of per capita rates of vehicle theft. The Cedar Rapids metro area ranked #175 (#1 = highest rate). Criteria: number of vehicle theft offenses per 100,000 inhabitants in 2018. *National Insurance Crime Bureau, "Hot Spots 2018," June 25, 2019*

Seniors/Retirement Rankings

- From its Best Cities for Successful Aging indexes, the Milken Institute generated rankings for metropolitan areas, weighing data in nine categories—health care, wellness, living arrangements, transportation and convenience, financial characteristics, education, employment, community engagement, and overall livability. The Cedar Rapids metro area was ranked #82 overall in the small metro area category. *Milken Institute, "Best Cities for Successful Aging, 2017" March 14, 2017*

Women/Minorities Rankings

- Personal finance website *WalletHub* compared more than 180 U.S. cities—including the 150 most populated U.S. cities, plus at least two of the most populated cities in each state—across two key dimensions, "Hispanic Business-Friendliness" and "Hispanic Purchasing Power", to arrive at the most favorable conditions for Hispanic entrepreneurs. Cedar Rapids was ranked #89 out of 182. Criteria includes: share of Hispanic-Owned Businesses; Hispanic entrepreneurship rate to median annual income of Hispanics; Small Business-Friendliness score; cost of living; and number of Hispanics with at least a bachelor's degree. *WalletHub.com, "2019's Best Cities for Hispanic Entrepreneurs," May 1, 2019*

Miscellaneous Rankings

- *WalletHub* compared the 150 most populated U.S. cities to determine their operating efficiency. A "Quality of Services" score was constructed for each city and then divided by the total budget per capita to reveal which were managed the best. Cedar Rapids ranked #15. Criteria: financial stability; economy; education; safety; health; infrastructure and pollution. *www.WalletHub.com, "2019's Best- & Worst-Run Cities in America," July 1, 2019*

Business Environment

CITY FINANCES

City Government Finances

Component	2017 ($000)	2017 ($ per capita)
Total Revenues	415,539	3,187
Total Expenditures	435,280	3,338
Debt Outstanding	489,631	3,755
Cash and Securities[1]	462,724	3,548

Note: (1) Cash and security holdings of a government at the close of its fiscal year, including those of its dependent agencies, utilities, and liquor stores.
Source: U.S. Census Bureau, State & Local Government Finances 2017

City Government Revenue by Source

Source	2017 ($000)	2017 ($ per capita)	2017 (%)
General Revenue			
From Federal Government	60,539	464	14.6
From State Government	38,079	292	9.2
From Local Governments	772	6	0.2
Taxes			
Property	97,949	751	23.6
Sales and Gross Receipts	36,926	283	8.9
Personal Income	0	0	0.0
Corporate Income	0	0	0.0
Motor Vehicle License	0	0	0.0
Other Taxes	2,644	20	0.6
Current Charges	111,605	856	26.9
Liquor Store	0	0	0.0
Utility	34,360	263	8.3
Employee Retirement	0	0	0.0

Source: U.S. Census Bureau, State & Local Government Finances 2017

City Government Expenditures by Function

Function	2017 ($000)	2017 ($ per capita)	2017 (%)
General Direct Expenditures			
Air Transportation	26,109	200	6.0
Corrections	0	0	0.0
Education	0	0	0.0
Employment Security Administration	0	0	0.0
Financial Administration	5,150	39	1.2
Fire Protection	20,748	159	4.8
General Public Buildings	1,127	8	0.3
Governmental Administration, Other	2,826	21	0.6
Health	1,198	9	0.3
Highways	19,315	148	4.4
Hospitals	0	0	0.0
Housing and Community Development	7,739	59	1.8
Interest on General Debt	14,516	111	3.3
Judicial and Legal	876	6	0.2
Libraries	5,710	43	1.3
Parking	1,033	7	0.2
Parks and Recreation	11,072	84	2.5
Police Protection	45,215	346	10.4
Public Welfare	0	0	0.0
Sewerage	38,095	292	8.8
Solid Waste Management	23,139	177	5.3
Veterans' Services	0	0	0.0
Liquor Store	0	0	0.0
Utility	47,466	364	10.9
Employee Retirement	0	0	0.0

Source: U.S. Census Bureau, State & Local Government Finances 2017

DEMOGRAPHICS

Population Growth

Area	1990 Census	2000 Census	2010 Census	2018* Estimate	Population Growth (%)	
					1990-2018	2010-2018
City	110,829	120,758	126,326	131,360	18.5	4.0
MSA[1]	210,640	237,230	257,940	268,315	27.4	4.0
U.S.	248,709,873	281,421,906	308,745,538	322,903,030	29.8	4.6

Note: (1) Figures cover the Cedar Rapids, IA Metropolitan Statistical Area—see Appendix B for areas included; (*) 2014-2018 5-year estimated population
Source: U.S. Census Bureau, 1990 Census, Census 2000, Census 2010, 2014-2018 American Community Survey 5-Year Estimates

Household Size

Area	One	Two	Three	Four	Five	Six	Seven or More	Average Household Size
City	33.5	33.9	14.3	11.5	4.0	2.1	0.6	2.40
MSA[1]	29.0	36.9	14.0	12.5	4.8	2.0	0.8	2.40
U.S.	27.7	33.9	15.7	13.0	6.0	2.3	1.4	2.60

Note: (1) Figures cover the Cedar Rapids, IA Metropolitan Statistical Area—see Appendix B for areas included
Source: U.S. Census Bureau, 2014-2018 American Community Survey 5-Year Estimates

Race

Area	White Alone[2] (%)	Black Alone[2] (%)	Asian Alone[2] (%)	AIAN[3] Alone[2] (%)	NHOPI[4] Alone[2] (%)	Other Race Alone[2] (%)	Two or More Races (%)
City	84.7	7.1	3.4	0.3	0.2	1.0	3.4
MSA[1]	89.8	4.7	2.1	0.2	0.1	0.7	2.5
U.S.	72.7	12.7	5.4	0.8	0.2	4.9	3.2

Note: (1) Figures cover the Cedar Rapids, IA Metropolitan Statistical Area—see Appendix B for areas included; (2) Alone is defined as not being in combination with one or more other races; (3) American Indian and Alaska Native; (4) Native Hawaiian and Other Pacific Islander
Source: U.S. Census Bureau, 2014-2018 American Community Survey 5-Year Estimates

Hispanic or Latino Origin

Area	Total (%)	Mexican (%)	Puerto Rican (%)	Cuban (%)	Other (%)
City	3.7	2.7	0.1	0.0	0.8
MSA[1]	2.9	2.1	0.1	0.0	0.7
U.S.	17.8	11.2	1.7	0.7	4.2

Note: Persons of Hispanic or Latino origin can be of any race; (1) Figures cover the Cedar Rapids, IA Metropolitan Statistical Area—see Appendix B for areas included
Source: U.S. Census Bureau, 2014-2018 American Community Survey 5-Year Estimates

Segregation

Type	1990	2000	2010	2010 Rank[2]	1990-2000	1990-2010	2000-2010
Black/White	n/a	n/a	n/a	n/a	n/a	n/a	n/a
Asian/White	n/a	n/a	n/a	n/a	n/a	n/a	n/a
Hispanic/White	n/a	n/a	n/a	n/a	n/a	n/a	n/a

Note: All figures cover the Metropolitan Statistical Area—see Appendix B for areas included; Figures are based on an analysis of 1990, 2000, and 2010 Census Decennial Census tract data by William H. Frey, Brookings Institution and the University of Michigan Social Science Data Analysis Network. In this analysis all racial groups (whites, blacks, and asians) are non-Hispanic members of those races. Hispanics are shown as a separate category; (1) Segregation Indices are Dissimilarity Indices that measure the degree to which the minority group is distributed differently than whites across census tracts. They range from 0 (complete integration) to 100 (complete segregation) where the value indicates the percentage of the minority group that needs to move to be distributed exactly like whites; (2) Ranges from 1 (most segregated) to 102 (least segregated); n/a not available.
Source: www.CensusScope.org

Ancestry

Area	German	Irish	English	American	Italian	Polish	French[2]	Scottish	Dutch
City	32.6	14.4	7.8	4.3	1.7	1.5	2.2	1.5	2.3
MSA[1]	35.7	14.8	7.8	4.8	1.8	1.3	2.3	1.5	2.1
U.S.	13.7	9.9	7.3	6.4	5.2	2.8	2.4	1.7	1.2

Note: Figures are the percentage of the total population reporting a particular ancestry. The nine most commonly reported ancestries in the U.S. are shown. Figures include multiple ancestries (e.g. if a person reported being Irish and Italian, they were included in both columns); (1) Figures cover the Cedar Rapids, IA Metropolitan Statistical Area—see Appendix B for areas included; (2) Excludes Basque
Source: U.S. Census Bureau, 2014-2018 American Community Survey 5-Year Estimates

Foreign-born Population

Area	Percent of Population Born in								
	Any Foreign Country	Asia	Mexico	Europe	Caribbean	Central America[2]	South America	Africa	Canada
City	5.5	2.8	0.7	0.5	0.2	0.1	0.1	0.9	0.1
MSA[1]	3.6	1.7	0.5	0.4	0.1	0.1	0.1	0.6	0.1
U.S.	13.5	4.1	3.5	1.5	1.3	1.1	0.9	0.7	0.3

Note: (1) Figures cover the Cedar Rapids, IA Metropolitan Statistical Area—see Appendix B for areas included; (2) Excludes Mexico.
Source: U.S. Census Bureau, 2014-2018 American Community Survey 5-Year Estimates

Marital Status

Area	Never Married	Now Married[2]	Separated	Widowed	Divorced
City	34.3	46.3	1.1	6.0	12.3
MSA[1]	29.2	52.7	1.0	5.9	11.2
U.S.	33.3	48.1	2.0	5.8	10.8

Note: Figures are percentages and cover the population 15 years of age and older; (1) Figures cover the Cedar Rapids, IA Metropolitan Statistical Area—see Appendix B for areas included; (2) Excludes separated
Source: U.S. Census Bureau, 2014-2018 American Community Survey 5-Year Estimates

Disability by Age

Area	All Ages	Under 18 Years Old	18 to 64 Years Old	65 Years and Over
City	10.3	3.5	8.2	30.4
MSA[1]	10.3	3.9	7.9	29.3
U.S.	12.6	4.2	10.3	35.0

Note: Figures show percent of the civilian noninstitutionalized population that reported having a disability. Disability status is determined from six types of difficulty: vision, hearing, cognitive, ambulatory, self-care, and independent living. For children under 5 years old, hearing and vision difficulty are used to determine disability status. For children between the ages of 5 and 14, disability status is determined from hearing, vision, cognitive, ambulatory, and self-care difficulties. For people aged 15 years and older, they are considered to have a disability if they have difficulty with any one of the six difficulty types; Note: (1) Figures cover the Cedar Rapids, IA Metropolitan Statistical Area—see Appendix B for areas included
Source: U.S. Census Bureau, 2014-2018 American Community Survey 5-Year Estimates

Age

Area	Percent of Population									Median Age
	Under Age 5	Age 5–19	Age 20–34	Age 35–44	Age 45–54	Age 55–64	Age 65–74	Age 75–84	Age 85+	
City	6.9	18.8	23.1	12.7	11.8	11.9	8.0	4.4	2.4	35.8
MSA[1]	6.2	19.7	19.6	12.6	13.3	12.8	8.7	4.8	2.3	38.2
U.S.	6.1	19.3	20.7	12.6	13.2	12.8	8.8	4.5	1.9	37.9

Note: (1) Figures cover the Cedar Rapids, IA Metropolitan Statistical Area—see Appendix B for areas included
Source: U.S. Census Bureau, 2014-2018 American Community Survey 5-Year Estimates

Gender

Area	Males	Females	Males per 100 Females
City	64,422	66,938	96.2
MSA[1]	132,908	135,407	98.2
U.S.	158,984,190	163,918,840	97.0

Note: (1) Figures cover the Cedar Rapids, IA Metropolitan Statistical Area—see Appendix B for areas included
Source: U.S. Census Bureau, 2014-2018 American Community Survey 5-Year Estimates

Religious Groups by Family

Area	Catholic	Baptist	Non-Den.	Methodist[2]	Lutheran	LDS[3]	Pentecostal	Presbyterian[4]	Muslim[5]	Judaism
MSA[1]	18.8	2.4	3.0	7.3	11.3	0.9	1.8	3.3	0.5	0.1
U.S.	19.1	9.3	4.0	4.0	2.3	2.0	1.9	1.6	0.8	0.7

Note: Figures are the number of adherents as a percentage of the total population; (1) Figures cover the Cedar Rapids, IA Metropolitan Statistical Area—see Appendix B for areas included; (2) Methodist/Pietist; (3) Latter Day Saints; (4) Reformed; (5) Figures are estimates
Source: Association of Statisticians of American Religious Bodies, 2010 U.S. Religion Census: Religious Congregations & Membership Study

Religious Groups by Tradition

Area	Catholic	Evangelical Protestant	Mainline Protestant	Other Tradition	Black Protestant	Orthodox
MSA[1]	18.8	13.7	17.5	2.0	0.2	0.2
U.S.	19.1	16.2	7.3	4.3	1.6	0.3

Note: Figures are the number of adherents as a percentage of the total population; (1) Figures cover the Cedar Rapids, IA Metropolitan Statistical Area—see Appendix B for areas included
Source: Association of Statisticians of American Religious Bodies, 2010 U.S. Religion Census: Religious Congregations & Membership Study

ECONOMY

Gross Metropolitan Product

Area	2017	2018	2019	2020	Rank[2]
MSA[1]	17.8	18.4	18.8	19.4	141

Note: Figures are in billions of dollars; (1) Figures cover the Cedar Rapids, IA Metropolitan Statistical Area—see Appendix B for areas included; (2) Rank is based on 2018 data and ranges from 1 to 381
Source: U.S. Conference of Mayors, U.S. Metro Economies: GMP & Employment 2018-2020, September 2019

Economic Growth

Area	2015-17 (%)	2018 (%)	2019 (%)	2020 (%)	Rank[2]
MSA[1]	-1.6	0.9	0.8	1.0	354
U.S.	1.9	2.9	2.3	2.1	–

Note: Figures are real gross metropolitan product (GMP) growth rates and represent average annual percent change; (1) Figures cover the Cedar Rapids, IA Metropolitan Statistical Area—see Appendix B for areas included; (2) Rank is based on 2017 2-year average annual percent change and ranges from 1 to 381
Source: U.S. Conference of Mayors, U.S. Metro Economies: GMP & Employment 2018-2020, September 2019

Metropolitan Area Exports

Area	2013	2014	2015	2016	2017	2018	Rank[2]
MSA[1]	930.2	879.0	873.5	945.0	1,071.6	1,025.0	160

Note: Figures are in millions of dollars; (1) Figures cover the Cedar Rapids, IA Metropolitan Statistical Area—see Appendix B for areas included; (2) Rank is based on 2018 data and ranges from 1 to 387
Source: U.S. Department of Commerce, International Trade Administration, Office of Trade and Economic Analysis, Industry and Analysis, Exports by Metropolitan Area, data extracted April 15, 2020

Building Permits

Area	Single-Family			Multi-Family			Total		
	2017	2018	Pct. Chg.	2017	2018	Pct. Chg.	2017	2018	Pct. Chg.
City	219	147	-32.9	313	325	3.8	532	472	-11.3
MSA[1]	537	490	-8.8	455	469	3.1	992	959	-3.3
U.S.	820,000	855,300	4.3	462,000	473,500	2.5	1,282,000	1,328,800	3.7

Note: (1) Figures cover the Cedar Rapids, IA Metropolitan Statistical Area—see Appendix B for areas included; Figures represent new, privately-owned housing units authorized (unadjusted data); All permit data are based on estimates with imputation
Source: U.S. Census Bureau, Manufacturing, Mining, and Construction Statistics, Building Permits, 2017, 2018

Bankruptcy Filings

Area	Business Filings			Nonbusiness Filings		
	2018	2019	% Chg.	2018	2019	% Chg.
Linn County	8	11	37.5	351	365	4.0
U.S.	22,232	22,780	2.5	751,186	752,160	0.1

Note: Business filings include Chapter 7, Chapter 9, Chapter 11, Chapter 12, Chapter 13, Chapter 15, and Section 304; Nonbusiness filings include Chapter 7, Chapter 11, and Chapter 13
Source: Administrative Office of the U.S. Courts, Business and Nonbusiness Bankruptcy, County Cases Commenced by Chapter of the Bankruptcy Code, During the 12-Month Period Ending December 31, 2018 and Business and Nonbusiness Bankruptcy, County Cases Commenced by Chapter of the Bankruptcy Code, During the 12-Month Period Ending December 31, 2019

Housing Vacancy Rates

Area	Gross Vacancy Rate[2] (%)			Year-Round Vacancy Rate[3] (%)			Rental Vacancy Rate[4] (%)			Homeowner Vacancy Rate[5] (%)		
	2017	2018	2019	2017	2018	2019	2017	2018	2019	2017	2018	2019
MSA[1]	n/a	n/a	n/a	n/a	n/a	n/a	n/a	n/a	n/a	n/a	n/a	n/a
U.S.	12.7	12.3	12.0	9.9	9.7	9.5	7.2	6.9	6.7	1.6	1.5	1.4

Note: (1) Figures cover the Cedar Rapids, IA Metropolitan Statistical Area—see Appendix B for areas included; (2) The percentage of the total housing inventory that is vacant; (3) The percentage of the housing inventory (excluding seasonal units) that is year-round vacant; (4) The percentage of rental inventory that is vacant for rent; (5) The percentage of homeowner inventory that is vacant for sale; n/a not available
Source: U.S. Census Bureau, Housing Vacancies and Homeownership Annual Statistics: 2017, 2018, 2019

INCOME

Income

Area	Per Capita ($)	Median Household ($)	Average Household ($)
City	32,625	59,152	76,644
MSA[1]	33,729	64,218	81,984
U.S.	32,621	60,293	84,938

Note: (1) Figures cover the Cedar Rapids, IA Metropolitan Statistical Area—see Appendix B for areas included
Source: U.S. Census Bureau, 2014-2018 American Community Survey 5-Year Estimates

Household Income Distribution

Area	Percent of Households Earning							
	Under $15,000	$15,000 -$24,999	$25,000 -$34,999	$35,000 -$49,999	$50,000 -$74,999	$75,000 -$99,999	$100,000 -$149,999	$150,000 and up
City	9.2	9.2	9.8	13.4	20.4	13.3	15.4	9.3
MSA[1]	8.0	8.5	9.0	13.1	19.3	14.4	16.6	11.2
U.S.	10.9	9.3	9.3	12.6	17.5	12.5	14.6	13.3

Note: (1) Figures cover the Cedar Rapids, IA Metropolitan Statistical Area—see Appendix B for areas included
Source: U.S. Census Bureau, 2014-2018 American Community Survey 5-Year Estimates

Poverty Rate

Area	All Ages	Under 18 Years Old	18 to 64 Years Old	65 Years and Over
City	11.6	15.1	11.7	5.9
MSA[1]	9.5	12.2	9.4	5.9
U.S.	14.1	19.5	13.2	9.3

Note: Figures are percentage of people whose income during the past 12 months was below the poverty level; (1) Figures cover the Cedar Rapids, IA Metropolitan Statistical Area—see Appendix B for areas included
Source: U.S. Census Bureau, 2014-2018 American Community Survey 5-Year Estimates

EMPLOYMENT

Labor Force and Employment

Area	Civilian Labor Force			Workers Employed		
	Dec. 2018	Dec. 2019	% Chg.	Dec. 2018	Dec. 2019	% Chg.
City	71,755	73,629	2.6	69,479	71,125	2.4
MSA[1]	144,931	148,694	2.6	140,627	143,975	2.4
U.S.	162,510,000	164,007,000	0.9	156,481,000	158,504,000	1.3

Note: Data is not seasonally adjusted and covers workers 16 years of age and older; (1) Figures cover the Cedar Rapids, IA Metropolitan Statistical Area—see Appendix B for areas included
Source: Bureau of Labor Statistics, Local Area Unemployment Statistics

Unemployment Rate

Area	2019											
	Jan.	Feb.	Mar.	Apr.	May	Jun.	Jul.	Aug.	Sep.	Oct.	Nov.	Dec.
City	3.7	3.3	3.4	2.7	2.7	3.2	3.2	3.3	2.9	2.8	3.1	3.4
MSA[1]	3.6	3.3	3.3	2.6	2.5	2.9	3.0	3.0	2.6	2.6	2.7	3.2
U.S.	4.4	4.1	3.9	3.3	3.4	3.8	4.0	3.8	3.3	3.3	3.3	3.4

*Note: Data is not seasonally adjusted and covers workers 16 years of age and older; (1) Figures cover the
Cedar Rapids, IA Metropolitan Statistical Area—see Appendix B for areas included*
Source: Bureau of Labor Statistics, Local Area Unemployment Statistics

Average Wages

Occupation	$/Hr.	Occupation	$/Hr.
Accountants and Auditors	34.50	Maintenance and Repair Workers	22.60
Automotive Mechanics	21.30	Marketing Managers	64.90
Bookkeepers	19.70	Network and Computer Systems Admin.	38.70
Carpenters	23.60	Nurses, Licensed Practical	20.70
Cashiers	11.00	Nurses, Registered	28.80
Computer Programmers	37.40	Nursing Assistants	14.40
Computer Systems Analysts	41.60	Office Clerks, General	17.70
Computer User Support Specialists	22.20	Physical Therapists	38.10
Construction Laborers	20.10	Physicians	111.00
Cooks, Restaurant	11.30	Plumbers, Pipefitters and Steamfitters	29.80
Customer Service Representatives	19.20	Police and Sheriff's Patrol Officers	30.40
Dentists	66.60	Postal Service Mail Carriers	25.10
Electricians	28.00	Real Estate Sales Agents	20.10
Engineers, Electrical	50.70	Retail Salespersons	13.60
Fast Food and Counter Workers	10.60	Sales Representatives, Technical/Scientific	46.50
Financial Managers	59.30	Secretaries, Exc. Legal/Medical/Executive	18.40
First-Line Supervisors of Office Workers	26.60	Security Guards	19.00
General and Operations Managers	53.80	Surgeons	n/a
Hairdressers/Cosmetologists	12.60	Teacher Assistants, Exc. Postsecondary*	12.70
Home Health and Personal Care Aides	13.20	Teachers, Secondary School, Exc. Sp. Ed.*	26.90
Janitors and Cleaners	15.20	Telemarketers	13.50
Landscaping/Groundskeeping Workers	15.70	Truck Drivers, Heavy/Tractor-Trailer	17.90
Lawyers	54.60	Truck Drivers, Light/Delivery Services	15.30
Maids and Housekeeping Cleaners	11.90	Waiters and Waitresses	10.50

*Note: Wage data covers the Cedar Rapids, IA Metropolitan Statistical Area—see Appendix B for areas
included; (*) Hourly wages were calculated from annual wage data based on a 40 hour work week; n/a not
available.*
Source: Bureau of Labor Statistics, Metro Area Occupational Employment & Wage Estimates, May 2019

Employment by Occupation

Occupation Classification	City (%)	MSA[1] (%)	U.S. (%)
Management, Business, Science, and Arts	37.0	37.8	37.9
Natural Resources, Construction, and Maintenance	7.5	8.7	8.9
Production, Transportation, and Material Moving	16.0	15.9	13.3
Sales and Office	23.2	22.4	22.1
Service	16.3	15.2	17.9

*Note: Figures cover employed civilians 16 years of age and older; (1) Figures cover the Cedar Rapids, IA
Metropolitan Statistical Area—see Appendix B for areas included*
Source: U.S. Census Bureau, 2014-2018 American Community Survey 5-Year Estimates

Employment by Industry

Sector	MSA[1]		U.S.
	Number of Employees	Percent of Total	Percent of Total
Construction, Mining, and Logging	7,900	5.4	5.4
Education and Health Services	21,400	14.6	16.1
Financial Activities	11,500	7.8	5.8
Government	17,300	11.8	15.0
Information	3,400	2.3	1.9
Leisure and Hospitality	12,000	8.2	10.8
Manufacturing	20,500	14.0	8.4
Other Services	5,200	3.5	3.9
Professional and Business Services	15,100	10.3	14.1
Retail Trade	15,000	10.2	10.6
Transportation, Warehousing, and Utilities	11,600	7.9	4.2
Wholesale Trade	5,900	4.0	3.9

Note: Figures are non-farm employment as of December 2019. Figures are not seasonally adjusted and include workers 16 years of age and older; (1) Figures cover the Cedar Rapids, IA Metropolitan Statistical Area—see Appendix B for areas included
Source: Bureau of Labor Statistics, Current Employment Statistics, Employment, Hours, and Earnings

Occupations with Greatest Projected Employment Growth: 2019 – 2021

Occupation[1]	2019 Employment	2021 Projected Employment	Numeric Employment Change	Percent Employment Change
Combined Food Preparation and Serving Workers, Including Fast Food	38,530	39,480	950	2.5
Heavy and Tractor-Trailer Truck Drivers	45,820	46,750	930	2.0
Registered Nurses	34,120	34,870	750	2.2
Personal Care Aides	11,780	12,230	450	3.8
Home Health Aides	8,050	8,490	440	5.5
Cooks, Restaurant	11,550	11,940	390	3.4
Laborers and Freight, Stock, and Material Movers, Hand	29,060	29,440	380	1.3
Janitors and Cleaners, Except Maids and Housekeeping Cleaners	26,660	26,980	320	1.2
Accountants and Auditors	12,170	12,430	260	2.1
Construction Laborers	13,390	13,640	250	1.9

Note: Projections cover Iowa; (1) Sorted by numeric employment change
Source: www.projectionscentral.com, State Occupational Projections, 2019–2021 Short-Term Projections

Fastest Growing Occupations: 2019 – 2021

Occupation[1]	2019 Employment	2021 Projected Employment	Numeric Employment Change	Percent Employment Change
Information Security Analysts	1,470	1,590	120	8.2
Home Health Aides	8,050	8,490	440	5.5
Veterinary Assistants and Laboratory Animal Caretakers	1,140	1,200	60	5.3
Woodworking Machine Setters, Operators, and Tenders, Except Sawing	1,490	1,560	70	4.7
Nurse Practitioners	1,330	1,390	60	4.5
Taxi Drivers and Chauffeurs	2,430	2,540	110	4.5
Health Specialties Teachers, Postsecondary	2,030	2,120	90	4.4
Paralegals and Legal Assistants	1,890	1,970	80	4.2
Speech-Language Pathologists	1,200	1,250	50	4.2
Gaming Dealers	1,210	1,260	50	4.1

Note: Projections cover Iowa; (1) Sorted by percent employment change and excludes occupations with numeric employment change less than 50
Source: www.projectionscentral.com, State Occupational Projections, 2019–2021 Short-Term Projections

TAXES

State Corporate Income Tax Rates

State	Tax Rate (%)	Income Brackets ($)	Num. of Brackets	Financial Institution Tax Rate (%)[a]	Federal Income Tax Ded.
Iowa	6.0 - 12.0	25,000 - 250,001	4	5.0	Yes (j)

Note: Tax rates as of January 1, 2020; (a) Rates listed are the corporate income tax rate applied to financial institutions or excise taxes based on income; (j) 50% of the federal income tax is deductible.
Source: Federation of Tax Administrators, State Corporate Income Tax Rates, January 1, 2020

State Individual Income Tax Rates

State	Tax Rate (%)	Income Brackets ($)	Personal Exemptions ($)			Standard Ded. ($)	
			Single	Married	Depend.	Single	Married
Iowa (a)	0.33 - 8.53	15,666 - 74,970	40 (c)	80 (c)	40 (c)	2,110	5,210 (a)

Note: Tax rates as of January 1, 2020; Local- and county-level taxes are not included; Federal income tax is deductible on state income tax returns; (a) 19 states have statutory provision for automatically adjusting to the rate of inflation the dollar values of the income tax brackets, standard deductions, and/or personal exemptions. Michigan indexes the personal exemption only. Oregon does not index the income brackets for $125,000 and over; (c) The personal exemption takes the form of a tax credit instead of a deduction
Source: Federation of Tax Administrators, State Individual Income Tax Rates, January 1, 2020

Various State Sales and Excise Tax Rates

State	State Sales Tax (%)	Gasoline[1] (¢/gal.)	Cigarette[2] ($/pack)	Spirits[3] ($/gal.)	Wine[4] ($/gal.)	Beer[5] ($/gal.)	Recreational Marijuana (%)
Iowa	6	30.5	1.36	13.03	1.75	0.19	Not legal

Note: All tax rates as of January 1, 2020; (1) The American Petroleum Institute has developed a methodology for determining the average tax rate on a gallon of fuel. Rates may include any of the following: excise taxes, environmental fees, storage tank fees, other fees or taxes, general sales tax, and local taxes; (2) The federal excise tax of $1.0066 per pack and local taxes are not included; (3) Rates are those applicable to off-premise sales of 40% alcohol by volume (a.b.v.) distilled spirits in 750ml containers. Local excise taxes are excluded; (4) Rates are those applicable to off-premise sales of 11% a.b.v. non-carbonated wine in 750ml containers; (5) Rates are those applicable to off-premise sales of 4.7% a.b.v. beer in 12 ounce containers.
Source: Tax Foundation, 2020 Facts & Figures: How Does Your State Compare?

State Business Tax Climate Index Rankings

State	Overall Rank	Corporate Tax Rank	Individual Income Tax Rank	Sales Tax Rank	Property Tax Rank	Unemployment Insurance Tax Rank
Iowa	42	48	42	15	35	35

Note: The index is a measure of how each state's tax laws affect economic performance. The lower the rank, the more favorable a state's tax system is for business. States without a given tax are given a ranking of 1. The scores/rankings for the District of Columbia do not affect other states. The 2020 index represents the tax climate as of July 1, 2019.
Source: Tax Foundation, State Business Tax Climate Index 2020

COMMERCIAL UTILITIES

Typical Monthly Electric Bills

Area	Commercial Service ($/month)		Industrial Service ($/month)	
	1,500 kWh	40 kW demand 14,000 kWh	1,000 kW demand 200,000 kWh	50,000 kW demand 32,500,000 kWh
City	n/a	n/a	n/a	n/a
Average[1]	203	1,612	25,706	2,520,671

Note: Figures are based on annualized rates; (1) Average based on 187 utilities surveyed; n/a not available
Source: Edison Electric Institute, Typical Bills and Average Rates Report, Summer 2019

TRANSPORTATION

Means of Transportation to Work

| Area | Car/Truck/Van | | Public Transportation | | | Bicycle | Walked | Other Means | Worked at Home |
	Drove Alone	Car-pooled	Bus	Subway	Railroad				
City	84.4	8.9	1.0	0.0	0.0	0.4	1.7	1.0	2.7
MSA[1]	84.4	8.3	0.6	0.0	0.0	0.3	2.0	0.7	3.7
U.S.	76.4	9.1	2.5	1.9	0.6	0.6	2.7	1.3	4.9

Note: Figures are percentages and cover workers 16 years of age and older; (1) Figures cover the Cedar Rapids, IA Metropolitan Statistical Area—see Appendix B for areas included
Source: U.S. Census Bureau, 2014-2018 American Community Survey 5-Year Estimates

Travel Time to Work

Area	Less Than 10 Minutes	10 to 19 Minutes	20 to 29 Minutes	30 to 44 Minutes	45 to 59 Minutes	60 to 89 Minutes	90 Minutes or More
City	17.7	49.8	18.2	9.5	2.1	1.5	1.1
MSA[1]	17.6	40.7	21.9	13.1	3.6	2.0	1.2
U.S.	12.5	28.7	20.9	20.7	8.2	6.3	2.8

Note: Note: Figures are percentages and include workers 16 years old and over; (1) Figures cover the Cedar Rapids, IA Metropolitan Statistical Area—see Appendix B for areas included
Source: U.S. Census Bureau, 2014-2018 American Community Survey 5-Year Estimates

Key Congestion Measures

Area	1982	1992	2002	2012	2017
Annual Hours of Delay, Total (000)	n/a	n/a	n/a	n/a	3,369
Annual Hours of Delay, Per Auto Commuter	n/a	n/a	n/a	n/a	17
Annual Congestion Cost, Total (million $)	n/a	n/a	n/a	n/a	69
Annual Congestion Cost, Per Auto Commuter ($)	n/a	n/a	n/a	n/a	346

Note: n/a not available
Source: Texas A&M Transportation Institute, 2019 Urban Mobility Report

Freeway Travel Time Index

Area	1982	1987	1992	1997	2002	2007	2012	2017
Urban Area Index[1]	n/a	n/a	n/a	n/a	n/a	n/a	n/a	1.08
Urban Area Rank[1,2]	n/a	n/a	n/a	n/a	n/a	n/a	n/a	n/a

Note: Freeway Travel Time Index—the ratio of travel time in the peak period to the travel time at free-flow conditions. For example, a value of 1.30 indicates a 20-minute free-flow trip takes 26 minutes in the peak (20 minutes x 1.30 = 26 minutes); (1) Covers the Cedar Rapids IA urban area; (2) Rank is based on 101 larger urban areas (#1 = highest travel time index); n/a not available
Source: Texas A&M Transportation Institute, 2019 Urban Mobility Report

Public Transportation

Agency Name / Mode of Transportation	Vehicles Operated in Maximum Service[1]	Annual Unlinked Passenger Trips[2] (in thous.)	Annual Passenger Miles[3] (in thous.)
Five Seasons Transportation and Parking (FSTP)			
Bus (directly operated)	23	1,265.7	5,806.4
Demand Response (purchased transportation)	12	86.7	495.5

Note: (1) Number of revenue vehicles operated by the given mode and type of service to meet the annual maximum service requirement. This is the revenue vehicle count during the peak season of the year; on the week and day that maximum service is provided. Vehicles operated in maximum service (VOMS) exclude atypical days and one-time special events; (2) Number of passengers who boarded public transportation vehicles. Passengers are counted each time they board a vehicle no matter how many vehicles they use to travel from their origin to their destination. (3) Sum of the distances ridden by all passengers during the entire fiscal year.
Source: Federal Transit Administration, National Transit Database, 2018

Air Transportation

Airport Name and Code / Type of Service	Passenger Airlines[1]	Passenger Enplanements	Freight Carriers[2]	Freight (lbs)
The Eastern Iowa (CID)				
Domestic service (U.S. carriers - 2019)	20	671,675	11	52,391,254
International service (U.S. carriers - 2018)	0	0	1	6,800

Note: (1) Includes all U.S.-based major, minor and commuter airlines that carried at least one passenger during the year; (2) Includes all U.S.-based airlines and freight carriers that transported at least one pound of freight during the year.
Source: Bureau of Transportation Statistics, The Intermodal Transportation Database, Air Carriers: T-100 Domestic Market (U.S. Carriers), 2019; Bureau of Transportation Statistics, The Intermodal Transportation Database, Air Carriers: T-100 International Market (U.S. Carriers), 2018

Other Transportation Statistics

Major Highways:	I-380
Amtrak Service:	No
Major Waterways/Ports:	Cedar River

Source: Amtrak.com; Google Maps

BUSINESSES

Major Business Headquarters

Company Name	Industry	Rankings Fortune[1]	Forbes[2]
Rockwell Collins	Aerospace and Defense	350	-

Note: (1) Companies that produce a 10-K are ranked 1 to 500 based on 2018 revenue; (2) All private companies with at least $2 billion in annual revenue through the end of their most current fiscal year are ranked 1 to 228; companies listed are headquartered in the city; dashes indicate no ranking
Source: Fortune, "Fortune 500," June 2019; Forbes, "America's Largest Private Companies," 2019 Rankings

Minority- and Women-Owned Businesses

Group	All Firms Firms	Sales ($000)	Firms with Paid Employees Firms	Sales ($000)	Employees	Payroll ($000)
AIAN[1]	34	574	0	0	0	0
Asian	288	71,587	86	64,737	515	16,645
Black	351	14,021	7	8,445	129	2,669
Hispanic	139	(s)	7	(s)	250 - 499	(s)
NHOPI[2]	n/a	n/a	n/a	n/a	n/a	n/a
Women	3,513	1,807,700	431	1,744,169	9,337	277,821
All Firms	9,807	27,778,483	2,763	27,473,339	88,551	4,137,794

Note: Figures cover firms located in the city; minority- and women-owned business are defined as firms in which the corresponding group own 51% or more of the stock or equity of the company; (1) American Indian and Alaska Native; (2) Native Hawaiian and Other Pacific Islander; (s) estimates are suppressed when publication standards are not met; n/a not available
Source: U.S. Census Bureau, 2012 Economic Census, Survey of Business Owners

HOTELS & CONVENTION CENTERS

Hotels, Motels and Vacation Rentals

Area	5 Star Num.	Pct.[3]	4 Star Num.	Pct.[3]	3 Star Num.	Pct.[3]	2 Star Num.	Pct.[3]	1 Star Num.	Pct.[3]	Not Rated Num.	Pct.[3]
City[1]	0	0.0	0	0.0	6	18.2	6	18.2	3	9.1	18	54.5
Total[2]	266	1.3	1,517	7.2	4,627	21.8	3,210	15.1	3,974	18.7	7,601	35.9

Note: (1) Figures cover Cedar Rapids and vicinity; (2) Figures cover all 100 cities in this book; (3) Percentage of hotels which have a given star rating; Star ratings are determined by priceline.com and offer an indication of the general quality of a particular hotel.
Source: priceline.com, April 27, 2020

Major Convention Centers

Name	Overall Space (sq. ft.)	Exhibit Space (sq. ft.)	Meeting Space (sq. ft.)	Meeting Rooms
Cedar Rapids Convention Complex	104,000	72,300	21,500	n/a

Note: Table includes convention centers located in the Cedar Rapids, IA metro area; n/a not available
Source: Original research

Living Environment

COST OF LIVING

Cost of Living Index

Composite Index	Groceries	Housing	Utilities	Trans- portation	Health Care	Misc. Goods/ Services
96.2	94.8	83.0	102.1	96.6	107.0	103.9

Note: The Cost of Living Index measures regional differences in the cost of consumer goods and services, excluding taxes and non-consumer expenditures, for professional and managerial households in the top income quintile. It is based on more than 50,000 prices covering almost 60 different items for which prices are collected three times a year by chambers of commerce, economic development organizations or university applied economic centers in each participating urban area. The numbers shown should be read as a percentage above or below the national average of 100. For example, a value of 115.4 in the groceries column indicates that grocery prices are 15.4% higher than the national average. Small differences in the index numbers should not be interpreted as significant; Figures cover the Cedar Rapids IA urban area.
Source: The Council for Community and Economic Research, ACCRA Cost of Living Index, 2019

Grocery Prices

Area[1]	T-Bone Steak ($/pound)	Frying Chicken ($/pound)	Whole Milk ($/half gal.)	Eggs ($/dozen)	Orange Juice ($/64 oz.)	Coffee ($/11.5 oz.)
City[2]	11.88	1.75	2.14	1.55	3.04	4.52
Avg.	11.40	1.41	1.93	1.54	3.51	4.30
Min.	7.40	0.92	0.85	0.58	2.67	2.90
Max.	15.58	2.68	4.09	4.18	5.57	8.10

Note: (1) Values for the local area are compared with the average, minimum and maximum values for all 290 areas in the Cost of Living Index; (2) Figures cover the Cedar Rapids IA urban area; T-Bone Steak (price per pound); Frying Chicken (price per pound, whole fryer); Whole Milk (half gallon carton); Eggs (price per dozen, Grade A, large); Orange Juice (64 oz. Tropicana or Florida Natural); Coffee (11.5 oz. can, vacuum-packed, Maxwell House, Hills Bros, or Folgers).
Source: The Council for Community and Economic Research, ACCRA Cost of Living Index, 2019

Housing and Utility Costs

Area[1]	New Home Price ($)	Apartment Rent ($/month)	All Electric ($/month)	Part Electric ($/month)	Other Energy ($/month)	Telephone ($/month)
City[2]	323,537	791	-	122.94	54.21	176.50
Avg.	362,090	1,142	174.35	100.00	67.76	179.60
Min.	198,329	501	91.58	31.44	28.51	165.30
Max.	2,074,561	5,050	388.18	239.41	306.15	207.90

Note: (1) Values for the local area are compared with the average, minimum and maximum values for all 290 areas in the Cost of Living Index; (2) Figures cover the Cedar Rapids IA urban area; New Home Price (2,400 sf living area, 8,000 sf lot, in urban area with full utilities); Apartment Rent (950 sf 2 bedroom/1.5 or 2 bath, unfurnished, excluding all utilities except water); All Electric (average monthly cost for an all-electric home); Part Electric (average monthly cost for a part-electric home); Other Energy (average monthly cost for natural gas, fuel oil, coal, wood, and any other forms of energy except electricity); Telephone (price includes the base monthly rate plus taxes and fees for three lines of mobile phone service).
Source: The Council for Community and Economic Research, ACCRA Cost of Living Index, 2019

Health Care, Transportation, and Other Costs

Area[1]	Doctor ($/visit)	Dentist ($/visit)	Optometrist ($/visit)	Gasoline ($/gallon)	Beauty Salon ($/visit)	Men's Shirt ($)
City[2]	111.14	113.18	113.67	2.44	37.05	31.85
Avg.	114.85	97.58	106.10	2.50	38.15	32.15
Min.	39.00	62.22	52.22	1.53	16.88	10.27
Max.	206.67	151.53	258.67	3.79	79.29	59.30

Note: (1) Values for the local area are compared with the average, minimum and maximum values for all 290 areas in the Cost of Living Index; (2) Figures cover the Cedar Rapids IA urban area; Doctor (general practitioners routine exam of an established patient); Dentist (adult teeth cleaning and periodic oral examination); Optometrist (full vision eye exam for established adult patient); Gasoline (one gallon regular unleaded, national brand, including all taxes, cash price at self-service pump if available); Beauty Salon (woman's shampoo, trim, and blow-dry); Men's Shirt (cotton/polyester dress shirt, pinpoint weave, long sleeves).
Source: The Council for Community and Economic Research, ACCRA Cost of Living Index, 2019

HOUSING

House Price Index (HPI)

Area	National Ranking[2]	Quarterly Change (%)	One-Year Change (%)	Five-Year Change (%)
MSA[1]	216	0.69	2.67	14.49
U.S.[3]	–	1.26	5.09	32.88

Note: The HPI is a weighted repeat sales index. It measures average price changes in repeat sales or refinancings on the same properties. This information is obtained by reviewing repeat mortgage transactions on single-family properties whose mortgages have been purchased or securitized by Fannie Mae or Freddie Mac in January 1975; (1) Figures cover the Cedar Rapids, IA Metropolitan Statistical Area—see Appendix B for areas included; (2) Rankings are based on annual percentage change for all metro areas containing at least 15,000 transactions over the last 10 years and ranges from 1 to 232; (3) figures based on a weighted average of Census Division estimates using a seasonally adjusted, purchase-only index; all figures are for the period ending December 31, 2019
Source: Federal Housing Finance Agency, House Price Index, February 25, 2020

Median Single-Family Home Prices

Area	2017	2018	2019p	Percent Change 2018 to 2019
MSA[1]	152.6	159.2	165.6	4.0
U.S. Average	248.8	261.6	274.6	5.0

Note: Figures are median sales prices of existing single-family homes in thousands of dollars; (p) preliminary; (1) Figures cover the Cedar Rapids, IA Metropolitan Statistical Area—see Appendix B for areas included
Source: National Association of Realtors, Median Sales Price of Existing Single-Family Homes for Metropolitan Areas, 4th Quarter 2019

Qualifying Income Based on Median Sales Price of Existing Single-Family Homes

Area	With 5% Down ($)	With 10% Down ($)	With 20% Down ($)
MSA[1]	34,549	32,730	29,094
U.S. Average	58,663	55,575	49,400

Note: Figures are preliminary; Qualifying income is based on a mortgage rate of 3.76%. Monthly principal and interest payment is limited to 25% of income; (1) Figures cover the Cedar Rapids, IA Metropolitan Statistical Area—see Appendix B for areas included
Source: National Association of Realtors, Qualifying Income Based on Median Sales Price of Existing Single-Family Homes for Metropolitan Areas, 4th Quarter 2019

Median Apartment Condo-Coop Home Prices

Area	2017	2018	2019p	Percent Change 2018 to 2019
MSA[1]	n/a	n/a	n/a	n/a
U.S. Average	234.3	241.0	249.5	3.5

Note: Figures are median sales prices of existing apartment condo-coop homes in thousands of dollars; (p) preliminary; n/a not available; (1) Figures cover the Cedar Rapids, IA Metropolitan Statistical Area—see Appendix B for areas included
Source: National Association of Realtors, Median Sales Price of Existing Apartment Condo-Coop Homes for Metropolitan Areas, 4th Quarter 2019

Home Value Distribution

Area	Under $50,000	$50,000 -$99,999	$100,000 -$149,999	$150,000 -$199,999	$200,000 -$299,999	$300,000 -$499,999	$500,000 -$999,999	$1,000,000 or more
City	5.3	16.8	35.0	20.3	15.7	5.1	1.4	0.3
MSA[1]	6.5	14.5	27.8	19.4	20.1	8.7	2.5	0.6
U.S.	7.6	13.0	14.0	14.3	19.2	18.3	10.5	3.1

Note: Figures are percentages and cover owner-occupied housing units; (1) Figures cover the Cedar Rapids, IA Metropolitan Statistical Area—see Appendix B for areas included
Source: U.S. Census Bureau, 2014-2018 American Community Survey 5-Year Estimates

Homeownership Rate

Area	2011 (%)	2012 (%)	2013 (%)	2014 (%)	2015 (%)	2016 (%)	2017 (%)	2018 (%)	2019 (%)
MSA[1]	n/a	n/a	n/a	n/a	n/a	n/a	n/a	n/a	n/a
U.S.	66.1	65.4	65.1	64.5	63.7	63.4	63.9	64.4	64.6

Note: (1) Figures cover the Cedar Rapids, IA Metropolitan Statistical Area—see Appendix B for areas included; n/a not available
Source: U.S. Census Bureau, Housing Vacancies and Homeownership Annual Statistics: 2011-2019

Year Housing Structure Built

Area	2010 or Later	2000 -2009	1990 -1999	1980 -1989	1970 -1979	1960 -1969	1950 -1959	1940 -1949	Before 1940	Median Year
City	5.3	11.6	13.2	8.2	14.6	14.6	12.4	4.2	15.8	1972
MSA[1]	5.5	14.6	14.6	7.4	13.8	12.5	10.0	3.8	17.8	1974
U.S.	4.1	14.3	13.9	13.5	15.3	10.7	10.4	5.0	12.8	1977

Note: Figures are percentages except for Median Year; Note: (1) Figures cover the Cedar Rapids, IA Metropolitan Statistical Area—see Appendix B for areas included
Source: U.S. Census Bureau, 2014-2018 American Community Survey 5-Year Estimates

Gross Monthly Rent

Area	Under $500	$500 -$999	$1,000 -$1,499	$1,500 -$1,999	$2,000 -$2,499	$2,500 -$2,999	$3,000 and up	Median ($)
City	18.2	62.3	16.5	2.0	0.5	0.1	0.3	751
MSA[1]	19.0	62.0	16.2	1.8	0.5	0.2	0.4	731
U.S.	9.8	38.5	29.6	12.9	5.1	2.1	2.0	1,023

Note: Figures are percentages except for Median; Gross rent is the contract rent plus the estimated average monthly cost of utilities (electricity, gas, and water and sewer) and fuels (oil, coal, kerosene, wood, etc.) if these are paid by the renter (or paid for the renter by someone else); (1) Figures cover the Cedar Rapids, IA Metropolitan Statistical Area—see Appendix B for areas included
Source: U.S. Census Bureau, 2014-2018 American Community Survey 5-Year Estimates

HEALTH

Health Risk Factors

Category	MSA[1] (%)	U.S. (%)
Adults aged 18–64 who have any kind of health care coverage	93.7	87.3
Adults who reported being in good or better health	86.4	82.4
Adults who have been told they have high blood cholesterol	36.1	33.0
Adults who have been told they have high blood pressure	28.4	32.3
Adults who are current smokers	18.1	17.1
Adults who currently use E-cigarettes	3.5	4.6
Adults who currently use chewing tobacco, snuff, or snus	6.7	4.0
Adults who are heavy drinkers[2]	5.9	6.3
Adults who are binge drinkers[3]	22.9	17.4
Adults who are overweight (BMI 25.0 - 29.9)	35.3	35.3
Adults who are obese (BMI 30.0 - 99.8)	34.2	31.3
Adults who participated in any physical activities in the past month	75.4	74.4
Adults who always or nearly always wears a seat belt	96.4	94.3

Note: (1) Figures cover the Cedar Rapids, IA Metropolitan Statistical Area—see Appendix B for areas included; (2) Heavy drinkers are classified as adult men having more than 14 drinks per week and adult women having more than 7 drinks per week; (3) Binge drinkers are classified as males having five or more drinks on one occasion or females having four or more drinks on one occasion
Source: Centers for Disease Control and Prevention, Behavioral Risk Factor Surveillance System, SMART: Selected Metropolitan Area Risk Trends, 2017

Acute and Chronic Health Conditions

Category	MSA[1] (%)	U.S. (%)
Adults who have ever been told they had a heart attack	3.4	4.2
Adults who have ever been told they have angina or coronary heart disease	3.7	3.9
Adults who have ever been told they had a stroke	2.8	3.0
Adults who have ever been told they have asthma	11.5	14.2
Adults who have ever been told they have arthritis	20.6	24.9
Adults who have ever been told they have diabetes[2]	8.4	10.5
Adults who have ever been told they had skin cancer	6.7	6.2
Adults who have ever been told they had any other types of cancer	9.3	7.1
Adults who have ever been told they have COPD	5.3	6.5
Adults who have ever been told they have kidney disease	2.3	3.0
Adults who have ever been told they have a form of depression	20.8	20.5

Note: (1) Figures cover the Cedar Rapids, IA Metropolitan Statistical Area—see Appendix B for areas included; (2) Figures do not include pregnancy-related, borderline, or pre-diabetes
Source: Centers for Disease Control and Prevention, Behaviorial Risk Factor Surveillance System, SMART: Selected Metropolitan Area Risk Trends, 2017

Health Screening and Vaccination Rates

Category	MSA[1] (%)	U.S. (%)
Adults aged 65+ who have had flu shot within the past year	71.4	60.7
Adults aged 65+ who have ever had a pneumonia vaccination	86.7	75.4
Adults who have ever been tested for HIV	27.8	36.1
Adults who have ever had the shingles or zoster vaccine?	38.8	28.9
Adults who have had their blood cholesterol checked within the last five years	85.3	85.9

Note: n/a not available; (1) Figures cover the Cedar Rapids, IA Metropolitan Statistical Area—see Appendix B for areas included.
Source: Centers for Disease Control and Prevention, Behaviorial Risk Factor Surveillance System, SMART: Selected Metropolitan Area Risk Trends, 2017

Disability Status

Category	MSA[1] (%)	U.S. (%)
Adults who reported being deaf	6.7	6.7
Are you blind or have serious difficulty seeing, even when wearing glasses?	4.2	4.5
Are you limited in any way in any of your usual activities due of arthritis?	9.8	12.9
Do you have difficulty doing errands alone?	5.2	6.8
Do you have difficulty dressing or bathing?	2.4	3.6
Do you have serious difficulty concentrating/remembering/making decisions?	8.6	10.7
Do you have serious difficulty walking or climbing stairs?	9.0	13.6

Note: (1) Figures cover the Cedar Rapids, IA Metropolitan Statistical Area—see Appendix B for areas included.
Source: Centers for Disease Control and Prevention, Behaviorial Risk Factor Surveillance System, SMART: Selected Metropolitan Area Risk Trends, 2017

Mortality Rates for the Top 10 Causes of Death in the U.S.

ICD-10[a] Sub-Chapter	ICD-10[a] Code	Age-Adjusted Mortality Rate[1] per 100,000 population	
		County[2]	U.S.
Malignant neoplasms	C00-C97	158.8	152.4
Ischaemic heart diseases	I20-I25	101.9	92.7
Other forms of heart disease	I30-I51	35.6	52.5
Chronic lower respiratory diseases	J40-J47	39.8	40.4
Cerebrovascular diseases	I60-I69	23.9	37.3
Other degenerative diseases of the nervous system	G30-G31	48.9	36.4
Other external causes of accidental injury	W00-X59	27.3	35.3
Organic, including symptomatic, mental disorders	F01-F09	26.9	30.0
Hypertensive diseases	I10-I15	13.5	22.9
Diabetes mellitus	E10-E14	16.0	21.3

Note: (a) ICD-10 = International Classification of Diseases 10th Revision; (1) Mortality rates are a three year average covering 2016-2018; (2) Figures cover Linn County.
Source: Centers for Disease Control and Prevention, National Center for Health Statistics. Underlying Cause of Death 1999-2018 on CDC WONDER Online Database

Mortality Rates for Selected Causes of Death

ICD-10[a] Sub-Chapter	ICD-10[a] Code	Age-Adjusted Mortality Rate[1] per 100,000 population	
		County[2]	U.S.
Assault	X85-Y09	3.2	6.0
Diseases of the liver	K70-K76	13.1	14.2
Human immunodeficiency virus (HIV) disease	B20-B24	Suppressed	1.6
Influenza and pneumonia	J09-J18	14.2	14.2
Intentional self-harm	X60-X84	17.7	13.9
Malnutrition	E40-E46	Unreliable	1.9
Obesity and other hyperalimentation	E65-E68	Suppressed	2.1
Renal failure	N17-N19	8.4	12.8
Transport accidents	V01-V99	10.6	12.5
Viral hepatitis	B15-B19	Suppressed	1.4

Note: (a) ICD-10 = International Classification of Diseases 10th Revision; (1) Mortality rates are a three year average covering 2016-2018; (2) Figures cover Linn County; Data are suppressed when the data meet the criteria for confidentiality constraints; Mortality rates are flagged as unreliable when the rate would be calculated with a numerator of 20 or less.
Source: Centers for Disease Control and Prevention, National Center for Health Statistics. Underlying Cause of Death 1999-2018 on CDC WONDER Online Database

Health Insurance Coverage

Area	With Health Insurance	With Private Health Insurance	With Public Health Insurance	Without Health Insurance	Population Under Age 19 Without Health Insurance
City	95.5	75.4	33.5	4.5	3.1
MSA[1]	96.3	77.6	32.5	3.7	2.3
U.S.	90.6	67.7	34.7	9.4	5.2

Note: Figures are percentages that cover the civilian noninstitutionalized population; (1) Figures cover the Cedar Rapids, IA Metropolitan Statistical Area—see Appendix B for areas included
Source: U.S. Census Bureau, 2014-2018 American Community Survey 5-Year Estimates

Number of Medical Professionals

Area	MDs[3]	DOs[3,4]	Dentists	Podiatrists	Chiropractors	Optometrists
County[1] (number)	411	49	163	17	129	39
County[1] (rate[2])	183.4	21.9	72.2	7.5	57.1	17.3
U.S. (rate[2])	281.9	23.4	69.1	6.0	27.5	16.4

Note: Data as of 2018 unless noted; (1) Data covers Linn County; (2) Rate per 100,000 population; (3) Data as of 2017 and includes all active, non-federal physicians; (4) Doctor of Osteopathic Medicine
Source: U.S. Department of Health and Human Services, Health Resources and Services Administration, Bureau of Health Professions, Area Resource File (ARF) 2018-2019

EDUCATION

Public School District Statistics

District Name	Schls	Pupils	Pupil/ Teacher Ratio	Minority Pupils[1] (%)	Free Lunch Eligible[2] (%)	IEP[3] (%)
Cedar Rapids CSD	31	16,717	15.1	37.2	48.3	15.7
College Comm School District	9	5,761	15.8	22.3	26.5	10.6

Note: Table includes school districts with 2,000 or more students; (1) Percentage of students that are not non-Hispanic white; (2) Percentage of students that are eligible for the free lunch program; (3) Percentage of students that have an Individualized Education Program.
Source: U.S. Department of Education, National Center for Education Statistics, Common Core of Data, Local Education Agency (School District) Universe Survey: School Year 2018-2019; U.S. Department of Education, National Center for Education Statistics, Common Core of Data, Public Elementary/Secondary School Universe Survey: School Year 2018-2019

Highest Level of Education

Area	Less than H.S.	H.S. Diploma	Some College, No Deg.	Associate Degree	Bachelor's Degree	Master's Degree	Prof. School Degree	Doctorate Degree
City	6.3	26.1	22.9	12.2	23.2	6.7	1.5	1.1
MSA[1]	5.7	29.0	22.1	12.4	21.8	6.8	1.4	0.9
U.S.	12.3	27.1	20.6	8.4	19.4	8.6	2.1	1.4

Note: Figures cover persons age 25 and over; (1) Figures cover the Cedar Rapids, IA Metropolitan Statistical Area—see Appendix B for areas included
Source: U.S. Census Bureau, 2014-2018 American Community Survey 5-Year Estimates

Educational Attainment by Race

Area	High School Graduate or Higher (%)					Bachelor's Degree or Higher (%)				
	Total	White	Black	Asian	Hisp.[2]	Total	White	Black	Asian	Hisp.[2]
City	93.7	94.9	82.9	86.1	76.5	32.5	33.2	15.8	51.3	20.4
MSA[1]	94.3	95.2	83.2	82.8	78.8	30.8	31.2	16.0	49.6	25.9
U.S.	87.7	89.6	85.4	86.8	67.7	31.5	32.9	21.1	53.5	15.8

Note: Figures shown cover persons 25 years old and over; (1) Figures cover the Cedar Rapids, IA Metropolitan Statistical Area—see Appendix B for areas included; (2) People of Hispanic origin can be of any race
Source: U.S. Census Bureau, 2014-2018 American Community Survey 5-Year Estimates

School Enrollment by Grade and Control

Area	Preschool (%)		Kindergarten (%)		Grades 1 - 4 (%)		Grades 5 - 8 (%)		Grades 9 - 12 (%)	
	Public	Private	Public	Private	Public	Private	Public	Private	Public	Private
City	65.4	34.6	85.9	14.1	88.1	11.9	92.3	7.7	92.6	7.4
MSA[1]	67.2	32.8	87.2	12.8	88.4	11.6	92.1	7.9	93.9	6.1
U.S.	59.0	41.0	87.7	12.3	89.6	10.4	89.5	10.5	90.2	9.8

Note: Figures shown cover persons 3 years old and over; (1) Figures cover the Cedar Rapids, IA Metropolitan Statistical Area—see Appendix B for areas included
Source: U.S. Census Bureau, 2014-2018 American Community Survey 5-Year Estimates

Average Salaries of Public School Teachers

Area	2016-17		2017-18		Change from 2016-17 to 2017-18	
	Dollars	Rank[1]	Dollars	Rank[1]	Percent	Rank[2]
Iowa	55,647	21	57,018	21	2.46	8
U.S. Average	59,539	–	60,477	–	1.58	–

Note: (1) Rank ranges from 1 to 51 where 1 indicates highest salary; (2) Rank ranges from 1 to 51 where 1 indicates highest percent change.
Source: National Education Association, Rankings & Estimates: Rankings of the States 2018 and Estimates of School Statistics 2019

Higher Education

Four-Year Colleges			Two-Year Colleges			Medical Schools[1]	Law Schools[2]	Voc/ Tech[3]
Public	Private Non-profit	Private For-profit	Public	Private Non-profit	Private For-profit			
1	2	0	1	1	1	0	0	0

Note: Figures cover institutions located within the city limits and include main campuses only; (1) includes schools accredited by the Liaison Committee on Medical Education and the American Osteopathic Association's Commission on Osteopathic College Accreditation; (2) includes ABA-accredited schools, schools with provisional ABA accreditation, and state accredited schools; (3) includes all schools with programs that are less than 2 years.
Source: National Center for Education Statistics, Integrated Postsecondary Education System (IPEDS), 2018-19; Wikipedia, List of Medical Schools in the United States, accessed May 1, 2020; Wikipedia, List of Law Schools in the United States, accessed May 1, 2020

According to *U.S. News & World Report,* the Cedar Rapids, IA metro area is home to one of the top 100 liberal arts colleges in the U.S.: **Cornell College** (#68 tie). The indicators used to capture academic quality fall into a number of categories: assessment by administrators at peer institutions; retention of students; faculty resources; student selectivity; financial resources; alumni giving; high school counselor ratings of colleges; and graduation rate. *U.S. News & World Report, "America's Best Colleges 2020"*

PRESIDENTIAL ELECTION

2016 Presidential Election Results

Area	Clinton	Trump	Johnson	Stein	Other
Linn County	50.3	41.3	4.7	0.9	2.7
U.S.	48.0	45.9	3.3	1.1	1.7

Note: Results are percentages and may not add to 100% due to rounding
Source: Dave Leip's Atlas of U.S. Presidential Elections

EMPLOYERS

Major Employers

Company Name	Industry
AEGON USA	Insurance
Alliant Energy	Energy
Amana Refrigeration Products	Appliances
Cedar Rapids Community School District	Education
City of Cedar Rapids	Government
Gazette Communications	Publishing
General Mills	Food products
Hy-Vee Food Stores	Grocery stores
Kirkwood Community College	Education
Linn County Offices	Government
Linn-Mar Community Schools	Education
Maytag Appliances	Appliances
MCI	Communications
McLeodUSA Incorporated	Communications
Mercy Medical Center	Healthcare
Nash Finch Company	Retail
Rockwell Collins	Aerospace/defense
St. Luke's Hospital	Education
Wal-Mart Stores	Retail
Yellowbook USA	Publisher

Note: Companies shown are located within the Cedar Rapids, IA Metropolitan Statistical Area.
Source: Hoovers.com; Wikipedia

Best Companies to Work For

Transamerica, headquartered in Cedar Rapids, is among the "100 Best Companies for Working Mothers." Criteria: paid time off and leaves; workforce profile; benefits; women's issues and advancement; flexible work; company culture and work life programs. *Working Mother, "100 Best Companies 2019"*

PUBLIC SAFETY

Crime Rate

Area	All Crimes	Violent Crimes				Property Crimes		
		Murder	Rape[3]	Robbery	Aggrav. Assault	Burglary	Larceny -Theft	Motor Vehicle Theft
City	4,035.5	4.5	25.8	91.8	158.5	704.4	2,791.2	259.3
Suburbs[1]	1,273.6	1.5	27.0	12.4	115.9	313.5	720.3	83.1
Metro[2]	2,627.4	3.0	26.4	51.3	136.8	505.1	1,735.4	169.5
U.S.	2,757.7	5.3	41.7	98.6	249.2	429.7	1,695.5	237.7

Note: Figures are crimes per 100,000 population; (1) All areas within the metro area that are located outside the city limits; (2) Figures cover the Cedar Rapids, IA Metropolitan Statistical Area—see Appendix B for areas included; (3) The city and U.S. figures shown were reported using the revised Uniform Crime Reporting (UCR) definition of rape. The suburban and metro area figures shown are an aggregate total of the data submitted using both the revised and legacy UCR definitions.
Source: FBI Uniform Crime Reports, 2017 (data for 2018 was not available)

Hate Crimes

Area	Number of Quarters Reported	Number of Incidents per Bias Motivation					
		Race/Ethnicity/ Ancestry	Religion	Sexual Orientation	Disability	Gender	Gender Identity
City	4	0	0	0	0	0	0
U.S.	4	4,047	1,419	1,196	159	47	168

Source: Federal Bureau of Investigation, Hate Crime Statistics 2018

Identity Theft Consumer Reports

Area	Reports	Reports per 100,000 Population	Rank[2]
MSA[1]	181	66	307
U.S.	650,572	198	-

Note: (1) Figures cover the Cedar Rapids, IA Metropolitan Statistical Area—see Appendix B for areas included; (2) Rank ranges from 1 to 386 where 1 indicates greatest number of identity theft reports per 100,000 population
Source: Federal Trade Commission, Consumer Sentinel Network Data Book for January–December 2019

Fraud and Other Consumer Reports

Area	Reports	Reports per 100,000 Population	Rank[2]
MSA[1]	1,588	583	153
U.S.	2,590,177	789	-

Note: (1) Figures cover the Cedar Rapids, IA Metropolitan Statistical Area—see Appendix B for areas included; (2) Rank ranges from 1 to 386 where 1 indicates greatest number of fraud and other consumer reports per 100,000 population
Source: Federal Trade Commission, Consumer Sentinel Network Data Book for January–December 2019

SPORTS

Professional Sports Teams

Team Name	League	Year Established
No teams are located in the metro area		

Source: Wikipedia, Major Professional Sports Teams of the United States and Canada, May 4, 2020

CLIMATE

Average and Extreme Temperatures

Temperature	Jan	Feb	Mar	Apr	May	Jun	Jul	Aug	Sep	Oct	Nov	Dec	Yr.
Extreme High (°F)	58	66	87	100	94	103	105	105	97	95	76	65	105
Average High (°F)	24	30	43	59	71	81	84	82	73	62	45	29	57
Average Temp. (°F)	15	21	34	48	60	69	73	71	62	50	36	21	47
Average Low (°F)	6	11	24	36	48	58	62	59	50	39	26	12	36
Extreme Low (°F)	-33	-29	-34	-4	25	38	42	38	22	11	-17	-27	-34

Note: Figures cover the years 1960-1995
Source: National Climatic Data Center, International Station Meteorological Climate Summary, 9/96

Average Precipitation/Snowfall/Humidity

Precip./Humidity	Jan	Feb	Mar	Apr	May	Jun	Jul	Aug	Sep	Oct	Nov	Dec	Yr.
Avg. Precip. (in.)	0.8	1.0	2.3	3.6	4.1	4.5	4.8	4.0	3.5	2.5	1.9	1.3	34.4
Avg. Snowfall (in.)	7	7	6	2	Tr	0	0	0	0	Tr	4	8	33
Avg. Rel. Hum. 6am (%)	77	80	82	81	81	83	87	90	89	84	83	82	83
Avg. Rel. Hum. 3pm (%)	68	66	62	52	51	51	55	55	55	52	62	70	58

Note: Figures cover the years 1960-1995; Tr = Trace amounts (<0.05 in. of rain; <0.5 in. of snow)
Source: National Climatic Data Center, International Station Meteorological Climate Summary, 9/96

Weather Conditions

Temperature			Daytime Sky			Precipitation		
5°F & below	32°F & below	90°F & above	Clear	Partly cloudy	Cloudy	0.01 inch or more precip.	0.1 inch or more snow/ice	Thunder-storms
38	156	16	89	132	144	109	28	42

Note: Figures are average number of days per year and cover the years 1960-1995
Source: National Climatic Data Center, International Station Meteorological Climate Summary, 9/96

HAZARDOUS WASTE

Superfund Sites

The Cedar Rapids, IA metro area has no sites on the EPA's Superfund Final National Priorities List. There are a total of 1,387 Superfund sites with a status of proposed or final on the list in the U.S.
U.S. Environmental Protection Agency, National Priorities List, May 5, 2020

AIR & WATER QUALITY

Air Quality Trends: Ozone

	1990	1995	2000	2005	2010	2012	2014	2016	2017	2018
MSA[1]	n/a	n/a	n/a	n/a	n/a	n/a	n/a	n/a	n/a	n/a
U.S.	0.088	0.089	0.082	0.080	0.073	0.075	0.067	0.069	0.068	0.069

Note: (1) Data covers the Cedar Rapids, IA Metropolitan Statistical Area—see Appendix B for areas included; n/a not available. The values shown are the composite ozone concentration averages among trend sites based on the highest fourth daily maximum 8-hour concentration in parts per million. These trends are based on sites having an adequate record of monitoring data during the trend period. Data from exceptional events are included.
Source: U.S. Environmental Protection Agency, Air Quality Monitoring Information, "Air Quality Trends by City, 1990-2018"

Air Quality Index

Area	Percent of Days when Air Quality was...[2]					AQI Statistics[2]	
	Good	Moderate	Unhealthy for Sensitive Groups	Unhealthy	Very Unhealthy	Maximum	Median
MSA[1]	68.2	30.7	1.1	0.0	0.0	129	44

Note: (1) Data covers the Cedar Rapids, IA Metropolitan Statistical Area—see Appendix B for areas included; (2) Based on 365 days with AQI data in 2018. Air Quality Index (AQI) is an index for reporting daily air quality. EPA calculates the AQI for five major air pollutants regulated by the Clean Air Act: ground-level ozone, particle pollution (aka particulate matter), carbon monoxide, sulfur dioxide, and nitrogen dioxide. The AQI runs from 0 to 500. The higher the AQI value, the greater the level of air pollution and the greater the health concern. There are six AQI categories: "Good" AQI is between 0 and 50. Air quality is considered satisfactory; "Moderate" AQI is between 51 and 100. Air quality is acceptable; "Unhealthy for Sensitive Groups" When AQI values are between 101 and 150, members of sensitive groups may experience health effects; "Unhealthy" When AQI values are between 151 and 200 everyone may begin to experience health effects; "Very Unhealthy" AQI values between 201 and 300 trigger a health alert; "Hazardous" AQI values over 300 trigger warnings of emergency conditions (not shown).
Source: U.S. Environmental Protection Agency, Air Quality Index Report, 2018

Air Quality Index Pollutants

Area	Percent of Days when AQI Pollutant was...[2]					
	Carbon Monoxide	Nitrogen Dioxide	Ozone	Sulfur Dioxide	Particulate Matter 2.5	Particulate Matter 10
MSA[1]	0.0	0.0	41.1	0.8	57.8	0.3

Note: (1) Data covers the Cedar Rapids, IA Metropolitan Statistical Area—see Appendix B for areas included; (2) Based on 365 days with AQI data in 2018. The Air Quality Index (AQI) is an index for reporting daily air quality. EPA calculates the AQI for five major air pollutants regulated by the Clean Air Act: ground-level ozone, particle pollution (also known as particulate matter), carbon monoxide, sulfur dioxide, and nitrogen dioxide. The AQI runs from 0 to 500. The higher the AQI value, the greater the level of air pollution and the greater the health concern.
Source: U.S. Environmental Protection Agency, Air Quality Index Report, 2018

Maximum Air Pollutant Concentrations: Particulate Matter, Ozone, CO and Lead

	Particulate Matter 10 (ug/m^3)	Particulate Matter 2.5 Wtd AM (ug/m^3)	Particulate Matter 2.5 24-Hr (ug/m^3)	Ozone (ppm)	Carbon Monoxide (ppm)	Lead (ug/m^3)
MSA[1] Level	54	8.4	20	0.069	1	n/a
NAAQS[2]	150	15	35	0.075	9	0.15
Met NAAQS[2]	Yes	Yes	Yes	Yes	Yes	n/a

Note: (1) Data covers the Cedar Rapids, IA Metropolitan Statistical Area—see Appendix B for areas included; Data from exceptional events are included; (2) National Ambient Air Quality Standards; ppm = parts per million; ug/m^3 = micrograms per cubic meter; n/a not available.
Concentrations: Particulate Matter 10 (coarse particulate)—highest second maximum 24-hour concentration; Particulate Matter 2.5 Wtd AM (fine particulate)—highest weighted annual mean concentration; Particulate Matter 2.5 24-Hour (fine particulate)—highest 98th percentile 24-hour concentration; Ozone—highest fourth daily maximum 8-hour concentration; Carbon Monoxide—highest second maximum non-overlapping 8-hour concentration; Lead—maximum running 3-month average
Source: U.S. Environmental Protection Agency, Air Quality Monitoring Information, "Air Quality Statistics by City, 2018"

Maximum Air Pollutant Concentrations: Nitrogen Dioxide and Sulfur Dioxide

	Nitrogen Dioxide AM (ppb)	Nitrogen Dioxide 1-Hr (ppb)	Sulfur Dioxide AM (ppb)	Sulfur Dioxide 1-Hr (ppb)	Sulfur Dioxide 24-Hr (ppb)
MSA[1] Level	n/a	n/a	n/a	28	n/a
NAAQS[2]	53	100	30	75	140
Met NAAQS[2]	n/a	n/a	n/a	Yes	n/a

Note: (1) Data covers the Cedar Rapids, IA Metropolitan Statistical Area—see Appendix B for areas included; Data from exceptional events are included; (2) National Ambient Air Quality Standards; ppm = parts per million; ug/m^3 = micrograms per cubic meter; n/a not available.
Concentrations: Nitrogen Dioxide AM—highest arithmetic mean concentration; Nitrogen Dioxide 1-Hr—highest 98th percentile 1-hour daily maximum concentration; Sulfur Dioxide AM—highest annual mean concentration; Sulfur Dioxide 1-Hr—highest 99th percentile 1-hour daily maximum concentration; Sulfur Dioxide 24-Hr—highest second maximum 24-hour concentration
Source: U.S. Environmental Protection Agency, Air Quality Monitoring Information, "Air Quality Statistics by City, 2018"

Drinking Water

Water System Name	Pop. Served	Primary Water Source Type	Violations[1]
Cedar Rapids Water Dept.	129,214	(2)	8

Note: (1) Total number of violations (both active and inactive) in the EPA database
Source: U.S. Environmental Protection Agency, Office of Ground Water and Drinking Water, Safe Drinking Water Information System (based on data extracted May 5, 2020)

Chicago, Illinois

Background

City of Big Shoulders, The Windy City, That Toddling Town, and The Second City, are some of Chicago's nicknames. Whatever one calls Chicago, it has always exemplified a great American city, from a bustling downtown with towering skyscrapers to a quaint collection of closely packed urban neighborhoods stretching into the suburban landscape, then into the fields of the Illinois prairie.

Innovation has been part of Chicago's history from the very start. Cyrus McCormick invented his McCormick Reaper in 1831 and put Chicago on the map, revolutionizing harvesting across the world. The first mail-order business, Montgomery Ward, was established in Chicago in 1872. The world's first skyscraper was built in Chicago in 1885 for the Home Insurance Company. In 1907, University of Chicago's Albert Michelson, received the first American Nobel Prize for science. In 1931, Enrico Fermi split the atom underneath the University of Chicago football field. In 1983, Motorola set up the first modern portable cellular phone system in Chicago. All of this is part of the same history that has given Chicago 78 Nobel Prize Winners, more than any city in the world.

Present-day Chicago is "greener" than ever before. It has 300 square miles of protected lands and is home to 131 plant species of global importance. The city is the nation's largest municipal marina with over 5,000 boat slips. Bicycling, walking trails, beaches and golf are all abundant and top notch. The Oceanarium is the world's largest indoor marine mammal pavilion.

Chicago, with the third largest gross metropolitan product in the nation, has been rated the most balanced economy in the United States, due to its high level of diversification. The Boeing Company relocated its corporate headquarters from Seattle to Chicago in 2001. The city is also a major convention destination. Chicago is first in the country and third worldwide, in number of conventions hosted annually. In addition, Chicago and its metro area are home to dozens of Fortune 500 companies.

When the Willis (formerly Sears) Tower was completed in 1973, it was the tallest building in North America. Chicago is also home to the tenth and twenty-second tallest buildings in the world, and the work of homegrown architects Frank Lloyd Wright, Louis Sullivan, and Helmut Jahn. In addition, Mies van der Rohe immigrated here and became one of the most influential architects of the post-World War II era.

Chicago boasts the Art Institute of Chicago, the Adler Planetarium, the Chicago Architecture Foundation, and the Hellenic Museum and Cultural Center. Classical musical offerings include the Chicago Symphony Orchestra, its Chamber Music Series, the Chicago Opera Theater, and the Lyric Opera of Chicago. The city is famous for its eclectic nightlife. You can hear music at dozens of clubs, and comedy at Second City, where such comics as John Belushi, John Candy, Chris Farley, and Stephen Colbert had their start.

Chicago professional sports have long been in the national spotlight. Chicago is home to two major league baseball teams, the Chicago Cubs who play at Wrigley Field in the city's North Side and the Chicago White Sox who play in the city's South Side at U.S. Cellular Field. The Cubs won the 2016 World Series, ending a 108-year record World Series Champion drought. The Chicago Bears, the city's NFL team, won thirteen NFL championships, and Chicago's professional basketball team, the Chicago Bulls, is one of the world's most recognized teams. The NHL's Chicago Blackhawks, who share the United Center on the Near West Side with the Bulls, hosted the 2008-2009 Winter Classic.

The Chicago Marathon, one of five world marathon events, has been held every October since 1977. Chicago is also the starting point for the Chicago Yacht Club Race to Mackinac—the longest annual freshwater sailboat race in the world. Considering Chicago's athletic legacy, it's not surprising that the city was selected by the International Olympic Committee as one of four candidates for the 2016 games, but lost the bid to Rio de Janeiro.

Outstanding educational institutions in Chicago include the University of Chicago (1891); Northwestern University (1851); DePaul University; Loyola University; and the School of the Art Institute of Chicago.

Located along the southwest shore of Lake Michigan, Chicago has four true seasons, with a white Christmas, spring flowers, a steamy summer, and the beautiful colors of fall. Summers can be very hot and winters are often quite cold.

Rankings

General Rankings

- In its eighth annual survey, *Travel + Leisure* readers nominated their favorite small cities and towns in America—those with 100,000 or fewer residents—voting on numerous attractive features in categories including culture, food and drink, quality of life, style, and people. After 50,000 votes, Chicago was ranked #6 among the proposed favorites. *www.travelandleisure.com, "America's Favorite Cities," October 20, 2017*

- Chicago was selected as one of the best places to live in America by *Outside Magazine*. Criteria included population, park acreage, neighborhood and resident diversity, new and upcoming things of interest, and opportunities for outdoor adventure. These places are home to a new breed of outdoor athletes and the new adventure capitals of America. *Outside Magazine, "The 12 Best Places to Live in 2019," July 11, 2019*

- The human resources consulting firm Mercer ranked 231 major cities worldwide in terms of overall quality of life. Chicago ranked #49. Criteria: political, social, economic, and socio-cultural factors; medical and health considerations; schools and education; public services and transportation; recreation; consumer goods; housing; and natural environment. *Mercer, "Mercer 2019 Quality of Living Survey," March 13, 2019*

- Chicago appeared on *Travel + Leisure's* list of the fifteen best cities in the United States. The city was ranked #6. Criteria: sights/landmarks; culture; food; friendliness; shopping; and overall value. *Travel + Leisure, "The World's Best Awards 2019" July 10, 2019*

- Based on more than 600,000 responses, *Condé Nast Traveler* ranked its readers' favorite cities in the U.S. The list was broken into cities over 350,000 and cities under 350,000. Chicago ranked #1 in the big city category. *Condé Nast Traveler, Readers' Choice Awards 2019, "Best Big Cities in the U.S." October 7, 2019*

Business/Finance Rankings

- Recognizing the sizeable percentage of American workers who are self-employed, NerdWallet editors assessed the country's cities according to percentage of freelancers, median rental costs, cell phone plans/taxes, and healthcare affordability and access. By these criteria, Chicago placed #16 among the best cities for independent workers. *www.nerdwallet.com, "Best Places for Freelance Workers," August 30, 2016*

- Based on metro area social media reviews, the employment opinion group Glassdoor surveyed 50 of the most populous U.S. metro areas and equally weighed cost of living, hiring opportunity, and job satisfaction to compose a list of "25 Best Cities for Jobs." Median pay and home value, and number of active job openings was also factored in. The Chicago metro area was ranked #15 in overall job satisfaction. *www.glassdoor.com, "Best Cities for Jobs," February 25, 2020*

- The Brookings Institution ranked the nation's largest cities based on income inequality. Chicago was ranked #22 (#1 = greatest inequality). Criteria: the "95/20 ratio," a figure representing the income at which a household earns more than 95 percent of all other households, divided by the income at which a household earns more than only 20 percent of all other households. *Brookings Institution, "Household Income Inequality, Largest Cities of 97 Large U.S. Metro Areas, 2014-2016," February 5, 2018*

- The Brookings Institution ranked the 100 largest metro areas in the U.S. based on income inequality. Chicago was ranked #15 (#1 = greatest inequality). Criteria: the "95/20 ratio," a figure representing the income at which a household earns more than 95 percent of all other households, divided by the income at which a household earns more than only 20 percent of all other households. *Brookings Institution, "Household Income Inequality, 100 Largest U.S. Metro Areas, 2014-2016," February 5, 2018*

- Payscale.com ranked the 32 largest metro areas in terms of wage growth. The Chicago metro area ranked #20. Criteria: private-sector and education professional wage growth between the 4th quarter of 2018 and the 4th quarter of 2019. *PayScale, "Wage Trends by Metro Area-4th Quarter," January 24, 2020*

- The Chicago metro area was identified as one of the most debt-ridden places in America by the finance site Credit.com. The metro area was ranked #12. Criteria: residents' average credit card debt as well as median income. *Credit.com, "25 Cities With the Most Credit Card Debt," February 28, 2018*

- Chicago was identified as one of the happiest cities to work in by CareerBliss.com, an online community for career advancement. The city ranked #2 out of 10. Criteria: an employee's relationship with his or her boss and co-workers; daily tasks; general work environment; compensation; opportunities for advancement; company culture and job reputation; and resources. *Businesswire.com, "CareerBliss Happiest Cities to Work 2019," February 12, 2019*

- The Chicago metro area appeared on the Milken Institute "2020 Best Performing Cities" list. Rank: #78 out of 200 large metro areas. Criteria: job growth; wage and salary growth; high-tech output growth. *Milken Institute, "Best-Performing Cities 2020," February 26, 2020*

- *Forbes* ranked the 200 most populous metro areas to determine the nation's "Best Places for Business and Careers." The Chicago metro area was ranked #75. Criteria: costs (business and living); job growth (past and projected); income growth; quality of life; educational attainment (college and high school); projected economic growth; cultural and leisure opportunities; workplace tolerance laws; net migration patterns. *Forbes, "The Best Places for Business and Careers 2019: Seattle Still On Top," October 30, 2019*

- Mercer Human Resources Consulting ranked 209 cities worldwide in terms of cost-of-living. Chicago ranked #37 (the lower the ranking, the higher the cost-of-living). The survey measured the comparative cost of over 200 items (such as housing, food, clothing, household goods, transportation, and entertainment) in each location. *Mercer, "2019 Cost of Living Survey," June 26, 2019*

Children/Family Rankings

- Chicago was selected as one of the most playful cities in the U.S. by KaBOOM! The organization's Playful City USA initiative honors cities and towns across the nation that have made their communities more playable. Criteria: pledging to integrate play as a solution to challenges in their communities; making it easy for children to get active and balanced play; creating more family-friendly and innovative communities as a result. *KaBOOM! National Campaign for Play, "2017 Playful City USA Communities"*

Culture/Performing Arts Rankings

- Chicago was selected as one of the twenty best large U.S. cities for moviemakers. Of cities with a population over 400,000, (NYC & LA intentionally not included) the city was ranked #2. Criteria: film community and culture; access to equipment and facilities; film activity in 2019; tax incentives; and standard of living. *MovieMaker Magazine, "Best Places to Live and Work as a Moviemaker: 2020," January 31, 2020*

- Chicago was selected as one of "America's Favorite Cities." The city ranked #10 in the "Culture" category. Respondents to an online survey were asked to rate 38 top urban destinations in the U.S. from a visitor's perspective. Criteria: theater scene and community; number of bookstores; live music; and sense of history. *Travelandleisure.com, "These Are America's 20 Most Cultured Cities," October 2016*

- Chicago was selected as one of "America's Favorite Cities." The city ranked #11 in the "Culture: Music Scene " category. Respondents to an online survey were asked to rate 38 top urban destinations in the U.S. from a visitor's perspective. *Travelandleisure.com, "From the Honkytonk Capital to Jazz's Birthplace: America's Best Music Scenes," October 2016*

- Chicago was selected as one of "America's Favorite Cities." The city ranked #3 in the "Architecture " category. Respondents to an online survey were asked to rate their favorite place (population over 100,000) in over 65 categories. *Travelandleisure.com, "America's Favorite Cities for Architecture 2016," March 2, 2017*

Education Rankings

- Personal finance website *WalletHub* analyzed the 150 largest U.S. metropolitan statistical areas to determine where the most educated Americans are choosing to settle. Criteria: education levels; percentage of workers with degrees; education quality and attainment gap; public school quality rankings; quality and size of each metro area's universities. Chicago was ranked #38 (#1 = most educated city). *www.WalletHub.com, "2019's Most and Least Educated Cities in America," July 22, 2019*

- Chicago was selected as one of the most well-read cities in America by Amazon.com. The city ranked #17 among the top 20. Cities with populations greater than 500,000 were evaluated based on per capita sales of books, magazines and newspapers (both print and Kindle format). *Amazon.com, "The 20 Most Well-Read Cities in America," May 24, 2016*

- Chicago was selected as one of America's most literate cities. The city ranked #22 out of the 82 largest U.S. cities. Criteria: number of booksellers; library resources; Internet resources; educational attainment; periodical publishing resources; newspaper circulation. *Central Connecticut State University, "America's Most Literate Cities, 2016," March 31, 2017*

Environmental Rankings

- The U.S. Environmental Protection Agency (EPA) released a list of U.S. metropolitan areas with the most ENERGY STAR certified buildings in 2017. The Chicago metro area was ranked #7 out of 25. *U.S. Environmental Protection Agency, "2018 Energy Star Top Cities," April 11, 2018*

- Chicago was highlighted as one of the 25 most ozone-polluted metro areas in the U.S. during 2015 through 2017. The area ranked #18. *American Lung Association, "State of the Air 2019," April 24, 2019*

- Chicago was highlighted as one of the 25 metro areas most polluted by year-round particle pollution (Annual PM 2.5) in the U.S. during 2015 through 2017. The area ranked #19. *American Lung Association, "State of the Air 2019," April 24, 2019*

Food/Drink Rankings

- The U.S. Chamber of Commerce Foundation conducted an in-depth study on local food truck regulations, surveyed 288 food truck owners, and ranked 20 major American cities based on how friendly they are for operating a food truck. The compiled index assessed the following: procedures for obtaining permits and licenses; complying with restrictions; and financial obligations associated with operating a food truck. Chicago ranked #13 overall (1 being the best) for ease in operating a food truck. *www.foodtrucknation.us, "Food Truck Nation," March 20, 2018*

- According to Fodor's Travel, Chicago placed among the 14 best U.S. cities for food-truck cuisine. *www.fodors.com, "America's Best Food Truck Cities," August 23, 2016*

Health/Fitness Rankings

- For each of the 100 largest cities in the United States, the American Fitness Index®, published by the American College of Sports Medicine and the Anthem Foundation, evaluated community infrastructure and 33 health behaviors including preventive health, levels of chronic disease conditions, pedestrian safety, air quality, and community resources that support physical activity. Chicago ranked #15 for "community fitness." *americanfitnessindex.org, "ACSM American Fitness Index Health and Community Fitness Status of the 100 Largest U.S. Cities," May 14, 2019*

- Chicago was identified as one of the 10 most walkable cities in the U.S. by Walk Score, a Seattle-based service that rates the convenience and transit access of 10,000 neighborhoods in more than 2,800 cities. The area ranked #6 out of the 50 largest U.S. cities. Walk Score measures walkability by analyzing hundreds of walking routes to nearby amenities, and also measures pedestrian friendliness by analyzing population density and road metrics such as block length and intersection density. *WalkScore.com, February 28, 2020*

- The Chicago metro area was identified as one of the worst cities for bed bugs in America by pest control company Orkin. The area ranked #12 out of 50 based on the number of bed bug treatments Orkin performed from December 2018 to November 2019. *Orkin, "Washington, D.C. Surpasses Baltimore to Secure Top Spot on Orkin's 2020 Bed Bug Cities List," January 13, 2020*

- Chicago was identified as a "2020 Spring Allergy Capital." The area ranked #74 out of 100. Three groups of factors were used to identify the most challenging cities for people with allergies during the spring season: annual spring pollen levels; over the counter medicine use; number of board-certified allergy specialists. *Asthma and Allergy Foundation of America, "Spring Allergy Capitals 2020," March 10, 2020*

- Chicago was identified as a "2020 Fall Allergy Capital." The area ranked #58 out of 100. Three groups of factors were used to identify the most challenging cities for people with allergies during the fall season: annual fall pollen levels; over the counter medicine use; number of board-certified allergy specialists. *Asthma and Allergy Foundation of America, "Fall Allergy Capitals 2020," March 10, 2020*

- Chicago was identified as a "2019 Asthma Capital." The area ranked #36 out of the nation's 100 largest metropolitan areas. Criteria: estimated asthma prevalence; crude death rate from asthma; and ER visits due to asthma. Risk factors that were analyzed but not factored in the rankings: annual pollen score; annual air quality; public smoking laws; number of board-certified asthma specialists; rescue medication use; controller medication use; uninsured rate; poverty rate. *Asthma and Allergy Foundation of America, "Asthma Capitals 2019: The Most Challenging Places to Live With Asthma," May 7, 2019*

- *Men's Health* ranked 100 major U.S. cities in terms of the best cities for men. Chicago ranked #55. Criteria: health; fitness; quality of life. *Men's Health, "The Best & Worst Cities for Men Who Want to Be Fit and Happy," January 1, 2016*

- The Chicago metro area ranked #95 out of 189 in The Gallup-Sharecare Well-Being Index. Criteria: purpose; social well being; financial health; community and physical health. Results are based on telephone interviews with adults, aged 18 and older, living in metropolitan areas in the 50 U.S. states and the District of Columbia. *Gallup-Sharecare, "State of American Well-Being, 2017 Community Well-Being Rankings" March 2018*

Pet Rankings

- Chicago appeared on *The Dogington Post* site as one of the top cities for dog lovers, ranking #2 out of 20. The real estate brokerage, Redfin and Rover, the largest pet sitter and dog walker network, compiled a list from over 14,000 U.S. cities to come up with a "Rover Rank". Criteria: highest count of dog walks, the city's Walk Score®, for-sale home listings that mention "dog", number of dog walkers and pet sitters and the hours spent and distance logged. *www.dogingtonpost.com, "The 20 Most Dog-Friendly Cities of 2019," April 4, 2019*

Real Estate Rankings

- FitSmallBusiness looked at 50 of the largest metropolitan areas in the U.S. to determine which metro was the best to start a real estate business. Data was compiled from such sources as: Zillow, Trulia, U.S. Census Bureau, and the Bureau of Labor Statistics. Criteria: location; inventory; annual wages; median sales price of homes; days on the market; median price cut percentage; and other factors that would influence real estate professional growth. The Chicago metro area ranked #4. *fitsmallbusiness.com, "The Best Cities to Become a Real Estate Agent in 2018," January 30, 2018*

- *WalletHub* compared the most populated U.S. cities, as well as at least two of the most populated cities in each state, for a total of 179, to determine which had the best markets for real estate agents. Chicago ranked #85 where demand was high and pay was the best. Criteria: sales per agent; annual median wage for real-estate agents; monthly average starting salary for real estate agents; real estate job density and competition; unemployment rate; home turnover rate; housing-market health index; and other relevant metrics. *www.WalletHub.com, "2019's Best Places to Be a Real Estate Agent," April 24, 2019*

- Chicago was ranked #135 out of 238 metro areas in terms of housing affordability in 2019 by the National Association of Home Builders (#1 = most affordable). Criteria: the share of homes sold in that area affordable to a family earning the local median income, based on standard mortgage underwriting criteria. *National Association of Home Builders®, NAHB-Wells Fargo Housing Opportunity Index, 4th Quarter 2019*

- The nation's largest metro areas were analyzed in terms of the percentage of households entering some stage of foreclosure in 2018. The Chicago metro area ranked #4 out of 10 (#1 = highest foreclosure rate). *ATTOM Data Solutions, "2018 Year-End U.S. Foreclosure Market Report™," January 17, 2019*

- The nation's largest metro areas were analyzed in terms of the percentage of households entering some stage of foreclosure in 2019. The Chicago metro area ranked #8 out of 10 (#1 = highest foreclosure rate). *ATTOM Data Solutions, "2019 Year-End U.S. Foreclosure Market Report™," January 14, 2020*

Safety Rankings

- To identify the most dangerous cities in America, 24/7 Wall Street focused on violent crime categories—murder, non-negligent manslaughter, rape, robbery, and aggravated assault—and property crime as reported in the FBI's 2018 annual Uniform Crime Report. Criteria also included median income from American Community Survey and unemployment figures from Bureau of Labor Statistics. For cities with populations over 100,000, Chicago was ranked #29. *247wallst.com, "America's Most Dangerous Cities" January 10, 2020*

- Allstate ranked the 200 largest cities in America in terms of driver safety. Chicago ranked #133. Criteria: internal property damage claims over a two-year period from January 2016 to December 2017. The report helps increase the importance of safety and awareness behind the wheel. *Allstate, "Allstate America's Best Drivers Report, 2019" June 24, 2019*

- Chicago was identified as one of the most dangerous cities in America by NeighborhoodScout. The city ranked #64 out of 100 (#1 = most dangerous). Criteria: number of violent crimes per 1,000 residents. The editors only considered cities with 25,000 or more residents. *NeighborhoodScout.com, "Top 100 Most Dangerous Cities in the U.S. 2020" January 2, 2020*

- The National Insurance Crime Bureau ranked 382 metro areas in the U.S. in terms of per capita rates of vehicle theft. The Chicago metro area ranked #193 (#1 = highest rate). Criteria: number of vehicle theft offenses per 100,000 inhabitants in 2018. *National Insurance Crime Bureau, "Hot Spots 2018," June 25, 2019*

Seniors/Retirement Rankings

- From its Best Cities for Successful Aging indexes, the Milken Institute generated rankings for metropolitan areas, weighing data in nine categories—health care, wellness, living arrangements, transportation and convenience, financial characteristics, education, employment, community engagement, and overall livability. The Chicago metro area was ranked #52 overall in the large metro area category. *Milken Institute, "Best Cities for Successful Aging, 2017" March 14, 2017*

Sports/Recreation Rankings

- Chicago was chosen as one of America's best cities for bicycling. The city ranked #6 out of 50. Criteria: cycling infrastructure that is safe and friendly for all ages; energy and bike culture. The editors only considered cities with populations of 100,000 or more. *Bicycling, "The 50 Best Bike Cities in America," October 10, 2018*

Transportation Rankings

- Business Insider presented an AllTransit Performance Score ranking of public transportation in major U.S. cities and towns, with populations over 250,000, in which Chicago earned the #6-ranked "Transit Score," awarded for frequency of service, access to jobs, quality and number of stops, and affordability. *www.businessinsider.com, "The 17 Major U.S. Cities with the Best Public Transportation," April 17, 2018*

- Chicago was identified as one of the most congested metro areas in the U.S. The area ranked #10 out of 10. Criteria: yearly delay per auto commuter in hours. *Texas A&M Transportation Institute, "2019 Urban Mobility Report," August 2019*

- According to the INRIX "2019 Global Traffic Scorecard," Chicago was identified as one of the most congested metro areas in the U.S. The area ranked #2 out of 10. Criteria: average annual time spent in traffic and average cost of congestion per motorist. *Inrix.com, "Congestion Costs Each American Nearly 100 hours, $1,400 A Year," March 9, 2020*

Women/Minorities Rankings

- The *Houston Chronicle* listed the Chicago metro area as #8 in top places for young Latinos to live in the U.S. Research was largely based on housing and occupational data from the largest metropolitan areas performed by *Forbes* and NBC Universo. Criteria: percentage of 18-34 year-olds; Latino college grad rates; and diversity. *blog.chron.com, "The 15 Best Big Cities for Latino Millenials," January 26, 2016*

- Personal finance website *WalletHub* compared more than 180 U.S. cities—including the 150 most populated U.S. cities, plus at least two of the most populated cities in each state—across two key dimensions, "Hispanic Business-Friendliness" and "Hispanic Purchasing Power", to arrive at the most favorable conditions for Hispanic entrepreneurs. Chicago was ranked #122 out of 182. Criteria includes: share of Hispanic-Owned Businesses; Hispanic entrepreneurship rate to median annual income of Hispanics; Small Business-Friendliness score; cost of living; and number of Hispanics with at least a bachelor's degree. *WalletHub.com, "2019's Best Cities for Hispanic Entrepreneurs," May 1, 2019*

Miscellaneous Rankings

- In its roundup of St. Patrick's Day parades "Gayot" listed the best festivals and parades of all things Irish. The festivities in Chicago as among the best. *www.gayot.com, "Best St. Patrick's Day Parades," March 2020*

- The watchdog site Charity Navigator conducts an annual study of charities in the nation's major markets both to analyze statistical differences in their financial, accountability, and transparency practices and to track year-to-year variations in individual philanthropic communities. Charity Navigator's analysis demonstrated that the financial, accountability and transparency behaviors of America's largest charities can be influenced by the metropolitan market within which the charity operates. The Chicago metro area was ranked #11 among the 30 metro markets in the rating category of Overall Score. *www.charitynavigator.org, "2017 Metro Market Study," May 1, 2017*

- The real estate site Zillow has compiled the 2017 Trick-or-Treat Index, which used its own Home Value Index and Walk Score along with single-family home density, age of residents, and cities with populations of at least 500,000 to determine that Chicago ranked #13 for "getting the best candy in the least amount of time." Zillow also zeroes in on the best neighborhoods in its top 20 cities. *www.zillow.com, "20 Best Cities for Trick or Treating in 2017," October 13, 2017*

- *WalletHub* compared the 150 most populated U.S. cities to determine their operating efficiency. A "Quality of Services" score was constructed for each city and then divided by the total budget per capita to reveal which were managed the best. Chicago ranked #140. Criteria: financial stability; economy; education; safety; health; infrastructure and pollution. *www.WalletHub.com, "2019's Best- & Worst-Run Cities in America," July 1, 2019*

- Chicago was selected as one of the 20 memorable places in the world during Thanksgiving by *Fodor's Travel*. Criteria: attractions; history; events. *Fodors.com, "Where to Go for Thanksgiving 2016," November 4, 2016*

- The National Alliance to End Homelessness listed the 25 most populous metro areas with the highest rate of homelessness. The Chicago metro area had a high rate of homelessness. Criteria: number of homeless people per 10,000 population in 2016. *National Alliance to End Homelessness, "Homelessness in the 25 Most Populous U.S. Metro Areas," September 1, 2017*

Business Environment

CITY FINANCES

City Government Finances

Component	2017 ($000)	2017 ($ per capita)
Total Revenues	9,903,182	3,640
Total Expenditures	10,401,108	3,823
Debt Outstanding	23,539,562	8,653
Cash and Securities[1]	16,038,297	5,895

Note: (1) Cash and security holdings of a government at the close of its fiscal year, including those of its dependent agencies, utilities, and liquor stores.
Source: U.S. Census Bureau, State & Local Government Finances 2017

City Government Revenue by Source

Source	2017 ($000)	2017 ($ per capita)	2017 (%)
General Revenue			
From Federal Government	619,242	228	6.3
From State Government	1,084,923	399	11.0
From Local Governments	6,583	2	0.1
Taxes			
Property	1,294,063	476	13.1
Sales and Gross Receipts	1,807,606	664	18.3
Personal Income	0	0	0.0
Corporate Income	0	0	0.0
Motor Vehicle License	24,335	9	0.2
Other Taxes	435,393	160	4.4
Current Charges	1,914,278	704	19.3
Liquor Store	0	0	0.0
Utility	760,638	280	7.7
Employee Retirement	881,784	324	8.9

Source: U.S. Census Bureau, State & Local Government Finances 2017

City Government Expenditures by Function

Function	2017 ($000)	2017 ($ per capita)	2017 (%)
General Direct Expenditures			
Air Transportation	1,279,601	470	12.3
Corrections	0	0	0.0
Education	0	0	0.0
Employment Security Administration	0	0	0.0
Financial Administration	146,554	53	1.4
Fire Protection	585,010	215	5.6
General Public Buildings	217,731	80	2.1
Governmental Administration, Other	64,026	23	0.6
Health	131,616	48	1.3
Highways	669,770	246	6.4
Hospitals	0	0	0.0
Housing and Community Development	241,747	88	2.3
Interest on General Debt	931,275	342	9.0
Judicial and Legal	29,525	10	0.3
Libraries	95,327	35	0.9
Parking	7,476	2	0.1
Parks and Recreation	28,506	10	0.3
Police Protection	1,456,302	535	14.0
Public Welfare	304,839	112	2.9
Sewerage	283,217	104	2.7
Solid Waste Management	159,572	58	1.5
Veterans' Services	0	0	0.0
Liquor Store	0	0	0.0
Utility	610,909	224	5.9
Employee Retirement	2,021,004	742	19.4

Source: U.S. Census Bureau, State & Local Government Finances 2017

DEMOGRAPHICS

Population Growth

Area	1990 Census	2000 Census	2010 Census	2018* Estimate	Population Growth (%) 1990-2018	2010-2018
City	2,783,726	2,896,016	2,695,598	2,718,555	-2.3	0.9
MSA[1]	8,182,076	9,098,316	9,461,105	9,536,428	16.6	0.8
U.S.	248,709,873	281,421,906	308,745,538	322,903,030	29.8	4.6

Note: (1) Figures cover the Chicago-Naperville-Elgin, IL-IN-WI Metropolitan Statistical Area—see Appendix B for areas included; (*) 2014-2018 5-year estimated population
Source: U.S. Census Bureau, 1990 Census, Census 2000, Census 2010, 2014-2018 American Community Survey 5-Year Estimates

Household Size

Area	Persons in Household (%) One	Two	Three	Four	Five	Six	Seven or More	Average Household Size
City	36.8	29.5	13.9	10.4	5.3	2.3	1.8	2.50
MSA[1]	28.6	31.0	15.7	14.0	6.8	2.5	1.5	2.70
U.S.	27.7	33.9	15.7	13.0	6.0	2.3	1.4	2.60

Note: (1) Figures cover the Chicago-Naperville-Elgin, IL-IN-WI Metropolitan Statistical Area—see Appendix B for areas included
Source: U.S. Census Bureau, 2014-2018 American Community Survey 5-Year Estimates

Race

Area	White Alone[2] (%)	Black Alone[2] (%)	Asian Alone[2] (%)	AIAN[3] Alone[2] (%)	NHOPI[4] Alone[2] (%)	Other Race Alone[2] (%)	Two or More Races (%)
City	49.4	30.1	6.4	0.3	0.0	10.9	2.7
MSA[1]	65.8	16.6	6.5	0.3	0.0	8.1	2.6
U.S.	72.7	12.7	5.4	0.8	0.2	4.9	3.2

Note: (1) Figures cover the Chicago-Naperville-Elgin, IL-IN-WI Metropolitan Statistical Area—see Appendix B for areas included; (2) Alone is defined as not being in combination with one or more other races; (3) American Indian and Alaska Native; (4) Native Hawaiian and Other Pacific Islander
Source: U.S. Census Bureau, 2014-2018 American Community Survey 5-Year Estimates

Hispanic or Latino Origin

Area	Total (%)	Mexican (%)	Puerto Rican (%)	Cuban (%)	Other (%)
City	29.0	21.6	3.8	0.3	3.3
MSA[1]	21.9	17.3	2.2	0.2	2.2
U.S.	17.8	11.2	1.7	0.7	4.2

Note: Persons of Hispanic or Latino origin can be of any race; (1) Figures cover the Chicago-Naperville-Elgin, IL-IN-WI Metropolitan Statistical Area—see Appendix B for areas included
Source: U.S. Census Bureau, 2014-2018 American Community Survey 5-Year Estimates

Segregation

Type	Segregation Indices[1] 1990	2000	2010	2010 Rank[2]	Percent Change 1990-2000	1990-2010	2000-2010
Black/White	84.4	81.2	76.4	3	-3.2	-8.0	-4.8
Asian/White	46.5	46.8	44.9	26	0.3	-1.6	-1.8
Hispanic/White	61.4	60.7	56.3	10	-0.8	-5.1	-4.3

Note: All figures cover the Metropolitan Statistical Area—see Appendix B for areas included; Figures are based on an analysis of 1990, 2000, and 2010 Census Decennial Census tract data by William H. Frey, Brookings Institution and the University of Michigan Social Science Data Analysis Network. In this analysis all racial groups (whites, blacks, and asians) are non-Hispanic members of those races. Hispanics are shown as a separate category; (1) Segregation Indices are Dissimilarity Indices that measure the degree to which the minority group is distributed differently than whites across census tracts. They range from 0 (complete integration) to 100 (complete segregation) where the value indicates the percentage of the minority group that needs to move to be distributed exactly like whites; (2) Ranges from 1 (most segregated) to 102 (least segregated); n/a not available.
Source: www.CensusScope.org

Ancestry

Area	German	Irish	English	American	Italian	Polish	French[2]	Scottish	Dutch
City	7.4	7.4	2.4	2.0	3.9	5.7	1.0	0.6	0.5
MSA[1]	14.6	10.9	4.2	2.7	6.7	8.9	1.5	0.9	1.2
U.S.	13.7	9.9	7.3	6.4	5.2	2.8	2.4	1.7	1.2

Note: Figures are the percentage of the total population reporting a particular ancestry. The nine most commonly reported ancestries in the U.S. are shown. Figures include multiple ancestries (e.g. if a person reported being Irish and Italian, they were included in both columns); (1) Figures cover the Chicago-Naperville-Elgin, IL-IN-WI Metropolitan Statistical Area—see Appendix B for areas included; (2) Excludes Basque
Source: U.S. Census Bureau, 2014-2018 American Community Survey 5-Year Estimates

Foreign-born Population

Area	Percent of Population Born in								
	Any Foreign Country	Asia	Mexico	Europe	Caribbean	Central America[2]	South America	Africa	Canada
City	20.6	5.1	8.6	3.5	0.4	0.8	1.0	0.9	0.2
MSA[1]	17.7	5.2	6.6	3.7	0.3	0.6	0.6	0.6	0.2
U.S.	13.5	4.1	3.5	1.5	1.3	1.1	0.9	0.7	0.3

Note: (1) Figures cover the Chicago-Naperville-Elgin, IL-IN-WI Metropolitan Statistical Area—see Appendix B for areas included; (2) Excludes Mexico.
Source: U.S. Census Bureau, 2014-2018 American Community Survey 5-Year Estimates

Marital Status

Area	Never Married	Now Married[2]	Separated	Widowed	Divorced
City	49.0	35.1	2.3	5.3	8.4
MSA[1]	37.0	46.9	1.7	5.5	8.9
U.S.	33.3	48.1	2.0	5.8	10.8

Note: Figures are percentages and cover the population 15 years of age and older; (1) Figures cover the Chicago-Naperville-Elgin, IL-IN-WI Metropolitan Statistical Area—see Appendix B for areas included; (2) Excludes separated
Source: U.S. Census Bureau, 2014-2018 American Community Survey 5-Year Estimates

Disability by Age

Area	All Ages	Under 18 Years Old	18 to 64 Years Old	65 Years and Over
City	10.4	3.0	8.2	36.5
MSA[1]	9.9	3.0	7.6	32.6
U.S.	12.6	4.2	10.3	35.0

Note: Figures show percent of the civilian noninstitutionalized population that reported having a disability. Disability status is determined from six types of difficulty: vision, hearing, cognitive, ambulatory, self-care, and independent living. For children under 5 years old, hearing and vision difficulty are used to determine disability status. For children between the ages of 5 and 14, disability status is determined from hearing, vision, cognitive, ambulatory, and self-care difficulties. For people aged 15 years and older, they are considered to have a disability if they have difficulty with any one of the six difficulty types; Note: (1) Figures cover the Chicago-Naperville-Elgin, IL-IN-WI Metropolitan Statistical Area—see Appendix B for areas included
Source: U.S. Census Bureau, 2014-2018 American Community Survey 5-Year Estimates

Age

Area	Percent of Population									Median Age
	Under Age 5	Age 5–19	Age 20–34	Age 35–44	Age 45–54	Age 55–64	Age 65–74	Age 75–84	Age 85+	
City	6.5	17.3	27.4	14.0	12.0	10.9	7.0	3.6	1.4	34.3
MSA[1]	6.2	19.7	21.1	13.3	13.5	12.6	7.9	4.0	1.8	37.2
U.S.	6.1	19.3	20.7	12.6	13.2	12.8	8.8	4.5	1.9	37.9

Note: (1) Figures cover the Chicago-Naperville-Elgin, IL-IN-WI Metropolitan Statistical Area—see Appendix B for areas included
Source: U.S. Census Bureau, 2014-2018 American Community Survey 5-Year Estimates

Gender

Area	Males	Females	Males per 100 Females
City	1,320,499	1,398,056	94.5
MSA[1]	4,666,894	4,869,534	95.8
U.S.	158,984,190	163,918,840	97.0

Note: (1) Figures cover the Chicago-Naperville-Elgin, IL-IN-WI Metropolitan Statistical Area—see Appendix B for areas included
Source: U.S. Census Bureau, 2014-2018 American Community Survey 5-Year Estimates

Religious Groups by Family

Area	Catholic	Baptist	Non-Den.	Methodist[2]	Lutheran	LDS[3]	Pente-costal	Presby-terian[4]	Muslim[5]	Judaism
MSA[1]	34.2	3.2	4.5	1.9	3.0	0.4	1.2	1.9	3.3	0.8
U.S.	19.1	9.3	4.0	4.0	2.3	2.0	1.9	1.6	0.8	0.7

Note: Figures are the number of adherents as a percentage of the total population; (1) Figures cover the Chicago-Naperville-Elgin, IL-IN-WI Metropolitan Statistical Area—see Appendix B for areas included; (2) Methodist/Pietist; (3) Latter Day Saints; (4) Reformed; (5) Figures are estimates
Source: Association of Statisticians of American Religious Bodies, 2010 U.S. Religion Census: Religious Congregations & Membership Study

Religious Groups by Tradition

Area	Catholic	Evangelical Protestant	Mainline Protestant	Other Tradition	Black Protestant	Orthodox
MSA[1]	34.2	9.8	5.1	5.1	2.1	0.9
U.S.	19.1	16.2	7.3	4.3	1.6	0.3

Note: Figures are the number of adherents as a percentage of the total population; (1) Figures cover the Chicago-Naperville-Elgin, IL-IN-WI Metropolitan Statistical Area—see Appendix B for areas included
Source: Association of Statisticians of American Religious Bodies, 2010 U.S. Religion Census: Religious Congregations & Membership Study

ECONOMY

Gross Metropolitan Product

Area	2017	2018	2019	2020	Rank[2]
MSA[1]	683.3	716.3	743.3	770.7	3

Note: Figures are in billions of dollars; (1) Figures cover the Chicago-Naperville-Elgin, IL-IN-WI Metropolitan Statistical Area—see Appendix B for areas included; (2) Rank is based on 2018 data and ranges from 1 to 381
Source: U.S. Conference of Mayors, U.S. Metro Economies: GMP & Employment 2018-2020, September 2019

Economic Growth

Area	2015-17 (%)	2018 (%)	2019 (%)	2020 (%)	Rank[2]
MSA[1]	0.8	2.3	2.0	1.6	247
U.S.	1.9	2.9	2.3	2.1	–

Note: Figures are real gross metropolitan product (GMP) growth rates and represent average annual percent change; (1) Figures cover the Chicago-Naperville-Elgin, IL-IN-WI Metropolitan Statistical Area—see Appendix B for areas included; (2) Rank is based on 2017 2-year average annual percent change and ranges from 1 to 381
Source: U.S. Conference of Mayors, U.S. Metro Economies: GMP & Employment 2018-2020, September 2019

Metropolitan Area Exports

Area	2013	2014	2015	2016	2017	2018	Rank[2]
MSA[1]	44,910.6	47,340.1	44,820.9	43,932.7	46,140.2	47,287.8	5

Note: Figures are in millions of dollars; (1) Figures cover the Chicago-Naperville-Elgin, IL-IN-WI Metropolitan Statistical Area—see Appendix B for areas included; (2) Rank is based on 2018 data and ranges from 1 to 387
Source: U.S. Department of Commerce, International Trade Administration, Office of Trade and Economic Analysis, Industry and Analysis, Exports by Metropolitan Area, data extracted April 15, 2020

Building Permits

Area	Single-Family			Multi-Family			Total		
	2017	2018	Pct. Chg.	2017	2018	Pct. Chg.	2017	2018	Pct. Chg.
City	525	439	-16.4	8,414	6,010	-28.6	8,939	6,449	-27.9
MSA[1]	8,416	8,546	1.5	13,716	9,135	-33.4	22,132	17,681	-20.1
U.S.	820,000	855,300	4.3	462,000	473,500	2.5	1,282,000	1,328,800	3.7

Note: (1) Figures cover the Chicago-Naperville-Elgin, IL-IN-WI Metropolitan Statistical Area—see Appendix B for areas included; Figures represent new, privately-owned housing units authorized (unadjusted data); All permit data are based on estimates with imputation
Source: U.S. Census Bureau, Manufacturing, Mining, and Construction Statistics, Building Permits, 2017, 2018

Bankruptcy Filings

Area	Business Filings			Nonbusiness Filings		
	2018	2019	% Chg.	2018	2019	% Chg.
Cook County	441	413	-6.3	27,072	27,789	2.6
U.S.	22,232	22,780	2.5	751,186	752,160	0.1

Note: Business filings include Chapter 7, Chapter 9, Chapter 11, Chapter 12, Chapter 13, Chapter 15, and Section 304; Nonbusiness filings include Chapter 7, Chapter 11, and Chapter 13
Source: Administrative Office of the U.S. Courts, Business and Nonbusiness Bankruptcy, County Cases Commenced by Chapter of the Bankruptcy Code, During the 12-Month Period Ending December 31, 2018 and Business and Nonbusiness Bankruptcy, County Cases Commenced by Chapter of the Bankruptcy Code, During the 12-Month Period Ending December 31, 2019

Housing Vacancy Rates

Area	Gross Vacancy Rate[2] (%)			Year-Round Vacancy Rate[3] (%)			Rental Vacancy Rate[4] (%)			Homeowner Vacancy Rate[5] (%)		
	2017	2018	2019	2017	2018	2019	2017	2018	2019	2017	2018	2019
MSA[1]	8.4	7.5	7.6	8.3	7.4	7.6	7.0	7.0	5.7	1.8	1.6	1.5
U.S.	12.7	12.3	12.0	9.9	9.7	9.5	7.2	6.9	6.7	1.6	1.5	1.4

Note: (1) Figures cover the Chicago-Naperville-Elgin, IL-IN-WI Metropolitan Statistical Area—see Appendix B for areas included; (2) The percentage of the total housing inventory that is vacant; (3) The percentage of the housing inventory (excluding seasonal units) that is year-round vacant; (4) The percentage of rental inventory that is vacant for rent; (5) The percentage of homeowner inventory that is vacant for sale
Source: U.S. Census Bureau, Housing Vacancies and Homeownership Annual Statistics: 2017, 2018, 2019

INCOME

Income

Area	Per Capita ($)	Median Household ($)	Average Household ($)
City	34,775	55,198	85,837
MSA[1]	36,368	68,715	96,140
U.S.	32,621	60,293	84,938

Note: (1) Figures cover the Chicago-Naperville-Elgin, IL-IN-WI Metropolitan Statistical Area—see Appendix B for areas included
Source: U.S. Census Bureau, 2014-2018 American Community Survey 5-Year Estimates

Household Income Distribution

Area	Percent of Households Earning							
	Under $15,000	$15,000 -$24,999	$25,000 -$34,999	$35,000 -$49,999	$50,000 -$74,999	$75,000 -$99,999	$100,000 -$149,999	$150,000 and up
City	14.7	10.7	9.0	11.5	15.6	11.0	13.2	14.3
MSA[1]	9.8	8.2	8.0	11.2	16.5	12.7	16.5	17.1
U.S.	10.9	9.3	9.3	12.6	17.5	12.5	14.6	13.3

Note: (1) Figures cover the Chicago-Naperville-Elgin, IL-IN-WI Metropolitan Statistical Area—see Appendix B for areas included
Source: U.S. Census Bureau, 2014-2018 American Community Survey 5-Year Estimates

Poverty Rate

Area	All Ages	Under 18 Years Old	18 to 64 Years Old	65 Years and Over
City	19.5	28.9	17.2	15.6
MSA[1]	12.5	17.6	11.3	9.2
U.S.	14.1	19.5	13.2	9.3

Note: Figures are percentage of people whose income during the past 12 months was below the poverty level;
(1) Figures cover the Chicago-Naperville-Elgin, IL-IN-WI Metropolitan Statistical Area—see Appendix B for areas included
Source: U.S. Census Bureau, 2014-2018 American Community Survey 5-Year Estimates

EMPLOYMENT

Labor Force and Employment

Area	Civilian Labor Force			Workers Employed		
	Dec. 2018	Dec. 2019	% Chg.	Dec. 2018	Dec. 2019	% Chg.
City	1,337,746	1,322,199	-1.2	1,284,655	1,281,869	-0.2
MD[1]	3,715,565	3,674,796	-1.1	3,577,585	3,570,383	-0.2
U.S.	162,510,000	164,007,000	0.9	156,481,000	158,504,000	1.3

Note: Data is not seasonally adjusted and covers workers 16 years of age and older; (1) Figures cover the Chicago-Naperville-Arlington Heights, IL Metropolitan Division—see Appendix B for areas included
Source: Bureau of Labor Statistics, Local Area Unemployment Statistics

Unemployment Rate

Area	2019											
	Jan.	Feb.	Mar.	Apr.	May	Jun.	Jul.	Aug.	Sep.	Oct.	Nov.	Dec.
City	4.9	4.4	4.0	3.8	3.7	4.4	4.5	4.3	3.6	3.6	3.3	3.1
MD[1]	4.7	4.2	3.9	3.5	3.3	4.1	4.1	3.8	3.2	3.2	3.0	2.8
U.S.	4.4	4.1	3.9	3.3	3.4	3.8	4.0	3.8	3.3	3.3	3.3	3.4

Note: Data is not seasonally adjusted and covers workers 16 years of age and older; (1) Figures cover the Chicago-Naperville-Arlington Heights, IL Metropolitan Division—see Appendix B for areas included
Source: Bureau of Labor Statistics, Local Area Unemployment Statistics

Average Wages

Occupation	$/Hr.	Occupation	$/Hr.
Accountants and Auditors	38.20	Maintenance and Repair Workers	22.30
Automotive Mechanics	23.10	Marketing Managers	65.10
Bookkeepers	21.90	Network and Computer Systems Admin.	42.60
Carpenters	33.70	Nurses, Licensed Practical	27.70
Cashiers	12.00	Nurses, Registered	37.20
Computer Programmers	46.40	Nursing Assistants	14.90
Computer Systems Analysts	43.60	Office Clerks, General	18.70
Computer User Support Specialists	26.10	Physical Therapists	45.30
Construction Laborers	31.20	Physicians	87.60
Cooks, Restaurant	14.40	Plumbers, Pipefitters and Steamfitters	43.00
Customer Service Representatives	19.30	Police and Sheriff's Patrol Officers	39.50
Dentists	88.60	Postal Service Mail Carriers	25.60
Electricians	39.10	Real Estate Sales Agents	20.20
Engineers, Electrical	47.00	Retail Salespersons	13.90
Fast Food and Counter Workers	11.50	Sales Representatives, Technical/Scientific	42.50
Financial Managers	74.00	Secretaries, Exc. Legal/Medical/Executive	20.00
First-Line Supervisors of Office Workers	31.00	Security Guards	16.20
General and Operations Managers	63.70	Surgeons	119.00
Hairdressers/Cosmetologists	14.90	Teacher Assistants, Exc. Postsecondary*	14.20
Home Health and Personal Care Aides	12.80	Teachers, Secondary School, Exc. Sp. Ed.*	38.20
Janitors and Cleaners	15.00	Telemarketers	13.80
Landscaping/Groundskeeping Workers	16.30	Truck Drivers, Heavy/Tractor-Trailer	24.50
Lawyers	78.10	Truck Drivers, Light/Delivery Services	22.30
Maids and Housekeeping Cleaners	14.00	Waiters and Waitresses	11.50

Note: Wage data covers the Chicago-Naperville-Elgin, IL-IN-WI Metropolitan Statistical Area—see Appendix B for areas included; (*) Hourly wages were calculated from annual wage data based on a 40 hour work week; n/a not available.
Source: Bureau of Labor Statistics, Metro Area Occupational Employment & Wage Estimates, May 2019

Employment by Occupation

Occupation Classification	City (%)	MSA[1] (%)	U.S. (%)
Management, Business, Science, and Arts	41.0	39.3	37.9
Natural Resources, Construction, and Maintenance	5.2	6.7	8.9
Production, Transportation, and Material Moving	13.3	14.4	13.3
Sales and Office	21.0	22.7	22.1
Service	19.5	16.8	17.9

Note: Figures cover employed civilians 16 years of age and older; (1) Figures cover the Chicago-Naperville-Elgin, IL-IN-WI Metropolitan Statistical Area—see Appendix B for areas included
Source: U.S. Census Bureau, 2014-2018 American Community Survey 5-Year Estimates

Employment by Industry

Sector	MD[1] Number of Employees	MD[1] Percent of Total	U.S. Percent of Total
Construction	127,800	3.3	4.9
Education and Health Services	617,200	16.1	16.1
Financial Activities	279,500	7.3	5.8
Government	425,300	11.1	15.0
Information	72,300	1.9	1.9
Leisure and Hospitality	384,300	10.0	10.8
Manufacturing	282,100	7.4	8.4
Mining and Logging	1,300	<0.1	0.5
Other Services	161,600	4.2	3.9
Professional and Business Services	706,100	18.4	14.1
Retail Trade	352,600	9.2	10.6
Transportation, Warehousing, and Utilities	229,600	6.0	4.2
Wholesale Trade	189,300	4.9	3.9

Note: Figures are non-farm employment as of December 2019. Figures are not seasonally adjusted and include workers 16 years of age and older; (1) Figures cover the Chicago-Naperville-Arlington Heights, IL Metropolitan Division—see Appendix B for areas included
Source: Bureau of Labor Statistics, Current Employment Statistics, Employment, Hours, and Earnings

Occupations with Greatest Projected Employment Growth: 2019 – 2021

Occupation[1]	2019 Employment	2021 Projected Employment	Numeric Employment Change	Percent Employment Change
Combined Food Preparation and Serving Workers, Including Fast Food	140,460	145,280	4,820	3.4
Registered Nurses	133,320	137,300	3,980	3.0
Personal Care Aides	56,160	59,830	3,670	6.5
Laborers and Freight, Stock, and Material Movers, Hand	158,620	162,170	3,550	2.2
Insurance Sales Agents	49,730	52,420	2,690	5.4
Heavy and Tractor-Trailer Truck Drivers	73,100	75,610	2,510	3.4
General and Operations Managers	120,880	123,200	2,320	1.9
Cooks, Restaurant	47,520	49,620	2,100	4.4
Janitors and Cleaners, Except Maids and Housekeeping Cleaners	85,160	86,710	1,550	1.8
Financial Managers	40,420	41,900	1,480	3.7

Note: Projections cover Illinois; (1) Sorted by numeric employment change
Source: www.projectionscentral.com, State Occupational Projections, 2019–2021 Short-Term Projections

Fastest Growing Occupations: 2019 – 2021

Occupation[1]	2019 Employment	2021 Projected Employment	Numeric Employment Change	Percent Employment Change
Actuaries	1,940	2,070	130	6.7
Personal Care Aides	56,160	59,830	3,670	6.5
Statisticians	1,910	2,030	120	6.3
Nurse Practitioners	8,130	8,610	480	5.9
Physician Assistants	3,800	4,020	220	5.8
Insurance Sales Agents	49,730	52,420	2,690	5.4
Operations Research Analysts	5,080	5,350	270	5.3
Computer Numerically Controlled Machine Tool Programmers, Metal and Plastic	1,150	1,210	60	5.2
Veterinary Technologists and Technicians	4,010	4,210	200	5.0
Massage Therapists	6,720	7,050	330	4.9

Note: Projections cover Illinois; (1) Sorted by percent employment change and excludes occupations with numeric employment change less than 50
Source: www.projectionscentral.com, State Occupational Projections, 2019–2021 Short-Term Projections

TAXES

State Corporate Income Tax Rates

State	Tax Rate (%)	Income Brackets ($)	Num. of Brackets	Financial Institution Tax Rate (%)[a]	Federal Income Tax Ded.
Illinois	9.5 (h)	Flat rate	1	9.5 (h)	No

Note: Tax rates as of January 1, 2020; (a) Rates listed are the corporate income tax rate applied to financial institutions or excise taxes based on income; (h) The Illinois rate of 9.5% is the sum of a corporate income tax rate of 7.0% plus a replacement tax of 2.5%.
Source: Federation of Tax Administrators, State Corporate Income Tax Rates, January 1, 2020

State Individual Income Tax Rates

State	Tax Rate (%)	Income Brackets ($)	Personal Exemptions ($)			Standard Ded. ($)	
			Single	Married	Depend.	Single	Married
Illinois (a)	4.95	Flat rate	2,275	4,550	2,275	–	–

Note: Tax rates as of January 1, 2020; Local- and county-level taxes are not included; Federal income tax is not deductible on state income tax returns; (a) 19 states have statutory provision for automatically adjusting to the rate of inflation the dollar values of the income tax brackets, standard deductions, and/or personal exemptions. Michigan indexes the personal exemption only. Oregon does not index the income brackets for $125,000 and over.
Source: Federation of Tax Administrators, State Individual Income Tax Rates, January 1, 2020

Various State Sales and Excise Tax Rates

State	State Sales Tax (%)	Gasoline[1] (¢/gal.)	Cigarette[2] ($/pack)	Spirits[3] ($/gal.)	Wine[4] ($/gal.)	Beer[5] ($/gal.)	Recreational Marijuana (%)
Illinois	6.25	53.65	2.98	8.55	1.39	0.23	(d)

Note: All tax rates as of January 1, 2020; (1) The American Petroleum Institute has developed a methodology for determining the average tax rate on a gallon of fuel. Rates may include any of the following: excise taxes, environmental fees, storage tank fees, other fees or taxes, general sales tax, and local taxes; (2) The federal excise tax of $1.0066 per pack and local taxes are not included; (3) Rates are those applicable to off-premise sales of 40% alcohol by volume (a.b.v.) distilled spirits in 750ml containers. Local excise taxes are excluded; (4) Rates are those applicable to off-premise sales of 11% a.b.v. non-carbonated wine in 750ml containers; (5) Rates are those applicable to off-premise sales of 4.7% a.b.v. beer in 12 ounce containers; (d) 7% excise tax of value at wholesale level, 10% tax on cannabis flower or products with less than 35% THC, 20% tax on products infused with cannabis, such as edible products, 25% tax on any product with a THC concentration higher than 35%
Source: Tax Foundation, 2020 Facts & Figures: How Does Your State Compare?

State Business Tax Climate Index Rankings

State	Overall Rank	Corporate Tax Rank	Individual Income Tax Rank	Sales Tax Rank	Property Tax Rank	Unemployment Insurance Tax Rank
Illinois	35	36	13	33	40	40

Note: The index is a measure of how each state's tax laws affect economic performance. The lower the rank, the more favorable a state's tax system is for business. States without a given tax are given a ranking of 1. The scores/rankings for the District of Columbia do not affect other states. The 2020 index represents the tax climate as of July 1, 2019.
Source: Tax Foundation, State Business Tax Climate Index 2020

COMMERCIAL REAL ESTATE

Office Market

Market Area	Inventory (sq. ft.)	Vacancy Rate (%)	Under Construction (sq. ft.)	YTD Net Absorption (sq. ft.)	Total Average Asking Rent ($/sq. ft./year)
Chicago	239,974,550	16.7	6,931,660	484,147	29.70
National	4,923,349,992	13.0	102,814,961	2,049,925	29.54

Source: Newmark Grubb Knight Frank, National Office Market Report, 1st Quarter 2020

Industrial/Warehouse/R&D Market

Market Area	Inventory (sq. ft.)	Vacancy Rate (%)	Under Construction (sq. ft.)	YTD Net Absorption (sq. ft.)	Total Average Asking Rent ($/sq. ft./year)
Chicago	1,130,976,313	6.6	9,523,059	2,450,122	5.69
National	15,332,123,451	5.4	322,705,045	48,296,842	7.54

Source: Newmark Grubb Knight Frank, National Industrial Market Report, 1st Quarter 2020

COMMERCIAL UTILITIES

Typical Monthly Electric Bills

Area	Commercial Service ($/month)		Industrial Service ($/month)	
	1,500 kWh	40 kW demand 14,000 kWh	1,000 kW demand 200,000 kWh	50,000 kW demand 32,500,000 kWh
City	167	1,410	n/a	n/a
Average[1]	203	1,612	25,706	2,520,671

Note: Figures are based on annualized rates; (1) Average based on 187 utilities surveyed; n/a not available
Source: Edison Electric Institute, Typical Bills and Average Rates Report, Summer 2019

TRANSPORTATION

Means of Transportation to Work

Area	Car/Truck/Van		Public Transportation			Bicycle	Walked	Other Means	Worked at Home
	Drove Alone	Car-pooled	Bus	Subway	Railroad				
City	49.0	7.8	13.5	12.9	1.8	1.7	6.5	2.0	4.8
MSA[1]	70.2	7.8	4.5	4.3	3.2	0.7	3.0	1.3	5.0
U.S.	76.4	9.1	2.5	1.9	0.6	0.6	2.7	1.3	4.9

Note: Figures are percentages and cover workers 16 years of age and older; (1) Figures cover the Chicago-Naperville-Elgin, IL-IN-WI Metropolitan Statistical Area—see Appendix B for areas included
Source: U.S. Census Bureau, 2014-2018 American Community Survey 5-Year Estimates

Travel Time to Work

Area	Less Than 10 Minutes	10 to 19 Minutes	20 to 29 Minutes	30 to 44 Minutes	45 to 59 Minutes	60 to 89 Minutes	90 Minutes or More
City	4.6	15.9	17.6	30.3	15.0	12.9	3.6
MSA[1]	8.4	21.6	18.4	25.0	12.4	10.8	3.4
U.S.	12.5	28.7	20.9	20.7	8.2	6.3	2.8

Note: Note: Figures are percentages and include workers 16 years old and over; (1) Figures cover the Chicago-Naperville-Elgin, IL-IN-WI Metropolitan Statistical Area—see Appendix B for areas included
Source: U.S. Census Bureau, 2014-2018 American Community Survey 5-Year Estimates

Key Congestion Measures

Area	1982	1992	2002	2012	2017
Annual Hours of Delay, Total (000)	99,294	160,710	254,740	319,661	352,759
Annual Hours of Delay, Per Auto Commuter	31	43	54	63	73
Annual Congestion Cost, Total (million $)	754	1,706	3,458	5,777	6,530
Annual Congestion Cost, Per Auto Commuter ($)	902	1,004	1,241	1,221	1,307

Source: Texas A&M Transportation Institute, 2019 Urban Mobility Report

Freeway Travel Time Index

Area	1982	1987	1992	1997	2002	2007	2012	2017
Urban Area Index[1]	1.16	1.19	1.22	1.25	1.27	1.30	1.29	1.32
Urban Area Rank[1,2]	7	8	6	9	14	13	17	16

Note: Freeway Travel Time Index—the ratio of travel time in the peak period to the travel time at free-flow conditions. For example, a value of 1.30 indicates a 20-minute free-flow trip takes 26 minutes in the peak (20 minutes x 1.30 = 26 minutes); (1) Covers the Chicago IL-IN urban area; (2) Rank is based on 101 larger urban areas (#1 = highest travel time index)
Source: Texas A&M Transportation Institute, 2019 Urban Mobility Report

Public Transportation

Agency Name / Mode of Transportation	Vehicles Operated in Maximum Service[1]	Annual Unlinked Passenger Trips[2] (in thous.)	Annual Passenger Miles[3] (in thous.)
Chicago Transit Authority (CTA)			
Bus (directly operated)	1,569	242,173.0	591,323.7
Heavy Rail (directly operated)	1,142	225,895.0	1,401,503.0
Northeast Illinois Regional Commuter Railroad (Metra)			
Commuter Rail (directly operated)	1,062	68,446.2	1,518,703.4

Note: (1) Number of revenue vehicles operated by the given mode and type of service to meet the annual maximum service requirement. This is the revenue vehicle count during the peak season of the year; on the week and day that maximum service is provided. Vehicles operated in maximum service (VOMS) exclude atypical days and one-time special events; (2) Number of passengers who boarded public transportation vehicles. Passengers are counted each time they board a vehicle no matter how many vehicles they use to travel from their origin to their destination. (3) Sum of the distances ridden by all passengers during the entire fiscal year.
Source: Federal Transit Administration, National Transit Database, 2018

Air Transportation

Airport Name and Code / Type of Service	Passenger Airlines[1]	Passenger Enplanements	Freight Carriers[2]	Freight (lbs)
O'Hare International (ORD)				
Domestic service (U.S. carriers - 2019)	29	34,060,492	15	492,006,280
International service (U.S. carriers - 2018)	15	3,227,012	9	132,953,724
Midway International (MDW)				
Domestic service (U.S. carriers - 2019)	19	9,685,613	3	19,961,649
International service (U.S. carriers - 2018)	5	163,036	0	0

Note: (1) Includes all U.S.-based major, minor and commuter airlines that carried at least one passenger during the year; (2) Includes all U.S.-based airlines and freight carriers that transported at least one pound of freight during the year.
Source: Bureau of Transportation Statistics, The Intermodal Transportation Database, Air Carriers: T-100 Domestic Market (U.S. Carriers), 2019; Bureau of Transportation Statistics, The Intermodal Transportation Database, Air Carriers: T-100 International Market (U.S. Carriers), 2018

Other Transportation Statistics

Major Highways:	I-55; I-57; I-80; I-88; I-90
Amtrak Service:	Yes
Major Waterways/Ports:	Port of Chicago (St. Lawrence Seaway)

Source: Amtrak.com; Google Maps

BUSINESSES

Major Business Headquarters

Company Name	Industry	Rankings	
		Fortune[1]	Forbes[2]
Amsted Industries	Capital Goods	-	142
Archer Daniels Midland	Food Production	49	-
Boeing	Aerospace and Defense	28	-
Conagra Brands	Food Consumer Products	386	-
Exelon	Utilities, Gas and Electric	93	-
Heico Cos	Capital Goods	-	176
Jones Lang LaSalle	Real Estate	189	-
Kirkland & Ellis	Services	-	118
LKQ	Wholesalers, Diversified	262	-
Northern Trust	Commercial Banks	453	-
Old Republic International	Insurance, Property and Casualty (Stock)	481	-
R.R. Donnelley & Sons	Publishing, Printing	445	-
Sidley Austin	Services	-	208
United Continental Holdings	Airlines	78	-
Walsh Group	Construction		105

Note: (1) Companies that produce a 10-K are ranked 1 to 500 based on 2018 revenue; (2) All private companies with at least $2 billion in annual revenue through the end of their most current fiscal year are ranked 1 to 228; companies listed are headquartered in the city; dashes indicate no ranking
Source: Fortune, "Fortune 500," June 2019; Forbes, "America's Largest Private Companies," 2019 Rankings

Fast-Growing Businesses

According to *Inc.*, Chicago is home to 14 of America's 500 fastest-growing private companies: **GForce Life Sciences** (#90); **ShipBob** (#99); **China Metal Solutions** (#130); **Arcalea** (#149); **UPshow** (#174); **Fitness Cubed** (#180); **RedShelf** (#231); **Cultivate Advisors** (#280); **OppLoans** (#321); **Wavicle Data Solutions** (#342); **First Stop Health** (#375); **Apogee Stores** (#400); **G2** (#408); **Era Transport** (#438). Criteria: must be an independent, privately-held, for-profit, U.S. corporation, proprietorship or partnership as of December 31, 2018; revenues must be at least $100,000 in 2015 and $2 million in 2018; must have four-year operating/sales history. *Inc., "America's 500 Fastest-Growing Private Companies," 2019*

According to *Fortune*, Chicago is home to two of the 100 fastest-growing companies in the world: **Grubhub** (#23); **CBOE Global Markets** (#65). Companies were ranked by their revenue growth rate; their EPS growth rate; and their three-year annualized total return to investors for the period ending June 30, 2019. Criteria for inclusion: a company, foreign or domestic, must trade on a major U.S. stock exchange; must file quarterly reports with the SEC; must have a minimum market capitalization of $250 million; must have a stock price of at least $5 on June 30, 2019; must have been trading continuously since June 30, 2016; must have revenue and net income for the four quarters ended on or before April 30, 2019, of at least $50 million and $10 million, respectively; and must have posted a compound annual growth in revenue and earnings per share of at least 15% annually over the three years ending on or before April 30, 2019. Real estate investment trusts, limited-liability companies, limited parterships, business development companies, closed-end investment firms, companies about to be acquired, and companies that lost money in the quarter ending April 30, 2019 were excluded. *Fortune, "100 Fastest-Growing Companies," 2019*

According to *Initiative for a Competitive Inner City (ICIC)*, Chicago is home to eight of America's 100 fastest-growing "inner city" companies: **Cloudbakers** (#10); **Trice Construction Company** (#29); **Gourmet Gorilla** (#40); **Transportation One** (#61); **LEEP Forward** (#62); **LaSalle Network** (#73); **Nova Driving School** (#82); **Sandstorm Design** (#92). Criteria for inclusion: company must be headquartered in or have 51 percent or more of its physical operations in an economically distressed urban area; must be an independent, for-profit corporation, partnership or proprietorship; must have 10 or more employees and have a five-year sales history that includes sales of at least $200,000 in the base year and at least $1 million in the current year with no decrease in sales over the two most recent years. Companies were ranked overall by revenue growth over the five-year period between 2014 and 2018. *Initiative for a Competitive Inner City (ICIC), "Inner City 100 Companies," 2019*

According to Deloitte, Chicago is home to 11 of North America's 500 fastest-growing high-technology companies: **Shipbob** (#50); **Fitness Cubed** (#57); **OppLoans** (#91); **G2** (#113); **ActiveCampaign** (#140); **Hireology** (#221); **Braviant Holdings** (#258); **Built In** (#261); **Snapsheet** (#284); **Origami Risk** (#380); **YCharts** (#463). Companies are ranked by percentage growth in revenue over a four-year period. Criteria for inclusion: company must be headquartered within North America; must own proprietary intellectual property or technology that is sold to customers in products that contributes to a significant portion of the company's operating revenue; must have been in business for a minumum of four years with 2015 operating revenues of at least $50,000 USD/CD and 2018 operating revenues of at least $5 million USD/CD. *Deloitte, 2019 Technology Fast 500*[TM]

Minority Business Opportunity

Chicago is home to two companies which are on the *Black Enterprise* Industrial/Service list (100 largest companies based on gross sales): **Harpo** (#52); **UJAMAA Construction** (#58). Criteria: operational in previous calendar year; at least 51% black-owned and manufactures/owns the product it sells or provides industrial or consumer services. Brokerages, real estate firms and firms that provide professional services are not eligible. *Black Enterprise, B.E. 100s, 2019*

Chicago is home to one company which is on the *Black Enterprise* Bank list (15 largest banks based on total assets, capital, deposits and loans, including mortgage-backed securities for the calendar year): **GN Bank** (#11). Only commercial banks or savings and loans that are classified by the Federal Reserve as black institutions and have been fully operational for the previous calendar year were considered. *Black Enterprise, B.E. 100s, 2019*

Chicago is home to three companies which are on the *Black Enterprise* Asset Manager list (10 largest asset management firms based on assets under management): **Ariel Investments** (#1); **Capri Capital Partners** (#7); **Channing Capital Management** (#10). Criteria: company must have been operational in previous calendar year and be at least 51% black-owned. *Black Enterprise, B.E. 100s, 2019*

Chicago is home to one company which is on the *Black Enterprise* Private Equity list (10 largest private equity firms based on capital under management): **Muller & Monroe Asset Management** (#7). Criteria: company must be operational in previous calendar year and be at least 51% black-owned. *Black Enterprise, B.E. 100s, 2019*

Chicago is home to 10 companies which are on the *Hispanic Business* 500 list (500 largest U.S. Hispanic-owned companies based on revenue): **Cardenas Marketing Network** (#93); **Primera Engineers Ltd.** (#212); **MZI Group** (#213); **Cristina Foods** (#227); **Monterrey Security** (#277); **Sanchez Daniels & Hoffman** (#299); **The San Jose Group Co.** (#333); **American Surveying & Engineering P.C.** (#356); **CivCon Services** (#392); **HCM Banners and Graphics** (#496). Companies included must show at least 51 percent ownership by Hispanic U.S. citizens, and must maintain headquarters in one of the 50 states or Washington, D.C. *Hispanic Business, "Hispanic Business 500," June 20, 2013*

Minority- and Women-Owned Businesses

Group	All Firms		Firms with Paid Employees			
	Firms	Sales ($000)	Firms	Sales ($000)	Employees	Payroll ($000)
AIAN[1]	1,655	(s)	112	(s)	250 - 499	(s)
Asian	23,333	6,696,989	5,069	6,105,786	37,844	1,155,038
Black	78,010	3,685,698	2,056	2,539,943	19,420	709,676
Hispanic	39,124	5,995,530	4,449	5,215,672	35,433	967,229
NHOPI[2]	334	44,951	50	40,051	389	8,984
Women	123,632	11,717,510	9,561	9,392,195	74,642	2,553,554
All Firms	291,007	395,746,404	48,499	387,004,804	1,183,301	71,043,548

Note: Figures cover firms located in the city; minority- and women-owned business are defined as firms in which the corresponding group own 51% or more of the stock or equity of the company; (1) American Indian and Alaska Native; (2) Native Hawaiian and Other Pacific Islander; (s) estimates are suppressed when publication standards are not met
Source: U.S. Census Bureau, 2012 Economic Census, Survey of Business Owners

**HOTELS &
CONVENTION
CENTERS**

Hotels, Motels and Vacation Rentals

Area	5 Star		4 Star		3 Star		2 Star		1 Star		Not Rated	
	Num.	Pct.[3]	Num.	Pct.[3]	Num.	Pct.[3]	Num.	Pct.[3]	Num.	Pct.[3]	Num.	Pct.[3]
City[1]	7	1.7	51	12.1	76	18.0	27	6.4	162	38.4	99	23.5
Total[2]	266	1.3	1,517	7.2	4,627	21.8	3,210	15.1	3,974	18.7	7,601	35.9

Note: (1) Figures cover Chicago and vicinity; (2) Figures cover all 100 cities in this book; (3) Percentage of hotels which have a given star rating; Star ratings are determined by priceline.com and offer an indication of the general quality of a particular hotel.
Source: priceline.com, April 27, 2020

The Chicago-Naperville-Arlington Heights, IL metro area is home to three of the best city hotels in the continental U.S. according to *Travel & Leisure*: **The Langham**; **Hotel Zachary**; **Viceroy Chicago**. Magazine readers were surveyed and asked to rate hotels on the following criteria: rooms/facilities; location; service; food; and value. The list includes the top 15 city hotels in the continental U.S. *Travel & Leisure, "The World's Best Awards 2019"*

The Chicago-Naperville-Arlington Heights, IL metro area is home to one of the best resort hotels in the continental U.S. according to *Travel & Leisure*: **Deer Path Inn**. Magazine readers were surveyed and asked to rate hotels on the following criteria: rooms/facilities; location; service; food; and value. The list includes the top 15 resort hotels in the continental U.S. *Travel & Leisure, "The World's Best Awards 2019"*

The Chicago-Naperville-Arlington Heights, IL metro area is home to one of the best hotels in the world according to *Condé Nast Traveler*: **The Langham, Chicago**. The selections are based on editors' picks. The list includes the top 17 hotels in the U.S. and Canada. *Condé Nast Traveler, "The Best Hotels and Resorts in the World: The 2020 Gold List"*

Major Convention Centers

Name	Overall Space (sq. ft.)	Exhibit Space (sq. ft.)	Meeting Space (sq. ft.)	Meeting Rooms
McCormick Place	n/a	2,670,000	600,000	173
Navy Pier-Festival Hall	n/a	170,100	44,000	36

Note: Table includes convention centers located in the Chicago-Naperville-Elgin, IL-IN-WI metro area; n/a not available
Source: Original research

Living Environment

COST OF LIVING

Cost of Living Index

Composite Index	Groceries	Housing	Utilities	Trans-portation	Health Care	Misc. Goods/Services
120.6	101.9	155.7	92.4	125.9	100.0	109.4

Note: The Cost of Living Index measures regional differences in the cost of consumer goods and services, excluding taxes and non-consumer expenditures, for professional and managerial households in the top income quintile. It is based on more than 50,000 prices covering almost 60 different items for which prices are collected three times a year by chambers of commerce, economic development organizations or university applied economic centers in each participating urban area. The numbers shown should be read as a percentage above or below the national average of 100. For example, a value of 115.4 in the groceries column indicates that grocery prices are 15.4% higher than the national average. Small differences in the index numbers should not be interpreted as significant; Figures cover the Chicago IL urban area.
Source: The Council for Community and Economic Research, ACCRA Cost of Living Index, 2019

Grocery Prices

Area[1]	T-Bone Steak ($/pound)	Frying Chicken ($/pound)	Whole Milk ($/half gal.)	Eggs ($/dozen)	Orange Juice ($/64 oz.)	Coffee ($/11.5 oz.)
City[2]	12.57	1.66	2.09	1.36	3.99	4.19
Avg.	11.40	1.41	1.93	1.54	3.51	4.30
Min.	7.40	0.92	0.85	0.58	2.67	2.90
Max.	15.58	2.68	4.09	4.18	5.57	8.10

*Note: (1) Values for the local area are compared with the average, minimum and maximum values for all 290 areas in the Cost of Living Index; (2) Figures cover the Chicago IL urban area; **T-Bone Steak** (price per pound); **Frying Chicken** (price per pound, whole fryer); **Whole Milk** (half gallon carton); **Eggs** (price per dozen, Grade A, large); **Orange Juice** (64 oz. Tropicana or Florida Natural); **Coffee** (11.5 oz. can, vacuum-packed, Maxwell House, Hills Bros, or Folgers).*
Source: The Council for Community and Economic Research, ACCRA Cost of Living Index, 2019

Housing and Utility Costs

Area[1]	New Home Price ($)	Apartment Rent ($/month)	All Electric ($/month)	Part Electric ($/month)	Other Energy ($/month)	Telephone ($/month)
City[2]	517,211	2,131	-	80.25	52.14	199.00
Avg.	362,090	1,142	174.35	100.00	67.76	179.60
Min.	198,329	501	91.58	31.44	28.51	165.30
Max.	2,074,561	5,050	388.18	239.41	306.15	207.90

*Note: (1) Values for the local area are compared with the average, minimum and maximum values for all 290 areas in the Cost of Living Index; (2) Figures cover the Chicago IL urban area; **New Home Price** (2,400 sf living area, 8,000 sf lot, in urban area with full utilities); **Apartment Rent** (950 sf 2 bedroom/1.5 or 2 bath, unfurnished, excluding all utilities except water); **All Electric** (average monthly cost for an all-electric home); **Part Electric** (average monthly cost for a part-electric home); **Other Energy** (average monthly cost for natural gas, fuel oil, coal, wood, and any other forms of energy except electricity); **Telephone** (price includes the base monthly rate plus taxes and fees for three lines of mobile phone service).*
Source: The Council for Community and Economic Research, ACCRA Cost of Living Index, 2019

Health Care, Transportation, and Other Costs

Area[1]	Doctor ($/visit)	Dentist ($/visit)	Optometrist ($/visit)	Gasoline ($/gallon)	Beauty Salon ($/visit)	Men's Shirt ($)
City[2]	105.00	102.00	97.00	3.25	69.77	32.00
Avg.	114.85	97.58	106.10	2.50	38.15	32.15
Min.	39.00	62.22	52.22	1.53	16.88	10.27
Max.	206.67	151.53	258.67	3.79	79.29	59.30

*Note: (1) Values for the local area are compared with the average, minimum and maximum values for all 290 areas in the Cost of Living Index; (2) Figures cover the Chicago IL urban area; **Doctor** (general practitioners routine exam of an established patient); **Dentist** (adult teeth cleaning and periodic oral examination); **Optometrist** (full vision eye exam for established adult patient); **Gasoline** (one gallon regular unleaded, national brand, including all taxes, cash price at self-service pump if available); **Beauty Salon** (woman's shampoo, trim, and blow-dry); **Men's Shirt** (cotton/polyester dress shirt, pinpoint weave, long sleeves).*
Source: The Council for Community and Economic Research, ACCRA Cost of Living Index, 2019

HOUSING

House Price Index (HPI)

Area	National Ranking[2]	Quarterly Change (%)	One-Year Change (%)	Five-Year Change (%)
MD[1]	169	0.81	3.97	20.01
U.S.[3]	–	1.26	5.09	32.88

Note: The HPI is a weighted repeat sales index. It measures average price changes in repeat sales or refinancings on the same properties. This information is obtained by reviewing repeat mortgage transactions on single-family properties whose mortgages have been purchased or securitized by Fannie Mae or Freddie Mac in January 1975; (1) Figures cover the Chicago-Naperville-Arlington Heights, IL Metropolitan Division—see Appendix B for areas included; (2) Rankings are based on annual percentage change for all metro areas containing at least 15,000 transactions over the last 10 years and ranges from 1 to 232; (3) figures based on a weighted average of Census Division estimates using a seasonally adjusted, purchase-only index; all figures are for the period ending December 31, 2019
Source: Federal Housing Finance Agency, House Price Index, February 25, 2020

Median Single-Family Home Prices

Area	2017	2018	2019p	Percent Change 2018 to 2019
MSA[1]	248.5	259.4	265.1	2.2
U.S. Average	248.8	261.6	274.6	5.0

Note: Figures are median sales prices of existing single-family homes in thousands of dollars; (p) preliminary; (1) Figures cover the Chicago-Naperville-Elgin, IL-IN-WI Metropolitan Statistical Area—see Appendix B for areas included
Source: National Association of Realtors, Median Sales Price of Existing Single-Family Homes for Metropolitan Areas, 4th Quarter 2019

Qualifying Income Based on Median Sales Price of Existing Single-Family Homes

Area	With 5% Down ($)	With 10% Down ($)	With 20% Down ($)
MSA[1]	54,352	51,491	45,770
U.S. Average	58,663	55,575	49,400

Note: Figures are preliminary; Qualifying income is based on a mortgage rate of 3.76%. Monthly principal and interest payment is limited to 25% of income; (1) Figures cover the Chicago-Naperville-Elgin, IL-IN-WI Metropolitan Statistical Area—see Appendix B for areas included
Source: National Association of Realtors, Qualifying Income Based on Median Sales Price of Existing Single-Family Homes for Metropolitan Areas, 4th Quarter 2019

Median Apartment Condo-Coop Home Prices

Area	2017	2018	2019p	Percent Change 2018 to 2019
MSA[1]	195.8	200.9	205.8	2.4
U.S. Average	234.3	241.0	249.5	3.5

Note: Figures are median sales prices of existing apartment condo-coop homes in thousands of dollars; (p) preliminary; (1) Figures cover the Chicago-Naperville-Elgin, IL-IN-WI Metropolitan Statistical Area—see Appendix B for areas included
Source: National Association of Realtors, Median Sales Price of Existing Apartment Condo-Coop Homes for Metropolitan Areas, 4th Quarter 2019

Home Value Distribution

Area	Under $50,000	$50,000 -$99,999	$100,000 -$149,999	$150,000 -$199,999	$200,000 -$299,999	$300,000 -$499,999	$500,000 -$999,999	$1,000,000 or more
City	3.2	7.8	12.0	15.3	23.4	23.0	11.5	3.8
MSA[1]	3.6	8.0	13.2	16.7	24.8	21.8	9.4	2.3
U.S.	7.6	13.0	14.0	14.3	19.2	18.3	10.5	3.1

Note: Figures are percentages and cover owner-occupied housing units; (1) Figures cover the Chicago-Naperville-Elgin, IL-IN-WI Metropolitan Statistical Area—see Appendix B for areas included
Source: U.S. Census Bureau, 2014-2018 American Community Survey 5-Year Estimates

Homeownership Rate

Area	2011 (%)	2012 (%)	2013 (%)	2014 (%)	2015 (%)	2016 (%)	2017 (%)	2018 (%)	2019 (%)
MSA[1]	67.7	67.1	68.2	66.3	64.3	64.5	64.1	64.6	63.4
U.S.	66.1	65.4	65.1	64.5	63.7	63.4	63.9	64.4	64.6

Note: (1) Figures cover the Chicago-Naperville-Elgin, IL-IN-WI Metropolitan Statistical Area—see Appendix B for areas included
Source: U.S. Census Bureau, Housing Vacancies and Homeownership Annual Statistics: 2011-2019

Year Housing Structure Built

Area	2010 or Later	2000 -2009	1990 -1999	1980 -1989	1970 -1979	1960 -1969	1950 -1959	1940 -1949	Before 1940	Median Year
City	2.0	8.1	4.7	4.2	7.2	9.7	12.1	9.3	42.7	1948
MSA[1]	1.9	11.6	11.1	8.9	14.1	11.7	13.1	6.2	21.4	1968
U.S.	4.1	14.3	13.9	13.5	15.3	10.7	10.4	5.0	12.8	1977

Note: Figures are percentages except for Median Year; Note: (1) Figures cover the Chicago-Naperville-Elgin, IL-IN-WI Metropolitan Statistical Area—see Appendix B for areas included
Source: U.S. Census Bureau, 2014-2018 American Community Survey 5-Year Estimates

Gross Monthly Rent

Area	Under $500	$500 -$999	$1,000 -$1,499	$1,500 -$1,999	$2,000 -$2,499	$2,500 -$2,999	$3,000 and up	Median ($)
City	9.6	34.6	30.9	14.7	5.9	2.5	1.9	1,077
MSA[1]	7.7	34.6	34.0	14.9	5.3	1.9	1.5	1,092
U.S.	9.8	38.5	29.6	12.9	5.1	2.1	2.0	1,023

Note: Figures are percentages except for Median; Gross rent is the contract rent plus the estimated average monthly cost of utilities (electricity, gas, and water and sewer) and fuels (oil, coal, kerosene, wood, etc.) if these are paid by the renter (or paid for the renter by someone else); (1) Figures cover the Chicago-Naperville-Elgin, IL-IN-WI Metropolitan Statistical Area—see Appendix B for areas included
Source: U.S. Census Bureau, 2014-2018 American Community Survey 5-Year Estimates

HEALTH

Health Risk Factors

Category	MSA[1] (%)	U.S. (%)
Adults aged 18–64 who have any kind of health care coverage	86.1	87.3
Adults who reported being in good or better health	82.6	82.4
Adults who have been told they have high blood cholesterol	31.6	33.0
Adults who have been told they have high blood pressure	31.5	32.3
Adults who are current smokers	13.6	17.1
Adults who currently use E-cigarettes	3.9	4.6
Adults who currently use chewing tobacco, snuff, or snus	2.1	4.0
Adults who are heavy drinkers[2]	6.3	6.3
Adults who are binge drinkers[3]	19.9	17.4
Adults who are overweight (BMI 25.0 - 29.9)	34.4	35.3
Adults who are obese (BMI 30.0 - 99.8)	30.1	31.3
Adults who participated in any physical activities in the past month	77.3	74.4
Adults who always or nearly always wears a seat belt	95.7	94.3

Note: (1) Figures cover the Chicago-Naperville-Elgin, IL-IN-WI Metropolitan Statistical Area—see Appendix B for areas included; (2) Heavy drinkers are classified as adult men having more than 14 drinks per week and adult women having more than 7 drinks per week; (3) Binge drinkers are classified as males having five or more drinks on one occasion or females having four or more drinks on one occasion
Source: Centers for Disease Control and Prevention, Behaviorial Risk Factor Surveillance System, SMART: Selected Metropolitan Area Risk Trends, 2017

Acute and Chronic Health Conditions

Category	MSA[1] (%)	U.S. (%)
Adults who have ever been told they had a heart attack	3.3	4.2
Adults who have ever been told they have angina or coronary heart disease	3.5	3.9
Adults who have ever been told they had a stroke	2.8	3.0
Adults who have ever been told they have asthma	13.1	14.2
Adults who have ever been told they have arthritis	22.5	24.9
Adults who have ever been told they have diabetes[2]	10.3	10.5
Adults who have ever been told they had skin cancer	3.9	6.2
Adults who have ever been told they had any other types of cancer	5.6	7.1
Adults who have ever been told they have COPD	6.1	6.5
Adults who have ever been told they have kidney disease	2.9	3.0
Adults who have ever been told they have a form of depression	16.3	20.5

Note: (1) Figures cover the Chicago-Naperville-Elgin, IL-IN-WI Metropolitan Statistical Area—see Appendix B for areas included; (2) Figures do not include pregnancy-related, borderline, or pre-diabetes
Source: Centers for Disease Control and Prevention, Behaviorial Risk Factor Surveillance System, SMART: Selected Metropolitan Area Risk Trends, 2017

Health Screening and Vaccination Rates

Category	MSA[1] (%)	U.S. (%)
Adults aged 65+ who have had flu shot within the past year	55.4	60.7
Adults aged 65+ who have ever had a pneumonia vaccination	71.8	75.4
Adults who have ever been tested for HIV	37.8	36.1
Adults who have ever had the shingles or zoster vaccine?	25.3	28.9
Adults who have had their blood cholesterol checked within the last five years	88.4	85.9

Note: n/a not available; (1) Figures cover the Chicago-Naperville-Elgin, IL-IN-WI Metropolitan Statistical Area—see Appendix B for areas included.
Source: Centers for Disease Control and Prevention, Behaviorial Risk Factor Surveillance System, SMART: Selected Metropolitan Area Risk Trends, 2017

Disability Status

Category	MSA[1] (%)	U.S. (%)
Adults who reported being deaf	3.2	6.7
Are you blind or have serious difficulty seeing, even when wearing glasses?	4.0	4.5
Are you limited in any way in any of your usual activities due of arthritis?	10.8	12.9
Do you have difficulty doing errands alone?	6.0	6.8
Do you have difficulty dressing or bathing?	3.2	3.6
Do you have serious difficulty concentrating/remembering/making decisions?	8.1	10.7
Do you have serious difficulty walking or climbing stairs?	11.8	13.6

Note: (1) Figures cover the Chicago-Naperville-Elgin, IL-IN-WI Metropolitan Statistical Area—see Appendix B for areas included.
Source: Centers for Disease Control and Prevention, Behaviorial Risk Factor Surveillance System, SMART: Selected Metropolitan Area Risk Trends, 2017

Mortality Rates for the Top 10 Causes of Death in the U.S.

ICD-10[a] Sub-Chapter	ICD-10[a] Code	Age-Adjusted Mortality Rate[1] per 100,000 population	
		County[2]	U.S.
Malignant neoplasms	C00-C97	156.4	152.4
Ischaemic heart diseases	I20-I25	83.9	92.7
Other forms of heart disease	I30-I51	59.2	52.5
Chronic lower respiratory diseases	J40-J47	28.3	40.4
Cerebrovascular diseases	I60-I69	40.6	37.3
Other degenerative diseases of the nervous system	G30-G31	25.9	36.4
Other external causes of accidental injury	W00-X59	32.7	35.3
Organic, including symptomatic, mental disorders	F01-F09	31.4	30.0
Hypertensive diseases	I10-I15	28.3	22.9
Diabetes mellitus	E10-E14	19.6	21.3

Note: (a) ICD-10 = International Classification of Diseases 10th Revision; (1) Mortality rates are a three year average covering 2016-2018; (2) Figures cover Cook County.
Source: Centers for Disease Control and Prevention, National Center for Health Statistics. Underlying Cause of Death 1999-2018 on CDC WONDER Online Database

Mortality Rates for Selected Causes of Death

ICD-10[a] Sub-Chapter	ICD-10[a] Code	Age-Adjusted Mortality Rate[1] per 100,000 population	
		County[2]	U.S.
Assault	X85-Y09	15.1	6.0
Diseases of the liver	K70-K76	11.3	14.2
Human immunodeficiency virus (HIV) disease	B20-B24	2.0	1.6
Influenza and pneumonia	J09-J18	15.7	14.2
Intentional self-harm	X60-X84	8.3	13.9
Malnutrition	E40-E46	1.7	1.9
Obesity and other hyperalimentation	E65-E68	2.2	2.1
Renal failure	N17-N19	16.8	12.8
Transport accidents	V01-V99	6.8	12.5
Viral hepatitis	B15-B19	1.0	1.4

Note: (a) ICD-10 = International Classification of Diseases 10th Revision; (1) Mortality rates are a three year average covering 2016-2018; (2) Figures cover Cook County; Data are suppressed when the data meet the criteria for confidentiality constraints; Mortality rates are flagged as unreliable when the rate would be calculated with a numerator of 20 or less.
Source: Centers for Disease Control and Prevention, National Center for Health Statistics. Underlying Cause of Death 1999-2018 on CDC WONDER Online Database

Health Insurance Coverage

Area	With Health Insurance	With Private Health Insurance	With Public Health Insurance	Without Health Insurance	Population Under Age 19 Without Health Insurance
City	89.3	58.8	37.2	10.7	3.4
MSA[1]	91.8	69.7	31.5	8.2	3.2
U.S.	90.6	67.7	34.7	9.4	5.2

Note: Figures are percentages that cover the civilian noninstitutionalized population; (1) Figures cover the Chicago-Naperville-Elgin, IL-IN-WI Metropolitan Statistical Area—see Appendix B for areas included
Source: U.S. Census Bureau, 2014-2018 American Community Survey 5-Year Estimates

Number of Medical Professionals

Area	MDs[3]	DOs[3,4]	Dentists	Podiatrists	Chiropractors	Optometrists
County[1] (number)	22,557	1,213	4,718	644	1,439	1,044
County[1] (rate[2])	432.9	23.3	91.1	12.4	27.8	20.2
U.S. (rate[2])	281.9	23.4	69.1	6.0	27.5	16.4

Note: Data as of 2018 unless noted; (1) Data covers Cook County; (2) Rate per 100,000 population; (3) Data as of 2017 and includes all active, non-federal physicians; (4) Doctor of Osteopathic Medicine
Source: U.S. Department of Health and Human Services, Health Resources and Services Administration, Bureau of Health Professions, Area Resource File (ARF) 2018-2019

Best Hospitals

According to *U.S. News,* the Chicago-Naperville-Arlington Heights, IL metro area is home to nine of the best hospitals in the U.S.: **Advocate Christ Medical Center** (1 pediatric specialty); **Amita Saints Mary and Elizabeth Medical Center Chicago** (1 adult specialty); **Loyola University Medical Center** (4 adult specialties); **NorthShore University HealthSystem-Metro Chicago** (2 adult specialties); **Northwestern Medicine Central DuPage Hospital** (1 adult specialty); **Northwestern Memorial Hospital** (Honor Roll/12 adult specialties); **Rush University Medical Center** (5 adult specialties); **Shirley Ryan AbilityLab (formerly Rehabilitation Institute of Chicago)** (1 adult specialty); **University of Chicago Medical Center** (6 adult specialties). The hospitals listed were nationally ranked in at least one of 16 adult or 10 pediatric specialties. Only 206 hospitals nationwide were nationally ranked in one or more adult or pediatric specialty. Twenty hospitals in the U.S. made the Honor Roll. The Best Hospitals Honor Roll takes both the national rankings and the procedure and condition ratings into account. Hospitals received points if they were nationally ranked in one of the 16 adult specialties—the higher they ranked, the more points they got—and how many ratings of "high performing" they earned in the nine procedures and conditions. *U.S. News Online, "America's Best Hospitals 2019-20"*

According to *U.S. News,* the Chicago-Naperville-Arlington Heights, IL metro area is home to three of the best children's hospitals in the U.S.: **Advocate Children's Hospital** (1 pediatric specialty); **Advocate Christ Medical Center** (1 pediatric specialty); **Ann and Robert H. Lurie Children's Hospital of Chicago** (10 pediatric specialties). The hospitals listed were highly ranked in at least one of 10 pediatric specialties. Ninety-one children's hospitals in the U.S. were nationally ranked in at least one specialty. Hospitals received points for being ranked in a specialty, and the 10 hospitals with the most points across the 10 specialties make up the Honor Roll. *U.S. News Online, "America's Best Children's Hospitals 2019-20"*

EDUCATION

Public School District Statistics

District Name	Schls	Pupils	Pupil/ Teacher Ratio	Minority Pupils[1] (%)	Free Lunch Eligible[2] (%)	IEP[3] (%)
City of Chicago SD 299	658	359,476	16.5	89.4	78.4	14.2

Note: Table includes school districts with 2,000 or more students; (1) Percentage of students that are not non-Hispanic white; (2) Percentage of students that are eligible for the free lunch program; (3) Percentage of students that have an Individualized Education Program.
Source: U.S. Department of Education, National Center for Education Statistics, Common Core of Data, Local Education Agency (School District) Universe Survey: School Year 2018-2019; U.S. Department of Education, National Center for Education Statistics, Common Core of Data, Public Elementary/Secondary School Universe Survey: School Year 2018-2019

Best High Schools

According to *U.S. News,* Chicago is home to eight of the top 500 high schools in the U.S.: **Payton College Preparatory High School** (#9); **Northside College Preparatory High School** (#38); **Jones College Prep High School** (#66); **Young Magnet High School** (#77); **Lane Technical**

High School (#81); **Lindblom Math and Science Academy** (#296); **Brooks College Prep Academy High School** (#304); **Lincoln Park High School** (#432). Nearly 18,000 public, magnet and charter schools were ranked based on their performance on state assessments and how well they prepare students for college. *U.S. News & World Report, "Best High Schools 2020"*

Highest Level of Education

Area	Less than H.S.	H.S. Diploma	Some College, No Deg.	Associate Degree	Bachelor's Degree	Master's Degree	Prof. School Degree	Doctorate Degree
City	15.5	22.9	17.6	5.7	22.7	10.9	3.2	1.6
MSA[1]	11.7	24.1	19.7	7.2	22.7	10.7	2.6	1.4
U.S.	12.3	27.1	20.6	8.4	19.4	8.6	2.1	1.4

Note: Figures cover persons age 25 and over; (1) Figures cover the Chicago-Naperville-Elgin, IL-IN-WI Metropolitan Statistical Area—see Appendix B for areas included
Source: U.S. Census Bureau, 2014-2018 American Community Survey 5-Year Estimates

Educational Attainment by Race

Area	High School Graduate or Higher (%)					Bachelor's Degree or Higher (%)				
	Total	White	Black	Asian	Hisp.[2]	Total	White	Black	Asian	Hisp.[2]
City	84.5	88.2	84.6	87.7	67.1	38.4	49.8	20.7	60.7	15.6
MSA[1]	88.3	91.1	87.4	90.8	66.7	37.4	40.9	22.3	64.4	14.4
U.S.	87.7	89.6	85.4	86.8	67.7	31.5	32.9	21.1	53.5	15.8

Note: Figures shown cover persons 25 years old and over; (1) Figures cover the Chicago-Naperville-Elgin, IL-IN-WI Metropolitan Statistical Area—see Appendix B for areas included; (2) People of Hispanic origin can be of any race
Source: U.S. Census Bureau, 2014-2018 American Community Survey 5-Year Estimates

School Enrollment by Grade and Control

Area	Preschool (%)		Kindergarten (%)		Grades 1 - 4 (%)		Grades 5 - 8 (%)		Grades 9 - 12 (%)	
	Public	Private	Public	Private	Public	Private	Public	Private	Public	Private
City	60.9	39.1	80.1	19.9	86.1	13.9	86.5	13.5	87.4	12.6
MSA[1]	59.0	41.0	84.3	15.7	89.0	11.0	89.2	10.8	90.5	9.5
U.S.	59.0	41.0	87.7	12.3	89.6	10.4	89.5	10.5	90.2	9.8

Note: Figures shown cover persons 3 years old and over; (1) Figures cover the Chicago-Naperville-Elgin, IL-IN-WI Metropolitan Statistical Area—see Appendix B for areas included
Source: U.S. Census Bureau, 2014-2018 American Community Survey 5-Year Estimates

Average Salaries of Public School Teachers

Area	2016-17		2017-18		Change from 2016-17 to 2017-18	
	Dollars	Rank[1]	Dollars	Rank[1]	Percent	Rank[2]
Illinois	64,516	11	65,721	11	1.87	20
U.S. Average	59,539	–	60,477	–	1.58	–

Note: (1) Rank ranges from 1 to 51 where 1 indicates highest salary; (2) Rank ranges from 1 to 51 where 1 indicates highest percent change.
Source: National Education Association, Rankings & Estimates: Rankings of the States 2018 and Estimates of School Statistics 2019

Higher Education

Four-Year Colleges			Two-Year Colleges			Medical Schools[1]	Law Schools[2]	Voc/ Tech[3]
Public	Private Non-profit	Private For-profit	Public	Private Non-profit	Private For-profit			
3	34	7	7	1	5	4	6	14

Note: Figures cover institutions located within the city limits and include main campuses only; (1) includes schools accredited by the Liaison Committee on Medical Education and the American Osteopathic Association's Commission on Osteopathic College Accreditation; (2) includes ABA-accredited schools, schools with provisional ABA accreditation, and state accredited schools; (3) includes all schools with programs that are less than 2 years.
Source: National Center for Education Statistics, Integrated Postsecondary Education System (IPEDS), 2018-19; Wikipedia, List of Medical Schools in the United States, accessed May 1, 2020; Wikipedia, List of Law Schools in the United States, accessed May 1, 2020

According to *U.S. News & World Report,* the Chicago-Naperville-Arlington Heights, IL metro division is home to six of the top 200 national universities in the U.S.: **University of Chicago** (#6 tie); **Northwestern University** (#9); **Loyola University Chicago** (#104 tie); **Illinois Institute of Technology** (#117 tie); **DePaul University** (#125 tie); **University of Illinois—Chicago** (#132 tie). The indicators used to capture academic quality fall into a number of categories: assessment by administrators at peer institutions; retention of students; faculty resources; student selectivity; financial resources; alumni giving; high school counselor ratings of colleges; and graduation rate. *U.S. News & World Report, "America's Best Colleges 2020"*

According to *U.S. News & World Report,* the Chicago-Naperville-Arlington Heights, IL metro division is home to one of the top 100 liberal arts colleges in the U.S.: **Wheaton College** (#58 tie). The indicators used to capture academic quality fall into a number of categories: assessment by administrators at peer institutions; retention of students; faculty resources; student selectivity; financial resources; alumni giving; high school counselor ratings of colleges; and graduation rate. *U.S. News & World Report, "America's Best Colleges 2020"*

According to *U.S. News & World Report,* the Chicago-Naperville-Arlington Heights, IL metro division is home to four of the top 100 law schools in the U.S.: **University of Chicago** (#4 tie); **Northwestern University (Pritzker)** (#9 tie); **Loyola University Chicago** (#70 tie); **Illinois Institute of Technology (Chicago-Kent)** (#83 tie). The rankings are based on a weighted average of 12 measures of quality: peer assessment score; assessment score by lawyers/judges; median LSAT scores; median undergrad GPA; acceptance rate; employment rates for graduates; placement success; bar passage rate; faculty resources; expenditures per student; student/faculty ratio; and library resources. *U.S. News & World Report, "America's Best Graduate Schools, Law, 2021"*

According to *U.S. News & World Report,* the Chicago-Naperville-Arlington Heights, IL metro division is home to four of the top 75 medical schools for research in the U.S.: **University of Chicago (Pritzker)** (#17); **Northwestern University (Feinberg)** (#18 tie); **University of Illinois** (#55 tie); **Rush University** (#58 tie). The rankings are based on a weighted average of 11 measures of quality: quality assessment; peer assessment score; assessment score by residency directors; research activity; total research activity; average research activity per faculty member; student selectivity; median MCAT total score; median undergraduate GPA; acceptance rate; and faculty resources. *U.S. News & World Report, "America's Best Graduate Schools, Medical, 2021"*

According to *U.S. News & World Report,* the Chicago-Naperville-Arlington Heights, IL metro division is home to two of the top 75 business schools in the U.S.: **Northwestern University (Kellogg)** (#3 tie); **University of Chicago (Booth)** (#3 tie). The rankings are based on a weighted average of the following nine measures: quality assessment; peer assessment; recruiter assessment; placement success; mean starting salary and bonus; student selectivity; mean GMAT and GRE scores; mean undergraduate GPA; and acceptance rate. *U.S. News & World Report, "America's Best Graduate Schools, Business, 2021"*

PRESIDENTIAL ELECTION

2016 Presidential Election Results

Area	Clinton	Trump	Johnson	Stein	Other
Cook County	73.9	20.8	2.7	1.5	1.1
U.S.	48.0	45.9	3.3	1.1	1.7

Note: Results are percentages and may not add to 100% due to rounding
Source: Dave Leip's Atlas of U.S. Presidential Elections

EMPLOYERS

Major Employers

Company Name	Industry
Abbott Laboratories	Pharmaceutical preparations
Addus HomeCare Corporation	Home health care services
Advocate Lutheran General Hospital	General medical & surgical hospitals
BMO Bankcorp	National commercial banks
City of Chicago	General government
Cook County Bureau of Health Services	Administration of public health programs, county govt
Graphic Packaging International	Folding boxboard
Loyola University Health System	General medical & surgical hospitals
Northshore University Healthsystem	General medical & surgical hospitals
Northwestern Memorial Hospital	General medical & surgical hospitals
SCC Holding Co.	Cups, plastics, except foam
Schneider Electric Holdings	Air transportation, scheduled
SOLO Cup Company	Cups, plastics, except foam
The Allstate Corporation	Fire, marine, & casualty insurance
The University of Chicago Medical Center	General medical & surgical hospitals
United Parcel Service	Mailing & messenger services
United States Steel Corporation	Steel foundries
WM Recycle America	Material recovery

Note: Companies shown are located within the Chicago-Naperville-Elgin, IL-IN-WI Metropolitan Statistical Area.
Source: Hoovers.com; Wikipedia

Best Companies to Work For

Crowe; Hyatt Hotels; West Monroe Partners, headquartered in Chicago, are among "The 100 Best Companies to Work For." To pick the best companies, *Fortune* partnered with the Great Place to Work Institute. Two-thirds of a company's score is based on the results of the Institute's Trust Index survey, which is sent to a random sample of employees from each company. The questions related to attitudes about management's credibility, job satisfaction, and camaraderie. The other third of the scoring is based on the company's responses to the Institute's Culture Audit, which includes detailed questions about pay and benefit programs, and a series of open-ended questions about hiring practices, internal communication, training, recognition programs, and diversity efforts. Any company that is at least five years old with more than 1,000 U.S. employees is eligible. *Fortune, "The 100 Best Companies to Work For," 2020*

A.T. Kearney; BDO USA; Grant Thornton; JLL; Katten; Leo Burnett Group; RSM U.S; Starcom USA, headquartered in Chicago, are among the "100 Best Companies for Working Mothers." Criteria: paid time off and leaves; workforce profile; benefits; women's issues and advancement; flexible work; company culture and work life programs. *Working Mother, "100 Best Companies 2019"*

A.T. Kearney, headquartered in Chicago, is among the "Best Companies for Multicultural Women." *Working Mother* selected 50 companies based on a detailed application completed by public and private firms based in the United States, excluding government agencies, companies in the human resources field and non-autonomous divisions. Companies supplied data about the hiring, pay, and promotion of multicultural employees. Applications focused on representation of multicultural women, recruitment, retention and advancement programs, and company culture. *Working Mother, "2019 Best Companies for Multicultural Women"*

CME Group; Enova International; Health Care Service Corp; Motorola Solutions; Nitel; RSM US, headquartered in Chicago, are among the "100 Best Places to Work in IT." To qualify, companies had to be U.S.-based organizations or be non-U.S.- based employers that met the following criteria: have a minimum of 300 total employees at a U.S. headquarters and a minimum of 30 IT employees in the U.S., with at least 50% of their IT employees based in the U.S. The best places to work were selected based on compensation, benefits, work/life balance, employee morale, and satisfaction with training and development programs. In addition, *Computerworld* looked at retention efforts, programs for recognizing and rewarding outstanding performances, and benefits such as flextime, elder care and child care, and reimbursement for college tuition and the cost of pursuing technology certifications. *Computerworld, "100 Best Places to Work in IT 2019"*

BDO USA; Grant Thornton; JLL; Katten, headquartered in Chicago, are among the "Top Companies for Executive Women." The 2020 National Association for Female Executives (NAFE) Top Companies application included more than 200 questions on topics including female representation at all levels, but especially the corporate officer and profit-and-loss leadership ranks.

The application tracked and examined how many employees have access to programs and policies that promote advancement of women and how many employees take advantage of them, plus how companies train managers to help women advance. To be considered, companies must have a minimum of two women on their boards of directors, a U.S.-based CEO and at least 1,000 U.S. employees. *National Association for Female Executives, "2020 NAFE Top 70 Companies for Executive Women"*

PUBLIC SAFETY

Crime Rate

Area	All Crimes	Violent Crimes				Property Crimes		
		Murder	Rape[3]	Robbery	Aggrav. Assault	Burglary	Larceny -Theft	Motor Vehicle Theft
City	4,187.7	20.7	66.1	356.1	563.1	429.8	2,379.2	372.6
Suburbs[1]	n/a	2.2	29.4	45.8	n/a	n/a	n/a	91.9
Metro[2]	n/a	9.2	43.3	163.5	n/a	n/a	n/a	198.4
U.S.	2,580.1	5.0	42.6	86.2	246.8	376.0	1,594.6	228.9

Note: Figures are crimes per 100,000 population; (1) All areas within the metro area that are located outside the city limits; (2) Figures cover the Chicago-Naperville-Arlington Heights, IL Metropolitan Division—see Appendix B for areas included; (3) The city and U.S. figures shown were reported using the revised Uniform Crime Reporting (UCR) definition of rape. The suburban and metro area figures shown are an aggregate total of the data submitted using both the revised and legacy UCR definitions.
Source: FBI Uniform Crime Reports, 2018

Hate Crimes

Area	Number of Quarters Reported	Number of Incidents per Bias Motivation					
		Race/Ethnicity/ Ancestry	Religion	Sexual Orientation	Disability	Gender	Gender Identity
City	4	36	10	13	0	0	3
U.S.	4	4,047	1,419	1,196	159	47	168

Source: Federal Bureau of Investigation, Hate Crime Statistics 2018

Identity Theft Consumer Reports

Area	Reports	Reports per 100,000 Population	Rank[2]
MSA[1]	20,245	213	40
U.S.	650,572	198	-

Note: (1) Figures cover the Chicago-Naperville-Elgin, IL-IN-WI Metropolitan Statistical Area—see Appendix B for areas included; (2) Rank ranges from 1 to 386 where 1 indicates greatest number of identity theft reports per 100,000 population
Source: Federal Trade Commission, Consumer Sentinel Network Data Book for January–December 2019

Fraud and Other Consumer Reports

Area	Reports	Reports per 100,000 Population	Rank[2]
MSA[1]	57,559	606	122
U.S.	2,590,177	789	-

Note: (1) Figures cover the Chicago-Naperville-Elgin, IL-IN-WI Metropolitan Statistical Area—see Appendix B for areas included; (2) Rank ranges from 1 to 386 where 1 indicates greatest number of fraud and other consumer reports per 100,000 population
Source: Federal Trade Commission, Consumer Sentinel Network Data Book for January–December 2019

SPORTS

Professional Sports Teams

Team Name	League	Year Established
Chicago Bears	National Football League (NFL)	1921
Chicago Blackhawks	National Hockey League (NHL)	1926
Chicago Bulls	National Basketball Association (NBA)	1966
Chicago Cubs	Major League Baseball (MLB)	1874
Chicago Fire	Major League Soccer (MLS)	1997
Chicago White Sox	Major League Baseball (MLB)	1900

Note: Includes teams located in the Chicago-Naperville-Elgin, IL-IN-WI Metropolitan Statistical Area.
Source: Wikipedia, Major Professional Sports Teams of the United States and Canada, May 4, 2020

CLIMATE

Average and Extreme Temperatures

Temperature	Jan	Feb	Mar	Apr	May	Jun	Jul	Aug	Sep	Oct	Nov	Dec	Yr.
Extreme High (°F)	65	71	88	91	93	104	102	100	99	91	78	71	104
Average High (°F)	29	33	45	59	70	79	84	82	75	63	48	34	59
Average Temp. (°F)	21	26	37	49	59	69	73	72	65	53	40	27	49
Average Low (°F)	13	17	28	39	48	57	63	62	54	42	32	19	40
Extreme Low (°F)	-27	-17	-8	7	24	36	40	41	28	17	1	-25	-27

Note: Figures cover the years 1958-1990
Source: National Climatic Data Center, International Station Meteorological Climate Summary, 9/96

Average Precipitation/Snowfall/Humidity

Precip./Humidity	Jan	Feb	Mar	Apr	May	Jun	Jul	Aug	Sep	Oct	Nov	Dec	Yr.
Avg. Precip. (in.)	1.6	1.4	2.7	3.6	3.3	3.7	3.7	4.1	3.7	2.4	2.8	2.3	35.4
Avg. Snowfall (in.)	11	8	7	2	Tr	0	0	0	0	1	2	9	39
Avg. Rel. Hum. 6am (%)	76	77	79	77	77	78	82	85	85	82	80	80	80
Avg. Rel. Hum. 3pm (%)	65	63	59	53	51	52	54	55	55	53	61	68	57

Note: Figures cover the years 1958-1990; Tr = Trace amounts (<0.05 in. of rain; <0.5 in. of snow)
Source: National Climatic Data Center, International Station Meteorological Climate Summary, 9/96

Weather Conditions

Temperature			Daytime Sky			Precipitation		
5°F & below	32°F & below	90°F & above	Clear	Partly cloudy	Cloudy	0.01 inch or more precip.	0.1 inch or more snow/ice	Thunder-storms
21	132	17	84	135	146	125	31	38

Note: Figures are average number of days per year and cover the years 1958-1990
Source: National Climatic Data Center, International Station Meteorological Climate Summary, 9/96

HAZARDOUS WASTE

Superfund Sites

The Chicago-Naperville-Arlington Heights, IL metro division is home to 11 sites on the EPA's Superfund National Priorities List: **Amoco Chemicals (Joliet Landfill)** (final); **Dupage County Landfill/Blackwell Forest Preserve** (final); **Estech General Chemical Company** (final); **Joliet Army Ammunition Plant (Load-Assembly-Packing Area)** (final); **Joliet Army Ammunition Plant (Manufacturing Area)** (final); **Kerr-Mcgee (Kress Creek/West Branch Of Dupage River)** (final); **Kerr-Mcgee (Residential Areas)** (final); **Lake Calumet Cluster** (final); **Lenz Oil Service, Inc.** (final); **Schroud Property** (final); **Woodstock Municipal Landfill** (final). There are a total of 1,387 Superfund sites with a status of proposed or final on the list in the U.S. *U.S. Environmental Protection Agency, National Priorities List, May 5, 2020*

AIR & WATER QUALITY

Air Quality Trends: Ozone

	1990	1995	2000	2005	2010	2012	2014	2016	2017	2018
MSA[1]	0.074	0.094	0.073	0.084	0.070	0.082	0.068	0.074	0.071	0.073
U.S.	0.088	0.089	0.082	0.080	0.073	0.075	0.067	0.069	0.068	0.069

Note: (1) Data covers the Chicago-Naperville-Elgin, IL-IN-WI Metropolitan Statistical Area—see Appendix B for areas included. The values shown are the composite ozone concentration averages among trend sites based on the highest fourth daily maximum 8-hour concentration in parts per million. These trends are based on sites having an adequate record of monitoring data during the trend period. Data from exceptional events are included.
Source: U.S. Environmental Protection Agency, Air Quality Monitoring Information, "Air Quality Trends by City, 1990-2018"

Air Quality Index

Area	Percent of Days when Air Quality was...[2]					AQI Statistics[2]	
	Good	Moderate	Unhealthy for Sensitive Groups	Unhealthy	Very Unhealthy	Maximum	Median
MSA[1]	32.1	60.8	5.5	1.6	0.0	177	57

Note: (1) Data covers the Chicago-Naperville-Elgin, IL-IN-WI Metropolitan Statistical Area—see Appendix B for areas included; (2) Based on 365 days with AQI data in 2018. Air Quality Index (AQI) is an index for reporting daily air quality. EPA calculates the AQI for five major air pollutants regulated by the Clean Air Act: ground-level ozone, particle pollution (aka particulate matter), carbon monoxide, sulfur dioxide, and nitrogen dioxide. The AQI runs from 0 to 500. The higher the AQI value, the greater the level of air pollution and the greater the health concern. There are six AQI categories: "Good" AQI is between 0 and 50. Air quality is considered satisfactory; "Moderate" AQI is between 51 and 100. Air quality is acceptable; "Unhealthy for Sensitive Groups" When AQI values are between 101 and 150, members of sensitive groups may experience health effects; "Unhealthy" When AQI values are between 151 and 200 everyone may begin to experience health effects; "Very Unhealthy" AQI values between 201 and 300 trigger a health alert; "Hazardous" AQI values over 300 trigger warnings of emergency conditions (not shown).
Source: U.S. Environmental Protection Agency, Air Quality Index Report, 2018

Air Quality Index Pollutants

Area	Percent of Days when AQI Pollutant was...[2]					
	Carbon Monoxide	Nitrogen Dioxide	Ozone	Sulfur Dioxide	Particulate Matter 2.5	Particulate Matter 10
MSA[1]	0.0	7.9	30.7	1.6	56.2	3.6

Note: (1) Data covers the Chicago-Naperville-Elgin, IL-IN-WI Metropolitan Statistical Area—see Appendix B for areas included; (2) Based on 365 days with AQI data in 2018. The Air Quality Index (AQI) is an index for reporting daily air quality. EPA calculates the AQI for five major air pollutants regulated by the Clean Air Act: ground-level ozone, particle pollution (also known as particulate matter), carbon monoxide, sulfur dioxide, and nitrogen dioxide. The AQI runs from 0 to 500. The higher the AQI value, the greater the level of air pollution and the greater the health concern.
Source: U.S. Environmental Protection Agency, Air Quality Index Report, 2018

Maximum Air Pollutant Concentrations: Particulate Matter, Ozone, CO and Lead

	Particulate Matter 10 (ug/m^3)	Particulate Matter 2.5 Wtd AM (ug/m^3)	Particulate Matter 2.5 24-Hr (ug/m^3)	Ozone (ppm)	Carbon Monoxide (ppm)	Lead (ug/m^3)
MSA[1] Level	78	11.2	27	0.084	2	0.31
NAAQS[2]	150	15	35	0.075	9	0.15
Met NAAQS[2]	Yes	Yes	Yes	No	Yes	No

Note: (1) Data covers the Chicago-Naperville-Elgin, IL-IN-WI Metropolitan Statistical Area—see Appendix B for areas included; Data from exceptional events are included; (2) National Ambient Air Quality Standards; ppm = parts per million; ug/m^3 = micrograms per cubic meter; n/a not available.
Concentrations: Particulate Matter 10 (coarse particulate)—highest second maximum 24-hour concentration; Particulate Matter 2.5 Wtd AM (fine particulate)—highest weighted annual mean concentration; Particulate Matter 2.5 24-Hour (fine particulate)—highest 98th percentile 24-hour concentration; Ozone—highest fourth daily maximum 8-hour concentration; Carbon Monoxide—highest second maximum non-overlapping 8-hour concentration; Lead—maximum running 3-month average
Source: U.S. Environmental Protection Agency, Air Quality Monitoring Information, "Air Quality Statistics by City, 2018"

Maximum Air Pollutant Concentrations: Nitrogen Dioxide and Sulfur Dioxide

	Nitrogen Dioxide AM (ppb)	Nitrogen Dioxide 1-Hr (ppb)	Sulfur Dioxide AM (ppb)	Sulfur Dioxide 1-Hr (ppb)	Sulfur Dioxide 24-Hr (ppb)
MSA[1] Level	18	61	n/a	28	n/a
NAAQS[2]	53	100	30	75	140
Met NAAQS[2]	Yes	Yes	n/a	Yes	n/a

Note: (1) Data covers the Chicago-Naperville-Elgin, IL-IN-WI Metropolitan Statistical Area—see Appendix B for areas included; Data from exceptional events are included; (2) National Ambient Air Quality Standards; ppm = parts per million; ug/m^3 = micrograms per cubic meter; n/a not available.
Concentrations: Nitrogen Dioxide AM—highest arithmetic mean concentration; Nitrogen Dioxide 1-Hr—highest 98th percentile 1-hour daily maximum concentration; Sulfur Dioxide AM—highest annual mean concentration; Sulfur Dioxide 1-Hr—highest 99th percentile 1-hour daily maximum concentration; Sulfur Dioxide 24-Hr—highest second maximum 24-hour concentration
Source: U.S. Environmental Protection Agency, Air Quality Monitoring Information, "Air Quality Statistics by City, 2018"

Drinking Water

Water System Name	Pop. Served	Primary Water Source Type	Violations[1]
Chicago	2,700,000	Surface	44

Note: (1) Total number of violations (both active and inactive) in the EPA database
Source: U.S. Environmental Protection Agency, Office of Ground Water and Drinking Water, Safe Drinking Water Information System (based on data extracted May 5, 2020)

Columbia, Missouri

Background

In the middle of the state, along its namesake river, Columbia is a college town teeming with the bright young minds and technological breakthroughs.

The city, located in Boone County, has ridden out the economic downturn with less trauma than the rest of Missouri. Recent surveys give the city high marks in general and for retirees.

The founding of its colleges and university dovetails with the growth and founding of the city itself. A settlement called Smithton grew from the Smithton Land Company's 2,000-acre land purchase on the other side of Flat Branch, not far from where Lewis and Clark passed by during their 1803 explorations. In 1821 the settlement moved across the river and Columbia was established. Daniel Boone and sons ran a salt lick about forty miles away.

Six counties competed for the right to host Missouri's university when it was founded in 1838, the first public university west of the Mississippi River. Boone County responded by raising more than $118,000 in land, cash and buildings. It was forced to repeat its largess decades later, when the academic hall burned down and talked turned to moving the university. The city responded by raising $50,000 to build Jesse Hall, now a local landmark.

Two other institutions of higher learning contributed to Columbia's focus on education. Stephens College, a private women's college, was founded in 1833, and Columbia College, now grown to 30,000 students, was founded as the Christian Female College in 1851. This school arrived as the first women's college west of the Mississippi chartered by a state legislature, and it went co-ed in 1970.

Although these three institutions help to define the historic downtown area, it is the state's massive flagship university—with a rare combination of law school, medical school, and veterinary school all on the same campus—that is Boone County's largest employer. As a major research institution, "Mizzou" conducts $435 million in research and even has a nuclear research reactor on campus. It is the nation's largest supplier of radioisotopes for diagnosing and treating cancer, and hosts interdisciplinary research in a range of scientific enterprises: biofuels, energy logistics, energy policy, wind, biomass and solar. The licensing of products invented by MU products by various companies is a huge market.

The MU Life Science Business Incubator, which opened in 2008, encourages and supports business based on these technologies. For instance, the Indian pharma company Shasun collaborated to create Shasun-NBI based in the incubator and to develop a cancer treatment. Another research park, Discovery Ridge, recently opened. Columbia is also home to several more state-certified sites under development.

The campus also houses a well-regarded journalism school and IRE, Investigative Reporters and Editors, Inc. The 1,250-acre campus is also home to a botanic garden and a number of cultural opportunities enjoyed by the community at large including the Missouri Theatre Center for the Arts, the Jesse Auditorium, and the university's Museum of Art and Architecture. The State Historical Society of Missouri also operates a research center at the university.

The county's other large employers include University Hospital and Clinics, Columbia Public Schools, Boone Hospital Center, the City of Columbia, and the U.S. Dept. of Veterans Affairs.

The city operates a regional airport, a short line railroad, and utilities for both water and electricity. It also has its own Office of Cultural Affairs, which distributes art guides and a cultural newsletter, funds local arts organizations, and underwrites advertising for local arts opportunities. Columbia offers a "percent for art" program that allows one percent of the cost of new city construction or renovation to be used for site-specific public art. The town is also full of galleries and various arts organizations.

Columbia has four distinct seasons, with highs in the upper 80s in July and August, lows below 20 degrees in January, and rainfall peaking in May.

Rankings

General Rankings

- In their sixth annual survey, Livability.com looked at data for more than 1,000 U.S. cities to determine the rankings for Livability's "Top 100 Best Places to Live" in 2019. Columbia ranked #6. Criteria: median home value capped at $250,000; affordable living; vibrant economy; education, demographics, health care options. transportation & infrastructure; abundant lifestyle amenities. *Livability.com, "Top 100 Best Places to Live 2019" March 2019*

Business/Finance Rankings

- The Columbia metro area appeared on the Milken Institute "2020 Best Performing Cities" list. Rank: #93 out of 201 small metro areas. Criteria: job growth; wage and salary growth; high-tech output growth. *Milken Institute, "Best-Performing Cities 2020," February 26, 2020*
- *Forbes* ranked 203 smaller metro areas (population under 268,000) to determine the nation's "Best Small Places for Business and Careers." The Columbia metro area was ranked #43. Criteria: costs (business and living); job growth (past and projected); income growth; quality of life; educational attainment (college and high school); projected economic growth; cultural and leisure opportunities; workplace tolerance laws; net migration patterns. *Forbes, "The Best Small Places for Business and Careers 2019," October 30, 2019*

Dating/Romance Rankings

- Columbia was selected as one of the most romantic cities in the U.S. by video-rental kiosk company Redbox. The city ranked #6 out of 20. Criteria: number of romance-related rentals in 2016. *Redbox, "20 Most Romantic Cities," February 6, 2017*

Environmental Rankings

- Columbia was highlighted as one of the cleanest metro areas for ozone air pollution in the U.S. during 2015 through 2017. The list represents cities with no monitored ozone air pollution in unhealthful ranges. *American Lung Association, "State of the Air 2019," April 24, 2019*

Real Estate Rankings

- The Columbia metro area was identified as one of the 20 best housing markets in the U.S. in 2019. The area ranked #12 out of 180 markets. Criteria: year-over-year change of median sales price of existing single-family homes between the 4th quarter of 2018 and the 4th quarter of 2019. *National Association of Realtors®, Median Sales Price of Existing Single-Family Homes for Metropolitan Areas, 4th Quarter 2019*

Safety Rankings

- The National Insurance Crime Bureau ranked 382 metro areas in the U.S. in terms of per capita rates of vehicle theft. The Columbia metro area ranked #157 (#1 = highest rate). Criteria: number of vehicle theft offenses per 100,000 inhabitants in 2018. *National Insurance Crime Bureau, "Hot Spots 2018," June 25, 2019*

Seniors/Retirement Rankings

- From its Best Cities for Successful Aging indexes, the Milken Institute generated rankings for metropolitan areas, weighing data in nine categories—health care, wellness, living arrangements, transportation and convenience, financial characteristics, education, employment, community engagement, and overall livability. The Columbia metro area was ranked #4 overall in the small metro area category. *Milken Institute, "Best Cities for Successful Aging, 2017" March 14, 2017*

■ Columbia made the 2019 *Forbes* list of "25 Best Places to Retire." Criteria focused on high-quality retirement living at an affordable price, include: housing/living costs compared to the national average and state taxes; air quality; crime rates; good economic outlook; home price appreciation; college presence; doctor availability; bikeability; walkability; healthy living. *Forbes.com, "The Best Places to Retire in 2019," April 23, 2019*

Sports/Recreation Rankings

■ Columbia was chosen as one of America's best cities for bicycling. The city ranked #46 out of 50. Criteria: cycling infrastructure that is safe and friendly for all ages; energy and bike culture. The editors only considered cities with populations of 100,000 or more. *Bicycling, "The 50 Best Bike Cities in America," October 10, 2018*

Miscellaneous Rankings

■ Columbia was selected as a 2019 Digital Cities Survey winner. The city ranked #3 in the small city (75,000 to 124,999 population) category. The survey examined and assessed how city governments are utilizing technology to improve transparency, enhance cybersecurity, and solve social challenges. Survey questions focused on ten characteristics: data governance, citizen-focused, leadership alignment, secure, staffed/supported, efficient, connected, resilient, best practices, and use of innovation. *Center for Digital Government, "2019 Digital Cities Survey," November 14, 2019*

Business Environment

CITY FINANCES

City Government Finances

Component	2017 ($000)	2017 ($ per capita)
Total Revenues	355,513	2,985
Total Expenditures	340,473	2,859
Debt Outstanding	365,171	3,066
Cash and Securities[1]	628,618	5,278

Note: (1) Cash and security holdings of a government at the close of its fiscal year, including those of its dependent agencies, utilities, and liquor stores.
Source: U.S. Census Bureau, State & Local Government Finances 2017

City Government Revenue by Source

Source	2017 ($000)	2017 ($ per capita)	2017 (%)
General Revenue			
From Federal Government	13,139	110	3.7
From State Government	4,995	42	1.4
From Local Governments	20,637	173	5.8
Taxes			
Property	12,015	101	3.4
Sales and Gross Receipts	58,981	495	16.6
Personal Income	0	0	0.0
Corporate Income	0	0	0.0
Motor Vehicle License	0	0	0.0
Other Taxes	2,496	21	0.7
Current Charges	54,879	461	15.4
Liquor Store	0	0	0.0
Utility	157,243	1,320	44.2
Employee Retirement	16,175	136	4.5

Source: U.S. Census Bureau, State & Local Government Finances 2017

City Government Expenditures by Function

Function	2017 ($000)	2017 ($ per capita)	2017 (%)
General Direct Expenditures			
Air Transportation	8,412	70	2.5
Corrections	0	0	0.0
Education	0	0	0.0
Employment Security Administration	0	0	0.0
Financial Administration	4,256	35	1.3
Fire Protection	13,013	109	3.8
General Public Buildings	1,962	16	0.6
Governmental Administration, Other	7,312	61	2.1
Health	5,388	45	1.6
Highways	20,767	174	6.1
Hospitals	0	0	0.0
Housing and Community Development	1,408	11	0.4
Interest on General Debt	4,990	41	1.5
Judicial and Legal	2,608	21	0.8
Libraries	0	0	0.0
Parking	2,714	22	0.8
Parks and Recreation	19,297	162	5.7
Police Protection	17,633	148	5.2
Public Welfare	875	7	0.3
Sewerage	17,027	143	5.0
Solid Waste Management	22,993	193	6.8
Veterans' Services	0	0	0.0
Liquor Store	0	0	0.0
Utility	172,488	1,448	50.7
Employee Retirement	11,264	94	3.3

Source: U.S. Census Bureau, State & Local Government Finances 2017

DEMOGRAPHICS

Population Growth

Area	1990 Census	2000 Census	2010 Census	2018* Estimate	Population Growth (%)	
					1990-2018	2010-2018
City	71,069	84,531	108,500	120,248	69.2	10.8
MSA[1]	122,010	145,666	172,786	176,515	44.7	2.2
U.S.	248,709,873	281,421,906	308,745,538	322,903,030	29.8	4.6

Note: (1) Figures cover the Columbia, MO Metropolitan Statistical Area—see Appendix B for areas included; (*) 2014-2018 5-year estimated population
Source: U.S. Census Bureau, 1990 Census, Census 2000, Census 2010, 2014-2018 American Community Survey 5-Year Estimates

Household Size

Area	Persons in Household (%)							Average Household Size
	One	Two	Three	Four	Five	Six	Seven or More	
City	33.1	33.7	14.6	12.4	4.5	1.2	0.5	2.30
MSA[1]	30.1	34.8	15.1	13.1	4.7	1.3	0.8	2.40
U.S.	27.7	33.9	15.7	13.0	6.0	2.3	1.4	2.60

Note: (1) Figures cover the Columbia, MO Metropolitan Statistical Area—see Appendix B for areas included
Source: U.S. Census Bureau, 2014-2018 American Community Survey 5-Year Estimates

Race

Area	White Alone[2] (%)	Black Alone[2] (%)	Asian Alone[2] (%)	AIAN[3] Alone[2] (%)	NHOPI[4] Alone[2] (%)	Other Race Alone[2] (%)	Two or More Races (%)
City	76.9	10.9	6.2	0.3	0.2	1.0	4.6
MSA[1]	81.1	8.8	4.5	0.3	0.1	1.0	4.2
U.S.	72.7	12.7	5.4	0.8	0.2	4.9	3.2

Note: (1) Figures cover the Columbia, MO Metropolitan Statistical Area—see Appendix B for areas included; (2) Alone is defined as not being in combination with one or more other races; (3) American Indian and Alaska Native; (4) Native Hawaiian and Other Pacific Islander
Source: U.S. Census Bureau, 2014-2018 American Community Survey 5-Year Estimates

Hispanic or Latino Origin

Area	Total (%)	Mexican (%)	Puerto Rican (%)	Cuban (%)	Other (%)
City	3.4	2.0	0.2	0.1	1.2
MSA[1]	3.4	2.1	0.1	0.1	1.0
U.S.	17.8	11.2	1.7	0.7	4.2

Note: Persons of Hispanic or Latino origin can be of any race; (1) Figures cover the Columbia, MO Metropolitan Statistical Area—see Appendix B for areas included
Source: U.S. Census Bureau, 2014-2018 American Community Survey 5-Year Estimates

Segregation

Type	Segregation Indices[1]				Percent Change		
	1990	2000	2010	2010 Rank[2]	1990-2000	1990-2010	2000-2010
Black/White	n/a	n/a	n/a	n/a	n/a	n/a	n/a
Asian/White	n/a	n/a	n/a	n/a	n/a	n/a	n/a
Hispanic/White	n/a	n/a	n/a	n/a	n/a	n/a	n/a

Note: All figures cover the Metropolitan Statistical Area—see Appendix B for areas included; Figures are based on an analysis of 1990, 2000, and 2010 Census Decennial Census tract data by William H. Frey, Brookings Institution and the University of Michigan Social Science Data Analysis Network. In this analysis all racial groups (whites, blacks, and asians) are non-Hispanic members of those races. Hispanics are shown as a separate category; (1) Segregation Indices are Dissimilarity Indices that measure the degree to which the minority group is distributed differently than whites across census tracts. They range from 0 (complete integration) to 100 (complete segregation) where the value indicates the percentage of the minority group that needs to move to be distributed exactly like whites; (2) Ranges from 1 (most segregated) to 102 (least segregated); n/a not available.
Source: www.CensusScope.org

Ancestry

Area	German	Irish	English	American	Italian	Polish	French[2]	Scottish	Dutch
City	24.4	12.4	9.0	5.1	3.6	2.4	2.7	2.1	1.1
MSA[1]	24.7	12.0	9.9	6.2	3.7	1.9	2.6	2.2	1.2
U.S.	13.7	9.9	7.3	6.4	5.2	2.8	2.4	1.7	1.2

Note: Figures are the percentage of the total population reporting a particular ancestry. The nine most commonly reported ancestries in the U.S. are shown. Figures include multiple ancestries (e.g. if a person reported being Irish and Italian, they were included in both columns); (1) Figures cover the Columbia, MO Metropolitan Statistical Area—see Appendix B for areas included; (2) Excludes Basque
Source: U.S. Census Bureau, 2014-2018 American Community Survey 5-Year Estimates

Foreign-born Population

Area	Any Foreign Country	Asia	Mexico	Europe	Caribbean	Central America[2]	South America	Africa	Canada
City	8.6	5.1	0.4	1.4	0.1	0.2	0.4	0.8	0.3
MSA[1]	6.6	3.7	0.4	1.2	0.1	0.1	0.3	0.6	0.2
U.S.	13.5	4.1	3.5	1.5	1.3	1.1	0.9	0.7	0.3

Note: (1) Figures cover the Columbia, MO Metropolitan Statistical Area—see Appendix B for areas included; (2) Excludes Mexico.
Source: U.S. Census Bureau, 2014-2018 American Community Survey 5-Year Estimates

Marital Status

Area	Never Married	Now Married[2]	Separated	Widowed	Divorced
City	47.7	39.2	1.1	3.2	8.8
MSA[1]	41.0	44.5	1.3	3.7	9.5
U.S.	33.3	48.1	2.0	5.8	10.8

Note: Figures are percentages and cover the population 15 years of age and older; (1) Figures cover the Columbia, MO Metropolitan Statistical Area—see Appendix B for areas included; (2) Excludes separated
Source: U.S. Census Bureau, 2014-2018 American Community Survey 5-Year Estimates

Disability by Age

Area	All Ages	Under 18 Years Old	18 to 64 Years Old	65 Years and Over
City	9.8	2.8	7.9	35.8
MSA[1]	11.2	3.7	9.4	36.3
U.S.	12.6	4.2	10.3	35.0

Note: Figures show percent of the civilian noninstitutionalized population that reported having a disability. Disability status is determined from six types of difficulty: vision, hearing, cognitive, ambulatory, self-care, and independent living. For children under 5 years old, hearing and vision difficulty are used to determine disability status. For children between the ages of 5 and 14, disability status is determined from hearing, vision, cognitive, ambulatory, and self-care difficulties. For people aged 15 years and older, they are considered to have a disability if they have difficulty with any one of the six difficulty types; Note: (1) Figures cover the Columbia, MO Metropolitan Statistical Area—see Appendix B for areas included
Source: U.S. Census Bureau, 2014-2018 American Community Survey 5-Year Estimates

Age

Area	Under Age 5	Age 5–19	Age 20–34	Age 35–44	Age 45–54	Age 55–64	Age 65–74	Age 75–84	Age 85+	Median Age
City	5.8	18.6	35.5	10.9	9.7	9.2	5.9	3.0	1.3	28.2
MSA[1]	5.9	19.3	30.3	11.5	10.8	10.7	6.8	3.4	1.3	30.8
U.S.	6.1	19.3	20.7	12.6	13.2	12.8	8.8	4.5	1.9	37.9

Note: (1) Figures cover the Columbia, MO Metropolitan Statistical Area—see Appendix B for areas included
Source: U.S. Census Bureau, 2014-2018 American Community Survey 5-Year Estimates

Gender

Area	Males	Females	Males per 100 Females
City	57,805	62,443	92.6
MSA[1]	85,827	90,688	94.6
U.S.	158,984,190	163,918,840	97.0

Note: (1) Figures cover the Columbia, MO Metropolitan Statistical Area—see Appendix B for areas included
Source: U.S. Census Bureau, 2014-2018 American Community Survey 5-Year Estimates

Religious Groups by Family

Area	Catholic	Baptist	Non-Den.	Methodist[2]	Lutheran	LDS[3]	Pente-costal	Presby-terian[4]	Muslim[5]	Judaism
MSA[1]	6.6	14.7	5.4	4.3	1.7	1.4	1.1	2.3	0.3	0.3
U.S.	19.1	9.3	4.0	4.0	2.3	2.0	1.9	1.6	0.8	0.7

Note: Figures are the number of adherents as a percentage of the total population; (1) Figures cover the Columbia, MO Metropolitan Statistical Area—see Appendix B for areas included; (2) Methodist/Pietist; (3) Latter Day Saints; (4) Reformed; (5) Figures are estimates
Source: Association of Statisticians of American Religious Bodies, 2010 U.S. Religion Census: Religious Congregations & Membership Study

Religious Groups by Tradition

Area	Catholic	Evangelical Protestant	Mainline Protestant	Other Tradition	Black Protestant	Orthodox
MSA[1]	6.6	19.9	10.5	2.3	0.5	0.1
U.S.	19.1	16.2	7.3	4.3	1.6	0.3

Note: Figures are the number of adherents as a percentage of the total population; (1) Figures cover the Columbia, MO Metropolitan Statistical Area—see Appendix B for areas included
Source: Association of Statisticians of American Religious Bodies, 2010 U.S. Religion Census: Religious Congregations & Membership Study

ECONOMY

Gross Metropolitan Product

Area	2017	2018	2019	2020	Rank[2]
MSA[1]	9.2	9.6	9.9	10.3	220

Note: Figures are in billions of dollars; (1) Figures cover the Columbia, MO Metropolitan Statistical Area—see Appendix B for areas included; (2) Rank is based on 2018 data and ranges from 1 to 381
Source: U.S. Conference of Mayors, U.S. Metro Economies: GMP & Employment 2018-2020, September 2019

Economic Growth

Area	2015-17 (%)	2018 (%)	2019 (%)	2020 (%)	Rank[2]
MSA[1]	0.9	1.6	1.5	1.8	242
U.S.	1.9	2.9	2.3	2.1	–

Note: Figures are real gross metropolitan product (GMP) growth rates and represent average annual percent change; (1) Figures cover the Columbia, MO Metropolitan Statistical Area—see Appendix B for areas included; (2) Rank is based on 2017 2-year average annual percent change and ranges from 1 to 381
Source: U.S. Conference of Mayors, U.S. Metro Economies: GMP & Employment 2018-2020, September 2019

Metropolitan Area Exports

Area	2013	2014	2015	2016	2017	2018	Rank[2]
MSA[1]	423.9	237.7	214.0	213.7	224.0	238.6	287

Note: Figures are in millions of dollars; (1) Figures cover the Columbia, MO Metropolitan Statistical Area—see Appendix B for areas included; (2) Rank is based on 2018 data and ranges from 1 to 387
Source: U.S. Department of Commerce, International Trade Administration, Office of Trade and Economic Analysis, Industry and Analysis, Exports by Metropolitan Area, data extracted April 15, 2020

Building Permits

Area	Single-Family			Multi-Family			Total		
	2017	2018	Pct. Chg.	2017	2018	Pct. Chg.	2017	2018	Pct. Chg.
City	403	261	-35.2	861	2	-99.8	1,264	263	-79.2
MSA[1]	769	555	-27.8	865	2	-99.8	1,634	557	-65.9
U.S.	820,000	855,300	4.3	462,000	473,500	2.5	1,282,000	1,328,800	3.7

Note: (1) Figures cover the Columbia, MO Metropolitan Statistical Area—see Appendix B for areas included; Figures represent new, privately-owned housing units authorized (unadjusted data); All permit data are based on estimates with imputation
Source: U.S. Census Bureau, Manufacturing, Mining, and Construction Statistics, Building Permits, 2017, 2018

Bankruptcy Filings

Area	Business Filings			Nonbusiness Filings		
	2018	2019	% Chg.	2018	2019	% Chg.
Boone County	7	6	-14.3	368	375	1.9
U.S.	22,232	22,780	2.5	751,186	752,160	0.1

Note: Business filings include Chapter 7, Chapter 9, Chapter 11, Chapter 12, Chapter 13, Chapter 15, and Section 304; Nonbusiness filings include Chapter 7, Chapter 11, and Chapter 13
Source: Administrative Office of the U.S. Courts, Business and Nonbusiness Bankruptcy, County Cases Commenced by Chapter of the Bankruptcy Code, During the 12-Month Period Ending December 31, 2018 and Business and Nonbusiness Bankruptcy, County Cases Commenced by Chapter of the Bankruptcy Code, During the 12-Month Period Ending December 31, 2019

Housing Vacancy Rates

Area	Gross Vacancy Rate[2] (%)			Year-Round Vacancy Rate[3] (%)			Rental Vacancy Rate[4] (%)			Homeowner Vacancy Rate[5] (%)		
	2017	2018	2019	2017	2018	2019	2017	2018	2019	2017	2018	2019
MSA[1]	n/a	n/a	n/a	n/a	n/a	n/a	n/a	n/a	n/a	n/a	n/a	n/a
U.S.	12.7	12.3	12.0	9.9	9.7	9.5	7.2	6.9	6.7	1.6	1.5	1.4

Note: (1) Figures cover the Columbia, MO Metropolitan Statistical Area—see Appendix B for areas included; (2) The percentage of the total housing inventory that is vacant; (3) The percentage of the housing inventory (excluding seasonal units) that is year-round vacant; (4) The percentage of rental inventory that is vacant for rent; (5) The percentage of homeowner inventory that is vacant for sale; n/a not available
Source: U.S. Census Bureau, Housing Vacancies and Homeownership Annual Statistics: 2017, 2018, 2019

INCOME

Income

Area	Per Capita ($)	Median Household ($)	Average Household ($)
City	28,962	49,277	71,311
MSA[1]	29,365	54,043	73,099
U.S.	32,621	60,293	84,938

Note: (1) Figures cover the Columbia, MO Metropolitan Statistical Area—see Appendix B for areas included
Source: U.S. Census Bureau, 2014-2018 American Community Survey 5-Year Estimates

Household Income Distribution

Area	Percent of Households Earning							
	Under $15,000	$15,000 -$24,999	$25,000 -$34,999	$35,000 -$49,999	$50,000 -$74,999	$75,000 -$99,999	$100,000 -$149,999	$150,000 and up
City	15.9	10.7	10.2	13.7	15.3	11.5	13.1	9.5
MSA[1]	13.2	9.8	10.2	13.7	17.3	12.6	14.0	9.4
U.S.	10.9	9.3	9.3	12.6	17.5	12.5	14.6	13.3

Note: (1) Figures cover the Columbia, MO Metropolitan Statistical Area—see Appendix B for areas included
Source: U.S. Census Bureau, 2014-2018 American Community Survey 5-Year Estimates

Poverty Rate

Area	All Ages	Under 18 Years Old	18 to 64 Years Old	65 Years and Over
City	22.2	15.6	26.7	4.3
MSA[1]	18.3	15.8	21.2	5.8
U.S.	14.1	19.5	13.2	9.3

Note: Figures are percentage of people whose income during the past 12 months was below the poverty level; (1) Figures cover the Columbia, MO Metropolitan Statistical Area—see Appendix B for areas included
Source: U.S. Census Bureau, 2014-2018 American Community Survey 5-Year Estimates

EMPLOYMENT

Labor Force and Employment

Area	Civilian Labor Force			Workers Employed		
	Dec. 2018	Dec. 2019	% Chg.	Dec. 2018	Dec. 2019	% Chg.
City	67,333	68,108	1.2	65,941	66,459	0.8
MSA[1]	98,400	99,481	1.1	96,312	97,069	0.8
U.S.	162,510,000	164,007,000	0.9	156,481,000	158,504,000	1.3

Note: Data is not seasonally adjusted and covers workers 16 years of age and older; (1) Figures cover the Columbia, MO Metropolitan Statistical Area—see Appendix B for areas included
Source: Bureau of Labor Statistics, Local Area Unemployment Statistics

Unemployment Rate

Area	2019											
	Jan.	Feb.	Mar.	Apr.	May	Jun.	Jul.	Aug.	Sep.	Oct.	Nov.	Dec.
City	2.7	2.5	2.5	2.0	2.3	2.7	3.0	2.8	1.9	1.9	2.3	2.4
MSA[1]	2.8	2.6	2.6	1.9	2.3	2.6	2.9	2.7	1.9	1.9	2.2	2.4
U.S.	4.4	4.1	3.9	3.3	3.4	3.8	4.0	3.8	3.3	3.3	3.3	3.4

Note: Data is not seasonally adjusted and covers workers 16 years of age and older; (1) Figures cover the Columbia, MO Metropolitan Statistical Area—see Appendix B for areas included
Source: Bureau of Labor Statistics, Local Area Unemployment Statistics

Average Wages

Occupation	$/Hr.	Occupation	$/Hr.
Accountants and Auditors	28.40	Maintenance and Repair Workers	15.00
Automotive Mechanics	21.40	Marketing Managers	47.60
Bookkeepers	16.90	Network and Computer Systems Admin.	33.30
Carpenters	23.40	Nurses, Licensed Practical	20.50
Cashiers	10.60	Nurses, Registered	33.20
Computer Programmers	32.10	Nursing Assistants	12.40
Computer Systems Analysts	38.90	Office Clerks, General	16.00
Computer User Support Specialists	22.40	Physical Therapists	39.00
Construction Laborers	19.50	Physicians	57.40
Cooks, Restaurant	12.00	Plumbers, Pipefitters and Steamfitters	25.90
Customer Service Representatives	15.20	Police and Sheriff's Patrol Officers	23.70
Dentists	97.90	Postal Service Mail Carriers	24.80
Electricians	23.10	Real Estate Sales Agents	25.50
Engineers, Electrical	41.90	Retail Salespersons	15.70
Fast Food and Counter Workers	12.10	Sales Representatives, Technical/Scientific	35.60
Financial Managers	62.00	Secretaries, Exc. Legal/Medical/Executive	17.70
First-Line Supervisors of Office Workers	26.90	Security Guards	14.40
General and Operations Managers	40.30	Surgeons	n/a
Hairdressers/Cosmetologists	14.90	Teacher Assistants, Exc. Postsecondary*	13.10
Home Health and Personal Care Aides	11.50	Teachers, Secondary School, Exc. Sp. Ed.*	25.80
Janitors and Cleaners	13.90	Telemarketers	n/a
Landscaping/Groundskeeping Workers	14.20	Truck Drivers, Heavy/Tractor-Trailer	20.10
Lawyers	43.40	Truck Drivers, Light/Delivery Services	17.90
Maids and Housekeeping Cleaners	11.10	Waiters and Waitresses	10.20

Note: Wage data covers the Columbia, MO Metropolitan Statistical Area—see Appendix B for areas included; (*) Hourly wages were calculated from annual wage data based on a 40 hour work week; n/a not available.
Source: Bureau of Labor Statistics, Metro Area Occupational Employment & Wage Estimates, May 2019

Employment by Occupation

Occupation Classification	City (%)	MSA[1] (%)	U.S. (%)
Management, Business, Science, and Arts	46.8	45.5	37.9
Natural Resources, Construction, and Maintenance	4.9	6.5	8.9
Production, Transportation, and Material Moving	7.9	8.9	13.3
Sales and Office	21.4	21.7	22.1
Service	19.0	17.4	17.9

Note: Figures cover employed civilians 16 years of age and older; (1) Figures cover the Columbia, MO Metropolitan Statistical Area—see Appendix B for areas included
Source: U.S. Census Bureau, 2014-2018 American Community Survey 5-Year Estimates

Employment by Industry

Sector	MSA[1]		U.S.
	Number of Employees	Percent of Total	Percent of Total
Construction, Mining, and Logging	n/a	n/a	5.4
Education and Health Services	n/a	n/a	16.1
Financial Activities	n/a	n/a	5.8
Government	30,900	30.4	15.0
Information	n/a	n/a	1.9
Leisure and Hospitality	n/a	n/a	10.8
Manufacturing	n/a	n/a	8.4
Other Services	n/a	n/a	3.9
Professional and Business Services	n/a	n/a	14.1
Retail Trade	10,600	10.4	10.6
Transportation, Warehousing, and Utilities	n/a	n/a	4.2
Wholesale Trade	n/a	n/a	3.9

Note: Figures are non-farm employment as of December 2019. Figures are not seasonally adjusted and include workers 16 years of age and older; (1) Figures cover the Columbia, MO Metropolitan Statistical Area—see Appendix B for areas included; n/a not available
Source: Bureau of Labor Statistics, Current Employment Statistics, Employment, Hours, and Earnings

Occupations with Greatest Projected Employment Growth: 2019 – 2021

Occupation[1]	2019 Employment	2021 Projected Employment	Numeric Employment Change	Percent Employment Change
Personal Care Aides	68,410	72,800	4,390	6.4
Combined Food Preparation and Serving Workers, Including Fast Food	78,960	81,510	2,550	3.2
Registered Nurses	75,470	77,450	1,980	2.6
Laborers and Freight, Stock, and Material Movers, Hand	48,110	49,400	1,290	2.7
Cooks, Restaurant	29,950	31,210	1,260	4.2
General and Operations Managers	49,940	50,750	810	1.6
Heavy and Tractor-Trailer Truck Drivers	49,310	50,100	790	1.6
Software Developers, Applications	16,180	16,950	770	4.8
Nursing Assistants	40,550	41,240	690	1.7
Waiters and Waitresses	49,780	50,460	680	1.4

Note: Projections cover Missouri; (1) Sorted by numeric employment change
Source: www.projectionscentral.com, State Occupational Projections, 2019–2021 Short-Term Projections

Fastest Growing Occupations: 2019 – 2021

Occupation[1]	2019 Employment	2021 Projected Employment	Numeric Employment Change	Percent Employment Change
Information Security Analysts	2,890	3,080	190	6.6
Personal Care Aides	68,410	72,800	4,390	6.4
Statisticians	930	980	50	5.4
Cargo and Freight Agents	2,430	2,560	130	5.3
Respiratory Therapists	3,410	3,580	170	5.0
Operations Research Analysts	1,620	1,700	80	4.9
Software Developers, Applications	16,180	16,950	770	4.8
Physician Assistants	1,120	1,170	50	4.5
Speech-Language Pathologists	3,570	3,730	160	4.5
Industrial Engineers	5,900	6,160	260	4.4

Note: Projections cover Missouri; (1) Sorted by percent employment change and excludes occupations with numeric employment change less than 50
Source: www.projectionscentral.com, State Occupational Projections, 2019–2021 Short-Term Projections

TAXES

State Corporate Income Tax Rates

State	Tax Rate (%)	Income Brackets ($)	Num. of Brackets	Financial Institution Tax Rate (%)[a]	Federal Income Tax Ded.
Missouri	4.0	Flat rate	1	7.0	Yes (j)

Note: Tax rates as of January 1, 2020; (a) Rates listed are the corporate income tax rate applied to financial institutions or excise taxes based on income; (j) 50% of the federal income tax is deductible.
Source: Federation of Tax Administrators, State Corporate Income Tax Rates, January 1, 2020

State Individual Income Tax Rates

State	Tax Rate (%)	Income Brackets ($)	Personal Exemptions ($)			Standard Ded. ($)	
			Single	Married	Depend.	Single	Married
Missouri (a)	1.5 - 5.4	1,053 - 8,424	(d)	(d)	(d)	12,400	24,800 (d)

Note: Tax rates as of January 1, 2020; Local- and county-level taxes are not included; The deduction for federal income tax is limited to $5,000 for individuals and $10,000 for joint returns in Missouri and Montana, and to $6,500 for all filers in Oregon; (a) 19 states have statutory provision for automatically adjusting to the rate of inflation the dollar values of the income tax brackets, standard deductions, and/or personal exemptions. Michigan indexes the personal exemption only. Oregon does not index the income brackets for $125,000 and over; (d) These states use the personal exemption/standard deduction amounts provided in the federal Internal Revenue Code.
Source: Federation of Tax Administrators, State Individual Income Tax Rates, January 1, 2020

Various State Sales and Excise Tax Rates

State	State Sales Tax (%)	Gasoline[1] (¢/gal.)	Cigarette[2] ($/pack)	Spirits[3] ($/gal.)	Wine[4] ($/gal.)	Beer[5] ($/gal.)	Recreational Marijuana (%)
Missouri	4.225	17.42	0.17	2.00	0.42	0.06	Not legal

Note: All tax rates as of January 1, 2020; (1) The American Petroleum Institute has developed a methodology for determining the average tax rate on a gallon of fuel. Rates may include any of the following: excise taxes, environmental fees, storage tank fees, other fees or taxes, general sales tax, and local taxes; (2) The federal excise tax of $1.0066 per pack and local taxes are not included; (3) Rates are those applicable to off-premise sales of 40% alcohol by volume (a.b.v.) distilled spirits in 750ml containers. Local excise taxes are excluded; (4) Rates are those applicable to off-premise sales of 11% a.b.v. non-carbonated wine in 750ml containers; (5) Rates are those applicable to off-premise sales of 4.7% a.b.v. beer in 12 ounce containers.
Source: Tax Foundation, 2020 Facts & Figures: How Does Your State Compare?

State Business Tax Climate Index Rankings

State	Overall Rank	Corporate Tax Rank	Individual Income Tax Rank	Sales Tax Rank	Property Tax Rank	Unemployment Insurance Tax Rank
Missouri	14	5	24	24	7	9

Note: The index is a measure of how each state's tax laws affect economic performance. The lower the rank, the more favorable a state's tax system is for business. States without a given tax are given a ranking of 1. The scores/rankings for the District of Columbia do not affect other states. The 2020 index represents the tax climate as of July 1, 2019.
Source: Tax Foundation, State Business Tax Climate Index 2020

COMMERCIAL UTILITIES

Typical Monthly Electric Bills

Area	Commercial Service ($/month)		Industrial Service ($/month)	
	1,500 kWh	40 kW demand 14,000 kWh	1,000 kW demand 200,000 kWh	50,000 kW demand 32,500,000 kWh
City	n/a	n/a	n/a	n/a
Average[1]	203	1,612	25,706	2,520,671

Note: Figures are based on annualized rates; (1) Average based on 187 utilities surveyed; n/a not available
Source: Edison Electric Institute, Typical Bills and Average Rates Report, Summer 2019

TRANSPORTATION

Means of Transportation to Work

Area	Car/Truck/Van		Public Transportation			Bicycle	Walked	Other Means	Worked at Home
	Drove Alone	Car-pooled	Bus	Subway	Railroad				
City	76.7	10.3	1.6	0.0	0.0	1.2	5.1	1.0	4.2
MSA[1]	78.5	10.6	1.1	0.0	0.0	0.8	3.8	0.9	4.3
U.S.	76.4	9.1	2.5	1.9	0.6	0.6	2.7	1.3	4.9

Note: Figures are percentages and cover workers 16 years of age and older; (1) Figures cover the Columbia, MO Metropolitan Statistical Area—see Appendix B for areas included
Source: U.S. Census Bureau, 2014-2018 American Community Survey 5-Year Estimates

Travel Time to Work

Area	Less Than 10 Minutes	10 to 19 Minutes	20 to 29 Minutes	30 to 44 Minutes	45 to 59 Minutes	60 to 89 Minutes	90 Minutes or More
City	19.7	55.1	13.0	7.7	2.7	0.9	0.9
MSA[1]	16.8	49.1	18.2	10.3	3.3	1.1	1.0
U.S.	12.5	28.7	20.9	20.7	8.2	6.3	2.8

Note: Note: Figures are percentages and include workers 16 years old and over; (1) Figures cover the Columbia, MO Metropolitan Statistical Area—see Appendix B for areas included
Source: U.S. Census Bureau, 2014-2018 American Community Survey 5-Year Estimates

Key Congestion Measures

Area	1982	1992	2002	2012	2017
Annual Hours of Delay, Total (000)	n/a	n/a	n/a	n/a	2,692
Annual Hours of Delay, Per Auto Commuter	n/a	n/a	n/a	n/a	19
Annual Congestion Cost, Total (million $)	n/a	n/a	n/a	n/a	56
Annual Congestion Cost, Per Auto Commuter ($)	n/a	n/a	n/a	n/a	404

Note: n/a not available
Source: Texas A&M Transportation Institute, 2019 Urban Mobility Report

Freeway Travel Time Index

Area	1982	1987	1992	1997	2002	2007	2012	2017
Urban Area Index[1]	n/a	n/a	n/a	n/a	n/a	n/a	n/a	1.10
Urban Area Rank[1,2]	n/a	n/a	n/a	n/a	n/a	n/a	n/a	n/a

Note: Freeway Travel Time Index—the ratio of travel time in the peak period to the travel time at free-flow conditions. For example, a value of 1.30 indicates a 20-minute free-flow trip takes 26 minutes in the peak (20 minutes x 1.30 = 26 minutes); (1) Covers the Columbia MO urban area; (2) Rank is based on 101 larger urban areas (#1 = highest travel time index); n/a not available
Source: Texas A&M Transportation Institute, 2019 Urban Mobility Report

Public Transportation

Agency Name / Mode of Transportation	Vehicles Operated in Maximum Service[1]	Annual Unlinked Passenger Trips[2] (in thous.)	Annual Passenger Miles[3] (in thous.)
Columbia Transit (CT)			
Bus (directly operated)	28	1,252.8	3,078.6
Demand Response (directly operated)	9	53.4	284.7

Note: (1) Number of revenue vehicles operated by the given mode and type of service to meet the annual maximum service requirement. This is the revenue vehicle count during the peak season of the year; on the week and day that maximum service is provided. Vehicles operated in maximum service (VOMS) exclude atypical days and one-time special events; (2) Number of passengers who boarded public transportation vehicles. Passengers are counted each time they board a vehicle no matter how many vehicles they use to travel from their origin to their destination. (3) Sum of the distances ridden by all passengers during the entire fiscal year.
Source: Federal Transit Administration, National Transit Database, 2018

Air Transportation

Airport Name and Code / Type of Service	Passenger Airlines[1]	Passenger Enplanements	Freight Carriers[2]	Freight (lbs)
Columbia Regional (COU)				
Domestic service (U.S. carriers - 2019)	13	129,459	3	6,225
International service (U.S. carriers - 2018)	0	0	0	0

Note: (1) Includes all U.S.-based major, minor and commuter airlines that carried at least one passenger during the year; (2) Includes all U.S.-based airlines and freight carriers that transported at least one pound of freight during the year.
Source: Bureau of Transportation Statistics, The Intermodal Transportation Database, Air Carriers: T-100 Domestic Market (U.S. Carriers), 2019; Bureau of Transportation Statistics, The Intermodal Transportation Database, Air Carriers: T-100 International Market (U.S. Carriers), 2018

Other Transportation Statistics

Major Highways:	I-70; SR-63
Amtrak Service:	No
Major Waterways/Ports:	Near the Missouri River (15 miles)

Source: Amtrak.com; Google Maps

BUSINESSES

Major Business Headquarters

Company Name	Industry	Rankings Fortune[1]	Forbes[2]
No companies listed	-	-	-

Note: (1) Companies that produce a 10-K are ranked 1 to 500 based on 2018 revenue; (2) All private companies with at least $2 billion in annual revenue through the end of their most current fiscal year are ranked 1 to 228; companies listed are headquartered in the city; dashes indicate no ranking
Source: Fortune, "Fortune 500," June 2019; Forbes, "America's Largest Private Companies," 2019 Rankings

Minority- and Women-Owned Businesses

Group	All Firms Firms	Sales ($000)	Firms with Paid Employees Firms	Sales ($000)	Employees	Payroll ($000)
AIAN[1]	47	24,456	16	23,452	109	9,444
Asian	395	90,432	92	76,643	715	10,907
Black	427	16,695	42	8,907	235	4,118
Hispanic	224	(s)	47	(s)	100 - 249	(s)
NHOPI[2]	n/a	n/a	n/a	n/a	n/a	n/a
Women	3,340	(s)	525	(s)	2,500 - 4,999	(s)
All Firms	10,543	12,132,769	3,219	11,714,258	53,511	1,918,079

Note: Figures cover firms located in the city; minority- and women-owned business are defined as firms in which the corresponding group own 51% or more of the stock or equity of the company; (1) American Indian and Alaska Native; (2) Native Hawaiian and Other Pacific Islander; (s) estimates are suppressed when publication standards are not met; n/a not available
Source: U.S. Census Bureau, 2012 Economic Census, Survey of Business Owners

HOTELS & CONVENTION CENTERS

Hotels, Motels and Vacation Rentals

Area	5 Star Num.	Pct.[3]	4 Star Num.	Pct.[3]	3 Star Num.	Pct.[3]	2 Star Num.	Pct.[3]	1 Star Num.	Pct.[3]	Not Rated Num.	Pct.[3]
City[1]	0	0.0	1	2.4	8	19.5	10	24.4	1	2.4	21	51.2
Total[2]	266	1.3	1,517	7.2	4,627	21.8	3,210	15.1	3,974	18.7	7,601	35.9

Note: (1) Figures cover Columbia and vicinity; (2) Figures cover all 100 cities in this book; (3) Percentage of hotels which have a given star rating; Star ratings are determined by priceline.com and offer an indication of the general quality of a particular hotel.
Source: priceline.com, April 27, 2020

Major Convention Centers

Name	Overall Space (sq. ft.)	Exhibit Space (sq. ft.)	Meeting Space (sq. ft.)	Meeting Rooms

There are no major convention centers located in the metro area
Source: Original research

Living Environment

COST OF LIVING

Cost of Living Index

Composite Index	Groceries	Housing	Utilities	Trans-portation	Health Care	Misc. Goods/Services
91.8	95.5	75.0	100.0	92.0	102.6	99.8

Note: The Cost of Living Index measures regional differences in the cost of consumer goods and services, excluding taxes and non-consumer expenditures, for professional and managerial households in the top income quintile. It is based on more than 50,000 prices covering almost 60 different items for which prices are collected three times a year by chambers of commerce, economic development organizations or university applied economic centers in each participating urban area. The numbers shown should be read as a percentage above or below the national average of 100. For example, a value of 115.4 in the groceries column indicates that grocery prices are 15.4% higher than the national average. Small differences in the index numbers should not be interpreted as significant; Figures cover the Columbia MO urban area.
Source: The Council for Community and Economic Research, ACCRA Cost of Living Index, 2019

Grocery Prices

Area[1]	T-Bone Steak ($/pound)	Frying Chicken ($/pound)	Whole Milk ($/half gal.)	Eggs ($/dozen)	Orange Juice ($/64 oz.)	Coffee ($/11.5 oz.)
City[2]	10.84	1.55	1.97	1.24	3.63	4.41
Avg.	11.40	1.41	1.93	1.54	3.51	4.30
Min.	7.40	0.92	0.85	0.58	2.67	2.90
Max.	15.58	2.68	4.09	4.18	5.57	8.10

*Note: (1) Values for the local area are compared with the average, minimum and maximum values for all 290 areas in the Cost of Living Index; (2) Figures cover the Columbia MO urban area; **T-Bone Steak** (price per pound); **Frying Chicken** (price per pound, whole fryer); **Whole Milk** (half gallon carton); **Eggs** (price per dozen, Grade A, large); **Orange Juice** (64 oz. Tropicana or Florida Natural); **Coffee** (11.5 oz. can, vacuum-packed, Maxwell House, Hills Bros, or Folgers).*
Source: The Council for Community and Economic Research, ACCRA Cost of Living Index, 2019

Housing and Utility Costs

Area[1]	New Home Price ($)	Apartment Rent ($/month)	All Electric ($/month)	Part Electric ($/month)	Other Energy ($/month)	Telephone ($/month)
City[2]	287,072	727	-	96.39	67.58	186.40
Avg.	362,090	1,142	174.35	100.00	67.76	179.60
Min.	198,329	501	91.58	31.44	28.51	165.30
Max.	2,074,561	5,050	388.18	239.41	306.15	207.90

*Note: (1) Values for the local area are compared with the average, minimum and maximum values for all 290 areas in the Cost of Living Index; (2) Figures cover the Columbia MO urban area; **New Home Price** (2,400 sf living area, 8,000 sf lot, in urban area with full utilities); **Apartment Rent** (950 sf 2 bedroom/1.5 or 2 bath, unfurnished, excluding all utilities except water); **All Electric** (average monthly cost for an all-electric home); **Part Electric** (average monthly cost for a part-electric home); **Other Energy** (average monthly cost for natural gas, fuel oil, coal, wood, and any other forms of energy except electricity); **Telephone** (price includes the base monthly rate plus taxes and fees for three lines of mobile phone service).*
Source: The Council for Community and Economic Research, ACCRA Cost of Living Index, 2019

Health Care, Transportation, and Other Costs

Area[1]	Doctor ($/visit)	Dentist ($/visit)	Optometrist ($/visit)	Gasoline ($/gallon)	Beauty Salon ($/visit)	Men's Shirt ($)
City[2]	137.89	88.73	98.53	2.34	37.29	33.87
Avg.	114.85	97.58	106.10	2.50	38.15	32.15
Min.	39.00	62.22	52.22	1.53	16.88	10.27
Max.	206.67	151.53	258.67	3.79	79.29	59.30

*Note: (1) Values for the local area are compared with the average, minimum and maximum values for all 290 areas in the Cost of Living Index; (2) Figures cover the Columbia MO urban area; **Doctor** (general practitioners routine exam of an established patient); **Dentist** (adult teeth cleaning and periodic oral examination); **Optometrist** (full vision eye exam for established adult patient); **Gasoline** (one gallon regular unleaded, national brand, including all taxes, cash price at self-service pump if available); **Beauty Salon** (woman's shampoo, trim, and blow-dry); **Men's Shirt** (cotton/polyester dress shirt, pinpoint weave, long sleeves).*
Source: The Council for Community and Economic Research, ACCRA Cost of Living Index, 2019

HOUSING

House Price Index (HPI)

Area	National Ranking[2]	Quarterly Change (%)	One-Year Change (%)	Five-Year Change (%)
MSA[1]	184	1.66	3.70	19.33
U.S.[3]	–	1.26	5.09	32.88

Note: The HPI is a weighted repeat sales index. It measures average price changes in repeat sales or refinancings on the same properties. This information is obtained by reviewing repeat mortgage transactions on single-family properties whose mortgages have been purchased or securitized by Fannie Mae or Freddie Mac in January 1975; (1) Figures cover the Columbia, MO Metropolitan Statistical Area—see Appendix B for areas included; (2) Rankings are based on annual percentage change for all metro areas containing at least 15,000 transactions over the last 10 years and ranges from 1 to 232; (3) figures based on a weighted average of Census Division estimates using a seasonally adjusted, purchase-only index; all figures are for the period ending December 31, 2019
Source: Federal Housing Finance Agency, House Price Index, February 25, 2020

Median Single-Family Home Prices

Area	2017	2018	2019p	Percent Change 2018 to 2019
MSA[1]	179.7	189.3	206.4	9.0
U.S. Average	248.8	261.6	274.6	5.0

Note: Figures are median sales prices of existing single-family homes in thousands of dollars; (p) preliminary; (1) Figures cover the Columbia, MO Metropolitan Statistical Area—see Appendix B for areas included
Source: National Association of Realtors, Median Sales Price of Existing Single-Family Homes for Metropolitan Areas, 4th Quarter 2019

Qualifying Income Based on Median Sales Price of Existing Single-Family Homes

Area	With 5% Down ($)	With 10% Down ($)	With 20% Down ($)
MSA[1]	44,002	41,686	37,055
U.S. Average	58,663	55,575	49,400

Note: Figures are preliminary; Qualifying income is based on a mortgage rate of 3.76%. Monthly principal and interest payment is limited to 25% of income; (1) Figures cover the Columbia, MO Metropolitan Statistical Area—see Appendix B for areas included
Source: National Association of Realtors, Qualifying Income Based on Median Sales Price of Existing Single-Family Homes for Metropolitan Areas, 4th Quarter 2019

Median Apartment Condo-Coop Home Prices

Area	2017	2018	2019p	Percent Change 2018 to 2019
MSA[1]	n/a	n/a	n/a	n/a
U.S. Average	234.3	241.0	249.5	3.5

Note: Figures are median sales prices of existing apartment condo-coop homes in thousands of dollars; (p) preliminary; n/a not available; (1) Figures cover the Columbia, MO Metropolitan Statistical Area—see Appendix B for areas included
Source: National Association of Realtors, Median Sales Price of Existing Apartment Condo-Coop Homes for Metropolitan Areas, 4th Quarter 2019

Home Value Distribution

Area	Under $50,000	$50,000 -$99,999	$100,000 -$149,999	$150,000 -$199,999	$200,000 -$299,999	$300,000 -$499,999	$500,000 -$999,999	$1,000,000 or more
City	3.3	8.5	20.1	23.2	25.2	15.8	3.7	0.1
MSA[1]	4.5	9.7	20.7	21.6	23.6	15.0	4.5	0.5
U.S.	7.6	13.0	14.0	14.3	19.2	18.3	10.5	3.1

Note: Figures are percentages and cover owner-occupied housing units; (1) Figures cover the Columbia, MO Metropolitan Statistical Area—see Appendix B for areas included
Source: U.S. Census Bureau, 2014-2018 American Community Survey 5-Year Estimates

Homeownership Rate

Area	2011 (%)	2012 (%)	2013 (%)	2014 (%)	2015 (%)	2016 (%)	2017 (%)	2018 (%)	2019 (%)
MSA[1]	n/a	n/a	n/a	n/a	n/a	n/a	n/a	n/a	n/a
U.S.	66.1	65.4	65.1	64.5	63.7	63.4	63.9	64.4	64.6

Note: (1) Figures cover the Columbia, MO Metropolitan Statistical Area—see Appendix B for areas included; n/a not available
Source: U.S. Census Bureau, Housing Vacancies and Homeownership Annual Statistics: 2011-2019

Year Housing Structure Built

Area	2010 or Later	2000 -2009	1990 -1999	1980 -1989	1970 -1979	1960 -1969	1950 -1959	1940 -1949	Before 1940	Median Year
City	10.0	21.9	17.7	13.6	12.7	10.4	5.6	2.4	5.7	1990
MSA[1]	8.3	20.6	18.8	13.9	16.0	9.6	5.1	2.2	5.5	1988
U.S.	4.1	14.3	13.9	13.5	15.3	10.7	10.4	5.0	12.8	1977

Note: Figures are percentages except for Median Year; Note: (1) Figures cover the Columbia, MO Metropolitan Statistical Area—see Appendix B for areas included
Source: U.S. Census Bureau, 2014-2018 American Community Survey 5-Year Estimates

Gross Monthly Rent

Area	Under $500	$500 -$999	$1,000 -$1,499	$1,500 -$1,999	$2,000 -$2,499	$2,500 -$2,999	$3,000 and up	Median ($)
City	6.8	60.3	24.2	5.1	3.0	0.5	0.2	854
MSA[1]	7.2	60.9	24.0	4.4	2.8	0.4	0.2	849
U.S.	9.8	38.5	29.6	12.9	5.1	2.1	2.0	1,023

Note: Figures are percentages except for Median; Gross rent is the contract rent plus the estimated average monthly cost of utilities (electricity, gas, and water and sewer) and fuels (oil, coal, kerosene, wood, etc.) if these are paid by the renter (or paid for the renter by someone else); (1) Figures cover the Columbia, MO Metropolitan Statistical Area—see Appendix B for areas included
Source: U.S. Census Bureau, 2014-2018 American Community Survey 5-Year Estimates

HEALTH

Health Risk Factors

Category	MSA[1] (%)	U.S. (%)
Adults aged 18–64 who have any kind of health care coverage	n/a	87.3
Adults who reported being in good or better health	n/a	82.4
Adults who have been told they have high blood cholesterol	n/a	33.0
Adults who have been told they have high blood pressure	n/a	32.3
Adults who are current smokers	n/a	17.1
Adults who currently use E-cigarettes	n/a	4.6
Adults who currently use chewing tobacco, snuff, or snus	n/a	4.0
Adults who are heavy drinkers[2]	n/a	6.3
Adults who are binge drinkers[3]	n/a	17.4
Adults who are overweight (BMI 25.0 - 29.9)	n/a	35.3
Adults who are obese (BMI 30.0 - 99.8)	n/a	31.3
Adults who participated in any physical activities in the past month	n/a	74.4
Adults who always or nearly always wears a seat belt	n/a	94.3

Note: n/a not available; (1) Figures cover the Columbia, MO Metropolitan Statistical Area—see Appendix B for areas included; (2) Heavy drinkers are classified as adult men having more than 14 drinks per week and adult women having more than 7 drinks per week; (3) Binge drinkers are classified as males having five or more drinks on one occasion or females having four or more drinks on one occasion
Source: Centers for Disease Control and Prevention, Behaviorial Risk Factor Surveillance System, SMART: Selected Metropolitan Area Risk Trends, 2017

Acute and Chronic Health Conditions

Category	MSA[1] (%)	U.S. (%)
Adults who have ever been told they had a heart attack	n/a	4.2
Adults who have ever been told they have angina or coronary heart disease	n/a	3.9
Adults who have ever been told they had a stroke	n/a	3.0
Adults who have ever been told they have asthma	n/a	14.2
Adults who have ever been told they have arthritis	n/a	24.9
Adults who have ever been told they have diabetes[2]	n/a	10.5
Adults who have ever been told they had skin cancer	n/a	6.2
Adults who have ever been told they had any other types of cancer	n/a	7.1
Adults who have ever been told they have COPD	n/a	6.5
Adults who have ever been told they have kidney disease	n/a	3.0
Adults who have ever been told they have a form of depression	n/a	20.5

Note: n/a not available; (1) Figures cover the Columbia, MO Metropolitan Statistical Area—see Appendix B for areas included; (2) Figures do not include pregnancy-related, borderline, or pre-diabetes
Source: Centers for Disease Control and Prevention, Behaviorial Risk Factor Surveillance System, SMART: Selected Metropolitan Area Risk Trends, 2017

Health Screening and Vaccination Rates

Category	MSA[1] (%)	U.S. (%)
Adults aged 65+ who have had flu shot within the past year	n/a	60.7
Adults aged 65+ who have ever had a pneumonia vaccination	n/a	75.4
Adults who have ever been tested for HIV	n/a	36.1
Adults who have ever had the shingles or zoster vaccine?	n/a	28.9
Adults who have had their blood cholesterol checked within the last five years	n/a	85.9

Note: n/a not available; (1) Figures cover the Columbia, MO Metropolitan Statistical Area—see Appendix B for areas included.
Source: Centers for Disease Control and Prevention, Behavioral Risk Factor Surveillance System, SMART: Selected Metropolitan Area Risk Trends, 2017

Disability Status

Category	MSA[1] (%)	U.S. (%)
Adults who reported being deaf	n/a	6.7
Are you blind or have serious difficulty seeing, even when wearing glasses?	n/a	4.5
Are you limited in any way in any of your usual activities due of arthritis?	n/a	12.9
Do you have difficulty doing errands alone?	n/a	6.8
Do you have difficulty dressing or bathing?	n/a	3.6
Do you have serious difficulty concentrating/remembering/making decisions?	n/a	10.7
Do you have serious difficulty walking or climbing stairs?	n/a	13.6

Note: n/a not available; (1) Figures cover the Columbia, MO Metropolitan Statistical Area—see Appendix B for areas included.
Source: Centers for Disease Control and Prevention, Behavioral Risk Factor Surveillance System, SMART: Selected Metropolitan Area Risk Trends, 2017

Mortality Rates for the Top 10 Causes of Death in the U.S.

ICD-10[a] Sub-Chapter	ICD-10[a] Code	Age-Adjusted Mortality Rate[1] per 100,000 population	
		County[2]	U.S.
Malignant neoplasms	C00-C97	144.9	152.4
Ischaemic heart diseases	I20-I25	67.1	92.7
Other forms of heart disease	I30-I51	56.2	52.5
Chronic lower respiratory diseases	J40-J47	36.2	40.4
Cerebrovascular diseases	I60-I69	42.7	37.3
Other degenerative diseases of the nervous system	G30-G31	30.9	36.4
Other external causes of accidental injury	W00-X59	27.5	35.3
Organic, including symptomatic, mental disorders	F01-F09	37.0	30.0
Hypertensive diseases	I10-I15	20.3	22.9
Diabetes mellitus	E10-E14	25.7	21.3

Note: (a) ICD-10 = International Classification of Diseases 10th Revision; (1) Mortality rates are a three year average covering 2016-2018; (2) Figures cover Boone County.
Source: Centers for Disease Control and Prevention, National Center for Health Statistics. Underlying Cause of Death 1999-2018 on CDC WONDER Online Database

Mortality Rates for Selected Causes of Death

ICD-10[a] Sub-Chapter	ICD-10[a] Code	Age-Adjusted Mortality Rate[1] per 100,000 population	
		County[2]	U.S.
Assault	X85-Y09	4.7	6.0
Diseases of the liver	K70-K76	11.9	14.2
Human immunodeficiency virus (HIV) disease	B20-B24	Suppressed	1.6
Influenza and pneumonia	J09-J18	12.7	14.2
Intentional self-harm	X60-X84	11.5	13.9
Malnutrition	E40-E46	Suppressed	1.9
Obesity and other hyperalimentation	E65-E68	Unreliable	2.1
Renal failure	N17-N19	11.5	12.8
Transport accidents	V01-V99	8.1	12.5
Viral hepatitis	B15-B19	Suppressed	1.4

Note: (a) ICD-10 = International Classification of Diseases 10th Revision; (1) Mortality rates are a three year average covering 2016-2018; (2) Figures cover Boone County; Data are suppressed when the data meet the criteria for confidentiality constraints; Mortality rates are flagged as unreliable when the rate would be calculated with a numerator of 20 or less.
Source: Centers for Disease Control and Prevention, National Center for Health Statistics. Underlying Cause of Death 1999-2018 on CDC WONDER Online Database

Health Insurance Coverage

Area	With Health Insurance	With Private Health Insurance	With Public Health Insurance	Without Health Insurance	Population Under Age 19 Without Health Insurance
City	93.4	82.7	20.1	6.6	3.1
MSA[1]	93.0	80.9	22.2	7.0	3.5
U.S.	90.6	67.7	34.7	9.4	5.2

Note: Figures are percentages that cover the civilian noninstitutionalized population; (1) Figures cover the Columbia, MO Metropolitan Statistical Area—see Appendix B for areas included
Source: U.S. Census Bureau, 2014-2018 American Community Survey 5-Year Estimates

Number of Medical Professionals

Area	MDs[3]	DOs[3,4]	Dentists	Podiatrists	Chiropractors	Optometrists
County[1] (number)	1,428	111	120	10	59	50
County[1] (rate[2])	801.0	62.3	66.7	5.6	32.8	27.8
U.S. (rate[2])	281.9	23.4	69.1	6.0	27.5	16.4

Note: Data as of 2018 unless noted; (1) Data covers Boone County; (2) Rate per 100,000 population; (3) Data as of 2017 and includes all active, non-federal physicians; (4) Doctor of Osteopathic Medicine
Source: U.S. Department of Health and Human Services, Health Resources and Services Administration, Bureau of Health Professions, Area Resource File (ARF) 2018-2019

EDUCATION

Public School District Statistics

District Name	Schls	Pupils	Pupil/ Teacher Ratio	Minority Pupils[1] (%)	Free Lunch Eligible[2] (%)	IEP[3] (%)
Columbia 93	35	18,499	13.3	40.9	39.7	10.8

Note: Table includes school districts with 2,000 or more students; (1) Percentage of students that are not non-Hispanic white; (2) Percentage of students that are eligible for the free lunch program; (3) Percentage of students that have an Individualized Education Program.
Source: U.S. Department of Education, National Center for Education Statistics, Common Core of Data, Local Education Agency (School District) Universe Survey: School Year 2018-2019; U.S. Department of Education, National Center for Education Statistics, Common Core of Data, Public Elementary/Secondary School Universe Survey: School Year 2018-2019

Highest Level of Education

Area	Less than H.S.	H.S. Diploma	Some College, No Deg.	Associate Degree	Bachelor's Degree	Master's Degree	Prof. School Degree	Doctorate Degree
City	5.0	17.6	18.3	6.3	27.5	15.7	4.7	4.8
MSA[1]	5.8	21.2	19.7	7.2	25.8	12.5	3.7	3.9
U.S.	12.3	27.1	20.6	8.4	19.4	8.6	2.1	1.4

Note: Figures cover persons age 25 and over; (1) Figures cover the Columbia, MO Metropolitan Statistical Area—see Appendix B for areas included
Source: U.S. Census Bureau, 2014-2018 American Community Survey 5-Year Estimates

Educational Attainment by Race

Area	High School Graduate or Higher (%)					Bachelor's Degree or Higher (%)				
	Total	White	Black	Asian	Hisp.[2]	Total	White	Black	Asian	Hisp.[2]
City	95.0	96.4	88.8	92.8	88.3	52.8	56.1	19.1	69.2	39.4
MSA[1]	94.2	95.2	87.6	92.9	80.5	46.0	47.7	18.1	67.2	35.1
U.S.	87.7	89.6	85.4	86.8	67.7	31.5	32.9	21.1	53.5	15.8

Note: Figures shown cover persons 25 years old and over; (1) Figures cover the Columbia, MO Metropolitan Statistical Area—see Appendix B for areas included; (2) People of Hispanic origin can be of any race
Source: U.S. Census Bureau, 2014-2018 American Community Survey 5-Year Estimates

School Enrollment by Grade and Control

Area	Preschool (%)		Kindergarten (%)		Grades 1 - 4 (%)		Grades 5 - 8 (%)		Grades 9 - 12 (%)	
	Public	Private	Public	Private	Public	Private	Public	Private	Public	Private
City	38.0	62.0	72.2	27.8	82.8	17.2	85.7	14.3	85.5	14.5
MSA[1]	44.5	55.5	77.9	22.1	85.3	14.7	88.3	11.7	88.7	11.3
U.S.	59.0	41.0	87.7	12.3	89.6	10.4	89.5	10.5	90.2	9.8

Note: Figures shown cover persons 3 years old and over; (1) Figures cover the Columbia, MO Metropolitan Statistical Area—see Appendix B for areas included
Source: U.S. Census Bureau, 2014-2018 American Community Survey 5-Year Estimates

Average Salaries of Public School Teachers

Area	2016-17 Dollars	2016-17 Rank[1]	2017-18 Dollars	2017-18 Rank[1]	Change from 2016-17 to 2017-18 Percent	Change from 2016-17 to 2017-18 Rank[2]
Missouri	48,620	41	49,304	43	1.41	27
U.S. Average	59,539	–	60,477	–	1.58	–

Note: (1) Rank ranges from 1 to 51 where 1 indicates highest salary; (2) Rank ranges from 1 to 51 where 1 indicates highest percent change.
Source: National Education Association, Rankings & Estimates: Rankings of the States 2018 and Estimates of School Statistics 2019

Higher Education

Four-Year Colleges Public	Four-Year Colleges Private Non-profit	Four-Year Colleges Private For-profit	Two-Year Colleges Public	Two-Year Colleges Private Non-profit	Two-Year Colleges Private For-profit	Medical Schools[1]	Law Schools[2]	Voc/ Tech[3]
1	2	0	0	0	1	1	1	2

Note: Figures cover institutions located within the city limits and include main campuses only; (1) includes schools accredited by the Liaison Committee on Medical Education and the American Osteopathic Association's Commission on Osteopathic College Accreditation; (2) includes ABA-accredited schools, schools with provisional ABA accreditation, and state accredited schools; (3) includes all schools with programs that are less than 2 years.
Source: National Center for Education Statistics, Integrated Postsecondary Education System (IPEDS), 2018-19; Wikipedia, List of Medical Schools in the United States, accessed May 1, 2020; Wikipedia, List of Law Schools in the United States, accessed May 1, 2020

According to *U.S. News & World Report,* the Columbia, MO metro area is home to one of the top 200 national universities in the U.S.: **University of Missouri** (#139 tie). The indicators used to capture academic quality fall into a number of categories: assessment by administrators at peer institutions; retention of students; faculty resources; student selectivity; financial resources; alumni giving; high school counselor ratings of colleges; and graduation rate. *U.S. News & World Report, "America's Best Colleges 2020"*

According to *U.S. News & World Report,* the Columbia, MO metro area is home to one of the top 100 law schools in the U.S.: **University of Missouri** (#67 tie). The rankings are based on a weighted average of 12 measures of quality: peer assessment score; assessment score by lawyers/judges; median LSAT scores; median undergrad GPA; acceptance rate; employment rates for graduates; placement success; bar passage rate; faculty resources; expenditures per student; student/faculty ratio; and library resources. *U.S. News & World Report, "America's Best Graduate Schools, Law, 2021"*

According to *U.S. News & World Report,* the Columbia, MO metro area is home to one of the top 75 business schools in the U.S.: **University of Missouri (Trulaske)** (#62 tie). The rankings are based on a weighted average of the following nine measures: quality assessment; peer assessment; recruiter assessment; placement success; mean starting salary and bonus; student selectivity; mean GMAT and GRE scores; mean undergraduate GPA; and acceptance rate. *U.S. News & World Report, "America's Best Graduate Schools, Business, 2021"*

PRESIDENTIAL ELECTION

2016 Presidential Election Results

Area	Clinton	Trump	Johnson	Stein	Other
Boone County	49.0	43.2	5.1	1.5	1.2
U.S.	48.0	45.9	3.3	1.1	1.7

Note: Results are percentages and may not add to 100% due to rounding
Source: Dave Leip's Atlas of U.S. Presidential Elections

EMPLOYERS

Major Employers

Company Name	Industry
BJC Health System	Hospital management
City of Columbia	Courts
Columbia College	Colleges & universities
Kraft Foods Global	Frankfurters, from purchased meat
MBS Textbook Exchange	Books, periodicals, & newspapers
MCI Worldcom Communications	Telephone communication, except radio
Regional Medical Pharmacy	Home health care services
Schneider Electric USA	Switchgear & switchboard apparatus
Shelter Insurance Companies	Fire, marine, & casualty insurance
State Farm Mutual Automobile Insurance	Insurance agents & brokers
University of Missouri Hospital	General medical & surgical hospitals
University of Missouri System	Colleges & universities
University Physicians Hospital	Gynecologist
Veterans Health Administration	Administration of veterans' affairs

Note: Companies shown are located within the Columbia, MO Metropolitan Statistical Area.
Source: Hoovers.com; Wikipedia

Best Companies to Work For

Veterans United Home Loans, headquartered in Columbia, is among "The 100 Best Companies to Work For." To pick the best companies, *Fortune* partnered with the Great Place to Work Institute. Two-thirds of a company's score is based on the results of the Institute's Trust Index survey, which is sent to a random sample of employees from each company. The questions related to attitudes about management's credibility, job satisfaction, and camaraderie. The other third of the scoring is based on the company's responses to the Institute's Culture Audit, which includes detailed questions about pay and benefit programs, and a series of open-ended questions about hiring practices, internal communication, training, recognition programs, and diversity efforts. Any company that is at least five years old with more than 1,000 U.S. employees is eligible. *Fortune, "The 100 Best Companies to Work For," 2020*

PUBLIC SAFETY

Crime Rate

Area	All Crimes	Violent Crimes				Property Crimes		
		Murder	Rape[3]	Robbery	Aggrav. Assault	Burglary	Larceny -Theft	Motor Vehicle Theft
City	3,179.2	4.0	72.0	84.2	200.7	444.2	2,142.6	231.4
Suburbs[1]	1,839.8	4.7	24.8	14.2	145.4	229.4	1,261.6	159.6
Metro[2]	2,635.0	4.3	52.8	55.7	178.2	356.9	1,784.7	202.2
U.S.	2,580.1	5.0	42.6	86.2	246.8	376.0	1,594.6	228.9

Note: Figures are crimes per 100,000 population; (1) All areas within the metro area that are located outside the city limits; (2) Figures cover the Columbia, MO Metropolitan Statistical Area—see Appendix B for areas included; (3) The city and U.S. figures shown were reported using the revised Uniform Crime Reporting (UCR) definition of rape. The suburban and metro area figures shown are an aggregate total of the data submitted using both the revised and legacy UCR definitions.
Source: FBI Uniform Crime Reports, 2018

Hate Crimes

Area	Number of Quarters Reported	Number of Incidents per Bias Motivation					
		Race/Ethnicity/ Ancestry	Religion	Sexual Orientation	Disability	Gender	Gender Identity
City	4	0	0	0	0	0	0
U.S.	4	4,047	1,419	1,196	159	47	168

Source: Federal Bureau of Investigation, Hate Crime Statistics 2018

Identity Theft Consumer Reports

Area	Reports	Reports per 100,000 Population	Rank[2]
MSA[1]	167	93	206
U.S.	650,572	198	-

Note: (1) Figures cover the Columbia, MO Metropolitan Statistical Area—see Appendix B for areas included; (2) Rank ranges from 1 to 386 where 1 indicates greatest number of identity theft reports per 100,000 population
Source: Federal Trade Commission, Consumer Sentinel Network Data Book for January–December 2019

Fraud and Other Consumer Reports

Area	Reports	Reports per 100,000 Population	Rank[2]
MSA[1]	923	513	229
U.S.	2,590,177	789	-

Note: (1) Figures cover the Columbia, MO Metropolitan Statistical Area—see Appendix B for areas included; (2) Rank ranges from 1 to 386 where 1 indicates greatest number of fraud and other consumer reports per 100,000 population
Source: Federal Trade Commission, Consumer Sentinel Network Data Book for January–December 2019

SPORTS

Professional Sports Teams

Team Name	League	Year Established
No teams are located in the metro area		

Source: Wikipedia, Major Professional Sports Teams of the United States and Canada, May 4, 2020

CLIMATE

Average and Extreme Temperatures

Temperature	Jan	Feb	Mar	Apr	May	Jun	Jul	Aug	Sep	Oct	Nov	Dec	Yr.
Extreme High (°F)	74	76	85	90	90	103	111	110	101	93	83	76	111
Average High (°F)	36	42	54	66	74	83	89	87	79	67	53	41	64
Average Temp. (°F)	28	33	44	55	64	73	78	76	68	56	44	33	54
Average Low (°F)	19	23	34	44	53	62	67	65	57	45	34	24	44
Extreme Low (°F)	-19	-15	-5	19	29	40	48	42	32	22	0	-20	-20

Note: Figures cover the years 1969-1995
Source: National Climatic Data Center, International Station Meteorological Climate Summary, 9/96

Average Precipitation/Snowfall/Humidity

Precip./Humidity	Jan	Feb	Mar	Apr	May	Jun	Jul	Aug	Sep	Oct	Nov	Dec	Yr.
Avg. Precip. (in.)	1.6	2.0	3.2	4.3	5.1	3.9	3.9	3.8	3.7	3.1	3.5	2.6	40.6
Avg. Snowfall (in.)	7	7	4	1	0	0	0	0	0	Tr	2	5	25
Avg. Rel. Hum. 6am (%)	80	80	79	79	85	86	87	89	88	84	82	81	83
Avg. Rel. Hum. 3pm (%)	62	59	53	52	57	56	53	52	54	53	59	64	56

Note: Figures cover the years 1969-1995; Tr = Trace amounts (<0.05 in. of rain; <0.5 in. of snow)
Source: National Climatic Data Center, International Station Meteorological Climate Summary, 9/96

Weather Conditions

Temperature			Daytime Sky			Precipitation		
10°F & below	32°F & below	90°F & above	Clear	Partly cloudy	Cloudy	0.01 inch or more precip.	0.1 inch or more snow/ice	Thunder-storms
17	108	36	99	127	139	110	17	52

Note: Figures are average number of days per year and cover the years 1969-1995
Source: National Climatic Data Center, International Station Meteorological Climate Summary, 9/96

HAZARDOUS WASTE

Superfund Sites

The Columbia, MO metro area has no sites on the EPA's Superfund Final National Priorities List. There are a total of 1,387 Superfund sites with a status of proposed or final on the list in the U.S.
U.S. Environmental Protection Agency, National Priorities List, May 5, 2020

**AIR & WATER
QUALITY**

Air Quality Trends: Ozone

	1990	1995	2000	2005	2010	2012	2014	2016	2017	2018
MSA[1]	n/a	n/a	n/a	n/a	n/a	n/a	n/a	n/a	n/a	n/a
U.S.	0.088	0.089	0.082	0.080	0.073	0.075	0.067	0.069	0.068	0.069

Note: (1) Data covers the Columbia, MO Metropolitan Statistical Area—see Appendix B for areas included; n/a not available. The values shown are the composite ozone concentration averages among trend sites based on the highest fourth daily maximum 8-hour concentration in parts per million. These trends are based on sites having an adequate record of monitoring data during the trend period. Data from exceptional events are included.
Source: U.S. Environmental Protection Agency, Air Quality Monitoring Information, "Air Quality Trends by City, 1990-2018"

Air Quality Index

Area	Percent of Days when Air Quality was...[2]					AQI Statistics[2]	
	Good	Moderate	Unhealthy for Sensitive Groups	Unhealthy	Very Unhealthy	Maximum	Median
MSA[1]	84.9	14.7	0.4	0.0	0.0	105	40

Note: (1) Data covers the Columbia, MO Metropolitan Statistical Area—see Appendix B for areas included; (2) Based on 245 days with AQI data in 2018. Air Quality Index (AQI) is an index for reporting daily air quality. EPA calculates the AQI for five major air pollutants regulated by the Clean Air Act: ground-level ozone, particle pollution (aka particulate matter), carbon monoxide, sulfur dioxide, and nitrogen dioxide. The AQI runs from 0 to 500. The higher the AQI value, the greater the level of air pollution and the greater the health concern. There are six AQI categories: "Good" AQI is between 0 and 50. Air quality is considered satisfactory; "Moderate" AQI is between 51 and 100. Air quality is acceptable; "Unhealthy for Sensitive Groups" When AQI values are between 101 and 150, members of sensitive groups may experience health effects; "Unhealthy" When AQI values are between 151 and 200 everyone may begin to experience health effects; "Very Unhealthy" AQI values between 201 and 300 trigger a health alert; "Hazardous" AQI values over 300 trigger warnings of emergency conditions (not shown).
Source: U.S. Environmental Protection Agency, Air Quality Index Report, 2018

Air Quality Index Pollutants

Area	Percent of Days when AQI Pollutant was...[2]					
	Carbon Monoxide	Nitrogen Dioxide	Ozone	Sulfur Dioxide	Particulate Matter 2.5	Particulate Matter 10
MSA[1]	0.0	0.0	100.0	0.0	0.0	0.0

Note: (1) Data covers the Columbia, MO Metropolitan Statistical Area—see Appendix B for areas included; (2) Based on 245 days with AQI data in 2018. The Air Quality Index (AQI) is an index for reporting daily air quality. EPA calculates the AQI for five major air pollutants regulated by the Clean Air Act: ground-level ozone, particle pollution (also known as particulate matter), carbon monoxide, sulfur dioxide, and nitrogen dioxide. The AQI runs from 0 to 500. The higher the AQI value, the greater the level of air pollution and the greater the health concern.
Source: U.S. Environmental Protection Agency, Air Quality Index Report, 2018

Maximum Air Pollutant Concentrations: Particulate Matter, Ozone, CO and Lead

	Particulate Matter 10 (ug/m^3)	Particulate Matter 2.5 Wtd AM (ug/m^3)	Particulate Matter 2.5 24-Hr (ug/m^3)	Ozone (ppm)	Carbon Monoxide (ppm)	Lead (ug/m^3)
MSA[1] Level	n/a	n/a	n/a	0.063	n/a	n/a
NAAQS[2]	150	15	35	0.075	9	0.15
Met NAAQS[2]	n/a	n/a	n/a	Yes	n/a	n/a

Note: (1) Data covers the Columbia, MO Metropolitan Statistical Area—see Appendix B for areas included; Data from exceptional events are included; (2) National Ambient Air Quality Standards; ppm = parts per million; ug/m^3 = micrograms per cubic meter; n/a not available.
Concentrations: Particulate Matter 10 (coarse particulate)—highest second maximum 24-hour concentration; Particulate Matter 2.5 Wtd AM (fine particulate)—highest weighted annual mean concentration; Particulate Matter 2.5 24-Hour (fine particulate)—highest 98th percentile 24-hour concentration; Ozone—highest fourth daily maximum 8-hour concentration; Carbon Monoxide—highest second maximum non-overlapping 8-hour concentration; Lead—maximum running 3-month average
Source: U.S. Environmental Protection Agency, Air Quality Monitoring Information, "Air Quality Statistics by City, 2018"

Maximum Air Pollutant Concentrations: Nitrogen Dioxide and Sulfur Dioxide

	Nitrogen Dioxide AM (ppb)	Nitrogen Dioxide 1-Hr (ppb)	Sulfur Dioxide AM (ppb)	Sulfur Dioxide 1-Hr (ppb)	Sulfur Dioxide 24-Hr (ppb)
MSA[1] Level	n/a	n/a	n/a	n/a	n/a
NAAQS[2]	53	100	30	75	140
Met NAAQS[2]	n/a	n/a	n/a	n/a	n/a

Note: (1) Data covers the Columbia, MO Metropolitan Statistical Area—see Appendix B for areas included; Data from exceptional events are included; (2) National Ambient Air Quality Standards; ppm = parts per million; ug/m³ = micrograms per cubic meter; n/a not available.
Concentrations: Nitrogen Dioxide AM—highest arithmetic mean concentration; Nitrogen Dioxide 1-Hr—highest 98th percentile 1-hour daily maximum concentration; Sulfur Dioxide AM—highest annual mean concentration; Sulfur Dioxide 1-Hr—highest 99th percentile 1-hour daily maximum concentration; Sulfur Dioxide 24-Hr—highest second maximum 24-hour concentration
Source: U.S. Environmental Protection Agency, Air Quality Monitoring Information, "Air Quality Statistics by City, 2018"

Drinking Water

Water System Name	Pop. Served	Primary Water Source Type	Violations[1]
Columbia PWS	100,733	Ground	3

Note: (1) Total number of violations (both active and inactive) in the EPA database
Source: U.S. Environmental Protection Agency, Office of Ground Water and Drinking Water, Safe Drinking Water Information System (based on data extracted May 5, 2020)

Davenport, Iowa

Background

The city of Davenport was first incorporated in 1836 on the site of the bloody "Black Hawk War," between the Native American Sac tribe and eastern settlers, intent on westward expansion. In 1828, John Quincy Adams had declared that all land east of the Mississippi would be sold to settlers. When Chief Black Hawk and his warriors refused to leave their land, the Black Hawk War ensued, resulting in a treaty now known as the Black Hawk Purchase. Credit Island, which had originally been a fur trading post, hosted the treaty signing between the Sac chief and Colonel George Davenport, from whom Davenport derives its name.

In 1856, a new bridge was constructed between Davenport and Rock Island, Illinois—the first railroad bridge to span the Mississippi. Only months later, a riverboat, the Effie Afton, struck and damaged the bridge. The ensuing court case, *Hurd v. Rock Island Railroad Company*, would remain the most notable court case in the law career of Abraham Lincoln.

The decade preceding the Civil War saw a major influx of German immigrants to Davenport, increasing the population fivefold; it is estimated that about 50% of today's Davenport citizenry are of German descent. Many of these immigrants were fleeing political persecution, and were instrumental in the creation of the Republican Party, which, within a decade, would provide the country with one of its most influential presidents. The culture and work ethic of these immigrants remains a key factor in the Davenport ethos of hard work and industry. At the turn of the 19th century, Davenport earned the rather amusing moniker of "Washing Machine Capital of the World."

In 1861, Rock Island had opened a munitions arsenal to help the Union war efforts. It is now home to the largest, government-owned weapons manufacturing facility in the United States, and is a designated national historic landmark. Today, Davenport supports a diverse base of manufacturing industries that include everything from farm and military machinery to publishing products and food processing. Its central, mid-continent location makes Davenport an important, inland U.S. Customs Port of Entry for freight distribution. It is also designated a Foreign Trade Zone.

The largest employers in the area comprise a veritable who's who of American manufacturing, including John Deere & Co., Aluminum Co. of America (ALCOA), Oscar Meyer Food Corp. and Eagle Food Center. Davenport is also home to the regional headquarters of the United Parcel Service, and serves as the headquarters of the Von Maur department stores.

Davenport is home to four institutes of higher learning, including the Catholic liberal arts school St. Ambrose University, the city's oldest college. The Palmer College of Chiropractic, the first college of its kind, was established by the inventor of chiropractic practice—Daniel David Palmer, a Davenport resident. Within commuting distance of Davenport are Augustana College (Rock Island), the University of Iowa (Iowa City), and Knox College (Galesburg).

Iowa's first municipal art museum, the Figge Museum, is home to the *Grant Wood Archive*. The collection features Wood's wire-rimmed glasses, his easel and painting tools, and the iconic cameo broach in both the portrait of his mother, *Woman with Plants*, 1929, and his most famous painting, *American Gothic*, 1930.

Given Davenport's central location in the heart of America's Midwest, the climate is relatively temperate. Temperatures can fluctuate considerably; summers are hot and winters severe, with an average snowfall just over 30 inches.

Rankings

Business/Finance Rankings

- The Davenport metro area appeared on the Milken Institute "2020 Best Performing Cities" list. Rank: #172 out of 200 large metro areas. Criteria: job growth; wage and salary growth; high-tech output growth. *Milken Institute, "Best-Performing Cities 2020," February 26, 2020*

- *Forbes* ranked the 200 most populous metro areas to determine the nation's "Best Places for Business and Careers." The Davenport metro area was ranked #175. Criteria: costs (business and living); job growth (past and projected); income growth; quality of life; educational attainment (college and high school); projected economic growth; cultural and leisure opportunities; workplace tolerance laws; net migration patterns. *Forbes, "The Best Places for Business and Careers 2019: Seattle Still On Top," October 30, 2019*

Children/Family Rankings

- Davenport was selected as one of the most playful cities in the U.S. by KaBOOM! The organization's Playful City USA initiative honors cities and towns across the nation that have made their communities more playable. Criteria: pledging to integrate play as a solution to challenges in their communities; making it easy for children to get active and balanced play; creating more family-friendly and innovative communities as a result. *KaBOOM! National Campaign for Play, "2017 Playful City USA Communities"*

Education Rankings

- Personal finance website *WalletHub* analyzed the 150 largest U.S. metropolitan statistical areas to determine where the most educated Americans are choosing to settle. Criteria: education levels; percentage of workers with degrees; education quality and attainment gap; public school quality rankings; quality and size of each metro area's universities. Davenport was ranked #115 (#1 = most educated city). *www.WalletHub.com, "2019's Most and Least Educated Cities in America," July 22, 2019*

Health/Fitness Rankings

- The Davenport metro area was identified as one of the worst cities for bed bugs in America by pest control company Orkin. The area ranked #37 out of 50 based on the number of bed bug treatments Orkin performed from December 2018 to November 2019. *Orkin, "Washington, D.C. Surpasses Baltimore to Secure Top Spot on Orkin's 2020 Bed Bug Cities List," January 13, 2020*

- The Davenport metro area ranked #115 out of 189 in The Gallup-Sharecare Well-Being Index. Criteria: purpose; social well being; financial health; community and physical health. Results are based on telephone interviews with adults, aged 18 and older, living in metropolitan areas in the 50 U.S. states and the District of Columbia. *Gallup-Sharecare, "State of American Well-Being, 2017 Community Well-Being Rankings" March 2018*

Real Estate Rankings

- The Davenport metro area was identified as one of the 20 worst housing markets in the U.S. in 2019. The area ranked #7 out of 180 markets. Criteria: year-over-year change of median sales price of existing single-family homes between the 4th quarter of 2018 and the 4th quarter of 2019. *National Association of Realtors®, Median Sales Price of Existing Single-Family Homes for Metropolitan Areas, 4th Quarter 2019*

- The Davenport metro area was identified as one of the 20 most affordable housing markets in the U.S. in 2019. The area ranked #12 out of 180 markets. Criteria: qualification for a mortgage loan with a 10% down payment on a typical home. *National Association of Realtors®, Qualifying Income Based on Sales Price of Existing Single-Family Homes for Metropolitan Areas, 2019*

- Davenport was ranked #4 out of 238 metro areas in terms of housing affordability in 2019 by the National Association of Home Builders (#1 = most affordable). Criteria: the share of homes sold in that area affordable to a family earning the local median income, based on standard mortgage underwriting criteria. *National Association of Home Builders®, NAHB-Wells Fargo Housing Opportunity Index, 4th Quarter 2019*

Safety Rankings

- The National Insurance Crime Bureau ranked 382 metro areas in the U.S. in terms of per capita rates of vehicle theft. The Davenport metro area ranked #75 (#1 = highest rate). Criteria: number of vehicle theft offenses per 100,000 inhabitants in 2018. *National Insurance Crime Bureau, "Hot Spots 2018," June 25, 2019*

Seniors/Retirement Rankings

- From its Best Cities for Successful Aging indexes, the Milken Institute generated rankings for metropolitan areas, weighing data in nine categories—health care, wellness, living arrangements, transportation and convenience, financial characteristics, education, employment, community engagement, and overall livability. The Davenport metro area was ranked #153 overall in the small metro area category. *Milken Institute, "Best Cities for Successful Aging, 2017" March 14, 2017*

Business Environment

CITY FINANCES

City Government Finances

Component	2017 ($000)	2017 ($ per capita)
Total Revenues	188,622	1,839
Total Expenditures	173,421	1,691
Debt Outstanding	317,307	3,093
Cash and Securities[1]	183,087	1,785

Note: (1) Cash and security holdings of a government at the close of its fiscal year, including those of its dependent agencies, utilities, and liquor stores.
Source: U.S. Census Bureau, State & Local Government Finances 2017

City Government Revenue by Source

Source	2017 ($000)	2017 ($ per capita)	2017 (%)
General Revenue			
From Federal Government	18,345	179	9.7
From State Government	22,413	218	11.9
From Local Governments	657	6	0.3
Taxes			
Property	73,111	713	38.8
Sales and Gross Receipts	22,798	222	12.1
Personal Income	0	0	0.0
Corporate Income	0	0	0.0
Motor Vehicle License	0	0	0.0
Other Taxes	2,461	24	1.3
Current Charges	40,522	395	21.5
Liquor Store	0	0	0.0
Utility	410	4	0.2
Employee Retirement	0	0	0.0

Source: U.S. Census Bureau, State & Local Government Finances 2017

City Government Expenditures by Function

Function	2017 ($000)	2017 ($ per capita)	2017 (%)
General Direct Expenditures			
Air Transportation	272	2	0.2
Corrections	0	0	0.0
Education	0	0	0.0
Employment Security Administration	0	0	0.0
Financial Administration	1,895	18	1.1
Fire Protection	18,360	179	10.6
General Public Buildings	944	9	0.5
Governmental Administration, Other	2,445	23	1.4
Health	0	0	0.0
Highways	17,356	169	10.0
Hospitals	0	0	0.0
Housing and Community Development	7,333	71	4.2
Interest on General Debt	9,038	88	5.2
Judicial and Legal	0	0	0.0
Libraries	4,779	46	2.8
Parking	977	9	0.6
Parks and Recreation	7,368	71	4.2
Police Protection	25,100	244	14.5
Public Welfare	0	0	0.0
Sewerage	15,588	152	9.0
Solid Waste Management	5,059	49	2.9
Veterans' Services	0	0	0.0
Liquor Store	0	0	0.0
Utility	6,319	61	3.6
Employee Retirement	0	0	0.0

Source: U.S. Census Bureau, State & Local Government Finances 2017

DEMOGRAPHICS

Population Growth

Area	1990 Census	2000 Census	2010 Census	2018* Estimate	Population Growth (%)	
					1990-2018	2010-2018
City	95,705	98,359	99,685	102,318	6.9	2.6
MSA[1]	368,151	376,019	379,690	382,720	4.0	0.8
U.S.	248,709,873	281,421,906	308,745,538	322,903,030	29.8	4.6

Note: (1) Figures cover the Davenport-Moline-Rock Island, IA-IL Metropolitan Statistical Area—see Appendix B for areas included; (*) 2014-2018 5-year estimated population
Source: U.S. Census Bureau, 1990 Census, Census 2000, Census 2010, 2014-2018 American Community Survey 5-Year Estimates

Household Size

Area	Persons in Household (%)							Average Household Size
	One	Two	Three	Four	Five	Six	Seven or More	
City	34.5	34.1	13.7	9.9	5.0	1.8	0.9	2.50
MSA[1]	31.0	35.7	13.6	12.0	5.1	1.8	0.7	2.40
U.S.	27.7	33.9	15.7	13.0	6.0	2.3	1.4	2.60

Note: (1) Figures cover the Davenport-Moline-Rock Island, IA-IL Metropolitan Statistical Area—see Appendix B for areas included
Source: U.S. Census Bureau, 2014-2018 American Community Survey 5-Year Estimates

Race

Area	White Alone[2] (%)	Black Alone[2] (%)	Asian Alone[2] (%)	AIAN[3] Alone[2] (%)	NHOPI[4] Alone[2] (%)	Other Race Alone[2] (%)	Two or More Races (%)
City	81.9	11.0	2.6	0.4	0.0	0.9	3.2
MSA[1]	85.5	7.4	2.3	0.3	0.0	1.5	3.0
U.S.	72.7	12.7	5.4	0.8	0.2	4.9	3.2

Note: (1) Figures cover the Davenport-Moline-Rock Island, IA-IL Metropolitan Statistical Area—see Appendix B for areas included; (2) Alone is defined as not being in combination with one or more other races; (3) American Indian and Alaska Native; (4) Native Hawaiian and Other Pacific Islander
Source: U.S. Census Bureau, 2014-2018 American Community Survey 5-Year Estimates

Hispanic or Latino Origin

Area	Total (%)	Mexican (%)	Puerto Rican (%)	Cuban (%)	Other (%)
City	8.5	7.5	0.4	0.0	0.5
MSA[1]	8.6	7.4	0.5	0.1	0.7
U.S.	17.8	11.2	1.7	0.7	4.2

Note: Persons of Hispanic or Latino origin can be of any race; (1) Figures cover the Davenport-Moline-Rock Island, IA-IL Metropolitan Statistical Area—see Appendix B for areas included
Source: U.S. Census Bureau, 2014-2018 American Community Survey 5-Year Estimates

Segregation

Type	Segregation Indices[1]				Percent Change		
	1990	2000	2010	2010 Rank[2]	1990-2000	1990-2010	2000-2010
Black/White	n/a	n/a	n/a	n/a	n/a	n/a	n/a
Asian/White	n/a	n/a	n/a	n/a	n/a	n/a	n/a
Hispanic/White	n/a	n/a	n/a	n/a	n/a	n/a	n/a

Note: All figures cover the Metropolitan Statistical Area—see Appendix B for areas included; Figures are based on an analysis of 1990, 2000, and 2010 Census Decennial Census tract data by William H. Frey, Brookings Institution and the University of Michigan Social Science Data Analysis Network. In this analysis all racial groups (whites, blacks, and asians) are non-Hispanic members of those races. Hispanics are shown as a separate category; (1) Segregation Indices are Dissimilarity Indices that measure the degree to which the minority group is distributed differently than whites across census tracts. They range from 0 (complete integration) to 100 (complete segregation) where the value indicates the percentage of the minority group that needs to move to be distributed exactly like whites; (2) Ranges from 1 (most segregated) to 102 (least segregated); n/a not available.
Source: www.CensusScope.org

Ancestry

Area	German	Irish	English	American	Italian	Polish	French[2]	Scottish	Dutch
City	27.8	14.6	6.2	4.2	2.0	1.9	1.6	1.4	1.7
MSA[1]	27.8	14.3	7.6	4.4	2.4	2.1	1.9	1.5	2.1
U.S.	13.7	9.9	7.3	6.4	5.2	2.8	2.4	1.7	1.2

Note: Figures are the percentage of the total population reporting a particular ancestry. The nine most commonly reported ancestries in the U.S. are shown. Figures include multiple ancestries (e.g. if a person reported being Irish and Italian, they were included in both columns); (1) Figures cover the Davenport-Moline-Rock Island, IA-IL Metropolitan Statistical Area—see Appendix B for areas included; (2) Excludes Basque
Source: U.S. Census Bureau, 2014-2018 American Community Survey 5-Year Estimates

Foreign-born Population

Area	Percent of Population Born in								
	Any Foreign Country	Asia	Mexico	Europe	Caribbean	Central America[2]	South America	Africa	Canada
City	4.5	1.8	1.5	0.5	0.3	0.0	0.1	0.2	0.1
MSA[1]	5.2	1.7	1.7	0.5	0.1	0.1	0.1	0.8	0.1
U.S.	13.5	4.1	3.5	1.5	1.3	1.1	0.9	0.7	0.3

Note: (1) Figures cover the Davenport-Moline-Rock Island, IA-IL Metropolitan Statistical Area—see Appendix B for areas included; (2) Excludes Mexico.
Source: U.S. Census Bureau, 2014-2018 American Community Survey 5-Year Estimates

Marital Status

Area	Never Married	Now Married[2]	Separated	Widowed	Divorced
City	37.0	43.1	1.5	6.2	12.3
MSA[1]	29.8	50.4	1.3	6.7	11.8
U.S.	33.3	48.1	2.0	5.8	10.8

Note: Figures are percentages and cover the population 15 years of age and older; (1) Figures cover the Davenport-Moline-Rock Island, IA-IL Metropolitan Statistical Area—see Appendix B for areas included; (2) Excludes separated
Source: U.S. Census Bureau, 2014-2018 American Community Survey 5-Year Estimates

Disability by Age

Area	All Ages	Under 18 Years Old	18 to 64 Years Old	65 Years and Over
City	11.9	4.2	9.9	33.9
MSA[1]	12.0	4.1	9.3	32.3
U.S.	12.6	4.2	10.3	35.0

Note: Figures show percent of the civilian noninstitutionalized population that reported having a disability. Disability status is determined from six types of difficulty: vision, hearing, cognitive, ambulatory, self-care, and independent living. For children under 5 years old, hearing and vision difficulty are used to determine disability status. For children between the ages of 5 and 14, disability status is determined from hearing, vision, cognitive, ambulatory, and self-care difficulties. For people aged 15 years and older, they are considered to have a disability if they have difficulty with any one of the six difficulty types; Note: (1) Figures cover the Davenport-Moline-Rock Island, IA-IL Metropolitan Statistical Area—see Appendix B for areas included
Source: U.S. Census Bureau, 2014-2018 American Community Survey 5-Year Estimates

Age

Area	Percent of Population									Median Age
	Under Age 5	Age 5–19	Age 20–34	Age 35–44	Age 45–54	Age 55–64	Age 65–74	Age 75–84	Age 85+	
City	6.6	19.2	22.6	12.1	12.4	12.6	8.0	4.1	2.4	36.1
MSA[1]	6.2	19.3	18.4	12.2	12.7	13.7	9.7	5.2	2.3	39.7
U.S.	6.1	19.3	20.7	12.6	13.2	12.8	8.8	4.5	1.9	37.9

Note: (1) Figures cover the Davenport-Moline-Rock Island, IA-IL Metropolitan Statistical Area—see Appendix B for areas included
Source: U.S. Census Bureau, 2014-2018 American Community Survey 5-Year Estimates

Gender

Area	Males	Females	Males per 100 Females
City	50,140	52,178	96.1
MSA[1]	188,445	194,275	97.0
U.S.	158,984,190	163,918,840	97.0

Note: (1) Figures cover the Davenport-Moline-Rock Island, IA-IL Metropolitan Statistical Area—see Appendix B for areas included
Source: U.S. Census Bureau, 2014-2018 American Community Survey 5-Year Estimates

Religious Groups by Family

Area	Catholic	Baptist	Non-Den.	Methodist[2]	Lutheran	LDS[3]	Pentecostal	Presbyterian[4]	Muslim[5]	Judaism
MSA[1]	14.9	5.0	2.7	5.3	8.7	0.8	1.4	3.0	0.9	0.1
U.S.	19.1	9.3	4.0	4.0	2.3	2.0	1.9	1.6	0.8	0.7

Note: Figures are the number of adherents as a percentage of the total population; (1) Figures cover the Davenport-Moline-Rock Island, IA-IL Metropolitan Statistical Area—see Appendix B for areas included; (2) Methodist/Pietist; (3) Latter Day Saints; (4) Reformed; (5) Figures are estimates
Source: Association of Statisticians of American Religious Bodies, 2010 U.S. Religion Census: Religious Congregations & Membership Study

Religious Groups by Tradition

Area	Catholic	Evangelical Protestant	Mainline Protestant	Other Tradition	Black Protestant	Orthodox
MSA[1]	14.9	11.4	15.1	2.4	1.6	0.1
U.S.	19.1	16.2	7.3	4.3	1.6	0.3

Note: Figures are the number of adherents as a percentage of the total population; (1) Figures cover the Davenport-Moline-Rock Island, IA-IL Metropolitan Statistical Area—see Appendix B for areas included
Source: Association of Statisticians of American Religious Bodies, 2010 U.S. Religion Census: Religious Congregations & Membership Study

ECONOMY

Gross Metropolitan Product

Area	2017	2018	2019	2020	Rank[2]
MSA[1]	19.8	20.7	21.6	22.3	124

Note: Figures are in billions of dollars; (1) Figures cover the Davenport-Moline-Rock Island, IA-IL Metropolitan Statistical Area—see Appendix B for areas included; (2) Rank is based on 2018 data and ranges from 1 to 381
Source: U.S. Conference of Mayors, U.S. Metro Economies: GMP & Employment 2018-2020, September 2019

Economic Growth

Area	2015-17 (%)	2018 (%)	2019 (%)	2020 (%)	Rank[2]
MSA[1]	-0.2	2.4	2.4	1.2	311
U.S.	1.9	2.9	2.3	2.1	–

Note: Figures are real gross metropolitan product (GMP) growth rates and represent average annual percent change; (1) Figures cover the Davenport-Moline-Rock Island, IA-IL Metropolitan Statistical Area—see Appendix B for areas included; (2) Rank is based on 2017 2-year average annual percent change and ranges from 1 to 381
Source: U.S. Conference of Mayors, U.S. Metro Economies: GMP & Employment 2018-2020, September 2019

Metropolitan Area Exports

Area	2013	2014	2015	2016	2017	2018	Rank[2]
MSA[1]	7,141.2	6,563.2	5,711.8	4,497.6	5,442.7	6,761.9	48

Note: Figures are in millions of dollars; (1) Figures cover the Davenport-Moline-Rock Island, IA-IL Metropolitan Statistical Area—see Appendix B for areas included; (2) Rank is based on 2018 data and ranges from 1 to 387
Source: U.S. Department of Commerce, International Trade Administration, Office of Trade and Economic Analysis, Industry and Analysis, Exports by Metropolitan Area, data extracted April 15, 2020

Building Permits

Area	Single-Family			Multi-Family			Total		
	2017	2018	Pct. Chg.	2017	2018	Pct. Chg.	2017	2018	Pct. Chg.
City	104	68	-34.6	0	0	0.0	104	68	-34.6
MSA[1]	443	490	10.6	307	69	-77.5	750	559	-25.5
U.S.	820,000	855,300	4.3	462,000	473,500	2.5	1,282,000	1,328,800	3.7

Note: (1) Figures cover the Davenport-Moline-Rock Island, IA-IL Metropolitan Statistical Area—see Appendix B for areas included; Figures represent new, privately-owned housing units authorized (unadjusted data); All permit data are based on estimates with imputation
Source: U.S. Census Bureau, Manufacturing, Mining, and Construction Statistics, Building Permits, 2017, 2018

Bankruptcy Filings

Area	Business Filings			Nonbusiness Filings		
	2018	2019	% Chg.	2018	2019	% Chg.
Scott County	20	10	-50.0	309	329	6.5
U.S.	22,232	22,780	2.5	751,186	752,160	0.1

Note: Business filings include Chapter 7, Chapter 9, Chapter 11, Chapter 12, Chapter 13, Chapter 15, and Section 304; Nonbusiness filings include Chapter 7, Chapter 11, and Chapter 13
Source: Administrative Office of the U.S. Courts, Business and Nonbusiness Bankruptcy, County Cases Commenced by Chapter of the Bankruptcy Code, During the 12-Month Period Ending December 31, 2018 and Business and Nonbusiness Bankruptcy, County Cases Commenced by Chapter of the Bankruptcy Code, During the 12-Month Period Ending December 31, 2019

Housing Vacancy Rates

Area	Gross Vacancy Rate[2] (%)			Year-Round Vacancy Rate[3] (%)			Rental Vacancy Rate[4] (%)			Homeowner Vacancy Rate[5] (%)		
	2017	2018	2019	2017	2018	2019	2017	2018	2019	2017	2018	2019
MSA[1]	n/a	n/a	n/a	n/a	n/a	n/a	n/a	n/a	n/a	n/a	n/a	n/a
U.S.	12.7	12.3	12.0	9.9	9.7	9.5	7.2	6.9	6.7	1.6	1.5	1.4

Note: (1) Figures cover the Davenport-Moline-Rock Island, IA-IL Metropolitan Statistical Area—see Appendix B for areas included; (2) The percentage of the total housing inventory that is vacant; (3) The percentage of the housing inventory (excluding seasonal units) that is year-round vacant; (4) The percentage of rental inventory that is vacant for rent; (5) The percentage of homeowner inventory that is vacant for sale; n/a not available
Source: U.S. Census Bureau, Housing Vacancies and Homeownership Annual Statistics: 2017, 2018, 2019

INCOME

Income

Area	Per Capita ($)	Median Household ($)	Average Household ($)
City	27,328	50,001	65,638
MSA[1]	30,141	55,941	72,778
U.S.	32,621	60,293	84,938

Note: (1) Figures cover the Davenport-Moline-Rock Island, IA-IL Metropolitan Statistical Area—see Appendix B for areas included
Source: U.S. Census Bureau, 2014-2018 American Community Survey 5-Year Estimates

Household Income Distribution

Area	Percent of Households Earning							
	Under $15,000	$15,000 -$24,999	$25,000 -$34,999	$35,000 -$49,999	$50,000 -$74,999	$75,000 -$99,999	$100,000 -$149,999	$150,000 and up
City	12.5	11.0	11.8	14.7	19.9	12.1	11.1	6.8
MSA[1]	10.6	9.8	10.2	13.7	19.5	13.4	14.2	8.5
U.S.	10.9	9.3	9.3	12.6	17.5	12.5	14.6	13.3

Note: (1) Figures cover the Davenport-Moline-Rock Island, IA-IL Metropolitan Statistical Area—see Appendix B for areas included
Source: U.S. Census Bureau, 2014-2018 American Community Survey 5-Year Estimates

Poverty Rate

Area	All Ages	Under 18 Years Old	18 to 64 Years Old	65 Years and Over
City	16.6	23.7	15.7	8.6
MSA[1]	13.1	19.3	12.0	8.1
U.S.	14.1	19.5	13.2	9.3

Note: Figures are percentage of people whose income during the past 12 months was below the poverty level;
(1) Figures cover the Davenport-Moline-Rock Island, IA-IL Metropolitan Statistical Area—see Appendix B for areas included
Source: U.S. Census Bureau, 2014-2018 American Community Survey 5-Year Estimates

EMPLOYMENT

Labor Force and Employment

Area	Civilian Labor Force			Workers Employed		
	Dec. 2018	Dec. 2019	% Chg.	Dec. 2018	Dec. 2019	% Chg.
City	50,579	51,918	2.6	48,734	49,753	2.1
MSA[1]	192,766	194,473	0.9	183,841	185,909	1.1
U.S.	162,510,000	164,007,000	0.9	156,481,000	158,504,000	1.3

Note: Data is not seasonally adjusted and covers workers 16 years of age and older; (1) Figures cover the Davenport-Moline-Rock Island, IA-IL Metropolitan Statistical Area—see Appendix B for areas included
Source: Bureau of Labor Statistics, Local Area Unemployment Statistics

Unemployment Rate

Area	2019											
	Jan.	Feb.	Mar.	Apr.	May	Jun.	Jul.	Aug.	Sep.	Oct.	Nov.	Dec.
City	4.4	3.8	4.2	3.3	3.3	4.2	3.9	4.2	3.7	3.7	3.9	4.2
MSA[1]	5.4	4.8	4.8	3.6	3.5	3.9	3.9	4.1	3.9	3.8	4.0	4.4
U.S.	4.4	4.1	3.9	3.3	3.4	3.8	4.0	3.8	3.3	3.3	3.3	3.4

Note: Data is not seasonally adjusted and covers workers 16 years of age and older; (1) Figures cover the Davenport-Moline-Rock Island, IA-IL Metropolitan Statistical Area—see Appendix B for areas included
Source: Bureau of Labor Statistics, Local Area Unemployment Statistics

Average Wages

Occupation	$/Hr.	Occupation	$/Hr.
Accountants and Auditors	34.10	Maintenance and Repair Workers	19.30
Automotive Mechanics	20.10	Marketing Managers	62.60
Bookkeepers	19.10	Network and Computer Systems Admin.	37.40
Carpenters	24.10	Nurses, Licensed Practical	21.50
Cashiers	10.90	Nurses, Registered	26.30
Computer Programmers	42.30	Nursing Assistants	13.40
Computer Systems Analysts	44.60	Office Clerks, General	15.50
Computer User Support Specialists	23.30	Physical Therapists	36.00
Construction Laborers	20.80	Physicians	117.50
Cooks, Restaurant	11.60	Plumbers, Pipefitters and Steamfitters	30.30
Customer Service Representatives	16.50	Police and Sheriff's Patrol Officers	29.20
Dentists	92.00	Postal Service Mail Carriers	24.60
Electricians	27.50	Real Estate Sales Agents	38.00
Engineers, Electrical	42.00	Retail Salespersons	14.70
Fast Food and Counter Workers	10.50	Sales Representatives, Technical/Scientific	37.60
Financial Managers	54.20	Secretaries, Exc. Legal/Medical/Executive	16.40
First-Line Supervisors of Office Workers	25.30	Security Guards	15.00
General and Operations Managers	47.00	Surgeons	133.10
Hairdressers/Cosmetologists	12.10	Teacher Assistants, Exc. Postsecondary*	13.00
Home Health and Personal Care Aides	12.40	Teachers, Secondary School, Exc. Sp. Ed.*	27.90
Janitors and Cleaners	13.70	Telemarketers	13.60
Landscaping/Groundskeeping Workers	14.90	Truck Drivers, Heavy/Tractor-Trailer	22.20
Lawyers	72.10	Truck Drivers, Light/Delivery Services	16.00
Maids and Housekeeping Cleaners	10.90	Waiters and Waitresses	10.80

Note: Wage data covers the Davenport-Moline-Rock Island, IA-IL Metropolitan Statistical Area—see Appendix B for areas included; (*) Hourly wages were calculated from annual wage data based on a 40 hour work week; n/a not available.
Source: Bureau of Labor Statistics, Metro Area Occupational Employment & Wage Estimates, May 2019

Employment by Occupation

Occupation Classification	City (%)	MSA[1] (%)	U.S. (%)
Management, Business, Science, and Arts	31.9	33.2	37.9
Natural Resources, Construction, and Maintenance	7.5	8.6	8.9
Production, Transportation, and Material Moving	17.9	18.6	13.3
Sales and Office	22.3	21.7	22.1
Service	20.3	17.9	17.9

Note: Figures cover employed civilians 16 years of age and older; (1) Figures cover the
Davenport-Moline-Rock Island, IA-IL Metropolitan Statistical Area—see Appendix B for areas included
Source: U.S. Census Bureau, 2014-2018 American Community Survey 5-Year Estimates

Employment by Industry

Sector	MSA[1]		U.S.
	Number of Employees	Percent of Total	Percent of Total
Construction, Mining, and Logging	n/a	n/a	5.4
Education and Health Services	n/a	n/a	16.1
Financial Activities	n/a	n/a	5.8
Government	n/a	n/a	15.0
Information	n/a	n/a	1.9
Leisure and Hospitality	n/a	n/a	10.8
Manufacturing	n/a	n/a	8.4
Other Services	n/a	n/a	3.9
Professional and Business Services	n/a	n/a	14.1
Retail Trade	n/a	n/a	10.6
Transportation, Warehousing, and Utilities	n/a	n/a	4.2
Wholesale Trade	n/a	n/a	3.9

Note: Figures are non-farm employment as of December 2019. Figures are not seasonally adjusted and include
workers 16 years of age and older; (1) Figures cover the Davenport-Moline-Rock Island, IA-IL Metropolitan
Statistical Area—see Appendix B for areas included; n/a not available
Source: Bureau of Labor Statistics, Current Employment Statistics, Employment, Hours, and Earnings

Occupations with Greatest Projected Employment Growth: 2019 – 2021

Occupation[1]	2019 Employment	2021 Projected Employment	Numeric Employment Change	Percent Employment Change
Combined Food Preparation and Serving Workers, Including Fast Food	38,530	39,480	950	2.5
Heavy and Tractor-Trailer Truck Drivers	45,820	46,750	930	2.0
Registered Nurses	34,120	34,870	750	2.2
Personal Care Aides	11,780	12,230	450	3.8
Home Health Aides	8,050	8,490	440	5.5
Cooks, Restaurant	11,550	11,940	390	3.4
Laborers and Freight, Stock, and Material Movers, Hand	29,060	29,440	380	1.3
Janitors and Cleaners, Except Maids and Housekeeping Cleaners	26,660	26,980	320	1.2
Accountants and Auditors	12,170	12,430	260	2.1
Construction Laborers	13,390	13,640	250	1.9

Note: Projections cover Iowa; (1) Sorted by numeric employment change
Source: www.projectionscentral.com, State Occupational Projections, 2019–2021 Short-Term Projections

Fastest Growing Occupations: 2019 – 2021

Occupation[1]	2019 Employment	2021 Projected Employment	Numeric Employment Change	Percent Employment Change
Information Security Analysts	1,470	1,590	120	8.2
Home Health Aides	8,050	8,490	440	5.5
Veterinary Assistants and Laboratory Animal Caretakers	1,140	1,200	60	5.3
Woodworking Machine Setters, Operators, and Tenders, Except Sawing	1,490	1,560	70	4.7
Nurse Practitioners	1,330	1,390	60	4.5
Taxi Drivers and Chauffeurs	2,430	2,540	110	4.5
Health Specialties Teachers, Postsecondary	2,030	2,120	90	4.4
Paralegals and Legal Assistants	1,890	1,970	80	4.2
Speech-Language Pathologists	1,200	1,250	50	4.2
Gaming Dealers	1,210	1,260	50	4.1

Note: Projections cover Iowa; (1) Sorted by percent employment change and excludes occupations with numeric employment change less than 50
Source: www.projectionscentral.com, State Occupational Projections, 2019–2021 Short-Term Projections

TAXES

State Corporate Income Tax Rates

State	Tax Rate (%)	Income Brackets ($)	Num. of Brackets	Financial Institution Tax Rate (%)[a]	Federal Income Tax Ded.
Iowa	6.0 - 12.0	25,000 - 250,001	4	5.0	Yes (j)

Note: Tax rates as of January 1, 2020; (a) Rates listed are the corporate income tax rate applied to financial institutions or excise taxes based on income; (j) 50% of the federal income tax is deductible.
Source: Federation of Tax Administrators, State Corporate Income Tax Rates, January 1, 2020

State Individual Income Tax Rates

State	Tax Rate (%)	Income Brackets ($)	Personal Exemptions ($) Single	Married	Depend.	Standard Ded. ($) Single	Married
Iowa (a)	0.33 - 8.53	15,666 - 74,970	40 (c)	80 (c)	40 (c)	2,110	5,210 (a)

Note: Tax rates as of January 1, 2020; Local- and county-level taxes are not included; Federal income tax is deductible on state income tax returns; (a) 19 states have statutory provision for automatically adjusting to the rate of inflation the dollar values of the income tax brackets, standard deductions, and/or personal exemptions. Michigan indexes the personal exemption only. Oregon does not index the income brackets for $125,000 and over; (c) The personal exemption takes the form of a tax credit instead of a deduction
Source: Federation of Tax Administrators, State Individual Income Tax Rates, January 1, 2020

Various State Sales and Excise Tax Rates

State	State Sales Tax (%)	Gasoline[1] (¢/gal.)	Cigarette[2] ($/pack)	Spirits[3] ($/gal.)	Wine[4] ($/gal.)	Beer[5] ($/gal.)	Recreational Marijuana (%)
Iowa	6	30.5	1.36	13.03	1.75	0.19	Not legal

Note: All tax rates as of January 1, 2020; (1) The American Petroleum Institute has developed a methodology for determining the average tax rate on a gallon of fuel. Rates may include any of the following: excise taxes, environmental fees, storage tank fees, other fees or taxes, general sales tax, and local taxes; (2) The federal excise tax of $1.0066 per pack and local taxes are not included; (3) Rates are those applicable to off-premise sales of 40% alcohol by volume (a.b.v.) distilled spirits in 750ml containers. Local excise taxes are excluded; (4) Rates are those applicable to off-premise sales of 11% a.b.v. non-carbonated wine in 750ml containers; (5) Rates are those applicable to off-premise sales of 4.7% a.b.v. beer in 12 ounce containers.
Source: Tax Foundation, 2020 Facts & Figures: How Does Your State Compare?

State Business Tax Climate Index Rankings

State	Overall Rank	Corporate Tax Rank	Individual Income Tax Rank	Sales Tax Rank	Property Tax Rank	Unemployment Insurance Tax Rank
Iowa	42	48	42	15	35	35

Note: The index is a measure of how each state's tax laws affect economic performance. The lower the rank, the more favorable a state's tax system is for business. States without a given tax are given a ranking of 1. The scores/rankings for the District of Columbia do not affect other states. The 2020 index represents the tax climate as of July 1, 2019.
Source: Tax Foundation, State Business Tax Climate Index 2020

**COMMERCIAL
UTILITIES**

Typical Monthly Electric Bills

Area	Commercial Service ($/month)		Industrial Service ($/month)	
	1,500 kWh	40 kW demand 14,000 kWh	1,000 kW demand 200,000 kWh	50,000 kW demand 32,500,000 kWh
City	151	1,071	15,699	1,713,210
Average[1]	203	1,612	25,706	2,520,671

Note: Figures are based on annualized rates; (1) Average based on 187 utilities surveyed
Source: Edison Electric Institute, Typical Bills and Average Rates Report, Summer 2019

TRANSPORTATION

Means of Transportation to Work

Area	Car/Truck/Van		Public Transportation			Bicycle	Walked	Other Means	Worked at Home
	Drove Alone	Car-pooled	Bus	Subway	Railroad				
City	84.7	7.2	1.2	0.0	0.0	0.4	2.2	0.5	3.9
MSA[1]	85.3	7.0	0.9	0.0	0.0	0.3	1.9	0.9	3.7
U.S.	76.4	9.1	2.5	1.9	0.6	0.6	2.7	1.3	4.9

Note: Figures are percentages and cover workers 16 years of age and older; (1) Figures cover the Davenport-Moline-Rock Island, IA-IL Metropolitan Statistical Area—see Appendix B for areas included
Source: U.S. Census Bureau, 2014-2018 American Community Survey 5-Year Estimates

Travel Time to Work

Area	Less Than 10 Minutes	10 to 19 Minutes	20 to 29 Minutes	30 to 44 Minutes	45 to 59 Minutes	60 to 89 Minutes	90 Minutes or More
City	17.1	47.8	19.7	9.6	3.2	1.4	1.2
MSA[1]	17.9	37.8	24.2	13.4	3.6	1.8	1.2
U.S.	12.5	28.7	20.9	20.7	8.2	6.3	2.8

Note: Note: Figures are percentages and include workers 16 years old and over; (1) Figures cover the Davenport-Moline-Rock Island, IA-IL Metropolitan Statistical Area—see Appendix B for areas included
Source: U.S. Census Bureau, 2014-2018 American Community Survey 5-Year Estimates

Key Congestion Measures

Area	1982	1992	2002	2012	2017
Annual Hours of Delay, Total (000)	n/a	n/a	n/a	n/a	4,102
Annual Hours of Delay, Per Auto Commuter	n/a	n/a	n/a	n/a	14
Annual Congestion Cost, Total (million $)	n/a	n/a	n/a	n/a	85
Annual Congestion Cost, Per Auto Commuter ($)	n/a	n/a	n/a	n/a	284

Note: n/a not available
Source: Texas A&M Transportation Institute, 2019 Urban Mobility Report

Freeway Travel Time Index

Area	1982	1987	1992	1997	2002	2007	2012	2017
Urban Area Index[1]	n/a	n/a	n/a	n/a	n/a	n/a	n/a	1.05
Urban Area Rank[1,2]	n/a	n/a	n/a	n/a	n/a	n/a	n/a	n/a

Note: Freeway Travel Time Index—the ratio of travel time in the peak period to the travel time at free-flow conditions. For example, a value of 1.30 indicates a 20-minute free-flow trip takes 26 minutes in the peak (20 minutes x 1.30 = 26 minutes); (1) Covers the Davenport IA-IL urban area; (2) Rank is based on 101 larger urban areas (#1 = highest travel time index); n/a not available
Source: Texas A&M Transportation Institute, 2019 Urban Mobility Report

Public Transportation

Agency Name / Mode of Transportation	Vehicles Operated in Maximum Service[1]	Annual Unlinked Passenger Trips[2] (in thous.)	Annual Passenger Miles[3] (in thous.)
Davenport Public Transit			
Bus (directly operated)	15	622.9	n/a

Note: (1) Number of revenue vehicles operated by the given mode and type of service to meet the annual maximum service requirement. This is the revenue vehicle count during the peak season of the year; on the week and day that maximum service is provided. Vehicles operated in maximum service (VOMS) exclude atypical days and one-time special events; (2) Number of passengers who boarded public transportation vehicles. Passengers are counted each time they board a vehicle no matter how many vehicles they use to travel from their origin to their destination. (3) Sum of the distances ridden by all passengers during the entire fiscal year.
Source: Federal Transit Administration, National Transit Database, 2018

Air Transportation

Airport Name and Code / Type of Service	Passenger Airlines[1]	Passenger Enplanements	Freight Carriers[2]	Freight (lbs)
Quad City International Airport (MLI)				
Domestic service (U.S. carriers - 2019)	15	355,455	2	1,575
International service (U.S. carriers - 2018)	0	0	1	24,701

Note: (1) Includes all U.S.-based major, minor and commuter airlines that carried at least one passenger during the year; (2) Includes all U.S.-based airlines and freight carriers that transported at least one pound of freight during the year.
Source: Bureau of Transportation Statistics, The Intermodal Transportation Database, Air Carriers: T-100 Domestic Market (U.S. Carriers), 2019; Bureau of Transportation Statistics, The Intermodal Transportation Database, Air Carriers: T-100 International Market (U.S. Carriers), 2018

Other Transportation Statistics

Major Highways:	I-74; I-80; I-280
Amtrak Service:	Bus connection
Major Waterways/Ports:	Mississippi River

Source: Amtrak.com; Google Maps

BUSINESSES

Major Business Headquarters

Company Name	Industry	Rankings	
		Fortune[1]	Forbes[2]
No companies listed	-	-	-

Note: (1) Companies that produce a 10-K are ranked 1 to 500 based on 2018 revenue; (2) All private companies with at least $2 billion in annual revenue through the end of their most current fiscal year are ranked 1 to 228; companies listed are headquartered in the city; dashes indicate no ranking
Source: Fortune, "Fortune 500," June 2019; Forbes, "America's Largest Private Companies," 2019 Rankings

Minority- and Women-Owned Businesses

Group	All Firms		Firms with Paid Employees			
	Firms	Sales ($000)	Firms	Sales ($000)	Employees	Payroll ($000)
AIAN[1]	59	5,302	2	(s)	100 - 249	(s)
Asian	256	37,598	68	30,217	304	5,187
Black	705	37,141	14	28,723	261	5,111
Hispanic	297	17,904	14	(s)	100 - 249	(s)
NHOPI[2]	n/a	n/a	n/a	n/a	n/a	n/a
Women	3,417	644,774	487	583,862	4,946	163,013
All Firms	7,994	14,327,565	2,383	14,115,279	62,284	2,234,073

Note: Figures cover firms located in the city; minority- and women-owned business are defined as firms in which the corresponding group own 51% or more of the stock or equity of the company; (1) American Indian and Alaska Native; (2) Native Hawaiian and Other Pacific Islander; (s) estimates are suppressed when publication standards are not met; n/a not available
Source: U.S. Census Bureau, 2012 Economic Census, Survey of Business Owners

**HOTELS &
CONVENTION
CENTERS**

Hotels, Motels and Vacation Rentals

Area	5 Star		4 Star		3 Star		2 Star		1 Star		Not Rated	
	Num.	Pct.[3]	Num.	Pct.[3]	Num.	Pct.[3]	Num.	Pct.[3]	Num.	Pct.[3]	Num.	Pct.[3]
City[1]	0	0.0	3	5.4	15	26.8	11	19.6	2	3.6	25	44.6
Total[2]	266	1.3	1,517	7.2	4,627	21.8	3,210	15.1	3,974	18.7	7,601	35.9

Note: (1) Figures cover Davenport and vicinity; (2) Figures cover all 100 cities in this book; (3) Percentage of hotels which have a given star rating; Star ratings are determined by priceline.com and offer an indication of the general quality of a particular hotel.
Source: priceline.com, April 27, 2020

Major Convention Centers

Name	Overall Space (sq. ft.)	Exhibit Space (sq. ft.)	Meeting Space (sq. ft.)	Meeting Rooms
The RiverCenter	100,000	n/a	n/a	n/a

Note: Table includes convention centers located in the Davenport-Moline-Rock Island, IA-IL metro area; n/a not available
Source: Original research

Living Environment

COST OF LIVING

Cost of Living Index

Composite Index	Groceries	Housing	Utilities	Trans- portation	Health Care	Misc. Goods/ Services
92.0	99.7	76.9	98.9	105.8	105.3	93.7

Note: The Cost of Living Index measures regional differences in the cost of consumer goods and services, excluding taxes and non-consumer expenditures, for professional and managerial households in the top income quintile. It is based on more than 50,000 prices covering almost 60 different items for which prices are collected three times a year by chambers of commerce, economic development organizations or university applied economic centers in each participating urban area. The numbers shown should be read as a percentage above or below the national average of 100. For example, a value of 115.4 in the groceries column indicates that grocery prices are 15.4% higher than the national average. Small differences in the index numbers should not be interpreted as significant; Figures cover the Davenport-Moline-Rock Is IA-IL urban area.
Source: The Council for Community and Economic Research, ACCRA Cost of Living Index, 2019

Grocery Prices

Area[1]	T-Bone Steak ($/pound)	Frying Chicken ($/pound)	Whole Milk ($/half gal.)	Eggs ($/dozen)	Orange Juice ($/64 oz.)	Coffee ($/11.5 oz.)
City[2]	11.55	1.66	2.30	1.36	2.98	4.58
Avg.	11.40	1.41	1.93	1.54	3.51	4.30
Min.	7.40	0.92	0.85	0.58	2.67	2.90
Max.	15.58	2.68	4.09	4.18	5.57	8.10

*Note: (1) Values for the local area are compared with the average, minimum and maximum values for all 290 areas in the Cost of Living Index; (2) Figures cover the Davenport-Moline-Rock Is IA-IL urban area; **T-Bone Steak** (price per pound); **Frying Chicken** (price per pound, whole fryer); **Whole Milk** (half gallon carton); **Eggs** (price per dozen, Grade A, large); **Orange Juice** (64 oz. Tropicana or Florida Natural); **Coffee** (11.5 oz. can, vacuum-packed, Maxwell House, Hills Bros, or Folgers).*
Source: The Council for Community and Economic Research, ACCRA Cost of Living Index, 2019

Housing and Utility Costs

Area[1]	New Home Price ($)	Apartment Rent ($/month)	All Electric ($/month)	Part Electric ($/month)	Other Energy ($/month)	Telephone ($/month)
City[2]	284,507	871	-	93.38	69.08	184.00
Avg.	362,090	1,142	174.35	100.00	67.76	179.60
Min.	198,329	501	91.58	31.44	28.51	165.30
Max.	2,074,561	5,050	388.18	239.41	306.15	207.90

*Note: (1) Values for the local area are compared with the average, minimum and maximum values for all 290 areas in the Cost of Living Index; (2) Figures cover the Davenport-Moline-Rock Is IA-IL urban area; **New Home Price** (2,400 sf living area, 8,000 sf lot, in urban area with full utilities); **Apartment Rent** (950 sf 2 bedroom/1.5 or 2 bath, unfurnished, excluding all utilities except water); **All Electric** (average monthly cost for an all-electric home); **Part Electric** (average monthly cost for a part-electric home); **Other Energy** (average monthly cost for natural gas, fuel oil, coal, wood, and any other forms of energy except electricity); **Telephone** (price includes the base monthly rate plus taxes and fees for three lines of mobile phone service).*
Source: The Council for Community and Economic Research, ACCRA Cost of Living Index, 2019

Health Care, Transportation, and Other Costs

Area[1]	Doctor ($/visit)	Dentist ($/visit)	Optometrist ($/visit)	Gasoline ($/gallon)	Beauty Salon ($/visit)	Men's Shirt ($)
City[2]	133.08	96.72	87.50	2.45	32.58	37.77
Avg.	114.85	97.58	106.10	2.50	38.15	32.15
Min.	39.00	62.22	52.22	1.53	16.88	10.27
Max.	206.67	151.53	258.67	3.79	79.29	59.30

*Note: (1) Values for the local area are compared with the average, minimum and maximum values for all 290 areas in the Cost of Living Index; (2) Figures cover the Davenport-Moline-Rock Is IA-IL urban area; **Doctor** (general practitioners routine exam of an established patient); **Dentist** (adult teeth cleaning and periodic oral examination); **Optometrist** (full vision eye exam for established adult patient); **Gasoline** (one gallon regular unleaded, national brand, including all taxes, cash price at self-service pump if available); **Beauty Salon** (woman's shampoo, trim, and blow-dry); **Men's Shirt** (cotton/polyester dress shirt, pinpoint weave, long sleeves).*
Source: The Council for Community and Economic Research, ACCRA Cost of Living Index, 2019

HOUSING

House Price Index (HPI)

Area	National Ranking[2]	Quarterly Change (%)	One-Year Change (%)	Five-Year Change (%)
MSA[1]	185	-1.22	3.68	13.08
U.S.[3]	–	1.26	5.09	32.88

Note: The HPI is a weighted repeat sales index. It measures average price changes in repeat sales or refinancings on the same properties. This information is obtained by reviewing repeat mortgage transactions on single-family properties whose mortgages have been purchased or securitized by Fannie Mae or Freddie Mac in January 1975; (1) Figures cover the Davenport-Moline-Rock Island, IA-IL Metropolitan Statistical Area—see Appendix B for areas included; (2) Rankings are based on annual percentage change for all metro areas containing at least 15,000 transactions over the last 10 years and ranges from 1 to 232; (3) figures based on a weighted average of Census Division estimates using a seasonally adjusted, purchase-only index; all figures are for the period ending December 31, 2019
Source: Federal Housing Finance Agency, House Price Index, February 25, 2020

Median Single-Family Home Prices

Area	2017	2018	2019p	Percent Change 2018 to 2019
MSA[1]	126.3	131.0	135.4	3.4
U.S. Average	248.8	261.6	274.6	5.0

Note: Figures are median sales prices of existing single-family homes in thousands of dollars; (p) preliminary; (1) Figures cover the Davenport-Moline-Rock Island, IA-IL Metropolitan Statistical Area—see Appendix B for areas included
Source: National Association of Realtors, Median Sales Price of Existing Single-Family Homes for Metropolitan Areas, 4th Quarter 2019

Qualifying Income Based on Median Sales Price of Existing Single-Family Homes

Area	With 5% Down ($)	With 10% Down ($)	With 20% Down ($)
MSA[1]	28,147	26,666	23,703
U.S. Average	58,663	55,575	49,400

Note: Figures are preliminary; Qualifying income is based on a mortgage rate of 3.76%. Monthly principal and interest payment is limited to 25% of income; (1) Figures cover the Davenport-Moline-Rock Island, IA-IL Metropolitan Statistical Area—see Appendix B for areas included
Source: National Association of Realtors, Qualifying Income Based on Median Sales Price of Existing Single-Family Homes for Metropolitan Areas, 4th Quarter 2019

Median Apartment Condo-Coop Home Prices

Area	2017	2018	2019p	Percent Change 2018 to 2019
MSA[1]	n/a	n/a	n/a	n/a
U.S. Average	234.3	241.0	249.5	3.5

Note: Figures are median sales prices of existing apartment condo-coop homes in thousands of dollars; (p) preliminary; n/a not available; (1) Figures cover the Davenport-Moline-Rock Island, IA-IL Metropolitan Statistical Area—see Appendix B for areas included
Source: National Association of Realtors, Median Sales Price of Existing Apartment Condo-Coop Homes for Metropolitan Areas, 4th Quarter 2019

Home Value Distribution

Area	Under $50,000	$50,000 -$99,999	$100,000 -$149,999	$150,000 -$199,999	$200,000 -$299,999	$300,000 -$499,999	$500,000 -$999,999	$1,000,000 or more
City	6.6	25.3	29.5	16.1	14.9	6.3	1.0	0.4
MSA[1]	7.9	24.3	25.0	17.1	15.2	8.2	1.9	0.4
U.S.	7.6	13.0	14.0	14.3	19.2	18.3	10.5	3.1

Note: Figures are percentages and cover owner-occupied housing units; (1) Figures cover the Davenport-Moline-Rock Island, IA-IL Metropolitan Statistical Area—see Appendix B for areas included
Source: U.S. Census Bureau, 2014-2018 American Community Survey 5-Year Estimates

Homeownership Rate

Area	2011 (%)	2012 (%)	2013 (%)	2014 (%)	2015 (%)	2016 (%)	2017 (%)	2018 (%)	2019 (%)
MSA[1]	n/a	n/a	n/a	n/a	n/a	n/a	n/a	n/a	n/a
U.S.	66.1	65.4	65.1	64.5	63.7	63.4	63.9	64.4	64.6

Note: (1) Figures cover the Davenport-Moline-Rock Island, IA-IL Metropolitan Statistical Area—see Appendix B for areas included; n/a not available
Source: U.S. Census Bureau, Housing Vacancies and Homeownership Annual Statistics: 2011-2019

Year Housing Structure Built

Area	2010 or Later	2000 -2009	1990 -1999	1980 -1989	1970 -1979	1960 -1969	1950 -1959	1940 -1949	Before 1940	Median Year
City	2.9	9.0	7.1	6.0	16.1	13.8	11.0	6.0	28.0	1964
MSA[1]	3.1	7.5	8.1	6.3	16.8	13.8	11.9	7.3	25.0	1964
U.S.	4.1	14.3	13.9	13.5	15.3	10.7	10.4	5.0	12.8	1977

Note: Figures are percentages except for Median Year; Note: (1) Figures cover the Davenport-Moline-Rock Island, IA-IL Metropolitan Statistical Area—see Appendix B for areas included
Source: U.S. Census Bureau, 2014-2018 American Community Survey 5-Year Estimates

Gross Monthly Rent

Area	Under $500	$500 -$999	$1,000 -$1,499	$1,500 -$1,999	$2,000 -$2,499	$2,500 -$2,999	$3,000 and up	Median ($)
City	9.4	68.0	17.6	2.9	0.6	1.0	0.5	757
MSA[1]	17.0	61.3	16.2	3.6	0.7	0.6	0.7	746
U.S.	9.8	38.5	29.6	12.9	5.1	2.1	2.0	1,023

Note: Figures are percentages except for Median; Gross rent is the contract rent plus the estimated average monthly cost of utilities (electricity, gas, and water and sewer) and fuels (oil, coal, kerosene, wood, etc.) if these are paid by the renter (or paid for the renter by someone else); (1) Figures cover the Davenport-Moline-Rock Island, IA-IL Metropolitan Statistical Area—see Appendix B for areas included
Source: U.S. Census Bureau, 2014-2018 American Community Survey 5-Year Estimates

HEALTH

Health Risk Factors

Category	MSA[1] (%)	U.S. (%)
Adults aged 18–64 who have any kind of health care coverage	n/a	87.3
Adults who reported being in good or better health	n/a	82.4
Adults who have been told they have high blood cholesterol	n/a	33.0
Adults who have been told they have high blood pressure	n/a	32.3
Adults who are current smokers	n/a	17.1
Adults who currently use E-cigarettes	n/a	4.6
Adults who currently use chewing tobacco, snuff, or snus	n/a	4.0
Adults who are heavy drinkers[2]	n/a	6.3
Adults who are binge drinkers[3]	n/a	17.4
Adults who are overweight (BMI 25.0 - 29.9)	n/a	35.3
Adults who are obese (BMI 30.0 - 99.8)	n/a	31.3
Adults who participated in any physical activities in the past month	n/a	74.4
Adults who always or nearly always wears a seat belt	n/a	94.3

Note: n/a not available; (1) Figures cover the Davenport-Moline-Rock Island, IA-IL Metropolitan Statistical Area—see Appendix B for areas included; (2) Heavy drinkers are classified as adult men having more than 14 drinks per week and adult women having more than 7 drinks per week; (3) Binge drinkers are classified as males having five or more drinks on one occasion or females having four or more drinks on one occasion
Source: Centers for Disease Control and Prevention, Behaviorial Risk Factor Surveillance System, SMART: Selected Metropolitan Area Risk Trends, 2017

Acute and Chronic Health Conditions

Category	MSA[1] (%)	U.S. (%)
Adults who have ever been told they had a heart attack	n/a	4.2
Adults who have ever been told they have angina or coronary heart disease	n/a	3.9
Adults who have ever been told they had a stroke	n/a	3.0
Adults who have ever been told they have asthma	n/a	14.2
Adults who have ever been told they have arthritis	n/a	24.9
Adults who have ever been told they have diabetes[2]	n/a	10.5
Adults who have ever been told they had skin cancer	n/a	6.2
Adults who have ever been told they had any other types of cancer	n/a	7.1
Adults who have ever been told they have COPD	n/a	6.5
Adults who have ever been told they have kidney disease	n/a	3.0
Adults who have ever been told they have a form of depression	n/a	20.5

Note: n/a not available; (1) Figures cover the Davenport-Moline-Rock Island, IA-IL Metropolitan Statistical Area—see Appendix B for areas included; (2) Figures do not include pregnancy-related, borderline, or pre-diabetes
Source: Centers for Disease Control and Prevention, Behaviorial Risk Factor Surveillance System, SMART: Selected Metropolitan Area Risk Trends, 2017

Health Screening and Vaccination Rates

Category	MSA[1] (%)	U.S. (%)
Adults aged 65+ who have had flu shot within the past year	n/a	60.7
Adults aged 65+ who have ever had a pneumonia vaccination	n/a	75.4
Adults who have ever been tested for HIV	n/a	36.1
Adults who have ever had the shingles or zoster vaccine?	n/a	28.9
Adults who have had their blood cholesterol checked within the last five years	n/a	85.9

Note: n/a not available; (1) Figures cover the Davenport-Moline-Rock Island, IA-IL Metropolitan Statistical Area—see Appendix B for areas included.
Source: Centers for Disease Control and Prevention, Behaviorial Risk Factor Surveillance System, SMART: Selected Metropolitan Area Risk Trends, 2017

Disability Status

Category	MSA[1] (%)	U.S. (%)
Adults who reported being deaf	n/a	6.7
Are you blind or have serious difficulty seeing, even when wearing glasses?	n/a	4.5
Are you limited in any way in any of your usual activities due of arthritis?	n/a	12.9
Do you have difficulty doing errands alone?	n/a	6.8
Do you have difficulty dressing or bathing?	n/a	3.6
Do you have serious difficulty concentrating/remembering/making decisions?	n/a	10.7
Do you have serious difficulty walking or climbing stairs?	n/a	13.6

Note: n/a not available; (1) Figures cover the Davenport-Moline-Rock Island, IA-IL Metropolitan Statistical Area—see Appendix B for areas included.
Source: Centers for Disease Control and Prevention, Behaviorial Risk Factor Surveillance System, SMART: Selected Metropolitan Area Risk Trends, 2017

Mortality Rates for the Top 10 Causes of Death in the U.S.

ICD-10[a] Sub-Chapter	ICD-10[a] Code	Age-Adjusted Mortality Rate[1] per 100,000 population	
		County[2]	U.S.
Malignant neoplasms	C00-C97	161.5	152.4
Ischaemic heart diseases	I20-I25	76.0	92.7
Other forms of heart disease	I30-I51	51.3	52.5
Chronic lower respiratory diseases	J40-J47	53.6	40.4
Cerebrovascular diseases	I60-I69	35.3	37.3
Other degenerative diseases of the nervous system	G30-G31	33.7	36.4
Other external causes of accidental injury	W00-X59	34.6	35.3
Organic, including symptomatic, mental disorders	F01-F09	39.3	30.0
Hypertensive diseases	I10-I15	25.7	22.9
Diabetes mellitus	E10-E14	20.8	21.3

Note: (a) ICD-10 = International Classification of Diseases 10th Revision; (1) Mortality rates are a three year average covering 2016-2018; (2) Figures cover Scott County.
Source: Centers for Disease Control and Prevention, National Center for Health Statistics. Underlying Cause of Death 1999-2018 on CDC WONDER Online Database

Mortality Rates for Selected Causes of Death

ICD-10[a] Sub-Chapter	ICD-10[a] Code	Age-Adjusted Mortality Rate[1] per 100,000 population	
		County[2]	U.S.
Assault	X85-Y09	4.1	6.0
Diseases of the liver	K70-K76	13.9	14.2
Human immunodeficiency virus (HIV) disease	B20-B24	Suppressed	1.6
Influenza and pneumonia	J09-J18	11.9	14.2
Intentional self-harm	X60-X84	14.4	13.9
Malnutrition	E40-E46	Unreliable	1.9
Obesity and other hyperalimentation	E65-E68	4.2	2.1
Renal failure	N17-N19	13.9	12.8
Transport accidents	V01-V99	10.4	12.5
Viral hepatitis	B15-B19	Suppressed	1.4

Note: (a) ICD-10 = International Classification of Diseases 10th Revision; (1) Mortality rates are a three year average covering 2016-2018; (2) Figures cover Scott County; Data are suppressed when the data meet the criteria for confidentiality constraints; Mortality rates are flagged as unreliable when the rate would be calculated with a numerator of 20 or less.
Source: Centers for Disease Control and Prevention, National Center for Health Statistics. Underlying Cause of Death 1999-2018 on CDC WONDER Online Database

Health Insurance Coverage

Area	With Health Insurance	With Private Health Insurance	With Public Health Insurance	Without Health Insurance	Population Under Age 19 Without Health Insurance
City	94.1	66.6	38.9	5.9	2.1
MSA[1]	94.9	72.8	36.9	5.1	2.1
U.S.	90.6	67.7	34.7	9.4	5.2

Note: Figures are percentages that cover the civilian noninstitutionalized population; (1) Figures cover the Davenport-Moline-Rock Island, IA-IL Metropolitan Statistical Area—see Appendix B for areas included
Source: U.S. Census Bureau, 2014-2018 American Community Survey 5-Year Estimates

Number of Medical Professionals

Area	MDs[3]	DOs[3,4]	Dentists	Podiatrists	Chiropractors	Optometrists
County[1] (number)	400	89	131	6	314	28
County[1] (rate[2])	231.9	51.6	75.6	3.5	181.2	16.2
U.S. (rate[2])	281.9	23.4	69.1	6.0	27.5	16.4

Note: Data as of 2018 unless noted; (1) Data covers Scott County; (2) Rate per 100,000 population; (3) Data as of 2017 and includes all active, non-federal physicians; (4) Doctor of Osteopathic Medicine
Source: U.S. Department of Health and Human Services, Health Resources and Services Administration, Bureau of Health Professions, Area Resource File (ARF) 2018-2019

EDUCATION

Public School District Statistics

District Name	Schls	Pupils	Pupil/ Teacher Ratio	Minority Pupils[1] (%)	Free Lunch Eligible[2] (%)	IEP[3] (%)
Davenport Comm School District	30	15,519	13.2	45.4	57.6	19.1

Note: Table includes school districts with 2,000 or more students; (1) Percentage of students that are not non-Hispanic white; (2) Percentage of students that are eligible for the free lunch program; (3) Percentage of students that have an Individualized Education Program.
Source: U.S. Department of Education, National Center for Education Statistics, Common Core of Data, Local Education Agency (School District) Universe Survey: School Year 2018-2019; U.S. Department of Education, National Center for Education Statistics, Common Core of Data, Public Elementary/Secondary School Universe Survey: School Year 2018-2019

Highest Level of Education

Area	Less than H.S.	H.S. Diploma	Some College, No Deg.	Associate Degree	Bachelor's Degree	Master's Degree	Prof. School Degree	Doctorate Degree
City	9.3	32.8	21.4	10.2	17.5	6.7	1.4	0.7
MSA[1]	9.0	30.8	23.0	10.4	17.1	7.3	1.6	0.8
U.S.	12.3	27.1	20.6	8.4	19.4	8.6	2.1	1.4

Note: Figures cover persons age 25 and over; (1) Figures cover the Davenport-Moline-Rock Island, IA-IL Metropolitan Statistical Area—see Appendix B for areas included
Source: U.S. Census Bureau, 2014-2018 American Community Survey 5-Year Estimates

Educational Attainment by Race

Area	High School Graduate or Higher (%)					Bachelor's Degree or Higher (%)				
	Total	White	Black	Asian	Hisp.[2]	Total	White	Black	Asian	Hisp.[2]
City	90.7	92.1	81.8	82.1	73.9	26.2	27.6	12.6	36.8	14.7
MSA[1]	91.0	92.4	79.9	83.8	72.6	26.7	27.2	16.1	48.0	15.7
U.S.	87.7	89.6	85.4	86.8	67.7	31.5	32.9	21.1	53.5	15.8

Note: Figures shown cover persons 25 years old and over; (1) Figures cover the Davenport-Moline-Rock Island, IA-IL Metropolitan Statistical Area—see Appendix B for areas included; (2) People of Hispanic origin can be of any race
Source: U.S. Census Bureau, 2014-2018 American Community Survey 5-Year Estimates

School Enrollment by Grade and Control

Area	Preschool (%)		Kindergarten (%)		Grades 1 - 4 (%)		Grades 5 - 8 (%)		Grades 9 - 12 (%)	
	Public	Private	Public	Private	Public	Private	Public	Private	Public	Private
City	68.6	31.4	86.3	13.7	88.4	11.6	85.7	14.3	94.0	6.0
MSA[1]	72.0	28.0	88.4	11.6	91.3	8.7	91.4	8.6	93.9	6.1
U.S.	59.0	41.0	87.7	12.3	89.6	10.4	89.5	10.5	90.2	9.8

Note: Figures shown cover persons 3 years old and over; (1) Figures cover the Davenport-Moline-Rock Island, IA-IL Metropolitan Statistical Area—see Appendix B for areas included
Source: U.S. Census Bureau, 2014-2018 American Community Survey 5-Year Estimates

Average Salaries of Public School Teachers

Area	2016-17		2017-18		Change from 2016-17 to 2017-18	
	Dollars	Rank[1]	Dollars	Rank[1]	Percent	Rank[2]
Iowa	55,647	21	57,018	21	2.46	8
U.S. Average	59,539	–	60,477	–	1.58	–

Note: (1) Rank ranges from 1 to 51 where 1 indicates highest salary; (2) Rank ranges from 1 to 51 where 1 indicates highest percent change.
Source: National Education Association, Rankings & Estimates: Rankings of the States 2018 and Estimates of School Statistics 2019

Higher Education

Four-Year Colleges			Two-Year Colleges			Medical Schools[1]	Law Schools[2]	Voc/ Tech[3]
Public	Private Non-profit	Private For-profit	Public	Private Non-profit	Private For-profit			
1	2	1	1	0	2	0	0	0

Note: Figures cover institutions located within the city limits and include main campuses only; (1) includes schools accredited by the Liaison Committee on Medical Education and the American Osteopathic Association's Commission on Osteopathic College Accreditation; (2) includes ABA-accredited schools, schools with provisional ABA accreditation, and state accredited schools; (3) includes all schools with programs that are less than 2 years.
Source: National Center for Education Statistics, Integrated Postsecondary Education System (IPEDS), 2018-19; Wikipedia, List of Medical Schools in the United States, accessed May 1, 2020; Wikipedia, List of Law Schools in the United States, accessed May 1, 2020

According to *U.S. News & World Report,* the Davenport-Moline-Rock Island, IA-IL metro area is home to one of the top 100 liberal arts colleges in the U.S.: **Augustana College** (#92 tie). The indicators used to capture academic quality fall into a number of categories: assessment by administrators at peer institutions; retention of students; faculty resources; student selectivity; financial resources; alumni giving; high school counselor ratings of colleges; and graduation rate. *U.S. News & World Report, "America's Best Colleges 2020"*

PRESIDENTIAL ELECTION

2016 Presidential Election Results

Area	Clinton	Trump	Johnson	Stein	Other
Scott County	46.9	45.4	4.1	0.9	2.7
U.S.	48.0	45.9	3.3	1.1	1.7

Note: Results are percentages and may not add to 100% due to rounding
Source: Dave Leip's Atlas of U.S. Presidential Elections

EMPLOYERS

Major Employers

Company Name	Industry
Alcoa	Manufacturer
Deere and Company	Manufacturer
Genesis Health System	Healthcare
HNI Corporation/The Hon Company/Allsteel	Manufacturer
Hy-Vee Food Stores	Grocery stores
Kraft Foods/Oscar Mayer	Food processing
Rock Island Arsenal	U.S. military
Trinity Regional Health System	Healthcare
Tyson Fresh Meats	Food processing
XPAC	Service, parts, packaging

Note: Companies shown are located within the Davenport-Moline-Rock Island, IA-IL Metropolitan Statistical Area.
Source: Hoovers.com; Wikipedia

PUBLIC SAFETY

Crime Rate

Area	All Crimes	Violent Crimes				Property Crimes		
		Murder	Rape[3]	Robbery	Aggrav. Assault	Burglary	Larceny -Theft	Motor Vehicle Theft
City	5,820.7	12.6	87.3	197.0	430.8	1,075.1	3,479.4	538.5
Suburbs[1]	2,285.2	1.8	45.4	24.0	213.6	396.8	1,486.5	117.0
Metro[2]	3,237.8	4.7	56.7	70.6	272.1	579.6	2,023.4	230.6
U.S.	2,757.7	5.3	41.7	98.6	249.2	429.7	1,695.5	237.7

Note: Figures are crimes per 100,000 population; (1) All areas within the metro area that are located outside the city limits; (2) Figures cover the Davenport-Moline-Rock Island, IA-IL Metropolitan Statistical Area—see Appendix B for areas included; (3) The city and U.S. figures shown were reported using the revised Uniform Crime Reporting (UCR) definition of rape. The suburban and metro area figures shown are an aggregate total of the data submitted using both the revised and legacy UCR definitions.
Source: FBI Uniform Crime Reports, 2017 (data for 2018 was not available)

Hate Crimes

Area	Number of Quarters Reported	Number of Incidents per Bias Motivation					
		Race/Ethnicity/ Ancestry	Religion	Sexual Orientation	Disability	Gender	Gender Identity
City	4	0	0	0	0	0	0
U.S.	4	4,047	1,419	1,196	159	47	168

Source: Federal Bureau of Investigation, Hate Crime Statistics 2018

Identity Theft Consumer Reports

Area	Reports	Reports per 100,000 Population	Rank[2]
MSA[1]	283	74	277
U.S.	650,572	198	-

Note: (1) Figures cover the Davenport-Moline-Rock Island, IA-IL Metropolitan Statistical Area—see Appendix B for areas included; (2) Rank ranges from 1 to 386 where 1 indicates greatest number of identity theft reports per 100,000 population
Source: Federal Trade Commission, Consumer Sentinel Network Data Book for January–December 2019

Fraud and Other Consumer Reports

Area	Reports	Reports per 100,000 Population	Rank[2]
MSA[1]	1,745	457	315
U.S.	2,590,177	789	-

Note: (1) Figures cover the Davenport-Moline-Rock Island, IA-IL Metropolitan Statistical Area—see Appendix B for areas included; (2) Rank ranges from 1 to 386 where 1 indicates greatest number of fraud and other consumer reports per 100,000 population
Source: Federal Trade Commission, Consumer Sentinel Network Data Book for January–December 2019

SPORTS

Professional Sports Teams

Team Name	League	Year Established
No teams are located in the metro area		

Source: Wikipedia, Major Professional Sports Teams of the United States and Canada, May 4, 2020

CLIMATE

Average and Extreme Temperatures

Temperature	Jan	Feb	Mar	Apr	May	Jun	Jul	Aug	Sep	Oct	Nov	Dec	Yr.
Extreme High (°F)	65	70	91	93	98	103	105	108	99	95	76	69	108
Average High (°F)	29	34	45	61	72	82	86	84	76	65	48	33	60
Average Temp. (°F)	20	25	36	51	62	72	76	74	65	54	39	25	50
Average Low (°F)	11	16	27	40	51	61	66	64	54	43	29	17	40
Extreme Low (°F)	-24	-20	-22	9	28	42	47	40	28	14	-3	-22	-24

Note: Figures cover the years 1945-1990
Source: National Climatic Data Center, International Station Meteorological Climate Summary, 9/96

Average Precipitation/Snowfall/Humidity

Precip./Humidity	Jan	Feb	Mar	Apr	May	Jun	Jul	Aug	Sep	Oct	Nov	Dec	Yr.
Avg. Precip. (in.)	1.1	1.1	2.3	3.1	3.8	4.4	3.5	3.9	3.1	2.4	1.7	1.2	31.8
Avg. Snowfall (in.)	8	7	7	2	Tr	0	0	0	Tr	Tr	3	7	33
Avg. Rel. Hum. 6am (%)	77	79	79	78	78	81	83	86	85	80	79	80	80
Avg. Rel. Hum. 3pm (%)	65	63	57	50	51	52	52	54	52	50	58	66	56

Note: Figures cover the years 1945-1990; Tr = Trace amounts (<0.05 in. of rain; <0.5 in. of snow)
Source: National Climatic Data Center, International Station Meteorological Climate Summary, 9/96

Weather Conditions

Temperature			Daytime Sky			Precipitation		
5°F & below	32°F & below	90°F & above	Clear	Partly cloudy	Cloudy	0.01 inch or more precip.	0.1 inch or more snow/ice	Thunder-storms
25	137	26	99	128	138	106	25	46

Note: Figures are average number of days per year and cover the years 1945-1990
Source: National Climatic Data Center, International Station Meteorological Climate Summary, 9/96

HAZARDOUS WASTE

Superfund Sites

The Davenport-Moline-Rock Island, IA-IL metro area has no sites on the EPA's Superfund Final National Priorities List. There are a total of 1,387 Superfund sites with a status of proposed or final on the list in the U.S. *U.S. Environmental Protection Agency, National Priorities List, May 5, 2020*

AIR & WATER QUALITY

Air Quality Trends: Ozone

	1990	1995	2000	2005	2010	2012	2014	2016	2017	2018
MSA[1]	n/a	n/a	n/a	n/a	n/a	n/a	n/a	n/a	n/a	n/a
U.S.	0.088	0.089	0.082	0.080	0.073	0.075	0.067	0.069	0.068	0.069

Note: (1) Data covers the Davenport-Moline-Rock Island, IA-IL Metropolitan Statistical Area—see Appendix B for areas included; n/a not available. The values shown are the composite ozone concentration averages among trend sites based on the highest fourth daily maximum 8-hour concentration in parts per million. These trends are based on sites having an adequate record of monitoring data during the trend period. Data from exceptional events are included.
Source: U.S. Environmental Protection Agency, Air Quality Monitoring Information, "Air Quality Trends by City, 1990-2018"

Air Quality Index

Area	Percent of Days when Air Quality was...[2]					AQI Statistics[2]	
	Good	Moderate	Unhealthy for Sensitive Groups	Unhealthy	Very Unhealthy	Maximum	Median
MSA[1]	47.1	51.8	1.1	0.0	0.0	108	52

Note: (1) Data covers the Davenport-Moline-Rock Island, IA-IL Metropolitan Statistical Area—see Appendix B for areas included; (2) Based on 365 days with AQI data in 2018. Air Quality Index (AQI) is an index for reporting daily air quality. EPA calculates the AQI for five major air pollutants regulated by the Clean Air Act: ground-level ozone, particle pollution (aka particulate matter), carbon monoxide, sulfur dioxide, and nitrogen dioxide. The AQI runs from 0 to 500. The higher the AQI value, the greater the level of air pollution and the greater the health concern. There are six AQI categories: "Good" AQI is between 0 and 50. Air quality is considered satisfactory; "Moderate" AQI is between 51 and 100. Air quality is acceptable; "Unhealthy for Sensitive Groups" When AQI values are between 101 and 150, members of sensitive groups may experience health effects; "Unhealthy" When AQI values are between 151 and 200 everyone may begin to experience health effects; "Very Unhealthy" AQI values between 201 and 300 trigger a health alert; "Hazardous" AQI values over 300 trigger warnings of emergency conditions (not shown).
Source: U.S. Environmental Protection Agency, Air Quality Index Report, 2018

Air Quality Index Pollutants

Area	Percent of Days when AQI Pollutant was...[2]					
	Carbon Monoxide	Nitrogen Dioxide	Ozone	Sulfur Dioxide	Particulate Matter 2.5	Particulate Matter 10
MSA[1]	0.0	0.3	22.5	0.0	52.9	24.4

Note: (1) Data covers the Davenport-Moline-Rock Island, IA-IL Metropolitan Statistical Area—see Appendix B for areas included; (2) Based on 365 days with AQI data in 2018. The Air Quality Index (AQI) is an index for reporting daily air quality. EPA calculates the AQI for five major air pollutants regulated by the Clean Air Act: ground-level ozone, particle pollution (also known as particulate matter), carbon monoxide, sulfur dioxide, and nitrogen dioxide. The AQI runs from 0 to 500. The higher the AQI value, the greater the level of air pollution and the greater the health concern.
Source: U.S. Environmental Protection Agency, Air Quality Index Report, 2018

Maximum Air Pollutant Concentrations: Particulate Matter, Ozone, CO and Lead

	Particulate Matter 10 (ug/m³)	Particulate Matter 2.5 Wtd AM (ug/m³)	Particulate Matter 2.5 24-Hr (ug/m³)	Ozone (ppm)	Carbon Monoxide (ppm)	Lead (ug/m³)
MSA[1] Level	140	8.8	21	0.071	1	n/a
NAAQS[2]	150	15	35	0.075	9	0.15
Met NAAQS[2]	Yes	Yes	Yes	Yes	Yes	n/a

Note: (1) Data covers the Davenport-Moline-Rock Island, IA-IL Metropolitan Statistical Area—see Appendix B for areas included; Data from exceptional events are included; (2) National Ambient Air Quality Standards; ppm = parts per million; ug/m³ = micrograms per cubic meter; n/a not available.
Concentrations: Particulate Matter 10 (coarse particulate)—highest second maximum 24-hour concentration; Particulate Matter 2.5 Wtd AM (fine particulate)—highest weighted annual mean concentration; Particulate Matter 2.5 24-Hour (fine particulate)—highest 98th percentile 24-hour concentration; Ozone—highest fourth daily maximum 8-hour concentration; Carbon Monoxide—highest second maximum non-overlapping 8-hour concentration; Lead—maximum running 3-month average
Source: U.S. Environmental Protection Agency, Air Quality Monitoring Information, "Air Quality Statistics by City, 2018"

Maximum Air Pollutant Concentrations: Nitrogen Dioxide and Sulfur Dioxide

	Nitrogen Dioxide AM (ppb)	Nitrogen Dioxide 1-Hr (ppb)	Sulfur Dioxide AM (ppb)	Sulfur Dioxide 1-Hr (ppb)	Sulfur Dioxide 24-Hr (ppb)
MSA[1] Level	6	30	n/a	5	n/a
NAAQS[2]	53	100	30	75	140
Met NAAQS[2]	Yes	Yes	n/a	Yes	n/a

Note: (1) Data covers the Davenport-Moline-Rock Island, IA-IL Metropolitan Statistical Area—see Appendix B for areas included; Data from exceptional events are included; (2) National Ambient Air Quality Standards; ppm = parts per million; ug/m³ = micrograms per cubic meter; n/a not available.
Concentrations: Nitrogen Dioxide AM—highest arithmetic mean concentration; Nitrogen Dioxide 1-Hr—highest 98th percentile 1-hour daily maximum concentration; Sulfur Dioxide AM—highest annual mean concentration; Sulfur Dioxide 1-Hr—highest 99th percentile 1-hour daily maximum concentration; Sulfur Dioxide 24-Hr—highest second maximum 24-hour concentration
Source: U.S. Environmental Protection Agency, Air Quality Monitoring Information, "Air Quality Statistics by City, 2018"

Drinking Water

Water System Name	Pop. Served	Primary Water Source Type	Violations[1]
Iowa-American Water Co.-Davenport	138,653	Surface	4

Note: (1) Total number of violations (both active and inactive) in the EPA database
Source: U.S. Environmental Protection Agency, Office of Ground Water and Drinking Water, Safe Drinking Water Information System (based on data extracted May 5, 2020)

Des Moines, Iowa

Background

In 1843, Fort Des Moines was founded at the confluence of the Des Moines and Raccoon rivers. Though the fort was initially established to protect local Native American populations, within two years the area was opened to white settlers. By 1857, the state capital was moved from Iowa City to Des Moines. Today, Des Moines remains the capital of Iowa and is its largest city.

The city frequently finds itself near the top of best-of lists extolling its reasonable cost of living, quality of life, or job opportunities. It has taken an active role in acquiring properties in its downtown for redevelopment, and also takes a progressive approach to planning, having joined with other counties and regional partners to plan for transportation and other future needs. The Capital Corridor encourages the development of creative high-value growth and development for industry, including animal science.

Des Moines's significant industries include the financial services industry; Greater Des Moines has the nation's highest concentration of employment in this sector. Additionally, logistics, bioscience, and data centers are significant economic sectors.

Greater Des Moines is home to the first statewide fiber optics network in the country. The city proper also boasts world-class architecture. The Des Moines Art Center was designed in 1944 by Eliel Saarinen, a Finnish architect and then-president of the renowned Cranbrook Academy of Art in Detroit. In 1968, I.M. Pei, architect of the Pyramid du Louvre and the East Wing of the National Gallery of Art in Washington, D.C., designed a gallery addition to the main Art Center structure. In 1985, Richard Meier, who had designed the Museum of Modern Art in Florence, Italy, designed an addition to the Art Center's north wing and went on to design the famed Getty Center in Los Angeles. The city's Home Federal Savings and Loan Building was designed by Mies van der Rohe, of the famous German Bauhaus School of Design, and a sculpture called The Crusoe Umbrella, designed by pop artist Claes Oldenberg, stands in the middle of Nollen Plaza, a wooded park and popular gathering place.

The Greater Des Moines Botanical Center has been renovated to include Iowa's first "living wall," a new office suite and lobby, and improvements to the center's gardens.

Des Moines Civic Center offers ballet, symphony and other performances. The Science Center of Iowa features hands-on science and technology exhibits, an IMAX theater, and a planetarium with an interactive program and laser light show.

Every four years, Des Moines becomes the center of national attention as correspondents from all over the U.S. and abroad arrive to cover the Iowa political caucuses, which has become a financial boon for the state.

Located in the heart of North America, Des Moines has a continental climate, resulting in a seasonal contrast in both temperature and precipitation. Exceptionally high summer rains have caused the nearby Des Moines River and Raccoon River to breach the city's levees on two occasions, in 1993 and again in 2008. The winter is a season of cold, dry air, interrupted by occasional storms of short duration. The autumn is characteristically sunny with diminishing precipitation.

Rankings

General Rankings

- *US News & World Report* conducted a survey of more than 2,000 people and analyzed the 125 largest metropolitan areas to determine what matters the most when selecting the next place to live. Des Moines ranked #5 out of the top 25 as having the best combination of desirable factors. Criteria: cost of living; quality of life; net migration; job market; desirability; and other factors. *realestate.usnews.com, "The 25 Best Places to Live in the U.S. in 2019," April 9, 2019*

- The Des Moines metro area was identified as one of America's fastest-growing areas in terms of population and business growth by *MagnifyMoney*. The area ranked #15 out of 35. The 100 most populous metro areas in the U.S. were evaluated on their change from 2011-2016 in the following categories: people and housing; workforce and employment opportunities; growing industry. *www.businessinsider.com, "The 35 Cities in the US with the Biggest Influx of People, the Most Work Opportunities, and the Hottest Business Growth," August 12, 2018*

- Des Moines was selected as one of the best places to live in the United States by *Money* magazine. The city ranked #62 out of 100. This year's list focused on cities with populations of 50,000 or greater. Beginning with a pool of 1,796 candidates, editors looked at 80 separate types of data, from local economy and housing market to education, diversity and ease of living—and then sent reporters to interview residents, search neighborhoods and look for other intangibles. *Money, "Best Places to Live, 2019" September 16, 2019*

- In their sixth annual survey, Livability.com looked at data for more than 1,000 U.S. cities to determine the rankings for Livability's "Top 100 Best Places to Live" in 2019. Des Moines ranked #96. Criteria: median home value capped at $250,000; affordable living; vibrant economy; education, demographics, health care options. transportation & infrastructure; abundant lifestyle amenities. *Livability.com, "Top 100 Best Places to Live 2019" March 2019*

Business/Finance Rankings

- Des Moines was the #10-ranked city for savers, according to a study by the finance site GOBankingRates, which considered the prospects for people trying to save money. Criteria: average monthly cost of grocery items; median home listing price; median rent; median income; transportation costs; gas prices; and the cost of eating out for an inexpensive and mid-range meal in 100 U.S. cities. *www.gobankingrates.com, "The 20 Best (and Worst) Places to Live If You're Trying to Save Money," August 27, 2019*

- Des Moines was ranked #10 among 100 U.S. cities for most difficult conditions for savers, according to a study by the finance site GOBankingRates. Criteria: average monthly cost of grocery items; median home listing price; median rent; median income; transportation costs; gas prices; and the cost of eating out for an inexpensive and mid-range meal. *www.gobankingrates.com, "The 20 Best (and Worst) Places to Live If You're Trying to Save Money," August 27, 2019*

- The Brookings Institution ranked the nation's largest cities based on income inequality. Des Moines was ranked #88 (#1 = greatest inequality). Criteria: the "95/20 ratio," a figure representing the income at which a household earns more than 95 percent of all other households, divided by the income at which a household earns more than only 20 percent of all other households. *Brookings Institution, "Household Income Inequality, Largest Cities of 97 Large U.S. Metro Areas, 2014-2016," February 5, 2018*

- The Brookings Institution ranked the 100 largest metro areas in the U.S. based on income inequality. Des Moines was ranked #93 (#1 = greatest inequality). Criteria: the "95/20 ratio," a figure representing the income at which a household earns more than 95 percent of all other households, divided by the income at which a household earns more than only 20 percent of all other households. *Brookings Institution, "Household Income Inequality, 100 Largest U.S. Metro Areas, 2014-2016," February 5, 2018*

- Des Moines was cited as one of America's top metros for new and expanded facility projects in 2019. The area ranked #5 in the mid-sized metro area category (population 200,000 to 1 million). *Site Selection, "Top Metros of 2019," March 2020*

- The Des Moines metro area appeared on the Milken Institute "2020 Best Performing Cities" list. Rank: #79 out of 200 large metro areas. Criteria: job growth; wage and salary growth; high-tech output growth. *Milken Institute, "Best-Performing Cities 2020," February 26, 2020*

- *Forbes* ranked the 200 most populous metro areas to determine the nation's "Best Places for Business and Careers." The Des Moines metro area was ranked #10. Criteria: costs (business and living); job growth (past and projected); income growth; quality of life; educational attainment (college and high school); projected economic growth; cultural and leisure opportunities; workplace tolerance laws; net migration patterns. *Forbes, "The Best Places for Business and Careers 2019: Seattle Still On Top," October 30, 2019*

Children/Family Rankings

- *Forbes* analyzed data on the 100 largest metropolitan areas in the United States to compile its 2016 ranking of the best cities for raising a family. The Des Moines metro area was ranked #11. Criteria: median income; childcare costs; percent of population under 18; commuting delays; crime rate; percentage of families owning homes; education quality (mainly test scores). Overall cost of living and housing affordability was also unofficially considered. *Forbes, "America's Best Cities for Raising a Family 2016," August 30, 2016*

Dating/Romance Rankings

- Des Moines was ranked #6 out of 25 cities that stood out for inspiring romance and attracting diners on the website OpenTable.com. Criteria: percentage of people who dined out on Valentine's Day in 2018; percentage of romantic restaurants as rated by OpenTable diner reviews; and percentage of tables seated for two. *OpenTable, "25 Most Romantic Cities in America for 2019," February 7, 2019*

Education Rankings

- Personal finance website *WalletHub* analyzed the 150 largest U.S. metropolitan statistical areas to determine where the most educated Americans are choosing to settle. Criteria: education levels; percentage of workers with degrees; education quality and attainment gap; public school quality rankings; quality and size of each metro area's universities. Des Moines was ranked #44 (#1 = most educated city). *www.WalletHub.com, "2019's Most and Least Educated Cities in America," July 22, 2019*

Environmental Rankings

- The U.S. Environmental Protection Agency (EPA) released a list of mid-size U.S. metropolitan areas with the most ENERGY STAR certified buildings in 2017. The Des Moines metro area was ranked #7 out of 10. *U.S. Environmental Protection Agency, "2018 Energy Star Top Cities," April 11, 2018*

- Des Moines was highlighted as one of the cleanest metro areas for ozone air pollution in the U.S. during 2015 through 2017. The list represents cities with no monitored ozone air pollution in unhealthful ranges. *American Lung Association, "State of the Air 2019," April 24, 2019*

Health/Fitness Rankings

- Des Moines was identified as a "2020 Spring Allergy Capital." The area ranked #57 out of 100. Three groups of factors were used to identify the most challenging cities for people with allergies during the spring season: annual spring pollen levels; over the counter medicine use; number of board-certified allergy specialists. *Asthma and Allergy Foundation of America, "Spring Allergy Capitals 2020," March 10, 2020*

- Des Moines was identified as a "2020 Fall Allergy Capital." The area ranked #44 out of 100. Three groups of factors were used to identify the most challenging cities for people with allergies during the fall season: annual fall pollen levels; over the counter medicine use; number of board-certified allergy specialists. *Asthma and Allergy Foundation of America, "Fall Allergy Capitals 2020," March 10, 2020*

- Des Moines was identified as a "2019 Asthma Capital." The area ranked #60 out of the nation's 100 largest metropolitan areas. Criteria: estimated asthma prevalence; crude death rate from asthma; and ER visits due to asthma. Risk factors that were analyzed but not factored in the rankings: annual pollen score; annual air quality; public smoking laws; number of board-certified asthma specialists; rescue medication use; controller medication use; uninsured rate; poverty rate. *Asthma and Allergy Foundation of America, "Asthma Capitals 2019: The Most Challenging Places to Live With Asthma," May 7, 2019*

- *Men's Health* ranked 100 major U.S. cities in terms of the best cities for men. Des Moines ranked #41. Criteria: health; fitness; quality of life. *Men's Health, "The Best & Worst Cities for Men Who Want to Be Fit and Happy," January 1, 2016*

- The Des Moines metro area ranked #52 out of 189 in The Gallup-Sharecare Well-Being Index. Criteria: purpose; social well being; financial health; community and physical health. Results are based on telephone interviews with adults, aged 18 and older, living in metropolitan areas in the 50 U.S. states and the District of Columbia. *Gallup-Sharecare, "State of American Well-Being, 2017 Community Well-Being Rankings" March 2018*

Real Estate Rankings

- *WalletHub* compared the most populated U.S. cities, as well as at least two of the most populated cities in each state, for a total of 179, to determine which had the best markets for real estate agents. Des Moines ranked #117 where demand was high and pay was the best. Criteria: sales per agent; annual median wage for real-estate agents; monthly average starting salary for real estate agents; real estate job density and competition; unemployment rate; home turnover rate; housing-market health index; and other relevant metrics. *www.WalletHub.com, "2019's Best Places to Be a Real Estate Agent," April 24, 2019*

Safety Rankings

- Allstate ranked the 200 largest cities in America in terms of driver safety. Des Moines ranked #38. Criteria: internal property damage claims over a two-year period from January 2016 to December 2017. The report helps increase the importance of safety and awareness behind the wheel. *Allstate, "Allstate America's Best Drivers Report, 2019" June 24, 2019*

- The National Insurance Crime Bureau ranked 382 metro areas in the U.S. in terms of per capita rates of vehicle theft. The Des Moines metro area ranked #105 (#1 = highest rate). Criteria: number of vehicle theft offenses per 100,000 inhabitants in 2018. *National Insurance Crime Bureau, "Hot Spots 2018," June 25, 2019*

Seniors/Retirement Rankings

- From its Best Cities for Successful Aging indexes, the Milken Institute generated rankings for metropolitan areas, weighing data in nine categories—health care, wellness, living arrangements, transportation and convenience, financial characteristics, education, employment, community engagement, and overall livability. The Des Moines metro area was ranked #5 overall in the large metro area category. *Milken Institute, "Best Cities for Successful Aging, 2017" March 14, 2017*

Sports/Recreation Rankings

- Des Moines was chosen as one of America's best cities for bicycling. The city ranked #38 out of 50. Criteria: cycling infrastructure that is safe and friendly for all ages; energy and bike culture. The editors only considered cities with populations of 100,000 or more. *Bicycling, "The 50 Best Bike Cities in America," October 10, 2018*

Women/Minorities Rankings

- Personal finance website *WalletHub* compared more than 180 U.S. cities—including the 150 most populated U.S. cities, plus at least two of the most populated cities in each state—across two key dimensions, "Hispanic Business-Friendliness" and "Hispanic Purchasing Power", to arrive at the most favorable conditions for Hispanic entrepreneurs. Des Moines was ranked #158 out of 182. Criteria includes: share of Hispanic-Owned Businesses; Hispanic entrepreneurship rate to median annual income of Hispanics; Small Business-Friendliness score; cost of living; and number of Hispanics with at least a bachelor's degree. *WalletHub.com, "2019's Best Cities for Hispanic Entrepreneurs," May 1, 2019*

Miscellaneous Rankings

- In *Condé Nast Traveler* magazine's 2018 Readers' Choice Survey, Des Moines made the top ten list of friendliest American cities. *www.cntraveler.com, "The Friendliest Cities in the U.S.," August 8, 2018*

- *WalletHub* compared the 150 most populated U.S. cities to determine their operating efficiency. A "Quality of Services" score was constructed for each city and then divided by the total budget per capita to reveal which were managed the best. Des Moines ranked #50. Criteria: financial stability; economy; education; safety; health; infrastructure and pollution. *www.WalletHub.com, "2019's Best- & Worst-Run Cities in America," July 1, 2019*

Business Environment

CITY FINANCES

City Government Finances

Component	2017 ($000)	2017 ($ per capita)
Total Revenues	528,256	2,512
Total Expenditures	483,529	2,299
Debt Outstanding	561,365	2,669
Cash and Securities[1]	350,621	1,667

Note: (1) Cash and security holdings of a government at the close of its fiscal year, including those of its dependent agencies, utilities, and liquor stores.
Source: U.S. Census Bureau, State & Local Government Finances 2017

City Government Revenue by Source

Source	2017 ($000)	2017 ($ per capita)	2017 (%)
General Revenue			
From Federal Government	46,747	222	8.8
From State Government	37,771	180	7.2
From Local Governments	11,529	55	2.2
Taxes			
Property	143,562	683	27.2
Sales and Gross Receipts	34,489	164	6.5
Personal Income	0	0	0.0
Corporate Income	0	0	0.0
Motor Vehicle License	0	0	0.0
Other Taxes	5,268	25	1.0
Current Charges	144,447	687	27.3
Liquor Store	0	0	0.0
Utility	59,915	285	11.3
Employee Retirement	4,666	22	0.9

Source: U.S. Census Bureau, State & Local Government Finances 2017

City Government Expenditures by Function

Function	2017 ($000)	2017 ($ per capita)	2017 (%)
General Direct Expenditures			
Air Transportation	35,144	167	7.3
Corrections	0	0	0.0
Education	0	0	0.0
Employment Security Administration	0	0	0.0
Financial Administration	3,428	16	0.7
Fire Protection	38,164	181	7.9
General Public Buildings	4,647	22	1.0
Governmental Administration, Other	3,223	15	0.7
Health	1,028	4	0.2
Highways	29,025	138	6.0
Hospitals	0	0	0.0
Housing and Community Development	19,989	95	4.1
Interest on General Debt	22,584	107	4.7
Judicial and Legal	1,821	8	0.4
Libraries	8,645	41	1.8
Parking	8,471	40	1.8
Parks and Recreation	10,271	48	2.1
Police Protection	64,042	304	13.2
Public Welfare	9,089	43	1.9
Sewerage	45,739	217	9.5
Solid Waste Management	11,691	55	2.4
Veterans' Services	0	0	0.0
Liquor Store	0	0	0.0
Utility	68,905	327	14.3
Employee Retirement	3,322	15	0.7

Source: U.S. Census Bureau, State & Local Government Finances 2017

DEMOGRAPHICS

Population Growth

Area	1990 Census	2000 Census	2010 Census	2018* Estimate	Population Growth (%)	
					1990-2018	2010-2018
City	193,569	198,682	203,433	215,932	11.6	6.1
MSA[1]	416,346	481,394	569,633	634,201	52.3	11.3
U.S.	248,709,873	281,421,906	308,745,538	322,903,030	29.8	4.6

Note: (1) Figures cover the Des Moines-West Des Moines, IA Metropolitan Statistical Area—see Appendix B for areas included; (*) 2014-2018 5-year estimated population
Source: U.S. Census Bureau, 1990 Census, Census 2000, Census 2010, 2014-2018 American Community Survey 5-Year Estimates

Household Size

Area	Persons in Household (%)							Average Household Size
	One	Two	Three	Four	Five	Six	Seven or More	
City	33.3	30.3	15.2	11.6	5.7	2.4	1.5	2.50
MSA[1]	27.8	34.0	15.0	13.7	6.5	2.2	0.9	2.50
U.S.	27.7	33.9	15.7	13.0	6.0	2.3	1.4	2.60

Note: (1) Figures cover the Des Moines-West Des Moines, IA Metropolitan Statistical Area—see Appendix B for areas included
Source: U.S. Census Bureau, 2014-2018 American Community Survey 5-Year Estimates

Race

Area	White Alone[2] (%)	Black Alone[2] (%)	Asian Alone[2] (%)	AIAN[3] Alone[2] (%)	NHOPI[4] Alone[2] (%)	Other Race Alone[2] (%)	Two or More Races (%)
City	75.4	11.3	6.5	0.4	0.1	2.3	4.0
MSA[1]	86.7	5.2	4.0	0.2	0.1	1.1	2.6
U.S.	72.7	12.7	5.4	0.8	0.2	4.9	3.2

Note: (1) Figures cover the Des Moines-West Des Moines, IA Metropolitan Statistical Area—see Appendix B for areas included; (2) Alone is defined as not being in combination with one or more other races; (3) American Indian and Alaska Native; (4) Native Hawaiian and Other Pacific Islander
Source: U.S. Census Bureau, 2014-2018 American Community Survey 5-Year Estimates

Hispanic or Latino Origin

Area	Total (%)	Mexican (%)	Puerto Rican (%)	Cuban (%)	Other (%)
City	13.3	10.6	0.3	0.1	2.2
MSA[1]	7.3	5.7	0.2	0.1	1.3
U.S.	17.8	11.2	1.7	0.7	4.2

Note: Persons of Hispanic or Latino origin can be of any race; (1) Figures cover the Des Moines-West Des Moines, IA Metropolitan Statistical Area—see Appendix B for areas included
Source: U.S. Census Bureau, 2014-2018 American Community Survey 5-Year Estimates

Segregation

Type	Segregation Indices[1]				Percent Change		
	1990	2000	2010	2010 Rank[2]	1990-2000	1990-2010	2000-2010
Black/White	65.2	58.6	51.6	66	-6.7	-13.7	-7.0
Asian/White	40.7	39.2	35.5	76	-1.5	-5.2	-3.8
Hispanic/White	32.6	47.5	46.7	40	14.9	14.1	-0.8

Note: All figures cover the Metropolitan Statistical Area—see Appendix B for areas included; Figures are based on an analysis of 1990, 2000, and 2010 Census Decennial Census tract data by William H. Frey, Brookings Institution and the University of Michigan Social Science Data Analysis Network. In this analysis all racial groups (whites, blacks, and asians) are non-Hispanic members of those races. Hispanics are shown as a separate category; (1) Segregation Indices are Dissimilarity Indices that measure the degree to which the minority group is distributed differently than whites across census tracts. They range from 0 (complete integration) to 100 (complete segregation) where the value indicates the percentage of the minority group that needs to move to be distributed exactly like whites; (2) Ranges from 1 (most segregated) to 102 (least segregated); n/a not available.
Source: www.CensusScope.org

Ancestry

Area	German	Irish	English	American	Italian	Polish	French[2]	Scottish	Dutch
City	20.4	11.5	6.6	3.9	3.8	1.0	1.9	1.4	2.7
MSA[1]	27.7	12.9	8.5	4.4	3.3	1.4	2.0	1.8	3.3
U.S.	13.7	9.9	7.3	6.4	5.2	2.8	2.4	1.7	1.2

Note: Figures are the percentage of the total population reporting a particular ancestry. The nine most commonly reported ancestries in the U.S. are shown. Figures include multiple ancestries (e.g. if a person reported being Irish and Italian, they were included in both columns); (1) Figures cover the Des Moines-West Des Moines, IA Metropolitan Statistical Area—see Appendix B for areas included; (2) Excludes Basque
Source: U.S. Census Bureau, 2014-2018 American Community Survey 5-Year Estimates

Foreign-born Population

Area	Percent of Population Born in								
	Any Foreign Country	Asia	Mexico	Europe	Caribbean	Central America[2]	South America	Africa	Canada
City	12.6	4.7	3.4	0.9	0.1	1.0	0.2	2.3	0.1
MSA[1]	7.9	3.1	1.6	1.2	0.1	0.5	0.2	1.2	0.1
U.S.	13.5	4.1	3.5	1.5	1.3	1.1	0.9	0.7	0.3

Note: (1) Figures cover the Des Moines-West Des Moines, IA Metropolitan Statistical Area—see Appendix B for areas included; (2) Excludes Mexico.
Source: U.S. Census Bureau, 2014-2018 American Community Survey 5-Year Estimates

Marital Status

Area	Never Married	Now Married[2]	Separated	Widowed	Divorced
City	38.4	40.4	1.9	5.3	13.9
MSA[1]	29.9	52.2	1.2	5.0	11.7
U.S.	33.3	48.1	2.0	5.8	10.8

Note: Figures are percentages and cover the population 15 years of age and older; (1) Figures cover the Des Moines-West Des Moines, IA Metropolitan Statistical Area—see Appendix B for areas included; (2) Excludes separated
Source: U.S. Census Bureau, 2014-2018 American Community Survey 5-Year Estimates

Disability by Age

Area	All Ages	Under 18 Years Old	18 to 64 Years Old	65 Years and Over
City	13.9	5.3	13.0	37.4
MSA[1]	10.5	3.8	9.1	31.4
U.S.	12.6	4.2	10.3	35.0

Note: Figures show percent of the civilian noninstitutionalized population that reported having a disability. Disability status is determined from six types of difficulty: vision, hearing, cognitive, ambulatory, self-care, and independent living. For children under 5 years old, hearing and vision difficulty are used to determine disability status. For children between the ages of 5 and 14, disability status is determined from hearing, vision, cognitive, ambulatory, and self-care difficulties. For people aged 15 years and older, they are considered to have a disability if they have difficulty with any one of the six difficulty types; Note: (1) Figures cover the Des Moines-West Des Moines, IA Metropolitan Statistical Area—see Appendix B for areas included
Source: U.S. Census Bureau, 2014-2018 American Community Survey 5-Year Estimates

Age

Area	Percent of Population									Median Age
	Under Age 5	Age 5–19	Age 20–34	Age 35–44	Age 45–54	Age 55–64	Age 65–74	Age 75–84	Age 85+	
City	6.9	20.5	24.2	13.1	12.0	11.7	6.7	3.3	1.6	33.9
MSA[1]	7.1	20.7	21.0	13.7	13.0	11.6	7.5	3.7	1.6	35.8
U.S.	6.1	19.3	20.7	12.6	13.2	12.8	8.8	4.5	1.9	37.9

Note: (1) Figures cover the Des Moines-West Des Moines, IA Metropolitan Statistical Area—see Appendix B for areas included
Source: U.S. Census Bureau, 2014-2018 American Community Survey 5-Year Estimates

Gender

Area	Males	Females	Males per 100 Females
City	106,266	109,666	96.9
MSA[1]	312,447	321,754	97.1
U.S.	158,984,190	163,918,840	97.0

Note: (1) Figures cover the Des Moines-West Des Moines, IA Metropolitan Statistical Area—see Appendix B for areas included
Source: U.S. Census Bureau, 2014-2018 American Community Survey 5-Year Estimates

Religious Groups by Family

Area	Catholic	Baptist	Non-Den.	Methodist[2]	Lutheran	LDS[3]	Pentecostal	Presbyterian[4]	Muslim[5]	Judaism
MSA[1]	13.6	4.8	3.3	7.0	8.2	1.0	2.4	3.0	0.3	0.3
U.S.	19.1	9.3	4.0	4.0	2.3	2.0	1.9	1.6	0.8	0.7

Note: Figures are the number of adherents as a percentage of the total population; (1) Figures cover the Des Moines-West Des Moines, IA Metropolitan Statistical Area—see Appendix B for areas included; (2) Methodist/Pietist; (3) Latter Day Saints; (4) Reformed; (5) Figures are estimates
Source: Association of Statisticians of American Religious Bodies, 2010 U.S. Religion Census: Religious Congregations & Membership Study

Religious Groups by Tradition

Area	Catholic	Evangelical Protestant	Mainline Protestant	Other Tradition	Black Protestant	Orthodox
MSA[1]	13.6	12.4	16.8	1.9	0.9	0.1
U.S.	19.1	16.2	7.3	4.3	1.6	0.3

Note: Figures are the number of adherents as a percentage of the total population; (1) Figures cover the Des Moines-West Des Moines, IA Metropolitan Statistical Area—see Appendix B for areas included
Source: Association of Statisticians of American Religious Bodies, 2010 U.S. Religion Census: Religious Congregations & Membership Study

ECONOMY

Gross Metropolitan Product

Area	2017	2018	2019	2020	Rank[2]
MSA[1]	55.0	57.7	60.3	62.8	58

Note: Figures are in billions of dollars; (1) Figures cover the Des Moines-West Des Moines, IA Metropolitan Statistical Area—see Appendix B for areas included; (2) Rank is based on 2018 data and ranges from 1 to 381
Source: U.S. Conference of Mayors, U.S. Metro Economies: GMP & Employment 2018-2020, September 2019

Economic Growth

Area	2015-17 (%)	2018 (%)	2019 (%)	2020 (%)	Rank[2]
MSA[1]	2.8	1.8	2.7	1.9	78
U.S.	1.9	2.9	2.3	2.1	–

Note: Figures are real gross metropolitan product (GMP) growth rates and represent average annual percent change; (1) Figures cover the Des Moines-West Des Moines, IA Metropolitan Statistical Area—see Appendix B for areas included; (2) Rank is based on 2017 2-year average annual percent change and ranges from 1 to 381
Source: U.S. Conference of Mayors, U.S. Metro Economies: GMP & Employment 2018-2020, September 2019

Metropolitan Area Exports

Area	2013	2014	2015	2016	2017	2018	Rank[2]
MSA[1]	1,279.4	1,361.8	1,047.8	1,052.2	1,141.2	1,293.7	136

Note: Figures are in millions of dollars; (1) Figures cover the Des Moines-West Des Moines, IA Metropolitan Statistical Area—see Appendix B for areas included; (2) Rank is based on 2018 data and ranges from 1 to 387
Source: U.S. Department of Commerce, International Trade Administration, Office of Trade and Economic Analysis, Industry and Analysis, Exports by Metropolitan Area, data extracted April 15, 2020

Building Permits

Area	Single-Family			Multi-Family			Total		
	2017	2018	Pct. Chg.	2017	2018	Pct. Chg.	2017	2018	Pct. Chg.
City	173	180	4.0	1,124	391	-65.2	1,297	571	-56.0
MSA[1]	3,697	3,233	-12.6	2,670	1,690	-36.7	6,367	4,923	-22.7
U.S.	820,000	855,300	4.3	462,000	473,500	2.5	1,282,000	1,328,800	3.7

Note: (1) Figures cover the Des Moines-West Des Moines, IA Metropolitan Statistical Area—see Appendix B for areas included; Figures represent new, privately-owned housing units authorized (unadjusted data); All permit data are based on estimates with imputation
Source: U.S. Census Bureau, Manufacturing, Mining, and Construction Statistics, Building Permits, 2017, 2018

Bankruptcy Filings

Area	Business Filings			Nonbusiness Filings		
	2018	2019	% Chg.	2018	2019	% Chg.
Polk County	22	28	27.3	848	962	13.4
U.S.	22,232	22,780	2.5	751,186	752,160	0.1

Note: Business filings include Chapter 7, Chapter 9, Chapter 11, Chapter 12, Chapter 13, Chapter 15, and
Section 304; Nonbusiness filings include Chapter 7, Chapter 11, and Chapter 13
Source: Administrative Office of the U.S. Courts, Business and Nonbusiness Bankruptcy, County Cases
Commenced by Chapter of the Bankruptcy Code, During the 12-Month Period Ending December 31, 2018 and
Business and Nonbusiness Bankruptcy, County Cases Commenced by Chapter of the Bankruptcy Code, During
the 12-Month Period Ending December 31, 2019

Housing Vacancy Rates

Area	Gross Vacancy Rate[2] (%)			Year-Round Vacancy Rate[3] (%)			Rental Vacancy Rate[4] (%)			Homeowner Vacancy Rate[5] (%)		
	2017	2018	2019	2017	2018	2019	2017	2018	2019	2017	2018	2019
MSA[1]	n/a	n/a	n/a	n/a	n/a	n/a	n/a	n/a	n/a	n/a	n/a	n/a
U.S.	12.7	12.3	12.0	9.9	9.7	9.5	7.2	6.9	6.7	1.6	1.5	1.4

Note: (1) Figures cover the Des Moines-West Des Moines, IA Metropolitan Statistical Area—see Appendix B for
areas included; (2) The percentage of the total housing inventory that is vacant; (3) The percentage of the
housing inventory (excluding seasonal units) that is year-round vacant; (4) The percentage of rental inventory
that is vacant for rent; (5) The percentage of homeowner inventory that is vacant for sale; n/a not available
Source: U.S. Census Bureau, Housing Vacancies and Homeownership Annual Statistics: 2017, 2018, 2019

INCOME

Income

Area	Per Capita ($)	Median Household ($)	Average Household ($)
City	27,325	52,251	67,235
MSA[1]	35,560	68,669	89,538
U.S.	32,621	60,293	84,938

Note: (1) Figures cover the Des Moines-West Des Moines, IA Metropolitan Statistical Area—see Appendix B for
areas included
Source: U.S. Census Bureau, 2014-2018 American Community Survey 5-Year Estimates

Household Income Distribution

Area	Percent of Households Earning							
	Under $15,000	$15,000 -$24,999	$25,000 -$34,999	$35,000 -$49,999	$50,000 -$74,999	$75,000 -$99,999	$100,000 -$149,999	$150,000 and up
City	13.0	10.6	10.3	14.1	20.3	13.3	12.0	6.4
MSA[1]	7.8	7.4	8.2	12.1	18.9	14.6	17.3	13.7
U.S.	10.9	9.3	9.3	12.6	17.5	12.5	14.6	13.3

Note: (1) Figures cover the Des Moines-West Des Moines, IA Metropolitan Statistical Area—see Appendix B for
areas included
Source: U.S. Census Bureau, 2014-2018 American Community Survey 5-Year Estimates

Poverty Rate

Area	All Ages	Under 18 Years Old	18 to 64 Years Old	65 Years and Over
City	17.2	25.4	15.3	10.4
MSA[1]	10.0	13.1	9.4	6.6
U.S.	14.1	19.5	13.2	9.3

Note: Figures are percentage of people whose income during the past 12 months was below the poverty level;
(1) Figures cover the Des Moines-West Des Moines, IA Metropolitan Statistical Area—see Appendix B for areas
included
Source: U.S. Census Bureau, 2014-2018 American Community Survey 5-Year Estimates

EMPLOYMENT

Labor Force and Employment

Area	Civilian Labor Force			Workers Employed		
	Dec. 2018	Dec. 2019	% Chg.	Dec. 2018	Dec. 2019	% Chg.
City	112,022	115,631	3.2	108,110	111,652	3.3
MSA[1]	354,790	366,728	3.4	345,318	356,630	3.3
U.S.	162,510,000	164,007,000	0.9	156,481,000	158,504,000	1.3

Note: Data is not seasonally adjusted and covers workers 16 years of age and older; (1) Figures cover the Des Moines-West Des Moines, IA Metropolitan Statistical Area—see Appendix B for areas included
Source: Bureau of Labor Statistics, Local Area Unemployment Statistics

Unemployment Rate

Area	2019											
	Jan.	Feb.	Mar.	Apr.	May	Jun.	Jul.	Aug.	Sep.	Oct.	Nov.	Dec.
City	4.5	4.1	4.3	3.2	3.0	3.4	3.2	3.3	2.9	2.9	3.0	3.4
MSA[1]	3.4	3.1	3.2	2.5	2.4	2.8	2.7	2.6	2.3	2.3	2.4	2.8
U.S.	4.4	4.1	3.9	3.3	3.4	3.8	4.0	3.8	3.3	3.3	3.3	3.4

Note: Data is not seasonally adjusted and covers workers 16 years of age and older; (1) Figures cover the Des Moines-West Des Moines, IA Metropolitan Statistical Area—see Appendix B for areas included
Source: Bureau of Labor Statistics, Local Area Unemployment Statistics

Average Wages

Occupation	$/Hr.	Occupation	$/Hr.
Accountants and Auditors	36.20	Maintenance and Repair Workers	20.40
Automotive Mechanics	22.70	Marketing Managers	61.20
Bookkeepers	21.30	Network and Computer Systems Admin.	40.20
Carpenters	21.30	Nurses, Licensed Practical	22.50
Cashiers	11.30	Nurses, Registered	30.20
Computer Programmers	39.10	Nursing Assistants	15.50
Computer Systems Analysts	41.20	Office Clerks, General	17.70
Computer User Support Specialists	25.90	Physical Therapists	41.80
Construction Laborers	18.70	Physicians	103.20
Cooks, Restaurant	13.90	Plumbers, Pipefitters and Steamfitters	28.40
Customer Service Representatives	20.40	Police and Sheriff's Patrol Officers	31.80
Dentists	105.40	Postal Service Mail Carriers	24.90
Electricians	26.20	Real Estate Sales Agents	23.40
Engineers, Electrical	37.90	Retail Salespersons	13.90
Fast Food and Counter Workers	11.00	Sales Representatives, Technical/Scientific	43.00
Financial Managers	63.60	Secretaries, Exc. Legal/Medical/Executive	19.60
First-Line Supervisors of Office Workers	30.80	Security Guards	16.30
General and Operations Managers	53.80	Surgeons	109.10
Hairdressers/Cosmetologists	15.40	Teacher Assistants, Exc. Postsecondary*	12.70
Home Health and Personal Care Aides	13.50	Teachers, Secondary School, Exc. Sp. Ed.*	29.10
Janitors and Cleaners	13.70	Telemarketers	15.30
Landscaping/Groundskeeping Workers	16.00	Truck Drivers, Heavy/Tractor-Trailer	24.30
Lawyers	63.20	Truck Drivers, Light/Delivery Services	17.60
Maids and Housekeeping Cleaners	12.10	Waiters and Waitresses	11.00

Note: Wage data covers the Des Moines-West Des Moines, IA Metropolitan Statistical Area—see Appendix B for areas included; (*) Hourly wages were calculated from annual wage data based on a 40 hour work week; n/a not available.
Source: Bureau of Labor Statistics, Metro Area Occupational Employment & Wage Estimates, May 2019

Employment by Occupation

Occupation Classification	City (%)	MSA[1] (%)	U.S. (%)
Management, Business, Science, and Arts	31.3	41.4	37.9
Natural Resources, Construction, and Maintenance	8.6	7.9	8.9
Production, Transportation, and Material Moving	16.1	11.8	13.3
Sales and Office	23.3	23.3	22.1
Service	20.8	15.6	17.9

Note: Figures cover employed civilians 16 years of age and older; (1) Figures cover the Des Moines-West Des Moines, IA Metropolitan Statistical Area—see Appendix B for areas included
Source: U.S. Census Bureau, 2014-2018 American Community Survey 5-Year Estimates

Employment by Industry

Sector	MSA[1]		U.S.
	Number of Employees	Percent of Total	Percent of Total
Construction, Mining, and Logging	20,400	5.4	5.4
Education and Health Services	54,000	14.4	16.1
Financial Activities	56,400	15.0	5.8
Government	46,500	12.4	15.0
Information	6,400	1.7	1.9
Leisure and Hospitality	35,900	9.6	10.8
Manufacturing	21,400	5.7	8.4
Other Services	13,900	3.7	3.9
Professional and Business Services	50,100	13.3	14.1
Retail Trade	40,500	10.8	10.6
Transportation, Warehousing, and Utilities	12,500	3.3	4.2
Wholesale Trade	17,900	4.8	3.9

Note: Figures are non-farm employment as of December 2019. Figures are not seasonally adjusted and include workers 16 years of age and older; (1) Figures cover the Des Moines-West Des Moines, IA Metropolitan Statistical Area—see Appendix B for areas included
Source: Bureau of Labor Statistics, Current Employment Statistics, Employment, Hours, and Earnings

Occupations with Greatest Projected Employment Growth: 2019 – 2021

Occupation[1]	2019 Employment	2021 Projected Employment	Numeric Employment Change	Percent Employment Change
Combined Food Preparation and Serving Workers, Including Fast Food	38,530	39,480	950	2.5
Heavy and Tractor-Trailer Truck Drivers	45,820	46,750	930	2.0
Registered Nurses	34,120	34,870	750	2.2
Personal Care Aides	11,780	12,230	450	3.8
Home Health Aides	8,050	8,490	440	5.5
Cooks, Restaurant	11,550	11,940	390	3.4
Laborers and Freight, Stock, and Material Movers, Hand	29,060	29,440	380	1.3
Janitors and Cleaners, Except Maids and Housekeeping Cleaners	26,660	26,980	320	1.2
Accountants and Auditors	12,170	12,430	260	2.1
Construction Laborers	13,390	13,640	250	1.9

Note: Projections cover Iowa; (1) Sorted by numeric employment change
Source: www.projectionscentral.com, State Occupational Projections, 2019–2021 Short-Term Projections

Fastest Growing Occupations: 2019 – 2021

Occupation[1]	2019 Employment	2021 Projected Employment	Numeric Employment Change	Percent Employment Change
Information Security Analysts	1,470	1,590	120	8.2
Home Health Aides	8,050	8,490	440	5.5
Veterinary Assistants and Laboratory Animal Caretakers	1,140	1,200	60	5.3
Woodworking Machine Setters, Operators, and Tenders, Except Sawing	1,490	1,560	70	4.7
Nurse Practitioners	1,330	1,390	60	4.5
Taxi Drivers and Chauffeurs	2,430	2,540	110	4.5
Health Specialties Teachers, Postsecondary	2,030	2,120	90	4.4
Paralegals and Legal Assistants	1,890	1,970	80	4.2
Speech-Language Pathologists	1,200	1,250	50	4.2
Gaming Dealers	1,210	1,260	50	4.1

Note: Projections cover Iowa; (1) Sorted by percent employment change and excludes occupations with numeric employment change less than 50
Source: www.projectionscentral.com, State Occupational Projections, 2019–2021 Short-Term Projections

TAXES

State Corporate Income Tax Rates

State	Tax Rate (%)	Income Brackets ($)	Num. of Brackets	Financial Institution Tax Rate (%)[a]	Federal Income Tax Ded.
Iowa	6.0 - 12.0	25,000 - 250,001	4	5.0	Yes (j)

Note: Tax rates as of January 1, 2020; (a) Rates listed are the corporate income tax rate applied to financial institutions or excise taxes based on income; (j) 50% of the federal income tax is deductible.
Source: Federation of Tax Administrators, State Corporate Income Tax Rates, January 1, 2020

State Individual Income Tax Rates

State	Tax Rate (%)	Income Brackets ($)	Personal Exemptions ($)			Standard Ded. ($)	
			Single	Married	Depend.	Single	Married
Iowa (a)	0.33 - 8.53	15,666 - 74,970	40 (c)	80 (c)	40 (c)	2,110	5,210 (a)

Note: Tax rates as of January 1, 2020; Local- and county-level taxes are not included; Federal income tax is deductible on state income tax returns; (a) 19 states have statutory provision for automatically adjusting to the rate of inflation the dollar values of the income tax brackets, standard deductions, and/or personal exemptions. Michigan indexes the personal exemption only. Oregon does not index the income brackets for $125,000 and over; (c) The personal exemption takes the form of a tax credit instead of a deduction
Source: Federation of Tax Administrators, State Individual Income Tax Rates, January 1, 2020

Various State Sales and Excise Tax Rates

State	State Sales Tax (%)	Gasoline[1] (¢/gal.)	Cigarette[2] ($/pack)	Spirits[3] ($/gal.)	Wine[4] ($/gal.)	Beer[5] ($/gal.)	Recreational Marijuana (%)
Iowa	6	30.5	1.36	13.03	1.75	0.19	Not legal

Note: All tax rates as of January 1, 2020; (1) The American Petroleum Institute has developed a methodology for determining the average tax rate on a gallon of fuel. Rates may include any of the following: excise taxes, environmental fees, storage tank fees, other fees or taxes, general sales tax, and local taxes; (2) The federal excise tax of $1.0066 per pack and local taxes are not included; (3) Rates are those applicable to off-premise sales of 40% alcohol by volume (a.b.v.) distilled spirits in 750ml containers. Local excise taxes are excluded; (4) Rates are those applicable to off-premise sales of 11% a.b.v. non-carbonated wine in 750ml containers; (5) Rates are those applicable to off-premise sales of 4.7% a.b.v. beer in 12 ounce containers.
Source: Tax Foundation, 2020 Facts & Figures: How Does Your State Compare?

State Business Tax Climate Index Rankings

State	Overall Rank	Corporate Tax Rank	Individual Income Tax Rank	Sales Tax Rank	Property Tax Rank	Unemployment Insurance Tax Rank
Iowa	42	48	42	15	35	35

Note: The index is a measure of how each state's tax laws affect economic performance. The lower the rank, the more favorable a state's tax system is for business. States without a given tax are given a ranking of 1. The scores/rankings for the District of Columbia do not affect other states. The 2020 index represents the tax climate as of July 1, 2019.
Source: Tax Foundation, State Business Tax Climate Index 2020

COMMERCIAL UTILITIES

Typical Monthly Electric Bills

Area	Commercial Service ($/month)		Industrial Service ($/month)	
	1,500 kWh	40 kW demand 14,000 kWh	1,000 kW demand 200,000 kWh	50,000 kW demand 32,500,000 kWh
City	n/a	n/a	n/a	n/a
Average[1]	203	1,612	25,706	2,520,671

Note: Figures are based on annualized rates; (1) Average based on 187 utilities surveyed; n/a not available
Source: Edison Electric Institute, Typical Bills and Average Rates Report, Summer 2019

TRANSPORTATION

Means of Transportation to Work

| Area | Car/Truck/Van | | Public Transportation | | | Bicycle | Walked | Other Means | Worked at Home |
	Drove Alone	Car-pooled	Bus	Subway	Railroad				
City	79.9	10.1	2.4	0.0	0.0	0.4	2.7	1.1	3.4
MSA[1]	83.7	8.0	1.2	0.0	0.0	0.2	1.8	0.7	4.5
U.S.	76.4	9.1	2.5	1.9	0.6	0.6	2.7	1.3	4.9

Note: Figures are percentages and cover workers 16 years of age and older; (1) Figures cover the Des Moines-West Des Moines, IA Metropolitan Statistical Area—see Appendix B for areas included
Source: U.S. Census Bureau, 2014-2018 American Community Survey 5-Year Estimates

Travel Time to Work

Area	Less Than 10 Minutes	10 to 19 Minutes	20 to 29 Minutes	30 to 44 Minutes	45 to 59 Minutes	60 to 89 Minutes	90 Minutes or More
City	13.3	44.0	26.5	11.6	2.2	1.4	1.1
MSA[1]	15.0	36.1	27.4	15.7	3.2	1.5	1.2
U.S.	12.5	28.7	20.9	20.7	8.2	6.3	2.8

Note: Note: Figures are percentages and include workers 16 years old and over; (1) Figures cover the Des Moines-West Des Moines, IA Metropolitan Statistical Area—see Appendix B for areas included
Source: U.S. Census Bureau, 2014-2018 American Community Survey 5-Year Estimates

Key Congestion Measures

Area	1982	1992	2002	2012	2017
Annual Hours of Delay, Total (000)	n/a	n/a	n/a	n/a	8,998
Annual Hours of Delay, Per Auto Commuter	n/a	n/a	n/a	n/a	18
Annual Congestion Cost, Total (million $)	n/a	n/a	n/a	n/a	184
Annual Congestion Cost, Per Auto Commuter ($)	n/a	n/a	n/a	n/a	371

Note: n/a not available
Source: Texas A&M Transportation Institute, 2019 Urban Mobility Report

Freeway Travel Time Index

Area	1982	1987	1992	1997	2002	2007	2012	2017
Urban Area Index[1]	n/a	n/a	n/a	n/a	n/a	n/a	n/a	1.08
Urban Area Rank[1,2]	n/a	n/a	n/a	n/a	n/a	n/a	n/a	n/a

Note: Freeway Travel Time Index—the ratio of travel time in the peak period to the travel time at free-flow conditions. For example, a value of 1.30 indicates a 20-minute free-flow trip takes 26 minutes in the peak (20 minutes x 1.30 = 26 minutes); (1) Covers the Des Moines IA urban area; (2) Rank is based on 101 larger urban areas (#1 = highest travel time index); n/a not available
Source: Texas A&M Transportation Institute, 2019 Urban Mobility Report

Public Transportation

Agency Name / Mode of Transportation	Vehicles Operated in Maximum Service[1]	Annual Unlinked Passenger Trips[2] (in thous.)	Annual Passenger Miles[3] (in thous.)
Des Moines Metropolitan Transit Authority (MTA)			
Bus (directly operated)	110	4,183.1	17,546.0
Demand Response (directly operated)	21	94.5	791.8
Demand Response Taxi (purchased transportation)	2	11.5	127.8
Vanpool (directly operated)	100	235.7	9,037.1

Note: (1) Number of revenue vehicles operated by the given mode and type of service to meet the annual maximum service requirement. This is the revenue vehicle count during the peak season of the year; on the week and day that maximum service is provided. Vehicles operated in maximum service (VOMS) exclude atypical days and one-time special events; (2) Number of passengers who boarded public transportation vehicles. Passengers are counted each time they board a vehicle no matter how many vehicles they use to travel from their origin to their destination. (3) Sum of the distances ridden by all passengers during the entire fiscal year.
Source: Federal Transit Administration, National Transit Database, 2018

Air Transportation

Airport Name and Code / Type of Service	Passenger Airlines[1]	Passenger Enplanements	Freight Carriers[2]	Freight (lbs)
Des Moines International (DSM)				
Domestic service (U.S. carriers - 2019)	25	1,426,052	10	32,866,411
International service (U.S. carriers - 2018)	2	305	0	0

Note: (1) Includes all U.S.-based major, minor and commuter airlines that carried at least one passenger during the year; (2) Includes all U.S.-based airlines and freight carriers that transported at least one pound of freight during the year.
Source: Bureau of Transportation Statistics, The Intermodal Transportation Database, Air Carriers: T-100 Domestic Market (U.S. Carriers), 2019; Bureau of Transportation Statistics, The Intermodal Transportation Database, Air Carriers: T-100 International Market (U.S. Carriers), 2018

Other Transportation Statistics

Major Highways:	I-35; I-80
Amtrak Service:	No
Major Waterways/Ports:	None

Source: Amtrak.com; Google Maps

BUSINESSES

Major Business Headquarters

Company Name	Industry	Rankings Fortune[1]	Rankings Forbes[2]
Principal Financial	Insurance, Life, Health (Stock)	219	-

Note: (1) Companies that produce a 10-K are ranked 1 to 500 based on 2018 revenue; (2) All private companies with at least $2 billion in annual revenue through the end of their most current fiscal year are ranked 1 to 228; companies listed are headquartered in the city; dashes indicate no ranking
Source: Fortune, "Fortune 500," June 2019; Forbes, "America's Largest Private Companies," 2019 Rankings

Minority Business Opportunity

Des Moines is home to one company which is on the *Black Enterprise* Industrial/Service list (100 largest companies based on gross sales): **Keystone Electrical Manufacturing Co.** (#73). Criteria: operational in previous calendar year; at least 51% black-owned and manufactures/owns the product it sells or provides industrial or consumer services. Brokerages, real estate firms and firms that provide professional services are not eligible. *Black Enterprise, B.E. 100s, 2019*

Minority- and Women-Owned Businesses

Group	All Firms Firms	All Firms Sales ($000)	Firms with Paid Employees Firms	Firms with Paid Employees Sales ($000)	Firms with Paid Employees Employees	Firms with Paid Employees Payroll ($000)
AIAN[1]	107	(s)	23	(s)	100 - 249	(s)
Asian	857	156,781	99	125,716	556	17,991
Black	1,197	82,259	22	60,836	920	14,023
Hispanic	931	70,008	65	39,733	450	8,919
NHOPI[2]	n/a	n/a	n/a	n/a	n/a	n/a
Women	5,681	708,100	428	597,154	4,000	121,008
All Firms	16,543	40,200,054	3,725	39,655,646	115,109	5,550,235

Note: Figures cover firms located in the city; minority- and women-owned business are defined as firms in which the corresponding group own 51% or more of the stock or equity of the company; (1) American Indian and Alaska Native; (2) Native Hawaiian and Other Pacific Islander; (s) estimates are suppressed when publication standards are not met; n/a not available
Source: U.S. Census Bureau, 2012 Economic Census, Survey of Business Owners

HOTELS & CONVENTION CENTERS

Hotels, Motels and Vacation Rentals

Area	5 Star Num.	5 Star Pct.[3]	4 Star Num.	4 Star Pct.[3]	3 Star Num.	3 Star Pct.[3]	2 Star Num.	2 Star Pct.[3]	1 Star Num.	1 Star Pct.[3]	Not Rated Num.	Not Rated Pct.[3]
City[1]	0	0.0	0	0.0	33	25.8	19	14.8	24	18.8	52	40.6
Total[2]	266	1.3	1,517	7.2	4,627	21.8	3,210	15.1	3,974	18.7	7,601	35.9

Note: (1) Figures cover Des Moines and vicinity; (2) Figures cover all 100 cities in this book; (3) Percentage of hotels which have a given star rating; Star ratings are determined by priceline.com and offer an indication of the general quality of a particular hotel.
Source: priceline.com, April 27, 2020

Major Convention Centers

Name	Overall Space (sq. ft.)	Exhibit Space (sq. ft.)	Meeting Space (sq. ft.)	Meeting Rooms
The Iowa Events Center	234,505	n/a	n/a	n/a

Note: Table includes convention centers located in the Des Moines-West Des Moines, IA metro area; n/a not available
Source: Original research

Living Environment

COST OF LIVING

Cost of Living Index

Composite Index	Groceries	Housing	Utilities	Trans-portation	Health Care	Misc. Goods/ Services
89.9	95.2	80.2	90.1	99.1	95.4	92.3

Note: The Cost of Living Index measures regional differences in the cost of consumer goods and services, excluding taxes and non-consumer expenditures, for professional and managerial households in the top income quintile. It is based on more than 50,000 prices covering almost 60 different items for which prices are collected three times a year by chambers of commerce, economic development organizations or university applied economic centers in each participating urban area. The numbers shown should be read as a percentage above or below the national average of 100. For example, a value of 115.4 in the groceries column indicates that grocery prices are 15.4% higher than the national average. Small differences in the index numbers should not be interpreted as significant; Figures cover the Des Moines IA urban area.
Source: The Council for Community and Economic Research, ACCRA Cost of Living Index, 2019

Grocery Prices

Area[1]	T-Bone Steak ($/pound)	Frying Chicken ($/pound)	Whole Milk ($/half gal.)	Eggs ($/dozen)	Orange Juice ($/64 oz.)	Coffee ($/11.5 oz.)
City[2]	10.37	1.76	2.13	1.56	2.99	4.22
Avg.	11.40	1.41	1.93	1.54	3.51	4.30
Min.	7.40	0.92	0.85	0.58	2.67	2.90
Max.	15.58	2.68	4.09	4.18	5.57	8.10

Note: (1) Values for the local area are compared with the average, minimum and maximum values for all 290 areas in the Cost of Living Index; (2) Figures cover the Des Moines IA urban area; T-Bone Steak (price per pound); Frying Chicken (price per pound, whole fryer); Whole Milk (half gallon carton); Eggs (price per dozen, Grade A, large); Orange Juice (64 oz. Tropicana or Florida Natural); Coffee (11.5 oz. can, vacuum-packed, Maxwell House, Hills Bros, or Folgers).
Source: The Council for Community and Economic Research, ACCRA Cost of Living Index, 2019

Housing and Utility Costs

Area[1]	New Home Price ($)	Apartment Rent ($/month)	All Electric ($/month)	Part Electric ($/month)	Other Energy ($/month)	Telephone ($/month)
City[2]	327,713	685	-	77.52	65.21	175.00
Avg.	362,090	1,142	174.35	100.00	67.76	179.60
Min.	198,329	501	91.58	31.44	28.51	165.30
Max.	2,074,561	5,050	388.18	239.41	306.15	207.90

Note: (1) Values for the local area are compared with the average, minimum and maximum values for all 290 areas in the Cost of Living Index; (2) Figures cover the Des Moines IA urban area; New Home Price (2,400 sf living area, 8,000 sf lot, in urban area with full utilities); Apartment Rent (950 sf 2 bedroom/1.5 or 2 bath, unfurnished, excluding all utilities except water); All Electric (average monthly cost for an all-electric home); Part Electric (average monthly cost for a part-electric home); Other Energy (average monthly cost for natural gas, fuel oil, coal, wood, and any other forms of energy except electricity); Telephone (price includes the base monthly rate plus taxes and fees for three lines of mobile phone service).
Source: The Council for Community and Economic Research, ACCRA Cost of Living Index, 2019

Health Care, Transportation, and Other Costs

Area[1]	Doctor ($/visit)	Dentist ($/visit)	Optometrist ($/visit)	Gasoline ($/gallon)	Beauty Salon ($/visit)	Men's Shirt ($)
City[2]	120.67	82.28	110.26	2.40	30.44	22.15
Avg.	114.85	97.58	106.10	2.50	38.15	32.15
Min.	39.00	62.22	52.22	1.53	16.88	10.27
Max.	206.67	151.53	258.67	3.79	79.29	59.30

Note: (1) Values for the local area are compared with the average, minimum and maximum values for all 290 areas in the Cost of Living Index; (2) Figures cover the Des Moines IA urban area; Doctor (general practitioners routine exam of an established patient); Dentist (adult teeth cleaning and periodic oral examination); Optometrist (full vision eye exam for established adult patient); Gasoline (one gallon regular unleaded, national brand, including all taxes, cash price at self-service pump if available); Beauty Salon (woman's shampoo, trim, and blow-dry); Men's Shirt (cotton/polyester dress shirt, pinpoint weave, long sleeves).
Source: The Council for Community and Economic Research, ACCRA Cost of Living Index, 2019

HOUSING

House Price Index (HPI)

Area	National Ranking[2]	Quarterly Change (%)	One-Year Change (%)	Five-Year Change (%)
MSA[1]	213	0.60	2.75	23.59
U.S.[3]	–	1.26	5.09	32.88

Note: The HPI is a weighted repeat sales index. It measures average price changes in repeat sales or refinancings on the same properties. This information is obtained by reviewing repeat mortgage transactions on single-family properties whose mortgages have been purchased or securitized by Fannie Mae or Freddie Mac in January 1975; (1) Figures cover the Des Moines-West Des Moines, IA Metropolitan Statistical Area—see Appendix B for areas included; (2) Rankings are based on annual percentage change for all metro areas containing at least 15,000 transactions over the last 10 years and ranges from 1 to 232; (3) figures based on a weighted average of Census Division estimates using a seasonally adjusted, purchase-only index; all figures are for the period ending December 31, 2019
Source: Federal Housing Finance Agency, House Price Index, February 25, 2020

Median Single-Family Home Prices

Area	2017	2018	2019[p]	Percent Change 2018 to 2019
MSA[1]	194.0	204.8	214.5	4.7
U.S. Average	248.8	261.6	274.6	5.0

Note: Figures are median sales prices of existing single-family homes in thousands of dollars; (p) preliminary; (1) Figures cover the Des Moines-West Des Moines, IA Metropolitan Statistical Area—see Appendix B for areas included
Source: National Association of Realtors, Median Sales Price of Existing Single-Family Homes for Metropolitan Areas, 4th Quarter 2019

Qualifying Income Based on Median Sales Price of Existing Single-Family Homes

Area	With 5% Down ($)	With 10% Down ($)	With 20% Down ($)
MSA[1]	44,536	42,192	37,504
U.S. Average	58,663	55,575	49,400

Note: Figures are preliminary; Qualifying income is based on a mortgage rate of 3.76%. Monthly principal and interest payment is limited to 25% of income; (1) Figures cover the Des Moines-West Des Moines, IA Metropolitan Statistical Area—see Appendix B for areas included
Source: National Association of Realtors, Qualifying Income Based on Median Sales Price of Existing Single-Family Homes for Metropolitan Areas, 4th Quarter 2019

Median Apartment Condo-Coop Home Prices

Area	2017	2018	2019[p]	Percent Change 2018 to 2019
MSA[1]	n/a	n/a	n/a	n/a
U.S. Average	234.3	241.0	249.5	3.5

Note: Figures are median sales prices of existing apartment condo-coop homes in thousands of dollars; (p) preliminary; n/a not available; (1) Figures cover the Des Moines-West Des Moines, IA Metropolitan Statistical Area—see Appendix B for areas included
Source: National Association of Realtors, Median Sales Price of Existing Apartment Condo-Coop Homes for Metropolitan Areas, 4th Quarter 2019

Home Value Distribution

Area	Under $50,000	$50,000 -$99,999	$100,000 -$149,999	$150,000 -$199,999	$200,000 -$299,999	$300,000 -$499,999	$500,000 -$999,999	$1,000,000 or more
City	6.5	23.7	34.7	19.4	10.0	4.2	1.4	0.1
MSA[1]	4.8	12.3	20.4	20.6	23.9	13.7	3.9	0.4
U.S.	7.6	13.0	14.0	14.3	19.2	18.3	10.5	3.1

Note: Figures are percentages and cover owner-occupied housing units; (1) Figures cover the Des Moines-West Des Moines, IA Metropolitan Statistical Area—see Appendix B for areas included
Source: U.S. Census Bureau, 2014-2018 American Community Survey 5-Year Estimates

Homeownership Rate

Area	2011 (%)	2012 (%)	2013 (%)	2014 (%)	2015 (%)	2016 (%)	2017 (%)	2018 (%)	2019 (%)
MSA[1]	n/a	n/a	n/a	n/a	n/a	n/a	n/a	n/a	n/a
U.S.	66.1	65.4	65.1	64.5	63.7	63.4	63.9	64.4	64.6

Note: (1) Figures cover the Des Moines-West Des Moines, IA Metropolitan Statistical Area—see Appendix B for areas included; n/a not available
Source: U.S. Census Bureau, Housing Vacancies and Homeownership Annual Statistics: 2011-2019

Year Housing Structure Built

Area	2010 or Later	2000 -2009	1990 -1999	1980 -1989	1970 -1979	1960 -1969	1950 -1959	1940 -1949	Before 1940	Median Year
City	2.5	7.3	6.8	6.2	13.5	10.7	16.0	8.4	28.6	1958
MSA[1]	9.1	17.7	12.9	8.7	13.7	8.8	9.3	4.3	15.5	1979
U.S.	4.1	14.3	13.9	13.5	15.3	10.7	10.4	5.0	12.8	1977

Note: Figures are percentages except for Median Year; Note: (1) Figures cover the Des Moines-West Des Moines, IA Metropolitan Statistical Area—see Appendix B for areas included
Source: U.S. Census Bureau, 2014-2018 American Community Survey 5-Year Estimates

Gross Monthly Rent

Area	Under $500	$500 -$999	$1,000 -$1,499	$1,500 -$1,999	$2,000 -$2,499	$2,500 -$2,999	$3,000 and up	Median ($)
City	9.7	63.1	22.5	3.7	0.7	0.1	0.1	822
MSA[1]	7.8	56.1	28.2	5.7	1.2	0.3	0.7	880
U.S.	9.8	38.5	29.6	12.9	5.1	2.1	2.0	1,023

Note: Figures are percentages except for Median; Gross rent is the contract rent plus the estimated average monthly cost of utilities (electricity, gas, and water and sewer) and fuels (oil, coal, kerosene, wood, etc.) if these are paid by the renter (or paid for the renter by someone else); (1) Figures cover the Des Moines-West Des Moines, IA Metropolitan Statistical Area—see Appendix B for areas included
Source: U.S. Census Bureau, 2014-2018 American Community Survey 5-Year Estimates

HEALTH

Health Risk Factors

Category	MSA[1] (%)	U.S. (%)
Adults aged 18–64 who have any kind of health care coverage	91.6	87.3
Adults who reported being in good or better health	86.3	82.4
Adults who have been told they have high blood cholesterol	33.4	33.0
Adults who have been told they have high blood pressure	29.4	32.3
Adults who are current smokers	14.4	17.1
Adults who currently use E-cigarettes	5.5	4.6
Adults who currently use chewing tobacco, snuff, or snus	4.0	4.0
Adults who are heavy drinkers[2]	7.2	6.3
Adults who are binge drinkers[3]	21.5	17.4
Adults who are overweight (BMI 25.0 - 29.9)	34.4	35.3
Adults who are obese (BMI 30.0 - 99.8)	34.4	31.3
Adults who participated in any physical activities in the past month	79.4	74.4
Adults who always or nearly always wears a seat belt	95.6	94.3

Note: (1) Figures cover the Des Moines-West Des Moines, IA Metropolitan Statistical Area—see Appendix B for areas included; (2) Heavy drinkers are classified as adult men having more than 14 drinks per week and adult women having more than 7 drinks per week; (3) Binge drinkers are classified as males having five or more drinks on one occasion or females having four or more drinks on one occasion
Source: Centers for Disease Control and Prevention, Behaviorial Risk Factor Surveillance System, SMART: Selected Metropolitan Area Risk Trends, 2017

Acute and Chronic Health Conditions

Category	MSA[1] (%)	U.S. (%)
Adults who have ever been told they had a heart attack	3.4	4.2
Adults who have ever been told they have angina or coronary heart disease	2.9	3.9
Adults who have ever been told they had a stroke	2.9	3.0
Adults who have ever been told they have asthma	12.9	14.2
Adults who have ever been told they have arthritis	22.8	24.9
Adults who have ever been told they have diabetes[2]	8.4	10.5
Adults who have ever been told they had skin cancer	6.3	6.2
Adults who have ever been told they had any other types of cancer	5.0	7.1
Adults who have ever been told they have COPD	5.6	6.5
Adults who have ever been told they have kidney disease	1.9	3.0
Adults who have ever been told they have a form of depression	20.1	20.5

Note: (1) Figures cover the Des Moines-West Des Moines, IA Metropolitan Statistical Area—see Appendix B for areas included; (2) Figures do not include pregnancy-related, borderline, or pre-diabetes
Source: Centers for Disease Control and Prevention, Behaviorial Risk Factor Surveillance System, SMART: Selected Metropolitan Area Risk Trends, 2017

Health Screening and Vaccination Rates

Category	MSA[1] (%)	U.S. (%)
Adults aged 65+ who have had flu shot within the past year	70.6	60.7
Adults aged 65+ who have ever had a pneumonia vaccination	83.0	75.4
Adults who have ever been tested for HIV	34.1	36.1
Adults who have ever had the shingles or zoster vaccine?	38.4	28.9
Adults who have had their blood cholesterol checked within the last five years	85.6	85.9

Note: n/a not available; (1) Figures cover the Des Moines-West Des Moines, IA Metropolitan Statistical Area—see Appendix B for areas included.
Source: Centers for Disease Control and Prevention, Behaviorial Risk Factor Surveillance System, SMART: Selected Metropolitan Area Risk Trends, 2017

Disability Status

Category	MSA[1] (%)	U.S. (%)
Adults who reported being deaf	5.4	6.7
Are you blind or have serious difficulty seeing, even when wearing glasses?	3.7	4.5
Are you limited in any way in any of your usual activities due of arthritis?	10.5	12.9
Do you have difficulty doing errands alone?	6.2	6.8
Do you have difficulty dressing or bathing?	2.5	3.6
Do you have serious difficulty concentrating/remembering/making decisions?	9.1	10.7
Do you have serious difficulty walking or climbing stairs?	10.1	13.6

Note: (1) Figures cover the Des Moines-West Des Moines, IA Metropolitan Statistical Area—see Appendix B for areas included.
Source: Centers for Disease Control and Prevention, Behaviorial Risk Factor Surveillance System, SMART: Selected Metropolitan Area Risk Trends, 2017

Mortality Rates for the Top 10 Causes of Death in the U.S.

ICD-10[a] Sub-Chapter	ICD-10[a] Code	Age-Adjusted Mortality Rate[1] per 100,000 population	
		County[2]	U.S.
Malignant neoplasms	C00-C97	158.7	152.4
Ischaemic heart diseases	I20-I25	93.8	92.7
Other forms of heart disease	I30-I51	45.3	52.5
Chronic lower respiratory diseases	J40-J47	51.9	40.4
Cerebrovascular diseases	I60-I69	30.0	37.3
Other degenerative diseases of the nervous system	G30-G31	42.8	36.4
Other external causes of accidental injury	W00-X59	40.3	35.3
Organic, including symptomatic, mental disorders	F01-F09	32.2	30.0
Hypertensive diseases	I10-I15	21.3	22.9
Diabetes mellitus	E10-E14	21.6	21.3

Note: (a) ICD-10 = International Classification of Diseases 10th Revision; (1) Mortality rates are a three year average covering 2016-2018; (2) Figures cover Polk County.
Source: Centers for Disease Control and Prevention, National Center for Health Statistics. Underlying Cause of Death 1999-2018 on CDC WONDER Online Database

Mortality Rates for Selected Causes of Death

ICD-10[a] Sub-Chapter	ICD-10[a] Code	Age-Adjusted Mortality Rate[1] per 100,000 population	
		County[2]	U.S.
Assault	X85-Y09	4.7	6.0
Diseases of the liver	K70-K76	14.5	14.2
Human immunodeficiency virus (HIV) disease	B20-B24	Unreliable	1.6
Influenza and pneumonia	J09-J18	13.1	14.2
Intentional self-harm	X60-X84	13.6	13.9
Malnutrition	E40-E46	4.4	1.9
Obesity and other hyperalimentation	E65-E68	1.8	2.1
Renal failure	N17-N19	7.7	12.8
Transport accidents	V01-V99	7.8	12.5
Viral hepatitis	B15-B19	Unreliable	1.4

Note: (a) ICD-10 = International Classification of Diseases 10th Revision; (1) Mortality rates are a three year average covering 2016-2018; (2) Figures cover Polk County; Data are suppressed when the data meet the criteria for confidentiality constraints; Mortality rates are flagged as unreliable when the rate would be calculated with a numerator of 20 or less.
Source: Centers for Disease Control and Prevention, National Center for Health Statistics. Underlying Cause of Death 1999-2018 on CDC WONDER Online Database

Health Insurance Coverage

Area	With Health Insurance	With Private Health Insurance	With Public Health Insurance	Without Health Insurance	Population Under Age 19 Without Health Insurance
City	92.8	64.0	40.9	7.2	3.8
MSA[1]	95.4	77.4	30.5	4.6	2.4
U.S.	90.6	67.7	34.7	9.4	5.2

Note: Figures are percentages that cover the civilian noninstitutionalized population; (1) Figures cover the Des Moines-West Des Moines, IA Metropolitan Statistical Area—see Appendix B for areas included
Source: U.S. Census Bureau, 2014-2018 American Community Survey 5-Year Estimates

Number of Medical Professionals

Area	MDs[3]	DOs[3,4]	Dentists	Podiatrists	Chiropractors	Optometrists
County[1] (number)	1,022	520	344	49	262	103
County[1] (rate[2])	212.1	107.9	70.6	10.1	53.8	21.1
U.S. (rate[2])	281.9	23.4	69.1	6.0	27.5	16.4

Note: Data as of 2018 unless noted; (1) Data covers Polk County; (2) Rate per 100,000 population; (3) Data as of 2017 and includes all active, non-federal physicians; (4) Doctor of Osteopathic Medicine
Source: U.S. Department of Health and Human Services, Health Resources and Services Administration, Bureau of Health Professions, Area Resource File (ARF) 2018-2019

EDUCATION

Public School District Statistics

District Name	Schls	Pupils	Pupil/ Teacher Ratio	Minority Pupils[1] (%)	Free Lunch Eligible[2] (%)	IEP[3] (%)
Des Moines Independent CSD	60	33,623	14.6	62.2	67.9	16.8

Note: Table includes school districts with 2,000 or more students; (1) Percentage of students that are not non-Hispanic white; (2) Percentage of students that are eligible for the free lunch program; (3) Percentage of students that have an Individualized Education Program.
Source: U.S. Department of Education, National Center for Education Statistics, Common Core of Data, Local Education Agency (School District) Universe Survey: School Year 2018-2019; U.S. Department of Education, National Center for Education Statistics, Common Core of Data, Public Elementary/Secondary School Universe Survey: School Year 2018-2019

Highest Level of Education

Area	Less than H.S.	H.S. Diploma	Some College, No Deg.	Associate Degree	Bachelor's Degree	Master's Degree	Prof. School Degree	Doctorate Degree
City	13.9	30.1	21.0	9.2	17.8	5.5	1.7	0.8
MSA[1]	7.6	24.9	20.3	10.4	25.5	8.0	2.4	1.0
U.S.	12.3	27.1	20.6	8.4	19.4	8.6	2.1	1.4

Note: Figures cover persons age 25 and over; (1) Figures cover the Des Moines-West Des Moines, IA Metropolitan Statistical Area—see Appendix B for areas included
Source: U.S. Census Bureau, 2014-2018 American Community Survey 5-Year Estimates

Educational Attainment by Race

Area	High School Graduate or Higher (%)					Bachelor's Degree or Higher (%)				
	Total	White	Black	Asian	Hisp.[2]	Total	White	Black	Asian	Hisp.[2]
City	86.1	89.3	81.4	61.7	56.5	25.8	28.3	13.9	19.8	8.3
MSA[1]	92.4	94.1	84.2	75.7	61.5	36.9	38.0	19.4	40.6	13.2
U.S.	87.7	89.6	85.4	86.8	67.7	31.5	32.9	21.1	53.5	15.8

Note: Figures shown cover persons 25 years old and over; (1) Figures cover the Des Moines-West Des Moines, IA Metropolitan Statistical Area—see Appendix B for areas included; (2) People of Hispanic origin can be of any race
Source: U.S. Census Bureau, 2014-2018 American Community Survey 5-Year Estimates

School Enrollment by Grade and Control

Area	Preschool (%)		Kindergarten (%)		Grades 1 - 4 (%)		Grades 5 - 8 (%)		Grades 9 - 12 (%)	
	Public	Private	Public	Private	Public	Private	Public	Private	Public	Private
City	76.1	23.9	92.6	7.4	90.0	10.0	90.6	9.4	91.3	8.7
MSA[1]	65.1	34.9	90.1	9.9	91.3	8.7	91.1	8.9	91.7	8.3
U.S.	59.0	41.0	87.7	12.3	89.6	10.4	89.5	10.5	90.2	9.8

Note: Figures shown cover persons 3 years old and over; (1) Figures cover the Des Moines-West Des Moines, IA Metropolitan Statistical Area—see Appendix B for areas included
Source: U.S. Census Bureau, 2014-2018 American Community Survey 5-Year Estimates

Average Salaries of Public School Teachers

Area	2016-17		2017-18		Change from 2016-17 to 2017-18	
	Dollars	Rank[1]	Dollars	Rank[1]	Percent	Rank[2]
Iowa	55,647	21	57,018	21	2.46	8
U.S. Average	59,539	–	60,477	–	1.58	–

Note: (1) Rank ranges from 1 to 51 where 1 indicates highest salary; (2) Rank ranges from 1 to 51 where 1 indicates highest percent change.
Source: National Education Association, Rankings & Estimates: Rankings of the States 2018 and Estimates of School Statistics 2019

Higher Education

Four-Year Colleges			Two-Year Colleges			Medical Schools[1]	Law Schools[2]	Voc/ Tech[3]
Public	Private Non-profit	Private For-profit	Public	Private Non-profit	Private For-profit			
0	4	0	0	1	3	1	1	0

Note: Figures cover institutions located within the city limits and include main campuses only; (1) includes schools accredited by the Liaison Committee on Medical Education and the American Osteopathic Association's Commission on Osteopathic College Accreditation; (2) includes ABA-accredited schools, schools with provisional ABA accreditation, and state accredited schools; (3) includes all schools with programs that are less than 2 years.
Source: National Center for Education Statistics, Integrated Postsecondary Education System (IPEDS), 2018-19; Wikipedia, List of Medical Schools in the United States, accessed May 1, 2020; Wikipedia, List of Law Schools in the United States, accessed May 1, 2020

According to *U.S. News & World Report,* the Des Moines-West Des Moines, IA metro area is home to one of the top 200 national universities in the U.S.: **Drake University** (#130 tie). The indicators used to capture academic quality fall into a number of categories: assessment by administrators at peer institutions; retention of students; faculty resources; student selectivity; financial resources; alumni giving; high school counselor ratings of colleges; and graduation rate. *U.S. News & World Report, "America's Best Colleges 2020"*

PRESIDENTIAL ELECTION

2016 Presidential Election Results

Area	Clinton	Trump	Johnson	Stein	Other
Polk County	51.7	40.4	4.3	0.8	2.8
U.S.	48.0	45.9	3.3	1.1	1.7

Note: Results are percentages and may not add to 100% due to rounding
Source: Dave Leip's Atlas of U.S. Presidential Elections

EMPLOYERS

Major Employers

Company Name	Industry
Bridgestone Americas Tire Operations	Global distribution center for tires
DuPont Pioneer	Crop inputs for worldwide agribusiness
Emerson Process Management Fisher Div	Control valves & systems, divisional headquarters
Grinnell Mutual Reinsurance Company	Reinsurance
Hy-Vee Food Stores	Retail grocery & drugstore chain
JBS USA	Pork processing & packaging
John Deere companies	Agricultural machinery, consumer financial services
Lennox Manufacturing	Heating & air conditioners
Mercer	Insurance
Mercy Medical Center	Healthcare
Meredith Corporation	Magazine, book publishing, tv, integrated marketing
Nationwide	Insurance
Principal Financial Group	Financial services
United Parcel Service	Logistics, distribution, transportation, freight
UnityPoint Health	Healthcare
Vermeer Manufacturing Company	Manufacturing
Wellmark	Health insurance
Wells Fargo	Financial services & home mortgage

Note: Companies shown are located within the Des Moines-West Des Moines, IA Metropolitan Statistical Area.
Source: Hoovers.com; Wikipedia

Best Companies to Work For

Principal, headquartered in Des Moines, is among the "100 Best Companies for Working Mothers." Criteria: paid time off and leaves; workforce profile; benefits; women's issues and advancement; flexible work; company culture and work life programs. *Working Mother, "100 Best Companies 2019"*

Principal Financial Group, headquartered in Des Moines, is among the "100 Best Places to Work in IT." To qualify, companies had to be U.S.-based organizations or be non-U.S.- based employers that met the following criteria: have a minimum of 300 total employees at a U.S. headquarters and a minimum of 30 IT employees in the U.S., with at least 50% of their IT employees based in the U.S. The best places to work were selected based on compensation, benefits, work/life balance, employee morale, and satisfaction with training and development programs. In addition, *Computerworld* looked at retention efforts, programs for recognizing and rewarding outstanding performances, and benefits such as flextime, elder care and child care, and reimbursement for college tuition and the cost of pursuing technology certifications. *Computerworld, "100 Best Places to Work in IT 2019"*

Principal, headquartered in Des Moines, is among the "Top Companies for Executive Women." The 2020 National Association for Female Executives (NAFE) Top Companies application included more than 200 questions on topics including female representation at all levels, but especially the corporate officer and profit-and-loss leadership ranks. The application tracked and examined how many employees have access to programs and policies that promote advancement of women and how many employees take advantage of them, plus how companies train managers to help women advance. To be considered, companies must have a minimum of two women on their boards of directors, a U.S.-based CEO and at least 1,000 U.S. employees. *National Association for Female Executives, "2020 NAFE Top 70 Companies for Executive Women"*

PUBLIC SAFETY

Crime Rate

Area	All Crimes	Violent Crimes				Property Crimes		
		Murder	Rape[3]	Robbery	Aggrav. Assault	Burglary	Larceny -Theft	Motor Vehicle Theft
City	5,083.4	12.9	33.6	167.5	456.1	1,099.1	2,734.3	579.9
Suburbs[1]	n/a	n/a	n/a	n/a	n/a	n/a	n/a	n/a
Metro[2]	n/a	n/a	n/a	n/a	n/a	n/a	n/a	n/a
U.S.	2,757.7	5.3	41.7	98.6	249.2	429.7	1,695.5	237.7

Note: Figures are crimes per 100,000 population; (1) All areas within the metro area that are located outside the city limits; (2) Figures cover the Des Moines-West Des Moines, IA Metropolitan Statistical Area—see Appendix B for areas included; n/a not available; (3) The city and U.S. figures shown were reported using the revised Uniform Crime Reporting (UCR) definition of rape. The suburban and metro area figures shown are an aggregate total of the data submitted using both the revised and legacy UCR definitions.
Source: FBI Uniform Crime Reports, 2017 (data for 2018 was not available)

Hate Crimes

Area	Number of Quarters Reported	Number of Incidents per Bias Motivation					
		Race/Ethnicity/ Ancestry	Religion	Sexual Orientation	Disability	Gender	Gender Identity
City	4	0	1	0	0	0	0
U.S.	4	4,047	1,419	1,196	159	47	168

Source: Federal Bureau of Investigation, Hate Crime Statistics 2018

Identity Theft Consumer Reports

Area	Reports	Reports per 100,000 Population	Rank[2]
MSA[1]	518	79	256
U.S.	650,572	198	-

Note: (1) Figures cover the Des Moines-West Des Moines, IA Metropolitan Statistical Area—see Appendix B for areas included; (2) Rank ranges from 1 to 386 where 1 indicates greatest number of identity theft reports per 100,000 population
Source: Federal Trade Commission, Consumer Sentinel Network Data Book for January–December 2019

Fraud and Other Consumer Reports

Area	Reports	Reports per 100,000 Population	Rank[2]
MSA[1]	3,295	503	245
U.S.	2,590,177	789	-

Note: (1) Figures cover the Des Moines-West Des Moines, IA Metropolitan Statistical Area—see Appendix B for areas included; (2) Rank ranges from 1 to 386 where 1 indicates greatest number of fraud and other consumer reports per 100,000 population
Source: Federal Trade Commission, Consumer Sentinel Network Data Book for January–December 2019

SPORTS

Professional Sports Teams

Team Name	League	Year Established

No teams are located in the metro area
Source: Wikipedia, Major Professional Sports Teams of the United States and Canada, May 4, 2020

CLIMATE

Average and Extreme Temperatures

Temperature	Jan	Feb	Mar	Apr	May	Jun	Jul	Aug	Sep	Oct	Nov	Dec	Yr.
Extreme High (°F)	65	70	91	93	98	103	105	108	99	95	76	69	108
Average High (°F)	29	34	45	61	72	82	86	84	76	65	48	33	60
Average Temp. (°F)	20	25	36	51	62	72	76	74	65	54	39	25	50
Average Low (°F)	11	16	27	40	51	61	66	64	54	43	29	17	40
Extreme Low (°F)	-24	-20	-22	9	28	42	47	40	28	14	-3	-22	-24

Note: Figures cover the years 1945-1990
Source: National Climatic Data Center, International Station Meteorological Climate Summary, 9/96

Average Precipitation/Snowfall/Humidity

Precip./Humidity	Jan	Feb	Mar	Apr	May	Jun	Jul	Aug	Sep	Oct	Nov	Dec	Yr.
Avg. Precip. (in.)	1.1	1.1	2.3	3.1	3.8	4.4	3.5	3.9	3.1	2.4	1.7	1.2	31.8
Avg. Snowfall (in.)	8	7	7	2	Tr	0	0	0	Tr	Tr	3	7	33
Avg. Rel. Hum. 6am (%)	77	79	79	78	78	81	83	86	85	80	79	80	80
Avg. Rel. Hum. 3pm (%)	65	63	57	50	51	52	52	54	52	50	58	66	56

Note: Figures cover the years 1945-1990; Tr = Trace amounts (<0.05 in. of rain; <0.5 in. of snow)
Source: National Climatic Data Center, International Station Meteorological Climate Summary, 9/96

Weather Conditions

Temperature			Daytime Sky			Precipitation		
5°F & below	32°F & below	90°F & above	Clear	Partly cloudy	Cloudy	0.01 inch or more precip.	0.1 inch or more snow/ice	Thunder-storms
25	137	26	99	128	138	106	25	46

Note: Figures are average number of days per year and cover the years 1945-1990
Source: National Climatic Data Center, International Station Meteorological Climate Summary, 9/96

HAZARDOUS WASTE

Superfund Sites

The Des Moines-West Des Moines, IA metro area is home to two sites on the EPA's Superfund National Priorities List: **Des Moines Tce** (final); **Railroad Avenue Groundwater Contamination** (final). There are a total of 1,387 Superfund sites with a status of proposed or final on the list in the U.S. *U.S. Environmental Protection Agency, National Priorities List, May 5, 2020*

**AIR & WATER
QUALITY**

Air Quality Trends: Ozone

	1990	1995	2000	2005	2010	2012	2014	2016	2017	2018
MSA[1]	n/a	n/a	n/a	n/a	n/a	n/a	n/a	n/a	n/a	n/a
U.S.	0.088	0.089	0.082	0.080	0.073	0.075	0.067	0.069	0.068	0.069

Note: (1) Data covers the Des Moines-West Des Moines, IA Metropolitan Statistical Area—see Appendix B for areas included; n/a not available. The values shown are the composite ozone concentration averages among trend sites based on the highest fourth daily maximum 8-hour concentration in parts per million. These trends are based on sites having an adequate record of monitoring data during the trend period. Data from exceptional events are included.
Source: U.S. Environmental Protection Agency, Air Quality Monitoring Information, "Air Quality Trends by City, 1990-2018"

Air Quality Index

Area	Percent of Days when Air Quality was...[2]					AQI Statistics[2]	
	Good	Moderate	Unhealthy for Sensitive Groups	Unhealthy	Very Unhealthy	Maximum	Median
MSA[1]	77.8	21.6	0.5	0.0	0.0	112	40

Note: (1) Data covers the Des Moines-West Des Moines, IA Metropolitan Statistical Area—see Appendix B for areas included; (2) Based on 365 days with AQI data in 2018. Air Quality Index (AQI) is an index for reporting daily air quality. EPA calculates the AQI for five major air pollutants regulated by the Clean Air Act: ground-level ozone, particle pollution (aka particulate matter), carbon monoxide, sulfur dioxide, and nitrogen dioxide. The AQI runs from 0 to 500. The higher the AQI value, the greater the level of air pollution and the greater the health concern. There are six AQI categories: "Good" AQI is between 0 and 50. Air quality is considered satisfactory; "Moderate" AQI is between 51 and 100. Air quality is acceptable; "Unhealthy for Sensitive Groups" When AQI values are between 101 and 150, members of sensitive groups may experience health effects; "Unhealthy" When AQI values are between 151 and 200 everyone may begin to experience health effects; "Very Unhealthy" AQI values between 201 and 300 trigger a health alert; "Hazardous" AQI values over 300 trigger warnings of emergency conditions (not shown).
Source: U.S. Environmental Protection Agency, Air Quality Index Report, 2018

Air Quality Index Pollutants

Area	Percent of Days when AQI Pollutant was...[2]					
	Carbon Monoxide	Nitrogen Dioxide	Ozone	Sulfur Dioxide	Particulate Matter 2.5	Particulate Matter 10
MSA[1]	0.0	1.4	61.6	0.0	37.0	0.0

Note: (1) Data covers the Des Moines-West Des Moines, IA Metropolitan Statistical Area—see Appendix B for areas included; (2) Based on 365 days with AQI data in 2018. The Air Quality Index (AQI) is an index for reporting daily air quality. EPA calculates the AQI for five major air pollutants regulated by the Clean Air Act: ground-level ozone, particle pollution (also known as particulate matter), carbon monoxide, sulfur dioxide, and nitrogen dioxide. The AQI runs from 0 to 500. The higher the AQI value, the greater the level of air pollution and the greater the health concern.
Source: U.S. Environmental Protection Agency, Air Quality Index Report, 2018

Maximum Air Pollutant Concentrations: Particulate Matter, Ozone, CO and Lead

	Particulate Matter 10 (ug/m³)	Particulate Matter 2.5 Wtd AM (ug/m³)	Particulate Matter 2.5 24-Hr (ug/m³)	Ozone (ppm)	Carbon Monoxide (ppm)	Lead (ug/m³)
MSA[1] Level	43	8	18	0.065	1	n/a
NAAQS[2]	150	15	35	0.075	9	0.15
Met NAAQS[2]	Yes	Yes	Yes	Yes	Yes	n/a

Note: (1) Data covers the Des Moines-West Des Moines, IA Metropolitan Statistical Area—see Appendix B for areas included; Data from exceptional events are included; (2) National Ambient Air Quality Standards; ppm = parts per million; ug/m³ = micrograms per cubic meter; n/a not available.
Concentrations: Particulate Matter 10 (coarse particulate)—highest second maximum 24-hour concentration; Particulate Matter 2.5 Wtd AM (fine particulate)—highest weighted annual mean concentration; Particulate Matter 2.5 24-Hour (fine particulate)—highest 98th percentile 24-hour concentration; Ozone—highest fourth daily maximum 8-hour concentration; Carbon Monoxide—highest second maximum non-overlapping 8-hour concentration; Lead—maximum running 3-month average
Source: U.S. Environmental Protection Agency, Air Quality Monitoring Information, "Air Quality Statistics by City, 2018"

Maximum Air Pollutant Concentrations: Nitrogen Dioxide and Sulfur Dioxide

	Nitrogen Dioxide AM (ppb)	Nitrogen Dioxide 1-Hr (ppb)	Sulfur Dioxide AM (ppb)	Sulfur Dioxide 1-Hr (ppb)	Sulfur Dioxide 24-Hr (ppb)
MSA[1] Level	7	34	n/a	1	n/a
NAAQS[2]	53	100	30	75	140
Met NAAQS[2]	Yes	Yes	n/a	Yes	n/a

Note: (1) Data covers the Des Moines-West Des Moines, IA Metropolitan Statistical Area—see Appendix B for areas included; Data from exceptional events are included; (2) National Ambient Air Quality Standards; ppm = parts per million; ug/m³ = micrograms per cubic meter; n/a not available.
Concentrations: Nitrogen Dioxide AM—highest arithmetic mean concentration; Nitrogen Dioxide 1-Hr—highest 98th percentile 1-hour daily maximum concentration; Sulfur Dioxide AM—highest annual mean concentration; Sulfur Dioxide 1-Hr—highest 99th percentile 1-hour daily maximum concentration; Sulfur Dioxide 24-Hr—highest second maximum 24-hour concentration
Source: U.S. Environmental Protection Agency, Air Quality Monitoring Information, "Air Quality Statistics by City, 2018"

Drinking Water

Water System Name	Pop. Served	Primary Water Source Type	Violations[1]
Des Moines Water Works	233,020	Surface	22

Note: (1) Total number of violations (both active and inactive) in the EPA database
Source: U.S. Environmental Protection Agency, Office of Ground Water and Drinking Water, Safe Drinking Water Information System (based on data extracted May 5, 2020)

Fargo, North Dakota

Background

Fargo sits on the western bank of the Red River in the Red River Valley in the southeastern part of the state. The city is in Cass County and about 300 miles northwest of Minneapolis.

Fargo was originally a stopping point for steamboats on the Red River in the later part of the 19th century. Founded in 1871, the city was first named Centralia, but renamed Fargo in honor of the Northern Pacific Railway director Wells Fargo. It began to flourish after the arrival of the railroad and became known as the Gateway to the West. During the 1880s, Fargo was also known for its lenient divorce laws.

A major fire in 1893 destroyed hundreds of homes and businesses but the city was quickly rebuilt with new brick buildings, new streets and a water system. The North Dakota State Agricultural College was founded in 1890 as the state's land-grant university, and was accredited by the North Central Association in 1915. The school eventually became known as North Dakota State University during the 1960s.

Fargo grew rapidly after World War II as the connection of two interstates, I-29 and I-94, revolutionized travel in the region and allowed for further expansion in the southern and western parts of the city. In 1972, the West Acres Shopping Center was constructed near the intersection of the two interstates and served as a catalyst for retail growth in the area.

Fargo is the crossroads and economic center of eastern North Dakota and western Minnesota. Though the economy of the region was historically dependent on agriculture, other sectors have become increasingly prevalent in recent years. Today, the city's growing economy is based on food processing, manufacturing, technology, retail trade, higher education, and healthcare. The University is the city's largest public sector employer.

A significant landmark in Fargo is the main campus of North Dakota State University, which has a full-time enrollment of nearly 9,000. The city also features a large number of public parks including Percy Godwin Park, Lindenwood Park, Mickelson Field, Island Park, Roosevelt Playground, and Oak Grove Park.

As the city continues to energize the downtown area, the Renaissance Zone and Storefront Rehab programs encourage new business, renovate deteriorating buildings, and increase the availability of housing in the downtown area. The renovated Fargo Public Library's main downtown branch is popular with the city's residents.

Fargo, an Academy Award-winning 1996 film named after the city, shows the city briefly at the film's opening scene set in a bar, and is mentioned twice in the film. *Fargo* the TV series based on the film, debuted on FX in 2014. The city was featured in its seventh episode of season 1, "Who Shaves the Barber?" and more prominently in season 2. The series was filmed in Calgary, Alberta, Canada.

Fargo has a moderate northern climate. Summer temperatures average 65 degrees, while winter averages fall to 10 degrees during of December and January. The city averages 2.5 inches of rainfall per month from April to October and 8 inches of snowfall per month from December to March. Natural disaster struck in 2009, when heavy snowfall caused the Red River to flood the area, followed by extended periods of freezing temperatures.

Rankings

General Rankings

- Fargo was selected as one of the best places to live in the United States by *Money* magazine. The city ranked #47 out of 100. This year's list focused on cities with populations of 50,000 or greater. Beginning with a pool of 1,796 candidates, editors looked at 80 separate types of data, from local economy and housing market to education, diversity and ease of living—and then sent reporters to interview residents, search neighborhoods and look for other intangibles. *Money, "Best Places to Live, 2019" September 16, 2019*

- In their sixth annual survey, Livability.com looked at data for more than 1,000 U.S. cities to determine the rankings for Livability's "Top 100 Best Places to Live" in 2019. Fargo ranked #11. Criteria: median home value capped at $250,000; affordable living; vibrant economy; education, demographics, health care options. transportation & infrastructure; abundant lifestyle amenities. *Livability.com, "Top 100 Best Places to Live 2019" March 2019*

Business/Finance Rankings

- The Fargo metro area appeared on the Milken Institute "2020 Best Performing Cities" list. Rank: #91 out of 201 small metro areas. Criteria: job growth; wage and salary growth; high-tech output growth. *Milken Institute, "Best-Performing Cities 2020," February 26, 2020*

- *Forbes* ranked 203 smaller metro areas (population under 268,000) to determine the nation's "Best Small Places for Business and Careers." The Fargo metro area was ranked #23. Criteria: costs (business and living); job growth (past and projected); income growth; quality of life; educational attainment (college and high school); projected economic growth; cultural and leisure opportunities; workplace tolerance laws; net migration patterns. *Forbes, "The Best Small Places for Business and Careers 2019," October 30, 2019*

Dating/Romance Rankings

- Fargo was selected as one of the most romantic cities in the U.S. by video-rental kiosk company Redbox. The city ranked #10 out of 20. Criteria: number of romance-related rentals in 2016. *Redbox, "20 Most Romantic Cities," February 6, 2017*

Environmental Rankings

- Niche compiled a list of the nation's snowiest cities, based on the National Oceanic and Atmospheric Administration's 30-year average snowfall data. Among cities with a population of at least 50,000, Fargo ranked #18. *Niche.com, Top 25 Snowiest Cities in America, December 10, 2018*

- Fargo was highlighted as one of the cleanest metro areas for ozone air pollution in the U.S. during 2015 through 2017. The list represents cities with no monitored ozone air pollution in unhealthful ranges. *American Lung Association, "State of the Air 2019," April 24, 2019*

Health/Fitness Rankings

- *Men's Health* ranked 100 major U.S. cities in terms of the best cities for men. Fargo ranked #20. Criteria: health; fitness; quality of life. *Men's Health, "The Best & Worst Cities for Men Who Want to Be Fit and Happy," January 1, 2016*

Real Estate Rankings

- *WalletHub* compared the most populated U.S. cities, as well as at least two of the most populated cities in each state, for a total of 179, to determine which had the best markets for real estate agents. Fargo ranked #13 where demand was high and pay was the best. Criteria: sales per agent; annual median wage for real-estate agents; monthly average starting salary for real estate agents; real estate job density and competition; unemployment rate; home turnover rate; housing-market health index; and other relevant metrics. *www.WalletHub.com, "2019's Best Places to Be a Real Estate Agent," April 24, 2019*

Safety Rankings

- The National Insurance Crime Bureau ranked 382 metro areas in the U.S. in terms of per capita rates of vehicle theft. The Fargo metro area ranked #218 (#1 = highest rate). Criteria: number of vehicle theft offenses per 100,000 inhabitants in 2018. *National Insurance Crime Bureau, "Hot Spots 2018," June 25, 2019*

Seniors/Retirement Rankings

- From its Best Cities for Successful Aging indexes, the Milken Institute generated rankings for metropolitan areas, weighing data in nine categories—health care, wellness, living arrangements, transportation and convenience, financial characteristics, education, employment, community engagement, and overall livability. The Fargo metro area was ranked #14 overall in the small metro area category. *Milken Institute, "Best Cities for Successful Aging, 2017" March 14, 2017*

- Fargo made the 2019 *Forbes* list of "25 Best Places to Retire." Criteria focused on high-quality retirement living at an affordable price, include: housing/living costs compared to the national average and state taxes; air quality; crime rates; good economic outlook; home price appreciation; college presence; doctor availability; bikeability; walkability; healthy living. *Forbes.com, "The Best Places to Retire in 2019," April 23, 2019*

Women/Minorities Rankings

- Personal finance website *WalletHub* compared more than 180 U.S. cities—including the 150 most populated U.S. cities, plus at least two of the most populated cities in each state—across two key dimensions, "Hispanic Business-Friendliness" and "Hispanic Purchasing Power", to arrive at the most favorable conditions for Hispanic entrepreneurs. Fargo was ranked #111 out of 182. Criteria includes: share of Hispanic-Owned Businesses; Hispanic entrepreneurship rate to median annual income of Hispanics; Small Business-Friendliness score; cost of living; and number of Hispanics with at least a bachelor's degree. *WalletHub.com, "2019's Best Cities for Hispanic Entrepreneurs," May 1, 2019*

Miscellaneous Rankings

- *WalletHub* compared the 150 most populated U.S. cities to determine their operating efficiency. A "Quality of Services" score was constructed for each city and then divided by the total budget per capita to reveal which were managed the best. Fargo ranked #10. Criteria: financial stability; economy; education; safety; health; infrastructure and pollution. *www.WalletHub.com, "2019's Best- & Worst-Run Cities in America," July 1, 2019*

Business Environment

CITY FINANCES

City Government Finances

Component	2017 ($000)	2017 ($ per capita)
Total Revenues	318,925	2,691
Total Expenditures	400,707	3,381
Debt Outstanding	795,379	6,711
Cash and Securities[1]	499,475	4,214

Note: (1) Cash and security holdings of a government at the close of its fiscal year, including those of its dependent agencies, utilities, and liquor stores.
Source: U.S. Census Bureau, State & Local Government Finances 2017

City Government Revenue by Source

Source	2017 ($000)	2017 ($ per capita)	2017 (%)
General Revenue			
From Federal Government	5,653	48	1.8
From State Government	71,530	604	22.4
From Local Governments	0	0	0.0
Taxes			
Property	26,914	227	8.4
Sales and Gross Receipts	58,288	492	18.3
Personal Income	0	0	0.0
Corporate Income	0	0	0.0
Motor Vehicle License	0	0	0.0
Other Taxes	6,596	56	2.1
Current Charges	59,221	500	18.6
Liquor Store	0	0	0.0
Utility	24,166	204	7.6
Employee Retirement	15,870	134	5.0

Source: U.S. Census Bureau, State & Local Government Finances 2017

City Government Expenditures by Function

Function	2017 ($000)	2017 ($ per capita)	2017 (%)
General Direct Expenditures			
Air Transportation	0	0	0.0
Corrections	805	6	0.2
Education	0	0	0.0
Employment Security Administration	0	0	0.0
Financial Administration	3,724	31	0.9
Fire Protection	12,355	104	3.1
General Public Buildings	1,838	15	0.5
Governmental Administration, Other	3,641	30	0.9
Health	10,971	92	2.7
Highways	110,683	933	27.6
Hospitals	0	0	0.0
Housing and Community Development	1,382	11	0.3
Interest on General Debt	23,414	197	5.8
Judicial and Legal	1,763	14	0.4
Libraries	4,154	35	1.0
Parking	1,796	15	0.4
Parks and Recreation	15,839	133	4.0
Police Protection	18,779	158	4.7
Public Welfare	328	2	0.1
Sewerage	7,188	60	1.8
Solid Waste Management	11,966	101	3.0
Veterans' Services	0	0	0.0
Liquor Store	0	0	0.0
Utility	18,457	155	4.6
Employee Retirement	9,106	76	2.3

Source: U.S. Census Bureau, State & Local Government Finances 2017

DEMOGRAPHICS

Population Growth

Area	1990 Census	2000 Census	2010 Census	2018* Estimate	Population Growth (%) 1990-2018	2010-2018
City	74,372	90,599	105,549	120,209	61.6	13.9
MSA[1]	153,296	174,367	208,777	237,003	54.6	13.5
U.S.	248,709,873	281,421,906	308,745,538	322,903,030	29.8	4.6

Note: (1) Figures cover the Fargo, ND-MN Metropolitan Statistical Area—see Appendix B for areas included; (*) 2014-2018 5-year estimated population
Source: U.S. Census Bureau, 1990 Census, Census 2000, Census 2010, 2014-2018 American Community Survey 5-Year Estimates

Household Size

Area	One	Two	Three	Four	Five	Six	Seven or More	Average Household Size
City	36.6	33.3	15.2	8.5	4.4	1.4	0.6	2.20
MSA[1]	30.9	34.8	15.0	11.8	5.0	1.6	0.9	2.30
U.S.	27.7	33.9	15.7	13.0	6.0	2.3	1.4	2.60

Note: (1) Figures cover the Fargo, ND-MN Metropolitan Statistical Area—see Appendix B for areas included
Source: U.S. Census Bureau, 2014-2018 American Community Survey 5-Year Estimates

Race

Area	White Alone[2] (%)	Black Alone[2] (%)	Asian Alone[2] (%)	AIAN[3] Alone[2] (%)	NHOPI[4] Alone[2] (%)	Other Race Alone[2] (%)	Two or More Races (%)
City	85.3	6.1	3.8	1.2	0.0	0.6	3.0
MSA[1]	88.4	4.6	2.5	1.1	0.0	0.6	2.7
U.S.	72.7	12.7	5.4	0.8	0.2	4.9	3.2

Note: (1) Figures cover the Fargo, ND-MN Metropolitan Statistical Area—see Appendix B for areas included; (2) Alone is defined as not being in combination with one or more other races; (3) American Indian and Alaska Native; (4) Native Hawaiian and Other Pacific Islander
Source: U.S. Census Bureau, 2014-2018 American Community Survey 5-Year Estimates

Hispanic or Latino Origin

Area	Total (%)	Mexican (%)	Puerto Rican (%)	Cuban (%)	Other (%)
City	2.8	1.8	0.3	0.0	0.7
MSA[1]	3.1	2.1	0.3	0.0	0.6
U.S.	17.8	11.2	1.7	0.7	4.2

Note: Persons of Hispanic or Latino origin can be of any race; (1) Figures cover the Fargo, ND-MN Metropolitan Statistical Area—see Appendix B for areas included
Source: U.S. Census Bureau, 2014-2018 American Community Survey 5-Year Estimates

Segregation

Type	1990	2000	2010	2010 Rank[2]	1990-2000	1990-2010	2000-2010
Black/White	n/a	n/a	n/a	n/a	n/a	n/a	n/a
Asian/White	n/a	n/a	n/a	n/a	n/a	n/a	n/a
Hispanic/White	n/a	n/a	n/a	n/a	n/a	n/a	n/a

Note: All figures cover the Metropolitan Statistical Area—see Appendix B for areas included; Figures are based on an analysis of 1990, 2000, and 2010 Census Decennial Census tract data by William H. Frey, Brookings Institution and the University of Michigan Social Science Data Analysis Network. In this analysis all racial groups (whites, blacks, and asians) are non-Hispanic members of those races. Hispanics are shown as a separate category; (1) Segregation Indices are Dissimilarity Indices that measure the degree to which the minority group is distributed differently than whites across census tracts. They range from 0 (complete integration) to 100 (complete segregation) where the value indicates the percentage of the minority group that needs to move to be distributed exactly like whites; (2) Ranges from 1 (most segregated) to 102 (least segregated); n/a not available.
Source: www.CensusScope.org

Ancestry

Area	German	Irish	English	American	Italian	Polish	French[2]	Scottish	Dutch
City	38.0	8.7	3.9	2.1	0.9	3.0	3.7	1.1	1.1
MSA[1]	38.5	8.1	4.1	2.0	1.1	2.9	3.3	1.2	1.2
U.S.	13.7	9.9	7.3	6.4	5.2	2.8	2.4	1.7	1.2

Note: Figures are the percentage of the total population reporting a particular ancestry. The nine most commonly reported ancestries in the U.S. are shown. Figures include multiple ancestries (e.g. if a person reported being Irish and Italian, they were included in both columns); (1) Figures cover the Fargo, ND-MN Metropolitan Statistical Area—see Appendix B for areas included; (2) Excludes Basque
Source: U.S. Census Bureau, 2014-2018 American Community Survey 5-Year Estimates

Foreign-born Population

Area	Percent of Population Born in								
	Any Foreign Country	Asia	Mexico	Europe	Caribbean	Central America[2]	South America	Africa	Canada
City	8.8	3.5	0.1	1.1	0.1	0.1	0.2	3.4	0.2
MSA[1]	6.4	2.7	0.2	0.7	0.1	0.1	0.2	2.2	0.3
U.S.	13.5	4.1	3.5	1.5	1.3	1.1	0.9	0.7	0.3

Note: (1) Figures cover the Fargo, ND-MN Metropolitan Statistical Area—see Appendix B for areas included; (2) Excludes Mexico.
Source: U.S. Census Bureau, 2014-2018 American Community Survey 5-Year Estimates

Marital Status

Area	Never Married	Now Married[2]	Separated	Widowed	Divorced
City	43.4	42.2	1.0	4.6	8.7
MSA[1]	37.3	49.2	0.9	4.3	8.3
U.S.	33.3	48.1	2.0	5.8	10.8

Note: Figures are percentages and cover the population 15 years of age and older; (1) Figures cover the Fargo, ND-MN Metropolitan Statistical Area—see Appendix B for areas included; (2) Excludes separated
Source: U.S. Census Bureau, 2014-2018 American Community Survey 5-Year Estimates

Disability by Age

Area	All Ages	Under 18 Years Old	18 to 64 Years Old	65 Years and Over
City	9.9	2.8	7.7	36.7
MSA[1]	9.5	3.1	7.5	34.0
U.S.	12.6	4.2	10.3	35.0

Note: Figures show percent of the civilian noninstitutionalized population that reported having a disability. Disability status is determined from six types of difficulty: vision, hearing, cognitive, ambulatory, self-care, and independent living. For children under 5 years old, hearing and vision difficulty are used to determine disability status. For children between the ages of 5 and 14, disability status is determined from hearing, vision, cognitive, ambulatory, and self-care difficulties. For people aged 15 years and older, they are considered to have a disability if they have difficulty with any one of the six difficulty types; Note: (1) Figures cover the Fargo, ND-MN Metropolitan Statistical Area—see Appendix B for areas included
Source: U.S. Census Bureau, 2014-2018 American Community Survey 5-Year Estimates

Age

Area	Percent of Population									Median Age
	Under Age 5	Age 5–19	Age 20–34	Age 35–44	Age 45–54	Age 55–64	Age 65–74	Age 75–84	Age 85+	
City	6.6	17.8	32.7	11.7	9.7	10.1	6.2	3.3	1.9	30.4
MSA[1]	7.1	19.4	27.8	12.4	10.8	10.8	6.4	3.4	1.9	32.3
U.S.	6.1	19.3	20.7	12.6	13.2	12.8	8.8	4.5	1.9	37.9

Note: (1) Figures cover the Fargo, ND-MN Metropolitan Statistical Area—see Appendix B for areas included
Source: U.S. Census Bureau, 2014-2018 American Community Survey 5-Year Estimates

Gender

Area	Males	Females	Males per 100 Females
City	60,770	59,439	102.2
MSA[1]	119,356	117,647	101.5
U.S.	158,984,190	163,918,840	97.0

Note: (1) Figures cover the Fargo, ND-MN Metropolitan Statistical Area—see Appendix B for areas included
Source: U.S. Census Bureau, 2014-2018 American Community Survey 5-Year Estimates

Religious Groups by Family

Area	Catholic	Baptist	Non-Den.	Methodist[2]	Lutheran	LDS[3]	Pentecostal	Presbyterian[4]	Muslim[5]	Judaism
MSA[1]	17.4	0.4	0.5	3.3	32.5	0.6	1.5	1.9	0.1	<0.1
U.S.	19.1	9.3	4.0	4.0	2.3	2.0	1.9	1.6	0.8	0.7

Note: Figures are the number of adherents as a percentage of the total population; (1) Figures cover the Fargo, ND-MN Metropolitan Statistical Area—see Appendix B for areas included; (2) Methodist/Pietist; (3) Latter Day Saints; (4) Reformed; (5) Figures are estimates
Source: Association of Statisticians of American Religious Bodies, 2010 U.S. Religion Census: Religious Congregations & Membership Study

Religious Groups by Tradition

Area	Catholic	Evangelical Protestant	Mainline Protestant	Other Tradition	Black Protestant	Orthodox
MSA[1]	17.4	10.7	30.8	0.9	<0.1	<0.1
U.S.	19.1	16.2	7.3	4.3	1.6	0.3

Note: Figures are the number of adherents as a percentage of the total population; (1) Figures cover the Fargo, ND-MN Metropolitan Statistical Area—see Appendix B for areas included
Source: Association of Statisticians of American Religious Bodies, 2010 U.S. Religion Census: Religious Congregations & Membership Study

ECONOMY

Gross Metropolitan Product

Area	2017	2018	2019	2020	Rank[2]
MSA[1]	15.3	16.1	16.8	17.5	156

Note: Figures are in billions of dollars; (1) Figures cover the Fargo, ND-MN Metropolitan Statistical Area—see Appendix B for areas included; (2) Rank is based on 2018 data and ranges from 1 to 381
Source: U.S. Conference of Mayors, U.S. Metro Economies: GMP & Employment 2018-2020, September 2019

Economic Growth

Area	2015-17 (%)	2018 (%)	2019 (%)	2020 (%)	Rank[2]
MSA[1]	0.4	2.1	2.6	2.0	283
U.S.	1.9	2.9	2.3	2.1	–

Note: Figures are real gross metropolitan product (GMP) growth rates and represent average annual percent change; (1) Figures cover the Fargo, ND-MN Metropolitan Statistical Area—see Appendix B for areas included; (2) Rank is based on 2017 2-year average annual percent change and ranges from 1 to 381
Source: U.S. Conference of Mayors, U.S. Metro Economies: GMP & Employment 2018-2020, September 2019

Metropolitan Area Exports

Area	2013	2014	2015	2016	2017	2018	Rank[2]
MSA[1]	817.9	782.8	543.2	474.5	519.5	553.5	208

Note: Figures are in millions of dollars; (1) Figures cover the Fargo, ND-MN Metropolitan Statistical Area—see Appendix B for areas included; (2) Rank is based on 2018 data and ranges from 1 to 387
Source: U.S. Department of Commerce, International Trade Administration, Office of Trade and Economic Analysis, Industry and Analysis, Exports by Metropolitan Area, data extracted April 15, 2020

Building Permits

Area	Single-Family			Multi-Family			Total		
	2017	2018	Pct. Chg.	2017	2018	Pct. Chg.	2017	2018	Pct. Chg.
City	444	313	-29.5	781	897	14.9	1,225	1,210	-1.2
MSA[1]	1,065	1,080	1.4	826	1,233	49.3	1,891	2,313	22.3
U.S.	820,000	855,300	4.3	462,000	473,500	2.5	1,282,000	1,328,800	3.7

Note: (1) Figures cover the Fargo, ND-MN Metropolitan Statistical Area—see Appendix B for areas included; Figures represent new, privately-owned housing units authorized (unadjusted data); All permit data are based on estimates with imputation
Source: U.S. Census Bureau, Manufacturing, Mining, and Construction Statistics, Building Permits, 2017, 2018

Bankruptcy Filings

Area	Business Filings			Nonbusiness Filings		
	2018	2019	% Chg.	2018	2019	% Chg.
Cass County	6	4	-33.3	187	198	5.9
U.S.	22,232	22,780	2.5	751,186	752,160	0.1

Note: Business filings include Chapter 7, Chapter 9, Chapter 11, Chapter 12, Chapter 13, Chapter 15, and Section 304; Nonbusiness filings include Chapter 7, Chapter 11, and Chapter 13
Source: Administrative Office of the U.S. Courts, Business and Nonbusiness Bankruptcy, County Cases Commenced by Chapter of the Bankruptcy Code, During the 12-Month Period Ending December 31, 2018 and Business and Nonbusiness Bankruptcy, County Cases Commenced by Chapter of the Bankruptcy Code, During the 12-Month Period Ending December 31, 2019

Housing Vacancy Rates

Area	Gross Vacancy Rate[2] (%)			Year-Round Vacancy Rate[3] (%)			Rental Vacancy Rate[4] (%)			Homeowner Vacancy Rate[5] (%)		
	2017	2018	2019	2017	2018	2019	2017	2018	2019	2017	2018	2019
MSA[1]	n/a	n/a	n/a	n/a	n/a	n/a	n/a	n/a	n/a	n/a	n/a	n/a
U.S.	12.7	12.3	12.0	9.9	9.7	9.5	7.2	6.9	6.7	1.6	1.5	1.4

Note: (1) Figures cover the Fargo, ND-MN Metropolitan Statistical Area—see Appendix B for areas included; (2) The percentage of the total housing inventory that is vacant; (3) The percentage of the housing inventory (excluding seasonal units) that is year-round vacant; (4) The percentage of rental inventory that is vacant for rent; (5) The percentage of homeowner inventory that is vacant for sale; n/a not available
Source: U.S. Census Bureau, Housing Vacancies and Homeownership Annual Statistics: 2017, 2018, 2019

INCOME

Income

Area	Per Capita ($)	Median Household ($)	Average Household ($)
City	33,985	53,309	76,065
MSA[1]	34,793	62,832	83,829
U.S.	32,621	60,293	84,938

Note: (1) Figures cover the Fargo, ND-MN Metropolitan Statistical Area—see Appendix B for areas included
Source: U.S. Census Bureau, 2014-2018 American Community Survey 5-Year Estimates

Household Income Distribution

Area	Percent of Households Earning							
	Under $15,000	$15,000 -$24,999	$25,000 -$34,999	$35,000 -$49,999	$50,000 -$74,999	$75,000 -$99,999	$100,000 -$149,999	$150,000 and up
City	11.1	10.5	10.6	14.4	18.1	13.5	12.4	9.4
MSA[1]	9.5	8.9	8.9	12.6	18.4	15.1	15.2	11.4
U.S.	10.9	9.3	9.3	12.6	17.5	12.5	14.6	13.3

Note: (1) Figures cover the Fargo, ND-MN Metropolitan Statistical Area—see Appendix B for areas included
Source: U.S. Census Bureau, 2014-2018 American Community Survey 5-Year Estimates

Poverty Rate

Area	All Ages	Under 18 Years Old	18 to 64 Years Old	65 Years and Over
City	13.0	12.2	14.1	8.0
MSA[1]	10.9	11.0	11.7	6.6
U.S.	14.1	19.5	13.2	9.3

Note: Figures are percentage of people whose income during the past 12 months was below the poverty level; (1) Figures cover the Fargo, ND-MN Metropolitan Statistical Area—see Appendix B for areas included
Source: U.S. Census Bureau, 2014-2018 American Community Survey 5-Year Estimates

EMPLOYMENT

Labor Force and Employment

Area	Civilian Labor Force			Workers Employed		
	Dec. 2018	Dec. 2019	% Chg.	Dec. 2018	Dec. 2019	% Chg.
City	69,345	69,702	0.5	67,902	68,423	0.8
MSA[1]	137,308	138,402	0.8	134,173	135,435	0.9
U.S.	162,510,000	164,007,000	0.9	156,481,000	158,504,000	1.3

Note: Data is not seasonally adjusted and covers workers 16 years of age and older; (1) Figures cover the Fargo, ND-MN Metropolitan Statistical Area—see Appendix B for areas included
Source: Bureau of Labor Statistics, Local Area Unemployment Statistics

Unemployment Rate

Area	2019											
	Jan.	Feb.	Mar.	Apr.	May	Jun.	Jul.	Aug.	Sep.	Oct.	Nov.	Dec.
City	2.8	2.6	2.6	2.1	1.8	2.2	1.9	1.9	1.7	1.4	1.7	1.8
MSA[1]	3.2	3.0	3.0	2.4	2.0	2.4	2.1	2.0	1.9	1.6	1.8	2.1
U.S.	4.4	4.1	3.9	3.3	3.4	3.8	4.0	3.8	3.3	3.3	3.3	3.4

Note: Data is not seasonally adjusted and covers workers 16 years of age and older; (1) Figures cover the
Fargo, ND-MN Metropolitan Statistical Area—see Appendix B for areas included
Source: Bureau of Labor Statistics, Local Area Unemployment Statistics

Average Wages

Occupation	$/Hr.	Occupation	$/Hr.
Accountants and Auditors	31.60	Maintenance and Repair Workers	19.70
Automotive Mechanics	22.40	Marketing Managers	58.10
Bookkeepers	19.00	Network and Computer Systems Admin.	35.50
Carpenters	21.20	Nurses, Licensed Practical	21.40
Cashiers	11.80	Nurses, Registered	32.80
Computer Programmers	37.10	Nursing Assistants	15.80
Computer Systems Analysts	38.00	Office Clerks, General	19.80
Computer User Support Specialists	22.30	Physical Therapists	38.20
Construction Laborers	20.90	Physicians	120.70
Cooks, Restaurant	14.10	Plumbers, Pipefitters and Steamfitters	26.00
Customer Service Representatives	17.80	Police and Sheriff's Patrol Officers	31.00
Dentists	93.20	Postal Service Mail Carriers	24.70
Electricians	27.00	Real Estate Sales Agents	24.30
Engineers, Electrical	41.90	Retail Salespersons	14.70
Fast Food and Counter Workers	12.30	Sales Representatives, Technical/Scientific	38.10
Financial Managers	69.10	Secretaries, Exc. Legal/Medical/Executive	18.50
First-Line Supervisors of Office Workers	26.50	Security Guards	16.00
General and Operations Managers	56.80	Surgeons	n/a
Hairdressers/Cosmetologists	17.00	Teacher Assistants, Exc. Postsecondary*	15.90
Home Health and Personal Care Aides	14.80	Teachers, Secondary School, Exc. Sp. Ed.*	30.30
Janitors and Cleaners	13.90	Telemarketers	n/a
Landscaping/Groundskeeping Workers	17.70	Truck Drivers, Heavy/Tractor-Trailer	23.70
Lawyers	52.20	Truck Drivers, Light/Delivery Services	18.90
Maids and Housekeeping Cleaners	12.80	Waiters and Waitresses	11.40

Note: Wage data covers the Fargo, ND-MN Metropolitan Statistical Area—see Appendix B for areas included;
(*) Hourly wages were calculated from annual wage data based on a 40 hour work week; n/a not available.
Source: Bureau of Labor Statistics, Metro Area Occupational Employment & Wage Estimates, May 2019

Employment by Occupation

Occupation Classification	City (%)	MSA[1] (%)	U.S. (%)
Management, Business, Science, and Arts	39.0	39.4	37.9
Natural Resources, Construction, and Maintenance	7.7	8.6	8.9
Production, Transportation, and Material Moving	12.6	12.7	13.3
Sales and Office	21.1	22.2	22.1
Service	19.5	17.2	17.9

Note: Figures cover employed civilians 16 years of age and older; (1) Figures cover the Fargo, ND-MN
Metropolitan Statistical Area—see Appendix B for areas included
Source: U.S. Census Bureau, 2014-2018 American Community Survey 5-Year Estimates

Employment by Industry

Sector	MSA[1] Number of Employees	MSA[1] Percent of Total	U.S. Percent of Total
Construction, Mining, and Logging	8,800	6.0	5.4
Education and Health Services	28,100	19.1	16.1
Financial Activities	11,600	7.9	5.8
Government	20,400	13.9	15.0
Information	3,200	2.2	1.9
Leisure and Hospitality	14,300	9.7	10.8
Manufacturing	10,200	6.9	8.4
Other Services	5,000	3.4	3.9
Professional and Business Services	14,600	9.9	14.1
Retail Trade	15,400	10.5	10.6
Transportation, Warehousing, and Utilities	6,100	4.2	4.2
Wholesale Trade	9,100	6.2	3.9

Note: Figures are non-farm employment as of December 2019. Figures are not seasonally adjusted and include workers 16 years of age and older; (1) Figures cover the Fargo, ND-MN Metropolitan Statistical Area—see Appendix B for areas included
Source: Bureau of Labor Statistics, Current Employment Statistics, Employment, Hours, and Earnings

Occupations with Greatest Projected Employment Growth: 2019 – 2021

Occupation[1]	2019 Employment	2021 Projected Employment	Numeric Employment Change	Percent Employment Change
Registered Nurses	9,890	10,300	410	4.1
Personal Care Aides	6,590	6,990	400	6.1
Combined Food Preparation and Serving Workers, Including Fast Food	7,660	7,900	240	3.1
Janitors and Cleaners, Except Maids and Housekeeping Cleaners	6,840	7,010	170	2.5
General and Operations Managers	7,590	7,740	150	2.0
Nursing Assistants	7,640	7,790	150	2.0
Teacher Assistants	5,020	5,160	140	2.8
Construction Laborers	5,750	5,880	130	2.3
Elementary School Teachers, Except Special Education	4,170	4,290	120	2.9
Cooks, Restaurant	2,920	3,040	120	4.1

Note: Projections cover North Dakota; (1) Sorted by numeric employment change
Source: www.projectionscentral.com, State Occupational Projections, 2019–2021 Short-Term Projections

Fastest Growing Occupations: 2019 – 2021

Occupation[1]	2019 Employment	2021 Projected Employment	Numeric Employment Change	Percent Employment Change
Personal Care Aides	6,590	6,990	400	6.1
Software Developers, Applications	1,130	1,190	60	5.3
Financial Managers	1,540	1,620	80	5.2
Coaches and Scouts	1,090	1,140	50	4.6
Civil Engineers	1,390	1,450	60	4.3
Preschool Teachers, Except Special Education	1,380	1,440	60	4.3
Registered Nurses	9,890	10,300	410	4.1
Cooks, Restaurant	2,920	3,040	120	4.1
Fitness Trainers and Aerobics Instructors	1,950	2,030	80	4.1
Social and Human Service Assistants	1,260	1,310	50	4.0

Note: Projections cover North Dakota; (1) Sorted by percent employment change and excludes occupations with numeric employment change less than 50
Source: www.projectionscentral.com, State Occupational Projections, 2019–2021 Short-Term Projections

TAXES

State Corporate Income Tax Rates

State	Tax Rate (%)	Income Brackets ($)	Num. of Brackets	Financial Institution Tax Rate (%)[a]	Federal Income Tax Ded.
North Dakota	1.41 - 4.31 (s)	25,000 - 50,001	3	1.41 - 4.31 (s)	No

Note: Tax rates as of January 1, 2020; (a) Rates listed are the corporate income tax rate applied to financial institutions or excise taxes based on income; (s) North Dakota imposes a 3.5% surtax for filers electing to use the water's edge method to apportion income.
Source: Federation of Tax Administrators, State Corporate Income Tax Rates, January 1, 2020

State Individual Income Tax Rates

State	Tax Rate (%)	Income Brackets ($)	Personal Exemptions ($) Single	Married	Depend.	Standard Ded. ($) Single	Married
North Dakota (a)	1.1 - 2.9	40,125 - 440,600 (r)	(d)	(d)	(d)	12,400	24,800 (d)

Note: Tax rates as of January 1, 2020; Local- and county-level taxes are not included; Federal income tax is not deductible on state income tax returns; (a) 19 states have statutory provision for automatically adjusting to the rate of inflation the dollar values of the income tax brackets, standard deductions, and/or personal exemptions. Michigan indexes the personal exemption only. Oregon does not index the income brackets for $125,000 and over; (d) These states use the personal exemption/standard deduction amounts provided in the federal Internal Revenue Code; (r) The income brackets reported for North Dakota are for single individuals. For married couples filing jointly, the same tax rates apply to income brackets ranging from $67,050 to $440,600.
Source: Federation of Tax Administrators, State Individual Income Tax Rates, January 1, 2020

Various State Sales and Excise Tax Rates

State	State Sales Tax (%)	Gasoline[1] (¢/gal.)	Cigarette[2] ($/pack)	Spirits[3] ($/gal.)	Wine[4] ($/gal.)	Beer[5] ($/gal.)	Recreational Marijuana (%)
North Dakota	5	23	0.44	5.12	1.22	0.45	Not legal

Note: All tax rates as of January 1, 2020; (1) The American Petroleum Institute has developed a methodology for determining the average tax rate on a gallon of fuel. Rates may include any of the following: excise taxes, environmental fees, storage tank fees, other fees or taxes, general sales tax, and local taxes; (2) The federal excise tax of $1.0066 per pack and local taxes are not included; (3) Rates are those applicable to off-premise sales of 40% alcohol by volume (a.b.v.) distilled spirits in 750ml containers. Local excise taxes are excluded; (4) Rates are those applicable to off-premise sales of 11% a.b.v. non-carbonated wine in 750ml containers; (5) Rates are those applicable to off-premise sales of 4.7% a.b.v. beer in 12 ounce containers.
Source: Tax Foundation, 2020 Facts & Figures: How Does Your State Compare?

State Business Tax Climate Index Rankings

State	Overall Rank	Corporate Tax Rank	Individual Income Tax Rank	Sales Tax Rank	Property Tax Rank	Unemployment Insurance Tax Rank
North Dakota	16	19	20	27	3	13

Note: The index is a measure of how each state's tax laws affect economic performance. The lower the rank, the more favorable a state's tax system is for business. States without a given tax are given a ranking of 1. The scores/rankings for the District of Columbia do not affect other states. The 2020 index represents the tax climate as of July 1, 2019.
Source: Tax Foundation, State Business Tax Climate Index 2020

COMMERCIAL UTILITIES

Typical Monthly Electric Bills

Area	Commercial Service ($/month) 1,500 kWh	40 kW demand 14,000 kWh	Industrial Service ($/month) 1,000 kW demand 200,000 kWh	50,000 kW demand 32,500,000 kWh
City	156	1,317	22,515	2,313,863
Average[1]	203	1,612	25,706	2,520,671

Note: Figures are based on annualized rates; (1) Average based on 187 utilities surveyed
Source: Edison Electric Institute, Typical Bills and Average Rates Report, Summer 2019

TRANSPORTATION

Means of Transportation to Work

Area	Car/Truck/Van		Public Transportation			Bicycle	Walked	Other Means	Worked at Home
	Drove Alone	Car-pooled	Bus	Subway	Railroad				
City	83.0	7.9	1.1	0.0	0.0	0.7	3.5	0.7	3.0
MSA[1]	82.5	8.2	0.8	0.0	0.0	0.6	2.9	0.8	4.2
U.S.	76.4	9.1	2.5	0.0	0.6	0.6	2.7	1.3	4.9

Note: Figures are percentages and cover workers 16 years of age and older; (1) Figures cover the Fargo, ND-MN Metropolitan Statistical Area—see Appendix B for areas included
Source: U.S. Census Bureau, 2014-2018 American Community Survey 5-Year Estimates

Travel Time to Work

Area	Less Than 10 Minutes	10 to 19 Minutes	20 to 29 Minutes	30 to 44 Minutes	45 to 59 Minutes	60 to 89 Minutes	90 Minutes or More
City	21.0	56.6	16.3	3.2	0.9	1.3	0.7
MSA[1]	19.0	51.2	18.5	7.1	1.8	1.5	1.0
U.S.	12.5	28.7	20.9	20.7	8.2	6.3	2.8

Note: Note: Figures are percentages and include workers 16 years old and over; (1) Figures cover the Fargo, ND-MN Metropolitan Statistical Area—see Appendix B for areas included
Source: U.S. Census Bureau, 2014-2018 American Community Survey 5-Year Estimates

Key Congestion Measures

Area	1982	1992	2002	2012	2017
Annual Hours of Delay, Total (000)	n/a	n/a	n/a	n/a	n/a
Annual Hours of Delay, Per Auto Commuter	n/a	n/a	n/a	n/a	n/a
Annual Congestion Cost, Total (million $)	n/a	n/a	n/a	n/a	n/a
Annual Congestion Cost, Per Auto Commuter ($)	n/a	n/a	n/a	n/a	n/a

Note: n/a not available
Source: Texas A&M Transportation Institute, 2019 Urban Mobility Report

Freeway Travel Time Index

Area	1982	1987	1992	1997	2002	2007	2012	2017
Urban Area Index[1]	n/a	n/a	n/a	n/a	n/a	n/a	n/a	n/a
Urban Area Rank[1,2]	n/a	n/a	n/a	n/a	n/a	n/a	n/a	n/a

Note: Freeway Travel Time Index—the ratio of travel time in the peak period to the travel time at free-flow conditions. For example, a value of 1.30 indicates a 20-minute free-flow trip takes 26 minutes in the peak (20 minutes x 1.30 = 26 minutes); (1) Data for the Fargo, ND-MN urban area was not available; (2) Rank is based on 101 larger urban areas (#1 = highest travel time index)
Source: Texas A&M Transportation Institute, 2019 Urban Mobility Report

Public Transportation

Agency Name / Mode of Transportation	Vehicles Operated in Maximum Service[1]	Annual Unlinked Passenger Trips[2] (in thous.)	Annual Passenger Miles[3] (in thous.)
Fargo Metropolitan Area Transit (MAT)			
Bus (purchased transportation)	24	1,439.0	5,852.5
Demand Response (purchased transportation)	13	52.7	303.1

Note: (1) Number of revenue vehicles operated by the given mode and type of service to meet the annual maximum service requirement. This is the revenue vehicle count during the peak season of the year; on the week and day that maximum service is provided. Vehicles operated in maximum service (VOMS) exclude atypical days and one-time special events; (2) Number of passengers who boarded public transportation vehicles. Passengers are counted each time they board a vehicle no matter how many vehicles they use to travel from their origin to their destination. (3) Sum of the distances ridden by all passengers during the entire fiscal year.
Source: Federal Transit Administration, National Transit Database, 2018

Air Transportation

Airport Name and Code / Type of Service	Passenger Airlines[1]	Passenger Enplanements	Freight Carriers[2]	Freight (lbs)
Hector International (FAR)				
Domestic service (U.S. carriers - 2019)	18	477,691	5	33,605,692
International service (U.S. carriers - 2018)	1	490	1	35,840

Note: (1) Includes all U.S.-based major, minor and commuter airlines that carried at least one passenger during the year; (2) Includes all U.S.-based airlines and freight carriers that transported at least one pound of freight during the year.
Source: Bureau of Transportation Statistics, The Intermodal Transportation Database, Air Carriers: T-100 Domestic Market (U.S. Carriers), 2019; Bureau of Transportation Statistics, The Intermodal Transportation Database, Air Carriers: T-100 International Market (U.S. Carriers), 2018

Other Transportation Statistics

Major Highways:	I-29; I-94
Amtrak Service:	Yes
Major Waterways/Ports:	North River

Source: Amtrak.com; Google Maps

BUSINESSES

Major Business Headquarters

Company Name	Industry	Rankings	
		Fortune[1]	Forbes[2]
No companies listed	-	-	-

Note: (1) Companies that produce a 10-K are ranked 1 to 500 based on 2018 revenue; (2) All private companies with at least $2 billion in annual revenue through the end of their most current fiscal year are ranked 1 to 228; companies listed are headquartered in the city; dashes indicate no ranking
Source: Fortune, "Fortune 500," June 2019; Forbes, "America's Largest Private Companies," 2019 Rankings

Fast-Growing Businesses

According to *Inc.*, Fargo is home to two of America's 500 fastest-growing private companies: **Haga Kommer** (#150); **PRx Performance** (#189). Criteria: must be an independent, privately-held, for-profit, U.S. corporation, proprietorship or partnership as of December 31, 2018; revenues must be at least $100,000 in 2015 and $2 million in 2018; must have four-year operating/sales history. *Inc., "America's 500 Fastest-Growing Private Companies," 2019*

Minority- and Women-Owned Businesses

Group	All Firms		Firms with Paid Employees			
	Firms	Sales ($000)	Firms	Sales ($000)	Employees	Payroll ($000)
AIAN[1]	73	(s)	29	(s)	100 - 249	(s)
Asian	251	128,405	80	116,765	948	23,616
Black	156	7,305	6	3,478	119	1,537
Hispanic	82	(s)	12	(s)	250 - 499	(s)
NHOPI[2]	n/a	n/a	n/a	n/a	n/a	n/a
Women	3,404	813,664	548	741,150	5,645	160,769
All Firms	11,347	21,269,902	3,362	20,817,554	84,294	3,584,192

Note: Figures cover firms located in the city; minority- and women-owned business are defined as firms in which the corresponding group own 51% or more of the stock or equity of the company; (1) American Indian and Alaska Native; (2) Native Hawaiian and Other Pacific Islander; (s) estimates are suppressed when publication standards are not met; n/a not available
Source: U.S. Census Bureau, 2012 Economic Census, Survey of Business Owners

HOTELS & CONVENTION CENTERS

Hotels, Motels and Vacation Rentals

Area	5 Star		4 Star		3 Star		2 Star		1 Star		Not Rated	
	Num.	Pct.[3]	Num.	Pct.[3]	Num.	Pct.[3]	Num.	Pct.[3]	Num.	Pct.[3]	Num.	Pct.[3]
City[1]	0	0.0	0	0.0	23	37.1	16	25.8	2	3.2	21	33.9
Total[2]	266	1.3	1,517	7.2	4,627	21.8	3,210	15.1	3,974	18.7	7,601	35.9

Note: (1) Figures cover Fargo and vicinity; (2) Figures cover all 100 cities in this book; (3) Percentage of hotels which have a given star rating; Star ratings are determined by priceline.com and offer an indication of the general quality of a particular hotel.
Source: priceline.com, April 27, 2020

Major Convention Centers

Name	Overall Space (sq. ft.)	Exhibit Space (sq. ft.)	Meeting Space (sq. ft.)	Meeting Rooms
Fargo Civic Center	n/a	n/a	40,000	4

Note: Table includes convention centers located in the Fargo, ND-MN metro area; n/a not available
Source: Original research

Living Environment

COST OF LIVING

Cost of Living Index

Composite Index	Groceries	Housing	Utilities	Trans-portation	Health Care	Misc. Goods/ Services
98.6	111.5	77.6	90.5	100.4	120.1	108.9

Note: The Cost of Living Index measures regional differences in the cost of consumer goods and services, excluding taxes and non-consumer expenditures, for professional and managerial households in the top income quintile. It is based on more than 50,000 prices covering almost 60 different items for which prices are collected three times a year by chambers of commerce, economic development organizations or university applied economic centers in each participating urban area. The numbers shown should be read as a percentage above or below the national average of 100. For example, a value of 115.4 in the groceries column indicates that grocery prices are 15.4% higher than the national average. Small differences in the index numbers should not be interpreted as significant; Figures cover the Fargo-Moorhead ND-MN urban area.
Source: The Council for Community and Economic Research, ACCRA Cost of Living Index, 2019

Grocery Prices

Area[1]	T-Bone Steak ($/pound)	Frying Chicken ($/pound)	Whole Milk ($/half gal.)	Eggs ($/dozen)	Orange Juice ($/64 oz.)	Coffee ($/11.5 oz.)
City[2]	13.65	1.95	2.59	1.81	4.01	4.14
Avg.	11.40	1.41	1.93	1.54	3.51	4.30
Min.	7.40	0.92	0.85	0.58	2.67	2.90
Max.	15.58	2.68	4.09	4.18	5.57	8.10

Note: (1) Values for the local area are compared with the average, minimum and maximum values for all 290 areas in the Cost of Living Index; (2) Figures cover the Fargo-Moorhead ND-MN urban area; T-Bone Steak (price per pound); Frying Chicken (price per pound, whole fryer); Whole Milk (half gallon carton); Eggs (price per dozen, Grade A, large); Orange Juice (64 oz. Tropicana or Florida Natural); Coffee (11.5 oz. can, vacuum-packed, Maxwell House, Hills Bros, or Folgers).
Source: The Council for Community and Economic Research, ACCRA Cost of Living Index, 2019

Housing and Utility Costs

Area[1]	New Home Price ($)	Apartment Rent ($/month)	All Electric ($/month)	Part Electric ($/month)	Other Energy ($/month)	Telephone ($/month)
City[2]	279,364	911	-	74.92	62.59	184.00
Avg.	362,090	1,142	174.35	100.00	67.76	179.60
Min.	198,329	501	91.58	31.44	28.51	165.30
Max.	2,074,561	5,050	388.18	239.41	306.15	207.90

Note: (1) Values for the local area are compared with the average, minimum and maximum values for all 290 areas in the Cost of Living Index; (2) Figures cover the Fargo-Moorhead ND-MN urban area; New Home Price (2,400 sf living area, 8,000 sf lot, in urban area with full utilities); Apartment Rent (950 sf 2 bedroom/1.5 or 2 bath, unfurnished, excluding all utilities except water); All Electric (average monthly cost for an all-electric home); Part Electric (average monthly cost for a part-electric home); Other Energy (average monthly cost for natural gas, fuel oil, coal, wood, and any other forms of energy except electricity); Telephone (price includes the base monthly rate plus taxes and fees for three lines of mobile phone service).
Source: The Council for Community and Economic Research, ACCRA Cost of Living Index, 2019

Health Care, Transportation, and Other Costs

Area[1]	Doctor ($/visit)	Dentist ($/visit)	Optometrist ($/visit)	Gasoline ($/gallon)	Beauty Salon ($/visit)	Men's Shirt ($)
City[2]	181.26	103.56	106.59	2.32	36.12	43.09
Avg.	114.85	97.58	106.10	2.50	38.15	32.15
Min.	39.00	62.22	52.22	1.53	16.88	10.27
Max.	206.67	151.53	258.67	3.79	79.29	59.30

Note: (1) Values for the local area are compared with the average, minimum and maximum values for all 290 areas in the Cost of Living Index; (2) Figures cover the Fargo-Moorhead ND-MN urban area; Doctor (general practitioners routine exam of an established patient); Dentist (adult teeth cleaning and periodic oral examination); Optometrist (full vision eye exam for established adult patient); Gasoline (one gallon regular unleaded, national brand, including all taxes, cash price at self-service pump if available); Beauty Salon (woman's shampoo, trim, and blow-dry); Men's Shirt (cotton/polyester dress shirt, pinpoint weave, long sleeves).
Source: The Council for Community and Economic Research, ACCRA Cost of Living Index, 2019

HOUSING

House Price Index (HPI)

Area	National Ranking[2]	Quarterly Change (%)	One-Year Change (%)	Five-Year Change (%)
MSA[1]	219	0.15	2.46	21.32
U.S.[3]	–	1.26	5.09	32.88

Note: The HPI is a weighted repeat sales index. It measures average price changes in repeat sales or refinancings on the same properties. This information is obtained by reviewing repeat mortgage transactions on single-family properties whose mortgages have been purchased or securitized by Fannie Mae or Freddie Mac in January 1975; (1) Figures cover the Fargo, ND-MN Metropolitan Statistical Area—see Appendix B for areas included; (2) Rankings are based on annual percentage change for all metro areas containing at least 15,000 transactions over the last 10 years and ranges from 1 to 232; (3) figures based on a weighted average of Census Division estimates using a seasonally adjusted, purchase-only index; all figures are for the period ending December 31, 2019
Source: Federal Housing Finance Agency, House Price Index, February 25, 2020

Median Single-Family Home Prices

Area	2017	2018	2019p	Percent Change 2018 to 2019
MSA[1]	208.5	217.5	221.0	1.6
U.S. Average	248.8	261.6	274.6	5.0

Note: Figures are median sales prices of existing single-family homes in thousands of dollars; (p) preliminary; (1) Figures cover the Fargo, ND-MN Metropolitan Statistical Area—see Appendix B for areas included
Source: National Association of Realtors, Median Sales Price of Existing Single-Family Homes for Metropolitan Areas, 4th Quarter 2019

Qualifying Income Based on Median Sales Price of Existing Single-Family Homes

Area	With 5% Down ($)	With 10% Down ($)	With 20% Down ($)
MSA[1]	48,356	45,810	40,720
U.S. Average	58,663	55,575	49,400

Note: Figures are preliminary; Qualifying income is based on a mortgage rate of 3.76%. Monthly principal and interest payment is limited to 25% of income; (1) Figures cover the Fargo, ND-MN Metropolitan Statistical Area—see Appendix B for areas included
Source: National Association of Realtors, Qualifying Income Based on Median Sales Price of Existing Single-Family Homes for Metropolitan Areas, 4th Quarter 2019

Median Apartment Condo-Coop Home Prices

Area	2017	2018	2019p	Percent Change 2018 to 2019
MSA[1]	n/a	n/a	n/a	n/a
U.S. Average	234.3	241.0	249.5	3.5

Note: Figures are median sales prices of existing apartment condo-coop homes in thousands of dollars; (p) preliminary; n/a not available; (1) Figures cover the Fargo, ND-MN Metropolitan Statistical Area—see Appendix B for areas included
Source: National Association of Realtors, Median Sales Price of Existing Apartment Condo-Coop Homes for Metropolitan Areas, 4th Quarter 2019

Home Value Distribution

Area	Under $50,000	$50,000 -$99,999	$100,000 -$149,999	$150,000 -$199,999	$200,000 -$299,999	$300,000 -$499,999	$500,000 -$999,999	$1,000,000 or more
City	3.6	5.6	16.1	24.9	30.0	15.9	3.5	0.5
MSA[1]	4.1	6.2	16.0	23.2	28.9	16.6	4.4	0.6
U.S.	7.6	13.0	14.0	14.3	19.2	18.3	10.5	3.1

Note: Figures are percentages and cover owner-occupied housing units; (1) Figures cover the Fargo, ND-MN Metropolitan Statistical Area—see Appendix B for areas included
Source: U.S. Census Bureau, 2014-2018 American Community Survey 5-Year Estimates

Homeownership Rate

Area	2011 (%)	2012 (%)	2013 (%)	2014 (%)	2015 (%)	2016 (%)	2017 (%)	2018 (%)	2019 (%)
MSA[1]	n/a	n/a	n/a	n/a	n/a	n/a	n/a	n/a	n/a
U.S.	66.1	65.4	65.1	64.5	63.7	63.4	63.9	64.4	64.6

Note: (1) Figures cover the Fargo, ND-MN Metropolitan Statistical Area—see Appendix B for areas included; n/a not available
Source: U.S. Census Bureau, Housing Vacancies and Homeownership Annual Statistics: 2011-2019

Year Housing Structure Built

Area	2010 or Later	2000 -2009	1990 -1999	1980 -1989	1970 -1979	1960 -1969	1950 -1959	1940 -1949	Before 1940	Median Year
City	12.6	15.7	18.4	14.3	13.9	6.6	6.9	2.7	9.0	1988
MSA[1]	12.1	18.7	15.4	11.5	15.1	7.4	7.7	2.8	9.4	1987
U.S.	4.1	14.3	13.9	13.5	15.3	10.7	10.4	5.0	12.8	1977

Note: Figures are percentages except for Median Year; Note: (1) Figures cover the Fargo, ND-MN Metropolitan Statistical Area—see Appendix B for areas included
Source: U.S. Census Bureau, 2014-2018 American Community Survey 5-Year Estimates

Gross Monthly Rent

Area	Under $500	$500 -$999	$1,000 -$1,499	$1,500 -$1,999	$2,000 -$2,499	$2,500 -$2,999	$3,000 and up	Median ($)
City	8.4	67.0	18.6	4.1	1.7	0.1	0.1	796
MSA[1]	9.1	64.2	18.8	5.5	1.8	0.3	0.2	806
U.S.	9.8	38.5	29.6	12.9	5.1	2.1	2.0	1,023

Note: Figures are percentages except for Median; Gross rent is the contract rent plus the estimated average monthly cost of utilities (electricity, gas, and water and sewer) and fuels (oil, coal, kerosene, wood, etc.) if these are paid by the renter (or paid for the renter by someone else); (1) Figures cover the Fargo, ND-MN Metropolitan Statistical Area—see Appendix B for areas included
Source: U.S. Census Bureau, 2014-2018 American Community Survey 5-Year Estimates

HEALTH

Health Risk Factors

Category	MSA[1] (%)	U.S. (%)
Adults aged 18–64 who have any kind of health care coverage	90.5	87.3
Adults who reported being in good or better health	86.1	82.4
Adults who have been told they have high blood cholesterol	29.8	33.0
Adults who have been told they have high blood pressure	25.4	32.3
Adults who are current smokers	16.7	17.1
Adults who currently use E-cigarettes	3.8	4.6
Adults who currently use chewing tobacco, snuff, or snus	5.9	4.0
Adults who are heavy drinkers[2]	8.4	6.3
Adults who are binge drinkers[3]	26.2	17.4
Adults who are overweight (BMI 25.0 - 29.9)	39.6	35.3
Adults who are obese (BMI 30.0 - 99.8)	29.0	31.3
Adults who participated in any physical activities in the past month	76.3	74.4
Adults who always or nearly always wears a seat belt	94.0	94.3

Note: (1) Figures cover the Fargo, ND-MN Metropolitan Statistical Area—see Appendix B for areas included; (2) Heavy drinkers are classified as adult men having more than 14 drinks per week and adult women having more than 7 drinks per week; (3) Binge drinkers are classified as males having five or more drinks on one occasion or females having four or more drinks on one occasion
Source: Centers for Disease Control and Prevention, Behaviorial Risk Factor Surveillance System, SMART: Selected Metropolitan Area Risk Trends, 2017

Acute and Chronic Health Conditions

Category	MSA[1] (%)	U.S. (%)
Adults who have ever been told they had a heart attack	2.8	4.2
Adults who have ever been told they have angina or coronary heart disease	3.2	3.9
Adults who have ever been told they had a stroke	1.6	3.0
Adults who have ever been told they have asthma	11.1	14.2
Adults who have ever been told they have arthritis	20.7	24.9
Adults who have ever been told they have diabetes[2]	7.4	10.5
Adults who have ever been told they had skin cancer	4.9	6.2
Adults who have ever been told they had any other types of cancer	5.7	7.1
Adults who have ever been told they have COPD	4.4	6.5
Adults who have ever been told they have kidney disease	2.4	3.0
Adults who have ever been told they have a form of depression	22.4	20.5

Note: (1) Figures cover the Fargo, ND-MN Metropolitan Statistical Area—see Appendix B for areas included; (2) Figures do not include pregnancy-related, borderline, or pre-diabetes
Source: Centers for Disease Control and Prevention, Behaviorial Risk Factor Surveillance System, SMART: Selected Metropolitan Area Risk Trends, 2017

Health Screening and Vaccination Rates

Category	MSA[1] (%)	U.S. (%)
Adults aged 65+ who have had flu shot within the past year	62.8	60.7
Adults aged 65+ who have ever had a pneumonia vaccination	78.5	75.4
Adults who have ever been tested for HIV	27.5	36.1
Adults who have ever had the shingles or zoster vaccine?	38.5	28.9
Adults who have had their blood cholesterol checked within the last five years	81.0	85.9

Note: n/a not available; (1) Figures cover the Fargo, ND-MN Metropolitan Statistical Area—see Appendix B for areas included.
Source: Centers for Disease Control and Prevention, Behavioral Risk Factor Surveillance System, SMART: Selected Metropolitan Area Risk Trends, 2017

Disability Status

Category	MSA[1] (%)	U.S. (%)
Adults who reported being deaf	5.0	6.7
Are you blind or have serious difficulty seeing, even when wearing glasses?	2.1	4.5
Are you limited in any way in any of your usual activities due of arthritis?	9.6	12.9
Do you have difficulty doing errands alone?	4.3	6.8
Do you have difficulty dressing or bathing?	n/a	3.6
Do you have serious difficulty concentrating/remembering/making decisions?	8.1	10.7
Do you have serious difficulty walking or climbing stairs?	8.6	13.6

Note: n/a not available; (1) Figures cover the Fargo, ND-MN Metropolitan Statistical Area—see Appendix B for areas included.
Source: Centers for Disease Control and Prevention, Behaviorial Risk Factor Surveillance System, SMART: Selected Metropolitan Area Risk Trends, 2017

Mortality Rates for the Top 10 Causes of Death in the U.S.

ICD-10[a] Sub-Chapter	ICD-10[a] Code	Age-Adjusted Mortality Rate[1] per 100,000 population	
		County[2]	U.S.
Malignant neoplasms	C00-C97	139.7	152.4
Ischaemic heart diseases	I20-I25	55.3	92.7
Other forms of heart disease	I30-I51	45.6	52.5
Chronic lower respiratory diseases	J40-J47	32.7	40.4
Cerebrovascular diseases	I60-I69	26.0	37.3
Other degenerative diseases of the nervous system	G30-G31	39.0	36.4
Other external causes of accidental injury	W00-X59	27.6	35.3
Organic, including symptomatic, mental disorders	F01-F09	27.2	30.0
Hypertensive diseases	I10-I15	20.0	22.9
Diabetes mellitus	E10-E14	18.9	21.3

Note: (a) ICD-10 = International Classification of Diseases 10th Revision; (1) Mortality rates are a three year average covering 2016-2018; (2) Figures cover Cass County.
Source: Centers for Disease Control and Prevention, National Center for Health Statistics. Underlying Cause of Death 1999-2018 on CDC WONDER Online Database

Mortality Rates for Selected Causes of Death

ICD-10[a] Sub-Chapter	ICD-10[a] Code	Age-Adjusted Mortality Rate[1] per 100,000 population	
		County[2]	U.S.
Assault	X85-Y09	Unreliable	6.0
Diseases of the liver	K70-K76	16.4	14.2
Human immunodeficiency virus (HIV) disease	B20-B24	Suppressed	1.6
Influenza and pneumonia	J09-J18	10.9	14.2
Intentional self-harm	X60-X84	17.3	13.9
Malnutrition	E40-E46	Suppressed	1.9
Obesity and other hyperalimentation	E65-E68	4.9	2.1
Renal failure	N17-N19	9.6	12.8
Transport accidents	V01-V99	6.6	12.5
Viral hepatitis	B15-B19	Suppressed	1.4

Note: (a) ICD-10 = International Classification of Diseases 10th Revision; (1) Mortality rates are a three year average covering 2016-2018; (2) Figures cover Cass County; Data are suppressed when the data meet the criteria for confidentiality constraints; Mortality rates are flagged as unreliable when the rate would be calculated with a numerator of 20 or less.
Source: Centers for Disease Control and Prevention, National Center for Health Statistics. Underlying Cause of Death 1999-2018 on CDC WONDER Online Database

Health Insurance Coverage

Area	With Health Insurance	With Private Health Insurance	With Public Health Insurance	Without Health Insurance	Population Under Age 19 Without Health Insurance
City	93.3	80.8	24.2	6.7	4.6
MSA[1]	94.4	82.1	24.4	5.6	4.5
U.S.	90.6	67.7	34.7	9.4	5.2

Note: Figures are percentages that cover the civilian noninstitutionalized population; (1) Figures cover the Fargo, ND-MN Metropolitan Statistical Area—see Appendix B for areas included
Source: U.S. Census Bureau, 2014-2018 American Community Survey 5-Year Estimates

Number of Medical Professionals

Area	MDs[3]	DOs[3,4]	Dentists	Podiatrists	Chiropractors	Optometrists
County[1] (number)	697	34	141	6	119	53
County[1] (rate[2])	392.0	19.1	77.7	3.3	65.6	29.2
U.S. (rate[2])	281.9	23.4	69.1	6.0	27.5	16.4

Note: Data as of 2018 unless noted; (1) Data covers Cass County; (2) Rate per 100,000 population; (3) Data as of 2017 and includes all active, non-federal physicians; (4) Doctor of Osteopathic Medicine
Source: U.S. Department of Health and Human Services, Health Resources and Services Administration, Bureau of Health Professions, Area Resource File (ARF) 2018-2019

EDUCATION

Public School District Statistics

District Name	Schls	Pupils	Pupil/ Teacher Ratio	Minority Pupils[1] (%)	Free Lunch Eligible[2] (%)	IEP[3] (%)
Fargo 1	22	11,514	13.4	28.1	25.5	14.2

Note: Table includes school districts with 2,000 or more students; (1) Percentage of students that are not non-Hispanic white; (2) Percentage of students that are eligible for the free lunch program; (3) Percentage of students that have an Individualized Education Program.
Source: U.S. Department of Education, National Center for Education Statistics, Common Core of Data, Local Education Agency (School District) Universe Survey: School Year 2018-2019; U.S. Department of Education, National Center for Education Statistics, Common Core of Data, Public Elementary/Secondary School Universe Survey: School Year 2018-2019

Highest Level of Education

Area	Less than H.S.	H.S. Diploma	Some College, No Deg.	Associate Degree	Bachelor's Degree	Master's Degree	Prof. School Degree	Doctorate Degree
City	6.1	20.1	19.9	14.5	27.8	7.6	2.2	1.9
MSA[1]	5.4	21.2	21.0	14.5	27.0	7.6	1.8	1.5
U.S.	12.3	27.1	20.6	8.4	19.4	8.6	2.1	1.4

Note: Figures cover persons age 25 and over; (1) Figures cover the Fargo, ND-MN Metropolitan Statistical Area—see Appendix B for areas included
Source: U.S. Census Bureau, 2014-2018 American Community Survey 5-Year Estimates

Educational Attainment by Race

Area	High School Graduate or Higher (%)					Bachelor's Degree or Higher (%)				
	Total	White	Black	Asian	Hisp.[2]	Total	White	Black	Asian	Hisp.[2]
City	93.9	95.7	80.4	76.5	81.9	39.5	40.6	22.4	51.1	17.3
MSA[1]	94.6	95.9	79.8	80.3	79.7	37.9	38.7	23.1	49.2	17.6
U.S.	87.7	89.6	85.4	86.8	67.7	31.5	32.9	21.1	53.5	15.8

Note: Figures shown cover persons 25 years old and over; (1) Figures cover the Fargo, ND-MN Metropolitan Statistical Area—see Appendix B for areas included; (2) People of Hispanic origin can be of any race
Source: U.S. Census Bureau, 2014-2018 American Community Survey 5-Year Estimates

School Enrollment by Grade and Control

Area	Preschool (%)		Kindergarten (%)		Grades 1 - 4 (%)		Grades 5 - 8 (%)		Grades 9 - 12 (%)	
	Public	Private	Public	Private	Public	Private	Public	Private	Public	Private
City	51.9	48.1	89.8	10.2	88.2	11.8	89.5	10.5	93.0	7.0
MSA[1]	56.9	43.1	91.6	8.4	88.8	11.2	89.2	10.8	93.0	7.0
U.S.	59.0	41.0	87.7	12.3	89.6	10.4	89.5	10.5	90.2	9.8

Note: Figures shown cover persons 3 years old and over; (1) Figures cover the Fargo, ND-MN Metropolitan Statistical Area—see Appendix B for areas included
Source: U.S. Census Bureau, 2014-2018 American Community Survey 5-Year Estimates

Average Salaries of Public School Teachers

Area	2016-17		2017-18		Change from 2016-17 to 2017-18	
	Dollars	Rank[1]	Dollars	Rank[1]	Percent	Rank[2]
North Dakota	52,536	26	52,850	29	0.60	38
U.S. Average	59,539	–	60,477	–	1.58	–

Note: (1) Rank ranges from 1 to 51 where 1 indicates highest salary; (2) Rank ranges from 1 to 51 where 1 indicates highest percent change.
Source: National Education Association, Rankings & Estimates: Rankings of the States 2018 and Estimates of School Statistics 2019

Higher Education

Four-Year Colleges			Two-Year Colleges			Medical Schools[1]	Law Schools[2]	Voc/ Tech[3]
Public	Private Non-profit	Private For-profit	Public	Private Non-profit	Private For-profit			
1	0	1	0	0	3	0	0	2

Note: Figures cover institutions located within the city limits and include main campuses only; (1) includes schools accredited by the Liaison Committee on Medical Education and the American Osteopathic Association's Commission on Osteopathic College Accreditation; (2) includes ABA-accredited schools, schools with provisional ABA accreditation, and state accredited schools; (3) includes all schools with programs that are less than 2 years.
Source: National Center for Education Statistics, Integrated Postsecondary Education System (IPEDS), 2018-19; Wikipedia, List of Medical Schools in the United States, accessed May 1, 2020; Wikipedia, List of Law Schools in the United States, accessed May 1, 2020

PRESIDENTIAL ELECTION

2016 Presidential Election Results

Area	Clinton	Trump	Johnson	Stein	Other
Cass County	38.8	49.3	7.5	1.5	2.9
U.S.	48.0	45.9	3.3	1.1	1.7

Note: Results are percentages and may not add to 100% due to rounding
Source: Dave Leip's Atlas of U.S. Presidential Elections

EMPLOYERS

Major Employers

Company Name	Industry
BlueCross BlueShield of North Dakota	Insurance
City of Fargo	Government
CNH Industrial America	Agriculture equipment
Concordia College	Education
Essentia Health	General medical & surgical hospitals
Fargo Public School District	Education
John Deere Electronic Solutions	Manufacturers
Microsoft	Computer software
Minnesota State University Moorhead	Education
Moorhead Area Public Schools	Education
Noridian Heathcare Solutions	Insurance
North Dakota State University	Education
Sanford Fargo Medical Center	Healthcare services
U.S. Bank	Financial services
Veterans Affairs	General medical & surgical hospitals
West Fargo Public School	Education

Note: Companies shown are located within the Fargo, ND-MN Metropolitan Statistical Area.
Source: Hoovers.com; Wikipedia

PUBLIC SAFETY

Crime Rate

Area	All Crimes	Violent Crimes				Property Crimes		
		Murder	Rape[3]	Robbery	Aggrav. Assault	Burglary	Larceny -Theft	Motor Vehicle Theft
City	3,565.1	4.0	84.1	50.4	279.4	556.4	2,343.4	247.4
Suburbs[1]	1,841.2	0.8	30.2	12.6	93.9	279.9	1,296.4	127.4
Metro[2]	2,722.8	2.5	57.7	31.9	188.8	421.3	1,831.9	188.8
U.S.	2,580.1	5.0	42.6	86.2	246.8	376.0	1,594.6	228.9

Note: Figures are crimes per 100,000 population; (1) All areas within the metro area that are located outside the city limits; (2) Figures cover the Fargo, ND-MN Metropolitan Statistical Area—see Appendix B for areas included; (3) The city and U.S. figures shown were reported using the revised Uniform Crime Reporting (UCR) definition of rape. The suburban and metro area figures shown are an aggregate total of the data submitted using both the revised and legacy UCR definitions.
Source: FBI Uniform Crime Reports, 2018

Hate Crimes

Area	Number of Quarters Reported	Number of Incidents per Bias Motivation					
		Race/Ethnicity/ Ancestry	Religion	Sexual Orientation	Disability	Gender	Gender Identity
City	4	0	1	1	0	0	0
U.S.	4	4,047	1,419	1,196	159	47	168

Source: Federal Bureau of Investigation, Hate Crime Statistics 2018

Identity Theft Consumer Reports

Area	Reports	Reports per 100,000 Population	Rank[2]
MSA[1]	138	56	346
U.S.	650,572	198	-

Note: (1) Figures cover the Fargo, ND-MN Metropolitan Statistical Area—see Appendix B for areas included; (2) Rank ranges from 1 to 386 where 1 indicates greatest number of identity theft reports per 100,000 population
Source: Federal Trade Commission, Consumer Sentinel Network Data Book for January–December 2019

Fraud and Other Consumer Reports

Area	Reports	Reports per 100,000 Population	Rank[2]
MSA[1]	980	399	355
U.S.	2,590,177	789	-

Note: (1) Figures cover the Fargo, ND-MN Metropolitan Statistical Area—see Appendix B for areas included; (2) Rank ranges from 1 to 386 where 1 indicates greatest number of fraud and other consumer reports per 100,000 population
Source: Federal Trade Commission, Consumer Sentinel Network Data Book for January–December 2019

SPORTS

Professional Sports Teams

Team Name	League	Year Established
No teams are located in the metro area		

Source: Wikipedia, Major Professional Sports Teams of the United States and Canada, May 4, 2020

CLIMATE

Average and Extreme Temperatures

Temperature	Jan	Feb	Mar	Apr	May	Jun	Jul	Aug	Sep	Oct	Nov	Dec	Yr.
Extreme High (°F)	52	66	78	100	98	100	106	106	102	93	74	57	106
Average High (°F)	15	21	34	54	69	77	83	81	70	57	36	21	52
Average Temp. (°F)	6	12	26	43	56	66	71	69	58	46	28	13	41
Average Low (°F)	-3	3	17	32	44	54	59	57	46	35	19	4	31
Extreme Low (°F)	-36	-34	-34	-7	20	30	36	33	19	5	-24	-32	-36

Note: Figures cover the years 1948-1995
Source: National Climatic Data Center, International Station Meteorological Climate Summary, 9/96

Average Precipitation/Snowfall/Humidity

Precip./Humidity	Jan	Feb	Mar	Apr	May	Jun	Jul	Aug	Sep	Oct	Nov	Dec	Yr.
Avg. Precip. (in.)	0.6	0.5	1.0	1.7	2.3	3.1	3.2	2.4	1.8	1.5	0.8	0.6	19.6
Avg. Snowfall (in.)	9	6	7	3	Tr	0	0	0	Tr	1	6	7	40
Avg. Rel. Hum. 6am (%)	75	77	82	79	77	82	86	86	85	80	81	78	81
Avg. Rel. Hum. 3pm (%)	70	71	67	51	45	50	50	47	49	51	65	73	57

Note: Figures cover the years 1948-1995; Tr = Trace amounts (<0.05 in. of rain; <0.5 in. of snow)
Source: National Climatic Data Center, International Station Meteorological Climate Summary, 9/96

Weather Conditions

Temperature			Daytime Sky			Precipitation		
5°F & below	32°F & below	90°F & above	Clear	Partly cloudy	Cloudy	0.01 inch or more precip.	0.1 inch or more snow/ice	Thunder-storms
65	180	15	81	145	139	100	38	31

Note: Figures are average number of days per year and cover the years 1948-1995
Source: National Climatic Data Center, International Station Meteorological Climate Summary, 9/96

HAZARDOUS WASTE

Superfund Sites

The Fargo, ND-MN metro area has no sites on the EPA's Superfund Final National Priorities List. There are a total of 1,387 Superfund sites with a status of proposed or final on the list in the U.S.
U.S. Environmental Protection Agency, National Priorities List, May 5, 2020

AIR & WATER QUALITY

Air Quality Trends: Ozone

	1990	1995	2000	2005	2010	2012	2014	2016	2017	2018
MSA[1]	n/a	n/a	n/a	n/a	n/a	n/a	n/a	n/a	n/a	n/a
U.S.	0.088	0.089	0.082	0.080	0.073	0.075	0.067	0.069	0.068	0.069

Note: (1) Data covers the Fargo, ND-MN Metropolitan Statistical Area—see Appendix B for areas included; n/a not available. The values shown are the composite ozone concentration averages among trend sites based on the highest fourth daily maximum 8-hour concentration in parts per million. These trends are based on sites having an adequate record of monitoring data during the trend period. Data from exceptional events are included.
Source: U.S. Environmental Protection Agency, Air Quality Monitoring Information, "Air Quality Trends by City, 1990-2018"

Air Quality Index

Area	Percent of Days when Air Quality was...[2]					AQI Statistics[2]	
	Good	Moderate	Unhealthy for Sensitive Groups	Unhealthy	Very Unhealthy	Maximum	Median
MSA[1]	87.5	12.2	0.3	0.0	0.0	121	35

Note: (1) Data covers the Fargo, ND-MN Metropolitan Statistical Area—see Appendix B for areas included; (2) Based on 360 days with AQI data in 2018. Air Quality Index (AQI) is an index for reporting daily air quality. EPA calculates the AQI for five major air pollutants regulated by the Clean Air Act: ground-level ozone, particle pollution (aka particulate matter), carbon monoxide, sulfur dioxide, and nitrogen dioxide. The AQI runs from 0 to 500. The higher the AQI value, the greater the level of air pollution and the greater the health concern. There are six AQI categories: "Good" AQI is between 0 and 50. Air quality is considered satisfactory; "Moderate" AQI is between 51 and 100. Air quality is acceptable; "Unhealthy for Sensitive Groups" When AQI values are between 101 and 150, members of sensitive groups may experience health effects; "Unhealthy" When AQI values are between 151 and 200 everyone may begin to experience health effects; "Very Unhealthy" AQI values between 201 and 300 trigger a health alert; "Hazardous" AQI values over 300 trigger warnings of emergency conditions (not shown).
Source: U.S. Environmental Protection Agency, Air Quality Index Report, 2018

Air Quality Index Pollutants

| Area | Percent of Days when AQI Pollutant was...[2] | | | | | |
	Carbon Monoxide	Nitrogen Dioxide	Ozone	Sulfur Dioxide	Particulate Matter 2.5	Particulate Matter 10
MSA[1]	0.0	2.5	66.4	0.0	28.6	2.5

Note: (1) Data covers the Fargo, ND-MN Metropolitan Statistical Area—see Appendix B for areas included; (2) Based on 360 days with AQI data in 2018. The Air Quality Index (AQI) is an index for reporting daily air quality. EPA calculates the AQI for five major air pollutants regulated by the Clean Air Act: ground-level ozone, particle pollution (also known as particulate matter), carbon monoxide, sulfur dioxide, and nitrogen dioxide. The AQI runs from 0 to 500. The higher the AQI value, the greater the level of air pollution and the greater the health concern.
Source: U.S. Environmental Protection Agency, Air Quality Index Report, 2018

Maximum Air Pollutant Concentrations: Particulate Matter, Ozone, CO and Lead

	Particulate Matter 10 (ug/m^3)	Particulate Matter 2.5 Wtd AM (ug/m^3)	Particulate Matter 2.5 24-Hr (ug/m^3)	Ozone (ppm)	Carbon Monoxide (ppm)	Lead (ug/m^3)
MSA[1] Level	74	7	22	0.063	n/a	n/a
NAAQS[2]	150	15	35	0.075	9	0.15
Met NAAQS[2]	Yes	Yes	Yes	Yes	n/a	n/a

Note: (1) Data covers the Fargo, ND-MN Metropolitan Statistical Area—see Appendix B for areas included; Data from exceptional events are included; (2) National Ambient Air Quality Standards; ppm = parts per million; ug/m^3 = micrograms per cubic meter; n/a not available.
Concentrations: Particulate Matter 10 (coarse particulate)—highest second maximum 24-hour concentration; Particulate Matter 2.5 Wtd AM (fine particulate)—highest weighted annual mean concentration; Particulate Matter 2.5 24-Hour (fine particulate)—highest 98th percentile 24-hour concentration; Ozone—highest fourth daily maximum 8-hour concentration; Carbon Monoxide—highest second maximum non-overlapping 8-hour concentration; Lead—maximum running 3-month average
Source: U.S. Environmental Protection Agency, Air Quality Monitoring Information, "Air Quality Statistics by City, 2018"

Maximum Air Pollutant Concentrations: Nitrogen Dioxide and Sulfur Dioxide

	Nitrogen Dioxide AM (ppb)	Nitrogen Dioxide 1-Hr (ppb)	Sulfur Dioxide AM (ppb)	Sulfur Dioxide 1-Hr (ppb)	Sulfur Dioxide 24-Hr (ppb)
MSA[1] Level	4	32	n/a	3	n/a
NAAQS[2]	53	100	30	75	140
Met NAAQS[2]	Yes	Yes	n/a	Yes	n/a

Note: (1) Data covers the Fargo, ND-MN Metropolitan Statistical Area—see Appendix B for areas included; Data from exceptional events are included; (2) National Ambient Air Quality Standards; ppm = parts per million; ug/m^3 = micrograms per cubic meter; n/a not available.
Concentrations: Nitrogen Dioxide AM—highest arithmetic mean concentration; Nitrogen Dioxide 1-Hr—highest 98th percentile 1-hour daily maximum concentration; Sulfur Dioxide AM—highest annual mean concentration; Sulfur Dioxide 1-Hr—highest 99th percentile 1-hour daily maximum concentration; Sulfur Dioxide 24-Hr—highest second maximum 24-hour concentration
Source: U.S. Environmental Protection Agency, Air Quality Monitoring Information, "Air Quality Statistics by City, 2018"

Drinking Water

Water System Name	Pop. Served	Primary Water Source Type	Violations[1]
City of Fargo	120,762	Surface	8

Note: (1) Total number of violations (both active and inactive) in the EPA database
Source: U.S. Environmental Protection Agency, Office of Ground Water and Drinking Water, Safe Drinking Water Information System (based on data extracted May 5, 2020)

Fort Wayne, Indiana

Background

Fort Wayne lies 100 miles northeast of Indianapolis, at the confluence of the St. Mary and St. Joseph rivers, which form the Maumee River. The waters, spanned by 21 bridges, divide the town into three parts.

Once the stronghold of the Miami tribe, the area was prominent in frontier history. The Miami Native Americans ruled the lower peninsula region, fighting against the Iroquois who had been armed by the English colonists. Later, the Miami tribe established itself in the Wabash Valley and built a village at the Lakeside district in Fort Wayne. They continued to side with the British during the American Revolution, after which President Washington ordered armies into the center of the Miami Territory to stop the Miami war parties, which had been encouraged to attack the new nation by the British. After Chief Little Turtle, one of the most feared and respected tribal leaders, defeated the army of General Arthur St. Clair, Washington sought the help of General "Mad" Anthony Wayne, who succeeded in defeating the rebellious tribes. Wayne marched on Miamitown and built the first American fort there. When the fort was turned over to Colonel John Hamtramck on October 21, 1794, the colonel immediately changed the name to Fort Wayne.

Fort Wayne's industrial growth began with the building of the Wabash and Erie Canal in the 1830s and was further stimulated in the 1850s when the railway came.

Nearly equidistant from Chicago, Cincinnati, and Detroit, the city is a regional transportation and communications center. Although the city is in an area rich in dairy, livestock, and vegetable farming, it is primarily a diversified industrial center, with several strong clusters of industry including advanced manufacturing, defense engineering, automotive-related development and production (home to the world's first full-size hybrid pickup truck), life science, higher education, aerospace/avionics-related, logistics and finance. Fort Wayne also enjoys additional prosperity due to its proximity to Warsaw, Indiana, termed the Orthopedic Capitol of the World due to its many orthopedic-implant manufacturers.

Institutions of higher education in the city include Indiana's Institute of Technology, Indiana University-Purdue University at Fort Wayne, and University of St. Francis. The city is also home to the Northeast Indiana Innovation Center, designed to attract high-tech businesses and to provide community outreach to local entrepreneurs and schools. Ongoing projects include the Core Incubation System, which specializes in biomedical, information systems, and advanced manufacturing plans, and the Digital Kids Initiative, which promotes early mastery of digital skills. The city has developed a blueprint for preservation and restoration of various downtown districts, including the Landing District, the Old Canal District, and the Barr Street District, which features an "International Marketplace," a cluster of businesses owned and operated by ethnic groups and supplemented by cultural centers serving them.

Fort Wayne is sometimes referred to as the "City of Churches," an unofficial moniker dating to the late-19th century when the city was the regional hub of Catholic, Lutheran, and Episcopal faiths. Today, there are nearly 400 churches in the city.

Parkview Field is home to the TinCaps, baseball's minor league team affiliated with the San Diegeo Padres. Not far from Parkview Field are condominiums, shops and a centrally located Courtyard Marriott hotel. Fort Wayne's renovated Grand Wayne Convention Center encompasses 225,000 square feet.

Fort Wayne's varied cultural and educational attractions combined with a low cost of living have earned Fort Wayne awards over the years, such as All-American City, Best Place to Live, and City Livability Outstanding Achievement. Arts events are held at the Allen County War Memorial Coliseum, Foellinger Outdoor Theater, and IPFW Performing Arts Center. Additional attractions include: the Foellinger-Freimann Botanical Conservatory with a Tropical House and cascading waterfall, Sonoran Desert House, Woody the talking tree, and hands-on exhibits; the Fort Wayne Museum of Art; the nationally acclaimed Fort Wayne Children's Zoo; and the Lincoln Museum with its award-winning permanent exhibit honoring the life and legacy of our 16th president.

The land surrounding the city is generally level to the south and east, rolling to the west and southwest, and quite hilly to the north and northwest. The climate is influenced by the Great Lakes, with rain fairly constant throughout the warmer months. Damaging hailstorms occur approximately twice a year, and severe flooding is possible. While snow generally covers the ground for about a month during the winter, heavy snowstorms are infrequent. With the exception of considerable cloudiness during the winter, Fort Wayne enjoys a good Midwestern average for sunshine.

Rankings

General Rankings

- Fort Wayne was selected as one of the best places to live in the United States by *Money* magazine. The city ranked #72 out of 100. This year's list focused on cities with populations of 50,000 or greater. Beginning with a pool of 1,796 candidates, editors looked at 80 separate types of data, from local economy and housing market to education, diversity and ease of living—and then sent reporters to interview residents, search neighborhoods and look for other intangibles. *Money, "Best Places to Live, 2019" September 16, 2019*

- In their sixth annual survey, Livability.com looked at data for more than 1,000 U.S. cities to determine the rankings for Livability's "Top 100 Best Places to Live" in 2019. Fort Wayne ranked #93. Criteria: median home value capped at $250,000; affordable living; vibrant economy; education, demographics, health care options. transportation & infrastructure; abundant lifestyle amenities. *Livability.com, "Top 100 Best Places to Live 2019" March 2019*

Business/Finance Rankings

- Fort Wayne was the #18-ranked city for savers, according to a study by the finance site GOBankingRates, which considered the prospects for people trying to save money. Criteria: average monthly cost of grocery items; median home listing price; median rent; median income; transportation costs; gas prices; and the cost of eating out for an inexpensive and mid-range meal in 100 U.S. cities. *www.gobankingrates.com, "The 20 Best (and Worst) Places to Live If You're Trying to Save Money," August 27, 2019*

- Fort Wayne was ranked #18 among 100 U.S. cities for most difficult conditions for savers, according to a study by the finance site GOBankingRates. Criteria: average monthly cost of grocery items; median home listing price; median rent; median income; transportation costs; gas prices; and the cost of eating out for an inexpensive and mid-range meal. *www.gobankingrates.com, "The 20 Best (and Worst) Places to Live If You're Trying to Save Money," August 27, 2019*

- The Fort Wayne metro area appeared on the Milken Institute "2020 Best Performing Cities" list. Rank: #111 out of 200 large metro areas. Criteria: job growth; wage and salary growth; high-tech output growth. *Milken Institute, "Best-Performing Cities 2020," February 26, 2020*

- *Forbes* ranked the 200 most populous metro areas to determine the nation's "Best Places for Business and Careers." The Fort Wayne metro area was ranked #122. Criteria: costs (business and living); job growth (past and projected); income growth; quality of life; educational attainment (college and high school); projected economic growth; cultural and leisure opportunities; workplace tolerance laws; net migration patterns. *Forbes, "The Best Places for Business and Careers 2019: Seattle Still On Top," October 30, 2019*

Children/Family Rankings

- Fort Wayne was selected as one of the most playful cities in the U.S. by KaBOOM! The organization's Playful City USA initiative honors cities and towns across the nation that have made their communities more playable. Criteria: pledging to integrate play as a solution to challenges in their communities; making it easy for children to get active and balanced play; creating more family-friendly and innovative communities as a result. *KaBOOM! National Campaign for Play, "2017 Playful City USA Communities"*

Education Rankings

- Personal finance website *WalletHub* analyzed the 150 largest U.S. metropolitan statistical areas to determine where the most educated Americans are choosing to settle. Criteria: education levels; percentage of workers with degrees; education quality and attainment gap; public school quality rankings; quality and size of each metro area's universities. Fort Wayne was ranked #104 (#1 = most educated city). *www.WalletHub.com, "2019's Most and Least Educated Cities in America," July 22, 2019*

- Fort Wayne was selected as one of America's most literate cities. The city ranked #49 out of the 82 largest U.S. cities. Criteria: number of booksellers; library resources; Internet resources; educational attainment; periodical publishing resources; newspaper circulation. *Central Connecticut State University, "America's Most Literate Cities, 2016," March 31, 2017*

Health/Fitness Rankings

- For each of the 100 largest cities in the United States, the American Fitness Index®, published by the American College of Sports Medicine and the Anthem Foundation, evaluated community infrastructure and 33 health behaviors including preventive health, levels of chronic disease conditions, pedestrian safety, air quality, and community resources that support physical activity. Fort Wayne ranked #86 for "community fitness." *americanfitnessindex.org, "ACSM American Fitness Index Health and Community Fitness Status of the 100 Largest U.S. Cities," May 14, 2019*

- The Fort Wayne metro area was identified as one of the worst cities for bed bugs in America by pest control company Orkin. The area ranked #46 out of 50 based on the number of bed bug treatments Orkin performed from December 2018 to November 2019. *Orkin, "Washington, D.C. Surpasses Baltimore to Secure Top Spot on Orkin's 2020 Bed Bug Cities List," January 13, 2020*

- *Men's Health* ranked 100 major U.S. cities in terms of the best cities for men. Fort Wayne ranked #66. Criteria: health; fitness; quality of life. *Men's Health, "The Best & Worst Cities for Men Who Want to Be Fit and Happy," January 1, 2016*

- The Fort Wayne metro area ranked #153 out of 189 in The Gallup-Sharecare Well-Being Index. Criteria: purpose; social well being; financial health; community and physical health. Results are based on telephone interviews with adults, aged 18 and older, living in metropolitan areas in the 50 U.S. states and the District of Columbia. *Gallup-Sharecare, "State of American Well-Being, 2017 Community Well-Being Rankings" March 2018*

Real Estate Rankings

- *WalletHub* compared the most populated U.S. cities, as well as at least two of the most populated cities in each state, for a total of 179, to determine which had the best markets for real estate agents. Fort Wayne ranked #108 where demand was high and pay was the best. Criteria: sales per agent; annual median wage for real-estate agents; monthly average starting salary for real estate agents; real estate job density and competition; unemployment rate; home turnover rate; housing-market health index; and other relevant metrics. *www.WalletHub.com, "2019's Best Places to Be a Real Estate Agent," April 24, 2019*

- The Fort Wayne metro area was identified as one of the nations's 20 hottest housing markets in 2020. Criteria: listing views as an indicator of demand and median days on the market as an indicator of supply. The area ranked #1. *Realtor.com, "January Top 20 Hottest Housing Markets," February 13, 2020*

Safety Rankings

- Allstate ranked the 200 largest cities in America in terms of driver safety. Fort Wayne ranked #36. Criteria: internal property damage claims over a two-year period from January 2016 to December 2017. The report helps increase the importance of safety and awareness behind the wheel. *Allstate, "Allstate America's Best Drivers Report, 2019" June 24, 2019*

- The National Insurance Crime Bureau ranked 382 metro areas in the U.S. in terms of per capita rates of vehicle theft. The Fort Wayne metro area ranked #224 (#1 = highest rate). Criteria: number of vehicle theft offenses per 100,000 inhabitants in 2018. *National Insurance Crime Bureau, "Hot Spots 2018," June 25, 2019*

Seniors/Retirement Rankings

- From its Best Cities for Successful Aging indexes, the Milken Institute generated rankings for metropolitan areas, weighing data in nine categories—health care, wellness, living arrangements, transportation and convenience, financial characteristics, education, employment, community engagement, and overall livability. The Fort Wayne metro area was ranked #115 overall in the small metro area category. *Milken Institute, "Best Cities for Successful Aging, 2017" March 14, 2017*

Women/Minorities Rankings

- Personal finance website *WalletHub* compared more than 180 U.S. cities—including the 150 most populated U.S. cities, plus at least two of the most populated cities in each state—across two key dimensions, "Hispanic Business-Friendliness" and "Hispanic Purchasing Power", to arrive at the most favorable conditions for Hispanic entrepreneurs. Fort Wayne was ranked #118 out of 182. Criteria includes: share of Hispanic-Owned Businesses; Hispanic entrepreneurship rate to median annual income of Hispanics; Small Business-Friendliness score; cost of living; and number of Hispanics with at least a bachelor's degree. *WalletHub.com, "2019's Best Cities for Hispanic Entrepreneurs," May 1, 2019*

Miscellaneous Rankings

- *WalletHub* compared the 150 most populated U.S. cities to determine their operating efficiency. A "Quality of Services" score was constructed for each city and then divided by the total budget per capita to reveal which were managed the best. Fort Wayne ranked #12. Criteria: financial stability; economy; education; safety; health; infrastructure and pollution. *www.WalletHub.com, "2019's Best- & Worst-Run Cities in America," July 1, 2019*

Business Environment

CITY FINANCES

City Government Finances

Component	2017 ($000)	2017 ($ per capita)
Total Revenues	285,215	1,096
Total Expenditures	183,365	704
Debt Outstanding	497,681	1,912
Cash and Securities[1]	168,604	648

Note: (1) Cash and security holdings of a government at the close of its fiscal year, including those of its dependent agencies, utilities, and liquor stores.
Source: U.S. Census Bureau, State & Local Government Finances 2017

City Government Revenue by Source

Source	2017 ($000)	2017 ($ per capita)	2017 (%)
General Revenue			
From Federal Government	0	0	0.0
From State Government	46,180	177	16.2
From Local Governments	0	0	0.0
Taxes			
Property	123,765	475	43.4
Sales and Gross Receipts	0	0	0.0
Personal Income	55,569	213	19.5
Corporate Income	0	0	0.0
Motor Vehicle License	4,558	18	1.6
Other Taxes	0	0	0.0
Current Charges	10,480	40	3.7
Liquor Store	0	0	0.0
Utility	44,642	171	15.7
Employee Retirement	0	0	0.0

Source: U.S. Census Bureau, State & Local Government Finances 2017

City Government Expenditures by Function

Function	2017 ($000)	2017 ($ per capita)	2017 (%)
General Direct Expenditures			
Air Transportation	0	0	0.0
Corrections	0	0	0.0
Education	0	0	0.0
Employment Security Administration	0	0	0.0
Financial Administration	7,070	27	3.9
Fire Protection	34,639	133	18.9
General Public Buildings	1,521	5	0.8
Governmental Administration, Other	974	3	0.5
Health	2,534	9	1.4
Highways	40,338	155	22.0
Hospitals	0	0	0.0
Housing and Community Development	10,089	38	5.5
Interest on General Debt	0	0	0.0
Judicial and Legal	533	2	0.3
Libraries	0	0	0.0
Parking	507	1	0.3
Parks and Recreation	13,320	51	7.3
Police Protection	62,459	239	34.1
Public Welfare	0	0	0.0
Sewerage	0	0	0.0
Solid Waste Management	9,255	35	5.0
Veterans' Services	0	0	0.0
Liquor Store	0	0	0.0
Utility	0	0	0.0
Employee Retirement	0	0	0.0

Source: U.S. Census Bureau, State & Local Government Finances 2017

DEMOGRAPHICS

Population Growth

Area	1990 Census	2000 Census	2010 Census	2018* Estimate	Population Growth (%)	
					1990-2018	2010-2018
City	205,671	205,727	253,691	264,052	28.4	4.1
MSA[1]	354,435	390,156	416,257	431,612	21.8	3.7
U.S.	248,709,873	281,421,906	308,745,538	322,903,030	29.8	4.6

Note: (1) Figures cover the Fort Wayne, IN Metropolitan Statistical Area—see Appendix B for areas included; (*) 2014-2018 5-year estimated population
Source: U.S. Census Bureau, 1990 Census, Census 2000, Census 2010, 2014-2018 American Community Survey 5-Year Estimates

Household Size

Area	Persons in Household (%)							Average Household Size
	One	Two	Three	Four	Five	Six	Seven or More	
City	32.0	32.6	14.9	11.2	5.9	2.2	1.2	2.50
MSA[1]	28.5	34.4	14.6	12.5	6.2	2.4	1.4	2.50
U.S.	27.7	33.9	15.7	13.0	6.0	2.3	1.4	2.60

Note: (1) Figures cover the Fort Wayne, IN Metropolitan Statistical Area—see Appendix B for areas included
Source: U.S. Census Bureau, 2014-2018 American Community Survey 5-Year Estimates

Race

Area	White Alone[2] (%)	Black Alone[2] (%)	Asian Alone[2] (%)	AIAN[3] Alone[2] (%)	NHOPI[4] Alone[2] (%)	Other Race Alone[2] (%)	Two or More Races (%)
City	73.8	14.9	4.6	0.2	0.0	1.9	4.5
MSA[1]	81.7	9.9	3.2	0.2	0.0	1.5	3.5
U.S.	72.7	12.7	5.4	0.8	0.2	4.9	3.2

Note: (1) Figures cover the Fort Wayne, IN Metropolitan Statistical Area—see Appendix B for areas included; (2) Alone is defined as not being in combination with one or more other races; (3) American Indian and Alaska Native; (4) Native Hawaiian and Other Pacific Islander
Source: U.S. Census Bureau, 2014-2018 American Community Survey 5-Year Estimates

Hispanic or Latino Origin

Area	Total (%)	Mexican (%)	Puerto Rican (%)	Cuban (%)	Other (%)
City	8.9	6.5	0.6	0.1	1.7
MSA[1]	6.6	4.9	0.4	0.1	1.3
U.S.	17.8	11.2	1.7	0.7	4.2

Note: Persons of Hispanic or Latino origin can be of any race; (1) Figures cover the Fort Wayne, IN Metropolitan Statistical Area—see Appendix B for areas included
Source: U.S. Census Bureau, 2014-2018 American Community Survey 5-Year Estimates

Segregation

Type	Segregation Indices[1]				Percent Change		
	1990	2000	2010	2010 Rank[2]	1990-2000	1990-2010	2000-2010
Black/White	n/a	n/a	n/a	n/a	n/a	n/a	n/a
Asian/White	n/a	n/a	n/a	n/a	n/a	n/a	n/a
Hispanic/White	n/a	n/a	n/a	n/a	n/a	n/a	n/a

Note: All figures cover the Metropolitan Statistical Area—see Appendix B for areas included; Figures are based on an analysis of 1990, 2000, and 2010 Census Decennial Census tract data by William H. Frey, Brookings Institution and the University of Michigan Social Science Data Analysis Network. In this analysis all racial groups (whites, blacks, and asians) are non-Hispanic members of those races. Hispanics are shown as a separate category; (1) Segregation Indices are Dissimilarity Indices that measure the degree to which the minority group is distributed differently than whites across census tracts. They range from 0 (complete integration) to 100 (complete segregation) where the value indicates the percentage of the minority group that needs to move to be distributed exactly like whites; (2) Ranges from 1 (most segregated) to 102 (least segregated); n/a not available.
Source: www.CensusScope.org

Ancestry

Area	German	Irish	English	American	Italian	Polish	French[2]	Scottish	Dutch
City	25.2	9.5	6.3	5.7	2.6	2.0	3.2	1.6	1.3
MSA[1]	27.8	9.5	6.9	7.1	2.7	1.9	3.5	1.7	1.5
U.S.	13.7	9.9	7.3	6.4	5.2	2.8	2.4	1.7	1.2

Note: Figures are the percentage of the total population reporting a particular ancestry. The nine most commonly reported ancestries in the U.S. are shown. Figures include multiple ancestries (e.g. if a person reported being Irish and Italian, they were included in both columns); (1) Figures cover the Fort Wayne, IN Metropolitan Statistical Area—see Appendix B for areas included; (2) Excludes Basque
Source: U.S. Census Bureau, 2014-2018 American Community Survey 5-Year Estimates

Foreign-born Population

Area	Percent of Population Born in								
	Any Foreign Country	Asia	Mexico	Europe	Caribbean	Central America[2]	South America	Africa	Canada
City	7.9	3.8	1.9	0.8	0.1	0.7	0.2	0.3	0.1
MSA[1]	5.8	2.7	1.3	0.6	0.1	0.5	0.2	0.2	0.1
U.S.	13.5	4.1	3.5	1.5	1.3	1.1	0.9	0.7	0.3

Note: (1) Figures cover the Fort Wayne, IN Metropolitan Statistical Area—see Appendix B for areas included; (2) Excludes Mexico.
Source: U.S. Census Bureau, 2014-2018 American Community Survey 5-Year Estimates

Marital Status

Area	Never Married	Now Married[2]	Separated	Widowed	Divorced
City	35.2	44.7	1.3	6.0	12.7
MSA[1]	30.8	50.5	1.1	5.9	11.7
U.S.	33.3	48.1	2.0	5.8	10.8

Note: Figures are percentages and cover the population 15 years of age and older; (1) Figures cover the Fort Wayne, IN Metropolitan Statistical Area—see Appendix B for areas included; (2) Excludes separated
Source: U.S. Census Bureau, 2014-2018 American Community Survey 5-Year Estimates

Disability by Age

Area	All Ages	Under 18 Years Old	18 to 64 Years Old	65 Years and Over
City	13.5	5.4	12.6	33.9
MSA[1]	12.8	4.5	11.5	33.6
U.S.	12.6	4.2	10.3	35.0

Note: Figures show percent of the civilian noninstitutionalized population that reported having a disability. Disability status is determined from six types of difficulty: vision, hearing, cognitive, ambulatory, self-care, and independent living. For children under 5 years old, hearing and vision difficulty are used to determine disability status. For children between the ages of 5 and 14, disability status is determined from hearing, vision, cognitive, ambulatory, and self-care difficulties. For people aged 15 years and older, they are considered to have a disability if they have difficulty with any one of the six difficulty types; Note: (1) Figures cover the Fort Wayne, IN Metropolitan Statistical Area—see Appendix B for areas included
Source: U.S. Census Bureau, 2014-2018 American Community Survey 5-Year Estimates

Age

Area	Percent of Population									Median Age
	Under Age 5	Age 5–19	Age 20–34	Age 35–44	Age 45–54	Age 55–64	Age 65–74	Age 75–84	Age 85+	
City	7.2	21.0	22.0	12.2	11.9	12.0	8.2	3.6	1.9	34.8
MSA[1]	7.0	21.1	19.9	12.3	12.6	12.7	8.4	4.0	2.0	36.5
U.S.	6.1	19.3	20.7	12.6	13.2	12.8	8.8	4.5	1.9	37.9

Note: (1) Figures cover the Fort Wayne, IN Metropolitan Statistical Area—see Appendix B for areas included
Source: U.S. Census Bureau, 2014-2018 American Community Survey 5-Year Estimates

Gender

Area	Males	Females	Males per 100 Females
City	127,627	136,425	93.6
MSA[1]	211,144	220,468	95.8
U.S.	158,984,190	163,918,840	97.0

Note: (1) Figures cover the Fort Wayne, IN Metropolitan Statistical Area—see Appendix B for areas included
Source: U.S. Census Bureau, 2014-2018 American Community Survey 5-Year Estimates

Religious Groups by Family

Area	Catholic	Baptist	Non-Den.	Methodist[2]	Lutheran	LDS[3]	Pente-costal	Presby-terian[4]	Muslim[5]	Judaism
MSA[1]	14.2	6.1	6.8	5.1	8.5	0.4	1.5	1.7	0.3	0.1
U.S.	19.1	9.3	4.0	4.0	2.3	2.0	1.9	1.6	0.8	0.7

Note: Figures are the number of adherents as a percentage of the total population; (1) Figures cover the Fort Wayne, IN Metropolitan Statistical Area—see Appendix B for areas included; (2) Methodist/Pietist; (3) Latter Day Saints; (4) Reformed; (5) Figures are estimates
Source: Association of Statisticians of American Religious Bodies, 2010 U.S. Religion Census: Religious Congregations & Membership Study

Religious Groups by Tradition

Area	Catholic	Evangelical Protestant	Mainline Protestant	Other Tradition	Black Protestant	Orthodox
MSA[1]	14.2	24.6	9.2	1.0	2.4	0.2
U.S.	19.1	16.2	7.3	4.3	1.6	0.3

Note: Figures are the number of adherents as a percentage of the total population; (1) Figures cover the Fort Wayne, IN Metropolitan Statistical Area—see Appendix B for areas included
Source: Association of Statisticians of American Religious Bodies, 2010 U.S. Religion Census: Religious Congregations & Membership Study

ECONOMY

Gross Metropolitan Product

Area	2017	2018	2019	2020	Rank[2]
MSA[1]	21.9	22.9	23.9	24.8	117

Note: Figures are in billions of dollars; (1) Figures cover the Fort Wayne, IN Metropolitan Statistical Area—see Appendix B for areas included; (2) Rank is based on 2018 data and ranges from 1 to 381
Source: U.S. Conference of Mayors, U.S. Metro Economies: GMP & Employment 2018-2020, September 2019

Economic Growth

Area	2015-17 (%)	2018 (%)	2019 (%)	2020 (%)	Rank[2]
MSA[1]	1.9	2.5	2.5	1.3	149
U.S.	1.9	2.9	2.3	2.1	–

Note: Figures are real gross metropolitan product (GMP) growth rates and represent average annual percent change; (1) Figures cover the Fort Wayne, IN Metropolitan Statistical Area—see Appendix B for areas included; (2) Rank is based on 2017 2-year average annual percent change and ranges from 1 to 381
Source: U.S. Conference of Mayors, U.S. Metro Economies: GMP & Employment 2018-2020, September 2019

Metropolitan Area Exports

Area	2013	2014	2015	2016	2017	2018	Rank[2]
MSA[1]	1,441.8	1,581.1	1,529.0	1,322.2	1,422.8	1,593.3	122

Note: Figures are in millions of dollars; (1) Figures cover the Fort Wayne, IN Metropolitan Statistical Area—see Appendix B for areas included; (2) Rank is based on 2018 data and ranges from 1 to 387
Source: U.S. Department of Commerce, International Trade Administration, Office of Trade and Economic Analysis, Industry and Analysis, Exports by Metropolitan Area, data extracted April 15, 2020

Building Permits

Area	Single-Family			Multi-Family			Total		
	2017	2018	Pct. Chg.	2017	2018	Pct. Chg.	2017	2018	Pct. Chg.
City	n/a	n/a	n/a	n/a	n/a	n/a	n/a	n/a	n/a
MSA[1]	1,222	1,343	9.9	500	541	8.2	1,722	1,884	9.4
U.S.	820,000	855,300	4.3	462,000	473,500	2.5	1,282,000	1,328,800	3.7

Note: (1) Figures cover the Fort Wayne, IN Metropolitan Statistical Area—see Appendix B for areas included; Figures represent new, privately-owned housing units authorized (unadjusted data); All permit data are based on estimates with imputation
Source: U.S. Census Bureau, Manufacturing, Mining, and Construction Statistics, Building Permits, 2017, 2018

Bankruptcy Filings

Area	Business Filings			Nonbusiness Filings		
	2018	2019	% Chg.	2018	2019	% Chg.
Allen County	16	15	-6.3	1,398	1,294	-7.4
U.S.	22,232	22,780	2.5	751,186	752,160	0.1

Note: Business filings include Chapter 7, Chapter 9, Chapter 11, Chapter 12, Chapter 13, Chapter 15, and Section 304; Nonbusiness filings include Chapter 7, Chapter 11, and Chapter 13
Source: Administrative Office of the U.S. Courts, Business and Nonbusiness Bankruptcy, County Cases Commenced by Chapter of the Bankruptcy Code, During the 12-Month Period Ending December 31, 2018 and Business and Nonbusiness Bankruptcy, County Cases Commenced by Chapter of the Bankruptcy Code, During the 12-Month Period Ending December 31, 2019

Housing Vacancy Rates

Area	Gross Vacancy Rate[2] (%)			Year-Round Vacancy Rate[3] (%)			Rental Vacancy Rate[4] (%)			Homeowner Vacancy Rate[5] (%)		
	2017	2018	2019	2017	2018	2019	2017	2018	2019	2017	2018	2019
MSA[1]	n/a	n/a	n/a	n/a	n/a	n/a	n/a	n/a	n/a	n/a	n/a	n/a
U.S.	12.7	12.3	12.0	9.9	9.7	9.5	7.2	6.9	6.7	1.6	1.5	1.4

Note: (1) Figures cover the Fort Wayne, IN Metropolitan Statistical Area—see Appendix B for areas included; (2) The percentage of the total housing inventory that is vacant; (3) The percentage of the housing inventory (excluding seasonal units) that is year-round vacant; (4) The percentage of rental inventory that is vacant for rent; (5) The percentage of homeowner inventory that is vacant for sale; n/a not available
Source: U.S. Census Bureau, Housing Vacancies and Homeownership Annual Statistics: 2017, 2018, 2019

INCOME

Income

Area	Per Capita ($)	Median Household ($)	Average Household ($)
City	26,213	48,023	63,932
MSA[1]	28,314	54,158	71,180
U.S.	32,621	60,293	84,938

Note: (1) Figures cover the Fort Wayne, IN Metropolitan Statistical Area—see Appendix B for areas included
Source: U.S. Census Bureau, 2014-2018 American Community Survey 5-Year Estimates

Household Income Distribution

Area	Percent of Households Earning							
	Under $15,000	$15,000 -$24,999	$25,000 -$34,999	$35,000 -$49,999	$50,000 -$74,999	$75,000 -$99,999	$100,000 -$149,999	$150,000 and up
City	12.6	11.9	12.0	15.3	20.0	12.3	10.1	5.9
MSA[1]	10.2	10.3	10.9	14.7	20.5	13.7	12.5	7.4
U.S.	10.9	9.3	9.3	12.6	17.5	12.5	14.6	13.3

Note: (1) Figures cover the Fort Wayne, IN Metropolitan Statistical Area—see Appendix B for areas included
Source: U.S. Census Bureau, 2014-2018 American Community Survey 5-Year Estimates

Poverty Rate

Area	All Ages	Under 18 Years Old	18 to 64 Years Old	65 Years and Over
City	17.3	26.7	15.4	7.3
MSA[1]	13.6	20.8	12.2	6.5
U.S.	14.1	19.5	13.2	9.3

Note: Figures are percentage of people whose income during the past 12 months was below the poverty level; (1) Figures cover the Fort Wayne, IN Metropolitan Statistical Area—see Appendix B for areas included
Source: U.S. Census Bureau, 2014-2018 American Community Survey 5-Year Estimates

EMPLOYMENT

Labor Force and Employment

Area	Civilian Labor Force			Workers Employed		
	Dec. 2018	Dec. 2019	% Chg.	Dec. 2018	Dec. 2019	% Chg.
City	128,555	128,470	-0.1	124,362	124,594	0.2
MSA[1]	217,241	216,998	-0.1	210,566	210,942	0.2
U.S.	162,510,000	164,007,000	0.9	156,481,000	158,504,000	1.3

Note: Data is not seasonally adjusted and covers workers 16 years of age and older; (1) Figures cover the Fort Wayne, IN Metropolitan Statistical Area—see Appendix B for areas included
Source: Bureau of Labor Statistics, Local Area Unemployment Statistics

Unemployment Rate

Area	2019											
	Jan.	Feb.	Mar.	Apr.	May	Jun.	Jul.	Aug.	Sep.	Oct.	Nov.	Dec.
City	4.0	3.7	3.4	2.6	2.9	3.3	3.5	3.3	2.8	3.5	3.3	3.0
MSA[1]	3.8	3.5	3.3	2.5	2.7	3.1	3.4	3.1	2.6	3.3	3.1	2.8
U.S.	4.4	4.1	3.9	3.3	3.4	3.8	4.0	3.8	3.3	3.3	3.3	3.4

Note: Data is not seasonally adjusted and covers workers 16 years of age and older; (1) Figures cover the Fort Wayne, IN Metropolitan Statistical Area—see Appendix B for areas included
Source: Bureau of Labor Statistics, Local Area Unemployment Statistics

Average Wages

Occupation	$/Hr.	Occupation	$/Hr.
Accountants and Auditors	32.10	Maintenance and Repair Workers	20.80
Automotive Mechanics	17.50	Marketing Managers	57.60
Bookkeepers	18.60	Network and Computer Systems Admin.	33.80
Carpenters	21.20	Nurses, Licensed Practical	22.10
Cashiers	10.50	Nurses, Registered	28.80
Computer Programmers	31.90	Nursing Assistants	13.80
Computer Systems Analysts	36.00	Office Clerks, General	16.40
Computer User Support Specialists	21.70	Physical Therapists	42.30
Construction Laborers	19.70	Physicians	111.10
Cooks, Restaurant	12.30	Plumbers, Pipefitters and Steamfitters	27.80
Customer Service Representatives	18.80	Police and Sheriff's Patrol Officers	28.30
Dentists	82.70	Postal Service Mail Carriers	24.90
Electricians	26.70	Real Estate Sales Agents	21.70
Engineers, Electrical	45.20	Retail Salespersons	12.60
Fast Food and Counter Workers	10.40	Sales Representatives, Technical/Scientific	43.10
Financial Managers	56.40	Secretaries, Exc. Legal/Medical/Executive	17.30
First-Line Supervisors of Office Workers	27.70	Security Guards	17.00
General and Operations Managers	51.50	Surgeons	n/a
Hairdressers/Cosmetologists	13.00	Teacher Assistants, Exc. Postsecondary*	12.00
Home Health and Personal Care Aides	11.40	Teachers, Secondary School, Exc. Sp. Ed.*	25.70
Janitors and Cleaners	12.00	Telemarketers	n/a
Landscaping/Groundskeeping Workers	13.50	Truck Drivers, Heavy/Tractor-Trailer	20.80
Lawyers	73.00	Truck Drivers, Light/Delivery Services	16.20
Maids and Housekeeping Cleaners	10.60	Waiters and Waitresses	12.20

Note: Wage data covers the Fort Wayne, IN Metropolitan Statistical Area—see Appendix B for areas included; (*) Hourly wages were calculated from annual wage data based on a 40 hour work week; n/a not available.
Source: Bureau of Labor Statistics, Metro Area Occupational Employment & Wage Estimates, May 2019

Employment by Occupation

Occupation Classification	City (%)	MSA[1] (%)	U.S. (%)
Management, Business, Science, and Arts	32.5	33.0	37.9
Natural Resources, Construction, and Maintenance	6.6	7.9	8.9
Production, Transportation, and Material Moving	19.9	20.4	13.3
Sales and Office	23.1	22.2	22.1
Service	17.8	16.5	17.9

Note: Figures cover employed civilians 16 years of age and older; (1) Figures cover the Fort Wayne, IN Metropolitan Statistical Area—see Appendix B for areas included
Source: U.S. Census Bureau, 2014-2018 American Community Survey 5-Year Estimates

Employment by Industry

Sector	MSA[1]		U.S.
	Number of Employees	Percent of Total	Percent of Total
Construction, Mining, and Logging	11,500	5.0	5.4
Education and Health Services	44,000	19.2	16.1
Financial Activities	12,500	5.4	5.8
Government	22,000	9.6	15.0
Information	2,200	1.0	1.9
Leisure and Hospitality	21,100	9.2	10.8
Manufacturing	38,000	16.6	8.4
Other Services	11,600	5.1	3.9
Professional and Business Services	22,000	9.6	14.1
Retail Trade	24,300	10.6	10.6
Transportation, Warehousing, and Utilities	9,500	4.1	4.2
Wholesale Trade	10,700	4.7	3.9

Note: Figures are non-farm employment as of December 2019. Figures are not seasonally adjusted and include workers 16 years of age and older; (1) Figures cover the Fort Wayne, IN Metropolitan Statistical Area—see Appendix B for areas included
Source: Bureau of Labor Statistics, Current Employment Statistics, Employment, Hours, and Earnings

Occupations with Greatest Projected Employment Growth: 2019 – 2021

Occupation[1]	2019 Employment	2021 Projected Employment	Numeric Employment Change	Percent Employment Change
Combined Food Preparation and Serving Workers, Including Fast Food	93,910	96,420	2,510	2.7
Registered Nurses	69,240	71,460	2,220	3.2
Personal Care Aides	29,510	31,560	2,050	6.9
Laborers and Freight, Stock, and Material Movers, Hand	95,190	96,990	1,800	1.9
General and Operations Managers	56,150	57,140	990	1.8
Home Health Aides	14,430	15,420	990	6.9
Cooks, Restaurant	27,660	28,650	990	3.6
Janitors and Cleaners, Except Maids and Housekeeping Cleaners	47,880	48,850	970	2.0
Maintenance and Repair Workers, General	36,930	37,670	740	2.0
Construction Laborers	27,060	27,790	730	2.7

Note: Projections cover Indiana; (1) Sorted by numeric employment change
Source: www.projectionscentral.com, State Occupational Projections, 2019–2021 Short-Term Projections

Fastest Growing Occupations: 2019 – 2021

Occupation[1]	2019 Employment	2021 Projected Employment	Numeric Employment Change	Percent Employment Change
Occupational Therapy Assistants	1,150	1,230	80	7.0
Home Health Aides	14,430	15,420	990	6.9
Personal Care Aides	29,510	31,560	2,050	6.9
Health Specialties Teachers, Postsecondary	3,490	3,710	220	6.3
Physician Assistants	1,630	1,730	100	6.1
Operations Research Analysts	1,160	1,230	70	6.0
Speech-Language Pathologists	2,500	2,650	150	6.0
Nurse Practitioners	4,980	5,270	290	5.8
Information Security Analysts	1,060	1,120	60	5.7
Hazardous Materials Removal Workers	900	950	50	5.6

Note: Projections cover Indiana; (1) Sorted by percent employment change and excludes occupations with numeric employment change less than 50
Source: www.projectionscentral.com, State Occupational Projections, 2019–2021 Short-Term Projections

TAXES

State Corporate Income Tax Rates

State	Tax Rate (%)	Income Brackets ($)	Num. of Brackets	Financial Institution Tax Rate (%)[a]	Federal Income Tax Ded.
Indiana	5.5 (i)	Flat rate	1	6.0	No

Note: Tax rates as of January 1, 2020; (a) Rates listed are the corporate income tax rate applied to financial institutions or excise taxes based on income; (i) The Indiana Corporate tax rate is scheduled to decrease to 5.25% on July 1, 2020. Bank tax rate is scheduled to decrease to 5.5% on 1/1/21.
Source: Federation of Tax Administrators, State Corporate Income Tax Rates, January 1, 2020

State Individual Income Tax Rates

State	Tax Rate (%)	Income Brackets ($)	Personal Exemptions ($) Single	Married	Depend.	Standard Ded. ($) Single	Married
Indiana	3.23	Flat rate	1,000	2,000	2,500 (j)	–	–

Note: Tax rates as of January 1, 2020; Local- and county-level taxes are not included; Federal income tax is not deductible on state income tax returns; (j) In Indiana, includes an additional exemption of $1,500 for each dependent child.
Source: Federation of Tax Administrators, State Individual Income Tax Rates, January 1, 2020

Various State Sales and Excise Tax Rates

State	State Sales Tax (%)	Gasoline[1] (¢/gal.)	Cigarette[2] ($/pack)	Spirits[3] ($/gal.)	Wine[4] ($/gal.)	Beer[5] ($/gal.)	Recreational Marijuana (%)
Indiana	7	46.62	0.995	2.68	0.47	0.12	Not legal

Note: All tax rates as of January 1, 2020; (1) The American Petroleum Institute has developed a methodology for determining the average tax rate on a gallon of fuel. Rates may include any of the following: excise taxes, environmental fees, storage tank fees, other fees or taxes, general sales tax, and local taxes; (2) The federal excise tax of $1.0066 per pack and local taxes are not included; (3) Rates are those applicable to off-premise sales of 40% alcohol by volume (a.b.v.) distilled spirits in 750ml containers. Local excise taxes are excluded; (4) Rates are those applicable to off-premise sales of 11% a.b.v. non-carbonated wine in 750ml containers; (5) Rates are those applicable to off-premise sales of 4.7% a.b.v. beer in 12 ounce containers.
Source: Tax Foundation, 2020 Facts & Figures: How Does Your State Compare?

State Business Tax Climate Index Rankings

State	Overall Rank	Corporate Tax Rank	Individual Income Tax Rank	Sales Tax Rank	Property Tax Rank	Unemployment Insurance Tax Rank
Indiana	10	11	15	20	2	25

Note: The index is a measure of how each state's tax laws affect economic performance. The lower the rank, the more favorable a state's tax system is for business. States without a given tax are given a ranking of 1. The scores/rankings for the District of Columbia do not affect other states. The 2020 index represents the tax climate as of July 1, 2019.
Source: Tax Foundation, State Business Tax Climate Index 2020

COMMERCIAL UTILITIES

Typical Monthly Electric Bills

Area	Commercial Service ($/month) 1,500 kWh	40 kW demand 14,000 kWh	Industrial Service ($/month) 1,000 kW demand 200,000 kWh	50,000 kW demand 32,500,000 kWh
City	226	1,858	27,873	2,000,332
Average[1]	203	1,612	25,706	2,520,671

Note: Figures are based on annualized rates; (1) Average based on 187 utilities surveyed
Source: Edison Electric Institute, Typical Bills and Average Rates Report, Summer 2019

TRANSPORTATION

Means of Transportation to Work

Area	Car/Truck/Van		Public Transportation			Bicycle	Walked	Other Means	Worked at Home
	Drove Alone	Car-pooled	Bus	Subway	Railroad				
City	83.7	9.2	0.8	0.0	0.0	0.3	1.4	0.8	3.8
MSA[1]	84.6	8.5	0.6	0.0	0.0	0.2	1.3	0.7	4.0
U.S.	76.4	9.1	2.5	1.9	0.6	0.6	2.7	1.3	4.9

Note: Figures are percentages and cover workers 16 years of age and older; (1) Figures cover the Fort Wayne, IN Metropolitan Statistical Area—see Appendix B for areas included
Source: U.S. Census Bureau, 2014-2018 American Community Survey 5-Year Estimates

Travel Time to Work

Area	Less Than 10 Minutes	10 to 19 Minutes	20 to 29 Minutes	30 to 44 Minutes	45 to 59 Minutes	60 to 89 Minutes	90 Minutes or More
City	13.1	39.9	27.7	12.2	3.2	2.2	1.7
MSA[1]	13.7	35.6	27.8	15.3	3.7	2.1	1.7
U.S.	12.5	28.7	20.9	20.7	8.2	6.3	2.8

Note: Note: Figures are percentages and include workers 16 years old and over; (1) Figures cover the Fort Wayne, IN Metropolitan Statistical Area—see Appendix B for areas included
Source: U.S. Census Bureau, 2014-2018 American Community Survey 5-Year Estimates

Key Congestion Measures

Area	1982	1992	2002	2012	2017
Annual Hours of Delay, Total (000)	n/a	n/a	n/a	n/a	5,892
Annual Hours of Delay, Per Auto Commuter	n/a	n/a	n/a	n/a	18
Annual Congestion Cost, Total (million $)	n/a	n/a	n/a	n/a	124
Annual Congestion Cost, Per Auto Commuter ($)	n/a	n/a	n/a	n/a	376

Note: n/a not available
Source: Texas A&M Transportation Institute, 2019 Urban Mobility Report

Freeway Travel Time Index

Area	1982	1987	1992	1997	2002	2007	2012	2017
Urban Area Index[1]	n/a	n/a	n/a	n/a	n/a	n/a	n/a	1.09
Urban Area Rank[1,2]	n/a	n/a	n/a	n/a	n/a	n/a	n/a	n/a

Note: Freeway Travel Time Index—the ratio of travel time in the peak period to the travel time at free-flow conditions. For example, a value of 1.30 indicates a 20-minute free-flow trip takes 26 minutes in the peak (20 minutes x 1.30 = 26 minutes); (1) Covers the Fort Wayne IN urban area; (2) Rank is based on 101 larger urban areas (#1 = highest travel time index); n/a not available
Source: Texas A&M Transportation Institute, 2019 Urban Mobility Report

Public Transportation

Agency Name / Mode of Transportation	Vehicles Operated in Maximum Service[1]	Annual Unlinked Passenger Trips[2] (in thous.)	Annual Passenger Miles[3] (in thous.)
Fort Wayne Public Transportation Corp. (Citilink)			
Bus (directly operated)	29	1,693.1	5,137.7
Demand Response (directly operated)	17	73.9	637.2

Note: (1) Number of revenue vehicles operated by the given mode and type of service to meet the annual maximum service requirement. This is the revenue vehicle count during the peak season of the year; on the week and day that maximum service is provided. Vehicles operated in maximum service (VOMS) exclude atypical days and one-time special events; (2) Number of passengers who boarded public transportation vehicles. Passengers are counted each time they board a vehicle no matter how many vehicles they use to travel from their origin to their destination. (3) Sum of the distances ridden by all passengers during the entire fiscal year.
Source: Federal Transit Administration, National Transit Database, 2018

Air Transportation

Airport Name and Code / Type of Service	Passenger Airlines[1]	Passenger Enplanements	Freight Carriers[2]	Freight (lbs)
Fort Wayne International (FWA)				
Domestic service (U.S. carriers - 2019)	9	402,255	8	25,397,579
International service (U.S. carriers - 2018)	0	0	4	127,409

Note: (1) Includes all U.S.-based major, minor and commuter airlines that carried at least one passenger during the year; (2) Includes all U.S.-based airlines and freight carriers that transported at least one pound of freight during the year.
Source: Bureau of Transportation Statistics, The Intermodal Transportation Database, Air Carriers: T-100 Domestic Market (U.S. Carriers), 2019; Bureau of Transportation Statistics, The Intermodal Transportation Database, Air Carriers: T-100 International Market (U.S. Carriers), 2018

Other Transportation Statistics

Major Highways:	I-69
Amtrak Service:	No
Major Waterways/Ports:	None

Source: Amtrak.com; Google Maps

BUSINESSES

Major Business Headquarters

Company Name	Industry	Rankings	
		Fortune[1]	Forbes[2]
Steel Dynamics	Metals	264	-

Note: (1) Companies that produce a 10-K are ranked 1 to 500 based on 2018 revenue; (2) All private companies with at least $2 billion in annual revenue through the end of their most current fiscal year are ranked 1 to 228; companies listed are headquartered in the city; dashes indicate no ranking
Source: Fortune, "Fortune 500," June 2019; Forbes, "America's Largest Private Companies," 2019 Rankings

Minority- and Women-Owned Businesses

Group	All Firms		Firms with Paid Employees			
	Firms	Sales ($000)	Firms	Sales ($000)	Employees	Payroll ($000)
AIAN[1]	178	(s)	62	(s)	100 - 249	(s)
Asian	848	346,698	277	315,177	2,330	65,979
Black	2,432	102,162	85	69,491	954	16,097
Hispanic	740	81,514	83	(s)	500 - 999	(s)
NHOPI[2]	31	5,314	21	5,115	51	1,057
Women	7,313	1,215,206	847	1,090,664	7,378	251,535
All Firms	20,502	33,229,404	5,545	32,720,966	126,993	4,909,699

Note: Figures cover firms located in the city; minority- and women-owned business are defined as firms in which the corresponding group own 51% or more of the stock or equity of the company; (1) American Indian and Alaska Native; (2) Native Hawaiian and Other Pacific Islander; (s) estimates are suppressed when publication standards are not met
Source: U.S. Census Bureau, 2012 Economic Census, Survey of Business Owners

**HOTELS &
CONVENTION
CENTERS**

Hotels, Motels and Vacation Rentals

Area	5 Star		4 Star		3 Star		2 Star		1 Star		Not Rated	
	Num.	Pct.[3]	Num.	Pct.[3]	Num.	Pct.[3]	Num.	Pct.[3]	Num.	Pct.[3]	Num.	Pct.[3]
City[1]	0	0.0	0	0.0	11	23.9	9	19.6	1	2.2	25	54.3
Total[2]	266	1.3	1,517	7.2	4,627	21.8	3,210	15.1	3,974	18.7	7,601	35.9

Note: (1) Figures cover Fort Wayne and vicinity; (2) Figures cover all 100 cities in this book; (3) Percentage of hotels which have a given star rating; Star ratings are determined by priceline.com and offer an indication of the general quality of a particular hotel.
Source: priceline.com, April 27, 2020

Major Convention Centers

Name	Overall Space (sq. ft.)	Exhibit Space (sq. ft.)	Meeting Space (sq. ft.)	Meeting Rooms
Grand Wayne Center	225,000	n/a	n/a	n/a

Note: Table includes convention centers located in the Fort Wayne, IN metro area; n/a not available
Source: Original research

Living Environment

COST OF LIVING

Cost of Living Index

Composite Index	Groceries	Housing	Utilities	Transportation	Health Care	Misc. Goods/ Services
86.9	86.7	62.3	95.7	99.5	101.5	98.6

Note: The Cost of Living Index measures regional differences in the cost of consumer goods and services, excluding taxes and non-consumer expenditures, for professional and managerial households in the top income quintile. It is based on more than 50,000 prices covering almost 60 different items for which prices are collected three times a year by chambers of commerce, economic development organizations or university applied economic centers in each participating urban area. The numbers shown should be read as a percentage above or below the national average of 100. For example, a value of 115.4 in the groceries column indicates that grocery prices are 15.4% higher than the national average. Small differences in the index numbers should not be interpreted as significant; Figures cover the Fort Wayne-Allen County IN urban area.
Source: The Council for Community and Economic Research, ACCRA Cost of Living Index, 2019

Grocery Prices

Area[1]	T-Bone Steak ($/pound)	Frying Chicken ($/pound)	Whole Milk ($/half gal.)	Eggs ($/dozen)	Orange Juice ($/64 oz.)	Coffee ($/11.5 oz.)
City[2]	12.87	0.96	1.37	0.84	3.24	3.97
Avg.	11.40	1.41	1.93	1.54	3.51	4.30
Min.	7.40	0.92	0.85	0.58	2.67	2.90
Max.	15.58	2.68	4.09	4.18	5.57	8.10

*Note: (1) Values for the local area are compared with the average, minimum and maximum values for all 290 areas in the Cost of Living Index; (2) Figures cover the Fort Wayne-Allen County IN urban area; **T-Bone Steak** (price per pound); **Frying Chicken** (price per pound, whole fryer); **Whole Milk** (half gallon carton); **Eggs** (price per dozen, Grade A, large); **Orange Juice** (64 oz. Tropicana or Florida Natural); **Coffee** (11.5 oz. can, vacuum-packed, Maxwell House, Hills Bros, or Folgers).*
Source: The Council for Community and Economic Research, ACCRA Cost of Living Index, 2019

Housing and Utility Costs

Area[1]	New Home Price ($)	Apartment Rent ($/month)	All Electric ($/month)	Part Electric ($/month)	Other Energy ($/month)	Telephone ($/month)
City[2]	211,226	780	-	96.48	59.30	179.90
Avg.	362,090	1,142	174.35	100.00	67.76	179.60
Min.	198,329	501	91.58	31.44	28.51	165.30
Max.	2,074,561	5,050	388.18	239.41	306.15	207.90

*Note: (1) Values for the local area are compared with the average, minimum and maximum values for all 290 areas in the Cost of Living Index; (2) Figures cover the Fort Wayne-Allen County IN urban area; **New Home Price** (2,400 sf living area, 8,000 sf lot, in urban area with full utilities); **Apartment Rent** (950 sf 2 bedroom/1.5 or 2 bath, unfurnished, excluding all utilities except water); **All Electric** (average monthly cost for an all-electric home); **Part Electric** (average monthly cost for a part-electric home); **Other Energy** (average monthly cost for natural gas, fuel oil, coal, wood, and any other forms of energy except electricity); **Telephone** (price includes the base monthly rate plus taxes and fees for three lines of mobile phone service).*
Source: The Council for Community and Economic Research, ACCRA Cost of Living Index, 2019

Health Care, Transportation, and Other Costs

Area[1]	Doctor ($/visit)	Dentist ($/visit)	Optometrist ($/visit)	Gasoline ($/gallon)	Beauty Salon ($/visit)	Men's Shirt ($)
City[2]	129.50	95.89	76.53	2.47	30.22	35.58
Avg.	114.85	97.58	106.10	2.50	38.15	32.15
Min.	39.00	62.22	52.22	1.53	16.88	10.27
Max.	206.67	151.53	258.67	3.79	79.29	59.30

*Note: (1) Values for the local area are compared with the average, minimum and maximum values for all 290 areas in the Cost of Living Index; (2) Figures cover the Fort Wayne-Allen County IN urban area; **Doctor** (general practitioners routine exam of an established patient); **Dentist** (adult teeth cleaning and periodic oral examination); **Optometrist** (full vision eye exam for established adult patient); **Gasoline** (one gallon regular unleaded, national brand, including all taxes, cash price at self-service pump if available); **Beauty Salon** (woman's shampoo, trim, and blow-dry); **Men's Shirt** (cotton/polyester dress shirt, pinpoint weave, long sleeves).*
Source: The Council for Community and Economic Research, ACCRA Cost of Living Index, 2019

HOUSING

House Price Index (HPI)

Area	National Ranking[2]	Quarterly Change (%)	One-Year Change (%)	Five-Year Change (%)
MSA[1]	155	0.24	4.26	33.61
U.S.[3]	–	1.26	5.09	32.88

Note: The HPI is a weighted repeat sales index. It measures average price changes in repeat sales or refinancings on the same properties. This information is obtained by reviewing repeat mortgage transactions on single-family properties whose mortgages have been purchased or securitized by Fannie Mae or Freddie Mac in January 1975; (1) Figures cover the Fort Wayne, IN Metropolitan Statistical Area—see Appendix B for areas included; (2) Rankings are based on annual percentage change for all metro areas containing at least 15,000 transactions over the last 10 years and ranges from 1 to 232; (3) figures based on a weighted average of Census Division estimates using a seasonally adjusted, purchase-only index; all figures are for the period ending December 31, 2019
Source: Federal Housing Finance Agency, House Price Index, February 25, 2020

Median Single-Family Home Prices

Area	2017	2018	2019p	Percent Change 2018 to 2019
MSA[1]	132.9	143.3	155.3	8.4
U.S. Average	248.8	261.6	274.6	5.0

Note: Figures are median sales prices of existing single-family homes in thousands of dollars; (p) preliminary; (1) Figures cover the Fort Wayne, IN Metropolitan Statistical Area—see Appendix B for areas included
Source: National Association of Realtors, Median Sales Price of Existing Single-Family Homes for Metropolitan Areas, 4th Quarter 2019

Qualifying Income Based on Median Sales Price of Existing Single-Family Homes

Area	With 5% Down ($)	With 10% Down ($)	With 20% Down ($)
MSA[1]	32,628	30,911	27,476
U.S. Average	58,663	55,575	49,400

Note: Figures are preliminary; Qualifying income is based on a mortgage rate of 3.76%. Monthly principal and interest payment is limited to 25% of income; (1) Figures cover the Fort Wayne, IN Metropolitan Statistical Area—see Appendix B for areas included
Source: National Association of Realtors, Qualifying Income Based on Median Sales Price of Existing Single-Family Homes for Metropolitan Areas, 4th Quarter 2019

Median Apartment Condo-Coop Home Prices

Area	2017	2018	2019p	Percent Change 2018 to 2019
MSA[1]	n/a	n/a	n/a	n/a
U.S. Average	234.3	241.0	249.5	3.5

Note: Figures are median sales prices of existing apartment condo-coop homes in thousands of dollars; (p) preliminary; n/a not available; (1) Figures cover the Fort Wayne, IN Metropolitan Statistical Area—see Appendix B for areas included
Source: National Association of Realtors, Median Sales Price of Existing Apartment Condo-Coop Homes for Metropolitan Areas, 4th Quarter 2019

Home Value Distribution

Area	Under $50,000	$50,000-$99,999	$100,000-$149,999	$150,000-$199,999	$200,000-$299,999	$300,000-$499,999	$500,000-$999,999	$1,000,000 or more
City	11.3	32.2	28.8	14.8	8.6	3.2	1.0	0.1
MSA[1]	9.3	26.4	26.7	16.2	12.9	6.4	1.8	0.4
U.S.	7.6	13.0	14.0	14.3	19.2	18.3	10.5	3.1

Note: Figures are percentages and cover owner-occupied housing units; (1) Figures cover the Fort Wayne, IN Metropolitan Statistical Area—see Appendix B for areas included
Source: U.S. Census Bureau, 2014-2018 American Community Survey 5-Year Estimates

Homeownership Rate

Area	2011 (%)	2012 (%)	2013 (%)	2014 (%)	2015 (%)	2016 (%)	2017 (%)	2018 (%)	2019 (%)
MSA[1]	n/a	n/a	n/a	n/a	n/a	n/a	n/a	n/a	n/a
U.S.	66.1	65.4	65.1	64.5	63.7	63.4	63.9	64.4	64.6

Note: (1) Figures cover the Fort Wayne, IN Metropolitan Statistical Area—see Appendix B for areas included; n/a not available
Source: U.S. Census Bureau, Housing Vacancies and Homeownership Annual Statistics: 2011-2019

Year Housing Structure Built

Area	2010 or Later	2000 -2009	1990 -1999	1980 -1989	1970 -1979	1960 -1969	1950 -1959	1940 -1949	Before 1940	Median Year
City	1.1	6.5	14.3	12.1	16.9	14.7	12.5	6.7	15.3	1970
MSA[1]	3.0	11.0	15.2	11.1	15.0	12.7	10.8	5.4	15.9	1973
U.S.	4.1	14.3	13.9	13.5	15.3	10.7	10.4	5.0	12.8	1977

Note: Figures are percentages except for Median Year; Note: (1) Figures cover the Fort Wayne, IN Metropolitan Statistical Area—see Appendix B for areas included
Source: U.S. Census Bureau, 2014-2018 American Community Survey 5-Year Estimates

Gross Monthly Rent

Area	Under $500	$500 -$999	$1,000 -$1,499	$1,500 -$1,999	$2,000 -$2,499	$2,500 -$2,999	$3,000 and up	Median ($)
City	13.5	71.5	12.5	1.6	0.6	0.2	0.1	735
MSA[1]	14.4	69.0	13.7	2.0	0.7	0.2	0.1	739
U.S.	9.8	38.5	29.6	12.9	5.1	2.1	2.0	1,023

Note: Figures are percentages except for Median; Gross rent is the contract rent plus the estimated average monthly cost of utilities (electricity, gas, and water and sewer) and fuels (oil, coal, kerosene, wood, etc.) if these are paid by the renter (or paid for the renter by someone else); (1) Figures cover the Fort Wayne, IN Metropolitan Statistical Area—see Appendix B for areas included
Source: U.S. Census Bureau, 2014-2018 American Community Survey 5-Year Estimates

HEALTH

Health Risk Factors

Category	MSA[1] (%)	U.S. (%)
Adults aged 18–64 who have any kind of health care coverage	85.9	87.3
Adults who reported being in good or better health	78.3	82.4
Adults who have been told they have high blood cholesterol	32.3	33.0
Adults who have been told they have high blood pressure	35.0	32.3
Adults who are current smokers	21.1	17.1
Adults who currently use E-cigarettes	3.9	4.6
Adults who currently use chewing tobacco, snuff, or snus	3.9	4.0
Adults who are heavy drinkers[2]	4.3	6.3
Adults who are binge drinkers[3]	15.5	17.4
Adults who are overweight (BMI 25.0 - 29.9)	30.4	35.3
Adults who are obese (BMI 30.0 - 99.8)	33.9	31.3
Adults who participated in any physical activities in the past month	72.6	74.4
Adults who always or nearly always wears a seat belt	94.7	94.3

Note: (1) Figures cover the Fort Wayne, IN Metropolitan Statistical Area—see Appendix B for areas included; (2) Heavy drinkers are classified as adult men having more than 14 drinks per week and adult women having more than 7 drinks per week; (3) Binge drinkers are classified as males having five or more drinks on one occasion or females having four or more drinks on one occasion
Source: Centers for Disease Control and Prevention, Behaviorial Risk Factor Surveillance System, SMART: Selected Metropolitan Area Risk Trends, 2017

Acute and Chronic Health Conditions

Category	MSA[1] (%)	U.S. (%)
Adults who have ever been told they had a heart attack	5.3	4.2
Adults who have ever been told they have angina or coronary heart disease	5.8	3.9
Adults who have ever been told they had a stroke	3.3	3.0
Adults who have ever been told they have asthma	14.7	14.2
Adults who have ever been told they have arthritis	29.3	24.9
Adults who have ever been told they have diabetes[2]	10.9	10.5
Adults who have ever been told they had skin cancer	3.9	6.2
Adults who have ever been told they had any other types of cancer	6.5	7.1
Adults who have ever been told they have COPD	7.8	6.5
Adults who have ever been told they have kidney disease	2.2	3.0
Adults who have ever been told they have a form of depression	24.7	20.5

Note: (1) Figures cover the Fort Wayne, IN Metropolitan Statistical Area—see Appendix B for areas included; (2) Figures do not include pregnancy-related, borderline, or pre-diabetes
Source: Centers for Disease Control and Prevention, Behaviorial Risk Factor Surveillance System, SMART: Selected Metropolitan Area Risk Trends, 2017

Health Screening and Vaccination Rates

Category	MSA[1] (%)	U.S. (%)
Adults aged 65+ who have had flu shot within the past year	46.3	60.7
Adults aged 65+ who have ever had a pneumonia vaccination	69.2	75.4
Adults who have ever been tested for HIV	31.9	36.1
Adults who have ever had the shingles or zoster vaccine?	22.5	28.9
Adults who have had their blood cholesterol checked within the last five years	83.5	85.9

Note: n/a not available; (1) Figures cover the Fort Wayne, IN Metropolitan Statistical Area—see Appendix B for areas included.
Source: Centers for Disease Control and Prevention, Behaviorial Risk Factor Surveillance System, SMART: Selected Metropolitan Area Risk Trends, 2017

Disability Status

Category	MSA[1] (%)	U.S. (%)
Adults who reported being deaf	4.4	6.7
Are you blind or have serious difficulty seeing, even when wearing glasses?	3.2	4.5
Are you limited in any way in any of your usual activities due of arthritis?	16.0	12.9
Do you have difficulty doing errands alone?	7.5	6.8
Do you have difficulty dressing or bathing?	3.8	3.6
Do you have serious difficulty concentrating/remembering/making decisions?	11.1	10.7
Do you have serious difficulty walking or climbing stairs?	14.7	13.6

Note: (1) Figures cover the Fort Wayne, IN Metropolitan Statistical Area—see Appendix B for areas included.
Source: Centers for Disease Control and Prevention, Behaviorial Risk Factor Surveillance System, SMART: Selected Metropolitan Area Risk Trends, 2017

Mortality Rates for the Top 10 Causes of Death in the U.S.

ICD-10[a] Sub-Chapter	ICD-10[a] Code	Age-Adjusted Mortality Rate[1] per 100,000 population	
		County[2]	U.S.
Malignant neoplasms	C00-C97	167.5	152.4
Ischaemic heart diseases	I20-I25	83.6	92.7
Other forms of heart disease	I30-I51	54.9	52.5
Chronic lower respiratory diseases	J40-J47	52.8	40.4
Cerebrovascular diseases	I60-I69	39.3	37.3
Other degenerative diseases of the nervous system	G30-G31	40.9	36.4
Other external causes of accidental injury	W00-X59	40.9	35.3
Organic, including symptomatic, mental disorders	F01-F09	44.7	30.0
Hypertensive diseases	I10-I15	41.7	22.9
Diabetes mellitus	E10-E14	30.2	21.3

Note: (a) ICD-10 = International Classification of Diseases 10th Revision; (1) Mortality rates are a three year average covering 2016-2018; (2) Figures cover Allen County.
Source: Centers for Disease Control and Prevention, National Center for Health Statistics. Underlying Cause of Death 1999-2018 on CDC WONDER Online Database

Mortality Rates for Selected Causes of Death

ICD-10[a] Sub-Chapter	ICD-10[a] Code	Age-Adjusted Mortality Rate[1] per 100,000 population	
		County[2]	U.S.
Assault	X85-Y09	12.2	6.0
Diseases of the liver	K70-K76	14.1	14.2
Human immunodeficiency virus (HIV) disease	B20-B24	Unreliable	1.6
Influenza and pneumonia	J09-J18	11.3	14.2
Intentional self-harm	X60-X84	14.1	13.9
Malnutrition	E40-E46	3.7	1.9
Obesity and other hyperalimentation	E65-E68	1.8	2.1
Renal failure	N17-N19	18.5	12.8
Transport accidents	V01-V99	11.7	12.5
Viral hepatitis	B15-B19	Unreliable	1.4

Note: (a) ICD-10 = International Classification of Diseases 10th Revision; (1) Mortality rates are a three year average covering 2016-2018; (2) Figures cover Allen County; Data are suppressed when the data meet the criteria for confidentiality constraints; Mortality rates are flagged as unreliable when the rate would be calculated with a numerator of 20 or less.
Source: Centers for Disease Control and Prevention, National Center for Health Statistics. Underlying Cause of Death 1999-2018 on CDC WONDER Online Database

Health Insurance Coverage

Area	With Health Insurance	With Private Health Insurance	With Public Health Insurance	Without Health Insurance	Population Under Age 19 Without Health Insurance
City	90.0	64.4	35.7	10.0	6.0
MSA[1]	91.0	69.4	32.5	9.0	6.4
U.S.	90.6	67.7	34.7	9.4	5.2

Note: Figures are percentages that cover the civilian noninstitutionalized population; (1) Figures cover the Fort Wayne, IN Metropolitan Statistical Area—see Appendix B for areas included
Source: U.S. Census Bureau, 2014-2018 American Community Survey 5-Year Estimates

Number of Medical Professionals

Area	MDs[3]	DOs[3,4]	Dentists	Podiatrists	Chiropractors	Optometrists
County[1] (number)	982	99	243	21	79	95
County[1] (rate[2])	263.4	26.6	64.7	5.6	21.0	25.3
U.S. (rate[2])	281.9	23.4	69.1	6.0	27.5	16.4

Note: Data as of 2018 unless noted; (1) Data covers Allen County; (2) Rate per 100,000 population; (3) Data as of 2017 and includes all active, non-federal physicians; (4) Doctor of Osteopathic Medicine
Source: U.S. Department of Health and Human Services, Health Resources and Services Administration, Bureau of Health Professions, Area Resource File (ARF) 2018-2019

EDUCATION

Public School District Statistics

District Name	Schls	Pupils	Pupil/Teacher Ratio	Minority Pupils[1] (%)	Free Lunch Eligible[2] (%)	IEP[3] (%)
Fort Wayne Community Schools	49	29,404	19.0	59.2	51.5	19.0
M S D Southwest Allen Co. Schls	9	7,471	17.7	20.6	13.3	10.1
Northwest Allen County Schools	11	7,722	17.6	15.9	13.2	14.6

Note: Table includes school districts with 2,000 or more students; (1) Percentage of students that are not non-Hispanic white; (2) Percentage of students that are eligible for the free lunch program; (3) Percentage of students that have an Individualized Education Program.
Source: U.S. Department of Education, National Center for Education Statistics, Common Core of Data, Local Education Agency (School District) Universe Survey: School Year 2018-2019; U.S. Department of Education, National Center for Education Statistics, Common Core of Data, Public Elementary/Secondary School Universe Survey: School Year 2018-2019

Highest Level of Education

Area	Less than H.S.	H.S. Diploma	Some College, No Deg.	Associate Degree	Bachelor's Degree	Master's Degree	Prof. School Degree	Doctorate Degree
City	11.5	28.7	22.2	10.0	18.1	7.0	1.7	0.9
MSA[1]	10.3	30.4	21.7	10.7	17.7	6.8	1.6	0.8
U.S.	12.3	27.1	20.6	8.4	19.4	8.6	2.1	1.4

Note: Figures cover persons age 25 and over; (1) Figures cover the Fort Wayne, IN Metropolitan Statistical Area—see Appendix B for areas included
Source: U.S. Census Bureau, 2014-2018 American Community Survey 5-Year Estimates

Educational Attainment by Race

Area	High School Graduate or Higher (%)					Bachelor's Degree or Higher (%)				
	Total	White	Black	Asian	Hisp.[2]	Total	White	Black	Asian	Hisp.[2]
City	88.5	91.7	83.2	58.9	60.0	27.6	30.5	13.7	32.5	9.6
MSA[1]	89.7	91.7	84.0	62.4	62.2	26.9	28.3	14.9	36.1	10.0
U.S.	87.7	89.6	85.4	86.8	67.7	31.5	32.9	21.1	53.5	15.8

Note: Figures shown cover persons 25 years old and over; (1) Figures cover the Fort Wayne, IN Metropolitan Statistical Area—see Appendix B for areas included; (2) People of Hispanic origin can be of any race
Source: U.S. Census Bureau, 2014-2018 American Community Survey 5-Year Estimates

School Enrollment by Grade and Control

Area	Preschool (%)		Kindergarten (%)		Grades 1 - 4 (%)		Grades 5 - 8 (%)		Grades 9 - 12 (%)	
	Public	Private	Public	Private	Public	Private	Public	Private	Public	Private
City	51.7	48.3	86.0	14.0	82.2	17.8	81.0	19.0	79.4	20.6
MSA[1]	48.1	51.9	80.4	19.6	79.6	20.4	79.2	20.8	81.0	19.0
U.S.	59.0	41.0	87.7	12.3	89.6	10.4	89.5	10.5	90.2	9.8

Note: Figures shown cover persons 3 years old and over; (1) Figures cover the Fort Wayne, IN Metropolitan Statistical Area—see Appendix B for areas included
Source: U.S. Census Bureau, 2014-2018 American Community Survey 5-Year Estimates

Average Salaries of Public School Teachers

Area	2016-17		2017-18		Change from 2016-17 to 2017-18	
	Dollars	Rank[1]	Dollars	Rank[1]	Percent	Rank[2]
Indiana	50,218	35	50,614	36	0.79	34
U.S. Average	59,539	–	60,477	–	1.58	–

Note: (1) Rank ranges from 1 to 51 where 1 indicates highest salary; (2) Rank ranges from 1 to 51 where 1 indicates highest percent change.
Source: National Education Association, Rankings & Estimates: Rankings of the States 2018 and Estimates of School Statistics 2019

Higher Education

Four-Year Colleges			Two-Year Colleges			Medical Schools[1]	Law Schools[2]	Voc/ Tech[3]
Public	Private Non-profit	Private For-profit	Public	Private Non-profit	Private For-profit			
1	5	0	0	0	2	0	1	2

Note: Figures cover institutions located within the city limits and include main campuses only; (1) includes schools accredited by the Liaison Committee on Medical Education and the American Osteopathic Association's Commission on Osteopathic College Accreditation; (2) includes ABA-accredited schools, schools with provisional ABA accreditation, and state accredited schools; (3) includes all schools with programs that are less than 2 years.
Source: National Center for Education Statistics, Integrated Postsecondary Education System (IPEDS), 2018-19; Wikipedia, List of Medical Schools in the United States, accessed May 1, 2020; Wikipedia, List of Law Schools in the United States, accessed May 1, 2020

PRESIDENTIAL ELECTION

2016 Presidential Election Results

Area	Clinton	Trump	Johnson	Stein	Other
Allen County	37.3	56.5	4.6	0.5	1.2
U.S.	48.0	45.9	3.3	1.1	1.7

Note: Results are percentages and may not add to 100% due to rounding
Source: Dave Leip's Atlas of U.S. Presidential Elections

EMPLOYERS

Major Employers

Company Name	Industry
Allen County Government	Government
BAE Systems Platform Solutions	Aircraft electronics
Benchmark Human Services	Services for people with disabilities
BFGoodrich	Rubber tire manufacturing
City of Fort Wayne	Government
Dana Corp.	Motor vehicle parts manufacturing
Edy's Grand Ice Cream	Ice cream & other frozen treats
Fort Wayne Community Schools	Elementary & secondary schools
Fort Wayne Metals Research Products Corp.	Wire for medical devices
Frontier Communications Corp.	Wired telecommunications carriers
General Motors	Motor vehicle manufacturing
Harris Corporation	Wireless networking systems & satellite imaging systems
IPFW	University
Ivy Tech Community College- Northeast	Community college
Lincoln Financial Group	Insurance carriers
Lutheran Health Network	General medical & surgical hospitals
Norfolk Southern Corp2	Rail transportation
Northwest Allen County Schools	Elementary & secondary schools
Parker Hannifin Corporation	Metal product manufacturing for a/c systems
Parkview Health Systems	General medical & surgical hospitals
Raytheon Systems Co.	Mission solutions for aerospace industry
Shambaugh & Son	Commercial building construction
Steel Dynamics1	Corporate headquarters & scrap metal processing
Sweetwater Sound	Sound recording studio & equipment distribution
Vera Bradley	Handbags, luggage, & accessories

Note: Companies shown are located within the Fort Wayne, IN Metropolitan Statistical Area.
Source: Hoovers.com; Wikipedia

PUBLIC SAFETY

Crime Rate

Area	All Crimes	Violent Crimes				Property Crimes		
		Murder	Rape[3]	Robbery	Aggrav. Assault	Burglary	Larceny -Theft	Motor Vehicle Theft
City	3,000.7	14.9	48.9	114.7	204.0	375.9	2,037.5	204.8
Suburbs[1]	1,159.6	1.4	26.2	29.0	114.5	195.2	713.4	79.9
Metro[2]	2,364.2	10.3	41.1	85.1	173.1	313.4	1,579.7	161.6
U.S.	2,580.1	5.0	42.6	86.2	246.8	376.0	1,594.6	228.9

Note: Figures are crimes per 100,000 population; (1) All areas within the metro area that are located outside the city limits; (2) Figures cover the Fort Wayne, IN Metropolitan Statistical Area—see Appendix B for areas included; (3) The city and U.S. figures shown were reported using the revised Uniform Crime Reporting (UCR) definition of rape. The suburban and metro area figures shown are an aggregate total of the data submitted using both the revised and legacy UCR definitions.
Source: FBI Uniform Crime Reports, 2018

Hate Crimes

Area	Number of Quarters Reported	Number of Incidents per Bias Motivation					
		Race/Ethnicity/ Ancestry	Religion	Sexual Orientation	Disability	Gender	Gender Identity
City	4	0	1	0	0	0	0
U.S.	4	4,047	1,419	1,196	159	47	168

Source: Federal Bureau of Investigation, Hate Crime Statistics 2018

Identity Theft Consumer Reports

Area	Reports	Reports per 100,000 Population	Rank[2]
MSA[1]	459	105	174
U.S.	650,572	198	-

Note: (1) Figures cover the Fort Wayne, IN Metropolitan Statistical Area—see Appendix B for areas included; (2) Rank ranges from 1 to 386 where 1 indicates greatest number of identity theft reports per 100,000 population
Source: Federal Trade Commission, Consumer Sentinel Network Data Book for January–December 2019

Fraud and Other Consumer Reports

Area	Reports	Reports per 100,000 Population	Rank[2]
MSA[1]	2,126	486	266
U.S.	2,590,177	789	-

Note: (1) Figures cover the Fort Wayne, IN Metropolitan Statistical Area—see Appendix B for areas included; (2) Rank ranges from 1 to 386 where 1 indicates greatest number of fraud and other consumer reports per 100,000 population
Source: Federal Trade Commission, Consumer Sentinel Network Data Book for January–December 2019

SPORTS

Professional Sports Teams

Team Name	League	Year Established
No teams are located in the metro area		

Source: Wikipedia, Major Professional Sports Teams of the United States and Canada, May 4, 2020

CLIMATE

Average and Extreme Temperatures

Temperature	Jan	Feb	Mar	Apr	May	Jun	Jul	Aug	Sep	Oct	Nov	Dec	Yr.
Extreme High (°F)	69	69	82	88	94	106	103	101	100	90	79	71	106
Average High (°F)	31	35	46	60	71	81	84	82	76	64	49	36	60
Average Temp. (°F)	24	27	37	49	60	70	74	72	65	53	41	29	50
Average Low (°F)	16	19	28	39	49	59	63	61	53	42	32	22	40
Extreme Low (°F)	-22	-18	-10	7	27	38	44	38	29	19	-1	-18	-22

Note: Figures cover the years 1948-1990
Source: National Climatic Data Center, International Station Meteorological Climate Summary, 9/96

Average Precipitation/Snowfall/Humidity

Precip./Humidity	Jan	Feb	Mar	Apr	May	Jun	Jul	Aug	Sep	Oct	Nov	Dec	Yr.
Avg. Precip. (in.)	2.3	2.1	2.9	3.4	3.6	3.8	3.6	3.4	2.6	2.7	2.8	2.7	35.9
Avg. Snowfall (in.)	8	8	5	2	Tr	0	0	0	0	Tr	3	7	33
Avg. Rel. Hum. 7am (%)	81	81	80	77	76	78	81	86	86	84	83	83	81
Avg. Rel. Hum. 4pm (%)	71	68	62	54	52	52	53	55	53	55	67	74	59

Note: Figures cover the years 1948-1990; Tr = Trace amounts (<0.05 in. of rain; <0.5 in. of snow)
Source: National Climatic Data Center, International Station Meteorological Climate Summary, 9/96

Weather Conditions

Temperature			Daytime Sky			Precipitation		
5°F & below	32°F & below	90°F & above	Clear	Partly cloudy	Cloudy	0.01 inch or more precip.	0.1 inch or more snow/ice	Thunder-storms
16	131	16	75	140	150	131	31	39

Note: Figures are average number of days per year and cover the years 1948-1990
Source: National Climatic Data Center, International Station Meteorological Climate Summary, 9/96

HAZARDOUS WASTE

Superfund Sites

The Fort Wayne, IN metro area is home to two sites on the EPA's Superfund National Priorities List: **Fort Wayne Reduction Dump** (final); **Wayne Waste Oil** (final). There are a total of 1,387 Superfund sites with a status of proposed or final on the list in the U.S. *U.S. Environmental Protection Agency, National Priorities List, May 5, 2020*

AIR & WATER QUALITY

Air Quality Trends: Ozone

	1990	1995	2000	2005	2010	2012	2014	2016	2017	2018
MSA[1]	0.086	0.094	0.086	0.081	0.067	0.076	0.063	0.068	0.063	0.071
U.S.	0.088	0.089	0.082	0.080	0.073	0.075	0.067	0.069	0.068	0.069

Note: (1) Data covers the Fort Wayne, IN Metropolitan Statistical Area—see Appendix B for areas included. The values shown are the composite ozone concentration averages among trend sites based on the highest fourth daily maximum 8-hour concentration in parts per million. These trends are based on sites having an adequate record of monitoring data during the trend period. Data from exceptional events are included.
Source: U.S. Environmental Protection Agency, Air Quality Monitoring Information, "Air Quality Trends by City, 1990-2018"

Air Quality Index

Area	Percent of Days when Air Quality was...[2]					AQI Statistics[2]	
	Good	Moderate	Unhealthy for Sensitive Groups	Unhealthy	Very Unhealthy	Maximum	Median
MSA[1]	66.6	31.8	1.6	0.0	0.0	122	44

Note: (1) Data covers the Fort Wayne, IN Metropolitan Statistical Area—see Appendix B for areas included; (2) Based on 365 days with AQI data in 2018. Air Quality Index (AQI) is an index for reporting daily air quality. EPA calculates the AQI for five major air pollutants regulated by the Clean Air Act: ground-level ozone, particle pollution (aka particulate matter), carbon monoxide, sulfur dioxide, and nitrogen dioxide. The AQI runs from 0 to 500. The higher the AQI value, the greater the level of air pollution and the greater the health concern. There are six AQI categories: "Good" AQI is between 0 and 50. Air quality is considered satisfactory; "Moderate" AQI is between 51 and 100. Air quality is acceptable; "Unhealthy for Sensitive Groups" When AQI values are between 101 and 150, members of sensitive groups may experience health effects; "Unhealthy" When AQI values are between 151 and 200 everyone may begin to experience health effects; "Very Unhealthy" AQI values between 201 and 300 trigger a health alert; "Hazardous" AQI values over 300 trigger warnings of emergency conditions (not shown).
Source: U.S. Environmental Protection Agency, Air Quality Index Report, 2018

Air Quality Index Pollutants

Area	Percent of Days when AQI Pollutant was...[2]					
	Carbon Monoxide	Nitrogen Dioxide	Ozone	Sulfur Dioxide	Particulate Matter 2.5	Particulate Matter 10
MSA[1]	0.0	0.0	52.3	0.0	47.7	0.0

Note: (1) Data covers the Fort Wayne, IN Metropolitan Statistical Area—see Appendix B for areas included; (2) Based on 365 days with AQI data in 2018. The Air Quality Index (AQI) is an index for reporting daily air quality. EPA calculates the AQI for five major air pollutants regulated by the Clean Air Act: ground-level ozone, particle pollution (also known as particulate matter), carbon monoxide, sulfur dioxide, and nitrogen dioxide. The AQI runs from 0 to 500. The higher the AQI value, the greater the level of air pollution and the greater the health concern.
Source: U.S. Environmental Protection Agency, Air Quality Index Report, 2018

Maximum Air Pollutant Concentrations: Particulate Matter, Ozone, CO and Lead

	Particulate Matter 10 (ug/m^3)	Particulate Matter 2.5 Wtd AM (ug/m^3)	Particulate Matter 2.5 24-Hr (ug/m^3)	Ozone (ppm)	Carbon Monoxide (ppm)	Lead (ug/m^3)
MSA[1] Level	n/a	9.1	22	0.072	n/a	n/a
NAAQS[2]	150	15	35	0.075	9	0.15
Met NAAQS[2]	n/a	Yes	Yes	Yes	n/a	n/a

Note: (1) Data covers the Fort Wayne, IN Metropolitan Statistical Area—see Appendix B for areas included; Data from exceptional events are included; (2) National Ambient Air Quality Standards; ppm = parts per million; ug/m^3 = micrograms per cubic meter; n/a not available.
Concentrations: Particulate Matter 10 (coarse particulate)—highest second maximum 24-hour concentration; Particulate Matter 2.5 Wtd AM (fine particulate)—highest weighted annual mean concentration; Particulate Matter 2.5 24-Hour (fine particulate)—highest 98th percentile 24-hour concentration; Ozone—highest fourth daily maximum 8-hour concentration; Carbon Monoxide—highest second maximum non-overlapping 8-hour concentration; Lead—maximum running 3-month average
Source: U.S. Environmental Protection Agency, Air Quality Monitoring Information, "Air Quality Statistics by City, 2018"

Maximum Air Pollutant Concentrations: Nitrogen Dioxide and Sulfur Dioxide

	Nitrogen Dioxide AM (ppb)	Nitrogen Dioxide 1-Hr (ppb)	Sulfur Dioxide AM (ppb)	Sulfur Dioxide 1-Hr (ppb)	Sulfur Dioxide 24-Hr (ppb)
MSA[1] Level	n/a	n/a	n/a	n/a	n/a
NAAQS[2]	53	100	30	75	140
Met NAAQS[2]	n/a	n/a	n/a	n/a	n/a

Note: (1) Data covers the Fort Wayne, IN Metropolitan Statistical Area—see Appendix B for areas included; Data from exceptional events are included; (2) National Ambient Air Quality Standards; ppm = parts per million; ug/m³ = micrograms per cubic meter; n/a not available.
Concentrations: Nitrogen Dioxide AM—highest arithmetic mean concentration; Nitrogen Dioxide 1-Hr—highest 98th percentile 1-hour daily maximum concentration; Sulfur Dioxide AM—highest annual mean concentration; Sulfur Dioxide 1-Hr—highest 99th percentile 1-hour daily maximum concentration; Sulfur Dioxide 24-Hr—highest second maximum 24-hour concentration
Source: U.S. Environmental Protection Agency, Air Quality Monitoring Information, "Air Quality Statistics by City, 2018"

Drinking Water

Water System Name	Pop. Served	Primary Water Source Type	Violations[1]
Ft. Wayne-3 Rivers Filtration Plant	266,000	Surface	15

Note: (1) Total number of violations (both active and inactive) in the EPA database
Source: U.S. Environmental Protection Agency, Office of Ground Water and Drinking Water, Safe Drinking Water Information System (based on data extracted May 5, 2020)

Grand Rapids, Michigan

Background

The city of Grand Rapids is located in the west-central part of Kent County in the picturesque Grand River Valley, about 30 miles east of Lake Michigan. It is known for its fine furniture making.

The presence of an abundant forest, as well as the hydropower and trade afforded by a powerful river, contributed to the reputation of a manufacturing industry that is known worldwide, producing not only furniture, but industrial machinery, metal, paper, plastics, and printing products. Food and information technology industries are also important to the economy of the city. There are 14 universities and colleges in Grand Rapids.

Before Grand Rapids became involved in making seating for churches, buses, and schools, among other furniture, the site was a Native American settlement of the Ottawa, Chippewa, and Potawatomi tribes. The earliest white settlers in the area were fur traders who bought pelts from the Native American tribes in the early nineteenth century. One by one, more white settlers found their way into the area on the rapids of the Grand River. A Baptist mission was established in 1825, and a year after that, Louis Campau erected a trading post. In 1833, the area's first permanent white settlement appeared, led by Samuel Dexter of Herkimer County, New York. In 1945, Grand Rapids became the first city in the United States to add fluoride to its drinking water.

Revitalization efforts have resulted in a thriving downtown district that includes restaurants, hotels, clubs, museums, and the 12,000-square foot Van Andel Arena. Also here is the DeVos Place Convention Center, with its 162,000-square foot, column-free exhibit hall, 40,000-square foot ballroom, 26 individual meeting rooms, and a 2,404-seat performing arts theater that is home to the Grand Rapids Symphony, the Grand Rapids Ballet Company, Opera Grand Rapids, and Broadway Grand Rapids.

The city's other attractions include a yearly Festival of the Arts held in June and featuring visual, performing and culinary arts, and annual jazz festival. Celebration on the Grand salutes summer with free concerts, West Michigan's largest fire works display and food booths. The annual Fulton Street Farmers Market has been held since 1922, and offers locally grown produce and handmade items.

The Frederik Meijer Gardens and Sculpture Park blends art and nature, maintaining outdoor (on 125 acres) and indoor exhibits. Each spring, visitors marvel at the thousands of butterflies, brought from all over the world and released into the Park's tropical conservatory.

Children enjoy the John Ball Zoo as well as the Grand Rapids Children's Museum, which offers a wide range of entertainment and educational programs.

Fall is a very colorful time of year in western Michigan, perhaps compensating for the late spring. During the winter, excessive cloudiness and numerous snow flurries occur with strong westerly winds. Lake Michigan has a tempering effect on cold waves coming in from the west in the winter. Prolonged, severe cold waves are infrequent. The snowfall season extends from mid-November to mid-March and some winters have had continuous snow cover throughout this period.

Rankings

General Rankings

- *US News & World Report* conducted a survey of more than 2,000 people and analyzed the 125 largest metropolitan areas to determine what matters the most when selecting the next place to live. Grand Rapids ranked #13 out of the top 25 as having the best combination of desirable factors. Criteria: cost of living; quality of life; net migration; job market; desirability; and other factors. *realestate.usnews.com, "The 25 Best Places to Live in the U.S. in 2019," April 9, 2019*

- The Grand Rapids metro area was identified as one of America's fastest-growing areas in terms of population and business growth by *MagnifyMoney*. The area ranked #27 out of 35. The 100 most populous metro areas in the U.S. were evaluated on their change from 2011-2016 in the following categories: people and housing; workforce and employment opportunities; growing industry. *www.businessinsider.com, "The 35 Cities in the US with the Biggest Influx of People, the Most Work Opportunities, and the Hottest Business Growth," August 12, 2018*

- The Grand Rapids metro area was identified as one of America's fastest-growing areas in terms of population and economy by *Forbes*. The area ranked #25 out of 25. The 100 most populous metro areas in the U.S. were evaluated on the following criteria: estimated population growth; employment; economic output; wages; home values. *Forbes, "America's Fastest-Growing Cities 2018," February 28, 2018*

- In their sixth annual survey, Livability.com looked at data for more than 1,000 U.S. cities to determine the rankings for Livability's "Top 100 Best Places to Live" in 2019. Grand Rapids ranked #45. Criteria: median home value capped at $250,000; affordable living; vibrant economy; education, demographics, health care options. transportation & infrastructure; abundant lifestyle amenities. *Livability.com, "Top 100 Best Places to Live 2019" March 2019*

Business/Finance Rankings

- The Brookings Institution ranked the nation's largest cities based on income inequality. Grand Rapids was ranked #85 (#1 = greatest inequality). Criteria: the "95/20 ratio," a figure representing the income at which a household earns more than 95 percent of all other households, divided by the income at which a household earns more than only 20 percent of all other households. *Brookings Institution, "Household Income Inequality, Largest Cities of 97 Large U.S. Metro Areas, 2014-2016," February 5, 2018*

- The Brookings Institution ranked the 100 largest metro areas in the U.S. based on income inequality. Grand Rapids was ranked #97 (#1 = greatest inequality). Criteria: the "95/20 ratio," a figure representing the income at which a household earns more than 95 percent of all other households, divided by the income at which a household earns more than only 20 percent of all other households. *Brookings Institution, "Household Income Inequality, 100 Largest U.S. Metro Areas, 2014-2016," February 5, 2018*

- The Grand Rapids metro area appeared on the Milken Institute "2020 Best Performing Cities" list. Rank: #73 out of 200 large metro areas. Criteria: job growth; wage and salary growth; high-tech output growth. *Milken Institute, "Best-Performing Cities 2020," February 26, 2020*

- *Forbes* ranked the 200 most populous metro areas to determine the nation's "Best Places for Business and Careers." The Grand Rapids metro area was ranked #68. Criteria: costs (business and living); job growth (past and projected); income growth; quality of life; educational attainment (college and high school); projected economic growth; cultural and leisure opportunities; workplace tolerance laws; net migration patterns. *Forbes, "The Best Places for Business and Careers 2019: Seattle Still On Top," October 30, 2019*

Dating/Romance Rankings

- *Apartment List* conducted its annual survey of renters to compile a list of cities that have the best opportunities for dating. More than 11,000 single respondents, from February 15, 2019 through the end of December 2019, rated their current city or neighborhood for opportunities to date. Grand Rapids ranked #10 out of 86 where single residents were very satisfied or somewhat satisfied, making it among the ten best metros for dating opportunities. Other criteria analyzed included gender and education levels of renters. *Apartment List, "The Best & Worst Metros for Dating 2020," February 4, 2020*

- Grand Rapids was ranked #7 out of 25 cities that stood out for inspiring romance and attracting diners on the website OpenTable.com. Criteria: percentage of people who dined out on Valentine's Day in 2018; percentage of romantic restaurants as rated by OpenTable diner reviews; and percentage of tables seated for two. *OpenTable, "25 Most Romantic Cities in America for 2019," February 7, 2019*

Education Rankings

- Personal finance website *WalletHub* analyzed the 150 largest U.S. metropolitan statistical areas to determine where the most educated Americans are choosing to settle. Criteria: education levels; percentage of workers with degrees; education quality and attainment gap; public school quality rankings; quality and size of each metro area's universities. Grand Rapids was ranked #62 (#1 = most educated city). *www.WalletHub.com, "2019's Most and Least Educated Cities in America," July 22, 2019*

Environmental Rankings

- Niche compiled a list of the nation's snowiest cities, based on the National Oceanic and Atmospheric Administration's 30-year average snowfall data. Among cities with a population of at least 50,000, Grand Rapids ranked #8. *Niche.com, Top 25 Snowiest Cities in America, December 10, 2018*

Health/Fitness Rankings

- The Grand Rapids metro area was identified as one of the worst cities for bed bugs in America by pest control company Orkin. The area ranked #18 out of 50 based on the number of bed bug treatments Orkin performed from December 2018 to November 2019. *Orkin, "Washington, D.C. Surpasses Baltimore to Secure Top Spot on Orkin's 2020 Bed Bug Cities List," January 13, 2020*

- Grand Rapids was identified as a "2020 Spring Allergy Capital." The area ranked #27 out of 100. Three groups of factors were used to identify the most challenging cities for people with allergies during the spring season: annual spring pollen levels; over the counter medicine use; number of board-certified allergy specialists. *Asthma and Allergy Foundation of America, "Spring Allergy Capitals 2020," March 10, 2020*

- Grand Rapids was identified as a "2020 Fall Allergy Capital." The area ranked #17 out of 100. Three groups of factors were used to identify the most challenging cities for people with allergies during the fall season: annual fall pollen levels; over the counter medicine use; number of board-certified allergy specialists. *Asthma and Allergy Foundation of America, "Fall Allergy Capitals 2020," March 10, 2020*

- Grand Rapids was identified as a "2019 Asthma Capital." The area ranked #62 out of the nation's 100 largest metropolitan areas. Criteria: estimated asthma prevalence; crude death rate from asthma; and ER visits due to asthma. Risk factors that were analyzed but not factored in the rankings: annual pollen score; annual air quality; public smoking laws; number of board-certified asthma specialists; rescue medication use; controller medication use; uninsured rate; poverty rate. *Asthma and Allergy Foundation of America, "Asthma Capitals 2019: The Most Challenging Places to Live With Asthma," May 7, 2019*

- The Grand Rapids metro area ranked #26 out of 189 in The Gallup-Sharecare Well-Being Index. Criteria: purpose; social well being; financial health; community and physical health. Results are based on telephone interviews with adults, aged 18 and older, living in metropolitan areas in the 50 U.S. states and the District of Columbia. *Gallup-Sharecare, "State of American Well-Being, 2017 Community Well-Being Rankings" March 2018*

Real Estate Rankings

- *WalletHub* compared the most populated U.S. cities, as well as at least two of the most populated cities in each state, for a total of 179, to determine which had the best markets for real estate agents. Grand Rapids ranked #49 where demand was high and pay was the best. Criteria: sales per agent; annual median wage for real-estate agents; monthly average starting salary for real estate agents; real estate job density and competition; unemployment rate; home turnover rate; housing-market health index; and other relevant metrics. *www.WalletHub.com, "2019's Best Places to Be a Real Estate Agent," April 24, 2019*

- Grand Rapids was ranked #17 in the top 20 out of the 100 largest metro areas in terms of house price appreciation in 2019 (#1 = highest rate). *Federal Housing Finance Agency, House Price Index, 4th Quarter 2019*

- Grand Rapids was ranked #37 out of 238 metro areas in terms of housing affordability in 2019 by the National Association of Home Builders (#1 = most affordable). Criteria: the share of homes sold in that area affordable to a family earning the local median income, based on standard mortgage underwriting criteria. *National Association of Home Builders®, NAHB-Wells Fargo Housing Opportunity Index, 4th Quarter 2019*

Safety Rankings

- Allstate ranked the 200 largest cities in America in terms of driver safety. Grand Rapids ranked #131. Criteria: internal property damage claims over a two-year period from January 2016 to December 2017. The report helps increase the importance of safety and awareness behind the wheel. *Allstate, "Allstate America's Best Drivers Report, 2019" June 24, 2019*

- The National Insurance Crime Bureau ranked 382 metro areas in the U.S. in terms of per capita rates of vehicle theft. The Grand Rapids metro area ranked #339 (#1 = highest rate). Criteria: number of vehicle theft offenses per 100,000 inhabitants in 2018. *National Insurance Crime Bureau, "Hot Spots 2018," June 25, 2019*

Women/Minorities Rankings

- Personal finance website *WalletHub* compared more than 180 U.S. cities—including the 150 most populated U.S. cities, plus at least two of the most populated cities in each state—across two key dimensions, "Hispanic Business-Friendliness" and "Hispanic Purchasing Power", to arrive at the most favorable conditions for Hispanic entrepreneurs. Grand Rapids was ranked #101 out of 182. Criteria includes: share of Hispanic-Owned Businesses; Hispanic entrepreneurship rate to median annual income of Hispanics; Small Business-Friendliness score; cost of living; and number of Hispanics with at least a bachelor's degree. *WalletHub.com, "2019's Best Cities for Hispanic Entrepreneurs," May 1, 2019*

Miscellaneous Rankings

- *MoveHub* ranked the coolest cities, appealing to young people, using its U.S. Hipster Index and Grand Rapids came out as #9. Criteria: number of thrift stores; density of tattoo parlors, vegan stores and microbreweries; and amount of rent increase. *www.thisisinsider.com, "The 20 Most Hipster Cities in the US-and Why You Should Consider Moving to One," April 10, 2018*

- *WalletHub* compared the 150 most populated U.S. cities to determine their operating efficiency. A "Quality of Services" score was constructed for each city and then divided by the total budget per capita to reveal which were managed the best. Grand Rapids ranked #37. Criteria: financial stability; economy; education; safety; health; infrastructure and pollution. *www.WalletHub.com, "2019's Best- & Worst-Run Cities in America," July 1, 2019*

- Grand Rapids was selected as one of "America's Friendliest Cities." The city ranked #13 in the "Friendliest" category. Respondents to an online survey were asked to rate 38 top urban destinations in the United States as to general friendliness, as well as manners, politeness and warm disposition. *Travel + Leisure, "America's Friendliest Cities," October 20, 2017*

Business Environment

CITY FINANCES

City Government Finances

Component	2017 ($000)	2017 ($ per capita)
Total Revenues	478,920	2,455
Total Expenditures	478,803	2,454
Debt Outstanding	676,126	3,466
Cash and Securities[1]	1,296,027	6,643

Note: (1) Cash and security holdings of a government at the close of its fiscal year, including those of its dependent agencies, utilities, and liquor stores.
Source: U.S. Census Bureau, State & Local Government Finances 2017

City Government Revenue by Source

Source	2017 ($000)	2017 ($ per capita)	2017 (%)
General Revenue			
From Federal Government	34,323	176	7.2
From State Government	39,306	201	8.2
From Local Governments	8,304	43	1.7
Taxes			
Property	55,540	285	11.6
Sales and Gross Receipts	0	0	0.0
Personal Income	93,951	482	19.6
Corporate Income	0	0	0.0
Motor Vehicle License	0	0	0.0
Other Taxes	5,110	26	1.1
Current Charges	108,871	558	22.7
Liquor Store	0	0	0.0
Utility	43,537	223	9.1
Employee Retirement	74,027	379	15.5

Source: U.S. Census Bureau, State & Local Government Finances 2017

City Government Expenditures by Function

Function	2017 ($000)	2017 ($ per capita)	2017 (%)
General Direct Expenditures			
Air Transportation	0	0	0.0
Corrections	0	0	0.0
Education	0	0	0.0
Employment Security Administration	0	0	0.0
Financial Administration	11,382	58	2.4
Fire Protection	28,775	147	6.0
General Public Buildings	0	0	0.0
Governmental Administration, Other	9,675	49	2.0
Health	578	3	0.1
Highways	20,547	105	4.3
Hospitals	0	0	0.0
Housing and Community Development	36,484	187	7.6
Interest on General Debt	20,409	104	4.3
Judicial and Legal	19,654	100	4.1
Libraries	9,036	46	1.9
Parking	15,311	78	3.2
Parks and Recreation	11,839	60	2.5
Police Protection	51,814	265	10.8
Public Welfare	0	0	0.0
Sewerage	38,566	197	8.1
Solid Waste Management	10,387	53	2.2
Veterans' Services	0	0	0.0
Liquor Store	0	0	0.0
Utility	44,804	229	9.4
Employee Retirement	62,328	319	13.0

Source: U.S. Census Bureau, State & Local Government Finances 2017

DEMOGRAPHICS

Population Growth

Area	1990 Census	2000 Census	2010 Census	2018* Estimate	Population Growth (%) 1990-2018	2010-2018
City	189,145	197,800	188,040	197,081	4.2	4.8
MSA[1]	645,914	740,482	774,160	1,050,440	62.6	35.7
U.S.	248,709,873	281,421,906	308,745,538	322,903,030	29.8	4.6

Note: (1) Figures cover the Grand Rapids-Wyoming, MI Metropolitan Statistical Area—see Appendix B for areas included; (*) 2014-2018 5-year estimated population
Source: U.S. Census Bureau, 1990 Census, Census 2000, Census 2010, 2014-2018 American Community Survey 5-Year Estimates

Household Size

Area	Persons in Household (%) One	Two	Three	Four	Five	Six	Seven or More	Average Household Size
City	32.6	31.8	13.8	11.1	6.2	2.6	2.0	2.60
MSA[1]	24.5	35.1	14.9	14.5	6.9	2.7	1.5	2.60
U.S.	27.7	33.9	15.7	13.0	6.0	2.3	1.4	2.60

Note: (1) Figures cover the Grand Rapids-Wyoming, MI Metropolitan Statistical Area—see Appendix B for areas included
Source: U.S. Census Bureau, 2014-2018 American Community Survey 5-Year Estimates

Race

Area	White Alone[2] (%)	Black Alone[2] (%)	Asian Alone[2] (%)	AIAN[3] Alone[2] (%)	NHOPI[4] Alone[2] (%)	Other Race Alone[2] (%)	Two or More Races (%)
City	67.5	19.2	2.3	0.4	0.1	5.5	5.0
MSA[1]	84.2	6.5	2.6	0.4	0.0	3.0	3.3
U.S.	72.7	12.7	5.4	0.8	0.2	4.9	3.2

Note: (1) Figures cover the Grand Rapids-Wyoming, MI Metropolitan Statistical Area—see Appendix B for areas included; (2) Alone is defined as not being in combination with one or more other races; (3) American Indian and Alaska Native; (4) Native Hawaiian and Other Pacific Islander
Source: U.S. Census Bureau, 2014-2018 American Community Survey 5-Year Estimates

Hispanic or Latino Origin

Area	Total (%)	Mexican (%)	Puerto Rican (%)	Cuban (%)	Other (%)
City	15.9	9.4	1.4	0.3	4.8
MSA[1]	9.4	6.6	0.8	0.3	1.7
U.S.	17.8	11.2	1.7	0.7	4.2

Note: Persons of Hispanic or Latino origin can be of any race; (1) Figures cover the Grand Rapids-Wyoming, MI Metropolitan Statistical Area—see Appendix B for areas included
Source: U.S. Census Bureau, 2014-2018 American Community Survey 5-Year Estimates

Segregation

Type	Segregation Indices[1] 1990	2000	2010	2010 Rank[2]	Percent Change 1990-2000	1990-2010	2000-2010
Black/White	72.7	66.7	64.3	26	-6.0	-8.4	-2.4
Asian/White	34.3	43.7	43.2	37	9.4	8.9	-0.5
Hispanic/White	42.4	52.7	50.4	23	10.3	8.0	-2.3

Note: All figures cover the Metropolitan Statistical Area—see Appendix B for areas included; Figures are based on an analysis of 1990, 2000, and 2010 Census Decennial Census tract data by William H. Frey, Brookings Institution and the University of Michigan Social Science Data Analysis Network. In this analysis all racial groups (whites, blacks, and asians) are non-Hispanic members of those races. Hispanics are shown as a separate category; (1) Segregation Indices are Dissimilarity Indices that measure the degree to which the minority group is distributed differently than whites across census tracts. They range from 0 (complete integration) to 100 (complete segregation) where the value indicates the percentage of the minority group that needs to move to be distributed exactly like whites; (2) Ranges from 1 (most segregated) to 102 (least segregated); n/a not available.
Source: www.CensusScope.org

Ancestry

Area	German	Irish	English	American	Italian	Polish	French[2]	Scottish	Dutch
City	15.5	9.1	6.8	2.7	2.9	6.8	2.5	1.7	14.1
MSA[1]	20.3	10.1	8.8	4.1	3.1	6.5	3.0	1.9	19.8
U.S.	13.7	9.9	7.3	6.4	5.2	2.8	2.4	1.7	1.2

Note: Figures are the percentage of the total population reporting a particular ancestry. The nine most commonly reported ancestries in the U.S. are shown. Figures include multiple ancestries (e.g. if a person reported being Irish and Italian, they were included in both columns); (1) Figures cover the Grand Rapids-Wyoming, MI Metropolitan Statistical Area—see Appendix B for areas included; (2) Excludes Basque
Source: U.S. Census Bureau, 2014-2018 American Community Survey 5-Year Estimates

Foreign-born Population

Area	Percent of Population Born in								
	Any Foreign Country	Asia	Mexico	Europe	Caribbean	Central America[2]	South America	Africa	Canada
City	10.5	2.0	3.2	1.2	0.5	1.8	0.1	1.4	0.3
MSA[1]	6.8	2.1	1.9	1.1	0.4	0.5	0.1	0.5	0.2
U.S.	13.5	4.1	3.5	1.5	1.3	1.1	0.9	0.7	0.3

Note: (1) Figures cover the Grand Rapids-Wyoming, MI Metropolitan Statistical Area—see Appendix B for areas included; (2) Excludes Mexico.
Source: U.S. Census Bureau, 2014-2018 American Community Survey 5-Year Estimates

Marital Status

Area	Never Married	Now Married[2]	Separated	Widowed	Divorced
City	46.6	36.4	1.4	5.3	10.3
MSA[1]	32.1	51.9	1.0	4.9	10.1
U.S.	33.3	48.1	2.0	5.8	10.8

Note: Figures are percentages and cover the population 15 years of age and older; (1) Figures cover the Grand Rapids-Wyoming, MI Metropolitan Statistical Area—see Appendix B for areas included; (2) Excludes separated
Source: U.S. Census Bureau, 2014-2018 American Community Survey 5-Year Estimates

Disability by Age

Area	All Ages	Under 18 Years Old	18 to 64 Years Old	65 Years and Over
City	13.3	5.6	11.8	38.8
MSA[1]	11.6	4.2	9.9	32.9
U.S.	12.6	4.2	10.3	35.0

Note: Figures show percent of the civilian noninstitutionalized population that reported having a disability. Disability status is determined from six types of difficulty: vision, hearing, cognitive, ambulatory, self-care, and independent living. For children under 5 years old, hearing and vision difficulty are used to determine disability status. For children between the ages of 5 and 14, disability status is determined from hearing, vision, cognitive, ambulatory, and self-care difficulties. For people aged 15 years and older, they are considered to have a disability if they have difficulty with any one of the six difficulty types; Note: (1) Figures cover the Grand Rapids-Wyoming, MI Metropolitan Statistical Area—see Appendix B for areas included
Source: U.S. Census Bureau, 2014-2018 American Community Survey 5-Year Estimates

Age

Area	Percent of Population									Median Age
	Under Age 5	Age 5–19	Age 20–34	Age 35–44	Age 45–54	Age 55–64	Age 65–74	Age 75–84	Age 85+	
City	7.1	19.3	30.2	11.1	10.1	10.5	6.1	3.3	2.3	31.0
MSA[1]	6.6	20.9	21.6	12.1	12.7	12.5	7.9	3.9	1.9	35.8
U.S.	6.1	19.3	20.7	12.6	13.2	12.8	8.8	4.5	1.9	37.9

Note: (1) Figures cover the Grand Rapids-Wyoming, MI Metropolitan Statistical Area—see Appendix B for areas included
Source: U.S. Census Bureau, 2014-2018 American Community Survey 5-Year Estimates

Gender

Area	Males	Females	Males per 100 Females
City	97,135	99,946	97.2
MSA[1]	519,862	530,578	98.0
U.S.	158,984,190	163,918,840	97.0

Note: (1) Figures cover the Grand Rapids-Wyoming, MI Metropolitan Statistical Area—see Appendix B for areas included
Source: U.S. Census Bureau, 2014-2018 American Community Survey 5-Year Estimates

Religious Groups by Family

Area	Catholic	Baptist	Non-Den.	Methodist[2]	Lutheran	LDS[3]	Pente-costal	Presby-terian[4]	Muslim[5]	Judaism
MSA[1]	17.2	1.7	8.4	3.1	2.1	0.6	1.1	10.0	1.1	0.1
U.S.	19.1	9.3	4.0	4.0	2.3	2.0	1.9	1.6	0.8	0.7

Note: Figures are the number of adherents as a percentage of the total population; (1) Figures cover the Grand Rapids-Wyoming, MI Metropolitan Statistical Area—see Appendix B for areas included; (2) Methodist/Pietist; (3) Latter Day Saints; (4) Reformed; (5) Figures are estimates
Source: Association of Statisticians of American Religious Bodies, 2010 U.S. Religion Census: Religious Congregations & Membership Study

Religious Groups by Tradition

Area	Catholic	Evangelical Protestant	Mainline Protestant	Other Tradition	Black Protestant	Orthodox
MSA[1]	17.2	20.7	7.6	2.2	1.1	0.2
U.S.	19.1	16.2	7.3	4.3	1.6	0.3

Note: Figures are the number of adherents as a percentage of the total population; (1) Figures cover the Grand Rapids-Wyoming, MI Metropolitan Statistical Area—see Appendix B for areas included
Source: Association of Statisticians of American Religious Bodies, 2010 U.S. Religion Census: Religious Congregations & Membership Study

ECONOMY

Gross Metropolitan Product

Area	2017	2018	2019	2020	Rank[2]
MSA[1]	60.6	63.6	66.2	68.3	54

Note: Figures are in billions of dollars; (1) Figures cover the Grand Rapids-Wyoming, MI Metropolitan Statistical Area—see Appendix B for areas included; (2) Rank is based on 2018 data and ranges from 1 to 381
Source: U.S. Conference of Mayors, U.S. Metro Economies: GMP & Employment 2018-2020, September 2019

Economic Growth

Area	2015-17 (%)	2018 (%)	2019 (%)	2020 (%)	Rank[2]
MSA[1]	1.9	3.4	2.3	1.2	139
U.S.	1.9	2.9	2.3	2.1	–

Note: Figures are real gross metropolitan product (GMP) growth rates and represent average annual percent change; (1) Figures cover the Grand Rapids-Wyoming, MI Metropolitan Statistical Area—see Appendix B for areas included; (2) Rank is based on 2017 2-year average annual percent change and ranges from 1 to 381
Source: U.S. Conference of Mayors, U.S. Metro Economies: GMP & Employment 2018-2020, September 2019

Metropolitan Area Exports

Area	2013	2014	2015	2016	2017	2018	Rank[2]
MSA[1]	5,314.8	5,244.5	5,143.0	5,168.5	5,385.8	5,420.9	54

Note: Figures are in millions of dollars; (1) Figures cover the Grand Rapids-Wyoming, MI Metropolitan Statistical Area—see Appendix B for areas included; (2) Rank is based on 2018 data and ranges from 1 to 387
Source: U.S. Department of Commerce, International Trade Administration, Office of Trade and Economic Analysis, Industry and Analysis, Exports by Metropolitan Area, data extracted April 15, 2020

Building Permits

Area	Single-Family 2017	2018	Pct. Chg.	Multi-Family 2017	2018	Pct. Chg.	Total 2017	2018	Pct. Chg.
City	101	124	22.8	777	690	-11.2	878	814	-7.3
MSA[1]	2,953	2,749	-6.9	1,886	1,105	-41.4	4,839	3,854	-20.4
U.S.	820,000	855,300	4.3	462,000	473,500	2.5	1,282,000	1,328,800	3.7

Note: (1) Figures cover the Grand Rapids-Wyoming, MI Metropolitan Statistical Area—see Appendix B for areas included; Figures represent new, privately-owned housing units authorized (unadjusted data); All permit data are based on estimates with imputation
Source: U.S. Census Bureau, Manufacturing, Mining, and Construction Statistics, Building Permits, 2017, 2018

Bankruptcy Filings

Area	Business Filings			Nonbusiness Filings		
	2018	2019	% Chg.	2018	2019	% Chg.
Kent County	28	35	25.0	928	935	0.8
U.S.	22,232	22,780	2.5	751,186	752,160	0.1

Note: Business filings include Chapter 7, Chapter 9, Chapter 11, Chapter 12, Chapter 13, Chapter 15, and Section 304; Nonbusiness filings include Chapter 7, Chapter 11, and Chapter 13
Source: Administrative Office of the U.S. Courts, Business and Nonbusiness Bankruptcy, County Cases Commenced by Chapter of the Bankruptcy Code, During the 12-Month Period Ending December 31, 2018 and Business and Nonbusiness Bankruptcy, County Cases Commenced by Chapter of the Bankruptcy Code, During the 12-Month Period Ending December 31, 2019

Housing Vacancy Rates

Area	Gross Vacancy Rate[2] (%)			Year-Round Vacancy Rate[3] (%)			Rental Vacancy Rate[4] (%)			Homeowner Vacancy Rate[5] (%)		
	2017	2018	2019	2017	2018	2019	2017	2018	2019	2017	2018	2019
MSA[1]	8.5	8.9	7.4	6.3	6.8	5.1	4.0	6.8	4.5	1.1	0.3	0.5
U.S.	12.7	12.3	12.0	9.9	9.7	9.5	7.2	6.9	6.7	1.6	1.5	1.4

Note: (1) Figures cover the Grand Rapids-Wyoming, MI Metropolitan Statistical Area—see Appendix B for areas included; (2) The percentage of the total housing inventory that is vacant; (3) The percentage of the housing inventory (excluding seasonal units) that is year-round vacant; (4) The percentage of rental inventory that is vacant for rent; (5) The percentage of homeowner inventory that is vacant for sale
Source: U.S. Census Bureau, Housing Vacancies and Homeownership Annual Statistics: 2017, 2018, 2019

INCOME

Income

Area	Per Capita ($)	Median Household ($)	Average Household ($)
City	24,852	47,173	62,979
MSA[1]	30,277	61,225	80,148
U.S.	32,621	60,293	84,938

Note: (1) Figures cover the Grand Rapids-Wyoming, MI Metropolitan Statistical Area—see Appendix B for areas included
Source: U.S. Census Bureau, 2014-2018 American Community Survey 5-Year Estimates

Household Income Distribution

Area	Percent of Households Earning							
	Under $15,000	$15,000 -$24,999	$25,000 -$34,999	$35,000 -$49,999	$50,000 -$74,999	$75,000 -$99,999	$100,000 -$149,999	$150,000 and up
City	13.8	12.4	10.9	15.3	19.0	11.9	11.0	5.7
MSA[1]	8.1	9.3	9.3	13.7	20.2	14.2	15.2	10.0
U.S.	10.9	9.3	9.3	12.6	17.5	12.5	14.6	13.3

Note: (1) Figures cover the Grand Rapids-Wyoming, MI Metropolitan Statistical Area—see Appendix B for areas included
Source: U.S. Census Bureau, 2014-2018 American Community Survey 5-Year Estimates

Poverty Rate

Area	All Ages	Under 18 Years Old	18 to 64 Years Old	65 Years and Over
City	21.2	29.7	20.2	10.0
MSA[1]	11.5	14.5	11.3	6.8
U.S.	14.1	19.5	13.2	9.3

Note: Figures are percentage of people whose income during the past 12 months was below the poverty level; (1) Figures cover the Grand Rapids-Wyoming, MI Metropolitan Statistical Area—see Appendix B for areas included
Source: U.S. Census Bureau, 2014-2018 American Community Survey 5-Year Estimates

EMPLOYMENT

Labor Force and Employment

Area	Civilian Labor Force			Workers Employed		
	Dec. 2018	Dec. 2019	% Chg.	Dec. 2018	Dec. 2019	% Chg.
City	105,185	103,987	-1.1	101,346	100,701	-0.6
MSA[1]	581,693	575,885	-1.0	565,324	561,939	-0.6
U.S.	162,510,000	164,007,000	0.9	156,481,000	158,504,000	1.3

Note: Data is not seasonally adjusted and covers workers 16 years of age and older; (1) Figures cover the Grand Rapids-Wyoming, MI Metropolitan Statistical Area—see Appendix B for areas included
Source: Bureau of Labor Statistics, Local Area Unemployment Statistics

Unemployment Rate

Area	2019											
	Jan.	Feb.	Mar.	Apr.	May	Jun.	Jul.	Aug.	Sep.	Oct.	Nov.	Dec.
City	4.4	4.1	4.3	3.4	3.7	4.3	5.2	4.0	3.4	3.1	3.1	3.2
MSA[1]	3.4	3.2	3.3	2.6	2.8	3.2	3.9	3.0	2.6	2.3	2.3	2.4
U.S.	4.4	4.1	3.9	3.3	3.4	3.8	4.0	3.8	3.3	3.3	3.3	3.4

Note: Data is not seasonally adjusted and covers workers 16 years of age and older; (1) Figures cover the Grand Rapids-Wyoming, MI Metropolitan Statistical Area—see Appendix B for areas included
Source: Bureau of Labor Statistics, Local Area Unemployment Statistics

Average Wages

Occupation	$/Hr.	Occupation	$/Hr.
Accountants and Auditors	33.00	Maintenance and Repair Workers	18.30
Automotive Mechanics	19.90	Marketing Managers	61.20
Bookkeepers	18.50	Network and Computer Systems Admin.	33.60
Carpenters	21.60	Nurses, Licensed Practical	22.50
Cashiers	11.60	Nurses, Registered	32.80
Computer Programmers	32.60	Nursing Assistants	14.20
Computer Systems Analysts	36.90	Office Clerks, General	17.90
Computer User Support Specialists	24.60	Physical Therapists	41.80
Construction Laborers	18.00	Physicians	98.50
Cooks, Restaurant	12.90	Plumbers, Pipefitters and Steamfitters	24.10
Customer Service Representatives	18.10	Police and Sheriff's Patrol Officers	30.00
Dentists	114.70	Postal Service Mail Carriers	24.90
Electricians	23.30	Real Estate Sales Agents	21.70
Engineers, Electrical	39.20	Retail Salespersons	13.60
Fast Food and Counter Workers	11.40	Sales Representatives, Technical/Scientific	41.90
Financial Managers	56.20	Secretaries, Exc. Legal/Medical/Executive	18.20
First-Line Supervisors of Office Workers	27.40	Security Guards	13.80
General and Operations Managers	56.60	Surgeons	n/a
Hairdressers/Cosmetologists	15.00	Teacher Assistants, Exc. Postsecondary*	13.70
Home Health and Personal Care Aides	12.60	Teachers, Secondary School, Exc. Sp. Ed.*	28.80
Janitors and Cleaners	13.40	Telemarketers	13.70
Landscaping/Groundskeeping Workers	15.40	Truck Drivers, Heavy/Tractor-Trailer	21.60
Lawyers	48.60	Truck Drivers, Light/Delivery Services	19.10
Maids and Housekeeping Cleaners	12.50	Waiters and Waitresses	14.50

Note: Wage data covers the Grand Rapids-Wyoming, MI Metropolitan Statistical Area—see Appendix B for areas included; (*) Hourly wages were calculated from annual wage data based on a 40 hour work week; n/a not available.
Source: Bureau of Labor Statistics, Metro Area Occupational Employment & Wage Estimates, May 2019

Employment by Occupation

Occupation Classification	City (%)	MSA[1] (%)	U.S. (%)
Management, Business, Science, and Arts	34.9	35.1	37.9
Natural Resources, Construction, and Maintenance	6.7	8.0	8.9
Production, Transportation, and Material Moving	17.9	19.3	13.3
Sales and Office	20.9	21.6	22.1
Service	19.6	16.0	17.9

Note: Figures cover employed civilians 16 years of age and older; (1) Figures cover the Grand Rapids-Wyoming, MI Metropolitan Statistical Area—see Appendix B for areas included
Source: U.S. Census Bureau, 2014-2018 American Community Survey 5-Year Estimates

Employment by Industry

| Sector | MSA[1] | | U.S. |
	Number of Employees	Percent of Total	Percent of Total
Construction, Mining, and Logging	25,800	4.6	5.4
Education and Health Services	95,100	16.8	16.1
Financial Activities	27,000	4.8	5.8
Government	50,300	8.9	15.0
Information	6,400	1.1	1.9
Leisure and Hospitality	48,400	8.5	10.8
Manufacturing	118,200	20.8	8.4
Other Services	22,700	4.0	3.9
Professional and Business Services	74,500	13.1	14.1
Retail Trade	48,500	8.6	10.6
Transportation, Warehousing, and Utilities	17,500	3.1	4.2
Wholesale Trade	32,600	5.7	3.9

Note: Figures are non-farm employment as of December 2019. Figures are not seasonally adjusted and include workers 16 years of age and older; (1) Figures cover the Grand Rapids-Wyoming, MI Metropolitan Statistical Area—see Appendix B for areas included
Source: Bureau of Labor Statistics, Current Employment Statistics, Employment, Hours, and Earnings

Occupations with Greatest Projected Employment Growth: 2019 – 2021

Occupation[1]	2019 Employment	2021 Projected Employment	Numeric Employment Change	Percent Employment Change
Combined Food Preparation and Serving Workers, Including Fast Food	126,900	131,480	4,580	3.6
Personal Care Aides	44,410	46,750	2,340	5.3
Registered Nurses	99,260	101,320	2,060	2.1
Laborers and Freight, Stock, and Material Movers, Hand	76,940	78,870	1,930	2.5
Cooks, Restaurant	37,590	39,390	1,800	4.8
Heavy and Tractor-Trailer Truck Drivers	61,220	62,880	1,660	2.7
Waiters and Waitresses	82,010	83,590	1,580	1.9
Software Developers, Applications	30,250	31,730	1,480	4.9
Home Health Aides	27,070	28,240	1,170	4.3
General and Operations Managers	61,080	62,190	1,110	1.8

Note: Projections cover Michigan; (1) Sorted by numeric employment change
Source: www.projectionscentral.com, State Occupational Projections, 2019–2021 Short-Term Projections

Fastest Growing Occupations: 2019 – 2021

Occupation[1]	2019 Employment	2021 Projected Employment	Numeric Employment Change	Percent Employment Change
Flight Attendants	3,640	3,980	340	9.3
Airline Pilots, Copilots, and Flight Engineers	3,210	3,480	270	8.4
Dental Laboratory Technicians	1,670	1,790	120	7.2
Veterinary Assistants and Laboratory Animal Caretakers	3,820	4,080	260	6.8
Commercial Pilots	1,350	1,440	90	6.7
Veterinarians	2,500	2,650	150	6.0
Veterinary Technologists and Technicians	2,630	2,780	150	5.7
Transportation Attendants, Except Flight Attendants	1,410	1,490	80	5.7
Statisticians	890	940	50	5.6
Personal Care Aides	44,410	46,750	2,340	5.3

Note: Projections cover Michigan; (1) Sorted by percent employment change and excludes occupations with numeric employment change less than 50
Source: www.projectionscentral.com, State Occupational Projections, 2019–2021 Short-Term Projections

TAXES

State Corporate Income Tax Rates

State	Tax Rate (%)	Income Brackets ($)	Num. of Brackets	Financial Institution Tax Rate (%)[a]	Federal Income Tax Ded.
Michigan	6.0	Flat rate	1	(a)	No

Note: Tax rates as of January 1, 2020; (a) Rates listed are the corporate income tax rate applied to financial institutions or excise taxes based on income.
Source: Federation of Tax Administrators, State Corporate Income Tax Rates, January 1, 2020

State Individual Income Tax Rates

State	Tax Rate (%)	Income Brackets ($)	Personal Exemptions ($)			Standard Ded. ($)	
			Single	Married	Depend.	Single	Married
Michigan (a)	4.25	Flat rate	4,400	8,800	4,050	–	–

Note: Tax rates as of January 1, 2020; Local- and county-level taxes are not included; Federal income tax is not deductible on state income tax returns; (a) 19 states have statutory provision for automatically adjusting to the rate of inflation the dollar values of the income tax brackets, standard deductions, and/or personal exemptions. Michigan indexes the personal exemption only. Oregon does not index the income brackets for $125,000 and over.
Source: Federation of Tax Administrators, State Individual Income Tax Rates, January 1, 2020

Various State Sales and Excise Tax Rates

State	State Sales Tax (%)	Gasoline[1] (¢/gal.)	Cigarette[2] ($/pack)	Spirits[3] ($/gal.)	Wine[4] ($/gal.)	Beer[5] ($/gal.)	Recreational Marijuana (%)
Michigan	6	41.98	2.00	11.95	0.51	0.20	10

Note: All tax rates as of January 1, 2020; (1) The American Petroleum Institute has developed a methodology for determining the average tax rate on a gallon of fuel. Rates may include any of the following: excise taxes, environmental fees, storage tank fees, other fees or taxes, general sales tax, and local taxes; (2) The federal excise tax of $1.0066 per pack and local taxes are not included; (3) Rates are those applicable to off-premise sales of 40% alcohol by volume (a.b.v.) distilled spirits in 750ml containers. Local excise taxes are excluded; (4) Rates are those applicable to off-premise sales of 11% a.b.v. non-carbonated wine in 750ml containers; (5) Rates are those applicable to off-premise sales of 4.7% a.b.v. beer in 12 ounce containers.
Source: Tax Foundation, 2020 Facts & Figures: How Does Your State Compare?

State Business Tax Climate Index Rankings

State	Overall Rank	Corporate Tax Rank	Individual Income Tax Rank	Sales Tax Rank	Property Tax Rank	Unemployment Insurance Tax Rank
Michigan	12	18	12	9	24	17

Note: The index is a measure of how each state's tax laws affect economic performance. The lower the rank, the more favorable a state's tax system is for business. States without a given tax are given a ranking of 1. The scores/rankings for the District of Columbia do not affect other states. The 2020 index represents the tax climate as of July 1, 2019.
Source: Tax Foundation, State Business Tax Climate Index 2020

COMMERCIAL UTILITIES

Typical Monthly Electric Bills

Area	Commercial Service ($/month)		Industrial Service ($/month)	
	1,500 kWh	40 kW demand 14,000 kWh	1,000 kW demand 200,000 kWh	50,000 kW demand 32,500,000 kWh
City	230	1,955	24,763	1,728,032
Average[1]	203	1,612	25,706	2,520,671

Note: Figures are based on annualized rates; (1) Average based on 187 utilities surveyed
Source: Edison Electric Institute, Typical Bills and Average Rates Report, Summer 2019

TRANSPORTATION

Means of Transportation to Work

| Area | Car/Truck/Van | | Public Transportation | | | Bicycle | Walked | Other Means | Worked at Home |
	Drove Alone	Car-pooled	Bus	Subway	Railroad				
City	75.3	10.7	3.9	0.1	0.0	1.0	4.0	1.4	3.7
MSA[1]	82.1	9.0	1.4	0.0	0.0	0.4	2.2	0.8	4.0
U.S.	76.4	9.1	2.5	1.9	0.6	0.6	2.7	1.3	4.9

Note: Figures are percentages and cover workers 16 years of age and older; (1) Figures cover the Grand Rapids-Wyoming, MI Metropolitan Statistical Area—see Appendix B for areas included
Source: U.S. Census Bureau, 2014-2018 American Community Survey 5-Year Estimates

Travel Time to Work

Area	Less Than 10 Minutes	10 to 19 Minutes	20 to 29 Minutes	30 to 44 Minutes	45 to 59 Minutes	60 to 89 Minutes	90 Minutes or More
City	15.7	42.5	23.8	11.8	3.1	2.1	1.0
MSA[1]	14.9	35.1	25.0	16.3	4.7	2.5	1.5
U.S.	12.5	28.7	20.9	20.7	8.2	6.3	2.8

Note: Note: Figures are percentages and include workers 16 years old and over; (1) Figures cover the Grand Rapids-Wyoming, MI Metropolitan Statistical Area—see Appendix B for areas included
Source: U.S. Census Bureau, 2014-2018 American Community Survey 5-Year Estimates

Key Congestion Measures

Area	1982	1992	2002	2012	2017
Annual Hours of Delay, Total (000)	1,467	6,052	11,749	16,557	19,417
Annual Hours of Delay, Per Auto Commuter	8	24	34	40	41
Annual Congestion Cost, Total (million $)	11	64	159	299	360
Annual Congestion Cost, Per Auto Commuter ($)	121	344	521	575	654

Source: Texas A&M Transportation Institute, 2019 Urban Mobility Report

Freeway Travel Time Index

Area	1982	1987	1992	1997	2002	2007	2012	2017
Urban Area Index[1]	1.03	1.07	1.11	1.14	1.14	1.15	1.14	1.13
Urban Area Rank[1,2]	76	55	49	47	69	72	79	83

Note: Freeway Travel Time Index—the ratio of travel time in the peak period to the travel time at free-flow conditions. For example, a value of 1.30 indicates a 20-minute free-flow trip takes 26 minutes in the peak (20 minutes x 1.30 = 26 minutes); (1) Covers the Grand Rapids MI urban area; (2) Rank is based on 101 larger urban areas (#1 = highest travel time index)
Source: Texas A&M Transportation Institute, 2019 Urban Mobility Report

Public Transportation

Agency Name / Mode of Transportation	Vehicles Operated in Maximum Service[1]	Annual Unlinked Passenger Trips[2] (in thous.)	Annual Passenger Miles[3] (in thous.)
Interurban Transit Partnership (The Rapid)			
Bus (directly operated)	123	9,229.7	31,104.2
Bus Rapid Transit (directly operated)	8	847.0	2,561.4
Demand Response (purchased transportation)	74	350.7	4,914.4
Vanpool (directly operated)	24	38.6	1,693.6

Note: (1) Number of revenue vehicles operated by the given mode and type of service to meet the annual maximum service requirement. This is the revenue vehicle count during the peak season of the year; on the week and day that maximum service is provided. Vehicles operated in maximum service (VOMS) exclude atypical days and one-time special events; (2) Number of passengers who boarded public transportation vehicles. Passengers are counted each time they board a vehicle no matter how many vehicles they use to travel from their origin to their destination. (3) Sum of the distances ridden by all passengers during the entire fiscal year.
Source: Federal Transit Administration, National Transit Database, 2018

Air Transportation

Airport Name and Code / Type of Service	Passenger Airlines[1]	Passenger Enplanements	Freight Carriers[2]	Freight (lbs)
Gerald R. Ford International (GRR)				
Domestic service (U.S. carriers - 2019)	24	1,786,656	10	47,622,110
International service (U.S. carriers - 2018)	2	90	0	0

Note: (1) Includes all U.S.-based major, minor and commuter airlines that carried at least one passenger during the year; (2) Includes all U.S.-based airlines and freight carriers that transported at least one pound of freight during the year.
Source: Bureau of Transportation Statistics, The Intermodal Transportation Database, Air Carriers: T-100 Domestic Market (U.S. Carriers), 2019; Bureau of Transportation Statistics, The Intermodal Transportation Database, Air Carriers: T-100 International Market (U.S. Carriers), 2018

Other Transportation Statistics

Major Highways:	I-96
Amtrak Service:	Yes
Major Waterways/Ports:	Grand River

Source: Amtrak.com; Google Maps

BUSINESSES

Major Business Headquarters

Company Name	Industry	Rankings	
		Fortune[1]	Forbes[2]
Gordon Food Service	Food, Drink & Tobacco	-	21
Meijer	Food Markets	-	19
SpartanNash	Wholesalers, Food and Grocery	377	-

Note: (1) Companies that produce a 10-K are ranked 1 to 500 based on 2018 revenue; (2) All private companies with at least $2 billion in annual revenue through the end of their most current fiscal year are ranked 1 to 228; companies listed are headquartered in the city; dashes indicate no ranking
Source: Fortune, "Fortune 500," June 2019; Forbes, "America's Largest Private Companies," 2019 Rankings

Fast-Growing Businesses

According to *Inc.*, Grand Rapids is home to two of America's 500 fastest-growing private companies: **Ally Logistics** (#120); **Jonas Paul Eyewear** (#166). Criteria: must be an independent, privately-held, for-profit, U.S. corporation, proprietorship or partnership as of December 31, 2018; revenues must be at least $100,000 in 2015 and $2 million in 2018; must have four-year operating/sales history. *Inc., "America's 500 Fastest-Growing Private Companies," 2019*

According to *Initiative for a Competitive Inner City (ICIC)*, Grand Rapids is home to one of America's 100 fastest-growing "inner city" companies: **DornerWorks** (#85). Criteria for inclusion: company must be headquartered in or have 51 percent or more of its physical operations in an economically distressed urban area; must be an independent, for-profit corporation, partnership or proprietorship; must have 10 or more employees and have a five-year sales history that includes sales of at least $200,000 in the base year and at least $1 million in the current year with no decrease in sales over the two most recent years. Companies were ranked overall by revenue growth over the five-year period between 2014 and 2018. *Initiative for a Competitive Inner City (ICIC), "Inner City 100 Companies," 2019*

Minority- and Women-Owned Businesses

Group	All Firms		Firms with Paid Employees			
	Firms	Sales ($000)	Firms	Sales ($000)	Employees	Payroll ($000)
AIAN[1]	142	104,324	2	(s)	100 - 249	(s)
Asian	509	129,401	147	115,947	1,260	32,363
Black	2,525	74,267	43	(s)	250 - 499	(s)
Hispanic	983	117,780	74	(s)	500 - 999	(s)
NHOPI[2]	n/a	n/a	n/a	n/a	n/a	n/a
Women	6,095	784,577	544	690,172	6,202	130,188
All Firms	16,153	28,419,322	3,518	27,970,918	106,476	4,605,805

Note: Figures cover firms located in the city; minority- and women-owned business are defined as firms in which the corresponding group own 51% or more of the stock or equity of the company; (1) American Indian and Alaska Native; (2) Native Hawaiian and Other Pacific Islander; (s) estimates are suppressed when publication standards are not met; n/a not available
Source: U.S. Census Bureau, 2012 Economic Census, Survey of Business Owners

HOTELS & CONVENTION CENTERS

Hotels, Motels and Vacation Rentals

Area	5 Star		4 Star		3 Star		2 Star		1 Star		Not Rated	
	Num.	Pct.[3]	Num.	Pct.[3]	Num.	Pct.[3]	Num.	Pct.[3]	Num.	Pct.[3]	Num.	Pct.[3]
City[1]	0	0.0	2	2.6	24	31.2	10	13.0	5	6.5	36	46.8
Total[2]	266	1.3	1,517	7.2	4,627	21.8	3,210	15.1	3,974	18.7	7,601	35.9

Note: (1) Figures cover Grand Rapids and vicinity; (2) Figures cover all 100 cities in this book; (3) Percentage of hotels which have a given star rating; Star ratings are determined by priceline.com and offer an indication of the general quality of a particular hotel.
Source: priceline.com, April 27, 2020

Major Convention Centers

Name	Overall Space (sq. ft.)	Exhibit Space (sq. ft.)	Meeting Space (sq. ft.)	Meeting Rooms
DeVos Place Convention Center	234,000	162,000	n/a	26

Note: Table includes convention centers located in the Grand Rapids-Wyoming, MI metro area; n/a not available
Source: Original research

Living Environment

COST OF LIVING

Cost of Living Index

Composite Index	Groceries	Housing	Utilities	Trans-portation	Health Care	Misc. Goods/ Services
94.1	92.8	87.4	98.5	104.1	92.3	96.3

Note: The Cost of Living Index measures regional differences in the cost of consumer goods and services, excluding taxes and non-consumer expenditures, for professional and managerial households in the top income quintile. It is based on more than 50,000 prices covering almost 60 different items for which prices are collected three times a year by chambers of commerce, economic development organizations or university applied economic centers in each participating urban area. The numbers shown should be read as a percentage above or below the national average of 100. For example, a value of 115.4 in the groceries column indicates that grocery prices are 15.4% higher than the national average. Small differences in the index numbers should not be interpreted as significant; Figures cover the Grand Rapids MI urban area.
Source: The Council for Community and Economic Research, ACCRA Cost of Living Index, 2019

Grocery Prices

Area[1]	T-Bone Steak ($/pound)	Frying Chicken ($/pound)	Whole Milk ($/half gal.)	Eggs ($/dozen)	Orange Juice ($/64 oz.)	Coffee ($/11.5 oz.)
City[2]	11.76	1.21	1.94	1.49	3.36	3.17
Avg.	11.40	1.41	1.93	1.54	3.51	4.30
Min.	7.40	0.92	0.85	0.58	2.67	2.90
Max.	15.58	2.68	4.09	4.18	5.57	8.10

*Note: (1) Values for the local area are compared with the average, minimum and maximum values for all 290 areas in the Cost of Living Index; (2) Figures cover the Grand Rapids MI urban area; **T-Bone Steak** (price per pound); **Frying Chicken** (price per pound, whole fryer); **Whole Milk** (half gallon carton); **Eggs** (price per dozen, Grade A, large); **Orange Juice** (64 oz. Tropicana or Florida Natural); **Coffee** (11.5 oz. can, vacuum-packed, Maxwell House, Hills Bros, or Folgers).*
Source: The Council for Community and Economic Research, ACCRA Cost of Living Index, 2019

Housing and Utility Costs

Area[1]	New Home Price ($)	Apartment Rent ($/month)	All Electric ($/month)	Part Electric ($/month)	Other Energy ($/month)	Telephone ($/month)
City[2]	281,576	1,182	-	97.35	69.16	176.70
Avg.	362,090	1,142	174.35	100.00	67.76	179.60
Min.	198,329	501	91.58	31.44	28.51	165.30
Max.	2,074,561	5,050	388.18	239.41	306.15	207.90

*Note: (1) Values for the local area are compared with the average, minimum and maximum values for all 290 areas in the Cost of Living Index; (2) Figures cover the Grand Rapids MI urban area; **New Home Price** (2,400 sf living area, 8,000 sf lot, in urban area with full utilities); **Apartment Rent** (950 sf 2 bedroom/1.5 or 2 bath, unfurnished, excluding all utilities except water); **All Electric** (average monthly cost for an all-electric home); **Part Electric** (average monthly cost for a part-electric home); **Other Energy** (average monthly cost for natural gas, fuel oil, coal, wood, and any other forms of energy except electricity); **Telephone** (price includes the base monthly rate plus taxes and fees for three lines of mobile phone service).*
Source: The Council for Community and Economic Research, ACCRA Cost of Living Index, 2019

Health Care, Transportation, and Other Costs

Area[1]	Doctor ($/visit)	Dentist ($/visit)	Optometrist ($/visit)	Gasoline ($/gallon)	Beauty Salon ($/visit)	Men's Shirt ($)
City[2]	97.28	91.25	96.06	2.66	36.78	17.74
Avg.	114.85	97.58	106.10	2.50	38.15	32.15
Min.	39.00	62.22	52.22	1.53	16.88	10.27
Max.	206.67	151.53	258.67	3.79	79.29	59.30

*Note: (1) Values for the local area are compared with the average, minimum and maximum values for all 290 areas in the Cost of Living Index; (2) Figures cover the Grand Rapids MI urban area; **Doctor** (general practitioners routine exam of an established patient); **Dentist** (adult teeth cleaning and periodic oral examination); **Optometrist** (full vision eye exam for established adult patient); **Gasoline** (one gallon regular unleaded, national brand, including all taxes, cash price at self-service pump if available); **Beauty Salon** (woman's shampoo, trim, and blow-dry); **Men's Shirt** (cotton/polyester dress shirt, pinpoint weave, long sleeves).*
Source: The Council for Community and Economic Research, ACCRA Cost of Living Index, 2019

HOUSING

House Price Index (HPI)

Area	National Ranking[2]	Quarterly Change (%)	One-Year Change (%)	Five-Year Change (%)
MSA[1]	79	0.27	5.50	46.00
U.S.[3]	–	1.26	5.09	32.88

Note: The HPI is a weighted repeat sales index. It measures average price changes in repeat sales or refinancings on the same properties. This information is obtained by reviewing repeat mortgage transactions on single-family properties whose mortgages have been purchased or securitized by Fannie Mae or Freddie Mac in January 1975; (1) Figures cover the Grand Rapids-Wyoming, MI Metropolitan Statistical Area—see Appendix B for areas included; (2) Rankings are based on annual percentage change for all metro areas containing at least 15,000 transactions over the last 10 years and ranges from 1 to 232; (3) figures based on a weighted average of Census Division estimates using a seasonally adjusted, purchase-only index; all figures are for the period ending December 31, 2019
Source: Federal Housing Finance Agency, House Price Index, February 25, 2020

Median Single-Family Home Prices

Area	2017	2018	2019p	Percent Change 2018 to 2019
MSA[1]	177.5	194.6	210.5	8.2
U.S. Average	248.8	261.6	274.6	5.0

Note: Figures are median sales prices of existing single-family homes in thousands of dollars; (p) preliminary; (1) Figures cover the Grand Rapids-Wyoming, MI Metropolitan Statistical Area—see Appendix B for areas included
Source: National Association of Realtors, Median Sales Price of Existing Single-Family Homes for Metropolitan Areas, 4th Quarter 2019

Qualifying Income Based on Median Sales Price of Existing Single-Family Homes

Area	With 5% Down ($)	With 10% Down ($)	With 20% Down ($)
MSA[1]	44,066	41,747	37,108
U.S. Average	58,663	55,575	49,400

Note: Figures are preliminary; Qualifying income is based on a mortgage rate of 3.76%. Monthly principal and interest payment is limited to 25% of income; (1) Figures cover the Grand Rapids-Wyoming, MI Metropolitan Statistical Area—see Appendix B for areas included
Source: National Association of Realtors, Qualifying Income Based on Median Sales Price of Existing Single-Family Homes for Metropolitan Areas, 4th Quarter 2019

Median Apartment Condo-Coop Home Prices

Area	2017	2018	2019p	Percent Change 2018 to 2019
MSA[1]	n/a	n/a	n/a	n/a
U.S. Average	234.3	241.0	249.5	3.5

Note: Figures are median sales prices of existing apartment condo-coop homes in thousands of dollars; (p) preliminary; n/a not available; (1) Figures cover the Grand Rapids-Wyoming, MI Metropolitan Statistical Area—see Appendix B for areas included
Source: National Association of Realtors, Median Sales Price of Existing Apartment Condo-Coop Homes for Metropolitan Areas, 4th Quarter 2019

Home Value Distribution

Area	Under $50,000	$50,000 -$99,999	$100,000 -$149,999	$150,000 -$199,999	$200,000 -$299,999	$300,000 -$499,999	$500,000 -$999,999	$1,000,000 or more
City	6.1	23.8	32.1	20.9	11.4	4.3	1.2	0.1
MSA[1]	7.3	13.4	22.2	21.0	20.4	11.6	3.2	0.7
U.S.	7.6	13.0	14.0	14.3	19.2	18.3	10.5	3.1

Note: Figures are percentages and cover owner-occupied housing units; (1) Figures cover the Grand Rapids-Wyoming, MI Metropolitan Statistical Area—see Appendix B for areas included
Source: U.S. Census Bureau, 2014-2018 American Community Survey 5-Year Estimates

Homeownership Rate

Area	2011 (%)	2012 (%)	2013 (%)	2014 (%)	2015 (%)	2016 (%)	2017 (%)	2018 (%)	2019 (%)
MSA[1]	76.4	76.9	73.7	71.6	75.8	76.2	71.7	73.0	75.2
U.S.	66.1	65.4	65.1	64.5	63.7	63.4	63.9	64.4	64.6

Note: (1) Figures cover the Grand Rapids-Wyoming, MI Metropolitan Statistical Area—see Appendix B for areas included
Source: U.S. Census Bureau, Housing Vacancies and Homeownership Annual Statistics: 2011-2019

Year Housing Structure Built

Area	2010 or Later	2000 -2009	1990 -1999	1980 -1989	1970 -1979	1960 -1969	1950 -1959	1940 -1949	Before 1940	Median Year
City	1.7	4.3	6.1	7.2	8.9	10.2	15.4	8.9	37.3	1952
MSA[1]	3.5	12.8	16.6	12.2	14.3	9.7	10.5	5.2	15.2	1977
U.S.	4.1	14.3	13.9	13.5	15.3	10.7	10.4	5.0	12.8	1977

Note: Figures are percentages except for Median Year; Note: (1) Figures cover the Grand Rapids-Wyoming, MI Metropolitan Statistical Area—see Appendix B for areas included
Source: U.S. Census Bureau, 2014-2018 American Community Survey 5-Year Estimates

Gross Monthly Rent

Area	Under $500	$500 -$999	$1,000 -$1,499	$1,500 -$1,999	$2,000 -$2,499	$2,500 -$2,999	$3,000 and up	Median ($)
City	10.4	53.2	26.8	6.9	2.3	0.3	0.1	895
MSA[1]	8.6	60.0	23.8	5.3	1.7	0.2	0.4	860
U.S.	9.8	38.5	29.6	12.9	5.1	2.1	2.0	1,023

Note: Figures are percentages except for Median; Gross rent is the contract rent plus the estimated average monthly cost of utilities (electricity, gas, and water and sewer) and fuels (oil, coal, kerosene, wood, etc.) if these are paid by the renter (or paid for the renter by someone else); (1) Figures cover the Grand Rapids-Wyoming, MI Metropolitan Statistical Area—see Appendix B for areas included
Source: U.S. Census Bureau, 2014-2018 American Community Survey 5-Year Estimates

HEALTH

Health Risk Factors

Category	MSA[1] (%)	U.S. (%)
Adults aged 18–64 who have any kind of health care coverage	90.2	87.3
Adults who reported being in good or better health	86.0	82.4
Adults who have been told they have high blood cholesterol	31.5	33.0
Adults who have been told they have high blood pressure	32.8	32.3
Adults who are current smokers	14.5	17.1
Adults who currently use E-cigarettes	5.0	4.6
Adults who currently use chewing tobacco, snuff, or snus	3.9	4.0
Adults who are heavy drinkers[2]	8.0	6.3
Adults who are binge drinkers[3]	19.9	17.4
Adults who are overweight (BMI 25.0 - 29.9)	32.2	35.3
Adults who are obese (BMI 30.0 - 99.8)	32.3	31.3
Adults who participated in any physical activities in the past month	75.2	74.4
Adults who always or nearly always wears a seat belt	94.5	94.3

Note: (1) Figures cover the Grand Rapids-Wyoming, MI Metropolitan Statistical Area—see Appendix B for areas included; (2) Heavy drinkers are classified as adult men having more than 14 drinks per week and adult women having more than 7 drinks per week; (3) Binge drinkers are classified as males having five or more drinks on one occasion or females having four or more drinks on one occasion
Source: Centers for Disease Control and Prevention, Behaviorial Risk Factor Surveillance System, SMART: Selected Metropolitan Area Risk Trends, 2017

Acute and Chronic Health Conditions

Category	MSA[1] (%)	U.S. (%)
Adults who have ever been told they had a heart attack	2.7	4.2
Adults who have ever been told they have angina or coronary heart disease	2.7	3.9
Adults who have ever been told they had a stroke	3.7	3.0
Adults who have ever been told they have asthma	14.5	14.2
Adults who have ever been told they have arthritis	25.6	24.9
Adults who have ever been told they have diabetes[2]	10.0	10.5
Adults who have ever been told they had skin cancer	6.4	6.2
Adults who have ever been told they had any other types of cancer	5.5	7.1
Adults who have ever been told they have COPD	6.8	6.5
Adults who have ever been told they have kidney disease	3.2	3.0
Adults who have ever been told they have a form of depression	25.0	20.5

Note: (1) Figures cover the Grand Rapids-Wyoming, MI Metropolitan Statistical Area—see Appendix B for areas included; (2) Figures do not include pregnancy-related, borderline, or pre-diabetes
Source: Centers for Disease Control and Prevention, Behaviorial Risk Factor Surveillance System, SMART: Selected Metropolitan Area Risk Trends, 2017

Health Screening and Vaccination Rates

Category	MSA[1] (%)	U.S. (%)
Adults aged 65+ who have had flu shot within the past year	58.8	60.7
Adults aged 65+ who have ever had a pneumonia vaccination	79.1	75.4
Adults who have ever been tested for HIV	37.3	36.1
Adults who have ever had the shingles or zoster vaccine?	32.2	28.9
Adults who have had their blood cholesterol checked within the last five years	92.5	85.9

Note: n/a not available; (1) Figures cover the Grand Rapids-Wyoming, MI Metropolitan Statistical Area—see Appendix B for areas included.
Source: Centers for Disease Control and Prevention, Behaviorial Risk Factor Surveillance System, SMART: Selected Metropolitan Area Risk Trends, 2017

Disability Status

Category	MSA[1] (%)	U.S. (%)
Adults who reported being deaf	6.8	6.7
Are you blind or have serious difficulty seeing, even when wearing glasses?	3.4	4.5
Are you limited in any way in any of your usual activities due of arthritis?	13.1	12.9
Do you have difficulty doing errands alone?	7.2	6.8
Do you have difficulty dressing or bathing?	4.3	3.6
Do you have serious difficulty concentrating/remembering/making decisions?	12.1	10.7
Do you have serious difficulty walking or climbing stairs?	14.4	13.6

Note: (1) Figures cover the Grand Rapids-Wyoming, MI Metropolitan Statistical Area—see Appendix B for areas included.
Source: Centers for Disease Control and Prevention, Behaviorial Risk Factor Surveillance System, SMART: Selected Metropolitan Area Risk Trends, 2017

Mortality Rates for the Top 10 Causes of Death in the U.S.

ICD-10[a] Sub-Chapter	ICD-10[a] Code	Age-Adjusted Mortality Rate[1] per 100,000 population	
		County[2]	U.S.
Malignant neoplasms	C00-C97	144.4	152.4
Ischaemic heart diseases	I20-I25	104.7	92.7
Other forms of heart disease	I30-I51	39.3	52.5
Chronic lower respiratory diseases	J40-J47	36.8	40.4
Cerebrovascular diseases	I60-I69	32.6	37.3
Other degenerative diseases of the nervous system	G30-G31	48.3	36.4
Other external causes of accidental injury	W00-X59	36.0	35.3
Organic, including symptomatic, mental disorders	F01-F09	32.5	30.0
Hypertensive diseases	I10-I15	27.2	22.9
Diabetes mellitus	E10-E14	12.4	21.3

Note: (a) ICD-10 = International Classification of Diseases 10th Revision; (1) Mortality rates are a three year average covering 2016-2018; (2) Figures cover Kent County.
Source: Centers for Disease Control and Prevention, National Center for Health Statistics. Underlying Cause of Death 1999-2018 on CDC WONDER Online Database

Mortality Rates for Selected Causes of Death

ICD-10[a] Sub-Chapter	ICD-10[a] Code	Age-Adjusted Mortality Rate[1] per 100,000 population	
		County[2]	U.S.
Assault	X85-Y09	3.3	6.0
Diseases of the liver	K70-K76	11.8	14.2
Human immunodeficiency virus (HIV) disease	B20-B24	Suppressed	1.6
Influenza and pneumonia	J09-J18	11.5	14.2
Intentional self-harm	X60-X84	12.2	13.9
Malnutrition	E40-E46	1.4	1.9
Obesity and other hyperalimentation	E65-E68	3.0	2.1
Renal failure	N17-N19	7.4	12.8
Transport accidents	V01-V99	10.9	12.5
Viral hepatitis	B15-B19	1.1	1.4

Note: (a) ICD-10 = International Classification of Diseases 10th Revision; (1) Mortality rates are a three year average covering 2016-2018; (2) Figures cover Kent County; Data are suppressed when the data meet the criteria for confidentiality constraints; Mortality rates are flagged as unreliable when the rate would be calculated with a numerator of 20 or less.
Source: Centers for Disease Control and Prevention, National Center for Health Statistics. Underlying Cause of Death 1999-2018 on CDC WONDER Online Database

Health Insurance Coverage

Area	With Health Insurance	With Private Health Insurance	With Public Health Insurance	Without Health Insurance	Population Under Age 19 Without Health Insurance
City	90.8	61.8	39.4	9.2	4.2
MSA[1]	94.1	75.2	31.2	5.9	3.2
U.S.	90.6	67.7	34.7	9.4	5.2

Note: Figures are percentages that cover the civilian noninstitutionalized population; (1) Figures cover the Grand Rapids-Wyoming, MI Metropolitan Statistical Area—see Appendix B for areas included
Source: U.S. Census Bureau, 2014-2018 American Community Survey 5-Year Estimates

Number of Medical Professionals

Area	MDs[3]	DOs[3,4]	Dentists	Podiatrists	Chiropractors	Optometrists
County[1] (number)	2,185	475	470	30	228	159
County[1] (rate[2])	336.9	73.2	71.9	4.6	34.9	24.3
U.S. (rate[2])	281.9	23.4	69.1	6.0	27.5	16.4

Note: Data as of 2018 unless noted; (1) Data covers Kent County; (2) Rate per 100,000 population; (3) Data as of 2017 and includes all active, non-federal physicians; (4) Doctor of Osteopathic Medicine
Source: U.S. Department of Health and Human Services, Health Resources and Services Administration, Bureau of Health Professions, Area Resource File (ARF) 2018-2019

Best Hospitals

According to *U.S. News,* the Grand Rapids-Wyoming, MI metro area is home to one of the best children's hospitals in the U.S.: **Spectrum Health Helen DeVos Children's Hospital** (4 pediatric specialties). The hospital listed was highly ranked in at least one of 10 pediatric specialties. Ninety-one children's hospitals in the U.S. were nationally ranked in at least one specialty. Hospitals received points for being ranked in a specialty, and the 10 hospitals with the most points across the 10 specialties make up the Honor Roll. *U.S. News Online, "America's Best Children's Hospitals 2019-20"*

EDUCATION

Public School District Statistics

District Name	Schls	Pupils	Pupil/Teacher Ratio	Minority Pupils[1] (%)	Free Lunch Eligible[2] (%)	IEP[3] (%)
East Grand Rapids Public Schools	6	2,886	16.9	14.3	5.6	5.7
Forest Hills Public Schools	18	9,772	19.3	21.2	10.2	8.9
Godwin Heights Public Schools	5	2,076	18.7	83.6	80.3	15.6
Grand Rapids Public Schools	59	15,803	15.2	77.8	70.7	19.6
Kelloggsville Public Schools	7	2,418	17.3	74.0	80.9	11.7
Kenowa Hills Public Schools	7	3,137	18.6	29.9	41.3	14.5
Kentwood Public Schools	18	9,276	18.3	69.2	62.0	13.6
Michigan Virtual Charter Academy	1	2,916	23.1	38.5	73.7	16.3
Northview Public Schools	7	3,327	18.4	24.8	34.7	13.2

Note: Table includes school districts with 2,000 or more students; (1) Percentage of students that are not non-Hispanic white; (2) Percentage of students that are eligible for the free lunch program; (3) Percentage of students that have an Individualized Education Program.
Source: U.S. Department of Education, National Center for Education Statistics, Common Core of Data, Local Education Agency (School District) Universe Survey: School Year 2018-2019; U.S. Department of Education, National Center for Education Statistics, Common Core of Data, Public Elementary/Secondary School Universe Survey: School Year 2018-2019

Best High Schools

According to *U.S. News,* Grand Rapids is home to one of the top 500 high schools in the U.S.: **City High Middle School** (#21). Nearly 18,000 public, magnet and charter schools were ranked based on their performance on state assessments and how well they prepare students for college. *U.S. News & World Report, "Best High Schools 2020"*

Highest Level of Education

Area	Less than H.S.	H.S. Diploma	Some College, No Deg.	Associate Degree	Bachelor's Degree	Master's Degree	Prof. School Degree	Doctorate Degree
City	13.4	22.4	20.8	7.8	23.4	8.9	1.9	1.4
MSA[1]	9.1	27.3	21.9	9.3	21.5	8.2	1.7	1.1
U.S.	12.3	27.1	20.6	8.4	19.4	8.6	2.1	1.4

Note: Figures cover persons age 25 and over; (1) Figures cover the Grand Rapids-Wyoming, MI Metropolitan Statistical Area—see Appendix B for areas included
Source: U.S. Census Bureau, 2014-2018 American Community Survey 5-Year Estimates

Educational Attainment by Race

Area	High School Graduate or Higher (%)					Bachelor's Degree or Higher (%)				
	Total	White	Black	Asian	Hisp.[2]	Total	White	Black	Asian	Hisp.[2]
City	86.6	90.9	81.6	71.5	50.8	35.6	42.3	16.6	42.4	10.7
MSA[1]	90.9	92.9	84.1	75.9	62.1	32.4	33.9	18.6	36.6	13.8
U.S.	87.7	89.6	85.4	86.8	67.7	31.5	32.9	21.1	53.5	15.8

Note: Figures shown cover persons 25 years old and over; (1) Figures cover the Grand Rapids-Wyoming, MI Metropolitan Statistical Area—see Appendix B for areas included; (2) People of Hispanic origin can be of any race
Source: U.S. Census Bureau, 2014-2018 American Community Survey 5-Year Estimates

School Enrollment by Grade and Control

Area	Preschool (%)		Kindergarten (%)		Grades 1 - 4 (%)		Grades 5 - 8 (%)		Grades 9 - 12 (%)	
	Public	Private	Public	Private	Public	Private	Public	Private	Public	Private
City	65.4	34.6	78.1	21.9	83.6	16.4	84.7	15.3	84.8	15.2
MSA[1]	63.0	37.0	82.8	17.2	84.9	15.1	85.5	14.5	86.2	13.8
U.S.	59.0	41.0	87.7	12.3	89.6	10.4	89.5	10.5	90.2	9.8

Note: Figures shown cover persons 3 years old and over; (1) Figures cover the Grand Rapids-Wyoming, MI Metropolitan Statistical Area—see Appendix B for areas included
Source: U.S. Census Bureau, 2014-2018 American Community Survey 5-Year Estimates

Average Salaries of Public School Teachers

Area	2016-17		2017-18		Change from 2016-17 to 2017-18	
	Dollars	Rank[1]	Dollars	Rank[1]	Percent	Rank[2]
Michigan	62,287	12	61,911	13	-0.6	49
U.S. Average	59,539	–	60,477	–	1.58	–

Note: (1) Rank ranges from 1 to 51 where 1 indicates highest salary; (2) Rank ranges from 1 to 51 where 1 indicates highest percent change.
Source: National Education Association, Rankings & Estimates: Rankings of the States 2018 and Estimates of School Statistics 2019

Higher Education

Four-Year Colleges			Two-Year Colleges			Medical Schools[1]	Law Schools[2]	Voc/ Tech[3]
Public	Private Non-profit	Private For-profit	Public	Private Non-profit	Private For-profit			
0	7	0	1	0	0	0	0	3

Note: Figures cover institutions located within the city limits and include main campuses only; (1) includes schools accredited by the Liaison Committee on Medical Education and the American Osteopathic Association's Commission on Osteopathic College Accreditation; (2) includes ABA-accredited schools, schools with provisional ABA accreditation, and state accredited schools; (3) includes all schools with programs that are less than 2 years.
Source: National Center for Education Statistics, Integrated Postsecondary Education System (IPEDS), 2018-19; Wikipedia, List of Medical Schools in the United States, accessed May 1, 2020; Wikipedia, List of Law Schools in the United States, accessed May 1, 2020

PRESIDENTIAL ELECTION

2016 Presidential Election Results

Area	Clinton	Trump	Johnson	Stein	Other
Kent County	44.6	47.7	4.6	1.3	1.9
U.S.	48.0	45.9	3.3	1.1	1.7

Note: Results are percentages and may not add to 100% due to rounding
Source: Dave Leip's Atlas of U.S. Presidential Elections

EMPLOYERS

Major Employers

Company Name	Industry
Alticor	Consumer products, multi-level marketing
Farmers Insurance Group	Insurance
Grand Rapids Public Schools	Public elementary & secondary schools
Herman Miller	Manufacturing & industrial supply
Johnson Controls	Automotive interiors, HVAC equipment
Meijer	Retail, grocery & discount
Spectrum Health	Healthcare
Steelcase	Furniture

Note: Companies shown are located within the Grand Rapids-Wyoming, MI Metropolitan Statistical Area.
Source: Hoovers.com; Wikipedia

PUBLIC SAFETY

Crime Rate

Area	All Crimes	Violent Crimes				Property Crimes		
		Murder	Rape[3]	Robbery	Aggrav. Assault	Burglary	Larceny -Theft	Motor Vehicle Theft
City	2,566.0	2.5	70.3	159.2	423.1	338.8	1,437.4	134.7
Suburbs[1]	1,513.3	2.4	94.3	22.1	137.9	196.6	984.6	75.4
Metro[2]	1,709.5	2.4	89.8	47.6	191.0	223.1	1,069.0	86.5
U.S.	2,580.1	5.0	42.6	86.2	246.8	376.0	1,594.6	228.9

Note: Figures are crimes per 100,000 population; (1) All areas within the metro area that are located outside the city limits; (2) Figures cover the Grand Rapids-Wyoming, MI Metropolitan Statistical Area—see Appendix B for areas included; (3) The city and U.S. figures shown were reported using the revised Uniform Crime Reporting (UCR) definition of rape. The suburban and metro area figures shown are an aggregate total of the data submitted using both the revised and legacy UCR definitions.
Source: FBI Uniform Crime Reports, 2018

Hate Crimes

Area	Number of Quarters Reported	Number of Incidents per Bias Motivation					
		Race/Ethnicity/ Ancestry	Religion	Sexual Orientation	Disability	Gender	Gender Identity
City	4	5	0	1	0	0	0
U.S.	4	4,047	1,419	1,196	159	47	168

Source: Federal Bureau of Investigation, Hate Crime Statistics 2018

Identity Theft Consumer Reports

Area	Reports	Reports per 100,000 Population	Rank[2]
MSA[1]	908	85	233
U.S.	650,572	198	-

Note: (1) Figures cover the Grand Rapids-Wyoming, MI Metropolitan Statistical Area—see Appendix B for areas included; (2) Rank ranges from 1 to 386 where 1 indicates greatest number of identity theft reports per 100,000 population
Source: Federal Trade Commission, Consumer Sentinel Network Data Book for January–December 2019

Fraud and Other Consumer Reports

Area	Reports	Reports per 100,000 Population	Rank[2]
MSA[1]	5,202	486	265
U.S.	2,590,177	789	-

Note: (1) Figures cover the Grand Rapids-Wyoming, MI Metropolitan Statistical Area—see Appendix B for areas included; (2) Rank ranges from 1 to 386 where 1 indicates greatest number of fraud and other consumer reports per 100,000 population
Source: Federal Trade Commission, Consumer Sentinel Network Data Book for January–December 2019

SPORTS

Professional Sports Teams

Team Name	League	Year Established

No teams are located in the metro area
Source: Wikipedia, Major Professional Sports Teams of the United States and Canada, May 4, 2020

CLIMATE

Average and Extreme Temperatures

Temperature	Jan	Feb	Mar	Apr	May	Jun	Jul	Aug	Sep	Oct	Nov	Dec	Yr.
Extreme High (°F)	66	67	80	88	92	102	100	100	97	87	81	67	102
Average High (°F)	30	32	42	57	69	79	83	81	73	61	46	34	57
Average Temp. (°F)	23	25	34	47	58	67	72	70	62	51	39	28	48
Average Low (°F)	15	16	25	36	46	56	60	59	51	41	31	21	38
Extreme Low (°F)	-22	-19	-8	3	22	33	41	39	28	18	-10	-18	-22

Note: Figures cover the years 1948-1990
Source: National Climatic Data Center, International Station Meteorological Climate Summary, 9/96

Average Precipitation/Snowfall/Humidity

Precip./Humidity	Jan	Feb	Mar	Apr	May	Jun	Jul	Aug	Sep	Oct	Nov	Dec	Yr.
Avg. Precip. (in.)	1.9	1.6	2.6	3.5	3.0	3.5	3.2	3.2	3.7	2.7	3.1	2.7	34.7
Avg. Snowfall (in.)	21	12	11	3	Tr	0	0	0	Tr	1	8	18	73
Avg. Rel. Hum. 7am (%)	81	80	80	79	79	81	84	88	89	85	83	83	83
Avg. Rel. Hum. 4pm (%)	71	66	61	54	50	52	52	55	58	60	68	74	60

Note: Figures cover the years 1948-1990; Tr = Trace amounts (<0.05 in. of rain; <0.5 in. of snow)
Source: National Climatic Data Center, International Station Meteorological Climate Summary, 9/96

Weather Conditions

Temperature			Daytime Sky			Precipitation		
5°F & below	32°F & below	90°F & above	Clear	Partly cloudy	Cloudy	0.01 inch or more precip.	0.1 inch or more snow/ice	Thunder-storms
15	146	11	67	119	179	142	57	34

Note: Figures are average number of days per year and cover the years 1948-1990
Source: National Climatic Data Center, International Station Meteorological Climate Summary, 9/96

HAZARDOUS WASTE

Superfund Sites

The Grand Rapids-Wyoming, MI metro area is home to nine sites on the EPA's Superfund National Priorities List: **Butterworth #2 Landfill** (final); **Chem Central** (final); **H. Brown Co., Inc.** (final); **Kentwood Landfill** (final); **Organic Chemicals, Inc.** (final); **Southwest Ottawa County Landfill** (final); **Sparta Landfill** (final); **Spartan Chemical Co.** (final); **State Disposal Landfill, Inc.** (final). There are a total of 1,387 Superfund sites with a status of proposed or final on the list in the U.S. *U.S. Environmental Protection Agency, National Priorities List, May 5, 2020*

AIR & WATER QUALITY

Air Quality Trends: Ozone

	1990	1995	2000	2005	2010	2012	2014	2016	2017	2018
MSA[1]	0.102	0.089	0.073	0.085	0.071	0.083	0.069	0.075	0.065	0.072
U.S.	0.088	0.089	0.082	0.080	0.073	0.075	0.067	0.069	0.068	0.069

Note: (1) Data covers the Grand Rapids-Wyoming, MI Metropolitan Statistical Area—see Appendix B for areas included. The values shown are the composite ozone concentration averages among trend sites based on the highest fourth daily maximum 8-hour concentration in parts per million. These trends are based on sites having an adequate record of monitoring data during the trend period. Data from exceptional events are included.
Source: U.S. Environmental Protection Agency, Air Quality Monitoring Information, "Air Quality Trends by City, 1990-2018"

Air Quality Index

Area	Percent of Days when Air Quality was...[2]					AQI Statistics[2]	
	Good	Moderate	Unhealthy for Sensitive Groups	Unhealthy	Very Unhealthy	Maximum	Median
MSA[1]	79.5	19.5	1.1	0.0	0.0	115	40

Note: (1) Data covers the Grand Rapids-Wyoming, MI Metropolitan Statistical Area—see Appendix B for areas included; (2) Based on 365 days with AQI data in 2018. Air Quality Index (AQI) is an index for reporting daily air quality. EPA calculates the AQI for five major air pollutants regulated by the Clean Air Act: ground-level ozone, particle pollution (aka particulate matter), carbon monoxide, sulfur dioxide, and nitrogen dioxide. The AQI runs from 0 to 500. The higher the AQI value, the greater the level of air pollution and the greater the health concern. There are six AQI categories: "Good" AQI is between 0 and 50. Air quality is considered satisfactory; "Moderate" AQI is between 51 and 100. Air quality is acceptable; "Unhealthy for Sensitive Groups" When AQI values are between 101 and 150, members of sensitive groups may experience health effects; "Unhealthy" When AQI values are between 151 and 200 everyone may begin to experience health effects; "Very Unhealthy" AQI values between 201 and 300 trigger a health alert; "Hazardous" AQI values over 300 trigger warnings of emergency conditions (not shown).
Source: U.S. Environmental Protection Agency, Air Quality Index Report, 2018

Air Quality Index Pollutants

Area	Percent of Days when AQI Pollutant was...[2]					
	Carbon Monoxide	Nitrogen Dioxide	Ozone	Sulfur Dioxide	Particulate Matter 2.5	Particulate Matter 10
MSA[1]	0.0	0.0	63.8	0.0	36.2	0.0

Note: (1) Data covers the Grand Rapids-Wyoming, MI Metropolitan Statistical Area—see Appendix B for areas included; (2) Based on 365 days with AQI data in 2018. The Air Quality Index (AQI) is an index for reporting daily air quality. EPA calculates the AQI for five major air pollutants regulated by the Clean Air Act: ground-level ozone, particle pollution (also known as particulate matter), carbon monoxide, sulfur dioxide, and nitrogen dioxide. The AQI runs from 0 to 500. The higher the AQI value, the greater the level of air pollution and the greater the health concern.
Source: U.S. Environmental Protection Agency, Air Quality Index Report, 2018

Maximum Air Pollutant Concentrations: Particulate Matter, Ozone, CO and Lead

	Particulate Matter 10 (ug/m^3)	Particulate Matter 2.5 Wtd AM (ug/m^3)	Particulate Matter 2.5 24-Hr (ug/m^3)	Ozone (ppm)	Carbon Monoxide (ppm)	Lead (ug/m^3)
MSA[1] Level	30	8.4	19	0.073	1	0
NAAQS[2]	150	15	35	0.075	9	0.15
Met NAAQS[2]	Yes	Yes	Yes	Yes	Yes	Yes

Note: (1) Data covers the Grand Rapids-Wyoming, MI Metropolitan Statistical Area—see Appendix B for areas included; Data from exceptional events are included; (2) National Ambient Air Quality Standards; ppm = parts per million; ug/m^3 = micrograms per cubic meter; n/a not available.
Concentrations: Particulate Matter 10 (coarse particulate)—highest second maximum 24-hour concentration; Particulate Matter 2.5 Wtd AM (fine particulate)—highest weighted annual mean concentration; Particulate Matter 2.5 24-Hour (fine particulate)—highest 98th percentile 24-hour concentration; Ozone—highest fourth daily maximum 8-hour concentration; Carbon Monoxide—highest second maximum non-overlapping 8-hour concentration; Lead—maximum running 3-month average
Source: U.S. Environmental Protection Agency, Air Quality Monitoring Information, "Air Quality Statistics by City, 2018"

Maximum Air Pollutant Concentrations: Nitrogen Dioxide and Sulfur Dioxide

	Nitrogen Dioxide AM (ppb)	Nitrogen Dioxide 1-Hr (ppb)	Sulfur Dioxide AM (ppb)	Sulfur Dioxide 1-Hr (ppb)	Sulfur Dioxide 24-Hr (ppb)
MSA[1] Level	n/a	n/a	n/a	13	n/a
NAAQS[2]	53	100	30	75	140
Met NAAQS[2]	n/a	n/a	n/a	Yes	n/a

Note: (1) Data covers the Grand Rapids-Wyoming, MI Metropolitan Statistical Area—see Appendix B for areas included; Data from exceptional events are included; (2) National Ambient Air Quality Standards; ppm = parts per million; ug/m^3 = micrograms per cubic meter; n/a not available.
Concentrations: Nitrogen Dioxide AM—highest arithmetic mean concentration; Nitrogen Dioxide 1-Hr—highest 98th percentile 1-hour daily maximum concentration; Sulfur Dioxide AM—highest annual mean concentration; Sulfur Dioxide 1-Hr—highest 99th percentile 1-hour daily maximum concentration; Sulfur Dioxide 24-Hr—highest second maximum 24-hour concentration
Source: U.S. Environmental Protection Agency, Air Quality Monitoring Information, "Air Quality Statistics by City, 2018"

Drinking Water

Water System Name	Pop. Served	Primary Water Source Type	Violations[1]
Grand Rapids	258,416	Surface	1

Note: (1) Total number of violations (both active and inactive) in the EPA database
Source: U.S. Environmental Protection Agency, Office of Ground Water and Drinking Water, Safe Drinking Water Information System (based on data extracted May 5, 2020)

Green Bay, Wisconsin

Background

The city of Green Bay takes its name from an inlet at the mouth of the Fox River, off Lake Michigan. Green Bay is the oldest city in Wisconsin, and the seat of Brown County. The city, laid out on high ground on either side of the river, has always been an important port and, in recent decades, is known to Americans as the home of the nation's oldest professional football team, the Green Bay Packers, who play in Lambeau Field, the longest continuously-occupied stadium in the NFL.

Prior to European settlement, the area had been home to Winnebago and other settled, horticultural tribes. The French explorer Jean Nicolet, who was seeking a route to the Pacific and thence to Asia, was the first recorded European visitor. He landed his canoe in 1634 about 10 miles south of the present city, finding there a community of friendly Winnebago or Oneida, who at first he thought to be Chinese.

Later explorers and traders, mostly French, established a trading post at the site, and in 1720, Fort St. Francis was completed at the mouth of the river. In 1745, the first permanent settlement was begun at "Le Baye" in what are the boundaries of the present city. The so-called "Tank House," built by the voyageur Joseph Roy in 1766, is thought to be the oldest house in the state. Green Bay is also home to the oldest Roman Catholic bishopric in the area. Although the French influence was paramount, many of the fur traders who came into the area were associated with the American fur baron John Jacob Astor, who constructed warehouses and other buildings on the site.

Settlers regarded themselves as French citizens until the fort was occupied by the British in 1763. From 1763 until the War of 1812, they were under British control. When the Americans garrisoned Fort Howard, the city was brought firmly under rule of the new republic. The first newspaper in the state, the *Green Bay Intelligencer,* was established in 1833. In 1854, the city of Green Bay was chartered, and in 1893, the adjoining Fort Howard was incorporated into it. In the late nineteenth century, Green Bay was a major port for the thriving lumber trade.

Forest products, particularly paper, are still a mainstay of the local economy, as are health care, finance, insurance and logistics. The Oneida Tribe of Indians of Wisconsin is headquartered in the region. Tourism is increasingly important, with visitors drawn to the city both for Green Bay Packers football, and for its proximity to some of the most attractive vacation spots in the state.

The city's downtown renaissance is still underway. Office space and dwelling units are now in place along the Fox River, as is a walking/biking trail along the river's east side. The CityDeck faces the water for four blocks. Similarly, the Broadway corridor has been revived. The KI Convention Center was expanded by 35,000 square feet and the 15,000-square foot Children's Museum of Green Bay is a relatively new addition to the city's downtown.

Other attractions include the National Railroad Museum, which includes the world's largest steam locomotive, and the NEW Zoo, with more than 200 animals of nearly 90 species.

Green Bay is home to a local campus (1965) of the University of Wisconsin and Bellin College (1909), which specializes in nursing and radiologic sciences.

The weather in Green Bay is a mild version of the general northern plains complex, with four seasons, warm summers, and considerable winter snowfall. High and low temperatures are modified by the city's location on Green Bay, as well as its proximity to Lake Superior and Lake Michigan.

Rankings

Business/Finance Rankings

- Experian's latest annual report on consumer credit ranked cities by the average credit score of its residents. Green Bay was ranked #5 among the ten cities with the highest average credit score, meaning that its residents showed strong credit management. *www.usatoday.com, "Minneapolis Tops List of Cities With Best Average Credit Score; Greenwood Miss., at the Bottom," January 11, 2018*

- The Green Bay metro area appeared on the Milken Institute "2020 Best Performing Cities" list. Rank: #122 out of 200 large metro areas. Criteria: job growth; wage and salary growth; high-tech output growth. *Milken Institute, "Best-Performing Cities 2020," February 26, 2020*

- *Forbes* ranked the 200 most populous metro areas to determine the nation's "Best Places for Business and Careers." The Green Bay metro area was ranked #100. Criteria: costs (business and living); job growth (past and projected); income growth; quality of life; educational attainment (college and high school); projected economic growth; cultural and leisure opportunities; workplace tolerance laws; net migration patterns. *Forbes, "The Best Places for Business and Careers 2019: Seattle Still On Top," October 30, 2019*

Environmental Rankings

- Green Bay was highlighted as one of the top 104 cleanest metro areas for short-term particle pollution (24-hour PM 2.5) in the U.S. during 2015 through 2017. Monitors in these cities reported no days with unhealthful PM 2.5 levels. *American Lung Association, "State of the Air 2019," April 24, 2019*

Health/Fitness Rankings

- The Green Bay metro area ranked #60 out of 189 in The Gallup-Sharecare Well-Being Index. Criteria: purpose; social well being; financial health; community and physical health. Results are based on telephone interviews with adults, aged 18 and older, living in metropolitan areas in the 50 U.S. states and the District of Columbia. *Gallup-Sharecare, "State of American Well-Being, 2017 Community Well-Being Rankings" March 2018*

Safety Rankings

- The National Insurance Crime Bureau ranked 382 metro areas in the U.S. in terms of per capita rates of vehicle theft. The Green Bay metro area ranked #335 (#1 = highest rate). Criteria: number of vehicle theft offenses per 100,000 inhabitants in 2018. *National Insurance Crime Bureau, "Hot Spots 2018," June 25, 2019*

Seniors/Retirement Rankings

- From its Best Cities for Successful Aging indexes, the Milken Institute generated rankings for metropolitan areas, weighing data in nine categories—health care, wellness, living arrangements, transportation and convenience, financial characteristics, education, employment, community engagement, and overall livability. The Green Bay metro area was ranked #162 overall in the small metro area category. *Milken Institute, "Best Cities for Successful Aging, 2017" March 14, 2017*

Business Environment

CITY FINANCES

City Government Finances

Component	2017 ($000)	2017 ($ per capita)
Total Revenues	185,002	1,758
Total Expenditures	185,784	1,766
Debt Outstanding	262,542	2,495
Cash and Securities[1]	12,017	114

Note: (1) Cash and security holdings of a government at the close of its fiscal year, including those of its dependent agencies, utilities, and liquor stores.
Source: U.S. Census Bureau, State & Local Government Finances 2017

City Government Revenue by Source

Source	2017 ($000)	2017 ($ per capita)	2017 (%)
General Revenue			
From Federal Government	3,493	33	1.9
From State Government	30,728	292	16.6
From Local Governments	7,983	76	4.3
Taxes			
Property	56,174	534	30.4
Sales and Gross Receipts	397	4	0.2
Personal Income	0	0	0.0
Corporate Income	0	0	0.0
Motor Vehicle License	0	0	0.0
Other Taxes	2,710	26	1.5
Current Charges	36,429	346	19.7
Liquor Store	0	0	0.0
Utility	37,336	355	20.2
Employee Retirement	0	0	0.0

Source: U.S. Census Bureau, State & Local Government Finances 2017

City Government Expenditures by Function

Function	2017 ($000)	2017 ($ per capita)	2017 (%)
General Direct Expenditures			
Air Transportation	0	0	0.0
Corrections	0	0	0.0
Education	0	0	0.0
Employment Security Administration	0	0	0.0
Financial Administration	1,841	17	1.0
Fire Protection	22,999	218	12.4
General Public Buildings	598	5	0.3
Governmental Administration, Other	3,786	36	2.0
Health	283	2	0.2
Highways	19,057	181	10.3
Hospitals	0	0	0.0
Housing and Community Development	863	8	0.5
Interest on General Debt	7,617	72	4.1
Judicial and Legal	1,083	10	0.6
Libraries	0	0	0.0
Parking	3,287	31	1.8
Parks and Recreation	11,664	110	6.3
Police Protection	26,764	254	14.4
Public Welfare	0	0	0.0
Sewerage	19,720	187	10.6
Solid Waste Management	8,131	77	4.4
Veterans' Services	0	0	0.0
Liquor Store	0	0	0.0
Utility	41,671	396	22.4
Employee Retirement	0	0	0.0

Source: U.S. Census Bureau, State & Local Government Finances 2017

DEMOGRAPHICS

Population Growth

Area	1990 Census	2000 Census	2010 Census	2018* Estimate	Population Growth (%) 1990-2018	Population Growth (%) 2010-2018
City	96,466	102,313	104,057	104,818	8.7	0.7
MSA[1]	243,698	282,599	306,241	317,702	30.4	3.7
U.S.	248,709,873	281,421,906	308,745,538	322,903,030	29.8	4.6

Note: (1) Figures cover the Green Bay, WI Metropolitan Statistical Area—see Appendix B for areas included; (*) 2014-2018 5-year estimated population
Source: U.S. Census Bureau, 1990 Census, Census 2000, Census 2010, 2014-2018 American Community Survey 5-Year Estimates

Household Size

Area	Persons in Household (%) One	Two	Three	Four	Five	Six	Seven or More	Average Household Size
City	34.0	32.4	12.4	11.1	7.0	1.4	1.6	2.40
MSA[1]	28.1	37.0	13.8	12.4	6.2	1.5	1.0	2.40
U.S.	27.7	33.9	15.7	13.0	6.0	2.3	1.4	2.60

Note: (1) Figures cover the Green Bay, WI Metropolitan Statistical Area—see Appendix B for areas included
Source: U.S. Census Bureau, 2014-2018 American Community Survey 5-Year Estimates

Race

Area	White Alone[2] (%)	Black Alone[2] (%)	Asian Alone[2] (%)	AIAN[3] Alone[2] (%)	NHOPI[4] Alone[2] (%)	Other Race Alone[2] (%)	Two or More Races (%)
City	76.7	4.0	4.2	3.6	0.0	6.3	5.2
MSA[1]	87.2	2.0	2.7	2.1	0.0	3.1	2.9
U.S.	72.7	12.7	5.4	0.8	0.2	4.9	3.2

Note: (1) Figures cover the Green Bay, WI Metropolitan Statistical Area—see Appendix B for areas included; (2) Alone is defined as not being in combination with one or more other races; (3) American Indian and Alaska Native; (4) Native Hawaiian and Other Pacific Islander
Source: U.S. Census Bureau, 2014-2018 American Community Survey 5-Year Estimates

Hispanic or Latino Origin

Area	Total (%)	Mexican (%)	Puerto Rican (%)	Cuban (%)	Other (%)
City	15.2	11.6	1.2	0.1	2.3
MSA[1]	7.3	5.6	0.6	0.1	0.9
U.S.	17.8	11.2	1.7	0.7	4.2

Note: Persons of Hispanic or Latino origin can be of any race; (1) Figures cover the Green Bay, WI Metropolitan Statistical Area—see Appendix B for areas included
Source: U.S. Census Bureau, 2014-2018 American Community Survey 5-Year Estimates

Segregation

Type	Segregation Indices[1] 1990	2000	2010	2010 Rank[2]	Percent Change 1990-2000	1990-2010	2000-2010
Black/White	n/a	n/a	n/a	n/a	n/a	n/a	n/a
Asian/White	n/a	n/a	n/a	n/a	n/a	n/a	n/a
Hispanic/White	n/a	n/a	n/a	n/a	n/a	n/a	n/a

Note: All figures cover the Metropolitan Statistical Area—see Appendix B for areas included; Figures are based on an analysis of 1990, 2000, and 2010 Census Decennial Census tract data by William H. Frey, Brookings Institution and the University of Michigan Social Science Data Analysis Network. In this analysis all racial groups (whites, blacks, and asians) are non-Hispanic members of those races. Hispanics are shown as a separate category; (1) Segregation Indices are Dissimilarity Indices that measure the degree to which the minority group is distributed differently than whites across census tracts. They range from 0 (complete integration) to 100 (complete segregation) where the value indicates the percentage of the minority group that needs to move to be distributed exactly like whites; (2) Ranges from 1 (most segregated) to 102 (least segregated); n/a not available.
Source: www.CensusScope.org

Ancestry

Area	German	Irish	English	American	Italian	Polish	French[2]	Scottish	Dutch
City	30.9	8.9	3.6	3.6	2.1	8.0	4.2	0.6	3.0
MSA[1]	37.1	9.7	4.0	3.9	2.2	9.6	4.4	0.8	4.6
U.S.	13.7	9.9	7.3	6.4	5.2	2.8	2.4	1.7	1.2

Note: Figures are the percentage of the total population reporting a particular ancestry. The nine most commonly reported ancestries in the U.S. are shown. Figures include multiple ancestries (e.g. if a person reported being Irish and Italian, they were included in both columns); (1) Figures cover the Green Bay, WI Metropolitan Statistical Area—see Appendix B for areas included; (2) Excludes Basque
Source: U.S. Census Bureau, 2014-2018 American Community Survey 5-Year Estimates

Foreign-born Population

Area	Percent of Population Born in								
	Any Foreign Country	Asia	Mexico	Europe	Caribbean	Central America[2]	South America	Africa	Canada
City	9.8	2.0	5.4	0.7	0.1	0.8	0.2	0.5	0.0
MSA[1]	5.1	1.4	2.4	0.5	0.0	0.3	0.1	0.2	0.1
U.S.	13.5	4.1	3.5	1.5	1.3	1.1	0.9	0.7	0.3

Note: (1) Figures cover the Green Bay, WI Metropolitan Statistical Area—see Appendix B for areas included; (2) Excludes Mexico.
Source: U.S. Census Bureau, 2014-2018 American Community Survey 5-Year Estimates

Marital Status

Area	Never Married	Now Married[2]	Separated	Widowed	Divorced
City	38.0	42.9	1.5	5.1	12.6
MSA[1]	30.2	53.0	1.0	5.1	10.7
U.S.	33.3	48.1	2.0	5.8	10.8

Note: Figures are percentages and cover the population 15 years of age and older; (1) Figures cover the Green Bay, WI Metropolitan Statistical Area—see Appendix B for areas included; (2) Excludes separated
Source: U.S. Census Bureau, 2014-2018 American Community Survey 5-Year Estimates

Disability by Age

Area	All Ages	Under 18 Years Old	18 to 64 Years Old	65 Years and Over
City	12.7	6.0	11.6	32.2
MSA[1]	11.2	4.7	9.2	30.1
U.S.	12.6	4.2	10.3	35.0

Note: Figures show percent of the civilian noninstitutionalized population that reported having a disability. Disability status is determined from six types of difficulty: vision, hearing, cognitive, ambulatory, self-care, and independent living. For children under 5 years old, hearing and vision difficulty are used to determine disability status. For children between the ages of 5 and 14, disability status is determined from hearing, vision, cognitive, ambulatory, and self-care difficulties. For people aged 15 years and older, they are considered to have a disability if they have difficulty with any one of the six difficulty types; Note: (1) Figures cover the Green Bay, WI Metropolitan Statistical Area—see Appendix B for areas included
Source: U.S. Census Bureau, 2014-2018 American Community Survey 5-Year Estimates

Age

Area	Percent of Population									Median Age
	Under Age 5	Age 5–19	Age 20–34	Age 35–44	Age 45–54	Age 55–64	Age 65–74	Age 75–84	Age 85+	
City	7.8	20.0	23.6	12.1	12.5	11.6	6.9	3.6	1.9	34.1
MSA[1]	6.3	19.7	19.3	12.4	13.8	13.6	8.6	4.5	1.8	38.7
U.S.	6.1	19.3	20.7	12.6	13.2	12.8	8.8	4.5	1.9	37.9

Note: (1) Figures cover the Green Bay, WI Metropolitan Statistical Area—see Appendix B for areas included
Source: U.S. Census Bureau, 2014-2018 American Community Survey 5-Year Estimates

Gender

Area	Males	Females	Males per 100 Females
City	52,255	52,563	99.4
MSA[1]	158,290	159,412	99.3
U.S.	158,984,190	163,918,840	97.0

Note: (1) Figures cover the Green Bay, WI Metropolitan Statistical Area—see Appendix B for areas included
Source: U.S. Census Bureau, 2014-2018 American Community Survey 5-Year Estimates

Religious Groups by Family

Area	Catholic	Baptist	Non-Den.	Methodist[2]	Lutheran	LDS[3]	Pente-costal	Presby-terian[4]	Muslim[5]	Judaism
MSA[1]	42.0	0.7	3.4	2.2	12.7	0.4	0.6	1.0	0.1	0.1
U.S.	19.1	9.3	4.0	4.0	2.3	2.0	1.9	1.6	0.8	0.7

Note: Figures are the number of adherents as a percentage of the total population; (1) Figures cover the Green Bay, WI Metropolitan Statistical Area—see Appendix B for areas included; (2) Methodist/Pietist; (3) Latter Day Saints; (4) Reformed; (5) Figures are estimates
Source: Association of Statisticians of American Religious Bodies, 2010 U.S. Religion Census: Religious Congregations & Membership Study

Religious Groups by Tradition

Area	Catholic	Evangelical Protestant	Mainline Protestant	Other Tradition	Black Protestant	Orthodox
MSA[1]	42.0	14.1	8.1	0.6	<0.1	<0.1
U.S.	19.1	16.2	7.3	4.3	1.6	0.3

Note: Figures are the number of adherents as a percentage of the total population; (1) Figures cover the Green Bay, WI Metropolitan Statistical Area—see Appendix B for areas included
Source: Association of Statisticians of American Religious Bodies, 2010 U.S. Religion Census: Religious Congregations & Membership Study

ECONOMY

Gross Metropolitan Product

Area	2017	2018	2019	2020	Rank[2]
MSA[1]	19.4	20.4	21.3	22.1	128

Note: Figures are in billions of dollars; (1) Figures cover the Green Bay, WI Metropolitan Statistical Area—see Appendix B for areas included; (2) Rank is based on 2018 data and ranges from 1 to 381
Source: U.S. Conference of Mayors, U.S. Metro Economies: GMP & Employment 2018-2020, September 2019

Economic Growth

Area	2015-17 (%)	2018 (%)	2019 (%)	2020 (%)	Rank[2]
MSA[1]	1.2	3.2	2.6	1.2	203
U.S.	1.9	2.9	2.3	2.1	–

Note: Figures are real gross metropolitan product (GMP) growth rates and represent average annual percent change; (1) Figures cover the Green Bay, WI Metropolitan Statistical Area—see Appendix B for areas included; (2) Rank is based on 2017 2-year average annual percent change and ranges from 1 to 381
Source: U.S. Conference of Mayors, U.S. Metro Economies: GMP & Employment 2018-2020, September 2019

Metropolitan Area Exports

Area	2013	2014	2015	2016	2017	2018	Rank[2]
MSA[1]	914.8	988.7	968.1	1,044.0	1,054.8	1,044.3	156

Note: Figures are in millions of dollars; (1) Figures cover the Green Bay, WI Metropolitan Statistical Area—see Appendix B for areas included; (2) Rank is based on 2018 data and ranges from 1 to 387
Source: U.S. Department of Commerce, International Trade Administration, Office of Trade and Economic Analysis, Industry and Analysis, Exports by Metropolitan Area, data extracted April 15, 2020

Building Permits

Area	Single-Family			Multi-Family			Total		
	2017	2018	Pct. Chg.	2017	2018	Pct. Chg.	2017	2018	Pct. Chg.
City	98	101	3.1	0	0	0.0	98	101	3.1
MSA[1]	828	766	-7.5	348	435	25.0	1,176	1,201	2.1
U.S.	820,000	855,300	4.3	462,000	473,500	2.5	1,282,000	1,328,800	3.7

Note: (1) Figures cover the Green Bay, WI Metropolitan Statistical Area—see Appendix B for areas included; Figures represent new, privately-owned housing units authorized (unadjusted data); All permit data are based on estimates with imputation
Source: U.S. Census Bureau, Manufacturing, Mining, and Construction Statistics, Building Permits, 2017, 2018

Bankruptcy Filings

Area	Business Filings			Nonbusiness Filings		
	2018	2019	% Chg.	2018	2019	% Chg.
Brown County	5	25	400.0	575	599	4.2
U.S.	22,232	22,780	2.5	751,186	752,160	0.1

Note: Business filings include Chapter 7, Chapter 9, Chapter 11, Chapter 12, Chapter 13, Chapter 15, and Section 304; Nonbusiness filings include Chapter 7, Chapter 11, and Chapter 13
Source: Administrative Office of the U.S. Courts, Business and Nonbusiness Bankruptcy, County Cases Commenced by Chapter of the Bankruptcy Code, During the 12-Month Period Ending December 31, 2018 and Business and Nonbusiness Bankruptcy, County Cases Commenced by Chapter of the Bankruptcy Code, During the 12-Month Period Ending December 31, 2019

Housing Vacancy Rates

Area	Gross Vacancy Rate[2] (%)			Year-Round Vacancy Rate[3] (%)			Rental Vacancy Rate[4] (%)			Homeowner Vacancy Rate[5] (%)		
	2017	2018	2019	2017	2018	2019	2017	2018	2019	2017	2018	2019
MSA[1]	n/a	n/a	n/a	n/a	n/a	n/a	n/a	n/a	n/a	n/a	n/a	n/a
U.S.	12.7	12.3	12.0	9.9	9.7	9.5	7.2	6.9	6.7	1.6	1.5	1.4

Note: (1) Figures cover the Green Bay, WI Metropolitan Statistical Area—see Appendix B for areas included; (2) The percentage of the total housing inventory that is vacant; (3) The percentage of the housing inventory (excluding seasonal units) that is year-round vacant; (4) The percentage of rental inventory that is vacant for rent; (5) The percentage of homeowner inventory that is vacant for sale; n/a not available
Source: U.S. Census Bureau, Housing Vacancies and Homeownership Annual Statistics: 2017, 2018, 2019

INCOME

Income

Area	Per Capita ($)	Median Household ($)	Average Household ($)
City	25,398	47,797	61,597
MSA[1]	30,926	59,830	75,756
U.S.	32,621	60,293	84,938

Note: (1) Figures cover the Green Bay, WI Metropolitan Statistical Area—see Appendix B for areas included
Source: U.S. Census Bureau, 2014-2018 American Community Survey 5-Year Estimates

Household Income Distribution

Area	Percent of Households Earning							
	Under $15,000	$15,000 -$24,999	$25,000 -$34,999	$35,000 -$49,999	$50,000 -$74,999	$75,000 -$99,999	$100,000 -$149,999	$150,000 and up
City	12.3	11.7	12.6	16.0	19.5	13.0	10.3	4.5
MSA[1]	8.6	9.0	10.1	13.9	19.6	15.0	15.1	8.7
U.S.	10.9	9.3	9.3	12.6	17.5	12.5	14.6	13.3

Note: (1) Figures cover the Green Bay, WI Metropolitan Statistical Area—see Appendix B for areas included
Source: U.S. Census Bureau, 2014-2018 American Community Survey 5-Year Estimates

Poverty Rate

Area	All Ages	Under 18 Years Old	18 to 64 Years Old	65 Years and Over
City	16.0	22.7	14.6	9.6
MSA[1]	10.1	13.6	9.3	7.7
U.S.	14.1	19.5	13.2	9.3

Note: Figures are percentage of people whose income during the past 12 months was below the poverty level; (1) Figures cover the Green Bay, WI Metropolitan Statistical Area—see Appendix B for areas included
Source: U.S. Census Bureau, 2014-2018 American Community Survey 5-Year Estimates

EMPLOYMENT

Labor Force and Employment

Area	Civilian Labor Force			Workers Employed		
	Dec. 2018	Dec. 2019	% Chg.	Dec. 2018	Dec. 2019	% Chg.
City	53,873	53,859	0.0	52,441	52,110	-0.6
MSA[1]	173,169	172,794	-0.2	168,711	167,575	-0.7
U.S.	162,510,000	164,007,000	0.9	156,481,000	158,504,000	1.3

Note: Data is not seasonally adjusted and covers workers 16 years of age and older; (1) Figures cover the Green Bay, WI Metropolitan Statistical Area—see Appendix B for areas included
Source: Bureau of Labor Statistics, Local Area Unemployment Statistics

Unemployment Rate

Area	2019											
	Jan.	Feb.	Mar.	Apr.	May	Jun.	Jul.	Aug.	Sep.	Oct.	Nov.	Dec.
City	3.4	3.6	3.6	3.2	3.2	3.8	3.8	3.4	3.0	2.9	3.2	3.2
MSA[1]	3.4	3.5	3.5	3.0	3.0	3.6	3.5	3.2	2.7	2.6	2.8	3.0
U.S.	4.4	4.1	3.9	3.3	3.4	3.8	4.0	3.8	3.3	3.3	3.3	3.4

Note: Data is not seasonally adjusted and covers workers 16 years of age and older; (1) Figures cover the Green Bay, WI Metropolitan Statistical Area—see Appendix B for areas included
Source: Bureau of Labor Statistics, Local Area Unemployment Statistics

Average Wages

Occupation	$/Hr.	Occupation	$/Hr.
Accountants and Auditors	33.30	Maintenance and Repair Workers	21.30
Automotive Mechanics	19.70	Marketing Managers	51.80
Bookkeepers	19.40	Network and Computer Systems Admin.	32.10
Carpenters	25.20	Nurses, Licensed Practical	20.50
Cashiers	10.90	Nurses, Registered	32.10
Computer Programmers	36.60	Nursing Assistants	14.80
Computer Systems Analysts	41.50	Office Clerks, General	17.70
Computer User Support Specialists	24.40	Physical Therapists	43.10
Construction Laborers	20.20	Physicians	127.10
Cooks, Restaurant	12.80	Plumbers, Pipefitters and Steamfitters	33.60
Customer Service Representatives	18.30	Police and Sheriff's Patrol Officers	33.90
Dentists	115.20	Postal Service Mail Carriers	24.90
Electricians	27.30	Real Estate Sales Agents	27.20
Engineers, Electrical	40.60	Retail Salespersons	14.10
Fast Food and Counter Workers	9.90	Sales Representatives, Technical/Scientific	42.10
Financial Managers	57.90	Secretaries, Exc. Legal/Medical/Executive	17.70
First-Line Supervisors of Office Workers	28.10	Security Guards	13.50
General and Operations Managers	59.70	Surgeons	n/a
Hairdressers/Cosmetologists	13.80	Teacher Assistants, Exc. Postsecondary*	15.50
Home Health and Personal Care Aides	12.10	Teachers, Secondary School, Exc. Sp. Ed.*	27.90
Janitors and Cleaners	13.70	Telemarketers	n/a
Landscaping/Groundskeeping Workers	15.20	Truck Drivers, Heavy/Tractor-Trailer	21.20
Lawyers	54.20	Truck Drivers, Light/Delivery Services	16.80
Maids and Housekeeping Cleaners	11.70	Waiters and Waitresses	9.50

Note: Wage data covers the Green Bay, WI Metropolitan Statistical Area—see Appendix B for areas included; (*) Hourly wages were calculated from annual wage data based on a 40 hour work week; n/a not available.
Source: Bureau of Labor Statistics, Metro Area Occupational Employment & Wage Estimates, May 2019

Employment by Occupation

Occupation Classification	City (%)	MSA[1] (%)	U.S. (%)
Management, Business, Science, and Arts	28.9	34.4	37.9
Natural Resources, Construction, and Maintenance	7.8	9.4	8.9
Production, Transportation, and Material Moving	21.9	18.7	13.3
Sales and Office	21.7	21.9	22.1
Service	19.7	15.6	17.9

Note: Figures cover employed civilians 16 years of age and older; (1) Figures cover the Green Bay, WI Metropolitan Statistical Area—see Appendix B for areas included
Source: U.S. Census Bureau, 2014-2018 American Community Survey 5-Year Estimates

Employment by Industry

Sector	MSA[1]		U.S.
	Number of Employees	Percent of Total	Percent of Total
Construction, Mining, and Logging	7,500	4.1	5.4
Education and Health Services	28,000	15.4	16.1
Financial Activities	12,200	6.7	5.8
Government	20,600	11.3	15.0
Information	1,500	0.8	1.9
Leisure and Hospitality	17,300	9.5	10.8
Manufacturing	31,800	17.5	8.4
Other Services	8,900	4.9	3.9
Professional and Business Services	19,100	10.5	14.1
Retail Trade	17,500	9.6	10.6
Transportation, Warehousing, and Utilities	8,700	4.8	4.2
Wholesale Trade	8,400	4.6	3.9

Note: Figures are non-farm employment as of December 2019. Figures are not seasonally adjusted and include workers 16 years of age and older; (1) Figures cover the Green Bay, WI Metropolitan Statistical Area—see Appendix B for areas included
Source: Bureau of Labor Statistics, Current Employment Statistics, Employment, Hours, and Earnings

Occupations with Greatest Projected Employment Growth: 2019 – 2021

Occupation[1]	2019 Employment	2021 Projected Employment	Numeric Employment Change	Percent Employment Change
Personal Care Aides	67,700	71,470	3,770	5.6
Combined Food Preparation and Serving Workers, Including Fast Food	76,450	78,390	1,940	2.5
Registered Nurses	57,510	58,900	1,390	2.4
Heavy and Tractor-Trailer Truck Drivers	53,400	54,730	1,330	2.5
Laborers and Freight, Stock, and Material Movers, Hand	54,370	55,330	960	1.8
Software Developers, Applications	16,690	17,520	830	5.0
Cooks, Restaurant	24,360	25,180	820	3.4
Janitors and Cleaners, Except Maids and Housekeeping Cleaners	49,840	50,600	760	1.5
Maintenance and Repair Workers, General	36,060	36,740	680	1.9
Elementary School Teachers, Except Special Education	35,490	36,150	660	1.9

Note: Projections cover Wisconsin; (1) Sorted by numeric employment change
Source: www.projectionscentral.com, State Occupational Projections, 2019–2021 Short-Term Projections

Fastest Growing Occupations: 2019 – 2021

Occupation[1]	2019 Employment	2021 Projected Employment	Numeric Employment Change	Percent Employment Change
Locomotive Engineers	880	990	110	12.5
Reservation and Transportation Ticket Agents and Travel Clerks	1,150	1,270	120	10.4
Railroad Conductors and Yardmasters	690	760	70	10.1
Nonfarm Animal Caretakers	7,590	8,180	590	7.8
Aircraft Mechanics and Service Technicians	850	910	60	7.1
Physician Assistants	2,040	2,180	140	6.9
Nurse Practitioners	3,080	3,270	190	6.2
Computer Numerically Controlled Machine Tool Programmers, Metal and Plastic	1,510	1,600	90	6.0
Taxi Drivers and Chauffeurs	9,130	9,670	540	5.9
Personal Care Aides	67,700	71,470	3,770	5.6

Note: Projections cover Wisconsin; (1) Sorted by percent employment change and excludes occupations with numeric employment change less than 50
Source: www.projectionscentral.com, State Occupational Projections, 2019–2021 Short-Term Projections

TAXES

State Corporate Income Tax Rates

State	Tax Rate (%)	Income Brackets ($)	Num. of Brackets	Financial Institution Tax Rate (%)[a]	Federal Income Tax Ded.
Wisconsin	7.9	Flat rate	1	7.9	No

Note: Tax rates as of January 1, 2020; (a) Rates listed are the corporate income tax rate applied to financial institutions or excise taxes based on income.
Source: Federation of Tax Administrators, State Corporate Income Tax Rates, January 1, 2020

State Individual Income Tax Rates

State	Tax Rate (%)	Income Brackets ($)	Personal Exemptions ($)			Standard Ded. ($)	
			Single	Married	Depend.	Single	Married
Wisconsin (a)	4.0 - 7.65	11,970 - 263,480 (w)	700	1,400	700	11,050	22,999 (y)

Note: Tax rates as of January 1, 2020; Local- and county-level taxes are not included; Federal income tax is not deductible on state income tax returns; (a) 19 states have statutory provision for automatically adjusting to the rate of inflation the dollar values of the income tax brackets, standard deductions, and/or personal exemptions. Michigan indexes the personal exemption only. Oregon does not index the income brackets for $125,000 and over; (w) The Wisconsin income brackets reported are for single individuals. For married taxpayers filing jointly, the same tax rates apply income brackets ranging from $15,960, to $351,310; (y) Alabama standard deduction is phased out for incomes over $23,000. Rhode Island exemptions & standard deductions phased out for incomes over $203,850; Wisconsin standard deduciton phases out for income over $15,939.
Source: Federation of Tax Administrators, State Individual Income Tax Rates, January 1, 2020

Various State Sales and Excise Tax Rates

State	State Sales Tax (%)	Gasoline[1] (¢/gal.)	Cigarette[2] ($/pack)	Spirits[3] ($/gal.)	Wine[4] ($/gal.)	Beer[5] ($/gal.)	Recreational Marijuana (%)
Wisconsin	5	32.9	2.52	3.25	0.25	0.06	Not legal

Note: All tax rates as of January 1, 2020; (1) The American Petroleum Institute has developed a methodology for determining the average tax rate on a gallon of fuel. Rates may include any of the following: excise taxes, environmental fees, storage tank fees, other fees or taxes, general sales tax, and local taxes; (2) The federal excise tax of $1.0066 per pack and local taxes are not included; (3) Rates are those applicable to off-premise sales of 40% alcohol by volume (a.b.v.) distilled spirits in 750ml containers. Local excise taxes are excluded; (4) Rates are those applicable to off-premise sales of 11% a.b.v. non-carbonated wine in 750ml containers; (5) Rates are those applicable to off-premise sales of 4.7% a.b.v. beer in 12 ounce containers.
Source: Tax Foundation, 2020 Facts & Figures: How Does Your State Compare?

State Business Tax Climate Index Rankings

State	Overall Rank	Corporate Tax Rank	Individual Income Tax Rank	Sales Tax Rank	Property Tax Rank	Unemployment Insurance Tax Rank
Wisconsin	26	30	37	7	23	37

Note: The index is a measure of how each state's tax laws affect economic performance. The lower the rank, the more favorable a state's tax system is for business. States without a given tax are given a ranking of 1. The scores/rankings for the District of Columbia do not affect other states. The 2020 index represents the tax climate as of July 1, 2019.
Source: Tax Foundation, State Business Tax Climate Index 2020

COMMERCIAL UTILITIES

Typical Monthly Electric Bills

Area	Commercial Service ($/month)		Industrial Service ($/month)	
	1,500 kWh	40 kW demand 14,000 kWh	1,000 kW demand 200,000 kWh	50,000 kW demand 32,500,000 kWh
City	174	1,340	21,338	1,956,816
Average[1]	203	1,612	25,706	2,520,671

Note: Figures are based on annualized rates; (1) Average based on 187 utilities surveyed
Source: Edison Electric Institute, Typical Bills and Average Rates Report, Summer 2019

TRANSPORTATION

Means of Transportation to Work

Area	Car/Truck/Van		Public Transportation			Bicycle	Walked	Other Means	Worked at Home
	Drove Alone	Car-pooled	Bus	Subway	Railroad				
City	79.5	10.5	1.1	0.0	0.0	0.6	2.7	2.1	3.5
MSA[1]	83.7	8.0	0.6	0.0	0.0	0.3	2.1	1.1	4.3
U.S.	76.4	9.1	2.5	1.9	0.6	0.6	2.7	1.3	4.9

Note: Figures are percentages and cover workers 16 years of age and older; (1) Figures cover the Green Bay, WI Metropolitan Statistical Area—see Appendix B for areas included
Source: U.S. Census Bureau, 2014-2018 American Community Survey 5-Year Estimates

Travel Time to Work

Area	Less Than 10 Minutes	10 to 19 Minutes	20 to 29 Minutes	30 to 44 Minutes	45 to 59 Minutes	60 to 89 Minutes	90 Minutes or More
City	17.9	48.7	19.6	7.6	3.3	1.7	1.3
MSA[1]	18.2	39.8	21.9	12.7	3.9	2.0	1.5
U.S.	12.5	28.7	20.9	20.7	8.2	6.3	2.8

Note: Note: Figures are percentages and include workers 16 years old and over; (1) Figures cover the Green Bay, WI Metropolitan Statistical Area—see Appendix B for areas included
Source: U.S. Census Bureau, 2014-2018 American Community Survey 5-Year Estimates

Key Congestion Measures

Area	1982	1992	2002	2012	2017
Annual Hours of Delay, Total (000)	n/a	n/a	n/a	n/a	3,421
Annual Hours of Delay, Per Auto Commuter	n/a	n/a	n/a	n/a	15
Annual Congestion Cost, Total (million $)	n/a	n/a	n/a	n/a	72
Annual Congestion Cost, Per Auto Commuter ($)	n/a	n/a	n/a	n/a	316

Note: n/a not available
Source: Texas A&M Transportation Institute, 2019 Urban Mobility Report

Freeway Travel Time Index

Area	1982	1987	1992	1997	2002	2007	2012	2017
Urban Area Index[1]	n/a	n/a	n/a	n/a	n/a	n/a	n/a	1.05
Urban Area Rank[1,2]	n/a	n/a	n/a	n/a	n/a	n/a	n/a	n/a

Note: Freeway Travel Time Index—the ratio of travel time in the peak period to the travel time at free-flow conditions. For example, a value of 1.30 indicates a 20-minute free-flow trip takes 26 minutes in the peak (20 minutes x 1.30 = 26 minutes); (1) Covers the Green Bay WI urban area; (2) Rank is based on 101 larger urban areas (#1 = highest travel time index); n/a not available
Source: Texas A&M Transportation Institute, 2019 Urban Mobility Report

Public Transportation

Agency Name / Mode of Transportation	Vehicles Operated in Maximum Service[1]	Annual Unlinked Passenger Trips[2] (in thous.)	Annual Passenger Miles[3] (in thous.)
Green Bay Metro			
Bus (directly operated)	23	1,275.8	3,765.1
Demand Response (purchased transportation)	11	34.6	273.8

Note: (1) Number of revenue vehicles operated by the given mode and type of service to meet the annual maximum service requirement. This is the revenue vehicle count during the peak season of the year; on the week and day that maximum service is provided. Vehicles operated in maximum service (VOMS) exclude atypical days and one-time special events; (2) Number of passengers who boarded public transportation vehicles. Passengers are counted each time they board a vehicle no matter how many vehicles they use to travel from their origin to their destination. (3) Sum of the distances ridden by all passengers during the entire fiscal year.
Source: Federal Transit Administration, National Transit Database, 2018

Air Transportation

Airport Name and Code / Type of Service	Passenger Airlines[1]	Passenger Enplanements	Freight Carriers[2]	Freight (lbs)
Austin-Bergstrom International (GRB)				
Domestic service (U.S. carriers - 2019)	19	347,008	4	41,564
International service (U.S. carriers - 2018)	0	0	0	0

Note: (1) Includes all U.S.-based major, minor and commuter airlines that carried at least one passenger during the year; (2) Includes all U.S.-based airlines and freight carriers that transported at least one pound of freight during the year.
Source: Bureau of Transportation Statistics, The Intermodal Transportation Database, Air Carriers: T-100 Domestic Market (U.S. Carriers), 2019; Bureau of Transportation Statistics, The Intermodal Transportation Database, Air Carriers: T-100 International Market (U.S. Carriers), 2018

Other Transportation Statistics

Major Highways:	I-43
Amtrak Service:	Bus connection
Major Waterways/Ports:	Green Bay

Source: Amtrak.com; Google Maps

BUSINESSES

Major Business Headquarters

Company Name	Industry	Rankings	
		Fortune[1]	Forbes[2]
Schreiber Foods	Food, Drink & Tobacco	-	85

Note: (1) Companies that produce a 10-K are ranked 1 to 500 based on 2018 revenue; (2) All private companies with at least $2 billion in annual revenue through the end of their most current fiscal year are ranked 1 to 228; companies listed are headquartered in the city; dashes indicate no ranking
Source: Fortune, "Fortune 500," June 2019; Forbes, "America's Largest Private Companies," 2019 Rankings

Fast-Growing Businesses

According to *Fortune*, Green Bay is home to one of the 100 fastest-growing companies in the world: **Nicolet Bankshares** (#76). Companies were ranked by their revenue growth rate; their EPS growth rate; and their three-year annualized total return to investors for the period ending June 30, 2019. Criteria for inclusion: a company, foreign or domestic, must trade on a major U.S. stock exchange; must file quarterly reports with the SEC; must have a minimum market capitalization of $250 million; must have a stock price of at least $5 on June 30, 2019; must have been trading continuously since June 30, 2016; must have revenue and net income for the four quarters ended on or before April 30, 2019, of at least $50 million and $10 million, respectively; and must have posted a compound annual growth in revenue and earnings per share of at least 15% annually over the three years ending on or before April 30, 2019. Real estate investment trusts, limited-liability companies, limited parterships, business development companies, closed-end investment firms, companies about to be acquired, and companies that lost money in the quarter ending April 30, 2019 were excluded. *Fortune, "100 Fastest-Growing Companies," 2019*

Minority- and Women-Owned Businesses

Group	All Firms		Firms with Paid Employees			
	Firms	Sales ($000)	Firms	Sales ($000)	Employees	Payroll ($000)
AIAN[1]	115	9,412	4	(s)	20 - 99	(s)
Asian	188	15,580	18	12,252	76	6,993
Black	225	8,788	3	4,982	104	2,161
Hispanic	138	13,471	23	(s)	100 - 249	(s)
NHOPI[2]	n/a	n/a	n/a	n/a	n/a	n/a
Women	1,753	244,342	213	206,608	2,681	70,498
All Firms	7,022	15,846,453	1,806	15,592,438	54,522	2,503,556

Note: Figures cover firms located in the city; minority- and women-owned business are defined as firms in which the corresponding group own 51% or more of the stock or equity of the company; (1) American Indian and Alaska Native; (2) Native Hawaiian and Other Pacific Islander; (s) estimates are suppressed when publication standards are not met; n/a not available
Source: U.S. Census Bureau, 2012 Economic Census, Survey of Business Owners

**HOTELS &
CONVENTION
CENTERS**

Hotels, Motels and Vacation Rentals

Area	5 Star		4 Star		3 Star		2 Star		1 Star		Not Rated	
	Num.	Pct.[3]	Num.	Pct.[3]	Num.	Pct.[3]	Num.	Pct.[3]	Num.	Pct.[3]	Num.	Pct.[3]
City[1]	0	0.0	0	0.0	22	26.2	18	21.4	8	9.5	36	42.9
Total[2]	266	1.3	1,517	7.2	4,627	21.8	3,210	15.1	3,974	18.7	7,601	35.9

Note: (1) Figures cover Green Bay and vicinity; (2) Figures cover all 100 cities in this book; (3) Percentage of hotels which have a given star rating; Star ratings are determined by priceline.com and offer an indication of the general quality of a particular hotel.
Source: priceline.com, April 27, 2020

Major Convention Centers

Name	Overall Space (sq. ft.)	Exhibit Space (sq. ft.)	Meeting Space (sq. ft.)	Meeting Rooms
KI Convention Center	80,000	35,000	n/a	19

Note: Table includes convention centers located in the Green Bay, WI metro area; n/a not available
Source: Original research

Living Environment

COST OF LIVING

Cost of Living Index

Composite Index	Groceries	Housing	Utilities	Trans-portation	Health Care	Misc. Goods/Services
91.1	91.0	77.9	97.4	97.7	101.8	96.6

Note: The Cost of Living Index measures regional differences in the cost of consumer goods and services, excluding taxes and non-consumer expenditures, for professional and managerial households in the top income quintile. It is based on more than 50,000 prices covering almost 60 different items for which prices are collected three times a year by chambers of commerce, economic development organizations or university applied economic centers in each participating urban area. The numbers shown should be read as a percentage above or below the national average of 100. For example, a value of 115.4 in the groceries column indicates that grocery prices are 15.4% higher than the national average. Small differences in the index numbers should not be interpreted as significant; Figures cover the Green Bay WI urban area.
Source: The Council for Community and Economic Research, ACCRA Cost of Living Index, 2019

Grocery Prices

Area[1]	T-Bone Steak ($/pound)	Frying Chicken ($/pound)	Whole Milk ($/half gal.)	Eggs ($/dozen)	Orange Juice ($/64 oz.)	Coffee ($/11.5 oz.)
City[2]	13.00	1.71	1.35	0.79	3.49	4.19
Avg.	11.40	1.41	1.93	1.54	3.51	4.30
Min.	7.40	0.92	0.85	0.58	2.67	2.90
Max.	15.58	2.68	4.09	4.18	5.57	8.10

Note: (1) Values for the local area are compared with the average, minimum and maximum values for all 290 areas in the Cost of Living Index; (2) Figures cover the Green Bay WI urban area; **T-Bone Steak** (price per pound); **Frying Chicken** (price per pound, whole fryer); **Whole Milk** (half gallon carton); **Eggs** (price per dozen, Grade A, large); **Orange Juice** (64 oz. Tropicana or Florida Natural); **Coffee** (11.5 oz. can, vacuum-packed, Maxwell House, Hills Bros, or Folgers).
Source: The Council for Community and Economic Research, ACCRA Cost of Living Index, 2019

Housing and Utility Costs

Area[1]	New Home Price ($)	Apartment Rent ($/month)	All Electric ($/month)	Part Electric ($/month)	Other Energy ($/month)	Telephone ($/month)
City[2]	294,559	803	-	80.66	83.63	175.30
Avg.	362,090	1,142	174.35	100.00	67.76	179.60
Min.	198,329	501	91.58	31.44	28.51	165.30
Max.	2,074,561	5,050	388.18	239.41	306.15	207.90

Note: (1) Values for the local area are compared with the average, minimum and maximum values for all 290 areas in the Cost of Living Index; (2) Figures cover the Green Bay WI urban area; **New Home Price** (2,400 sf living area, 8,000 sf lot, in urban area with full utilities); **Apartment Rent** (950 sf 2 bedroom/1.5 or 2 bath, unfurnished, excluding all utilities except water); **All Electric** (average monthly cost for an all-electric home); **Part Electric** (average monthly cost for a part-electric home); **Other Energy** (average monthly cost for natural gas, fuel oil, coal, wood, and any other forms of energy except electricity); **Telephone** (price includes the base monthly rate plus taxes and fees for three lines of mobile phone service).
Source: The Council for Community and Economic Research, ACCRA Cost of Living Index, 2019

Health Care, Transportation, and Other Costs

Area[1]	Doctor ($/visit)	Dentist ($/visit)	Optometrist ($/visit)	Gasoline ($/gallon)	Beauty Salon ($/visit)	Men's Shirt ($)
City[2]	156.95	88.29	63.24	2.26	25.17	30.64
Avg.	114.85	97.58	106.10	2.50	38.15	32.15
Min.	39.00	62.22	52.22	1.53	16.88	10.27
Max.	206.67	151.53	258.67	3.79	79.29	59.30

Note: (1) Values for the local area are compared with the average, minimum and maximum values for all 290 areas in the Cost of Living Index; (2) Figures cover the Green Bay WI urban area; **Doctor** (general practitioners routine exam of an established patient); **Dentist** (adult teeth cleaning and periodic oral examination); **Optometrist** (full vision eye exam for established adult patient); **Gasoline** (one gallon regular unleaded, national brand, including all taxes, cash price at self-service pump if available); **Beauty Salon** (woman's shampoo, trim, and blow-dry); **Men's Shirt** (cotton/polyester dress shirt, pinpoint weave, long sleeves).
Source: The Council for Community and Economic Research, ACCRA Cost of Living Index, 2019

HOUSING

House Price Index (HPI)

Area	National Ranking[2]	Quarterly Change (%)	One-Year Change (%)	Five-Year Change (%)
MSA[1]	118	1.11	4.88	29.23
U.S.[3]	–	1.26	5.09	32.88

Note: The HPI is a weighted repeat sales index. It measures average price changes in repeat sales or refinancings on the same properties. This information is obtained by reviewing repeat mortgage transactions on single-family properties whose mortgages have been purchased or securitized by Fannie Mae or Freddie Mac in January 1975; (1) Figures cover the Green Bay, WI Metropolitan Statistical Area—see Appendix B for areas included; (2) Rankings are based on annual percentage change for all metro areas containing at least 15,000 transactions over the last 10 years and ranges from 1 to 232; (3) figures based on a weighted average of Census Division estimates using a seasonally adjusted, purchase-only index; all figures are for the period ending December 31, 2019
Source: Federal Housing Finance Agency, House Price Index, February 25, 2020

Median Single-Family Home Prices

Area	2017	2018	2019p	Percent Change 2018 to 2019
MSA[1]	163.2	177.3	189.4	6.8
U.S. Average	248.8	261.6	274.6	5.0

Note: Figures are median sales prices of existing single-family homes in thousands of dollars; (p) preliminary; (1) Figures cover the Green Bay, WI Metropolitan Statistical Area—see Appendix B for areas included
Source: National Association of Realtors, Median Sales Price of Existing Single-Family Homes for Metropolitan Areas, 4th Quarter 2019

Qualifying Income Based on Median Sales Price of Existing Single-Family Homes

Area	With 5% Down ($)	With 10% Down ($)	With 20% Down ($)
MSA[1]	40,076	37,967	33,748
U.S. Average	58,663	55,575	49,400

Note: Figures are preliminary; Qualifying income is based on a mortgage rate of 3.76%. Monthly principal and interest payment is limited to 25% of income; (1) Figures cover the Green Bay, WI Metropolitan Statistical Area—see Appendix B for areas included
Source: National Association of Realtors, Qualifying Income Based on Median Sales Price of Existing Single-Family Homes for Metropolitan Areas, 4th Quarter 2019

Median Apartment Condo-Coop Home Prices

Area	2017	2018	2019p	Percent Change 2018 to 2019
MSA[1]	n/a	n/a	n/a	n/a
U.S. Average	234.3	241.0	249.5	3.5

Note: Figures are median sales prices of existing apartment condo-coop homes in thousands of dollars; (p) preliminary; n/a not available; (1) Figures cover the Green Bay, WI Metropolitan Statistical Area—see Appendix B for areas included
Source: National Association of Realtors, Median Sales Price of Existing Apartment Condo-Coop Homes for Metropolitan Areas, 4th Quarter 2019

Home Value Distribution

Area	Under $50,000	$50,000 -$99,999	$100,000 -$149,999	$150,000 -$199,999	$200,000 -$299,999	$300,000 -$499,999	$500,000 -$999,999	$1,000,000 or more
City	3.3	22.5	37.0	19.4	11.4	4.8	1.3	0.3
MSA[1]	4.3	13.0	24.4	22.8	23.1	9.5	2.4	0.6
U.S.	7.6	13.0	14.0	14.3	19.2	18.3	10.5	3.1

Note: Figures are percentages and cover owner-occupied housing units; (1) Figures cover the Green Bay, WI Metropolitan Statistical Area—see Appendix B for areas included
Source: U.S. Census Bureau, 2014-2018 American Community Survey 5-Year Estimates

Homeownership Rate

Area	2011 (%)	2012 (%)	2013 (%)	2014 (%)	2015 (%)	2016 (%)	2017 (%)	2018 (%)	2019 (%)
MSA[1]	n/a	n/a	n/a	n/a	n/a	n/a	n/a	n/a	n/a
U.S.	66.1	65.4	65.1	64.5	63.7	63.4	63.9	64.4	64.6

Note: (1) Figures cover the Green Bay, WI Metropolitan Statistical Area—see Appendix B for areas included; n/a not available
Source: U.S. Census Bureau, Housing Vacancies and Homeownership Annual Statistics: 2011-2019

Year Housing Structure Built

Area	2010 or Later	2000 -2009	1990 -1999	1980 -1989	1970 -1979	1960 -1969	1950 -1959	1940 -1949	Before 1940	Median Year
City	1.6	7.6	9.6	12.6	18.0	13.3	14.7	6.2	16.4	1970
MSA[1]	4.1	15.4	16.2	12.1	15.7	9.9	9.3	4.4	12.8	1979
U.S.	4.1	14.3	13.9	13.5	15.3	10.7	10.4	5.0	12.8	1977

Note: Figures are percentages except for Median Year; Note: (1) Figures cover the Green Bay, WI Metropolitan Statistical Area—see Appendix B for areas included
Source: U.S. Census Bureau, 2014-2018 American Community Survey 5-Year Estimates

Gross Monthly Rent

Area	Under $500	$500 -$999	$1,000 -$1,499	$1,500 -$1,999	$2,000 -$2,499	$2,500 -$2,999	$3,000 and up	Median ($)
City	13.5	72.7	12.8	0.5	0.3	0.0	0.1	701
MSA[1]	10.9	71.2	16.1	1.1	0.3	0.0	0.3	760
U.S.	9.8	38.5	29.6	12.9	5.1	2.1	2.0	1,023

Note: Figures are percentages except for Median; Gross rent is the contract rent plus the estimated average monthly cost of utilities (electricity, gas, and water and sewer) and fuels (oil, coal, kerosene, wood, etc.) if these are paid by the renter (or paid for the renter by someone else); (1) Figures cover the Green Bay, WI Metropolitan Statistical Area—see Appendix B for areas included
Source: U.S. Census Bureau, 2014-2018 American Community Survey 5-Year Estimates

HEALTH

Health Risk Factors

Category	MSA[1] (%)	U.S. (%)
Adults aged 18–64 who have any kind of health care coverage	n/a	87.3
Adults who reported being in good or better health	n/a	82.4
Adults who have been told they have high blood cholesterol	n/a	33.0
Adults who have been told they have high blood pressure	n/a	32.3
Adults who are current smokers	n/a	17.1
Adults who currently use E-cigarettes	n/a	4.6
Adults who currently use chewing tobacco, snuff, or snus	n/a	4.0
Adults who are heavy drinkers[2]	n/a	6.3
Adults who are binge drinkers[3]	n/a	17.4
Adults who are overweight (BMI 25.0 - 29.9)	n/a	35.3
Adults who are obese (BMI 30.0 - 99.8)	n/a	31.3
Adults who participated in any physical activities in the past month	n/a	74.4
Adults who always or nearly always wears a seat belt	n/a	94.3

Note: n/a not available; (1) Figures cover the Green Bay, WI Metropolitan Statistical Area—see Appendix B for areas included; (2) Heavy drinkers are classified as adult men having more than 14 drinks per week and adult women having more than 7 drinks per week; (3) Binge drinkers are classified as males having five or more drinks on one occasion or females having four or more drinks on one occasion
Source: Centers for Disease Control and Prevention, Behavioral Risk Factor Surveillance System, SMART: Selected Metropolitan Area Risk Trends, 2017

Acute and Chronic Health Conditions

Category	MSA[1] (%)	U.S. (%)
Adults who have ever been told they had a heart attack	n/a	4.2
Adults who have ever been told they have angina or coronary heart disease	n/a	3.9
Adults who have ever been told they had a stroke	n/a	3.0
Adults who have ever been told they have asthma	n/a	14.2
Adults who have ever been told they have arthritis	n/a	24.9
Adults who have ever been told they have diabetes[2]	n/a	10.5
Adults who have ever been told they had skin cancer	n/a	6.2
Adults who have ever been told they had any other types of cancer	n/a	7.1
Adults who have ever been told they have COPD	n/a	6.5
Adults who have ever been told they have kidney disease	n/a	3.0
Adults who have ever been told they have a form of depression	n/a	20.5

Note: n/a not available; (1) Figures cover the Green Bay, WI Metropolitan Statistical Area—see Appendix B for areas included; (2) Figures do not include pregnancy-related, borderline, or pre-diabetes
Source: Centers for Disease Control and Prevention, Behaviorial Risk Factor Surveillance System, SMART: Selected Metropolitan Area Risk Trends, 2017

Health Screening and Vaccination Rates

Category	MSA[1] (%)	U.S. (%)
Adults aged 65+ who have had flu shot within the past year	n/a	60.7
Adults aged 65+ who have ever had a pneumonia vaccination	n/a	75.4
Adults who have ever been tested for HIV	n/a	36.1
Adults who have ever had the shingles or zoster vaccine?	n/a	28.9
Adults who have had their blood cholesterol checked within the last five years	n/a	85.9

Note: n/a not available; (1) Figures cover the Green Bay, WI Metropolitan Statistical Area—see Appendix B for areas included.
Source: Centers for Disease Control and Prevention, Behaviorial Risk Factor Surveillance System, SMART: Selected Metropolitan Area Risk Trends, 2017

Disability Status

Category	MSA[1] (%)	U.S. (%)
Adults who reported being deaf	n/a	6.7
Are you blind or have serious difficulty seeing, even when wearing glasses?	n/a	4.5
Are you limited in any way in any of your usual activities due of arthritis?	n/a	12.9
Do you have difficulty doing errands alone?	n/a	6.8
Do you have difficulty dressing or bathing?	n/a	3.6
Do you have serious difficulty concentrating/remembering/making decisions?	n/a	10.7
Do you have serious difficulty walking or climbing stairs?	n/a	13.6

Note: n/a not available; (1) Figures cover the Green Bay, WI Metropolitan Statistical Area—see Appendix B for areas included.
Source: Centers for Disease Control and Prevention, Behaviorial Risk Factor Surveillance System, SMART: Selected Metropolitan Area Risk Trends, 2017

Mortality Rates for the Top 10 Causes of Death in the U.S.

ICD-10[a] Sub-Chapter	ICD-10[a] Code	Age-Adjusted Mortality Rate[1] per 100,000 population	
		County[2]	U.S.
Malignant neoplasms	C00-C97	150.9	152.4
Ischaemic heart diseases	I20-I25	104.9	92.7
Other forms of heart disease	I30-I51	45.1	52.5
Chronic lower respiratory diseases	J40-J47	31.6	40.4
Cerebrovascular diseases	I60-I69	30.2	37.3
Other degenerative diseases of the nervous system	G30-G31	41.1	36.4
Other external causes of accidental injury	W00-X59	39.4	35.3
Organic, including symptomatic, mental disorders	F01-F09	46.3	30.0
Hypertensive diseases	I10-I15	18.1	22.9
Diabetes mellitus	E10-E14	17.9	21.3

Note: (a) ICD-10 = International Classification of Diseases 10th Revision; (1) Mortality rates are a three year average covering 2016-2018; (2) Figures cover Brown County.
Source: Centers for Disease Control and Prevention, National Center for Health Statistics. Underlying Cause of Death 1999-2018 on CDC WONDER Online Database

Mortality Rates for Selected Causes of Death

ICD-10[a] Sub-Chapter	ICD-10[a] Code	Age-Adjusted Mortality Rate[1] per 100,000 population	
		County[2]	U.S.
Assault	X85-Y09	Unreliable	6.0
Diseases of the liver	K70-K76	12.3	14.2
Human immunodeficiency virus (HIV) disease	B20-B24	Suppressed	1.6
Influenza and pneumonia	J09-J18	11.5	14.2
Intentional self-harm	X60-X84	16.2	13.9
Malnutrition	E40-E46	Unreliable	1.9
Obesity and other hyperalimentation	E65-E68	2.7	2.1
Renal failure	N17-N19	10.1	12.8
Transport accidents	V01-V99	8.7	12.5
Viral hepatitis	B15-B19	Suppressed	1.4

Note: (a) ICD-10 = International Classification of Diseases 10th Revision; (1) Mortality rates are a three year average covering 2016-2018; (2) Figures cover Brown County; Data are suppressed when the data meet the criteria for confidentiality constraints; Mortality rates are flagged as unreliable when the rate would be calculated with a numerator of 20 or less.
Source: Centers for Disease Control and Prevention, National Center for Health Statistics. Underlying Cause of Death 1999-2018 on CDC WONDER Online Database

Health Insurance Coverage

Area	With Health Insurance	With Private Health Insurance	With Public Health Insurance	Without Health Insurance	Population Under Age 19 Without Health Insurance
City	91.6	65.9	35.8	8.4	4.0
MSA[1]	94.3	75.2	30.3	5.7	3.6
U.S.	90.6	67.7	34.7	9.4	5.2

Note: Figures are percentages that cover the civilian noninstitutionalized population; (1) Figures cover the Green Bay, WI Metropolitan Statistical Area—see Appendix B for areas included
Source: U.S. Census Bureau, 2014-2018 American Community Survey 5-Year Estimates

Number of Medical Professionals

Area	MDs[3]	DOs[3,4]	Dentists	Podiatrists	Chiropractors	Optometrists
County[1] (number)	635	61	201	8	119	48
County[1] (rate[2])	242.3	23.3	76.3	3.0	45.2	18.2
U.S. (rate[2])	281.9	23.4	69.1	6.0	27.5	16.4

Note: Data as of 2018 unless noted; (1) Data covers Brown County; (2) Rate per 100,000 population; (3) Data as of 2017 and includes all active, non-federal physicians; (4) Doctor of Osteopathic Medicine
Source: U.S. Department of Health and Human Services, Health Resources and Services Administration, Bureau of Health Professions, Area Resource File (ARF) 2018-2019

EDUCATION

Public School District Statistics

District Name	Schls	Pupils	Pupil/Teacher Ratio	Minority Pupils[1] (%)	Free Lunch Eligible[2] (%)	IEP[3] (%)
Ashwaubenon School District	5	3,313	15.4	23.6	26.9	12.3
Green Bay Area PSD	42	20,391	13.6	55.5	54.9	14.7
Howard-Suamico School District	9	6,103	15.7	11.3	15.8	11.8

Note: Table includes school districts with 2,000 or more students; (1) Percentage of students that are not non-Hispanic white; (2) Percentage of students that are eligible for the free lunch program; (3) Percentage of students that have an Individualized Education Program.
Source: U.S. Department of Education, National Center for Education Statistics, Common Core of Data, Local Education Agency (School District) Universe Survey: School Year 2018-2019; U.S. Department of Education, National Center for Education Statistics, Common Core of Data, Public Elementary/Secondary School Universe Survey: School Year 2018-2019

Highest Level of Education

Area	Less than H.S.	H.S. Diploma	Some College, No Deg.	Associate Degree	Bachelor's Degree	Master's Degree	Prof. School Degree	Doctorate Degree
City	12.6	31.4	20.0	11.2	17.7	5.4	1.0	0.7
MSA[1]	8.2	32.6	19.6	12.4	19.1	6.0	1.4	0.6
U.S.	12.3	27.1	20.6	8.4	19.4	8.6	2.1	1.4

Note: Figures cover persons age 25 and over; (1) Figures cover the Green Bay, WI Metropolitan Statistical Area—see Appendix B for areas included
Source: U.S. Census Bureau, 2014-2018 American Community Survey 5-Year Estimates

Educational Attainment by Race

Area	High School Graduate or Higher (%)					Bachelor's Degree or Higher (%)				
	Total	White	Black	Asian	Hisp.[2]	Total	White	Black	Asian	Hisp.[2]
City	87.4	90.7	85.8	70.5	49.3	24.8	27.4	11.6	17.9	6.1
MSA[1]	91.8	93.4	86.0	81.1	55.8	27.2	28.0	13.2	39.5	8.4
U.S.	87.7	89.6	85.4	86.8	67.7	31.5	32.9	21.1	53.5	15.8

Note: Figures shown cover persons 25 years old and over; (1) Figures cover the Green Bay, WI Metropolitan Statistical Area—see Appendix B for areas included; (2) People of Hispanic origin can be of any race
Source: U.S. Census Bureau, 2014-2018 American Community Survey 5-Year Estimates

School Enrollment by Grade and Control

Area	Preschool (%)		Kindergarten (%)		Grades 1 - 4 (%)		Grades 5 - 8 (%)		Grades 9 - 12 (%)	
	Public	Private	Public	Private	Public	Private	Public	Private	Public	Private
City	70.9	29.1	88.6	11.4	92.0	8.0	88.1	11.9	91.1	8.9
MSA[1]	68.9	31.1	86.6	13.4	89.9	10.1	89.5	10.5	93.5	6.5
U.S.	59.0	41.0	87.7	12.3	89.6	10.4	89.5	10.5	90.2	9.8

Note: Figures shown cover persons 3 years old and over; (1) Figures cover the Green Bay, WI Metropolitan Statistical Area—see Appendix B for areas included
Source: U.S. Census Bureau, 2014-2018 American Community Survey 5-Year Estimates

Average Salaries of Public School Teachers

Area	2016-17		2017-18		Change from 2016-17 to 2017-18	
	Dollars	Rank[1]	Dollars	Rank[1]	Percent	Rank[2]
Wisconsin	51,439	32	51,469	33	0.06	47
U.S. Average	59,539	–	60,477	–	1.58	–

Note: (1) Rank ranges from 1 to 51 where 1 indicates highest salary; (2) Rank ranges from 1 to 51 where 1 indicates highest percent change.
Source: National Education Association, Rankings & Estimates: Rankings of the States 2018 and Estimates of School Statistics 2019

Higher Education

Four-Year Colleges			Two-Year Colleges			Medical Schools[1]	Law Schools[2]	Voc/ Tech[3]
Public	Private Non-profit	Private For-profit	Public	Private Non-profit	Private For-profit			
1	1	1	1	0	0	0	0	1

Note: Figures cover institutions located within the city limits and include main campuses only; (1) includes schools accredited by the Liaison Committee on Medical Education and the American Osteopathic Association's Commission on Osteopathic College Accreditation; (2) includes ABA-accredited schools, schools with provisional ABA accreditation, and state accredited schools; (3) includes all schools with programs that are less than 2 years.
Source: National Center for Education Statistics, Integrated Postsecondary Education System (IPEDS), 2018-19; Wikipedia, List of Medical Schools in the United States, accessed May 1, 2020; Wikipedia, List of Law Schools in the United States, accessed May 1, 2020

PRESIDENTIAL ELECTION

2016 Presidential Election Results

Area	Clinton	Trump	Johnson	Stein	Other
Brown County	41.4	52.1	3.9	1.1	1.6
U.S.	48.0	45.9	3.3	1.1	1.7

Note: Results are percentages and may not add to 100% due to rounding
Source: Dave Leip's Atlas of U.S. Presidential Elections

EMPLOYERS

Major Employers

Company Name	Industry
American Foods Group	Food manufacturing
APAC Customer Services	Business management
Associated Bank	Financial services
Aurora Health Care	Healthcare
Bellin Health	Healthcare
Georgia-Pacific	Paper manufacturing
Green Bay Packaging	Paper manufacturing
Green Bay Packers	NFL franchise
H.J. Martin and Son	Interior design
JBS	Food manufacturing
Nicolet National Bank	Financial services
Procter & Gamble Paper Products	Paper manufacturing
Schreiber Foods	Food manufacturing
Schwabe North America	Health products
St. Mary's Hospital Medical Center	Healthcare
St. Vincent Hospital	Healthcare
Wal-Mart Stores	Retail
Wisconsin Public Service	Utilities

Note: Companies shown are located within the Green Bay, WI Metropolitan Statistical Area.
Source: Hoovers.com; Wikipedia

PUBLIC SAFETY

Crime Rate

Area	All Crimes	Violent Crimes				Property Crimes		
		Murder	Rape[3]	Robbery	Aggrav. Assault	Burglary	Larceny -Theft	Motor Vehicle Theft
City	2,166.6	0.9	74.1	53.2	330.5	237.5	1,375.4	95.0
Suburbs[1]	972.5	0.0	34.1	4.2	50.3	105.6	737.3	41.0
Metro[2]	1,362.7	0.3	47.2	20.2	141.9	148.7	945.8	58.7
U.S.	2,580.1	5.0	42.6	86.2	246.8	376.0	1,594.6	228.9

Note: Figures are crimes per 100,000 population; (1) All areas within the metro area that are located outside the city limits; (2) Figures cover the Green Bay, WI Metropolitan Statistical Area—see Appendix B for areas included; (3) The city and U.S. figures shown were reported using the revised Uniform Crime Reporting (UCR) definition of rape. The suburban and metro area figures shown are an aggregate total of the data submitted using both the revised and legacy UCR definitions.
Source: FBI Uniform Crime Reports, 2018

Hate Crimes

Area	Number of Quarters Reported	Number of Incidents per Bias Motivation					
		Race/Ethnicity/ Ancestry	Religion	Sexual Orientation	Disability	Gender	Gender Identity
City	4	0	0	0	0	0	0
U.S.	4	4,047	1,419	1,196	159	47	168

Source: Federal Bureau of Investigation, Hate Crime Statistics 2018

Identity Theft Consumer Reports

Area	Reports	Reports per 100,000 Population	Rank[2]
MSA[1]	249	77	262
U.S.	650,572	198	-

Note: (1) Figures cover the Green Bay, WI Metropolitan Statistical Area—see Appendix B for areas included; (2) Rank ranges from 1 to 386 where 1 indicates greatest number of identity theft reports per 100,000 population
Source: Federal Trade Commission, Consumer Sentinel Network Data Book for January–December 2019

Fraud and Other Consumer Reports

Area	Reports	Reports per 100,000 Population	Rank[2]
MSA[1]	1,566	487	264
U.S.	2,590,177	789	-

Note: (1) Figures cover the Green Bay, WI Metropolitan Statistical Area—see Appendix B for areas included; (2) Rank ranges from 1 to 386 where 1 indicates greatest number of fraud and other consumer reports per 100,000 population
Source: Federal Trade Commission, Consumer Sentinel Network Data Book for January–December 2019

SPORTS

Professional Sports Teams

Team Name	League	Year Established
Green Bay Packers	National Football League (NFL)	1921

Note: Includes teams located in the Green Bay, WI Metropolitan Statistical Area.
Source: Wikipedia, Major Professional Sports Teams of the United States and Canada, May 4, 2020

CLIMATE

Average and Extreme Temperatures

Temperature	Jan	Feb	Mar	Apr	May	Jun	Jul	Aug	Sep	Oct	Nov	Dec	Yr.
Extreme High (°F)	50	55	77	89	91	98	99	99	95	88	72	62	99
Average High (°F)	23	27	38	54	67	76	81	78	70	58	42	28	54
Average Temp. (°F)	15	19	29	44	55	65	70	68	59	48	34	21	44
Average Low (°F)	6	10	21	34	44	53	58	56	48	38	26	13	34
Extreme Low (°F)	-31	-26	-29	7	21	32	40	38	24	15	-9	-27	-31

Note: Figures cover the years 1949-1990
Source: National Climatic Data Center, International Station Meteorological Climate Summary, 9/96

Average Precipitation/Snowfall/Humidity

Precip./Humidity	Jan	Feb	Mar	Apr	May	Jun	Jul	Aug	Sep	Oct	Nov	Dec	Yr.
Avg. Precip. (in.)	1.1	1.1	1.9	2.6	2.9	3.2	3.3	3.3	3.2	2.2	2.0	1.4	28.3
Avg. Snowfall (in.)	11	8	9	2	Tr	0	0	0	Tr	Tr	5	11	46
Avg. Rel. Hum. 6am (%)	77	79	81	79	79	82	86	90	89	85	82	80	83
Avg. Rel. Hum. 3pm (%)	68	65	63	54	52	55	55	58	59	59	67	71	60

Note: Figures cover the years 1949-1990; Tr = Trace amounts (<0.05 in. of rain; <0.5 in. of snow)
Source: National Climatic Data Center, International Station Meteorological Climate Summary, 9/96

Weather Conditions

Temperature			Daytime Sky			Precipitation		
5°F & below	32°F & below	90°F & above	Clear	Partly cloudy	Cloudy	0.01 inch or more precip.	0.1 inch or more snow/ice	Thunder-storms
39	163	7	86	125	154	120	40	33

Note: Figures are average number of days per year and cover the years 1949-1990
Source: National Climatic Data Center, International Station Meteorological Climate Summary, 9/96

HAZARDOUS WASTE

Superfund Sites

The Green Bay, WI metro area is home to three sites on the EPA's Superfund National Priorities List: **Algoma Municipal Landfill** (final); **Better Brite Plating Co. Chrome and Zinc Shops** (final); **Fox River Nrda/Pcb Releases** (proposed). There are a total of 1,387 Superfund sites with a status of proposed or final on the list in the U.S. *U.S. Environmental Protection Agency, National Priorities List, May 5, 2020*

**AIR & WATER
QUALITY**

Air Quality Trends: Ozone

	1990	1995	2000	2005	2010	2012	2014	2016	2017	2018
MSA[1]	n/a	n/a	n/a	n/a	n/a	n/a	n/a	n/a	n/a	n/a
U.S.	0.088	0.089	0.082	0.080	0.073	0.075	0.067	0.069	0.068	0.069

Note: (1) Data covers the Green Bay, WI Metropolitan Statistical Area—see Appendix B for areas included; n/a not available. The values shown are the composite ozone concentration averages among trend sites based on the highest fourth daily maximum 8-hour concentration in parts per million. These trends are based on sites having an adequate record of monitoring data during the trend period. Data from exceptional events are included.
Source: U.S. Environmental Protection Agency, Air Quality Monitoring Information, "Air Quality Trends by City, 1990-2018"

Air Quality Index

Area	Percent of Days when Air Quality was...[2]					AQI Statistics[2]	
	Good	Moderate	Unhealthy for Sensitive Groups	Unhealthy	Very Unhealthy	Maximum	Median
MSA[1]	78.9	19.5	1.4	0.3	0.0	151	41

Note: (1) Data covers the Green Bay, WI Metropolitan Statistical Area—see Appendix B for areas included; (2) Based on 365 days with AQI data in 2018. Air Quality Index (AQI) is an index for reporting daily air quality. EPA calculates the AQI for five major air pollutants regulated by the Clean Air Act: ground-level ozone, particle pollution (aka particulate matter), carbon monoxide, sulfur dioxide, and nitrogen dioxide. The AQI runs from 0 to 500. The higher the AQI value, the greater the level of air pollution and the greater the health concern. There are six AQI categories: "Good" AQI is between 0 and 50. Air quality is considered satisfactory; "Moderate" AQI is between 51 and 100. Air quality is acceptable; "Unhealthy for Sensitive Groups" When AQI values are between 101 and 150, members of sensitive groups may experience health effects; "Unhealthy" When AQI values are between 151 and 200 everyone may begin to experience health effects; "Very Unhealthy" AQI values between 201 and 300 trigger a health alert; "Hazardous" AQI values over 300 trigger warnings of emergency conditions (not shown).
Source: U.S. Environmental Protection Agency, Air Quality Index Report, 2018

Air Quality Index Pollutants

Area	Percent of Days when AQI Pollutant was...[2]					
	Carbon Monoxide	Nitrogen Dioxide	Ozone	Sulfur Dioxide	Particulate Matter 2.5	Particulate Matter 10
MSA[1]	0.0	0.0	61.1	1.9	37.0	0.0

Note: (1) Data covers the Green Bay, WI Metropolitan Statistical Area—see Appendix B for areas included; (2) Based on 365 days with AQI data in 2018. The Air Quality Index (AQI) is an index for reporting daily air quality. EPA calculates the AQI for five major air pollutants regulated by the Clean Air Act: ground-level ozone, particle pollution (also known as particulate matter), carbon monoxide, sulfur dioxide, and nitrogen dioxide. The AQI runs from 0 to 500. The higher the AQI value, the greater the level of air pollution and the greater the health concern.
Source: U.S. Environmental Protection Agency, Air Quality Index Report, 2018

Maximum Air Pollutant Concentrations: Particulate Matter, Ozone, CO and Lead

	Particulate Matter 10 (ug/m^3)	Particulate Matter 2.5 Wtd AM (ug/m^3)	Particulate Matter 2.5 24-Hr (ug/m^3)	Ozone (ppm)	Carbon Monoxide (ppm)	Lead (ug/m^3)
MSA[1] Level	n/a	6.4	19	0.072	n/a	n/a
NAAQS[2]	150	15	35	0.075	9	0.15
Met NAAQS[2]	n/a	Yes	Yes	Yes	n/a	n/a

Note: (1) Data covers the Green Bay, WI Metropolitan Statistical Area—see Appendix B for areas included; Data from exceptional events are included; (2) National Ambient Air Quality Standards; ppm = parts per million; ug/m³ = micrograms per cubic meter; n/a not available.
Concentrations: Particulate Matter 10 (coarse particulate)—highest second maximum 24-hour concentration; Particulate Matter 2.5 Wtd AM (fine particulate)—highest weighted annual mean concentration; Particulate Matter 2.5 24-Hour (fine particulate)—highest 98th percentile 24-hour concentration; Ozone—highest fourth daily maximum 8-hour concentration; Carbon Monoxide—highest second maximum non-overlapping 8-hour concentration; Lead—maximum running 3-month average
Source: U.S. Environmental Protection Agency, Air Quality Monitoring Information, "Air Quality Statistics by City, 2018"

Maximum Air Pollutant Concentrations: Nitrogen Dioxide and Sulfur Dioxide

	Nitrogen Dioxide AM (ppb)	Nitrogen Dioxide 1-Hr (ppb)	Sulfur Dioxide AM (ppb)	Sulfur Dioxide 1-Hr (ppb)	Sulfur Dioxide 24-Hr (ppb)
MSA[1] Level	n/a	n/a	n/a	12	n/a
NAAQS[2]	53	100	30	75	140
Met NAAQS[2]	n/a	n/a	n/a	Yes	n/a

Note: (1) Data covers the Green Bay, WI Metropolitan Statistical Area—see Appendix B for areas included; Data from exceptional events are included; (2) National Ambient Air Quality Standards; ppm = parts per million; ug/m³ = micrograms per cubic meter; n/a not available.
Concentrations: Nitrogen Dioxide AM—highest arithmetic mean concentration; Nitrogen Dioxide 1-Hr—highest 98th percentile 1-hour daily maximum concentration; Sulfur Dioxide AM—highest annual mean concentration; Sulfur Dioxide 1-Hr—highest 99th percentile 1-hour daily maximum concentration; Sulfur Dioxide 24-Hr—highest second maximum 24-hour concentration
Source: U.S. Environmental Protection Agency, Air Quality Monitoring Information, "Air Quality Statistics by City, 2018"

Drinking Water

Water System Name	Pop. Served	Primary Water Source Type	Violations[1]
Green Bay Waterworks	104,057	Surface	6

Note: (1) Total number of violations (both active and inactive) in the EPA database
Source: U.S. Environmental Protection Agency, Office of Ground Water and Drinking Water, Safe Drinking Water Information System (based on data extracted May 5, 2020)

Indianapolis, Indiana

Background

Indianapolis sits within the boundaries of the Northern manufacturing belt and the midwestern Corn Belt, and its economy reflects both influences. On one side lies the Indianapolis industrial sector, including transportation, airplane and truck parts, paper and rubber products, and computer software. On the other side lies agriculture. Indianapolis is a leading grain market, as well as the largest meat-processing center outside of Chicago.

Despite pollution and other problems of urban decay in the late twentieth century, Indianapolis has made significant strides in this area, completing dozens of major downtown projects, including Dolphin Adventure at the Indianapolis Zoo, Eiteljorg Museum of American Indians and Western Art expansion, Eli Lilly and Company Insulin Finishing Building, the Indianapolis Museum of Art expansion, and Circle Centre, a retail and entertainment complex that draws one million visitors a month.

Known as the "Crossroads of America," Indianapolis is bisected by more interstate highways than any other city in the nation, making it accessible from many locations and within a day's drive of half the country's population. As a result, the city is a popular choice for conventions and offers excellent facilities at the Indiana Convention Center & RCA Dome. The Indianapolis Artsgarden, offering more than 300 free performances and exhibits each year, is linked to the Convention Center by a skywalk, and is a world-class venue for the arts.

The city is home to one of the finest children's museums in the United States, and its 85 parks offer many outdoor activities.

Indianapolis has been called by many the rising food star of the Midwest, with top-notch restaurants in the Fletcher Place neighborhood and a number of city chefs and restaurateurs recent semifinalists in the James Beard Foundation Awards. Microbreweries are a staple in the city, with more than 50 craft brewers.

Known as the "Racing Capital of the World," Indianapolis hosts the world's three biggest single-day sporting events at the world-famous Indianapolis Motor Speedway: Indy 500; Brickyard 400; and SAP United States Grand Prix. The National Collegiate Athletic Association is also in Indianapolis, as is the NCAA Hall of Champions. Housing divisions of both Indiana and Purdue Universities make for a lively learning center.

Indianapolis's Conseco Fieldhouse hosted the Big Ten college basketball tournament from 2008 through 2012. The city hosted the Women's NCAA basketball tournament Final Fours in 2011 and 2016, and the 2012 Super Bowl.

The Indianapolis Art Museum is one of the largest general museums in the United States. Collections include works of Gaugin, Seurat, and Turner. The museum has integrated its galleries with other properties on its campus, including the Virginia B. Fairbanks Art & Nature Park and the Oldfields-Lilly House.

Indianapolis was initially planned by Alexander Ralston, the American engineer who assisted French architect Pierre L'Enfant in planning Washington, D.C. Thus, like the nation's capital, Indianapolis is laid out on a mile-square grid and is easily navigable. Its centerpiece is Monument Circle, home of the 284-foot Soldiers and Sailors Monument, with a 32-story panoramic view of the Indianapolis skyline.

Indianapolis has a temperate climate, with very warm summers and no dry season. Very cold winter weather sometime occurs with the invasion of continental polar air from northern latitudes. In the summer, tropical air from the Gulf of Mexico brings warm temperatures and moderate humidity.

Rankings

General Rankings

- In its eighth annual survey, *Travel + Leisure* readers nominated their favorite small cities and towns in America—those with 100,000 or fewer residents—voting on numerous attractive features in categories including culture, food and drink, quality of life, style, and people. After 50,000 votes, Indianapolis was ranked #7 among the proposed favorites. *www.travelandleisure.com, "America's Favorite Cities," October 20, 2017*

- In their sixth annual survey, Livability.com looked at data for more than 1,000 U.S. cities to determine the rankings for Livability's "Top 100 Best Places to Live" in 2019. Indianapolis ranked #75. Criteria: median home value capped at $250,000; affordable living; vibrant economy; education, demographics, health care options. transportation & infrastructure; abundant lifestyle amenities. *Livability.com, "Top 100 Best Places to Live 2019" March 2019*

Business/Finance Rankings

- Based on metro area social media reviews, the employment opinion group Glassdoor surveyed 50 of the most populous U.S. metro areas and equally weighed cost of living, hiring opportunity, and job satisfaction to compose a list of "25 Best Cities for Jobs." Median pay and home value, and number of active job openings was also factored in. The Indianapolis metro area was ranked #3 in overall job satisfaction. *www.glassdoor.com, "Best Cities for Jobs," February 25, 2020*

- The Brookings Institution ranked the nation's largest cities based on income inequality. Indianapolis was ranked #72 (#1 = greatest inequality). Criteria: the "95/20 ratio," a figure representing the income at which a household earns more than 95 percent of all other households, divided by the income at which a household earns more than only 20 percent of all other households. *Brookings Institution, "Household Income Inequality, Largest Cities of 97 Large U.S. Metro Areas, 2014-2016," February 5, 2018*

- The Brookings Institution ranked the 100 largest metro areas in the U.S. based on income inequality. Indianapolis was ranked #58 (#1 = greatest inequality). Criteria: the "95/20 ratio," a figure representing the income at which a household earns more than 95 percent of all other households, divided by the income at which a household earns more than only 20 percent of all other households. *Brookings Institution, "Household Income Inequality, 100 Largest U.S. Metro Areas, 2014-2016," February 5, 2018*

- *Forbes* ranked the 100 largest metro areas in the U.S. in terms of the "Best Cities for Young Professionals." The Indianapolis metro area ranked #11 out of 25. (Large metro areas were divided into metro divisions.) Criteria: median rent of a two-bedroom apartment; job growth and unemployment rate; median salary of college graduates with 5 or less years of work experience; networking opportunities; social outlook; percentage of population 25 years of age and older with college degrees. *Forbes.com, "America's 25 Best Cities for Young Professionals in 2017," May 22, 2017*

- Indianapolis was identified as one of America's most frugal metro areas by *Coupons.com*. The city ranked #17 out of 25. Criteria: digital coupon usage. *Coupons.com, "America's Most Frugal Cities of 2017," March 22, 2018*

- Indianapolis was cited as one of America's top metros for new and expanded facility projects in 2019. The area ranked #9 in the large metro area category (population over 1 million). *Site Selection, "Top Metros of 2019," March 2020*

- Indianapolis was identified as one of the happiest cities to work in by CareerBliss.com, an online community for career advancement. The city ranked #7 out of 10. Criteria: an employee's relationship with his or her boss and co-workers; daily tasks; general work environment; compensation; opportunities for advancement; company culture and job reputation; and resources. *Businesswire.com, "CareerBliss Happiest Cities to Work 2019," February 12, 2019*

- The Indianapolis metro area appeared on the Milken Institute "2020 Best Performing Cities" list. Rank: #106 out of 200 large metro areas. Criteria: job growth; wage and salary growth; high-tech output growth. *Milken Institute, "Best-Performing Cities 2020," February 26, 2020*

- *Forbes* ranked the 200 most populous metro areas to determine the nation's "Best Places for Business and Careers." The Indianapolis metro area was ranked #58. Criteria: costs (business and living); job growth (past and projected); income growth; quality of life; educational attainment (college and high school); projected economic growth; cultural and leisure opportunities; workplace tolerance laws; net migration patterns. *Forbes, "The Best Places for Business and Careers 2019: Seattle Still On Top," October 30, 2019*

Education Rankings

- Personal finance website *WalletHub* analyzed the 150 largest U.S. metropolitan statistical areas to determine where the most educated Americans are choosing to settle. Criteria: education levels; percentage of workers with degrees; education quality and attainment gap; public school quality rankings; quality and size of each metro area's universities. Indianapolis was ranked #70 (#1 = most educated city). *www.WalletHub.com, "2019's Most and Least Educated Cities in America, " July 22, 2019*

- Indianapolis was selected as one of the most well-read cities in America by Amazon.com. The city ranked #18 among the top 20. Cities with populations greater than 500,000 were evaluated based on per capita sales of books, magazines and newspapers (both print and Kindle format). *Amazon.com, "The 20 Most Well-Read Cities in America," May 24, 2016*

- Indianapolis was selected as one of America's most literate cities. The city ranked #29 out of the 82 largest U.S. cities. Criteria: number of booksellers; library resources; Internet resources; educational attainment; periodical publishing resources; newspaper circulation. *Central Connecticut State University, "America's Most Literate Cities, 2016," March 31, 2017*

Environmental Rankings

- The U.S. Environmental Protection Agency (EPA) released a list of U.S. metropolitan areas with the most ENERGY STAR certified buildings in 2017. The Indianapolis metro area was ranked #24 out of 25. *U.S. Environmental Protection Agency, "2018 Energy Star Top Cities," April 11, 2018*

- Indianapolis was highlighted as one of the 25 metro areas most polluted by year-round particle pollution (Annual PM 2.5) in the U.S. during 2015 through 2017. The area ranked #19. *American Lung Association, "State of the Air 2019," April 24, 2019*

Food/Drink Rankings

- The U.S. Chamber of Commerce Foundation conducted an in-depth study on local food truck regulations, surveyed 288 food truck owners, and ranked 20 major American cities based on how friendly they are for operating a food truck. The compiled index assessed the following: procedures for obtaining permits and licenses; complying with restrictions; and financial obligations associated with operating a food truck. Indianapolis ranked #5 overall (1 being the best) for ease in operating a food truck. *www.foodtrucknation.us, "Food Truck Nation," March 20, 2018*

Health/Fitness Rankings

- For each of the 100 largest cities in the United States, the American Fitness Index®, published by the American College of Sports Medicine and the Anthem Foundation, evaluated community infrastructure and 33 health behaviors including preventive health, levels of chronic disease conditions, pedestrian safety, air quality, and community resources that support physical activity. Indianapolis ranked #96 for "community fitness." *americanfitnessindex.org, "ACSM American Fitness Index Health and Community Fitness Status of the 100 Largest U.S. Cities," May 14, 2019*

- The Indianapolis metro area was identified as one of the worst cities for bed bugs in America by pest control company Orkin. The area ranked #9 out of 50 based on the number of bed bug treatments Orkin performed from December 2018 to November 2019. *Orkin, "Washington, D.C. Surpasses Baltimore to Secure Top Spot on Orkin's 2020 Bed Bug Cities List," January 13, 2020*

- Indianapolis was identified as a "2020 Spring Allergy Capital." The area ranked #75 out of 100. Three groups of factors were used to identify the most challenging cities for people with allergies during the spring season: annual spring pollen levels; over the counter medicine use; number of board-certified allergy specialists. *Asthma and Allergy Foundation of America, "Spring Allergy Capitals 2020," March 10, 2020*

- Indianapolis was identified as a "2020 Fall Allergy Capital." The area ranked #65 out of 100. Three groups of factors were used to identify the most challenging cities for people with allergies during the fall season: annual fall pollen levels; over the counter medicine use; number of board-certified allergy specialists. *Asthma and Allergy Foundation of America, "Fall Allergy Capitals 2020," March 10, 2020*

- Indianapolis was identified as a "2019 Asthma Capital." The area ranked #48 out of the nation's 100 largest metropolitan areas. Criteria: estimated asthma prevalence; crude death rate from asthma; and ER visits due to asthma. Risk factors that were analyzed but not factored in the rankings: annual pollen score; annual air quality; public smoking laws; number of board-certified asthma specialists; rescue medication use; controller medication use; uninsured rate; poverty rate. *Asthma and Allergy Foundation of America, "Asthma Capitals 2019: The Most Challenging Places to Live With Asthma," May 7, 2019*

- *Men's Health* ranked 100 major U.S. cities in terms of the best cities for men. Indianapolis ranked #91. Criteria: health; fitness; quality of life. *Men's Health, "The Best & Worst Cities for Men Who Want to Be Fit and Happy," January 1, 2016*

- The Indianapolis metro area ranked #133 out of 189 in The Gallup-Sharecare Well-Being Index. Criteria: purpose; social well being; financial health; community and physical health. Results are based on telephone interviews with adults, aged 18 and older, living in metropolitan areas in the 50 U.S. states and the District of Columbia. *Gallup-Sharecare, "State of American Well-Being, 2017 Community Well-Being Rankings" March 2018*

Real Estate Rankings

- *WalletHub* compared the most populated U.S. cities, as well as at least two of the most populated cities in each state, for a total of 179, to determine which had the best markets for real estate agents. Indianapolis ranked #142 where demand was high and pay was the best. Criteria: sales per agent; annual median wage for real-estate agents; monthly average starting salary for real estate agents; real estate job density and competition; unemployment rate; home turnover rate; housing-market health index; and other relevant metrics. *www.WalletHub.com, "2019's Best Places to Be a Real Estate Agent," April 24, 2019*

- The Indianapolis metro area was identified as one of the top 20 housing markets to invest in for 2019 by *Forbes*. Criteria: strong job and population growth; stable local economy; anticipated home price appreciation; and other factors. *Forbes.com, "The Best Markets for Real Estate Investments In 2019," January 7, 2019*

- Indianapolis was ranked #6 in the top 20 out of the 100 largest metro areas in terms of house price appreciation in 2019 (#1 = highest rate). *Federal Housing Finance Agency, House Price Index, 4th Quarter 2019*

- The Indianapolis metro area was identified as one of the 10 best condo markets in the U.S. in 2019. The area ranked #3 out of 61 markets. Criteria: year-over-year change of median sales price of existing apartment condo-coop homes between the 4th quarter of 2018 and the 4th quarter of 2019. *National Association of Realtors®, Median Sales Price of Existing Apartment Condo-Coops Homes for Metropolitan Areas, 4th Quarter 2019*

- Indianapolis was ranked #12 out of 238 metro areas in terms of housing affordability in 2019 by the National Association of Home Builders (#1 = most affordable). Criteria: the share of homes sold in that area affordable to a family earning the local median income, based on standard mortgage underwriting criteria. *National Association of Home Builders®, NAHB-Wells Fargo Housing Opportunity Index, 4th Quarter 2019*

Safety Rankings

- To identify the most dangerous cities in America, 24/7 Wall Street focused on violent crime categories—murder, non-negligent manslaughter, rape, robbery, and aggravated assault—and property crime as reported in the FBI's 2018 annual Uniform Crime Report. Criteria also included median income from American Community Survey and unemployment figures from Bureau of Labor Statistics. For cities with populations over 100,000, Indianapolis was ranked #17. *247wallst.com, "America's Most Dangerous Cities" January 10, 2020*

- Allstate ranked the 200 largest cities in America in terms of driver safety. Indianapolis ranked #75. Criteria: internal property damage claims over a two-year period from January 2016 to December 2017. The report helps increase the importance of safety and awareness behind the wheel. *Allstate, "Allstate America's Best Drivers Report, 2019" June 24, 2019*

- Indianapolis was identified as one of the most dangerous cities in America by NeighborhoodScout. The city ranked #31 out of 100 (#1 = most dangerous). Criteria: number of violent crimes per 1,000 residents. The editors only considered cities with 25,000 or more residents. *NeighborhoodScout.com, "Top 100 Most Dangerous Cities in the U.S. 2020" January 2, 2020*

- The National Insurance Crime Bureau ranked 382 metro areas in the U.S. in terms of per capita rates of vehicle theft. The Indianapolis metro area ranked #50 (#1 = highest rate). Criteria: number of vehicle theft offenses per 100,000 inhabitants in 2018. *National Insurance Crime Bureau, "Hot Spots 2018," June 25, 2019*

Seniors/Retirement Rankings

- From its Best Cities for Successful Aging indexes, the Milken Institute generated rankings for metropolitan areas, weighing data in nine categories—health care, wellness, living arrangements, transportation and convenience, financial characteristics, education, employment, community engagement, and overall livability. The Indianapolis metro area was ranked #44 overall in the large metro area category. *Milken Institute, "Best Cities for Successful Aging, 2017" March 14, 2017*

Sports/Recreation Rankings

- Indianapolis was selected as one of "America's Most Miserable Sports Cities" by *Forbes*. The city was ranked #10. Criteria: postseason losses/misery; years since last title; and number of teams lost to relocation. Contenders were limited to cities with at least 75 cumulative pro seasons of NFL, NBA, NHL, MLS and MLB play. *Forbes, "America's Most Miserable Sports Cities 2016," April 20, 2016*

- Indianapolis was chosen as a bicycle friendly community by the League of American Bicyclists. A "Bicycle Friendly Community" welcomes cyclists by providing safe and supportive accommodation for cycling and encouraging people to bike for transportation and recreation. There are five award levels: Diamond; Platinum; Gold; Silver; and Bronze. The community achieved an award level of Bronze. *League of American Bicyclists, "Fall 2019 Awards-Bicycle Friendly Community Master List," November 21, 2019*

- Indianapolis was chosen as one of America's best cities for bicycling. The city ranked #30 out of 50. Criteria: cycling infrastructure that is safe and friendly for all ages; energy and bike culture. The editors only considered cities with populations of 100,000 or more. *Bicycling, "The 50 Best Bike Cities in America," October 10, 2018*

Women/Minorities Rankings

- Personal finance website *WalletHub* compared more than 180 U.S. cities—including the 150 most populated U.S. cities, plus at least two of the most populated cities in each state—across two key dimensions, "Hispanic Business-Friendliness" and "Hispanic Purchasing Power", to arrive at the most favorable conditions for Hispanic entrepreneurs. Indianapolis was ranked #121 out of 182. Criteria includes: share of Hispanic-Owned Businesses; Hispanic entrepreneurship rate to median annual income of Hispanics; Small Business-Friendliness score; cost of living; and number of Hispanics with at least a bachelor's degree. *WalletHub.com, "2019's Best Cities for Hispanic Entrepreneurs," May 1, 2019*

Miscellaneous Rankings

- Based on the advice of plugged-in travel influencers and experts, Indianapolis appeared on a *Forbes* list of 25 U.S. cities that should be on anyone's travel wish list. Whether it be quirky things to see and do, historic cities, or mountain getaways, these places are emerging as must-see destinations. *Forbes, "U.S. Travel: 25 Best Places to Visit in 2020," December 19, 2019*

- The watchdog site Charity Navigator conducts an annual study of charities in the nation's major markets both to analyze statistical differences in their financial, accountability, and transparency practices and to track year-to-year variations in individual philanthropic communities. Charity Navigator's analysis demonstrated that the financial, accountability and transparency behaviors of America's largest charities can be influenced by the metropolitan market within which the charity operates. The Indianapolis metro area was ranked #29 among the 30 metro markets in the rating category of Overall Score. *www.charitynavigator.org, "2017 Metro Market Study," May 1, 2017*

- *WalletHub* compared the 150 most populated U.S. cities to determine their operating efficiency. A "Quality of Services" score was constructed for each city and then divided by the total budget per capita to reveal which were managed the best. Indianapolis ranked #99. Criteria: financial stability; economy; education; safety; health; infrastructure and pollution. *www.WalletHub.com, "2019's Best- & Worst-Run Cities in America," July 1, 2019*

- Indianapolis was selected as one of "America's Friendliest Cities." The city ranked #6 in the "Friendliest" category. Respondents to an online survey were asked to rate 38 top urban destinations in the United States as to general friendliness, as well as manners, politeness and warm disposition. *Travel + Leisure, "America's Friendliest Cities," October 20, 2017*

Business Environment

CITY FINANCES

City Government Finances

Component	2017 ($000)	2017 ($ per capita)
Total Revenues	3,565,593	4,179
Total Expenditures	3,331,544	3,905
Debt Outstanding	3,572,605	4,187
Cash and Securities[1]	2,775,016	3,253

Note: (1) Cash and security holdings of a government at the close of its fiscal year, including those of its dependent agencies, utilities, and liquor stores.
Source: U.S. Census Bureau, State & Local Government Finances 2017

City Government Revenue by Source

Source	2017 ($000)	2017 ($ per capita)	2017 (%)
General Revenue			
From Federal Government	116,677	137	3.3
From State Government	569,241	667	16.0
From Local Governments	233,296	273	6.5
Taxes			
Property	280,887	329	7.9
Sales and Gross Receipts	0	0	0.0
Personal Income	138,814	163	3.9
Corporate Income	0	0	0.0
Motor Vehicle License	0	0	0.0
Other Taxes	4,944	6	0.1
Current Charges	1,539,093	1,804	43.2
Liquor Store	0	0	0.0
Utility	528,130	619	14.8
Employee Retirement	28,968	34	0.8

Source: U.S. Census Bureau, State & Local Government Finances 2017

City Government Expenditures by Function

Function	2017 ($000)	2017 ($ per capita)	2017 (%)
General Direct Expenditures			
Air Transportation	107,339	125	3.2
Corrections	142,805	167	4.3
Education	0	0	0.0
Employment Security Administration	0	0	0.0
Financial Administration	18,767	22	0.6
Fire Protection	158,006	185	4.7
General Public Buildings	0	0	0.0
Governmental Administration, Other	19,952	23	0.6
Health	105,846	124	3.2
Highways	0	0	0.0
Hospitals	1,217,062	1,426	36.5
Housing and Community Development	0	0	0.0
Interest on General Debt	203,833	238	6.1
Judicial and Legal	103,854	121	3.1
Libraries	0	0	0.0
Parking	0	0	0.0
Parks and Recreation	83,254	97	2.5
Police Protection	220,425	258	6.6
Public Welfare	0	0	0.0
Sewerage	0	0	0.0
Solid Waste Management	44,390	52	1.3
Veterans' Services	0	0	0.0
Liquor Store	0	0	0.0
Utility	857,838	1,005	25.7
Employee Retirement	11,648	13	0.3

Source: U.S. Census Bureau, State & Local Government Finances 2017

DEMOGRAPHICS

Population Growth

Area	1990 Census	2000 Census	2010 Census	2018* Estimate	Population Growth (%) 1990-2018	Population Growth (%) 2010-2018
City	730,993	781,870	820,445	857,637	17.3	4.5
MSA[1]	1,294,217	1,525,104	1,756,241	2,007,497	55.1	14.3
U.S.	248,709,873	281,421,906	308,745,538	322,903,030	29.8	4.6

Note: (1) Figures cover the Indianapolis-Carmel-Anderson, IN Metropolitan Statistical Area—see Appendix B for areas included; (*) 2014-2018 5-year estimated population
Source: U.S. Census Bureau, 1990 Census, Census 2000, Census 2010, 2014-2018 American Community Survey 5-Year Estimates

Household Size

Area	One	Two	Three	Four	Five	Six	Seven or More	Average Household Size
City	36.9	31.4	13.6	10.3	4.8	1.9	1.1	2.50
MSA[1]	29.5	33.5	15.2	13.0	5.7	2.0	1.0	2.60
U.S.	27.7	33.9	15.7	13.0	6.0	2.3	1.4	2.60

Note: (1) Figures cover the Indianapolis-Carmel-Anderson, IN Metropolitan Statistical Area—see Appendix B for areas included
Source: U.S. Census Bureau, 2014-2018 American Community Survey 5-Year Estimates

Race

Area	White Alone[2] (%)	Black Alone[2] (%)	Asian Alone[2] (%)	AIAN[3] Alone[2] (%)	NHOPI[4] Alone[2] (%)	Other Race Alone[2] (%)	Two or More Races (%)
City	61.4	28.3	3.2	0.3	0.1	3.5	3.2
MSA[1]	77.1	15.1	3.1	0.2	0.0	2.0	2.6
U.S.	72.7	12.7	5.4	0.8	0.2	4.9	3.2

Note: (1) Figures cover the Indianapolis-Carmel-Anderson, IN Metropolitan Statistical Area—see Appendix B for areas included; (2) Alone is defined as not being in combination with one or more other races; (3) American Indian and Alaska Native; (4) Native Hawaiian and Other Pacific Islander
Source: U.S. Census Bureau, 2014-2018 American Community Survey 5-Year Estimates

Hispanic or Latino Origin

Area	Total (%)	Mexican (%)	Puerto Rican (%)	Cuban (%)	Other (%)
City	10.2	7.2	0.6	0.1	2.4
MSA[1]	6.6	4.5	0.4	0.1	1.6
U.S.	17.8	11.2	1.7	0.7	4.2

Note: Persons of Hispanic or Latino origin can be of any race; (1) Figures cover the Indianapolis-Carmel-Anderson, IN Metropolitan Statistical Area—see Appendix B for areas included
Source: U.S. Census Bureau, 2014-2018 American Community Survey 5-Year Estimates

Segregation

Type	1990	2000	2010	2010 Rank[2]	1990-2000	1990-2010	2000-2010
Black/White	74.4	72.1	66.4	15	-2.4	-8.0	-5.7
Asian/White	37.8	40.6	41.6	47	2.9	3.9	1.0
Hispanic/White	25.8	43.8	47.3	37	18.0	21.5	3.5

Note: All figures cover the Metropolitan Statistical Area—see Appendix B for areas included; Figures are based on an analysis of 1990, 2000, and 2010 Census Decennial Census tract data by William H. Frey, Brookings Institution and the University of Michigan Social Science Data Analysis Network. In this analysis all racial groups (whites, blacks, and asians) are non-Hispanic members of those races. Hispanics are shown as a separate category; (1) Segregation Indices are Dissimilarity Indices that measure the degree to which the minority group is distributed differently than whites across census tracts. They range from 0 (complete integration) to 100 (complete segregation) where the value indicates the percentage of the minority group that needs to move to be distributed exactly like whites; (2) Ranges from 1 (most segregated) to 102 (least segregated); n/a not available.
Source: www.CensusScope.org

Ancestry

Area	German	Irish	English	American	Italian	Polish	French[2]	Scottish	Dutch
City	14.5	8.9	6.1	6.0	2.2	1.5	1.6	1.5	1.1
MSA[1]	18.6	10.4	8.0	9.5	2.6	2.0	1.9	1.8	1.5
U.S.	13.7	9.9	7.3	6.4	5.2	2.8	2.4	1.7	1.2

Note: Figures are the percentage of the total population reporting a particular ancestry. The nine most commonly reported ancestries in the U.S. are shown. Figures include multiple ancestries (e.g. if a person reported being Irish and Italian, they were included in both columns); (1) Figures cover the Indianapolis-Carmel-Anderson, IN Metropolitan Statistical Area—see Appendix B for areas included; (2) Excludes Basque
Source: U.S. Census Bureau, 2014-2018 American Community Survey 5-Year Estimates

Foreign-born Population

Area	Any Foreign Country	Asia	Mexico	Europe	Caribbean	Central America[2]	South America	Africa	Canada
City	9.5	2.7	3.1	0.6	0.4	1.0	0.3	1.4	0.1
MSA[1]	6.8	2.5	1.8	0.6	0.2	0.6	0.2	0.8	0.1
U.S.	13.5	4.1	3.5	1.5	1.3	1.1	0.9	0.7	0.3

Note: (1) Figures cover the Indianapolis-Carmel-Anderson, IN Metropolitan Statistical Area—see Appendix B for areas included; (2) Excludes Mexico.
Source: U.S. Census Bureau, 2014-2018 American Community Survey 5-Year Estimates

Marital Status

Area	Never Married	Now Married[2]	Separated	Widowed	Divorced
City	42.1	37.9	1.9	5.1	13.0
MSA[1]	32.9	48.2	1.5	5.3	12.2
U.S.	33.3	48.1	2.0	5.8	10.8

Note: Figures are percentages and cover the population 15 years of age and older; (1) Figures cover the Indianapolis-Carmel-Anderson, IN Metropolitan Statistical Area—see Appendix B for areas included; (2) Excludes separated
Source: U.S. Census Bureau, 2014-2018 American Community Survey 5-Year Estimates

Disability by Age

Area	All Ages	Under 18 Years Old	18 to 64 Years Old	65 Years and Over
City	13.6	5.3	12.3	38.2
MSA[1]	12.4	4.6	10.8	35.8
U.S.	12.6	4.2	10.3	35.0

Note: Figures show percent of the civilian noninstitutionalized population that reported having a disability. Disability status is determined from six types of difficulty: vision, hearing, cognitive, ambulatory, self-care, and independent living. For children under 5 years old, hearing and vision difficulty are used to determine disability status. For children between the ages of 5 and 14, disability status is determined from hearing, vision, cognitive, ambulatory, and self-care difficulties. For people aged 15 years and older, they are considered to have a disability if they have difficulty with any one of the six difficulty types; Note: (1) Figures cover the Indianapolis-Carmel-Anderson, IN Metropolitan Statistical Area—see Appendix B for areas included
Source: U.S. Census Bureau, 2014-2018 American Community Survey 5-Year Estimates

Age

Area	Under Age 5	Age 5–19	Age 20–34	Age 35–44	Age 45–54	Age 55–64	Age 65–74	Age 75–84	Age 85+	Median Age
City	7.3	19.6	24.1	12.9	12.3	11.9	6.9	3.4	1.5	34.2
MSA[1]	6.7	20.6	20.7	13.3	13.4	12.3	7.7	3.8	1.6	36.4
U.S.	6.1	19.3	20.7	12.6	13.2	12.8	8.8	4.5	1.9	37.9

Note: (1) Figures cover the Indianapolis-Carmel-Anderson, IN Metropolitan Statistical Area—see Appendix B for areas included
Source: U.S. Census Bureau, 2014-2018 American Community Survey 5-Year Estimates

Gender

Area	Males	Females	Males per 100 Females
City	413,806	443,831	93.2
MSA[1]	980,534	1,026,963	95.5
U.S.	158,984,190	163,918,840	97.0

Note: (1) Figures cover the Indianapolis-Carmel-Anderson, IN Metropolitan Statistical Area—see Appendix B for areas included
Source: U.S. Census Bureau, 2014-2018 American Community Survey 5-Year Estimates

Religious Groups by Family

Area	Catholic	Baptist	Non-Den.	Methodist[2]	Lutheran	LDS[3]	Pente-costal	Presby-terian[4]	Muslim[5]	Judaism
MSA[1]	10.5	10.3	7.2	5.0	1.7	0.7	1.6	1.7	0.2	0.4
U.S.	19.1	9.3	4.0	4.0	2.3	2.0	1.9	1.6	0.8	0.7

Note: Figures are the number of adherents as a percentage of the total population; (1) Figures cover the Indianapolis-Carmel-Anderson, IN Metropolitan Statistical Area—see Appendix B for areas included; (2) Methodist/Pietist; (3) Latter Day Saints; (4) Reformed; (5) Figures are estimates
Source: Association of Statisticians of American Religious Bodies, 2010 U.S. Religion Census: Religious Congregations & Membership Study

Religious Groups by Tradition

Area	Catholic	Evangelical Protestant	Mainline Protestant	Other Tradition	Black Protestant	Orthodox
MSA[1]	10.5	18.3	9.6	1.7	1.9	0.3
U.S.	19.1	16.2	7.3	4.3	1.6	0.3

Note: Figures are the number of adherents as a percentage of the total population; (1) Figures cover the Indianapolis-Carmel-Anderson, IN Metropolitan Statistical Area—see Appendix B for areas included
Source: Association of Statisticians of American Religious Bodies, 2010 U.S. Religion Census: Religious Congregations & Membership Study

ECONOMY

Gross Metropolitan Product

Area	2017	2018	2019	2020	Rank[2]
MSA[1]	140.6	147.0	152.8	159.1	27

Note: Figures are in billions of dollars; (1) Figures cover the Indianapolis-Carmel-Anderson, IN Metropolitan Statistical Area—see Appendix B for areas included; (2) Rank is based on 2018 data and ranges from 1 to 381
Source: U.S. Conference of Mayors, U.S. Metro Economies: GMP & Employment 2018-2020, September 2019

Economic Growth

Area	2015-17 (%)	2018 (%)	2019 (%)	2020 (%)	Rank[2]
MSA[1]	2.5	1.9	2.1	2.0	101
U.S.	1.9	2.9	2.3	2.1	–

Note: Figures are real gross metropolitan product (GMP) growth rates and represent average annual percent change; (1) Figures cover the Indianapolis-Carmel-Anderson, IN Metropolitan Statistical Area—see Appendix B for areas included; (2) Rank is based on 2017 2-year average annual percent change and ranges from 1 to 381
Source: U.S. Conference of Mayors, U.S. Metro Economies: GMP & Employment 2018-2020, September 2019

Metropolitan Area Exports

Area	2013	2014	2015	2016	2017	2018	Rank[2]
MSA[1]	9,747.5	9,539.4	9,809.4	9,655.4	10,544.2	11,069.9	31

Note: Figures are in millions of dollars; (1) Figures cover the Indianapolis-Carmel-Anderson, IN Metropolitan Statistical Area—see Appendix B for areas included; (2) Rank is based on 2018 data and ranges from 1 to 387
Source: U.S. Department of Commerce, International Trade Administration, Office of Trade and Economic Analysis, Industry and Analysis, Exports by Metropolitan Area, data extracted April 15, 2020

Building Permits

Area	Single-Family			Multi-Family			Total		
	2017	2018	Pct. Chg.	2017	2018	Pct. Chg.	2017	2018	Pct. Chg.
City	914	1,090	19.3	645	1,196	85.4	1,559	2,286	46.6
MSA[1]	6,755	7,291	7.9	2,324	1,603	-31.0	9,079	8,894	-2.0
U.S.	820,000	855,300	4.3	462,000	473,500	2.5	1,282,000	1,328,800	3.7

Note: (1) Figures cover the Indianapolis-Carmel-Anderson, IN Metropolitan Statistical Area—see Appendix B for areas included; Figures represent new, privately-owned housing units authorized (unadjusted data); All permit data are based on estimates with imputation
Source: U.S. Census Bureau, Manufacturing, Mining, and Construction Statistics, Building Permits, 2017, 2018

Bankruptcy Filings

Area	Business Filings			Nonbusiness Filings		
	2018	2019	% Chg.	2018	2019	% Chg.
Marion County	57	100	75.4	4,546	4,465	-1.8
U.S.	22,232	22,780	2.5	751,186	752,160	0.1

Note: Business filings include Chapter 7, Chapter 9, Chapter 11, Chapter 12, Chapter 13, Chapter 15, and Section 304; Nonbusiness filings include Chapter 7, Chapter 11, and Chapter 13
Source: Administrative Office of the U.S. Courts, Business and Nonbusiness Bankruptcy, County Cases Commenced by Chapter of the Bankruptcy Code, During the 12-Month Period Ending December 31, 2018 and Business and Nonbusiness Bankruptcy, County Cases Commenced by Chapter of the Bankruptcy Code, During the 12-Month Period Ending December 31, 2019

Housing Vacancy Rates

Area	Gross Vacancy Rate[2] (%)			Year-Round Vacancy Rate[3] (%)			Rental Vacancy Rate[4] (%)			Homeowner Vacancy Rate[5] (%)		
	2017	2018	2019	2017	2018	2019	2017	2018	2019	2017	2018	2019
MSA[1]	10.9	8.7	7.2	10.8	8.6	6.7	11.9	9.9	7.0	1.5	1.5	1.5
U.S.	12.7	12.3	12.0	9.9	9.7	9.5	7.2	6.9	6.7	1.6	1.5	1.4

Note: (1) Figures cover the Indianapolis-Carmel-Anderson, IN Metropolitan Statistical Area—see Appendix B for areas included; (2) The percentage of the total housing inventory that is vacant; (3) The percentage of the housing inventory (excluding seasonal units) that is year-round vacant; (4) The percentage of rental inventory that is vacant for rent; (5) The percentage of homeowner inventory that is vacant for sale
Source: U.S. Census Bureau, Housing Vacancies and Homeownership Annual Statistics: 2017, 2018, 2019

INCOME

Income

Area	Per Capita ($)	Median Household ($)	Average Household ($)
City	27,119	46,442	65,566
MSA[1]	31,953	59,232	81,060
U.S.	32,621	60,293	84,938

Note: (1) Figures cover the Indianapolis-Carmel-Anderson, IN Metropolitan Statistical Area—see Appendix B for areas included
Source: U.S. Census Bureau, 2014-2018 American Community Survey 5-Year Estimates

Household Income Distribution

Area	Percent of Households Earning							
	Under $15,000	$15,000 -$24,999	$25,000 -$34,999	$35,000 -$49,999	$50,000 -$74,999	$75,000 -$99,999	$100,000 -$149,999	$150,000 and up
City	14.3	11.7	11.8	15.4	18.2	10.8	10.6	7.4
MSA[1]	10.1	9.2	9.7	13.5	18.3	13.0	14.8	11.5
U.S.	10.9	9.3	9.3	12.6	17.5	12.5	14.6	13.3

Note: (1) Figures cover the Indianapolis-Carmel-Anderson, IN Metropolitan Statistical Area—see Appendix B for areas included
Source: U.S. Census Bureau, 2014-2018 American Community Survey 5-Year Estimates

Poverty Rate

Area	All Ages	Under 18 Years Old	18 to 64 Years Old	65 Years and Over
City	19.1	28.7	17.1	9.8
MSA[1]	13.2	18.9	12.2	7.0
U.S.	14.1	19.5	13.2	9.3

Note: Figures are percentage of people whose income during the past 12 months was below the poverty level;
(1) Figures cover the Indianapolis-Carmel-Anderson, IN Metropolitan Statistical Area—see Appendix B for
areas included
Source: U.S. Census Bureau, 2014-2018 American Community Survey 5-Year Estimates

EMPLOYMENT

Labor Force and Employment

Area	Civilian Labor Force			Workers Employed		
	Dec. 2018	Dec. 2019	% Chg.	Dec. 2018	Dec. 2019	% Chg.
City	446,378	446,151	-0.1	430,884	433,373	0.6
MSA[1]	1,060,308	1,060,176	0.0	1,026,584	1,032,445	0.6
U.S.	162,510,000	164,007,000	0.9	156,481,000	158,504,000	1.3

Note: Data is not seasonally adjusted and covers workers 16 years of age and older; (1) Figures cover the
Indianapolis-Carmel-Anderson, IN Metropolitan Statistical Area—see Appendix B for areas included
Source: Bureau of Labor Statistics, Local Area Unemployment Statistics

Unemployment Rate

Area	2019											
	Jan.	Feb.	Mar.	Apr.	May	Jun.	Jul.	Aug.	Sep.	Oct.	Nov.	Dec.
City	4.1	3.8	3.6	2.8	3.0	3.4	3.5	3.4	2.9	3.0	3.1	2.9
MSA[1]	3.8	3.5	3.3	2.6	2.8	3.1	3.2	3.1	2.6	2.7	2.8	2.6
U.S.	4.4	4.1	3.9	3.3	3.4	3.8	4.0	3.8	3.3	3.3	3.3	3.4

Note: Data is not seasonally adjusted and covers workers 16 years of age and older; (1) Figures cover the
Indianapolis-Carmel-Anderson, IN Metropolitan Statistical Area—see Appendix B for areas included
Source: Bureau of Labor Statistics, Local Area Unemployment Statistics

Average Wages

Occupation	$/Hr.	Occupation	$/Hr.
Accountants and Auditors	37.00	Maintenance and Repair Workers	19.80
Automotive Mechanics	21.10	Marketing Managers	57.80
Bookkeepers	20.60	Network and Computer Systems Admin.	42.00
Carpenters	24.40	Nurses, Licensed Practical	22.80
Cashiers	10.90	Nurses, Registered	34.10
Computer Programmers	44.70	Nursing Assistants	14.30
Computer Systems Analysts	40.60	Office Clerks, General	17.30
Computer User Support Specialists	23.60	Physical Therapists	42.40
Construction Laborers	18.50	Physicians	118.30
Cooks, Restaurant	12.80	Plumbers, Pipefitters and Steamfitters	26.70
Customer Service Representatives	18.40	Police and Sheriff's Patrol Officers	30.00
Dentists	75.80	Postal Service Mail Carriers	25.20
Electricians	28.30	Real Estate Sales Agents	24.80
Engineers, Electrical	45.10	Retail Salespersons	14.20
Fast Food and Counter Workers	10.10	Sales Representatives, Technical/Scientific	50.50
Financial Managers	64.00	Secretaries, Exc. Legal/Medical/Executive	17.80
First-Line Supervisors of Office Workers	29.90	Security Guards	14.80
General and Operations Managers	58.90	Surgeons	81.40
Hairdressers/Cosmetologists	14.80	Teacher Assistants, Exc. Postsecondary*	12.80
Home Health and Personal Care Aides	11.70	Teachers, Secondary School, Exc. Sp. Ed.*	26.60
Janitors and Cleaners	13.40	Telemarketers	17.30
Landscaping/Groundskeeping Workers	15.50	Truck Drivers, Heavy/Tractor-Trailer	22.00
Lawyers	53.90	Truck Drivers, Light/Delivery Services	18.40
Maids and Housekeeping Cleaners	11.40	Waiters and Waitresses	12.20

Note: Wage data covers the Indianapolis-Carmel-Anderson, IN Metropolitan Statistical Area—see Appendix B
for areas included; (*) Hourly wages were calculated from annual wage data based on a 40 hour work week;
n/a not available.
Source: Bureau of Labor Statistics, Metro Area Occupational Employment & Wage Estimates, May 2019

Employment by Occupation

Occupation Classification	City (%)	MSA[1] (%)	U.S. (%)
Management, Business, Science, and Arts	34.8	39.1	37.9
Natural Resources, Construction, and Maintenance	7.1	7.6	8.9
Production, Transportation, and Material Moving	17.4	14.8	13.3
Sales and Office	23.4	22.9	22.1
Service	17.2	15.6	17.9

Note: Figures cover employed civilians 16 years of age and older; (1) Figures cover the Indianapolis-Carmel-Anderson, IN Metropolitan Statistical Area—see Appendix B for areas included
Source: U.S. Census Bureau, 2014-2018 American Community Survey 5-Year Estimates

Employment by Industry

Sector	MSA[1] Number of Employees	MSA[1] Percent of Total	U.S. Percent of Total
Construction	53,600	4.9	4.9
Education and Health Services	164,900	15.1	16.1
Financial Activities	70,700	6.5	5.8
Government	137,300	12.6	15.0
Information	13,600	1.2	1.9
Leisure and Hospitality	108,200	9.9	10.8
Manufacturing	92,700	8.5	8.4
Mining and Logging	700	0.1	0.5
Other Services	45,400	4.2	3.9
Professional and Business Services	174,100	15.9	14.1
Retail Trade	104,300	9.5	10.6
Transportation, Warehousing, and Utilities	77,200	7.1	4.2
Wholesale Trade	50,600	4.6	3.9

Note: Figures are non-farm employment as of December 2019. Figures are not seasonally adjusted and include workers 16 years of age and older; (1) Figures cover the Indianapolis-Carmel-Anderson, IN Metropolitan Statistical Area—see Appendix B for areas included
Source: Bureau of Labor Statistics, Current Employment Statistics, Employment, Hours, and Earnings

Occupations with Greatest Projected Employment Growth: 2019 – 2021

Occupation[1]	2019 Employment	2021 Projected Employment	Numeric Employment Change	Percent Employment Change
Combined Food Preparation and Serving Workers, Including Fast Food	93,910	96,420	2,510	2.7
Registered Nurses	69,240	71,460	2,220	3.2
Personal Care Aides	29,510	31,560	2,050	6.9
Laborers and Freight, Stock, and Material Movers, Hand	95,190	96,990	1,800	1.9
General and Operations Managers	56,150	57,140	990	1.8
Home Health Aides	14,430	15,420	990	6.9
Cooks, Restaurant	27,660	28,650	990	3.6
Janitors and Cleaners, Except Maids and Housekeeping Cleaners	47,880	48,850	970	2.0
Maintenance and Repair Workers, General	36,930	37,670	740	2.0
Construction Laborers	27,060	27,790	730	2.7

Note: Projections cover Indiana; (1) Sorted by numeric employment change
Source: www.projectionscentral.com, State Occupational Projections, 2019–2021 Short-Term Projections

Fastest Growing Occupations: 2019 – 2021

Occupation[1]	2019 Employment	2021 Projected Employment	Numeric Employment Change	Percent Employment Change
Occupational Therapy Assistants	1,150	1,230	80	7.0
Home Health Aides	14,430	15,420	990	6.9
Personal Care Aides	29,510	31,560	2,050	6.9
Health Specialties Teachers, Postsecondary	3,490	3,710	220	6.3
Physician Assistants	1,630	1,730	100	6.1
Operations Research Analysts	1,160	1,230	70	6.0
Speech-Language Pathologists	2,500	2,650	150	6.0
Nurse Practitioners	4,980	5,270	290	5.8
Information Security Analysts	1,060	1,120	60	5.7
Hazardous Materials Removal Workers	900	950	50	5.6

Note: Projections cover Indiana; (1) Sorted by percent employment change and excludes occupations with numeric employment change less than 50
Source: www.projectionscentral.com, State Occupational Projections, 2019–2021 Short-Term Projections

TAXES

State Corporate Income Tax Rates

State	Tax Rate (%)	Income Brackets ($)	Num. of Brackets	Financial Institution Tax Rate (%)[a]	Federal Income Tax Ded.
Indiana	5.5 (i)	Flat rate	1	6.0	No

Note: Tax rates as of January 1, 2020; (a) Rates listed are the corporate income tax rate applied to financial institutions or excise taxes based on income; (i) The Indiana Corporate tax rate is scheduled to decrease to 5.25% on July 1, 2020. Bank tax rate is scheduled to decrease to 5.5% on 1/1/21.
Source: Federation of Tax Administrators, State Corporate Income Tax Rates, January 1, 2020

State Individual Income Tax Rates

State	Tax Rate (%)	Income Brackets ($)	Personal Exemptions ($)			Standard Ded. ($)	
			Single	Married	Depend.	Single	Married
Indiana	3.23	Flat rate	1,000	2,000	2,500 (j)	–	–

Note: Tax rates as of January 1, 2020; Local- and county-level taxes are not included; Federal income tax is not deductible on state income tax returns; (j) In Indiana, includes an additional exemption of $1,500 for each dependent child.
Source: Federation of Tax Administrators, State Individual Income Tax Rates, January 1, 2020

Various State Sales and Excise Tax Rates

State	State Sales Tax (%)	Gasoline[1] (¢/gal.)	Cigarette[2] ($/pack)	Spirits[3] ($/gal.)	Wine[4] ($/gal.)	Beer[5] ($/gal.)	Recreational Marijuana (%)
Indiana	7	46.62	0.995	2.68	0.47	0.12	Not legal

Note: All tax rates as of January 1, 2020; (1) The American Petroleum Institute has developed a methodology for determining the average tax rate on a gallon of fuel. Rates may include any of the following: excise taxes, environmental fees, storage tank fees, other fees or taxes, general sales tax, and local taxes; (2) The federal excise tax of $1.0066 per pack and local taxes are not included; (3) Rates are those applicable to off-premise sales of 40% alcohol by volume (a.b.v.) distilled spirits in 750ml containers. Local excise taxes are excluded; (4) Rates are those applicable to off-premise sales of 11% a.b.v. non-carbonated wine in 750ml containers; (5) Rates are those applicable to off-premise sales of 4.7% a.b.v. beer in 12 ounce containers.
Source: Tax Foundation, 2020 Facts & Figures: How Does Your State Compare?

State Business Tax Climate Index Rankings

State	Overall Rank	Corporate Tax Rank	Individual Income Tax Rank	Sales Tax Rank	Property Tax Rank	Unemployment Insurance Tax Rank
Indiana	10	11	15	20	2	25

Note: The index is a measure of how each state's tax laws affect economic performance. The lower the rank, the more favorable a state's tax system is for business. States without a given tax are given a ranking of 1. The scores/rankings for the District of Columbia do not affect other states. The 2020 index represents the tax climate as of July 1, 2019.
Source: Tax Foundation, State Business Tax Climate Index 2020

COMMERCIAL REAL ESTATE

Office Market

Market Area	Inventory (sq. ft.)	Vacancy Rate (%)	Under Construction (sq. ft.)	YTD Net Absorption (sq. ft.)	Total Average Asking Rent ($/sq. ft./year)
Indianapolis	61,959,469	10.9	0	-322,970	19.74
National	4,923,349,992	13.0	102,814,961	2,049,925	29.54

Source: Newmark Grubb Knight Frank, National Office Market Report, 1st Quarter 2020

Industrial/Warehouse/R&D Market

Market Area	Inventory (sq. ft.)	Vacancy Rate (%)	Under Construction (sq. ft.)	YTD Net Absorption (sq. ft.)	Total Average Asking Rent ($/sq. ft./year)
Indianapolis	338,069,691	4.6	11,615,347	-2,215,598	4.12
National	15,332,123,451	5.4	322,705,045	48,296,842	7.54

Source: Newmark Grubb Knight Frank, National Industrial Market Report, 1st Quarter 2020

COMMERCIAL UTILITIES

Typical Monthly Electric Bills

Area	Commercial Service ($/month)		Industrial Service ($/month)	
	1,500 kWh	40 kW demand 14,000 kWh	1,000 kW demand 200,000 kWh	50,000 kW demand 32,500,000 kWh
City	196	1,375	28,891	2,318,765
Average[1]	203	1,612	25,706	2,520,671

Note: Figures are based on annualized rates; (1) Average based on 187 utilities surveyed
Source: Edison Electric Institute, Typical Bills and Average Rates Report, Summer 2019

TRANSPORTATION

Means of Transportation to Work

Area	Car/Truck/Van		Public Transportation			Bicycle	Walked	Other Means	Worked at Home
	Drove Alone	Car-pooled	Bus	Subway	Railroad				
City	82.3	9.0	1.9	0.0	0.0	0.5	1.9	1.1	3.3
MSA[1]	83.9	8.0	0.9	0.0	0.0	0.3	1.5	0.9	4.5
U.S.	76.4	9.1	2.5	1.9	0.6	0.6	2.7	1.3	4.9

Note: Figures are percentages and cover workers 16 years of age and older; (1) Figures cover the Indianapolis-Carmel-Anderson, IN Metropolitan Statistical Area—see Appendix B for areas included
Source: U.S. Census Bureau, 2014-2018 American Community Survey 5-Year Estimates

Travel Time to Work

Area	Less Than 10 Minutes	10 to 19 Minutes	20 to 29 Minutes	30 to 44 Minutes	45 to 59 Minutes	60 to 89 Minutes	90 Minutes or More
City	9.9	30.2	30.1	21.6	4.1	2.5	1.5
MSA[1]	11.5	27.8	24.6	23.7	7.4	3.5	1.5
U.S.	12.5	28.7	20.9	20.7	8.2	6.3	2.8

Note: Note: Figures are percentages and include workers 16 years old and over; (1) Figures cover the Indianapolis-Carmel-Anderson, IN Metropolitan Statistical Area—see Appendix B for areas included
Source: U.S. Census Bureau, 2014-2018 American Community Survey 5-Year Estimates

Key Congestion Measures

Area	1982	1992	2002	2012	2017
Annual Hours of Delay, Total (000)	6,965	13,196	23,514	37,744	43,003
Annual Hours of Delay, Per Auto Commuter	18	29	40	43	48
Annual Congestion Cost, Total (million $)	53	140	319	687	801
Annual Congestion Cost, Per Auto Commuter ($)	295	385	535	673	743

Source: Texas A&M Transportation Institute, 2019 Urban Mobility Report

Freeway Travel Time Index

Area	1982	1987	1992	1997	2002	2007	2012	2017
Urban Area Index[1]	1.08	1.10	1.12	1.15	1.17	1.18	1.18	1.18
Urban Area Rank[1,2]	28	36	40	41	41	44	40	45

Note: Freeway Travel Time Index—the ratio of travel time in the peak period to the travel time at free-flow conditions. For example, a value of 1.30 indicates a 20-minute free-flow trip takes 26 minutes in the peak (20 minutes x 1.30 = 26 minutes); (1) Covers the Indianapolis IN urban area; (2) Rank is based on 101 larger urban areas (#1 = highest travel time index)
Source: Texas A&M Transportation Institute, 2019 Urban Mobility Report

Public Transportation

Agency Name / Mode of Transportation	Vehicles Operated in Maximum Service[1]	Annual Unlinked Passenger Trips[2] (in thous.)	Annual Passenger Miles[3] (in thous.)
Indianapolis and Marion County Public Transportation (IndyGo)			
Bus (directly operated)	137	8,816.0	41,887.2
Demand Response (purchased transportation)	74	303.1	3,701.8

Note: (1) Number of revenue vehicles operated by the given mode and type of service to meet the annual maximum service requirement. This is the revenue vehicle count during the peak season of the year; on the week and day that maximum service is provided. Vehicles operated in maximum service (VOMS) exclude atypical days and one-time special events; (2) Number of passengers who boarded public transportation vehicles. Passengers are counted each time they board a vehicle no matter how many vehicles they use to travel from their origin to their destination. (3) Sum of the distances ridden by all passengers during the entire fiscal year.
Source: Federal Transit Administration, National Transit Database, 2018

Air Transportation

Airport Name and Code / Type of Service	Passenger Airlines[1]	Passenger Enplanements	Freight Carriers[2]	Freight (lbs)
Indianapolis International (IND)				
Domestic service (U.S. carriers - 2019)	31	4,616,432	15	945,081,880
International service (U.S. carriers - 2018)	7	39,641	5	52,830,713

Note: (1) Includes all U.S.-based major, minor and commuter airlines that carried at least one passenger during the year; (2) Includes all U.S.-based airlines and freight carriers that transported at least one pound of freight during the year.
Source: Bureau of Transportation Statistics, The Intermodal Transportation Database, Air Carriers: T-100 Domestic Market (U.S. Carriers), 2019; Bureau of Transportation Statistics, The Intermodal Transportation Database, Air Carriers: T-100 International Market (U.S. Carriers), 2018

Other Transportation Statistics

Major Highways:	I-65; I-69; I-70; I-74
Amtrak Service:	Yes
Major Waterways/Ports:	White River

Source: Amtrak.com; Google Maps

BUSINESSES

Major Business Headquarters

Company Name	Industry	Rankings Fortune[1]	Rankings Forbes[2]
Anthem	Health Care, Insurance and Managed Care	33	-
Eli Lilly	Pharmaceuticals	123	-
Simon Property Group	Real Estate	496	-

Note: (1) Companies that produce a 10-K are ranked 1 to 500 based on 2018 revenue; (2) All private companies with at least $2 billion in annual revenue through the end of their most current fiscal year are ranked 1 to 228; companies listed are headquartered in the city; dashes indicate no ranking
Source: Fortune, "Fortune 500," June 2019; Forbes, "America's Largest Private Companies," 2019 Rankings

Fast-Growing Businesses

According to *Inc.*, Indianapolis is home to two of America's 500 fastest-growing private companies: **Vespa Group** (#250); **Prosper Group** (#466). Criteria: must be an independent, privately-held, for-profit, U.S. corporation, proprietorship or partnership as of December 31, 2018; revenues must be at least $100,000 in 2015 and $2 million in 2018; must have four-year operating/sales history. *Inc., "America's 500 Fastest-Growing Private Companies," 2019*

According to Deloitte, Indianapolis is home to one of North America's 500 fastest-growing high-technology companies: **Journey Holding Corp. (dba Ride Systems and D** (#404).

Companies are ranked by percentage growth in revenue over a four-year period. Criteria for inclusion: company must be headquartered within North America; must own proprietary intellectual property or technology that is sold to customers in products that contributes to a significant portion of the company's operating revenue; must have been in business for a minumum of four years with 2015 operating revenues of at least $50,000 USD/CD and 2018 operating revenues of at least $5 million USD/CD. *Deloitte, 2019 Technology Fast 500*[TM]

Minority Business Opportunity

Indianapolis is home to two companies which are on the *Black Enterprise* Industrial/Service list (100 largest companies based on gross sales): **Harris & Ford** (#21); **Mays Chemical Co.** (#43). Criteria: operational in previous calendar year; at least 51% black-owned and manufactures/owns the product it sells or provides industrial or consumer services. Brokerages, real estate firms and firms that provide professional services are not eligible. *Black Enterprise, B.E. 100s, 2019*

Indianapolis is home to two companies which are on the *Hispanic Business* 500 list (500 largest U.S. Hispanic-owned companies based on revenue): **Morales Group** (#150); **Garcia Construction Group** (#205). Companies included must show at least 51 percent ownership by Hispanic U.S. citizens, and must maintain headquarters in one of the 50 states or Washington, D.C. *Hispanic Business, "Hispanic Business 500," June 20, 2013*

Minority- and Women-Owned Businesses

Group	All Firms		Firms with Paid Employees			
	Firms	Sales ($000)	Firms	Sales ($000)	Employees	Payroll ($000)
AIAN[1]	441	49,971	28	39,396	246	10,419
Asian	2,101	1,076,911	651	1,003,996	5,305	132,640
Black	13,322	977,881	521	757,937	7,840	262,939
Hispanic	3,395	617,641	339	512,149	4,224	97,914
NHOPI[2]	48	(s)	12	(s)	20 - 99	(s)
Women	27,668	4,729,023	2,600	4,232,733	28,874	1,054,998
All Firms	69,366	141,782,909	15,252	139,642,415	474,109	23,195,994

Note: Figures cover firms located in the city; minority- and women-owned business are defined as firms in which the corresponding group own 51% or more of the stock or equity of the company; (1) American Indian and Alaska Native; (2) Native Hawaiian and Other Pacific Islander; (s) estimates are suppressed when publication standards are not met
Source: U.S. Census Bureau, 2012 Economic Census, Survey of Business Owners

HOTELS & CONVENTION CENTERS

Hotels, Motels and Vacation Rentals

Area	5 Star		4 Star		3 Star		2 Star		1 Star		Not Rated	
	Num.	Pct.[3]	Num.	Pct.[3]	Num.	Pct.[3]	Num.	Pct.[3]	Num.	Pct.[3]	Num.	Pct.[3]
City[1]	0	0.0	10	4.1	59	24.3	24	9.9	46	18.9	104	42.8
Total[2]	266	1.3	1,517	7.2	4,627	21.8	3,210	15.1	3,974	18.7	7,601	35.9

Note: (1) Figures cover Indianapolis and vicinity; (2) Figures cover all 100 cities in this book; (3) Percentage of hotels which have a given star rating; Star ratings are determined by priceline.com and offer an indication of the general quality of a particular hotel.
Source: priceline.com, April 27, 2020

Major Convention Centers

Name	Overall Space (sq. ft.)	Exhibit Space (sq. ft.)	Meeting Space (sq. ft.)	Meeting Rooms
Indiana Convention Center	n/a	400,000	140,000	48

Note: Table includes convention centers located in the Indianapolis-Carmel-Anderson, IN metro area; n/a not available
Source: Original research

Living Environment

COST OF LIVING

Cost of Living Index

Composite Index	Groceries	Housing	Utilities	Trans-portation	Health Care	Misc. Goods/Services
92.4	94.1	78.4	105.4	97.9	90.6	98.0

Note: The Cost of Living Index measures regional differences in the cost of consumer goods and services, excluding taxes and non-consumer expenditures, for professional and managerial households in the top income quintile. It is based on more than 50,000 prices covering almost 60 different items for which prices are collected three times a year by chambers of commerce, economic development organizations or university applied economic centers in each participating urban area. The numbers shown should be read as a percentage above or below the national average of 100. For example, a value of 115.4 in the groceries column indicates that grocery prices are 15.4% higher than the national average. Small differences in the index numbers should not be interpreted as significant; Figures cover the Indianapolis IN urban area.
Source: The Council for Community and Economic Research, ACCRA Cost of Living Index, 2019

Grocery Prices

Area[1]	T-Bone Steak ($/pound)	Frying Chicken ($/pound)	Whole Milk ($/half gal.)	Eggs ($/dozen)	Orange Juice ($/64 oz.)	Coffee ($/11.5 oz.)
City[2]	11.62	1.36	1.48	1.04	3.47	4.26
Avg.	11.40	1.41	1.93	1.54	3.51	4.30
Min.	7.40	0.92	0.85	0.58	2.67	2.90
Max.	15.58	2.68	4.09	4.18	5.57	8.10

*Note: (1) Values for the local area are compared with the average, minimum and maximum values for all 290 areas in the Cost of Living Index; (2) Figures cover the Indianapolis IN urban area; **T-Bone Steak** (price per pound); **Frying Chicken** (price per pound, whole fryer); **Whole Milk** (half gallon carton); **Eggs** (price per dozen, Grade A, large); **Orange Juice** (64 oz. Tropicana or Florida Natural); **Coffee** (11.5 oz. can, vacuum-packed, Maxwell House, Hills Bros, or Folgers).*
Source: The Council for Community and Economic Research, ACCRA Cost of Living Index, 2019

Housing and Utility Costs

Area[1]	New Home Price ($)	Apartment Rent ($/month)	All Electric ($/month)	Part Electric ($/month)	Other Energy ($/month)	Telephone ($/month)
City[2]	258,287	1,062	-	108.07	76.54	179.90
Avg.	362,090	1,142	174.35	100.00	67.76	179.60
Min.	198,329	501	91.58	31.44	28.51	165.30
Max.	2,074,561	5,050	388.18	239.41	306.15	207.90

*Note: (1) Values for the local area are compared with the average, minimum and maximum values for all 290 areas in the Cost of Living Index; (2) Figures cover the Indianapolis IN urban area; **New Home Price** (2,400 sf living area, 8,000 sf lot, in urban area with full utilities); **Apartment Rent** (950 sf 2 bedroom/1.5 or 2 bath, unfurnished, excluding all utilities except water); **All Electric** (average monthly cost for an all-electric home); **Part Electric** (average monthly cost for a part-electric home); **Other Energy** (average monthly cost for natural gas, fuel oil, coal, wood, and any other forms of energy except electricity); **Telephone** (price includes the base monthly rate plus taxes and fees for three lines of mobile phone service).*
Source: The Council for Community and Economic Research, ACCRA Cost of Living Index, 2019

Health Care, Transportation, and Other Costs

Area[1]	Doctor ($/visit)	Dentist ($/visit)	Optometrist ($/visit)	Gasoline ($/gallon)	Beauty Salon ($/visit)	Men's Shirt ($)
City[2]	94.37	93.20	58.27	2.56	39.63	46.29
Avg.	114.85	97.58	106.10	2.50	38.15	32.15
Min.	39.00	62.22	52.22	1.53	16.88	10.27
Max.	206.67	151.53	258.67	3.79	79.29	59.30

*Note: (1) Values for the local area are compared with the average, minimum and maximum values for all 290 areas in the Cost of Living Index; (2) Figures cover the Indianapolis IN urban area; **Doctor** (general practitioners routine exam of an established patient); **Dentist** (adult teeth cleaning and periodic oral examination); **Optometrist** (full vision eye exam for established adult patient); **Gasoline** (one gallon regular unleaded, national brand, including all taxes, cash price at self-service pump if available); **Beauty Salon** (woman's shampoo, trim, and blow-dry); **Men's Shirt** (cotton/polyester dress shirt, pinpoint weave, long sleeves).*
Source: The Council for Community and Economic Research, ACCRA Cost of Living Index, 2019

HOUSING

House Price Index (HPI)

Area	National Ranking[2]	Quarterly Change (%)	One-Year Change (%)	Five-Year Change (%)
MSA[1]	59	0.98	6.06	33.98
U.S.[3]	–	1.26	5.09	32.88

Note: The HPI is a weighted repeat sales index. It measures average price changes in repeat sales or refinancings on the same properties. This information is obtained by reviewing repeat mortgage transactions on single-family properties whose mortgages have been purchased or securitized by Fannie Mae or Freddie Mac in January 1975; (1) Figures cover the Indianapolis-Carmel-Anderson, IN Metropolitan Statistical Area—see Appendix B for areas included; (2) Rankings are based on annual percentage change for all metro areas containing at least 15,000 transactions over the last 10 years and ranges from 1 to 232; (3) figures based on a weighted average of Census Division estimates using a seasonally adjusted, purchase-only index; all figures are for the period ending December 31, 2019
Source: Federal Housing Finance Agency, House Price Index, February 25, 2020

Median Single-Family Home Prices

Area	2017	2018	2019[p]	Percent Change 2018 to 2019
MSA[1]	171.5	187.1	200.1	6.9
U.S. Average	248.8	261.6	274.6	5.0

Note: Figures are median sales prices of existing single-family homes in thousands of dollars; (p) preliminary; (1) Figures cover the Indianapolis-Carmel-Anderson, IN Metropolitan Statistical Area—see Appendix B for areas included
Source: National Association of Realtors, Median Sales Price of Existing Single-Family Homes for Metropolitan Areas, 4th Quarter 2019

Qualifying Income Based on Median Sales Price of Existing Single-Family Homes

Area	With 5% Down ($)	With 10% Down ($)	With 20% Down ($)
MSA[1]	42,765	40,514	36,012
U.S. Average	58,663	55,575	49,400

Note: Figures are preliminary; Qualifying income is based on a mortgage rate of 3.76%. Monthly principal and interest payment is limited to 25% of income; (1) Figures cover the Indianapolis-Carmel-Anderson, IN Metropolitan Statistical Area—see Appendix B for areas included
Source: National Association of Realtors, Qualifying Income Based on Median Sales Price of Existing Single-Family Homes for Metropolitan Areas, 4th Quarter 2019

Median Apartment Condo-Coop Home Prices

Area	2017	2018	2019[p]	Percent Change 2018 to 2019
MSA[1]	139.8	147.7	162.6	10.1
U.S. Average	234.3	241.0	249.5	3.5

Note: Figures are median sales prices of existing apartment condo-coop homes in thousands of dollars; (p) preliminary; (1) Figures cover the Indianapolis-Carmel-Anderson, IN Metropolitan Statistical Area—see Appendix B for areas included
Source: National Association of Realtors, Median Sales Price of Existing Apartment Condo-Coop Homes for Metropolitan Areas, 4th Quarter 2019

Home Value Distribution

Area	Under $50,000	$50,000 -$99,999	$100,000 -$149,999	$150,000 -$199,999	$200,000 -$299,999	$300,000 -$499,999	$500,000 -$999,999	$1,000,000 or more
City	8.2	24.6	28.5	17.4	10.5	7.3	2.7	0.6
MSA[1]	6.3	17.7	23.8	18.4	17.0	12.1	4.0	0.8
U.S.	7.6	13.0	14.0	14.3	19.2	18.3	10.5	3.1

Note: Figures are percentages and cover owner-occupied housing units; (1) Figures cover the Indianapolis-Carmel-Anderson, IN Metropolitan Statistical Area—see Appendix B for areas included
Source: U.S. Census Bureau, 2014-2018 American Community Survey 5-Year Estimates

Homeownership Rate

Area	2011 (%)	2012 (%)	2013 (%)	2014 (%)	2015 (%)	2016 (%)	2017 (%)	2018 (%)	2019 (%)
MSA[1]	68.3	67.1	67.5	66.9	64.6	63.9	63.9	64.3	66.2
U.S.	66.1	65.4	65.1	64.5	63.7	63.4	63.9	64.4	64.6

Note: (1) Figures cover the Indianapolis-Carmel-Anderson, IN Metropolitan Statistical Area—see Appendix B for areas included
Source: U.S. Census Bureau, Housing Vacancies and Homeownership Annual Statistics: 2011-2019

Year Housing Structure Built

Area	2010 or Later	2000 -2009	1990 -1999	1980 -1989	1970 -1979	1960 -1969	1950 -1959	1940 -1949	Before 1940	Median Year
City	2.7	9.5	13.1	11.9	14.1	13.4	12.5	6.0	16.6	1971
MSA[1]	5.2	16.0	16.7	10.6	12.9	10.9	10.4	4.5	12.9	1979
U.S.	4.1	14.3	13.9	13.5	15.3	10.7	10.4	5.0	12.8	1977

Note: Figures are percentages except for Median Year; Note: (1) Figures cover the Indianapolis-Carmel-Anderson, IN Metropolitan Statistical Area—see Appendix B for areas included
Source: U.S. Census Bureau, 2014-2018 American Community Survey 5-Year Estimates

Gross Monthly Rent

Area	Under $500	$500 -$999	$1,000 -$1,499	$1,500 -$1,999	$2,000 -$2,499	$2,500 -$2,999	$3,000 and up	Median ($)
City	6.8	61.8	25.6	4.5	0.8	0.2	0.3	865
MSA[1]	6.8	57.6	28.1	5.6	1.2	0.4	0.4	888
U.S.	9.8	38.5	29.6	12.9	5.1	2.1	2.0	1,023

Note: Figures are percentages except for Median; Gross rent is the contract rent plus the estimated average monthly cost of utilities (electricity, gas, and water and sewer) and fuels (oil, coal, kerosene, wood, etc.) if these are paid by the renter (or paid for the renter by someone else); (1) Figures cover the Indianapolis-Carmel-Anderson, IN Metropolitan Statistical Area—see Appendix B for areas included
Source: U.S. Census Bureau, 2014-2018 American Community Survey 5-Year Estimates

HEALTH

Health Risk Factors

Category	MSA[1] (%)	U.S. (%)
Adults aged 18–64 who have any kind of health care coverage	88.5	87.3
Adults who reported being in good or better health	81.9	82.4
Adults who have been told they have high blood cholesterol	33.0	33.0
Adults who have been told they have high blood pressure	34.6	32.3
Adults who are current smokers	19.4	17.1
Adults who currently use E-cigarettes	6.3	4.6
Adults who currently use chewing tobacco, snuff, or snus	3.8	4.0
Adults who are heavy drinkers[2]	6.4	6.3
Adults who are binge drinkers[3]	17.1	17.4
Adults who are overweight (BMI 25.0 - 29.9)	34.3	35.3
Adults who are obese (BMI 30.0 - 99.8)	32.0	31.3
Adults who participated in any physical activities in the past month	71.6	74.4
Adults who always or nearly always wears a seat belt	93.8	94.3

Note: (1) Figures cover the Indianapolis-Carmel-Anderson, IN Metropolitan Statistical Area—see Appendix B for areas included; (2) Heavy drinkers are classified as adult men having more than 14 drinks per week and adult women having more than 7 drinks per week; (3) Binge drinkers are classified as males having five or more drinks on one occasion or females having four or more drinks on one occasion
Source: Centers for Disease Control and Prevention, Behaviorial Risk Factor Surveillance System, SMART: Selected Metropolitan Area Risk Trends, 2017

Acute and Chronic Health Conditions

Category	MSA[1] (%)	U.S. (%)
Adults who have ever been told they had a heart attack	4.3	4.2
Adults who have ever been told they have angina or coronary heart disease	4.2	3.9
Adults who have ever been told they had a stroke	3.4	3.0
Adults who have ever been told they have asthma	14.8	14.2
Adults who have ever been told they have arthritis	25.6	24.9
Adults who have ever been told they have diabetes[2]	11.8	10.5
Adults who have ever been told they had skin cancer	6.6	6.2
Adults who have ever been told they had any other types of cancer	6.9	7.1
Adults who have ever been told they have COPD	7.2	6.5
Adults who have ever been told they have kidney disease	3.4	3.0
Adults who have ever been told they have a form of depression	22.6	20.5

Note: (1) Figures cover the Indianapolis-Carmel-Anderson, IN Metropolitan Statistical Area—see Appendix B for areas included; (2) Figures do not include pregnancy-related, borderline, or pre-diabetes
Source: Centers for Disease Control and Prevention, Behaviorial Risk Factor Surveillance System, SMART: Selected Metropolitan Area Risk Trends, 2017

Health Screening and Vaccination Rates

Category	MSA[1] (%)	U.S. (%)
Adults aged 65+ who have had flu shot within the past year	59.1	60.7
Adults aged 65+ who have ever had a pneumonia vaccination	81.2	75.4
Adults who have ever been tested for HIV	39.3	36.1
Adults who have ever had the shingles or zoster vaccine?	28.3	28.9
Adults who have had their blood cholesterol checked within the last five years	85.3	85.9

Note: n/a not available; (1) Figures cover the Indianapolis-Carmel-Anderson, IN Metropolitan Statistical Area—see Appendix B for areas included.
Source: Centers for Disease Control and Prevention, Behaviorial Risk Factor Surveillance System, SMART: Selected Metropolitan Area Risk Trends, 2017

Disability Status

Category	MSA[1] (%)	U.S. (%)
Adults who reported being deaf	5.1	6.7
Are you blind or have serious difficulty seeing, even when wearing glasses?	4.5	4.5
Are you limited in any way in any of your usual activities due of arthritis?	13.1	12.9
Do you have difficulty doing errands alone?	7.6	6.8
Do you have difficulty dressing or bathing?	3.7	3.6
Do you have serious difficulty concentrating/remembering/making decisions?	10.9	10.7
Do you have serious difficulty walking or climbing stairs?	12.6	13.6

Note: (1) Figures cover the Indianapolis-Carmel-Anderson, IN Metropolitan Statistical Area—see Appendix B for areas included.
Source: Centers for Disease Control and Prevention, Behaviorial Risk Factor Surveillance System, SMART: Selected Metropolitan Area Risk Trends, 2017

Mortality Rates for the Top 10 Causes of Death in the U.S.

ICD-10[a] Sub-Chapter	ICD-10[a] Code	Age-Adjusted Mortality Rate[1] per 100,000 population	
		County[2]	U.S.
Malignant neoplasms	C00-C97	175.4	152.4
Ischaemic heart diseases	I20-I25	97.7	92.7
Other forms of heart disease	I30-I51	59.6	52.5
Chronic lower respiratory diseases	J40-J47	59.5	40.4
Cerebrovascular diseases	I60-I69	39.7	37.3
Other degenerative diseases of the nervous system	G30-G31	33.5	36.4
Other external causes of accidental injury	W00-X59	51.8	35.3
Organic, including symptomatic, mental disorders	F01-F09	42.0	30.0
Hypertensive diseases	I10-I15	26.7	22.9
Diabetes mellitus	E10-E14	26.7	21.3

Note: (a) ICD-10 = International Classification of Diseases 10th Revision; (1) Mortality rates are a three year average covering 2016-2018; (2) Figures cover Marion County.
Source: Centers for Disease Control and Prevention, National Center for Health Statistics. Underlying Cause of Death 1999-2018 on CDC WONDER Online Database

Mortality Rates for Selected Causes of Death

ICD-10[a] Sub-Chapter	ICD-10[a] Code	Age-Adjusted Mortality Rate[1] per 100,000 population	
		County[2]	U.S.
Assault	X85-Y09	18.2	6.0
Diseases of the liver	K70-K76	17.4	14.2
Human immunodeficiency virus (HIV) disease	B20-B24	2.1	1.6
Influenza and pneumonia	J09-J18	12.0	14.2
Intentional self-harm	X60-X84	15.3	13.9
Malnutrition	E40-E46	2.8	1.9
Obesity and other hyperalimentation	E65-E68	2.2	2.1
Renal failure	N17-N19	20.1	12.8
Transport accidents	V01-V99	12.8	12.5
Viral hepatitis	B15-B19	1.8	1.4

Note: (a) ICD-10 = International Classification of Diseases 10th Revision; (1) Mortality rates are a three year average covering 2016-2018; (2) Figures cover Marion County; Data are suppressed when the data meet the criteria for confidentiality constraints; Mortality rates are flagged as unreliable when the rate would be calculated with a numerator of 20 or less.
Source: Centers for Disease Control and Prevention, National Center for Health Statistics. Underlying Cause of Death 1999-2018 on CDC WONDER Online Database

Health Insurance Coverage

Area	With Health Insurance	With Private Health Insurance	With Public Health Insurance	Without Health Insurance	Population Under Age 19 Without Health Insurance
City	88.7	61.6	36.3	11.3	6.2
MSA[1]	91.2	71.1	30.6	8.8	5.6
U.S.	90.6	67.7	34.7	9.4	5.2

Note: Figures are percentages that cover the civilian noninstitutionalized population; (1) Figures cover the Indianapolis-Carmel-Anderson, IN Metropolitan Statistical Area—see Appendix B for areas included
Source: U.S. Census Bureau, 2014-2018 American Community Survey 5-Year Estimates

Number of Medical Professionals

Area	MDs[3]	DOs[3,4]	Dentists	Podiatrists	Chiropractors	Optometrists
County[1] (number)	4,141	205	848	61	149	190
County[1] (rate[2])	435.9	21.6	88.8	6.4	15.6	19.9
U.S. (rate[2])	281.9	23.4	69.1	6.0	27.5	16.4

Note: Data as of 2018 unless noted; (1) Data covers Marion County; (2) Rate per 100,000 population; (3) Data as of 2017 and includes all active, non-federal physicians; (4) Doctor of Osteopathic Medicine
Source: U.S. Department of Health and Human Services, Health Resources and Services Administration, Bureau of Health Professions, Area Resource File (ARF) 2018-2019

Best Hospitals

According to *U.S. News,* the Indianapolis-Carmel-Anderson, IN metro area is home to one of the best hospitals in the U.S.: **Indiana University Health Medical Center** (1 adult specialty and 9 pediatric specialties). The hospital listed was nationally ranked in at least one of 16 adult or 10 pediatric specialties. Only 206 hospitals nationwide were nationally ranked in one or more adult or pediatric specialty. Twenty hospitals in the U.S. made the Honor Roll. The Best Hospitals Honor Roll takes both the national rankings and the procedure and condition ratings into account. Hospitals received points if they were nationally ranked in one of the 16 adult specialties—the higher they ranked, the more points they got—and how many ratings of "high performing" they earned in the nine procedures and conditions. *U.S. News Online, "America's Best Hospitals 2019-20"*

According to *U.S. News,* the Indianapolis-Carmel-Anderson, IN metro area is home to one of the best children's hospitals in the U.S.: **Riley Hospital for Children at IU Health** (9 pediatric specialties). The hospital listed was highly ranked in at least one of 10 pediatric specialties. Ninety-one children's hospitals in the U.S. were nationally ranked in at least one specialty. Hospitals received points for being ranked in a specialty, and the 10 hospitals with the most points across the 10 specialties make up the Honor Roll. *U.S. News Online, "America's Best Children's Hospitals 2019-20"*

EDUCATION

Public School District Statistics

District Name	Schls	Pupils	Pupil/ Teacher Ratio	Minority Pupils[1] (%)	Free Lunch Eligible[2] (%)	IEP[3] (%)
Franklin Township Com Sch Corp	10	9,654	20.1	29.7	30.4	19.1
Indiana Connections Academy	1	4,852	41.4	20.4	31.8	17.2
Indiana Virtual Pathways Academy	1	6,266	120.1	34.0	73.9	4.5
Indianapolis Public Schools	59	26,410	14.0	79.0	63.9	22.0
M S D Decatur Township	9	6,810	18.2	34.0	56.5	16.7
M S D Lawrence Township	17	16,035	20.1	77.9	54.8	13.8
M S D Pike Township	13	11,150	17.1	91.6	60.9	15.2
M S D Warren Township	18	12,188	22.7	77.8	65.7	16.8
M S D Washington Township	13	11,140	18.1	70.3	49.9	17.8
M S D Wayne Township	18	16,484	15.8	71.2	62.6	14.6
Perry Township Schools	17	16,610	19.3	55.9	57.3	15.8

Note: Table includes school districts with 2,000 or more students; (1) Percentage of students that are not non-Hispanic white; (2) Percentage of students that are eligible for the free lunch program; (3) Percentage of students that have an Individualized Education Program.
Source: U.S. Department of Education, National Center for Education Statistics, Common Core of Data, Local Education Agency (School District) Universe Survey: School Year 2018-2019; U.S. Department of Education, National Center for Education Statistics, Common Core of Data, Public Elementary/Secondary School Universe Survey: School Year 2018-2019

Best High Schools

According to *U.S. News,* Indianapolis is home to one of the top 500 high schools in the U.S.: **Herron High School** (#218). Nearly 18,000 public, magnet and charter schools were ranked based on their performance on state assessments and how well they prepare students for college. *U.S. News & World Report, "Best High Schools 2020"*

Highest Level of Education

Area	Less than H.S.	H.S. Diploma	Some College, No Deg.	Associate Degree	Bachelor's Degree	Master's Degree	Prof. School Degree	Doctorate Degree
City	14.5	28.0	19.9	7.3	19.7	7.5	2.1	1.1
MSA[1]	10.6	28.0	19.7	7.8	21.9	8.7	2.1	1.2
U.S.	12.3	27.1	20.6	8.4	19.4	8.6	2.1	1.4

Note: Figures cover persons age 25 and over; (1) Figures cover the Indianapolis-Carmel-Anderson, IN Metropolitan Statistical Area—see Appendix B for areas included
Source: U.S. Census Bureau, 2014-2018 American Community Survey 5-Year Estimates

Educational Attainment by Race

Area	High School Graduate or Higher (%)					Bachelor's Degree or Higher (%)				
	Total	White	Black	Asian	Hisp.[2]	Total	White	Black	Asian	Hisp.[2]
City	85.5	87.7	84.1	75.0	55.9	30.4	35.4	17.6	46.1	11.6
MSA[1]	89.4	91.0	85.2	82.7	61.5	33.9	36.0	19.8	55.0	16.1
U.S.	87.7	89.6	85.4	86.8	67.7	31.5	32.9	21.1	53.5	15.8

Note: Figures shown cover persons 25 years old and over; (1) Figures cover the Indianapolis-Carmel-Anderson, IN Metropolitan Statistical Area—see Appendix B for areas included; (2) People of Hispanic origin can be of any race
Source: U.S. Census Bureau, 2014-2018 American Community Survey 5-Year Estimates

School Enrollment by Grade and Control

Area	Preschool (%)		Kindergarten (%)		Grades 1 - 4 (%)		Grades 5 - 8 (%)		Grades 9 - 12 (%)	
	Public	Private	Public	Private	Public	Private	Public	Private	Public	Private
City	57.0	43.0	84.7	15.3	88.5	11.5	86.1	13.9	88.5	11.5
MSA[1]	50.8	49.2	86.8	13.2	89.3	10.7	88.6	11.4	89.1	10.9
U.S.	59.0	41.0	87.7	12.3	89.6	10.4	89.5	10.5	90.2	9.8

Note: Figures shown cover persons 3 years old and over; (1) Figures cover the Indianapolis-Carmel-Anderson, IN Metropolitan Statistical Area—see Appendix B for areas included
Source: U.S. Census Bureau, 2014-2018 American Community Survey 5-Year Estimates

Average Salaries of Public School Teachers

Area	2016-17		2017-18		Change from 2016-17 to 2017-18	
	Dollars	Rank[1]	Dollars	Rank[1]	Percent	Rank[2]
Indiana	50,218	35	50,614	36	0.79	34
U.S. Average	59,539	–	60,477	–	1.58	–

Note: (1) Rank ranges from 1 to 51 where 1 indicates highest salary; (2) Rank ranges from 1 to 51 where 1 indicates highest percent change.
Source: National Education Association, Rankings & Estimates: Rankings of the States 2018 and Estimates of School Statistics 2019

Higher Education

Four-Year Colleges			Two-Year Colleges			Medical Schools[1]	Law Schools[2]	Voc/ Tech[3]
Public	Private Non-profit	Private For-profit	Public	Private Non-profit	Private For-profit			
2	7	6	1	0	5	2	1	8

Note: Figures cover institutions located within the city limits and include main campuses only; (1) includes schools accredited by the Liaison Committee on Medical Education and the American Osteopathic Association's Commission on Osteopathic College Accreditation; (2) includes ABA-accredited schools, schools with provisional ABA accreditation, and state accredited schools; (3) includes all schools with programs that are less than 2 years.
Source: National Center for Education Statistics, Integrated Postsecondary Education System (IPEDS), 2018-19; Wikipedia, List of Medical Schools in the United States, accessed May 1, 2020; Wikipedia, List of Law Schools in the United States, accessed May 1, 2020

According to *U.S. News & World Report,* the Indianapolis-Carmel-Anderson, IN metro area is home to one of the top 100 liberal arts colleges in the U.S.: **DePauw University** (#46 tie). The indicators used to capture academic quality fall into a number of categories: assessment by administrators at peer institutions; retention of students; faculty resources; student selectivity;

financial resources; alumni giving; high school counselor ratings of colleges; and graduation rate. *U.S. News & World Report, "America's Best Colleges 2020"*

According to *U.S. News & World Report,* the Indianapolis-Carmel-Anderson, IN metro area is home to one of the top 75 medical schools for research in the U.S.: **Indiana University—Indianapolis** (#47 tie). The rankings are based on a weighted average of 11 measures of quality: quality assessment; peer assessment score; assessment score by residency directors; research activity; total research activity; average research activity per faculty member; student selectivity; median MCAT total score; median undergraduate GPA; acceptance rate; and faculty resources. *U.S. News & World Report, "America's Best Graduate Schools, Medical, 2021"*

PRESIDENTIAL ELECTION

2016 Presidential Election Results

Area	Clinton	Trump	Johnson	Stein	Other
Marion County	58.0	35.5	5.0	0.2	1.3
U.S.	48.0	45.9	3.3	1.1	1.7

Note: Results are percentages and may not add to 100% due to rounding
Source: Dave Leip's Atlas of U.S. Presidential Elections

EMPLOYERS

Major Employers

Company Name	Industry
Allison Transmission	Motor vehicle parts & accessories
Ameritech	Local and long distance telephone
Apple American Indiana	Restaurant/family chain
Automotive Components Holdings	Steering mechanisms, motor vehicle
Celadon Trucking Service	Trucking, except local
CNO Financial Group	Insurance services
Communikty Hospitals of Indiana	General medical & surgical hospitals
Conseco Variable Ins Company	Life insurance
Defense Finance and Accounting Services	Accounting, auditing, & bookkeeping
Eli Lilly and Company	Pharmaceutical preparations
Family & Social Svcs Admin	Administration of social and human resources
Federal Express Corporation	Air cargo carrier
GEICO	Auto insurance
Hewlett-Packard Co.	Computer terminals
Indiana Department of Transportation	Regulation administration of transportation
Indiana Police State	General government, state government
Liberty Mutual	Insurance services
Meridian Citizens Mutual Ins Company	Assessment associations: fire, marine & casualty ins
Methodist Hospital	General medical & surgical hospitals
Navient	Financial services
Rolls Royce Corporation	Aircraft engines & engine parts
St. Vincent Hospital and Healthcare Center	General medical & surgical hospitals
The Health Hospital of Marion County	General medical & surgical hospitals
Trustees of indiana University	University
United States Postal Service	U.S. postal service

Note: Companies shown are located within the Indianapolis-Carmel-Anderson, IN Metropolitan Statistical Area.
Source: Hoovers.com; Wikipedia

Best Companies to Work For

Anthem, headquartered in Indianapolis, is among the "Best Companies for Multicultural Women." *Working Mother* selected 50 companies based on a detailed application completed by public and private firms based in the United States, excluding government agencies, companies in the human resources field and non-autonomous divisions. Companies supplied data about the hiring, pay, and promotion of multicultural employees. Applications focused on representation of multicultural women, recruitment, retention and advancement programs, and company culture. *Working Mother, "2019 Best Companies for Multicultural Women"*

NCAA, headquartered in Indianapolis, is among the "100 Best Places to Work in IT." To qualify, companies had to be U.S.-based organizations or be non-U.S.- based employers that met the following criteria: have a minimum of 300 total employees at a U.S. headquarters and a minimum of 30 IT employees in the U.S., with at least 50% of their IT employees based in the U.S. The best places to work were selected based on compensation, benefits, work/life balance, employee morale, and satisfaction with training and development programs. In addition, *Computerworld* looked at retention efforts, programs for recognizing and rewarding outstanding performances, and benefits such as flextime, elder care and child care, and reimbursement for college tuition and the cost of pursuing technology certifications. *Computerworld, "100 Best Places to Work in IT 2019"*

Anthem; Eli Lilly and Company, headquartered in Indianapolis, are among the "Top Companies for Executive Women." The 2020 National Association for Female Executives (NAFE) Top Companies application included more than 200 questions on topics including female representation at all levels, but especially the corporate officer and profit-and-loss leadership ranks. The application tracked and examined how many employees have access to programs and policies that promote advancement of women and how many employees take advantage of them, plus how companies train managers to help women advance. To be considered, companies must have a minimum of two women on their boards of directors, a U.S.-based CEO and at least 1,000 U.S. employees. *National Association for Female Executives, "2020 NAFE Top 70 Companies for Executive Women"*

PUBLIC SAFETY

Crime Rate

Area	All Crimes	Violent Crimes				Property Crimes		
		Murder	Rape[3]	Robbery	Aggrav. Assault	Burglary	Larceny -Theft	Motor Vehicle Theft
City	5,402.0	18.5	77.1	351.1	826.1	893.6	2,671.9	563.7
Suburbs[1]	1,699.1	2.5	23.1	28.7	114.1	199.2	1,200.7	130.7
Metro[2]	3,285.3	9.3	46.3	166.8	419.1	496.7	1,830.9	316.2
U.S.	2,580.1	5.0	42.6	86.2	246.8	376.0	1,594.6	228.9

Note: Figures are crimes per 100,000 population; (1) All areas within the metro area that are located outside the city limits; (2) Figures cover the Indianapolis-Carmel-Anderson, IN Metropolitan Statistical Area—see Appendix B for areas included; (3) The city and U.S. figures shown were reported using the revised Uniform Crime Reporting (UCR) definition of rape. The suburban and metro area figures shown are an aggregate total of the data submitted using both the revised and legacy UCR definitions.
Source: FBI Uniform Crime Reports, 2018

Hate Crimes

Area	Number of Quarters Reported	Number of Incidents per Bias Motivation					
		Race/Ethnicity/ Ancestry	Religion	Sexual Orientation	Disability	Gender	Gender Identity
City[1]	4	22	5	5	0	2	0
U.S.	4	4,047	1,419	1,196	159	47	168

Note: (1) Figures include one incident reported with more than one bias motivation.
Source: Federal Bureau of Investigation, Hate Crime Statistics 2018

Identity Theft Consumer Reports

Area	Reports	Reports per 100,000 Population	Rank[2]
MSA[1]	2,831	138	109
U.S.	650,572	198	-

Note: (1) Figures cover the Indianapolis-Carmel-Anderson, IN Metropolitan Statistical Area—see Appendix B for areas included; (2) Rank ranges from 1 to 386 where 1 indicates greatest number of identity theft reports per 100,000 population
Source: Federal Trade Commission, Consumer Sentinel Network Data Book for January–December 2019

Fraud and Other Consumer Reports

Area	Reports	Reports per 100,000 Population	Rank[2]
MSA[1]	11,962	584	150
U.S.	2,590,177	789	-

Note: (1) Figures cover the Indianapolis-Carmel-Anderson, IN Metropolitan Statistical Area—see Appendix B for areas included; (2) Rank ranges from 1 to 386 where 1 indicates greatest number of fraud and other consumer reports per 100,000 population
Source: Federal Trade Commission, Consumer Sentinel Network Data Book for January–December 2019

SPORTS

Professional Sports Teams

Team Name	League	Year Established
Indiana Pacers	National Basketball Association (NBA)	1967
Indianapolis Colts	National Football League (NFL)	1984

Note: Includes teams located in the Indianapolis-Carmel-Anderson, IN Metropolitan Statistical Area.
Source: Wikipedia, Major Professional Sports Teams of the United States and Canada, May 4, 2020

CLIMATE

Average and Extreme Temperatures

Temperature	Jan	Feb	Mar	Apr	May	Jun	Jul	Aug	Sep	Oct	Nov	Dec	Yr.
Extreme High (°F)	71	72	85	89	93	102	104	102	100	90	81	74	104
Average High (°F)	35	39	50	63	73	82	85	84	78	66	51	39	62
Average Temp. (°F)	27	31	41	52	63	72	76	73	67	55	43	31	53
Average Low (°F)	18	22	31	41	52	61	65	63	55	44	33	23	42
Extreme Low (°F)	-22	-21	-7	18	28	39	48	41	34	20	-2	-23	-23

Note: Figures cover the years 1948-1990
Source: National Climatic Data Center, International Station Meteorological Climate Summary, 9/96

Average Precipitation/Snowfall/Humidity

Precip./Humidity	Jan	Feb	Mar	Apr	May	Jun	Jul	Aug	Sep	Oct	Nov	Dec	Yr.
Avg. Precip. (in.)	2.8	2.5	3.6	3.6	4.0	3.9	4.3	3.4	2.9	2.6	3.3	3.3	40.2
Avg. Snowfall (in.)	7	6	4	1	Tr	0	0	0	0	Tr	2	5	25
Avg. Rel. Hum. 7am (%)	81	81	79	77	79	80	84	87	87	85	83	83	82
Avg. Rel. Hum. 4pm (%)	68	64	59	53	53	53	56	56	53	53	63	70	59

Note: Figures cover the years 1948-1990; Tr = Trace amounts (<0.05 in. of rain; <0.5 in. of snow)
Source: National Climatic Data Center, International Station Meteorological Climate Summary, 9/96

Weather Conditions

Temperature			Daytime Sky			Precipitation		
10°F & below	32°F & below	90°F & above	Clear	Partly cloudy	Cloudy	0.01 inch or more precip.	0.1 inch or more snow/ice	Thunder-storms
19	119	19	83	128	154	127	24	43

Note: Figures are average number of days per year and cover the years 1948-1990
Source: National Climatic Data Center, International Station Meteorological Climate Summary, 9/96

HAZARDOUS WASTE

Superfund Sites

The Indianapolis-Carmel-Anderson, IN metro area is home to seven sites on the EPA's Superfund National Priorities List: **Broadway Street Corridor Groundwater Contamination** (final); **Envirochem Corp.** (final); **Keystone Corridor Ground Water Contamination** (final); **Northside Sanitary Landfill, Inc** (final); **Pike and Mulberry Streets PCE Plume** (final); **Reilly Tar & Chemical Corp. (Indianapolis Plant)** (final); **Riverside Ground Water Contamination** (proposed). There are a total of 1,387 Superfund sites with a status of proposed or final on the list in the U.S. *U.S. Environmental Protection Agency, National Priorities List, May 5, 2020*

AIR & WATER QUALITY

Air Quality Trends: Ozone

	1990	1995	2000	2005	2010	2012	2014	2016	2017	2018
MSA[1]	0.084	0.094	0.081	0.080	0.069	0.078	0.066	0.070	0.067	0.073
U.S.	0.088	0.089	0.082	0.080	0.073	0.075	0.067	0.069	0.068	0.069

Note: (1) Data covers the Indianapolis-Carmel-Anderson, IN Metropolitan Statistical Area—see Appendix B for areas included. The values shown are the composite ozone concentration averages among trend sites based on the highest fourth daily maximum 8-hour concentration in parts per million. These trends are based on sites having an adequate record of monitoring data during the trend period. Data from exceptional events are included.
Source: U.S. Environmental Protection Agency, Air Quality Monitoring Information, "Air Quality Trends by City, 1990-2018"

Air Quality Index

Area	Percent of Days when Air Quality was...[2]					AQI Statistics[2]	
	Good	Moderate	Unhealthy for Sensitive Groups	Unhealthy	Very Unhealthy	Maximum	Median
MSA[1]	51.2	44.4	4.1	0.3	0.0	156	50

Note: (1) Data covers the Indianapolis-Carmel-Anderson, IN Metropolitan Statistical Area—see Appendix B for areas included; (2) Based on 365 days with AQI data in 2018. Air Quality Index (AQI) is an index for reporting daily air quality. EPA calculates the AQI for five major air pollutants regulated by the Clean Air Act: ground-level ozone, particle pollution (aka particulate matter), carbon monoxide, sulfur dioxide, and nitrogen dioxide. The AQI runs from 0 to 500. The higher the AQI value, the greater the level of air pollution and the greater the health concern. There are six AQI categories: "Good" AQI is between 0 and 50. Air quality is considered satisfactory; "Moderate" AQI is between 51 and 100. Air quality is acceptable; "Unhealthy for Sensitive Groups" When AQI values are between 101 and 150, members of sensitive groups may experience health effects; "Unhealthy" When AQI values are between 151 and 200 everyone may begin to experience health effects; "Very Unhealthy" AQI values between 201 and 300 trigger a health alert; "Hazardous" AQI values over 300 trigger warnings of emergency conditions (not shown).
Source: U.S. Environmental Protection Agency, Air Quality Index Report, 2018

Air Quality Index Pollutants

Area	Percent of Days when AQI Pollutant was...[2]					
	Carbon Monoxide	Nitrogen Dioxide	Ozone	Sulfur Dioxide	Particulate Matter 2.5	Particulate Matter 10
MSA[1]	0.0	0.3	39.7	3.0	57.0	0.0

Note: (1) Data covers the Indianapolis-Carmel-Anderson, IN Metropolitan Statistical Area—see Appendix B for areas included; (2) Based on 365 days with AQI data in 2018. The Air Quality Index (AQI) is an index for reporting daily air quality. EPA calculates the AQI for five major air pollutants regulated by the Clean Air Act: ground-level ozone, particle pollution (also known as particulate matter), carbon monoxide, sulfur dioxide, and nitrogen dioxide. The AQI runs from 0 to 500. The higher the AQI value, the greater the level of air pollution and the greater the health concern.
Source: U.S. Environmental Protection Agency, Air Quality Index Report, 2018

Maximum Air Pollutant Concentrations: Particulate Matter, Ozone, CO and Lead

	Particulate Matter 10 (ug/m^3)	Particulate Matter 2.5 Wtd AM (ug/m^3)	Particulate Matter 2.5 24-Hr (ug/m^3)	Ozone (ppm)	Carbon Monoxide (ppm)	Lead (ug/m^3)
MSA[1] Level	55	10.8	28	0.076	2	n/a
NAAQS[2]	150	15	35	0.075	9	0.15
Met NAAQS[2]	Yes	Yes	Yes	No	Yes	n/a

Note: (1) Data covers the Indianapolis-Carmel-Anderson, IN Metropolitan Statistical Area—see Appendix B for areas included; Data from exceptional events are included; (2) National Ambient Air Quality Standards; ppm = parts per million; ug/m^3 = micrograms per cubic meter; n/a not available.
Concentrations: Particulate Matter 10 (coarse particulate)—highest second maximum 24-hour concentration; Particulate Matter 2.5 Wtd AM (fine particulate)—highest weighted annual mean concentration; Particulate Matter 2.5 24-Hour (fine particulate)—highest 98th percentile 24-hour concentration; Ozone—highest fourth daily maximum 8-hour concentration; Carbon Monoxide—highest second maximum non-overlapping 8-hour concentration; Lead—maximum running 3-month average
Source: U.S. Environmental Protection Agency, Air Quality Monitoring Information, "Air Quality Statistics by City, 2018"

Maximum Air Pollutant Concentrations: Nitrogen Dioxide and Sulfur Dioxide

	Nitrogen Dioxide AM (ppb)	Nitrogen Dioxide 1-Hr (ppb)	Sulfur Dioxide AM (ppb)	Sulfur Dioxide 1-Hr (ppb)	Sulfur Dioxide 24-Hr (ppb)
MSA[1] Level	14	n/a	n/a	55	n/a
NAAQS[2]	53	100	30	75	140
Met NAAQS[2]	Yes	n/a	n/a	Yes	n/a

Note: (1) Data covers the Indianapolis-Carmel-Anderson, IN Metropolitan Statistical Area—see Appendix B for areas included; Data from exceptional events are included; (2) National Ambient Air Quality Standards; ppm = parts per million; ug/m^3 = micrograms per cubic meter; n/a not available.
Concentrations: Nitrogen Dioxide AM—highest arithmetic mean concentration; Nitrogen Dioxide 1-Hr—highest 98th percentile 1-hour daily maximum concentration; Sulfur Dioxide AM—highest annual mean concentration; Sulfur Dioxide 1-Hr—highest 99th percentile 1-hour daily maximum concentration; Sulfur Dioxide 24-Hr—highest second maximum 24-hour concentration
Source: U.S. Environmental Protection Agency, Air Quality Monitoring Information, "Air Quality Statistics by City, 2018"

Drinking Water

Water System Name	Pop. Served	Primary Water Source Type	Violations[1]
Citizens Water-Indianapolis	825,173	Surface	15

Note: (1) Total number of violations (both active and inactive) in the EPA database
Source: U.S. Environmental Protection Agency, Office of Ground Water and Drinking Water, Safe Drinking Water Information System (based on data extracted May 5, 2020)

Kansas City, Missouri

Background

Kansas City lies on the western boundary of the state. With its sister city of the same name on the other side of the Kansas/Missouri border, both Kansas Cities make up the greater Kansas City metropolitan area.

The territory of the Kansa (or Kaw) tribe received intermittent visits from white settlers during the eighteenth and nineteenth centuries. In 1724, a fort was built in the general vicinity, and in 1804, Meriwether Lewis and William Clark explored the area on behalf of President Jefferson for the Louisiana Purchase. In 1821, the site was a trading post established by François Chouteau, who established the American Fur Company.

A combination of gold prospectors passing through on their way to California, via steamboat, rail, and coach, and the migration of would-be settlers to California and the Southwest stimulated economic activity in Kansas City during the 1800s. Three major trails—Santa Fe, California, and Oregon—all originated in Jackson County.

It was in this solid Midwestern city that the jazz clubs on 18th Street and Vine gave birth to the careers of Charlie Parker and Count Basie. Today a new generation of artists upholds Kansas City's reputation for great jazz, performing in dozens of clubs featuring live jazz nightly.

Kansas City is also home to more than 100 barbecue restaurants in the metropolitan area and each fall hosts what it claims is the world's biggest barbecue contest.

As one might expect from the heartland of America, Kansas City's major industries are hard wheat and cattle. This is not how to picture all of Kansas City. Downtown Kansas City continues to transform its skyline by incorporating modern skyscrapers among the more traditional nineteenth-century buildings. The city boasts over 100 parks and playgrounds, suburban areas with an above-average living standard, European statues that line wide stretching boulevards, and a foreign trade zone where foreign countries can store their goods free of import duties. It offers something for everyone, from cultural and sporting events to casinos and gaming, from hot barbecue to even hotter jazz. The Sprint Center arena is a world class home for major league sports, concerts, and events.

The Stowers Institute for Medical Research is home to genetic studies that help explain the relationship between cellular and molecular changes and disease.

The Kansas City International Airport and historic Union Station are modern transportation hubs. The station's restored grand hall, with its 95-foot ceilings, shares space with the Science City Museum, theaters, restaurants, and shops.

The city maintains its own symphony, lyric opera and ballet. It boasts dozens of museums and art galleries, many with free admission. The Kansas City Zoo offers over 200 acres of exhibits, including the Orangutan Primadome and a penguin exhibit. Visitors to the Harley-Davidson plant can see how a "Hog" is built; other attractions include the Children's Peace Pavilion, the Kansas City Renaissance Festival, and Fiesta Hispana, a yearly celebration of Hispanic heritage. And the National Football League's Kansas City Chiefs won Super Bowl LIV in 2020.

The National Weather Service office at Kansas City is very near the geographical center of the United States. The gently rolling terrain with no topographic impediments allows a free sweep of air from all directions, often with conflict between warm, moist air from the Gulf of Mexico and cold polar air from the north. The summer season is characterized by warm days, mild nights, and moderate humidity. Winters are not severely cold, and sizeable snowfalls are rare.

Rankings

General Rankings

- In their sixth annual survey, Livability.com looked at data for more than 1,000 U.S. cities to determine the rankings for Livability's "Top 100 Best Places to Live" in 2019. Kansas City ranked #49. Criteria: median home value capped at $250,000; affordable living; vibrant economy; education, demographics, health care options. transportation & infrastructure; abundant lifestyle amenities. *Livability.com, "Top 100 Best Places to Live 2019" March 2019*

Business/Finance Rankings

- According to *Business Insider*, the Kansas City metro area is where conditions are prime to run a startup. It ranked #10. The software company Volusion analyzed 50 of the most populous metro areas, to assign an entrepreneurship score, based on the 2017 U.S. Census Bureau Annual Survey of Entrepreneurs (ASE). Criteria: cost of living; startup density; availability of venture capital investment; percentage of self-employed workers; small business density; percentage of workers employed by startups; and startup motivation. *www.businessinsider.com, "From San Diego to Austin and Seattle, These are the 15 Best U.S. Cities to Launch a Startup," July 9, 2019*

- Recognizing the sizeable percentage of American workers who are self-employed, NerdWallet editors assessed the country's cities according to percentage of freelancers, median rental costs, cell phone plans/taxes, and healthcare affordability and access. By these criteria, Kansas City placed #13 among the best cities for independent workers. *www.nerdwallet.com, "Best Places for Freelance Workers," August 30, 2016*

- Based on metro area social media reviews, the employment opinion group Glassdoor surveyed 50 of the most populous U.S. metro areas and equally weighed cost of living, hiring opportunity, and job satisfaction to compose a list of "25 Best Cities for Jobs." Median pay and home value, and number of active job openings was also factored in. The Kansas City metro area was ranked #11 in overall job satisfaction. *www.glassdoor.com, "Best Cities for Jobs," February 25, 2020*

- The Brookings Institution ranked the nation's largest cities based on income inequality. Kansas City was ranked #77 (#1 = greatest inequality). Criteria: the "95/20 ratio," a figure representing the income at which a household earns more than 95 percent of all other households, divided by the income at which a household earns more than only 20 percent of all other households. *Brookings Institution, "Household Income Inequality, Largest Cities of 97 Large U.S. Metro Areas, 2014-2016," February 5, 2018*

- The Brookings Institution ranked the 100 largest metro areas in the U.S. based on income inequality. Kansas City was ranked #81 (#1 = greatest inequality). Criteria: the "95/20 ratio," a figure representing the income at which a household earns more than 95 percent of all other households, divided by the income at which a household earns more than only 20 percent of all other households. *Brookings Institution, "Household Income Inequality, 100 Largest U.S. Metro Areas, 2014-2016," February 5, 2018*

- Payscale.com ranked the 32 largest metro areas in terms of wage growth. The Kansas City metro area ranked #20. Criteria: private-sector and education professional wage growth between the 4th quarter of 2018 and the 4th quarter of 2019. *PayScale, "Wage Trends by Metro Area-4th Quarter," January 24, 2020*

- Kansas City was identified as one of America's most frugal metro areas by *Coupons.com*. The city ranked #18 out of 25. Criteria: digital coupon usage. *Coupons.com, "America's Most Frugal Cities of 2017," March 22, 2018*

- The Kansas City metro area appeared on the Milken Institute "2020 Best Performing Cities" list. Rank: #95 out of 200 large metro areas. Criteria: job growth; wage and salary growth; high-tech output growth. *Milken Institute, "Best-Performing Cities 2020," February 26, 2020*

- *Forbes* ranked the 200 most populous metro areas to determine the nation's "Best Places for Business and Careers." The Kansas City metro area was ranked #51. Criteria: costs (business and living); job growth (past and projected); income growth; quality of life; educational attainment (college and high school); projected economic growth; cultural and leisure opportunities; workplace tolerance laws; net migration patterns. *Forbes, "The Best Places for Business and Careers 2019: Seattle Still On Top," October 30, 2019*

Culture/Performing Arts Rankings

- Kansas City was selected as one of the twenty best large U.S. cities for moviemakers. Of cities with a population over 400,000, (NYC & LA intentionally not included) the city was ranked #17. Criteria: film community and culture; access to equipment and facilities; film activity in 2019; tax incentives; and standard of living. *MovieMaker Magazine, "Best Places to Live and Work as a Moviemaker: 2020," January 31, 2020*

- Kansas City was selected as one of "America's Favorite Cities." The city ranked #4 in the "Culture" category. Respondents to an online survey were asked to rate 38 top urban destinations in the U.S. from a visitor's perspective. Criteria: theater scene and community; number of bookstores; live music; and sense of history. *Travelandleisure.com, "These Are America's 20 Most Cultured Cities," October 2016*

- Kansas City was selected as one of "America's Favorite Cities." The city ranked #12 in the "Culture: Music Scene " category. Respondents to an online survey were asked to rate 38 top urban destinations in the U.S. from a visitor's perspective. *Travelandleisure.com, "From the Honkytonk Capital to Jazz's Birthplace: America's Best Music Scenes," October 2016*

Dating/Romance Rankings

- Kansas City was selected as one of the best cities for post grads by *Rent.com*. The city ranked among the top 10. Criteria: jobs per capita; unemployment rate; mean annual income; cost of living; rental inventory. *Rent.com, "Best Cities for College Grads," December 11, 2018*

Education Rankings

- Personal finance website *WalletHub* analyzed the 150 largest U.S. metropolitan statistical areas to determine where the most educated Americans are choosing to settle. Criteria: education levels; percentage of workers with degrees; education quality and attainment gap; public school quality rankings; quality and size of each metro area's universities. Kansas City was ranked #33 (#1 = most educated city). *www.WalletHub.com, "2019's Most and Least Educated Cities in America, " July 22, 2019*

- Kansas City was selected as one of America's most literate cities. The city ranked #16 out of the 82 largest U.S. cities. Criteria: number of booksellers; library resources; Internet resources; educational attainment; periodical publishing resources; newspaper circulation. *Central Connecticut State University, "America's Most Literate Cities, 2016," March 31, 2017*

Food/Drink Rankings

- Kauffman Stadium was selected as one of PETA's "Top 10 Vegan-Friendly Ballparks" for 2019. The park ranked #9. *People for the Ethical Treatment of Animals, "Top 10 Vegan-Friendly Ballparks, " May 23, 2019*

Health/Fitness Rankings

- For each of the 100 largest cities in the United States, the American Fitness Index®, published by the American College of Sports Medicine and the Anthem Foundation, evaluated community infrastructure and 33 health behaviors including preventive health, levels of chronic disease conditions, pedestrian safety, air quality, and community resources that support physical activity. Kansas City ranked #67 for "community fitness." *americanfitnessindex.org, "ACSM American Fitness Index Health and Community Fitness Status of the 100 Largest U.S. Cities," May 14, 2019*

- Kansas City was identified as a "2020 Spring Allergy Capital." The area ranked #66 out of 100. Three groups of factors were used to identify the most challenging cities for people with allergies during the spring season: annual spring pollen levels; over the counter medicine use; number of board-certified allergy specialists. *Asthma and Allergy Foundation of America, "Spring Allergy Capitals 2020," March 10, 2020*

- Kansas City was identified as a "2020 Fall Allergy Capital." The area ranked #62 out of 100. Three groups of factors were used to identify the most challenging cities for people with allergies during the fall season: annual fall pollen levels; over the counter medicine use; number of board-certified allergy specialists. *Asthma and Allergy Foundation of America, "Fall Allergy Capitals 2020," March 10, 2020*

- Kansas City was identified as a "2019 Asthma Capital." The area ranked #41 out of the nation's 100 largest metropolitan areas. Criteria: estimated asthma prevalence; crude death rate from asthma; and ER visits due to asthma. Risk factors that were analyzed but not factored in the rankings: annual pollen score; annual air quality; public smoking laws; number of board-certified asthma specialists; rescue medication use; controller medication use; uninsured rate; poverty rate. *Asthma and Allergy Foundation of America, "Asthma Capitals 2019: The Most Challenging Places to Live With Asthma," May 7, 2019*

- *Men's Health* ranked 100 major U.S. cities in terms of the best cities for men. Kansas City ranked #81. Criteria: health; fitness; quality of life. *Men's Health, "The Best & Worst Cities for Men Who Want to Be Fit and Happy," January 1, 2016*

- The Kansas City metro area ranked #87 out of 189 in The Gallup-Sharecare Well-Being Index. Criteria: purpose; social well being; financial health; community and physical health. Results are based on telephone interviews with adults, aged 18 and older, living in metropolitan areas in the 50 U.S. states and the District of Columbia. *Gallup-Sharecare, "State of American Well-Being, 2017 Community Well-Being Rankings" March 2018*

Real Estate Rankings

- FitSmallBusiness looked at 50 of the largest metropolitan areas in the U.S. to determine which metro was the best to start a real estate business. Data was compiled from such sources as: Zillow, Trulia, U.S. Census Bureau, and the Bureau of Labor Statistics. Criteria: location; inventory; annual wages; median sales price of homes; days on the market; median price cut percentage; and other factors that would influence real estate professional growth. The Kansas City metro area ranked #41. *fitsmallbusiness.com, "The Best Cities to Become a Real Estate Agent in 2018," January 30, 2018*

- *WalletHub* compared the most populated U.S. cities, as well as at least two of the most populated cities in each state, for a total of 179, to determine which had the best markets for real estate agents. Kansas City ranked #118 where demand was high and pay was the best. Criteria: sales per agent; annual median wage for real-estate agents; monthly average starting salary for real estate agents; real estate job density and competition; unemployment rate; home turnover rate; housing-market health index; and other relevant metrics. *www.WalletHub.com, "2019's Best Places to Be a Real Estate Agent," April 24, 2019*

- The Kansas City metro area was identified as one of the top 20 housing markets to invest in for 2019 by *Forbes*. Criteria: strong job and population growth; stable local economy; anticipated home price appreciation; and other factors. *Forbes.com, "The Best Markets for Real Estate Investments In 2019," January 7, 2019*

- Kansas City was ranked #12 in the top 20 out of the 100 largest metro areas in terms of house price appreciation in 2019 (#1 = highest rate). *Federal Housing Finance Agency, House Price Index, 4th Quarter 2019*

- Kansas City was ranked #104 out of 238 metro areas in terms of housing affordability in 2019 by the National Association of Home Builders (#1 = most affordable). Criteria: the share of homes sold in that area affordable to a family earning the local median income, based on standard mortgage underwriting criteria. *National Association of Home Builders®, NAHB-Wells Fargo Housing Opportunity Index, 4th Quarter 2019*

Safety Rankings

- To identify the most dangerous cities in America, 24/7 Wall Street focused on violent crime categories—murder, non-negligent manslaughter, rape, robbery, and aggravated assault—and property crime as reported in the FBI's 2018 annual Uniform Crime Report. Criteria also included median income from American Community Survey and unemployment figures from Bureau of Labor Statistics. For cities with populations over 100,000, Kansas City was ranked #6. *247wallst.com, "America's Most Dangerous Cities" January 10, 2020*

- Allstate ranked the 200 largest cities in America in terms of driver safety. Kansas City ranked #37. Criteria: internal property damage claims over a two-year period from January 2016 to December 2017. The report helps increase the importance of safety and awareness behind the wheel. *Allstate, "Allstate America's Best Drivers Report, 2019" June 24, 2019*

- Kansas City was identified as one of the most dangerous cities in America by NeighborhoodScout. The city ranked #12 out of 100 (#1 = most dangerous). Criteria: number of violent crimes per 1,000 residents. The editors only considered cities with 25,000 or more residents. *NeighborhoodScout.com, "Top 100 Most Dangerous Cities in the U.S. 2020" January 2, 2020*

- The National Insurance Crime Bureau ranked 382 metro areas in the U.S. in terms of per capita rates of vehicle theft. The Kansas City metro area ranked #29 (#1 = highest rate). Criteria: number of vehicle theft offenses per 100,000 inhabitants in 2018. *National Insurance Crime Bureau, "Hot Spots 2018," June 25, 2019*

Seniors/Retirement Rankings

- From its Best Cities for Successful Aging indexes, the Milken Institute generated rankings for metropolitan areas, weighing data in nine categories—health care, wellness, living arrangements, transportation and convenience, financial characteristics, education, employment, community engagement, and overall livability. The Kansas City metro area was ranked #26 overall in the large metro area category. *Milken Institute, "Best Cities for Successful Aging, 2017" March 14, 2017*

Women/Minorities Rankings

- Personal finance website *WalletHub* compared more than 180 U.S. cities—including the 150 most populated U.S. cities, plus at least two of the most populated cities in each state—across two key dimensions, "Hispanic Business-Friendliness" and "Hispanic Purchasing Power", to arrive at the most favorable conditions for Hispanic entrepreneurs. Kansas City was ranked #84 out of 182. Criteria includes: share of Hispanic-Owned Businesses; Hispanic entrepreneurship rate to median annual income of Hispanics; Small Business-Friendliness score; cost of living; and number of Hispanics with at least a bachelor's degree. *WalletHub.com, "2019's Best Cities for Hispanic Entrepreneurs," May 1, 2019*

Miscellaneous Rankings

- Kansas City was selected as a 2019 Digital Cities Survey winner. The city ranked #5 in the large city (250,000 to 499,999 population) category. The survey examined and assessed how city governments are utilizing technology to improve transparency, enhance cybersecurity, and solve social challenges. Survey questions focused on ten characteristics: data governance, citizen-focused, leadership alignment, secure, staffed/supported, efficient, connected, resilient, best practices, and use of innovation. *Center for Digital Government, "2019 Digital Cities Survey," November 14, 2019*

- The watchdog site Charity Navigator conducts an annual study of charities in the nation's major markets both to analyze statistical differences in their financial, accountability, and transparency practices and to track year-to-year variations in individual philanthropic communities. Charity Navigator's analysis demonstrated that the financial, accountability and transparency behaviors of America's largest charities can be influenced by the metropolitan market within which the charity operates. The Kansas City metro area was ranked #9 among the 30 metro markets in the rating category of Overall Score. *www.charitynavigator.org, "2017 Metro Market Study," May 1, 2017*

- *WalletHub* compared the 150 most populated U.S. cities to determine their operating efficiency. A "Quality of Services" score was constructed for each city and then divided by the total budget per capita to reveal which were managed the best. Kansas City ranked #102. Criteria: financial stability; economy; education; safety; health; infrastructure and pollution. *www.WalletHub.com, "2019's Best- & Worst-Run Cities in America," July 1, 2019*

- Kansas City was selected as one of "America's Friendliest Cities." The city ranked #16 in the "Friendliest" category. Respondents to an online survey were asked to rate 38 top urban destinations in the United States as to general friendliness, as well as manners, politeness and warm disposition. *Travel + Leisure, "America's Friendliest Cities," October 20, 2017*

Business Environment

CITY FINANCES

City Government Finances

Component	2017 ($000)	2017 ($ per capita)
Total Revenues	2,092,987	4,403
Total Expenditures	1,985,767	4,177
Debt Outstanding	3,583,786	7,539
Cash and Securities[1]	4,926,544	10,363

Note: (1) Cash and security holdings of a government at the close of its fiscal year, including those of its dependent agencies, utilities, and liquor stores.
Source: U.S. Census Bureau, State & Local Government Finances 2017

City Government Revenue by Source

Source	2017 ($000)	2017 ($ per capita)	2017 (%)
General Revenue			
From Federal Government	51,758	109	2.5
From State Government	40,071	84	1.9
From Local Governments	9,166	19	0.4
Taxes			
Property	123,811	260	5.9
Sales and Gross Receipts	325,898	686	15.6
Personal Income	236,637	498	11.3
Corporate Income	37,856	80	1.8
Motor Vehicle License	5,682	12	0.3
Other Taxes	9,145	19	0.4
Current Charges	433,529	912	20.7
Liquor Store	0	0	0.0
Utility	165,358	348	7.9
Employee Retirement	310,088	652	14.8

Source: U.S. Census Bureau, State & Local Government Finances 2017

City Government Expenditures by Function

Function	2017 ($000)	2017 ($ per capita)	2017 (%)
General Direct Expenditures			
Air Transportation	135,206	284	6.8
Corrections	0	0	0.0
Education	0	0	0.0
Employment Security Administration	0	0	0.0
Financial Administration	20,750	43	1.0
Fire Protection	154,793	325	7.8
General Public Buildings	0	0	0.0
Governmental Administration, Other	54,193	114	2.7
Health	54,541	114	2.7
Highways	73,823	155	3.7
Hospitals	0	0	0.0
Housing and Community Development	56,358	118	2.8
Interest on General Debt	77,995	164	3.9
Judicial and Legal	19,204	40	1.0
Libraries	0	0	0.0
Parking	4,067	8	0.2
Parks and Recreation	71,517	150	3.6
Police Protection	224,426	472	11.3
Public Welfare	11,749	24	0.6
Sewerage	221,655	466	11.2
Solid Waste Management	0	0	0.0
Veterans' Services	0	0	0.0
Liquor Store	0	0	0.0
Utility	99,477	209	5.0
Employee Retirement	175,405	369	8.8

Source: U.S. Census Bureau, State & Local Government Finances 2017

DEMOGRAPHICS

Population Growth

Area	1990 Census	2000 Census	2010 Census	2018* Estimate	Population Growth (%)	
					1990-2018	2010-2018
City	434,967	441,545	459,787	481,417	10.7	4.7
MSA[1]	1,636,528	1,836,038	2,035,334	2,106,632	28.7	3.5
U.S.	248,709,873	281,421,906	308,745,538	322,903,030	29.8	4.6

Note: (1) Figures cover the Kansas City, MO-KS Metropolitan Statistical Area—see Appendix B for areas included; (*) 2014-2018 5-year estimated population
Source: U.S. Census Bureau, 1990 Census, Census 2000, Census 2010, 2014-2018 American Community Survey 5-Year Estimates

Household Size

Area	Persons in Household (%)							Average Household Size
	One	Two	Three	Four	Five	Six	Seven or More	
City	37.1	31.6	13.7	10.0	4.8	1.8	1.2	2.40
MSA[1]	29.0	33.9	15.2	12.9	5.8	2.0	1.1	2.50
U.S.	27.7	33.9	15.7	13.0	6.0	2.3	1.4	2.60

Note: (1) Figures cover the Kansas City, MO-KS Metropolitan Statistical Area—see Appendix B for areas included
Source: U.S. Census Bureau, 2014-2018 American Community Survey 5-Year Estimates

Race

Area	White Alone[2] (%)	Black Alone[2] (%)	Asian Alone[2] (%)	AIAN[3] Alone[2] (%)	NHOPI[4] Alone[2] (%)	Other Race Alone[2] (%)	Two or More Races (%)
City	60.1	29.0	2.7	0.4	0.1	4.1	3.5
MSA[1]	78.4	12.4	2.8	0.4	0.2	2.6	3.2
U.S.	72.7	12.7	5.4	0.8	0.2	4.9	3.2

Note: (1) Figures cover the Kansas City, MO-KS Metropolitan Statistical Area—see Appendix B for areas included; (2) Alone is defined as not being in combination with one or more other races; (3) American Indian and Alaska Native; (4) Native Hawaiian and Other Pacific Islander
Source: U.S. Census Bureau, 2014-2018 American Community Survey 5-Year Estimates

Hispanic or Latino Origin

Area	Total (%)	Mexican (%)	Puerto Rican (%)	Cuban (%)	Other (%)
City	10.2	7.7	0.3	0.3	1.9
MSA[1]	8.9	6.9	0.3	0.2	1.5
U.S.	17.8	11.2	1.7	0.7	4.2

Note: Persons of Hispanic or Latino origin can be of any race; (1) Figures cover the Kansas City, MO-KS Metropolitan Statistical Area—see Appendix B for areas included
Source: U.S. Census Bureau, 2014-2018 American Community Survey 5-Year Estimates

Segregation

Type	Segregation Indices[1]				Percent Change		
	1990	2000	2010	2010 Rank[2]	1990-2000	1990-2010	2000-2010
Black/White	72.9	70.9	61.2	39	-2.0	-11.7	-9.7
Asian/White	34.4	38.3	38.4	65	3.9	4.0	0.1
Hispanic/White	39.5	45.5	44.4	48	6.0	4.9	-1.2

Note: All figures cover the Metropolitan Statistical Area—see Appendix B for areas included; Figures are based on an analysis of 1990, 2000, and 2010 Census Decennial Census tract data by William H. Frey, Brookings Institution and the University of Michigan Social Science Data Analysis Network. In this analysis all racial groups (whites, blacks, and asians) are non-Hispanic members of those races. Hispanics are shown as a separate category; (1) Segregation Indices are Dissimilarity Indices that measure the degree to which the minority group is distributed differently than whites across census tracts. They range from 0 (complete integration) to 100 (complete segregation) where the value indicates the percentage of the minority group that needs to move to be distributed exactly like whites; (2) Ranges from 1 (most segregated) to 102 (least segregated); n/a not available.
Source: www.CensusScope.org

Ancestry

Area	German	Irish	English	American	Italian	Polish	French[2]	Scottish	Dutch
City	16.0	10.7	7.2	4.1	3.6	1.4	2.1	1.6	1.2
MSA[1]	21.3	12.5	9.6	5.7	3.3	1.5	2.3	1.9	1.5
U.S.	13.7	9.9	7.3	6.4	5.2	2.8	2.4	1.7	1.2

Note: Figures are the percentage of the total population reporting a particular ancestry. The nine most commonly reported ancestries in the U.S. are shown. Figures include multiple ancestries (e.g. if a person reported being Irish and Italian, they were included in both columns); (1) Figures cover the Kansas City, MO-KS Metropolitan Statistical Area—see Appendix B for areas included; (2) Excludes Basque
Source: U.S. Census Bureau, 2014-2018 American Community Survey 5-Year Estimates

Foreign-born Population

Area	Any Foreign Country	Asia	Mexico	Europe	Caribbean	Central America[2]	South America	Africa	Canada
City	7.7	2.3	2.3	0.5	0.4	0.6	0.2	1.2	0.1
MSA[1]	6.7	2.3	2.1	0.6	0.2	0.5	0.2	0.7	0.1
U.S.	13.5	4.1	3.5	1.5	1.3	1.1	0.9	0.7	0.3

Note: (1) Figures cover the Kansas City, MO-KS Metropolitan Statistical Area—see Appendix B for areas included; (2) Excludes Mexico.
Source: U.S. Census Bureau, 2014-2018 American Community Survey 5-Year Estimates

Marital Status

Area	Never Married	Now Married[2]	Separated	Widowed	Divorced
City	40.1	39.5	2.1	5.4	12.9
MSA[1]	30.5	50.4	1.6	5.4	12.0
U.S.	33.3	48.1	2.0	5.8	10.8

Note: Figures are percentages and cover the population 15 years of age and older; (1) Figures cover the Kansas City, MO-KS Metropolitan Statistical Area—see Appendix B for areas included; (2) Excludes separated
Source: U.S. Census Bureau, 2014-2018 American Community Survey 5-Year Estimates

Disability by Age

Area	All Ages	Under 18 Years Old	18 to 64 Years Old	65 Years and Over
City	12.6	4.0	11.2	36.3
MSA[1]	12.2	4.1	10.5	34.6
U.S.	12.6	4.2	10.3	35.0

Note: Figures show percent of the civilian noninstitutionalized population that reported having a disability. Disability status is determined from six types of difficulty: vision, hearing, cognitive, ambulatory, self-care, and independent living. For children under 5 years old, hearing and vision difficulty are used to determine disability status. For children between the ages of 5 and 14, disability status is determined from hearing, vision, cognitive, ambulatory, and self-care difficulties. For people aged 15 years and older, they are considered to have a disability if they have difficulty with any one of the six difficulty types; Note: (1) Figures cover the Kansas City, MO-KS Metropolitan Statistical Area—see Appendix B for areas included
Source: U.S. Census Bureau, 2014-2018 American Community Survey 5-Year Estimates

Age

Area	Under Age 5	Age 5–19	Age 20–34	Age 35–44	Age 45–54	Age 55–64	Age 65–74	Age 75–84	Age 85+	Median Age
City	6.9	18.4	24.5	13.2	12.4	12.0	7.4	3.6	1.7	35.1
MSA[1]	6.6	20.1	20.1	13.2	13.2	12.8	8.2	4.1	1.8	37.3
U.S.	6.1	19.3	20.7	12.6	13.2	12.8	8.8	4.5	1.9	37.9

Note: (1) Figures cover the Kansas City, MO-KS Metropolitan Statistical Area—see Appendix B for areas included
Source: U.S. Census Bureau, 2014-2018 American Community Survey 5-Year Estimates

Gender

Area	Males	Females	Males per 100 Females
City	233,915	247,502	94.5
MSA[1]	1,033,710	1,072,922	96.3
U.S.	158,984,190	163,918,840	97.0

Note: (1) Figures cover the Kansas City, MO-KS Metropolitan Statistical Area—see Appendix B for areas included
Source: U.S. Census Bureau, 2014-2018 American Community Survey 5-Year Estimates

Religious Groups by Family

Area	Catholic	Baptist	Non-Den.	Methodist[2]	Lutheran	LDS[3]	Pentecostal	Presbyterian[4]	Muslim[5]	Judaism
MSA[1]	12.7	13.2	5.2	5.9	2.3	2.5	2.6	1.6	0.3	0.4
U.S.	19.1	9.3	4.0	4.0	2.3	2.0	1.9	1.6	0.8	0.7

Note: Figures are the number of adherents as a percentage of the total population; (1) Figures cover the Kansas City, MO-KS Metropolitan Statistical Area—see Appendix B for areas included; (2) Methodist/Pietist; (3) Latter Day Saints; (4) Reformed; (5) Figures are estimates
Source: Association of Statisticians of American Religious Bodies, 2010 U.S. Religion Census: Religious Congregations & Membership Study

Religious Groups by Tradition

Area	Catholic	Evangelical Protestant	Mainline Protestant	Other Tradition	Black Protestant	Orthodox
MSA[1]	12.7	20.6	10.0	3.7	2.6	0.1
U.S.	19.1	16.2	7.3	4.3	1.6	0.3

Note: Figures are the number of adherents as a percentage of the total population; (1) Figures cover the Kansas City, MO-KS Metropolitan Statistical Area—see Appendix B for areas included
Source: Association of Statisticians of American Religious Bodies, 2010 U.S. Religion Census: Religious Congregations & Membership Study

ECONOMY

Gross Metropolitan Product

Area	2017	2018	2019	2020	Rank[2]
MSA[1]	131.8	138.2	144.1	149.7	33

Note: Figures are in billions of dollars; (1) Figures cover the Kansas City, MO-KS Metropolitan Statistical Area—see Appendix B for areas included; (2) Rank is based on 2018 data and ranges from 1 to 381
Source: U.S. Conference of Mayors, U.S. Metro Economies: GMP & Employment 2018-2020, September 2019

Economic Growth

Area	2015-17 (%)	2018 (%)	2019 (%)	2020 (%)	Rank[2]
MSA[1]	0.6	2.6	2.4	1.7	263
U.S.	1.9	2.9	2.3	2.1	–

Note: Figures are real gross metropolitan product (GMP) growth rates and represent average annual percent change; (1) Figures cover the Kansas City, MO-KS Metropolitan Statistical Area—see Appendix B for areas included; (2) Rank is based on 2017 2-year average annual percent change and ranges from 1 to 381
Source: U.S. Conference of Mayors, U.S. Metro Economies: GMP & Employment 2018-2020, September 2019

Metropolitan Area Exports

Area	2013	2014	2015	2016	2017	2018	Rank[2]
MSA[1]	8,012.1	8,262.9	6,723.2	6,709.8	7,015.0	7,316.9	47

Note: Figures are in millions of dollars; (1) Figures cover the Kansas City, MO-KS Metropolitan Statistical Area—see Appendix B for areas included; (2) Rank is based on 2018 data and ranges from 1 to 387
Source: U.S. Department of Commerce, International Trade Administration, Office of Trade and Economic Analysis, Industry and Analysis, Exports by Metropolitan Area, data extracted April 15, 2020

Building Permits

Area	Single-Family			Multi-Family			Total		
	2017	2018	Pct. Chg.	2017	2018	Pct. Chg.	2017	2018	Pct. Chg.
City	824	813	-1.3	1,542	1,341	-13.0	2,366	2,154	-9.0
MSA[1]	5,951	5,608	-5.8	3,900	4,660	19.5	9,851	10,268	4.2
U.S.	820,000	855,300	4.3	462,000	473,500	2.5	1,282,000	1,328,800	3.7

Note: (1) Figures cover the Kansas City, MO-KS Metropolitan Statistical Area—see Appendix B for areas included; Figures represent new, privately-owned housing units authorized (unadjusted data); All permit data are based on estimates with imputation
Source: U.S. Census Bureau, Manufacturing, Mining, and Construction Statistics, Building Permits, 2017, 2018

Bankruptcy Filings

Area	Business Filings			Nonbusiness Filings		
	2018	2019	% Chg.	2018	2019	% Chg.
Jackson County	22	36	63.6	2,192	2,080	-5.1
U.S.	22,232	22,780	2.5	751,186	752,160	0.1

Note: Business filings include Chapter 7, Chapter 9, Chapter 11, Chapter 12, Chapter 13, Chapter 15, and Section 304; Nonbusiness filings include Chapter 7, Chapter 11, and Chapter 13
Source: Administrative Office of the U.S. Courts, Business and Nonbusiness Bankruptcy, County Cases Commenced by Chapter of the Bankruptcy Code, During the 12-Month Period Ending December 31, 2018 and Business and Nonbusiness Bankruptcy, County Cases Commenced by Chapter of the Bankruptcy Code, During the 12-Month Period Ending December 31, 2019

Housing Vacancy Rates

Area	Gross Vacancy Rate[2] (%)			Year-Round Vacancy Rate[3] (%)			Rental Vacancy Rate[4] (%)			Homeowner Vacancy Rate[5] (%)		
	2017	2018	2019	2017	2018	2019	2017	2018	2019	2017	2018	2019
MSA[1]	8.1	7.8	8.9	7.9	7.7	8.7	9.4	7.9	10.0	0.8	1.2	1.4
U.S.	12.7	12.3	12.0	9.9	9.7	9.5	7.2	6.9	6.7	1.6	1.5	1.4

Note: (1) Figures cover the Kansas City, MO-KS Metropolitan Statistical Area—see Appendix B for areas included; (2) The percentage of the total housing inventory that is vacant; (3) The percentage of the housing inventory (excluding seasonal units) that is year-round vacant; (4) The percentage of rental inventory that is vacant for rent; (5) The percentage of homeowner inventory that is vacant for sale
Source: U.S. Census Bureau, Housing Vacancies and Homeownership Annual Statistics: 2017, 2018, 2019

INCOME

Income

Area	Per Capita ($)	Median Household ($)	Average Household ($)
City	31,143	52,405	72,418
MSA[1]	34,444	64,020	86,106
U.S.	32,621	60,293	84,938

Note: (1) Figures cover the Kansas City, MO-KS Metropolitan Statistical Area—see Appendix B for areas included
Source: U.S. Census Bureau, 2014-2018 American Community Survey 5-Year Estimates

Household Income Distribution

Area	Percent of Households Earning							
	Under $15,000	$15,000 -$24,999	$25,000 -$34,999	$35,000 -$49,999	$50,000 -$74,999	$75,000 -$99,999	$100,000 -$149,999	$150,000 and up
City	13.1	10.7	10.4	13.9	18.1	11.6	12.9	9.2
MSA[1]	8.9	8.2	9.0	13.0	18.2	13.6	16.1	12.9
U.S.	10.9	9.3	9.3	12.6	17.5	12.5	14.6	13.3

Note: (1) Figures cover the Kansas City, MO-KS Metropolitan Statistical Area—see Appendix B for areas included
Source: U.S. Census Bureau, 2014-2018 American Community Survey 5-Year Estimates

Poverty Rate

Area	All Ages	Under 18 Years Old	18 to 64 Years Old	65 Years and Over
City	16.5	24.8	14.9	9.5
MSA[1]	11.0	15.6	10.0	6.8
U.S.	14.1	19.5	13.2	9.3

Note: Figures are percentage of people whose income during the past 12 months was below the poverty level; (1) Figures cover the Kansas City, MO-KS Metropolitan Statistical Area—see Appendix B for areas included
Source: U.S. Census Bureau, 2014-2018 American Community Survey 5-Year Estimates

EMPLOYMENT

Labor Force and Employment

Area	Civilian Labor Force			Workers Employed		
	Dec. 2018	Dec. 2019	% Chg.	Dec. 2018	Dec. 2019	% Chg.
City	257,417	262,205	1.9	249,062	252,990	1.6
MSA[1]	1,123,499	1,145,405	1.9	1,089,301	1,109,920	1.9
U.S.	162,510,000	164,007,000	0.9	156,481,000	158,504,000	1.3

Note: Data is not seasonally adjusted and covers workers 16 years of age and older; (1) Figures cover the Kansas City, MO-KS Metropolitan Statistical Area—see Appendix B for areas included
Source: Bureau of Labor Statistics, Local Area Unemployment Statistics

Unemployment Rate

Area	2019											
	Jan.	Feb.	Mar.	Apr.	May	Jun.	Jul.	Aug.	Sep.	Oct.	Nov.	Dec.
City	4.1	3.6	3.8	2.9	3.2	3.7	4.7	4.1	2.9	3.3	3.3	3.5
MSA[1]	3.8	3.6	3.6	2.8	3.0	3.3	4.0	3.5	2.7	2.9	2.9	3.1
U.S.	4.4	4.1	3.9	3.3	3.4	3.8	4.0	3.8	3.3	3.3	3.3	3.4

Note: Data is not seasonally adjusted and covers workers 16 years of age and older; (1) Figures cover the Kansas City, MO-KS Metropolitan Statistical Area—see Appendix B for areas included
Source: Bureau of Labor Statistics, Local Area Unemployment Statistics

Average Wages

Occupation	$/Hr.	Occupation	$/Hr.
Accountants and Auditors	34.10	Maintenance and Repair Workers	20.20
Automotive Mechanics	22.70	Marketing Managers	70.80
Bookkeepers	20.10	Network and Computer Systems Admin.	40.50
Carpenters	26.90	Nurses, Licensed Practical	22.40
Cashiers	11.40	Nurses, Registered	32.80
Computer Programmers	41.70	Nursing Assistants	13.70
Computer Systems Analysts	37.20	Office Clerks, General	16.50
Computer User Support Specialists	25.00	Physical Therapists	40.20
Construction Laborers	21.20	Physicians	86.40
Cooks, Restaurant	13.60	Plumbers, Pipefitters and Steamfitters	33.10
Customer Service Representatives	18.10	Police and Sheriff's Patrol Officers	26.40
Dentists	83.40	Postal Service Mail Carriers	24.70
Electricians	27.90	Real Estate Sales Agents	22.80
Engineers, Electrical	42.90	Retail Salespersons	13.00
Fast Food and Counter Workers	11.00	Sales Representatives, Technical/Scientific	38.30
Financial Managers	69.70	Secretaries, Exc. Legal/Medical/Executive	18.40
First-Line Supervisors of Office Workers	29.00	Security Guards	18.70
General and Operations Managers	53.10	Surgeons	128.90
Hairdressers/Cosmetologists	15.00	Teacher Assistants, Exc. Postsecondary*	12.90
Home Health and Personal Care Aides	11.50	Teachers, Secondary School, Exc. Sp. Ed.*	27.20
Janitors and Cleaners	14.40	Telemarketers	14.30
Landscaping/Groundskeeping Workers	18.00	Truck Drivers, Heavy/Tractor-Trailer	23.60
Lawyers	57.70	Truck Drivers, Light/Delivery Services	18.30
Maids and Housekeeping Cleaners	11.30	Waiters and Waitresses	10.90

Note: Wage data covers the Kansas City, MO-KS Metropolitan Statistical Area—see Appendix B for areas included; (*) Hourly wages were calculated from annual wage data based on a 40 hour work week; n/a not available.
Source: Bureau of Labor Statistics, Metro Area Occupational Employment & Wage Estimates, May 2019

Employment by Occupation

Occupation Classification	City (%)	MSA[1] (%)	U.S. (%)
Management, Business, Science, and Arts	39.5	40.3	37.9
Natural Resources, Construction, and Maintenance	6.6	7.9	8.9
Production, Transportation, and Material Moving	13.4	13.0	13.3
Sales and Office	22.7	22.9	22.1
Service	17.8	15.9	17.9

Note: Figures cover employed civilians 16 years of age and older; (1) Figures cover the Kansas City, MO-KS Metropolitan Statistical Area—see Appendix B for areas included
Source: U.S. Census Bureau, 2014-2018 American Community Survey 5-Year Estimates

Employment by Industry

Sector	MSA[1]		U.S.
	Number of Employees	Percent of Total	Percent of Total
Construction, Mining, and Logging	54,500	4.9	5.4
Education and Health Services	158,500	14.3	16.1
Financial Activities	78,900	7.1	5.8
Government	151,400	13.7	15.0
Information	16,000	1.4	1.9
Leisure and Hospitality	111,500	10.1	10.8
Manufacturing	79,700	7.2	8.4
Other Services	42,700	3.9	3.9
Professional and Business Services	191,600	17.3	14.1
Retail Trade	113,300	10.2	10.6
Transportation, Warehousing, and Utilities	58,800	5.3	4.2
Wholesale Trade	52,200	4.7	3.9

Note: Figures are non-farm employment as of December 2019. Figures are not seasonally adjusted and include workers 16 years of age and older; (1) Figures cover the Kansas City, MO-KS Metropolitan Statistical Area—see Appendix B for areas included
Source: Bureau of Labor Statistics, Current Employment Statistics, Employment, Hours, and Earnings

Occupations with Greatest Projected Employment Growth: 2019 – 2021

Occupation[1]	2019 Employment	2021 Projected Employment	Numeric Employment Change	Percent Employment Change
Personal Care Aides	68,410	72,800	4,390	6.4
Combined Food Preparation and Serving Workers, Including Fast Food	78,960	81,510	2,550	3.2
Registered Nurses	75,470	77,450	1,980	2.6
Laborers and Freight, Stock, and Material Movers, Hand	48,110	49,400	1,290	2.7
Cooks, Restaurant	29,950	31,210	1,260	4.2
General and Operations Managers	49,940	50,750	810	1.6
Heavy and Tractor-Trailer Truck Drivers	49,310	50,100	790	1.6
Software Developers, Applications	16,180	16,950	770	4.8
Nursing Assistants	40,550	41,240	690	1.7
Waiters and Waitresses	49,780	50,460	680	1.4

Note: Projections cover Missouri; (1) Sorted by numeric employment change
Source: www.projectionscentral.com, State Occupational Projections, 2019–2021 Short-Term Projections

Fastest Growing Occupations: 2019 – 2021

Occupation[1]	2019 Employment	2021 Projected Employment	Numeric Employment Change	Percent Employment Change
Information Security Analysts	2,890	3,080	190	6.6
Personal Care Aides	68,410	72,800	4,390	6.4
Statisticians	930	980	50	5.4
Cargo and Freight Agents	2,430	2,560	130	5.3
Respiratory Therapists	3,410	3,580	170	5.0
Operations Research Analysts	1,620	1,700	80	4.9
Software Developers, Applications	16,180	16,950	770	4.8
Physician Assistants	1,120	1,170	50	4.5
Speech-Language Pathologists	3,570	3,730	160	4.5
Industrial Engineers	5,900	6,160	260	4.4

Note: Projections cover Missouri; (1) Sorted by percent employment change and excludes occupations with numeric employment change less than 50
Source: www.projectionscentral.com, State Occupational Projections, 2019–2021 Short-Term Projections

TAXES

State Corporate Income Tax Rates

State	Tax Rate (%)	Income Brackets ($)	Num. of Brackets	Financial Institution Tax Rate (%)[a]	Federal Income Tax Ded.
Missouri	4.0	Flat rate	1	7.0	Yes (j)

Note: Tax rates as of January 1, 2020; (a) Rates listed are the corporate income tax rate applied to financial institutions or excise taxes based on income; (j) 50% of the federal income tax is deductible.
Source: Federation of Tax Administrators, State Corporate Income Tax Rates, January 1, 2020

State Individual Income Tax Rates

State	Tax Rate (%)	Income Brackets ($)	Personal Exemptions ($)			Standard Ded. ($)	
			Single	Married	Depend.	Single	Married
Missouri (a)	1.5 - 5.4	1,053 - 8,424	(d)	(d)	(d)	12,400	24,800 (d)

Note: Tax rates as of January 1, 2020; Local- and county-level taxes are not included; The deduction for federal income tax is limited to $5,000 for individuals and $10,000 for joint returns in Missouri and Montana, and to $6,500 for all filers in Oregon; (a) 19 states have statutory provision for automatically adjusting to the rate of inflation the dollar values of the income tax brackets, standard deductions, and/or personal exemptions. Michigan indexes the personal exemption only. Oregon does not index the income brackets for $125,000 and over; (d) These states use the personal exemption/standard deduction amounts provided in the federal Internal Revenue Code.
Source: Federation of Tax Administrators, State Individual Income Tax Rates, January 1, 2020

Various State Sales and Excise Tax Rates

State	State Sales Tax (%)	Gasoline[1] (¢/gal.)	Cigarette[2] ($/pack)	Spirits[3] ($/gal.)	Wine[4] ($/gal.)	Beer[5] ($/gal.)	Recreational Marijuana (%)
Missouri	4.225	17.42	0.17	2.00	0.42	0.06	Not legal

Note: All tax rates as of January 1, 2020; (1) The American Petroleum Institute has developed a methodology for determining the average tax rate on a gallon of fuel. Rates may include any of the following: excise taxes, environmental fees, storage tank fees, other fees or taxes, general sales tax, and local taxes; (2) The federal excise tax of $1.0066 per pack and local taxes are not included; (3) Rates are those applicable to off-premise sales of 40% alcohol by volume (a.b.v.) distilled spirits in 750ml containers. Local excise taxes are excluded; (4) Rates are those applicable to off-premise sales of 11% a.b.v. non-carbonated wine in 750ml containers; (5) Rates are those applicable to off-premise sales of 4.7% a.b.v. beer in 12 ounce containers.
Source: Tax Foundation, 2020 Facts & Figures: How Does Your State Compare?

State Business Tax Climate Index Rankings

State	Overall Rank	Corporate Tax Rank	Individual Income Tax Rank	Sales Tax Rank	Property Tax Rank	Unemployment Insurance Tax Rank
Missouri	14	5	24	24	7	9

Note: The index is a measure of how each state's tax laws affect economic performance. The lower the rank, the more favorable a state's tax system is for business. States without a given tax are given a ranking of 1. The scores/rankings for the District of Columbia do not affect other states. The 2020 index represents the tax climate as of July 1, 2019.
Source: Tax Foundation, State Business Tax Climate Index 2020

COMMERCIAL REAL ESTATE

Office Market

Market Area	Inventory (sq. ft.)	Vacancy Rate (%)	Under Construction (sq. ft.)	YTD Net Absorption (sq. ft.)	Total Average Asking Rent ($/sq. ft./year)
Kansas City	75,384,716	9.5	277,028	-261,043	21.11
National	4,923,349,992	13.0	102,814,961	2,049,925	29.54

Source: Newmark Grubb Knight Frank, National Office Market Report, 1st Quarter 2020

Industrial/Warehouse/R&D Market

Market Area	Inventory (sq. ft.)	Vacancy Rate (%)	Under Construction (sq. ft.)	YTD Net Absorption (sq. ft.)	Total Average Asking Rent ($/sq. ft./year)
Kansas City	284,707,933	4.1	7,144,232	2,021,459	4.62
National	15,332,123,451	5.4	322,705,045	48,296,842	7.54

Source: Newmark Grubb Knight Frank, National Industrial Market Report, 1st Quarter 2020

COMMERCIAL UTILITIES

Typical Monthly Electric Bills

Area	Commercial Service ($/month)		Industrial Service ($/month)	
	1,500 kWh	40 kW demand 14,000 kWh	1,000 kW demand 200,000 kWh	50,000 kW demand 32,500,000 kWh
City	n/a	1,710	31,111	2,389,367
Average[1]	203	1,612	25,706	2,520,671

Note: Figures are based on annualized rates; (1) Average based on 187 utilities surveyed; n/a not available
Source: Edison Electric Institute, Typical Bills and Average Rates Report, Summer 2019

TRANSPORTATION

Means of Transportation to Work

Area	Car/Truck/Van		Public Transportation			Bicycle	Walked	Other Means	Worked at Home
	Drove Alone	Car-pooled	Bus	Subway	Railroad				
City	81.0	8.1	2.7	0.0	0.0	0.2	1.9	1.3	4.8
MSA[1]	83.5	8.1	0.9	0.0	0.0	0.2	1.3	0.9	5.1
U.S.	76.4	9.1	2.5	1.9	0.6	0.6	2.7	1.3	4.9

Note: Figures are percentages and cover workers 16 years of age and older; (1) Figures cover the Kansas City, MO-KS Metropolitan Statistical Area—see Appendix B for areas included
Source: U.S. Census Bureau, 2014-2018 American Community Survey 5-Year Estimates

Travel Time to Work

Area	Less Than 10 Minutes	10 to 19 Minutes	20 to 29 Minutes	30 to 44 Minutes	45 to 59 Minutes	60 to 89 Minutes	90 Minutes or More
City	11.4	33.5	28.3	19.5	4.7	1.7	1.0
MSA[1]	12.3	30.9	25.3	21.4	6.7	2.5	1.0
U.S.	12.5	28.7	20.9	20.7	8.2	6.3	2.8

Note: Note: Figures are percentages and include workers 16 years old and over; (1) Figures cover the Kansas City, MO-KS Metropolitan Statistical Area—see Appendix B for areas included
Source: U.S. Census Bureau, 2014-2018 American Community Survey 5-Year Estimates

Key Congestion Measures

Area	1982	1992	2002	2012	2017
Annual Hours of Delay, Total (000)	6,319	18,760	32,336	43,434	48,328
Annual Hours of Delay, Per Auto Commuter	11	28	35	42	47
Annual Congestion Cost, Total (million $)	48	197	436	775	889
Annual Congestion Cost, Per Auto Commuter ($)	245	501	673	709	764

Source: Texas A&M Transportation Institute, 2019 Urban Mobility Report

Freeway Travel Time Index

Area	1982	1987	1992	1997	2002	2007	2012	2017
Urban Area Index[1]	1.04	1.08	1.11	1.12	1.14	1.14	1.15	1.15
Urban Area Rank[1,2]	61	44	49	69	69	80	71	71

Note: Freeway Travel Time Index—the ratio of travel time in the peak period to the travel time at free-flow conditions. For example, a value of 1.30 indicates a 20-minute free-flow trip takes 26 minutes in the peak (20 minutes x 1.30 = 26 minutes); (1) Covers the Kansas City MO-KS urban area; (2) Rank is based on 101 larger urban areas (#1 = highest travel time index)
Source: Texas A&M Transportation Institute, 2019 Urban Mobility Report

Public Transportation

Agency Name / Mode of Transportation	Vehicles Operated in Maximum Service[1]	Annual Unlinked Passenger Trips[2] (in thous.)	Annual Passenger Miles[3] (in thous.)
Kansas City Area Transportation Authority (KCATA)			
Bus (directly operated)	160	11,365.4	41,682.0
Bus Rapid Transit (directly operated)	11	1,160.2	3,193.5
Demand Response (directly operated)	9	73.6	306.9
Demand Response (purchased transportation)	57	214.8	1,750.4
Demand Response Taxi (purchased transportation)	47	89.4	532.6
Vanpool (purchased transportation)	27	54.0	1,919.6

Note: (1) Number of revenue vehicles operated by the given mode and type of service to meet the annual maximum service requirement. This is the revenue vehicle count during the peak season of the year; on the week and day that maximum service is provided. Vehicles operated in maximum service (VOMS) exclude atypical days and one-time special events; (2) Number of passengers who boarded public transportation vehicles. Passengers are counted each time they board a vehicle no matter how many vehicles they use to travel from their origin to their destination. (3) Sum of the distances ridden by all passengers during the entire fiscal year. Source: Federal Transit Administration, National Transit Database, 2018

Air Transportation

Airport Name and Code / Type of Service	Passenger Airlines[1]	Passenger Enplanements	Freight Carriers[2]	Freight (lbs)
Kansas City International (MCI)				
Domestic service (U.S. carriers - 2019)	30	5,719,811	17	104,487,071
International service (U.S. carriers - 2018)	6	19,397	3	73,907

*Note: (1) Includes all U.S.-based major, minor and commuter airlines that carried at least one passenger during the year; (2) Includes all U.S.-based airlines and freight carriers that transported at least one pound of freight during the year.
Source: Bureau of Transportation Statistics, The Intermodal Transportation Database, Air Carriers: T-100 Domestic Market (U.S. Carriers), 2019; Bureau of Transportation Statistics, The Intermodal Transportation Database, Air Carriers: T-100 International Market (U.S. Carriers), 2018*

Other Transportation Statistics

Major Highways:	I-29; I-35; I-70
Amtrak Service:	Yes
Major Waterways/Ports:	Kansas River; Missouri River

Source: Amtrak.com; Google Maps

BUSINESSES

Major Business Headquarters

Company Name	Industry	Rankings	
		Fortune[1]	Forbes[2]
Hallmark Cards	Media	-	108
JE Dunn Construction Group	Construction	-	130

*Note: (1) Companies that produce a 10-K are ranked 1 to 500 based on 2018 revenue; (2) All private companies with at least $2 billion in annual revenue through the end of their most current fiscal year are ranked 1 to 228; companies listed are headquartered in the city; dashes indicate no ranking
Source: Fortune, "Fortune 500," June 2019; Forbes, "America's Largest Private Companies," 2019 Rankings*

Fast-Growing Businesses

According to *Inc.*, Kansas City is home to one of America's 500 fastest-growing private companies: **Axiom Strategies** (#201). Criteria: must be an independent, privately-held, for-profit, U.S. corporation, proprietorship or partnership as of December 31, 2018; revenues must be at least $100,000 in 2015 and $2 million in 2018; must have four-year operating/sales history. *Inc., "America's 500 Fastest-Growing Private Companies,"* 2019

Minority Business Opportunity

Kansas City is home to one company which is on the *Hispanic Business* 500 list (500 largest U.S. Hispanic-owned companies based on revenue): **ECCO Select Corp.** (#255). Companies included must show at least 51 percent ownership by Hispanic U.S. citizens, and must maintain headquarters in one of the 50 states or Washington, D.C. *Hispanic Business, "Hispanic Business 500," June 20, 2013*

Minority- and Women-Owned Businesses

Group	All Firms		Firms with Paid Employees			
	Firms	Sales ($000)	Firms	Sales ($000)	Employees	Payroll ($000)
AIAN[1]	383	28,439	40	19,096	212	6,131
Asian	1,655	449,804	394	397,022	2,641	55,413
Black	6,399	285,544	446	184,710	3,071	65,508
Hispanic	1,699	280,269	193	242,365	2,021	62,147
NHOPI[2]	n/a	n/a	n/a	n/a	n/a	n/a
Women	14,564	3,136,838	1,555	2,791,200	12,646	498,565
All Firms	39,486	88,819,944	9,034	87,638,564	287,462	13,831,669

Note: Figures cover firms located in the city; minority- and women-owned business are defined as firms in which the corresponding group own 51% or more of the stock or equity of the company; (1) American Indian and Alaska Native; (2) Native Hawaiian and Other Pacific Islander; n/a not available
Source: U.S. Census Bureau, 2012 Economic Census, Survey of Business Owners

HOTELS & CONVENTION CENTERS

Hotels, Motels and Vacation Rentals

Area	5 Star		4 Star		3 Star		2 Star		1 Star		Not Rated	
	Num.	Pct.[3]	Num.	Pct.[3]	Num.	Pct.[3]	Num.	Pct.[3]	Num.	Pct.[3]	Num.	Pct.[3]
City[1]	0	0.0	14	4.5	60	19.4	47	15.2	60	19.4	129	41.6
Total[2]	266	1.3	1,517	7.2	4,627	21.8	3,210	15.1	3,974	18.7	7,601	35.9

Note: (1) Figures cover Kansas City and vicinity; (2) Figures cover all 100 cities in this book; (3) Percentage of hotels which have a given star rating; Star ratings are determined by priceline.com and offer an indication of the general quality of a particular hotel.
Source: priceline.com, April 27, 2020

Major Convention Centers

Name	Overall Space (sq. ft.)	Exhibit Space (sq. ft.)	Meeting Space (sq. ft.)	Meeting Rooms
Kansas City Convention Center	n/a	388,000	n/a	48
Overland Park Convention Center	140,000	60,000	15,000	n/a

Note: Table includes convention centers located in the Kansas City, MO-KS metro area; n/a not available
Source: Original research

Living Environment

COST OF LIVING

Cost of Living Index

Composite Index	Groceries	Housing	Utilities	Trans- portation	Health Care	Misc. Goods/ Services
95.8	102.4	82.6	100.6	92.6	105.9	101.7

Note: The Cost of Living Index measures regional differences in the cost of consumer goods and services, excluding taxes and non-consumer expenditures, for professional and managerial households in the top income quintile. It is based on more than 50,000 prices covering almost 60 different items for which prices are collected three times a year by chambers of commerce, economic development organizations or university applied economic centers in each participating urban area. The numbers shown should be read as a percentage above or below the national average of 100. For example, a value of 115.4 in the groceries column indicates that grocery prices are 15.4% higher than the national average. Small differences in the index numbers should not be interpreted as significant; Figures cover the Kansas City MO-KS urban area.
Source: The Council for Community and Economic Research, ACCRA Cost of Living Index, 2019

Grocery Prices

Area[1]	T-Bone Steak ($/pound)	Frying Chicken ($/pound)	Whole Milk ($/half gal.)	Eggs ($/dozen)	Orange Juice ($/64 oz.)	Coffee ($/11.5 oz.)
City[2]	12.07	1.73	2.02	1.33	3.27	4.27
Avg.	11.40	1.41	1.93	1.54	3.51	4.30
Min.	7.40	0.92	0.85	0.58	2.67	2.90
Max.	15.58	2.68	4.09	4.18	5.57	8.10

*Note: (1) Values for the local area are compared with the average, minimum and maximum values for all 290 areas in the Cost of Living Index; (2) Figures cover the Kansas City MO-KS urban area; **T-Bone Steak** (price per pound); **Frying Chicken** (price per pound, whole fryer); **Whole Milk** (half gallon carton); **Eggs** (price per dozen, Grade A, large); **Orange Juice** (64 oz. Tropicana or Florida Natural); **Coffee** (11.5 oz. can, vacuum-packed, Maxwell House, Hills Bros, or Folgers).*
Source: The Council for Community and Economic Research, ACCRA Cost of Living Index, 2019

Housing and Utility Costs

Area[1]	New Home Price ($)	Apartment Rent ($/month)	All Electric ($/month)	Part Electric ($/month)	Other Energy ($/month)	Telephone ($/month)
City[2]	268,109	1,141	-	100.21	66.26	185.40
Avg.	362,090	1,142	174.35	100.00	67.76	179.60
Min.	198,329	501	91.58	31.44	28.51	165.30
Max.	2,074,561	5,050	388.18	239.41	306.15	207.90

*Note: (1) Values for the local area are compared with the average, minimum and maximum values for all 290 areas in the Cost of Living Index; (2) Figures cover the Kansas City MO-KS urban area; **New Home Price** (2,400 sf living area, 8,000 sf lot, in urban area with full utilities); **Apartment Rent** (950 sf 2 bedroom/1.5 or 2 bath, unfurnished, excluding all utilities except water); **All Electric** (average monthly cost for an all-electric home); **Part Electric** (average monthly cost for a part-electric home); **Other Energy** (average monthly cost for natural gas, fuel oil, coal, wood, and any other forms of energy except electricity); **Telephone** (price includes the base monthly rate plus taxes and fees for three lines of mobile phone service).*
Source: The Council for Community and Economic Research, ACCRA Cost of Living Index, 2019

Health Care, Transportation, and Other Costs

Area[1]	Doctor ($/visit)	Dentist ($/visit)	Optometrist ($/visit)	Gasoline ($/gallon)	Beauty Salon ($/visit)	Men's Shirt ($)
City[2]	130.62	101.33	107.23	2.28	33.57	41.26
Avg.	114.85	97.58	106.10	2.50	38.15	32.15
Min.	39.00	62.22	52.22	1.53	16.88	10.27
Max.	206.67	151.53	258.67	3.79	79.29	59.30

*Note: (1) Values for the local area are compared with the average, minimum and maximum values for all 290 areas in the Cost of Living Index; (2) Figures cover the Kansas City MO-KS urban area; **Doctor** (general practitioners routine exam of an established patient); **Dentist** (adult teeth cleaning and periodic oral examination); **Optometrist** (full vision eye exam for established adult patient); **Gasoline** (one gallon regular unleaded, national brand, including all taxes, cash price at self-service pump if available); **Beauty Salon** (woman's shampoo, trim, and blow-dry); **Men's Shirt** (cotton/polyester dress shirt, pinpoint weave, long sleeves).*
Source: The Council for Community and Economic Research, ACCRA Cost of Living Index, 2019

HOUSING

House Price Index (HPI)

Area	National Ranking[2]	Quarterly Change (%)	One-Year Change (%)	Five-Year Change (%)
MSA[1]	101	1.32	5.21	37.34
U.S.[3]	—	1.26	5.09	32.88

Note: The HPI is a weighted repeat sales index. It measures average price changes in repeat sales or refinancings on the same properties. This information is obtained by reviewing repeat mortgage transactions on single-family properties whose mortgages have been purchased or securitized by Fannie Mae or Freddie Mac in January 1975; (1) Figures cover the Kansas City, MO-KS Metropolitan Statistical Area—see Appendix B for areas included; (2) Rankings are based on annual percentage change for all metro areas containing at least 15,000 transactions over the last 10 years and ranges from 1 to 232; (3) figures based on a weighted average of Census Division estimates using a seasonally adjusted, purchase-only index; all figures are for the period ending December 31, 2019
Source: Federal Housing Finance Agency, House Price Index, February 25, 2020

Median Single-Family Home Prices

Area	2017	2018	2019p	Percent Change 2018 to 2019
MSA[1]	194.8	206.5	219.4	6.2
U.S. Average	248.8	261.6	274.6	5.0

Note: Figures are median sales prices of existing single-family homes in thousands of dollars; (p) preliminary; (1) Figures cover the Kansas City, MO-KS Metropolitan Statistical Area—see Appendix B for areas included
Source: National Association of Realtors, Median Sales Price of Existing Single-Family Homes for Metropolitan Areas, 4th Quarter 2019

Qualifying Income Based on Median Sales Price of Existing Single-Family Homes

Area	With 5% Down ($)	With 10% Down ($)	With 20% Down ($)
MSA[1]	46,008	43,587	38,744
U.S. Average	58,663	55,575	49,400

Note: Figures are preliminary; Qualifying income is based on a mortgage rate of 3.76%. Monthly principal and interest payment is limited to 25% of income; (1) Figures cover the Kansas City, MO-KS Metropolitan Statistical Area—see Appendix B for areas included
Source: National Association of Realtors, Qualifying Income Based on Median Sales Price of Existing Single-Family Homes for Metropolitan Areas, 4th Quarter 2019

Median Apartment Condo-Coop Home Prices

Area	2017	2018	2019p	Percent Change 2018 to 2019
MSA[1]	n/a	n/a	n/a	n/a
U.S. Average	234.3	241.0	249.5	3.5

Note: Figures are median sales prices of existing apartment condo-coop homes in thousands of dollars; (p) preliminary; n/a not available; (1) Figures cover the Kansas City, MO-KS Metropolitan Statistical Area—see Appendix B for areas included
Source: National Association of Realtors, Median Sales Price of Existing Apartment Condo-Coop Homes for Metropolitan Areas, 4th Quarter 2019

Home Value Distribution

Area	Under $50,000	$50,000 -$99,999	$100,000 -$149,999	$150,000 -$199,999	$200,000 -$299,999	$300,000 -$499,999	$500,000 -$999,999	$1,000,000 or more
City	11.7	19.2	19.8	18.2	18.0	9.3	3.2	0.7
MSA[1]	6.8	14.2	18.7	19.1	21.5	14.4	4.5	0.8
U.S.	7.6	13.0	14.0	14.3	19.2	18.3	10.5	3.1

Note: Figures are percentages and cover owner-occupied housing units; (1) Figures cover the Kansas City, MO-KS Metropolitan Statistical Area—see Appendix B for areas included
Source: U.S. Census Bureau, 2014-2018 American Community Survey 5-Year Estimates

Homeownership Rate

Area	2011 (%)	2012 (%)	2013 (%)	2014 (%)	2015 (%)	2016 (%)	2017 (%)	2018 (%)	2019 (%)
MSA[1]	68.5	65.1	65.6	66.1	65.0	62.4	62.4	64.3	65.0
U.S.	66.1	65.4	65.1	64.5	63.7	63.4	63.9	64.4	64.6

Note: (1) Figures cover the Kansas City, MO-KS Metropolitan Statistical Area—see Appendix B for areas included
Source: U.S. Census Bureau, Housing Vacancies and Homeownership Annual Statistics: 2011-2019

Year Housing Structure Built

Area	2010 or Later	2000 -2009	1990 -1999	1980 -1989	1970 -1979	1960 -1969	1950 -1959	1940 -1949	Before 1940	Median Year
City	3.6	10.3	9.3	8.5	12.4	13.1	14.4	6.7	21.7	1965
MSA[1]	3.7	14.0	14.5	12.3	15.8	11.9	11.6	4.6	11.7	1976
U.S.	4.1	14.3	13.9	13.5	15.3	10.7	10.4	5.0	12.8	1977

Note: Figures are percentages except for Median Year; Note: (1) Figures cover the Kansas City, MO-KS
Metropolitan Statistical Area—see Appendix B for areas included
Source: U.S. Census Bureau, 2014-2018 American Community Survey 5-Year Estimates

Gross Monthly Rent

Area	Under $500	$500 -$999	$1,000 -$1,499	$1,500 -$1,999	$2,000 -$2,499	$2,500 -$2,999	$3,000 and up	Median ($)
City	9.7	51.8	30.1	6.2	1.4	0.3	0.5	899
MSA[1]	8.8	49.4	31.9	7.1	1.8	0.4	0.6	929
U.S.	9.8	38.5	29.6	12.9	5.1	2.1	2.0	1,023

Note: Figures are percentages except for Median; Gross rent is the contract rent plus the estimated average
monthly cost of utilities (electricity, gas, and water and sewer) and fuels (oil, coal, kerosene, wood, etc.) if these
are paid by the renter (or paid for the renter by someone else); (1) Figures cover the Kansas City, MO-KS
Metropolitan Statistical Area—see Appendix B for areas included
Source: U.S. Census Bureau, 2014-2018 American Community Survey 5-Year Estimates

HEALTH

Health Risk Factors

Category	MSA[1] (%)	U.S. (%)
Adults aged 18–64 who have any kind of health care coverage	85.0	87.3
Adults who reported being in good or better health	85.8	82.4
Adults who have been told they have high blood cholesterol	34.1	33.0
Adults who have been told they have high blood pressure	29.6	32.3
Adults who are current smokers	17.1	17.1
Adults who currently use E-cigarettes	4.5	4.6
Adults who currently use chewing tobacco, snuff, or snus	4.0	4.0
Adults who are heavy drinkers[2]	6.0	6.3
Adults who are binge drinkers[3]	20.7	17.4
Adults who are overweight (BMI 25.0 - 29.9)	36.1	35.3
Adults who are obese (BMI 30.0 - 99.8)	31.2	31.3
Adults who participated in any physical activities in the past month	73.7	74.4
Adults who always or nearly always wears a seat belt	94.9	94.3

Note: (1) Figures cover the Kansas City, MO-KS Metropolitan Statistical Area—see Appendix B for areas
included; (2) Heavy drinkers are classified as adult men having more than 14 drinks per week and adult women
having more than 7 drinks per week; (3) Binge drinkers are classified as males having five or more drinks on
one occasion or females having four or more drinks on one occasion
Source: Centers for Disease Control and Prevention, Behaviorial Risk Factor Surveillance System, SMART:
Selected Metropolitan Area Risk Trends, 2017

Acute and Chronic Health Conditions

Category	MSA[1] (%)	U.S. (%)
Adults who have ever been told they had a heart attack	3.9	4.2
Adults who have ever been told they have angina or coronary heart disease	3.8	3.9
Adults who have ever been told they had a stroke	3.4	3.0
Adults who have ever been told they have asthma	13.2	14.2
Adults who have ever been told they have arthritis	23.7	24.9
Adults who have ever been told they have diabetes[2]	9.7	10.5
Adults who have ever been told they had skin cancer	7.0	6.2
Adults who have ever been told they had any other types of cancer	6.4	7.1
Adults who have ever been told they have COPD	6.0	6.5
Adults who have ever been told they have kidney disease	2.5	3.0
Adults who have ever been told they have a form of depression	20.5	20.5

Note: (1) Figures cover the Kansas City, MO-KS Metropolitan Statistical Area—see Appendix B for areas
included; (2) Figures do not include pregnancy-related, borderline, or pre-diabetes
Source: Centers for Disease Control and Prevention, Behaviorial Risk Factor Surveillance System, SMART:
Selected Metropolitan Area Risk Trends, 2017

Health Screening and Vaccination Rates

Category	MSA[1] (%)	U.S. (%)
Adults aged 65+ who have had flu shot within the past year	60.6	60.7
Adults aged 65+ who have ever had a pneumonia vaccination	78.2	75.4
Adults who have ever been tested for HIV	36.9	36.1
Adults who have ever had the shingles or zoster vaccine?	27.7	28.9
Adults who have had their blood cholesterol checked within the last five years	87.4	85.9

Note: n/a not available; (1) Figures cover the Kansas City, MO-KS Metropolitan Statistical Area—see Appendix B for areas included.
Source: Centers for Disease Control and Prevention, Behaviorial Risk Factor Surveillance System, SMART: Selected Metropolitan Area Risk Trends, 2017

Disability Status

Category	MSA[1] (%)	U.S. (%)
Adults who reported being deaf	5.6	6.7
Are you blind or have serious difficulty seeing, even when wearing glasses?	3.7	4.5
Are you limited in any way in any of your usual activities due of arthritis?	11.2	12.9
Do you have difficulty doing errands alone?	6.5	6.8
Do you have difficulty dressing or bathing?	3.1	3.6
Do you have serious difficulty concentrating/remembering/making decisions?	9.4	10.7
Do you have serious difficulty walking or climbing stairs?	13.0	13.6

Note: (1) Figures cover the Kansas City, MO-KS Metropolitan Statistical Area—see Appendix B for areas included.
Source: Centers for Disease Control and Prevention, Behaviorial Risk Factor Surveillance System, SMART: Selected Metropolitan Area Risk Trends, 2017

Mortality Rates for the Top 10 Causes of Death in the U.S.

ICD-10[a] Sub-Chapter	ICD-10[a] Code	Age-Adjusted Mortality Rate[1] per 100,000 population	
		County[2]	U.S.
Malignant neoplasms	C00-C97	161.6	152.4
Ischaemic heart diseases	I20-I25	76.0	92.7
Other forms of heart disease	I30-I51	72.1	52.5
Chronic lower respiratory diseases	J40-J47	46.6	40.4
Cerebrovascular diseases	I60-I69	39.0	37.3
Other degenerative diseases of the nervous system	G30-G31	26.0	36.4
Other external causes of accidental injury	W00-X59	36.9	35.3
Organic, including symptomatic, mental disorders	F01-F09	46.4	30.0
Hypertensive diseases	I10-I15	25.1	22.9
Diabetes mellitus	E10-E14	18.3	21.3

Note: (a) ICD-10 = International Classification of Diseases 10th Revision; (1) Mortality rates are a three year average covering 2016-2018; (2) Figures cover Jackson County.
Source: Centers for Disease Control and Prevention, National Center for Health Statistics. Underlying Cause of Death 1999-2018 on CDC WONDER Online Database

Mortality Rates for Selected Causes of Death

ICD-10[a] Sub-Chapter	ICD-10[a] Code	Age-Adjusted Mortality Rate[1] per 100,000 population	
		County[2]	U.S.
Assault	X85-Y09	22.2	6.0
Diseases of the liver	K70-K76	13.3	14.2
Human immunodeficiency virus (HIV) disease	B20-B24	1.7	1.6
Influenza and pneumonia	J09-J18	13.8	14.2
Intentional self-harm	X60-X84	20.2	13.9
Malnutrition	E40-E46	3.2	1.9
Obesity and other hyperalimentation	E65-E68	1.3	2.1
Renal failure	N17-N19	23.2	12.8
Transport accidents	V01-V99	14.4	12.5
Viral hepatitis	B15-B19	1.5	1.4

Note: (a) ICD-10 = International Classification of Diseases 10th Revision; (1) Mortality rates are a three year average covering 2016-2018; (2) Figures cover Jackson County; Data are suppressed when the data meet the criteria for confidentiality constraints; Mortality rates are flagged as unreliable when the rate would be calculated with a numerator of 20 or less.
Source: Centers for Disease Control and Prevention, National Center for Health Statistics. Underlying Cause of Death 1999-2018 on CDC WONDER Online Database

Health Insurance Coverage

Area	With Health Insurance	With Private Health Insurance	With Public Health Insurance	Without Health Insurance	Population Under Age 19 Without Health Insurance
City	87.6	68.0	29.1	12.4	7.2
MSA[1]	90.9	75.2	27.1	9.1	5.4
U.S.	90.6	67.7	34.7	9.4	5.2

Note: Figures are percentages that cover the civilian noninstitutionalized population; (1) Figures cover the Kansas City, MO-KS Metropolitan Statistical Area—see Appendix B for areas included
Source: U.S. Census Bureau, 2014-2018 American Community Survey 5-Year Estimates

Number of Medical Professionals

Area	MDs[3]	DOs[3,4]	Dentists	Podiatrists	Chiropractors	Optometrists
County[1] (number)	2,106	408	610	43	308	138
County[1] (rate[2])	301.3	58.4	87.1	6.1	44.0	19.7
U.S. (rate[2])	281.9	23.4	69.1	6.0	27.5	16.4

Note: Data as of 2018 unless noted; (1) Data covers Jackson County; (2) Rate per 100,000 population; (3) Data as of 2017 and includes all active, non-federal physicians; (4) Doctor of Osteopathic Medicine
Source: U.S. Department of Health and Human Services, Health Resources and Services Administration, Bureau of Health Professions, Area Resource File (ARF) 2018-2019

Best Hospitals

According to *U.S. News,* the Kansas City, MO-KS metro area is home to two of the best hospitals in the U.S.: **St. Luke's Hospital of Kansas City** (2 adult specialties); **University of Kansas Hospital** (8 adult specialties). The hospitals listed were nationally ranked in at least one of 16 adult or 10 pediatric specialties. Only 206 hospitals nationwide were nationally ranked in one or more adult or pediatric specialty. Twenty hospitals in the U.S. made the Honor Roll. The Best Hospitals Honor Roll takes both the national rankings and the procedure and condition ratings into account. Hospitals received points if they were nationally ranked in one of the 16 adult specialties—the higher they ranked, the more points they got—and how many ratings of "high performing" they earned in the nine procedures and conditions. *U.S. News Online, "America's Best Hospitals 2019-20"*

According to *U.S. News,* the Kansas City, MO-KS metro area is home to one of the best children's hospitals in the U.S.: **Children's Mercy Kansas City** (10 pediatric specialties). The hospital listed was highly ranked in at least one of 10 pediatric specialties. Ninety-one children's hospitals in the U.S. were nationally ranked in at least one specialty. Hospitals received points for being ranked in a specialty, and the 10 hospitals with the most points across the 10 specialties make up the Honor Roll. *U.S. News Online, "America's Best Children's Hospitals 2019-20"*

EDUCATION

Public School District Statistics

District Name	Schls	Pupils	Pupil/ Teacher Ratio	Minority Pupils[1] (%)	Free Lunch Eligible[2] (%)	IEP[3] (%)
Center 58	8	2,639	11.8	80.1	67.9	15.3
Hickman Mills C-1	14	5,830	13.2	90.8	99.3	14.2
Kansas City 33	35	15,345	14.1	90.3	99.5	12.6
North Kansas City 74	32	20,763	15.1	43.6	40.5	11.8
Park Hill	18	12,038	15.0	32.6	22.8	11.0

Note: Table includes school districts with 2,000 or more students; (1) Percentage of students that are not non-Hispanic white; (2) Percentage of students that are eligible for the free lunch program; (3) Percentage of students that have an Individualized Education Program.
Source: U.S. Department of Education, National Center for Education Statistics, Common Core of Data, Local Education Agency (School District) Universe Survey: School Year 2018-2019; U.S. Department of Education, National Center for Education Statistics, Common Core of Data, Public Elementary/Secondary School Universe Survey: School Year 2018-2019

Best High Schools

According to *U.S. News,* Kansas City is home to one of the top 500 high schools in the U.S.: **Lincoln College Prep.** (#294). Nearly 18,000 public, magnet and charter schools were ranked based on their performance on state assessments and how well they prepare students for college. *U.S. News & World Report, "Best High Schools 2020"*

Highest Level of Education

Area	Less than H.S.	H.S. Diploma	Some College, No Deg.	Associate Degree	Bachelor's Degree	Master's Degree	Prof. School Degree	Doctorate Degree
City	10.4	25.5	22.5	7.3	21.4	9.3	2.4	1.2
MSA[1]	8.2	25.6	22.1	7.6	23.1	9.9	2.3	1.1
U.S.	12.3	27.1	20.6	8.4	19.4	8.6	2.1	1.4

Note: Figures cover persons age 25 and over; (1) Figures cover the Kansas City, MO-KS Metropolitan Statistical Area—see Appendix B for areas included
Source: U.S. Census Bureau, 2014-2018 American Community Survey 5-Year Estimates

Educational Attainment by Race

Area	High School Graduate or Higher (%)					Bachelor's Degree or Higher (%)				
	Total	White	Black	Asian	Hisp.[2]	Total	White	Black	Asian	Hisp.[2]
City	89.6	93.1	86.1	80.1	69.6	34.3	42.6	16.0	47.1	17.2
MSA[1]	91.8	93.3	88.3	85.7	68.0	36.4	38.9	20.0	54.6	16.7
U.S.	87.7	89.6	85.4	86.8	67.7	31.5	32.9	21.1	53.5	15.8

Note: Figures shown cover persons 25 years old and over; (1) Figures cover the Kansas City, MO-KS Metropolitan Statistical Area—see Appendix B for areas included; (2) People of Hispanic origin can be of any race
Source: U.S. Census Bureau, 2014-2018 American Community Survey 5-Year Estimates

School Enrollment by Grade and Control

Area	Preschool (%)		Kindergarten (%)		Grades 1 - 4 (%)		Grades 5 - 8 (%)		Grades 9 - 12 (%)	
	Public	Private	Public	Private	Public	Private	Public	Private	Public	Private
City	58.7	41.3	87.1	12.9	90.3	9.7	87.4	12.6	85.9	14.1
MSA[1]	55.9	44.1	88.9	11.1	89.2	10.8	88.8	11.2	89.7	10.3
U.S.	59.0	41.0	87.7	12.3	89.6	10.4	89.5	10.5	90.2	9.8

Note: Figures shown cover persons 3 years old and over; (1) Figures cover the Kansas City, MO-KS Metropolitan Statistical Area—see Appendix B for areas included
Source: U.S. Census Bureau, 2014-2018 American Community Survey 5-Year Estimates

Average Salaries of Public School Teachers

Area	2016-17		2017-18		Change from 2016-17 to 2017-18	
	Dollars	Rank[1]	Dollars	Rank[1]	Percent	Rank[2]
Missouri	48,620	41	49,304	43	1.41	27
U.S. Average	59,539	–	60,477	–	1.58	–

Note: (1) Rank ranges from 1 to 51 where 1 indicates highest salary; (2) Rank ranges from 1 to 51 where 1 indicates highest percent change.
Source: National Education Association, Rankings & Estimates: Rankings of the States 2018 and Estimates of School Statistics 2019

Higher Education

Four-Year Colleges			Two-Year Colleges			Medical Schools[1]	Law Schools[2]	Voc/ Tech[3]
Public	Private Non-profit	Private For-profit	Public	Private Non-profit	Private For-profit			
1	9	4	1	0	6	2	1	3

Note: Figures cover institutions located within the city limits and include main campuses only; (1) includes schools accredited by the Liaison Committee on Medical Education and the American Osteopathic Association's Commission on Osteopathic College Accreditation; (2) includes ABA-accredited schools, schools with provisional ABA accreditation, and state accredited schools; (3) includes all schools with programs that are less than 2 years.
Source: National Center for Education Statistics, Integrated Postsecondary Education System (IPEDS), 2018-19; Wikipedia, List of Medical Schools in the United States, accessed May 1, 2020; Wikipedia, List of Law Schools in the United States, accessed May 1, 2020

According to *U.S. News & World Report,* the Kansas City, MO-KS metro area is home to one of the top 75 medical schools for research in the U.S.: **University of Kansas Medical Center** (#62 tie). The rankings are based on a weighted average of 11 measures of quality: quality assessment; peer assessment score; assessment score by residency directors; research activity; total research activity; average research activity per faculty member; student selectivity; median MCAT total score; median undergraduate GPA; acceptance rate; and faculty resources. *U.S. News & World Report, "America's Best Graduate Schools, Medical, 2021"*

PRESIDENTIAL ELECTION

2016 Presidential Election Results

Area	Clinton	Trump	Johnson	Stein	Other
Jackson County	55.5	38.1	3.6	1.2	1.7
U.S.	48.0	45.9	3.3	1.1	1.7

Note: Results are percentages and may not add to 100% due to rounding
Source: Dave Leip's Atlas of U.S. Presidential Elections

EMPLOYERS

Major Employers

Company Name	Industry
B&V Baker Guam JV	Engineering services
Black and Veatch Corp	Engineering services
DST Systems	Data processing
Embarq Corporation	Telephone communications
Ford Motor Company	Automobile assembly
Hallmark Cards	Greeting cards
HCA Midwest Division	Hospital management
Honeywell International	Search & navigation equipment
Internal Revenue Service	Taxation department, government
North Kansas City Hospital	General medical & surgical hospitals
Park University	Colleges & universities
Performance Contracting	Drywall
St. Lukes Hospital of Kansas	General medical & surgical hospitals
United Auto Workers	Labor union
University of Kansas	Medical centers
University of Missouri System	General medical & surgical hospitals

Note: Companies shown are located within the Kansas City, MO-KS Metropolitan Statistical Area.
Source: Hoovers.com; Wikipedia

Best Companies to Work For

Burns & McDonnell, headquartered in Kansas City, is among "The 100 Best Companies to Work For." To pick the best companies, *Fortune* partnered with the Great Place to Work Institute. Two-thirds of a company's score is based on the results of the Institute's Trust Index survey, which is sent to a random sample of employees from each company. The questions related to attitudes about management's credibility, job satisfaction, and camaraderie. The other third of the scoring is based on the company's responses to the Institute's Culture Audit, which includes detailed questions about pay and benefit programs, and a series of open-ended questions about hiring practices, internal communication, training, recognition programs, and diversity efforts. Any company that is at least five years old with more than 1,000 U.S. employees is eligible. *Fortune*, "The 100 Best Companies to Work For," 2020

PUBLIC SAFETY

Crime Rate

Area	All Crimes	Violent Crimes				Property Crimes		
		Murder	Rape[3]	Robbery	Aggrav. Assault	Burglary	Larceny-Theft	Motor Vehicle Theft
City	5,896.8	27.8	81.7	332.0	1,148.8	753.8	2,698.2	854.6
Suburbs[1]	n/a	n/a	n/a	n/a	n/a	n/a	n/a	n/a
Metro[2]	n/a	n/a	n/a	n/a	n/a	n/a	n/a	n/a
U.S.	2,580.1	5.0	42.6	86.2	246.8	376.0	1,594.6	228.9

Note: Figures are crimes per 100,000 population; (1) All areas within the metro area that are located outside the city limits; (2) Figures cover the Kansas City, MO-KS Metropolitan Statistical Area—see Appendix B for areas included; n/a not available; (3) The city and U.S. figures shown were reported using the revised Uniform Crime Reporting (UCR) definition of rape. The suburban and metro area figures shown are an aggregate total of the data submitted using both the revised and legacy UCR definitions.
Source: FBI Uniform Crime Reports, 2018

Hate Crimes

Area	Number of Quarters Reported	Number of Incidents per Bias Motivation					
		Race/Ethnicity/Ancestry	Religion	Sexual Orientation	Disability	Gender	Gender Identity
City	4	29	0	3	0	0	1
U.S.	4	4,047	1,419	1,196	159	47	168

Source: Federal Bureau of Investigation, Hate Crime Statistics 2018

Identity Theft Consumer Reports

Area	Reports	Reports per 100,000 Population	Rank[2]
MSA[1]	2,355	110	159
U.S.	650,572	198	-

Note: (1) Figures cover the Kansas City, MO-KS Metropolitan Statistical Area—see Appendix B for areas included; (2) Rank ranges from 1 to 386 where 1 indicates greatest number of identity theft reports per 100,000 population
Source: Federal Trade Commission, Consumer Sentinel Network Data Book for January–December 2019

Fraud and Other Consumer Reports

Area	Reports	Reports per 100,000 Population	Rank[2]
MSA[1]	13,810	644	80
U.S.	2,590,177	789	-

Note: (1) Figures cover the Kansas City, MO-KS Metropolitan Statistical Area—see Appendix B for areas included; (2) Rank ranges from 1 to 386 where 1 indicates greatest number of fraud and other consumer reports per 100,000 population
Source: Federal Trade Commission, Consumer Sentinel Network Data Book for January–December 2019

SPORTS

Professional Sports Teams

Team Name	League	Year Established
Kansas City Chiefs	National Football League (NFL)	1963
Kansas City Royals	Major League Baseball (MLB)	1969
Sporting Kansas City	Major League Soccer (MLS)	1996

Note: Includes teams located in the Kansas City, MO-KS Metropolitan Statistical Area.
Source: Wikipedia, Major Professional Sports Teams of the United States and Canada, May 4, 2020

CLIMATE

Average and Extreme Temperatures

Temperature	Jan	Feb	Mar	Apr	May	Jun	Jul	Aug	Sep	Oct	Nov	Dec	Yr.
Extreme High (°F)	69	76	86	93	92	105	107	109	102	92	82	70	109
Average High (°F)	35	40	54	65	74	84	90	87	79	66	52	39	64
Average Temp. (°F)	26	31	44	55	64	74	79	77	68	56	43	30	54
Average Low (°F)	17	22	34	44	54	63	69	66	58	45	34	21	44
Extreme Low (°F)	-17	-19	-10	12	30	42	54	43	33	21	1	-23	-23

Note: Figures cover the years 1972-1990
Source: National Climatic Data Center, International Station Meteorological Climate Summary, 9/96

Average Precipitation/Snowfall/Humidity

Precip./Humidity	Jan	Feb	Mar	Apr	May	Jun	Jul	Aug	Sep	Oct	Nov	Dec	Yr.
Avg. Precip. (in.)	1.1	1.2	2.8	3.0	5.5	4.1	3.8	4.1	4.9	3.6	2.1	1.6	38.1
Avg. Snowfall (in.)	6	5	3	1	0	0	0	0	0	Tr	1	5	21
Avg. Rel. Hum. 6am (%)	76	77	78	77	82	84	84	86	86	80	79	78	80
Avg. Rel. Hum. 3pm (%)	58	59	54	50	54	54	51	53	53	51	57	60	54

Note: Figures cover the years 1972-1990; Tr = Trace amounts (<0.05 in. of rain; <0.5 in. of snow)
Source: National Climatic Data Center, International Station Meteorological Climate Summary, 9/96

Weather Conditions

Temperature			Daytime Sky			Precipitation		
10°F & below	32°F & below	90°F & above	Clear	Partly cloudy	Cloudy	0.01 inch or more precip.	0.1 inch or more snow/ice	Thunder-storms
22	110	39	112	134	119	103	17	51

Note: Figures are average number of days per year and cover the years 1972-1990
Source: National Climatic Data Center, International Station Meteorological Climate Summary, 9/96

HAZARDOUS WASTE

Superfund Sites

The Kansas City, MO-KS metro area is home to six sites on the EPA's Superfund National Priorities List: **Armour Road** (final); **Chemical Commodities, Inc.** (final); **Conservation Chemical Co.** (final); **Doepke Disposal (Holliday)** (final); **Lake City Army Ammunition Plant (Northwest Lagoon)** (final); **Lee Chemical** (final). There are a total of 1,387 Superfund sites with a status of proposed or final on the list in the U.S. *U.S. Environmental Protection Agency, National Priorities List, May 5, 2020*

AIR & WATER QUALITY

Air Quality Trends: Ozone

	1990	1995	2000	2005	2010	2012	2014	2016	2017	2018
MSA[1]	0.075	0.098	0.088	0.084	0.072	0.085	0.066	0.066	0.069	0.073
U.S.	0.088	0.089	0.088	0.082	0.073	0.075	0.067	0.069	0.068	0.069

Note: (1) Data covers the Kansas City, MO-KS Metropolitan Statistical Area—see Appendix B for areas included. The values shown are the composite ozone concentration averages among trend sites based on the highest fourth daily maximum 8-hour concentration in parts per million. These trends are based on sites having an adequate record of monitoring data during the trend period. Data from exceptional events are included.
Source: U.S. Environmental Protection Agency, Air Quality Monitoring Information, "Air Quality Trends by City, 1990-2018"

Air Quality Index

Area	Percent of Days when Air Quality was...[2]					AQI Statistics[2]	
	Good	Moderate	Unhealthy for Sensitive Groups	Unhealthy	Very Unhealthy	Maximum	Median
MSA[1]	57.8	38.6	3.3	0.3	0.0	172	47

Note: (1) Data covers the Kansas City, MO-KS Metropolitan Statistical Area—see Appendix B for areas included; (2) Based on 365 days with AQI data in 2018. Air Quality Index (AQI) is an index for reporting daily air quality. EPA calculates the AQI for five major air pollutants regulated by the Clean Air Act: ground-level ozone, particle pollution (aka particulate matter), carbon monoxide, sulfur dioxide, and nitrogen dioxide. The AQI runs from 0 to 500. The higher the AQI value, the greater the level of air pollution and the greater the health concern. There are six AQI categories: "Good" AQI is between 0 and 50. Air quality is considered satisfactory; "Moderate" AQI is between 51 and 100. Air quality is acceptable; "Unhealthy for Sensitive Groups" When AQI values are between 101 and 150, members of sensitive groups may experience health effects; "Unhealthy" When AQI values are between 151 and 200 everyone may begin to experience health effects; "Very Unhealthy" AQI values between 201 and 300 trigger a health alert; "Hazardous" AQI values over 300 trigger warnings of emergency conditions (not shown).
Source: U.S. Environmental Protection Agency, Air Quality Index Report, 2018

Air Quality Index Pollutants

Area	Percent of Days when AQI Pollutant was...[2]					
	Carbon Monoxide	Nitrogen Dioxide	Ozone	Sulfur Dioxide	Particulate Matter 2.5	Particulate Matter 10
MSA[1]	0.0	3.6	51.0	0.0	43.6	1.9

Note: (1) Data covers the Kansas City, MO-KS Metropolitan Statistical Area—see Appendix B for areas included; (2) Based on 365 days with AQI data in 2018. The Air Quality Index (AQI) is an index for reporting daily air quality. EPA calculates the AQI for five major air pollutants regulated by the Clean Air Act: ground-level ozone, particle pollution (also known as particulate matter), carbon monoxide, sulfur dioxide, and nitrogen dioxide. The AQI runs from 0 to 500. The higher the AQI value, the greater the level of air pollution and the greater the health concern.
Source: U.S. Environmental Protection Agency, Air Quality Index Report, 2018

Maximum Air Pollutant Concentrations: Particulate Matter, Ozone, CO and Lead

	Particulate Matter 10 (ug/m³)	Particulate Matter 2.5 Wtd AM (ug/m³)	Particulate Matter 2.5 24-Hr (ug/m³)	Ozone (ppm)	Carbon Monoxide (ppm)	Lead (ug/m³)
MSA[1] Level	61	8.2	17	0.074	1	n/a
NAAQS[2]	150	15	35	0.075	9	0.15
Met NAAQS[2]	Yes	Yes	Yes	Yes	Yes	n/a

Note: (1) Data covers the Kansas City, MO-KS Metropolitan Statistical Area—see Appendix B for areas included; Data from exceptional events are included; (2) National Ambient Air Quality Standards; ppm = parts per million; ug/m³ = micrograms per cubic meter; n/a not available.
Concentrations: Particulate Matter 10 (coarse particulate)—highest second maximum 24-hour concentration; Particulate Matter 2.5 Wtd AM (fine particulate)—highest weighted annual mean concentration; Particulate Matter 2.5 24-Hour (fine particulate)—highest 98th percentile 24-hour concentration; Ozone—highest fourth daily maximum 8-hour concentration; Carbon Monoxide—highest second maximum non-overlapping 8-hour concentration; Lead—maximum running 3-month average
Source: U.S. Environmental Protection Agency, Air Quality Monitoring Information, "Air Quality Statistics by City, 2018"

Maximum Air Pollutant Concentrations: Nitrogen Dioxide and Sulfur Dioxide

	Nitrogen Dioxide AM (ppb)	Nitrogen Dioxide 1-Hr (ppb)	Sulfur Dioxide AM (ppb)	Sulfur Dioxide 1-Hr (ppb)	Sulfur Dioxide 24-Hr (ppb)
MSA[1] Level	12	48	n/a	6	n/a
NAAQS[2]	53	100	30	75	140
Met NAAQS[2]	Yes	Yes	n/a	Yes	n/a

Note: (1) Data covers the Kansas City, MO-KS Metropolitan Statistical Area—see Appendix B for areas included; Data from exceptional events are included; (2) National Ambient Air Quality Standards; ppm = parts per million; ug/m³ = micrograms per cubic meter; n/a not available.
Concentrations: Nitrogen Dioxide AM—highest arithmetic mean concentration; Nitrogen Dioxide 1-Hr—highest 98th percentile 1-hour daily maximum concentration; Sulfur Dioxide AM—highest annual mean concentration; Sulfur Dioxide 1-Hr—highest 99th percentile 1-hour daily maximum concentration; Sulfur Dioxide 24-Hr—highest second maximum 24-hour concentration
Source: U.S. Environmental Protection Agency, Air Quality Monitoring Information, "Air Quality Statistics by City, 2018"

Drinking Water

Water System Name	Pop. Served	Primary Water Source Type	Violations[1]
Kansas City	471,767	Surface	15

Note: (1) Total number of violations (both active and inactive) in the EPA database
Source: U.S. Environmental Protection Agency, Office of Ground Water and Drinking Water, Safe Drinking Water Information System (based on data extracted May 5, 2020)

Lincoln, Nebraska

Background

Lincoln, the capital of Nebraska and the seat of Lancaster County is located in the southeastern part of the state. It is a thriving and multifaceted city with a fascinating history and a dynamic and expanding contemporary economy and cultural life. Lincoln today is the second-largest city in Nebraska.

The site first attracted the attention of settlers in 1856 when commercial explorers found saline deposits on the banks of the Salt Creek, and what is today known as Capitol Beach Lake. Salt, in fact, constituted the first major commercial activity in the city, with two large salt "boilers," Cox and Peckham, supplying this vital resource to farmers and townspeople in a wide stretch of the Plains region. Captain W.T. Donovan came to the area as a salt company representative, settling there permanently in 1867. He named his claim Lancaster after his home in Pennsylvania, which became the county name.

Omaha had been the capital of Nebraska, but with statehood, a drive began to move the capital south of the Platte River. The new capital, originally to be called simply Capitol City, was sited at Lancaster. State Senator J.H.N. Patrick proposed changing the name to Lincoln, largely because he thought it would discourage Democratic support.

In the 1880s—a dynamic period of Lincoln's early economic growth—William Jennings Bryan came to town as a lawyer and budding politician, and two years later was elected to the U.S. Congress. Another Lincoln luminary from this period was General John J. Pershing, who was an instructor in military science at the recently established University of Nebraska.

Designated as a "refugee-friendly" city by the U.S. Department of State in the 1970s, the city was the twelfth-largest resettlement site per capita in the United States by 2000. Refugee Vietnamese, Karen (Burmese ethnic minority), Sudanese and Yazidi (Iraqi ethnic minority) people, as well as refugees from the Middle East, have been resettled in the city. Lincoln Public Schools took in more than 3,000 students speaking 50 languages during the 2017-2018 school year.

The city's downtown is a modern entertainment, commercial, and office center, and on its west edge is the historic Haymarket District. The state capitol building, designed by Bertram Grosvenor Goodhue in 1919, is an architectural attraction of international repute, and its modernist central white stone column, visible from surrounding prairie hilltops for miles, still uniquely defines the Lincoln skyline. Lincoln is also a city of parks, with 100 parks covering more than 6,000 acres, including a children's zoo and, in cooperation with Lancaster County, a wilderness park. Recent years saw restoration and enhancement to the downtown and improved flood control measures.

The University of Nebraska is city's largest institution of higher learning and its football team attracts crowds of 78,000 to Memorial Stadium. The University of Nebraska is a major hub of cultural activity in the city, and is the site of the State Museum of Natural History. Nebraska Wesleyan University and Union College are also located in Lincoln.

The city offers rich cultural resources that draw on its increasingly cosmopolitan character, as well as on the rural traditions of the state as a whole. The Lied Center for Performing Arts, on the University of Nebraska's downtown campus, features a full range of musical and dramatic performances, and the city also hosts the Nebraska State Fair in early September. In 2010, Lincoln hosted the Special Olympics USA National Games.

Government is the largest employer in Lincoln, with health services the largest non-industrial private sector employer. The city hosts operations of many major employers, and Bryan Medical Center is one of the largest.

The joint County-City Building houses the mayor's office, the city council, Lancaster County commissioner's office, and county, district, and juvenile courts, and the judicial center is connected to the County-City Building by elevated walkways.

The climate in Lincoln is characterized by the robust and dramatic range of the Great Plains area as a whole. Most precipitation falls during April through September, and thunderstorms are predominant in the summer months. Lincoln lies in a valley that affords considerable protection against tornadoes, although more than 25 Federal Signal warning sirens throughout the city are still tested every Wednesday morning, except in the winter months.

Rankings

General Rankings

- For its "Best for Vets: Places to Live 2019" rankings, *Military Times* evaluated 599 cities (83 large, 234 medium, 282 small) and compared the locations across three broad categories: veteran and military culture/services; economic indicators; and livability factors such as health, crime, traffic, and school quality. Lincoln ranked #12 out of the top 25, in the large city category (populations of more than 250,000). Data points more specific to veterans and the military weighed more heavily than the rest. *rebootcamp.militarytimes.com, "Military Times Best Places to Live 2019," September 10, 2018*

- In their sixth annual survey, Livability.com looked at data for more than 1,000 U.S. cities to determine the rankings for Livability's "Top 100 Best Places to Live" in 2019. Lincoln ranked #9. Criteria: median home value capped at $250,000; affordable living; vibrant economy; education, demographics, health care options. transportation & infrastructure; abundant lifestyle amenities. *Livability.com, "Top 100 Best Places to Live 2019" March 2019*

Business/Finance Rankings

- Lincoln was the #11-ranked city for savers, according to a study by the finance site GOBankingRates, which considered the prospects for people trying to save money. Criteria: average monthly cost of grocery items; median home listing price; median rent; median income; transportation costs; gas prices; and the cost of eating out for an inexpensive and mid-range meal in 100 U.S. cities. *www.gobankingrates.com, "The 20 Best (and Worst) Places to Live If You're Trying to Save Money," August 27, 2019*

- Lincoln was ranked #11 among 100 U.S. cities for most difficult conditions for savers, according to a study by the finance site GOBankingRates. Criteria: average monthly cost of grocery items; median home listing price; median rent; median income; transportation costs; gas prices; and the cost of eating out for an inexpensive and mid-range meal. *www.gobankingrates.com, "The 20 Best (and Worst) Places to Live If You're Trying to Save Money," August 27, 2019*

- The Lincoln metro area appeared on the Milken Institute "2020 Best Performing Cities" list. Rank: #139 out of 200 large metro areas. Criteria: job growth; wage and salary growth; high-tech output growth. *Milken Institute, "Best-Performing Cities 2020," February 26, 2020*

- *Forbes* ranked the 200 most populous metro areas to determine the nation's "Best Places for Business and Careers." The Lincoln metro area was ranked #36. Criteria: costs (business and living); job growth (past and projected); income growth; quality of life; educational attainment (college and high school); projected economic growth; cultural and leisure opportunities; workplace tolerance laws; net migration patterns. *Forbes, "The Best Places for Business and Careers 2019: Seattle Still On Top," October 30, 2019*

Children/Family Rankings

- Lincoln was selected as one of the most playful cities in the U.S. by KaBOOM! The organization's Playful City USA initiative honors cities and towns across the nation that have made their communities more playable. Criteria: pledging to integrate play as a solution to challenges in their communities; making it easy for children to get active and balanced play; creating more family-friendly and innovative communities as a result. *KaBOOM! National Campaign for Play, "2017 Playful City USA Communities"*

- Lincoln was selected as one of the best cities for newlyweds by *Rent.com*. The city ranked #8 of 15. Criteria: cost of living; availability of affordable rental inventory; annual household income; activities and restaurant options; percentage of married couples; concentration of millennials; safety. *Rent.com, "The 15 Best Cities for Newlyweds," December 11, 2018*

Dating/Romance Rankings

- Lincoln was selected as one of the most romantic cities in the U.S. by video-rental kiosk company Redbox. The city ranked #8 out of 20. Criteria: number of romance-related rentals in 2016. *Redbox, "20 Most Romantic Cities," February 6, 2017*

Education Rankings

- Lincoln was selected as one of America's most literate cities. The city ranked #24 out of the 82 largest U.S. cities. Criteria: number of booksellers; library resources; Internet resources; educational attainment; periodical publishing resources; newspaper circulation. *Central Connecticut State University, "America's Most Literate Cities, 2016," March 31, 2017*

Environmental Rankings

- Lincoln was highlighted as one of the cleanest metro areas for ozone air pollution in the U.S. during 2015 through 2017. The list represents cities with no monitored ozone air pollution in unhealthful ranges. *American Lung Association, "State of the Air 2019," April 24, 2019*

- Lincoln was highlighted as one of the top 25 cleanest metro areas for year-round particle pollution (Annual PM 2.5) in the U.S. during 2015 through 2017. The area ranked #23. *American Lung Association, "State of the Air 2019," April 24, 2019*

- Lincoln was highlighted as one of the top 104 cleanest metro areas for short-term particle pollution (24-hour PM 2.5) in the U.S. during 2015 through 2017. Monitors in these cities reported no days with unhealthful PM 2.5 levels. *American Lung Association, "State of the Air 2019," April 24, 2019*

Health/Fitness Rankings

- For each of the 100 largest cities in the United States, the American Fitness Index®, published by the American College of Sports Medicine and the Anthem Foundation, evaluated community infrastructure and 33 health behaviors including preventive health, levels of chronic disease conditions, pedestrian safety, air quality, and community resources that support physical activity. Lincoln ranked #17 for "community fitness." *americanfitnessindex.org, "ACSM American Fitness Index Health and Community Fitness Status of the 100 Largest U.S. Cities," May 14, 2019*

- *Men's Health* ranked 100 major U.S. cities in terms of the best cities for men. Lincoln ranked #11. Criteria: health; fitness; quality of life. *Men's Health, "The Best & Worst Cities for Men Who Want to Be Fit and Happy," January 1, 2016*

- The Lincoln metro area ranked #58 out of 189 in The Gallup-Sharecare Well-Being Index. Criteria: purpose; social well being; financial health; community and physical health. Results are based on telephone interviews with adults, aged 18 and older, living in metropolitan areas in the 50 U.S. states and the District of Columbia. *Gallup-Sharecare, "State of American Well-Being, 2017 Community Well-Being Rankings" March 2018*

Real Estate Rankings

- *WalletHub* compared the most populated U.S. cities, as well as at least two of the most populated cities in each state, for a total of 179, to determine which had the best markets for real estate agents. Lincoln ranked #126 where demand was high and pay was the best. Criteria: sales per agent; annual median wage for real-estate agents; monthly average starting salary for real estate agents; real estate job density and competition; unemployment rate; home turnover rate; housing-market health index; and other relevant metrics. *www.WalletHub.com, "2019's Best Places to Be a Real Estate Agent," April 24, 2019*

Safety Rankings

- Allstate ranked the 200 largest cities in America in terms of driver safety. Lincoln ranked #21. Criteria: internal property damage claims over a two-year period from January 2016 to December 2017. The report helps increase the importance of safety and awareness behind the wheel. *Allstate, "Allstate America's Best Drivers Report, 2019" June 24, 2019*

- The National Insurance Crime Bureau ranked 382 metro areas in the U.S. in terms of per capita rates of vehicle theft. The Lincoln metro area ranked #252 (#1 = highest rate). Criteria: number of vehicle theft offenses per 100,000 inhabitants in 2018. *National Insurance Crime Bureau, "Hot Spots 2018," June 25, 2019*

Seniors/Retirement Rankings

- From its Best Cities for Successful Aging indexes, the Milken Institute generated rankings for metropolitan areas, weighing data in nine categories—health care, wellness, living arrangements, transportation and convenience, financial characteristics, education, employment, community engagement, and overall livability. The Lincoln metro area was ranked #35 overall in the small metro area category. *Milken Institute, "Best Cities for Successful Aging, 2017" March 14, 2017*

Sports/Recreation Rankings

- Lincoln was chosen as a bicycle friendly community by the League of American Bicyclists. A "Bicycle Friendly Community" welcomes cyclists by providing safe and supportive accommodation for cycling and encouraging people to bike for transportation and recreation. There are five award levels: Diamond; Platinum; Gold; Silver; and Bronze. The community achieved an award level of Silver. *League of American Bicyclists, "Fall 2019 Awards-Bicycle Friendly Community Master List," November 21, 2019*

- Lincoln was chosen as one of America's best cities for bicycling. The city ranked #35 out of 50. Criteria: cycling infrastructure that is safe and friendly for all ages; energy and bike culture. The editors only considered cities with populations of 100,000 or more. *Bicycling, "The 50 Best Bike Cities in America," October 10, 2018*

Women/Minorities Rankings

- Personal finance website *WalletHub* compared more than 180 U.S. cities—including the 150 most populated U.S. cities, plus at least two of the most populated cities in each state—across two key dimensions, "Hispanic Business-Friendliness" and "Hispanic Purchasing Power", to arrive at the most favorable conditions for Hispanic entrepreneurs. Lincoln was ranked #106 out of 182. Criteria includes: share of Hispanic-Owned Businesses; Hispanic entrepreneurship rate to median annual income of Hispanics; Small Business-Friendliness score; cost of living; and number of Hispanics with at least a bachelor's degree. *WalletHub.com, "2019's Best Cities for Hispanic Entrepreneurs," May 1, 2019*

Miscellaneous Rankings

- *WalletHub* compared the 150 most populated U.S. cities to determine their operating efficiency. A "Quality of Services" score was constructed for each city and then divided by the total budget per capita to reveal which were managed the best. Lincoln ranked #25. Criteria: financial stability; economy; education; safety; health; infrastructure and pollution. *www.WalletHub.com, "2019's Best- & Worst-Run Cities in America," July 1, 2019*

Business Environment

CITY FINANCES

City Government Finances

Component	2017 ($000)	2017 ($ per capita)
Total Revenues	424,642	1,531
Total Expenditures	477,060	1,720
Debt Outstanding	1,368,810	4,935
Cash and Securities[1]	739,649	2,667

Note: (1) Cash and security holdings of a government at the close of its fiscal year, including those of its dependent agencies, utilities, and liquor stores.
Source: U.S. Census Bureau, State & Local Government Finances 2017

City Government Revenue by Source

Source	2017 ($000)	2017 ($ per capita)	2017 (%)
General Revenue			
From Federal Government	43,639	157	10.3
From State Government	24,735	89	5.8
From Local Governments	2,212	8	0.5
Taxes			
Property	71,254	257	16.8
Sales and Gross Receipts	74,546	269	17.6
Personal Income	0	0	0.0
Corporate Income	0	0	0.0
Motor Vehicle License	0	0	0.0
Other Taxes	25,052	90	5.9
Current Charges	76,816	277	18.1
Liquor Store	0	0	0.0
Utility	58,176	210	13.7
Employee Retirement	16,168	58	3.8

Source: U.S. Census Bureau, State & Local Government Finances 2017

City Government Expenditures by Function

Function	2017 ($000)	2017 ($ per capita)	2017 (%)
General Direct Expenditures			
Air Transportation	0	0	0.0
Corrections	0	0	0.0
Education	0	0	0.0
Employment Security Administration	0	0	0.0
Financial Administration	5,321	19	1.1
Fire Protection	26,166	94	5.5
General Public Buildings	1,064	3	0.2
Governmental Administration, Other	6,918	24	1.5
Health	28,979	104	6.1
Highways	62,909	226	13.2
Hospitals	0	0	0.0
Housing and Community Development	4,849	17	1.0
Interest on General Debt	50,005	180	10.5
Judicial and Legal	0	0	0.0
Libraries	5,756	20	1.2
Parking	6,204	22	1.3
Parks and Recreation	17,265	62	3.6
Police Protection	40,927	147	8.6
Public Welfare	8,279	29	1.7
Sewerage	28,450	102	6.0
Solid Waste Management	12,370	44	2.6
Veterans' Services	0	0	0.0
Liquor Store	0	0	0.0
Utility	91,315	329	19.1
Employee Retirement	12,134	43	2.5

Source: U.S. Census Bureau, State & Local Government Finances 2017

DEMOGRAPHICS

Population Growth

Area	1990 Census	2000 Census	2010 Census	2018* Estimate	Population Growth (%) 1990-2018	2010-2018
City	193,629	225,581	258,379	280,849	45.0	8.7
MSA[1]	229,091	266,787	302,157	327,221	42.8	8.3
U.S.	248,709,873	281,421,906	308,745,538	322,903,030	29.8	4.6

Note: (1) Figures cover the Lincoln, NE Metropolitan Statistical Area—see Appendix B for areas included; (*) 2014-2018 5-year estimated population
Source: U.S. Census Bureau, 1990 Census, Census 2000, Census 2010, 2014-2018 American Community Survey 5-Year Estimates

Household Size

Area	One	Two	Three	Four	Five	Six	Seven or More	Average Household Size
City	31.6	35.0	13.8	11.5	5.1	2.0	0.9	2.40
MSA[1]	30.1	35.8	13.8	12.1	5.3	2.0	1.0	2.40
U.S.	27.7	33.9	15.7	13.0	6.0	2.3	1.4	2.60

Note: (1) Figures cover the Lincoln, NE Metropolitan Statistical Area—see Appendix B for areas included
Source: U.S. Census Bureau, 2014-2018 American Community Survey 5-Year Estimates

Race

Area	White Alone[2] (%)	Black Alone[2] (%)	Asian Alone[2] (%)	AIAN[3] Alone[2] (%)	NHOPI[4] Alone[2] (%)	Other Race Alone[2] (%)	Two or More Races (%)
City	85.2	4.4	4.7	0.6	0.1	1.4	3.6
MSA[1]	86.9	3.8	4.1	0.6	0.1	1.3	3.3
U.S.	72.7	12.7	5.4	0.8	0.2	4.9	3.2

Note: (1) Figures cover the Lincoln, NE Metropolitan Statistical Area—see Appendix B for areas included; (2) Alone is defined as not being in combination with one or more other races; (3) American Indian and Alaska Native; (4) Native Hawaiian and Other Pacific Islander
Source: U.S. Census Bureau, 2014-2018 American Community Survey 5-Year Estimates

Hispanic or Latino Origin

Area	Total (%)	Mexican (%)	Puerto Rican (%)	Cuban (%)	Other (%)
City	7.4	5.5	0.2	0.2	1.5
MSA[1]	6.6	4.8	0.3	0.1	1.4
U.S.	17.8	11.2	1.7	0.7	4.2

Note: Persons of Hispanic or Latino origin can be of any race; (1) Figures cover the Lincoln, NE Metropolitan Statistical Area—see Appendix B for areas included
Source: U.S. Census Bureau, 2014-2018 American Community Survey 5-Year Estimates

Segregation

Type	1990	2000	2010	2010 Rank[2]	1990-2000	1990-2010	2000-2010
Black/White	n/a	n/a	n/a	n/a	n/a	n/a	n/a
Asian/White	n/a	n/a	n/a	n/a	n/a	n/a	n/a
Hispanic/White	n/a	n/a	n/a	n/a	n/a	n/a	n/a

Note: All figures cover the Metropolitan Statistical Area—see Appendix B for areas included; Figures are based on an analysis of 1990, 2000, and 2010 Census Decennial Census tract data by William H. Frey, Brookings Institution and the University of Michigan Social Science Data Analysis Network. In this analysis all racial groups (whites, blacks, and asians) are non-Hispanic members of those races. Hispanics are shown as a separate category; (1) Segregation Indices are Dissimilarity Indices that measure the degree to which the minority group is distributed differently than whites across census tracts. They range from 0 (complete integration) to 100 (complete segregation) where the value indicates the percentage of the minority group that needs to move to be distributed exactly like whites; (2) Ranges from 1 (most segregated) to 102 (least segregated); n/a not available.
Source: www.CensusScope.org

Ancestry

Area	German	Irish	English	American	Italian	Polish	French[2]	Scottish	Dutch
City	34.7	12.0	8.5	3.7	2.1	2.6	2.1	1.5	2.1
MSA[1]	36.6	11.9	8.4	3.8	2.0	2.7	2.1	1.5	2.4
U.S.	13.7	9.9	7.3	6.4	5.2	2.8	2.4	1.7	1.2

Note: Figures are the percentage of the total population reporting a particular ancestry. The nine most commonly reported ancestries in the U.S. are shown. Figures include multiple ancestries (e.g. if a person reported being Irish and Italian, they were included in both columns); (1) Figures cover the Lincoln, NE Metropolitan Statistical Area—see Appendix B for areas included; (2) Excludes Basque
Source: U.S. Census Bureau, 2014-2018 American Community Survey 5-Year Estimates

Foreign-born Population

Area	Any Foreign Country	Asia	Mexico	Europe	Caribbean	Central America[2]	South America	Africa	Canada
City	8.4	4.5	1.2	0.9	0.2	0.3	0.3	0.7	0.1
MSA[1]	7.4	3.9	1.1	0.9	0.2	0.3	0.3	0.7	0.1
U.S.	13.5	4.1	3.5	1.5	1.3	1.1	0.9	0.7	0.3

Note: (1) Figures cover the Lincoln, NE Metropolitan Statistical Area—see Appendix B for areas included; (2) Excludes Mexico.
Source: U.S. Census Bureau, 2014-2018 American Community Survey 5-Year Estimates

Marital Status

Area	Never Married	Now Married[2]	Separated	Widowed	Divorced
City	39.0	45.1	1.1	4.4	10.4
MSA[1]	36.8	47.8	1.1	4.4	10.0
U.S.	33.3	48.1	2.0	5.8	10.8

Note: Figures are percentages and cover the population 15 years of age and older; (1) Figures cover the Lincoln, NE Metropolitan Statistical Area—see Appendix B for areas included; (2) Excludes separated
Source: U.S. Census Bureau, 2014-2018 American Community Survey 5-Year Estimates

Disability by Age

Area	All Ages	Under 18 Years Old	18 to 64 Years Old	65 Years and Over
City	10.9	4.5	8.7	33.5
MSA[1]	10.7	4.2	8.4	33.1
U.S.	12.6	4.2	10.3	35.0

Note: Figures show percent of the civilian noninstitutionalized population that reported having a disability. Disability status is determined from six types of difficulty: vision, hearing, cognitive, ambulatory, self-care, and independent living. For children under 5 years old, hearing and vision difficulty are used to determine disability status. For children between the ages of 5 and 14, disability status is determined from hearing, vision, cognitive, ambulatory, and self-care difficulties. For people aged 15 years and older, they are considered to have a disability if they have difficulty with any one of the six difficulty types; Note: (1) Figures cover the Lincoln, NE Metropolitan Statistical Area—see Appendix B for areas included
Source: U.S. Census Bureau, 2014-2018 American Community Survey 5-Year Estimates

Age

Area	Under Age 5	Age 5–19	Age 20–34	Age 35–44	Age 45–54	Age 55–64	Age 65–74	Age 75–84	Age 85+	Median Age
City	6.6	19.8	26.9	12.2	10.7	10.9	7.5	3.6	1.7	32.6
MSA[1]	6.5	20.3	25.2	12.2	11.1	11.5	7.8	3.7	1.7	33.5
U.S.	6.1	19.3	20.7	12.6	13.2	12.8	8.8	4.5	1.9	37.9

Note: (1) Figures cover the Lincoln, NE Metropolitan Statistical Area—see Appendix B for areas included
Source: U.S. Census Bureau, 2014-2018 American Community Survey 5-Year Estimates

Gender

Area	Males	Females	Males per 100 Females
City	140,897	139,952	100.7
MSA[1]	164,425	162,796	101.0
U.S.	158,984,190	163,918,840	97.0

Note: (1) Figures cover the Lincoln, NE Metropolitan Statistical Area—see Appendix B for areas included
Source: U.S. Census Bureau, 2014-2018 American Community Survey 5-Year Estimates

Religious Groups by Family

Area	Catholic	Baptist	Non-Den.	Methodist[2]	Lutheran	LDS[3]	Pente-costal	Presby-terian[4]	Muslim[5]	Judaism
MSA[1]	14.8	2.4	1.9	7.2	11.3	1.2	1.4	3.9	0.2	0.2
U.S.	19.1	9.3	4.0	4.0	2.3	2.0	1.9	1.6	0.8	0.7

Note: Figures are the number of adherents as a percentage of the total population; (1) Figures cover the Lincoln, NE Metropolitan Statistical Area—see Appendix B for areas included; (2) Methodist/Pietist; (3) Latter Day Saints; (4) Reformed; (5) Figures are estimates
Source: Association of Statisticians of American Religious Bodies, 2010 U.S. Religion Census: Religious Congregations & Membership Study

Religious Groups by Tradition

Area	Catholic	Evangelical Protestant	Mainline Protestant	Other Tradition	Black Protestant	Orthodox
MSA[1]	14.8	14.8	16.2	2.0	0.1	0.1
U.S.	19.1	16.2	7.3	4.3	1.6	0.3

Note: Figures are the number of adherents as a percentage of the total population; (1) Figures cover the Lincoln, NE Metropolitan Statistical Area—see Appendix B for areas included
Source: Association of Statisticians of American Religious Bodies, 2010 U.S. Religion Census: Religious Congregations & Membership Study

ECONOMY

Gross Metropolitan Product

Area	2017	2018	2019	2020	Rank[2]
MSA[1]	19.7	20.6	21.2	22.0	125

Note: Figures are in billions of dollars; (1) Figures cover the Lincoln, NE Metropolitan Statistical Area—see Appendix B for areas included; (2) Rank is based on 2018 data and ranges from 1 to 381
Source: U.S. Conference of Mayors, U.S. Metro Economies: GMP & Employment 2018-2020, September 2019

Economic Growth

Area	2015-17 (%)	2018 (%)	2019 (%)	2020 (%)	Rank[2]
MSA[1]	0.3	2.1	1.3	1.5	287
U.S.	1.9	2.9	2.3	2.1	–

Note: Figures are real gross metropolitan product (GMP) growth rates and represent average annual percent change; (1) Figures cover the Lincoln, NE Metropolitan Statistical Area—see Appendix B for areas included; (2) Rank is based on 2017 2-year average annual percent change and ranges from 1 to 381
Source: U.S. Conference of Mayors, U.S. Metro Economies: GMP & Employment 2018-2020, September 2019

Metropolitan Area Exports

Area	2013	2014	2015	2016	2017	2018	Rank[2]
MSA[1]	818.4	1,173.9	1,189.3	796.9	860.9	885.6	170

Note: Figures are in millions of dollars; (1) Figures cover the Lincoln, NE Metropolitan Statistical Area—see Appendix B for areas included; (2) Rank is based on 2018 data and ranges from 1 to 387
Source: U.S. Department of Commerce, International Trade Administration, Office of Trade and Economic Analysis, Industry and Analysis, Exports by Metropolitan Area, data extracted April 15, 2020

Building Permits

Area	Single-Family			Multi-Family			Total		
	2017	2018	Pct. Chg.	2017	2018	Pct. Chg.	2017	2018	Pct. Chg.
City	994	859	-13.6	1,231	673	-45.3	2,225	1,532	-31.1
MSA[1]	1,271	1,117	-12.1	1,237	687	-44.5	2,508	1,804	-28.1
U.S.	820,000	855,300	4.3	462,000	473,500	2.5	1,282,000	1,328,800	3.7

Note: (1) Figures cover the Lincoln, NE Metropolitan Statistical Area—see Appendix B for areas included; Figures represent new, privately-owned housing units authorized (unadjusted data); All permit data are based on estimates with imputation
Source: U.S. Census Bureau, Manufacturing, Mining, and Construction Statistics, Building Permits, 2017, 2018

Bankruptcy Filings

Area	Business Filings			Nonbusiness Filings		
	2018	2019	% Chg.	2018	2019	% Chg.
Lancaster County	9	16	77.8	665	653	-1.8
U.S.	22,232	22,780	2.5	751,186	752,160	0.1

Note: Business filings include Chapter 7, Chapter 9, Chapter 11, Chapter 12, Chapter 13, Chapter 15, and Section 304; Nonbusiness filings include Chapter 7, Chapter 11, and Chapter 13
Source: Administrative Office of the U.S. Courts, Business and Nonbusiness Bankruptcy, County Cases Commenced by Chapter of the Bankruptcy Code, During the 12-Month Period Ending December 31, 2018 and Business and Nonbusiness Bankruptcy, County Cases Commenced by Chapter of the Bankruptcy Code, During the 12-Month Period Ending December 31, 2019

Housing Vacancy Rates

Area	Gross Vacancy Rate[2] (%)			Year-Round Vacancy Rate[3] (%)			Rental Vacancy Rate[4] (%)			Homeowner Vacancy Rate[5] (%)		
	2017	2018	2019	2017	2018	2019	2017	2018	2019	2017	2018	2019
MSA[1]	n/a	n/a	n/a	n/a	n/a	n/a	n/a	n/a	n/a	n/a	n/a	n/a
U.S.	12.7	12.3	12.0	9.9	9.7	9.5	7.2	6.9	6.7	1.6	1.5	1.4

Note: (1) Figures cover the Lincoln, NE Metropolitan Statistical Area—see Appendix B for areas included; (2) The percentage of the total housing inventory that is vacant; (3) The percentage of the housing inventory (excluding seasonal units) that is year-round vacant; (4) The percentage of rental inventory that is vacant for rent; (5) The percentage of homeowner inventory that is vacant for sale; n/a not available
Source: U.S. Census Bureau, Housing Vacancies and Homeownership Annual Statistics: 2017, 2018, 2019

INCOME

Income

Area	Per Capita ($)	Median Household ($)	Average Household ($)
City	30,013	55,224	73,422
MSA[1]	30,917	58,478	76,653
U.S.	32,621	60,293	84,938

Note: (1) Figures cover the Lincoln, NE Metropolitan Statistical Area—see Appendix B for areas included
Source: U.S. Census Bureau, 2014-2018 American Community Survey 5-Year Estimates

Household Income Distribution

Area	Percent of Households Earning							
	Under $15,000	$15,000 -$24,999	$25,000 -$34,999	$35,000 -$49,999	$50,000 -$74,999	$75,000 -$99,999	$100,000 -$149,999	$150,000 and up
City	9.9	9.9	10.8	14.4	19.2	12.5	15.0	8.4
MSA[1]	9.2	9.4	10.3	13.9	19.0	13.0	16.0	9.3
U.S.	10.9	9.3	9.3	12.6	17.5	12.5	14.6	13.3

Note: (1) Figures cover the Lincoln, NE Metropolitan Statistical Area—see Appendix B for areas included
Source: U.S. Census Bureau, 2014-2018 American Community Survey 5-Year Estimates

Poverty Rate

Area	All Ages	Under 18 Years Old	18 to 64 Years Old	65 Years and Over
City	14.2	15.8	15.4	6.1
MSA[1]	12.8	14.0	14.0	5.5
U.S.	14.1	19.5	13.2	9.3

Note: Figures are percentage of people whose income during the past 12 months was below the poverty level; (1) Figures cover the Lincoln, NE Metropolitan Statistical Area—see Appendix B for areas included
Source: U.S. Census Bureau, 2014-2018 American Community Survey 5-Year Estimates

EMPLOYMENT

Labor Force and Employment

Area	Civilian Labor Force			Workers Employed		
	Dec. 2018	Dec. 2019	% Chg.	Dec. 2018	Dec. 2019	% Chg.
City	158,114	160,552	1.5	154,188	156,783	1.7
MSA[1]	184,089	186,998	1.6	179,515	182,613	1.7
U.S.	162,510,000	164,007,000	0.9	156,481,000	158,504,000	1.3

Note: Data is not seasonally adjusted and covers workers 16 years of age and older; (1) Figures cover the Lincoln, NE Metropolitan Statistical Area—see Appendix B for areas included
Source: Bureau of Labor Statistics, Local Area Unemployment Statistics

Unemployment Rate

Area	2019											
	Jan.	Feb.	Mar.	Apr.	May	Jun.	Jul.	Aug.	Sep.	Oct.	Nov.	Dec.
City	2.9	2.9	3.0	2.7	2.8	3.2	3.0	2.8	2.6	2.5	2.5	2.3
MSA[1]	2.9	2.9	3.0	2.7	2.8	3.2	3.0	2.8	2.6	2.5	2.5	2.3
U.S.	4.4	4.1	3.9	3.3	3.4	3.8	4.0	3.8	3.3	3.3	3.3	3.4

Note: Data is not seasonally adjusted and covers workers 16 years of age and older; (1) Figures cover the Lincoln, NE Metropolitan Statistical Area—see Appendix B for areas included
Source: Bureau of Labor Statistics, Local Area Unemployment Statistics

Average Wages

Occupation	$/Hr.	Occupation	$/Hr.
Accountants and Auditors	32.50	Maintenance and Repair Workers	20.90
Automotive Mechanics	22.20	Marketing Managers	43.70
Bookkeepers	18.40	Network and Computer Systems Admin.	34.40
Carpenters	20.00	Nurses, Licensed Practical	21.10
Cashiers	11.30	Nurses, Registered	31.70
Computer Programmers	34.10	Nursing Assistants	14.60
Computer Systems Analysts	35.90	Office Clerks, General	14.80
Computer User Support Specialists	22.80	Physical Therapists	40.90
Construction Laborers	16.50	Physicians	101.80
Cooks, Restaurant	14.10	Plumbers, Pipefitters and Steamfitters	25.20
Customer Service Representatives	15.90	Police and Sheriff's Patrol Officers	30.80
Dentists	58.00	Postal Service Mail Carriers	24.80
Electricians	24.40	Real Estate Sales Agents	23.40
Engineers, Electrical	44.80	Retail Salespersons	13.20
Fast Food and Counter Workers	11.20	Sales Representatives, Technical/Scientific	43.30
Financial Managers	57.20	Secretaries, Exc. Legal/Medical/Executive	17.60
First-Line Supervisors of Office Workers	26.40	Security Guards	17.80
General and Operations Managers	48.00	Surgeons	n/a
Hairdressers/Cosmetologists	12.10	Teacher Assistants, Exc. Postsecondary*	14.60
Home Health and Personal Care Aides	12.90	Teachers, Secondary School, Exc. Sp. Ed.*	30.10
Janitors and Cleaners	13.50	Telemarketers	11.70
Landscaping/Groundskeeping Workers	13.90	Truck Drivers, Heavy/Tractor-Trailer	24.90
Lawyers	46.70	Truck Drivers, Light/Delivery Services	18.20
Maids and Housekeeping Cleaners	13.10	Waiters and Waitresses	12.00

Note: Wage data covers the Lincoln, NE Metropolitan Statistical Area—see Appendix B for areas included;
(*) Hourly wages were calculated from annual wage data based on a 40 hour work week; n/a not available.
Source: Bureau of Labor Statistics, Metro Area Occupational Employment & Wage Estimates, May 2019

Employment by Occupation

Occupation Classification	City (%)	MSA[1] (%)	U.S. (%)
Management, Business, Science, and Arts	40.2	40.5	37.9
Natural Resources, Construction, and Maintenance	7.2	7.8	8.9
Production, Transportation, and Material Moving	12.1	12.2	13.3
Sales and Office	22.8	22.4	22.1
Service	17.8	17.1	17.9

Note: Figures cover employed civilians 16 years of age and older; (1) Figures cover the Lincoln, NE Metropolitan Statistical Area—see Appendix B for areas included
Source: U.S. Census Bureau, 2014-2018 American Community Survey 5-Year Estimates

Employment by Industry

Sector	MSA[1]		U.S.
	Number of Employees	Percent of Total	Percent of Total
Construction, Mining, and Logging	9,100	4.6	5.4
Education and Health Services	31,500	16.0	16.1
Financial Activities	13,400	6.8	5.8
Government	43,200	21.9	15.0
Information	3,300	1.7	1.9
Leisure and Hospitality	20,100	10.2	10.8
Manufacturing	13,600	6.9	8.4
Other Services	7,200	3.6	3.9
Professional and Business Services	22,000	11.1	14.1
Retail Trade	18,300	9.3	10.6
Transportation, Warehousing, and Utilities	11,400	5.8	4.2
Wholesale Trade	4,300	2.2	3.9

Note: Figures are non-farm employment as of December 2019. Figures are not seasonally adjusted and include workers 16 years of age and older; (1) Figures cover the Lincoln, NE Metropolitan Statistical Area—see Appendix B for areas included
Source: Bureau of Labor Statistics, Current Employment Statistics, Employment, Hours, and Earnings

Occupations with Greatest Projected Employment Growth: 2019 – 2021

Occupation[1]	2019 Employment	2021 Projected Employment	Numeric Employment Change	Percent Employment Change
Combined Food Preparation and Serving Workers, Including Fast Food	25,070	25,830	760	3.0
Heavy and Tractor-Trailer Truck Drivers	29,660	30,420	760	2.6
Registered Nurses	26,550	27,250	700	2.6
Carpenters	11,090	11,530	440	4.0
General and Operations Managers	17,490	17,860	370	2.1
Nursing Assistants	15,650	15,980	330	2.1
Laborers and Freight, Stock, and Material Movers, Hand	16,670	17,000	330	2.0
Janitors and Cleaners, Except Maids and Housekeeping Cleaners	16,450	16,750	300	1.8
Personal Care Aides	7,200	7,500	300	4.2
Electricians	5,720	6,020	300	5.2

Note: Projections cover Nebraska; (1) Sorted by numeric employment change
Source: www.projectionscentral.com, State Occupational Projections, 2019–2021 Short-Term Projections

Fastest Growing Occupations: 2019 – 2021

Occupation[1]	2019 Employment	2021 Projected Employment	Numeric Employment Change	Percent Employment Change
Heating, Air Conditioning, and Refrigeration Mechanics and Installers	2,870	3,060	190	6.6
Roofers	1,230	1,310	80	6.5
Veterinary Technologists and Technicians	880	930	50	5.7
Physical Therapist Assistants	900	950	50	5.6
Cement Masons and Concrete Finishers	3,550	3,740	190	5.4
Operations Research Analysts	1,130	1,190	60	5.3
Physician Assistants	1,330	1,400	70	5.3
Electricians	5,720	6,020	300	5.2
Taxi Drivers and Chauffeurs	2,580	2,710	130	5.0
Software Developers, Applications	4,880	5,120	240	4.9

Note: Projections cover Nebraska; (1) Sorted by percent employment change and excludes occupations with numeric employment change less than 50
Source: www.projectionscentral.com, State Occupational Projections, 2019–2021 Short-Term Projections

TAXES

State Corporate Income Tax Rates

State	Tax Rate (%)	Income Brackets ($)	Num. of Brackets	Financial Institution Tax Rate (%)[a]	Federal Income Tax Ded.
Nebraska	5.58 - 7.81	100,000	2	(a)	No

Note: Tax rates as of January 1, 2020; (a) Rates listed are the corporate income tax rate applied to financial institutions or excise taxes based on income.
Source: Federation of Tax Administrators, State Corporate Income Tax Rates, January 1, 2020

State Individual Income Tax Rates

State	Tax Rate (%)	Income Brackets ($)	Personal Exemptions ($)			Standard Ded. ($)	
			Single	Married	Depend.	Single	Married
Nebraska (a)	2.46 - 6.84	3,230 - 31,160 (b)	140	280 (c)	140 (c)	7,000	14,000

Note: Tax rates as of January 1, 2020; Local- and county-level taxes are not included; Federal income tax is not deductible on state income tax returns; (a) 19 states have statutory provision for automatically adjusting to the rate of inflation the dollar values of the income tax brackets, standard deductions, and/or personal exemptions. Michigan indexes the personal exemption only. Oregon does not index the income brackets for $125,000 and over; (b) For joint returns, taxes are twice the tax on half the couple's income; (c) The personal exemption takes the form of a tax credit instead of a deduction
Source: Federation of Tax Administrators, State Individual Income Tax Rates, January 1, 2020

Various State Sales and Excise Tax Rates

State	State Sales Tax (%)	Gasoline[1] (¢/gal.)	Cigarette[2] ($/pack)	Spirits[3] ($/gal.)	Wine[4] ($/gal.)	Beer[5] ($/gal.)	Recreational Marijuana (%)
Nebraska	5.5	30.2	0.64	3.75	0.95	0.31	Not legal

Note: All tax rates as of January 1, 2020; (1) The American Petroleum Institute has developed a methodology for determining the average tax rate on a gallon of fuel. Rates may include any of the following: excise taxes, environmental fees, storage tank fees, other fees or taxes, general sales tax, and local taxes; (2) The federal excise tax of $1.0066 per pack and local taxes are not included; (3) Rates are those applicable to off-premise sales of 40% alcohol by volume (a.b.v.) distilled spirits in 750ml containers. Local excise taxes are excluded; (4) Rates are those applicable to off-premise sales of 11% a.b.v. non-carbonated wine in 750ml containers; (5) Rates are those applicable to off-premise sales of 4.7% a.b.v. beer in 12 ounce containers.
Source: Tax Foundation, 2020 Facts & Figures: How Does Your State Compare?

State Business Tax Climate Index Rankings

State	Overall Rank	Corporate Tax Rank	Individual Income Tax Rank	Sales Tax Rank	Property Tax Rank	Unemployment Insurance Tax Rank
Nebraska	28	31	21	10	41	11

Note: The index is a measure of how each state's tax laws affect economic performance. The lower the rank, the more favorable a state's tax system is for business. States without a given tax are given a ranking of 1. The scores/rankings for the District of Columbia do not affect other states. The 2020 index represents the tax climate as of July 1, 2019.
Source: Tax Foundation, State Business Tax Climate Index 2020

COMMERCIAL UTILITIES

Typical Monthly Electric Bills

Area	General Service, Light ($/month)		General Service, Heavy ($/month)	
	40 kW demand 5,000 kWh	100 kW demand 10,000 kWh	500 kW demand 100,000 kWh	1,500 kW demand 500,000 kWh
City	n/a	n/a	n/a	n/a

Note: Figures are based on rates in effect January 1, 2019
Source: Memphis Light, Gas and Water, 2019 Utility Bill Comparisons for Selected U.S. Cities

TRANSPORTATION

Means of Transportation to Work

Area	Car/Truck/Van		Public Transportation			Bicycle	Walked	Other Means	Worked at Home
	Drove Alone	Car-pooled	Bus	Subway	Railroad				
City	81.0	9.1	1.3	0.0	0.0	1.3	3.3	0.6	3.3
MSA[1]	81.3	8.9	1.1	0.0	0.0	1.1	3.3	0.6	3.7
U.S.	76.4	9.1	2.5	1.9	0.6	0.6	2.7	1.3	4.9

Note: Figures are percentages and cover workers 16 years of age and older; (1) Figures cover the Lincoln, NE Metropolitan Statistical Area—see Appendix B for areas included
Source: U.S. Census Bureau, 2014-2018 American Community Survey 5-Year Estimates

Travel Time to Work

Area	Less Than 10 Minutes	10 to 19 Minutes	20 to 29 Minutes	30 to 44 Minutes	45 to 59 Minutes	60 to 89 Minutes	90 Minutes or More
City	17.0	44.8	22.8	9.5	2.7	2.1	1.0
MSA[1]	17.0	41.7	23.5	11.5	3.0	2.1	1.1
U.S.	12.5	28.7	20.9	20.7	8.2	6.3	2.8

Note: Note: Figures are percentages and include workers 16 years old and over; (1) Figures cover the Lincoln, NE Metropolitan Statistical Area—see Appendix B for areas included
Source: U.S. Census Bureau, 2014-2018 American Community Survey 5-Year Estimates

Key Congestion Measures

Area	1982	1992	2002	2012	2017
Annual Hours of Delay, Total (000)	n/a	n/a	n/a	n/a	4,733
Annual Hours of Delay, Per Auto Commuter	n/a	n/a	n/a	n/a	16
Annual Congestion Cost, Total (million $)	n/a	n/a	n/a	n/a	97
Annual Congestion Cost, Per Auto Commuter ($)	n/a	n/a	n/a	n/a	334

Note: n/a not available
Source: Texas A&M Transportation Institute, 2019 Urban Mobility Report

Freeway Travel Time Index

Area	1982	1987	1992	1997	2002	2007	2012	2017
Urban Area Index[1]	n/a	n/a	n/a	n/a	n/a	n/a	n/a	1.09
Urban Area Rank[1,2]	n/a	n/a	n/a	n/a	n/a	n/a	n/a	n/a

Note: Freeway Travel Time Index—the ratio of travel time in the peak period to the travel time at free-flow conditions. For example, a value of 1.30 indicates a 20-minute free-flow trip takes 26 minutes in the peak (20 minutes x 1.30 = 26 minutes); (1) Covers the Lincoln NE urban area; (2) Rank is based on 101 larger urban areas (#1 = highest travel time index); n/a not available
Source: Texas A&M Transportation Institute, 2019 Urban Mobility Report

Public Transportation

Agency Name / Mode of Transportation	Vehicles Operated in Maximum Service[1]	Annual Unlinked Passenger Trips[2] (in thous.)	Annual Passenger Miles[3] (in thous.)
StarTran			
Bus (directly operated)	56	2,395.8	7,144.6
Demand Response (directly operated)	9	41.2	220.4
Demand Response Taxi (purchased transportation)	13	26.8	172.6

Note: (1) Number of revenue vehicles operated by the given mode and type of service to meet the annual maximum service requirement. This is the revenue vehicle count during the peak season of the year; on the week and day that maximum service is provided. Vehicles operated in maximum service (VOMS) exclude atypical days and one-time special events; (2) Number of passengers who boarded public transportation vehicles. Passengers are counted each time they board a vehicle no matter how many vehicles they use to travel from their origin to their destination. (3) Sum of the distances ridden by all passengers during the entire fiscal year.
Source: Federal Transit Administration, National Transit Database, 2018

Air Transportation

Airport Name and Code / Type of Service	Passenger Airlines[1]	Passenger Enplanements	Freight Carriers[2]	Freight (lbs)
Lincoln Municipal (LNK)				
Domestic service (U.S. carriers - 2019)	18	166,051	3	61,237
International service (U.S. carriers - 2018)	0	0	2	50,323

Note: (1) Includes all U.S.-based major, minor and commuter airlines that carried at least one passenger during the year; (2) Includes all U.S.-based airlines and freight carriers that transported at least one pound of freight during the year.
Source: Bureau of Transportation Statistics, The Intermodal Transportation Database, Air Carriers: T-100 Domestic Market (U.S. Carriers), 2019; Bureau of Transportation Statistics, The Intermodal Transportation Database, Air Carriers: T-100 International Market (U.S. Carriers), 2018

Other Transportation Statistics

Major Highways:	I-80
Amtrak Service:	Yes
Major Waterways/Ports:	None

Source: Amtrak.com; Google Maps

Major Business Headquarters

Company Name	Industry	Rankings	
		Fortune[1]	Forbes[2]
No companies listed	-	-	-

Note: (1) Companies that produce a 10-K are ranked 1 to 500 based on 2018 revenue; (2) All private companies with at least $2 billion in annual revenue through the end of their most current fiscal year are ranked 1 to 228; companies listed are headquartered in the city; dashes indicate no ranking
Source: Fortune, "Fortune 500," June 2019; Forbes, "America's Largest Private Companies," 2019 Rankings

Fast-Growing Businesses

According to *Inc.*, Lincoln is home to one of America's 500 fastest-growing private companies: **Mobile Text Alerts** (#399). Criteria: must be an independent, privately-held, for-profit, U.S. corporation, proprietorship or partnership as of December 31, 2018; revenues must be at least $100,000 in 2015 and $2 million in 2018; must have four-year operating/sales history. *Inc., "America's 500 Fastest-Growing Private Companies," 2019*

Minority- and Women-Owned Businesses

Group	All Firms		Firms with Paid Employees			
	Firms	Sales ($000)	Firms	Sales ($000)	Employees	Payroll ($000)
AIAN[1]	130	29,599	23	27,877	38	928
Asian	806	105,738	119	87,598	1,339	23,272
Black	455	(s)	38	(s)	250 - 499	(s)
Hispanic	717	136,533	77	116,899	739	16,332
NHOPI[2]	n/a	n/a	n/a	n/a	n/a	n/a
Women	8,174	1,096,265	1,000	930,979	8,882	272,596
All Firms	22,687	27,446,594	5,367	26,843,772	116,653	4,292,071

Note: Figures cover firms located in the city; minority- and women-owned business are defined as firms in which the corresponding group own 51% or more of the stock or equity of the company; (1) American Indian and Alaska Native; (2) Native Hawaiian and Other Pacific Islander; (s) estimates are suppressed when publication standards are not met; n/a not available
Source: U.S. Census Bureau, 2012 Economic Census, Survey of Business Owners

Hotels, Motels and Vacation Rentals

Area	5 Star		4 Star		3 Star		2 Star		1 Star		Not Rated	
	Num.	Pct.[3]	Num.	Pct.[3]	Num.	Pct.[3]	Num.	Pct.[3]	Num.	Pct.[3]	Num.	Pct.[3]
City[1]	0	0.0	0	0.0	9	16.7	15	27.8	3	5.6	27	50.0
Total[2]	266	1.3	1,517	7.2	4,627	21.8	3,210	15.1	3,974	18.7	7,601	35.9

Note: (1) Figures cover Lincoln and vicinity; (2) Figures cover all 100 cities in this book; (3) Percentage of hotels which have a given star rating; Star ratings are determined by priceline.com and offer an indication of the general quality of a particular hotel.
Source: priceline.com, April 27, 2020

Major Convention Centers

Name	Overall Space (sq. ft.)	Exhibit Space (sq. ft.)	Meeting Space (sq. ft.)	Meeting Rooms
Lancaster Events Center	400,000	11,500	n/a	n/a

Note: Table includes convention centers located in the Lincoln, NE metro area; n/a not available
Source: Original research

Living Environment

COST OF LIVING

Cost of Living Index

Composite Index	Groceries	Housing	Utilities	Trans-portation	Health Care	Misc. Goods/Services
93.0	95.6	78.7	90.2	93.4	105.8	102.2

Note: The Cost of Living Index measures regional differences in the cost of consumer goods and services, excluding taxes and non-consumer expenditures, for professional and managerial households in the top income quintile. It is based on more than 50,000 prices covering almost 60 different items for which prices are collected three times a year by chambers of commerce, economic development organizations or university applied economic centers in each participating urban area. The numbers shown should be read as a percentage above or below the national average of 100. For example, a value of 115.4 in the groceries column indicates that grocery prices are 15.4% higher than the national average. Small differences in the index numbers should not be interpreted as significant; Figures cover the Lincoln NE urban area.
Source: The Council for Community and Economic Research, ACCRA Cost of Living Index, 2019

Grocery Prices

Area[1]	T-Bone Steak ($/pound)	Frying Chicken ($/pound)	Whole Milk ($/half gal.)	Eggs ($/dozen)	Orange Juice ($/64 oz.)	Coffee ($/11.5 oz.)
City[2]	10.97	1.47	2.35	1.70	3.12	3.91
Avg.	11.40	1.41	1.93	1.54	3.51	4.30
Min.	7.40	0.92	0.85	0.58	2.67	2.90
Max.	15.58	2.68	4.09	4.18	5.57	8.10

Note: (1) Values for the local area are compared with the average, minimum and maximum values for all 290 areas in the Cost of Living Index; (2) Figures cover the Lincoln NE urban area; T-Bone Steak (price per pound); Frying Chicken (price per pound, whole fryer); Whole Milk (half gallon carton); Eggs (price per dozen, Grade A, large); Orange Juice (64 oz. Tropicana or Florida Natural); Coffee (11.5 oz. can, vacuum-packed, Maxwell House, Hills Bros, or Folgers).
Source: The Council for Community and Economic Research, ACCRA Cost of Living Index, 2019

Housing and Utility Costs

Area[1]	New Home Price ($)	Apartment Rent ($/month)	All Electric ($/month)	Part Electric ($/month)	Other Energy ($/month)	Telephone ($/month)
City[2]	285,102	868	-	69.68	62.56	190.10
Avg.	362,090	1,142	174.35	100.00	67.76	179.60
Min.	198,329	501	91.58	31.44	28.51	165.30
Max.	2,074,561	5,050	388.18	239.41	306.15	207.90

Note: (1) Values for the local area are compared with the average, minimum and maximum values for all 290 areas in the Cost of Living Index; (2) Figures cover the Lincoln NE urban area; New Home Price (2,400 sf living area, 8,000 sf lot, in urban area with full utilities); Apartment Rent (950 sf 2 bedroom/1.5 or 2 bath, unfurnished, excluding all utilities except water); All Electric (average monthly cost for an all-electric home); Part Electric (average monthly cost for a part-electric home); Other Energy (average monthly cost for natural gas, fuel oil, coal, wood, and any other forms of energy except electricity); Telephone (price includes the base monthly rate plus taxes and fees for three lines of mobile phone service).
Source: The Council for Community and Economic Research, ACCRA Cost of Living Index, 2019

Health Care, Transportation, and Other Costs

Area[1]	Doctor ($/visit)	Dentist ($/visit)	Optometrist ($/visit)	Gasoline ($/gallon)	Beauty Salon ($/visit)	Men's Shirt ($)
City[2]	139.62	93.77	102.20	2.42	40.02	47.22
Avg.	114.85	97.58	106.10	2.50	38.15	32.15
Min.	39.00	62.22	52.22	1.53	16.88	10.27
Max.	206.67	151.53	258.67	3.79	79.29	59.30

Note: (1) Values for the local area are compared with the average, minimum and maximum values for all 290 areas in the Cost of Living Index; (2) Figures cover the Lincoln NE urban area; Doctor (general practitioners routine exam of an established patient); Dentist (adult teeth cleaning and periodic oral examination); Optometrist (full vision eye exam for established adult patient); Gasoline (one gallon regular unleaded, national brand, including all taxes, cash price at self-service pump if available); Beauty Salon (woman's shampoo, trim, and blow-dry); Men's Shirt (cotton/polyester dress shirt, pinpoint weave, long sleeves).
Source: The Council for Community and Economic Research, ACCRA Cost of Living Index, 2019

HOUSING

House Price Index (HPI)

Area	National Ranking[2]	Quarterly Change (%)	One-Year Change (%)	Five-Year Change (%)
MSA[1]	180	0.34	3.84	30.88
U.S.[3]	–	1.26	5.09	32.88

Note: The HPI is a weighted repeat sales index. It measures average price changes in repeat sales or refinancings on the same properties. This information is obtained by reviewing repeat mortgage transactions on single-family properties whose mortgages have been purchased or securitized by Fannie Mae or Freddie Mac in January 1975; (1) Figures cover the Lincoln, NE Metropolitan Statistical Area—see Appendix B for areas included; (2) Rankings are based on annual percentage change for all metro areas containing at least 15,000 transactions over the last 10 years and ranges from 1 to 232; (3) figures based on a weighted average of Census Division estimates using a seasonally adjusted, purchase-only index; all figures are for the period ending December 31, 2019
Source: Federal Housing Finance Agency, House Price Index, February 25, 2020

Median Single-Family Home Prices

Area	2017	2018	2019[p]	Percent Change 2018 to 2019
MSA[1]	175.4	189.0	198.4	5.0
U.S. Average	248.8	261.6	274.6	5.0

Note: Figures are median sales prices of existing single-family homes in thousands of dollars; (p) preliminary; (1) Figures cover the Lincoln, NE Metropolitan Statistical Area—see Appendix B for areas included
Source: National Association of Realtors, Median Sales Price of Existing Single-Family Homes for Metropolitan Areas, 4th Quarter 2019

Qualifying Income Based on Median Sales Price of Existing Single-Family Homes

Area	With 5% Down ($)	With 10% Down ($)	With 20% Down ($)
MSA[1]	42,444	40,211	35,743
U.S. Average	58,663	55,575	49,400

Note: Figures are preliminary; Qualifying income is based on a mortgage rate of 3.76%. Monthly principal and interest payment is limited to 25% of income; (1) Figures cover the Lincoln, NE Metropolitan Statistical Area—see Appendix B for areas included
Source: National Association of Realtors, Qualifying Income Based on Median Sales Price of Existing Single-Family Homes for Metropolitan Areas, 4th Quarter 2019

Median Apartment Condo-Coop Home Prices

Area	2017	2018	2019[p]	Percent Change 2018 to 2019
MSA[1]	n/a	n/a	n/a	n/a
U.S. Average	234.3	241.0	249.5	3.5

Note: Figures are median sales prices of existing apartment condo-coop homes in thousands of dollars; (p) preliminary; n/a not available; (1) Figures cover the Lincoln, NE Metropolitan Statistical Area—see Appendix B for areas included
Source: National Association of Realtors, Median Sales Price of Existing Apartment Condo-Coop Homes for Metropolitan Areas, 4th Quarter 2019

Home Value Distribution

Area	Under $50,000	$50,000 -$99,999	$100,000 -$149,999	$150,000 -$199,999	$200,000 -$299,999	$300,000 -$499,999	$500,000 -$999,999	$1,000,000 or more
City	4.1	11.1	28.4	23.7	20.7	9.6	2.0	0.4
MSA[1]	3.9	10.6	26.1	22.5	21.3	12.1	3.0	0.5
U.S.	7.6	13.0	14.0	14.3	19.2	18.3	10.5	3.1

Note: Figures are percentages and cover owner-occupied housing units; (1) Figures cover the Lincoln, NE Metropolitan Statistical Area—see Appendix B for areas included
Source: U.S. Census Bureau, 2014-2018 American Community Survey 5-Year Estimates

Homeownership Rate

Area	2011 (%)	2012 (%)	2013 (%)	2014 (%)	2015 (%)	2016 (%)	2017 (%)	2018 (%)	2019 (%)
MSA[1]	n/a	n/a	n/a	n/a	n/a	n/a	n/a	n/a	n/a
U.S.	66.1	65.4	65.1	64.5	63.7	63.4	63.9	64.4	64.6

Note: (1) Figures cover the Lincoln, NE Metropolitan Statistical Area—see Appendix B for areas included; n/a not available
Source: U.S. Census Bureau, Housing Vacancies and Homeownership Annual Statistics: 2011-2019

Year Housing Structure Built

Area	2010 or Later	2000 -2009	1990 -1999	1980 -1989	1970 -1979	1960 -1969	1950 -1959	1940 -1949	Before 1940	Median Year
City	5.8	14.2	15.0	10.6	15.1	10.7	11.2	3.3	14.1	1977
MSA[1]	5.9	14.7	15.0	10.2	15.4	10.4	10.3	3.1	14.9	1977
U.S.	4.1	14.3	13.9	13.5	15.3	10.7	10.4	5.0	12.8	1977

Note: Figures are percentages except for Median Year; Note: (1) Figures cover the Lincoln, NE Metropolitan Statistical Area—see Appendix B for areas included
Source: U.S. Census Bureau, 2014-2018 American Community Survey 5-Year Estimates

Gross Monthly Rent

Area	Under $500	$500 -$999	$1,000 -$1,499	$1,500 -$1,999	$2,000 -$2,499	$2,500 -$2,999	$3,000 and up	Median ($)
City	11.5	59.8	22.4	4.3	0.7	0.3	1.0	822
MSA[1]	11.8	59.7	22.4	4.1	0.7	0.3	1.0	819
U.S.	9.8	38.5	29.6	12.9	5.1	2.1	2.0	1,023

Note: Figures are percentages except for Median; Gross rent is the contract rent plus the estimated average monthly cost of utilities (electricity, gas, and water and sewer) and fuels (oil, coal, kerosene, wood, etc.) if these are paid by the renter (or paid for the renter by someone else); (1) Figures cover the Lincoln, NE Metropolitan Statistical Area—see Appendix B for areas included
Source: U.S. Census Bureau, 2014-2018 American Community Survey 5-Year Estimates

HEALTH

Health Risk Factors

Category	MSA[1] (%)	U.S. (%)
Adults aged 18–64 who have any kind of health care coverage	87.5	87.3
Adults who reported being in good or better health	86.9	82.4
Adults who have been told they have high blood cholesterol	29.3	33.0
Adults who have been told they have high blood pressure	26.5	32.3
Adults who are current smokers	12.2	17.1
Adults who currently use E-cigarettes	3.4	4.6
Adults who currently use chewing tobacco, snuff, or snus	3.3	4.0
Adults who are heavy drinkers[2]	7.5	6.3
Adults who are binge drinkers[3]	24.2	17.4
Adults who are overweight (BMI 25.0 - 29.9)	38.1	35.3
Adults who are obese (BMI 30.0 - 99.8)	28.9	31.3
Adults who participated in any physical activities in the past month	80.1	74.4
Adults who always or nearly always wears a seat belt	92.3	94.3

Note: (1) Figures cover the Lincoln, NE Metropolitan Statistical Area—see Appendix B for areas included; (2) Heavy drinkers are classified as adult men having more than 14 drinks per week and adult women having more than 7 drinks per week; (3) Binge drinkers are classified as males having five or more drinks on one occasion or females having four or more drinks on one occasion
Source: Centers for Disease Control and Prevention, Behavioral Risk Factor Surveillance System, SMART: Selected Metropolitan Area Risk Trends, 2017

Acute and Chronic Health Conditions

Category	MSA[1] (%)	U.S. (%)
Adults who have ever been told they had a heart attack	3.7	4.2
Adults who have ever been told they have angina or coronary heart disease	3.5	3.9
Adults who have ever been told they had a stroke	2.3	3.0
Adults who have ever been told they have asthma	13.2	14.2
Adults who have ever been told they have arthritis	21.0	24.9
Adults who have ever been told they have diabetes[2]	8.3	10.5
Adults who have ever been told they had skin cancer	5.8	6.2
Adults who have ever been told they had any other types of cancer	6.4	7.1
Adults who have ever been told they have COPD	5.5	6.5
Adults who have ever been told they have kidney disease	2.9	3.0
Adults who have ever been told they have a form of depression	20.7	20.5

Note: (1) Figures cover the Lincoln, NE Metropolitan Statistical Area—see Appendix B for areas included; (2) Figures do not include pregnancy-related, borderline, or pre-diabetes
Source: Centers for Disease Control and Prevention, Behavioral Risk Factor Surveillance System, SMART: Selected Metropolitan Area Risk Trends, 2017

Health Screening and Vaccination Rates

Category	MSA[1] (%)	U.S. (%)
Adults aged 65+ who have had flu shot within the past year	68.4	60.7
Adults aged 65+ who have ever had a pneumonia vaccination	82.1	75.4
Adults who have ever been tested for HIV	27.1	36.1
Adults who have ever had the shingles or zoster vaccine?	37.7	28.9
Adults who have had their blood cholesterol checked within the last five years	86.2	85.9

Note: n/a not available; (1) Figures cover the Lincoln, NE Metropolitan Statistical Area—see Appendix B for areas included.
Source: Centers for Disease Control and Prevention, Behaviorial Risk Factor Surveillance System, SMART: Selected Metropolitan Area Risk Trends, 2017

Disability Status

Category	MSA[1] (%)	U.S. (%)
Adults who reported being deaf	5.7	6.7
Are you blind or have serious difficulty seeing, even when wearing glasses?	2.5	4.5
Are you limited in any way in any of your usual activities due of arthritis?	9.5	12.9
Do you have difficulty doing errands alone?	3.7	6.8
Do you have difficulty dressing or bathing?	2.4	3.6
Do you have serious difficulty concentrating/remembering/making decisions?	8.0	10.7
Do you have serious difficulty walking or climbing stairs?	8.9	13.6

Note: (1) Figures cover the Lincoln, NE Metropolitan Statistical Area—see Appendix B for areas included.
Source: Centers for Disease Control and Prevention, Behaviorial Risk Factor Surveillance System, SMART: Selected Metropolitan Area Risk Trends, 2017

Mortality Rates for the Top 10 Causes of Death in the U.S.

ICD-10[a] Sub-Chapter	ICD-10[a] Code	Age-Adjusted Mortality Rate[1] per 100,000 population	
		County[2]	U.S.
Malignant neoplasms	C00-C97	147.6	152.4
Ischaemic heart diseases	I20-I25	62.7	92.7
Other forms of heart disease	I30-I51	52.1	52.5
Chronic lower respiratory diseases	J40-J47	52.4	40.4
Cerebrovascular diseases	I60-I69	35.3	37.3
Other degenerative diseases of the nervous system	G30-G31	39.9	36.4
Other external causes of accidental injury	W00-X59	21.8	35.3
Organic, including symptomatic, mental disorders	F01-F09	35.5	30.0
Hypertensive diseases	I10-I15	19.7	22.9
Diabetes mellitus	E10-E14	17.6	21.3

Note: (a) ICD-10 = International Classification of Diseases 10th Revision; (1) Mortality rates are a three year average covering 2016-2018; (2) Figures cover Lancaster County.
Source: Centers for Disease Control and Prevention, National Center for Health Statistics. Underlying Cause of Death 1999-2018 on CDC WONDER Online Database

Mortality Rates for Selected Causes of Death

ICD-10[a] Sub-Chapter	ICD-10[a] Code	Age-Adjusted Mortality Rate[1] per 100,000 population	
		County[2]	U.S.
Assault	X85-Y09	Unreliable	6.0
Diseases of the liver	K70-K76	13.0	14.2
Human immunodeficiency virus (HIV) disease	B20-B24	Suppressed	1.6
Influenza and pneumonia	J09-J18	12.4	14.2
Intentional self-harm	X60-X84	14.0	13.9
Malnutrition	E40-E46	3.7	1.9
Obesity and other hyperalimentation	E65-E68	3.0	2.1
Renal failure	N17-N19	7.7	12.8
Transport accidents	V01-V99	7.2	12.5
Viral hepatitis	B15-B19	Unreliable	1.4

Note: (a) ICD-10 = International Classification of Diseases 10th Revision; (1) Mortality rates are a three year average covering 2016-2018; (2) Figures cover Lancaster County; Data are suppressed when the data meet the criteria for confidentiality constraints; Mortality rates are flagged as unreliable when the rate would be calculated with a numerator of 20 or less.
Source: Centers for Disease Control and Prevention, National Center for Health Statistics. Underlying Cause of Death 1999-2018 on CDC WONDER Online Database

Health Insurance Coverage

Area	With Health Insurance	With Private Health Insurance	With Public Health Insurance	Without Health Insurance	Population Under Age 19 Without Health Insurance
City	92.2	78.1	25.6	7.8	4.4
MSA[1]	92.8	79.3	25.1	7.2	4.1
U.S.	90.6	67.7	34.7	9.4	5.2

Note: Figures are percentages that cover the civilian noninstitutionalized population; (1) Figures cover the Lincoln, NE Metropolitan Statistical Area—see Appendix B for areas included
Source: U.S. Census Bureau, 2014-2018 American Community Survey 5-Year Estimates

Number of Medical Professionals

Area	MDs[3]	DOs[3,4]	Dentists	Podiatrists	Chiropractors	Optometrists
County[1] (number)	678	37	310	17	137	66
County[1] (rate[2])	215.7	11.8	97.7	5.4	43.2	20.8
U.S. (rate[2])	281.9	23.4	69.1	6.0	27.5	16.4

Note: Data as of 2018 unless noted; (1) Data covers Lancaster County; (2) Rate per 100,000 population; (3) Data as of 2017 and includes all active, non-federal physicians; (4) Doctor of Osteopathic Medicine
Source: U.S. Department of Health and Human Services, Health Resources and Services Administration, Bureau of Health Professions, Area Resource File (ARF) 2018-2019

EDUCATION

Public School District Statistics

District Name	Schls	Pupils	Pupil/ Teacher Ratio	Minority Pupils[1] (%)	Free Lunch Eligible[2] (%)	IEP[3] (%)
Lincoln Public Schools	74	42,020	13.5	33.8	37.8	17.5

Note: Table includes school districts with 2,000 or more students; (1) Percentage of students that are not non-Hispanic white; (2) Percentage of students that are eligible for the free lunch program; (3) Percentage of students that have an Individualized Education Program.
Source: U.S. Department of Education, National Center for Education Statistics, Common Core of Data, Local Education Agency (School District) Universe Survey: School Year 2018-2019; U.S. Department of Education, National Center for Education Statistics, Common Core of Data, Public Elementary/Secondary School Universe Survey: School Year 2018-2019

Highest Level of Education

Area	Less than H.S.	H.S. Diploma	Some College, No Deg.	Associate Degree	Bachelor's Degree	Master's Degree	Prof. School Degree	Doctorate Degree
City	6.8	21.8	21.7	10.9	24.8	9.2	2.2	2.6
MSA[1]	6.5	22.2	21.6	11.5	24.5	9.1	2.2	2.5
U.S.	12.3	27.1	20.6	8.4	19.4	8.6	2.1	1.4

Note: Figures cover persons age 25 and over; (1) Figures cover the Lincoln, NE Metropolitan Statistical Area—see Appendix B for areas included
Source: U.S. Census Bureau, 2014-2018 American Community Survey 5-Year Estimates

Educational Attainment by Race

Area	High School Graduate or Higher (%)					Bachelor's Degree or Higher (%)				
	Total	White	Black	Asian	Hisp.[2]	Total	White	Black	Asian	Hisp.[2]
City	93.2	94.8	87.8	78.7	70.6	38.8	39.9	23.0	45.2	20.2
MSA[1]	93.5	95.0	87.8	78.5	70.9	38.3	39.1	23.1	45.0	20.5
U.S.	87.7	89.6	85.4	86.8	67.7	31.5	32.9	21.1	53.5	15.8

Note: Figures shown cover persons 25 years old and over; (1) Figures cover the Lincoln, NE Metropolitan Statistical Area—see Appendix B for areas included; (2) People of Hispanic origin can be of any race
Source: U.S. Census Bureau, 2014-2018 American Community Survey 5-Year Estimates

School Enrollment by Grade and Control

Area	Preschool (%)		Kindergarten (%)		Grades 1 - 4 (%)		Grades 5 - 8 (%)		Grades 9 - 12 (%)	
	Public	Private	Public	Private	Public	Private	Public	Private	Public	Private
City	51.0	49.0	76.1	23.9	85.2	14.8	86.1	13.9	85.6	14.4
MSA[1]	49.6	50.4	77.1	22.9	84.4	15.6	86.1	13.9	86.3	13.7
U.S.	59.0	41.0	87.7	12.3	89.6	10.4	89.5	10.5	90.2	9.8

Note: Figures shown cover persons 3 years old and over; (1) Figures cover the Lincoln, NE Metropolitan Statistical Area—see Appendix B for areas included
Source: U.S. Census Bureau, 2014-2018 American Community Survey 5-Year Estimates

Average Salaries of Public School Teachers

Area	2016-17		2017-18		Change from 2016-17 to 2017-18	
	Dollars	Rank[1]	Dollars	Rank[1]	Percent	Rank[2]
Nebraska	52,338	29	54,213	25	3.58	3
U.S. Average	59,539	–	60,477	–	1.58	–

Note: (1) Rank ranges from 1 to 51 where 1 indicates highest salary; (2) Rank ranges from 1 to 51 where 1 indicates highest percent change.
Source: National Education Association, Rankings & Estimates: Rankings of the States 2018 and Estimates of School Statistics 2019

Higher Education

Four-Year Colleges			Two-Year Colleges			Medical Schools[1]	Law Schools[2]	Voc/ Tech[3]
Public	Private Non-profit	Private For-profit	Public	Private Non-profit	Private For-profit			
2	4	0	1	0	5	0	1	0

Note: Figures cover institutions located within the city limits and include main campuses only; (1) includes schools accredited by the Liaison Committee on Medical Education and the American Osteopathic Association's Commission on Osteopathic College Accreditation; (2) includes ABA-accredited schools, schools with provisional ABA accreditation, and state accredited schools; (3) includes all schools with programs that are less than 2 years.
Source: National Center for Education Statistics, Integrated Postsecondary Education System (IPEDS), 2018-19; Wikipedia, List of Medical Schools in the United States, accessed May 1, 2020; Wikipedia, List of Law Schools in the United States, accessed May 1, 2020

According to *U.S. News & World Report,* the Lincoln, NE metro area is home to one of the top 200 national universities in the U.S.: **University of Nebraska—Lincoln** (#139 tie). The indicators used to capture academic quality fall into a number of categories: assessment by administrators at peer institutions; retention of students; faculty resources; student selectivity; financial resources; alumni giving; high school counselor ratings of colleges; and graduation rate. *U.S. News & World Report, "America's Best Colleges 2020"*

According to *U.S. News & World Report,* the Lincoln, NE metro area is home to one of the top 100 law schools in the U.S.: **University of Nebraska—Lincoln** (#76 tie). The rankings are based on a weighted average of 12 measures of quality: peer assessment score; assessment score by lawyers/judges; median LSAT scores; median undergrad GPA; acceptance rate; employment rates for graduates; placement success; bar passage rate; faculty resources; expenditures per student; student/faculty ratio; and library resources. *U.S. News & World Report, "America's Best Graduate Schools, Law, 2021"*

PRESIDENTIAL ELECTION

2016 Presidential Election Results

Area	Clinton	Trump	Johnson	Stein	Other
Lancaster County	45.4	45.2	5.2	1.4	2.7
U.S.	48.0	45.9	3.3	1.1	1.7

Note: Results are percentages and may not add to 100% due to rounding
Source: Dave Leip's Atlas of U.S. Presidential Elections

EMPLOYERS

Major Employers

Company Name	Industry
Bank of the West	Financial services
Cargill Meat Solutions	Food processing
CHI Health Bergan Mercy	Healthcare
CHI Health Saint Elizabeth	Healthcare
Con Agra Foods Inc	Food manufacturing
Creighton University	Education
First Data	Commerce
Health & Human Svc Dept	Government
JBS USA	Food processing
Methodist Hospital	Healthcare
Mutual of Omaha Insurance Co	Insurance
Nebraska Medical Center	Healthcare
Nebraska Medicine	Healthcare
Offutt AFB	U.S. military
Pay Pal	Payment services
Smithfield Farmland	Agriculture
Tyson Fresh Meats	Food processing
Union Pacific Railroad Co	Railroad
University of NE Medical Ctr	Healthcare
University of Nebraska	Education
West Corp	Communications

Note: Companies shown are located within the Lincoln, NE Metropolitan Statistical Area.
Source: Hoovers.com; Wikipedia

PUBLIC SAFETY

Crime Rate

Area	All Crimes	Violent Crimes				Property Crimes		
		Murder	Rape[3]	Robbery	Aggrav. Assault	Burglary	Larceny -Theft	Motor Vehicle Theft
City	3,240.6	2.1	98.1	56.1	205.8	409.6	2,319.6	149.3
Suburbs[1]	1,240.2	0.0	84.0	4.3	47.4	155.0	859.1	90.4
Metro[2]	2,963.3	1.8	96.1	49.0	183.9	374.3	2,117.1	141.2
U.S.	2,580.1	5.0	42.6	86.2	246.8	376.0	1,594.6	228.9

Note: Figures are crimes per 100,000 population; (1) All areas within the metro area that are located outside the city limits; (2) Figures cover the Lincoln, NE Metropolitan Statistical Area—see Appendix B for areas included; (3) The city and U.S. figures shown were reported using the revised Uniform Crime Reporting (UCR) definition of rape. The suburban and metro area figures shown are an aggregate total of the data submitted using both the revised and legacy UCR definitions.
Source: FBI Uniform Crime Reports, 2018

Hate Crimes

Area	Number of Quarters Reported	Number of Incidents per Bias Motivation					
		Race/Ethnicity/ Ancestry	Religion	Sexual Orientation	Disability	Gender	Gender Identity
City	4	10	0	1	0	0	1
U.S.	4	4,047	1,419	1,196	159	47	168

Source: Federal Bureau of Investigation, Hate Crime Statistics 2018

Identity Theft Consumer Reports

Area	Reports	Reports per 100,000 Population	Rank[2]
MSA[1]	180	54	349
U.S.	650,572	198	-

Note: (1) Figures cover the Lincoln, NE Metropolitan Statistical Area—see Appendix B for areas included; (2) Rank ranges from 1 to 386 where 1 indicates greatest number of identity theft reports per 100,000 population
Source: Federal Trade Commission, Consumer Sentinel Network Data Book for January–December 2019

Fraud and Other Consumer Reports

Area	Reports	Reports per 100,000 Population	Rank[2]
MSA[1]	1,428	427	342
U.S.	2,590,177	789	-

Note: (1) Figures cover the Lincoln, NE Metropolitan Statistical Area—see Appendix B for areas included; (2) Rank ranges from 1 to 386 where 1 indicates greatest number of fraud and other consumer reports per 100,000 population
Source: Federal Trade Commission, Consumer Sentinel Network Data Book for January–December 2019

SPORTS

Professional Sports Teams

Team Name	League	Year Established
No teams are located in the metro area		

Source: Wikipedia, Major Professional Sports Teams of the United States and Canada, May 4, 2020

CLIMATE

Average and Extreme Temperatures

Temperature	Jan	Feb	Mar	Apr	May	Jun	Jul	Aug	Sep	Oct	Nov	Dec	Yr.
Extreme High (°F)	73	77	89	97	99	107	108	107	101	93	82	69	108
Average High (°F)	33	38	50	64	74	85	89	86	78	66	49	36	62
Average Temp. (°F)	22	28	39	52	62	73	78	75	66	53	38	26	51
Average Low (°F)	11	16	27	39	50	60	66	64	53	40	27	16	39
Extreme Low (°F)	-33	-24	-19	3	24	39	45	39	26	11	-5	-27	-33

Note: Figures cover the years 1948-1995
Source: National Climatic Data Center, International Station Meteorological Climate Summary, 9/96

Average Precipitation/Snowfall/Humidity

Precip./Humidity	Jan	Feb	Mar	Apr	May	Jun	Jul	Aug	Sep	Oct	Nov	Dec	Yr.
Avg. Precip. (in.)	0.8	0.8	2.4	2.9	4.1	3.7	3.7	3.4	3.1	1.9	1.4	0.9	29.1
Avg. Snowfall (in.)	6	5	6	1	Tr	0	0	0	Tr	Tr	3	6	27
Avg. Rel. Hum. 6am (%)	78	81	81	80	83	83	83	86	84	80	80	80	82
Avg. Rel. Hum. 3pm (%)	61	60	55	47	51	49	48	51	49	46	54	60	53

Note: Figures cover the years 1948-1995; Tr = Trace amounts (<0.05 in. of rain; <0.5 in. of snow)
Source: National Climatic Data Center, International Station Meteorological Climate Summary, 9/96

Weather Conditions

Temperature			Daytime Sky			Precipitation		
5°F & below	32°F & below	90°F & above	Clear	Partly cloudy	Cloudy	0.01 inch or more precip.	0.1 inch or more snow/ice	Thunder-storms
25	145	40	108	135	122	94	19	46

Note: Figures are average number of days per year and cover the years 1948-1995
Source: National Climatic Data Center, International Station Meteorological Climate Summary, 9/96

HAZARDOUS WASTE

Superfund Sites

The Lincoln, NE metro area has no sites on the EPA's Superfund Final National Priorities List. There are a total of 1,387 Superfund sites with a status of proposed or final on the list in the U.S.
U.S. Environmental Protection Agency, National Priorities List, May 5, 2020

**AIR & WATER
QUALITY**

Air Quality Trends: Ozone

	1990	1995	2000	2005	2010	2012	2014	2016	2017	2018
MSA[1]	0.057	0.060	0.057	0.056	0.050	0.058	0.061	0.058	0.062	0.062
U.S.	0.088	0.089	0.082	0.080	0.073	0.075	0.067	0.069	0.068	0.069

Note: (1) Data covers the Lincoln, NE Metropolitan Statistical Area—see Appendix B for areas included. The values shown are the composite ozone concentration averages among trend sites based on the highest fourth daily maximum 8-hour concentration in parts per million. These trends are based on sites having an adequate record of monitoring data during the trend period. Data from exceptional events are included.
Source: U.S. Environmental Protection Agency, Air Quality Monitoring Information, "Air Quality Trends by City, 1990-2018"

Air Quality Index

Area	Percent of Days when Air Quality was...[2]					AQI Statistics[2]	
	Good	Moderate	Unhealthy for Sensitive Groups	Unhealthy	Very Unhealthy	Maximum	Median
MSA[1]	90.4	9.6	0.0	0.0	0.0	78	31

Note: (1) Data covers the Lincoln, NE Metropolitan Statistical Area—see Appendix B for areas included; (2) Based on 365 days with AQI data in 2018. Air Quality Index (AQI) is an index for reporting daily air quality. EPA calculates the AQI for five major air pollutants regulated by the Clean Air Act: ground-level ozone, particle pollution (aka particulate matter), carbon monoxide, sulfur dioxide, and nitrogen dioxide. The AQI runs from 0 to 500. The higher the AQI value, the greater the level of air pollution and the greater the health concern. There are six AQI categories: "Good" AQI is between 0 and 50. Air quality is considered satisfactory; "Moderate" AQI is between 51 and 100. Air quality is acceptable; "Unhealthy for Sensitive Groups" When AQI values are between 101 and 150, members of sensitive groups may experience health effects; "Unhealthy" When AQI values are between 151 and 200 everyone may begin to experience health effects; "Very Unhealthy" AQI values between 201 and 300 trigger a health alert; "Hazardous" AQI values over 300 trigger warnings of emergency conditions (not shown).
Source: U.S. Environmental Protection Agency, Air Quality Index Report, 2018

Air Quality Index Pollutants

Area	Percent of Days when AQI Pollutant was...[2]					
	Carbon Monoxide	Nitrogen Dioxide	Ozone	Sulfur Dioxide	Particulate Matter 2.5	Particulate Matter 10
MSA[1]	0.0	0.0	62.7	21.1	16.2	0.0

Note: (1) Data covers the Lincoln, NE Metropolitan Statistical Area—see Appendix B for areas included; (2) Based on 365 days with AQI data in 2018. The Air Quality Index (AQI) is an index for reporting daily air quality. EPA calculates the AQI for five major air pollutants regulated by the Clean Air Act: ground-level ozone, particle pollution (also known as particulate matter), carbon monoxide, sulfur dioxide, and nitrogen dioxide. The AQI runs from 0 to 500. The higher the AQI value, the greater the level of air pollution and the greater the health concern.
Source: U.S. Environmental Protection Agency, Air Quality Index Report, 2018

Maximum Air Pollutant Concentrations: Particulate Matter, Ozone, CO and Lead

	Particulate Matter 10 (ug/m³)	Particulate Matter 2.5 Wtd AM (ug/m³)	Particulate Matter 2.5 24-Hr (ug/m³)	Ozone (ppm)	Carbon Monoxide (ppm)	Lead (ug/m³)
MSA[1] Level	n/a	7.1	19	0.062	n/a	n/a
NAAQS[2]	150	15	35	0.075	9	0.15
Met NAAQS[2]	n/a	Yes	Yes	Yes	n/a	n/a

Note: (1) Data covers the Lincoln, NE Metropolitan Statistical Area—see Appendix B for areas included; Data from exceptional events are included; (2) National Ambient Air Quality Standards; ppm = parts per million; ug/m³ = micrograms per cubic meter; n/a not available.
Concentrations: Particulate Matter 10 (coarse particulate)—highest second maximum 24-hour concentration; Particulate Matter 2.5 Wtd AM (fine particulate)—highest weighted annual mean concentration; Particulate Matter 2.5 24-Hour (fine particulate)—highest 98th percentile 24-hour concentration; Ozone—highest fourth daily maximum 8-hour concentration; Carbon Monoxide—highest second maximum non-overlapping 8-hour concentration; Lead—maximum running 3-month average
Source: U.S. Environmental Protection Agency, Air Quality Monitoring Information, "Air Quality Statistics by City, 2018"

Maximum Air Pollutant Concentrations: Nitrogen Dioxide and Sulfur Dioxide

	Nitrogen Dioxide AM (ppb)	Nitrogen Dioxide 1-Hr (ppb)	Sulfur Dioxide AM (ppb)	Sulfur Dioxide 1-Hr (ppb)	Sulfur Dioxide 24-Hr (ppb)
MSA[1] Level	n/a	n/a	n/a	10	n/a
NAAQS[2]	53	100	30	75	140
Met NAAQS[2]	n/a	n/a	n/a	Yes	n/a

Note: (1) Data covers the Lincoln, NE Metropolitan Statistical Area—see Appendix B for areas included; Data from exceptional events are included; (2) National Ambient Air Quality Standards; ppm = parts per million; ug/m³ = micrograms per cubic meter; n/a not available.
Concentrations: Nitrogen Dioxide AM—highest arithmetic mean concentration; Nitrogen Dioxide 1-Hr—highest 98th percentile 1-hour daily maximum concentration; Sulfur Dioxide AM—highest annual mean concentration; Sulfur Dioxide 1-Hr—highest 99th percentile 1-hour daily maximum concentration; Sulfur Dioxide 24-Hr—highest second maximum 24-hour concentration
Source: U.S. Environmental Protection Agency, Air Quality Monitoring Information, "Air Quality Statistics by City, 2018"

Drinking Water

Water System Name	Pop. Served	Primary Water Source Type	Violations[1]
City of Lincoln	280,369	(2)	2

Note: (1) Total number of violations (both active and inactive) in the EPA database
Source: U.S. Environmental Protection Agency, Office of Ground Water and Drinking Water, Safe Drinking Water Information System (based on data extracted May 5, 2020)

Little Rock, Arkansas

Background

Little Rock is the capital of Arkansas and the most populous city in the state. It is located along the banks of the Arkansas River and marks the point where the flat Mississippi Delta ends and the foothills of the Quachita Mountains begin. The city is best known for its place in the history of the United States Civil Rights Movement and for its connection to former President William Jefferson Clinton, who served as the Governor of Arkansas before being elected our forty-second President.

The area that is now Little Rock was originally inhabited by Native American tribes including the Quapaw, Choctaw and Cherokee, but the first Europeans in the area were the Spanish, who passed through in the mid-sixteenth century. The city got its name from a rock formation on the southern side of the Arkansas River that was a landmark for river crossings. When French explorer Jean-Baptiste Benard de la Harpe arrived in the area in 1722, he called the area Le petite roche, or "the little rock," and the nickname stuck. La Harpe built a trading post on the site, but it would be more than 100 years before the city is officially incorporated in 1831. When Arkansas became the 25th American State in 1836, Little Rock was chosen as its capital. Initially the city grew quickly, but many projects, including the railroad between Little Rock and Memphis, were put on hold when the Civil War broke out. Post-war reconstruction, however, brought a wealth of new development so that by the turn of the century, its transformation from a small, sleepy frontier town to a thriving, modern city was complete. After the Great Depression ended in the early 1930s, many residents began to move out to the suburbs and many new roads were built to accommodate the city's changing layout.

In 1957 the city was thrown into the national spotlight with Little Rock Nine—nine African-American students who enrolled in the all-white Central High School, claiming it was their right, based on the U.S. Supreme Court's ruling on *Brown v. Board of Education*. Governor Orval Faubus sent the National Guard to prevent the students from entering the school, but they were eventually admitted under the protection of the U.S. Army sent by President Eisenhower.

Little Rock was again brought to national prominence when then-Governor Bill Clinton started his presidential election campaign in 1992, and gave his election-night acceptance speech from the steps of the Old State House in downtown Little Rock. Clinton has since solidified his link to the city through the William J. Clinton Presidential Center and Park.

Today, the city has a diverse economy built upon manufacturing, education, healthcare and commercial trade. Many major corporations have headquarters in the city. The Little Rock Port is part of a comprehensive industrial business zone on the Arkansas River. In 2016, Little Rock was chosen to join "What Works Cities," a national initiative to help American cities enhance their use of data, improve services, and engage residents.

The Pulaski County Pedestrian and Bicycle Bridge, at 3,463 feet, is the world's longest bridge for pedestrians and bicyclists only. Prominent charitable organization Heifer International has its world headquarters in Little Rock. Dickey-Stephens Park, a 7,000-seat baseball park, is home to minor league team Arkansas Travelers.

Attractions in the city include the MacArthur Museum of Arkansas Military History, the Arkansas Museum of Discovery, and the Old State House Museum. In addition, the William J. Clinton Presidential Center and Park houses the Clinton Presidential Library and the headquarters of the Clinton Foundation. A section of downtown's Main Street, called Creative Corridor, combines the arts, entertainment, business and culture, and is home to the Arkansas Repertory Theatre, Arkansas Symphony Orchestra, and Ballet Arkansas. Other cultural attractions in Little Rock include the Arkansas Arts Center, the Robinson Center Music Hall, and Wildwood Center for the Performing Arts. The city's major institutions of higher learning are the University of Arkansas at Little Rock and the University of Arkansas for Medical Sciences.

Little Rock has a humid subtropical climate, typical of the southern United States. Summers are generally hot, while winters are cooler, but high humidity persists all year round. Rainfall can be heavy at times during the spring and fall but the city rarely receives any snow. In April of 2017, a deadly flood devastated the city. The highest temperature recorded is 114 degrees. A deadly tornado touched down 10 miles west of the city in 2014, when powerful storms killed 16 people in three states.

Rankings

General Rankings

- In their sixth annual survey, Livability.com looked at data for more than 1,000 U.S. cities to determine the rankings for Livability's "Top 100 Best Places to Live" in 2019. Little Rock ranked #90. Criteria: median home value capped at $250,000; affordable living; vibrant economy; education, demographics, health care options. transportation & infrastructure; abundant lifestyle amenities. *Livability.com, "Top 100 Best Places to Live 2019" March 2019*

Business/Finance Rankings

- The Brookings Institution ranked the nation's largest cities based on income inequality. Little Rock was ranked #19 (#1 = greatest inequality). Criteria: the "95/20 ratio," a figure representing the income at which a household earns more than 95 percent of all other households, divided by the income at which a household earns more than only 20 percent of all other households. *Brookings Institution, "Household Income Inequality, Largest Cities of 97 Large U.S. Metro Areas, 2014-2016," February 5, 2018*

- The Brookings Institution ranked the 100 largest metro areas in the U.S. based on income inequality. Little Rock was ranked #48 (#1 = greatest inequality). Criteria: the "95/20 ratio," a figure representing the income at which a household earns more than 95 percent of all other households, divided by the income at which a household earns more than only 20 percent of all other households. *Brookings Institution, "Household Income Inequality, 100 Largest U.S. Metro Areas, 2014-2016," February 5, 2018*

- The Little Rock metro area appeared on the Milken Institute "2020 Best Performing Cities" list. Rank: #177 out of 200 large metro areas. Criteria: job growth; wage and salary growth; high-tech output growth. *Milken Institute, "Best-Performing Cities 2020," February 26, 2020*

- *Forbes* ranked the 200 most populous metro areas to determine the nation's "Best Places for Business and Careers." The Little Rock metro area was ranked #132. Criteria: costs (business and living); job growth (past and projected); income growth; quality of life; educational attainment (college and high school); projected economic growth; cultural and leisure opportunities; workplace tolerance laws; net migration patterns. *Forbes, "The Best Places for Business and Careers 2019: Seattle Still On Top," October 30, 2019*

Education Rankings

- Personal finance website *WalletHub* analyzed the 150 largest U.S. metropolitan statistical areas to determine where the most educated Americans are choosing to settle. Criteria: education levels; percentage of workers with degrees; education quality and attainment gap; public school quality rankings; quality and size of each metro area's universities. Little Rock was ranked #76 (#1 = most educated city). *www.WalletHub.com, "2019's Most and Least Educated Cities in America, " July 22, 2019*

Environmental Rankings

- Little Rock was highlighted as one of the top 104 cleanest metro areas for short-term particle pollution (24-hour PM 2.5) in the U.S. during 2015 through 2017. Monitors in these cities reported no days with unhealthful PM 2.5 levels. *American Lung Association, "State of the Air 2019," April 24, 2019*

Health/Fitness Rankings

- Little Rock was identified as a "2020 Spring Allergy Capital." The area ranked #36 out of 100. Three groups of factors were used to identify the most challenging cities for people with allergies during the spring season: annual spring pollen levels; over the counter medicine use; number of board-certified allergy specialists. *Asthma and Allergy Foundation of America, "Spring Allergy Capitals 2020," March 10, 2020*

- Little Rock was identified as a "2020 Fall Allergy Capital." The area ranked #52 out of 100. Three groups of factors were used to identify the most challenging cities for people with allergies during the fall season: annual fall pollen levels; over the counter medicine use; number of board-certified allergy specialists. *Asthma and Allergy Foundation of America, "Fall Allergy Capitals 2020," March 10, 2020*

- Little Rock was identified as a "2019 Asthma Capital." The area ranked #56 out of the nation's 100 largest metropolitan areas. Criteria: estimated asthma prevalence; crude death rate from asthma; and ER visits due to asthma. Risk factors that were analyzed but not factored in the rankings: annual pollen score; annual air quality; public smoking laws; number of board-certified asthma specialists; rescue medication use; controller medication use; uninsured rate; poverty rate. *Asthma and Allergy Foundation of America, "Asthma Capitals 2019: The Most Challenging Places to Live With Asthma," May 7, 2019*

- *Men's Health* ranked 100 major U.S. cities in terms of the best cities for men. Little Rock ranked #89. Criteria: health; fitness; quality of life. *Men's Health, "The Best & Worst Cities for Men Who Want to Be Fit and Happy," January 1, 2016*

- The Little Rock metro area ranked #161 out of 189 in The Gallup-Sharecare Well-Being Index. Criteria: purpose; social well being; financial health; community and physical health. Results are based on telephone interviews with adults, aged 18 and older, living in metropolitan areas in the 50 U.S. states and the District of Columbia. *Gallup-Sharecare, "State of American Well-Being, 2017 Community Well-Being Rankings" March 2018*

Real Estate Rankings

- *WalletHub* compared the most populated U.S. cities, as well as at least two of the most populated cities in each state, for a total of 179, to determine which had the best markets for real estate agents. Little Rock ranked #157 where demand was high and pay was the best. Criteria: sales per agent; annual median wage for real-estate agents; monthly average starting salary for real estate agents; real estate job density and competition; unemployment rate; home turnover rate; housing-market health index; and other relevant metrics. *www.WalletHub.com, "2019's Best Places to Be a Real Estate Agent," April 24, 2019*

Safety Rankings

- To identify the most dangerous cities in America, 24/7 Wall Street focused on violent crime categories—murder, non-negligent manslaughter, rape, robbery, and aggravated assault—and property crime as reported in the FBI's 2018 annual Uniform Crime Report. Criteria also included median income from American Community Survey and unemployment figures from Bureau of Labor Statistics. For cities with populations over 100,000, Little Rock was ranked #8. *247wallst.com, "America's Most Dangerous Cities" January 10, 2020*

- Allstate ranked the 200 largest cities in America in terms of driver safety. Little Rock ranked #112. Criteria: internal property damage claims over a two-year period from January 2016 to December 2017. The report helps increase the importance of safety and awareness behind the wheel. *Allstate, "Allstate America's Best Drivers Report, 2019" June 24, 2019*

- Little Rock was identified as one of the most dangerous cities in America by NeighborhoodScout. The city ranked #15 out of 100 (#1 = most dangerous). Criteria: number of violent crimes per 1,000 residents. The editors only considered cities with 25,000 or more residents. *NeighborhoodScout.com, "Top 100 Most Dangerous Cities in the U.S. 2020" January 2, 2020*

- The National Insurance Crime Bureau ranked 382 metro areas in the U.S. in terms of per capita rates of vehicle theft. The Little Rock metro area ranked #42 (#1 = highest rate). Criteria: number of vehicle theft offenses per 100,000 inhabitants in 2018. *National Insurance Crime Bureau, "Hot Spots 2018," June 25, 2019*

Seniors/Retirement Rankings

- From its Best Cities for Successful Aging indexes, the Milken Institute generated rankings for metropolitan areas, weighing data in nine categories—health care, wellness, living arrangements, transportation and convenience, financial characteristics, education, employment, community engagement, and overall livability. The Little Rock metro area was ranked #47 overall in the large metro area category. *Milken Institute, "Best Cities for Successful Aging, 2017" March 14, 2017*

Women/Minorities Rankings

- Personal finance website *WalletHub* compared more than 180 U.S. cities—including the 150 most populated U.S. cities, plus at least two of the most populated cities in each state—across two key dimensions, "Hispanic Business-Friendliness" and "Hispanic Purchasing Power", to arrive at the most favorable conditions for Hispanic entrepreneurs. Little Rock was ranked #135 out of 182. Criteria includes: share of Hispanic-Owned Businesses; Hispanic entrepreneurship rate to median annual income of Hispanics; Small Business-Friendliness score; cost of living; and number of Hispanics with at least a bachelor's degree. *WalletHub.com, "2019's Best Cities for Hispanic Entrepreneurs," May 1, 2019*

Miscellaneous Rankings

- *WalletHub* compared the 150 most populated U.S. cities to determine their operating efficiency. A "Quality of Services" score was constructed for each city and then divided by the total budget per capita to reveal which were managed the best. Little Rock ranked #68. Criteria: financial stability; economy; education; safety; health; infrastructure and pollution. *www.WalletHub.com, "2019's Best- & Worst-Run Cities in America," July 1, 2019*

Business Environment

CITY FINANCES

City Government Finances

Component	2017 ($000)	2017 ($ per capita)
Total Revenues	470,624	2,377
Total Expenditures	526,047	2,657
Debt Outstanding	592,815	2,994
Cash and Securities[1]	451,118	2,278

Note: (1) Cash and security holdings of a government at the close of its fiscal year, including those of its dependent agencies, utilities, and liquor stores.
Source: U.S. Census Bureau, State & Local Government Finances 2017

City Government Revenue by Source

Source	2017 ($000)	2017 ($ per capita)	2017 (%)
General Revenue			
From Federal Government	14,181	72	3.0
From State Government	22,046	111	4.7
From Local Governments	54,161	274	11.5
Taxes			
Property	54,738	276	11.6
Sales and Gross Receipts	122,173	617	26.0
Personal Income	0	0	0.0
Corporate Income	0	0	0.0
Motor Vehicle License	0	0	0.0
Other Taxes	9,277	47	2.0
Current Charges	167,720	847	35.6
Liquor Store	0	0	0.0
Utility	0	0	0.0
Employee Retirement	9,255	47	2.0

Source: U.S. Census Bureau, State & Local Government Finances 2017

City Government Expenditures by Function

Function	2017 ($000)	2017 ($ per capita)	2017 (%)
General Direct Expenditures			
Air Transportation	42,799	216	8.1
Corrections	0	0	0.0
Education	0	0	0.0
Employment Security Administration	0	0	0.0
Financial Administration	8,744	44	1.7
Fire Protection	50,120	253	9.5
General Public Buildings	983	5	0.2
Governmental Administration, Other	5,635	28	1.1
Health	37,819	191	7.2
Highways	42,142	212	8.0
Hospitals	0	0	0.0
Housing and Community Development	7,106	35	1.4
Interest on General Debt	21,316	107	4.1
Judicial and Legal	5,036	25	1.0
Libraries	9,990	50	1.9
Parking	1,344	6	0.3
Parks and Recreation	42,911	216	8.2
Police Protection	71,608	361	13.6
Public Welfare	0	0	0.0
Sewerage	50,250	253	9.6
Solid Waste Management	16,095	81	3.1
Veterans' Services	0	0	0.0
Liquor Store	0	0	0.0
Utility	0	0	0.0
Employee Retirement	12,706	64	2.4

Source: U.S. Census Bureau, State & Local Government Finances 2017

DEMOGRAPHICS

Population Growth

Area	1990 Census	2000 Census	2010 Census	2018* Estimate	Population Growth (%)	
					1990-2018	2010-2018
City	177,519	183,133	193,524	198,135	11.6	2.4
MSA[1]	535,034	610,518	699,757	734,502	37.3	5.0
U.S.	248,709,873	281,421,906	308,745,538	322,903,030	29.8	4.6

Note: (1) Figures cover the Little Rock-North Little Rock-Conway, AR Metropolitan Statistical Area—see Appendix B for areas included; (*) 2014-2018 5-year estimated population
Source: U.S. Census Bureau, 1990 Census, Census 2000, Census 2010, 2014-2018 American Community Survey 5-Year Estimates

Household Size

Area	Persons in Household (%)							Average Household Size
	One	Two	Three	Four	Five	Six	Seven or More	
City	36.8	32.4	13.7	10.1	4.5	1.8	0.7	2.40
MSA[1]	29.6	34.6	16.3	11.7	5.0	1.8	0.9	2.60
U.S.	27.7	33.9	15.7	13.0	6.0	2.3	1.4	2.60

Note: (1) Figures cover the Little Rock-North Little Rock-Conway, AR Metropolitan Statistical Area—see Appendix B for areas included
Source: U.S. Census Bureau, 2014-2018 American Community Survey 5-Year Estimates

Race

Area	White Alone[2] (%)	Black Alone[2] (%)	Asian Alone[2] (%)	AIAN[3] Alone[2] (%)	NHOPI[4] Alone[2] (%)	Other Race Alone[2] (%)	Two or More Races (%)
City	50.6	41.7	3.1	0.2	0.1	1.8	2.4
MSA[1]	70.7	23.3	1.7	0.3	0.1	1.5	2.5
U.S.	72.7	12.7	5.4	0.8	0.2	4.9	3.2

Note: (1) Figures cover the Little Rock-North Little Rock-Conway, AR Metropolitan Statistical Area—see Appendix B for areas included; (2) Alone is defined as not being in combination with one or more other races; (3) American Indian and Alaska Native; (4) Native Hawaiian and Other Pacific Islander
Source: U.S. Census Bureau, 2014-2018 American Community Survey 5-Year Estimates

Hispanic or Latino Origin

Area	Total (%)	Mexican (%)	Puerto Rican (%)	Cuban (%)	Other (%)
City	7.3	4.7	0.3	0.2	2.0
MSA[1]	5.2	3.7	0.3	0.1	1.2
U.S.	17.8	11.2	1.7	0.7	4.2

Note: Persons of Hispanic or Latino origin can be of any race; (1) Figures cover the Little Rock-North Little Rock-Conway, AR Metropolitan Statistical Area—see Appendix B for areas included
Source: U.S. Census Bureau, 2014-2018 American Community Survey 5-Year Estimates

Segregation

Type	Segregation Indices[1]				Percent Change		
	1990	2000	2010	2010 Rank[2]	1990-2000	1990-2010	2000-2010
Black/White	61.1	61.3	58.8	42	0.3	-2.3	-2.5
Asian/White	37.5	38.8	39.7	59	1.3	2.2	0.9
Hispanic/White	23.2	34.7	39.7	68	11.5	16.5	5.0

Note: All figures cover the Metropolitan Statistical Area—see Appendix B for areas included; Figures are based on an analysis of 1990, 2000, and 2010 Census Decennial Census tract data by William H. Frey, Brookings Institution and the University of Michigan Social Science Data Analysis Network. In this analysis all racial groups (whites, blacks, and asians) are non-Hispanic members of those races. Hispanics are shown as a separate category; (1) Segregation Indices are Dissimilarity Indices that measure the degree to which the minority group is distributed differently than whites across census tracts. They range from 0 (complete integration) to 100 (complete segregation) where the value indicates the percentage of the minority group that needs to move to be distributed exactly like whites; (2) Ranges from 1 (most segregated) to 102 (least segregated); n/a not available.
Source: www.CensusScope.org

Ancestry

Area	German	Irish	English	American	Italian	Polish	French[2]	Scottish	Dutch
City	7.1	7.2	7.7	6.1	1.4	1.0	1.7	1.8	0.7
MSA[1]	9.7	9.2	8.2	8.3	1.5	1.0	1.7	2.0	1.1
U.S.	13.7	9.9	7.3	6.4	5.2	2.8	2.4	1.7	1.2

Note: Figures are the percentage of the total population reporting a particular ancestry. The nine most commonly reported ancestries in the U.S. are shown. Figures include multiple ancestries (e.g. if a person reported being Irish and Italian, they were included in both columns); (1) Figures cover the Little Rock-North Little Rock-Conway, AR Metropolitan Statistical Area—see Appendix B for areas included; (2) Excludes Basque
Source: U.S. Census Bureau, 2014-2018 American Community Survey 5-Year Estimates

Foreign-born Population

Area	Any Foreign Country	Asia	Mexico	Europe	Caribbean	Central America[2]	South America	Africa	Canada
City	7.8	2.8	2.1	0.7	0.1	1.1	0.4	0.4	0.1
MSA[1]	4.2	1.4	1.3	0.4	0.1	0.5	0.2	0.2	0.1
U.S.	13.5	4.1	3.5	1.5	1.3	1.1	0.9	0.7	0.3

Note: (1) Figures cover the Little Rock-North Little Rock-Conway, AR Metropolitan Statistical Area—see Appendix B for areas included; (2) Excludes Mexico.
Source: U.S. Census Bureau, 2014-2018 American Community Survey 5-Year Estimates

Marital Status

Area	Never Married	Now Married[2]	Separated	Widowed	Divorced
City	37.7	40.2	2.8	6.2	13.2
MSA[1]	30.6	47.5	2.3	6.1	13.5
U.S.	33.3	48.1	2.0	5.8	10.8

Note: Figures are percentages and cover the population 15 years of age and older; (1) Figures cover the Little Rock-North Little Rock-Conway, AR Metropolitan Statistical Area—see Appendix B for areas included; (2) Excludes separated
Source: U.S. Census Bureau, 2014-2018 American Community Survey 5-Year Estimates

Disability by Age

Area	All Ages	Under 18 Years Old	18 to 64 Years Old	65 Years and Over
City	13.3	5.8	11.5	35.4
MSA[1]	15.6	6.1	13.6	40.3
U.S.	12.6	4.2	10.3	35.0

Note: Figures show percent of the civilian noninstitutionalized population that reported having a disability. Disability status is determined from six types of difficulty: vision, hearing, cognitive, ambulatory, self-care, and independent living. For children under 5 years old, hearing and vision difficulty are used to determine disability status. For children between the ages of 5 and 14, disability status is determined from hearing, vision, cognitive, ambulatory, and self-care difficulties. For people aged 15 years and older, they are considered to have a disability if they have difficulty with any one of the six difficulty types; Note: (1) Figures cover the Little Rock-North Little Rock-Conway, AR Metropolitan Statistical Area—see Appendix B for areas included
Source: U.S. Census Bureau, 2014-2018 American Community Survey 5-Year Estimates

Age

Area	Under Age 5	Age 5–19	Age 20–34	Age 35–44	Age 45–54	Age 55–64	Age 65–74	Age 75–84	Age 85+	Median Age
City	6.5	19.3	22.2	13.3	11.9	13.1	8.0	3.6	2.0	36.3
MSA[1]	6.5	19.7	21.4	13.0	12.6	12.4	8.7	4.1	1.7	36.7
U.S.	6.1	19.3	20.7	12.6	13.2	12.8	8.8	4.5	1.9	37.9

Note: (1) Figures cover the Little Rock-North Little Rock-Conway, AR Metropolitan Statistical Area—see Appendix B for areas included
Source: U.S. Census Bureau, 2014-2018 American Community Survey 5-Year Estimates

Gender

Area	Males	Females	Males per 100 Females
City	94,389	103,746	91.0
MSA[1]	356,158	378,344	94.1
U.S.	158,984,190	163,918,840	97.0

Note: (1) Figures cover the Little Rock-North Little Rock-Conway, AR Metropolitan Statistical Area—see Appendix B for areas included
Source: U.S. Census Bureau, 2014-2018 American Community Survey 5-Year Estimates

Religious Groups by Family

Area	Catholic	Baptist	Non-Den.	Methodist[2]	Lutheran	LDS[3]	Pentecostal	Presbyterian[4]	Muslim[5]	Judaism
MSA[1]	4.5	25.9	6.1	7.3	0.5	0.9	2.9	0.9	0.1	0.1
U.S.	19.1	9.3	4.0	4.0	2.3	2.0	1.9	1.6	0.8	0.7

Note: Figures are the number of adherents as a percentage of the total population; (1) Figures cover the Little Rock-North Little Rock-Conway, AR Metropolitan Statistical Area—see Appendix B for areas included; (2) Methodist/Pietist; (3) Latter Day Saints; (4) Reformed; (5) Figures are estimates
Source: Association of Statisticians of American Religious Bodies, 2010 U.S. Religion Census: Religious Congregations & Membership Study

Religious Groups by Tradition

Area	Catholic	Evangelical Protestant	Mainline Protestant	Other Tradition	Black Protestant	Orthodox
MSA[1]	4.5	33.9	8.2	1.7	3.5	0.1
U.S.	19.1	16.2	7.3	4.3	1.6	0.3

Note: Figures are the number of adherents as a percentage of the total population; (1) Figures cover the Little Rock-North Little Rock-Conway, AR Metropolitan Statistical Area—see Appendix B for areas included
Source: Association of Statisticians of American Religious Bodies, 2010 U.S. Religion Census: Religious Congregations & Membership Study

ECONOMY

Gross Metropolitan Product

Area	2017	2018	2019	2020	Rank[2]
MSA[1]	38.5	39.8	41.1	42.7	76

Note: Figures are in billions of dollars; (1) Figures cover the Little Rock-North Little Rock-Conway, AR Metropolitan Statistical Area—see Appendix B for areas included; (2) Rank is based on 2018 data and ranges from 1 to 381
Source: U.S. Conference of Mayors, U.S. Metro Economies: GMP & Employment 2018-2020, September 2019

Economic Growth

Area	2015-17 (%)	2018 (%)	2019 (%)	2020 (%)	Rank[2]
MSA[1]	0.4	0.9	1.6	1.5	286
U.S.	1.9	2.9	2.3	2.1	–

Note: Figures are real gross metropolitan product (GMP) growth rates and represent average annual percent change; (1) Figures cover the Little Rock-North Little Rock-Conway, AR Metropolitan Statistical Area—see Appendix B for areas included; (2) Rank is based on 2017 2-year average annual percent change and ranges from 1 to 381
Source: U.S. Conference of Mayors, U.S. Metro Economies: GMP & Employment 2018-2020, September 2019

Metropolitan Area Exports

Area	2013	2014	2015	2016	2017	2018	Rank[2]
MSA[1]	2,497.5	2,463.5	1,777.5	1,871.0	2,146.1	1,607.4	120

Note: Figures are in millions of dollars; (1) Figures cover the Little Rock-North Little Rock-Conway, AR Metropolitan Statistical Area—see Appendix B for areas included; (2) Rank is based on 2018 data and ranges from 1 to 387
Source: U.S. Department of Commerce, International Trade Administration, Office of Trade and Economic Analysis, Industry and Analysis, Exports by Metropolitan Area, data extracted April 15, 2020

Building Permits

Area	Single-Family			Multi-Family			Total		
	2017	2018	Pct. Chg.	2017	2018	Pct. Chg.	2017	2018	Pct. Chg.
City	592	325	-45.1	508	145	-71.5	1,100	470	-57.3
MSA[1]	2,087	1,819	-12.8	1,128	355	-68.5	3,215	2,174	-32.4
U.S.	820,000	855,300	4.3	462,000	473,500	2.5	1,282,000	1,328,800	3.7

Note: (1) Figures cover the Little Rock-North Little Rock-Conway, AR Metropolitan Statistical Area—see Appendix B for areas included; Figures represent new, privately-owned housing units authorized (unadjusted data); All permit data are based on estimates with imputation
Source: U.S. Census Bureau, Manufacturing, Mining, and Construction Statistics, Building Permits, 2017, 2018

Bankruptcy Filings

Area	Business Filings			Nonbusiness Filings		
	2018	2019	% Chg.	2018	2019	% Chg.
Pulaski County	24	233	870.8	2,420	2,318	-4.2
U.S.	22,232	22,780	2.5	751,186	752,160	0.1

Note: Business filings include Chapter 7, Chapter 9, Chapter 11, Chapter 12, Chapter 13, Chapter 15, and Section 304; Nonbusiness filings include Chapter 7, Chapter 11, and Chapter 13
Source: Administrative Office of the U.S. Courts, Business and Nonbusiness Bankruptcy, County Cases Commenced by Chapter of the Bankruptcy Code, During the 12-Month Period Ending December 31, 2018 and Business and Nonbusiness Bankruptcy, County Cases Commenced by Chapter of the Bankruptcy Code, During the 12-Month Period Ending December 31, 2019

Housing Vacancy Rates

Area	Gross Vacancy Rate[2] (%)			Year-Round Vacancy Rate[3] (%)			Rental Vacancy Rate[4] (%)			Homeowner Vacancy Rate[5] (%)		
	2017	2018	2019	2017	2018	2019	2017	2018	2019	2017	2018	2019
MSA[1]	10.3	10.5	9.9	10.0	10.2	9.6	11.3	10.9	11.4	2.0	1.8	1.7
U.S.	12.7	12.3	12.0	9.9	9.7	9.5	7.2	6.9	6.7	1.6	1.5	1.4

Note: (1) Figures cover the Little Rock-North Little Rock-Conway, AR Metropolitan Statistical Area—see Appendix B for areas included; (2) The percentage of the total housing inventory that is vacant; (3) The percentage of the housing inventory (excluding seasonal units) that is year-round vacant; (4) The percentage of rental inventory that is vacant for rent; (5) The percentage of homeowner inventory that is vacant for sale
Source: U.S. Census Bureau, Housing Vacancies and Homeownership Annual Statistics: 2017, 2018, 2019

INCOME

Income

Area	Per Capita ($)	Median Household ($)	Average Household ($)
City	34,546	49,957	80,455
MSA[1]	29,397	53,008	73,205
U.S.	32,621	60,293	84,938

Note: (1) Figures cover the Little Rock-North Little Rock-Conway, AR Metropolitan Statistical Area—see Appendix B for areas included
Source: U.S. Census Bureau, 2014-2018 American Community Survey 5-Year Estimates

Household Income Distribution

Area	Percent of Households Earning							
	Under $15,000	$15,000 -$24,999	$25,000 -$34,999	$35,000 -$49,999	$50,000 -$74,999	$75,000 -$99,999	$100,000 -$149,999	$150,000 and up
City	13.0	11.4	10.8	14.8	16.2	10.2	11.2	12.3
MSA[1]	12.2	10.2	10.7	14.4	18.0	12.0	13.5	9.1
U.S.	10.9	9.3	9.3	12.6	17.5	12.5	14.6	13.3

Note: (1) Figures cover the Little Rock-North Little Rock-Conway, AR Metropolitan Statistical Area—see Appendix B for areas included
Source: U.S. Census Bureau, 2014-2018 American Community Survey 5-Year Estimates

Poverty Rate

Area	All Ages	Under 18 Years Old	18 to 64 Years Old	65 Years and Over
City	17.4	25.7	15.8	10.0
MSA[1]	15.1	20.7	14.3	9.2
U.S.	14.1	19.5	13.2	9.3

Note: Figures are percentage of people whose income during the past 12 months was below the poverty level; (1) Figures cover the Little Rock-North Little Rock-Conway, AR Metropolitan Statistical Area—see Appendix B for areas included
Source: U.S. Census Bureau, 2014-2018 American Community Survey 5-Year Estimates

EMPLOYMENT

Labor Force and Employment

Area	Civilian Labor Force			Workers Employed		
	Dec. 2018	Dec. 2019	% Chg.	Dec. 2018	Dec. 2019	% Chg.
City	97,191	96,600	-0.6	94,024	93,594	-0.5
MSA[1]	356,666	354,854	-0.5	345,501	343,794	-0.5
U.S.	162,510,000	164,007,000	0.9	156,481,000	158,504,000	1.3

Note: Data is not seasonally adjusted and covers workers 16 years of age and older; (1) Figures cover the Little Rock-North Little Rock-Conway, AR Metropolitan Statistical Area—see Appendix B for areas included
Source: Bureau of Labor Statistics, Local Area Unemployment Statistics

Unemployment Rate

Area	2019											
	Jan.	Feb.	Mar.	Apr.	May	Jun.	Jul.	Aug.	Sep.	Oct.	Nov.	Dec.
City	3.8	3.7	3.2	2.9	3.2	3.6	3.8	3.4	3.1	3.0	3.0	3.1
MSA[1]	3.7	3.6	3.1	2.7	3.0	3.4	3.7	3.3	3.1	2.9	2.9	3.1
U.S.	4.4	4.1	3.9	3.3	3.4	3.8	4.0	3.8	3.3	3.3	3.3	3.4

Note: Data is not seasonally adjusted and covers workers 16 years of age and older; (1) Figures cover the Little Rock-North Little Rock-Conway, AR Metropolitan Statistical Area—see Appendix B for areas included
Source: Bureau of Labor Statistics, Local Area Unemployment Statistics

Average Wages

Occupation	$/Hr.	Occupation	$/Hr.
Accountants and Auditors	32.50	Maintenance and Repair Workers	16.00
Automotive Mechanics	19.80	Marketing Managers	59.60
Bookkeepers	18.60	Network and Computer Systems Admin.	34.40
Carpenters	19.20	Nurses, Licensed Practical	21.20
Cashiers	11.10	Nurses, Registered	31.90
Computer Programmers	36.50	Nursing Assistants	13.20
Computer Systems Analysts	35.20	Office Clerks, General	16.40
Computer User Support Specialists	23.10	Physical Therapists	39.90
Construction Laborers	13.40	Physicians	74.10
Cooks, Restaurant	11.50	Plumbers, Pipefitters and Steamfitters	23.10
Customer Service Representatives	16.40	Police and Sheriff's Patrol Officers	23.30
Dentists	86.90	Postal Service Mail Carriers	25.00
Electricians	20.40	Real Estate Sales Agents	n/a
Engineers, Electrical	43.80	Retail Salespersons	13.30
Fast Food and Counter Workers	10.00	Sales Representatives, Technical/Scientific	30.80
Financial Managers	51.40	Secretaries, Exc. Legal/Medical/Executive	15.90
First-Line Supervisors of Office Workers	24.80	Security Guards	14.20
General and Operations Managers	46.70	Surgeons	n/a
Hairdressers/Cosmetologists	11.90	Teacher Assistants, Exc. Postsecondary*	10.80
Home Health and Personal Care Aides	11.20	Teachers, Secondary School, Exc. Sp. Ed.*	27.00
Janitors and Cleaners	11.50	Telemarketers	11.20
Landscaping/Groundskeeping Workers	13.30	Truck Drivers, Heavy/Tractor-Trailer	22.40
Lawyers	44.30	Truck Drivers, Light/Delivery Services	13.60
Maids and Housekeeping Cleaners	10.40	Waiters and Waitresses	10.50

Note: Wage data covers the Little Rock-North Little Rock-Conway, AR Metropolitan Statistical Area—see Appendix B for areas included; (*) Hourly wages were calculated from annual wage data based on a 40 hour work week; n/a not available.
Source: Bureau of Labor Statistics, Metro Area Occupational Employment & Wage Estimates, May 2019

Employment by Occupation

Occupation Classification	City (%)	MSA[1] (%)	U.S. (%)
Management, Business, Science, and Arts	44.2	39.1	37.9
Natural Resources, Construction, and Maintenance	5.3	8.3	8.9
Production, Transportation, and Material Moving	11.3	12.8	13.3
Sales and Office	23.3	23.5	22.1
Service	15.8	16.3	17.9

Note: Figures cover employed civilians 16 years of age and older; (1) Figures cover the Little Rock-North Little Rock-Conway, AR Metropolitan Statistical Area—see Appendix B for areas included
Source: U.S. Census Bureau, 2014-2018 American Community Survey 5-Year Estimates

Employment by Industry

Sector	MSA[1]		U.S.
	Number of Employees	Percent of Total	Percent of Total
Construction, Mining, and Logging	17,800	4.9	5.4
Education and Health Services	58,800	16.0	16.1
Financial Activities	21,600	5.9	5.8
Government	70,700	19.3	15.0
Information	4,300	1.2	1.9
Leisure and Hospitality	33,600	9.2	10.8
Manufacturing	20,700	5.6	8.4
Other Services	18,400	5.0	3.9
Professional and Business Services	48,400	13.2	14.1
Retail Trade	38,900	10.6	10.6
Transportation, Warehousing, and Utilities	17,300	4.7	4.2
Wholesale Trade	15,900	4.3	3.9

Note: Figures are non-farm employment as of December 2019. Figures are not seasonally adjusted and include workers 16 years of age and older; (1) Figures cover the Little Rock-North Little Rock-Conway, AR Metropolitan Statistical Area—see Appendix B for areas included
Source: Bureau of Labor Statistics, Current Employment Statistics, Employment, Hours, and Earnings

Occupations with Greatest Projected Employment Growth: 2019 – 2021

Occupation[1]	2019 Employment	2021 Projected Employment	Numeric Employment Change	Percent Employment Change
Combined Food Preparation and Serving Workers, Including Fast Food	38,590	40,380	1,790	4.6
Heavy and Tractor-Trailer Truck Drivers	38,360	39,540	1,180	3.1
Insurance Sales Agents	15,010	16,120	1,110	7.4
Personal Care Aides	18,460	19,290	830	4.5
Registered Nurses	26,400	27,110	710	2.7
Cooks, Restaurant	10,940	11,570	630	5.8
General and Operations Managers	20,940	21,490	550	2.6
Clergy	13,520	14,030	510	3.8
Waiters and Waitresses	18,640	19,140	500	2.7
Janitors and Cleaners, Except Maids and Housekeeping Cleaners	19,050	19,510	460	2.4

Note: Projections cover Arkansas; (1) Sorted by numeric employment change
Source: www.projectionscentral.com, State Occupational Projections, 2019–2021 Short-Term Projections

Fastest Growing Occupations: 2019 – 2021

Occupation[1]	2019 Employment	2021 Projected Employment	Numeric Employment Change	Percent Employment Change
Sewing Machine Operators	1,060	1,250	190	17.9
Fundraisers	760	850	90	11.8
Fiberglass Laminators and Fabricators	540	600	60	11.1
Veterinary Assistants and Laboratory Animal Caretakers	1,030	1,140	110	10.7
Nonfarm Animal Caretakers	3,050	3,290	240	7.9
Speech-Language Pathologists	2,200	2,370	170	7.7
Ushers, Lobby Attendants, and Ticket Takers	650	700	50	7.7
Veterinarians	670	720	50	7.5
Insurance Sales Agents	15,010	16,120	1,110	7.4
Cargo and Freight Agents	970	1,040	70	7.2

Note: Projections cover Arkansas; (1) Sorted by percent employment change and excludes occupations with numeric employment change less than 50
Source: www.projectionscentral.com, State Occupational Projections, 2019–2021 Short-Term Projections

TAXES

State Corporate Income Tax Rates

State	Tax Rate (%)	Income Brackets ($)	Num. of Brackets	Financial Institution Tax Rate (%)[a]	Federal Income Tax Ded.
Arkansas	1.0 - 6.5	3,000 - 100,001	6	1.0 - 6.5	No

Note: Tax rates as of January 1, 2020; (a) Rates listed are the corporate income tax rate applied to financial institutions or excise taxes based on income.
Source: Federation of Tax Administrators, State Corporate Income Tax Rates, January 1, 2020

State Individual Income Tax Rates

State	Tax Rate (%)	Income Brackets ($)	Personal Exemptions ($)			Standard Ded. ($)	
			Single	Married	Depend.	Single	Married
Arkansas (a)	2.0 - 6.6 (f)	4,600 - 80,801	26	52 (c)	26 (c)	2,200	4,400

Note: Tax rates as of January 1, 2020; Local- and county-level taxes are not included; Federal income tax is not deductible on state income tax returns; (a) 19 states have statutory provision for automatically adjusting to the rate of inflation the dollar values of the income tax brackets, standard deductions, and/or personal exemptions. Michigan indexes the personal exemption only. Oregon does not index the income brackets for $125,000 and over; (c) The personal exemption takes the form of a tax credit instead of a deduction; (f) Arkansas has separate brackets for taxpayers with income under $75,000 and $21,000.
Source: Federation of Tax Administrators, State Individual Income Tax Rates, January 1, 2020

Various State Sales and Excise Tax Rates

State	State Sales Tax (%)	Gasoline[1] (¢/gal.)	Cigarette[2] ($/pack)	Spirits[3] ($/gal.)	Wine[4] ($/gal.)	Beer[5] ($/gal.)	Recreational Marijuana (%)
Arkansas	6.5	24.8	1.15	8.41	1.41	0.34	Not legal

Note: All tax rates as of January 1, 2020; (1) The American Petroleum Institute has developed a methodology for determining the average tax rate on a gallon of fuel. Rates may include any of the following: excise taxes, environmental fees, storage tank fees, other fees or taxes, general sales tax, and local taxes; (2) The federal excise tax of $1.0066 per pack and local taxes are not included; (3) Rates are those applicable to off-premise sales of 40% alcohol by volume (a.b.v.) distilled spirits in 750ml containers. Local excise taxes are excluded; (4) Rates are those applicable to off-premise sales of 11% a.b.v. non-carbonated wine in 750ml containers; (5) Rates are those applicable to off-premise sales of 4.7% a.b.v. beer in 12 ounce containers.
Source: Tax Foundation, 2020 Facts & Figures: How Does Your State Compare?

State Business Tax Climate Index Rankings

State	Overall Rank	Corporate Tax Rank	Individual Income Tax Rank	Sales Tax Rank	Property Tax Rank	Unemployment Insurance Tax Rank
Arkansas	46	34	40	46	29	23

Note: The index is a measure of how each state's tax laws affect economic performance. The lower the rank, the more favorable a state's tax system is for business. States without a given tax are given a ranking of 1. The scores/rankings for the District of Columbia do not affect other states. The 2020 index represents the tax climate as of July 1, 2019.
Source: Tax Foundation, State Business Tax Climate Index 2020

COMMERCIAL UTILITIES

Typical Monthly Electric Bills

Area	Commercial Service ($/month)		Industrial Service ($/month)	
	1,500 kWh	40 kW demand 14,000 kWh	1,000 kW demand 200,000 kWh	50,000 kW demand 32,500,000 kWh
City	144	1,244	21,141	1,858,863
Average[1]	203	1,612	25,706	2,520,671

Note: Figures are based on annualized rates; (1) Average based on 187 utilities surveyed
Source: Edison Electric Institute, Typical Bills and Average Rates Report, Summer 2019

TRANSPORTATION

Means of Transportation to Work

Area	Car/Truck/Van Drove Alone	Car-pooled	Public Transportation Bus	Subway	Railroad	Bicycle	Walked	Other Means	Worked at Home
City	82.6	9.4	0.8	0.0	0.0	0.1	1.6	1.4	4.1
MSA[1]	84.1	9.6	0.5	0.0	0.0	0.1	1.3	1.1	3.4
U.S.	76.4	9.1	2.5	1.9	0.6	0.6	2.7	1.3	4.9

Note: Figures are percentages and cover workers 16 years of age and older; (1) Figures cover the Little Rock-North Little Rock-Conway, AR Metropolitan Statistical Area—see Appendix B for areas included
Source: U.S. Census Bureau, 2014-2018 American Community Survey 5-Year Estimates

Travel Time to Work

Area	Less Than 10 Minutes	10 to 19 Minutes	20 to 29 Minutes	30 to 44 Minutes	45 to 59 Minutes	60 to 89 Minutes	90 Minutes or More
City	13.8	43.7	27.5	10.8	1.9	1.2	1.1
MSA[1]	12.9	32.4	24.1	19.7	6.9	2.9	1.3
U.S.	12.5	28.7	20.9	20.7	8.2	6.3	2.8

Note: Note: Figures are percentages and include workers 16 years old and over; (1) Figures cover the Little Rock-North Little Rock-Conway, AR Metropolitan Statistical Area—see Appendix B for areas included
Source: U.S. Census Bureau, 2014-2018 American Community Survey 5-Year Estimates

Key Congestion Measures

Area	1982	1992	2002	2012	2017
Annual Hours of Delay, Total (000)	964	2,401	7,468	13,278	14,823
Annual Hours of Delay, Per Auto Commuter	6	12	31	36	43
Annual Congestion Cost, Total (million $)	7	25	100	233	269
Annual Congestion Cost, Per Auto Commuter ($)	109	187	454	632	684

Source: Texas A&M Transportation Institute, 2019 Urban Mobility Report

Freeway Travel Time Index

Area	1982	1987	1992	1997	2002	2007	2012	2017
Urban Area Index[1]	1.02	1.03	1.04	1.07	1.11	1.13	1.13	1.13
Urban Area Rank[1,2]	90	93	97	94	84	85	85	83

Note: Freeway Travel Time Index—the ratio of travel time in the peak period to the travel time at free-flow conditions. For example, a value of 1.30 indicates a 20-minute free-flow trip takes 26 minutes in the peak (20 minutes x 1.30 = 26 minutes); (1) Covers the Little Rock AR urban area; (2) Rank is based on 101 larger urban areas (#1 = highest travel time index)
Source: Texas A&M Transportation Institute, 2019 Urban Mobility Report

Public Transportation

Agency Name / Mode of Transportation	Vehicles Operated in Maximum Service[1]	Annual Unlinked Passenger Trips[2] (in thous.)	Annual Passenger Miles[3] (in thous.)
Central Arkansas Transit Authority (CATA)			
Bus (directly operated)	49	2,215.0	10,652.8
Demand Response (directly operated)	21	93.5	753.2
Streetcar Rail (directly operated)	3	42.9	110.5

Note: (1) Number of revenue vehicles operated by the given mode and type of service to meet the annual maximum service requirement. This is the revenue vehicle count during the peak season of the year; on the week and day that maximum service is provided. Vehicles operated in maximum service (VOMS) exclude atypical days and one-time special events; (2) Number of passengers who boarded public transportation vehicles. Passengers are counted each time they board a vehicle no matter how many vehicles they use to travel from their origin to their destination. (3) Sum of the distances ridden by all passengers during the entire fiscal year.
Source: Federal Transit Administration, National Transit Database, 2018

Air Transportation

Airport Name and Code / Type of Service	Passenger Airlines[1]	Passenger Enplanements	Freight Carriers[2]	Freight (lbs)
Little Rock National Airport (LIT)				
Domestic service (U.S. carriers - 2019)	21	1,086,394	14	13,063,041
International service (U.S. carriers - 2018)	0	0	2	16,139

Note: (1) Includes all U.S.-based major, minor and commuter airlines that carried at least one passenger during the year; (2) Includes all U.S.-based airlines and freight carriers that transported at least one pound of freight during the year.
Source: Bureau of Transportation Statistics, The Intermodal Transportation Database, Air Carriers: T-100 Domestic Market (U.S. Carriers), 2019; Bureau of Transportation Statistics, The Intermodal Transportation Database, Air Carriers: T-100 International Market (U.S. Carriers), 2018

Other Transportation Statistics

Major Highways:	I-30; I-40
Amtrak Service:	Yes
Major Waterways/Ports:	David D. Terry Lake

Source: Amtrak.com; Google Maps

BUSINESSES

Major Business Headquarters

Company Name	Industry	Rankings Fortune[1]	Forbes[2]
Dillard's	General Merchandisers	458	-
Windstream Holdings	Telecommunications	493	-

Note: (1) Companies that produce a 10-K are ranked 1 to 500 based on 2018 revenue; (2) All private companies with at least $2 billion in annual revenue through the end of their most current fiscal year are ranked 1 to 228; companies listed are headquartered in the city; dashes indicate no ranking
Source: Fortune, "Fortune 500," June 2019; Forbes, "America's Largest Private Companies," 2019 Rankings

Fast-Growing Businesses

According to *Initiative for a Competitive Inner City (ICIC)*, Little Rock is home to one of America's 100 fastest-growing "inner city" companies: **Team SI** (#18). Criteria for inclusion: company must be headquartered in or have 51 percent or more of its physical operations in an economically distressed urban area; must be an independent, for-profit corporation, partnership or proprietorship; must have 10 or more employees and have a five-year sales history that includes sales of at least $200,000 in the base year and at least $1 million in the current year with no decrease in sales over the two most recent years. Companies were ranked overall by revenue growth over the five-year period between 2014 and 2018. *Initiative for a Competitive Inner City (ICIC), "Inner City 100 Companies," 2019*

Minority- and Women-Owned Businesses

Group	All Firms		Firms with Paid Employees			
	Firms	Sales ($000)	Firms	Sales ($000)	Employees	Payroll ($000)
AIAN[1]	146	12,532	25	9,855	103	4,700
Asian	661	641,144	262	623,037	2,252	75,888
Black	4,180	230,893	254	160,948	1,785	37,032
Hispanic	632	142,238	63	121,498	888	18,975
NHOPI[2]	26	(s)	0	(s)	0 - 19	(s)
Women	7,174	972,045	958	852,140	6,026	191,780
All Firms	20,934	42,281,113	6,235	41,457,610	131,640	6,069,077

Note: Figures cover firms located in the city; minority- and women-owned business are defined as firms in which the corresponding group own 51% or more of the stock or equity of the company; (1) American Indian and Alaska Native; (2) Native Hawaiian and Other Pacific Islander; (s) estimates are suppressed when publication standards are not met
Source: U.S. Census Bureau, 2012 Economic Census, Survey of Business Owners

HOTELS & CONVENTION CENTERS

Hotels, Motels and Vacation Rentals

Area	5 Star		4 Star		3 Star		2 Star		1 Star		Not Rated	
	Num.	Pct.[3]	Num.	Pct.[3]	Num.	Pct.[3]	Num.	Pct.[3]	Num.	Pct.[3]	Num.	Pct.[3]
City[1]	0	0.0	3	2.8	26	24.5	26	24.5	5	4.7	46	43.4
Total[2]	266	1.3	1,517	7.2	4,627	21.8	3,210	15.1	3,974	18.7	7,601	35.9

Note: (1) Figures cover Little Rock and vicinity; (2) Figures cover all 100 cities in this book; (3) Percentage of hotels which have a given star rating; Star ratings are determined by priceline.com and offer an indication of the general quality of a particular hotel.
Source: priceline.com, April 27, 2020

Major Convention Centers

Name	Overall Space (sq. ft.)	Exhibit Space (sq. ft.)	Meeting Space (sq. ft.)	Meeting Rooms
Alltell Arena	370,000	n/a	28,000	n/a
Statehouse Convention Center	220,000	n/a	n/a	n/a

Note: Table includes convention centers located in the Little Rock-North Little Rock-Conway, AR metro area; n/a not available
Source: Original research

Living Environment

COST OF LIVING

Cost of Living Index

Composite Index	Groceries	Housing	Utilities	Trans-portation	Health Care	Misc. Goods/ Services
96.0	95.1	88.1	97.4	94.7	89.6	103.2

Note: The Cost of Living Index measures regional differences in the cost of consumer goods and services, excluding taxes and non-consumer expenditures, for professional and managerial households in the top income quintile. It is based on more than 50,000 prices covering almost 60 different items for which prices are collected three times a year by chambers of commerce, economic development organizations or university applied economic centers in each participating urban area. The numbers shown should be read as a percentage above or below the national average of 100. For example, a value of 115.4 in the groceries column indicates that grocery prices are 15.4% higher than the national average. Small differences in the index numbers should not be interpreted as significant; Figures cover the Little Rock-North Little Rock AR urban area.
Source: The Council for Community and Economic Research, ACCRA Cost of Living Index, 2019

Grocery Prices

Area[1]	T-Bone Steak ($/pound)	Frying Chicken ($/pound)	Whole Milk ($/half gal.)	Eggs ($/dozen)	Orange Juice ($/64 oz.)	Coffee ($/11.5 oz.)
City[2]	11.27	1.22	1.81	1.33	2.91	4.01
Avg.	11.40	1.41	1.93	1.54	3.51	4.30
Min.	7.40	0.92	0.85	0.58	2.67	2.90
Max.	15.58	2.68	4.09	4.18	5.57	8.10

Note: (1) Values for the local area are compared with the average, minimum and maximum values for all 290 areas in the Cost of Living Index; (2) Figures cover the Little Rock-North Little Rock AR urban area; T-Bone Steak (price per pound); Frying Chicken (price per pound, whole fryer); Whole Milk (half gallon carton); Eggs (price per dozen, Grade A, large); Orange Juice (64 oz. Tropicana or Florida Natural); Coffee (11.5 oz. can, vacuum-packed, Maxwell House, Hills Bros, or Folgers).
Source: The Council for Community and Economic Research, ACCRA Cost of Living Index, 2019

Housing and Utility Costs

Area[1]	New Home Price ($)	Apartment Rent ($/month)	All Electric ($/month)	Part Electric ($/month)	Other Energy ($/month)	Telephone ($/month)
City[2]	350,708	763	-	91.46	64.82	186.50
Avg.	362,090	1,142	174.35	100.00	67.76	179.60
Min.	198,329	501	91.58	31.44	28.51	165.30
Max.	2,074,561	5,050	388.18	239.41	306.15	207.90

Note: (1) Values for the local area are compared with the average, minimum and maximum values for all 290 areas in the Cost of Living Index; (2) Figures cover the Little Rock-North Little Rock AR urban area; New Home Price (2,400 sf living area, 8,000 sf lot, in urban area with full utilities); Apartment Rent (950 sf 2 bedroom/1.5 or 2 bath, unfurnished, excluding all utilities except water); All Electric (average monthly cost for an all-electric home); Part Electric (average monthly cost for a part-electric home); Other Energy (average monthly cost for natural gas, fuel oil, coal, wood, and any other forms of energy except electricity); Telephone (price includes the base monthly rate plus taxes and fees for three lines of mobile phone service).
Source: The Council for Community and Economic Research, ACCRA Cost of Living Index, 2019

Health Care, Transportation, and Other Costs

Area[1]	Doctor ($/visit)	Dentist ($/visit)	Optometrist ($/visit)	Gasoline ($/gallon)	Beauty Salon ($/visit)	Men's Shirt ($)
City[2]	124.17	65.61	97.00	2.19	41.80	33.55
Avg.	114.85	97.58	106.10	2.50	38.15	32.15
Min.	39.00	62.22	52.22	1.53	16.88	10.27
Max.	206.67	151.53	258.67	3.79	79.29	59.30

Note: (1) Values for the local area are compared with the average, minimum and maximum values for all 290 areas in the Cost of Living Index; (2) Figures cover the Little Rock-North Little Rock AR urban area; Doctor (general practitioners routine exam of an established patient); Dentist (adult teeth cleaning and periodic oral examination); Optometrist (full vision eye exam for established adult patient); Gasoline (one gallon regular unleaded, national brand, including all taxes, cash price at self-service pump if available); Beauty Salon (woman's shampoo, trim, and blow-dry); Men's Shirt (cotton/polyester dress shirt, pinpoint weave, long sleeves).
Source: The Council for Community and Economic Research, ACCRA Cost of Living Index, 2019

HOUSING

House Price Index (HPI)

Area	National Ranking[2]	Quarterly Change (%)	One-Year Change (%)	Five-Year Change (%)
MSA[1]	186	1.04	3.58	13.81
U.S.[3]	–	1.26	5.09	32.88

Note: The HPI is a weighted repeat sales index. It measures average price changes in repeat sales or refinancings on the same properties. This information is obtained by reviewing repeat mortgage transactions on single-family properties whose mortgages have been purchased or securitized by Fannie Mae or Freddie Mac in January 1975; (1) Figures cover the Little Rock-North Little Rock-Conway, AR Metropolitan Statistical Area—see Appendix B for areas included; (2) Rankings are based on annual percentage change for all metro areas containing at least 15,000 transactions over the last 10 years and ranges from 1 to 232; (3) figures based on a weighted average of Census Division estimates using a seasonally adjusted, purchase-only index; all figures are for the period ending December 31, 2019
Source: Federal Housing Finance Agency, House Price Index, February 25, 2020

Median Single-Family Home Prices

Area	2017	2018	2019[p]	Percent Change 2018 to 2019
MSA[1]	141.7	146.4	152.5	4.2
U.S. Average	248.8	261.6	274.6	5.0

Note: Figures are median sales prices of existing single-family homes in thousands of dollars; (p) preliminary; (1) Figures cover the Little Rock-North Little Rock-Conway, AR Metropolitan Statistical Area—see Appendix B for areas included
Source: National Association of Realtors, Median Sales Price of Existing Single-Family Homes for Metropolitan Areas, 4th Quarter 2019

Qualifying Income Based on Median Sales Price of Existing Single-Family Homes

Area	With 5% Down ($)	With 10% Down ($)	With 20% Down ($)
MSA[1]	32,543	30,830	27,405
U.S. Average	58,663	55,575	49,400

Note: Figures are preliminary; Qualifying income is based on a mortgage rate of 3.76%. Monthly principal and interest payment is limited to 25% of income; (1) Figures cover the Little Rock-North Little Rock-Conway, AR Metropolitan Statistical Area—see Appendix B for areas included
Source: National Association of Realtors, Qualifying Income Based on Median Sales Price of Existing Single-Family Homes for Metropolitan Areas, 4th Quarter 2019

Median Apartment Condo-Coop Home Prices

Area	2017	2018	2019[p]	Percent Change 2018 to 2019
MSA[1]	n/a	n/a	n/a	n/a
U.S. Average	234.3	241.0	249.5	3.5

Note: Figures are median sales prices of existing apartment condo-coop homes in thousands of dollars; (p) preliminary; n/a not available; (1) Figures cover the Little Rock-North Little Rock-Conway, AR Metropolitan Statistical Area—see Appendix B for areas included
Source: National Association of Realtors, Median Sales Price of Existing Apartment Condo-Coop Homes for Metropolitan Areas, 4th Quarter 2019

Home Value Distribution

Area	Under $50,000	$50,000 -$99,999	$100,000 -$149,999	$150,000 -$199,999	$200,000 -$299,999	$300,000 -$499,999	$500,000 -$999,999	$1,000,000 or more
City	7.0	20.1	17.4	17.5	15.4	14.8	6.3	1.4
MSA[1]	8.6	18.5	22.7	19.5	17.5	9.5	3.0	0.8
U.S.	7.6	13.0	14.0	14.3	19.2	18.3	10.5	3.1

Note: Figures are percentages and cover owner-occupied housing units; (1) Figures cover the Little Rock-North Little Rock-Conway, AR Metropolitan Statistical Area—see Appendix B for areas included
Source: U.S. Census Bureau, 2014-2018 American Community Survey 5-Year Estimates

Homeownership Rate

Area	2011 (%)	2012 (%)	2013 (%)	2014 (%)	2015 (%)	2016 (%)	2017 (%)	2018 (%)	2019 (%)
MSA[1]	n/a	n/a	n/a	n/a	65.8	64.9	61.0	62.2	65.0
U.S.	66.1	65.4	65.1	64.5	63.7	63.4	63.9	64.4	64.6

Note: (1) Figures cover the Little Rock-North Little Rock-Conway, AR Metropolitan Statistical Area—see Appendix B for areas included
Source: U.S. Census Bureau, Housing Vacancies and Homeownership Annual Statistics: 2011-2019

Year Housing Structure Built

Area	2010 or Later	2000 -2009	1990 -1999	1980 -1989	1970 -1979	1960 -1969	1950 -1959	1940 -1949	Before 1940	Median Year
City	4.9	10.9	12.5	15.4	19.9	14.1	9.7	4.9	7.7	1977
MSA[1]	7.7	18.7	17.2	14.4	17.2	10.6	7.0	3.3	3.9	1986
U.S.	4.1	14.3	13.9	13.5	15.3	10.7	10.4	5.0	12.8	1977

Note: Figures are percentages except for Median Year; Note: (1) Figures cover the Little Rock-North Little Rock-Conway, AR Metropolitan Statistical Area—see Appendix B for areas included
Source: U.S. Census Bureau, 2014-2018 American Community Survey 5-Year Estimates

Gross Monthly Rent

Area	Under $500	$500 -$999	$1,000 -$1,499	$1,500 -$1,999	$2,000 -$2,499	$2,500 -$2,999	$3,000 and up	Median ($)
City	9.8	58.4	25.8	3.9	1.1	0.5	0.5	850
MSA[1]	10.4	61.7	22.9	3.9	0.6	0.3	0.2	826
U.S.	9.8	38.5	29.6	12.9	5.1	2.1	2.0	1,023

Note: Figures are percentages except for Median; Gross rent is the contract rent plus the estimated average monthly cost of utilities (electricity, gas, and water and sewer) and fuels (oil, coal, kerosene, wood, etc.) if these are paid by the renter (or paid for the renter by someone else); (1) Figures cover the Little Rock-North Little Rock-Conway, AR Metropolitan Statistical Area—see Appendix B for areas included
Source: U.S. Census Bureau, 2014-2018 American Community Survey 5-Year Estimates

HEALTH

Health Risk Factors

Category	MSA[1] (%)	U.S. (%)
Adults aged 18–64 who have any kind of health care coverage	85.8	87.3
Adults who reported being in good or better health	76.7	82.4
Adults who have been told they have high blood cholesterol	37.3	33.0
Adults who have been told they have high blood pressure	39.8	32.3
Adults who are current smokers	24.8	17.1
Adults who currently use E-cigarettes	9.1	4.6
Adults who currently use chewing tobacco, snuff, or snus	5.2	4.0
Adults who are heavy drinkers[2]	6.1	6.3
Adults who are binge drinkers[3]	18.2	17.4
Adults who are overweight (BMI 25.0 - 29.9)	31.2	35.3
Adults who are obese (BMI 30.0 - 99.8)	35.4	31.3
Adults who participated in any physical activities in the past month	69.3	74.4
Adults who always or nearly always wears a seat belt	95.2	94.3

Note: (1) Figures cover the Little Rock-North Little Rock-Conway, AR Metropolitan Statistical Area—see Appendix B for areas included; (2) Heavy drinkers are classified as adult men having more than 14 drinks per week and adult women having more than 7 drinks per week; (3) Binge drinkers are classified as males having five or more drinks on one occasion or females having four or more drinks on one occasion
Source: Centers for Disease Control and Prevention, Behaviorial Risk Factor Surveillance System, SMART: Selected Metropolitan Area Risk Trends, 2017

Acute and Chronic Health Conditions

Category	MSA[1] (%)	U.S. (%)
Adults who have ever been told they had a heart attack	4.9	4.2
Adults who have ever been told they have angina or coronary heart disease	5.3	3.9
Adults who have ever been told they had a stroke	3.5	3.0
Adults who have ever been told they have asthma	16.1	14.2
Adults who have ever been told they have arthritis	27.5	24.9
Adults who have ever been told they have diabetes[2]	11.1	10.5
Adults who have ever been told they had skin cancer	7.5	6.2
Adults who have ever been told they had any other types of cancer	8.3	7.1
Adults who have ever been told they have COPD	7.0	6.5
Adults who have ever been told they have kidney disease	4.0	3.0
Adults who have ever been told they have a form of depression	23.3	20.5

Note: (1) Figures cover the Little Rock-North Little Rock-Conway, AR Metropolitan Statistical Area—see Appendix B for areas included; (2) Figures do not include pregnancy-related, borderline, or pre-diabetes
Source: Centers for Disease Control and Prevention, Behaviorial Risk Factor Surveillance System, SMART: Selected Metropolitan Area Risk Trends, 2017

Health Screening and Vaccination Rates

Category	MSA[1] (%)	U.S. (%)
Adults aged 65+ who have had flu shot within the past year	61.5	60.7
Adults aged 65+ who have ever had a pneumonia vaccination	76.1	75.4
Adults who have ever been tested for HIV	40.0	36.1
Adults who have ever had the shingles or zoster vaccine?	32.4	28.9
Adults who have had their blood cholesterol checked within the last five years	83.3	85.9

Note: n/a not available; (1) Figures cover the Little Rock-North Little Rock-Conway, AR Metropolitan Statistical Area—see Appendix B for areas included.
Source: Centers for Disease Control and Prevention, Behaviorial Risk Factor Surveillance System, SMART: Selected Metropolitan Area Risk Trends, 2017

Disability Status

Category	MSA[1] (%)	U.S. (%)
Adults who reported being deaf	7.3	6.7
Are you blind or have serious difficulty seeing, even when wearing glasses?	5.9	4.5
Are you limited in any way in any of your usual activities due of arthritis?	16.7	12.9
Do you have difficulty doing errands alone?	9.5	6.8
Do you have difficulty dressing or bathing?	4.8	3.6
Do you have serious difficulty concentrating/remembering/making decisions?	14.0	10.7
Do you have serious difficulty walking or climbing stairs?	18.7	13.6

Note: (1) Figures cover the Little Rock-North Little Rock-Conway, AR Metropolitan Statistical Area—see Appendix B for areas included.
Source: Centers for Disease Control and Prevention, Behaviorial Risk Factor Surveillance System, SMART: Selected Metropolitan Area Risk Trends, 2017

Mortality Rates for the Top 10 Causes of Death in the U.S.

ICD-10[a] Sub-Chapter	ICD-10[a] Code	Age-Adjusted Mortality Rate[1] per 100,000 population	
		County[2]	U.S.
Malignant neoplasms	C00-C97	158.4	152.4
Ischaemic heart diseases	I20-I25	116.9	92.7
Other forms of heart disease	I30-I51	50.8	52.5
Chronic lower respiratory diseases	J40-J47	44.7	40.4
Cerebrovascular diseases	I60-I69	45.9	37.3
Other degenerative diseases of the nervous system	G30-G31	70.2	36.4
Other external causes of accidental injury	W00-X59	31.0	35.3
Organic, including symptomatic, mental disorders	F01-F09	16.6	30.0
Hypertensive diseases	I10-I15	28.9	22.9
Diabetes mellitus	E10-E14	30.0	21.3

Note: (a) ICD-10 = International Classification of Diseases 10th Revision; (1) Mortality rates are a three year average covering 2016-2018; (2) Figures cover Pulaski County.
Source: Centers for Disease Control and Prevention, National Center for Health Statistics. Underlying Cause of Death 1999-2018 on CDC WONDER Online Database

Mortality Rates for Selected Causes of Death

ICD-10[a] Sub-Chapter	ICD-10[a] Code	Age-Adjusted Mortality Rate[1] per 100,000 population	
		County[2]	U.S.
Assault	X85-Y09	17.5	6.0
Diseases of the liver	K70-K76	14.3	14.2
Human immunodeficiency virus (HIV) disease	B20-B24	2.6	1.6
Influenza and pneumonia	J09-J18	15.8	14.2
Intentional self-harm	X60-X84	17.2	13.9
Malnutrition	E40-E46	4.1	1.9
Obesity and other hyperalimentation	E65-E68	3.4	2.1
Renal failure	N17-N19	18.9	12.8
Transport accidents	V01-V99	15.0	12.5
Viral hepatitis	B15-B19	Unreliable	1.4

Note: (a) ICD-10 = International Classification of Diseases 10th Revision; (1) Mortality rates are a three year average covering 2016-2018; (2) Figures cover Pulaski County; Data are suppressed when the data meet the criteria for confidentiality constraints; Mortality rates are flagged as unreliable when the rate would be calculated with a numerator of 20 or less.
Source: Centers for Disease Control and Prevention, National Center for Health Statistics. Underlying Cause of Death 1999-2018 on CDC WONDER Online Database

Health Insurance Coverage

Area	With Health Insurance	With Private Health Insurance	With Public Health Insurance	Without Health Insurance	Population Under Age 19 Without Health Insurance
City	90.6	65.8	36.2	9.4	5.8
MSA[1]	91.8	67.3	37.8	8.2	4.8
U.S.	90.6	67.7	34.7	9.4	5.2

Note: Figures are percentages that cover the civilian noninstitutionalized population; (1) Figures cover the Little Rock-North Little Rock-Conway, AR Metropolitan Statistical Area—see Appendix B for areas included
Source: U.S. Census Bureau, 2014-2018 American Community Survey 5-Year Estimates

Number of Medical Professionals

Area	MDs[3]	DOs[3,4]	Dentists	Podiatrists	Chiropractors	Optometrists
County[1] (number)	2,925	60	295	20	85	82
County[1] (rate[2])	742.5	15.2	75.1	5.1	21.6	20.9
U.S. (rate[2])	281.9	23.4	69.1	6.0	27.5	16.4

Note: Data as of 2018 unless noted; (1) Data covers Pulaski County; (2) Rate per 100,000 population; (3) Data as of 2017 and includes all active, non-federal physicians; (4) Doctor of Osteopathic Medicine
Source: U.S. Department of Health and Human Services, Health Resources and Services Administration, Bureau of Health Professions, Area Resource File (ARF) 2018-2019

Best Hospitals

According to *U.S. News,* the Little Rock-North Little Rock-Conway, AR metro area is home to one of the best hospitals in the U.S.: **UAMS Medical Center** (1 adult specialty). The hospital listed was nationally ranked in at least one of 16 adult or 10 pediatric specialties. Only 206 hospitals nationwide were nationally ranked in one or more adult or pediatric specialty. Twenty hospitals in the U.S. made the Honor Roll. The Best Hospitals Honor Roll takes both the national rankings and the procedure and condition ratings into account. Hospitals received points if they were nationally ranked in one of the 16 adult specialties—the higher they ranked, the more points they got—and how many ratings of "high performing" they earned in the nine procedures and conditions. *U.S. News Online, "America's Best Hospitals 2019-20"*

According to *U.S. News,* the Little Rock-North Little Rock-Conway, AR metro area is home to one of the best children's hospitals in the U.S.: **Arkansas Children's Hospital** (5 pediatric specialties). The hospital listed was highly ranked in at least one of 10 pediatric specialties. Ninety-one children's hospitals in the U.S. were nationally ranked in at least one specialty. Hospitals received points for being ranked in a specialty, and the 10 hospitals with the most points across the 10 specialties make up the Honor Roll. *U.S. News Online, "America's Best Children's Hospitals 2019-20"*

EDUCATION

Public School District Statistics

District Name	Schls	Pupils	Pupil/ Teacher Ratio	Minority Pupils[1] (%)	Free Lunch Eligible[2] (%)	IEP[3] (%)
Arkansas Virtual Academy	3	2,361	26.7	21.5	54.1	15.6
Estem High Charter	5	3,070	17.3	73.7	38.6	9.5
Lisa Academy Charter	6	2,218	14.6	78.9	49.0	10.2
Little Rock School District	43	23,368	14.4	81.2	62.9	14.9
Pulaski Co. Spec. School Dist.	24	12,383	14.6	58.3	43.3	14.8

Note: Table includes school districts with 2,000 or more students; (1) Percentage of students that are not non-Hispanic white; (2) Percentage of students that are eligible for the free lunch program; (3) Percentage of students that have an Individualized Education Program.
Source: U.S. Department of Education, National Center for Education Statistics, Common Core of Data, Local Education Agency (School District) Universe Survey: School Year 2018-2019; U.S. Department of Education, National Center for Education Statistics, Common Core of Data, Public Elementary/Secondary School Universe Survey: School Year 2018-2019

Highest Level of Education

Area	Less than H.S.	H.S. Diploma	Some College, No Deg.	Associate Degree	Bachelor's Degree	Master's Degree	Prof. School Degree	Doctorate Degree
City	8.7	22.1	21.8	6.1	24.3	10.0	4.1	2.9
MSA[1]	9.7	29.3	23.4	7.6	18.8	7.6	2.1	1.5
U.S.	12.3	27.1	20.6	8.4	19.4	8.6	2.1	1.4

Note: Figures cover persons age 25 and over; (1) Figures cover the Little Rock-North Little Rock-Conway, AR Metropolitan Statistical Area—see Appendix B for areas included
Source: U.S. Census Bureau, 2014-2018 American Community Survey 5-Year Estimates

Educational Attainment by Race

Area	High School Graduate or Higher (%)					Bachelor's Degree or Higher (%)				
	Total	White	Black	Asian	Hisp.[2]	Total	White	Black	Asian	Hisp.[2]
City	91.3	93.8	88.4	94.4	61.8	41.3	54.1	21.5	73.0	10.1
MSA[1]	90.3	91.6	87.4	89.1	67.3	30.1	32.5	20.9	55.1	13.5
U.S.	87.7	89.6	85.4	86.8	67.7	31.5	32.9	21.1	53.5	15.8

Note: Figures shown cover persons 25 years old and over; (1) Figures cover the Little Rock-North Little Rock-Conway, AR Metropolitan Statistical Area—see Appendix B for areas included; (2) People of Hispanic origin can be of any race
Source: U.S. Census Bureau, 2014-2018 American Community Survey 5-Year Estimates

School Enrollment by Grade and Control

Area	Preschool (%)		Kindergarten (%)		Grades 1 - 4 (%)		Grades 5 - 8 (%)		Grades 9 - 12 (%)	
	Public	Private	Public	Private	Public	Private	Public	Private	Public	Private
City	52.2	47.8	78.8	21.2	83.8	16.2	80.0	20.0	78.6	21.4
MSA[1]	60.2	39.8	86.8	13.2	89.7	10.3	88.4	11.6	87.1	12.9
U.S.	59.0	41.0	87.7	12.3	89.6	10.4	89.5	10.5	90.2	9.8

Note: Figures shown cover persons 3 years old and over; (1) Figures cover the Little Rock-North Little Rock-Conway, AR Metropolitan Statistical Area—see Appendix B for areas included
Source: U.S. Census Bureau, 2014-2018 American Community Survey 5-Year Estimates

Average Salaries of Public School Teachers

Area	2016-17		2017-18		Change from 2016-17 to 2017-18	
	Dollars	Rank[1]	Dollars	Rank[1]	Percent	Rank[2]
Arkansas	48,304	43	50,544	38	4.64	1
U.S. Average	59,539	–	60,477	–	1.58	–

Note: (1) Rank ranges from 1 to 51 where 1 indicates highest salary; (2) Rank ranges from 1 to 51 where 1 indicates highest percent change.
Source: National Education Association, Rankings & Estimates: Rankings of the States 2018 and Estimates of School Statistics 2019

Higher Education

Four-Year Colleges			Two-Year Colleges			Medical Schools[1]	Law Schools[2]	Voc/ Tech[3]
Public	Private Non-profit	Private For-profit	Public	Private Non-profit	Private For-profit			
2	2	2	0	2	0	1	1	5

Note: Figures cover institutions located within the city limits and include main campuses only; (1) includes schools accredited by the Liaison Committee on Medical Education and the American Osteopathic Association's Commission on Osteopathic College Accreditation; (2) includes ABA-accredited schools, schools with provisional ABA accreditation, and state accredited schools; (3) includes all schools with programs that are less than 2 years.
Source: National Center for Education Statistics, Integrated Postsecondary Education System (IPEDS), 2018-19; Wikipedia, List of Medical Schools in the United States, accessed May 1, 2020; Wikipedia, List of Law Schools in the United States, accessed May 1, 2020

According to *U.S. News & World Report,* the Little Rock-North Little Rock-Conway, AR metro area is home to one of the top 100 liberal arts colleges in the U.S.: **Hendrix College** (#92 tie). The indicators used to capture academic quality fall into a number of categories: assessment by administrators at peer institutions; retention of students; faculty resources; student selectivity; financial resources; alumni giving; high school counselor ratings of colleges; and graduation rate. *U.S. News & World Report, "America's Best Colleges 2020"*

PRESIDENTIAL ELECTION

2016 Presidential Election Results

Area	Clinton	Trump	Johnson	Stein	Other
Pulaski County	56.1	38.3	2.7	1.0	1.9
U.S.	48.0	45.9	3.3	1.1	1.7

Note: Results are percentages and may not add to 100% due to rounding
Source: Dave Leip's Atlas of U.S. Presidential Elections

EMPLOYERS

Major Employers

Company Name	Industry
Arkansas Blue Cross and Blue Shield	Hospitals and medical service plans
Arkansas Childrens Hospital	Specialty hospitals, except psychiatric
Baptist Health Systems	General medical & surgical hospitals
Dassault Falcon Jet Corp	Aviation and or aeronautical engineering
Dept of Highway and Trans Arkansas	Regulation, administration of transportation
Dept of Finance & Admin Arkansas	Finance, taxation, and monetary policy
Fidelity Information Systems	Data processing services
Loreal USA	Toilet preparations
Mountaire Farms	Broiler, fryer and roaster chickens
Pulaski County	General practice, attorney
St. Vincent Health System	Medical services organization
United States Dept of Veteran Affairs	General medical & surgical hospitals
University of Arkansas System	Colleges & universities
Valor Telecommunications	Voice telephone communications
Veterans Health Administration	Administration of veterans affairs

Note: Companies shown are located within the Little Rock-North Little Rock-Conway, AR Metropolitan Statistical Area.
Source: Hoovers.com; Wikipedia

PUBLIC SAFETY

Crime Rate

Area	All Crimes	Violent Crimes				Property Crimes		
		Murder	Rape[3]	Robbery	Aggrav. Assault	Burglary	Larceny -Theft	Motor Vehicle Theft
City	7,994.0	20.1	109.4	186.2	1,130.5	1,043.2	4,942.6	562.0
Suburbs[1]	n/a	5.2	50.2	53.5	369.5	n/a	1,994.8	258.0
Metro[2]	n/a	9.2	66.1	89.1	573.7	n/a	2,785.7	339.5
U.S.	2,580.1	5.0	42.6	86.2	246.8	376.0	1,594.6	228.9

Note: Figures are crimes per 100,000 population; (1) All areas within the metro area that are located outside the city limits; (2) Figures cover the Little Rock-North Little Rock-Conway, AR Metropolitan Statistical Area—see Appendix B for areas included; (3) The city and U.S. figures shown were reported using the revised Uniform Crime Reporting (UCR) definition of rape. The suburban and metro area figures shown are an aggregate total of the data submitted using both the revised and legacy UCR definitions.
Source: FBI Uniform Crime Reports, 2018

Hate Crimes

Area	Number of Quarters Reported	Number of Incidents per Bias Motivation					
		Race/Ethnicity/ Ancestry	Religion	Sexual Orientation	Disability	Gender	Gender Identity
City	4	0	0	0	0	0	0
U.S.	4	4,047	1,419	1,196	159	47	168

Source: Federal Bureau of Investigation, Hate Crime Statistics 2018

Identity Theft Consumer Reports

Area	Reports	Reports per 100,000 Population	Rank[2]
MSA[1]	2,347	317	13
U.S.	650,572	198	-

Note: (1) Figures cover the Little Rock-North Little Rock-Conway, AR Metropolitan Statistical Area—see Appendix B for areas included; (2) Rank ranges from 1 to 386 where 1 indicates greatest number of identity theft reports per 100,000 population
Source: Federal Trade Commission, Consumer Sentinel Network Data Book for January–December 2019

Fraud and Other Consumer Reports

Area	Reports	Reports per 100,000 Population	Rank[2]
MSA[1]	4,358	588	140
U.S.	2,590,177	789	-

Note: (1) Figures cover the Little Rock-North Little Rock-Conway, AR Metropolitan Statistical Area—see Appendix B for areas included; (2) Rank ranges from 1 to 386 where 1 indicates greatest number of fraud and other consumer reports per 100,000 population
Source: Federal Trade Commission, Consumer Sentinel Network Data Book for January–December 2019

SPORTS

Professional Sports Teams

Team Name	League	Year Established
No teams are located in the metro area		

Source: Wikipedia, Major Professional Sports Teams of the United States and Canada, May 4, 2020

CLIMATE

Average and Extreme Temperatures

Temperature	Jan	Feb	Mar	Apr	May	Jun	Jul	Aug	Sep	Oct	Nov	Dec	Yr.
Extreme High (°F)	83	85	91	95	98	105	112	108	103	97	86	80	112
Average High (°F)	50	54	63	73	81	89	92	91	85	75	62	53	73
Average Temp. (°F)	40	45	53	63	71	79	82	81	74	63	52	43	62
Average Low (°F)	30	34	42	51	60	68	72	70	63	51	41	34	51
Extreme Low (°F)	-4	-5	17	28	40	46	54	52	38	29	17	-1	-5

Note: Figures cover the years 1948-1990
Source: National Climatic Data Center, International Station Meteorological Climate Summary, 9/96

Average Precipitation/Snowfall/Humidity

Precip./Humidity	Jan	Feb	Mar	Apr	May	Jun	Jul	Aug	Sep	Oct	Nov	Dec	Yr.
Avg. Precip. (in.)	4.1	4.2	4.9	5.2	5.4	3.6	3.5	3.2	3.8	3.5	4.8	4.5	50.7
Avg. Snowfall (in.)	3	2	1	Tr	0	0	0	0	0	0	Tr	1	5
Avg. Rel. Hum. 6am (%)	80	80	78	81	86	86	87	88	87	86	82	80	84
Avg. Rel. Hum. 3pm (%)	57	54	50	50	53	52	54	52	52	48	52	57	53

Note: Figures cover the years 1948-1990; Tr = Trace amounts (<0.05 in. of rain; <0.5 in. of snow)
Source: National Climatic Data Center, International Station Meteorological Climate Summary, 9/96

Weather Conditions

Temperature			Daytime Sky			Precipitation		
10°F & below	32°F & below	90°F & above	Clear	Partly cloudy	Cloudy	0.01 inch or more precip.	0.1 inch or more snow/ice	Thunder-storms
1	57	73	110	142	113	104	4	57

Note: Figures are average number of days per year and cover the years 1948-1990
Source: National Climatic Data Center, International Station Meteorological Climate Summary, 9/96

HAZARDOUS WASTE

Superfund Sites

The Little Rock-North Little Rock-Conway, AR metro area is home to one site on the EPA's Superfund National Priorities List: **Vertac, Inc.** (final). There are a total of 1,387 Superfund sites with a status of proposed or final on the list in the U.S. U.S. Environmental Protection Agency, National Priorities List, May 5, 2020

**AIR & WATER
QUALITY**

Air Quality Trends: Ozone

	1990	1995	2000	2005	2010	2012	2014	2016	2017	2018
MSA[1]	0.080	0.086	0.090	0.083	0.072	0.078	0.066	0.064	0.060	0.066
U.S.	0.088	0.089	0.082	0.080	0.073	0.075	0.067	0.069	0.068	0.069

Note: (1) Data covers the Little Rock-North Little Rock-Conway, AR Metropolitan Statistical Area—see Appendix B for areas included. The values shown are the composite ozone concentration averages among trend sites based on the highest fourth daily maximum 8-hour concentration in parts per million. These trends are based on sites having an adequate record of monitoring data during the trend period. Data from exceptional events are included.
Source: U.S. Environmental Protection Agency, Air Quality Monitoring Information, "Air Quality Trends by City, 1990-2018"

Air Quality Index

Area	Percent of Days when Air Quality was...[2]					AQI Statistics[2]	
	Good	Moderate	Unhealthy for Sensitive Groups	Unhealthy	Very Unhealthy	Maximum	Median
MSA[1]	70.4	29.0	0.5	0.0	0.0	122	43

Note: (1) Data covers the Little Rock-North Little Rock-Conway, AR Metropolitan Statistical Area—see Appendix B for areas included; (2) Based on 365 days with AQI data in 2018. Air Quality Index (AQI) is an index for reporting daily air quality. EPA calculates the AQI for five major air pollutants regulated by the Clean Air Act: ground-level ozone, particle pollution (aka particulate matter), carbon monoxide, sulfur dioxide, and nitrogen dioxide. The AQI runs from 0 to 500. The higher the AQI value, the greater the level of air pollution and the greater the health concern. There are six AQI categories: "Good" AQI is between 0 and 50. Air quality is considered satisfactory; "Moderate" AQI is between 51 and 100. Air quality is acceptable; "Unhealthy for Sensitive Groups" When AQI values are between 101 and 150, members of sensitive groups may experience health effects; "Unhealthy" When AQI values are between 151 and 200 everyone may begin to experience health effects; "Very Unhealthy" AQI values between 201 and 300 trigger a health alert; "Hazardous" AQI values over 300 trigger warnings of emergency conditions (not shown).
Source: U.S. Environmental Protection Agency, Air Quality Index Report, 2018

Air Quality Index Pollutants

Area	Percent of Days when AQI Pollutant was...[2]					
	Carbon Monoxide	Nitrogen Dioxide	Ozone	Sulfur Dioxide	Particulate Matter 2.5	Particulate Matter 10
MSA[1]	0.0	0.3	40.0	0.0	59.7	0.0

Note: (1) Data covers the Little Rock-North Little Rock-Conway, AR Metropolitan Statistical Area—see Appendix B for areas included; (2) Based on 365 days with AQI data in 2018. The Air Quality Index (AQI) is an index for reporting daily air quality. EPA calculates the AQI for five major air pollutants regulated by the Clean Air Act: ground-level ozone, particle pollution (also known as particulate matter), carbon monoxide, sulfur dioxide, and nitrogen dioxide. The AQI runs from 0 to 500. The higher the AQI value, the greater the level of air pollution and the greater the health concern.
Source: U.S. Environmental Protection Agency, Air Quality Index Report, 2018

Maximum Air Pollutant Concentrations: Particulate Matter, Ozone, CO and Lead

	Particulate Matter 10 (ug/m^3)	Particulate Matter 2.5 Wtd AM (ug/m^3)	Particulate Matter 2.5 24-Hr (ug/m^3)	Ozone (ppm)	Carbon Monoxide (ppm)	Lead (ug/m^3)
MSA[1] Level	51	9.7	22	0.067	1	n/a
NAAQS[2]	150	15	35	0.075	9	0.15
Met NAAQS[2]	Yes	Yes	Yes	Yes	Yes	n/a

Note: (1) Data covers the Little Rock-North Little Rock-Conway, AR Metropolitan Statistical Area—see Appendix B for areas included; Data from exceptional events are included; (2) National Ambient Air Quality Standards; ppm = parts per million; ug/m^3 = micrograms per cubic meter; n/a not available.
Concentrations: Particulate Matter 10 (coarse particulate)—highest second maximum 24-hour concentration; Particulate Matter 2.5 Wtd AM (fine particulate)—highest weighted annual mean concentration; Particulate Matter 2.5 24-Hour (fine particulate)—highest 98th percentile 24-hour concentration; Ozone—highest fourth daily maximum 8-hour concentration; Carbon Monoxide—highest second maximum non-overlapping 8-hour concentration; Lead—maximum running 3-month average
Source: U.S. Environmental Protection Agency, Air Quality Monitoring Information, "Air Quality Statistics by City, 2018"

Maximum Air Pollutant Concentrations: Nitrogen Dioxide and Sulfur Dioxide

	Nitrogen Dioxide AM (ppb)	Nitrogen Dioxide 1-Hr (ppb)	Sulfur Dioxide AM (ppb)	Sulfur Dioxide 1-Hr (ppb)	Sulfur Dioxide 24-Hr (ppb)
MSA[1] Level	7	42	n/a	6	n/a
NAAQS[2]	53	100	30	75	140
Met NAAQS[2]	Yes	Yes	n/a	Yes	n/a

Note: (1) Data covers the Little Rock-North Little Rock-Conway, AR Metropolitan Statistical Area—see Appendix B for areas included; Data from exceptional events are included; (2) National Ambient Air Quality Standards; ppm = parts per million; ug/m³ = micrograms per cubic meter; n/a not available.
Concentrations: Nitrogen Dioxide AM—highest arithmetic mean concentration; Nitrogen Dioxide 1-Hr—highest 98th percentile 1-hour daily maximum concentration; Sulfur Dioxide AM—highest annual mean concentration; Sulfur Dioxide 1-Hr—highest 99th percentile 1-hour daily maximum concentration; Sulfur Dioxide 24-Hr—highest second maximum 24-hour concentration
Source: U.S. Environmental Protection Agency, Air Quality Monitoring Information, "Air Quality Statistics by City, 2018"

Drinking Water

Water System Name	Pop. Served	Primary Water Source Type	Violations[1]
Central Arkansas Water	330,667	Surface	1

Note: (1) Total number of violations (both active and inactive) in the EPA database
Source: U.S. Environmental Protection Agency, Office of Ground Water and Drinking Water, Safe Drinking Water Information System (based on data extracted May 5, 2020)

Madison, Wisconsin

Background

Madison was selected as Wisconsin's territorial capital in 1836 before construction of the city began in 1838. Despite repeated threats to move the capital elsewhere by members of the legislature, it has maintained its status. It was named for President James Madison in 1836, and incorporated into a village in 1856. When Wisconsin attained statehood in 1848, the University of Wisconsin (one of the largest in the country) was established.

Most of the city, including its business center, is situated on an isthmus between Lake Mendota and Lake Minona in the south-central part of the state. Two other lakes, Kengonsa and Waubesa, lie to the south. By ordinance, the city's skyline is dominated by the capitol dome, which weighs 2,500 tons.

Madison serves as the trade center of a rich agricultural and dairy region. Food processing is a major industry. Batteries, dairy equipment, and machine tools are produced there as well.

Wisconsin state government and the University of Wisconsin-Madison remain the two largest Madison employers. However, Madison continues to evolve from a government-based economy to consumer services and a base for high-tech, particularly in the health, biotech, and advertising sectors. Beginning in the early 1990s, the city experienced a steady economic boom fostered by the development of high-tech companies and UW-Madison working with local businesses and entrepreneurs to transfer the results of academic research into real-world applications, especially bio-tech applications. Businesses are attracted to Madison's skill base, taking advantage of the area's high level of education.

The city has received numerous awards, beginning as early as 1948 when it was named Best Place to Live in America by *Life* magazine. Although Madison is a progressive, eclectic city, it also offers the atmosphere of a small town with many picturesque communities, four lakes, and over 200 parks. There are a total of 29,000 acres designated for recreational use, including 46 miles of hiking trails, over 150 miles of bicycle trails, 92 miles of shoreline for swimming and boating, and 20 golf courses. Bicycle tourism is an $800 million industry in Wisconsin, which has 20 percent of the nation's bicycling industry manufacturing capacity.

Madison's many restaurants boast a large variety of ethnic food, from Greek and Italian to Japanese, Mexican, and Middle Eastern, as well as many brew pubs.

Cultural life in Madison has long had a center in the downtown, at the Madison Civic Center and its associated sites. Project Overture renovated and redeveloped a variety of cultural venues, including the Madison Museum of Contemporary Art with innovative design and sculpture-garden rooftop. A 2,250-seat hall houses the Madison Symphony Orchestra, whose old home, the Oscar Meyer Theater, is used by groups such as the CTM Family Theatre and the Wisconsin Chamber group. Keeping the goal of architectural integration in mind, facades of nearby buildings have been refurbished and preserved.

Another major attraction in Madison is the Olbrich Botanical Gardens, with 16 acres of outdoor display gardens, including sunken, perennial, rose, rock, herb, and wildflower gardens. Over 250,000 visitors a year enjoy the gardens, which include a lush, tropical conservatory filled with exotic plants, bright flowers, a rushing waterfall, and free-flying birds.

Madison is home to many institutions of higher learning, including the University of Wisconsin-Madison, Edgewood College, Herzing College, Lakeland College, and Madison Media Institute.

The area has the typical continental climate of interior North America with a large annual temperature range and frequent short-period temperature changes. The city lies in the path of the frequent cyclones and anticyclones, which move eastward over this area during fall, winter, and spring. The most frequent air masses are of polar origin, with occasional influxes of arctic air affecting this area during the winter months. Summers are pleasant, with only occasional periods of extreme heat or high humidity.

Rankings

General Rankings

- *US News & World Report* conducted a survey of more than 2,000 people and analyzed the 125 largest metropolitan areas to determine what matters the most when selecting the next place to live. Madison ranked #12 out of the top 25 as having the best combination of desirable factors. Criteria: cost of living; quality of life; net migration; job market; desirability; and other factors. *realestate.usnews.com, "The 25 Best Places to Live in the U.S. in 2019," April 9, 2019*

- Madison was selected as one of the best places to live in the United States by *Money* magazine. The city ranked #8 out of 100. This year's list focused on cities with populations of 50,000 or greater. Beginning with a pool of 1,796 candidates, editors looked at 80 separate types of data, from local economy and housing market to education, diversity and ease of living—and then sent reporters to interview residents, search neighborhoods and look for other intangibles. *Money, "Best Places to Live, 2019" September 16, 2019*

- In their sixth annual survey, Livability.com looked at data for more than 1,000 U.S. cities to determine the rankings for Livability's "Top 100 Best Places to Live" in 2019. Madison ranked #3. Criteria: median home value capped at $250,000; affordable living; vibrant economy; education, demographics, health care options. transportation & infrastructure; abundant lifestyle amenities. *Livability.com, "Top 100 Best Places to Live 2019" March 2019*

Business/Finance Rankings

- Experian's latest annual report on consumer credit ranked cities by the average credit score of its residents. Madison was ranked #10 among the ten cities with the highest average credit score, meaning that its residents showed strong credit management. *www.usatoday.com, "Minneapolis Tops List of Cities With Best Average Credit Score; Greenwood Miss., at the Bottom," January 11, 2018*

- The Brookings Institution ranked the nation's largest cities based on income inequality. Madison was ranked #86 (#1 = greatest inequality). Criteria: the "95/20 ratio," a figure representing the income at which a household earns more than 95 percent of all other households, divided by the income at which a household earns more than only 20 percent of all other households. *Brookings Institution, "Household Income Inequality, Largest Cities of 97 Large U.S. Metro Areas, 2014-2016," February 5, 2018*

- The Brookings Institution ranked the 100 largest metro areas in the U.S. based on income inequality. Madison was ranked #95 (#1 = greatest inequality). Criteria: the "95/20 ratio," a figure representing the income at which a household earns more than 95 percent of all other households, divided by the income at which a household earns more than only 20 percent of all other households. *Brookings Institution, "Household Income Inequality, 100 Largest U.S. Metro Areas, 2014-2016," February 5, 2018*

- Livability.com rated Madison as #10 of ten cities where new college grads' job prospects are brightest. Criteria included: number of 22- to 29-year olds; good job opportunities; affordable housing options; public transportation users; educational attainment; variety of fun things to do. *Livability.com, "2018 Top 10 Best Cities for Recent College Grads," April 26, 2018*

- The Madison metro area appeared on the Milken Institute "2020 Best Performing Cities" list. Rank: #93 out of 200 large metro areas. Criteria: job growth; wage and salary growth; high-tech output growth. *Milken Institute, "Best-Performing Cities 2020," February 26, 2020*

- *Forbes* ranked the 200 most populous metro areas to determine the nation's "Best Places for Business and Careers." The Madison metro area was ranked #57. Criteria: costs (business and living); job growth (past and projected); income growth; quality of life; educational attainment (college and high school); projected economic growth; cultural and leisure opportunities; workplace tolerance laws; net migration patterns. *Forbes, "The Best Places for Business and Careers 2019: Seattle Still On Top," October 30, 2019*

Children/Family Rankings

- *Forbes* analyzed data on the 100 largest metropolitan areas in the United States to compile its 2016 ranking of the best cities for raising a family. The Madison metro area was ranked #12. Criteria: median income; childcare costs; percent of population under 18; commuting delays; crime rate; percentage of families owning homes; education quality (mainly test scores). Overall cost of living and housing affordability was also unofficially considered. *Forbes, "America's Best Cities for Raising a Family 2016," August 30, 2016*

Dating/Romance Rankings

- Madison was ranked #15 out of 25 cities that stood out for inspiring romance and attracting diners on the website OpenTable.com. Criteria: percentage of people who dined out on Valentine's Day in 2018; percentage of romantic restaurants as rated by OpenTable diner reviews; and percentage of tables seated for two. *OpenTable, "25 Most Romantic Cities in America for 2019," February 7, 2019*

- Madison was selected as one of America's best cities for singles by the readers of *Travel + Leisure* in their annual "America's Favorite Cities" survey. Criteria included good-looking locals, cool shopping, an active bar scene and hipster-magnet coffee bars. *Travel + Leisure, "Best Cities in America for Singles," July 21, 2017*

Education Rankings

- Personal finance website *WalletHub* analyzed the 150 largest U.S. metropolitan statistical areas to determine where the most educated Americans are choosing to settle. Criteria: education levels; percentage of workers with degrees; education quality and attainment gap; public school quality rankings; quality and size of each metro area's universities. Madison was ranked #5 (#1 = most educated city). *www.WalletHub.com, "2019's Most and Least Educated Cities in America," July 22, 2019*

Environmental Rankings

- Madison was highlighted as one of the top 104 cleanest metro areas for short-term particle pollution (24-hour PM 2.5) in the U.S. during 2015 through 2017. Monitors in these cities reported no days with unhealthful PM 2.5 levels. *American Lung Association, "State of the Air 2019," April 24, 2019*

Health/Fitness Rankings

- For each of the 100 largest cities in the United States, the American Fitness Index®, published by the American College of Sports Medicine and the Anthem Foundation, evaluated community infrastructure and 33 health behaviors including preventive health, levels of chronic disease conditions, pedestrian safety, air quality, and community resources that support physical activity. Madison ranked #5 for "community fitness." *americanfitnessindex.org, "ACSM American Fitness Index Health and Community Fitness Status of the 100 Largest U.S. Cities," May 14, 2019*

- Madison was identified as a "2020 Spring Allergy Capital." The area ranked #89 out of 100. Three groups of factors were used to identify the most challenging cities for people with allergies during the spring season: annual spring pollen levels; over the counter medicine use; number of board-certified allergy specialists. *Asthma and Allergy Foundation of America, "Spring Allergy Capitals 2020," March 10, 2020*

- Madison was identified as a "2020 Fall Allergy Capital." The area ranked #85 out of 100. Three groups of factors were used to identify the most challenging cities for people with allergies during the fall season: annual fall pollen levels; over the counter medicine use; number of board-certified allergy specialists. *Asthma and Allergy Foundation of America, "Fall Allergy Capitals 2020," March 10, 2020*

- Madison was identified as a "2019 Asthma Capital." The area ranked #66 out of the nation's 100 largest metropolitan areas. Criteria: estimated asthma prevalence; crude death rate from asthma; and ER visits due to asthma. Risk factors that were analyzed but not factored in the rankings: annual pollen score; annual air quality; public smoking laws; number of board-certified asthma specialists; rescue medication use; controller medication use; uninsured rate; poverty rate. *Asthma and Allergy Foundation of America, "Asthma Capitals 2019: The Most Challenging Places to Live With Asthma," May 7, 2019*

- *Men's Health* ranked 100 major U.S. cities in terms of the best cities for men. Madison ranked #3. Criteria: health; fitness; quality of life. *Men's Health, "The Best & Worst Cities for Men Who Want to Be Fit and Happy," January 1, 2016*

- The Madison metro area ranked #61 out of 189 in The Gallup-Sharecare Well-Being Index. Criteria: purpose; social well being; financial health; community and physical health. Results are based on telephone interviews with adults, aged 18 and older, living in metropolitan areas in the 50 U.S. states and the District of Columbia. *Gallup-Sharecare, "State of American Well-Being, 2017 Community Well-Being Rankings" March 2018*

Real Estate Rankings

- *WalletHub* compared the most populated U.S. cities, as well as at least two of the most populated cities in each state, for a total of 179, to determine which had the best markets for real estate agents. Madison ranked #107 where demand was high and pay was the best. Criteria: sales per agent; annual median wage for real-estate agents; monthly average starting salary for real estate agents; real estate job density and competition; unemployment rate; home turnover rate; housing-market health index; and other relevant metrics. *www.WalletHub.com, "2019's Best Places to Be a Real Estate Agent," April 24, 2019*

- The Madison metro area was identified as one of the 10 best condo markets in the U.S. in 2019. The area ranked #5 out of 61 markets. Criteria: year-over-year change of median sales price of existing apartment condo-coop homes between the 4th quarter of 2018 and the 4th quarter of 2019. *National Association of Realtors®, Median Sales Price of Existing Apartment Condo-Coops Homes for Metropolitan Areas, 4th Quarter 2019*

- Madison was ranked #83 out of 238 metro areas in terms of housing affordability in 2019 by the National Association of Home Builders (#1 = most affordable). Criteria: the share of homes sold in that area affordable to a family earning the local median income, based on standard mortgage underwriting criteria. *National Association of Home Builders®, NAHB-Wells Fargo Housing Opportunity Index, 4th Quarter 2019*

Safety Rankings

- Allstate ranked the 200 largest cities in America in terms of driver safety. Madison ranked #11. Criteria: internal property damage claims over a two-year period from January 2016 to December 2017. The report helps increase the importance of safety and awareness behind the wheel. *Allstate, "Allstate America's Best Drivers Report, 2019" June 24, 2019*

- The National Insurance Crime Bureau ranked 382 metro areas in the U.S. in terms of per capita rates of vehicle theft. The Madison metro area ranked #253 (#1 = highest rate). Criteria: number of vehicle theft offenses per 100,000 inhabitants in 2018. *National Insurance Crime Bureau, "Hot Spots 2018," June 25, 2019*

Seniors/Retirement Rankings

- From its Best Cities for Successful Aging indexes, the Milken Institute generated rankings for metropolitan areas, weighing data in nine categories—health care, wellness, living arrangements, transportation and convenience, financial characteristics, education, employment, community engagement, and overall livability. The Madison metro area was ranked #2 overall in the large metro area category. *Milken Institute, "Best Cities for Successful Aging, 2017" March 14, 2017*

Sports/Recreation Rankings

- Madison was chosen as a bicycle friendly community by the League of American Bicyclists. A "Bicycle Friendly Community" welcomes cyclists by providing safe and supportive accommodation for cycling and encouraging people to bike for transportation and recreation. There are five award levels: Diamond; Platinum; Gold; Silver; and Bronze. The community achieved an award level of Platinum. *League of American Bicyclists, "Fall 2019 Awards-Bicycle Friendly Community Master List," November 21, 2019*

- Madison was chosen as one of America's best cities for bicycling. The city ranked #8 out of 50. Criteria: cycling infrastructure that is safe and friendly for all ages; energy and bike culture. The editors only considered cities with populations of 100,000 or more. *Bicycling, "The 50 Best Bike Cities in America," October 10, 2018*

Women/Minorities Rankings

- Personal finance website *WalletHub* compared more than 180 U.S. cities—including the 150 most populated U.S. cities, plus at least two of the most populated cities in each state—across two key dimensions, "Hispanic Business-Friendliness" and "Hispanic Purchasing Power", to arrive at the most favorable conditions for Hispanic entrepreneurs. Madison was ranked #100 out of 182. Criteria includes: share of Hispanic-Owned Businesses; Hispanic entrepreneurship rate to median annual income of Hispanics; Small Business-Friendliness score; cost of living; and number of Hispanics with at least a bachelor's degree. *WalletHub.com, "2019's Best Cities for Hispanic Entrepreneurs," May 1, 2019*

Miscellaneous Rankings

- Madison was selected as a 2019 Digital Cities Survey winner. The city ranked #6 in the large city (250,000 to 499,999 population) category. The survey examined and assessed how city governments are utilizing technology to improve transparency, enhance cybersecurity, and solve social challenges. Survey questions focused on ten characteristics: data governance, citizen-focused, leadership alignment, secure, staffed/supported, efficient, connected, resilient, best practices, and use of innovation. *Center for Digital Government, "2019 Digital Cities Survey," November 14, 2019*

- *WalletHub* compared the 150 most populated U.S. cities to determine their operating efficiency. A "Quality of Services" score was constructed for each city and then divided by the total budget per capita to reveal which were managed the best. Madison ranked #22. Criteria: financial stability; economy; education; safety; health; infrastructure and pollution. *www.WalletHub.com, "2019's Best- & Worst-Run Cities in America," July 1, 2019*

Business Environment

CITY FINANCES

City Government Finances

Component	2017 ($000)	2017 ($ per capita)
Total Revenues	526,216	2,114
Total Expenditures	508,836	2,044
Debt Outstanding	906,358	3,641
Cash and Securities[1]	895,615	3,598

Note: (1) Cash and security holdings of a government at the close of its fiscal year, including those of its dependent agencies, utilities, and liquor stores.
Source: U.S. Census Bureau, State & Local Government Finances 2017

City Government Revenue by Source

Source	2017 ($000)	2017 ($ per capita)	2017 (%)
General Revenue			
From Federal Government	27,724	111	5.3
From State Government	70,119	282	13.3
From Local Governments	7,180	29	1.4
Taxes			
Property	223,443	898	42.5
Sales and Gross Receipts	14,556	58	2.8
Personal Income	0	0	0.0
Corporate Income	0	0	0.0
Motor Vehicle License	0	0	0.0
Other Taxes	7,954	32	1.5
Current Charges	101,908	409	19.4
Liquor Store	0	0	0.0
Utility	44,703	180	8.5
Employee Retirement	0	0	0.0

Source: U.S. Census Bureau, State & Local Government Finances 2017

City Government Expenditures by Function

Function	2017 ($000)	2017 ($ per capita)	2017 (%)
General Direct Expenditures			
Air Transportation	0	0	0.0
Corrections	0	0	0.0
Education	0	0	0.0
Employment Security Administration	0	0	0.0
Financial Administration	6,310	25	1.2
Fire Protection	52,238	209	10.3
General Public Buildings	5,162	20	1.0
Governmental Administration, Other	8,266	33	1.6
Health	13,699	55	2.7
Highways	57,332	230	11.3
Hospitals	0	0	0.0
Housing and Community Development	43,131	173	8.5
Interest on General Debt	23,162	93	4.6
Judicial and Legal	2,737	11	0.5
Libraries	16,294	65	3.2
Parking	9,116	36	1.8
Parks and Recreation	41,309	165	8.1
Police Protection	73,348	294	14.4
Public Welfare	0	0	0.0
Sewerage	7,875	31	1.5
Solid Waste Management	15,617	62	3.1
Veterans' Services	0	0	0.0
Liquor Store	0	0	0.0
Utility	85,735	344	16.8
Employee Retirement	0	0	0.0

Source: U.S. Census Bureau, State & Local Government Finances 2017

DEMOGRAPHICS

Population Growth

Area	1990 Census	2000 Census	2010 Census	2018* Estimate	Population Growth (%) 1990-2018	Population Growth (%) 2010-2018
City	193,451	208,054	233,209	252,086	30.3	8.1
MSA[1]	432,323	501,774	568,593	647,281	49.7	13.8
U.S.	248,709,873	281,421,906	308,745,538	322,903,030	29.8	4.6

Note: (1) Figures cover the Madison, WI Metropolitan Statistical Area—see Appendix B for areas included; (*) 2014-2018 5-year estimated population
Source: U.S. Census Bureau, 1990 Census, Census 2000, Census 2010, 2014-2018 American Community Survey 5-Year Estimates

Household Size

Area	Persons in Household (%) One	Two	Three	Four	Five	Six	Seven or More	Average Household Size
City	34.7	36.4	13.6	9.9	3.9	1.0	0.5	2.20
MSA[1]	29.5	37.1	14.2	12.3	4.7	1.4	0.8	2.40
U.S.	27.7	33.9	15.7	13.0	6.0	2.3	1.4	2.60

Note: (1) Figures cover the Madison, WI Metropolitan Statistical Area—see Appendix B for areas included
Source: U.S. Census Bureau, 2014-2018 American Community Survey 5-Year Estimates

Race

Area	White Alone[2] (%)	Black Alone[2] (%)	Asian Alone[2] (%)	AIAN[3] Alone[2] (%)	NHOPI[4] Alone[2] (%)	Other Race Alone[2] (%)	Two or More Races (%)
City	78.4	6.8	9.0	0.4	0.0	1.8	3.6
MSA[1]	85.9	4.4	4.9	0.3	0.0	1.6	2.9
U.S.	72.7	12.7	5.4	0.8	0.2	4.9	3.2

Note: (1) Figures cover the Madison, WI Metropolitan Statistical Area—see Appendix B for areas included; (2) Alone is defined as not being in combination with one or more other races; (3) American Indian and Alaska Native; (4) Native Hawaiian and Other Pacific Islander
Source: U.S. Census Bureau, 2014-2018 American Community Survey 5-Year Estimates

Hispanic or Latino Origin

Area	Total (%)	Mexican (%)	Puerto Rican (%)	Cuban (%)	Other (%)
City	6.9	4.3	0.6	0.2	1.8
MSA[1]	5.7	3.7	0.5	0.2	1.4
U.S.	17.8	11.2	1.7	0.7	4.2

Note: Persons of Hispanic or Latino origin can be of any race; (1) Figures cover the Madison, WI Metropolitan Statistical Area—see Appendix B for areas included
Source: U.S. Census Bureau, 2014-2018 American Community Survey 5-Year Estimates

Segregation

Type	Segregation Indices[1] 1990	2000	2010	2010 Rank[2]	Percent Change 1990-2000	1990-2010	2000-2010
Black/White	52.1	49.9	49.6	71	-2.2	-2.6	-0.3
Asian/White	54.5	49.5	44.2	29	-5.0	-10.3	-5.3
Hispanic/White	31.1	38.7	40.1	65	7.7	9.1	1.4

Note: All figures cover the Metropolitan Statistical Area—see Appendix B for areas included; Figures are based on an analysis of 1990, 2000, and 2010 Census Decennial Census tract data by William H. Frey, Brookings Institution and the University of Michigan Social Science Data Analysis Network. In this analysis all racial groups (whites, blacks, and asians) are non-Hispanic members of those races. Hispanics are shown as a separate category; (1) Segregation Indices are Dissimilarity Indices that measure the degree to which the minority group is distributed differently than whites across census tracts. They range from 0 (complete integration) to 100 (complete segregation) where the value indicates the percentage of the minority group that needs to move to be distributed exactly like whites; (2) Ranges from 1 (most segregated) to 102 (least segregated); n/a not available.
Source: www.CensusScope.org

Ancestry

Area	German	Irish	English	American	Italian	Polish	French[2]	Scottish	Dutch
City	32.0	13.1	8.1	1.9	4.1	5.8	3.0	1.5	1.8
MSA[1]	37.7	13.5	8.6	2.8	3.9	5.4	2.9	1.5	2.0
U.S.	13.7	9.9	7.3	6.4	5.2	2.8	2.4	1.7	1.2

Note: Figures are the percentage of the total population reporting a particular ancestry. The nine most commonly reported ancestries in the U.S. are shown. Figures include multiple ancestries (e.g. if a person reported being Irish and Italian, they were included in both columns); (1) Figures cover the Madison, WI Metropolitan Statistical Area—see Appendix B for areas included; (2) Excludes Basque
Source: U.S. Census Bureau, 2014-2018 American Community Survey 5-Year Estimates

Foreign-born Population

Area	Percent of Population Born in								
	Any Foreign Country	Asia	Mexico	Europe	Caribbean	Central America[2]	South America	Africa	Canada
City	12.0	6.5	1.7	1.4	0.1	0.3	0.8	0.8	0.2
MSA[1]	7.5	3.5	1.4	1.0	0.1	0.2	0.5	0.5	0.2
U.S.	13.5	4.1	3.5	1.5	1.3	1.1	0.9	0.7	0.3

Note: (1) Figures cover the Madison, WI Metropolitan Statistical Area—see Appendix B for areas included; (2) Excludes Mexico.
Source: U.S. Census Bureau, 2014-2018 American Community Survey 5-Year Estimates

Marital Status

Area	Never Married	Now Married[2]	Separated	Widowed	Divorced
City	49.5	37.8	0.8	3.3	8.5
MSA[1]	36.2	49.2	0.9	4.2	9.6
U.S.	33.3	48.1	2.0	5.8	10.8

Note: Figures are percentages and cover the population 15 years of age and older; (1) Figures cover the Madison, WI Metropolitan Statistical Area—see Appendix B for areas included; (2) Excludes separated
Source: U.S. Census Bureau, 2014-2018 American Community Survey 5-Year Estimates

Disability by Age

Area	All Ages	Under 18 Years Old	18 to 64 Years Old	65 Years and Over
City	8.1	3.5	6.2	26.8
MSA[1]	9.0	3.6	7.0	27.6
U.S.	12.6	4.2	10.3	35.0

Note: Figures show percent of the civilian noninstitutionalized population that reported having a disability. Disability status is determined from six types of difficulty: vision, hearing, cognitive, ambulatory, self-care, and independent living. For children under 5 years old, hearing and vision difficulty are used to determine disability status. For children between the ages of 5 and 14, disability status is determined from hearing, vision, cognitive, ambulatory, and self-care difficulties. For people aged 15 years and older, they are considered to have a disability if they have difficulty with any one of the six difficulty types; Note: (1) Figures cover the Madison, WI Metropolitan Statistical Area—see Appendix B for areas included
Source: U.S. Census Bureau, 2014-2018 American Community Survey 5-Year Estimates

Age

Area	Percent of Population									Median Age
	Under Age 5	Age 5–19	Age 20–34	Age 35–44	Age 45–54	Age 55–64	Age 65–74	Age 75–84	Age 85+	
City	5.2	16.4	35.4	12.0	9.9	9.7	6.6	3.1	1.6	30.8
MSA[1]	5.7	18.3	24.4	12.8	12.7	12.4	8.2	3.7	1.7	36.0
U.S.	6.1	19.3	20.7	12.6	13.2	12.8	8.8	4.5	1.9	37.9

Note: (1) Figures cover the Madison, WI Metropolitan Statistical Area—see Appendix B for areas included
Source: U.S. Census Bureau, 2014-2018 American Community Survey 5-Year Estimates

Gender

Area	Males	Females	Males per 100 Females
City	124,658	127,428	97.8
MSA[1]	322,491	324,790	99.3
U.S.	158,984,190	163,918,840	97.0

Note: (1) Figures cover the Madison, WI Metropolitan Statistical Area—see Appendix B for areas included
Source: U.S. Census Bureau, 2014-2018 American Community Survey 5-Year Estimates

Religious Groups by Family

Area	Catholic	Baptist	Non-Den.	Methodist[2]	Lutheran	LDS[3]	Pente-costal	Presby-terian[4]	Muslim[5]	Judaism
MSA[1]	21.8	1.1	1.6	3.7	12.8	0.5	0.4	2.2	0.5	0.5
U.S.	19.1	9.3	4.0	4.0	2.3	2.0	1.9	1.6	0.8	0.7

Note: Figures are the number of adherents as a percentage of the total population; (1) Figures cover the Madison, WI Metropolitan Statistical Area—see Appendix B for areas included; (2) Methodist/Pietist; (3) Latter Day Saints; (4) Reformed; (5) Figures are estimates
Source: Association of Statisticians of American Religious Bodies, 2010 U.S. Religion Census: Religious Congregations & Membership Study

Religious Groups by Tradition

Area	Catholic	Evangelical Protestant	Mainline Protestant	Other Tradition	Black Protestant	Orthodox
MSA[1]	21.8	7.3	15.4	2.3	0.1	0.1
U.S.	19.1	16.2	7.3	4.3	1.6	0.3

Note: Figures are the number of adherents as a percentage of the total population; (1) Figures cover the Madison, WI Metropolitan Statistical Area—see Appendix B for areas included
Source: Association of Statisticians of American Religious Bodies, 2010 U.S. Religion Census: Religious Congregations & Membership Study

ECONOMY

Gross Metropolitan Product

Area	2017	2018	2019	2020	Rank[2]
MSA[1]	49.5	52.1	54.5	56.5	61

Note: Figures are in billions of dollars; (1) Figures cover the Madison, WI Metropolitan Statistical Area—see Appendix B for areas included; (2) Rank is based on 2018 data and ranges from 1 to 381
Source: U.S. Conference of Mayors, U.S. Metro Economies: GMP & Employment 2018-2020, September 2019

Economic Growth

Area	2015-17 (%)	2018 (%)	2019 (%)	2020 (%)	Rank[2]
MSA[1]	2.4	3.2	2.8	1.7	107
U.S.	1.9	2.9	2.3	2.1	–

Note: Figures are real gross metropolitan product (GMP) growth rates and represent average annual percent change; (1) Figures cover the Madison, WI Metropolitan Statistical Area—see Appendix B for areas included; (2) Rank is based on 2017 2-year average annual percent change and ranges from 1 to 381
Source: U.S. Conference of Mayors, U.S. Metro Economies: GMP & Employment 2018-2020, September 2019

Metropolitan Area Exports

Area	2013	2014	2015	2016	2017	2018	Rank[2]
MSA[1]	2,292.1	2,369.5	2,280.4	2,204.8	2,187.7	2,460.2	91

Note: Figures are in millions of dollars; (1) Figures cover the Madison, WI Metropolitan Statistical Area—see Appendix B for areas included; (2) Rank is based on 2018 data and ranges from 1 to 387
Source: U.S. Department of Commerce, International Trade Administration, Office of Trade and Economic Analysis, Industry and Analysis, Exports by Metropolitan Area, data extracted April 15, 2020

Building Permits

Area	Single-Family 2017	2018	Pct. Chg.	Multi-Family 2017	2018	Pct. Chg.	Total 2017	2018	Pct. Chg.
City	379	334	-11.9	1,809	1,109	-38.7	2,188	1,443	-34.0
MSA[1]	1,656	1,623	-2.0	2,976	2,029	-31.8	4,632	3,652	-21.2
U.S.	820,000	855,300	4.3	462,000	473,500	2.5	1,282,000	1,328,800	3.7

Note: (1) Figures cover the Madison, WI Metropolitan Statistical Area—see Appendix B for areas included; Figures represent new, privately-owned housing units authorized (unadjusted data); All permit data are based on estimates with imputation
Source: U.S. Census Bureau, Manufacturing, Mining, and Construction Statistics, Building Permits, 2017, 2018

Bankruptcy Filings

Area	Business Filings			Nonbusiness Filings		
	2018	2019	% Chg.	2018	2019	% Chg.
Dane County	22	34	54.5	772	773	0.1
U.S.	22,232	22,780	2.5	751,186	752,160	0.1

Note: Business filings include Chapter 7, Chapter 9, Chapter 11, Chapter 12, Chapter 13, Chapter 15, and Section 304; Nonbusiness filings include Chapter 7, Chapter 11, and Chapter 13
Source: Administrative Office of the U.S. Courts, Business and Nonbusiness Bankruptcy, County Cases Commenced by Chapter of the Bankruptcy Code, During the 12-Month Period Ending December 31, 2018 and Business and Nonbusiness Bankruptcy, County Cases Commenced by Chapter of the Bankruptcy Code, During the 12-Month Period Ending December 31, 2019

Housing Vacancy Rates

Area	Gross Vacancy Rate[2] (%)			Year-Round Vacancy Rate[3] (%)			Rental Vacancy Rate[4] (%)			Homeowner Vacancy Rate[5] (%)		
	2017	2018	2019	2017	2018	2019	2017	2018	2019	2017	2018	2019
MSA[1]	n/a	n/a	n/a	n/a	n/a	n/a	n/a	n/a	n/a	n/a	n/a	n/a
U.S.	12.7	12.3	12.0	9.9	9.7	9.5	7.2	6.9	6.7	1.6	1.5	1.4

Note: (1) Figures cover the Madison, WI Metropolitan Statistical Area—see Appendix B for areas included; (2) The percentage of the total housing inventory that is vacant; (3) The percentage of the housing inventory (excluding seasonal units) that is year-round vacant; (4) The percentage of rental inventory that is vacant for rent; (5) The percentage of homeowner inventory that is vacant for sale; n/a not available
Source: U.S. Census Bureau, Housing Vacancies and Homeownership Annual Statistics: 2017, 2018, 2019

INCOME

Income

Area	Per Capita ($)	Median Household ($)	Average Household ($)
City	36,372	62,906	83,233
MSA[1]	37,679	69,372	90,098
U.S.	32,621	60,293	84,938

Note: (1) Figures cover the Madison, WI Metropolitan Statistical Area—see Appendix B for areas included
Source: U.S. Census Bureau, 2014-2018 American Community Survey 5-Year Estimates

Household Income Distribution

Area	Percent of Households Earning							
	Under $15,000	$15,000 -$24,999	$25,000 -$34,999	$35,000 -$49,999	$50,000 -$74,999	$75,000 -$99,999	$100,000 -$149,999	$150,000 and up
City	11.0	8.1	8.7	12.7	18.0	13.3	15.8	12.4
MSA[1]	7.8	7.3	8.3	12.4	18.0	14.3	17.7	14.1
U.S.	10.9	9.3	9.3	12.6	17.5	12.5	14.6	13.3

Note: (1) Figures cover the Madison, WI Metropolitan Statistical Area—see Appendix B for areas included
Source: U.S. Census Bureau, 2014-2018 American Community Survey 5-Year Estimates

Poverty Rate

Area	All Ages	Under 18 Years Old	18 to 64 Years Old	65 Years and Over
City	17.9	15.6	20.4	5.7
MSA[1]	11.2	10.9	12.4	5.6
U.S.	14.1	19.5	13.2	9.3

Note: Figures are percentage of people whose income during the past 12 months was below the poverty level; (1) Figures cover the Madison, WI Metropolitan Statistical Area—see Appendix B for areas included
Source: U.S. Census Bureau, 2014-2018 American Community Survey 5-Year Estimates

EMPLOYMENT

Labor Force and Employment

Area	Civilian Labor Force			Workers Employed		
	Dec. 2018	Dec. 2019	% Chg.	Dec. 2018	Dec. 2019	% Chg.
City	155,501	157,534	1.3	152,428	154,347	1.3
MSA[1]	384,805	390,192	1.4	376,892	381,370	1.2
U.S.	162,510,000	164,007,000	0.9	156,481,000	158,504,000	1.3

Note: Data is not seasonally adjusted and covers workers 16 years of age and older; (1) Figures cover the Madison, WI Metropolitan Statistical Area—see Appendix B for areas included
Source: Bureau of Labor Statistics, Local Area Unemployment Statistics

Unemployment Rate

Area	2019											
	Jan.	Feb.	Mar.	Apr.	May	Jun.	Jul.	Aug.	Sep.	Oct.	Nov.	Dec.
City	2.4	2.4	2.5	2.2	2.6	3.1	2.6	2.5	2.2	2.1	2.1	2.0
MSA[1]	2.7	2.8	2.8	2.4	2.6	3.1	2.7	2.5	2.2	2.2	2.2	2.3
U.S.	4.4	4.1	3.9	3.3	3.4	3.8	4.0	3.8	3.3	3.3	3.3	3.4

Note: Data is not seasonally adjusted and covers workers 16 years of age and older; (1) Figures cover the Madison, WI Metropolitan Statistical Area—see Appendix B for areas included
Source: Bureau of Labor Statistics, Local Area Unemployment Statistics

Average Wages

Occupation	$/Hr.	Occupation	$/Hr.
Accountants and Auditors	34.10	Maintenance and Repair Workers	21.20
Automotive Mechanics	22.80	Marketing Managers	60.00
Bookkeepers	20.30	Network and Computer Systems Admin.	37.90
Carpenters	26.60	Nurses, Licensed Practical	23.50
Cashiers	11.60	Nurses, Registered	38.70
Computer Programmers	40.00	Nursing Assistants	16.30
Computer Systems Analysts	45.10	Office Clerks, General	17.70
Computer User Support Specialists	27.70	Physical Therapists	41.30
Construction Laborers	21.10	Physicians	99.00
Cooks, Restaurant	12.70	Plumbers, Pipefitters and Steamfitters	31.20
Customer Service Representatives	19.50	Police and Sheriff's Patrol Officers	31.10
Dentists	116.70	Postal Service Mail Carriers	24.90
Electricians	26.50	Real Estate Sales Agents	25.40
Engineers, Electrical	45.00	Retail Salespersons	13.40
Fast Food and Counter Workers	10.50	Sales Representatives, Technical/Scientific	36.20
Financial Managers	66.60	Secretaries, Exc. Legal/Medical/Executive	19.00
First-Line Supervisors of Office Workers	29.90	Security Guards	16.60
General and Operations Managers	62.60	Surgeons	n/a
Hairdressers/Cosmetologists	14.80	Teacher Assistants, Exc. Postsecondary*	15.30
Home Health and Personal Care Aides	13.30	Teachers, Secondary School, Exc. Sp. Ed.*	27.50
Janitors and Cleaners	15.00	Telemarketers	11.50
Landscaping/Groundskeeping Workers	16.90	Truck Drivers, Heavy/Tractor-Trailer	25.10
Lawyers	58.00	Truck Drivers, Light/Delivery Services	17.60
Maids and Housekeeping Cleaners	13.10	Waiters and Waitresses	12.20

Note: Wage data covers the Madison, WI Metropolitan Statistical Area—see Appendix B for areas included; (*) Hourly wages were calculated from annual wage data based on a 40 hour work week; n/a not available.
Source: Bureau of Labor Statistics, Metro Area Occupational Employment & Wage Estimates, May 2019

Employment by Occupation

Occupation Classification	City (%)	MSA[1] (%)	U.S. (%)
Management, Business, Science, and Arts	53.8	47.7	37.9
Natural Resources, Construction, and Maintenance	3.4	6.7	8.9
Production, Transportation, and Material Moving	7.8	10.4	13.3
Sales and Office	18.2	19.9	22.1
Service	16.8	15.3	17.9

Note: Figures cover employed civilians 16 years of age and older; (1) Figures cover the Madison, WI Metropolitan Statistical Area—see Appendix B for areas included
Source: U.S. Census Bureau, 2014-2018 American Community Survey 5-Year Estimates

Employment by Industry

| Sector | MSA[1] | | U.S. |
	Number of Employees	Percent of Total	Percent of Total
Construction, Mining, and Logging	18,100	4.3	5.4
Education and Health Services	51,200	12.3	16.1
Financial Activities	24,100	5.8	5.8
Government	90,300	21.7	15.0
Information	17,800	4.3	1.9
Leisure and Hospitality	37,700	9.1	10.8
Manufacturing	36,500	8.8	8.4
Other Services	20,500	4.9	3.9
Professional and Business Services	53,700	12.9	14.1
Retail Trade	41,300	9.9	10.6
Transportation, Warehousing, and Utilities	9,800	2.4	4.2
Wholesale Trade	15,100	3.6	3.9

Note: Figures are non-farm employment as of December 2019. Figures are not seasonally adjusted and include workers 16 years of age and older; (1) Figures cover the Madison, WI Metropolitan Statistical Area—see Appendix B for areas included
Source: Bureau of Labor Statistics, Current Employment Statistics, Employment, Hours, and Earnings

Occupations with Greatest Projected Employment Growth: 2019 – 2021

Occupation[1]	2019 Employment	2021 Projected Employment	Numeric Employment Change	Percent Employment Change
Personal Care Aides	67,700	71,470	3,770	5.6
Combined Food Preparation and Serving Workers, Including Fast Food	76,450	78,390	1,940	2.5
Registered Nurses	57,510	58,900	1,390	2.4
Heavy and Tractor-Trailer Truck Drivers	53,400	54,730	1,330	2.5
Laborers and Freight, Stock, and Material Movers, Hand	54,370	55,330	960	1.8
Software Developers, Applications	16,690	17,520	830	5.0
Cooks, Restaurant	24,360	25,180	820	3.4
Janitors and Cleaners, Except Maids and Housekeeping Cleaners	49,840	50,600	760	1.5
Maintenance and Repair Workers, General	36,060	36,740	680	1.9
Elementary School Teachers, Except Special Education	35,490	36,150	660	1.9

Note: Projections cover Wisconsin; (1) Sorted by numeric employment change
Source: www.projectionscentral.com, State Occupational Projections, 2019–2021 Short-Term Projections

Fastest Growing Occupations: 2019 – 2021

Occupation[1]	2019 Employment	2021 Projected Employment	Numeric Employment Change	Percent Employment Change
Locomotive Engineers	880	990	110	12.5
Reservation and Transportation Ticket Agents and Travel Clerks	1,150	1,270	120	10.4
Railroad Conductors and Yardmasters	690	760	70	10.1
Nonfarm Animal Caretakers	7,590	8,180	590	7.8
Aircraft Mechanics and Service Technicians	850	910	60	7.1
Physician Assistants	2,040	2,180	140	6.9
Nurse Practitioners	3,080	3,270	190	6.2
Computer Numerically Controlled Machine Tool Programmers, Metal and Plastic	1,510	1,600	90	6.0
Taxi Drivers and Chauffeurs	9,130	9,670	540	5.9
Personal Care Aides	67,700	71,470	3,770	5.6

Note: Projections cover Wisconsin; (1) Sorted by percent employment change and excludes occupations with numeric employment change less than 50
Source: www.projectionscentral.com, State Occupational Projections, 2019–2021 Short-Term Projections

TAXES

State Corporate Income Tax Rates

State	Tax Rate (%)	Income Brackets ($)	Num. of Brackets	Financial Institution Tax Rate (%)[a]	Federal Income Tax Ded.
Wisconsin	7.9	Flat rate	1	7.9	No

Note: Tax rates as of January 1, 2020; (a) Rates listed are the corporate income tax rate applied to financial institutions or excise taxes based on income.
Source: Federation of Tax Administrators, State Corporate Income Tax Rates, January 1, 2020

State Individual Income Tax Rates

State	Tax Rate (%)	Income Brackets ($)	Personal Exemptions ($)			Standard Ded. ($)	
			Single	Married	Depend.	Single	Married
Wisconsin (a)	4.0 - 7.65	11,970 - 263,480 (w)	700	1,400	700	11,050	22,999 (y)

Note: Tax rates as of January 1, 2020; Local- and county-level taxes are not included; Federal income tax is not deductible on state income tax returns; (a) 19 states have statutory provision for automatically adjusting to the rate of inflation the dollar values of the income tax brackets, standard deductions, and/or personal exemptions. Michigan indexes the personal exemption only. Oregon does not index the income brackets for $125,000 and over; (w) The Wisconsin income brackets reported are for single individuals. For married taxpayers filing jointly, the same tax rates apply income brackets ranging from $15,960, to $351,310; (y) Alabama standard deduction is phased out for incomes over $23,000. Rhode Island exemptions & standard deductions phased out for incomes over $203,850; Wisconsin standard deduciton phases out for income over $15,939.
Source: Federation of Tax Administrators, State Individual Income Tax Rates, January 1, 2020

Various State Sales and Excise Tax Rates

State	State Sales Tax (%)	Gasoline[1] (¢/gal.)	Cigarette[2] ($/pack)	Spirits[3] ($/gal.)	Wine[4] ($/gal.)	Beer[5] ($/gal.)	Recreational Marijuana (%)
Wisconsin	5	32.9	2.52	3.25	0.25	0.06	Not legal

Note: All tax rates as of January 1, 2020; (1) The American Petroleum Institute has developed a methodology for determining the average tax rate on a gallon of fuel. Rates may include any of the following: excise taxes, environmental fees, storage tank fees, other fees or taxes, general sales tax, and local taxes; (2) The federal excise tax of $1.0066 per pack and local taxes are not included; (3) Rates are those applicable to off-premise sales of 40% alcohol by volume (a.b.v.) distilled spirits in 750ml containers. Local excise taxes are excluded; (4) Rates are those applicable to off-premise sales of 11% a.b.v. non-carbonated wine in 750ml containers; (5) Rates are those applicable to off-premise sales of 4.7% a.b.v. beer in 12 ounce containers.
Source: Tax Foundation, 2020 Facts & Figures: How Does Your State Compare?

State Business Tax Climate Index Rankings

State	Overall Rank	Corporate Tax Rank	Individual Income Tax Rank	Sales Tax Rank	Property Tax Rank	Unemployment Insurance Tax Rank
Wisconsin	26	30	37	7	23	37

Note: The index is a measure of how each state's tax laws affect economic performance. The lower the rank, the more favorable a state's tax system is for business. States without a given tax are given a ranking of 1. The scores/rankings for the District of Columbia do not affect other states. The 2020 index represents the tax climate as of July 1, 2019.
Source: Tax Foundation, State Business Tax Climate Index 2020

COMMERCIAL UTILITIES

Typical Monthly Electric Bills

Area	Commercial Service ($/month)		Industrial Service ($/month)	
	1,500 kWh	40 kW demand 14,000 kWh	1,000 kW demand 200,000 kWh	50,000 kW demand 32,500,000 kWh
City	200	1,731	29,333	2,817,675
Average[1]	203	1,612	25,706	2,520,671

Note: Figures are based on annualized rates; (1) Average based on 187 utilities surveyed
Source: Edison Electric Institute, Typical Bills and Average Rates Report, Summer 2019

TRANSPORTATION

Means of Transportation to Work

Area	Car/Truck/Van		Public Transportation			Bicycle	Walked	Other Means	Worked at Home
	Drove Alone	Car-pooled	Bus	Subway	Railroad				
City	64.2	7.1	9.2	0.0	0.0	4.7	9.4	1.2	4.2
MSA[1]	74.7	7.8	4.3	0.0	0.0	2.3	5.1	1.0	4.9
U.S.	76.4	9.1	2.5	1.9	0.6	0.6	2.7	1.3	4.9

Note: Figures are percentages and cover workers 16 years of age and older; (1) Figures cover the Madison, WI Metropolitan Statistical Area—see Appendix B for areas included
Source: U.S. Census Bureau, 2014-2018 American Community Survey 5-Year Estimates

Travel Time to Work

Area	Less Than 10 Minutes	10 to 19 Minutes	20 to 29 Minutes	30 to 44 Minutes	45 to 59 Minutes	60 to 89 Minutes	90 Minutes or More
City	15.0	40.9	23.8	15.0	2.7	1.8	0.8
MSA[1]	16.1	32.6	24.0	18.8	5.0	2.3	1.1
U.S.	12.5	28.7	20.9	20.7	8.2	6.3	2.8

Note: Note: Figures are percentages and include workers 16 years old and over; (1) Figures cover the Madison, WI Metropolitan Statistical Area—see Appendix B for areas included
Source: U.S. Census Bureau, 2014-2018 American Community Survey 5-Year Estimates

Key Congestion Measures

Area	1982	1992	2002	2012	2017
Annual Hours of Delay, Total (000)	1,612	2,292	4,604	8,400	9,664
Annual Hours of Delay, Per Auto Commuter	15	17	26	34	38
Annual Congestion Cost, Total (million $)	12	24	63	152	179
Annual Congestion Cost, Per Auto Commuter ($)	236	231	362	518	577

Source: Texas A&M Transportation Institute, 2019 Urban Mobility Report

Freeway Travel Time Index

Area	1982	1987	1992	1997	2002	2007	2012	2017
Urban Area Index[1]	1.07	1.08	1.08	1.10	1.13	1.15	1.15	1.15
Urban Area Rank[1,2]	35	44	76	80	75	72	71	71

Note: Freeway Travel Time Index—the ratio of travel time in the peak period to the travel time at free-flow conditions. For example, a value of 1.30 indicates a 20-minute free-flow trip takes 26 minutes in the peak (20 minutes x 1.30 = 26 minutes); (1) Covers the Madison WI urban area; (2) Rank is based on 101 larger urban areas (#1 = highest travel time index)
Source: Texas A&M Transportation Institute, 2019 Urban Mobility Report

Public Transportation

Agency Name / Mode of Transportation	Vehicles Operated in Maximum Service[1]	Annual Unlinked Passenger Trips[2] (in thous.)	Annual Passenger Miles[3] (in thous.)
Metro Transit System (Metro)			
Bus (directly operated)	182	13,230.7	52,239.9
Demand Response (directly operated)	12	16.7	93.2
Demand Response (purchased transportation)	60	138.3	1,145.5

Note: (1) Number of revenue vehicles operated by the given mode and type of service to meet the annual maximum service requirement. This is the revenue vehicle count during the peak season of the year; on the week and day that maximum service is provided. Vehicles operated in maximum service (VOMS) exclude atypical days and one-time special events; (2) Number of passengers who boarded public transportation vehicles. Passengers are counted each time they board a vehicle no matter how many vehicles they use to travel from their origin to their destination. (3) Sum of the distances ridden by all passengers during the entire fiscal year.
Source: Federal Transit Administration, National Transit Database, 2018

Air Transportation

Airport Name and Code / Type of Service	Passenger Airlines[1]	Passenger Enplanements	Freight Carriers[2]	Freight (lbs)
Dane County Regional-Truax Field (MSN)				
Domestic service (U.S. carriers - 2019)	26	1,161,451	9	25,433,892
International service (U.S. carriers - 2018)	3	163	0	0

Note: (1) Includes all U.S.-based major, minor and commuter airlines that carried at least one passenger during the year; (2) Includes all U.S.-based airlines and freight carriers that transported at least one pound of freight during the year.
Source: Bureau of Transportation Statistics, The Intermodal Transportation Database, Air Carriers: T-100 Domestic Market (U.S. Carriers), 2019; Bureau of Transportation Statistics, The Intermodal Transportation Database, Air Carriers: T-100 International Market (U.S. Carriers), 2018

Other Transportation Statistics

Major Highways:	I-90; I-94
Amtrak Service:	Bus connection
Major Waterways/Ports:	None

Source: Amtrak.com; Google Maps

BUSINESSES

Major Business Headquarters

Company Name	Industry	Rankings Fortune[1]	Forbes[2]
American Family Insurance Group	Insurance, Property and Casualty (Stock)	306	-

Note: (1) Companies that produce a 10-K are ranked 1 to 500 based on 2018 revenue; (2) All private companies with at least $2 billion in annual revenue through the end of their most current fiscal year are ranked 1 to 228; companies listed are headquartered in the city; dashes indicate no ranking
Source: Fortune, "Fortune 500," June 2019; Forbes, "America's Largest Private Companies," 2019 Rankings

Fast-Growing Businesses

According to *Inc.*, Madison is home to two of America's 500 fastest-growing private companies: **SwanLeap** (#35); **Fetch Rewards** (#68). Criteria: must be an independent, privately-held, for-profit, U.S. corporation, proprietorship or partnership as of December 31, 2018; revenues must be at least $100,000 in 2015 and $2 million in 2018; must have four-year operating/sales history. *Inc., "America's 500 Fastest-Growing Private Companies," 2019*

According to Deloitte, Madison is home to three of North America's 500 fastest-growing high-technology companies: **SwanLeap** (#15); **Exact Sciences Corp** (#117); **EyeKor** (#299). Companies are ranked by percentage growth in revenue over a four-year period. Criteria for inclusion: company must be headquartered within North America; must own proprietary intellectual property or technology that is sold to customers in products that contributes to a significant portion of the company's operating revenue; must have been in business for a minumum of four years with 2015 operating revenues of at least $50,000 USD/CD and 2018 operating revenues of at least $5 million USD/CD. *Deloitte, 2019 Technology Fast 500™*

Minority Business Opportunity

Madison is home to one company which is on the *Hispanic Business* 500 list (500 largest U.S. Hispanic-owned companies based on revenue): **Cartridge Savers** (#193). Companies included must show at least 51 percent ownership by Hispanic U.S. citizens, and must maintain headquarters in one of the 50 states or Washington, D.C. *Hispanic Business, "Hispanic Business 500," June 20, 2013*

Minority- and Women-Owned Businesses

Group	All Firms		Firms with Paid Employees			
	Firms	Sales ($000)	Firms	Sales ($000)	Employees	Payroll ($000)
AIAN[1]	96	(s)	6	(s)	0 - 19	(s)
Asian	1,073	293,249	185	240,561	1,693	67,928
Black	1,028	38,193	36	25,015	442	8,135
Hispanic	648	492,586	130	(s)	500 - 999	(s)
NHOPI[2]	34	(s)	2	(s)	0 - 19	(s)
Women	7,329	1,379,723	722	1,212,701	8,343	292,151
All Firms	20,714	31,747,001	4,811	31,054,781	133,370	6,237,901

Note: Figures cover firms located in the city; minority- and women-owned business are defined as firms in which the corresponding group own 51% or more of the stock or equity of the company; (1) American Indian and Alaska Native; (2) Native Hawaiian and Other Pacific Islander; (s) estimates are suppressed when publication standards are not met
Source: U.S. Census Bureau, 2012 Economic Census, Survey of Business Owners

HOTELS & CONVENTION CENTERS

Hotels, Motels and Vacation Rentals

Area	5 Star		4 Star		3 Star		2 Star		1 Star		Not Rated	
	Num.	Pct.[3]	Num.	Pct.[3]	Num.	Pct.[3]	Num.	Pct.[3]	Num.	Pct.[3]	Num.	Pct.[3]
City[1]	0	0.0	2	2.1	28	29.5	18	18.9	4	4.2	43	45.3
Total[2]	266	1.3	1,517	7.2	4,627	21.8	3,210	15.1	3,974	18.7	7,601	35.9

Note: (1) Figures cover Madison and vicinity; (2) Figures cover all 100 cities in this book; (3) Percentage of hotels which have a given star rating; Star ratings are determined by priceline.com and offer an indication of the general quality of a particular hotel.
Source: priceline.com, April 27, 2020

Major Convention Centers

Name	Overall Space (sq. ft.)	Exhibit Space (sq. ft.)	Meeting Space (sq. ft.)	Meeting Rooms
Monona Terrace Convention Center	250,000	37,200	28,000	21

Note: Table includes convention centers located in the Madison, WI metro area
Source: Original research

Living Environment

COST OF LIVING

Cost of Living Index

Composite Index	Groceries	Housing	Utilities	Trans-portation	Health Care	Misc. Goods/ Services
107.0	107.6	108.6	99.8	104.4	124.0	106.0

Note: The Cost of Living Index measures regional differences in the cost of consumer goods and services, excluding taxes and non-consumer expenditures, for professional and managerial households in the top income quintile. It is based on more than 50,000 prices covering almost 60 different items for which prices are collected three times a year by chambers of commerce, economic development organizations or university applied economic centers in each participating urban area. The numbers shown should be read as a percentage above or below the national average of 100. For example, a value of 115.4 in the groceries column indicates that grocery prices are 15.4% higher than the national average. Small differences in the index numbers should not be interpreted as significant; Figures cover the Madison WI urban area.
Source: The Council for Community and Economic Research, ACCRA Cost of Living Index, 2019

Grocery Prices

Area[1]	T-Bone Steak ($/pound)	Frying Chicken ($/pound)	Whole Milk ($/half gal.)	Eggs ($/dozen)	Orange Juice ($/64 oz.)	Coffee ($/11.5 oz.)
City[2]	14.20	1.67	2.11	1.18	3.32	4.81
Avg.	11.40	1.41	1.93	1.54	3.51	4.30
Min.	7.40	0.92	0.85	0.58	2.67	2.90
Max.	15.58	2.68	4.09	4.18	5.57	8.10

Note: (1) Values for the local area are compared with the average, minimum and maximum values for all 290 areas in the Cost of Living Index; (2) Figures cover the Madison WI urban area; T-Bone Steak (price per pound); Frying Chicken (price per pound, whole fryer); Whole Milk (half gallon carton); Eggs (price per dozen, Grade A, large); Orange Juice (64 oz. Tropicana or Florida Natural); Coffee (11.5 oz. can, vacuum-packed, Maxwell House, Hills Bros, or Folgers).
Source: The Council for Community and Economic Research, ACCRA Cost of Living Index, 2019

Housing and Utility Costs

Area[1]	New Home Price ($)	Apartment Rent ($/month)	All Electric ($/month)	Part Electric ($/month)	Other Energy ($/month)	Telephone ($/month)
City[2]	417,025	1,091	-	103.44	68.68	174.30
Avg.	362,090	1,142	174.35	100.00	67.76	179.60
Min.	198,329	501	91.58	31.44	28.51	165.30
Max.	2,074,561	5,050	388.18	239.41	306.15	207.90

Note: (1) Values for the local area are compared with the average, minimum and maximum values for all 290 areas in the Cost of Living Index; (2) Figures cover the Madison WI urban area; New Home Price (2,400 sf living area, 8,000 sf lot, in urban area with full utilities); Apartment Rent (950 sf 2 bedroom/1.5 or 2 bath, unfurnished, excluding all utilities except water); All Electric (average monthly cost for an all-electric home); Part Electric (average monthly cost for a part-electric home); Other Energy (average monthly cost for natural gas, fuel oil, coal, wood, and any other forms of energy except electricity); Telephone (price includes the base monthly rate plus taxes and fees for three lines of mobile phone service).
Source: The Council for Community and Economic Research, ACCRA Cost of Living Index, 2019

Health Care, Transportation, and Other Costs

Area[1]	Doctor ($/visit)	Dentist ($/visit)	Optometrist ($/visit)	Gasoline ($/gallon)	Beauty Salon ($/visit)	Men's Shirt ($)
City[2]	196.00	107.89	60.55	2.49	41.89	30.94
Avg.	114.85	97.58	106.10	2.50	38.15	32.15
Min.	39.00	62.22	52.22	1.53	16.88	10.27
Max.	206.67	151.53	258.67	3.79	79.29	59.30

Note: (1) Values for the local area are compared with the average, minimum and maximum values for all 290 areas in the Cost of Living Index; (2) Figures cover the Madison WI urban area; Doctor (general practitioners routine exam of an established patient); Dentist (adult teeth cleaning and periodic oral examination); Optometrist (full vision eye exam for established adult patient); Gasoline (one gallon regular unleaded, national brand, including all taxes, cash price at self-service pump if available); Beauty Salon (woman's shampoo, trim, and blow-dry); Men's Shirt (cotton/polyester dress shirt, pinpoint weave, long sleeves).
Source: The Council for Community and Economic Research, ACCRA Cost of Living Index, 2019

HOUSING

House Price Index (HPI)

Area	National Ranking[2]	Quarterly Change (%)	One-Year Change (%)	Five-Year Change (%)
MSA[1]	156	0.56	4.26	28.02
U.S.[3]	–	1.26	5.09	32.88

Note: The HPI is a weighted repeat sales index. It measures average price changes in repeat sales or refinancings on the same properties. This information is obtained by reviewing repeat mortgage transactions on single-family properties whose mortgages have been purchased or securitized by Fannie Mae or Freddie Mac in January 1975; (1) Figures cover the Madison, WI Metropolitan Statistical Area—see Appendix B for areas included; (2) Rankings are based on annual percentage change for all metro areas containing at least 15,000 transactions over the last 10 years and ranges from 1 to 232; (3) figures based on a weighted average of Census Division estimates using a seasonally adjusted, purchase-only index; all figures are for the period ending December 31, 2019
Source: Federal Housing Finance Agency, House Price Index, February 25, 2020

Median Single-Family Home Prices

Area	2017	2018	2019p	Percent Change 2018 to 2019
MSA[1]	267.9	283.7	299.2	5.5
U.S. Average	248.8	261.6	274.6	5.0

Note: Figures are median sales prices of existing single-family homes in thousands of dollars; (p) preliminary; (1) Figures cover the Madison, WI Metropolitan Statistical Area—see Appendix B for areas included
Source: National Association of Realtors, Median Sales Price of Existing Single-Family Homes for Metropolitan Areas, 4th Quarter 2019

Qualifying Income Based on Median Sales Price of Existing Single-Family Homes

Area	With 5% Down ($)	With 10% Down ($)	With 20% Down ($)
MSA[1]	64,040	60,670	53,929
U.S. Average	58,663	55,575	49,400

Note: Figures are preliminary; Qualifying income is based on a mortgage rate of 3.76%. Monthly principal and interest payment is limited to 25% of income; (1) Figures cover the Madison, WI Metropolitan Statistical Area—see Appendix B for areas included
Source: National Association of Realtors, Qualifying Income Based on Median Sales Price of Existing Single-Family Homes for Metropolitan Areas, 4th Quarter 2019

Median Apartment Condo-Coop Home Prices

Area	2017	2018	2019p	Percent Change 2018 to 2019
MSA[1]	183.1	195.0	205.3	5.3
U.S. Average	234.3	241.0	249.5	3.5

Note: Figures are median sales prices of existing apartment condo-coop homes in thousands of dollars; (p) preliminary; (1) Figures cover the Madison, WI Metropolitan Statistical Area—see Appendix B for areas included
Source: National Association of Realtors, Median Sales Price of Existing Apartment Condo-Coop Homes for Metropolitan Areas, 4th Quarter 2019

Home Value Distribution

Area	Under $50,000	$50,000 -$99,999	$100,000 -$149,999	$150,000 -$199,999	$200,000 -$299,999	$300,000 -$499,999	$500,000 -$999,999	$1,000,000 or more
City	1.9	2.6	9.4	21.5	35.4	23.1	5.6	0.6
MSA[1]	2.4	4.0	10.7	18.3	32.4	24.5	6.6	1.1
U.S.	7.6	13.0	14.0	14.3	19.2	18.3	10.5	3.1

Note: Figures are percentages and cover owner-occupied housing units; (1) Figures cover the Madison, WI Metropolitan Statistical Area—see Appendix B for areas included
Source: U.S. Census Bureau, 2014-2018 American Community Survey 5-Year Estimates

Homeownership Rate

Area	2011 (%)	2012 (%)	2013 (%)	2014 (%)	2015 (%)	2016 (%)	2017 (%)	2018 (%)	2019 (%)
MSA[1]	n/a	n/a	n/a	n/a	n/a	n/a	n/a	n/a	n/a
U.S.	66.1	65.4	65.1	64.5	63.7	63.4	63.9	64.4	64.6

Note: (1) Figures cover the Madison, WI Metropolitan Statistical Area—see Appendix B for areas included; n/a not available
Source: U.S. Census Bureau, Housing Vacancies and Homeownership Annual Statistics: 2011-2019

Year Housing Structure Built

Area	2010 or Later	2000 -2009	1990 -1999	1980 -1989	1970 -1979	1960 -1969	1950 -1959	1940 -1949	Before 1940	Median Year
City	5.5	15.2	13.2	11.1	14.1	11.4	10.6	4.9	14.0	1976
MSA[1]	5.1	16.6	15.8	11.1	15.4	9.4	8.0	3.7	14.8	1979
U.S.	4.1	14.3	13.9	13.5	15.3	10.7	10.4	5.0	12.8	1977

Note: Figures are percentages except for Median Year; Note: (1) Figures cover the Madison, WI Metropolitan Statistical Area—see Appendix B for areas included
Source: U.S. Census Bureau, 2014-2018 American Community Survey 5-Year Estimates

Gross Monthly Rent

Area	Under $500	$500 -$999	$1,000 -$1,499	$1,500 -$1,999	$2,000 -$2,499	$2,500 -$2,999	$3,000 and up	Median ($)
City	3.8	39.7	38.4	12.4	3.8	1.4	0.6	1,068
MSA[1]	5.2	45.3	35.3	10.2	2.7	0.8	0.4	996
U.S.	9.8	38.5	29.6	12.9	5.1	2.1	2.0	1,023

Note: Figures are percentages except for Median; Gross rent is the contract rent plus the estimated average monthly cost of utilities (electricity, gas, and water and sewer) and fuels (oil, coal, kerosene, wood, etc.) if these are paid by the renter (or paid for the renter by someone else); (1) Figures cover the Madison, WI Metropolitan Statistical Area—see Appendix B for areas included
Source: U.S. Census Bureau, 2014-2018 American Community Survey 5-Year Estimates

HEALTH

Health Risk Factors

Category	MSA[1] (%)	U.S. (%)
Adults aged 18–64 who have any kind of health care coverage	n/a	87.3
Adults who reported being in good or better health	n/a	82.4
Adults who have been told they have high blood cholesterol	n/a	33.0
Adults who have been told they have high blood pressure	n/a	32.3
Adults who are current smokers	n/a	17.1
Adults who currently use E-cigarettes	n/a	4.6
Adults who currently use chewing tobacco, snuff, or snus	n/a	4.0
Adults who are heavy drinkers[2]	n/a	6.3
Adults who are binge drinkers[3]	n/a	17.4
Adults who are overweight (BMI 25.0 - 29.9)	n/a	35.3
Adults who are obese (BMI 30.0 - 99.8)	n/a	31.3
Adults who participated in any physical activities in the past month	n/a	74.4
Adults who always or nearly always wears a seat belt	n/a	94.3

Note: n/a not available; (1) Figures cover the Madison, WI Metropolitan Statistical Area—see Appendix B for areas included; (2) Heavy drinkers are classified as adult men having more than 14 drinks per week and adult women having more than 7 drinks per week; (3) Binge drinkers are classified as males having five or more drinks on one occasion or females having four or more drinks on one occasion
Source: Centers for Disease Control and Prevention, Behaviorial Risk Factor Surveillance System, SMART: Selected Metropolitan Area Risk Trends, 2017

Acute and Chronic Health Conditions

Category	MSA[1] (%)	U.S. (%)
Adults who have ever been told they had a heart attack	n/a	4.2
Adults who have ever been told they have angina or coronary heart disease	n/a	3.9
Adults who have ever been told they had a stroke	n/a	3.0
Adults who have ever been told they have asthma	n/a	14.2
Adults who have ever been told they have arthritis	n/a	24.9
Adults who have ever been told they have diabetes[2]	n/a	10.5
Adults who have ever been told they had skin cancer	n/a	6.2
Adults who have ever been told they had any other types of cancer	n/a	7.1
Adults who have ever been told they have COPD	n/a	6.5
Adults who have ever been told they have kidney disease	n/a	3.0
Adults who have ever been told they have a form of depression	n/a	20.5

Note: n/a not available; (1) Figures cover the Madison, WI Metropolitan Statistical Area—see Appendix B for areas included; (2) Figures do not include pregnancy-related, borderline, or pre-diabetes
Source: Centers for Disease Control and Prevention, Behaviorial Risk Factor Surveillance System, SMART: Selected Metropolitan Area Risk Trends, 2017

Health Screening and Vaccination Rates

Category	MSA[1] (%)	U.S. (%)
Adults aged 65+ who have had flu shot within the past year	n/a	60.7
Adults aged 65+ who have ever had a pneumonia vaccination	n/a	75.4
Adults who have ever been tested for HIV	n/a	36.1
Adults who have ever had the shingles or zoster vaccine?	n/a	28.9
Adults who have had their blood cholesterol checked within the last five years	n/a	85.9

Note: n/a not available; (1) Figures cover the Madison, WI Metropolitan Statistical Area—see Appendix B for areas included.
Source: Centers for Disease Control and Prevention, Behaviorial Risk Factor Surveillance System, SMART: Selected Metropolitan Area Risk Trends, 2017

Disability Status

Category	MSA[1] (%)	U.S. (%)
Adults who reported being deaf	n/a	6.7
Are you blind or have serious difficulty seeing, even when wearing glasses?	n/a	4.5
Are you limited in any way in any of your usual activities due of arthritis?	n/a	12.9
Do you have difficulty doing errands alone?	n/a	6.8
Do you have difficulty dressing or bathing?	n/a	3.6
Do you have serious difficulty concentrating/remembering/making decisions?	n/a	10.7
Do you have serious difficulty walking or climbing stairs?	n/a	13.6

Note: n/a not available; (1) Figures cover the Madison, WI Metropolitan Statistical Area—see Appendix B for areas included.
Source: Centers for Disease Control and Prevention, Behaviorial Risk Factor Surveillance System, SMART: Selected Metropolitan Area Risk Trends, 2017

Mortality Rates for the Top 10 Causes of Death in the U.S.

ICD-10[a] Sub-Chapter	ICD-10[a] Code	Age-Adjusted Mortality Rate[1] per 100,000 population	
		County[2]	U.S.
Malignant neoplasms	C00-C97	135.9	152.4
Ischaemic heart diseases	I20-I25	66.5	92.7
Other forms of heart disease	I30-I51	43.7	52.5
Chronic lower respiratory diseases	J40-J47	23.7	40.4
Cerebrovascular diseases	I60-I69	27.7	37.3
Other degenerative diseases of the nervous system	G30-G31	39.9	36.4
Other external causes of accidental injury	W00-X59	49.1	35.3
Organic, including symptomatic, mental disorders	F01-F09	36.8	30.0
Hypertensive diseases	I10-I15	13.1	22.9
Diabetes mellitus	E10-E14	13.2	21.3

Note: (a) ICD-10 = International Classification of Diseases 10th Revision; (1) Mortality rates are a three year average covering 2016-2018; (2) Figures cover Dane County.
Source: Centers for Disease Control and Prevention, National Center for Health Statistics. Underlying Cause of Death 1999-2018 on CDC WONDER Online Database

Mortality Rates for Selected Causes of Death

ICD-10[a] Sub-Chapter	ICD-10[a] Code	Age-Adjusted Mortality Rate[1] per 100,000 population	
		County[2]	U.S.
Assault	X85-Y09	1.8	6.0
Diseases of the liver	K70-K76	7.9	14.2
Human immunodeficiency virus (HIV) disease	B20-B24	Suppressed	1.6
Influenza and pneumonia	J09-J18	10.3	14.2
Intentional self-harm	X60-X84	12.8	13.9
Malnutrition	E40-E46	Suppressed	1.9
Obesity and other hyperalimentation	E65-E68	1.8	2.1
Renal failure	N17-N19	7.5	12.8
Transport accidents	V01-V99	7.7	12.5
Viral hepatitis	B15-B19	Suppressed	1.4

Note: (a) ICD-10 = International Classification of Diseases 10th Revision; (1) Mortality rates are a three year average covering 2016-2018; (2) Figures cover Dane County; Data are suppressed when the data meet the criteria for confidentiality constraints; Mortality rates are flagged as unreliable when the rate would be calculated with a numerator of 20 or less.
Source: Centers for Disease Control and Prevention, National Center for Health Statistics. Underlying Cause of Death 1999-2018 on CDC WONDER Online Database

Health Insurance Coverage

Area	With Health Insurance	With Private Health Insurance	With Public Health Insurance	Without Health Insurance	Population Under Age 19 Without Health Insurance
City	95.6	83.3	22.4	4.4	2.3
MSA[1]	95.7	82.9	24.7	4.3	2.3
U.S.	90.6	67.7	34.7	9.4	5.2

Note: Figures are percentages that cover the civilian noninstitutionalized population; (1) Figures cover the Madison, WI Metropolitan Statistical Area—see Appendix B for areas included
Source: U.S. Census Bureau, 2014-2018 American Community Survey 5-Year Estimates

Number of Medical Professionals

Area	MDs[3]	DOs[3,4]	Dentists	Podiatrists	Chiropractors	Optometrists
County[1] (number)	3,222	110	387	24	231	118
County[1] (rate[2])	600.7	20.5	71.4	4.4	42.6	21.8
U.S. (rate[2])	281.9	23.4	69.1	6.0	27.5	16.4

Note: Data as of 2018 unless noted; (1) Data covers Dane County; (2) Rate per 100,000 population; (3) Data as of 2017 and includes all active, non-federal physicians; (4) Doctor of Osteopathic Medicine
Source: U.S. Department of Health and Human Services, Health Resources and Services Administration, Bureau of Health Professions, Area Resource File (ARF) 2018-2019

Best Hospitals

According to *U.S. News,* the Madison, WI metro area is home to one of the best hospitals in the U.S.: **University of Wisconsin Hospitals** (Honor Roll/12 adult specialties and 4 pediatric specialties). The hospital listed was nationally ranked in at least one of 16 adult or 10 pediatric specialties. Only 206 hospitals nationwide were nationally ranked in one or more adult or pediatric specialty. Twenty hospitals in the U.S. made the Honor Roll. The Best Hospitals Honor Roll takes both the national rankings and the procedure and condition ratings into account. Hospitals received points if they were nationally ranked in one of the 16 adult specialties—the higher they ranked, the more points they got—and how many ratings of "high performing" they earned in the nine procedures and conditions. *U.S. News Online, "America's Best Hospitals 2019-20"*

According to *U.S. News,* the Madison, WI metro area is home to one of the best children's hospitals in the U.S.: **American Family Children's Hospital** (4 pediatric specialties). The hospital listed was highly ranked in at least one of 10 pediatric specialties. Ninety-one children's hospitals in the U.S. were nationally ranked in at least one specialty. Hospitals received points for being ranked in a specialty, and the 10 hospitals with the most points across the 10 specialties make up the Honor Roll. *U.S. News Online, "America's Best Children's Hospitals 2019-20"*

EDUCATION

Public School District Statistics

District Name	Schls	Pupils	Pupil/Teacher Ratio	Minority Pupils[1] (%)	Free Lunch Eligible[2] (%)	IEP[3] (%)
Madison Metropolitan SD	54	26,917	12.0	57.8	44.0	14.6

Note: Table includes school districts with 2,000 or more students; (1) Percentage of students that are not non-Hispanic white; (2) Percentage of students that are eligible for the free lunch program; (3) Percentage of students that have an Individualized Education Program.
Source: U.S. Department of Education, National Center for Education Statistics, Common Core of Data, Local Education Agency (School District) Universe Survey: School Year 2018-2019; U.S. Department of Education, National Center for Education Statistics, Common Core of Data, Public Elementary/Secondary School Universe Survey: School Year 2018-2019

Highest Level of Education

Area	Less than H.S.	H.S. Diploma	Some College, No Deg.	Associate Degree	Bachelor's Degree	Master's Degree	Prof. School Degree	Doctorate Degree
City	4.7	14.0	15.3	8.1	32.6	15.7	4.4	5.2
MSA[1]	4.8	21.1	18.2	10.4	27.6	11.7	3.0	3.1
U.S.	12.3	27.1	20.6	8.4	19.4	8.6	2.1	1.4

Note: Figures cover persons age 25 and over; (1) Figures cover the Madison, WI Metropolitan Statistical Area—see Appendix B for areas included
Source: U.S. Census Bureau, 2014-2018 American Community Survey 5-Year Estimates

Educational Attainment by Race

Area	High School Graduate or Higher (%)					Bachelor's Degree or Higher (%)				
	Total	White	Black	Asian	Hisp.[2]	Total	White	Black	Asian	Hisp.[2]
City	95.3	96.9	87.6	90.4	76.9	57.9	60.1	20.6	70.5	34.0
MSA[1]	95.2	96.2	88.9	90.2	75.6	45.5	45.8	21.5	67.9	25.5
U.S.	87.7	89.6	85.4	86.8	67.7	31.5	32.9	21.1	53.5	15.8

Note: Figures shown cover persons 25 years old and over; (1) Figures cover the Madison, WI Metropolitan Statistical Area—see Appendix B for areas included; (2) People of Hispanic origin can be of any race
Source: U.S. Census Bureau, 2014-2018 American Community Survey 5-Year Estimates

School Enrollment by Grade and Control

Area	Preschool (%)		Kindergarten (%)		Grades 1 - 4 (%)		Grades 5 - 8 (%)		Grades 9 - 12 (%)	
	Public	Private	Public	Private	Public	Private	Public	Private	Public	Private
City	55.7	44.3	85.4	14.6	89.6	10.4	85.0	15.0	92.4	7.6
MSA[1]	64.4	35.6	88.2	11.8	90.4	9.6	89.4	10.6	94.4	5.6
U.S.	59.0	41.0	87.7	12.3	89.6	10.4	89.5	10.5	90.2	9.8

Note: Figures shown cover persons 3 years old and over; (1) Figures cover the Madison, WI Metropolitan Statistical Area—see Appendix B for areas included
Source: U.S. Census Bureau, 2014-2018 American Community Survey 5-Year Estimates

Average Salaries of Public School Teachers

Area	2016-17		2017-18		Change from 2016-17 to 2017-18	
	Dollars	Rank[1]	Dollars	Rank[1]	Percent	Rank[2]
Wisconsin	51,439	32	51,469	33	0.06	47
U.S. Average	59,539	–	60,477	–	1.58	–

Note: (1) Rank ranges from 1 to 51 where 1 indicates highest salary; (2) Rank ranges from 1 to 51 where 1 indicates highest percent change.
Source: National Education Association, Rankings & Estimates: Rankings of the States 2018 and Estimates of School Statistics 2019

Higher Education

Four-Year Colleges			Two-Year Colleges			Medical Schools[1]	Law Schools[2]	Voc/ Tech[3]
Public	Private Non-profit	Private For-profit	Public	Private Non-profit	Private For-profit			
3	2	0	1	0	1	1	1	4

Note: Figures cover institutions located within the city limits and include main campuses only; (1) includes schools accredited by the Liaison Committee on Medical Education and the American Osteopathic Association's Commission on Osteopathic College Accreditation; (2) includes ABA-accredited schools, schools with provisional ABA accreditation, and state accredited schools; (3) includes all schools with programs that are less than 2 years.
Source: National Center for Education Statistics, Integrated Postsecondary Education System (IPEDS), 2018-19; Wikipedia, List of Medical Schools in the United States, accessed May 1, 2020; Wikipedia, List of Law Schools in the United States, accessed May 1, 2020

According to *U.S. News & World Report,* the Madison, WI metro area is home to one of the top 200 national universities in the U.S.: **University of Wisconsin—Madison** (#46 tie). The indicators used to capture academic quality fall into a number of categories: assessment by administrators at peer institutions; retention of students; faculty resources; student selectivity; financial resources; alumni giving; high school counselor ratings of colleges; and graduation rate. *U.S. News & World Report, "America's Best Colleges 2020"*

According to *U.S. News & World Report,* the Madison, WI metro area is home to one of the top 100 law schools in the U.S.: **University of Wisconsin—Madison** (#38 tie). The rankings are based on a weighted average of 12 measures of quality: peer assessment score; assessment score by lawyers/judges; median LSAT scores; median undergrad GPA; acceptance rate; employment rates for graduates; placement success; bar passage rate; faculty resources; expenditures per student; student/faculty ratio; and library resources. *U.S. News & World Report, "America's Best Graduate Schools, Law, 2021"*

According to *U.S. News & World Report,* the Madison, WI metro area is home to one of the top 75 medical schools for research in the U.S.: **University of Wisconsin—Madison** (#27). The rankings are based on a weighted average of 11 measures of quality: quality assessment; peer assessment score; assessment score by residency directors; research activity; total research activity; average research activity per faculty member; student selectivity; median MCAT total score; median undergraduate GPA; acceptance rate; and faculty resources. *U.S. News & World Report, "America's Best Graduate Schools, Medical, 2021"*

According to *U.S. News & World Report,* the Madison, WI metro area is home to one of the top 75 business schools in the U.S.: **University of Wisconsin—Madison** (#37 tie). The rankings are based on a weighted average of the following nine measures: quality assessment; peer assessment; recruiter assessment; placement success; mean starting salary and bonus; student selectivity; mean GMAT and GRE scores; mean undergraduate GPA; and acceptance rate. *U.S. News & World Report, "America's Best Graduate Schools, Business, 2021"*

PRESIDENTIAL ELECTION

2016 Presidential Election Results

Area	Clinton	Trump	Johnson	Stein	Other
Dane County	70.4	23.0	3.4	1.4	1.8
U.S.	48.0	45.9	3.3	1.1	1.7

Note: Results are percentages and may not add to 100% due to rounding
Source: Dave Leip's Atlas of U.S. Presidential Elections

EMPLOYERS

Major Employers

Company Name	Industry
American Family Mutual Insurance Company	Fire, marine, & casualty insurance
Community Living Alliance	Social services for the handicapped
Covence Laboratories	Druggists preparations
CUNA Mutual Insurance Society	Telephone communication, except radio
Kraft Foods Global	Luncheon meat from purchased meat
University of Wisconsin Hospitals	General medical & surgical hospitals
Veterans Health Administration	General medical & surgical hospitals
WI Dept of Workforce Development	Administration of social & manpower programs
Wisconsin Department of Administration	Administration of general economic programs
Wisconsin Department of Health Services	Administration of public health programs
Wisconsin Department of Natural Resources	Land, mineral, & wildlife conservation
Wisconsin Department of Transportation	Regulation, administration of transportation
Wisconsin Dept of Natural Resources	Land, mineral, & wildlife conservation
Wisconsin Physicians Srvc Ins Corp	Hospital & medical services plans

Note: Companies shown are located within the Madison, WI Metropolitan Statistical Area.
Source: Hoovers.com; Wikipedia

PUBLIC SAFETY

Crime Rate

Area	All Crimes	Violent Crimes				Property Crimes		
		Murder	Rape[3]	Robbery	Aggrav. Assault	Burglary	Larceny -Theft	Motor Vehicle Theft
City	3,004.4	1.9	44.9	92.9	263.9	410.5	1,984.5	205.8
Suburbs[1]	1,377.6	1.2	25.3	18.1	94.7	163.7	1,001.2	73.4
Metro[2]	2,013.1	1.5	32.9	47.3	160.8	260.1	1,385.3	125.1
U.S.	2,580.1	5.0	42.6	86.2	246.8	376.0	1,594.6	228.9

Note: Figures are crimes per 100,000 population; (1) All areas within the metro area that are located outside the city limits; (2) Figures cover the Madison, WI Metropolitan Statistical Area—see Appendix B for areas included; (3) The city and U.S. figures shown were reported using the revised Uniform Crime Reporting (UCR) definition of rape. The suburban and metro area figures shown are an aggregate total of the data submitted using both the revised and legacy UCR definitions.
Source: FBI Uniform Crime Reports, 2018

Hate Crimes

Area	Number of Quarters Reported	Number of Incidents per Bias Motivation					
		Race/Ethnicity/ Ancestry	Religion	Sexual Orientation	Disability	Gender	Gender Identity
City	4	0	0	0	0	0	0
U.S.	4	4,047	1,419	1,196	159	47	168

Source: Federal Bureau of Investigation, Hate Crime Statistics 2018

Identity Theft Consumer Reports

Area	Reports	Reports per 100,000 Population	Rank[2]
MSA[1]	505	76	265
U.S.	650,572	198	-

Note: (1) Figures cover the Madison, WI Metropolitan Statistical Area—see Appendix B for areas included;
(2) Rank ranges from 1 to 386 where 1 indicates greatest number of identity theft reports per 100,000
population
Source: Federal Trade Commission, Consumer Sentinel Network Data Book for January–December 2019

Fraud and Other Consumer Reports

Area	Reports	Reports per 100,000 Population	Rank[2]
MSA[1]	3,453	523	221
U.S.	2,590,177	789	-

Note: (1) Figures cover the Madison, WI Metropolitan Statistical Area—see Appendix B for areas included;
(2) Rank ranges from 1 to 386 where 1 indicates greatest number of fraud and other consumer reports per
100,000 population
Source: Federal Trade Commission, Consumer Sentinel Network Data Book for January–December 2019

SPORTS

Professional Sports Teams

Team Name	League	Year Established

No teams are located in the metro area
Source: Wikipedia, Major Professional Sports Teams of the United States and Canada, May 4, 2020

CLIMATE

Average and Extreme Temperatures

Temperature	Jan	Feb	Mar	Apr	May	Jun	Jul	Aug	Sep	Oct	Nov	Dec	Yr.
Extreme High (°F)	56	61	82	94	93	101	104	102	99	90	76	62	104
Average High (°F)	26	30	42	58	70	79	84	81	72	61	44	30	57
Average Temp. (°F)	17	21	32	46	57	67	72	69	61	50	36	23	46
Average Low (°F)	8	12	22	35	45	54	59	57	49	38	27	14	35
Extreme Low (°F)	-37	-28	-29	0	19	31	36	35	25	13	-8	-25	-37

Note: Figures cover the years 1948-1990
Source: National Climatic Data Center, International Station Meteorological Climate Summary, 9/96

Average Precipitation/Snowfall/Humidity

Precip./Humidity	Jan	Feb	Mar	Apr	May	Jun	Jul	Aug	Sep	Oct	Nov	Dec	Yr.
Avg. Precip. (in.)	1.1	1.1	2.1	2.9	3.2	3.8	3.9	3.9	3.0	2.3	2.0	1.7	31.1
Avg. Snowfall (in.)	10	7	9	2	Tr	0	0	0	Tr	Tr	4	11	42
Avg. Rel. Hum. 6am (%)	78	80	81	80	79	81	85	89	90	85	84	82	83
Avg. Rel. Hum. 3pm (%)	66	63	59	50	50	51	53	55	55	54	64	69	57

Note: Figures cover the years 1948-1990; Tr = Trace amounts (<0.05 in. of rain; <0.5 in. of snow)
Source: National Climatic Data Center, International Station Meteorological Climate Summary, 9/96

Weather Conditions

Temperature			Daytime Sky			Precipitation		
5°F & below	32°F & below	90°F & above	Clear	Partly cloudy	Cloudy	0.01 inch or more precip.	0.1 inch or more snow/ice	Thunder-storms
35	161	14	88	119	158	118	38	40

Note: Figures are average number of days per year and cover the years 1948-1990
Source: National Climatic Data Center, International Station Meteorological Climate Summary, 9/96

HAZARDOUS WASTE

Superfund Sites

The Madison, WI metro area is home to five sites on the EPA's Superfund National Priorities List: **City Disposal Corp. Landfill** (final); **Hagen Farm** (final); **Madison Metropolitan Sewerage District Lagoons** (final); **Refuse Hideaway Landfill** (final); **Stoughton City Landfill** (final). There are a total of 1,387 Superfund sites with a status of proposed or final on the list in the U.S. *U.S. Environmental Protection Agency, National Priorities List, May 5, 2020*

AIR & WATER QUALITY

Air Quality Trends: Ozone

	1990	1995	2000	2005	2010	2012	2014	2016	2017	2018
MSA[1]	0.077	0.084	0.072	0.079	0.062	0.074	0.068	0.068	0.064	0.066
U.S.	0.088	0.089	0.082	0.080	0.073	0.075	0.067	0.069	0.068	0.069

Note: (1) Data covers the Madison, WI Metropolitan Statistical Area—see Appendix B for areas included. The values shown are the composite ozone concentration averages among trend sites based on the highest fourth daily maximum 8-hour concentration in parts per million. These trends are based on sites having an adequate record of monitoring data during the trend period. Data from exceptional events are included.
Source: U.S. Environmental Protection Agency, Air Quality Monitoring Information, "Air Quality Trends by City, 1990-2018"

Air Quality Index

Area	Percent of Days when Air Quality was...[2]					AQI Statistics[2]	
	Good	Moderate	Unhealthy for Sensitive Groups	Unhealthy	Very Unhealthy	Maximum	Median
MSA[1]	74.2	25.2	0.5	0.0	0.0	122	42

Note: (1) Data covers the Madison, WI Metropolitan Statistical Area—see Appendix B for areas included; (2) Based on 365 days with AQI data in 2018. Air Quality Index (AQI) is an index for reporting daily air quality. EPA calculates the AQI for five major air pollutants regulated by the Clean Air Act: ground-level ozone, particle pollution (aka particulate matter), carbon monoxide, sulfur dioxide, and nitrogen dioxide. The AQI runs from 0 to 500. The higher the AQI value, the greater the level of air pollution and the greater the health concern. There are six AQI categories: "Good" AQI is between 0 and 50. Air quality is considered satisfactory; "Moderate" AQI is between 51 and 100. Air quality is acceptable; "Unhealthy for Sensitive Groups" When AQI values are between 101 and 150, members of sensitive groups may experience health effects; "Unhealthy" When AQI values are between 151 and 200 everyone may begin to experience health effects; "Very Unhealthy" AQI values between 201 and 300 trigger a health alert; "Hazardous" AQI values over 300 trigger warnings of emergency conditions (not shown).
Source: U.S. Environmental Protection Agency, Air Quality Index Report, 2018

Air Quality Index Pollutants

Area	Percent of Days when AQI Pollutant was...[2]					
	Carbon Monoxide	Nitrogen Dioxide	Ozone	Sulfur Dioxide	Particulate Matter 2.5	Particulate Matter 10
MSA[1]	0.0	0.0	49.9	0.0	49.9	0.3

Note: (1) Data covers the Madison, WI Metropolitan Statistical Area—see Appendix B for areas included; (2) Based on 365 days with AQI data in 2018. The Air Quality Index (AQI) is an index for reporting daily air quality. EPA calculates the AQI for five major air pollutants regulated by the Clean Air Act: ground-level ozone, particle pollution (also known as particulate matter), carbon monoxide, sulfur dioxide, and nitrogen dioxide. The AQI runs from 0 to 500. The higher the AQI value, the greater the level of air pollution and the greater the health concern.
Source: U.S. Environmental Protection Agency, Air Quality Index Report, 2018

Maximum Air Pollutant Concentrations: Particulate Matter, Ozone, CO and Lead

	Particulate Matter 10 (ug/m³)	Particulate Matter 2.5 Wtd AM (ug/m³)	Particulate Matter 2.5 24-Hr (ug/m³)	Ozone (ppm)	Carbon Monoxide (ppm)	Lead (ug/m³)
MSA[1] Level	42	8.6	23	0.066	n/a	n/a
NAAQS[2]	150	15	35	0.075	9	0.15
Met NAAQS[2]	Yes	Yes	Yes	Yes	n/a	n/a

Note: (1) Data covers the Madison, WI Metropolitan Statistical Area—see Appendix B for areas included; Data from exceptional events are included; (2) National Ambient Air Quality Standards; ppm = parts per million; ug/m³ = micrograms per cubic meter; n/a not available.
Concentrations: Particulate Matter 10 (coarse particulate)—highest second maximum 24-hour concentration; Particulate Matter 2.5 Wtd AM (fine particulate)—highest weighted annual mean concentration; Particulate Matter 2.5 24-Hour (fine particulate)—highest 98th percentile 24-hour concentration; Ozone—highest fourth daily maximum 8-hour concentration; Carbon Monoxide—highest second maximum non-overlapping 8-hour concentration; Lead—maximum running 3-month average
Source: U.S. Environmental Protection Agency, Air Quality Monitoring Information, "Air Quality Statistics by City, 2018"

Maximum Air Pollutant Concentrations: Nitrogen Dioxide and Sulfur Dioxide

	Nitrogen Dioxide AM (ppb)	Nitrogen Dioxide 1-Hr (ppb)	Sulfur Dioxide AM (ppb)	Sulfur Dioxide 1-Hr (ppb)	Sulfur Dioxide 24-Hr (ppb)
MSA[1] Level	n/a	n/a	n/a	3	n/a
NAAQS[2]	53	100	30	75	140
Met NAAQS[2]	n/a	n/a	n/a	Yes	n/a

Note: (1) Data covers the Madison, WI Metropolitan Statistical Area—see Appendix B for areas included; Data from exceptional events are included; (2) National Ambient Air Quality Standards; ppm = parts per million; ug/m³ = micrograms per cubic meter; n/a not available.
Concentrations: Nitrogen Dioxide AM—highest arithmetic mean concentration; Nitrogen Dioxide 1-Hr—highest 98th percentile 1-hour daily maximum concentration; Sulfur Dioxide AM—highest annual mean concentration; Sulfur Dioxide 1-Hr—highest 99th percentile 1-hour daily maximum concentration; Sulfur Dioxide 24-Hr—highest second maximum 24-hour concentration
Source: U.S. Environmental Protection Agency, Air Quality Monitoring Information, "Air Quality Statistics by City, 2018"

Drinking Water

Water System Name	Pop. Served	Primary Water Source Type	Violations[1]
Madison Water Utility	235,000	Ground	68

Note: (1) Total number of violations (both active and inactive) in the EPA database
Source: U.S. Environmental Protection Agency, Office of Ground Water and Drinking Water, Safe Drinking Water Information System (based on data extracted May 5, 2020)

Milwaukee, Wisconsin

Background

Many people associate Milwaukee with beer, perhaps due to the 1970s television show *Laverne and Shirley*, where the main characters worked in a brewery, or to the large influx of German immigrants during the 1840s who left an indelible mark upon the city. However, there is a lot more Wisconsin's largest city than these superficial images suggest.

Milwaukee originally began as a trading post for French fur traders. Its favorable location on the western shore of Lake Michigan and at the confluence of the Milwaukee, Menomonee, and Kinnickinnic rivers made the site a natural meeting place. In 1818, Solomon Laurent Juneau, a son-in-law of a French fur trader, became Milwaukee's first founder and permanent white settler.

During the 1840s, Milwaukee saw a wave of German immigrants hit its shores. Many of these exiles were unsuccessful revolutionaries in the overthrow of the German monarchy. Despite their lack of success back home, these immigrants managed to impart considerable influences in the new country, including: political, with three socialist mayors; economical, with Pabst and Schlitz breweries located in Milwaukee; and cultural, with the Goethe House cultural resource center located in the central library of the Milwaukee Public Library system.

Today, Milwaukee is diverse in many ways. The city is home to many nationalities, including people of Irish, Mexican, Serbian, Scandinavian, Polish, Italian, German, and Puerto Rican descent, as well as a large and thriving African American population. And while the brewing industry does remain a major employer in the city that was once the number one producer of beer worldwide, Milwaukee's economy has widely diversified in recent years. Six Fortune 500 companies—Johnson Controls, Northwestern Mutual, Manpower, Rockwell Automation, Harley-Davidson, and Joy Global—have their headquarters in the city. Among the most prominent industries in Milwaukee today include healthcare, financial services, education, and manufacturing.

Culture and entertainment thrive in Milwaukee. The Milwaukee Public Museum features exhibits devoted to science, technology, and natural history, and includes the first IMAX(r) theater in Wisconsin. The city is also home to the Florentine Opera Company, the Milwaukee Symphony Orchestra, the Milwaukee Ballet, the Milwaukee Repertory Theater, and the Milwaukee Shakespeare Company. The annual lakefront music festival Summerfest is considered the largest music festival in the world with nearly a million people attending yearly. The Milwaukee Art Museum is known worldwide; its Quadracci Pavilion, designed by Santiago Calatrava, is breathtaking. Discovery World, the city's largest science museum, is known for its high-tech, hands-on exhibits. Milwaukee is also home to numerous colleges and universities, including Marquette University and the University of Wisconsin-Milwaukee.

Milwaukee is home to two professional sports teams, the Brewers of Major League Baseball and the Bucks of the National Basketball Association. Both have fielded highly competitive teams in recent years, each featuring a central, Most Valuable Player award-winning star, Christian Yelich and Giannis Antetokounmpo, respectively. In addition, Milwaukee is considered a home market for the popular football team, the Green Bay Packers, who play a little over an hour away. Among college sports, Marquette University's men's basketball team, the Golden Eagles, is a popular draw, playing in the competitive Big East conference.

Milwaukee has a continental climate, and its weather is quite changeable. Temperatures vary widely through the year. In winter, arctic air masses from Canada bring frigid winter temperatures, while in summer high temperatures occur with brisk, hot winds from the southwest. Lake Michigan mitigates against these extremes, as do the other Great Lakes to a lesser extent: in late autumn and winter, the coldest air masses from the northwest are often warmed by the lakes before they can reach the city.

Rankings

General Rankings

- As part of its *Next Stop* series, *Insider* listed 10 places in the U.S. that were either a classic vacation destination experiencing a renaissance or a new up-and-coming hot spot. Whether it is the exploding food scene, experiencing the great outdoors, where cool people are moving to, and not overrun with tourists, according to the website insider.com Milwaukee is a place to visit in 2020. *Insider, "10 Places in the U.S. You Need to Visit in 2020," December 23, 2019*

Business/Finance Rankings

- Based on metro area social media reviews, the employment opinion group Glassdoor surveyed 50 of the most populous U.S. metro areas and equally weighed cost of living, hiring opportunity, and job satisfaction to compose a list of "25 Best Cities for Jobs." Median pay and home value, and number of active job openings was also factored in. The Milwaukee metro area was ranked #19 in overall job satisfaction. *www.glassdoor.com, "Best Cities for Jobs," February 25, 2020*

- The Brookings Institution ranked the nation's largest cities based on income inequality. Milwaukee was ranked #46 (#1 = greatest inequality). Criteria: the "95/20 ratio," a figure representing the income at which a household earns more than 95 percent of all other households, divided by the income at which a household earns more than only 20 percent of all other households. *Brookings Institution, "Household Income Inequality, Largest Cities of 97 Large U.S. Metro Areas, 2014-2016," February 5, 2018*

- The Brookings Institution ranked the 100 largest metro areas in the U.S. based on income inequality. Milwaukee was ranked #17 (#1 = greatest inequality). Criteria: the "95/20 ratio," a figure representing the income at which a household earns more than 95 percent of all other households, divided by the income at which a household earns more than only 20 percent of all other households. *Brookings Institution, "Household Income Inequality, 100 Largest U.S. Metro Areas, 2014-2016," February 5, 2018*

- Payscale.com ranked the 32 largest metro areas in terms of wage growth. The Milwaukee metro area ranked #18. Criteria: private-sector and education professional wage growth between the 4th quarter of 2018 and the 4th quarter of 2019. *PayScale, "Wage Trends by Metro Area-4th Quarter," January 24, 2020*

- The Milwaukee metro area appeared on the Milken Institute "2020 Best Performing Cities" list. Rank: #160 out of 200 large metro areas. Criteria: job growth; wage and salary growth; high-tech output growth. *Milken Institute, "Best-Performing Cities 2020," February 26, 2020*

- *Forbes* ranked the 200 most populous metro areas to determine the nation's "Best Places for Business and Careers." The Milwaukee metro area was ranked #89. Criteria: costs (business and living); job growth (past and projected); income growth; quality of life; educational attainment (college and high school); projected economic growth; cultural and leisure opportunities; workplace tolerance laws; net migration patterns. *Forbes, "The Best Places for Business and Careers 2019: Seattle Still On Top," October 30, 2019*

Education Rankings

- Personal finance website *WalletHub* analyzed the 150 largest U.S. metropolitan statistical areas to determine where the most educated Americans are choosing to settle. Criteria: education levels; percentage of workers with degrees; education quality and attainment gap; public school quality rankings; quality and size of each metro area's universities. Milwaukee was ranked #59 (#1 = most educated city). *www.WalletHub.com, "2019's Most and Least Educated Cities in America," July 22, 2019*

- Milwaukee was selected as one of America's most literate cities. The city ranked #47 out of the 82 largest U.S. cities. Criteria: number of booksellers; library resources; Internet resources; educational attainment; periodical publishing resources; newspaper circulation. *Central Connecticut State University, "America's Most Literate Cities, 2016," March 31, 2017*

Health/Fitness Rankings

- For each of the 100 largest cities in the United States, the American Fitness Index®, published by the American College of Sports Medicine and the Anthem Foundation, evaluated community infrastructure and 33 health behaviors including preventive health, levels of chronic disease conditions, pedestrian safety, air quality, and community resources that support physical activity. Milwaukee ranked #25 for "community fitness." *americanfitnessindex.org, "ACSM American Fitness Index Health and Community Fitness Status of the 100 Largest U.S. Cities," May 14, 2019*

- The Milwaukee metro area was identified as one of the worst cities for bed bugs in America by pest control company Orkin. The area ranked #33 out of 50 based on the number of bed bug treatments Orkin performed from December 2018 to November 2019. *Orkin, "Washington, D.C. Surpasses Baltimore to Secure Top Spot on Orkin's 2020 Bed Bug Cities List," January 13, 2020*

- Milwaukee was identified as a "2020 Spring Allergy Capital." The area ranked #98 out of 100. Three groups of factors were used to identify the most challenging cities for people with allergies during the spring season: annual spring pollen levels; over the counter medicine use; number of board-certified allergy specialists. *Asthma and Allergy Foundation of America, "Spring Allergy Capitals 2020," March 10, 2020*

- Milwaukee was identified as a "2020 Fall Allergy Capital." The area ranked #92 out of 100. Three groups of factors were used to identify the most challenging cities for people with allergies during the fall season: annual fall pollen levels; over the counter medicine use; number of board-certified allergy specialists. *Asthma and Allergy Foundation of America, "Fall Allergy Capitals 2020," March 10, 2020*

- Milwaukee was identified as a "2019 Asthma Capital." The area ranked #10 out of the nation's 100 largest metropolitan areas. Criteria: estimated asthma prevalence; crude death rate from asthma; and ER visits due to asthma. Risk factors that were analyzed but not factored in the rankings: annual pollen score; annual air quality; public smoking laws; number of board-certified asthma specialists; rescue medication use; controller medication use; uninsured rate; poverty rate. *Asthma and Allergy Foundation of America, "Asthma Capitals 2019: The Most Challenging Places to Live With Asthma," May 7, 2019*

- *Men's Health* ranked 100 major U.S. cities in terms of the best cities for men. Milwaukee ranked #82. Criteria: health; fitness; quality of life. *Men's Health, "The Best & Worst Cities for Men Who Want to Be Fit and Happy," January 1, 2016*

- The Milwaukee metro area ranked #102 out of 189 in The Gallup-Sharecare Well-Being Index. Criteria: purpose; social well being; financial health; community and physical health. Results are based on telephone interviews with adults, aged 18 and older, living in metropolitan areas in the 50 U.S. states and the District of Columbia. *Gallup-Sharecare, "State of American Well-Being, 2017 Community Well-Being Rankings" March 2018*

Real Estate Rankings

- FitSmallBusiness looked at 50 of the largest metropolitan areas in the U.S. to determine which metro was the best to start a real estate business. Data was compiled from such sources as: Zillow, Trulia, U.S. Census Bureau, and the Bureau of Labor Statistics. Criteria: location; inventory; annual wages; median sales price of homes; days on the market; median price cut percentage; and other factors that would influence real estate professional growth. The Milwaukee metro area ranked #43. *fitsmallbusiness.com, "The Best Cities to Become a Real Estate Agent in 2018," January 30, 2018*

- *WalletHub* compared the most populated U.S. cities, as well as at least two of the most populated cities in each state, for a total of 179, to determine which had the best markets for real estate agents. Milwaukee ranked #96 where demand was high and pay was the best. Criteria: sales per agent; annual median wage for real-estate agents; monthly average starting salary for real estate agents; real estate job density and competition; unemployment rate; home turnover rate; housing-market health index; and other relevant metrics. *www.WalletHub.com, "2019's Best Places to Be a Real Estate Agent," April 24, 2019*

- Milwaukee was ranked #92 out of 238 metro areas in terms of housing affordability in 2019 by the National Association of Home Builders (#1 = most affordable). Criteria: the share of homes sold in that area affordable to a family earning the local median income, based on standard mortgage underwriting criteria. *National Association of Home Builders®, NAHB-Wells Fargo Housing Opportunity Index, 4th Quarter 2019*

Safety Rankings

- To identify the most dangerous cities in America, 24/7 Wall Street focused on violent crime categories—murder, non-negligent manslaughter, rape, robbery, and aggravated assault—and property crime as reported in the FBI's 2018 annual Uniform Crime Report. Criteria also included median income from American Community Survey and unemployment figures from Bureau of Labor Statistics. For cities with populations over 100,000, Milwaukee was ranked #9. *247wallst.com, "America's Most Dangerous Cities" January 10, 2020*

- Allstate ranked the 200 largest cities in America in terms of driver safety. Milwaukee ranked #61. Criteria: internal property damage claims over a two-year period from January 2016 to December 2017. The report helps increase the importance of safety and awareness behind the wheel. *Allstate, "Allstate America's Best Drivers Report, 2019" June 24, 2019*

- Milwaukee was identified as one of the most dangerous cities in America by NeighborhoodScout. The city ranked #17 out of 100 (#1 = most dangerous). Criteria: number of violent crimes per 1,000 residents. The editors only considered cities with 25,000 or more residents. *NeighborhoodScout.com, "Top 100 Most Dangerous Cities in the U.S. 2020" January 2, 2020*

- The National Insurance Crime Bureau ranked 382 metro areas in the U.S. in terms of per capita rates of vehicle theft. The Milwaukee metro area ranked #56 (#1 = highest rate). Criteria: number of vehicle theft offenses per 100,000 inhabitants in 2018. *National Insurance Crime Bureau, "Hot Spots 2018," June 25, 2019*

Seniors/Retirement Rankings

- From its Best Cities for Successful Aging indexes, the Milken Institute generated rankings for metropolitan areas, weighing data in nine categories—health care, wellness, living arrangements, transportation and convenience, financial characteristics, education, employment, community engagement, and overall livability. The Milwaukee metro area was ranked #33 overall in the large metro area category. *Milken Institute, "Best Cities for Successful Aging, 2017" March 14, 2017*

Sports/Recreation Rankings

- Milwaukee was chosen as one of America's best cities for bicycling. The city ranked #36 out of 50. Criteria: cycling infrastructure that is safe and friendly for all ages; energy and bike culture. The editors only considered cities with populations of 100,000 or more. *Bicycling, "The 50 Best Bike Cities in America," October 10, 2018*

Women/Minorities Rankings

- *Women's Health*, together with the site Yelp, identified the 15 "Wellthiest" spots in the U.S. Milwaukee appeared among the top for happiest, healthiest, outdoorsiest and Zen-iest. *Women's Health, "The 15 Wellthiest Cities in the U.S." July 5, 2017*

- Personal finance website *WalletHub* compared more than 180 U.S. cities—including the 150 most populated U.S. cities, plus at least two of the most populated cities in each state—across two key dimensions, "Hispanic Business-Friendliness" and "Hispanic Purchasing Power", to arrive at the most favorable conditions for Hispanic entrepreneurs. Milwaukee was ranked #165 out of 182. Criteria includes: share of Hispanic-Owned Businesses; Hispanic entrepreneurship rate to median annual income of Hispanics; Small Business-Friendliness score; cost of living; and number of Hispanics with at least a bachelor's degree. *WalletHub.com, "2019's Best Cities for Hispanic Entrepreneurs," May 1, 2019*

Miscellaneous Rankings

- Based on the advice of plugged-in travel influencers and experts, Milwaukee appeared on a *Forbes* list of 25 U.S. cities that should be on anyone's travel wish list. Whether it be quirky things to see and do, historic cities, or mountain getaways, these places are emerging as must-see destinations. *Forbes, "U.S. Travel: 25 Best Places to Visit in 2020," December 19, 2019*

- The watchdog site Charity Navigator conducts an annual study of charities in the nation's major markets both to analyze statistical differences in their financial, accountability, and transparency practices and to track year-to-year variations in individual philanthropic communities. Charity Navigator's analysis demonstrated that the financial, accountability and transparency behaviors of America's largest charities can be influenced by the metropolitan market within which the charity operates. The Milwaukee metro area was ranked #12 among the 30 metro markets in the rating category of Overall Score. *www.charitynavigator.org, "2017 Metro Market Study," May 1, 2017*

- The real estate site Zillow has compiled the 2017 Trick-or-Treat Index, which used its own Home Value Index and Walk Score along with single-family home density, age of residents, and cities with populations of at least 500,000 to determine that Milwaukee ranked #9 for "getting the best candy in the least amount of time." Zillow also zeroes in on the best neighborhoods in its top 20 cities. *www.zillow.com, "20 Best Cities for Trick or Treating in 2017," October 13, 2017*

- *WalletHub* compared the 150 most populated U.S. cities to determine their operating efficiency. A "Quality of Services" score was constructed for each city and then divided by the total budget per capita to reveal which were managed the best. Milwaukee ranked #113. Criteria: financial stability; economy; education; safety; health; infrastructure and pollution. *www.WalletHub.com, "2019's Best- & Worst-Run Cities in America," July 1, 2019*

- Milwaukee was selected as one of "America's Friendliest Cities." The city ranked #10 in the "Friendliest" category. Respondents to an online survey were asked to rate 38 top urban destinations in the United States as to general friendliness, as well as manners, politeness and warm disposition. *Travel + Leisure, "America's Friendliest Cities," October 20, 2017*

Business Environment

CITY FINANCES

City Government Finances

Component	2017 ($000)	2017 ($ per capita)
Total Revenues	1,554,524	2,590
Total Expenditures	1,541,532	2,569
Debt Outstanding	1,506,976	2,511
Cash and Securities[1]	5,325,249	8,873

Note: (1) Cash and security holdings of a government at the close of its fiscal year, including those of its dependent agencies, utilities, and liquor stores.
Source: U.S. Census Bureau, State & Local Government Finances 2017

City Government Revenue by Source

Source	2017 ($000)	2017 ($ per capita)	2017 (%)
General Revenue			
From Federal Government	44,384	74	2.9
From State Government	288,396	481	18.6
From Local Governments	45,531	76	2.9
Taxes			
Property	269,486	449	17.3
Sales and Gross Receipts	0	0	0.0
Personal Income	0	0	0.0
Corporate Income	0	0	0.0
Motor Vehicle License	0	0	0.0
Other Taxes	16,767	28	1.1
Current Charges	233,499	389	15.0
Liquor Store	0	0	0.0
Utility	80,043	133	5.1
Employee Retirement	533,972	890	34.3

Source: U.S. Census Bureau, State & Local Government Finances 2017

City Government Expenditures by Function

Function	2017 ($000)	2017 ($ per capita)	2017 (%)
General Direct Expenditures			
Air Transportation	0	0	0.0
Corrections	6,332	10	0.4
Education	0	0	0.0
Employment Security Administration	0	0	0.0
Financial Administration	18,302	30	1.2
Fire Protection	110,894	184	7.2
General Public Buildings	36,832	61	2.4
Governmental Administration, Other	120,316	200	7.8
Health	22,926	38	1.5
Highways	152,415	254	9.9
Hospitals	0	0	0.0
Housing and Community Development	32,553	54	2.1
Interest on General Debt	48,554	80	3.1
Judicial and Legal	20,129	33	1.3
Libraries	27,976	46	1.8
Parking	24,506	40	1.6
Parks and Recreation	3,852	6	0.2
Police Protection	315,980	526	20.5
Public Welfare	0	0	0.0
Sewerage	53,002	88	3.4
Solid Waste Management	36,713	61	2.4
Veterans' Services	0	0	0.0
Liquor Store	0	0	0.0
Utility	73,447	122	4.8
Employee Retirement	351,338	585	22.8

Source: U.S. Census Bureau, State & Local Government Finances 2017

DEMOGRAPHICS

Population Growth

Area	1990 Census	2000 Census	2010 Census	2018* Estimate	Population Growth (%) 1990-2018	Population Growth (%) 2010-2018
City	628,095	596,974	594,833	596,886	-5.0	0.3
MSA[1]	1,432,149	1,500,741	1,555,908	1,575,907	10.0	1.3
U.S.	248,709,873	281,421,906	308,745,538	322,903,030	29.8	4.6

Note: (1) Figures cover the Milwaukee-Waukesha-West Allis, WI Metropolitan Statistical Area—see Appendix B for areas included; (*) 2014-2018 5-year estimated population
Source: U.S. Census Bureau, 1990 Census, Census 2000, Census 2010, 2014-2018 American Community Survey 5-Year Estimates

Household Size

Area	Persons in Household (%) One	Two	Three	Four	Five	Six	Seven or More	Average Household Size
City	36.0	29.2	14.3	10.6	5.9	2.4	1.7	2.50
MSA[1]	31.3	34.1	14.3	12.1	5.3	1.8	1.0	2.50
U.S.	27.7	33.9	15.7	13.0	6.0	2.3	1.4	2.60

Note: (1) Figures cover the Milwaukee-Waukesha-West Allis, WI Metropolitan Statistical Area—see Appendix B for areas included
Source: U.S. Census Bureau, 2014-2018 American Community Survey 5-Year Estimates

Race

Area	White Alone[2] (%)	Black Alone[2] (%)	Asian Alone[2] (%)	AIAN[3] Alone[2] (%)	NHOPI[4] Alone[2] (%)	Other Race Alone[2] (%)	Two or More Races (%)
City	44.6	38.8	4.3	0.6	0.0	7.7	4.0
MSA[1]	72.9	16.6	3.7	0.4	0.0	3.6	2.7
U.S.	72.7	12.7	5.4	0.8	0.2	4.9	3.2

Note: (1) Figures cover the Milwaukee-Waukesha-West Allis, WI Metropolitan Statistical Area—see Appendix B for areas included; (2) Alone is defined as not being in combination with one or more other races; (3) American Indian and Alaska Native; (4) Native Hawaiian and Other Pacific Islander
Source: U.S. Census Bureau, 2014-2018 American Community Survey 5-Year Estimates

Hispanic or Latino Origin

Area	Total (%)	Mexican (%)	Puerto Rican (%)	Cuban (%)	Other (%)
City	18.8	13.0	4.5	0.2	1.1
MSA[1]	10.5	7.1	2.3	0.1	0.9
U.S.	17.8	11.2	1.7	0.7	4.2

Note: Persons of Hispanic or Latino origin can be of any race; (1) Figures cover the Milwaukee-Waukesha-West Allis, WI Metropolitan Statistical Area—see Appendix B for areas included
Source: U.S. Census Bureau, 2014-2018 American Community Survey 5-Year Estimates

Segregation

Type	Segregation Indices[1] 1990	2000	2010	2010 Rank[2]	Percent Change 1990-2000	Percent Change 1990-2010	Percent Change 2000-2010
Black/White	82.8	83.3	81.5	1	0.6	-1.2	-1.8
Asian/White	42.2	43.4	40.7	52	1.2	-1.5	-2.7
Hispanic/White	56.4	59.5	57.0	9	3.2	0.7	-2.5

Note: All figures cover the Metropolitan Statistical Area—see Appendix B for areas included; Figures are based on an analysis of 1990, 2000, and 2010 Census Decennial Census tract data by William H. Frey, Brookings Institution and the University of Michigan Social Science Data Analysis Network. In this analysis all racial groups (whites, blacks, and asians) are non-Hispanic members of those races. Hispanics are shown as a separate category; (1) Segregation Indices are Dissimilarity Indices that measure the degree to which the minority group is distributed differently than whites across census tracts. They range from 0 (complete integration) to 100 (complete segregation) where the value indicates the percentage of the minority group that needs to move to be distributed exactly like whites; (2) Ranges from 1 (most segregated) to 102 (least segregated); n/a not available.
Source: www.CensusScope.org

Ancestry

Area	German	Irish	English	American	Italian	Polish	French[2]	Scottish	Dutch
City	16.5	5.9	2.2	1.2	2.7	6.7	1.3	0.5	0.7
MSA[1]	33.6	9.9	4.3	2.2	4.3	10.8	2.5	0.9	1.3
U.S.	13.7	9.9	7.3	6.4	5.2	2.8	2.4	1.7	1.2

Note: Figures are the percentage of the total population reporting a particular ancestry. The nine most commonly reported ancestries in the U.S. are shown. Figures include multiple ancestries (e.g. if a person reported being Irish and Italian, they were included in both columns); (1) Figures cover the Milwaukee-Waukesha-West Allis, WI Metropolitan Statistical Area—see Appendix B for areas included; (2) Excludes Basque
Source: U.S. Census Bureau, 2014-2018 American Community Survey 5-Year Estimates

Foreign-born Population

Area	Percent of Population Born in								
	Any Foreign Country	Asia	Mexico	Europe	Caribbean	Central America[2]	South America	Africa	Canada
City	9.8	2.8	4.8	0.8	0.3	0.2	0.2	0.7	0.1
MSA[1]	7.3	2.7	2.3	1.3	0.2	0.2	0.2	0.4	0.1
U.S.	13.5	4.1	3.5	1.5	1.3	1.1	0.9	0.7	0.3

Note: (1) Figures cover the Milwaukee-Waukesha-West Allis, WI Metropolitan Statistical Area—see Appendix B for areas included; (2) Excludes Mexico.
Source: U.S. Census Bureau, 2014-2018 American Community Survey 5-Year Estimates

Marital Status

Area	Never Married	Now Married[2]	Separated	Widowed	Divorced
City	53.0	29.9	2.0	4.7	10.4
MSA[1]	36.8	46.3	1.2	5.5	10.1
U.S.	33.3	48.1	2.0	5.8	10.8

Note: Figures are percentages and cover the population 15 years of age and older; (1) Figures cover the Milwaukee-Waukesha-West Allis, WI Metropolitan Statistical Area—see Appendix B for areas included; (2) Excludes separated
Source: U.S. Census Bureau, 2014-2018 American Community Survey 5-Year Estimates

Disability by Age

Area	All Ages	Under 18 Years Old	18 to 64 Years Old	65 Years and Over
City	13.3	5.9	12.1	39.7
MSA[1]	11.5	4.4	9.4	32.4
U.S.	12.6	4.2	10.3	35.0

Note: Figures show percent of the civilian noninstitutionalized population that reported having a disability. Disability status is determined from six types of difficulty: vision, hearing, cognitive, ambulatory, self-care, and independent living. For children under 5 years old, hearing and vision difficulty are used to determine disability status. For children between the ages of 5 and 14, disability status is determined from hearing, vision, cognitive, ambulatory, and self-care difficulties. For people aged 15 years and older, they are considered to have a disability if they have difficulty with any one of the six difficulty types; Note: (1) Figures cover the Milwaukee-Waukesha-West Allis, WI Metropolitan Statistical Area—see Appendix B for areas included
Source: U.S. Census Bureau, 2014-2018 American Community Survey 5-Year Estimates

Age

Area	Percent of Population									Median Age
	Under Age 5	Age 5–19	Age 20–34	Age 35–44	Age 45–54	Age 55–64	Age 65–74	Age 75–84	Age 85+	
City	7.6	21.9	25.7	12.6	11.4	10.6	6.0	2.7	1.5	31.4
MSA[1]	6.3	19.7	20.4	12.4	13.2	13.3	8.3	4.2	2.2	37.7
U.S.	6.1	19.3	20.7	12.6	13.2	12.8	8.8	4.5	1.9	37.9

Note: (1) Figures cover the Milwaukee-Waukesha-West Allis, WI Metropolitan Statistical Area—see Appendix B for areas included
Source: U.S. Census Bureau, 2014-2018 American Community Survey 5-Year Estimates

Gender

Area	Males	Females	Males per 100 Females
City	287,646	309,240	93.0
MSA[1]	767,869	808,038	95.0
U.S.	158,984,190	163,918,840	97.0

Note: (1) Figures cover the Milwaukee-Waukesha-West Allis, WI Metropolitan Statistical Area—see Appendix B for areas included
Source: U.S. Census Bureau, 2014-2018 American Community Survey 5-Year Estimates

Religious Groups by Family

Area	Catholic	Baptist	Non-Den.	Methodist[2]	Lutheran	LDS[3]	Pente-costal	Presby-terian[4]	Muslim[5]	Judaism
MSA[1]	24.6	3.1	3.9	1.6	10.8	0.4	2.0	1.6	0.6	0.6
U.S.	19.1	9.3	4.0	4.0	2.3	2.0	1.9	1.6	0.8	0.7

Note: Figures are the number of adherents as a percentage of the total population; (1) Figures cover the Milwaukee-Waukesha-West Allis, WI Metropolitan Statistical Area—see Appendix B for areas included; (2) Methodist/Pietist; (3) Latter Day Saints; (4) Reformed; (5) Figures are estimates
Source: Association of Statisticians of American Religious Bodies, 2010 U.S. Religion Census: Religious Congregations & Membership Study

Religious Groups by Tradition

Area	Catholic	Evangelical Protestant	Mainline Protestant	Other Tradition	Black Protestant	Orthodox
MSA[1]	24.6	14.6	7.2	2.3	2.5	0.6
U.S.	19.1	16.2	7.3	4.3	1.6	0.3

Note: Figures are the number of adherents as a percentage of the total population; (1) Figures cover the Milwaukee-Waukesha-West Allis, WI Metropolitan Statistical Area—see Appendix B for areas included
Source: Association of Statisticians of American Religious Bodies, 2010 U.S. Religion Census: Religious Congregations & Membership Study

ECONOMY

Gross Metropolitan Product

Area	2017	2018	2019	2020	Rank[2]
MSA[1]	104.6	109.2	112.8	116.2	37

Note: Figures are in billions of dollars; (1) Figures cover the Milwaukee-Waukesha-West Allis, WI Metropolitan Statistical Area—see Appendix B for areas included; (2) Rank is based on 2018 data and ranges from 1 to 381
Source: U.S. Conference of Mayors, U.S. Metro Economies: GMP & Employment 2018-2020, September 2019

Economic Growth

Area	2015-17 (%)	2018 (%)	2019 (%)	2020 (%)	Rank[2]
MSA[1]	0.9	2.1	1.5	0.9	243
U.S.	1.9	2.9	2.3	2.1	–

Note: Figures are real gross metropolitan product (GMP) growth rates and represent average annual percent change; (1) Figures cover the Milwaukee-Waukesha-West Allis, WI Metropolitan Statistical Area—see Appendix B for areas included; (2) Rank is based on 2017 2-year average annual percent change and ranges from 1 to 381
Source: U.S. Conference of Mayors, U.S. Metro Economies: GMP & Employment 2018-2020, September 2019

Metropolitan Area Exports

Area	2013	2014	2015	2016	2017	2018	Rank[2]
MSA[1]	8,874.6	8,696.0	7,953.6	7,256.2	7,279.1	7,337.6	46

Note: Figures are in millions of dollars; (1) Figures cover the Milwaukee-Waukesha-West Allis, WI Metropolitan Statistical Area—see Appendix B for areas included; (2) Rank is based on 2018 data and ranges from 1 to 387
Source: U.S. Department of Commerce, International Trade Administration, Office of Trade and Economic Analysis, Industry and Analysis, Exports by Metropolitan Area, data extracted April 15, 2020

Building Permits

Area	Single-Family			Multi-Family			Total		
	2017	2018	Pct. Chg.	2017	2018	Pct. Chg.	2017	2018	Pct. Chg.
City	7	39	457.1	708	717	1.3	715	756	5.7
MSA[1]	1,559	1,712	9.8	2,085	2,057	-1.3	3,644	3,769	3.4
U.S.	820,000	855,300	4.3	462,000	473,500	2.5	1,282,000	1,328,800	3.7

Note: (1) Figures cover the Milwaukee-Waukesha-West Allis, WI Metropolitan Statistical Area—see Appendix B for areas included; Figures represent new, privately-owned housing units authorized (unadjusted data); All permit data are based on estimates with imputation
Source: U.S. Census Bureau, Manufacturing, Mining, and Construction Statistics, Building Permits, 2017, 2018

Bankruptcy Filings

Area	Business Filings			Nonbusiness Filings		
	2018	2019	% Chg.	2018	2019	% Chg.
Milwaukee County	35	43	22.9	6,116	6,315	3.3
U.S.	22,232	22,780	2.5	751,186	752,160	0.1

Note: Business filings include Chapter 7, Chapter 9, Chapter 11, Chapter 12, Chapter 13, Chapter 15, and Section 304; Nonbusiness filings include Chapter 7, Chapter 11, and Chapter 13
Source: Administrative Office of the U.S. Courts, Business and Nonbusiness Bankruptcy, County Cases Commenced by Chapter of the Bankruptcy Code, During the 12-Month Period Ending December 31, 2018 and Business and Nonbusiness Bankruptcy, County Cases Commenced by Chapter of the Bankruptcy Code, During the 12-Month Period Ending December 31, 2019

Housing Vacancy Rates

Area	Gross Vacancy Rate[2] (%)			Year-Round Vacancy Rate[3] (%)			Rental Vacancy Rate[4] (%)			Homeowner Vacancy Rate[5] (%)		
	2017	2018	2019	2017	2018	2019	2017	2018	2019	2017	2018	2019
MSA[1]	7.9	8.1	8.0	7.0	7.8	7.8	6.5	5.9	6.6	0.9	1.4	0.6
U.S.	12.7	12.3	12.0	9.9	9.7	9.5	7.2	6.9	6.7	1.6	1.5	1.4

Note: (1) Figures cover the Milwaukee-Waukesha-West Allis, WI Metropolitan Statistical Area—see Appendix B for areas included; (2) The percentage of the total housing inventory that is vacant; (3) The percentage of the housing inventory (excluding seasonal units) that is year-round vacant; (4) The percentage of rental inventory that is vacant for rent; (5) The percentage of homeowner inventory that is vacant for sale
Source: U.S. Census Bureau, Housing Vacancies and Homeownership Annual Statistics: 2017, 2018, 2019

INCOME

Income

Area	Per Capita ($)	Median Household ($)	Average Household ($)
City	22,605	40,036	55,556
MSA[1]	34,141	59,751	83,215
U.S.	32,621	60,293	84,938

Note: (1) Figures cover the Milwaukee-Waukesha-West Allis, WI Metropolitan Statistical Area—see Appendix B for areas included
Source: U.S. Census Bureau, 2014-2018 American Community Survey 5-Year Estimates

Household Income Distribution

Area	Percent of Households Earning							
	Under $15,000	$15,000 -$24,999	$25,000 -$34,999	$35,000 -$49,999	$50,000 -$74,999	$75,000 -$99,999	$100,000 -$149,999	$150,000 and up
City	19.0	13.4	12.2	14.6	17.3	10.2	9.0	4.3
MSA[1]	11.0	9.6	9.1	12.8	17.4	12.8	15.3	12.1
U.S.	10.9	9.3	9.3	12.6	17.5	12.5	14.6	13.3

Note: (1) Figures cover the Milwaukee-Waukesha-West Allis, WI Metropolitan Statistical Area—see Appendix B for areas included
Source: U.S. Census Bureau, 2014-2018 American Community Survey 5-Year Estimates

Poverty Rate

Area	All Ages	Under 18 Years Old	18 to 64 Years Old	65 Years and Over
City	26.6	38.4	23.7	14.2
MSA[1]	14.0	20.3	12.9	8.4
U.S.	14.1	19.5	13.2	9.3

Note: Figures are percentage of people whose income during the past 12 months was below the poverty level; (1) Figures cover the Milwaukee-Waukesha-West Allis, WI Metropolitan Statistical Area—see Appendix B for areas included
Source: U.S. Census Bureau, 2014-2018 American Community Survey 5-Year Estimates

EMPLOYMENT

Labor Force and Employment

Area	Civilian Labor Force			Workers Employed		
	Dec. 2018	Dec. 2019	% Chg.	Dec. 2018	Dec. 2019	% Chg.
City	270,854	271,222	0.1	261,547	260,380	-0.4
MSA[1]	811,245	811,069	0.0	788,833	785,335	-0.4
U.S.	162,510,000	164,007,000	0.9	156,481,000	158,504,000	1.3

Note: Data is not seasonally adjusted and covers workers 16 years of age and older; (1) Figures cover the Milwaukee-Waukesha-West Allis, WI Metropolitan Statistical Area—see Appendix B for areas included
Source: Bureau of Labor Statistics, Local Area Unemployment Statistics

Unemployment Rate

Area	2019											
	Jan.	Feb.	Mar.	Apr.	May	Jun.	Jul.	Aug.	Sep.	Oct.	Nov.	Dec.
City	4.4	4.5	4.5	4.0	4.1	5.2	5.3	5.1	4.3	4.0	4.2	4.0
MSA[1]	3.6	3.6	3.7	3.2	3.3	4.1	4.0	3.8	3.3	3.2	3.3	3.2
U.S.	4.4	4.1	3.9	3.3	3.4	3.8	4.0	3.8	3.3	3.3	3.3	3.4

Note: Data is not seasonally adjusted and covers workers 16 years of age and older; (1) Figures cover the Milwaukee-Waukesha-West Allis, WI Metropolitan Statistical Area—see Appendix B for areas included
Source: Bureau of Labor Statistics, Local Area Unemployment Statistics

Average Wages

Occupation	$/Hr.	Occupation	$/Hr.
Accountants and Auditors	34.90	Maintenance and Repair Workers	20.80
Automotive Mechanics	20.50	Marketing Managers	64.00
Bookkeepers	20.20	Network and Computer Systems Admin.	37.80
Carpenters	27.20	Nurses, Licensed Practical	24.10
Cashiers	11.20	Nurses, Registered	35.60
Computer Programmers	40.70	Nursing Assistants	14.90
Computer Systems Analysts	39.10	Office Clerks, General	18.20
Computer User Support Specialists	25.50	Physical Therapists	42.20
Construction Laborers	23.60	Physicians	113.60
Cooks, Restaurant	13.20	Plumbers, Pipefitters and Steamfitters	36.30
Customer Service Representatives	20.00	Police and Sheriff's Patrol Officers	35.00
Dentists	103.20	Postal Service Mail Carriers	25.10
Electricians	33.40	Real Estate Sales Agents	25.90
Engineers, Electrical	42.00	Retail Salespersons	13.10
Fast Food and Counter Workers	10.20	Sales Representatives, Technical/Scientific	43.70
Financial Managers	70.60	Secretaries, Exc. Legal/Medical/Executive	18.90
First-Line Supervisors of Office Workers	30.20	Security Guards	14.70
General and Operations Managers	70.80	Surgeons	n/a
Hairdressers/Cosmetologists	15.30	Teacher Assistants, Exc. Postsecondary*	15.40
Home Health and Personal Care Aides	11.80	Teachers, Secondary School, Exc. Sp. Ed.*	30.10
Janitors and Cleaners	13.80	Telemarketers	15.30
Landscaping/Groundskeeping Workers	16.20	Truck Drivers, Heavy/Tractor-Trailer	23.70
Lawyers	70.50	Truck Drivers, Light/Delivery Services	16.70
Maids and Housekeeping Cleaners	12.40	Waiters and Waitresses	11.10

Note: Wage data covers the Milwaukee-Waukesha-West Allis, WI Metropolitan Statistical Area—see Appendix B for areas included; (*) Hourly wages were calculated from annual wage data based on a 40 hour work week; n/a not available.
Source: Bureau of Labor Statistics, Metro Area Occupational Employment & Wage Estimates, May 2019

Employment by Occupation

Occupation Classification	City (%)	MSA[1] (%)	U.S. (%)
Management, Business, Science, and Arts	31.2	40.0	37.9
Natural Resources, Construction, and Maintenance	6.0	6.3	8.9
Production, Transportation, and Material Moving	19.0	15.0	13.3
Sales and Office	20.1	21.7	22.1
Service	23.6	17.0	17.9

Note: Figures cover employed civilians 16 years of age and older; (1) Figures cover the Milwaukee-Waukesha-West Allis, WI Metropolitan Statistical Area—see Appendix B for areas included
Source: U.S. Census Bureau, 2014-2018 American Community Survey 5-Year Estimates

Employment by Industry

Sector	MSA[1] Number of Employees	MSA[1] Percent of Total	U.S. Percent of Total
Construction	31,500	3.6	4.9
Education and Health Services	178,200	20.3	16.1
Financial Activities	50,400	5.7	5.8
Government	87,200	9.9	15.0
Information	13,300	1.5	1.9
Leisure and Hospitality	78,800	9.0	10.8
Manufacturing	118,500	13.5	8.4
Mining and Logging	400	<0.1	0.5
Other Services	46,600	5.3	3.9
Professional and Business Services	124,300	14.1	14.1
Retail Trade	78,900	9.0	10.6
Transportation, Warehousing, and Utilities	32,000	3.6	4.2
Wholesale Trade	39,000	4.4	3.9

Note: Figures are non-farm employment as of December 2019. Figures are not seasonally adjusted and include workers 16 years of age and older; (1) Figures cover the Milwaukee-Waukesha-West Allis, WI Metropolitan Statistical Area—see Appendix B for areas included
Source: Bureau of Labor Statistics, Current Employment Statistics, Employment, Hours, and Earnings

Occupations with Greatest Projected Employment Growth: 2019 – 2021

Occupation[1]	2019 Employment	2021 Projected Employment	Numeric Employment Change	Percent Employment Change
Personal Care Aides	67,700	71,470	3,770	5.6
Combined Food Preparation and Serving Workers, Including Fast Food	76,450	78,390	1,940	2.5
Registered Nurses	57,510	58,900	1,390	2.4
Heavy and Tractor-Trailer Truck Drivers	53,400	54,730	1,330	2.5
Laborers and Freight, Stock, and Material Movers, Hand	54,370	55,330	960	1.8
Software Developers, Applications	16,690	17,520	830	5.0
Cooks, Restaurant	24,360	25,180	820	3.4
Janitors and Cleaners, Except Maids and Housekeeping Cleaners	49,840	50,600	760	1.5
Maintenance and Repair Workers, General	36,060	36,740	680	1.9
Elementary School Teachers, Except Special Education	35,490	36,150	660	1.9

Note: Projections cover Wisconsin; (1) Sorted by numeric employment change
Source: www.projectionscentral.com, State Occupational Projections, 2019–2021 Short-Term Projections

Fastest Growing Occupations: 2019 – 2021

Occupation[1]	2019 Employment	2021 Projected Employment	Numeric Employment Change	Percent Employment Change
Locomotive Engineers	880	990	110	12.5
Reservation and Transportation Ticket Agents and Travel Clerks	1,150	1,270	120	10.4
Railroad Conductors and Yardmasters	690	760	70	10.1
Nonfarm Animal Caretakers	7,590	8,180	590	7.8
Aircraft Mechanics and Service Technicians	850	910	60	7.1
Physician Assistants	2,040	2,180	140	6.9
Nurse Practitioners	3,080	3,270	190	6.2
Computer Numerically Controlled Machine Tool Programmers, Metal and Plastic	1,510	1,600	90	6.0
Taxi Drivers and Chauffeurs	9,130	9,670	540	5.9
Personal Care Aides	67,700	71,470	3,770	5.6

Note: Projections cover Wisconsin; (1) Sorted by percent employment change and excludes occupations with numeric employment change less than 50
Source: www.projectionscentral.com, State Occupational Projections, 2019–2021 Short-Term Projections

TAXES

State Corporate Income Tax Rates

State	Tax Rate (%)	Income Brackets ($)	Num. of Brackets	Financial Institution Tax Rate (%)[a]	Federal Income Tax Ded.
Wisconsin	7.9	Flat rate	1	7.9	No

Note: Tax rates as of January 1, 2020; (a) Rates listed are the corporate income tax rate applied to financial institutions or excise taxes based on income.
Source: Federation of Tax Administrators, State Corporate Income Tax Rates, January 1, 2020

State Individual Income Tax Rates

State	Tax Rate (%)	Income Brackets ($)	Personal Exemptions ($) Single	Married	Depend.	Standard Ded. ($) Single	Married
Wisconsin (a)	4.0 - 7.65	11,970 - 263,480 (w)	700	1,400	700	11,050	22,999 (y)

Note: Tax rates as of January 1, 2020; Local- and county-level taxes are not included; Federal income tax is not deductible on state income tax returns; (a) 19 states have statutory provision for automatically adjusting to the rate of inflation the dollar values of the income tax brackets, standard deductions, and/or personal exemptions. Michigan indexes the personal exemption only. Oregon does not index the income brackets for $125,000 and over; (w) The Wisconsin income brackets reported are for single individuals. For married taxpayers filing jointly, the same tax rates apply income brackets ranging from $15,960, to $351,310; (y) Alabama standard deduction is phased out for incomes over $23,000. Rhode Island exemptions & standard deductions phased out for incomes over $203,850; Wisconsin standard deduciton phases out for income over $15,939.
Source: Federation of Tax Administrators, State Individual Income Tax Rates, January 1, 2020

Various State Sales and Excise Tax Rates

State	State Sales Tax (%)	Gasoline[1] (¢/gal.)	Cigarette[2] ($/pack)	Spirits[3] ($/gal.)	Wine[4] ($/gal.)	Beer[5] ($/gal.)	Recreational Marijuana (%)
Wisconsin	5	32.9	2.52	3.25	0.25	0.06	Not legal

Note: All tax rates as of January 1, 2020; (1) The American Petroleum Institute has developed a methodology for determining the average tax rate on a gallon of fuel. Rates may include any of the following: excise taxes, environmental fees, storage tank fees, other fees or taxes, general sales tax, and local taxes; (2) The federal excise tax of $1.0066 per pack and local taxes are not included; (3) Rates are those applicable to off-premise sales of 40% alcohol by volume (a.b.v.) distilled spirits in 750ml containers. Local excise taxes are excluded; (4) Rates are those applicable to off-premise sales of 11% a.b.v. non-carbonated wine in 750ml containers; (5) Rates are those applicable to off-premise sales of 4.7% a.b.v. beer in 12 ounce containers.
Source: Tax Foundation, 2020 Facts & Figures: How Does Your State Compare?

State Business Tax Climate Index Rankings

State	Overall Rank	Corporate Tax Rank	Individual Income Tax Rank	Sales Tax Rank	Property Tax Rank	Unemployment Insurance Tax Rank
Wisconsin	26	30	37	7	23	37

Note: The index is a measure of how each state's tax laws affect economic performance. The lower the rank, the more favorable a state's tax system is for business. States without a given tax are given a ranking of 1. The scores/rankings for the District of Columbia do not affect other states. The 2020 index represents the tax climate as of July 1, 2019.
Source: Tax Foundation, State Business Tax Climate Index 2020

COMMERCIAL REAL ESTATE

Office Market

Market Area	Inventory (sq. ft.)	Vacancy Rate (%)	Under Construction (sq. ft.)	YTD Net Absorption (sq. ft.)	Total Average Asking Rent ($/sq. ft./year)
Milwaukee	36,027,933	16.4	835,282	117,111	18.58
National	4,923,349,992	13.0	102,814,961	2,049,925	29.54

Source: Newmark Grubb Knight Frank, National Office Market Report, 1st Quarter 2020

Industrial/Warehouse/R&D Market

Market Area	Inventory (sq. ft.)	Vacancy Rate (%)	Under Construction (sq. ft.)	YTD Net Absorption (sq. ft.)	Total Average Asking Rent ($/sq. ft./year)
Milwaukee	241,712,104	4.1	4,467,505	522,844	4.33
National	15,332,123,451	5.4	322,705,045	48,296,842	7.54

Source: Newmark Grubb Knight Frank, National Industrial Market Report, 1st Quarter 2020

COMMERCIAL UTILITIES

Typical Monthly Electric Bills

Area	Commercial Service ($/month)		Industrial Service ($/month)	
	1,500 kWh	40 kW demand 14,000 kWh	1,000 kW demand 200,000 kWh	50,000 kW demand 32,500,000 kWh
City	213	1,724	27,445	2,686,559
Average[1]	203	1,612	25,706	2,520,671

Note: Figures are based on annualized rates; (1) Average based on 187 utilities surveyed
Source: Edison Electric Institute, Typical Bills and Average Rates Report, Summer 2019

TRANSPORTATION

Means of Transportation to Work

Area	Car/Truck/Van Drove Alone	Car/Truck/Van Car-pooled	Public Transportation Bus	Public Transportation Subway	Public Transportation Railroad	Bicycle	Walked	Other Means	Worked at Home
City	72.3	10.3	7.5	0.0	0.1	0.9	4.7	0.9	3.4
MSA[1]	80.8	7.9	3.3	0.0	0.1	0.5	2.6	0.8	4.1
U.S.	76.4	9.1	2.5	1.9	0.6	0.6	2.7	1.3	4.9

Note: Figures are percentages and cover workers 16 years of age and older; (1) Figures cover the Milwaukee-Waukesha-West Allis, WI Metropolitan Statistical Area—see Appendix B for areas included
Source: U.S. Census Bureau, 2014-2018 American Community Survey 5-Year Estimates

Travel Time to Work

Area	Less Than 10 Minutes	10 to 19 Minutes	20 to 29 Minutes	30 to 44 Minutes	45 to 59 Minutes	60 to 89 Minutes	90 Minutes or More
City	10.4	36.6	25.5	19.0	4.1	2.9	1.4
MSA[1]	12.1	31.6	25.6	21.1	5.6	2.6	1.3
U.S.	12.5	28.7	20.9	20.7	8.2	6.3	2.8

Note: Note: Figures are percentages and include workers 16 years old and over; (1) Figures cover the Milwaukee-Waukesha-West Allis, WI Metropolitan Statistical Area—see Appendix B for areas included
Source: U.S. Census Bureau, 2014-2018 American Community Survey 5-Year Estimates

Key Congestion Measures

Area	1982	1992	2002	2012	2017
Annual Hours of Delay, Total (000)	8,634	20,774	30,159	37,638	42,146
Annual Hours of Delay, Per Auto Commuter	13	28	34	41	46
Annual Congestion Cost, Total (million $)	67	222	414	691	788
Annual Congestion Cost, Per Auto Commuter ($)	398	658	744	728	790

Source: Texas A&M Transportation Institute, 2019 Urban Mobility Report

Freeway Travel Time Index

Area	1982	1987	1992	1997	2002	2007	2012	2017
Urban Area Index[1]	1.06	1.10	1.13	1.15	1.15	1.16	1.17	1.17
Urban Area Rank[1,2]	43	36	37	41	61	63	50	49

Note: Freeway Travel Time Index—the ratio of travel time in the peak period to the travel time at free-flow conditions. For example, a value of 1.30 indicates a 20-minute free-flow trip takes 26 minutes in the peak (20 minutes x 1.30 = 26 minutes); (1) Covers the Milwaukee WI urban area; (2) Rank is based on 101 larger urban areas (#1 = highest travel time index)
Source: Texas A&M Transportation Institute, 2019 Urban Mobility Report

Public Transportation

Agency Name / Mode of Transportation	Vehicles Operated in Maximum Service[1]	Annual Unlinked Passenger Trips[2] (in thous.)	Annual Passenger Miles[3] (in thous.)
Milwaukee County Transit System (MCTS)			
Bus (purchased transportation)	321	30,429.8	106,718.1
Demand Response (purchased transportation)	84	454.9	3,099.2

Note: (1) Number of revenue vehicles operated by the given mode and type of service to meet the annual maximum service requirement. This is the revenue vehicle count during the peak season of the year; on the week and day that maximum service is provided. Vehicles operated in maximum service (VOMS) exclude atypical days and one-time special events; (2) Number of passengers who boarded public transportation vehicles. Passengers are counted each time they board a vehicle no matter how many vehicles they use to travel from their origin to their destination. (3) Sum of the distances ridden by all passengers during the entire fiscal year.
Source: Federal Transit Administration, National Transit Database, 2018

Air Transportation

Airport Name and Code / Type of Service	Passenger Airlines[1]	Passenger Enplanements	Freight Carriers[2]	Freight (lbs)
General Mitchell International (MKE)				
Domestic service (U.S. carriers - 2019)	31	3,346,013	14	77,163,562
International service (U.S. carriers - 2018)	2	3,378	2	2,229,330

Note: (1) Includes all U.S.-based major, minor and commuter airlines that carried at least one passenger during the year; (2) Includes all U.S.-based airlines and freight carriers that transported at least one pound of freight during the year.
Source: Bureau of Transportation Statistics, The Intermodal Transportation Database, Air Carriers: T-100 Domestic Market (U.S. Carriers), 2019; Bureau of Transportation Statistics, The Intermodal Transportation Database, Air Carriers: T-100 International Market (U.S. Carriers), 2018

Other Transportation Statistics

Major Highways:	I-43; I-94
Amtrak Service:	Yes
Major Waterways/Ports:	Port of Milwaukee; Lake Michigan; Milwaukee River

Source: Amtrak.com; Google Maps

BUSINESSES

Major Business Headquarters

Company Name	Industry	Rankings Fortune[1]	Forbes[2]
Harley-Davidson	Transportation Equipment	492	-
ManpowerGroup	Temporary Help	141	-
Northwestern Mutual	Insurance, Life, Health (Mutual)	111	-
Rockwell Automation	Electronics, Electrical Equip.	452	-
WEC Energy Group	Utilities, Gas and Electric	398	-

Note: (1) Companies that produce a 10-K are ranked 1 to 500 based on 2018 revenue; (2) All private companies with at least $2 billion in annual revenue through the end of their most current fiscal year are ranked 1 to 228; companies listed are headquartered in the city; dashes indicate no ranking
Source: Fortune, "Fortune 500," June 2019; Forbes, "America's Largest Private Companies," 2019 Rankings

Fast-Growing Businesses

According to *Inc.*, Milwaukee is home to one of America's 500 fastest-growing private companies: **Spike Brewing Equipment** (#426). Criteria: must be an independent, privately-held, for-profit, U.S. corporation, proprietorship or partnership as of December 31, 2018; revenues must be at least $100,000 in 2015 and $2 million in 2018; must have four-year operating/sales history. *Inc., "America's 500 Fastest-Growing Private Companies," 2019*

Minority Business Opportunity

Milwaukee is home to one company which is on the *Black Enterprise* Industrial/Service list (100 largest companies based on gross sales): **V & J Holding Cos.** (#45). Criteria: operational in previous calendar year; at least 51% black-owned and manufactures/owns the product it sells or provides industrial or consumer services. Brokerages, real estate firms and firms that provide professional services are not eligible. *Black Enterprise, B.E. 100s, 2019*

Milwaukee is home to two companies which are on the *Hispanic Business* 500 list (500 largest U.S. Hispanic-owned companies based on revenue): **Thomas A. Mason Co.** (#323); **Barrientos Design & Consulting** (#469). Companies included must show at least 51 percent ownership by Hispanic U.S. citizens, and must maintain headquarters in one of the 50 states or Washington, D.C. *Hispanic Business, "Hispanic Business 500," June 20, 2013*

Minority- and Women-Owned Businesses

Group	All Firms		Firms with Paid Employees			
	Firms	Sales ($000)	Firms	Sales ($000)	Employees	Payroll ($000)
AIAN[1]	364	11,345	36	7,141	139	2,295
Asian	1,891	797,548	605	716,931	4,396	100,111
Black	13,219	582,195	696	391,493	6,168	137,611
Hispanic	2,685	367,055	267	309,221	5,922	92,362
NHOPI[2]	27	4,851	6	(s)	0 - 19	(s)
Women	17,101	1,860,758	1,430	1,608,982	15,413	412,755
All Firms	38,017	83,930,464	8,275	82,880,037	266,273	13,659,239

Note: Figures cover firms located in the city; minority- and women-owned business are defined as firms in which the corresponding group own 51% or more of the stock or equity of the company; (1) American Indian and Alaska Native; (2) Native Hawaiian and Other Pacific Islander; (s) estimates are suppressed when publication standards are not met
Source: U.S. Census Bureau, 2012 Economic Census, Survey of Business Owners

HOTELS & CONVENTION CENTERS

Hotels, Motels and Vacation Rentals

Area	5 Star		4 Star		3 Star		2 Star		1 Star		Not Rated	
	Num.	Pct.[3]	Num.	Pct.[3]	Num.	Pct.[3]	Num.	Pct.[3]	Num.	Pct.[3]	Num.	Pct.[3]
City[1]	0	0.0	9	4.8	39	21.0	15	8.1	43	23.1	80	43.0
Total[2]	266	1.3	1,517	7.2	4,627	21.8	3,210	15.1	3,974	18.7	7,601	35.9

Note: (1) Figures cover Milwaukee and vicinity; (2) Figures cover all 100 cities in this book; (3) Percentage of hotels which have a given star rating; Star ratings are determined by priceline.com and offer an indication of the general quality of a particular hotel.
Source: priceline.com, April 27, 2020

Major Convention Centers

Name	Overall Space (sq. ft.)	Exhibit Space (sq. ft.)	Meeting Space (sq. ft.)	Meeting Rooms
Wisconsin Center	n/a	188,695	39,364	28

Note: Table includes convention centers located in the Milwaukee-Waukesha-West Allis, WI metro area; n/a not available
Source: Original research

Living Environment

COST OF LIVING

Cost of Living Index

Composite Index	Groceries	Housing	Utilities	Trans-portation	Health Care	Misc. Goods/ Services
n/a	n/a	n/a	n/a	n/a	n/a	n/a

Note: The Cost of Living Index measures regional differences in the cost of consumer goods and services, excluding taxes and non-consumer expenditures, for professional and managerial households in the top income quintile. It is based on more than 50,000 prices covering almost 60 different items for which prices are collected three times a year by chambers of commerce, economic development organizations or university applied economic centers in each participating urban area. The numbers shown should be read as a percentage above or below the national average of 100. For example, a value of 115.4 in the groceries column indicates that grocery prices are 15.4% higher than the national average. Small differences in the index numbers should not be interpreted as significant; n/a not available.
Source: The Council for Community and Economic Research, ACCRA Cost of Living Index, 2019

Grocery Prices

Area[1]	T-Bone Steak ($/pound)	Frying Chicken ($/pound)	Whole Milk ($/half gal.)	Eggs ($/dozen)	Orange Juice ($/64 oz.)	Coffee ($/11.5 oz.)
City[2]	291.00	291.00	291.00	291.00	291.00	291.00
Avg.	11.40	1.41	1.93	1.54	3.51	4.30
Min.	7.40	0.92	0.85	0.58	2.67	2.90
Max.	15.58	2.68	4.09	4.18	5.57	8.10

Note: (1) Values for the local area are compared with the average, minimum and maximum values for all 290 areas in the Cost of Living Index; (2) Figures cover the urban area; **T-Bone Steak** (price per pound); **Frying Chicken** (price per pound, whole fryer); **Whole Milk** (half gallon carton); **Eggs** (price per dozen, Grade A, large); **Orange Juice** (64 oz. Tropicana or Florida Natural); **Coffee** (11.5 oz. can, vacuum-packed, Maxwell House, Hills Bros, or Folgers).
Source: The Council for Community and Economic Research, ACCRA Cost of Living Index, 2019

Housing and Utility Costs

Area[1]	New Home Price ($)	Apartment Rent ($/month)	All Electric ($/month)	Part Electric ($/month)	Other Energy ($/month)	Telephone ($/month)
City[2]	291	291	n/a	n/a	n/a	291.00
Avg.	362,090	1,142	174.35	100.00	67.76	179.60
Min.	198,329	501	91.58	31.44	28.51	165.30
Max.	2,074,561	5,050	388.18	239.41	306.15	207.90

Note: (1) Values for the local area are compared with the average, minimum and maximum values for all 290 areas in the Cost of Living Index; (2) Figures cover the urban area; **New Home Price** (2,400 sf living area, 8,000 sf lot, in urban area with full utilities); **Apartment Rent** (950 sf 2 bedroom/1.5 or 2 bath, unfurnished, excluding all utilities except water); **All Electric** (average monthly cost for an all-electric home); **Part Electric** (average monthly cost for a part-electric home); **Other Energy** (average monthly cost for natural gas, fuel oil, coal, wood, and any other forms of energy except electricity); **Telephone** (price includes the base monthly rate plus taxes and fees for three lines of mobile phone service).
Source: The Council for Community and Economic Research, ACCRA Cost of Living Index, 2019

Health Care, Transportation, and Other Costs

Area[1]	Doctor ($/visit)	Dentist ($/visit)	Optometrist ($/visit)	Gasoline ($/gallon)	Beauty Salon ($/visit)	Men's Shirt ($)
City[2]	291.00	291.00	291.00	291.00	291.00	291.00
Avg.	114.85	97.58	106.10	2.50	38.15	32.15
Min.	39.00	62.22	52.22	1.53	16.88	10.27
Max.	206.67	151.53	258.67	3.79	79.29	59.30

Note: (1) Values for the local area are compared with the average, minimum and maximum values for all 290 areas in the Cost of Living Index; (2) Figures cover the urban area; **Doctor** (general practitioners routine exam of an established patient); **Dentist** (adult teeth cleaning and periodic oral examination); **Optometrist** (full vision eye exam for established adult patient); **Gasoline** (one gallon regular unleaded, national brand, including all taxes, cash price at self-service pump if available); **Beauty Salon** (woman's shampoo, trim, and blow-dry); **Men's Shirt** (cotton/polyester dress shirt, pinpoint weave, long sleeves).
Source: The Council for Community and Economic Research, ACCRA Cost of Living Index, 2019

HOUSING

House Price Index (HPI)

Area	National Ranking[2]	Quarterly Change (%)	One-Year Change (%)	Five-Year Change (%)
MSA[1]	165	0.46	4.06	25.49
U.S.[3]	–	1.26	5.09	32.88

Note: The HPI is a weighted repeat sales index. It measures average price changes in repeat sales or refinancings on the same properties. This information is obtained by reviewing repeat mortgage transactions on single-family properties whose mortgages have been purchased or securitized by Fannie Mae or Freddie Mac in January 1975; (1) Figures cover the Milwaukee-Waukesha-West Allis, WI Metropolitan Statistical Area—see Appendix B for areas included; (2) Rankings are based on annual percentage change for all metro areas containing at least 15,000 transactions over the last 10 years and ranges from 1 to 232; (3) figures based on a weighted average of Census Division estimates using a seasonally adjusted, purchase-only index; all figures are for the period ending December 31, 2019
Source: Federal Housing Finance Agency, House Price Index, February 25, 2020

Median Single-Family Home Prices

Area	2017	2018	2019[p]	Percent Change 2018 to 2019
MSA[1]	239.6	250.3	268.4	7.2
U.S. Average	248.8	261.6	274.6	5.0

Note: Figures are median sales prices of existing single-family homes in thousands of dollars; (p) preliminary; (1) Figures cover the Milwaukee-Waukesha-West Allis, WI Metropolitan Statistical Area—see Appendix B for areas included
Source: National Association of Realtors, Median Sales Price of Existing Single-Family Homes for Metropolitan Areas, 4th Quarter 2019

Qualifying Income Based on Median Sales Price of Existing Single-Family Homes

Area	With 5% Down ($)	With 10% Down ($)	With 20% Down ($)
MSA[1]	56,059	53,109	47,208
U.S. Average	58,663	55,575	49,400

Note: Figures are preliminary; Qualifying income is based on a mortgage rate of 3.76%. Monthly principal and interest payment is limited to 25% of income; (1) Figures cover the Milwaukee-Waukesha-West Allis, WI Metropolitan Statistical Area—see Appendix B for areas included
Source: National Association of Realtors, Qualifying Income Based on Median Sales Price of Existing Single-Family Homes for Metropolitan Areas, 4th Quarter 2019

Median Apartment Condo-Coop Home Prices

Area	2017	2018	2019[p]	Percent Change 2018 to 2019
MSA[1]	169.0	177.6	197.8	11.4
U.S. Average	234.3	241.0	249.5	3.5

Note: Figures are median sales prices of existing apartment condo-coop homes in thousands of dollars; (p) preliminary; (1) Figures cover the Milwaukee-Waukesha-West Allis, WI Metropolitan Statistical Area—see Appendix B for areas included
Source: National Association of Realtors, Median Sales Price of Existing Apartment Condo-Coop Homes for Metropolitan Areas, 4th Quarter 2019

Home Value Distribution

Area	Under $50,000	$50,000 -$99,999	$100,000 -$149,999	$150,000 -$199,999	$200,000 -$299,999	$300,000 -$499,999	$500,000 -$999,999	$1,000,000 or more
City	9.5	29.3	29.5	17.2	9.5	3.2	1.5	0.3
MSA[1]	4.1	9.7	15.9	18.9	26.6	18.5	5.4	1.0
U.S.	7.6	13.0	14.0	14.3	19.2	18.3	10.5	3.1

Note: Figures are percentages and cover owner-occupied housing units; (1) Figures cover the Milwaukee-Waukesha-West Allis, WI Metropolitan Statistical Area—see Appendix B for areas included
Source: U.S. Census Bureau, 2014-2018 American Community Survey 5-Year Estimates

Homeownership Rate

Area	2011 (%)	2012 (%)	2013 (%)	2014 (%)	2015 (%)	2016 (%)	2017 (%)	2018 (%)	2019 (%)
MSA[1]	62.3	61.9	60.0	55.9	57.0	60.4	63.9	62.3	56.9
U.S.	66.1	65.4	65.1	64.5	63.7	63.4	63.9	64.4	64.6

Note: (1) Figures cover the Milwaukee-Waukesha-West Allis, WI Metropolitan Statistical Area—see Appendix B for areas included
Source: U.S. Census Bureau, Housing Vacancies and Homeownership Annual Statistics: 2011-2019

Year Housing Structure Built

Area	2010 or Later	2000 -2009	1990 -1999	1980 -1989	1970 -1979	1960 -1969	1950 -1959	1940 -1949	Before 1940	Median Year
City	1.3	3.4	2.8	4.0	8.4	10.5	20.9	9.8	38.9	1951
MSA[1]	2.1	8.3	10.7	8.1	12.9	11.4	16.7	6.9	23.0	1963
U.S.	4.1	14.3	13.9	13.5	15.3	10.7	10.4	5.0	12.8	1977

Note: Figures are percentages except for Median Year; Note: (1) Figures cover the Milwaukee-Waukesha-West Allis, WI Metropolitan Statistical Area—see Appendix B for areas included
Source: U.S. Census Bureau, 2014-2018 American Community Survey 5-Year Estimates

Gross Monthly Rent

Area	Under $500	$500 -$999	$1,000 -$1,499	$1,500 -$1,999	$2,000 -$2,499	$2,500 -$2,999	$3,000 and up	Median ($)
City	9.9	61.2	23.3	4.1	1.1	0.3	0.2	842
MSA[1]	8.2	56.0	27.7	5.8	1.6	0.4	0.3	885
U.S.	9.8	38.5	29.6	12.9	5.1	2.1	2.0	1,023

Note: Figures are percentages except for Median; Gross rent is the contract rent plus the estimated average monthly cost of utilities (electricity, gas, and water and sewer) and fuels (oil, coal, kerosene, wood, etc.) if these are paid by the renter (or paid for the renter by someone else); (1) Figures cover the Milwaukee-Waukesha-West Allis, WI Metropolitan Statistical Area—see Appendix B for areas included
Source: U.S. Census Bureau, 2014-2018 American Community Survey 5-Year Estimates

HEALTH

Health Risk Factors

Category	MSA[1] (%)	U.S. (%)
Adults aged 18–64 who have any kind of health care coverage	91.4	87.3
Adults who reported being in good or better health	81.0	82.4
Adults who have been told they have high blood cholesterol	34.2	33.0
Adults who have been told they have high blood pressure	30.5	32.3
Adults who are current smokers	14.5	17.1
Adults who currently use E-cigarettes	4.5	4.6
Adults who currently use chewing tobacco, snuff, or snus	2.8	4.0
Adults who are heavy drinkers[2]	7.7	6.3
Adults who are binge drinkers[3]	21.0	17.4
Adults who are overweight (BMI 25.0 - 29.9)	38.3	35.3
Adults who are obese (BMI 30.0 - 99.8)	29.1	31.3
Adults who participated in any physical activities in the past month	75.2	74.4
Adults who always or nearly always wears a seat belt	93.3	94.3

Note: (1) Figures cover the Milwaukee-Waukesha-West Allis, WI Metropolitan Statistical Area—see Appendix B for areas included; (2) Heavy drinkers are classified as adult men having more than 14 drinks per week and adult women having more than 7 drinks per week; (3) Binge drinkers are classified as males having five or more drinks on one occasion or females having four or more drinks on one occasion
Source: Centers for Disease Control and Prevention, Behaviorial Risk Factor Surveillance System, SMART: Selected Metropolitan Area Risk Trends, 2017

Acute and Chronic Health Conditions

Category	MSA[1] (%)	U.S. (%)
Adults who have ever been told they had a heart attack	3.2	4.2
Adults who have ever been told they have angina or coronary heart disease	3.7	3.9
Adults who have ever been told they had a stroke	2.3	3.0
Adults who have ever been told they have asthma	13.3	14.2
Adults who have ever been told they have arthritis	26.7	24.9
Adults who have ever been told they have diabetes[2]	10.3	10.5
Adults who have ever been told they had skin cancer	4.4	6.2
Adults who have ever been told they had any other types of cancer	7.0	7.1
Adults who have ever been told they have COPD	5.0	6.5
Adults who have ever been told they have kidney disease	3.5	3.0
Adults who have ever been told they have a form of depression	19.3	20.5

Note: (1) Figures cover the Milwaukee-Waukesha-West Allis, WI Metropolitan Statistical Area—see Appendix B for areas included; (2) Figures do not include pregnancy-related, borderline, or pre-diabetes
Source: Centers for Disease Control and Prevention, Behaviorial Risk Factor Surveillance System, SMART: Selected Metropolitan Area Risk Trends, 2017

Health Screening and Vaccination Rates

Category	MSA[1] (%)	U.S. (%)
Adults aged 65+ who have had flu shot within the past year	49.8	60.7
Adults aged 65+ who have ever had a pneumonia vaccination	77.9	75.4
Adults who have ever been tested for HIV	37.6	36.1
Adults who have ever had the shingles or zoster vaccine?	29.5	28.9
Adults who have had their blood cholesterol checked within the last five years	87.5	85.9

Note: n/a not available; (1) Figures cover the Milwaukee-Waukesha-West Allis, WI Metropolitan Statistical Area—see Appendix B for areas included.
Source: Centers for Disease Control and Prevention, Behaviorial Risk Factor Surveillance System, SMART: Selected Metropolitan Area Risk Trends, 2017

Disability Status

Category	MSA[1] (%)	U.S. (%)
Adults who reported being deaf	5.3	6.7
Are you blind or have serious difficulty seeing, even when wearing glasses?	3.3	4.5
Are you limited in any way in any of your usual activities due of arthritis?	12.8	12.9
Do you have difficulty doing errands alone?	6.8	6.8
Do you have difficulty dressing or bathing?	4.3	3.6
Do you have serious difficulty concentrating/remembering/making decisions?	10.5	10.7
Do you have serious difficulty walking or climbing stairs?	12.2	13.6

Note: (1) Figures cover the Milwaukee-Waukesha-West Allis, WI Metropolitan Statistical Area—see Appendix B for areas included.
Source: Centers for Disease Control and Prevention, Behaviorial Risk Factor Surveillance System, SMART: Selected Metropolitan Area Risk Trends, 2017

Mortality Rates for the Top 10 Causes of Death in the U.S.

ICD-10[a] Sub-Chapter	ICD-10[a] Code	Age-Adjusted Mortality Rate[1] per 100,000 population	
		County[2]	U.S.
Malignant neoplasms	C00-C97	173.7	152.4
Ischaemic heart diseases	I20-I25	106.1	92.7
Other forms of heart disease	I30-I51	52.6	52.5
Chronic lower respiratory diseases	J40-J47	39.1	40.4
Cerebrovascular diseases	I60-I69	34.8	37.3
Other degenerative diseases of the nervous system	G30-G31	26.8	36.4
Other external causes of accidental injury	W00-X59	66.3	35.3
Organic, including symptomatic, mental disorders	F01-F09	39.7	30.0
Hypertensive diseases	I10-I15	28.9	22.9
Diabetes mellitus	E10-E14	23.8	21.3

Note: (a) ICD-10 = International Classification of Diseases 10th Revision; (1) Mortality rates are a three year average covering 2016-2018; (2) Figures cover Milwaukee County.
Source: Centers for Disease Control and Prevention, National Center for Health Statistics. Underlying Cause of Death 1999-2018 on CDC WONDER Online Database

Mortality Rates for Selected Causes of Death

ICD-10[a] Sub-Chapter	ICD-10[a] Code	Age-Adjusted Mortality Rate[1] per 100,000 population	
		County[2]	U.S.
Assault	X85-Y09	14.7	6.0
Diseases of the liver	K70-K76	15.5	14.2
Human immunodeficiency virus (HIV) disease	B20-B24	1.2	1.6
Influenza and pneumonia	J09-J18	12.6	14.2
Intentional self-harm	X60-X84	13.3	13.9
Malnutrition	E40-E46	2.4	1.9
Obesity and other hyperalimentation	E65-E68	2.5	2.1
Renal failure	N17-N19	16.1	12.8
Transport accidents	V01-V99	10.1	12.5
Viral hepatitis	B15-B19	0.7	1.4

Note: (a) ICD-10 = International Classification of Diseases 10th Revision; (1) Mortality rates are a three year average covering 2016-2018; (2) Figures cover Milwaukee County; Data are suppressed when the data meet the criteria for confidentiality constraints; Mortality rates are flagged as unreliable when the rate would be calculated with a numerator of 20 or less.
Source: Centers for Disease Control and Prevention, National Center for Health Statistics. Underlying Cause of Death 1999-2018 on CDC WONDER Online Database

Health Insurance Coverage

Area	With Health Insurance	With Private Health Insurance	With Public Health Insurance	Without Health Insurance	Population Under Age 19 Without Health Insurance
City	90.3	53.7	44.8	9.7	3.3
MSA[1]	94.0	71.5	33.9	6.0	2.6
U.S.	90.6	67.7	34.7	9.4	5.2

Note: Figures are percentages that cover the civilian noninstitutionalized population; (1) Figures cover the Milwaukee-Waukesha-West Allis, WI Metropolitan Statistical Area—see Appendix B for areas included
Source: U.S. Census Bureau, 2014-2018 American Community Survey 5-Year Estimates

Number of Medical Professionals

Area	MDs[3]	DOs[3,4]	Dentists	Podiatrists	Chiropractors	Optometrists
County[1] (number)	3,466	212	750	67	186	101
County[1] (rate[2])	364.0	22.3	79.1	7.1	19.6	10.7
U.S. (rate[2])	281.9	23.4	69.1	6.0	27.5	16.4

Note: Data as of 2018 unless noted; (1) Data covers Milwaukee County; (2) Rate per 100,000 population; (3) Data as of 2017 and includes all active, non-federal physicians; (4) Doctor of Osteopathic Medicine
Source: U.S. Department of Health and Human Services, Health Resources and Services Administration, Bureau of Health Professions, Area Resource File (ARF) 2018-2019

Best Hospitals

According to *U.S. News,* the Milwaukee-Waukesha-West Allis, WI metro area is home to one of the best hospitals in the U.S.: **Froedtert West Bend Hospital** (1 adult specialty). The hospital listed was nationally ranked in at least one of 16 adult or 10 pediatric specialties. Only 206 hospitals nationwide were nationally ranked in one or more adult or pediatric specialty. Twenty hospitals in the U.S. made the Honor Roll. The Best Hospitals Honor Roll takes both the national rankings and the procedure and condition ratings into account. Hospitals received points if they were nationally ranked in one of the 16 adult specialties—the higher they ranked, the more points they got—and how many ratings of "high performing" they earned in the nine procedures and conditions. *U.S. News Online, "America's Best Hospitals 2019-20"*

According to *U.S. News,* the Milwaukee-Waukesha-West Allis, WI metro area is home to one of the best children's hospitals in the U.S.: **Children's Hospital of Wisconsin** (9 pediatric specialties). The hospital listed was highly ranked in at least one of 10 pediatric specialties. Ninety-one children's hospitals in the U.S. were nationally ranked in at least one specialty. Hospitals received points for being ranked in a specialty, and the 10 hospitals with the most points across the 10 specialties make up the Honor Roll. *U.S. News Online, "America's Best Children's Hospitals 2019-20"*

EDUCATION

Public School District Statistics

District Name	Schls	Pupils	Pupil/ Teacher Ratio	Minority Pupils[1] (%)	Free Lunch Eligible[2] (%)	IEP[3] (%)
Milwaukee School District	161	75,431	17.2	89.5	73.9	20.0

Note: Table includes school districts with 2,000 or more students; (1) Percentage of students that are not non-Hispanic white; (2) Percentage of students that are eligible for the free lunch program; (3) Percentage of students that have an Individualized Education Program.
Source: U.S. Department of Education, National Center for Education Statistics, Common Core of Data, Local Education Agency (School District) Universe Survey: School Year 2018-2019; U.S. Department of Education, National Center for Education Statistics, Common Core of Data, Public Elementary/Secondary School Universe Survey: School Year 2018-2019

Best High Schools

According to *U.S. News,* Milwaukee is home to two of the top 500 high schools in the U.S.: **Reagan College Preparatory High** (#223); **Carmen High School of Science and Technology** (#406). Nearly 18,000 public, magnet and charter schools were ranked based on their performance on state assessments and how well they prepare students for college. *U.S. News & World Report, "Best High Schools 2020"*

Highest Level of Education

Area	Less than H.S.	H.S. Diploma	Some College, No Deg.	Associate Degree	Bachelor's Degree	Master's Degree	Prof. School Degree	Doctorate Degree
City	16.6	29.9	22.1	7.2	15.5	6.4	1.3	0.9
MSA[1]	8.9	26.6	20.9	8.6	22.6	8.9	2.3	1.3
U.S.	12.3	27.1	20.6	8.4	19.4	8.6	2.1	1.4

Note: Figures cover persons age 25 and over; (1) Figures cover the Milwaukee-Waukesha-West Allis, WI Metropolitan Statistical Area—see Appendix B for areas included
Source: U.S. Census Bureau, 2014-2018 American Community Survey 5-Year Estimates

Educational Attainment by Race

Area	High School Graduate or Higher (%)					Bachelor's Degree or Higher (%)				
	Total	White	Black	Asian	Hisp.[2]	Total	White	Black	Asian	Hisp.[2]
City	83.4	88.8	82.0	70.2	60.6	24.2	34.5	12.4	28.2	8.9
MSA[1]	91.1	94.1	82.8	83.5	67.8	35.1	39.2	14.1	51.4	14.1
U.S.	87.7	89.6	85.4	86.8	67.7	31.5	32.9	21.1	53.5	15.8

Note: Figures shown cover persons 25 years old and over; (1) Figures cover the Milwaukee-Waukesha-West Allis, WI Metropolitan Statistical Area—see Appendix B for areas included; (2) People of Hispanic origin can be of any race
Source: U.S. Census Bureau, 2014-2018 American Community Survey 5-Year Estimates

School Enrollment by Grade and Control

Area	Preschool (%)		Kindergarten (%)		Grades 1 - 4 (%)		Grades 5 - 8 (%)		Grades 9 - 12 (%)	
	Public	Private	Public	Private	Public	Private	Public	Private	Public	Private
City	75.2	24.8	76.3	23.7	75.7	24.3	76.4	23.6	81.6	18.4
MSA[1]	56.4	43.6	78.4	21.6	79.4	20.6	80.2	19.8	85.1	14.9
U.S.	59.0	41.0	87.7	12.3	89.6	10.4	89.5	10.5	90.2	9.8

Note: Figures shown cover persons 3 years old and over; (1) Figures cover the Milwaukee-Waukesha-West Allis, WI Metropolitan Statistical Area—see Appendix B for areas included
Source: U.S. Census Bureau, 2014-2018 American Community Survey 5-Year Estimates

Average Salaries of Public School Teachers

Area	2016-17		2017-18		Change from 2016-17 to 2017-18	
	Dollars	Rank[1]	Dollars	Rank[1]	Percent	Rank[2]
Wisconsin	51,439	32	51,469	33	0.06	47
U.S. Average	59,539	–	60,477	–	1.58	–

Note: (1) Rank ranges from 1 to 51 where 1 indicates highest salary; (2) Rank ranges from 1 to 51 where 1 indicates highest percent change.
Source: National Education Association, Rankings & Estimates: Rankings of the States 2018 and Estimates of School Statistics 2019

Higher Education

Four-Year Colleges			Two-Year Colleges			Medical Schools[1]	Law Schools[2]	Voc/ Tech[3]
Public	Private Non-profit	Private For-profit	Public	Private Non-profit	Private For-profit			
3	10	2	1	0	1	1	1	2

Note: Figures cover institutions located within the city limits and include main campuses only; (1) includes schools accredited by the Liaison Committee on Medical Education and the American Osteopathic Association's Commission on Osteopathic College Accreditation; (2) includes ABA-accredited schools, schools with provisional ABA accreditation, and state accredited schools; (3) includes all schools with programs that are less than 2 years.
Source: National Center for Education Statistics, Integrated Postsecondary Education System (IPEDS), 2018-19; Wikipedia, List of Medical Schools in the United States, accessed May 1, 2020; Wikipedia, List of Law Schools in the United States, accessed May 1, 2020

According to *U.S. News & World Report*, the Milwaukee-Waukesha-West Allis, WI metro area is home to one of the top 200 national universities in the U.S.: **Marquette University** (#84 tie). The indicators used to capture academic quality fall into a number of categories: assessment by administrators at peer institutions; retention of students; faculty resources; student selectivity; financial resources; alumni giving; high school counselor ratings of colleges; and graduation rate. *U.S. News & World Report, "America's Best Colleges 2020"*

PRESIDENTIAL ELECTION

2016 Presidential Election Results

Area	Clinton	Trump	Johnson	Stein	Other
Milwaukee County	65.5	28.6	3.1	1.0	1.8
U.S.	48.0	45.9	3.3	1.1	1.7

Note: Results are percentages and may not add to 100% due to rounding
Source: Dave Leip's Atlas of U.S. Presidential Elections

EMPLOYERS

Major Employers

Company Name	Industry
Ascension Wisconsin	Health care system
Aurora Health	Health care system
Children's Hospital of Wisconsin	Pediatric health care services
Froedtert Health	Health care services
GE Healthcare Technologies	Medical imaging & information systems
Kohl's	Department stores
Kroger Co./Roundy's	Food distributor & retailer
Medical College of Wisconsin	Medical school
Northwestern Mutual	Life insurance & investment services
ProHealth Care Inc.	Health care system
Quad/Graphics	Commercial printing and print mgmt
WEC Energy	Electric & natural gas utility

Note: Companies shown are located within the Milwaukee-Waukesha-West Allis, WI Metropolitan Statistical Area.
Source: Hoovers.com; Wikipedia

Best Companies to Work For

Baird, headquartered in Milwaukee, is among "The 100 Best Companies to Work For." To pick the best companies, *Fortune* partnered with the Great Place to Work Institute. Two-thirds of a company's score is based on the results of the Institute's Trust Index survey, which is sent to a random sample of employees from each company. The questions related to attitudes about management's credibility, job satisfaction, and camaraderie. The other third of the scoring is based on the company's responses to the Institute's Culture Audit, which includes detailed questions about pay and benefit programs, and a series of open-ended questions about hiring practices, internal communication, training, recognition programs, and diversity efforts. Any company that is at least five years old with more than 1,000 U.S. employees is eligible. *Fortune, "The 100 Best Companies to Work For," 2020*

Robert W. Baird and Co, headquartered in Milwaukee, is among the "100 Best Places to Work in IT." To qualify, companies had to be U.S.-based organizations or be non-U.S.- based employers that met the following criteria: have a minimum of 300 total employees at a U.S. headquarters and a minimum of 30 IT employees in the U.S., with at least 50% of their IT employees based in the U.S. The best places to work were selected based on compensation, benefits, work/life balance, employee morale, and satisfaction with training and development programs. In addition, *Computerworld* looked at retention efforts, programs for recognizing and rewarding outstanding performances, and benefits such as flextime, elder care and child care, and reimbursement for college tuition and the cost of pursuing technology certifications. *Computerworld, "100 Best Places to Work in IT 2019"*

PUBLIC SAFETY

Crime Rate

Area	All Crimes	Violent Crimes				Property Crimes		
		Murder	Rape[3]	Robbery	Aggrav. Assault	Burglary	Larceny -Theft	Motor Vehicle Theft
City	4,384.5	16.6	82.1	382.6	931.6	715.1	1,486.0	770.5
Suburbs[1]	1,663.9	1.4	20.4	33.2	68.4	137.4	1,299.1	104.0
Metro[2]	2,689.7	7.2	43.7	165.0	393.9	355.2	1,369.6	355.3
U.S.	2,580.1	5.0	42.6	86.2	246.8	376.0	1,594.6	228.9

Note: Figures are crimes per 100,000 population; (1) All areas within the metro area that are located outside the city limits; (2) Figures cover the Milwaukee-Waukesha-West Allis, WI Metropolitan Statistical Area—see Appendix B for areas included; (3) The city and U.S. figures shown were reported using the revised Uniform Crime Reporting (UCR) definition of rape. The suburban and metro area figures shown are an aggregate total of the data submitted using both the revised and legacy UCR definitions.
Source: FBI Uniform Crime Reports, 2018

Hate Crimes

Area	Number of Quarters Reported	Number of Incidents per Bias Motivation					
		Race/Ethnicity/ Ancestry	Religion	Sexual Orientation	Disability	Gender	Gender Identity
City	4	2	0	1	0	0	0
U.S.	4	4,047	1,419	1,196	159	47	168

Source: Federal Bureau of Investigation, Hate Crime Statistics 2018

Identity Theft Consumer Reports

Area	Reports	Reports per 100,000 Population	Rank[2]
MSA[1]	2,490	158	88
U.S.	650,572	198	-

Note: (1) Figures cover the Milwaukee-Waukesha-West Allis, WI Metropolitan Statistical Area—see Appendix B for areas included; (2) Rank ranges from 1 to 386 where 1 indicates greatest number of identity theft reports per 100,000 population
Source: Federal Trade Commission, Consumer Sentinel Network Data Book for January–December 2019

Fraud and Other Consumer Reports

Area	Reports	Reports per 100,000 Population	Rank[2]
MSA[1]	9,688	615	111
U.S.	2,590,177	789	-

Note: (1) Figures cover the Milwaukee-Waukesha-West Allis, WI Metropolitan Statistical Area—see Appendix B for areas included; (2) Rank ranges from 1 to 386 where 1 indicates greatest number of fraud and other consumer reports per 100,000 population
Source: Federal Trade Commission, Consumer Sentinel Network Data Book for January–December 2019

SPORTS

Professional Sports Teams

Team Name	League	Year Established
Milwaukee Brewers	Major League Baseball (MLB)	1970
Milwaukee Bucks	National Basketball Association (NBA)	1968

Note: Includes teams located in the Milwaukee-Waukesha-West Allis, WI Metropolitan Statistical Area.
Source: Wikipedia, Major Professional Sports Teams of the United States and Canada, May 4, 2020

CLIMATE

Average and Extreme Temperatures

Temperature	Jan	Feb	Mar	Apr	May	Jun	Jul	Aug	Sep	Oct	Nov	Dec	Yr.
Extreme High (°F)	60	65	82	91	92	101	101	103	98	89	77	63	103
Average High (°F)	27	31	40	54	65	76	80	79	71	60	45	32	55
Average Temp. (°F)	20	24	33	45	55	66	71	70	62	51	38	25	47
Average Low (°F)	12	16	26	36	45	55	62	61	53	42	30	18	38
Extreme Low (°F)	-26	-19	-10	12	21	36	40	44	28	18	-5	-20	-26

Note: Figures cover the years 1948-1990
Source: National Climatic Data Center, International Station Meteorological Climate Summary, 9/96

Average Precipitation/Snowfall/Humidity

Precip./Humidity	Jan	Feb	Mar	Apr	May	Jun	Jul	Aug	Sep	Oct	Nov	Dec	Yr.
Avg. Precip. (in.)	1.6	1.4	2.6	3.3	2.9	3.4	3.6	3.4	2.9	2.3	2.3	2.2	32.0
Avg. Snowfall (in.)	13	10	9	2	Tr	0	0	0	0	Tr	3	11	49
Avg. Rel. Hum. 6am (%)	76	77	78	78	77	79	82	86	86	82	80	80	80
Avg. Rel. Hum. 3pm (%)	68	66	64	58	58	58	59	62	61	61	66	70	63

Note: Figures cover the years 1948-1990; Tr = Trace amounts (<0.05 in. of rain; <0.5 in. of snow)
Source: National Climatic Data Center, International Station Meteorological Climate Summary, 9/96

Weather Conditions

Temperature			Daytime Sky			Precipitation		
5°F & below	32°F & below	90°F & above	Clear	Partly cloudy	Cloudy	0.01 inch or more precip.	0.1 inch or more snow/ice	Thunder-storms
22	141	10	90	118	157	126	38	35

Note: Figures are average number of days per year and cover the years 1948-1990
Source: National Climatic Data Center, International Station Meteorological Climate Summary, 9/96

HAZARDOUS WASTE

Superfund Sites

The Milwaukee-Waukesha-West Allis, WI metro area is home to six sites on the EPA's Superfund National Priorities List: **Amcast Industrial Corporation** (final); **Lauer I Sanitary Landfill** (final); **Master Disposal Service Landfill** (final); **Moss-American Co., Inc. (Kerr-Mcgee Oil Co.)** (final); **Muskego Sanitary Landfill** (final); **Waste Management of Wisconsin, Inc. (Brookfield Sanitary Landfill)** (final). There are a total of 1,387 Superfund sites with a status of proposed or final on the list in the U.S. *U.S. Environmental Protection Agency, National Priorities List, May 5, 2020*

AIR & WATER QUALITY

Air Quality Trends: Ozone

	1990	1995	2000	2005	2010	2012	2014	2016	2017	2018
MSA[1]	0.095	0.106	0.082	0.092	0.079	0.092	0.072	0.074	0.072	0.073
U.S.	0.088	0.089	0.082	0.080	0.073	0.075	0.067	0.069	0.068	0.069

Note: (1) Data covers the Milwaukee-Waukesha-West Allis, WI Metropolitan Statistical Area—see Appendix B for areas included. The values shown are the composite ozone concentration averages among trend sites based on the highest fourth daily maximum 8-hour concentration in parts per million. These trends are based on sites having an adequate record of monitoring data during the trend period. Data from exceptional events are included.
Source: U.S. Environmental Protection Agency, Air Quality Monitoring Information, "Air Quality Trends by City, 1990-2018"

Air Quality Index

Area	Percent of Days when Air Quality was...[2]					AQI Statistics[2]	
	Good	Moderate	Unhealthy for Sensitive Groups	Unhealthy	Very Unhealthy	Maximum	Median
MSA[1]	64.7	32.9	1.9	0.5	0.0	169	44

Note: (1) Data covers the Milwaukee-Waukesha-West Allis, WI Metropolitan Statistical Area—see Appendix B for areas included; (2) Based on 365 days with AQI data in 2018. Air Quality Index (AQI) is an index for reporting daily air quality. EPA calculates the AQI for five major air pollutants regulated by the Clean Air Act: ground-level ozone, particle pollution (aka particulate matter), carbon monoxide, sulfur dioxide, and nitrogen dioxide. The AQI runs from 0 to 500. The higher the AQI value, the greater the level of air pollution and the greater the health concern. There are six AQI categories: "Good" AQI is between 0 and 50. Air quality is considered satisfactory; "Moderate" AQI is between 51 and 100. Air quality is acceptable; "Unhealthy for Sensitive Groups" When AQI values are between 101 and 150, members of sensitive groups may experience health effects; "Unhealthy" When AQI values are between 151 and 200 everyone may begin to experience health effects; "Very Unhealthy" AQI values between 201 and 300 trigger a health alert; "Hazardous" AQI values over 300 trigger warnings of emergency conditions (not shown).
Source: U.S. Environmental Protection Agency, Air Quality Index Report, 2018

Air Quality Index Pollutants

Area	Percent of Days when AQI Pollutant was...[2]					
	Carbon Monoxide	Nitrogen Dioxide	Ozone	Sulfur Dioxide	Particulate Matter 2.5	Particulate Matter 10
MSA[1]	0.0	3.3	52.1	0.0	44.7	0.0

Note: (1) Data covers the Milwaukee-Waukesha-West Allis, WI Metropolitan Statistical Area—see Appendix B for areas included; (2) Based on 365 days with AQI data in 2018. The Air Quality Index (AQI) is an index for reporting daily air quality. EPA calculates the AQI for five major air pollutants regulated by the Clean Air Act: ground-level ozone, particle pollution (also known as particulate matter), carbon monoxide, sulfur dioxide, and nitrogen dioxide. The AQI runs from 0 to 500. The higher the AQI value, the greater the level of air pollution and the greater the health concern.
Source: U.S. Environmental Protection Agency, Air Quality Index Report, 2018

Maximum Air Pollutant Concentrations: Particulate Matter, Ozone, CO and Lead

	Particulate Matter 10 (ug/m³)	Particulate Matter 2.5 Wtd AM (ug/m³)	Particulate Matter 2.5 24-Hr (ug/m³)	Ozone (ppm)	Carbon Monoxide (ppm)	Lead (ug/m³)
MSA[1] Level	40	9.1	22	0.073	1	n/a
NAAQS[2]	150	15	35	0.075	9	0.15
Met NAAQS[2]	Yes	Yes	Yes	Yes	Yes	n/a

Note: (1) Data covers the Milwaukee-Waukesha-West Allis, WI Metropolitan Statistical Area—see Appendix B for areas included; Data from exceptional events are included; (2) National Ambient Air Quality Standards; ppm = parts per million; ug/m³ = micrograms per cubic meter; n/a not available.
Concentrations: Particulate Matter 10 (coarse particulate)—highest second maximum 24-hour concentration; Particulate Matter 2.5 Wtd AM (fine particulate)—highest weighted annual mean concentration; Particulate Matter 2.5 24-Hour (fine particulate)—highest 98th percentile 24-hour concentration; Ozone—highest fourth daily maximum 8-hour concentration; Carbon Monoxide—highest second maximum non-overlapping 8-hour concentration; Lead—maximum running 3-month average
Source: U.S. Environmental Protection Agency, Air Quality Monitoring Information, "Air Quality Statistics by City, 2018"

Maximum Air Pollutant Concentrations: Nitrogen Dioxide and Sulfur Dioxide

	Nitrogen Dioxide AM (ppb)	Nitrogen Dioxide 1-Hr (ppb)	Sulfur Dioxide AM (ppb)	Sulfur Dioxide 1-Hr (ppb)	Sulfur Dioxide 24-Hr (ppb)
MSA[1] Level	14	47	n/a	4	n/a
NAAQS[2]	53	100	30	75	140
Met NAAQS[2]	Yes	Yes	n/a	Yes	n/a

Note: (1) Data covers the Milwaukee-Waukesha-West Allis, WI Metropolitan Statistical Area—see Appendix B for areas included; Data from exceptional events are included; (2) National Ambient Air Quality Standards; ppm = parts per million; ug/m³ = micrograms per cubic meter; n/a not available.
Concentrations: Nitrogen Dioxide AM—highest arithmetic mean concentration; Nitrogen Dioxide 1-Hr—highest 98th percentile 1-hour daily maximum concentration; Sulfur Dioxide AM—highest annual mean concentration; Sulfur Dioxide 1-Hr—highest 99th percentile 1-hour daily maximum concentration; Sulfur Dioxide 24-Hr—highest second maximum 24-hour concentration
Source: U.S. Environmental Protection Agency, Air Quality Monitoring Information, "Air Quality Statistics by City, 2018"

Drinking Water

Water System Name	Pop. Served	Primary Water Source Type	Violations[1]
Milwaukee Waterworks	590,547	Surface	11

Note: (1) Total number of violations (both active and inactive) in the EPA database
Source: U.S. Environmental Protection Agency, Office of Ground Water and Drinking Water, Safe Drinking Water Information System (based on data extracted May 5, 2020)

Minneapolis, Minnesota

Background

Minneapolis is a vibrant, cosmopolitan city that boasts sunlit skyscrapers and sparkling lakes, as well as theater, museums and abundant recreation. Known for its offerings of performing arts, visual arts, education, finance, advertising, and manufacturing, Minneapolis is also a hub of trade, industry, transportation and finance for the Upper Midwest.

In 1680, a French Franciscan priest, Father Louis Hennepin, was the area's first white man to arrive. In 1819, Fort Snelling was established to protect fur traders from the Sioux and Chippewa tribes. In 1848, two towns, St. Anthony (later named St. Paul), and Minneapolis, grew simultaneously, thus forming the metropolitan area known today as the Twin Cities. A tide of Swedish, German, and Norwegian immigrants came in the late nineteenth century, giving the city a decidedly Scandinavian flavor. Its many lakes gave Minneapolis its name, which comes from the Dakota word "minne," or "of the waters," and the Greek "polis," or city.

Minneapolis's traditional industries were lumber and flour milling. Since the 1950s, technology, including electronics, computers, and other related science industries, has played a vital role in the city's economy, as has printing and advertising.

The city's economy is fueled by an influx of urban dwellers and rapid growth of rental units to house them. The Pillsbury A-Mill Apartment Complex, and the 26 Story Apartment Building are just two of the city's multi-million dollar housing projects.

In addition, the U.S. Bank Stadium was funded by its NFL tenants, the Minnesota Vikings, and the state. During construction of the stadium—built on the site of the old Metrodome—the team played its 2014 and 2015 seasons in the TCF Bank Stadium at the University of Minnesota. Called "Minnesota's biggest-ever public works project," the stadium opened in 2016 with 66,000 seats, and expanded to 70,000 for the 2018 Super Bowl.

Minneapolis has the fourth-highest percentage of gay, lesbian, or bisexual people in the adult population, behind San Francisco, Seattle, and Atlanta. In 2013, the city was among 25 U.S. cities to receive the highest possible score from the Human Rights Campaign, signifying its support for LGBTQ residents.

Well-known for its cultural and artistic offerings, Minneapolis occupies more theater seats per capita than any U.S. city outside of New York. The Minneapolis Institute of Arts has more than 100,000 pieces of art with renovated African Art galleries. A Michael Graves-designed wing holds contemporary and modern works. Other area attractions include the Science Museum of Minnesota, the Minneapolis Zoo and the Charles A. Lindbergh Historic Site.

More than five miles of downtown Minneapolis are connected by comfortable, climate-controlled glass "skyways" one flight above ground.

Minneapolis is home to award-winning restaurants and chefs. As of 2018, six Minneapolis-based chefs have won James Beard Foundation Awards, causing the city to be named one of the ten best places to visit in the world.

Minneapolis is a major transportation hub. The Minneapolis-St. Paul International Airport is the 16th busiest in North America in terms of number of travelers served, and supports $10.1 billion in business revenue.

The city also hosts a Northstar Corridor commuter line between downtown and Big Lake on existing railroad tracks, and a Green Line linking downtown, the University of Minnesota, and downtown St. Paul. Old rail lines and bridges within the city have been converted for bicycles and pedestrians.

Minneapolis is located at the confluence of the Mississippi and Minnesota rivers. Numerous lakes mark the surrounding region, with 22 within the city park system. The climate is predominantly continental, with extreme swings in seasonal temperatures. Blizzards, freezing rain, tornadoes, wind, and hail storms do occur. Due to the spring snow melt and excessive rain, the Mississippi River sees its share of floods.

Rankings

General Rankings

- *US News & World Report* conducted a survey of more than 2,000 people and analyzed the 125 largest metropolitan areas to determine what matters the most when selecting the next place to live. Minneapolis ranked #6 out of the top 25 as having the best combination of desirable factors. Criteria: cost of living; quality of life; net migration; job market; desirability; and other factors. *realestate.usnews.com, "The 25 Best Places to Live in the U.S. in 2019," April 9, 2019*

- In its eighth annual survey, *Travel + Leisure* readers nominated their favorite small cities and towns in America—those with 100,000 or fewer residents—voting on numerous attractive features in categories including culture, food and drink, quality of life, style, and people. After 50,000 votes, Minneapolis was ranked #12 among the proposed favorites. *www.travelandleisure.com, "America's Favorite Cities," October 20, 2017*

- Minneapolis was selected as one of the best places to live in America by *Outside Magazine.* Criteria included population, park acreage, neighborhood and resident diversity, new and upcoming things of interest, and opportunities for outdoor adventure. These places are home to a new breed of outdoor athletes and the new adventure capitals of America. *Outside Magazine, "The 12 Best Places to Live in 2019," July 11, 2019*

- Minneapolis was selected as one of the "The 10 Best Places to Live" by *Men's Journal. Men's Journal, "The 10 Best Places to Live," March 8, 2016*

- The human resources consulting firm Mercer ranked 231 major cities worldwide in terms of overall quality of life. Minneapolis ranked #61. Criteria: political, social, economic, and socio-cultural factors; medical and health considerations; schools and education; public services and transportation; recreation; consumer goods; housing; and natural environment. *Mercer, "Mercer 2019 Quality of Living Survey," March 13, 2019*

- Based on more than 600,000 responses, *Condé Nast Traveler* ranked its readers' favorite cities in the U.S. The list was broken into cities over 350,000 and cities under 350,000. Minneapolis ranked #2 in the big city category. *Condé Nast Traveler, Readers' Choice Awards 2019, "Best Big Cities in the U.S." October 7, 2019*

- In their sixth annual survey, Livability.com looked at data for more than 1,000 U.S. cities to determine the rankings for Livability's "Top 100 Best Places to Live" in 2019. Minneapolis ranked #13. Criteria: median home value capped at $250,000; affordable living; vibrant economy; education, demographics, health care options. transportation & infrastructure; abundant lifestyle amenities. *Livability.com, "Top 100 Best Places to Live 2019" March 2019*

Business/Finance Rankings

- According to *Business Insider*, the Minneapolis metro area is where conditions are prime to run a startup. It ranked #15. The software company Volusion analyzed 50 of the most populous metro areas, to assign an entrepreneurship score, based on the 2017 U.S. Census Bureau Annual Survey of Entrepreneurs (ASE). Criteria: cost of living; startup density; availability of venture capital investment; percentage of self-employed workers; small business density; percentage of workers employed by startups; and startup motivation. *www.businessinsider.com, "From San Diego to Austin and Seattle, These are the 15 Best U.S. Cities to Launch a Startup," July 9, 2019*

- Experian's latest annual report on consumer credit ranked cities by the average credit score of its residents. Minneapolis was ranked #1 among the ten cities with the highest average credit score, meaning that its residents showed strong credit management. *www.usatoday.com, "Minneapolis Tops List of Cities With Best Average Credit Score; Greenwood Miss., at the Bottom," January 11, 2018*

- Based on metro area social media reviews, the employment opinion group Glassdoor surveyed 50 of the most populous U.S. metro areas and equally weighed cost of living, hiring opportunity, and job satisfaction to compose a list of "25 Best Cities for Jobs." Median pay and home value, and number of active job openings was also factored in. The Minneapolis metro area was ranked #21 in overall job satisfaction. *www.glassdoor.com, "Best Cities for Jobs," February 25, 2020*

- The Brookings Institution ranked the nation's largest cities based on income inequality. Minneapolis was ranked #31 (#1 = greatest inequality). Criteria: the "95/20 ratio," a figure representing the income at which a household earns more than 95 percent of all other households, divided by the income at which a household earns more than only 20 percent of all other households. *Brookings Institution, "Household Income Inequality, Largest Cities of 97 Large U.S. Metro Areas, 2014-2016," February 5, 2018*

- The Brookings Institution ranked the 100 largest metro areas in the U.S. based on income inequality. Minneapolis was ranked #85 (#1 = greatest inequality). Criteria: the "95/20 ratio," a figure representing the income at which a household earns more than 95 percent of all other households, divided by the income at which a household earns more than only 20 percent of all other households. *Brookings Institution, "Household Income Inequality, 100 Largest U.S. Metro Areas, 2014-2016," February 5, 2018*

- *Forbes* ranked the 100 largest metro areas in the U.S. in terms of the "Best Cities for Young Professionals." The Minneapolis metro area ranked #13 out of 25. (Large metro areas were divided into metro divisions.) Criteria: median rent of a two-bedroom apartment; job growth and unemployment rate; median salary of college graduates with 5 or less years of work experience; networking opportunities; social outlook; percentage of population 25 years of age and older with college degrees. *Forbes.com, "America's 25 Best Cities for Young Professionals in 2017," May 22, 2017*

- Payscale.com ranked the 32 largest metro areas in terms of wage growth. The Minneapolis metro area ranked #32. Criteria: private-sector and education professional wage growth between the 4th quarter of 2018 and the 4th quarter of 2019. *PayScale, "Wage Trends by Metro Area-4th Quarter," January 24, 2020*

- The Minneapolis metro area was identified as one of the most debt-ridden places in America by the finance site Credit.com. The metro area was ranked #22. Criteria: residents' average credit card debt as well as median income. *Credit.com, "25 Cities With the Most Credit Card Debt," February 28, 2018*

- The Minneapolis metro area appeared on the Milken Institute "2020 Best Performing Cities" list. Rank: #98 out of 200 large metro areas. Criteria: job growth; wage and salary growth; high-tech output growth. *Milken Institute, "Best-Performing Cities 2020," February 26, 2020*

- *Forbes* ranked the 200 most populous metro areas to determine the nation's "Best Places for Business and Careers." The Minneapolis metro area was ranked #32. Criteria: costs (business and living); job growth (past and projected); income growth; quality of life; educational attainment (college and high school); projected economic growth; cultural and leisure opportunities; workplace tolerance laws; net migration patterns. *Forbes, "The Best Places for Business and Careers 2019: Seattle Still On Top," October 30, 2019*

- Mercer Human Resources Consulting ranked 209 cities worldwide in terms of cost-of-living. Minneapolis ranked #78 (the lower the ranking, the higher the cost-of-living). The survey measured the comparative cost of over 200 items (such as housing, food, clothing, household goods, transportation, and entertainment) in each location. *Mercer, "2019 Cost of Living Survey," June 26, 2019*

Children/Family Rankings

- *Forbes* analyzed data on the 100 largest metropolitan areas in the United States to compile its 2016 ranking of the best cities for raising a family. The Minneapolis metro area was ranked #15. Criteria: median income; childcare costs; percent of population under 18; commuting delays; crime rate; percentage of families owning homes; education quality (mainly test scores). Overall cost of living and housing affordability was also unofficially considered. *Forbes, "America's Best Cities for Raising a Family 2016," August 30, 2016*

Culture/Performing Arts Rankings

■ Minneapolis was selected as one of "America's Favorite Cities." The city ranked #8 in the "Culture" category. Respondents to an online survey were asked to rate 38 top urban destinations in the U.S. from a visitor's perspective. Criteria: theater scene and community; number of bookstores; live music; and sense of history. *Travelandleisure.com, "These Are America's 20 Most Cultured Cities," October 2016*

■ Minneapolis was selected as one of "America's Favorite Cities." The city ranked #5 in the "Culture: Music Scene " category. Respondents to an online survey were asked to rate 38 top urban destinations in the U.S. from a visitor's perspective. *Travelandleisure.com, "From the Honkytonk Capital to Jazz's Birthplace: America's Best Music Scenes," October 2016*

Dating/Romance Rankings

■ Minneapolis was selected as one of the best cities for post grads by *Rent.com*. The city ranked among the top 10. Criteria: jobs per capita; unemployment rate; mean annual income; cost of living; rental inventory. *Rent.com, "Best Cities for College Grads," December 11, 2018*

Education Rankings

■ Personal finance website *WalletHub* analyzed the 150 largest U.S. metropolitan statistical areas to determine where the most educated Americans are choosing to settle. Criteria: education levels; percentage of workers with degrees; education quality and attainment gap; public school quality rankings; quality and size of each metro area's universities. Minneapolis was ranked #19 (#1 = most educated city). *www.WalletHub.com, "2019's Most and Least Educated Cities in America, " July 22, 2019*

■ Minneapolis was selected as one of America's most literate cities. The city ranked #3 out of the 82 largest U.S. cities. Criteria: number of booksellers; library resources; Internet resources; educational attainment; periodical publishing resources; newspaper circulation. *Central Connecticut State University, "America's Most Literate Cities, 2016," March 31, 2017*

Environmental Rankings

■ Niche compiled a list of the nation's snowiest cities, based on the National Oceanic and Atmospheric Administration's 30-year average snowfall data. Among cities with a population of at least 50,000, Minneapolis ranked #24. *Niche.com, Top 25 Snowiest Cities in America, December 10, 2018*

■ Sperling's BestPlaces assessed the 50 largest metropolitan areas of the United States for the likelihood of dangerously extreme weather events or earthquakes. In general the Southeast and South-Central regions have the highest risk of weather extremes and earthquakes, while the Pacific Northwest enjoys the lowest risk. Of the least risky metropolitan areas, the Minneapolis metro area was ranked #7. *www.bestplaces.net, "Avoid Natural Disasters: BestPlaces Reveals The Top 10 Safest Places to Live," October 25, 2017*

■ The U.S. Environmental Protection Agency (EPA) released a list of U.S. metropolitan areas with the most ENERGY STAR certified buildings in 2017. The Minneapolis metro area was ranked #19 out of 25. *U.S. Environmental Protection Agency, "2018 Energy Star Top Cities," April 11, 2018*

■ The U.S. Conference of Mayors and Walmart Stores sponsor the Mayors' Climate Protection Awards Program which recognize mayors for outstanding and innovative practices that mayors are taking to increase energy efficiency in their cities, reduce carbon emissions and expand renewable energy. Minneapolis received an Honorable Mention in the large city category. *U.S. Conference of Mayors, "2019 Mayors' Climate Protection Awards Program," June 28, 2019*

Food/Drink Rankings

- The U.S. Chamber of Commerce Foundation conducted an in-depth study on local food truck regulations, surveyed 288 food truck owners, and ranked 20 major American cities based on how friendly they are for operating a food truck. The compiled index assessed the following: procedures for obtaining permits and licenses; complying with restrictions; and financial obligations associated with operating a food truck. Minneapolis ranked #16 overall (1 being the best) for ease in operating a food truck. *www.foodtrucknation.us, "Food Truck Nation," March 20, 2018*

- According to Fodor's Travel, Minneapolis placed among the 14 best U.S. cities for food-truck cuisine. *www.fodors.com, "America's Best Food Truck Cities," August 23, 2016*

- Target Field was selected as one of PETA's "Top 10 Vegan-Friendly Ballparks" for 2019. The park ranked #3. *People for the Ethical Treatment of Animals, "Top 10 Vegan-Friendly Ballparks," May 23, 2019*

Health/Fitness Rankings

- For each of the 100 largest cities in the United States, the American Fitness Index®, published by the American College of Sports Medicine and the Anthem Foundation, evaluated community infrastructure and 33 health behaviors including preventive health, levels of chronic disease conditions, pedestrian safety, air quality, and community resources that support physical activity. Minneapolis ranked #3 for "community fitness." *americanfitnessindex.org, "ACSM American Fitness Index Health and Community Fitness Status of the 100 Largest U.S. Cities," May 14, 2019*

- Minneapolis was identified as a "2020 Spring Allergy Capital." The area ranked #72 out of 100. Three groups of factors were used to identify the most challenging cities for people with allergies during the spring season: annual spring pollen levels; over the counter medicine use; number of board-certified allergy specialists. *Asthma and Allergy Foundation of America, "Spring Allergy Capitals 2020," March 10, 2020*

- Minneapolis was identified as a "2020 Fall Allergy Capital." The area ranked #76 out of 100. Three groups of factors were used to identify the most challenging cities for people with allergies during the fall season: annual fall pollen levels; over the counter medicine use; number of board-certified allergy specialists. *Asthma and Allergy Foundation of America, "Fall Allergy Capitals 2020," March 10, 2020*

- Minneapolis was identified as a "2019 Asthma Capital." The area ranked #87 out of the nation's 100 largest metropolitan areas. Criteria: estimated asthma prevalence; crude death rate from asthma; and ER visits due to asthma. Risk factors that were analyzed but not factored in the rankings: annual pollen score; annual air quality; public smoking laws; number of board-certified asthma specialists; rescue medication use; controller medication use; uninsured rate; poverty rate. *Asthma and Allergy Foundation of America, "Asthma Capitals 2019: The Most Challenging Places to Live With Asthma," May 7, 2019*

- *Men's Health* ranked 100 major U.S. cities in terms of the best cities for men. Minneapolis ranked #14. Criteria: health; fitness; quality of life. *Men's Health, "The Best & Worst Cities for Men Who Want to Be Fit and Happy," January 1, 2016*

- The Minneapolis metro area ranked #41 out of 189 in The Gallup-Sharecare Well-Being Index. Criteria: purpose; social well being; financial health; community and physical health. Results are based on telephone interviews with adults, aged 18 and older, living in metropolitan areas in the 50 U.S. states and the District of Columbia. *Gallup-Sharecare, "State of American Well-Being, 2017 Community Well-Being Rankings" March 2018*

Pet Rankings

- Minneapolis appeared on *The Dogington Post* site as one of the top cities for dog lovers, ranking #15 out of 20. The real estate brokerage, Redfin and Rover, the largest pet sitter and dog walker network, compiled a list from over 14,000 U.S. cities to come up with a "Rover Rank". Criteria: highest count of dog walks, the city's Walk Score®, for-sale home listings that mention "dog", number of dog walkers and pet sitters and the hours spent and distance logged. *www.dogingtonpost.com, "The 20 Most Dog-Friendly Cities of 2019," April 4, 2019*

Real Estate Rankings

- FitSmallBusiness looked at 50 of the largest metropolitan areas in the U.S. to determine which metro was the best to start a real estate business. Data was compiled from such sources as: Zillow, Trulia, U.S. Census Bureau, and the Bureau of Labor Statistics. Criteria: location; inventory; annual wages; median sales price of homes; days on the market; median price cut percentage; and other factors that would influence real estate professional growth. The Minneapolis metro area ranked #22. *fitsmallbusiness.com, "The Best Cities to Become a Real Estate Agent in 2018," January 30, 2018*

- *WalletHub* compared the most populated U.S. cities, as well as at least two of the most populated cities in each state, for a total of 179, to determine which had the best markets for real estate agents. Minneapolis ranked #89 where demand was high and pay was the best. Criteria: sales per agent; annual median wage for real-estate agents; monthly average starting salary for real estate agents; real estate job density and competition; unemployment rate; home turnover rate; housing-market health index; and other relevant metrics. *www.WalletHub.com, "2019's Best Places to Be a Real Estate Agent," April 24, 2019*

- The Minneapolis metro area was identified as one of the top 20 housing markets to invest in for 2019 by *Forbes*. Criteria: strong job and population growth; stable local economy; anticipated home price appreciation; and other factors. *Forbes.com, "The Best Markets for Real Estate Investments In 2019," January 7, 2019*

- Minneapolis was ranked #78 out of 238 metro areas in terms of housing affordability in 2019 by the National Association of Home Builders (#1 = most affordable). Criteria: the share of homes sold in that area affordable to a family earning the local median income, based on standard mortgage underwriting criteria. *National Association of Home Builders®, NAHB-Wells Fargo Housing Opportunity Index, 4th Quarter 2019*

Safety Rankings

- Allstate ranked the 200 largest cities in America in terms of driver safety. Minneapolis ranked #137. Criteria: internal property damage claims over a two-year period from January 2016 to December 2017. The report helps increase the importance of safety and awareness behind the wheel. *Allstate, "Allstate America's Best Drivers Report, 2019" June 24, 2019*

- The National Insurance Crime Bureau ranked 382 metro areas in the U.S. in terms of per capita rates of vehicle theft. The Minneapolis metro area ranked #130 (#1 = highest rate). Criteria: number of vehicle theft offenses per 100,000 inhabitants in 2018. *National Insurance Crime Bureau, "Hot Spots 2018," June 25, 2019*

Seniors/Retirement Rankings

- From its Best Cities for Successful Aging indexes, the Milken Institute generated rankings for metropolitan areas, weighing data in nine categories—health care, wellness, living arrangements, transportation and convenience, financial characteristics, education, employment, community engagement, and overall livability. The Minneapolis metro area was ranked #14 overall in the large metro area category. *Milken Institute, "Best Cities for Successful Aging, 2017" March 14, 2017*

Sports/Recreation Rankings

- Minneapolis was selected as one of "America's Most Miserable Sports Cities" by *Forbes*. The city was ranked #4. Criteria: postseason losses/misery; years since last title; and number of teams lost to relocation. Contenders were limited to cities with at least 75 cumulative pro seasons of NFL, NBA, NHL, MLS and MLB play. *Forbes, "America's Most Miserable Sports Cities 2016," April 20, 2016*

- Minneapolis was chosen as a bicycle friendly community by the League of American Bicyclists. A "Bicycle Friendly Community" welcomes cyclists by providing safe and supportive accommodation for cycling and encouraging people to bike for transportation and recreation. There are five award levels: Diamond; Platinum; Gold; Silver; and Bronze. The community achieved an award level of Gold. *League of American Bicyclists, "Fall 2019 Awards-Bicycle Friendly Community Master List," November 21, 2019*

- Minneapolis was chosen as one of America's best cities for bicycling. The city ranked #4 out of 50. Criteria: cycling infrastructure that is safe and friendly for all ages; energy and bike culture. The editors only considered cities with populations of 100,000 or more. *Bicycling, "The 50 Best Bike Cities in America," October 10, 2018*

Transportation Rankings

- Business Insider presented an AllTransit Performance Score ranking of public transportation in major U.S. cities and towns, with populations over 250,000, in which Minneapolis earned the #12-ranked "Transit Score," awarded for frequency of service, access to jobs, quality and number of stops, and affordability. *www.businessinsider.com, "The 17 Major U.S. Cities with the Best Public Transportation," April 17, 2018*

Women/Minorities Rankings

- NerdWallet examined data for 529 U.S. cities and ranked them based on the environment for working women. Minneapolis ranked #2. Criteria: women's earnings; labor force participation rate; cost of living; unemployment rate. *www.nerdwallet.com, "Best Cities for Women in the Workforce 2016," April 4, 2016*

- Minneapolis was selected as one of the gayest cities in America by *The Advocate*. The city ranked #22 out of 25. Criteria, among many: Trans Pride parades/festivals; gay rugby teams; lesbian bars; LGBT centers; theater screenings of "Moonlight"; LGBT-inclusive nondiscrimination ordinances; and gay bowling teams. *The Advocate, "Queerest Cities in America 2017" January 12, 2017*

- Personal finance website *WalletHub* compared more than 180 U.S. cities—including the 150 most populated U.S. cities, plus at least two of the most populated cities in each state—across two key dimensions, "Hispanic Business-Friendliness" and "Hispanic Purchasing Power", to arrive at the most favorable conditions for Hispanic entrepreneurs. Minneapolis was ranked #131 out of 182. Criteria includes: share of Hispanic-Owned Businesses; Hispanic entrepreneurship rate to median annual income of Hispanics; Small Business-Friendliness score; cost of living; and number of Hispanics with at least a bachelor's degree. *WalletHub.com, "2019's Best Cities for Hispanic Entrepreneurs," May 1, 2019*

Miscellaneous Rankings

- The watchdog site Charity Navigator conducts an annual study of charities in the nation's major markets both to analyze statistical differences in their financial, accountability, and transparency practices and to track year-to-year variations in individual philanthropic communities. Charity Navigator's analysis demonstrated that the financial, accountability and transparency behaviors of America's largest charities can be influenced by the metropolitan market within which the charity operates. The Minneapolis metro area was ranked #8 among the 30 metro markets in the rating category of Overall Score. *www.charitynavigator.org, "2017 Metro Market Study," May 1, 2017*

- *WalletHub* compared the 150 most populated U.S. cities to determine their operating efficiency. A "Quality of Services" score was constructed for each city and then divided by the total budget per capita to reveal which were managed the best. Minneapolis ranked #91. Criteria: financial stability; economy; education; safety; health; infrastructure and pollution. *www.WalletHub.com, "2019's Best- & Worst-Run Cities in America," July 1, 2019*

- Minneapolis was selected as one of "America's Friendliest Cities." The city ranked #18 in the "Friendliest" category. Respondents to an online survey were asked to rate 38 top urban destinations in the United States as to general friendliness, as well as manners, politeness and warm disposition. *Travel + Leisure, "America's Friendliest Cities," October 20, 2017*

- The National Alliance to End Homelessness listed the 25 most populous metro areas with the highest rate of homelessness. The Minneapolis metro area had a high rate of homelessness. Criteria: number of homeless people per 10,000 population in 2016. *National Alliance to End Homelessness, "Homelessness in the 25 Most Populous U.S. Metro Areas," September 1, 2017*

Business Environment

CITY FINANCES

City Government Finances

Component	2017 ($000)	2017 ($ per capita)
Total Revenues	1,295,426	3,152
Total Expenditures	1,652,051	4,020
Debt Outstanding	2,903,428	7,065
Cash and Securities[1]	2,942,802	7,161

Note: (1) Cash and security holdings of a government at the close of its fiscal year,
including those of its dependent agencies, utilities, and liquor stores.
Source: U.S. Census Bureau, State & Local Government Finances 2017

City Government Revenue by Source

Source	2017 ($000)	2017 ($ per capita)	2017 (%)
General Revenue			
From Federal Government	26,803	65	2.1
From State Government	92,021	224	7.1
From Local Governments	104,276	254	8.0
Taxes			
Property	313,081	762	24.2
Sales and Gross Receipts	112,060	273	8.7
Personal Income	0	0	0.0
Corporate Income	0	0	0.0
Motor Vehicle License	0	0	0.0
Other Taxes	46,114	112	3.6
Current Charges	384,162	935	29.7
Liquor Store	0	0	0.0
Utility	79,840	194	6.2
Employee Retirement	0	0	0.0

Source: U.S. Census Bureau, State & Local Government Finances 2017

City Government Expenditures by Function

Function	2017 ($000)	2017 ($ per capita)	2017 (%)
General Direct Expenditures			
Air Transportation	0	0	0.0
Corrections	0	0	0.0
Education	0	0	0.0
Employment Security Administration	0	0	0.0
Financial Administration	28,578	69	1.7
Fire Protection	62,357	151	3.8
General Public Buildings	0	0	0.0
Governmental Administration, Other	17,748	43	1.1
Health	25,494	62	1.5
Highways	186,498	453	11.3
Hospitals	0	0	0.0
Housing and Community Development	187,867	457	11.4
Interest on General Debt	105,161	255	6.4
Judicial and Legal	9,396	22	0.6
Libraries	7,544	18	0.5
Parking	43,608	106	2.6
Parks and Recreation	107,109	260	6.5
Police Protection	160,137	389	9.7
Public Welfare	0	0	0.0
Sewerage	90,039	219	5.5
Solid Waste Management	33,312	81	2.0
Veterans' Services	0	0	0.0
Liquor Store	0	0	0.0
Utility	69,757	169	4.2
Employee Retirement	0	0	0.0

Source: U.S. Census Bureau, State & Local Government Finances 2017

DEMOGRAPHICS

Population Growth

Area	1990 Census	2000 Census	2010 Census	2018* Estimate	Population Growth (%)	
					1990-2018	2010-2018
City	368,383	382,618	382,578	416,021	12.9	8.7
MSA[1]	2,538,834	2,968,806	3,279,833	3,557,528	40.1	8.5
U.S.	248,709,873	281,421,906	308,745,538	322,903,030	29.8	4.6

Note: (1) Figures cover the Minneapolis-St. Paul-Bloomington, MN-WI Metropolitan Statistical Area—see Appendix B for areas included; (*) 2014-2018 5-year estimated population
Source: U.S. Census Bureau, 1990 Census, Census 2000, Census 2010, 2014-2018 American Community Survey 5-Year Estimates

Household Size

Area	Persons in Household (%)							Average Household Size
	One	Two	Three	Four	Five	Six	Seven or More	
City	40.3	30.8	12.2	9.5	3.7	1.8	1.8	2.30
MSA[1]	27.8	34.2	14.9	13.8	5.9	2.1	1.4	2.60
U.S.	27.7	33.9	15.7	13.0	6.0	2.3	1.4	2.60

Note: (1) Figures cover the Minneapolis-St. Paul-Bloomington, MN-WI Metropolitan Statistical Area—see Appendix B for areas included
Source: U.S. Census Bureau, 2014-2018 American Community Survey 5-Year Estimates

Race

Area	White Alone[2] (%)	Black Alone[2] (%)	Asian Alone[2] (%)	AIAN[3] Alone[2] (%)	NHOPI[4] Alone[2] (%)	Other Race Alone[2] (%)	Two or More Races (%)
City	63.8	19.4	6.1	1.4	0.0	4.7	4.6
MSA[1]	79.2	8.3	6.5	0.6	0.0	2.1	3.3
U.S.	72.7	12.7	5.4	0.8	0.2	4.9	3.2

Note: (1) Figures cover the Minneapolis-St. Paul-Bloomington, MN-WI Metropolitan Statistical Area—see Appendix B for areas included; (2) Alone is defined as not being in combination with one or more other races; (3) American Indian and Alaska Native; (4) Native Hawaiian and Other Pacific Islander
Source: U.S. Census Bureau, 2014-2018 American Community Survey 5-Year Estimates

Hispanic or Latino Origin

Area	Total (%)	Mexican (%)	Puerto Rican (%)	Cuban (%)	Other (%)
City	9.6	5.9	0.5	0.2	3.1
MSA[1]	5.8	3.9	0.3	0.1	1.5
U.S.	17.8	11.2	1.7	0.7	4.2

Note: Persons of Hispanic or Latino origin can be of any race; (1) Figures cover the Minneapolis-St. Paul-Bloomington, MN-WI Metropolitan Statistical Area—see Appendix B for areas included
Source: U.S. Census Bureau, 2014-2018 American Community Survey 5-Year Estimates

Segregation

Type	Segregation Indices[1]				Percent Change		
	1990	2000	2010	2010 Rank[2]	1990-2000	1990-2010	2000-2010
Black/White	62.3	60.1	52.9	60	-2.3	-9.4	-7.2
Asian/White	41.6	44.8	42.8	39	3.2	1.2	-2.0
Hispanic/White	35.5	46.5	42.5	54	11.0	7.0	-4.0

Note: All figures cover the Metropolitan Statistical Area—see Appendix B for areas included; Figures are based on an analysis of 1990, 2000, and 2010 Census Decennial Census tract data by William H. Frey, Brookings Institution and the University of Michigan Social Science Data Analysis Network. In this analysis all racial groups (whites, blacks, and asians) are non-Hispanic members of those races. Hispanics are shown as a separate category; (1) Segregation Indices are Dissimilarity Indices that measure the degree to which the minority group is distributed differently than whites across census tracts. They range from 0 (complete integration) to 100 (complete segregation) where the value indicates the percentage of the minority group that needs to move to be distributed exactly like whites; (2) Ranges from 1 (most segregated) to 102 (least segregated); n/a not available.
Source: www.CensusScope.org

Ancestry

Area	German	Irish	English	American	Italian	Polish	French[2]	Scottish	Dutch
City	21.6	10.1	5.5	1.9	2.8	3.8	2.6	1.4	1.4
MSA[1]	30.1	11.0	5.6	3.0	2.7	4.4	3.4	1.3	1.5
U.S.	13.7	9.9	7.3	6.4	5.2	2.8	2.4	1.7	1.2

Note: Figures are the percentage of the total population reporting a particular ancestry. The nine most commonly reported ancestries in the U.S. are shown. Figures include multiple ancestries (e.g. if a person reported being Irish and Italian, they were included in both columns); (1) Figures cover the Minneapolis-St. Paul-Bloomington, MN-WI Metropolitan Statistical Area—see Appendix B for areas included; (2) Excludes Basque
Source: U.S. Census Bureau, 2014-2018 American Community Survey 5-Year Estimates

Foreign-born Population

Area	Percent of Population Born in								
	Any Foreign Country	Asia	Mexico	Europe	Caribbean	Central America[2]	South America	Africa	Canada
City	15.7	4.1	2.6	1.2	0.3	0.4	1.3	5.6	0.3
MSA[1]	10.6	4.2	1.3	1.1	0.2	0.4	0.5	2.6	0.2
U.S.	13.5	4.1	3.5	1.5	1.3	1.1	0.9	0.7	0.3

Note: (1) Figures cover the Minneapolis-St. Paul-Bloomington, MN-WI Metropolitan Statistical Area—see Appendix B for areas included; (2) Excludes Mexico.
Source: U.S. Census Bureau, 2014-2018 American Community Survey 5-Year Estimates

Marital Status

Area	Never Married	Now Married[2]	Separated	Widowed	Divorced
City	50.6	34.4	1.7	3.0	10.3
MSA[1]	33.1	51.4	1.1	4.4	10.0
U.S.	33.3	48.1	2.0	5.8	10.8

Note: Figures are percentages and cover the population 15 years of age and older; (1) Figures cover the Minneapolis-St. Paul-Bloomington, MN-WI Metropolitan Statistical Area—see Appendix B for areas included; (2) Excludes separated
Source: U.S. Census Bureau, 2014-2018 American Community Survey 5-Year Estimates

Disability by Age

Area	All Ages	Under 18 Years Old	18 to 64 Years Old	65 Years and Over
City	11.2	4.7	10.2	33.8
MSA[1]	9.9	3.7	8.0	30.5
U.S.	12.6	4.2	10.3	35.0

Note: Figures show percent of the civilian noninstitutionalized population that reported having a disability. Disability status is determined from six types of difficulty: vision, hearing, cognitive, ambulatory, self-care, and independent living. For children under 5 years old, hearing and vision difficulty are used to determine disability status. For children between the ages of 5 and 14, disability status is determined from hearing, vision, cognitive, ambulatory, and self-care difficulties. For people aged 15 years and older, they are considered to have a disability if they have difficulty with any one of the six difficulty types; Note: (1) Figures cover the Minneapolis-St. Paul-Bloomington, MN-WI Metropolitan Statistical Area—see Appendix B for areas included
Source: U.S. Census Bureau, 2014-2018 American Community Survey 5-Year Estimates

Age

Area	Percent of Population									Median Age
	Under Age 5	Age 5–19	Age 20–34	Age 35–44	Age 45–54	Age 55–64	Age 65–74	Age 75–84	Age 85+	
City	6.7	16.9	32.1	13.6	11.1	9.9	6.0	2.4	1.2	32.1
MSA[1]	6.5	19.8	20.9	13.2	13.7	12.8	7.7	3.7	1.7	36.9
U.S.	6.1	19.3	20.7	12.6	13.2	12.8	8.8	4.5	1.9	37.9

Note: (1) Figures cover the Minneapolis-St. Paul-Bloomington, MN-WI Metropolitan Statistical Area—see Appendix B for areas included
Source: U.S. Census Bureau, 2014-2018 American Community Survey 5-Year Estimates

Gender

Area	Males	Females	Males per 100 Females
City	211,095	204,926	103.0
MSA[1]	1,762,345	1,795,183	98.2
U.S.	158,984,190	163,918,840	97.0

Note: (1) Figures cover the Minneapolis-St. Paul-Bloomington, MN-WI Metropolitan Statistical Area—see Appendix B for areas included
Source: U.S. Census Bureau, 2014-2018 American Community Survey 5-Year Estimates

Religious Groups by Family

Area	Catholic	Baptist	Non-Den.	Methodist[2]	Lutheran	LDS[3]	Pente-costal	Presby-terian[4]	Muslim[5]	Judaism
MSA[1]	21.7	2.5	3.0	2.8	14.5	0.6	1.8	1.9	0.4	0.7
U.S.	19.1	9.3	4.0	4.0	2.3	2.0	1.9	1.6	0.8	0.7

Note: Figures are the number of adherents as a percentage of the total population; (1) Figures cover the Minneapolis-St. Paul-Bloomington, MN-WI Metropolitan Statistical Area—see Appendix B for areas included; (2) Methodist/Pietist; (3) Latter Day Saints; (4) Reformed; (5) Figures are estimates
Source: Association of Statisticians of American Religious Bodies, 2010 U.S. Religion Census: Religious Congregations & Membership Study

Religious Groups by Tradition

Area	Catholic	Evangelical Protestant	Mainline Protestant	Other Tradition	Black Protestant	Orthodox
MSA[1]	21.7	12.9	14.5	2.3	0.5	0.2
U.S.	19.1	16.2	7.3	4.3	1.6	0.3

Note: Figures are the number of adherents as a percentage of the total population; (1) Figures cover the Minneapolis-St. Paul-Bloomington, MN-WI Metropolitan Statistical Area—see Appendix B for areas included
Source: Association of Statisticians of American Religious Bodies, 2010 U.S. Religion Census: Religious Congregations & Membership Study

ECONOMY

Gross Metropolitan Product

Area	2017	2018	2019	2020	Rank[2]
MSA[1]	260.9	273.1	284.6	296.0	14

Note: Figures are in billions of dollars; (1) Figures cover the Minneapolis-St. Paul-Bloomington, MN-WI Metropolitan Statistical Area—see Appendix B for areas included; (2) Rank is based on 2018 data and ranges from 1 to 381
Source: U.S. Conference of Mayors, U.S. Metro Economies: GMP & Employment 2018-2020, September 2019

Economic Growth

Area	2015-17 (%)	2018 (%)	2019 (%)	2020 (%)	Rank[2]
MSA[1]	1.9	2.3	2.5	1.9	144
U.S.	1.9	2.9	2.3	2.1	–

Note: Figures are real gross metropolitan product (GMP) growth rates and represent average annual percent change; (1) Figures cover the Minneapolis-St. Paul-Bloomington, MN-WI Metropolitan Statistical Area—see Appendix B for areas included; (2) Rank is based on 2017 2-year average annual percent change and ranges from 1 to 381
Source: U.S. Conference of Mayors, U.S. Metro Economies: GMP & Employment 2018-2020, September 2019

Metropolitan Area Exports

Area	2013	2014	2015	2016	2017	2018	Rank[2]
MSA[1]	23,747.5	21,198.2	19,608.6	18,329.2	19,070.9	20,016.2	21

Note: Figures are in millions of dollars; (1) Figures cover the Minneapolis-St. Paul-Bloomington, MN-WI Metropolitan Statistical Area—see Appendix B for areas included; (2) Rank is based on 2018 data and ranges from 1 to 387
Source: U.S. Department of Commerce, International Trade Administration, Office of Trade and Economic Analysis, Industry and Analysis, Exports by Metropolitan Area, data extracted April 15, 2020

Building Permits

Area	Single-Family			Multi-Family			Total		
	2017	2018	Pct. Chg.	2017	2018	Pct. Chg.	2017	2018	Pct. Chg.
City	137	162	18.2	2,117	3,463	63.6	2,254	3,625	60.8
MSA[1]	8,782	8,985	2.3	6,318	9,221	45.9	15,100	18,206	20.6
U.S.	820,000	855,300	4.3	462,000	473,500	2.5	1,282,000	1,328,800	3.7

Note: (1) Figures cover the Minneapolis-St. Paul-Bloomington, MN-WI Metropolitan Statistical Area—see
Appendix B for areas included; Figures represent new, privately-owned housing units authorized (unadjusted
data); All permit data are based on estimates with imputation
Source: U.S. Census Bureau, Manufacturing, Mining, and Construction Statistics, Building Permits, 2017, 2018

Bankruptcy Filings

Area	Business Filings			Nonbusiness Filings		
	2018	2019	% Chg.	2018	2019	% Chg.
Hennepin County	61	62	1.6	2,124	2,032	-4.3
U.S.	22,232	22,780	2.5	751,186	752,160	0.1

Note: Business filings include Chapter 7, Chapter 9, Chapter 11, Chapter 12, Chapter 13, Chapter 15, and
Section 304; Nonbusiness filings include Chapter 7, Chapter 11, and Chapter 13
Source: Administrative Office of the U.S. Courts, Business and Nonbusiness Bankruptcy, County Cases
Commenced by Chapter of the Bankruptcy Code, During the 12-Month Period Ending December 31, 2018 and
Business and Nonbusiness Bankruptcy, County Cases Commenced by Chapter of the Bankruptcy Code, During
the 12-Month Period Ending December 31, 2019

Housing Vacancy Rates

Area	Gross Vacancy Rate[2] (%)			Year-Round Vacancy Rate[3] (%)			Rental Vacancy Rate[4] (%)			Homeowner Vacancy Rate[5] (%)		
	2017	2018	2019	2017	2018	2019	2017	2018	2019	2017	2018	2019
MSA[1]	4.5	3.9	4.4	4.1	3.3	3.8	4.2	4.1	4.1	0.9	0.4	0.5
U.S.	12.7	12.3	12.0	9.9	9.7	9.5	7.2	6.9	6.7	1.6	1.5	1.4

Note: (1) Figures cover the Minneapolis-St. Paul-Bloomington, MN-WI Metropolitan Statistical Area—see
Appendix B for areas included; (2) The percentage of the total housing inventory that is vacant; (3) The
percentage of the housing inventory (excluding seasonal units) that is year-round vacant; (4) The percentage of
rental inventory that is vacant for rent; (5) The percentage of homeowner inventory that is vacant for sale
Source: U.S. Census Bureau, Housing Vacancies and Homeownership Annual Statistics: 2017, 2018, 2019

INCOME

Income

Area	Per Capita ($)	Median Household ($)	Average Household ($)
City	37,071	58,993	85,887
MSA[1]	39,647	76,870	101,071
U.S.	32,621	60,293	84,938

Note: (1) Figures cover the Minneapolis-St. Paul-Bloomington, MN-WI Metropolitan Statistical Area—see
Appendix B for areas included
Source: U.S. Census Bureau, 2014-2018 American Community Survey 5-Year Estimates

Household Income Distribution

Area	Percent of Households Earning							
	Under $15,000	$15,000 -$24,999	$25,000 -$34,999	$35,000 -$49,999	$50,000 -$74,999	$75,000 -$99,999	$100,000 -$149,999	$150,000 and up
City	14.2	9.0	8.6	11.9	16.3	11.5	14.3	14.3
MSA[1]	7.1	6.6	7.2	11.0	17.0	14.0	19.0	18.2
U.S.	10.9	9.3	9.3	12.6	17.5	12.5	14.6	13.3

Note: (1) Figures cover the Minneapolis-St. Paul-Bloomington, MN-WI Metropolitan Statistical Area—see
Appendix B for areas included
Source: U.S. Census Bureau, 2014-2018 American Community Survey 5-Year Estimates

Poverty Rate

Area	All Ages	Under 18 Years Old	18 to 64 Years Old	65 Years and Over
City	19.9	26.4	19.0	13.2
MSA[1]	9.0	11.7	8.5	6.6
U.S.	14.1	19.5	13.2	9.3

Note: Figures are percentage of people whose income during the past 12 months was below the poverty level; (1) Figures cover the Minneapolis-St. Paul-Bloomington, MN-WI Metropolitan Statistical Area—see Appendix B for areas included
Source: U.S. Census Bureau, 2014-2018 American Community Survey 5-Year Estimates

EMPLOYMENT

Labor Force and Employment

Area	Civilian Labor Force			Workers Employed		
	Dec. 2018	Dec. 2019	% Chg.	Dec. 2018	Dec. 2019	% Chg.
City	242,642	245,206	1.1	236,426	238,869	1.0
MSA[1]	2,015,207	2,037,880	1.1	1,957,633	1,976,964	1.0
U.S.	162,510,000	164,007,000	0.9	156,481,000	158,504,000	1.3

Note: Data is not seasonally adjusted and covers workers 16 years of age and older; (1) Figures cover the Minneapolis-St. Paul-Bloomington, MN-WI Metropolitan Statistical Area—see Appendix B for areas included
Source: Bureau of Labor Statistics, Local Area Unemployment Statistics

Unemployment Rate

Area	2019											
	Jan.	Feb.	Mar.	Apr.	May	Jun.	Jul.	Aug.	Sep.	Oct.	Nov.	Dec.
City	3.1	2.9	3.0	2.5	2.6	3.2	3.1	3.0	2.6	2.7	2.5	2.6
MSA[1]	3.7	3.4	3.4	2.7	2.6	3.1	3.0	2.9	2.5	2.6	2.6	3.0
U.S.	4.4	4.1	3.9	3.3	3.4	3.8	4.0	3.8	3.3	3.3	3.3	3.4

Note: Data is not seasonally adjusted and covers workers 16 years of age and older; (1) Figures cover the Minneapolis-St. Paul-Bloomington, MN-WI Metropolitan Statistical Area—see Appendix B for areas included
Source: Bureau of Labor Statistics, Local Area Unemployment Statistics

Average Wages

Occupation	$/Hr.	Occupation	$/Hr.
Accountants and Auditors	36.40	Maintenance and Repair Workers	23.00
Automotive Mechanics	23.10	Marketing Managers	71.50
Bookkeepers	22.60	Network and Computer Systems Admin.	43.10
Carpenters	28.40	Nurses, Licensed Practical	24.50
Cashiers	12.70	Nurses, Registered	40.60
Computer Programmers	40.40	Nursing Assistants	17.80
Computer Systems Analysts	46.90	Office Clerks, General	19.90
Computer User Support Specialists	27.80	Physical Therapists	40.20
Construction Laborers	27.50	Physicians	111.80
Cooks, Restaurant	15.30	Plumbers, Pipefitters and Steamfitters	38.80
Customer Service Representatives	20.60	Police and Sheriff's Patrol Officers	37.30
Dentists	105.30	Postal Service Mail Carriers	25.40
Electricians	35.60	Real Estate Sales Agents	22.30
Engineers, Electrical	49.80	Retail Salespersons	14.60
Fast Food and Counter Workers	12.30	Sales Representatives, Technical/Scientific	41.10
Financial Managers	69.30	Secretaries, Exc. Legal/Medical/Executive	20.70
First-Line Supervisors of Office Workers	31.80	Security Guards	17.40
General and Operations Managers	61.70	Surgeons	n/a
Hairdressers/Cosmetologists	16.60	Teacher Assistants, Exc. Postsecondary*	16.10
Home Health and Personal Care Aides	13.80	Teachers, Secondary School, Exc. Sp. Ed.*	32.40
Janitors and Cleaners	16.10	Telemarketers	16.30
Landscaping/Groundskeeping Workers	17.80	Truck Drivers, Heavy/Tractor-Trailer	25.50
Lawyers	61.90	Truck Drivers, Light/Delivery Services	21.00
Maids and Housekeeping Cleaners	14.50	Waiters and Waitresses	14.40

Note: Wage data covers the Minneapolis-St. Paul-Bloomington, MN-WI Metropolitan Statistical Area—see Appendix B for areas included; (*) Hourly wages were calculated from annual wage data based on a 40 hour work week; n/a not available.
Source: Bureau of Labor Statistics, Metro Area Occupational Employment & Wage Estimates, May 2019

Employment by Occupation

Occupation Classification	City (%)	MSA[1] (%)	U.S. (%)
Management, Business, Science, and Arts	49.8	43.9	37.9
Natural Resources, Construction, and Maintenance	3.8	6.6	8.9
Production, Transportation, and Material Moving	9.3	12.3	13.3
Sales and Office	18.9	21.8	22.1
Service	18.2	15.4	17.9

Note: Figures cover employed civilians 16 years of age and older; (1) Figures cover the Minneapolis-St. Paul-Bloomington, MN-WI Metropolitan Statistical Area—see Appendix B for areas included
Source: U.S. Census Bureau, 2014-2018 American Community Survey 5-Year Estimates

Employment by Industry

Sector	MSA[1] Number of Employees	MSA[1] Percent of Total	U.S. Percent of Total
Construction, Mining, and Logging	80,900	4.0	5.4
Education and Health Services	345,500	17.0	16.1
Financial Activities	157,900	7.8	5.8
Government	254,500	12.5	15.0
Information	35,500	1.7	1.9
Leisure and Hospitality	185,000	9.1	10.8
Manufacturing	199,400	9.8	8.4
Other Services	80,100	3.9	3.9
Professional and Business Services	329,000	16.2	14.1
Retail Trade	194,100	9.5	10.6
Transportation, Warehousing, and Utilities	80,000	3.9	4.2
Wholesale Trade	91,600	4.5	3.9

Note: Figures are non-farm employment as of December 2019. Figures are not seasonally adjusted and include workers 16 years of age and older; (1) Figures cover the Minneapolis-St. Paul-Bloomington, MN-WI Metropolitan Statistical Area—see Appendix B for areas included
Source: Bureau of Labor Statistics, Current Employment Statistics, Employment, Hours, and Earnings

Occupations with Greatest Projected Employment Growth: 2019 – 2021

Occupation[1]	2019 Employment	2021 Projected Employment	Numeric Employment Change	Percent Employment Change
Personal Care Aides	77,670	81,800	4,130	5.3
Registered Nurses	69,170	71,020	1,850	2.7
Combined Food Preparation and Serving Workers, Including Fast Food	65,670	66,730	1,060	1.6
Light Truck or Delivery Services Drivers	17,520	18,560	1,040	5.9
Janitors and Cleaners, Except Maids and Housekeeping Cleaners	47,900	48,820	920	1.9
Cooks, Restaurant	28,290	28,980	690	2.4
Teacher Assistants	36,820	37,490	670	1.8
Home Health Aides	22,450	22,980	530	2.4
Carpenters	18,170	18,660	490	2.7
Financial Managers	16,170	16,630	460	2.8

Note: Projections cover Minnesota; (1) Sorted by numeric employment change
Source: www.projectionscentral.com, State Occupational Projections, 2019–2021 Short-Term Projections

Fastest Growing Occupations: 2019 – 2021

Occupation[1]	2019 Employment	2021 Projected Employment	Numeric Employment Change	Percent Employment Change
Couriers and Messengers	950	1,010	60	6.3
Physician Assistants	2,020	2,140	120	5.9
Light Truck or Delivery Services Drivers	17,520	18,560	1,040	5.9
Respiratory Therapists	1,900	2,000	100	5.3
Personal Care Aides	77,670	81,800	4,130	5.3
Massage Therapists	2,290	2,410	120	5.2
Operations Research Analysts	3,480	3,640	160	4.6
Nurse Practitioners	3,900	4,080	180	4.6
Information Security Analysts	2,890	3,020	130	4.5
Medical Assistants	10,230	10,660	430	4.2

Note: Projections cover Minnesota; (1) Sorted by percent employment change and excludes occupations with numeric employment change less than 50
Source: www.projectionscentral.com, State Occupational Projections, 2019–2021 Short-Term Projections

TAXES

State Corporate Income Tax Rates

State	Tax Rate (%)	Income Brackets ($)	Num. of Brackets	Financial Institution Tax Rate (%)[a]	Federal Income Tax Ded.
Minnesota	9.8 (n)	Flat rate	1	9.8 (n)	No

Note: Tax rates as of January 1, 2020; (a) Rates listed are the corporate income tax rate applied to financial institutions or excise taxes based on income; (n) In addition, Minnesota levies a 5.8% tentative minimum tax on Alternative Minimum Taxable Income. Minnesota also imposes a surtax ranging up to $10,380.
Source: Federation of Tax Administrators, State Corporate Income Tax Rates, January 1, 2020

State Individual Income Tax Rates

State	Tax Rate (%)	Income Brackets ($)	Personal Exemptions ($)			Standard Ded. ($)	
			Single	Married	Depend.	Single	Married
Minnesota (a)	5.35 - 9.85	26,960 - 164,401 (n)	(d)	(d)	4,250	12,400	24,800 (d)

Note: Tax rates as of January 1, 2020; Local- and county-level taxes are not included; Federal income tax is not deductible on state income tax returns; (a) 19 states have statutory provision for automatically adjusting to the rate of inflation the dollar values of the income tax brackets, standard deductions, and/or personal exemptions. Michigan indexes the personal exemption only. Oregon does not index the income brackets for $125,000 and over; (d) These states use the personal exemption/standard deduction amounts provided in the federal Internal Revenue Code; (n) The income brackets reported for Minnesota are for single individuals. For married couples filing jointly, the same tax rates apply to income brackets ranging from $39,410 to $273,470.
Source: Federation of Tax Administrators, State Individual Income Tax Rates, January 1, 2020

Various State Sales and Excise Tax Rates

State	State Sales Tax (%)	Gasoline[1] (¢/gal.)	Cigarette[2] ($/pack)	Spirits[3] ($/gal.)	Wine[4] ($/gal.)	Beer[5] ($/gal.)	Recreational Marijuana (%)
Minnesota	6.875	28.6	3.04	9.01	1.22	0.51	Not legal

Note: All tax rates as of January 1, 2020; (1) The American Petroleum Institute has developed a methodology for determining the average tax rate on a gallon of fuel. Rates may include any of the following: excise taxes, environmental fees, storage tank fees, other fees or taxes, general sales tax, and local taxes; (2) The federal excise tax of $1.0066 per pack and local taxes are not included; (3) Rates are those applicable to off-premise sales of 40% alcohol by volume (a.b.v.) distilled spirits in 750ml containers. Local excise taxes are excluded; (4) Rates are those applicable to off-premise sales of 11% a.b.v. non-carbonated wine in 750ml containers; (5) Rates are those applicable to off-premise sales of 4.7% a.b.v. beer in 12 ounce containers.
Source: Tax Foundation, 2020 Facts & Figures: How Does Your State Compare?

State Business Tax Climate Index Rankings

State	Overall Rank	Corporate Tax Rank	Individual Income Tax Rank	Sales Tax Rank	Property Tax Rank	Unemployment Insurance Tax Rank
Minnesota	45	44	46	28	26	34

Note: The index is a measure of how each state's tax laws affect economic performance. The lower the rank, the more favorable a state's tax system is for business. States without a given tax are given a ranking of 1. The scores/rankings for the District of Columbia do not affect other states. The 2020 index represents the tax climate as of July 1, 2019.
Source: Tax Foundation, State Business Tax Climate Index 2020

COMMERCIAL REAL ESTATE

Office Market

Market Area	Inventory (sq. ft.)	Vacancy Rate (%)	Under Construction (sq. ft.)	YTD Net Absorption (sq. ft.)	Total Average Asking Rent ($/sq. ft./year)
Minneapolis	119,353,811	10.7	1,192,300	842,835	24.62
National	4,923,349,992	13.0	102,814,961	2,049,925	29.54

Source: Newmark Grubb Knight Frank, National Office Market Report, 1st Quarter 2020

Industrial/Warehouse/R&D Market

Market Area	Inventory (sq. ft.)	Vacancy Rate (%)	Under Construction (sq. ft.)	YTD Net Absorption (sq. ft.)	Total Average Asking Rent ($/sq. ft./year)
Minneapolis	393,636,360	3.4	2,565,407	-1,255,362	5.71
National	15,332,123,451	5.4	322,705,045	48,296,842	7.54

Source: Newmark Grubb Knight Frank, National Industrial Market Report, 1st Quarter 2020

COMMERCIAL UTILITIES

Typical Monthly Electric Bills

Area	Commercial Service ($/month)		Industrial Service ($/month)	
	1,500 kWh	40 kW demand 14,000 kWh	1,000 kW demand 200,000 kWh	50,000 kW demand 32,500,000 kWh
City	193	1,507	25,833	2,585,742
Average[1]	203	1,612	25,706	2,520,671

Note: Figures are based on annualized rates; (1) Average based on 187 utilities surveyed
Source: Edison Electric Institute, Typical Bills and Average Rates Report, Summer 2019

TRANSPORTATION

Means of Transportation to Work

Area	Car/Truck/Van		Public Transportation			Bicycle	Walked	Other Means	Worked at Home
	Drove Alone	Car-pooled	Bus	Subway	Railroad				
City	60.7	7.5	11.8	1.2	0.3	4.1	7.3	1.8	5.4
MSA[1]	77.6	8.2	4.2	0.2	0.2	0.9	2.3	1.0	5.5
U.S.	76.4	9.1	2.5	1.9	0.6	0.6	2.7	1.3	4.9

Note: Figures are percentages and cover workers 16 years of age and older; (1) Figures cover the
Minneapolis-St. Paul-Bloomington, MN-WI Metropolitan Statistical Area—see Appendix B for areas included
Source: U.S. Census Bureau, 2014-2018 American Community Survey 5-Year Estimates

Travel Time to Work

Area	Less Than 10 Minutes	10 to 19 Minutes	20 to 29 Minutes	30 to 44 Minutes	45 to 59 Minutes	60 to 89 Minutes	90 Minutes or More
City	8.3	32.2	30.8	20.3	4.2	3.0	1.2
MSA[1]	10.4	27.4	25.1	23.5	8.1	4.3	1.4
U.S.	12.5	28.7	20.9	20.7	8.2	6.3	2.8

Note: Note: Figures are percentages and include workers 16 years old and over; (1) Figures cover the
Minneapolis-St. Paul-Bloomington, MN-WI Metropolitan Statistical Area—see Appendix B for areas included
Source: U.S. Census Bureau, 2014-2018 American Community Survey 5-Year Estimates

Key Congestion Measures

Area	1982	1992	2002	2012	2017
Annual Hours of Delay, Total (000)	11,029	34,442	73,265	90,573	103,695
Annual Hours of Delay, Per Auto Commuter	12	30	48	50	56
Annual Congestion Cost, Total (million $)	82	361	981	1,601	1,896
Annual Congestion Cost, Per Auto Commuter ($)	233	501	831	805	894

Source: Texas A&M Transportation Institute, 2019 Urban Mobility Report

Freeway Travel Time Index

Area	1982	1987	1992	1997	2002	2007	2012	2017
Urban Area Index[1]	1.07	1.11	1.16	1.24	1.27	1.27	1.26	1.25
Urban Area Rank[1,2]	35	29	23	11	14	20	21	25

Note: Freeway Travel Time Index—the ratio of travel time in the peak period to the travel time at free-flow conditions. For example, a value of 1.30 indicates a 20-minute free-flow trip takes 26 minutes in the peak (20 minutes x 1.30 = 26 minutes); (1) Covers the Minneapolis-St. Paul MN-WI urban area; (2) Rank is based on 101 larger urban areas (#1 = highest travel time index)
Source: Texas A&M Transportation Institute, 2019 Urban Mobility Report

Public Transportation

Agency Name / Mode of Transportation	Vehicles Operated in Maximum Service[1]	Annual Unlinked Passenger Trips[2] (in thous.)	Annual Passenger Miles[3] (in thous.)
Metro Transit			
Bus (directly operated)	758	54,910.5	260,030.3
Commuter Rail (purchased transportation)	20	787.3	19,441.5
Light Rail (directly operated)	76	24,955.6	100,276.9

Note: (1) Number of revenue vehicles operated by the given mode and type of service to meet the annual maximum service requirement. This is the revenue vehicle count during the peak season of the year; on the week and day that maximum service is provided. Vehicles operated in maximum service (VOMS) exclude atypical days and one-time special events; (2) Number of passengers who boarded public transportation vehicles. Passengers are counted each time they board a vehicle no matter how many vehicles they use to travel from their origin to their destination. (3) Sum of the distances ridden by all passengers during the entire fiscal year.
Source: Federal Transit Administration, National Transit Database, 2018

Air Transportation

Airport Name and Code / Type of Service	Passenger Airlines[1]	Passenger Enplanements	Freight Carriers[2]	Freight (lbs)
Minneapolis-St. Paul International (MSP)				
Domestic service (U.S. carriers - 2019)	32	17,567,847	17	184,510,152
International service (U.S. carriers - 2018)	11	1,292,256	4	23,155,376

Note: (1) Includes all U.S.-based major, minor and commuter airlines that carried at least one passenger during the year; (2) Includes all U.S.-based airlines and freight carriers that transported at least one pound of freight during the year.
Source: Bureau of Transportation Statistics, The Intermodal Transportation Database, Air Carriers: T-100 Domestic Market (U.S. Carriers), 2019; Bureau of Transportation Statistics, The Intermodal Transportation Database, Air Carriers: T-100 International Market (U.S. Carriers), 2018

Other Transportation Statistics

Major Highways:	I-35; I-94
Amtrak Service:	Yes (station is located in St. Paul)
Major Waterways/Ports:	Port of Minneapolis

Source: Amtrak.com; Google Maps

BUSINESSES

Major Business Headquarters

Company Name	Industry	Rankings	
		Fortune[1]	Forbes[2]
Ameriprise Financial	Diversified Financials	249	-
Cargill	Food, Drink & Tobacco	-	1
General Mills	Food Consumer Products	200	-
Mortenson	Construction	-	98
Target	General Merchandisers	39	-
Thrivent Financial for Lutherans	Insurance, Life, Health (Mutual)	351	-
U.S. Bancorp	Commercial Banks	117	-
Xcel Energy	Utilities, Gas and Electric	274	-

Note: (1) Companies that produce a 10-K are ranked 1 to 500 based on 2018 revenue; (2) All private companies with at least $2 billion in annual revenue through the end of their most current fiscal year are ranked 1 to 228; companies listed are headquartered in the city; dashes indicate no ranking
Source: Fortune, "Fortune 500," June 2019; Forbes, "America's Largest Private Companies," 2019 Rankings

Fast-Growing Businesses

According to *Inc.*, Minneapolis is home to two of America's 500 fastest-growing private companies: **phData** (#48); **Park Financial Group** (#252). Criteria: must be an independent, privately-held, for-profit, U.S. corporation, proprietorship or partnership as of December 31, 2018; revenues must be at least $100,000 in 2015 and $2 million in 2018; must have four-year operating/sales history. *Inc., "America's 500 Fastest-Growing Private Companies," 2019*

According to *Initiative for a Competitive Inner City (ICIC)*, Minneapolis is home to one of America's 100 fastest-growing "inner city" companies: **On-Demand Services Group** (#59). Criteria for inclusion: company must be headquartered in or have 51 percent or more of its physical operations in an economically distressed urban area; must be an independent, for-profit corporation, partnership or proprietorship; must have 10 or more employees and have a five-year sales history that includes sales of at least $200,000 in the base year and at least $1 million in the current year with no decrease in sales over the two most recent years. Companies were ranked overall by revenue growth over the five-year period between 2014 and 2018. *Initiative for a Competitive Inner City (ICIC), "Inner City 100 Companies," 2019*

Minority- and Women-Owned Businesses

Group	All Firms		Firms with Paid Employees			
	Firms	Sales ($000)	Firms	Sales ($000)	Employees	Payroll ($000)
AIAN[1]	629	56,171	31	(s)	500 - 999	(s)
Asian	1,633	483,166	420	448,249	3,658	93,512
Black	6,009	641,492	294	(s)	5,000 - 9,999	(s)
Hispanic	1,333	163,280	145	120,458	1,620	33,314
NHOPI[2]	59	(s)	0	(s)	0 - 19	(s)
Women	16,547	1,901,149	1,602	1,479,305	19,696	549,893
All Firms	44,702	95,129,881	9,209	93,644,436	299,777	18,398,078

Note: Figures cover firms located in the city; minority- and women-owned business are defined as firms in which the corresponding group own 51% or more of the stock or equity of the company; (1) American Indian and Alaska Native; (2) Native Hawaiian and Other Pacific Islander; (s) estimates are suppressed when publication standards are not met
Source: U.S. Census Bureau, 2012 Economic Census, Survey of Business Owners

HOTELS & CONVENTION CENTERS

Hotels, Motels and Vacation Rentals

Area	5 Star		4 Star		3 Star		2 Star		1 Star		Not Rated	
	Num.	Pct.[3]	Num.	Pct.[3]	Num.	Pct.[3]	Num.	Pct.[3]	Num.	Pct.[3]	Num.	Pct.[3]
City[1]	0	0.0	17	4.6	86	23.1	38	10.2	93	24.9	139	37.3
Total[2]	266	1.3	1,517	7.2	4,627	21.8	3,210	15.1	3,974	18.7	7,601	35.9

Note: (1) Figures cover Minneapolis and vicinity; (2) Figures cover all 100 cities in this book; (3) Percentage of hotels which have a given star rating; Star ratings are determined by priceline.com and offer an indication of the general quality of a particular hotel.
Source: priceline.com, April 27, 2020

Major Convention Centers

Name	Overall Space (sq. ft.)	Exhibit Space (sq. ft.)	Meeting Space (sq. ft.)	Meeting Rooms
Minneapolis Convention Center	n/a	475,000	95,458	87
Saint Paul River Centre	n/a	100,000	n/a	15

Note: Table includes convention centers located in the Minneapolis-St. Paul-Bloomington, MN-WI metro area; n/a not available
Source: Original research

Living Environment

COST OF LIVING

Cost of Living Index

Composite Index	Groceries	Housing	Utilities	Trans-portation	Health Care	Misc. Goods/ Services
106.6	103.6	102.9	97.5	104.4	105.6	113.9

Note: The Cost of Living Index measures regional differences in the cost of consumer goods and services, excluding taxes and non-consumer expenditures, for professional and managerial households in the top income quintile. It is based on more than 50,000 prices covering almost 60 different items for which prices are collected three times a year by chambers of commerce, economic development organizations or university applied economic centers in each participating urban area. The numbers shown should be read as a percentage above or below the national average of 100. For example, a value of 115.4 in the groceries column indicates that grocery prices are 15.4% higher than the national average. Small differences in the index numbers should not be interpreted as significant; Figures cover the Minneapolis MN urban area.
Source: The Council for Community and Economic Research, ACCRA Cost of Living Index, 2019

Grocery Prices

Area[1]	T-Bone Steak ($/pound)	Frying Chicken ($/pound)	Whole Milk ($/half gal.)	Eggs ($/dozen)	Orange Juice ($/64 oz.)	Coffee ($/11.5 oz.)
City[2]	13.60	2.12	2.58	1.82	3.70	4.69
Avg.	11.40	1.41	1.93	1.54	3.51	4.30
Min.	7.40	0.92	0.85	0.58	2.67	2.90
Max.	15.58	2.68	4.09	4.18	5.57	8.10

*Note: (1) Values for the local area are compared with the average, minimum and maximum values for all 290 areas in the Cost of Living Index; (2) Figures cover the Minneapolis MN urban area; **T-Bone Steak** (price per pound); **Frying Chicken** (price per pound, whole fryer); **Whole Milk** (half gallon carton); **Eggs** (price per dozen, Grade A, large); **Orange Juice** (64 oz. Tropicana or Florida Natural); **Coffee** (11.5 oz. can, vacuum-packed, Maxwell House, Hills Bros, or Folgers).*
Source: The Council for Community and Economic Research, ACCRA Cost of Living Index, 2019

Housing and Utility Costs

Area[1]	New Home Price ($)	Apartment Rent ($/month)	All Electric ($/month)	Part Electric ($/month)	Other Energy ($/month)	Telephone ($/month)
City[2]	371,899	1,192	-	94.84	68.83	176.60
Avg.	362,090	1,142	174.35	100.00	67.76	179.60
Min.	198,329	501	91.58	31.44	28.51	165.30
Max.	2,074,561	5,050	388.18	239.41	306.15	207.90

*Note: (1) Values for the local area are compared with the average, minimum and maximum values for all 290 areas in the Cost of Living Index; (2) Figures cover the Minneapolis MN urban area; **New Home Price** (2,400 sf living area, 8,000 sf lot, in urban area with full utilities); **Apartment Rent** (950 sf 2 bedroom/1.5 or 2 bath, unfurnished, excluding all utilities except water); **All Electric** (average monthly cost for an all-electric home); **Part Electric** (average monthly cost for a part-electric home); **Other Energy** (average monthly cost for natural gas, fuel oil, coal, wood, and any other forms of energy except electricity); **Telephone** (price includes the base monthly rate plus taxes and fees for three lines of mobile phone service).*
Source: The Council for Community and Economic Research, ACCRA Cost of Living Index, 2019

Health Care, Transportation, and Other Costs

Area[1]	Doctor ($/visit)	Dentist ($/visit)	Optometrist ($/visit)	Gasoline ($/gallon)	Beauty Salon ($/visit)	Men's Shirt ($)
City[2]	150.35	87.29	90.36	2.41	35.33	37.08
Avg.	114.85	97.58	106.10	2.50	38.15	32.15
Min.	39.00	62.22	52.22	1.53	16.88	10.27
Max.	206.67	151.53	258.67	3.79	79.29	59.30

*Note: (1) Values for the local area are compared with the average, minimum and maximum values for all 290 areas in the Cost of Living Index; (2) Figures cover the Minneapolis MN urban area; **Doctor** (general practitioners routine exam of an established patient); **Dentist** (adult teeth cleaning and periodic oral examination); **Optometrist** (full vision eye exam for established adult patient); **Gasoline** (one gallon regular unleaded, national brand, including all taxes, cash price at self-service pump if available); **Beauty Salon** (woman's shampoo, trim, and blow-dry); **Men's Shirt** (cotton/polyester dress shirt, pinpoint weave, long sleeves).*
Source: The Council for Community and Economic Research, ACCRA Cost of Living Index, 2019

HOUSING

House Price Index (HPI)

Area	National Ranking[2]	Quarterly Change (%)	One-Year Change (%)	Five-Year Change (%)
MSA[1]	119	0.32	4.85	31.56
U.S.[3]	–	1.26	5.09	32.88

Note: The HPI is a weighted repeat sales index. It measures average price changes in repeat sales or refinancings on the same properties. This information is obtained by reviewing repeat mortgage transactions on single-family properties whose mortgages have been purchased or securitized by Fannie Mae or Freddie Mac in January 1975; (1) Figures cover the Minneapolis-St. Paul-Bloomington, MN-WI Metropolitan Statistical Area—see Appendix B for areas included; (2) Rankings are based on annual percentage change for all metro areas containing at least 15,000 transactions over the last 10 years and ranges from 1 to 232; (3) figures based on a weighted average of Census Division estimates using a seasonally adjusted, purchase-only index; all figures are for the period ending December 31, 2019
Source: Federal Housing Finance Agency, House Price Index, February 25, 2020

Median Single-Family Home Prices

Area	2017	2018	2019[p]	Percent Change 2018 to 2019
MSA[1]	252.1	273.4	288.6	5.6
U.S. Average	248.8	261.6	274.6	5.0

Note: Figures are median sales prices of existing single-family homes in thousands of dollars; (p) preliminary; (1) Figures cover the Minneapolis-St. Paul-Bloomington, MN-WI Metropolitan Statistical Area—see Appendix B for areas included
Source: National Association of Realtors, Median Sales Price of Existing Single-Family Homes for Metropolitan Areas, 4th Quarter 2019

Qualifying Income Based on Median Sales Price of Existing Single-Family Homes

Area	With 5% Down ($)	With 10% Down ($)	With 20% Down ($)
MSA[1]	61,245	58,021	51,574
U.S. Average	58,663	55,575	49,400

Note: Figures are preliminary; Qualifying income is based on a mortgage rate of 3.76%. Monthly principal and interest payment is limited to 25% of income; (1) Figures cover the Minneapolis-St. Paul-Bloomington, MN-WI Metropolitan Statistical Area—see Appendix B for areas included
Source: National Association of Realtors, Qualifying Income Based on Median Sales Price of Existing Single-Family Homes for Metropolitan Areas, 4th Quarter 2019

Median Apartment Condo-Coop Home Prices

Area	2017	2018	2019[p]	Percent Change 2018 to 2019
MSA[1]	n/a	n/a	n/a	n/a
U.S. Average	234.3	241.0	249.5	3.5

Note: Figures are median sales prices of existing apartment condo-coop homes in thousands of dollars; (p) preliminary; n/a not available; (1) Figures cover the Minneapolis-St. Paul-Bloomington, MN-WI Metropolitan Statistical Area—see Appendix B for areas included
Source: National Association of Realtors, Median Sales Price of Existing Apartment Condo-Coop Homes for Metropolitan Areas, 4th Quarter 2019

Home Value Distribution

Area	Under $50,000	$50,000 -$99,999	$100,000 -$149,999	$150,000 -$199,999	$200,000 -$299,999	$300,000 -$499,999	$500,000 -$999,999	$1,000,000 or more
City	1.8	5.1	12.1	18.0	30.5	21.7	8.9	1.8
MSA[1]	3.1	3.4	9.7	18.5	31.7	24.3	7.9	1.3
U.S.	7.6	13.0	14.0	14.3	19.2	18.3	10.5	3.1

Note: Figures are percentages and cover owner-occupied housing units; (1) Figures cover the Minneapolis-St. Paul-Bloomington, MN-WI Metropolitan Statistical Area—see Appendix B for areas included
Source: U.S. Census Bureau, 2014-2018 American Community Survey 5-Year Estimates

Homeownership Rate

Area	2011 (%)	2012 (%)	2013 (%)	2014 (%)	2015 (%)	2016 (%)	2017 (%)	2018 (%)	2019 (%)
MSA[1]	69.1	70.8	71.7	69.7	67.9	69.1	70.1	67.8	70.2
U.S.	66.1	65.4	65.1	64.5	63.7	63.4	63.9	64.4	64.6

Note: (1) Figures cover the Minneapolis-St. Paul-Bloomington, MN-WI Metropolitan Statistical Area—see Appendix B for areas included
Source: U.S. Census Bureau, Housing Vacancies and Homeownership Annual Statistics: 2011-2019

Year Housing Structure Built

Area	2010 or Later	2000 -2009	1990 -1999	1980 -1989	1970 -1979	1960 -1969	1950 -1959	1940 -1949	Before 1940	Median Year
City	4.5	6.9	3.5	6.5	9.2	7.6	10.0	6.9	44.8	1948
MSA[1]	4.0	14.7	14.3	14.6	14.8	9.9	9.8	3.7	14.2	1978
U.S.	4.1	14.3	13.9	13.5	15.3	10.7	10.4	5.0	12.8	1977

Note: Figures are percentages except for Median Year; Note: (1) Figures cover the Minneapolis-St. Paul-Bloomington, MN-WI Metropolitan Statistical Area—see Appendix B for areas included
Source: U.S. Census Bureau, 2014-2018 American Community Survey 5-Year Estimates

Gross Monthly Rent

Area	Under $500	$500 -$999	$1,000 -$1,499	$1,500 -$1,999	$2,000 -$2,499	$2,500 -$2,999	$3,000 and up	Median ($)
City	13.8	37.8	30.0	12.4	4.0	1.2	0.8	985
MSA[1]	9.5	36.3	34.4	14.3	3.7	1.0	0.8	1,052
U.S.	9.8	38.5	29.6	12.9	5.1	2.1	2.0	1,023

Note: Figures are percentages except for Median; Gross rent is the contract rent plus the estimated average monthly cost of utilities (electricity, gas, and water and sewer) and fuels (oil, coal, kerosene, wood, etc.) if these are paid by the renter (or paid for the renter by someone else); (1) Figures cover the Minneapolis-St. Paul-Bloomington, MN-WI Metropolitan Statistical Area—see Appendix B for areas included
Source: U.S. Census Bureau, 2014-2018 American Community Survey 5-Year Estimates

HEALTH

Health Risk Factors

Category	MSA[1] (%)	U.S. (%)
Adults aged 18–64 who have any kind of health care coverage	91.0	87.3
Adults who reported being in good or better health	88.5	82.4
Adults who have been told they have high blood cholesterol	28.1	33.0
Adults who have been told they have high blood pressure	24.8	32.3
Adults who are current smokers	13.2	17.1
Adults who currently use E-cigarettes	3.4	4.6
Adults who currently use chewing tobacco, snuff, or snus	3.9	4.0
Adults who are heavy drinkers[2]	6.6	6.3
Adults who are binge drinkers[3]	20.5	17.4
Adults who are overweight (BMI 25.0 - 29.9)	35.6	35.3
Adults who are obese (BMI 30.0 - 99.8)	26.0	31.3
Adults who participated in any physical activities in the past month	78.1	74.4
Adults who always or nearly always wears a seat belt	97.3	94.3

Note: (1) Figures cover the Minneapolis-St. Paul-Bloomington, MN-WI Metropolitan Statistical Area—see Appendix B for areas included; (2) Heavy drinkers are classified as adult men having more than 14 drinks per week and adult women having more than 7 drinks per week; (3) Binge drinkers are classified as males having five or more drinks on one occasion or females having four or more drinks on one occasion
Source: Centers for Disease Control and Prevention, Behaviorial Risk Factor Surveillance System, SMART: Selected Metropolitan Area Risk Trends, 2017

Acute and Chronic Health Conditions

Category	MSA[1] (%)	U.S. (%)
Adults who have ever been told they had a heart attack	3.0	4.2
Adults who have ever been told they have angina or coronary heart disease	3.0	3.9
Adults who have ever been told they had a stroke	2.0	3.0
Adults who have ever been told they have asthma	10.8	14.2
Adults who have ever been told they have arthritis	17.4	24.9
Adults who have ever been told they have diabetes[2]	6.7	10.5
Adults who have ever been told they had skin cancer	5.7	6.2
Adults who have ever been told they had any other types of cancer	6.3	7.1
Adults who have ever been told they have COPD	3.9	6.5
Adults who have ever been told they have kidney disease	2.5	3.0
Adults who have ever been told they have a form of depression	19.2	20.5

Note: (1) Figures cover the Minneapolis-St. Paul-Bloomington, MN-WI Metropolitan Statistical Area—see Appendix B for areas included; (2) Figures do not include pregnancy-related, borderline, or pre-diabetes
Source: Centers for Disease Control and Prevention, Behaviorial Risk Factor Surveillance System, SMART: Selected Metropolitan Area Risk Trends, 2017

Health Screening and Vaccination Rates

Category	MSA[1] (%)	U.S. (%)
Adults aged 65+ who have had flu shot within the past year	65.7	60.7
Adults aged 65+ who have ever had a pneumonia vaccination	78.7	75.4
Adults who have ever been tested for HIV	35.8	36.1
Adults who have ever had the shingles or zoster vaccine?	33.6	28.9
Adults who have had their blood cholesterol checked within the last five years	87.9	85.9

Note: n/a not available; (1) Figures cover the Minneapolis-St. Paul-Bloomington, MN-WI Metropolitan Statistical Area—see Appendix B for areas included.
Source: Centers for Disease Control and Prevention, Behaviorial Risk Factor Surveillance System, SMART: Selected Metropolitan Area Risk Trends, 2017

Disability Status

Category	MSA[1] (%)	U.S. (%)
Adults who reported being deaf	5.6	6.7
Are you blind or have serious difficulty seeing, even when wearing glasses?	2.6	4.5
Are you limited in any way in any of your usual activities due of arthritis?	8.1	12.9
Do you have difficulty doing errands alone?	4.8	6.8
Do you have difficulty dressing or bathing?	2.5	3.6
Do you have serious difficulty concentrating/remembering/making decisions?	9.2	10.7
Do you have serious difficulty walking or climbing stairs?	9.1	13.6

Note: (1) Figures cover the Minneapolis-St. Paul-Bloomington, MN-WI Metropolitan Statistical Area—see Appendix B for areas included.
Source: Centers for Disease Control and Prevention, Behaviorial Risk Factor Surveillance System, SMART: Selected Metropolitan Area Risk Trends, 2017

Mortality Rates for the Top 10 Causes of Death in the U.S.

ICD-10[a] Sub-Chapter	ICD-10[a] Code	Age-Adjusted Mortality Rate[1] per 100,000 population	
		County[2]	U.S.
Malignant neoplasms	C00-C97	138.1	152.4
Ischaemic heart diseases	I20-I25	49.6	92.7
Other forms of heart disease	I30-I51	38.8	52.5
Chronic lower respiratory diseases	J40-J47	31.9	40.4
Cerebrovascular diseases	I60-I69	31.8	37.3
Other degenerative diseases of the nervous system	G30-G31	34.8	36.4
Other external causes of accidental injury	W00-X59	42.5	35.3
Organic, including symptomatic, mental disorders	F01-F09	48.6	30.0
Hypertensive diseases	I10-I15	16.5	22.9
Diabetes mellitus	E10-E14	17.9	21.3

Note: (a) ICD-10 = International Classification of Diseases 10th Revision; (1) Mortality rates are a three year average covering 2016-2018; (2) Figures cover Hennepin County.
Source: Centers for Disease Control and Prevention, National Center for Health Statistics. Underlying Cause of Death 1999-2018 on CDC WONDER Online Database

Mortality Rates for Selected Causes of Death

ICD-10[a] Sub-Chapter	ICD-10[a] Code	Age-Adjusted Mortality Rate[1] per 100,000 population	
		County[2]	U.S.
Assault	X85-Y09	3.6	6.0
Diseases of the liver	K70-K76	12.7	14.2
Human immunodeficiency virus (HIV) disease	B20-B24	1.5	1.6
Influenza and pneumonia	J09-J18	9.2	14.2
Intentional self-harm	X60-X84	10.5	13.9
Malnutrition	E40-E46	1.4	1.9
Obesity and other hyperalimentation	E65-E68	2.1	2.1
Renal failure	N17-N19	8.2	12.8
Transport accidents	V01-V99	5.6	12.5
Viral hepatitis	B15-B19	0.8	1.4

Note: (a) ICD-10 = International Classification of Diseases 10th Revision; (1) Mortality rates are a three year average covering 2016-2018; (2) Figures cover Hennepin County; Data are suppressed when the data meet the criteria for confidentiality constraints; Mortality rates are flagged as unreliable when the rate would be calculated with a numerator of 20 or less.
Source: Centers for Disease Control and Prevention, National Center for Health Statistics. Underlying Cause of Death 1999-2018 on CDC WONDER Online Database

Health Insurance Coverage

Area	With Health Insurance	With Private Health Insurance	With Public Health Insurance	Without Health Insurance	Population Under Age 19 Without Health Insurance
City	93.0	67.0	33.9	7.0	3.9
MSA[1]	95.5	78.1	29.1	4.5	3.2
U.S.	90.6	67.7	34.7	9.4	5.2

Note: Figures are percentages that cover the civilian noninstitutionalized population; (1) Figures cover the Minneapolis-St. Paul-Bloomington, MN-WI Metropolitan Statistical Area—see Appendix B for areas included Source: U.S. Census Bureau, 2014-2018 American Community Survey 5-Year Estimates

Number of Medical Professionals

Area	MDs[3]	DOs[3,4]	Dentists	Podiatrists	Chiropractors	Optometrists
County[1] (number)	6,433	256	1,201	57	900	257
County[1] (rate[2])	513.8	20.4	95.4	4.5	71.5	20.4
U.S. (rate[2])	281.9	23.4	69.1	6.0	27.5	16.4

Note: Data as of 2018 unless noted; (1) Data covers Hennepin County; (2) Rate per 100,000 population; (3) Data as of 2017 and includes all active, non-federal physicians; (4) Doctor of Osteopathic Medicine Source: U.S. Department of Health and Human Services, Health Resources and Services Administration, Bureau of Health Professions, Area Resource File (ARF) 2018-2019

Best Hospitals

According to *U.S. News,* the Minneapolis-St. Paul-Bloomington, MN-WI metro area is home to six of the best hospitals in the U.S.: **Abbott Northwestern Hospital** (8 adult specialties); **Fairview Ridges Hospital** (1 adult specialty); **Mercy Hospital-Coon Rapids** (1 adult specialty); **Minneapolis Heart Institute at Abbott Northwestern Hospital** (8 adult specialties); **Park Nicollet Methodist Hospital** (1 adult specialty); **University of Minnesota Medical Center** (1 adult specialty and 5 pediatric specialties). The hospitals listed were nationally ranked in at least one of 16 adult or 10 pediatric specialties. Only 206 hospitals nationwide were nationally ranked in one or more adult or pediatric specialty. Twenty hospitals in the U.S. made the Honor Roll. The Best Hospitals Honor Roll takes both the national rankings and the procedure and condition ratings into account. Hospitals received points if they were nationally ranked in one of the 16 adult specialties—the higher they ranked, the more points they got—and how many ratings of "high performing" they earned in the nine procedures and conditions. *U.S. News Online, "America's Best Hospitals 2019-20"*

According to *U.S. News,* the Minneapolis-St. Paul-Bloomington, MN-WI metro area is home to two of the best children's hospitals in the U.S.: **Children's Minnesota** (3 pediatric specialties); **University of Minnesota Masonic Children's Hospital** (5 pediatric specialties). The hospitals listed were highly ranked in at least one of 10 pediatric specialties. Ninety-one children's hospitals in the U.S. were nationally ranked in at least one specialty. Hospitals received points for being ranked in a specialty, and the 10 hospitals with the most points across the 10 specialties make up the Honor Roll. *U.S. News Online, "America's Best Children's Hospitals 2019-20"*

EDUCATION

Public School District Statistics

District Name	Schls	Pupils	Pupil/ Teacher Ratio	Minority Pupils[1] (%)	Free Lunch Eligible[2] (%)	IEP[3] (%)
Minneapolis Public School District	102	35,580	14.0	64.6	50.4	18.7
Minnesota Transitions Charter	7	3,423	19.4	38.0	48.4	17.4

Note: Table includes school districts with 2,000 or more students; (1) Percentage of students that are not non-Hispanic white; (2) Percentage of students that are eligible for the free lunch program; (3) Percentage of students that have an Individualized Education Program.
Source: U.S. Department of Education, National Center for Education Statistics, Common Core of Data, Local Education Agency (School District) Universe Survey: School Year 2018-2019; U.S. Department of Education, National Center for Education Statistics, Common Core of Data, Public Elementary/Secondary School Universe Survey: School Year 2018-2019

Highest Level of Education

Area	Less than H.S.	H.S. Diploma	Some College, No Deg.	Associate Degree	Bachelor's Degree	Master's Degree	Prof. School Degree	Doctorate Degree
City	10.3	15.7	17.3	7.2	29.9	13.2	3.9	2.4
MSA[1]	6.5	21.5	20.3	10.5	26.9	10.1	2.5	1.6
U.S.	12.3	27.1	20.6	8.4	19.4	8.6	2.1	1.4

Note: Figures cover persons age 25 and over; (1) Figures cover the Minneapolis-St. Paul-Bloomington, MN-WI Metropolitan Statistical Area—see Appendix B for areas included
Source: U.S. Census Bureau, 2014-2018 American Community Survey 5-Year Estimates

Educational Attainment by Race

Area	High School Graduate or Higher (%)					Bachelor's Degree or Higher (%)				
	Total	White	Black	Asian	Hisp.[2]	Total	White	Black	Asian	Hisp.[2]
City	89.7	95.9	75.0	82.2	57.5	49.4	59.9	14.2	53.0	18.4
MSA[1]	93.5	96.1	82.4	80.8	67.2	41.2	43.4	21.4	44.6	18.7
U.S.	87.7	89.6	85.4	86.8	67.7	31.5	32.9	21.1	53.5	15.8

Note: Figures shown cover persons 25 years old and over; (1) Figures cover the Minneapolis-St. Paul-Bloomington, MN-WI Metropolitan Statistical Area—see Appendix B for areas included; (2) People of Hispanic origin can be of any race
Source: U.S. Census Bureau, 2014-2018 American Community Survey 5-Year Estimates

School Enrollment by Grade and Control

Area	Preschool (%)		Kindergarten (%)		Grades 1 - 4 (%)		Grades 5 - 8 (%)		Grades 9 - 12 (%)	
	Public	Private	Public	Private	Public	Private	Public	Private	Public	Private
City	57.0	43.0	85.7	14.3	87.6	12.4	87.2	12.8	87.2	12.8
MSA[1]	59.6	40.4	88.3	11.7	89.2	10.8	89.7	10.3	91.3	8.7
U.S.	59.0	41.0	87.7	12.3	89.6	10.4	89.5	10.5	90.2	9.8

Note: Figures shown cover persons 3 years old and over; (1) Figures cover the Minneapolis-St. Paul-Bloomington, MN-WI Metropolitan Statistical Area—see Appendix B for areas included
Source: U.S. Census Bureau, 2014-2018 American Community Survey 5-Year Estimates

Average Salaries of Public School Teachers

Area	2016-17		2017-18		Change from 2016-17 to 2017-18	
	Dollars	Rank[1]	Dollars	Rank[1]	Percent	Rank[2]
Minnesota	57,346	19	57,782	20	0.76	35
U.S. Average	59,539	–	60,477	–	1.58	–

Note: (1) Rank ranges from 1 to 51 where 1 indicates highest salary; (2) Rank ranges from 1 to 51 where 1 indicates highest percent change.
Source: National Education Association, Rankings & Estimates: Rankings of the States 2018 and Estimates of School Statistics 2019

Higher Education

Four-Year Colleges			Two-Year Colleges			Medical Schools[1]	Law Schools[2]	Voc/ Tech[3]
Public	Private Non-profit	Private For-profit	Public	Private Non-profit	Private For-profit			
1	5	3	1	0	0	1	2	3

Note: Figures cover institutions located within the city limits and include main campuses only; (1) includes schools accredited by the Liaison Committee on Medical Education and the American Osteopathic Association's Commission on Osteopathic College Accreditation; (2) includes ABA-accredited schools, schools with provisional ABA accreditation, and state accredited schools; (3) includes all schools with programs that are less than 2 years.
Source: National Center for Education Statistics, Integrated Postsecondary Education System (IPEDS), 2018-19; Wikipedia, List of Medical Schools in the United States, accessed May 1, 2020; Wikipedia, List of Law Schools in the United States, accessed May 1, 2020

According to *U.S. News & World Report*, the Minneapolis-St. Paul-Bloomington, MN-WI metro area is home to three of the top 200 national universities in the U.S.: **University of Minnesota—Twin Cities** (#70 tie); **University of St. Thomas** (#139 tie); **Bethel University** (#197 tie). The indicators used to capture academic quality fall into a number of categories: assessment by administrators at peer institutions; retention of students; faculty resources; student selectivity; financial resources; alumni giving; high school counselor ratings of colleges; and graduation rate. *U.S. News & World Report, "America's Best Colleges 2020"*

According to *U.S. News & World Report*, the Minneapolis-St. Paul-Bloomington, MN-WI metro area is home to three of the top 100 liberal arts colleges in the U.S.: **Carleton College** (#7 tie); **Macalester College** (#25 tie); **St. Olaf College** (#62 tie). The indicators used to capture academic quality fall into a number of categories: assessment by administrators at peer institutions; retention of students; faculty resources; student selectivity; financial resources; alumni giving; high school counselor ratings of colleges; and graduation rate. *U.S. News & World Report, "America's Best Colleges 2020"*

According to *U.S. News & World Report,* the Minneapolis-St. Paul-Bloomington, MN-WI metro area is home to one of the top 100 law schools in the U.S.: **University of Minnesota** (#21). The rankings are based on a weighted average of 12 measures of quality: peer assessment score; assessment score by lawyers/judges; median LSAT scores; median undergrad GPA; acceptance rate; employment rates for graduates; placement success; bar passage rate; faculty resources; expenditures per student; student/faculty ratio; and library resources. *U.S. News & World Report, "America's Best Graduate Schools, Law, 2021"*

According to *U.S. News & World Report,* the Minneapolis-St. Paul-Bloomington, MN-WI metro area is home to one of the top 75 medical schools for research in the U.S.: **University of Minnesota** (#40 tie). The rankings are based on a weighted average of 11 measures of quality: quality assessment; peer assessment score; assessment score by residency directors; research activity; total research activity; average research activity per faculty member; student selectivity; median MCAT total score; median undergraduate GPA; acceptance rate; and faculty resources. *U.S. News & World Report, "America's Best Graduate Schools, Medical, 2021"*

According to *U.S. News & World Report,* the Minneapolis-St. Paul-Bloomington, MN-WI metro area is home to one of the top 75 business schools in the U.S.: **University of Minnesota—Twin Cities (Carlson)** (#28 tie). The rankings are based on a weighted average of the following nine measures: quality assessment; peer assessment; recruiter assessment; placement success; mean starting salary and bonus; student selectivity; mean GMAT and GRE scores; mean undergraduate GPA; and acceptance rate. *U.S. News & World Report, "America's Best Graduate Schools, Business, 2021"*

PRESIDENTIAL ELECTION

2016 Presidential Election Results

Area	Clinton	Trump	Johnson	Stein	Other
Hennepin County	63.1	28.2	3.6	1.5	3.6
U.S.	48.0	45.9	3.3	1.1	1.7

Note: Results are percentages and may not add to 100% due to rounding
Source: Dave Leip's Atlas of U.S. Presidential Elections

EMPLOYERS

Major Employers

Company Name	Industry
3M Company	Adhesives, sealants
Ameriprise Financial	Investment advice
Anderson Corporation	Millwork
Aware Integrated	Hospital & medical services plans
Bethesda Healtheast Hospital	General medical & surgical hospitals
Carlson Holdings	Hotels & motels
City of Minneapolis	General government, local government
County of Hennepin	General government, county government
Hennepin County	County government
Honeywell International	Aircraft engines & engine parts
Lawson Software	Application computer software
Medtronic	Electromedical equipment
Minnesota Department of Human Services	Family services agency
Minnesota Department of Transportation	Regulation, administration of transportation
North Memorial Hospital	General medical & surgical hospitals
Regents of the University of Minnesota	Specialty outpatient clinics, nec
Rosemount Apple Valley and Eagan	Personal service agents, brokers, & bureaus
St. Paul Fire and marine Insurance Company	Fire, marine, & casualty insurance
Thomson Legal Regulatory	Books, publishing & printing
United Parcel Service	Package delivery services
Wells Fargo	Mortgage bankers
West Publishing Corporation	Data base information retrieval

Note: Companies shown are located within the Minneapolis-St. Paul-Bloomington, MN-WI Metropolitan Statistical Area.
Source: Hoovers.com; Wikipedia

Best Companies to Work For

Allianz Life Insurance Co. of N. America, headquartered in Minneapolis, is among "The 100 Best Companies to Work For." To pick the best companies, *Fortune* partnered with the Great Place to Work Institute. Two-thirds of a company's score is based on the results of the Institute's Trust Index survey, which is sent to a random sample of employees from each company. The questions related to attitudes about management's credibility, job satisfaction, and camaraderie. The other third of the scoring is based on the company's responses to the Institute's Culture Audit, which includes detailed questions about pay and benefit programs, and a series of open-ended questions about hiring practices, internal communication, training, recognition programs, and diversity efforts. Any company that is at least five years old with more than 1,000 U.S. employees is eligible. *Fortune, "The 100 Best Companies to Work For," 2020*

Ceridian; General Mills, headquartered in Minneapolis, are among the "100 Best Companies for Working Mothers." Criteria: paid time off and leaves; workforce profile; benefits; women's issues and advancement; flexible work; company culture and work life programs. *Working Mother, "100 Best Companies 2019"*

General Mills; Target; U.S. Bank, headquartered in Minneapolis, are among the "Best Companies for Multicultural Women." *Working Mother* selected 50 companies based on a detailed application completed by public and private firms based in the United States, excluding government agencies, companies in the human resources field and non-autonomous divisions. Companies supplied data about the hiring, pay, and promotion of multicultural employees. Applications focused on representation of multicultural women, recruitment, retention and advancement programs, and company culture. *Working Mother, "2019 Best Companies for Multicultural Women"*

General Mills, headquartered in Minneapolis, is among the "Top Companies for Executive Women." The 2020 National Association for Female Executives (NAFE) Top Companies application included more than 200 questions on topics including female representation at all levels, but especially the corporate officer and profit-and-loss leadership ranks. The application tracked and examined how many employees have access to programs and policies that promote advancement of women and how many employees take advantage of them, plus how companies train managers to help women advance. To be considered, companies must have a minimum of two women on their boards of directors, a U.S.-based CEO and at least 1,000 U.S. employees. *National Association for Female Executives, "2020 NAFE Top 70 Companies for Executive Women"*

PUBLIC SAFETY

Crime Rate

Area	All Crimes	Violent Crimes				Property Crimes		
		Murder	Rape[3]	Robbery	Aggrav. Assault	Burglary	Larceny -Theft	Motor Vehicle Theft
City	4,703.9	7.2	100.9	276.5	408.2	721.3	2,678.5	511.4
Suburbs[1]	2,106.6	1.2	38.5	45.7	95.6	236.9	1,512.5	176.2
Metro[2]	2,413.9	1.9	45.9	73.0	132.6	294.2	1,650.5	215.8
U.S.	2,580.1	5.0	42.6	86.2	246.8	376.0	1,594.6	228.9

Note: Figures are crimes per 100,000 population; (1) All areas within the metro area that are located outside the city limits; (2) Figures cover the Minneapolis-St. Paul-Bloomington, MN-WI Metropolitan Statistical Area—see Appendix B for areas included; (3) The city and U.S. figures shown were reported using the revised Uniform Crime Reporting (UCR) definition of rape. The suburban and metro area figures shown are an aggregate total of the data submitted using both the revised and legacy UCR definitions.
Source: FBI Uniform Crime Reports, 2018

Hate Crimes

Area	Number of Quarters Reported	Number of Incidents per Bias Motivation					
		Race/Ethnicity/ Ancestry	Religion	Sexual Orientation	Disability	Gender	Gender Identity
City	4	8	1	14	0	0	0
U.S.	4	4,047	1,419	1,196	159	47	168

Source: Federal Bureau of Investigation, Hate Crime Statistics 2018

Identity Theft Consumer Reports

Area	Reports	Reports per 100,000 Population	Rank[2]
MSA[1]	3,591	99	191
U.S.	650,572	198	-

Note: (1) Figures cover the Minneapolis-St. Paul-Bloomington, MN-WI Metropolitan Statistical Area—see Appendix B for areas included; (2) Rank ranges from 1 to 386 where 1 indicates greatest number of identity theft reports per 100,000 population
Source: Federal Trade Commission, Consumer Sentinel Network Data Book for January–December 2019

Fraud and Other Consumer Reports

Area	Reports	Reports per 100,000 Population	Rank[2]
MSA[1]	20,523	565	166
U.S.	2,590,177	789	-

Note: (1) Figures cover the Minneapolis-St. Paul-Bloomington, MN-WI Metropolitan Statistical Area—see Appendix B for areas included; (2) Rank ranges from 1 to 386 where 1 indicates greatest number of fraud and other consumer reports per 100,000 population
Source: Federal Trade Commission, Consumer Sentinel Network Data Book for January–December 2019

SPORTS

Professional Sports Teams

Team Name	League	Year Established
Minnesota Timberwolves	National Basketball Association (NBA)	1989
Minnesota Twins	Major League Baseball (MLB)	1961
Minnesota United FC	Major League Soccer (MLS)	2017
Minnesota Vikings	National Football League (NFL)	1961
Minnesota Wild	National Hockey League (NHL)	2000

Note: Includes teams located in the Minneapolis-St. Paul-Bloomington, MN-WI Metropolitan Statistical Area.
Source: Wikipedia, Major Professional Sports Teams of the United States and Canada, May 4, 2020

CLIMATE

Average and Extreme Temperatures

Temperature	Jan	Feb	Mar	Apr	May	Jun	Jul	Aug	Sep	Oct	Nov	Dec	Yr.
Extreme High (°F)	57	60	83	95	96	102	105	101	98	89	74	63	105
Average High (°F)	21	27	38	56	69	79	84	81	71	59	41	26	54
Average Temp. (°F)	12	18	30	46	59	69	74	71	61	50	33	19	45
Average Low (°F)	3	9	21	36	48	58	63	61	50	39	25	11	35
Extreme Low (°F)	-34	-28	-32	2	18	37	43	39	26	15	-17	-29	-34

Note: Figures cover the years 1948-1990
Source: National Climatic Data Center, International Station Meteorological Climate Summary, 9/96

Average Precipitation/Snowfall/Humidity

Precip./Humidity	Jan	Feb	Mar	Apr	May	Jun	Jul	Aug	Sep	Oct	Nov	Dec	Yr.
Avg. Precip. (in.)	0.8	0.8	1.9	2.2	3.1	4.0	3.8	3.6	2.5	1.9	1.4	1.0	27.1
Avg. Snowfall (in.)	11	9	12	3	Tr	0	0	0	Tr	Tr	7	10	52
Avg. Rel. Hum. 6am (%)	75	76	77	75	75	79	81	84	85	81	80	79	79
Avg. Rel. Hum. 3pm (%)	64	62	58	48	47	50	50	52	53	52	62	68	55

Note: Figures cover the years 1948-1990; Tr = Trace amounts (<0.05 in. of rain; <0.5 in. of snow)
Source: National Climatic Data Center, International Station Meteorological Climate Summary, 9/96

Weather Conditions

Temperature			Daytime Sky			Precipitation		
5°F & below	32°F & below	90°F & above	Clear	Partly cloudy	Cloudy	0.01 inch or more precip.	0.1 inch or more snow/ice	Thunder-storms
45	156	16	93	125	147	113	41	37

Note: Figures are average number of days per year and cover the years 1948-1990
Source: National Climatic Data Center, International Station Meteorological Climate Summary, 9/96

HAZARDOUS WASTE

Superfund Sites

The Minneapolis-St. Paul-Bloomington, MN-WI metro area is home to 17 sites on the EPA's Superfund National Priorities List: **Baytown Township Ground Water Plume** (final); **FMC Corp. (Fridley Plant)** (final); **Freeway Sanitary Landfill** (final); **Fridley Commons Park Well Field** (final); **General Mills/Henkel Corp.** (final); **Highway 100 and County Road 3 Groundwater Plume** (proposed); **Joslyn Manufacturing & Supply Co.** (final); **Koppers Coke** (final); **Kurt Manufacturing Co.** (final); **Macgillis & Gibbs Co./Bell Lumber & Pole Co.** (final); **Naval Industrial Reserve Ordnance Plant** (final); **New Brighton/Arden Hills/Tcaap (USARMY)** (final); **Oakdale Dump** (final); **Reilly Tar & Chemical Corp. (Saint Louis Park Plant)** (final); **South Andover Site** (final); **South Minneapolis Residential Soil Contamination** (final); **Spring Park Municipal Well Field** (final). There are a total of 1,387 Superfund sites with a status of proposed or final on the list in the U.S. *U.S. Environmental Protection Agency, National Priorities List, May 5, 2020*

AIR & WATER QUALITY

Air Quality Trends: Ozone

	1990	1995	2000	2005	2010	2012	2014	2016	2017	2018
MSA[1]	0.068	0.084	0.065	0.074	0.066	0.073	0.063	0.061	0.062	0.065
U.S.	0.088	0.089	0.082	0.080	0.073	0.075	0.067	0.069	0.068	0.069

Note: (1) Data covers the Minneapolis-St. Paul-Bloomington, MN-WI Metropolitan Statistical Area—see Appendix B for areas included. The values shown are the composite ozone concentration averages among trend sites based on the highest fourth daily maximum 8-hour concentration in parts per million. These trends are based on sites having an adequate record of monitoring data during the trend period. Data from exceptional events are included.
Source: U.S. Environmental Protection Agency, Air Quality Monitoring Information, "Air Quality Trends by City, 1990-2018"

Air Quality Index

Area	Percent of Days when Air Quality was...[2]					AQI Statistics[2]	
	Good	Moderate	Unhealthy for Sensitive Groups	Unhealthy	Very Unhealthy	Maximum	Median
MSA[1]	47.4	51.2	1.4	0.0	0.0	122	51

Note: (1) Data covers the Minneapolis-St. Paul-Bloomington, MN-WI Metropolitan Statistical Area—see Appendix B for areas included; (2) Based on 365 days with AQI data in 2018. Air Quality Index (AQI) is an index for reporting daily air quality. EPA calculates the AQI for five major air pollutants regulated by the Clean Air Act: ground-level ozone, particle pollution (aka particulate matter), carbon monoxide, sulfur dioxide, and nitrogen dioxide. The AQI runs from 0 to 500. The higher the AQI value, the greater the level of air pollution and the greater the health concern. There are six AQI categories: "Good" AQI is between 0 and 50. Air quality is considered satisfactory; "Moderate" AQI is between 51 and 100. Air quality is acceptable; "Unhealthy for Sensitive Groups" When AQI values are between 101 and 150, members of sensitive groups may experience health effects; "Unhealthy" When AQI values are between 151 and 200 everyone may begin to experience health effects; "Very Unhealthy" AQI values between 201 and 300 trigger a health alert; "Hazardous" AQI values over 300 trigger warnings of emergency conditions (not shown).
Source: U.S. Environmental Protection Agency, Air Quality Index Report, 2018

Air Quality Index Pollutants

Area	Percent of Days when AQI Pollutant was...[2]					
	Carbon Monoxide	Nitrogen Dioxide	Ozone	Sulfur Dioxide	Particulate Matter 2.5	Particulate Matter 10
MSA[1]	1.1	1.9	28.2	0.3	40.8	27.7

Note: (1) Data covers the Minneapolis-St. Paul-Bloomington, MN-WI Metropolitan Statistical Area—see Appendix B for areas included; (2) Based on 365 days with AQI data in 2018. The Air Quality Index (AQI) is an index for reporting daily air quality. EPA calculates the AQI for five major air pollutants regulated by the Clean Air Act: ground-level ozone, particle pollution (also known as particulate matter), carbon monoxide, sulfur dioxide, and nitrogen dioxide. The AQI runs from 0 to 500. The higher the AQI value, the greater the level of air pollution and the greater the health concern.
Source: U.S. Environmental Protection Agency, Air Quality Index Report, 2018

Maximum Air Pollutant Concentrations: Particulate Matter, Ozone, CO and Lead

	Particulate Matter 10 (ug/m³)	Particulate Matter 2.5 Wtd AM (ug/m³)	Particulate Matter 2.5 24-Hr (ug/m³)	Ozone (ppm)	Carbon Monoxide (ppm)	Lead (ug/m³)
MSA[1] Level	144	8.9	25	0.069	4	0.08
NAAQS[2]	150	15	35	0.075	9	0.15
Met NAAQS[2]	Yes	Yes	Yes	Yes	Yes	Yes

Note: (1) Data covers the Minneapolis-St. Paul-Bloomington, MN-WI Metropolitan Statistical Area—see Appendix B for areas included; Data from exceptional events are included; (2) National Ambient Air Quality Standards; ppm = parts per million; ug/m³ = micrograms per cubic meter; n/a not available.
Concentrations: Particulate Matter 10 (coarse particulate)—highest second maximum 24-hour concentration; Particulate Matter 2.5 Wtd AM (fine particulate)—highest weighted annual mean concentration; Particulate Matter 2.5 24-Hour (fine particulate)—highest 98th percentile 24-hour concentration; Ozone—highest fourth daily maximum 8-hour concentration; Carbon Monoxide—highest second maximum non-overlapping 8-hour concentration; Lead—maximum running 3-month average
Source: U.S. Environmental Protection Agency, Air Quality Monitoring Information, "Air Quality Statistics by City, 2018"

Maximum Air Pollutant Concentrations: Nitrogen Dioxide and Sulfur Dioxide

	Nitrogen Dioxide AM (ppb)	Nitrogen Dioxide 1-Hr (ppb)	Sulfur Dioxide AM (ppb)	Sulfur Dioxide 1-Hr (ppb)	Sulfur Dioxide 24-Hr (ppb)
MSA[1] Level	13	45	n/a	17	n/a
NAAQS[2]	53	100	30	75	140
Met NAAQS[2]	Yes	Yes	n/a	Yes	n/a

Note: (1) Data covers the Minneapolis-St. Paul-Bloomington, MN-WI Metropolitan Statistical Area—see Appendix B for areas included; Data from exceptional events are included; (2) National Ambient Air Quality Standards; ppm = parts per million; ug/m³ = micrograms per cubic meter; n/a not available.
Concentrations: Nitrogen Dioxide AM—highest arithmetic mean concentration; Nitrogen Dioxide 1-Hr—highest 98th percentile 1-hour daily maximum concentration; Sulfur Dioxide AM—highest annual mean concentration; Sulfur Dioxide 1-Hr—highest 99th percentile 1-hour daily maximum concentration; Sulfur Dioxide 24-Hr—highest second maximum 24-hour concentration
Source: U.S. Environmental Protection Agency, Air Quality Monitoring Information, "Air Quality Statistics by City, 2018"

Drinking Water

Water System Name	Pop. Served	Primary Water Source Type	Violations[1]
Minneapolis	423,990	Surface	2

Note: (1) Total number of violations (both active and inactive) in the EPA database
Source: U.S. Environmental Protection Agency, Office of Ground Water and Drinking Water, Safe Drinking Water Information System (based on data extracted May 5, 2020)

Oklahoma City, Oklahoma

Background

The 1992 film *Far and Away,* directed by Ron Howard, shows Tom Cruise charging away on his horse to claim land in the Oklahoma Territory. That dramatic scene depicted a true event from the great Oklahoma land run of 1889. A pistol was fired from the Oklahoma Station house of the Santa Fe Railroad and 10,000 homesteaders raced away to stake land claims in central Oklahoma territory. Overnight, Oklahoma City, "OKC" as the locals like to call their town, had been founded.

The town grew quickly along the tracks of the Santa Fe Railroad. Soon it became a distribution center for the territory's crops and livestock. Today, the city still functions as a major transportation center for the state's farm produce and livestock industry. By 1910 the city had become the state capital, which also furthered growth. But in 1928, growth went through the ceiling when oil was discovered within the city limits, forever changing the economic face of Oklahoma City from one of livestock and feed to one of livestock, feed, and oil.

After World War II, Oklahoma City, like many other cities, entered industry, most notably aircraft and related industries. The Tinker Air Force Base and the Federal Aviation Administration's Mike Monroney Aeronautical Center—home to the largest concentration of Dept. of Transportation personnel outside of Washington, D.C.—have made Oklahoma City a leading aviation center and, combined, employ more than 30,000 federal and civil contract workers. Major economic sectors for the Greater Oklahoma City region—the geographic center of the continent—also include energy, bioscience, and logistics.

The area caters to a Western lifestyle. The town is the home of the National Cowboy and Western Heritage Museum, with its famous 18-foot tall sculpture, "End of the Trail," by James Earle Fraser. The Oklahoma History Center, affiliated with the Smithsonian Institute, occupies a 215,000 square foot building on an 18-acre campus. The Red Earth Museum features 1,400 items of Native American art and a research center. To the north of Oklahoma City's Capitol building is the Tribal Flag Plaza, displaying the 39 native tribal flags of Oklahoma. Each September the State Fair is held in Oklahoma City, and each January the International Finals Rodeo is held at the State Fair Park. If swinging a bat is more your style than riding a bronco, there's the National Softball Hall of Fame and Museum.

Oklahoma City hired famous architect I.M. Pei to redesign its downtown area. Taking inspiration from the Tivoli Gardens of Copenhagen, the downtown boasts of the Myriad Gardens, a 12-acre recreational park with gardens, an amphitheater, and the seven-story Crystal Bridge Tropical Conservatory.

The city is also home to the Oklahoma City Thunder, a team that's become a leading NBA contender in recent years, often making the playoffs.

A national tragedy that played out in Oklahoma City remains present in the memory of the city and the country. On April 19, 1995, Oklahoma City suffered a deadly terrorist incident when a truck bomb destroyed part of the Alfred P. Murray Federal Building in the downtown area, leaving 168 people dead and more than 500 injured. In the face of such tragedy, the world marveled at how Oklahoma City and the state of Oklahoma carried itself with dignity and generosity. The Oklahoma City National Memorial commemorates those people whose lives were ended or forever changed on that day.

Oklahoma City's weather is changeable. There are pronounced daily and seasonal temperature changes and considerable variation in seasonal and annual precipitation. Summers are long and usually hot, while winters are comparatively mild and short. The city is located in Tornado Alley, which is frequently visited in the springtime by violent thunderstorms producing damaging winds, large hail, and tornadoes.

Rankings

General Rankings

- For its "Best for Vets: Places to Live 2019" rankings, *Military Times* evaluated 599 cities (83 large, 234 medium, 282 small) and compared the locations across three broad categories: veteran and military culture/services; economic indicators; and livability factors such as health, crime, traffic, and school quality. Oklahoma City ranked #6 out of the top 25, in the large city category (populations of more than 250,000). Data points more specific to veterans and the military weighed more heavily than the rest. *rebootcamp.militarytimes.com, "Military Times Best Places to Live 2019," September 10, 2018*

- The Oklahoma City metro area was identified as one of America's fastest-growing areas in terms of population and business growth by *MagnifyMoney*. The area ranked #31 out of 35. The 100 most populous metro areas in the U.S. were evaluated on their change from 2011-2016 in the following categories: people and housing; workforce and employment opportunities; growing industry. *www.businessinsider.com, "The 35 Cities in the US with the Biggest Influx of People, the Most Work Opportunities, and the Hottest Business Growth," August 12, 2018*

- In their sixth annual survey, Livability.com looked at data for more than 1,000 U.S. cities to determine the rankings for Livability's "Top 100 Best Places to Live" in 2019. Oklahoma City ranked #89. Criteria: median home value capped at $250,000; affordable living; vibrant economy; education, demographics, health care options. transportation & infrastructure; abundant lifestyle amenities. *Livability.com, "Top 100 Best Places to Live 2019" March 2019*

Business/Finance Rankings

- Oklahoma City was the #2-ranked city for savers, according to a study by the finance site GOBankingRates, which considered the prospects for people trying to save money. Criteria: average monthly cost of grocery items; median home listing price; median rent; median income; transportation costs; gas prices; and the cost of eating out for an inexpensive and mid-range meal in 100 U.S. cities. *www.gobankingrates.com, "The 20 Best (and Worst) Places to Live If You're Trying to Save Money," August 27, 2019*

- Oklahoma City was ranked #2 among 100 U.S. cities for most difficult conditions for savers, according to a study by the finance site GOBankingRates. Criteria: average monthly cost of grocery items; median home listing price; median rent; median income; transportation costs; gas prices; and the cost of eating out for an inexpensive and mid-range meal. *www.gobankingrates.com, "The 20 Best (and Worst) Places to Live If You're Trying to Save Money," August 27, 2019*

- Recognizing the sizeable percentage of American workers who are self-employed, NerdWallet editors assessed the country's cities according to percentage of freelancers, median rental costs, cell phone plans/taxes, and healthcare affordability and access. By these criteria, Oklahoma City placed #14 among the best cities for independent workers. *www.nerdwallet.com, "Best Places for Freelance Workers," August 30, 2016*

- Based on metro area social media reviews, the employment opinion group Glassdoor surveyed 50 of the most populous U.S. metro areas and equally weighed cost of living, hiring opportunity, and job satisfaction to compose a list of "25 Best Cities for Jobs." Median pay and home value, and number of active job openings was also factored in. The Oklahoma City metro area was ranked #12 in overall job satisfaction. *www.glassdoor.com, "Best Cities for Jobs," February 25, 2020*

- The Brookings Institution ranked the nation's largest cities based on income inequality. Oklahoma City was ranked #70 (#1 = greatest inequality). Criteria: the "95/20 ratio," a figure representing the income at which a household earns more than 95 percent of all other households, divided by the income at which a household earns more than only 20 percent of all other households. *Brookings Institution, "Household Income Inequality, Largest Cities of 97 Large U.S. Metro Areas, 2014-2016," February 5, 2018*

- The Brookings Institution ranked the 100 largest metro areas in the U.S. based on income inequality. Oklahoma City was ranked #47 (#1 = greatest inequality). Criteria: the "95/20 ratio," a figure representing the income at which a household earns more than 95 percent of all other households, divided by the income at which a household earns more than only 20 percent of all other households. *Brookings Institution, "Household Income Inequality, 100 Largest U.S. Metro Areas, 2014-2016," February 5, 2018*

- For its annual survey of the "Cheapest U.S. Cities to Live In," Kiplinger applied Cost of Living Index statistics developed by the Council for Community and Economic Research to U.S. Census Bureau population and median household income data for 270 urban areas. In the resulting ranking, Oklahoma City ranked #13. *Kiplinger.com, "25 Cheapest U.S. Cities to Live In," April 28, 2019*

- The Oklahoma City metro area appeared on the Milken Institute "2020 Best Performing Cities" list. Rank: #116 out of 200 large metro areas. Criteria: job growth; wage and salary growth; high-tech output growth. *Milken Institute, "Best-Performing Cities 2020," February 26, 2020*

- *Forbes* ranked the 200 most populous metro areas to determine the nation's "Best Places for Business and Careers." The Oklahoma City metro area was ranked #54. Criteria: costs (business and living); job growth (past and projected); income growth; quality of life; educational attainment (college and high school); projected economic growth; cultural and leisure opportunities; workplace tolerance laws; net migration patterns. *Forbes, "The Best Places for Business and Careers 2019: Seattle Still On Top," October 30, 2019*

Dating/Romance Rankings

- Oklahoma City was ranked #18 out of 25 cities that stood out for inspiring romance and attracting diners on the website OpenTable.com. Criteria: percentage of people who dined out on Valentine's Day in 2018; percentage of romantic restaurants as rated by OpenTable diner reviews; and percentage of tables seated for two. *OpenTable, "25 Most Romantic Cities in America for 2019," February 7, 2019*

Education Rankings

- Personal finance website *WalletHub* analyzed the 150 largest U.S. metropolitan statistical areas to determine where the most educated Americans are choosing to settle. Criteria: education levels; percentage of workers with degrees; education quality and attainment gap; public school quality rankings; quality and size of each metro area's universities. Oklahoma City was ranked #84 (#1 = most educated city). *www.WalletHub.com, "2019's Most and Least Educated Cities in America," July 22, 2019*

- Oklahoma City was selected as one of America's most literate cities. The city ranked #41 out of the 82 largest U.S. cities. Criteria: number of booksellers; library resources; Internet resources; educational attainment; periodical publishing resources; newspaper circulation. *Central Connecticut State University, "America's Most Literate Cities, 2016," March 31, 2017*

Environmental Rankings

- Sperling's BestPlaces assessed the 50 largest metropolitan areas of the United States for the likelihood of dangerously extreme weather events or earthquakes. In general the Southeast and South-Central regions have the highest risk of weather extremes and earthquakes, while the Pacific Northwest enjoys the lowest risk. Of the most risky metropolitan areas, the Oklahoma City metro area was ranked #3. *www.bestplaces.net, "Avoid Natural Disasters: BestPlaces Reveals The Top 10 Safest Places to Live," October 25, 2017*

- Oklahoma City was highlighted as one of the top 104 cleanest metro areas for short-term particle pollution (24-hour PM 2.5) in the U.S. during 2015 through 2017. Monitors in these cities reported no days with unhealthful PM 2.5 levels. *American Lung Association, "State of the Air 2019," April 24, 2019*

Health/Fitness Rankings

- For each of the 100 largest cities in the United States, the American Fitness Index®, published by the American College of Sports Medicine and the Anthem Foundation, evaluated community infrastructure and 33 health behaviors including preventive health, levels of chronic disease conditions, pedestrian safety, air quality, and community resources that support physical activity. Oklahoma City ranked #100 for "community fitness." *americanfitnessindex.org, "ACSM American Fitness Index Health and Community Fitness Status of the 100 Largest U.S. Cities," May 14, 2019*

- Oklahoma City was identified as a "2020 Spring Allergy Capital." The area ranked #8 out of 100. Three groups of factors were used to identify the most challenging cities for people with allergies during the spring season: annual spring pollen levels; over the counter medicine use; number of board-certified allergy specialists. *Asthma and Allergy Foundation of America, "Spring Allergy Capitals 2020," March 10, 2020*

- Oklahoma City was identified as a "2020 Fall Allergy Capital." The area ranked #5 out of 100. Three groups of factors were used to identify the most challenging cities for people with allergies during the fall season: annual fall pollen levels; over the counter medicine use; number of board-certified allergy specialists. *Asthma and Allergy Foundation of America, "Fall Allergy Capitals 2020," March 10, 2020*

- Oklahoma City was identified as a "2019 Asthma Capital." The area ranked #32 out of the nation's 100 largest metropolitan areas. Criteria: estimated asthma prevalence; crude death rate from asthma; and ER visits due to asthma. Risk factors that were analyzed but not factored in the rankings: annual pollen score; annual air quality; public smoking laws; number of board-certified asthma specialists; rescue medication use; controller medication use; uninsured rate; poverty rate. *Asthma and Allergy Foundation of America, "Asthma Capitals 2019: The Most Challenging Places to Live With Asthma," May 7, 2019*

- *Men's Health* ranked 100 major U.S. cities in terms of the best cities for men. Oklahoma City ranked #86. Criteria: health; fitness; quality of life. *Men's Health, "The Best & Worst Cities for Men Who Want to Be Fit and Happy," January 1, 2016*

- The Oklahoma City metro area ranked #173 out of 189 in The Gallup-Sharecare Well-Being Index. Criteria: purpose; social well being; financial health; community and physical health. Results are based on telephone interviews with adults, aged 18 and older, living in metropolitan areas in the 50 U.S. states and the District of Columbia. *Gallup-Sharecare, "State of American Well-Being, 2017 Community Well-Being Rankings" March 2018*

Real Estate Rankings

- FitSmallBusiness looked at 50 of the largest metropolitan areas in the U.S. to determine which metro was the best to start a real estate business. Data was compiled from such sources as: Zillow, Trulia, U.S. Census Bureau, and the Bureau of Labor Statistics. Criteria: location; inventory; annual wages; median sales price of homes; days on the market; median price cut percentage; and other factors that would influence real estate professional growth. The Oklahoma City metro area ranked #35. *fitsmallbusiness.com, "The Best Cities to Become a Real Estate Agent in 2018," January 30, 2018*

- *WalletHub* compared the most populated U.S. cities, as well as at least two of the most populated cities in each state, for a total of 179, to determine which had the best markets for real estate agents. Oklahoma City ranked #166 where demand was high and pay was the best. Criteria: sales per agent; annual median wage for real-estate agents; monthly average starting salary for real estate agents; real estate job density and competition; unemployment rate; home turnover rate; housing-market health index; and other relevant metrics. *www.WalletHub.com, "2019's Best Places to Be a Real Estate Agent," April 24, 2019*

- Oklahoma City was ranked #19 in the top 20 out of the 100 largest metro areas in terms of house price appreciation in 2019 (#1 = highest rate). *Federal Housing Finance Agency, House Price Index, 4th Quarter 2019*

- The Oklahoma City metro area was identified as one of the 20 worst housing markets in the U.S. in 2019. The area ranked #5 out of 180 markets. Criteria: year-over-year change of median sales price of existing single-family homes between the 4th quarter of 2018 and the 4th quarter of 2019. *National Association of Realtors®, Median Sales Price of Existing Single-Family Homes for Metropolitan Areas, 4th Quarter 2019*

- Oklahoma City was ranked #55 out of 238 metro areas in terms of housing affordability in 2019 by the National Association of Home Builders (#1 = most affordable). Criteria: the share of homes sold in that area affordable to a family earning the local median income, based on standard mortgage underwriting criteria. *National Association of Home Builders®, NAHB-Wells Fargo Housing Opportunity Index, 4th Quarter 2019*

Safety Rankings

- To identify the most dangerous cities in America, 24/7 Wall Street focused on violent crime categories—murder, non-negligent manslaughter, rape, robbery, and aggravated assault—and property crime as reported in the FBI's 2018 annual Uniform Crime Report. Criteria also included median income from American Community Survey and unemployment figures from Bureau of Labor Statistics. For cities with populations over 100,000, Oklahoma City was ranked #43. *247wallst.com, "America's Most Dangerous Cities" January 10, 2020*

- Allstate ranked the 200 largest cities in America in terms of driver safety. Oklahoma City ranked #45. Criteria: internal property damage claims over a two-year period from January 2016 to December 2017. The report helps increase the importance of safety and awareness behind the wheel. *Allstate, "Allstate America's Best Drivers Report, 2019" June 24, 2019*

- Oklahoma City was identified as one of the most dangerous cities in America by NeighborhoodScout. The city ranked #94 out of 100 (#1 = most dangerous). Criteria: number of violent crimes per 1,000 residents. The editors only considered cities with 25,000 or more residents. *NeighborhoodScout.com, "Top 100 Most Dangerous Cities in the U.S. 2020" January 2, 2020*

- The National Insurance Crime Bureau ranked 382 metro areas in the U.S. in terms of per capita rates of vehicle theft. The Oklahoma City metro area ranked #43 (#1 = highest rate). Criteria: number of vehicle theft offenses per 100,000 inhabitants in 2018. *National Insurance Crime Bureau, "Hot Spots 2018," June 25, 2019*

Seniors/Retirement Rankings

- From its Best Cities for Successful Aging indexes, the Milken Institute generated rankings for metropolitan areas, weighing data in nine categories—health care, wellness, living arrangements, transportation and convenience, financial characteristics, education, employment, community engagement, and overall livability. The Oklahoma City metro area was ranked #28 overall in the large metro area category. *Milken Institute, "Best Cities for Successful Aging, 2017" March 14, 2017*

Women/Minorities Rankings

- Personal finance website *WalletHub* compared more than 180 U.S. cities—including the 150 most populated U.S. cities, plus at least two of the most populated cities in each state—across two key dimensions, "Hispanic Business-Friendliness" and "Hispanic Purchasing Power", to arrive at the most favorable conditions for Hispanic entrepreneurs. Oklahoma City was ranked #16 out of 182. Criteria includes: share of Hispanic-Owned Businesses; Hispanic entrepreneurship rate to median annual income of Hispanics; Small Business-Friendliness score; cost of living; and number of Hispanics with at least a bachelor's degree. *WalletHub.com, "2019's Best Cities for Hispanic Entrepreneurs," May 1, 2019*

Miscellaneous Rankings

- *WalletHub* compared the 150 most populated U.S. cities to determine their operating efficiency. A "Quality of Services" score was constructed for each city and then divided by the total budget per capita to reveal which were managed the best. Oklahoma City ranked #20. Criteria: financial stability; economy; education; safety; health; infrastructure and pollution. *www.WalletHub.com, "2019's Best- & Worst-Run Cities in America," July 1, 2019*

Business Environment

CITY FINANCES

City Government Finances

Component	2017 ($000)	2017 ($ per capita)
Total Revenues	1,516,466	2,402
Total Expenditures	1,362,700	2,158
Debt Outstanding	1,836,790	2,909
Cash and Securities[1]	2,727,642	4,320

Note: (1) Cash and security holdings of a government at the close of its fiscal year, including those of its dependent agencies, utilities, and liquor stores.
Source: U.S. Census Bureau, State & Local Government Finances 2017

City Government Revenue by Source

Source	2017 ($000)	2017 ($ per capita)	2017 (%)
General Revenue			
From Federal Government	55,396	88	3.7
From State Government	87,648	139	5.8
From Local Governments	54,532	86	3.6
Taxes			
Property	103,227	164	6.8
Sales and Gross Receipts	472,619	749	31.2
Personal Income	0	0	0.0
Corporate Income	0	0	0.0
Motor Vehicle License	0	0	0.0
Other Taxes	66,634	106	4.4
Current Charges	273,900	434	18.1
Liquor Store	0	0	0.0
Utility	161,785	256	10.7
Employee Retirement	86,474	137	5.7

Source: U.S. Census Bureau, State & Local Government Finances 2017

City Government Expenditures by Function

Function	2017 ($000)	2017 ($ per capita)	2017 (%)
General Direct Expenditures			
Air Transportation	78,558	124	5.8
Corrections	7,188	11	0.5
Education	0	0	0.0
Employment Security Administration	0	0	0.0
Financial Administration	36,489	57	2.7
Fire Protection	129,112	204	9.5
General Public Buildings	0	0	0.0
Governmental Administration, Other	14,772	23	1.1
Health	5,580	8	0.4
Highways	77,227	122	5.7
Hospitals	0	0	0.0
Housing and Community Development	50,468	79	3.7
Interest on General Debt	36,151	57	2.7
Judicial and Legal	29,843	47	2.2
Libraries	0	0	0.0
Parking	4,242	6	0.3
Parks and Recreation	230,879	365	16.9
Police Protection	183,966	291	13.5
Public Welfare	0	0	0.0
Sewerage	31,812	50	2.3
Solid Waste Management	42,925	68	3.2
Veterans' Services	0	0	0.0
Liquor Store	0	0	0.0
Utility	301,993	478	22.2
Employee Retirement	34,727	55	2.5

Source: U.S. Census Bureau, State & Local Government Finances 2017

DEMOGRAPHICS

Population Growth

Area	1990 Census	2000 Census	2010 Census	2018* Estimate	Population Growth (%) 1990-2018	2010-2018
City	445,065	506,132	579,999	637,284	43.2	9.9
MSA[1]	971,042	1,095,421	1,252,987	1,369,759	41.1	9.3
U.S.	248,709,873	281,421,906	308,745,538	322,903,030	29.8	4.6

Note: (1) Figures cover the Oklahoma City, OK Metropolitan Statistical Area—see Appendix B for areas included; (*) 2014-2018 5-year estimated population
Source: U.S. Census Bureau, 1990 Census, Census 2000, Census 2010, 2014-2018 American Community Survey 5-Year Estimates

Household Size

Area	Persons in Household (%) One	Two	Three	Four	Five	Six	Seven or More	Average Household Size
City	30.9	32.2	14.7	12.3	6.0	2.6	1.2	2.60
MSA[1]	28.0	34.3	15.6	12.7	5.9	2.4	1.2	2.60
U.S.	27.7	33.9	15.7	13.0	6.0	2.3	1.4	2.60

Note: (1) Figures cover the Oklahoma City, OK Metropolitan Statistical Area—see Appendix B for areas included
Source: U.S. Census Bureau, 2014-2018 American Community Survey 5-Year Estimates

Race

Area	White Alone[2] (%)	Black Alone[2] (%)	Asian Alone[2] (%)	AIAN[3] Alone[2] (%)	NHOPI[4] Alone[2] (%)	Other Race Alone[2] (%)	Two or More Races (%)
City	67.5	14.6	4.6	2.8	0.1	4.0	6.4
MSA[1]	73.7	10.3	3.2	3.4	0.1	2.8	6.6
U.S.	72.7	12.7	5.4	0.8	0.2	4.9	3.2

Note: (1) Figures cover the Oklahoma City, OK Metropolitan Statistical Area—see Appendix B for areas included; (2) Alone is defined as not being in combination with one or more other races; (3) American Indian and Alaska Native; (4) Native Hawaiian and Other Pacific Islander
Source: U.S. Census Bureau, 2014-2018 American Community Survey 5-Year Estimates

Hispanic or Latino Origin

Area	Total (%)	Mexican (%)	Puerto Rican (%)	Cuban (%)	Other (%)
City	19.2	16.1	0.3	0.1	2.7
MSA[1]	13.1	10.7	0.3	0.1	2.0
U.S.	17.8	11.2	1.7	0.7	4.2

Note: Persons of Hispanic or Latino origin can be of any race; (1) Figures cover the Oklahoma City, OK Metropolitan Statistical Area—see Appendix B for areas included
Source: U.S. Census Bureau, 2014-2018 American Community Survey 5-Year Estimates

Segregation

Type	Segregation Indices[1] 1990	2000	2010	2010 Rank[2]	Percent Change 1990-2000	1990-2010	2000-2010
Black/White	60.2	55.3	51.4	67	-4.8	-8.8	-4.0
Asian/White	39.8	40.8	39.2	60	1.0	-0.6	-1.7
Hispanic/White	33.4	44.2	47.0	38	10.7	13.6	2.9

Note: All figures cover the Metropolitan Statistical Area—see Appendix B for areas included; Figures are based on an analysis of 1990, 2000, and 2010 Census Decennial Census tract data by William H. Frey, Brookings Institution and the University of Michigan Social Science Data Analysis Network. In this analysis all racial groups (whites, blacks, and asians) are non-Hispanic members of those races. Hispanics are shown as a separate category; (1) Segregation Indices are Dissimilarity Indices that measure the degree to which the minority group is distributed differently than whites across census tracts. They range from 0 (complete integration) to 100 (complete segregation) where the value indicates the percentage of the minority group that needs to move to be distributed exactly like whites; (2) Ranges from 1 (most segregated) to 102 (least segregated); n/a not available.
Source: www.CensusScope.org

Ancestry

Area	German	Irish	English	American	Italian	Polish	French[2]	Scottish	Dutch
City	11.1	8.6	6.4	5.8	2.0	0.8	1.7	1.5	1.1
MSA[1]	12.7	9.6	7.3	7.6	2.0	0.9	1.8	1.7	1.3
U.S.	13.7	9.9	7.3	6.4	5.2	2.8	2.4	1.7	1.2

Note: Figures are the percentage of the total population reporting a particular ancestry. The nine most commonly reported ancestries in the U.S. are shown. Figures include multiple ancestries (e.g. if a person reported being Irish and Italian, they were included in both columns); (1) Figures cover the Oklahoma City, OK Metropolitan Statistical Area—see Appendix B for areas included; (2) Excludes Basque
Source: U.S. Census Bureau, 2014-2018 American Community Survey 5-Year Estimates

Foreign-born Population

Area	Percent of Population Born in								
	Any Foreign Country	Asia	Mexico	Europe	Caribbean	Central America[2]	South America	Africa	Canada
City	12.0	3.5	6.0	0.4	0.1	1.0	0.3	0.6	0.1
MSA[1]	8.0	2.5	3.6	0.4	0.1	0.6	0.2	0.4	0.1
U.S.	13.5	4.1	3.5	1.5	1.3	1.1	0.9	0.7	0.3

Note: (1) Figures cover the Oklahoma City, OK Metropolitan Statistical Area—see Appendix B for areas included; (2) Excludes Mexico.
Source: U.S. Census Bureau, 2014-2018 American Community Survey 5-Year Estimates

Marital Status

Area	Never Married	Now Married[2]	Separated	Widowed	Divorced
City	33.1	45.9	2.3	5.4	13.3
MSA[1]	31.0	48.7	2.0	5.5	12.7
U.S.	33.3	48.1	2.0	5.8	10.8

Note: Figures are percentages and cover the population 15 years of age and older; (1) Figures cover the Oklahoma City, OK Metropolitan Statistical Area—see Appendix B for areas included; (2) Excludes separated
Source: U.S. Census Bureau, 2014-2018 American Community Survey 5-Year Estimates

Disability by Age

Area	All Ages	Under 18 Years Old	18 to 64 Years Old	65 Years and Over
City	13.4	4.6	12.2	39.1
MSA[1]	13.8	4.4	12.2	39.5
U.S.	12.6	4.2	10.3	35.0

Note: Figures show percent of the civilian noninstitutionalized population that reported having a disability. Disability status is determined from six types of difficulty: vision, hearing, cognitive, ambulatory, self-care, and independent living. For children under 5 years old, hearing and vision difficulty are used to determine disability status. For children between the ages of 5 and 14, disability status is determined from hearing, vision, cognitive, ambulatory, and self-care difficulties. For people aged 15 years and older, they are considered to have a disability if they have difficulty with any one of the six difficulty types; Note: (1) Figures cover the Oklahoma City, OK Metropolitan Statistical Area—see Appendix B for areas included
Source: U.S. Census Bureau, 2014-2018 American Community Survey 5-Year Estimates

Age

Area	Percent of Population									Median Age
	Under Age 5	Age 5–19	Age 20–34	Age 35–44	Age 45–54	Age 55–64	Age 65–74	Age 75–84	Age 85+	
City	7.7	20.6	23.1	13.4	11.7	11.5	7.2	3.4	1.5	34.1
MSA[1]	7.0	20.5	22.4	12.9	12.0	11.9	7.9	3.8	1.5	35.0
U.S.	6.1	19.3	20.7	12.6	13.2	12.8	8.8	4.5	1.9	37.9

Note: (1) Figures cover the Oklahoma City, OK Metropolitan Statistical Area—see Appendix B for areas included
Source: U.S. Census Bureau, 2014-2018 American Community Survey 5-Year Estimates

Gender

Area	Males	Females	Males per 100 Females
City	313,370	323,914	96.7
MSA[1]	675,536	694,223	97.3
U.S.	158,984,190	163,918,840	97.0

Note: (1) Figures cover the Oklahoma City, OK Metropolitan Statistical Area—see Appendix B for areas included
Source: U.S. Census Bureau, 2014-2018 American Community Survey 5-Year Estimates

Religious Groups by Family

Area	Catholic	Baptist	Non-Den.	Methodist[2]	Lutheran	LDS[3]	Pente-costal	Presby-terian[4]	Muslim[5]	Judaism
MSA[1]	6.4	25.4	7.1	10.6	0.7	1.3	3.2	1.0	0.2	0.1
U.S.	19.1	9.3	4.0	4.0	2.3	2.0	1.9	1.6	0.8	0.7

Note: Figures are the number of adherents as a percentage of the total population; (1) Figures cover the Oklahoma City, OK Metropolitan Statistical Area—see Appendix B for areas included; (2) Methodist/Pietist; (3) Latter Day Saints; (4) Reformed; (5) Figures are estimates
Source: Association of Statisticians of American Religious Bodies, 2010 U.S. Religion Census: Religious Congregations & Membership Study

Religious Groups by Tradition

Area	Catholic	Evangelical Protestant	Mainline Protestant	Other Tradition	Black Protestant	Orthodox
MSA[1]	6.4	39.1	9.9	2.8	1.9	0.2
U.S.	19.1	16.2	7.3	4.3	1.6	0.3

Note: Figures are the number of adherents as a percentage of the total population; (1) Figures cover the Oklahoma City, OK Metropolitan Statistical Area—see Appendix B for areas included
Source: Association of Statisticians of American Religious Bodies, 2010 U.S. Religion Census: Religious Congregations & Membership Study

ECONOMY

Gross Metropolitan Product

Area	2017	2018	2019	2020	Rank[2]
MSA[1]	74.2	79.6	83.2	88.3	47

Note: Figures are in billions of dollars; (1) Figures cover the Oklahoma City, OK Metropolitan Statistical Area—see Appendix B for areas included; (2) Rank is based on 2018 data and ranges from 1 to 381
Source: U.S. Conference of Mayors, U.S. Metro Economies: GMP & Employment 2018-2020, September 2019

Economic Growth

Area	2015-17 (%)	2018 (%)	2019 (%)	2020 (%)	Rank[2]
MSA[1]	0.7	2.8	2.9	2.2	259
U.S.	1.9	2.9	2.3	2.1	–

Note: Figures are real gross metropolitan product (GMP) growth rates and represent average annual percent change; (1) Figures cover the Oklahoma City, OK Metropolitan Statistical Area—see Appendix B for areas included; (2) Rank is based on 2017 2-year average annual percent change and ranges from 1 to 381
Source: U.S. Conference of Mayors, U.S. Metro Economies: GMP & Employment 2018-2020, September 2019

Metropolitan Area Exports

Area	2013	2014	2015	2016	2017	2018	Rank[2]
MSA[1]	1,581.7	1,622.0	1,353.1	1,260.0	1,278.8	1,489.4	127

Note: Figures are in millions of dollars; (1) Figures cover the Oklahoma City, OK Metropolitan Statistical Area—see Appendix B for areas included; (2) Rank is based on 2018 data and ranges from 1 to 387
Source: U.S. Department of Commerce, International Trade Administration, Office of Trade and Economic Analysis, Industry and Analysis, Exports by Metropolitan Area, data extracted April 15, 2020

Building Permits

Area	Single-Family			Multi-Family			Total		
	2017	2018	Pct. Chg.	2017	2018	Pct. Chg.	2017	2018	Pct. Chg.
City	2,707	2,955	9.2	48	142	195.8	2,755	3,097	12.4
MSA[1]	5,132	5,430	5.8	287	300	4.5	5,419	5,730	5.7
U.S.	820,000	855,300	4.3	462,000	473,500	2.5	1,282,000	1,328,800	3.7

Note: (1) Figures cover the Oklahoma City, OK Metropolitan Statistical Area—see Appendix B for areas included; Figures represent new, privately-owned housing units authorized (unadjusted data); All permit data are based on estimates with imputation
Source: U.S. Census Bureau, Manufacturing, Mining, and Construction Statistics, Building Permits, 2017, 2018

Bankruptcy Filings

Area	Business Filings			Nonbusiness Filings		
	2018	2019	% Chg.	2018	2019	% Chg.
Oklahoma County	63	89	41.3	2,255	2,147	-4.8
U.S.	22,232	22,780	2.5	751,186	752,160	0.1

Note: Business filings include Chapter 7, Chapter 9, Chapter 11, Chapter 12, Chapter 13, Chapter 15, and Section 304; Nonbusiness filings include Chapter 7, Chapter 11, and Chapter 13
Source: Administrative Office of the U.S. Courts, Business and Nonbusiness Bankruptcy, County Cases Commenced by Chapter of the Bankruptcy Code, During the 12-Month Period Ending December 31, 2018 and Business and Nonbusiness Bankruptcy, County Cases Commenced by Chapter of the Bankruptcy Code, During the 12-Month Period Ending December 31, 2019

Housing Vacancy Rates

Area	Gross Vacancy Rate[2] (%)			Year-Round Vacancy Rate[3] (%)			Rental Vacancy Rate[4] (%)			Homeowner Vacancy Rate[5] (%)		
	2017	2018	2019	2017	2018	2019	2017	2018	2019	2017	2018	2019
MSA[1]	11.1	11.5	10.8	10.8	11.2	10.4	9.9	11.8	8.6	1.9	2.7	2.7
U.S.	12.7	12.3	12.0	9.9	9.7	9.5	7.2	6.9	6.7	1.6	1.5	1.4

Note: (1) Figures cover the Oklahoma City, OK Metropolitan Statistical Area—see Appendix B for areas included; (2) The percentage of the total housing inventory that is vacant; (3) The percentage of the housing inventory (excluding seasonal units) that is year-round vacant; (4) The percentage of rental inventory that is vacant for rent; (5) The percentage of homeowner inventory that is vacant for sale
Source: U.S. Census Bureau, Housing Vacancies and Homeownership Annual Statistics: 2017, 2018, 2019

INCOME

Income

Area	Per Capita ($)	Median Household ($)	Average Household ($)
City	29,581	54,034	75,485
MSA[1]	30,159	57,072	77,916
U.S.	32,621	60,293	84,938

Note: (1) Figures cover the Oklahoma City, OK Metropolitan Statistical Area—see Appendix B for areas included
Source: U.S. Census Bureau, 2014-2018 American Community Survey 5-Year Estimates

Household Income Distribution

Area	Percent of Households Earning							
	Under $15,000	$15,000 -$24,999	$25,000 -$34,999	$35,000 -$49,999	$50,000 -$74,999	$75,000 -$99,999	$100,000 -$149,999	$150,000 and up
City	11.6	9.7	10.8	14.3	18.2	12.3	12.9	10.2
MSA[1]	10.6	9.4	10.2	13.9	18.9	13.0	13.6	10.4
U.S.	10.9	9.3	9.3	12.6	17.5	12.5	14.6	13.3

Note: (1) Figures cover the Oklahoma City, OK Metropolitan Statistical Area—see Appendix B for areas included
Source: U.S. Census Bureau, 2014-2018 American Community Survey 5-Year Estimates

Poverty Rate

Area	All Ages	Under 18 Years Old	18 to 64 Years Old	65 Years and Over
City	16.8	25.2	14.8	8.3
MSA[1]	14.4	20.2	13.7	7.1
U.S.	14.1	19.5	13.2	9.3

Note: Figures are percentage of people whose income during the past 12 months was below the poverty level; (1) Figures cover the Oklahoma City, OK Metropolitan Statistical Area—see Appendix B for areas included
Source: U.S. Census Bureau, 2014-2018 American Community Survey 5-Year Estimates

EMPLOYMENT

Labor Force and Employment

Area	Civilian Labor Force			Workers Employed		
	Dec. 2018	Dec. 2019	% Chg.	Dec. 2018	Dec. 2019	% Chg.
City	318,621	322,420	1.2	309,247	313,116	1.3
MSA[1]	679,720	687,962	1.2	660,322	668,536	1.2
U.S.	162,510,000	164,007,000	0.9	156,481,000	158,504,000	1.3

Note: Data is not seasonally adjusted and covers workers 16 years of age and older; (1) Figures cover the Oklahoma City, OK Metropolitan Statistical Area—see Appendix B for areas included
Source: Bureau of Labor Statistics, Local Area Unemployment Statistics

Unemployment Rate

Area	2019											
	Jan.	Feb.	Mar.	Apr.	May	Jun.	Jul.	Aug.	Sep.	Oct.	Nov.	Dec.
City	3.6	3.3	3.1	2.7	3.0	3.3	3.2	3.1	2.9	3.1	3.0	2.9
MSA[1]	3.5	3.2	3.0	2.6	3.0	3.3	3.1	3.1	2.9	3.0	2.9	2.8
U.S.	4.4	4.1	3.9	3.3	3.4	3.8	4.0	3.8	3.3	3.3	3.3	3.4

Note: Data is not seasonally adjusted and covers workers 16 years of age and older; (1) Figures cover the Oklahoma City, OK Metropolitan Statistical Area—see Appendix B for areas included
Source: Bureau of Labor Statistics, Local Area Unemployment Statistics

Average Wages

Occupation	$/Hr.	Occupation	$/Hr.
Accountants and Auditors	37.10	Maintenance and Repair Workers	17.60
Automotive Mechanics	22.20	Marketing Managers	61.40
Bookkeepers	19.30	Network and Computer Systems Admin.	37.00
Carpenters	20.40	Nurses, Licensed Practical	20.90
Cashiers	10.60	Nurses, Registered	32.00
Computer Programmers	38.10	Nursing Assistants	12.90
Computer Systems Analysts	36.40	Office Clerks, General	14.60
Computer User Support Specialists	23.60	Physical Therapists	43.60
Construction Laborers	16.00	Physicians	68.40
Cooks, Restaurant	12.50	Plumbers, Pipefitters and Steamfitters	25.70
Customer Service Representatives	16.40	Police and Sheriff's Patrol Officers	27.10
Dentists	83.50	Postal Service Mail Carriers	24.90
Electricians	24.60	Real Estate Sales Agents	25.80
Engineers, Electrical	45.20	Retail Salespersons	14.00
Fast Food and Counter Workers	10.20	Sales Representatives, Technical/Scientific	42.90
Financial Managers	55.40	Secretaries, Exc. Legal/Medical/Executive	16.00
First-Line Supervisors of Office Workers	26.10	Security Guards	16.60
General and Operations Managers	54.40	Surgeons	n/a
Hairdressers/Cosmetologists	12.90	Teacher Assistants, Exc. Postsecondary*	10.70
Home Health and Personal Care Aides	11.90	Teachers, Secondary School, Exc. Sp. Ed.*	22.70
Janitors and Cleaners	12.20	Telemarketers	12.70
Landscaping/Groundskeeping Workers	13.90	Truck Drivers, Heavy/Tractor-Trailer	22.00
Lawyers	56.70	Truck Drivers, Light/Delivery Services	16.60
Maids and Housekeeping Cleaners	10.70	Waiters and Waitresses	10.40

Note: Wage data covers the Oklahoma City, OK Metropolitan Statistical Area—see Appendix B for areas included; (*) Hourly wages were calculated from annual wage data based on a 40 hour work week; n/a not available.
Source: Bureau of Labor Statistics, Metro Area Occupational Employment & Wage Estimates, May 2019

Employment by Occupation

Occupation Classification	City (%)	MSA[1] (%)	U.S. (%)
Management, Business, Science, and Arts	36.5	37.2	37.9
Natural Resources, Construction, and Maintenance	10.8	10.6	8.9
Production, Transportation, and Material Moving	11.8	11.9	13.3
Sales and Office	23.6	23.4	22.1
Service	17.4	16.9	17.9

Note: Figures cover employed civilians 16 years of age and older; (1) Figures cover the Oklahoma City, OK Metropolitan Statistical Area—see Appendix B for areas included
Source: U.S. Census Bureau, 2014-2018 American Community Survey 5-Year Estimates

Employment by Industry

| Sector | MSA[1] | | U.S. |
	Number of Employees	Percent of Total	Percent of Total
Construction	32,900	4.9	4.9
Education and Health Services	98,300	14.7	16.1
Financial Activities	34,700	5.2	5.8
Government	134,900	20.2	15.0
Information	7,100	1.1	1.9
Leisure and Hospitality	74,500	11.1	10.8
Manufacturing	33,900	5.1	8.4
Mining and Logging	16,700	2.5	0.5
Other Services	29,300	4.4	3.9
Professional and Business Services	88,500	13.2	14.1
Retail Trade	67,600	10.1	10.6
Transportation, Warehousing, and Utilities	27,200	4.1	4.2
Wholesale Trade	23,500	3.5	3.9

Note: Figures are non-farm employment as of December 2019. Figures are not seasonally adjusted and include workers 16 years of age and older; (1) Figures cover the Oklahoma City, OK Metropolitan Statistical Area—see Appendix B for areas included
Source: Bureau of Labor Statistics, Current Employment Statistics, Employment, Hours, and Earnings

Occupations with Greatest Projected Employment Growth: 2019 – 2021

Occupation[1]	2019 Employment	2021 Projected Employment	Numeric Employment Change	Percent Employment Change
Combined Food Preparation and Serving Workers, Including Fast Food	32,200	33,740	1,540	4.8
Laborers and Freight, Stock, and Material Movers, Hand	30,640	32,090	1,450	4.7
Cooks, Restaurant	16,980	17,960	980	5.8
Waiters and Waitresses	29,590	30,450	860	2.9
Personal Care Aides	15,510	16,360	850	5.5
Registered Nurses	35,540	36,290	750	2.1
First-Line Supervisors of Food Preparation and Serving Workers	15,820	16,380	560	3.5
Heavy and Tractor-Trailer Truck Drivers	28,410	28,920	510	1.8
General and Operations Managers	27,980	28,330	350	1.3
Home Health Aides	7,370	7,720	350	4.7

Note: Projections cover Oklahoma; (1) Sorted by numeric employment change
Source: www.projectionscentral.com, State Occupational Projections, 2019–2021 Short-Term Projections

Fastest Growing Occupations: 2019 – 2021

Occupation[1]	2019 Employment	2021 Projected Employment	Numeric Employment Change	Percent Employment Change
Cooks, Restaurant	16,980	17,960	980	5.8
Personal Care Aides	15,510	16,360	850	5.5
Veterinary Technologists and Technicians	1,130	1,190	60	5.3
Slaughterers and Meat Packers	1,310	1,380	70	5.3
Veterinary Assistants and Laboratory Animal Caretakers	1,540	1,620	80	5.2
Speech-Language Pathologists	1,960	2,060	100	5.1
Combined Food Preparation and Serving Workers, Including Fast Food	32,200	33,740	1,540	4.8
Veterinarians	1,270	1,330	60	4.7
Home Health Aides	7,370	7,720	350	4.7
Laborers and Freight, Stock, and Material Movers, Hand	30,640	32,090	1,450	4.7

Note: Projections cover Oklahoma; (1) Sorted by percent employment change and excludes occupations with numeric employment change less than 50
Source: www.projectionscentral.com, State Occupational Projections, 2019–2021 Short-Term Projections

TAXES

State Corporate Income Tax Rates

State	Tax Rate (%)	Income Brackets ($)	Num. of Brackets	Financial Institution Tax Rate (%)[a]	Federal Income Tax Ded.
Oklahoma	6.0	Flat rate	1	6.0	No

Note: Tax rates as of January 1, 2020; (a) Rates listed are the corporate income tax rate applied to financial institutions or excise taxes based on income.
Source: Federation of Tax Administrators, State Corporate Income Tax Rates, January 1, 2020

State Individual Income Tax Rates

State	Tax Rate (%)	Income Brackets ($)	Personal Exemptions ($)			Standard Ded. ($)	
			Single	Married	Depend.	Single	Married
Oklahoma	0.5 - 5.0	1,000 - 7,200 (t)	1,000	2,000	1,000	6,350	12,700

Note: Tax rates as of January 1, 2020; Local- and county-level taxes are not included; Federal income tax is not deductible on state income tax returns; (t) The income brackets reported for Oklahoma are for single persons. For married persons filing jointly, the same tax rates apply to income brackets ranging from $2,000, to $12,200.
Source: Federation of Tax Administrators, State Individual Income Tax Rates, January 1, 2020

Various State Sales and Excise Tax Rates

State	State Sales Tax (%)	Gasoline[1] (¢/gal.)	Cigarette[2] ($/pack)	Spirits[3] ($/gal.)	Wine[4] ($/gal.)	Beer[5] ($/gal.)	Recreational Marijuana (%)
Oklahoma	4.5	20	2.03	5.56	0.72	0.40	Not legal

Note: All tax rates as of January 1, 2020; (1) The American Petroleum Institute has developed a methodology for determining the average tax rate on a gallon of fuel. Rates may include any of the following: excise taxes, environmental fees, storage tank fees, other fees or taxes, general sales tax, and local taxes; (2) The federal excise tax of $1.0066 per pack and local taxes are not included; (3) Rates are those applicable to off-premise sales of 40% alcohol by volume (a.b.v.) distilled spirits in 750ml containers. Local excise taxes are excluded; (4) Rates are those applicable to off-premise sales of 11% a.b.v. non-carbonated wine in 750ml containers; (5) Rates are those applicable to off-premise sales of 4.7% a.b.v. beer in 12 ounce containers.
Source: Tax Foundation, 2020 Facts & Figures: How Does Your State Compare?

State Business Tax Climate Index Rankings

State	Overall Rank	Corporate Tax Rank	Individual Income Tax Rank	Sales Tax Rank	Property Tax Rank	Unemployment Insurance Tax Rank
Oklahoma	27	8	33	39	19	1

Note: The index is a measure of how each state's tax laws affect economic performance. The lower the rank, the more favorable a state's tax system is for business. States without a given tax are given a ranking of 1. The scores/rankings for the District of Columbia do not affect other states. The 2020 index represents the tax climate as of July 1, 2019.
Source: Tax Foundation, State Business Tax Climate Index 2020

COMMERCIAL REAL ESTATE

Office Market

Market Area	Inventory (sq. ft.)	Vacancy Rate (%)	Under Construction (sq. ft.)	YTD Net Absorption (sq. ft.)	Total Average Asking Rent ($/sq. ft./year)
Oklahoma City	15,029,565	26.9	153,000	-261,376	20.05
National	4,923,349,992	13.0	102,814,961	2,049,925	29.54

Source: Newmark Grubb Knight Frank, National Office Market Report, 1st Quarter 2020

COMMERCIAL UTILITIES

Typical Monthly Electric Bills

Area	Commercial Service ($/month)		Industrial Service ($/month)	
	1,500 kWh	40 kW demand 14,000 kWh	1,000 kW demand 200,000 kWh	50,000 kW demand 32,500,000 kWh
City	165	1,022	14,209	1,248,885
Average[1]	203	1,612	25,706	2,520,671

Note: Figures are based on annualized rates; (1) Average based on 187 utilities surveyed
Source: Edison Electric Institute, Typical Bills and Average Rates Report, Summer 2019

TRANSPORTATION

Means of Transportation to Work

Area	Car/Truck/Van		Public Transportation			Bicycle	Walked	Other Means	Worked at Home
	Drove Alone	Car-pooled	Bus	Subway	Railroad				
City	82.0	11.0	0.5	0.0	0.0	0.1	1.6	1.0	3.7
MSA[1]	82.9	9.7	0.4	0.0	0.0	0.3	1.7	1.0	4.0
U.S.	76.4	9.1	2.5	1.9	0.6	0.6	2.7	1.3	4.9

Note: Figures are percentages and cover workers 16 years of age and older; (1) Figures cover the Oklahoma City, OK Metropolitan Statistical Area—see Appendix B for areas included
Source: U.S. Census Bureau, 2014-2018 American Community Survey 5-Year Estimates

Travel Time to Work

Area	Less Than 10 Minutes	10 to 19 Minutes	20 to 29 Minutes	30 to 44 Minutes	45 to 59 Minutes	60 to 89 Minutes	90 Minutes or More
City	11.2	35.9	29.4	17.5	3.1	1.5	1.5
MSA[1]	12.6	32.3	25.7	20.1	5.5	2.3	1.5
U.S.	12.5	28.7	20.9	20.7	8.2	6.3	2.8

Note: Note: Figures are percentages and include workers 16 years old and over; (1) Figures cover the Oklahoma City, OK Metropolitan Statistical Area—see Appendix B for areas included
Source: U.S. Census Bureau, 2014-2018 American Community Survey 5-Year Estimates

Key Congestion Measures

Area	1982	1992	2002	2012	2017
Annual Hours of Delay, Total (000)	4,550	10,361	25,336	36,587	43,448
Annual Hours of Delay, Per Auto Commuter	11	20	39	45	50
Annual Congestion Cost, Total (million $)	34	109	341	653	798
Annual Congestion Cost, Per Auto Commuter ($)	197	309	589	667	768

Source: Texas A&M Transportation Institute, 2019 Urban Mobility Report

Freeway Travel Time Index

Area	1982	1987	1992	1997	2002	2007	2012	2017
Urban Area Index[1]	1.05	1.07	1.09	1.13	1.17	1.18	1.18	1.19
Urban Area Rank[1,2]	51	55	70	62	41	44	40	41

Note: Freeway Travel Time Index—the ratio of travel time in the peak period to the travel time at free-flow conditions. For example, a value of 1.30 indicates a 20-minute free-flow trip takes 26 minutes in the peak (20 minutes x 1.30 = 26 minutes); (1) Covers the Oklahoma City OK urban area; (2) Rank is based on 101 larger urban areas (#1 = highest travel time index)
Source: Texas A&M Transportation Institute, 2019 Urban Mobility Report

Public Transportation

Agency Name / Mode of Transportation	Vehicles Operated in Maximum Service[1]	Annual Unlinked Passenger Trips[2] (in thous.)	Annual Passenger Miles[3] (in thous.)
Central Oklahoma Transportation & Parking Authority (COTPA)			
Bus (directly operated)	49	2,958.9	14,805.4
Demand Response (directly operated)	17	53.2	474.3
Demand Response Taxi (purchased transportation)	5	6.9	41.6
Ferryboat (purchased transportation)	2	8.9	21.1
Vanpool (purchased transportation)	2	3.5	108.7

Note: (1) Number of revenue vehicles operated by the given mode and type of service to meet the annual maximum service requirement. This is the revenue vehicle count during the peak season of the year; on the week and day that maximum service is provided. Vehicles operated in maximum service (VOMS) exclude atypical days and one-time special events; (2) Number of passengers who boarded public transportation vehicles. Passengers are counted each time they board a vehicle no matter how many vehicles they use to travel from their origin to their destination. (3) Sum of the distances ridden by all passengers during the entire fiscal year.
Source: Federal Transit Administration, National Transit Database, 2018

Air Transportation

Airport Name and Code / Type of Service	Passenger Airlines[1]	Passenger Enplanements	Freight Carriers[2]	Freight (lbs)
Will Rogers World Airport (OKC)				
Domestic service (U.S. carriers - 2019)	28	2,141,240	13	27,321,403
International service (U.S. carriers - 2018)	2	160	2	61,608

Note: (1) Includes all U.S.-based major, minor and commuter airlines that carried at least one passenger during the year; (2) Includes all U.S.-based airlines and freight carriers that transported at least one pound of freight during the year.
Source: Bureau of Transportation Statistics, The Intermodal Transportation Database, Air Carriers: T-100 Domestic Market (U.S. Carriers), 2019; Bureau of Transportation Statistics, The Intermodal Transportation Database, Air Carriers: T-100 International Market (U.S. Carriers), 2018

Other Transportation Statistics

Major Highways:	I-35; I-40; I-44;
Amtrak Service:	Yes
Major Waterways/Ports:	None

Source: Amtrak.com; Google Maps

BUSINESSES

Major Business Headquarters

Company Name	Industry	Rankings	
		Fortune[1]	Forbes[2]
Chesapeake Energy	Mining, Crude-Oil Production	309	-
Devon Energy	Mining, Crude-Oil Production	297	-
Hobby Lobby Stores	Retailing	-	89
Love's Travel Stops & Country Stores	Convenience Stores & Gas Stations	-	17

Note: (1) Companies that produce a 10-K are ranked 1 to 500 based on 2018 revenue; (2) All private companies with at least $2 billion in annual revenue through the end of their most current fiscal year are ranked 1 to 228; companies listed are headquartered in the city; dashes indicate no ranking
Source: Fortune, "Fortune 500," June 2019; Forbes, "America's Largest Private Companies," 2019 Rankings

Fast-Growing Businesses

According to *Fortune*, Oklahoma City is home to one of the 100 fastest-growing companies in the world: **Paycom Software** (#6). Companies were ranked by their revenue growth rate; their EPS growth rate; and their three-year annualized total return to investors for the period ending June 30, 2019. Criteria for inclusion: a company, foreign or domestic, must trade on a major U.S. stock exchange; must file quarterly reports with the SEC; must have a minimum market capitalization of $250 million; must have a stock price of at least $5 on June 30, 2019; must have been trading continuously since June 30, 2016; must have revenue and net income for the four quarters ended on or before April 30, 2019, of at least $50 million and $10 million, respectively; and must have posted a compound annual growth in revenue and earnings per share of at least 15% annually over the three years ending on or before April 30, 2019. Real estate investment trusts, limited-liability companies, limited parterships, business development companies, closed-end investment firms, companies about to be acquired, and companies that lost money in the quarter ending April 30, 2019 were excluded. *Fortune, "100 Fastest-Growing Companies," 2019*

Minority Business Opportunity

Oklahoma City is home to one company which is on the *Hispanic Business* 500 list (500 largest U.S. Hispanic-owned companies based on revenue): **Lopez Foods** (#17). Companies included must show at least 51 percent ownership by Hispanic U.S. citizens, and must maintain headquarters in one of the 50 states or Washington, D.C. *Hispanic Business, "Hispanic Business 500," June 20, 2013*

Minority- and Women-Owned Businesses

Group	All Firms		Firms with Paid Employees			
	Firms	Sales ($000)	Firms	Sales ($000)	Employees	Payroll ($000)
AIAN[1]	2,870	716,870	413	596,089	4,227	193,808
Asian	3,475	714,106	630	589,326	5,443	102,323
Black	5,208	305,422	289	215,201	3,043	89,435
Hispanic	4,920	1,092,474	430	885,775	3,845	111,618
NHOPI[2]	35	3,784	6	(s)	20 - 99	(s)
Women	20,163	5,106,277	2,624	4,596,994	24,353	933,230
All Firms	58,815	132,726,309	14,488	130,383,497	301,903	13,914,882

Note: Figures cover firms located in the city; minority- and women-owned business are defined as firms in which the corresponding group own 51% or more of the stock or equity of the company; (1) American Indian and Alaska Native; (2) Native Hawaiian and Other Pacific Islander; (s) estimates are suppressed when publication standards are not met
Source: U.S. Census Bureau, 2012 Economic Census, Survey of Business Owners

HOTELS & CONVENTION CENTERS

Hotels, Motels and Vacation Rentals

Area	5 Star		4 Star		3 Star		2 Star		1 Star		Not Rated	
	Num.	Pct.[3]	Num.	Pct.[3]	Num.	Pct.[3]	Num.	Pct.[3]	Num.	Pct.[3]	Num.	Pct.[3]
City[1]	0	0.0	8	3.6	45	20.3	44	19.8	10	4.5	115	51.8
Total[2]	266	1.3	1,517	7.2	4,627	21.8	3,210	15.1	3,974	18.7	7,601	35.9

Note: (1) Figures cover Oklahoma City and vicinity; (2) Figures cover all 100 cities in this book; (3) Percentage of hotels which have a given star rating; Star ratings are determined by priceline.com and offer an indication of the general quality of a particular hotel.
Source: priceline.com, April 27, 2020

Major Convention Centers

Name	Overall Space (sq. ft.)	Exhibit Space (sq. ft.)	Meeting Space (sq. ft.)	Meeting Rooms
Cox Convention Center	n/a	100,000	30,000	26

Note: Table includes convention centers located in the Oklahoma City, OK metro area; n/a not available
Source: Original research

Living Environment

COST OF LIVING

Cost of Living Index

Composite Index	Groceries	Housing	Utilities	Trans- portation	Health Care	Misc. Goods/ Services
86.0	93.3	69.6	95.3	86.2	95.0	92.1

Note: The Cost of Living Index measures regional differences in the cost of consumer goods and services, excluding taxes and non-consumer expenditures, for professional and managerial households in the top income quintile. It is based on more than 50,000 prices covering almost 60 different items for which prices are collected three times a year by chambers of commerce, economic development organizations or university applied economic centers in each participating urban area. The numbers shown should be read as a percentage above or below the national average of 100. For example, a value of 115.4 in the groceries column indicates that grocery prices are 15.4% higher than the national average. Small differences in the index numbers should not be interpreted as significant; Figures cover the Oklahoma City OK urban area.
Source: The Council for Community and Economic Research, ACCRA Cost of Living Index, 2019

Grocery Prices

Area[1]	T-Bone Steak ($/pound)	Frying Chicken ($/pound)	Whole Milk ($/half gal.)	Eggs ($/dozen)	Orange Juice ($/64 oz.)	Coffee ($/11.5 oz.)
City[2]	10.39	1.49	1.84	1.33	3.15	4.07
Avg.	11.40	1.41	1.93	1.54	3.51	4.30
Min.	7.40	0.92	0.85	0.58	2.67	2.90
Max.	15.58	2.68	4.09	4.18	5.57	8.10

Note: (1) Values for the local area are compared with the average, minimum and maximum values for all 290 areas in the Cost of Living Index; (2) Figures cover the Oklahoma City OK urban area; T-Bone Steak (price per pound); Frying Chicken (price per pound, whole fryer); Whole Milk (half gallon carton); Eggs (price per dozen, Grade A, large); Orange Juice (64 oz. Tropicana or Florida Natural); Coffee (11.5 oz. can, vacuum-packed, Maxwell House, Hills Bros, or Folgers).
Source: The Council for Community and Economic Research, ACCRA Cost of Living Index, 2019

Housing and Utility Costs

Area[1]	New Home Price ($)	Apartment Rent ($/month)	All Electric ($/month)	Part Electric ($/month)	Other Energy ($/month)	Telephone ($/month)
City[2]	241,727	850	-	93.97	60.92	179.40
Avg.	362,090	1,142	174.35	100.00	67.76	179.60
Min.	198,329	501	91.58	31.44	28.51	165.30
Max.	2,074,561	5,050	388.18	239.41	306.15	207.90

Note: (1) Values for the local area are compared with the average, minimum and maximum values for all 290 areas in the Cost of Living Index; (2) Figures cover the Oklahoma City OK urban area; New Home Price (2,400 sf living area, 8,000 sf lot, in urban area with full utilities); Apartment Rent (950 sf 2 bedroom/1.5 or 2 bath, unfurnished, excluding all utilities except water); All Electric (average monthly cost for an all-electric home); Part Electric (average monthly cost for a part-electric home); Other Energy (average monthly cost for natural gas, fuel oil, coal, wood, and any other forms of energy except electricity); Telephone (price includes the base monthly rate plus taxes and fees for three lines of mobile phone service).
Source: The Council for Community and Economic Research, ACCRA Cost of Living Index, 2019

Health Care, Transportation, and Other Costs

Area[1]	Doctor ($/visit)	Dentist ($/visit)	Optometrist ($/visit)	Gasoline ($/gallon)	Beauty Salon ($/visit)	Men's Shirt ($)
City[2]	101.98	91.50	102.51	2.12	39.79	20.91
Avg.	114.85	97.58	106.10	2.50	38.15	32.15
Min.	39.00	62.22	52.22	1.53	16.88	10.27
Max.	206.67	151.53	258.67	3.79	79.29	59.30

Note: (1) Values for the local area are compared with the average, minimum and maximum values for all 290 areas in the Cost of Living Index; (2) Figures cover the Oklahoma City OK urban area; Doctor (general practitioners routine exam of an established patient); Dentist (adult teeth cleaning and periodic oral examination); Optometrist (full vision eye exam for established adult patient); Gasoline (one gallon regular unleaded, national brand, including all taxes, cash price at self-service pump if available); Beauty Salon (woman's shampoo, trim, and blow-dry); Men's Shirt (cotton/polyester dress shirt, pinpoint weave, long sleeves).
Source: The Council for Community and Economic Research, ACCRA Cost of Living Index, 2019

HOUSING

House Price Index (HPI)

Area	National Ranking[2]	Quarterly Change (%)	One-Year Change (%)	Five-Year Change (%)
MSA[1]	55	0.60	6.13	22.05
U.S.[3]	–	1.26	5.09	32.88

Note: The HPI is a weighted repeat sales index. It measures average price changes in repeat sales or refinancings on the same properties. This information is obtained by reviewing repeat mortgage transactions on single-family properties whose mortgages have been purchased or securitized by Fannie Mae or Freddie Mac in January 1975; (1) Figures cover the Oklahoma City, OK Metropolitan Statistical Area—see Appendix B for areas included; (2) Rankings are based on annual percentage change for all metro areas containing at least 15,000 transactions over the last 10 years and ranges from 1 to 232; (3) figures based on a weighted average of Census Division estimates using a seasonally adjusted, purchase-only index; all figures are for the period ending December 31, 2019
Source: Federal Housing Finance Agency, House Price Index, February 25, 2020

Median Single-Family Home Prices

Area	2017	2018	2019p	Percent Change 2018 to 2019
MSA[1]	154.3	159.5	158.9	-0.4
U.S. Average	248.8	261.6	274.6	5.0

Note: Figures are median sales prices of existing single-family homes in thousands of dollars; (p) preliminary; (1) Figures cover the Oklahoma City, OK Metropolitan Statistical Area—see Appendix B for areas included
Source: National Association of Realtors, Median Sales Price of Existing Single-Family Homes for Metropolitan Areas, 4th Quarter 2019

Qualifying Income Based on Median Sales Price of Existing Single-Family Homes

Area	With 5% Down ($)	With 10% Down ($)	With 20% Down ($)
MSA[1]	33,845	32,063	28,501
U.S. Average	58,663	55,575	49,400

Note: Figures are preliminary; Qualifying income is based on a mortgage rate of 3.76%. Monthly principal and interest payment is limited to 25% of income; (1) Figures cover the Oklahoma City, OK Metropolitan Statistical Area—see Appendix B for areas included
Source: National Association of Realtors, Qualifying Income Based on Median Sales Price of Existing Single-Family Homes for Metropolitan Areas, 4th Quarter 2019

Median Apartment Condo-Coop Home Prices

Area	2017	2018	2019p	Percent Change 2018 to 2019
MSA[1]	n/a	n/a	n/a	n/a
U.S. Average	234.3	241.0	249.5	3.5

Note: Figures are median sales prices of existing apartment condo-coop homes in thousands of dollars; (p) preliminary; n/a not available; (1) Figures cover the Oklahoma City, OK Metropolitan Statistical Area—see Appendix B for areas included
Source: National Association of Realtors, Median Sales Price of Existing Apartment Condo-Coop Homes for Metropolitan Areas, 4th Quarter 2019

Home Value Distribution

Area	Under $50,000	$50,000 -$99,999	$100,000 -$149,999	$150,000 -$199,999	$200,000 -$299,999	$300,000 -$499,999	$500,000 -$999,999	$1,000,000 or more
City	8.5	18.8	20.9	20.3	18.0	9.7	3.2	0.6
MSA[1]	8.2	18.9	22.0	19.3	17.5	9.9	3.3	0.9
U.S.	7.6	13.0	14.0	14.3	19.2	18.3	10.5	3.1

Note: Figures are percentages and cover owner-occupied housing units; (1) Figures cover the Oklahoma City, OK Metropolitan Statistical Area—see Appendix B for areas included
Source: U.S. Census Bureau, 2014-2018 American Community Survey 5-Year Estimates

Homeownership Rate

Area	2011 (%)	2012 (%)	2013 (%)	2014 (%)	2015 (%)	2016 (%)	2017 (%)	2018 (%)	2019 (%)
MSA[1]	69.6	67.3	67.6	65.7	61.4	63.1	64.7	64.6	64.3
U.S.	66.1	65.4	65.1	64.5	63.7	63.4	63.9	64.4	64.6

Note: (1) Figures cover the Oklahoma City, OK Metropolitan Statistical Area—see Appendix B for areas included
Source: U.S. Census Bureau, Housing Vacancies and Homeownership Annual Statistics: 2011-2019

Year Housing Structure Built

Area	2010 or Later	2000 -2009	1990 -1999	1980 -1989	1970 -1979	1960 -1969	1950 -1959	1940 -1949	Before 1940	Median Year
City	8.0	13.4	10.0	15.3	15.9	12.6	10.7	5.7	8.4	1978
MSA[1]	7.8	15.2	11.5	15.0	17.2	12.2	9.8	4.9	6.3	1980
U.S.	4.1	14.3	13.9	13.5	15.3	10.7	10.4	5.0	12.8	1977

Note: Figures are percentages except for Median Year; Note: (1) Figures cover the Oklahoma City, OK Metropolitan Statistical Area—see Appendix B for areas included
Source: U.S. Census Bureau, 2014-2018 American Community Survey 5-Year Estimates

Gross Monthly Rent

Area	Under $500	$500 -$999	$1,000 -$1,499	$1,500 -$1,999	$2,000 -$2,499	$2,500 -$2,999	$3,000 and up	Median ($)
City	8.3	59.7	24.6	5.6	1.1	0.3	0.4	849
MSA[1]	8.4	58.6	25.5	5.8	1.1	0.3	0.3	858
U.S.	9.8	38.5	29.6	12.9	5.1	2.1	2.0	1,023

Note: Figures are percentages except for Median; Gross rent is the contract rent plus the estimated average monthly cost of utilities (electricity, gas, and water and sewer) and fuels (oil, coal, kerosene, wood, etc.) if these are paid by the renter (or paid for the renter by someone else); (1) Figures cover the Oklahoma City, OK Metropolitan Statistical Area—see Appendix B for areas included
Source: U.S. Census Bureau, 2014-2018 American Community Survey 5-Year Estimates

HEALTH

Health Risk Factors

Category	MSA[1] (%)	U.S. (%)
Adults aged 18–64 who have any kind of health care coverage	80.7	87.3
Adults who reported being in good or better health	80.8	82.4
Adults who have been told they have high blood cholesterol	35.9	33.0
Adults who have been told they have high blood pressure	34.7	32.3
Adults who are current smokers	17.1	17.1
Adults who currently use E-cigarettes	6.6	4.6
Adults who currently use chewing tobacco, snuff, or snus	5.8	4.0
Adults who are heavy drinkers[2]	4.4	6.3
Adults who are binge drinkers[3]	14.7	17.4
Adults who are overweight (BMI 25.0 - 29.9)	33.5	35.3
Adults who are obese (BMI 30.0 - 99.8)	34.6	31.3
Adults who participated in any physical activities in the past month	71.9	74.4
Adults who always or nearly always wears a seat belt	94.9	94.3

Note: (1) Figures cover the Oklahoma City, OK Metropolitan Statistical Area—see Appendix B for areas included; (2) Heavy drinkers are classified as adult men having more than 14 drinks per week and adult women having more than 7 drinks per week; (3) Binge drinkers are classified as males having five or more drinks on one occasion or females having four or more drinks on one occasion
Source: Centers for Disease Control and Prevention, Behaviorial Risk Factor Surveillance System, SMART: Selected Metropolitan Area Risk Trends, 2017

Acute and Chronic Health Conditions

Category	MSA[1] (%)	U.S. (%)
Adults who have ever been told they had a heart attack	4.9	4.2
Adults who have ever been told they have angina or coronary heart disease	5.1	3.9
Adults who have ever been told they had a stroke	3.4	3.0
Adults who have ever been told they have asthma	14.2	14.2
Adults who have ever been told they have arthritis	26.9	24.9
Adults who have ever been told they have diabetes[2]	12.1	10.5
Adults who have ever been told they had skin cancer	5.9	6.2
Adults who have ever been told they had any other types of cancer	7.0	7.1
Adults who have ever been told they have COPD	7.2	6.5
Adults who have ever been told they have kidney disease	4.1	3.0
Adults who have ever been told they have a form of depression	23.1	20.5

Note: (1) Figures cover the Oklahoma City, OK Metropolitan Statistical Area—see Appendix B for areas included; (2) Figures do not include pregnancy-related, borderline, or pre-diabetes
Source: Centers for Disease Control and Prevention, Behaviorial Risk Factor Surveillance System, SMART: Selected Metropolitan Area Risk Trends, 2017

Health Screening and Vaccination Rates

Category	MSA[1] (%)	U.S. (%)
Adults aged 65+ who have had flu shot within the past year	70.4	60.7
Adults aged 65+ who have ever had a pneumonia vaccination	82.0	75.4
Adults who have ever been tested for HIV	32.8	36.1
Adults who have ever had the shingles or zoster vaccine?	30.7	28.9
Adults who have had their blood cholesterol checked within the last five years	83.2	85.9

Note: n/a not available; (1) Figures cover the Oklahoma City, OK Metropolitan Statistical Area—see Appendix B for areas included.
Source: Centers for Disease Control and Prevention, Behaviorial Risk Factor Surveillance System, SMART: Selected Metropolitan Area Risk Trends, 2017

Disability Status

Category	MSA[1] (%)	U.S. (%)
Adults who reported being deaf	7.9	6.7
Are you blind or have serious difficulty seeing, even when wearing glasses?	6.3	4.5
Are you limited in any way in any of your usual activities due of arthritis?	15.0	12.9
Do you have difficulty doing errands alone?	9.9	6.8
Do you have difficulty dressing or bathing?	5.9	3.6
Do you have serious difficulty concentrating/remembering/making decisions?	14.7	10.7
Do you have serious difficulty walking or climbing stairs?	17.4	13.6

Note: (1) Figures cover the Oklahoma City, OK Metropolitan Statistical Area—see Appendix B for areas included.
Source: Centers for Disease Control and Prevention, Behaviorial Risk Factor Surveillance System, SMART: Selected Metropolitan Area Risk Trends, 2017

Mortality Rates for the Top 10 Causes of Death in the U.S.

ICD-10[a] Sub-Chapter	ICD-10[a] Code	Age-Adjusted Mortality Rate[1] per 100,000 population	
		County[2]	U.S.
Malignant neoplasms	C00-C97	177.0	152.4
Ischaemic heart diseases	I20-I25	114.6	92.7
Other forms of heart disease	I30-I51	49.7	52.5
Chronic lower respiratory diseases	J40-J47	59.6	40.4
Cerebrovascular diseases	I60-I69	44.5	37.3
Other degenerative diseases of the nervous system	G30-G31	51.7	36.4
Other external causes of accidental injury	W00-X59	49.7	35.3
Organic, including symptomatic, mental disorders	F01-F09	31.9	30.0
Hypertensive diseases	I10-I15	50.7	22.9
Diabetes mellitus	E10-E14	33.2	21.3

Note: (a) ICD-10 = International Classification of Diseases 10th Revision; (1) Mortality rates are a three year average covering 2016-2018; (2) Figures cover Oklahoma County.
Source: Centers for Disease Control and Prevention, National Center for Health Statistics. Underlying Cause of Death 1999-2018 on CDC WONDER Online Database

Mortality Rates for Selected Causes of Death

ICD-10[a] Sub-Chapter	ICD-10[a] Code	Age-Adjusted Mortality Rate[1] per 100,000 population	
		County[2]	U.S.
Assault	X85-Y09	10.8	6.0
Diseases of the liver	K70-K76	20.2	14.2
Human immunodeficiency virus (HIV) disease	B20-B24	2.6	1.6
Influenza and pneumonia	J09-J18	12.7	14.2
Intentional self-harm	X60-X84	18.6	13.9
Malnutrition	E40-E46	2.5	1.9
Obesity and other hyperalimentation	E65-E68	2.0	2.1
Renal failure	N17-N19	10.7	12.8
Transport accidents	V01-V99	14.5	12.5
Viral hepatitis	B15-B19	2.9	1.4

Note: (a) ICD-10 = International Classification of Diseases 10th Revision; (1) Mortality rates are a three year average covering 2016-2018; (2) Figures cover Oklahoma County; Data are suppressed when the data meet the criteria for confidentiality constraints; Mortality rates are flagged as unreliable when the rate would be calculated with a numerator of 20 or less.
Source: Centers for Disease Control and Prevention, National Center for Health Statistics. Underlying Cause of Death 1999-2018 on CDC WONDER Online Database

Health Insurance Coverage

Area	With Health Insurance	With Private Health Insurance	With Public Health Insurance	Without Health Insurance	Population Under Age 19 Without Health Insurance
City	85.0	63.7	31.7	15.0	6.9
MSA[1]	87.2	68.4	30.6	12.8	6.3
U.S.	90.6	67.7	34.7	9.4	5.2

Note: Figures are percentages that cover the civilian noninstitutionalized population; (1) Figures cover the Oklahoma City, OK Metropolitan Statistical Area—see Appendix B for areas included
Source: U.S. Census Bureau, 2014-2018 American Community Survey 5-Year Estimates

Number of Medical Professionals

Area	MDs[3]	DOs[3,4]	Dentists	Podiatrists	Chiropractors	Optometrists
County[1] (number)	3,250	348	811	39	213	147
County[1] (rate[2])	412.5	44.2	102.3	4.9	26.9	18.5
U.S. (rate[2])	281.9	23.4	69.1	6.0	27.5	16.4

Note: Data as of 2018 unless noted; (1) Data covers Oklahoma County; (2) Rate per 100,000 population; (3) Data as of 2017 and includes all active, non-federal physicians; (4) Doctor of Osteopathic Medicine
Source: U.S. Department of Health and Human Services, Health Resources and Services Administration, Bureau of Health Professions, Area Resource File (ARF) 2018-2019

Best Hospitals

According to *U.S. News,* the Oklahoma City, OK metro area is home to two of the best hospitals in the U.S.: **Dean McGee Eye Institute, OU Medical Center** (1 adult specialty); **OU Medical Center** (1 adult specialty). The hospitals listed were nationally ranked in at least one of 16 adult or 10 pediatric specialties. Only 206 hospitals nationwide were nationally ranked in one or more adult or pediatric specialty. Twenty hospitals in the U.S. made the Honor Roll. The Best Hospitals Honor Roll takes both the national rankings and the procedure and condition ratings into account. Hospitals received points if they were nationally ranked in one of the 16 adult specialties—the higher they ranked, the more points they got—and how many ratings of "high performing" they earned in the nine procedures and conditions. *U.S. News Online, "America's Best Hospitals 2019-20"*

EDUCATION

Public School District Statistics

District Name	Schls	Pupils	Pupil/ Teacher Ratio	Minority Pupils[1] (%)	Free Lunch Eligible[2] (%)	IEP[3] (%)
Epic Blended Learning Charter	6	7,773	23.6	42.2	n/a	14.6
Epic One On One Charter School	3	13,532	27.4	32.8	n/a	18.3
Oklahoma City	78	37,530	16.7	86.6	n/a	15.1
Santa Fe South (charter)	7	3,278	17.9	97.3	n/a	10.6
Western Heights	8	3,363	14.8	78.5	n/a	13.1

Note: Table includes school districts with 2,000 or more students; (1) Percentage of students that are not non-Hispanic white; (2) Percentage of students that are eligible for the free lunch program; (3) Percentage of students that have an Individualized Education Program.
Source: U.S. Department of Education, National Center for Education Statistics, Common Core of Data, Local Education Agency (School District) Universe Survey: School Year 2018-2019; U.S. Department of Education, National Center for Education Statistics, Common Core of Data, Public Elementary/Secondary School Universe Survey: School Year 2018-2019

Best High Schools

According to *U.S. News,* Oklahoma City is home to two of the top 500 high schools in the U.S.: **Classen High School of Advanced Studies** (#84); **Harding Charter Preparatory High School** (#96). Nearly 18,000 public, magnet and charter schools were ranked based on their performance on state assessments and how well they prepare students for college. *U.S. News & World Report, "Best High Schools 2020"*

Highest Level of Education

Area	Less than H.S.	H.S. Diploma	Some College, No Deg.	Associate Degree	Bachelor's Degree	Master's Degree	Prof. School Degree	Doctorate Degree
City	13.8	25.3	23.3	7.3	19.8	7.4	2.1	1.1
MSA[1]	11.1	27.2	24.1	7.5	19.5	7.5	1.9	1.2
U.S.	12.3	27.1	20.6	8.4	19.4	8.6	2.1	1.4

Note: Figures cover persons age 25 and over; (1) Figures cover the Oklahoma City, OK Metropolitan Statistical Area—see Appendix B for areas included
Source: U.S. Census Bureau, 2014-2018 American Community Survey 5-Year Estimates

Educational Attainment by Race

Area	High School Graduate or Higher (%)					Bachelor's Degree or Higher (%)				
	Total	White	Black	Asian	Hisp.[2]	Total	White	Black	Asian	Hisp.[2]
City	86.2	87.5	89.2	81.3	54.0	30.3	32.8	20.3	42.4	9.9
MSA[1]	88.9	89.9	90.2	84.5	60.1	30.1	31.5	21.3	46.1	12.5
U.S.	87.7	89.6	85.4	86.8	67.7	31.5	32.9	21.1	53.5	15.8

Note: Figures shown cover persons 25 years old and over; (1) Figures cover the Oklahoma City, OK Metropolitan Statistical Area—see Appendix B for areas included; (2) People of Hispanic origin can be of any race
Source: U.S. Census Bureau, 2014-2018 American Community Survey 5-Year Estimates

School Enrollment by Grade and Control

Area	Preschool (%)		Kindergarten (%)		Grades 1 - 4 (%)		Grades 5 - 8 (%)		Grades 9 - 12 (%)	
	Public	Private	Public	Private	Public	Private	Public	Private	Public	Private
City	73.4	26.6	91.6	8.4	91.7	8.3	89.5	10.5	90.7	9.3
MSA[1]	72.3	27.7	90.7	9.3	91.3	8.7	90.2	9.8	91.4	8.6
U.S.	59.0	41.0	87.7	12.3	89.6	10.4	89.5	10.5	90.2	9.8

Note: Figures shown cover persons 3 years old and over; (1) Figures cover the Oklahoma City, OK Metropolitan Statistical Area—see Appendix B for areas included
Source: U.S. Census Bureau, 2014-2018 American Community Survey 5-Year Estimates

Average Salaries of Public School Teachers

Area	2016-17		2017-18		Change from 2016-17 to 2017-18	
	Dollars	Rank[1]	Dollars	Rank[1]	Percent	Rank[2]
Oklahoma	45,292	50	46,300	49	2.23	10
U.S. Average	59,539	–	60,477	–	1.58	–

Note: (1) Rank ranges from 1 to 51 where 1 indicates highest salary; (2) Rank ranges from 1 to 51 where 1 indicates highest percent change.
Source: National Education Association, Rankings & Estimates: Rankings of the States 2018 and Estimates of School Statistics 2019

Higher Education

Four-Year Colleges			Two-Year Colleges			Medical Schools[1]	Law Schools[2]	Voc/ Tech[3]
Public	Private Non-profit	Private For-profit	Public	Private Non-profit	Private For-profit			
2	2	1	2	0	1	1	1	5

Note: Figures cover institutions located within the city limits and include main campuses only; (1) includes schools accredited by the Liaison Committee on Medical Education and the American Osteopathic Association's Commission on Osteopathic College Accreditation; (2) includes ABA-accredited schools, schools with provisional ABA accreditation, and state accredited schools; (3) includes all schools with programs that are less than 2 years.
Source: National Center for Education Statistics, Integrated Postsecondary Education System (IPEDS), 2018-19; Wikipedia, List of Medical Schools in the United States, accessed May 1, 2020; Wikipedia, List of Law Schools in the United States, accessed May 1, 2020

According to U.S. News & World Report, the Oklahoma City, OK metro area is home to one of the top 200 national universities in the U.S.: **University of Oklahoma** (#132 tie). The indicators used to capture academic quality fall into a number of categories: assessment by administrators at peer institutions; retention of students; faculty resources; student selectivity; financial resources; alumni giving; high school counselor ratings of colleges; and graduation rate. U.S. News & World Report, "America's Best Colleges 2020"

According to U.S. News & World Report, the Oklahoma City, OK metro area is home to one of the top 100 law schools in the U.S.: **University of Oklahoma** (#76 tie). The rankings are based on a weighted average of 12 measures of quality: peer assessment score; assessment score by lawyers/judges; median LSAT scores; median undergrad GPA; acceptance rate; employment rates for graduates; placement success; bar passage rate; faculty resources; expenditures per student; student/faculty ratio; and library resources. *U.S. News & World Report, "America's Best Graduate Schools, Law, 2021"*

According to *U.S. News & World Report,* the Oklahoma City, OK metro area is home to one of the top 75 medical schools for research in the U.S.: **University of Oklahoma** (#70 tie). The rankings are based on a weighted average of 11 measures of quality: quality assessment; peer assessment score; assessment score by residency directors; research activity; total research activity; average research activity per faculty member; student selectivity; median MCAT total score; median undergraduate GPA; acceptance rate; and faculty resources. *U.S. News & World Report, "America's Best Graduate Schools, Medical, 2021"*

PRESIDENTIAL ELECTION

2016 Presidential Election Results

Area	Clinton	Trump	Johnson	Stein	Other
Oklahoma County	41.2	51.7	7.1	0.0	0.0
U.S.	48.0	45.9	3.3	1.1	1.7

Note: Results are percentages and may not add to 100% due to rounding
Source: Dave Leip's Atlas of U.S. Presidential Elections

EMPLOYERS

Major Employers

Company Name	Industry
AT&T	Telecommunications
Chesapeake Energy Corp	Oil & gas
City of Oklahoma City	Government
Devon Energy Corp	Oil & gas
FAA Mike Monroney Aeronautical Center	Aerospace
Hobby Lobby Stores	Wholesale & retail
INTEGRIS Health	Health care
Mercy Health Center	Health care
Norman Regional Hospital	Health care
OGE Energy Corp	Utility
Oklahoma City Community College	Education
OU Medical Center	Health care
Sonic Corp	Wholesale & retail
SSM Health Care of Oklahoma	Health care
State of Oklahoma	State government
The Boeing Company	Aerospace
Tinker Air Force Base	U.S. military
University of Central Oklahoma	Higher education
University of Oklahoma - Norman	Higher education
University of Oklahoma Health Sci Ctr	Higher education

Note: Companies shown are located within the Oklahoma City, OK Metropolitan Statistical Area.
Source: Hoovers.com; Wikipedia

Best Companies to Work For

American Fidelity Assurance, headquartered in Oklahoma City, is among "The 100 Best Companies to Work For." To pick the best companies, *Fortune* partnered with the Great Place to Work Institute. Two-thirds of a company's score is based on the results of the Institute's Trust Index survey, which is sent to a random sample of employees from each company. The questions related to attitudes about management's credibility, job satisfaction, and camaraderie. The other third of the scoring is based on the company's responses to the Institute's Culture Audit, which includes detailed questions about pay and benefit programs, and a series of open-ended questions about hiring practices, internal communication, training, recognition programs, and diversity efforts. Any company that is at least five years old with more than 1,000 U.S. employees is eligible. *Fortune, "The 100 Best Companies to Work For," 2020*

American Fidelity Assurance, headquartered in Oklahoma City, is among the "100 Best Places to Work in IT." To qualify, companies had to be U.S.-based organizations or be non-U.S.-based employers that met the following criteria: have a minimum of 300 total employees at a U.S. headquarters and a minimum of 30 IT employees in the U.S., with at least 50% of their IT employees based in the U.S. The best places to work were selected based on compensation, benefits, work/life balance, employee morale, and satisfaction with training and development

programs. In addition, *Computerworld* looked at retention efforts, programs for recognizing and rewarding outstanding performances, and benefits such as flextime, elder care and child care, and reimbursement for college tuition and the cost of pursuing technology certifications.
Computerworld, "100 Best Places to Work in IT 2019"

PUBLIC SAFETY

Crime Rate

Area	All Crimes	Violent Crimes				Property Crimes		
		Murder	Rape[3]	Robbery	Aggrav. Assault	Burglary	Larceny -Theft	Motor Vehicle Theft
City	4,895.0	8.0	83.0	165.7	610.6	918.9	2,552.8	556.0
Suburbs[1]	2,478.1	2.7	42.5	33.7	154.5	478.9	1,522.7	243.1
Metro[2]	3,606.9	5.2	61.4	95.4	367.5	684.4	2,003.8	389.2
U.S.	2,580.1	5.0	42.6	86.2	246.8	376.0	1,594.6	228.9

Note: Figures are crimes per 100,000 population; (1) All areas within the metro area that are located outside the city limits; (2) Figures cover the Oklahoma City, OK Metropolitan Statistical Area—see Appendix B for areas included; (3) The city and U.S. figures shown were reported using the revised Uniform Crime Reporting (UCR) definition of rape. The suburban and metro area figures shown are an aggregate total of the data submitted using both the revised and legacy UCR definitions.
Source: FBI Uniform Crime Reports, 2018

Hate Crimes

Area	Number of Quarters Reported	Number of Incidents per Bias Motivation					
		Race/Ethnicity/ Ancestry	Religion	Sexual Orientation	Disability	Gender	Gender Identity
City	4	1	0	0	0	0	0
U.S.	4	4,047	1,419	1,196	159	47	168

Source: Federal Bureau of Investigation, Hate Crime Statistics 2018

Identity Theft Consumer Reports

Area	Reports	Reports per 100,000 Population	Rank[2]
MSA[1]	1,609	115	147
U.S.	650,572	198	-

Note: (1) Figures cover the Oklahoma City, OK Metropolitan Statistical Area—see Appendix B for areas included; (2) Rank ranges from 1 to 386 where 1 indicates greatest number of identity theft reports per 100,000 population
Source: Federal Trade Commission, Consumer Sentinel Network Data Book for January–December 2019

Fraud and Other Consumer Reports

Area	Reports	Reports per 100,000 Population	Rank[2]
MSA[1]	6,942	497	251
U.S.	2,590,177	789	-

Note: (1) Figures cover the Oklahoma City, OK Metropolitan Statistical Area—see Appendix B for areas included; (2) Rank ranges from 1 to 386 where 1 indicates greatest number of fraud and other consumer reports per 100,000 population
Source: Federal Trade Commission, Consumer Sentinel Network Data Book for January–December 2019

SPORTS

Professional Sports Teams

Team Name	League	Year Established
Oklahoma City Thunder	National Basketball Association (NBA)	2008

Note: Includes teams located in the Oklahoma City, OK Metropolitan Statistical Area.
Source: Wikipedia, Major Professional Sports Teams of the United States and Canada, May 4, 2020

CLIMATE

Average and Extreme Temperatures

Temperature	Jan	Feb	Mar	Apr	May	Jun	Jul	Aug	Sep	Oct	Nov	Dec	Yr.
Extreme High (°F)	80	84	93	100	104	105	109	110	104	96	87	86	110
Average High (°F)	47	52	61	72	79	87	93	92	84	74	60	50	71
Average Temp. (°F)	36	41	50	60	69	77	82	81	73	62	49	40	60
Average Low (°F)	26	30	38	49	58	66	71	70	62	51	38	29	49
Extreme Low (°F)	-4	-3	1	20	32	47	53	51	36	22	11	-8	-8

Note: Figures cover the years 1948-1990
Source: National Climatic Data Center, International Station Meteorological Climate Summary, 9/96

Average Precipitation/Snowfall/Humidity

Precip./Humidity	Jan	Feb	Mar	Apr	May	Jun	Jul	Aug	Sep	Oct	Nov	Dec	Yr.
Avg. Precip. (in.)	1.2	1.5	2.5	2.8	5.6	4.4	2.8	2.5	3.5	3.1	1.6	1.3	32.8
Avg. Snowfall (in.)	3	3	2	Tr	0	0	0	0	0	Tr	1	2	10
Avg. Rel. Hum. 6am (%)	78	78	76	77	84	84	81	81	82	79	78	77	80
Avg. Rel. Hum. 3pm (%)	53	52	47	46	52	51	46	44	47	46	48	52	49

Note: Figures cover the years 1948-1990; Tr = Trace amounts (<0.05 in. of rain; <0.5 in. of snow)
Source: National Climatic Data Center, International Station Meteorological Climate Summary, 9/96

Weather Conditions

Temperature			Daytime Sky			Precipitation		
10°F & below	32°F & below	90°F & above	Clear	Partly cloudy	Cloudy	0.01 inch or more precip.	0.1 inch or more snow/ice	Thunder-storms
5	79	70	124	131	110	80	8	50

Note: Figures are average number of days per year and cover the years 1948-1990
Source: National Climatic Data Center, International Station Meteorological Climate Summary, 9/96

HAZARDOUS WASTE

Superfund Sites

The Oklahoma City, OK metro area is home to three sites on the EPA's Superfund National Priorities List: **Eagle Industries** (final); **Hardage/Criner** (final); **Tinker Air Force Base (Soldier Creek/Building 3001)** (final). There are a total of 1,387 Superfund sites with a status of proposed or final on the list in the U.S. *U.S. Environmental Protection Agency, National Priorities List, May 5, 2020*

AIR & WATER QUALITY

Air Quality Trends: Ozone

	1990	1995	2000	2005	2010	2012	2014	2016	2017	2018
MSA[1]	0.078	0.086	0.082	0.077	0.071	0.080	0.068	0.066	0.069	0.072
U.S.	0.088	0.089	0.082	0.080	0.073	0.075	0.067	0.069	0.068	0.069

Note: (1) Data covers the Oklahoma City, OK Metropolitan Statistical Area—see Appendix B for areas included. The values shown are the composite ozone concentration averages among trend sites based on the highest fourth daily maximum 8-hour concentration in parts per million. These trends are based on sites having an adequate record of monitoring data during the trend period. Data from exceptional events are included.
Source: U.S. Environmental Protection Agency, Air Quality Monitoring Information, "Air Quality Trends by City, 1990-2018"

Air Quality Index

Area	Percent of Days when Air Quality was...[2]					AQI Statistics[2]	
	Good	Moderate	Unhealthy for Sensitive Groups	Unhealthy	Very Unhealthy	Maximum	Median
MSA[1]	58.1	38.6	3.3	0.0	0.0	150	47

Note: (1) Data covers the Oklahoma City, OK Metropolitan Statistical Area—see Appendix B for areas included; (2) Based on 365 days with AQI data in 2018. Air Quality Index (AQI) is an index for reporting daily air quality. EPA calculates the AQI for five major air pollutants regulated by the Clean Air Act: ground-level ozone, particle pollution (aka particulate matter), carbon monoxide, sulfur dioxide, and nitrogen dioxide. The AQI runs from 0 to 500. The higher the AQI value, the greater the level of air pollution and the greater the health concern. There are six AQI categories: "Good" AQI is between 0 and 50. Air quality is considered satisfactory; "Moderate" AQI is between 51 and 100. Air quality is acceptable; "Unhealthy for Sensitive Groups" When AQI values are between 101 and 150, members of sensitive groups may experience health effects; "Unhealthy" When AQI values are between 151 and 200 everyone may begin to experience health effects; "Very Unhealthy" AQI values between 201 and 300 trigger a health alert; "Hazardous" AQI values over 300 trigger warnings of emergency conditions (not shown).
Source: U.S. Environmental Protection Agency, Air Quality Index Report, 2018

Air Quality Index Pollutants

Area	Percent of Days when AQI Pollutant was...[2]					
	Carbon Monoxide	Nitrogen Dioxide	Ozone	Sulfur Dioxide	Particulate Matter 2.5	Particulate Matter 10
MSA[1]	0.0	1.6	49.9	0.0	47.4	1.1

Note: (1) Data covers the Oklahoma City, OK Metropolitan Statistical Area—see Appendix B for areas included; (2) Based on 365 days with AQI data in 2018. The Air Quality Index (AQI) is an index for reporting daily air quality. EPA calculates the AQI for five major air pollutants regulated by the Clean Air Act: ground-level ozone, particle pollution (also known as particulate matter), carbon monoxide, sulfur dioxide, and nitrogen dioxide. The AQI runs from 0 to 500. The higher the AQI value, the greater the level of air pollution and the greater the health concern.
Source: U.S. Environmental Protection Agency, Air Quality Index Report, 2018

Maximum Air Pollutant Concentrations: Particulate Matter, Ozone, CO and Lead

	Particulate Matter 10 (ug/m^3)	Particulate Matter 2.5 Wtd AM (ug/m^3)	Particulate Matter 2.5 24-Hr (ug/m^3)	Ozone (ppm)	Carbon Monoxide (ppm)	Lead (ug/m^3)
MSA[1] Level	92	10.1	24	0.076	2	n/a
NAAQS[2]	150	15	35	0.075	9	0.15
Met NAAQS[2]	Yes	Yes	Yes	No	Yes	n/a

Note: (1) Data covers the Oklahoma City, OK Metropolitan Statistical Area—see Appendix B for areas included; Data from exceptional events are included; (2) National Ambient Air Quality Standards; ppm = parts per million; ug/m³ = micrograms per cubic meter; n/a not available.
Concentrations: Particulate Matter 10 (coarse particulate)—highest second maximum 24-hour concentration; Particulate Matter 2.5 Wtd AM (fine particulate)—highest weighted annual mean concentration; Particulate Matter 2.5 24-Hour (fine particulate)—highest 98th percentile 24-hour concentration; Ozone—highest fourth daily maximum 8-hour concentration; Carbon Monoxide—highest second maximum non-overlapping 8-hour concentration; Lead—maximum running 3-month average
Source: U.S. Environmental Protection Agency, Air Quality Monitoring Information, "Air Quality Statistics by City, 2018"

Maximum Air Pollutant Concentrations: Nitrogen Dioxide and Sulfur Dioxide

	Nitrogen Dioxide AM (ppb)	Nitrogen Dioxide 1-Hr (ppb)	Sulfur Dioxide AM (ppb)	Sulfur Dioxide 1-Hr (ppb)	Sulfur Dioxide 24-Hr (ppb)
MSA[1] Level	13	41	n/a	3	n/a
NAAQS[2]	53	100	30	75	140
Met NAAQS[2]	Yes	Yes	n/a	Yes	n/a

Note: (1) Data covers the Oklahoma City, OK Metropolitan Statistical Area—see Appendix B for areas included; Data from exceptional events are included; (2) National Ambient Air Quality Standards; ppm = parts per million; ug/m³ = micrograms per cubic meter; n/a not available.
Concentrations: Nitrogen Dioxide AM—highest arithmetic mean concentration; Nitrogen Dioxide 1-Hr—highest 98th percentile 1-hour daily maximum concentration; Sulfur Dioxide AM—highest annual mean concentration; Sulfur Dioxide 1-Hr—highest 99th percentile 1-hour daily maximum concentration; Sulfur Dioxide 24-Hr—highest second maximum 24-hour concentration
Source: U.S. Environmental Protection Agency, Air Quality Monitoring Information, "Air Quality Statistics by City, 2018"

Drinking Water

Water System Name	Pop. Served	Primary Water Source Type	Violations[1]
Oklahoma City	644,000	Surface	9

Note: (1) Total number of violations (both active and inactive) in the EPA database
Source: U.S. Environmental Protection Agency, Office of Ground Water and Drinking Water, Safe Drinking Water Information System (based on data extracted May 5, 2020)

Omaha, Nebraska

Background

Omaha's central location in the heartland of the United States has been important to its strong economy. Located on the western banks of the Missouri River, the city has been a significant agricultural and transportation center since its establishment in 1854. In its earliest history, Omaha was a trading center and "Gateway to the West." From these roots, Omaha has seen steady growth.

There are nearly 20,000 businesses located in the metropolitan area, including Fortune 500 companies such as ConAgra Foods, Mutual of Omaha, Union Pacific Railroad, Kiewit Corporation, and Berkshire Hathaway, the last of which is headed by Omaha's most prominent businessman, Warren Buffet, famously recognized as one of the richest men in the world.

Additional Fortune 500 companies have manufacturing plants or service centers in the metropolitan area. The headquarters of insurance companies, direct response/telemarketing centers and other national and international firms call Omaha home. The city is also a regional service and trade center. Services and trade combined comprise 57 percent of metro area employment.

Omaha is large enough to offer a variety of cosmopolitan attractions, yet small enough to provide a relaxed lifestyle. Recreational activities abound, and Omaha residents enjoy a low cost of living, outstanding health care and a low crime rate.

The Omaha metropolitan area is served by several public and private school systems, and offers 11 colleges and universities, including Gallup University, offering courses that support leaders, managers, and sales professionals.

The community also has access to excellent cultural programs worthy of a much larger city, including the professional Omaha Symphony, Omaha Theater Ballet, and Opera Omaha. Performances by these groups and other touring companies are held in the magnificent Orpheum Theater, a restored 1920s vaudeville house. The Bemis Center for Contemporary Arts, the largest urban artist colony in the world, plays host to artists from all over the world.

Omaha is home to world-famous Father Flanagan's Boys and Girls Town, and the award-winning Henry Doorly Zoo, which includes the world's largest indoor rainforest and a collection of rare white tigers. Other attractions include the Strategic Air & Space Museum and the birthplaces of Malcom X and former President Gerald R. Ford.

Omaha celebrated its 150th birthday in 2004, and continues to devote much effort to new projects. The acreage fronting the Missouri River, is home to several new developments including a 2,700-foot bridge with a 506-foot span across the river connecting nearly 150 miles of trails in Nebraska and Iowa. The Midwestern headquarters for the National Park Service is in Omaha, the first building in Nebraska to be rated tops under the Leadership in Energy and Environmental Design system, or LEED. The nearby Riverfront Place is a six-acre urban neighborhood that includes residential units, commercial space, a public plaza, riverfront access, and connections to miles of walking trails.

Omaha's weather shows the usual contrasts of a continental climate, with cold, dry winters and warm summers. The city is situated between two climatic zones, the humid east and the dry west, and fluctuation between these zones produce for weather periods characteristic of either zone or combinations of both. Most precipitation falls between April and September in the form of sharp thunderstorms or evening lightning shows.

Rankings

General Rankings

- For its "Best for Vets: Places to Live 2019" rankings, *Military Times* evaluated 599 cities (83 large, 234 medium, 282 small) and compared the locations across three broad categories: veteran and military culture/services; economic indicators; and livability factors such as health, crime, traffic, and school quality. Omaha ranked #9 out of the top 25, in the large city category (populations of more than 250,000). Data points more specific to veterans and the military weighed more heavily than the rest. *rebootcamp.militarytimes.com, "Military Times Best Places to Live 2019," September 10, 2018*

- The Omaha metro area was identified as one of America's fastest-growing areas in terms of population and business growth by *MagnifyMoney*. The area ranked #33 out of 35. The 100 most populous metro areas in the U.S. were evaluated on their change from 2011-2016 in the following categories: people and housing; workforce and employment opportunities; growing industry. *www.businessinsider.com, "The 35 Cities in the US with the Biggest Influx of People, the Most Work Opportunities, and the Hottest Business Growth," August 12, 2018*

- In their sixth annual survey, Livability.com looked at data for more than 1,000 U.S. cities to determine the rankings for Livability's "Top 100 Best Places to Live" in 2019. Omaha ranked #20. Criteria: median home value capped at $250,000; affordable living; vibrant economy; education, demographics, health care options. transportation & infrastructure; abundant lifestyle amenities. *Livability.com, "Top 100 Best Places to Live 2019" March 2019*

Business/Finance Rankings

- Omaha was the #8-ranked city for savers, according to a study by the finance site GOBankingRates, which considered the prospects for people trying to save money. Criteria: average monthly cost of grocery items; median home listing price; median rent; median income; transportation costs; gas prices; and the cost of eating out for an inexpensive and mid-range meal in 100 U.S. cities. *www.gobankingrates.com, "The 20 Best (and Worst) Places to Live If You're Trying to Save Money," August 27, 2019*

- Omaha was ranked #8 among 100 U.S. cities for most difficult conditions for savers, according to a study by the finance site GOBankingRates. Criteria: average monthly cost of grocery items; median home listing price; median rent; median income; transportation costs; gas prices; and the cost of eating out for an inexpensive and mid-range meal. *www.gobankingrates.com, "The 20 Best (and Worst) Places to Live If You're Trying to Save Money," August 27, 2019*

- Recognizing the sizeable percentage of American workers who are self-employed, NerdWallet editors assessed the country's cities according to percentage of freelancers, median rental costs, cell phone plans/taxes, and healthcare affordability and access. By these criteria, Omaha placed #11 among the best cities for independent workers. *www.nerdwallet.com, "Best Places for Freelance Workers," August 30, 2016*

- The Brookings Institution ranked the nation's largest cities based on income inequality. Omaha was ranked #67 (#1 = greatest inequality). Criteria: the "95/20 ratio," a figure representing the income at which a household earns more than 95 percent of all other households, divided by the income at which a household earns more than only 20 percent of all other households. *Brookings Institution, "Household Income Inequality, Largest Cities of 97 Large U.S. Metro Areas, 2014-2016," February 5, 2018*

- The Brookings Institution ranked the 100 largest metro areas in the U.S. based on income inequality. Omaha was ranked #90 (#1 = greatest inequality). Criteria: the "95/20 ratio," a figure representing the income at which a household earns more than 95 percent of all other households, divided by the income at which a household earns more than only 20 percent of all other households. *Brookings Institution, "Household Income Inequality, 100 Largest U.S. Metro Areas, 2014-2016," February 5, 2018*

- *Forbes* ranked the 100 largest metro areas in the U.S. in terms of the "Best Cities for Young Professionals." The Omaha metro area ranked #19 out of 25. (Large metro areas were divided into metro divisions.) Criteria: median rent of a two-bedroom apartment; job growth and unemployment rate; median salary of college graduates with 5 or less years of work experience; networking opportunities; social outlook; percentage of population 25 years of age and older with college degrees. *Forbes.com, "America's 25 Best Cities for Young Professionals in 2017," May 22, 2017*

- Omaha was cited as one of America's top metros for new and expanded facility projects in 2019. The area ranked #3 in the mid-sized metro area category (population 200,000 to 1 million). *Site Selection, "Top Metros of 2019," March 2020*

- The Omaha metro area appeared on the Milken Institute "2020 Best Performing Cities" list. Rank: #127 out of 200 large metro areas. Criteria: job growth; wage and salary growth; high-tech output growth. *Milken Institute, "Best-Performing Cities 2020," February 26, 2020*

- *Forbes* ranked the 200 most populous metro areas to determine the nation's "Best Places for Business and Careers." The Omaha metro area was ranked #38. Criteria: costs (business and living); job growth (past and projected); income growth; quality of life; educational attainment (college and high school); projected economic growth; cultural and leisure opportunities; workplace tolerance laws; net migration patterns. *Forbes, "The Best Places for Business and Careers 2019: Seattle Still On Top," October 30, 2019*

Dating/Romance Rankings

- Omaha was ranked #19 out of 25 cities that stood out for inspiring romance and attracting diners on the website OpenTable.com. Criteria: percentage of people who dined out on Valentine's Day in 2018; percentage of romantic restaurants as rated by OpenTable diner reviews; and percentage of tables seated for two. *OpenTable, "25 Most Romantic Cities in America for 2019," February 7, 2019*

Education Rankings

- Personal finance website *WalletHub* analyzed the 150 largest U.S. metropolitan statistical areas to determine where the most educated Americans are choosing to settle. Criteria: education levels; percentage of workers with degrees; education quality and attainment gap; public school quality rankings; quality and size of each metro area's universities. Omaha was ranked #35 (#1 = most educated city). *www.WalletHub.com, "2019's Most and Least Educated Cities in America," July 22, 2019*

- Omaha was selected as one of America's most literate cities. The city ranked #33 out of the 82 largest U.S. cities. Criteria: number of booksellers; library resources; Internet resources; educational attainment; periodical publishing resources; newspaper circulation. *Central Connecticut State University, "America's Most Literate Cities, 2016," March 31, 2017*

Health/Fitness Rankings

- For each of the 100 largest cities in the United States, the American Fitness Index®, published by the American College of Sports Medicine and the Anthem Foundation, evaluated community infrastructure and 33 health behaviors including preventive health, levels of chronic disease conditions, pedestrian safety, air quality, and community resources that support physical activity. Omaha ranked #45 for "community fitness." *americanfitnessindex.org, "ACSM American Fitness Index Health and Community Fitness Status of the 100 Largest U.S. Cities," May 14, 2019*

- The Omaha metro area was identified as one of the worst cities for bed bugs in America by pest control company Orkin. The area ranked #35 out of 50 based on the number of bed bug treatments Orkin performed from December 2018 to November 2019. *Orkin, "Washington, D.C. Surpasses Baltimore to Secure Top Spot on Orkin's 2020 Bed Bug Cities List," January 13, 2020*

- Omaha was identified as a "2020 Spring Allergy Capital." The area ranked #73 out of 100. Three groups of factors were used to identify the most challenging cities for people with allergies during the spring season: annual spring pollen levels; over the counter medicine use; number of board-certified allergy specialists. *Asthma and Allergy Foundation of America, "Spring Allergy Capitals 2020," March 10, 2020*

- Omaha was identified as a "2020 Fall Allergy Capital." The area ranked #63 out of 100. Three groups of factors were used to identify the most challenging cities for people with allergies during the fall season: annual fall pollen levels; over the counter medicine use; number of board-certified allergy specialists. *Asthma and Allergy Foundation of America, "Fall Allergy Capitals 2020," March 10, 2020*

- Omaha was identified as a "2019 Asthma Capital." The area ranked #9 out of the nation's 100 largest metropolitan areas. Criteria: estimated asthma prevalence; crude death rate from asthma; and ER visits due to asthma. Risk factors that were analyzed but not factored in the rankings: annual pollen score; annual air quality; public smoking laws; number of board-certified asthma specialists; rescue medication use; controller medication use; uninsured rate; poverty rate. *Asthma and Allergy Foundation of America, "Asthma Capitals 2019: The Most Challenging Places to Live With Asthma," May 7, 2019*

- *Men's Health* ranked 100 major U.S. cities in terms of the best cities for men. Omaha ranked #33. Criteria: health; fitness; quality of life. *Men's Health, "The Best & Worst Cities for Men Who Want to Be Fit and Happy," January 1, 2016*

- The Omaha metro area ranked #82 out of 189 in The Gallup-Sharecare Well-Being Index. Criteria: purpose; social well being; financial health; community and physical health. Results are based on telephone interviews with adults, aged 18 and older, living in metropolitan areas in the 50 U.S. states and the District of Columbia. *Gallup-Sharecare, "State of American Well-Being, 2017 Community Well-Being Rankings" March 2018*

Real Estate Rankings

- *WalletHub* compared the most populated U.S. cities, as well as at least two of the most populated cities in each state, for a total of 179, to determine which had the best markets for real estate agents. Omaha ranked #86 where demand was high and pay was the best. Criteria: sales per agent; annual median wage for real-estate agents; monthly average starting salary for real estate agents; real estate job density and competition; unemployment rate; home turnover rate; housing-market health index; and other relevant metrics. *www.WalletHub.com, "2019's Best Places to Be a Real Estate Agent," April 24, 2019*

Safety Rankings

- Allstate ranked the 200 largest cities in America in terms of driver safety. Omaha ranked #33. Criteria: internal property damage claims over a two-year period from January 2016 to December 2017. The report helps increase the importance of safety and awareness behind the wheel. *Allstate, "Allstate America's Best Drivers Report, 2019" June 24, 2019*

- The National Insurance Crime Bureau ranked 382 metro areas in the U.S. in terms of per capita rates of vehicle theft. The Omaha metro area ranked #47 (#1 = highest rate). Criteria: number of vehicle theft offenses per 100,000 inhabitants in 2018. *National Insurance Crime Bureau, "Hot Spots 2018," June 25, 2019*

Seniors/Retirement Rankings

- From its Best Cities for Successful Aging indexes, the Milken Institute generated rankings for metropolitan areas, weighing data in nine categories—health care, wellness, living arrangements, transportation and convenience, financial characteristics, education, employment, community engagement, and overall livability. The Omaha metro area was ranked #7 overall in the large metro area category. *Milken Institute, "Best Cities for Successful Aging, 2017" March 14, 2017*

Sports/Recreation Rankings

- Omaha was chosen as a bicycle friendly community by the League of American Bicyclists. A "Bicycle Friendly Community" welcomes cyclists by providing safe and supportive accommodation for cycling and encouraging people to bike for transportation and recreation. There are five award levels: Diamond; Platinum; Gold; Silver; and Bronze. The community achieved an award level of Bronze. *League of American Bicyclists, "Fall 2019 Awards-Bicycle Friendly Community Master List," November 21, 2019*

- Omaha was chosen as one of America's best cities for bicycling. The city ranked #45 out of 50. Criteria: cycling infrastructure that is safe and friendly for all ages; energy and bike culture. The editors only considered cities with populations of 100,000 or more. *Bicycling, "The 50 Best Bike Cities in America," October 10, 2018*

Women/Minorities Rankings

- Personal finance website *WalletHub* compared more than 180 U.S. cities—including the 150 most populated U.S. cities, plus at least two of the most populated cities in each state—across two key dimensions, "Hispanic Business-Friendliness" and "Hispanic Purchasing Power", to arrive at the most favorable conditions for Hispanic entrepreneurs. Omaha was ranked #108 out of 182. Criteria includes: share of Hispanic-Owned Businesses; Hispanic entrepreneurship rate to median annual income of Hispanics; Small Business-Friendliness score; cost of living; and number of Hispanics with at least a bachelor's degree. *WalletHub.com, "2019's Best Cities for Hispanic Entrepreneurs," May 1, 2019*

Miscellaneous Rankings

- *WalletHub* compared the 150 most populated U.S. cities to determine their operating efficiency. A "Quality of Services" score was constructed for each city and then divided by the total budget per capita to reveal which were managed the best. Omaha ranked #78. Criteria: financial stability; economy; education; safety; health; infrastructure and pollution. *www.WalletHub.com, "2019's Best- & Worst-Run Cities in America," July 1, 2019*

Business Environment

CITY FINANCES

City Government Finances

Component	2017 ($000)	2017 ($ per capita)
Total Revenues	821,214	1,850
Total Expenditures	644,976	1,453
Debt Outstanding	1,386,723	3,124
Cash and Securities[1]	908,653	2,047

Note: (1) Cash and security holdings of a government at the close of its fiscal year,
including those of its dependent agencies, utilities, and liquor stores.
Source: U.S. Census Bureau, State & Local Government Finances 2017

City Government Revenue by Source

Source	2017 ($000)	2017 ($ per capita)	2017 (%)
General Revenue			
From Federal Government	15,571	35	1.9
From State Government	46,051	104	5.6
From Local Governments	8,934	20	1.1
Taxes			
Property	155,281	350	18.9
Sales and Gross Receipts	154,989	349	18.9
Personal Income	0	0	0.0
Corporate Income	0	0	0.0
Motor Vehicle License	32,186	73	3.9
Other Taxes	85,355	192	10.4
Current Charges	216,550	488	26.4
Liquor Store	0	0	0.0
Utility	0	0	0.0
Employee Retirement	103,379	233	12.6

Source: U.S. Census Bureau, State & Local Government Finances 2017

City Government Expenditures by Function

Function	2017 ($000)	2017 ($ per capita)	2017 (%)
General Direct Expenditures			
Air Transportation	0	0	0.0
Corrections	0	0	0.0
Education	0	0	0.0
Employment Security Administration	0	0	0.0
Financial Administration	3,788	8	0.6
Fire Protection	79,033	178	12.3
General Public Buildings	14,998	33	2.3
Governmental Administration, Other	14,360	32	2.2
Health	0	0	0.0
Highways	79,362	178	12.3
Hospitals	0	0	0.0
Housing and Community Development	756	1	0.1
Interest on General Debt	52,969	119	8.2
Judicial and Legal	4,045	9	0.6
Libraries	13,875	31	2.2
Parking	1,924	4	0.3
Parks and Recreation	27,576	62	4.3
Police Protection	130,435	293	20.2
Public Welfare	0	0	0.0
Sewerage	34,707	78	5.4
Solid Waste Management	22,090	49	3.4
Veterans' Services	0	0	0.0
Liquor Store	0	0	0.0
Utility	0	0	0.0
Employee Retirement	104,783	236	16.2

Source: U.S. Census Bureau, State & Local Government Finances 2017

DEMOGRAPHICS

Population Growth

Area	1990 Census	2000 Census	2010 Census	2018* Estimate	Population Growth (%) 1990-2018	Population Growth (%) 2010-2018
City	371,972	390,007	408,958	465,112	25.0	13.7
MSA[1]	685,797	767,041	865,350	922,891	34.6	6.6
U.S.	248,709,873	281,421,906	308,745,538	322,903,030	29.8	4.6

Note: (1) Figures cover the Omaha-Council Bluffs, NE-IA Metropolitan Statistical Area—see Appendix B for areas included; (*) 2014-2018 5-year estimated population
Source: U.S. Census Bureau, 1990 Census, Census 2000, Census 2010, 2014-2018 American Community Survey 5-Year Estimates

Household Size

Area	One	Two	Three	Four	Five	Six	Seven or More	Average Household Size
City	32.7	31.8	14.1	11.3	5.9	2.6	1.6	2.50
MSA[1]	28.4	33.6	14.6	13.0	6.3	2.6	1.5	2.50
U.S.	27.7	33.9	15.7	13.0	6.0	2.3	1.4	2.60

Note: (1) Figures cover the Omaha-Council Bluffs, NE-IA Metropolitan Statistical Area—see Appendix B for areas included
Source: U.S. Census Bureau, 2014-2018 American Community Survey 5-Year Estimates

Race

Area	White Alone[2] (%)	Black Alone[2] (%)	Asian Alone[2] (%)	AIAN[3] Alone[2] (%)	NHOPI[4] Alone[2] (%)	Other Race Alone[2] (%)	Two or More Races (%)
City	77.8	12.3	3.7	0.7	0.1	2.2	3.2
MSA[1]	84.3	7.6	2.8	0.5	0.1	1.8	2.9
U.S.	72.7	12.7	5.4	0.8	0.2	4.9	3.2

Note: (1) Figures cover the Omaha-Council Bluffs, NE-IA Metropolitan Statistical Area—see Appendix B for areas included; (2) Alone is defined as not being in combination with one or more other races; (3) American Indian and Alaska Native; (4) Native Hawaiian and Other Pacific Islander
Source: U.S. Census Bureau, 2014-2018 American Community Survey 5-Year Estimates

Hispanic or Latino Origin

Area	Total (%)	Mexican (%)	Puerto Rican (%)	Cuban (%)	Other (%)
City	13.9	10.8	0.3	0.2	2.7
MSA[1]	10.2	7.8	0.4	0.1	1.9
U.S.	17.8	11.2	1.7	0.7	4.2

Note: Persons of Hispanic or Latino origin can be of any race; (1) Figures cover the Omaha-Council Bluffs, NE-IA Metropolitan Statistical Area—see Appendix B for areas included
Source: U.S. Census Bureau, 2014-2018 American Community Survey 5-Year Estimates

Segregation

Type	1990	2000	2010	2010 Rank[2]	1990-2000	1990-2010	2000-2010
Black/White	71.4	67.3	61.3	38	-4.1	-10.1	-6.0
Asian/White	34.2	36.0	36.3	74	1.8	2.1	0.3
Hispanic/White	38.5	48.9	48.8	30	10.4	10.3	-0.1

Note: All figures cover the Metropolitan Statistical Area—see Appendix B for areas included; Figures are based on an analysis of 1990, 2000, and 2010 Census Decennial Census tract data by William H. Frey, Brookings Institution and the University of Michigan Social Science Data Analysis Network. In this analysis all racial groups (whites, blacks, and asians) are non-Hispanic members of those races. Hispanics are shown as a separate category; (1) Segregation Indices are Dissimilarity Indices that measure the degree to which the minority group is distributed differently than whites across census tracts. They range from 0 (complete integration) to 100 (complete segregation) where the value indicates the percentage of the minority group that needs to move to be distributed exactly like whites; (2) Ranges from 1 (most segregated) to 102 (least segregated); n/a not available.
Source: www.CensusScope.org

Ancestry

Area	German	Irish	English	American	Italian	Polish	French[2]	Scottish	Dutch
City	25.2	13.6	6.6	3.1	4.3	3.6	2.2	1.2	1.5
MSA[1]	29.5	14.1	7.8	3.7	4.1	3.7	2.3	1.3	1.7
U.S.	13.7	9.9	7.3	6.4	5.2	2.8	2.4	1.7	1.2

Note: Figures are the percentage of the total population reporting a particular ancestry. The nine most commonly reported ancestries in the U.S. are shown. Figures include multiple ancestries (e.g. if a person reported being Irish and Italian, they were included in both columns); (1) Figures cover the Omaha-Council Bluffs, NE-IA Metropolitan Statistical Area—see Appendix B for areas included; (2) Excludes Basque
Source: U.S. Census Bureau, 2014-2018 American Community Survey 5-Year Estimates

Foreign-born Population

Area	Percent of Population Born in								
	Any Foreign Country	Asia	Mexico	Europe	Caribbean	Central America[2]	South America	Africa	Canada
City	10.5	3.2	4.0	0.7	0.2	1.1	0.2	1.1	0.1
MSA[1]	7.3	2.3	2.6	0.6	0.1	0.7	0.2	0.7	0.1
U.S.	13.5	4.1	3.5	1.5	1.3	1.1	0.9	0.7	0.3

Note: (1) Figures cover the Omaha-Council Bluffs, NE-IA Metropolitan Statistical Area—see Appendix B for areas included; (2) Excludes Mexico.
Source: U.S. Census Bureau, 2014-2018 American Community Survey 5-Year Estimates

Marital Status

Area	Never Married	Now Married[2]	Separated	Widowed	Divorced
City	36.1	45.8	1.6	5.0	11.4
MSA[1]	31.0	51.8	1.3	5.0	10.9
U.S.	33.3	48.1	2.0	5.8	10.8

Note: Figures are percentages and cover the population 15 years of age and older; (1) Figures cover the Omaha-Council Bluffs, NE-IA Metropolitan Statistical Area—see Appendix B for areas included; (2) Excludes separated
Source: U.S. Census Bureau, 2014-2018 American Community Survey 5-Year Estimates

Disability by Age

Area	All Ages	Under 18 Years Old	18 to 64 Years Old	65 Years and Over
City	11.0	3.5	9.6	33.5
MSA[1]	10.9	3.5	9.4	32.9
U.S.	12.6	4.2	10.3	35.0

Note: Figures show percent of the civilian noninstitutionalized population that reported having a disability. Disability status is determined from six types of difficulty: vision, hearing, cognitive, ambulatory, self-care, and independent living. For children under 5 years old, hearing and vision difficulty are used to determine disability status. For children between the ages of 5 and 14, disability status is determined from hearing, vision, cognitive, ambulatory, and self-care difficulties. For people aged 15 years and older, they are considered to have a disability if they have difficulty with any one of the six difficulty types; Note: (1) Figures cover the Omaha-Council Bluffs, NE-IA Metropolitan Statistical Area—see Appendix B for areas included
Source: U.S. Census Bureau, 2014-2018 American Community Survey 5-Year Estimates

Age

Area	Percent of Population									Median Age
	Under Age 5	Age 5–19	Age 20–34	Age 35–44	Age 45–54	Age 55–64	Age 65–74	Age 75–84	Age 85+	
City	7.3	20.3	23.1	12.6	12.1	11.9	7.4	3.4	1.8	34.5
MSA[1]	7.3	20.9	21.0	13.0	12.6	12.1	7.7	3.6	1.7	35.5
U.S.	6.1	19.3	20.7	12.6	13.2	12.8	8.8	4.5	1.9	37.9

Note: (1) Figures cover the Omaha-Council Bluffs, NE-IA Metropolitan Statistical Area—see Appendix B for areas included
Source: U.S. Census Bureau, 2014-2018 American Community Survey 5-Year Estimates

Gender

Area	Males	Females	Males per 100 Females
City	229,987	235,125	97.8
MSA[1]	456,815	466,076	98.0
U.S.	158,984,190	163,918,840	97.0

Note: (1) Figures cover the Omaha-Council Bluffs, NE-IA Metropolitan Statistical Area—see Appendix B for areas included
Source: U.S. Census Bureau, 2014-2018 American Community Survey 5-Year Estimates

Religious Groups by Family

Area	Catholic	Baptist	Non-Den.	Methodist[2]	Lutheran	LDS[3]	Pente-costal	Presby-terian[4]	Muslim[5]	Judaism
MSA[1]	21.6	4.6	1.8	3.9	7.9	1.8	1.3	2.3	0.5	0.4
U.S.	19.1	9.3	4.0	4.0	2.3	2.0	1.9	1.6	0.8	0.7

Note: Figures are the number of adherents as a percentage of the total population; (1) Figures cover the Omaha-Council Bluffs, NE-IA Metropolitan Statistical Area—see Appendix B for areas included; (2) Methodist/Pietist; (3) Latter Day Saints; (4) Reformed; (5) Figures are estimates
Source: Association of Statisticians of American Religious Bodies, 2010 U.S. Religion Census: Religious Congregations & Membership Study

Religious Groups by Tradition

Area	Catholic	Evangelical Protestant	Mainline Protestant	Other Tradition	Black Protestant	Orthodox
MSA[1]	21.6	12.1	10.8	3.3	1.5	0.1
U.S.	19.1	16.2	7.3	4.3	1.6	0.3

Note: Figures are the number of adherents as a percentage of the total population; (1) Figures cover the Omaha-Council Bluffs, NE-IA Metropolitan Statistical Area—see Appendix B for areas included
Source: Association of Statisticians of American Religious Bodies, 2010 U.S. Religion Census: Religious Congregations & Membership Study

ECONOMY

Gross Metropolitan Product

Area	2017	2018	2019	2020	Rank[2]
MSA[1]	63.3	65.9	68.5	71.0	52

Note: Figures are in billions of dollars; (1) Figures cover the Omaha-Council Bluffs, NE-IA Metropolitan Statistical Area—see Appendix B for areas included; (2) Rank is based on 2018 data and ranges from 1 to 381
Source: U.S. Conference of Mayors, U.S. Metro Economies: GMP & Employment 2018-2020, September 2019

Economic Growth

Area	2015-17 (%)	2018 (%)	2019 (%)	2020 (%)	Rank[2]
MSA[1]	0.6	1.7	2.2	1.5	272
U.S.	1.9	2.9	2.3	2.1	–

Note: Figures are real gross metropolitan product (GMP) growth rates and represent average annual percent change; (1) Figures cover the Omaha-Council Bluffs, NE-IA Metropolitan Statistical Area—see Appendix B for areas included; (2) Rank is based on 2017 2-year average annual percent change and ranges from 1 to 381
Source: U.S. Conference of Mayors, U.S. Metro Economies: GMP & Employment 2018-2020, September 2019

Metropolitan Area Exports

Area	2013	2014	2015	2016	2017	2018	Rank[2]
MSA[1]	4,255.9	4,528.5	3,753.4	3,509.7	3,756.2	4,371.6	64

Note: Figures are in millions of dollars; (1) Figures cover the Omaha-Council Bluffs, NE-IA Metropolitan Statistical Area—see Appendix B for areas included; (2) Rank is based on 2018 data and ranges from 1 to 387
Source: U.S. Department of Commerce, International Trade Administration, Office of Trade and Economic Analysis, Industry and Analysis, Exports by Metropolitan Area, data extracted April 15, 2020

Building Permits

Area	Single-Family			Multi-Family			Total		
	2017	2018	Pct. Chg.	2017	2018	Pct. Chg.	2017	2018	Pct. Chg.
City	1,533	1,237	-19.3	1,697	1,650	-2.8	3,230	2,887	-10.6
MSA[1]	3,158	2,791	-11.6	1,797	1,997	11.1	4,955	4,788	-3.4
U.S.	820,000	855,300	4.3	462,000	473,500	2.5	1,282,000	1,328,800	3.7

Note: (1) Figures cover the Omaha-Council Bluffs, NE-IA Metropolitan Statistical Area—see Appendix B for areas included; Figures represent new, privately-owned housing units authorized (unadjusted data); All permit data are based on estimates with imputation
Source: U.S. Census Bureau, Manufacturing, Mining, and Construction Statistics, Building Permits, 2017, 2018

Bankruptcy Filings

Area	Business Filings			Nonbusiness Filings		
	2018	2019	% Chg.	2018	2019	% Chg.
Douglas County	23	39	69.6	1,189	1,283	7.9
U.S.	22,232	22,780	2.5	751,186	752,160	0.1

Note: Business filings include Chapter 7, Chapter 9, Chapter 11, Chapter 12, Chapter 13, Chapter 15, and Section 304; Nonbusiness filings include Chapter 7, Chapter 11, and Chapter 13
Source: Administrative Office of the U.S. Courts, Business and Nonbusiness Bankruptcy, County Cases Commenced by Chapter of the Bankruptcy Code, During the 12-Month Period Ending December 31, 2018 and Business and Nonbusiness Bankruptcy, County Cases Commenced by Chapter of the Bankruptcy Code, During the 12-Month Period Ending December 31, 2019

Housing Vacancy Rates

Area	Gross Vacancy Rate[2] (%)			Year-Round Vacancy Rate[3] (%)			Rental Vacancy Rate[4] (%)			Homeowner Vacancy Rate[5] (%)		
	2017	2018	2019	2017	2018	2019	2017	2018	2019	2017	2018	2019
MSA[1]	5.9	7.1	5.6	5.4	6.1	4.8	4.7	7.1	6.3	0.9	0.7	0.6
U.S.	12.7	12.3	12.0	9.9	9.7	9.5	7.2	6.9	6.7	1.6	1.5	1.4

Note: (1) Figures cover the Omaha-Council Bluffs, NE-IA Metropolitan Statistical Area—see Appendix B for areas included; (2) The percentage of the total housing inventory that is vacant; (3) The percentage of the housing inventory (excluding seasonal units) that is year-round vacant; (4) The percentage of rental inventory that is vacant for rent; (5) The percentage of homeowner inventory that is vacant for sale
Source: U.S. Census Bureau, Housing Vacancies and Homeownership Annual Statistics: 2017, 2018, 2019

INCOME

Income

Area	Per Capita ($)	Median Household ($)	Average Household ($)
City	31,798	56,780	78,728
MSA[1]	33,453	65,227	85,142
U.S.	32,621	60,293	84,938

Note: (1) Figures cover the Omaha-Council Bluffs, NE-IA Metropolitan Statistical Area—see Appendix B for areas included
Source: U.S. Census Bureau, 2014-2018 American Community Survey 5-Year Estimates

Household Income Distribution

Area	Percent of Households Earning							
	Under $15,000	$15,000 -$24,999	$25,000 -$34,999	$35,000 -$49,999	$50,000 -$74,999	$75,000 -$99,999	$100,000 -$149,999	$150,000 and up
City	11.2	9.3	9.3	14.3	18.5	12.9	13.7	10.8
MSA[1]	8.9	7.9	8.5	13.0	18.5	14.0	16.9	12.5
U.S.	10.9	9.3	9.3	12.6	17.5	12.5	14.6	13.3

Note: (1) Figures cover the Omaha-Council Bluffs, NE-IA Metropolitan Statistical Area—see Appendix B for areas included
Source: U.S. Census Bureau, 2014-2018 American Community Survey 5-Year Estimates

Poverty Rate

Area	All Ages	Under 18 Years Old	18 to 64 Years Old	65 Years and Over
City	14.3	19.9	13.2	8.2
MSA[1]	10.6	14.0	10.0	6.8
U.S.	14.1	19.5	13.2	9.3

Note: Figures are percentage of people whose income during the past 12 months was below the poverty level; (1) Figures cover the Omaha-Council Bluffs, NE-IA Metropolitan Statistical Area—see Appendix B for areas included
Source: U.S. Census Bureau, 2014-2018 American Community Survey 5-Year Estimates

EMPLOYMENT

Labor Force and Employment

Area	Civilian Labor Force			Workers Employed		
	Dec. 2018	Dec. 2019	% Chg.	Dec. 2018	Dec. 2019	% Chg.
City	241,394	243,405	0.8	233,531	236,406	1.2
MSA[1]	490,069	496,578	1.3	475,528	483,022	1.6
U.S.	162,510,000	164,007,000	0.9	156,481,000	158,504,000	1.3

Note: Data is not seasonally adjusted and covers workers 16 years of age and older; (1) Figures cover the Omaha-Council Bluffs, NE-IA Metropolitan Statistical Area—see Appendix B for areas included
Source: Bureau of Labor Statistics, Local Area Unemployment Statistics

Unemployment Rate

Area	2019											
	Jan.	Feb.	Mar.	Apr.	May	Jun.	Jul.	Aug.	Sep.	Oct.	Nov.	Dec.
City	3.7	3.7	3.7	3.2	3.2	3.6	3.6	3.3	3.0	2.9	2.8	2.9
MSA[1]	3.5	3.4	3.5	3.0	3.0	3.3	3.3	3.0	2.8	2.7	2.6	2.7
U.S.	4.4	4.1	3.9	3.3	3.4	3.8	4.0	3.8	3.3	3.3	3.3	3.4

Note: Data is not seasonally adjusted and covers workers 16 years of age and older; (1) Figures cover the Omaha-Council Bluffs, NE-IA Metropolitan Statistical Area—see Appendix B for areas included
Source: Bureau of Labor Statistics, Local Area Unemployment Statistics

Average Wages

Occupation	$/Hr.	Occupation	$/Hr.
Accountants and Auditors	35.10	Maintenance and Repair Workers	20.70
Automotive Mechanics	21.90	Marketing Managers	52.50
Bookkeepers	19.90	Network and Computer Systems Admin.	40.20
Carpenters	19.90	Nurses, Licensed Practical	22.10
Cashiers	11.70	Nurses, Registered	32.30
Computer Programmers	39.00	Nursing Assistants	15.00
Computer Systems Analysts	39.70	Office Clerks, General	16.80
Computer User Support Specialists	26.30	Physical Therapists	39.40
Construction Laborers	18.50	Physicians	80.90
Cooks, Restaurant	13.70	Plumbers, Pipefitters and Steamfitters	30.80
Customer Service Representatives	17.60	Police and Sheriff's Patrol Officers	31.80
Dentists	86.30	Postal Service Mail Carriers	25.00
Electricians	27.60	Real Estate Sales Agents	24.90
Engineers, Electrical	43.80	Retail Salespersons	14.10
Fast Food and Counter Workers	11.20	Sales Representatives, Technical/Scientific	26.10
Financial Managers	58.00	Secretaries, Exc. Legal/Medical/Executive	17.80
First-Line Supervisors of Office Workers	27.50	Security Guards	17.20
General and Operations Managers	50.00	Surgeons	131.50
Hairdressers/Cosmetologists	16.50	Teacher Assistants, Exc. Postsecondary*	14.10
Home Health and Personal Care Aides	13.10	Teachers, Secondary School, Exc. Sp. Ed.*	29.40
Janitors and Cleaners	13.70	Telemarketers	12.30
Landscaping/Groundskeeping Workers	16.20	Truck Drivers, Heavy/Tractor-Trailer	21.50
Lawyers	59.10	Truck Drivers, Light/Delivery Services	17.20
Maids and Housekeeping Cleaners	12.10	Waiters and Waitresses	12.70

Note: Wage data covers the Omaha-Council Bluffs, NE-IA Metropolitan Statistical Area—see Appendix B for areas included; (*) Hourly wages were calculated from annual wage data based on a 40 hour work week; n/a not available.
Source: Bureau of Labor Statistics, Metro Area Occupational Employment & Wage Estimates, May 2019

Employment by Occupation

Occupation Classification	City (%)	MSA[1] (%)	U.S. (%)
Management, Business, Science, and Arts	38.9	39.9	37.9
Natural Resources, Construction, and Maintenance	7.8	8.5	8.9
Production, Transportation, and Material Moving	12.1	12.1	13.3
Sales and Office	24.0	23.4	22.1
Service	17.2	16.1	17.9

Note: Figures cover employed civilians 16 years of age and older; (1) Figures cover the Omaha-Council Bluffs, NE-IA Metropolitan Statistical Area—see Appendix B for areas included
Source: U.S. Census Bureau, 2014-2018 American Community Survey 5-Year Estimates

Employment by Industry

Sector	MSA[1]		U.S.
	Number of Employees	Percent of Total	Percent of Total
Construction, Mining, and Logging	31,200	6.1	5.4
Education and Health Services	81,100	15.7	16.1
Financial Activities	46,600	9.0	5.8
Government	67,900	13.2	15.0
Information	10,400	2.0	1.9
Leisure and Hospitality	52,500	10.2	10.8
Manufacturing	34,200	6.6	8.4
Other Services	18,800	3.6	3.9
Professional and Business Services	73,100	14.2	14.1
Retail Trade	53,700	10.4	10.6
Transportation, Warehousing, and Utilities	29,000	5.6	4.2
Wholesale Trade	16,700	3.2	3.9

Note: Figures are non-farm employment as of December 2019. Figures are not seasonally adjusted and include workers 16 years of age and older; (1) Figures cover the Omaha-Council Bluffs, NE-IA Metropolitan Statistical Area—see Appendix B for areas included
Source: Bureau of Labor Statistics, Current Employment Statistics, Employment, Hours, and Earnings

Occupations with Greatest Projected Employment Growth: 2019 – 2021

Occupation[1]	2019 Employment	2021 Projected Employment	Numeric Employment Change	Percent Employment Change
Combined Food Preparation and Serving Workers, Including Fast Food	25,070	25,830	760	3.0
Heavy and Tractor-Trailer Truck Drivers	29,660	30,420	760	2.6
Registered Nurses	26,550	27,250	700	2.6
Carpenters	11,090	11,530	440	4.0
General and Operations Managers	17,490	17,860	370	2.1
Nursing Assistants	15,650	15,980	330	2.1
Laborers and Freight, Stock, and Material Movers, Hand	16,670	17,000	330	2.0
Janitors and Cleaners, Except Maids and Housekeeping Cleaners	16,450	16,750	300	1.8
Personal Care Aides	7,200	7,500	300	4.2
Electricians	5,720	6,020	300	5.2

Note: Projections cover Nebraska; (1) Sorted by numeric employment change
Source: www.projectionscentral.com, State Occupational Projections, 2019–2021 Short-Term Projections

Fastest Growing Occupations: 2019 – 2021

Occupation[1]	2019 Employment	2021 Projected Employment	Numeric Employment Change	Percent Employment Change
Heating, Air Conditioning, and Refrigeration Mechanics and Installers	2,870	3,060	190	6.6
Roofers	1,230	1,310	80	6.5
Veterinary Technologists and Technicians	880	930	50	5.7
Physical Therapist Assistants	900	950	50	5.6
Cement Masons and Concrete Finishers	3,550	3,740	190	5.4
Operations Research Analysts	1,130	1,190	60	5.3
Physician Assistants	1,330	1,400	70	5.3
Electricians	5,720	6,020	300	5.2
Taxi Drivers and Chauffeurs	2,580	2,710	130	5.0
Software Developers, Applications	4,880	5,120	240	4.9

Note: Projections cover Nebraska; (1) Sorted by percent employment change and excludes occupations with numeric employment change less than 50
Source: www.projectionscentral.com, State Occupational Projections, 2019–2021 Short-Term Projections

TAXES

State Corporate Income Tax Rates

State	Tax Rate (%)	Income Brackets ($)	Num. of Brackets	Financial Institution Tax Rate (%)[a]	Federal Income Tax Ded.
Nebraska	5.58 - 7.81	100,000	2	(a)	No

Note: Tax rates as of January 1, 2020; (a) Rates listed are the corporate income tax rate applied to financial institutions or excise taxes based on income.
Source: Federation of Tax Administrators, State Corporate Income Tax Rates, January 1, 2020

State Individual Income Tax Rates

State	Tax Rate (%)	Income Brackets ($)	Personal Exemptions ($)			Standard Ded. ($)	
			Single	Married	Depend.	Single	Married
Nebraska (a)	2.46 - 6.84	3,230 - 31,160 (b)	140	280 (c)	140 (c)	7,000	14,000

Note: Tax rates as of January 1, 2020; Local- and county-level taxes are not included; Federal income tax is not deductible on state income tax returns; (a) 19 states have statutory provision for automatically adjusting to the rate of inflation the dollar values of the income tax brackets, standard deductions, and/or personal exemptions. Michigan indexes the personal exemption only. Oregon does not index the income brackets for $125,000 and over; (b) For joint returns, taxes are twice the tax on half the couple's income; (c) The personal exemption takes the form of a tax credit instead of a deduction
Source: Federation of Tax Administrators, State Individual Income Tax Rates, January 1, 2020

Various State Sales and Excise Tax Rates

State	State Sales Tax (%)	Gasoline[1] (¢/gal.)	Cigarette[2] ($/pack)	Spirits[3] ($/gal.)	Wine[4] ($/gal.)	Beer[5] ($/gal.)	Recreational Marijuana (%)
Nebraska	5.5	30.2	0.64	3.75	0.95	0.31	Not legal

Note: All tax rates as of January 1, 2020; (1) The American Petroleum Institute has developed a methodology for determining the average tax rate on a gallon of fuel. Rates may include any of the following: excise taxes, environmental fees, storage tank fees, other fees or taxes, general sales tax, and local taxes; (2) The federal excise tax of $1.0066 per pack and local taxes are not included; (3) Rates are those applicable to off-premise sales of 40% alcohol by volume (a.b.v.) distilled spirits in 750ml containers. Local excise taxes are excluded; (4) Rates are those applicable to off-premise sales of 11% a.b.v. non-carbonated wine in 750ml containers; (5) Rates are those applicable to off-premise sales of 4.7% a.b.v. beer in 12 ounce containers.
Source: Tax Foundation, 2020 Facts & Figures: How Does Your State Compare?

State Business Tax Climate Index Rankings

State	Overall Rank	Corporate Tax Rank	Individual Income Tax Rank	Sales Tax Rank	Property Tax Rank	Unemployment Insurance Tax Rank
Nebraska	28	31	21	10	41	11

Note: The index is a measure of how each state's tax laws affect economic performance. The lower the rank, the more favorable a state's tax system is for business. States without a given tax are given a ranking of 1. The scores/rankings for the District of Columbia do not affect other states. The 2020 index represents the tax climate as of July 1, 2019.
Source: Tax Foundation, State Business Tax Climate Index 2020

COMMERCIAL UTILITIES

Typical Monthly Electric Bills

Area	General Service, Light ($/month)		General Service, Heavy ($/month)	
	40 kW demand 5,000 kWh	100 kW demand 10,000 kWh	500 kW demand 100,000 kWh	1,500 kW demand 500,000 kWh
City	384	1,186	8,996	36,640

Note: Figures are based on rates in effect January 1, 2019
Source: Memphis Light, Gas and Water, 2019 Utility Bill Comparisons for Selected U.S. Cities

TRANSPORTATION

Means of Transportation to Work

Area	Car/Truck/Van		Public Transportation			Bicycle	Walked	Other Means	Worked at Home
	Drove Alone	Car-pooled	Bus	Subway	Railroad				
City	82.1	9.1	1.3	0.0	0.0	0.3	2.3	1.2	3.7
MSA[1]	84.2	8.1	0.8	0.0	0.0	0.2	1.8	1.0	3.8
U.S.	76.4	9.1	2.5	1.9	0.6	0.6	2.7	1.3	4.9

Note: Figures are percentages and cover workers 16 years of age and older; (1) Figures cover the Omaha-Council Bluffs, NE-IA Metropolitan Statistical Area—see Appendix B for areas included
Source: U.S. Census Bureau, 2014-2018 American Community Survey 5-Year Estimates

Travel Time to Work

Area	Less Than 10 Minutes	10 to 19 Minutes	20 to 29 Minutes	30 to 44 Minutes	45 to 59 Minutes	60 to 89 Minutes	90 Minutes or More
City	14.4	41.4	27.5	12.3	2.1	1.4	0.9
MSA[1]	14.4	36.6	27.1	15.7	3.5	1.7	1.0
U.S.	12.5	28.7	20.9	20.7	8.2	6.3	2.8

Note: Note: Figures are percentages and include workers 16 years old and over; (1) Figures cover the Omaha-Council Bluffs, NE-IA Metropolitan Statistical Area—see Appendix B for areas included
Source: U.S. Census Bureau, 2014-2018 American Community Survey 5-Year Estimates

Key Congestion Measures

Area	1982	1992	2002	2012	2017
Annual Hours of Delay, Total (000)	2,280	5,374	11,017	16,444	19,117
Annual Hours of Delay, Per Auto Commuter	9	18	28	34	38
Annual Congestion Cost, Total (million $)	17	57	150	298	355
Annual Congestion Cost, Per Auto Commuter ($)	180	292	468	547	616

Source: Texas A&M Transportation Institute, 2019 Urban Mobility Report

Freeway Travel Time Index

Area	1982	1987	1992	1997	2002	2007	2012	2017
Urban Area Index[1]	1.04	1.06	1.09	1.11	1.14	1.15	1.16	1.17
Urban Area Rank[1,2]	61	66	70	72	69	72	60	49

Note: Freeway Travel Time Index—the ratio of travel time in the peak period to the travel time at free-flow conditions. For example, a value of 1.30 indicates a 20-minute free-flow trip takes 26 minutes in the peak (20 minutes x 1.30 = 26 minutes); (1) Covers the Omaha NE-IA urban area; (2) Rank is based on 101 larger urban areas (#1 = highest travel time index)
Source: Texas A&M Transportation Institute, 2019 Urban Mobility Report

Public Transportation

Agency Name / Mode of Transportation	Vehicles Operated in Maximum Service[1]	Annual Unlinked Passenger Trips[2] (in thous.)	Annual Passenger Miles[3] (in thous.)
Transit Authority of Omaha (MAT)			
Bus (directly operated)	88	3,409.2	12,569.5
Demand Response (directly operated)	25	106.9	771.0

Note: (1) Number of revenue vehicles operated by the given mode and type of service to meet the annual maximum service requirement. This is the revenue vehicle count during the peak season of the year; on the week and day that maximum service is provided. Vehicles operated in maximum service (VOMS) exclude atypical days and one-time special events; (2) Number of passengers who boarded public transportation vehicles. Passengers are counted each time they board a vehicle no matter how many vehicles they use to travel from their origin to their destination. (3) Sum of the distances ridden by all passengers during the entire fiscal year.
Source: Federal Transit Administration, National Transit Database, 2018

Air Transportation

Airport Name and Code / Type of Service	Passenger Airlines[1]	Passenger Enplanements	Freight Carriers[2]	Freight (lbs)
Eppley Airfield (OMA)				
Domestic service (U.S. carriers - 2019)	27	2,448,116	12	61,593,251
International service (U.S. carriers - 2018)	4	617	0	0

Note: (1) Includes all U.S.-based major, minor and commuter airlines that carried at least one passenger during the year; (2) Includes all U.S.-based airlines and freight carriers that transported at least one pound of freight during the year.
Source: Bureau of Transportation Statistics, The Intermodal Transportation Database, Air Carriers: T-100 Domestic Market (U.S. Carriers), 2019; Bureau of Transportation Statistics, The Intermodal Transportation Database, Air Carriers: T-100 International Market (U.S. Carriers), 2018

Other Transportation Statistics

Major Highways:	I-80
Amtrak Service:	Yes
Major Waterways/Ports:	Port of Omaha (serves the Missouri River basin)

Source: Amtrak.com; Google Maps

BUSINESSES

Major Business Headquarters

Company Name	Industry	Rankings	
		Fortune[1]	Forbes[2]
Berkshire Hathaway	Insurance, Property and Casualty (Stock)	4	-
Kiewit Corporation	Construction	-	43
Mutual of Omaha Insurance	Insurance, Life, Health (Stock)	336	-
Peter Kiewit Sons'	Engineering, Construction	340	-
Scoular	Food, Drink & Tobacco	-	106
Tenaska	Multicompany	-	26
Union Pacific	Railroads	134	-

Note: (1) Companies that produce a 10-K are ranked 1 to 500 based on 2018 revenue; (2) All private companies with at least $2 billion in annual revenue through the end of their most current fiscal year are ranked 1 to 228; companies listed are headquartered in the city; dashes indicate no ranking
Source: Fortune, "Fortune 500," June 2019; Forbes, "America's Largest Private Companies," 2019 Rankings

Fast-Growing Businesses

According to *Inc.*, Omaha is home to one of America's 500 fastest-growing private companies: **City Ventures** (#207). Criteria: must be an independent, privately-held, for-profit, U.S. corporation, proprietorship or partnership as of December 31, 2018; revenues must be at least $100,000 in 2015 and $2 million in 2018; must have four-year operating/sales history. *Inc., "America's 500 Fastest-Growing Private Companies," 2019*

According to *Fortune*, Omaha is home to one of the 100 fastest-growing companies in the world: **TD Ameritrade Holding** (#96). Companies were ranked by their revenue growth rate; their EPS growth rate; and their three-year annualized total return to investors for the period ending June 30, 2019. Criteria for inclusion: a company, foreign or domestic, must trade on a major U.S. stock exchange; must file quarterly reports with the SEC; must have a minimum market capitalization of $250 million; must have a stock price of at least $5 on June 30, 2019; must have been trading continuously since June 30, 2016; must have revenue and net income for the four quarters ended on or before April 30, 2019, of at least $50 million and $10 million, respectively; and must have posted a compound annual growth in revenue and earnings per share of at least 15% annually over the three years ending on or before April 30, 2019. Real estate investment trusts, limited-liability companies, limited parterships, business development companies, closed-end investment firms, companies about to be acquired, and companies that lost money in the quarter ending April 30, 2019 were excluded. *Fortune, "100 Fastest-Growing Companies," 2019*

According to Deloitte, Omaha is home to one of North America's 500 fastest-growing high-technology companies: **Buildertrend** (#390). Companies are ranked by percentage growth in revenue over a four-year period. Criteria for inclusion: company must be headquartered within North America; must own proprietary intellectual property or technology that is sold to customers in products that contributes to a significant portion of the company's operating revenue; must have been in business for a minumum of four years with 2015 operating revenues of at least $50,000 USD/CD and 2018 operating revenues of at least $5 million USD/CD. *Deloitte, 2019 Technology Fast 500™*

Minority Business Opportunity

Omaha is home to one company which is on the *Black Enterprise* Industrial/Service list (100 largest companies based on gross sales): **All American Meats** (#48). Criteria: operational in previous calendar year; at least 51% black-owned and manufactures/owns the product it sells or provides industrial or consumer services. Brokerages, real estate firms and firms that provide professional services are not eligible. *Black Enterprise, B.E. 100s, 2019*

Omaha is home to one company which is on the *Hispanic Business* 500 list (500 largest U.S. Hispanic-owned companies based on revenue): **Midwest Maintenance Co.** (#317). Companies included must show at least 51 percent ownership by Hispanic U.S. citizens, and must maintain headquarters in one of the 50 states or Washington, D.C. *Hispanic Business, "Hispanic Business 500," June 20, 2013*

Minority- and Women-Owned Businesses

Group	All Firms		Firms with Paid Employees			
	Firms	Sales ($000)	Firms	Sales ($000)	Employees	Payroll ($000)
AIAN[1]	254	9,161	15	3,675	32	371
Asian	1,150	224,709	230	194,717	1,913	44,163
Black	3,349	137,711	168	77,071	918	18,750
Hispanic	2,021	447,845	170	356,891	1,709	49,522
NHOPI[2]	n/a	n/a	n/a	n/a	n/a	n/a
Women	12,869	2,379,340	1,494	2,107,314	13,828	479,154
All Firms	37,664	91,113,564	10,126	89,879,746	320,226	14,447,769

Note: Figures cover firms located in the city; minority- and women-owned business are defined as firms in which the corresponding group own 51% or more of the stock or equity of the company; (1) American Indian and Alaska Native; (2) Native Hawaiian and Other Pacific Islander; n/a not available
Source: U.S. Census Bureau, 2012 Economic Census, Survey of Business Owners

HOTELS & CONVENTION CENTERS

Hotels, Motels and Vacation Rentals

Area	5 Star		4 Star		3 Star		2 Star		1 Star		Not Rated	
	Num.	Pct.[3]	Num.	Pct.[3]	Num.	Pct.[3]	Num.	Pct.[3]	Num.	Pct.[3]	Num.	Pct.[3]
City[1]	0	0.0	3	2.5	28	23.1	20	16.5	4	3.3	66	54.5
Total[2]	266	1.3	1,517	7.2	4,627	21.8	3,210	15.1	3,974	18.7	7,601	35.9

Note: (1) Figures cover Omaha and vicinity; (2) Figures cover all 100 cities in this book; (3) Percentage of hotels which have a given star rating; Star ratings are determined by priceline.com and offer an indication of the general quality of a particular hotel.
Source: priceline.com, April 27, 2020

Major Convention Centers

Name	Overall Space (sq. ft.)	Exhibit Space (sq. ft.)	Meeting Space (sq. ft.)	Meeting Rooms
Quest Center Omaha	n/a	194,000	63,000	n/a

Note: Table includes convention centers located in the Omaha-Council Bluffs, NE-IA metro area; n/a not available
Source: Original research

Living Environment

COST OF LIVING

Cost of Living Index

Composite Index	Groceries	Housing	Utilities	Trans-portation	Health Care	Misc. Goods/ Services
92.3	96.8	83.6	99.4	98.3	96.4	93.3

Note: The Cost of Living Index measures regional differences in the cost of consumer goods and services, excluding taxes and non-consumer expenditures, for professional and managerial households in the top income quintile. It is based on more than 50,000 prices covering almost 60 different items for which prices are collected three times a year by chambers of commerce, economic development organizations or university applied economic centers in each participating urban area. The numbers shown should be read as a percentage above or below the national average of 100. For example, a value of 115.4 in the groceries column indicates that grocery prices are 15.4% higher than the national average. Small differences in the index numbers should not be interpreted as significant; Figures cover the Omaha NE urban area.
Source: The Council for Community and Economic Research, ACCRA Cost of Living Index, 2019

Grocery Prices

Area[1]	T-Bone Steak ($/pound)	Frying Chicken ($/pound)	Whole Milk ($/half gal.)	Eggs ($/dozen)	Orange Juice ($/64 oz.)	Coffee ($/11.5 oz.)
City[2]	11.14	1.59	1.63	1.33	3.28	4.31
Avg.	11.40	1.41	1.93	1.54	3.51	4.30
Min.	7.40	0.92	0.85	0.58	2.67	2.90
Max.	15.58	2.68	4.09	4.18	5.57	8.10

*Note: (1) Values for the local area are compared with the average, minimum and maximum values for all 290 areas in the Cost of Living Index; (2) Figures cover the Omaha NE urban area; **T-Bone Steak** (price per pound); **Frying Chicken** (price per pound, whole fryer); **Whole Milk** (half gallon carton); **Eggs** (price per dozen, Grade A, large); **Orange Juice** (64 oz. Tropicana or Florida Natural); **Coffee** (11.5 oz. can, vacuum-packed, Maxwell House, Hills Bros, or Folgers).*
Source: The Council for Community and Economic Research, ACCRA Cost of Living Index, 2019

Housing and Utility Costs

Area[1]	New Home Price ($)	Apartment Rent ($/month)	All Electric ($/month)	Part Electric ($/month)	Other Energy ($/month)	Telephone ($/month)
City[2]	282,378	1,042	-	89.71	69.48	190.50
Avg.	362,090	1,142	174.35	100.00	67.76	179.60
Min.	198,329	501	91.58	31.44	28.51	165.30
Max.	2,074,561	5,050	388.18	239.41	306.15	207.90

*Note: (1) Values for the local area are compared with the average, minimum and maximum values for all 290 areas in the Cost of Living Index; (2) Figures cover the Omaha NE urban area; **New Home Price** (2,400 sf living area, 8,000 sf lot, in urban area with full utilities); **Apartment Rent** (950 sf 2 bedroom/1.5 or 2 bath, unfurnished, excluding all utilities except water); **All Electric** (average monthly cost for an all-electric home); **Part Electric** (average monthly cost for a part-electric home); **Other Energy** (average monthly cost for natural gas, fuel oil, coal, wood, and any other forms of energy except electricity); **Telephone** (price includes the base monthly rate plus taxes and fees for three lines of mobile phone service).*
Source: The Council for Community and Economic Research, ACCRA Cost of Living Index, 2019

Health Care, Transportation, and Other Costs

Area[1]	Doctor ($/visit)	Dentist ($/visit)	Optometrist ($/visit)	Gasoline ($/gallon)	Beauty Salon ($/visit)	Men's Shirt ($)
City[2]	129.23	75.22	111.77	2.36	34.09	21.25
Avg.	114.85	97.58	106.10	2.50	38.15	32.15
Min.	39.00	62.22	52.22	1.53	16.88	10.27
Max.	206.67	151.53	258.67	3.79	79.29	59.30

*Note: (1) Values for the local area are compared with the average, minimum and maximum values for all 290 areas in the Cost of Living Index; (2) Figures cover the Omaha NE urban area; **Doctor** (general practitioners routine exam of an established patient); **Dentist** (adult teeth cleaning and periodic oral examination); **Optometrist** (full vision eye exam for established adult patient); **Gasoline** (one gallon regular unleaded, national brand, including all taxes, cash price at self-service pump if available); **Beauty Salon** (woman's shampoo, trim, and blow-dry); **Men's Shirt** (cotton/polyester dress shirt, pinpoint weave, long sleeves).*
Source: The Council for Community and Economic Research, ACCRA Cost of Living Index, 2019

HOUSING

House Price Index (HPI)

Area	National Ranking[2]	Quarterly Change (%)	One-Year Change (%)	Five-Year Change (%)
MSA[1]	75	1.03	5.58	32.31
U.S.[3]	–	1.26	5.09	32.88

Note: The HPI is a weighted repeat sales index. It measures average price changes in repeat sales or refinancings on the same properties. This information is obtained by reviewing repeat mortgage transactions on single-family properties whose mortgages have been purchased or securitized by Fannie Mae or Freddie Mac in January 1975; (1) Figures cover the Omaha-Council Bluffs, NE-IA Metropolitan Statistical Area—see Appendix B for areas included; (2) Rankings are based on annual percentage change for all metro areas containing at least 15,000 transactions over the last 10 years and ranges from 1 to 232; (3) figures based on a weighted average of Census Division estimates using a seasonally adjusted, purchase-only index; all figures are for the period ending December 31, 2019
Source: Federal Housing Finance Agency, House Price Index, February 25, 2020

Median Single-Family Home Prices

Area	2017	2018	2019[p]	Percent Change 2018 to 2019
MSA[1]	175.9	191.7	200.7	4.7
U.S. Average	248.8	261.6	274.6	5.0

Note: Figures are median sales prices of existing single-family homes in thousands of dollars; (p) preliminary; (1) Figures cover the Omaha-Council Bluffs, NE-IA Metropolitan Statistical Area—see Appendix B for areas included
Source: National Association of Realtors, Median Sales Price of Existing Single-Family Homes for Metropolitan Areas, 4th Quarter 2019

Qualifying Income Based on Median Sales Price of Existing Single-Family Homes

Area	With 5% Down ($)	With 10% Down ($)	With 20% Down ($)
MSA[1]	42,466	40,231	35,761
U.S. Average	58,663	55,575	49,400

Note: Figures are preliminary; Qualifying income is based on a mortgage rate of 3.76%. Monthly principal and interest payment is limited to 25% of income; (1) Figures cover the Omaha-Council Bluffs, NE-IA Metropolitan Statistical Area—see Appendix B for areas included
Source: National Association of Realtors, Qualifying Income Based on Median Sales Price of Existing Single-Family Homes for Metropolitan Areas, 4th Quarter 2019

Median Apartment Condo-Coop Home Prices

Area	2017	2018	2019[p]	Percent Change 2018 to 2019
MSA[1]	n/a	n/a	n/a	n/a
U.S. Average	234.3	241.0	249.5	3.5

Note: Figures are median sales prices of existing apartment condo-coop homes in thousands of dollars; (p) preliminary; n/a not available; (1) Figures cover the Omaha-Council Bluffs, NE-IA Metropolitan Statistical Area—see Appendix B for areas included
Source: National Association of Realtors, Median Sales Price of Existing Apartment Condo-Coop Homes for Metropolitan Areas, 4th Quarter 2019

Home Value Distribution

Area	Under $50,000	$50,000 -$99,999	$100,000 -$149,999	$150,000 -$199,999	$200,000 -$299,999	$300,000 -$499,999	$500,000 -$999,999	$1,000,000 or more
City	4.9	16.2	28.4	20.7	17.4	9.0	2.8	0.7
MSA[1]	4.5	13.1	25.7	20.4	20.6	12.1	3.0	0.6
U.S.	7.6	13.0	14.0	14.3	19.2	18.3	10.5	3.1

Note: Figures are percentages and cover owner-occupied housing units; (1) Figures cover the Omaha-Council Bluffs, NE-IA Metropolitan Statistical Area—see Appendix B for areas included
Source: U.S. Census Bureau, 2014-2018 American Community Survey 5-Year Estimates

Homeownership Rate

Area	2011 (%)	2012 (%)	2013 (%)	2014 (%)	2015 (%)	2016 (%)	2017 (%)	2018 (%)	2019 (%)
MSA[1]	71.6	72.4	70.6	68.7	69.6	69.2	65.5	67.8	66.9
U.S.	66.1	65.4	65.1	64.5	63.7	63.4	63.9	64.4	64.6

Note: (1) Figures cover the Omaha-Council Bluffs, NE-IA Metropolitan Statistical Area—see Appendix B for areas included
Source: U.S. Census Bureau, Housing Vacancies and Homeownership Annual Statistics: 2011-2019

Year Housing Structure Built

Area	2010 or Later	2000 -2009	1990 -1999	1980 -1989	1970 -1979	1960 -1969	1950 -1959	1940 -1949	Before 1940	Median Year
City	2.7	6.6	12.5	11.0	15.8	14.8	11.5	4.4	20.6	1969
MSA[1]	5.4	14.8	12.8	10.0	14.7	12.0	8.9	3.6	17.6	1975
U.S.	4.1	14.3	13.9	13.5	15.3	10.7	10.4	5.0	12.8	1977

Note: Figures are percentages except for Median Year; Note: (1) Figures cover the Omaha-Council Bluffs, NE-IA Metropolitan Statistical Area—see Appendix B for areas included
Source: U.S. Census Bureau, 2014-2018 American Community Survey 5-Year Estimates

Gross Monthly Rent

Area	Under $500	$500 -$999	$1,000 -$1,499	$1,500 -$1,999	$2,000 -$2,499	$2,500 -$2,999	$3,000 and up	Median ($)
City	8.3	53.5	30.1	5.8	1.2	0.5	0.6	896
MSA[1]	8.6	53.0	29.7	6.3	1.3	0.5	0.7	900
U.S.	9.8	38.5	29.6	12.9	5.1	2.1	2.0	1,023

Note: Figures are percentages except for Median; Gross rent is the contract rent plus the estimated average monthly cost of utilities (electricity, gas, and water and sewer) and fuels (oil, coal, kerosene, wood, etc.) if these are paid by the renter (or paid for the renter by someone else); (1) Figures cover the Omaha-Council Bluffs, NE-IA Metropolitan Statistical Area—see Appendix B for areas included
Source: U.S. Census Bureau, 2014-2018 American Community Survey 5-Year Estimates

HEALTH

Health Risk Factors

Category	MSA[1] (%)	U.S. (%)
Adults aged 18–64 who have any kind of health care coverage	86.6	87.3
Adults who reported being in good or better health	85.7	82.4
Adults who have been told they have high blood cholesterol	33.2	33.0
Adults who have been told they have high blood pressure	31.8	32.3
Adults who are current smokers	16.6	17.1
Adults who currently use E-cigarettes	4.9	4.6
Adults who currently use chewing tobacco, snuff, or snus	4.1	4.0
Adults who are heavy drinkers[2]	7.5	6.3
Adults who are binge drinkers[3]	20.6	17.4
Adults who are overweight (BMI 25.0 - 29.9)	35.2	35.3
Adults who are obese (BMI 30.0 - 99.8)	33.3	31.3
Adults who participated in any physical activities in the past month	76.9	74.4
Adults who always or nearly always wears a seat belt	91.6	94.3

Note: (1) Figures cover the Omaha-Council Bluffs, NE-IA Metropolitan Statistical Area—see Appendix B for areas included; (2) Heavy drinkers are classified as adult men having more than 14 drinks per week and adult women having more than 7 drinks per week; (3) Binge drinkers are classified as males having five or more drinks on one occasion or females having four or more drinks on one occasion
Source: Centers for Disease Control and Prevention, Behaviorial Risk Factor Surveillance System, SMART: Selected Metropolitan Area Risk Trends, 2017

Acute and Chronic Health Conditions

Category	MSA[1] (%)	U.S. (%)
Adults who have ever been told they had a heart attack	3.7	4.2
Adults who have ever been told they have angina or coronary heart disease	3.5	3.9
Adults who have ever been told they had a stroke	2.8	3.0
Adults who have ever been told they have asthma	12.0	14.2
Adults who have ever been told they have arthritis	23.1	24.9
Adults who have ever been told they have diabetes[2]	10.3	10.5
Adults who have ever been told they had skin cancer	5.5	6.2
Adults who have ever been told they had any other types of cancer	5.7	7.1
Adults who have ever been told they have COPD	5.9	6.5
Adults who have ever been told they have kidney disease	2.5	3.0
Adults who have ever been told they have a form of depression	20.6	20.5

Note: (1) Figures cover the Omaha-Council Bluffs, NE-IA Metropolitan Statistical Area—see Appendix B for areas included; (2) Figures do not include pregnancy-related, borderline, or pre-diabetes
Source: Centers for Disease Control and Prevention, Behaviorial Risk Factor Surveillance System, SMART: Selected Metropolitan Area Risk Trends, 2017

Health Screening and Vaccination Rates

Category	MSA[1] (%)	U.S. (%)
Adults aged 65+ who have had flu shot within the past year	67.3	60.7
Adults aged 65+ who have ever had a pneumonia vaccination	81.9	75.4
Adults who have ever been tested for HIV	31.2	36.1
Adults who have ever had the shingles or zoster vaccine?	35.0	28.9
Adults who have had their blood cholesterol checked within the last five years	86.0	85.9

Note: n/a not available; (1) Figures cover the Omaha-Council Bluffs, NE-IA Metropolitan Statistical Area—see Appendix B for areas included.
Source: Centers for Disease Control and Prevention, Behaviorial Risk Factor Surveillance System, SMART: Selected Metropolitan Area Risk Trends, 2017

Disability Status

Category	MSA[1] (%)	U.S. (%)
Adults who reported being deaf	5.9	6.7
Are you blind or have serious difficulty seeing, even when wearing glasses?	3.5	4.5
Are you limited in any way in any of your usual activities due of arthritis?	11.2	12.9
Do you have difficulty doing errands alone?	6.1	6.8
Do you have difficulty dressing or bathing?	3.4	3.6
Do you have serious difficulty concentrating/remembering/making decisions?	10.0	10.7
Do you have serious difficulty walking or climbing stairs?	11.4	13.6

Note: (1) Figures cover the Omaha-Council Bluffs, NE-IA Metropolitan Statistical Area—see Appendix B for areas included.
Source: Centers for Disease Control and Prevention, Behaviorial Risk Factor Surveillance System, SMART: Selected Metropolitan Area Risk Trends, 2017

Mortality Rates for the Top 10 Causes of Death in the U.S.

ICD-10[a] Sub-Chapter	ICD-10[a] Code	Age-Adjusted Mortality Rate[1] per 100,000 population	
		County[2]	U.S.
Malignant neoplasms	C00-C97	157.3	152.4
Ischaemic heart diseases	I20-I25	64.6	92.7
Other forms of heart disease	I30-I51	52.4	52.5
Chronic lower respiratory diseases	J40-J47	48.8	40.4
Cerebrovascular diseases	I60-I69	34.5	37.3
Other degenerative diseases of the nervous system	G30-G31	40.0	36.4
Other external causes of accidental injury	W00-X59	25.6	35.3
Organic, including symptomatic, mental disorders	F01-F09	38.7	30.0
Hypertensive diseases	I10-I15	22.9	22.9
Diabetes mellitus	E10-E14	28.6	21.3

Note: (a) ICD-10 = International Classification of Diseases 10th Revision; (1) Mortality rates are a three year average covering 2016-2018; (2) Figures cover Douglas County.
Source: Centers for Disease Control and Prevention, National Center for Health Statistics. Underlying Cause of Death 1999-2018 on CDC WONDER Online Database

Mortality Rates for Selected Causes of Death

ICD-10[a] Sub-Chapter	ICD-10[a] Code	Age-Adjusted Mortality Rate[1] per 100,000 population	
		County[2]	U.S.
Assault	X85-Y09	4.7	6.0
Diseases of the liver	K70-K76	14.9	14.2
Human immunodeficiency virus (HIV) disease	B20-B24	1.1	1.6
Influenza and pneumonia	J09-J18	15.0	14.2
Intentional self-harm	X60-X84	11.7	13.9
Malnutrition	E40-E46	3.2	1.9
Obesity and other hyperalimentation	E65-E68	2.8	2.1
Renal failure	N17-N19	10.8	12.8
Transport accidents	V01-V99	9.3	12.5
Viral hepatitis	B15-B19	1.6	1.4

Note: (a) ICD-10 = International Classification of Diseases 10th Revision; (1) Mortality rates are a three year average covering 2016-2018; (2) Figures cover Douglas County; Data are suppressed when the data meet the criteria for confidentiality constraints; Mortality rates are flagged as unreliable when the rate would be calculated with a numerator of 20 or less.
Source: Centers for Disease Control and Prevention, National Center for Health Statistics. Underlying Cause of Death 1999-2018 on CDC WONDER Online Database

Health Insurance Coverage

Area	With Health Insurance	With Private Health Insurance	With Public Health Insurance	Without Health Insurance	Population Under Age 19 Without Health Insurance
City	89.3	70.5	28.1	10.7	5.9
MSA[1]	92.0	75.9	26.8	8.0	4.3
U.S.	90.6	67.7	34.7	9.4	5.2

Note: Figures are percentages that cover the civilian noninstitutionalized population; (1) Figures cover the Omaha-Council Bluffs, NE-IA Metropolitan Statistical Area—see Appendix B for areas included
Source: U.S. Census Bureau, 2014-2018 American Community Survey 5-Year Estimates

Number of Medical Professionals

Area	MDs[3]	DOs[3,4]	Dentists	Podiatrists	Chiropractors	Optometrists
County[1] (number)	3,015	161	537	30	228	111
County[1] (rate[2])	536.8	28.7	94.7	5.3	40.2	19.6
U.S. (rate[2])	281.9	23.4	69.1	6.0	27.5	16.4

Note: Data as of 2018 unless noted; (1) Data covers Douglas County; (2) Rate per 100,000 population; (3) Data as of 2017 and includes all active, non-federal physicians; (4) Doctor of Osteopathic Medicine
Source: U.S. Department of Health and Human Services, Health Resources and Services Administration, Bureau of Health Professions, Area Resource File (ARF) 2018-2019

Best Hospitals

According to *U.S. News,* the Omaha-Council Bluffs, NE-IA metro area is home to one of the best hospitals in the U.S.: **Nebraska Medicine-Nebraska Medical Center** (1 adult specialty). The hospital listed was nationally ranked in at least one of 16 adult or 10 pediatric specialties. Only 206 hospitals nationwide were nationally ranked in one or more adult or pediatric specialty. Twenty hospitals in the U.S. made the Honor Roll. The Best Hospitals Honor Roll takes both the national rankings and the procedure and condition ratings into account. Hospitals received points if they were nationally ranked in one of the 16 adult specialties—the higher they ranked, the more points they got—and how many ratings of "high performing" they earned in the nine procedures and conditions. *U.S. News Online, "America's Best Hospitals 2019-20"*

According to *U.S. News,* the Omaha-Council Bluffs, NE-IA metro area is home to one of the best children's hospitals in the U.S.: **Children's Hospital and Medical Center** (5 pediatric specialties). The hospital listed was highly ranked in at least one of 10 pediatric specialties. Ninety-one children's hospitals in the U.S. were nationally ranked in at least one specialty. Hospitals received points for being ranked in a specialty, and the 10 hospitals with the most points across the 10 specialties make up the Honor Roll. *U.S. News Online, "America's Best Children's Hospitals 2019-20"*

EDUCATION

Public School District Statistics

District Name	Schls	Pupils	Pupil/ Teacher Ratio	Minority Pupils[1] (%)	Free Lunch Eligible[2] (%)	IEP[3] (%)
Millard Public Schools	36	24,104	16.4	22.9	15.8	11.6
Omaha Public Schools	106	53,194	14.9	73.6	61.5	19.7
Westside Community Schools	14	5,942	13.6	30.2	27.2	11.0

Note: Table includes school districts with 2,000 or more students; (1) Percentage of students that are not non-Hispanic white; (2) Percentage of students that are eligible for the free lunch program; (3) Percentage of students that have an Individualized Education Program.
Source: U.S. Department of Education, National Center for Education Statistics, Common Core of Data, Local Education Agency (School District) Universe Survey: School Year 2018-2019; U.S. Department of Education, National Center for Education Statistics, Common Core of Data, Public Elementary/Secondary School Universe Survey: School Year 2018-2019

Best High Schools

According to *U.S. News,* Omaha is home to one of the top 500 high schools in the U.S.: **Elkhorn South High School** (#203). Nearly 18,000 public, magnet and charter schools were ranked based on their performance on state assessments and how well they prepare students for college. *U.S. News & World Report, "Best High Schools 2020"*

Highest Level of Education

Area	Less than H.S.	H.S. Diploma	Some College, No Deg.	Associate Degree	Bachelor's Degree	Master's Degree	Prof. School Degree	Doctorate Degree
City	11.2	22.3	22.3	7.7	23.7	8.6	2.7	1.5
MSA[1]	8.6	23.7	22.9	8.9	23.6	8.8	2.1	1.3
U.S.	12.3	27.1	20.6	8.4	19.4	8.6	2.1	1.4

Note: Figures cover persons age 25 and over; (1) Figures cover the Omaha-Council Bluffs, NE-IA
Metropolitan Statistical Area—see Appendix B for areas included
Source: U.S. Census Bureau, 2014-2018 American Community Survey 5-Year Estimates

Educational Attainment by Race

Area	High School Graduate or Higher (%)					Bachelor's Degree or Higher (%)				
	Total	White	Black	Asian	Hisp.[2]	Total	White	Black	Asian	Hisp.[2]
City	88.8	90.9	86.0	67.7	52.0	36.6	39.3	19.2	47.9	11.5
MSA[1]	91.4	92.8	87.4	75.2	59.5	35.8	37.1	22.2	49.1	14.4
U.S.	87.7	89.6	85.4	86.8	67.7	31.5	32.9	21.1	53.5	15.8

Note: Figures shown cover persons 25 years old and over; (1) Figures cover the Omaha-Council Bluffs, NE-IA
Metropolitan Statistical Area—see Appendix B for areas included; (2) People of Hispanic origin can be of any
race
Source: U.S. Census Bureau, 2014-2018 American Community Survey 5-Year Estimates

School Enrollment by Grade and Control

Area	Preschool (%)		Kindergarten (%)		Grades 1 - 4 (%)		Grades 5 - 8 (%)		Grades 9 - 12 (%)	
	Public	Private	Public	Private	Public	Private	Public	Private	Public	Private
City	56.1	43.9	81.7	18.3	86.1	13.9	85.9	14.1	85.3	14.7
MSA[1]	57.8	42.2	85.6	14.4	87.6	12.4	87.4	12.6	87.4	12.6
U.S.	59.0	41.0	87.7	12.3	89.6	10.4	89.5	10.5	90.2	9.8

Note: Figures shown cover persons 3 years old and over; (1) Figures cover the Omaha-Council Bluffs, NE-IA
Metropolitan Statistical Area—see Appendix B for areas included
Source: U.S. Census Bureau, 2014-2018 American Community Survey 5-Year Estimates

Average Salaries of Public School Teachers

Area	2016-17		2017-18		Change from 2016-17 to 2017-18	
	Dollars	Rank[1]	Dollars	Rank[1]	Percent	Rank[2]
Nebraska	52,338	29	54,213	25	3.58	3
U.S. Average	59,539	–	60,477	–	1.58	–

Note: (1) Rank ranges from 1 to 51 where 1 indicates highest salary; (2) Rank ranges from 1 to 51 where 1
indicates highest percent change.
Source: National Education Association, Rankings & Estimates: Rankings of the States 2018 and Estimates of
School Statistics 2019

Higher Education

Four-Year Colleges			Two-Year Colleges			Medical Schools[1]	Law Schools[2]	Voc/ Tech[3]
Public	Private Non-profit	Private For-profit	Public	Private Non-profit	Private For-profit			
3	4	1	1	1	3	2	1	0

Note: Figures cover institutions located within the city limits and include main campuses only; (1) includes
schools accredited by the Liaison Committee on Medical Education and the American Osteopathic
Association's Commission on Osteopathic College Accreditation; (2) includes ABA-accredited schools, schools
with provisional ABA accreditation, and state accredited schools; (3) includes all schools with programs that
are less than 2 years.
Source: National Center for Education Statistics, Integrated Postsecondary Education System (IPEDS),
2018-19; Wikipedia, List of Medical Schools in the United States, accessed May 1, 2020; Wikipedia, List of Law
Schools in the United States, accessed May 1, 2020

According to *U.S. News & World Report,* the Omaha-Council Bluffs, NE-IA metro area is home to
one of the top 200 national universities in the U.S.: **Creighton University** (#104 tie). The
indicators used to capture academic quality fall into a number of categories: assessment by
administrators at peer institutions; retention of students; faculty resources; student selectivity;
financial resources; alumni giving; high school counselor ratings of colleges; and graduation rate.
U.S. News & World Report, "America's Best Colleges 2020"

According to *U.S. News & World Report,* the Omaha-Council Bluffs, NE-IA metro area is home to
one of the top 75 medical schools for research in the U.S.: **University of Nebraska Medical
Center** (#62 tie). The rankings are based on a weighted average of 11 measures of quality: quality
assessment; peer assessment score; assessment score by residency directors; research activity; total

research activity; average research activity per faculty member; student selectivity; median MCAT total score; median undergraduate GPA; acceptance rate; and faculty resources. *U.S. News & World Report, "America's Best Graduate Schools, Medical, 2021"*

PRESIDENTIAL ELECTION

2016 Presidential Election Results

Area	Clinton	Trump	Johnson	Stein	Other
Douglas County	47.3	45.0	4.3	1.2	2.2
U.S.	48.0	45.9	3.3	1.1	1.7

Note: Results are percentages and may not add to 100% due to rounding
Source: Dave Leip's Atlas of U.S. Presidential Elections

EMPLOYERS

Major Employers

Company Name	Industry
Alegent Health	General medical & surgical hospitals
City of Omaha	City & town managers' office
Creighton St. Joseph Reg Healthcare Sys	General medical & surgical hospitals
Creighton University	Colleges & universities
Drivers Management	Truck driver services
First Data Resources	Data processing service
Harveys Iowa Management Company	Casino hotels
Kiewit Offshore Services	Fabricated structural metal
Metropolitan Community College	Community college
Mutual of Omaha Insurance Company	Life insurance
Nebraska Furniture Mart	Furniture stores
Omaha Public Power District	Electric services
The Archbishop Bergan Mercy Hospital	General medical & surgical hospitals
The Nebraska Medical Center	General medical & surgical hospitals
The Pacesetter Corporation	General remodeling, single-family houses
Tyson Foods	Meats & meat products
Valmont Industries	Irrigation equipment, self-propelled

Note: Companies shown are located within the Omaha-Council Bluffs, NE-IA Metropolitan Statistical Area.
Source: Hoovers.com; Wikipedia

Best Companies to Work For

TD Ameritrade, headquartered in Omaha, is among the "100 Best Places to Work in IT." To qualify, companies had to be U.S.-based organizations or be non-U.S.- based employers that met the following criteria: have a minimum of 300 total employees at a U.S. headquarters and a minimum of 30 IT employees in the U.S., with at least 50% of their IT employees based in the U.S. The best places to work were selected based on compensation, benefits, work/life balance, employee morale, and satisfaction with training and development programs. In addition, *Computerworld* looked at retention efforts, programs for recognizing and rewarding outstanding performances, and benefits such as flextime, elder care and child care, and reimbursement for college tuition and the cost of pursuing technology certifications. *Computerworld, "100 Best Places to Work in IT 2019"*

PUBLIC SAFETY

Crime Rate

Area	All Crimes	Violent Crimes				Property Crimes		
		Murder	Rape[3]	Robbery	Aggrav. Assault	Burglary	Larceny -Theft	Motor Vehicle Theft
City	4,035.8	4.7	85.9	97.2	372.2	393.7	2,416.7	665.4
Suburbs[1]	n/a	n/a	n/a	n/a	n/a	n/a	n/a	n/a
Metro[2]	n/a	n/a	n/a	n/a	n/a	n/a	n/a	n/a
U.S.	2,580.1	5.0	42.6	86.2	246.8	376.0	1,594.6	228.9

Note: Figures are crimes per 100,000 population; (1) All areas within the metro area that are located outside the city limits; (2) Figures cover the Omaha-Council Bluffs, NE-IA Metropolitan Statistical Area—see Appendix B for areas included; n/a not available; (3) The city and U.S. figures shown were reported using the revised Uniform Crime Reporting (UCR) definition of rape. The suburban and metro area figures shown are an aggregate total of the data submitted using both the revised and legacy UCR definitions.
Source: FBI Uniform Crime Reports, 2018

Hate Crimes

Area	Number of Quarters Reported	Number of Incidents per Bias Motivation					
		Race/Ethnicity/ Ancestry	Religion	Sexual Orientation	Disability	Gender	Gender Identity
City	4	3	2	0	0	0	0
U.S.	4	4,047	1,419	1,196	159	47	168

Source: Federal Bureau of Investigation, Hate Crime Statistics 2018

Identity Theft Consumer Reports

Area	Reports	Reports per 100,000 Population	Rank[2]
MSA[1]	889	94	201
U.S.	650,572	198	-

Note: (1) Figures cover the Omaha-Council Bluffs, NE-IA Metropolitan Statistical Area—see Appendix B for areas included; (2) Rank ranges from 1 to 386 where 1 indicates greatest number of identity theft reports per 100,000 population
Source: Federal Trade Commission, Consumer Sentinel Network Data Book for January–December 2019

Fraud and Other Consumer Reports

Area	Reports	Reports per 100,000 Population	Rank[2]
MSA[1]	5,110	542	199
U.S.	2,590,177	789	-

Note: (1) Figures cover the Omaha-Council Bluffs, NE-IA Metropolitan Statistical Area—see Appendix B for areas included; (2) Rank ranges from 1 to 386 where 1 indicates greatest number of fraud and other consumer reports per 100,000 population
Source: Federal Trade Commission, Consumer Sentinel Network Data Book for January–December 2019

SPORTS

Professional Sports Teams

Team Name	League	Year Established
No teams are located in the metro area		

Source: Wikipedia, Major Professional Sports Teams of the United States and Canada, May 4, 2020

CLIMATE

Average and Extreme Temperatures

Temperature	Jan	Feb	Mar	Apr	May	Jun	Jul	Aug	Sep	Oct	Nov	Dec	Yr.
Extreme High (°F)	67	77	89	97	98	105	110	107	103	95	80	69	110
Average High (°F)	31	37	48	64	74	84	88	85	77	66	49	36	62
Average Temp. (°F)	22	27	38	52	63	73	77	75	66	54	39	27	51
Average Low (°F)	11	17	27	40	52	61	66	64	54	42	29	17	40
Extreme Low (°F)	-23	-21	-16	5	27	38	44	43	25	13	-9	-23	-23

Note: Figures cover the years 1948-1992
Source: National Climatic Data Center, International Station Meteorological Climate Summary, 9/96

Average Precipitation/Snowfall/Humidity

Precip./Humidity	Jan	Feb	Mar	Apr	May	Jun	Jul	Aug	Sep	Oct	Nov	Dec	Yr.
Avg. Precip. (in.)	0.8	0.9	2.0	2.8	4.3	4.0	3.7	3.8	3.4	2.1	1.5	0.9	30.1
Avg. Snowfall (in.)	7	6	7	1	Tr	0	0	0	Tr	Tr	3	6	29
Avg. Rel. Hum. 6am (%)	78	80	79	77	80	82	84	86	85	81	79	80	81
Avg. Rel. Hum. 3pm (%)	61	59	54	46	49	50	51	53	51	47	55	61	53

Note: Figures cover the years 1948-1992; Tr = Trace amounts (<0.05 in. of rain; <0.5 in. of snow)
Source: National Climatic Data Center, International Station Meteorological Climate Summary, 9/96

Weather Conditions

Temperature			Daytime Sky			Precipitation		
5°F & below	32°F & below	90°F & above	Clear	Partly cloudy	Cloudy	0.01 inch or more precip.	0.1 inch or more snow/ice	Thunder-storms
23	139	35	100	142	123	97	20	46

Note: Figures are average number of days per year and cover the years 1948-1992
Source: National Climatic Data Center, International Station Meteorological Climate Summary, 9/96

HAZARDOUS WASTE

Superfund Sites

The Omaha-Council Bluffs, NE-IA metro area is home to three sites on the EPA's Superfund National Priorities List: **Nebraska Ordnance Plant (Former)** (final); **Old Hwy 275 and N 288th Street** (final); **Omaha Lead** (final). There are a total of 1,387 Superfund sites with a status of proposed or final on the list in the U.S. *U.S. Environmental Protection Agency, National Priorities List, May 5, 2020*

AIR & WATER QUALITY

Air Quality Trends: Ozone

	1990	1995	2000	2005	2010	2012	2014	2016	2017	2018
MSA[1]	0.054	0.075	0.063	0.069	0.058	0.066	0.059	0.063	0.061	0.063
U.S.	0.088	0.089	0.082	0.080	0.073	0.075	0.067	0.069	0.068	0.069

Note: (1) Data covers the Omaha-Council Bluffs, NE-IA Metropolitan Statistical Area—see Appendix B for areas included. The values shown are the composite ozone concentration averages among trend sites based on the highest fourth daily maximum 8-hour concentration in parts per million. These trends are based on sites having an adequate record of monitoring data during the trend period. Data from exceptional events are included.
Source: U.S. Environmental Protection Agency, Air Quality Monitoring Information, "Air Quality Trends by City, 1990-2018"

Air Quality Index

Area	Percent of Days when Air Quality was...[2]					AQI Statistics[2]	
	Good	Moderate	Unhealthy for Sensitive Groups	Unhealthy	Very Unhealthy	Maximum	Median
MSA[1]	62.7	35.9	1.4	0.0	0.0	108	46

Note: (1) Data covers the Omaha-Council Bluffs, NE-IA Metropolitan Statistical Area—see Appendix B for areas included; (2) Based on 365 days with AQI data in 2018. Air Quality Index (AQI) is an index for reporting daily air quality. EPA calculates the AQI for five major air pollutants regulated by the Clean Air Act: ground-level ozone, particle pollution (aka particulate matter), carbon monoxide, sulfur dioxide, and nitrogen dioxide. The AQI runs from 0 to 500. The higher the AQI value, the greater the level of air pollution and the greater the health concern. There are six AQI categories: "Good" AQI is between 0 and 50. Air quality is considered satisfactory; "Moderate" AQI is between 51 and 100. Air quality is acceptable; "Unhealthy for Sensitive Groups" When AQI values are between 101 and 150, members of sensitive groups may experience health effects; "Unhealthy" When AQI values are between 151 and 200 everyone may begin to experience health effects; "Very Unhealthy" AQI values between 201 and 300 trigger a health alert; "Hazardous" AQI values over 300 trigger warnings of emergency conditions (not shown).
Source: U.S. Environmental Protection Agency, Air Quality Index Report, 2018

Air Quality Index Pollutants

| Area | Percent of Days when AQI Pollutant was...[2] | | | | | |
	Carbon Monoxide	Nitrogen Dioxide	Ozone	Sulfur Dioxide	Particulate Matter 2.5	Particulate Matter 10
MSA[1]	0.0	0.0	39.2	3.0	54.0	3.8

Note: (1) Data covers the Omaha-Council Bluffs, NE-IA Metropolitan Statistical Area—see Appendix B for areas included; (2) Based on 365 days with AQI data in 2018. The Air Quality Index (AQI) is an index for reporting daily air quality. EPA calculates the AQI for five major air pollutants regulated by the Clean Air Act: ground-level ozone, particle pollution (also known as particulate matter), carbon monoxide, sulfur dioxide, and nitrogen dioxide. The AQI runs from 0 to 500. The higher the AQI value, the greater the level of air pollution and the greater the health concern.
Source: U.S. Environmental Protection Agency, Air Quality Index Report, 2018

Maximum Air Pollutant Concentrations: Particulate Matter, Ozone, CO and Lead

	Particulate Matter 10 (ug/m^3)	Particulate Matter 2.5 Wtd AM (ug/m^3)	Particulate Matter 2.5 24-Hr (ug/m^3)	Ozone (ppm)	Carbon Monoxide (ppm)	Lead (ug/m^3)
MSA[1] Level	62	9.1	22	0.07	1	0.08
NAAQS[2]	150	15	35	0.075	9	0.15
Met NAAQS[2]	Yes	Yes	Yes	Yes	Yes	Yes

Note: (1) Data covers the Omaha-Council Bluffs, NE-IA Metropolitan Statistical Area—see Appendix B for areas included; Data from exceptional events are included; (2) National Ambient Air Quality Standards; ppm = parts per million; ug/m^3 = micrograms per cubic meter; n/a not available.
Concentrations: Particulate Matter 10 (coarse particulate)—highest second maximum 24-hour concentration; Particulate Matter 2.5 Wtd AM (fine particulate)—highest weighted annual mean concentration; Particulate Matter 2.5 24-Hour (fine particulate)—highest 98th percentile 24-hour concentration; Ozone—highest fourth daily maximum 8-hour concentration; Carbon Monoxide—highest second maximum non-overlapping 8-hour concentration; Lead—maximum running 3-month average
Source: U.S. Environmental Protection Agency, Air Quality Monitoring Information, "Air Quality Statistics by City, 2018"

Maximum Air Pollutant Concentrations: Nitrogen Dioxide and Sulfur Dioxide

	Nitrogen Dioxide AM (ppb)	Nitrogen Dioxide 1-Hr (ppb)	Sulfur Dioxide AM (ppb)	Sulfur Dioxide 1-Hr (ppb)	Sulfur Dioxide 24-Hr (ppb)
MSA[1] Level	n/a	n/a	n/a	37	n/a
NAAQS[2]	53	100	30	75	140
Met NAAQS[2]	n/a	n/a	n/a	Yes	n/a

Note: (1) Data covers the Omaha-Council Bluffs, NE-IA Metropolitan Statistical Area—see Appendix B for areas included; Data from exceptional events are included; (2) National Ambient Air Quality Standards; ppm = parts per million; ug/m^3 = micrograms per cubic meter; n/a not available.
Concentrations: Nitrogen Dioxide AM—highest arithmetic mean concentration; Nitrogen Dioxide 1-Hr—highest 98th percentile 1-hour daily maximum concentration; Sulfur Dioxide AM—highest annual mean concentration; Sulfur Dioxide 1-Hr—highest 99th percentile 1-hour daily maximum concentration; Sulfur Dioxide 24-Hr—highest second maximum 24-hour concentration
Source: U.S. Environmental Protection Agency, Air Quality Monitoring Information, "Air Quality Statistics by City, 2018"

Drinking Water

Water System Name	Pop. Served	Primary Water Source Type	Violations[1]
Metropolitan Utilities District	554,091	Surface	2

Note: (1) Total number of violations (both active and inactive) in the EPA database
Source: U.S. Environmental Protection Agency, Office of Ground Water and Drinking Water, Safe Drinking Water Information System (based on data extracted May 5, 2020)

Peoria, Illinois

Background

Like most Midwestern cities at the turn of the 19th century, Peoria started out as a military fort. Originally built in 1680 by French explorers, Fort Clark burned to the ground only to be rebuilt in 1813, following the War of 1812. By 1825, Fort Clark was renamed Peoria—the name of a local tribe of Native Americans. By 1845, Peoria was incorporated as a city.

Industry came to Peoria in 1830 when John Hamlin constructed a flour mill. Other industries soon followed including foundries, carriage factories, and furniture makers. In 1837, Andrew Eitle and Almiron S. Cole founded a distillery that made Peoria a world leader in liquor production, with the greatest liquor tax revenues of any other district in the country. In fact, at the turn of the century, the federal government received 42 percent of its revenue from liquor taxes—a major factor in the prohibition debate. And nobody produced more liquor than Peoria. According to The Peoria Historical Society, between the years of 1837 and 1919, Peoria had 24 breweries and 73 distilleries. The city took a huge financial hit during prohibition, although it became a bootleg capital with the dubious distinction of being home to mobsters such as the Shelton Brothers. This economic growth due to tax revenues would draw other industries to the area, the largest being farm equipment manufacturing, which included everything from wire fencing to wheels. Today, Keystone Steel & Wire is still the nation's leader in wire manufacturing after more than 120 years. Other top manufacturers in Peoria include Caterpillar Tractor Company and Komatsu-Dresser.

The health care industry employs over 25 percent of Peoria's work force, and reflects some of Peoria's greatest contributions to national health. During World War II, the "Peoria Plan for Human Rehabilitation" called for the creation of the Institute of Physical Medicine and Rehabilitation, one of the first such institutions designed to rehabilitate polio victims, and to help injured veterans integrate back into civilian life and work. In 1943, a moldy cantaloupe found in Peoria would produce the world's first Penicillium chrysogenum, used in producing industrial penicillin at the USDA's National Center for Agricultural Utilization Research, located in Peoria.

In the 1850s, German immigrants brought the concept of the public hall to Peoria, providing theater, music and the concomitant lectures and debates. At the time it was considered great success if an act could "play in Peoria." Perhaps Peoria's reputation for theater and debate is what brought Abraham Lincoln to the city in October of 1864, a first step in his journey to the White House and the Emancipation Proclamation in his three-hour response to the Kansas-Nebraska Act.

Peoria citizenry was largely divided during the Civil War. However, a local merchant, Moses Pettengill, opened his home to the Underground Railroad, and Peoria's Camp Lyon was a Union training ground for over 7500 Union soldiers.

Other notable events include Charles Lindbergh's connection with his first airmail route. Locals debate that, had Peoria provided backing for his transatlantic flight, Lindbergh's plane might have been called the "Spirit of Peoria." Music icon, Richard Whiting was from Peoria, and wrote an extraordinary number of hits, including "Til We Meet Again," "On the Good Ship Lollipop," "Hooray for Hollywood," and "Ain't We Got Fun." He died at 46.

The Glen Oak Park is a 100-acre park featuring a zoo, conservatory and gardens. Peoria has numerous performing arts venues that include the Peoria Symphony (the 10th oldest in the nation), Peoria Ballet Company, and Opera Illinois. The Lakeview Museum of Arts and Sciences displays folk art and African art, and also features a planetarium and children's science museum. A new museum square, The Block, houses the Peoria Riverfront Museum, a planetarium, and the Caterpillar World Visitors Center.

The best time to visit Peoria is between May and October when the weather is usually mild and dry.

Rankings

Business/Finance Rankings

- The Peoria metro area appeared on the Milken Institute "2020 Best Performing Cities" list. Rank: #189 out of 200 large metro areas. Criteria: job growth; wage and salary growth; high-tech output growth. *Milken Institute, "Best-Performing Cities 2020," February 26, 2020*

- *Forbes* ranked the 200 most populous metro areas to determine the nation's "Best Places for Business and Careers." The Peoria metro area was ranked #167. Criteria: costs (business and living); job growth (past and projected); income growth; quality of life; educational attainment (college and high school); projected economic growth; cultural and leisure opportunities; workplace tolerance laws; net migration patterns. *Forbes, "The Best Places for Business and Careers 2019: Seattle Still On Top," October 30, 2019*

Education Rankings

- Personal finance website *WalletHub* analyzed the 150 largest U.S. metropolitan statistical areas to determine where the most educated Americans are choosing to settle. Criteria: education levels; percentage of workers with degrees; education quality and attainment gap; public school quality rankings; quality and size of each metro area's universities. Peoria was ranked #93 (#1 = most educated city). *www.WalletHub.com, "2019's Most and Least Educated Cities in America," July 22, 2019*

Environmental Rankings

- Peoria was highlighted as one of the top 104 cleanest metro areas for short-term particle pollution (24-hour PM 2.5) in the U.S. during 2015 through 2017. Monitors in these cities reported no days with unhealthful PM 2.5 levels. *American Lung Association, "State of the Air 2019," April 24, 2019*

Health/Fitness Rankings

- The Peoria metro area ranked #139 out of 189 in The Gallup-Sharecare Well-Being Index. Criteria: purpose; social well being; financial health; community and physical health. Results are based on telephone interviews with adults, aged 18 and older, living in metropolitan areas in the 50 U.S. states and the District of Columbia. *Gallup-Sharecare, "State of American Well-Being, 2017 Community Well-Being Rankings" March 2018*

Real Estate Rankings

- The Peoria metro area was identified as one of the 20 most affordable housing markets in the U.S. in 2019. The area ranked #6 out of 180 markets. Criteria: qualification for a mortgage loan with a 10% down payment on a typical home. *National Association of Realtors®, Qualifying Income Based on Sales Price of Existing Single-Family Homes for Metropolitan Areas, 2019*

- Peoria was ranked #18 out of 238 metro areas in terms of housing affordability in 2019 by the National Association of Home Builders (#1 = most affordable). Criteria: the share of homes sold in that area affordable to a family earning the local median income, based on standard mortgage underwriting criteria. *National Association of Home Builders®, NAHB-Wells Fargo Housing Opportunity Index, 4th Quarter 2019*

- The nation's largest metro areas were analyzed in terms of the percentage of households entering some stage of foreclosure in 2018. The Peoria metro area ranked #5 out of 10 (#1 = highest foreclosure rate). *ATTOM Data Solutions, "2018 Year-End U.S. Foreclosure Market Report™," January 17, 2019*

Safety Rankings

- The National Insurance Crime Bureau ranked 382 metro areas in the U.S. in terms of per capita rates of vehicle theft. The Peoria metro area ranked #223 (#1 = highest rate). Criteria: number of vehicle theft offenses per 100,000 inhabitants in 2018. *National Insurance Crime Bureau, "Hot Spots 2018," June 25, 2019*

Seniors/Retirement Rankings

- From its Best Cities for Successful Aging indexes, the Milken Institute generated rankings for metropolitan areas, weighing data in nine categories—health care, wellness, living arrangements, transportation and convenience, financial characteristics, education, employment, community engagement, and overall livability. The Peoria metro area was ranked #134 overall in the small metro area category. *Milken Institute, "Best Cities for Successful Aging, 2017" March 14, 2017*

Business Environment

CITY FINANCES

City Government Finances

Component	2017 ($000)	2017 ($ per capita)
Total Revenues	207,363	1,802
Total Expenditures	225,369	1,959
Debt Outstanding	191,860	1,667
Cash and Securities[1]	323,297	2,810

Note: (1) Cash and security holdings of a government at the close of its fiscal year, including those of its dependent agencies, utilities, and liquor stores.
Source: U.S. Census Bureau, State & Local Government Finances 2017

City Government Revenue by Source

Source	2017 ($000)	2017 ($ per capita)	2017 (%)
General Revenue			
From Federal Government	4,379	38	2.1
From State Government	50,838	442	24.5
From Local Governments	0	0	0.0
Taxes			
Property	36,361	316	17.5
Sales and Gross Receipts	44,953	391	21.7
Personal Income	0	0	0.0
Corporate Income	0	0	0.0
Motor Vehicle License	0	0	0.0
Other Taxes	3,324	29	1.6
Current Charges	38,615	336	18.6
Liquor Store	0	0	0.0
Utility	0	0	0.0
Employee Retirement	21,476	187	10.4

Source: U.S. Census Bureau, State & Local Government Finances 2017

City Government Expenditures by Function

Function	2017 ($000)	2017 ($ per capita)	2017 (%)
General Direct Expenditures			
Air Transportation	0	0	0.0
Corrections	0	0	0.0
Education	0	0	0.0
Employment Security Administration	0	0	0.0
Financial Administration	0	0	0.0
Fire Protection	31,045	269	13.8
General Public Buildings	0	0	0.0
Governmental Administration, Other	11,631	101	5.2
Health	0	0	0.0
Highways	27,827	241	12.3
Hospitals	0	0	0.0
Housing and Community Development	243	2	0.1
Interest on General Debt	8,248	71	3.7
Judicial and Legal	0	0	0.0
Libraries	7,680	66	3.4
Parking	0	0	0.0
Parks and Recreation	0	0	0.0
Police Protection	39,593	344	17.6
Public Welfare	0	0	0.0
Sewerage	1,341	11	0.6
Solid Waste Management	8,999	78	4.0
Veterans' Services	0	0	0.0
Liquor Store	0	0	0.0
Utility	0	0	0.0
Employee Retirement	27,570	239	12.2

Source: U.S. Census Bureau, State & Local Government Finances 2017

DEMOGRAPHICS

Population Growth

Area	1990 Census	2000 Census	2010 Census	2018* Estimate	Population Growth (%) 1990-2018	2010-2018
City	114,341	112,936	115,007	114,512	0.1	-0.4
MSA[1]	358,552	366,899	379,186	374,426	4.4	-1.3
U.S.	248,709,873	281,421,906	308,745,538	322,903,030	29.8	4.6

Note: (1) Figures cover the Peoria, IL Metropolitan Statistical Area—see Appendix B for areas included; (*) 2014-2018 5-year estimated population
Source: U.S. Census Bureau, 1990 Census, Census 2000, Census 2010, 2014-2018 American Community Survey 5-Year Estimates

Household Size

Area	Persons in Household (%) One	Two	Three	Four	Five	Six	Seven or More	Average Household Size
City	37.5	31.4	13.8	9.7	4.6	2.0	1.0	2.40
MSA[1]	30.6	35.8	14.2	11.4	4.9	2.2	1.0	2.40
U.S.	27.7	33.9	15.7	13.0	6.0	2.3	1.4	2.60

Note: (1) Figures cover the Peoria, IL Metropolitan Statistical Area—see Appendix B for areas included
Source: U.S. Census Bureau, 2014-2018 American Community Survey 5-Year Estimates

Race

Area	White Alone[2] (%)	Black Alone[2] (%)	Asian Alone[2] (%)	AIAN[3] Alone[2] (%)	NHOPI[4] Alone[2] (%)	Other Race Alone[2] (%)	Two or More Races (%)
City	59.9	27.0	5.9	0.4	0.0	2.4	4.5
MSA[1]	84.7	9.2	2.4	0.2	0.0	0.9	2.5
U.S.	72.7	12.7	5.4	0.8	0.2	4.9	3.2

Note: (1) Figures cover the Peoria, IL Metropolitan Statistical Area—see Appendix B for areas included; (2) Alone is defined as not being in combination with one or more other races; (3) American Indian and Alaska Native; (4) Native Hawaiian and Other Pacific Islander
Source: U.S. Census Bureau, 2014-2018 American Community Survey 5-Year Estimates

Hispanic or Latino Origin

Area	Total (%)	Mexican (%)	Puerto Rican (%)	Cuban (%)	Other (%)
City	6.0	4.4	0.4	0.1	1.1
MSA[1]	3.4	2.5	0.2	0.1	0.6
U.S.	17.8	11.2	1.7	0.7	4.2

Note: Persons of Hispanic or Latino origin can be of any race; (1) Figures cover the Peoria, IL Metropolitan Statistical Area—see Appendix B for areas included
Source: U.S. Census Bureau, 2014-2018 American Community Survey 5-Year Estimates

Segregation

Type	Segregation Indices[1] 1990	2000	2010	2010 Rank[2]	Percent Change 1990-2000	1990-2010	2000-2010
Black/White	n/a	n/a	n/a	n/a	n/a	n/a	n/a
Asian/White	n/a	n/a	n/a	n/a	n/a	n/a	n/a
Hispanic/White	n/a	n/a	n/a	n/a	n/a	n/a	n/a

Note: All figures cover the Metropolitan Statistical Area—see Appendix B for areas included; Figures are based on an analysis of 1990, 2000, and 2010 Census Decennial Census tract data by William H. Frey, Brookings Institution and the University of Michigan Social Science Data Analysis Network. In this analysis all racial groups (whites, blacks, and asians) are non-Hispanic members of those races. Hispanics are shown as a separate category; (1) Segregation Indices are Dissimilarity Indices that measure the degree to which the minority group is distributed differently than whites across census tracts. They range from 0 (complete integration) to 100 (complete segregation) where the value indicates the percentage of the minority group that needs to move to be distributed exactly like whites; (2) Ranges from 1 (most segregated) to 102 (least segregated); n/a not available.
Source: www.CensusScope.org

Ancestry

Area	German	Irish	English	American	Italian	Polish	French[2]	Scottish	Dutch
City	19.1	11.8	7.0	5.1	3.3	2.1	1.9	1.2	1.1
MSA[1]	28.3	12.9	8.7	6.8	4.0	2.1	2.3	1.9	1.5
U.S.	13.7	9.9	7.3	6.4	5.2	2.8	2.4	1.7	1.2

Note: Figures are the percentage of the total population reporting a particular ancestry. The nine most commonly reported ancestries in the U.S. are shown. Figures include multiple ancestries (e.g. if a person reported being Irish and Italian, they were included in both columns); (1) Figures cover the Peoria, IL Metropolitan Statistical Area—see Appendix B for areas included; (2) Excludes Basque
Source: U.S. Census Bureau, 2014-2018 American Community Survey 5-Year Estimates

Foreign-born Population

Area	Any Foreign Country	Asia	Mexico	Europe	Caribbean	Central America[2]	South America	Africa	Canada
City	7.9	4.7	1.4	0.7	0.1	0.2	0.4	0.3	0.1
MSA[1]	3.6	1.9	0.6	0.5	0.0	0.1	0.2	0.1	0.1
U.S.	13.5	4.1	3.5	1.5	1.3	1.1	0.9	0.7	0.3

Note: (1) Figures cover the Peoria, IL Metropolitan Statistical Area—see Appendix B for areas included; (2) Excludes Mexico.
Source: U.S. Census Bureau, 2014-2018 American Community Survey 5-Year Estimates

Marital Status

Area	Never Married	Now Married[2]	Separated	Widowed	Divorced
City	40.4	40.0	1.5	5.9	12.3
MSA[1]	29.8	50.9	1.1	6.6	11.5
U.S.	33.3	48.1	2.0	5.8	10.8

Note: Figures are percentages and cover the population 15 years of age and older; (1) Figures cover the Peoria, IL Metropolitan Statistical Area—see Appendix B for areas included; (2) Excludes separated
Source: U.S. Census Bureau, 2014-2018 American Community Survey 5-Year Estimates

Disability by Age

Area	All Ages	Under 18 Years Old	18 to 64 Years Old	65 Years and Over
City	12.3	2.8	11.0	33.7
MSA[1]	11.7	3.2	9.3	32.8
U.S.	12.6	4.2	10.3	35.0

Note: Figures show percent of the civilian noninstitutionalized population that reported having a disability. Disability status is determined from six types of difficulty: vision, hearing, cognitive, ambulatory, self-care, and independent living. For children under 5 years old, hearing and vision difficulty are used to determine disability status. For children between the ages of 5 and 14, disability status is determined from hearing, vision, cognitive, ambulatory, and self-care difficulties. For people aged 15 years and older, they are considered to have a disability if they have difficulty with any one of the six difficulty types; Note: (1) Figures cover the Peoria, IL Metropolitan Statistical Area—see Appendix B for areas included
Source: U.S. Census Bureau, 2014-2018 American Community Survey 5-Year Estimates

Age

Area	Under Age 5	Age 5–19	Age 20–34	Age 35–44	Age 45–54	Age 55–64	Age 65–74	Age 75–84	Age 85+	Median Age
City	7.7	19.6	22.8	12.0	11.3	11.7	8.2	4.3	2.3	34.9
MSA[1]	6.5	19.4	18.8	12.3	12.7	13.5	9.4	5.1	2.5	39.2
U.S.	6.1	19.3	20.7	12.6	13.2	12.8	8.8	4.5	1.9	37.9

Note: (1) Figures cover the Peoria, IL Metropolitan Statistical Area—see Appendix B for areas included
Source: U.S. Census Bureau, 2014-2018 American Community Survey 5-Year Estimates

Gender

Area	Males	Females	Males per 100 Females
City	54,734	59,778	91.6
MSA[1]	183,307	191,119	95.9
U.S.	158,984,190	163,918,840	97.0

Note: (1) Figures cover the Peoria, IL Metropolitan Statistical Area—see Appendix B for areas included
Source: U.S. Census Bureau, 2014-2018 American Community Survey 5-Year Estimates

Religious Groups by Family

Area	Catholic	Baptist	Non-Den.	Methodist[2]	Lutheran	LDS[3]	Pente-costal	Presby-terian[4]	Muslim[5]	Judaism
MSA[1]	11.5	5.5	5.3	5.0	6.1	0.5	1.5	2.8	5.2	0.1
U.S.	19.1	9.3	4.0	4.0	2.3	2.0	1.9	1.6	0.8	0.7

Note: Figures are the number of adherents as a percentage of the total population; (1) Figures cover the Peoria, IL Metropolitan Statistical Area—see Appendix B for areas included; (2) Methodist/Pietist; (3) Latter Day Saints; (4) Reformed; (5) Figures are estimates
Source: Association of Statisticians of American Religious Bodies, 2010 U.S. Religion Census: Religious Congregations & Membership Study

Religious Groups by Tradition

Area	Catholic	Evangelical Protestant	Mainline Protestant	Other Tradition	Black Protestant	Orthodox
MSA[1]	11.5	18.9	11.1	6.2	0.9	0.1
U.S.	19.1	16.2	7.3	4.3	1.6	0.3

Note: Figures are the number of adherents as a percentage of the total population; (1) Figures cover the Peoria, IL Metropolitan Statistical Area—see Appendix B for areas included
Source: Association of Statisticians of American Religious Bodies, 2010 U.S. Religion Census: Religious Congregations & Membership Study

ECONOMY

Gross Metropolitan Product

Area	2017	2018	2019	2020	Rank[2]
MSA[1]	19.2	20.1	20.9	21.6	133

Note: Figures are in billions of dollars; (1) Figures cover the Peoria, IL Metropolitan Statistical Area—see Appendix B for areas included; (2) Rank is based on 2018 data and ranges from 1 to 381
Source: U.S. Conference of Mayors, U.S. Metro Economies: GMP & Employment 2018-2020, September 2019

Economic Growth

Area	2015-17 (%)	2018 (%)	2019 (%)	2020 (%)	Rank[2]
MSA[1]	-4.0	2.5	2.0	1.3	376
U.S.	1.9	2.9	2.3	2.1	–

Note: Figures are real gross metropolitan product (GMP) growth rates and represent average annual percent change; (1) Figures cover the Peoria, IL Metropolitan Statistical Area—see Appendix B for areas included; (2) Rank is based on 2017 2-year average annual percent change and ranges from 1 to 381
Source: U.S. Conference of Mayors, U.S. Metro Economies: GMP & Employment 2018-2020, September 2019

Metropolitan Area Exports

Area	2013	2014	2015	2016	2017	2018	Rank[2]
MSA[1]	12,184.5	11,234.8	9,826.9	7,260.1	9,403.6	9,683.6	39

Note: Figures are in millions of dollars; (1) Figures cover the Peoria, IL Metropolitan Statistical Area—see Appendix B for areas included; (2) Rank is based on 2018 data and ranges from 1 to 387
Source: U.S. Department of Commerce, International Trade Administration, Office of Trade and Economic Analysis, Industry and Analysis, Exports by Metropolitan Area, data extracted April 15, 2020

Building Permits

Area	Single-Family			Multi-Family			Total		
	2017	2018	Pct. Chg.	2017	2018	Pct. Chg.	2017	2018	Pct. Chg.
City	32	32	0.0	0	0	0.0	32	32	0.0
MSA[1]	247	228	-7.7	10	106	960.0	257	334	30.0
U.S.	820,000	855,300	4.3	462,000	473,500	2.5	1,282,000	1,328,800	3.7

Note: (1) Figures cover the Peoria, IL Metropolitan Statistical Area—see Appendix B for areas included; Figures represent new, privately-owned housing units authorized (unadjusted data); All permit data are based on estimates with imputation
Source: U.S. Census Bureau, Manufacturing, Mining, and Construction Statistics, Building Permits, 2017, 2018

Bankruptcy Filings

Area	Business Filings			Nonbusiness Filings		
	2018	2019	% Chg.	2018	2019	% Chg.
Peoria County	14	16	14.3	555	548	-1.3
U.S.	22,232	22,780	2.5	751,186	752,160	0.1

Note: Business filings include Chapter 7, Chapter 9, Chapter 11, Chapter 12, Chapter 13, Chapter 15, and Section 304; Nonbusiness filings include Chapter 7, Chapter 11, and Chapter 13
Source: Administrative Office of the U.S. Courts, Business and Nonbusiness Bankruptcy, County Cases Commenced by Chapter of the Bankruptcy Code, During the 12-Month Period Ending December 31, 2018 and Business and Nonbusiness Bankruptcy, County Cases Commenced by Chapter of the Bankruptcy Code, During the 12-Month Period Ending December 31, 2019

Housing Vacancy Rates

Area	Gross Vacancy Rate[2] (%)			Year-Round Vacancy Rate[3] (%)			Rental Vacancy Rate[4] (%)			Homeowner Vacancy Rate[5] (%)		
	2017	2018	2019	2017	2018	2019	2017	2018	2019	2017	2018	2019
MSA[1]	n/a	n/a	n/a	n/a	n/a	n/a	n/a	n/a	n/a	n/a	n/a	n/a
U.S.	12.7	12.3	12.0	9.9	9.7	9.5	7.2	6.9	6.7	1.6	1.5	1.4

Note: (1) Figures cover the Peoria, IL Metropolitan Statistical Area—see Appendix B for areas included; (2) The percentage of the total housing inventory that is vacant; (3) The percentage of the housing inventory (excluding seasonal units) that is year-round vacant; (4) The percentage of rental inventory that is vacant for rent; (5) The percentage of homeowner inventory that is vacant for sale; n/a not available
Source: U.S. Census Bureau, Housing Vacancies and Homeownership Annual Statistics: 2017, 2018, 2019

INCOME

Income

Area	Per Capita ($)	Median Household ($)	Average Household ($)
City	30,158	50,688	72,101
MSA[1]	31,998	59,047	77,892
U.S.	32,621	60,293	84,938

Note: (1) Figures cover the Peoria, IL Metropolitan Statistical Area—see Appendix B for areas included
Source: U.S. Census Bureau, 2014-2018 American Community Survey 5-Year Estimates

Household Income Distribution

Area	Percent of Households Earning							
	Under $15,000	$15,000 -$24,999	$25,000 -$34,999	$35,000 -$49,999	$50,000 -$74,999	$75,000 -$99,999	$100,000 -$149,999	$150,000 and up
City	16.6	11.5	9.5	11.9	17.8	11.3	11.6	9.7
MSA[1]	10.2	9.2	9.2	13.4	19.6	13.6	14.8	10.1
U.S.	10.9	9.3	9.3	12.6	17.5	12.5	14.6	13.3

Note: (1) Figures cover the Peoria, IL Metropolitan Statistical Area—see Appendix B for areas included
Source: U.S. Census Bureau, 2014-2018 American Community Survey 5-Year Estimates

Poverty Rate

Area	All Ages	Under 18 Years Old	18 to 64 Years Old	65 Years and Over
City	20.7	26.3	20.7	11.2
MSA[1]	12.4	16.6	12.3	6.9
U.S.	14.1	19.5	13.2	9.3

Note: Figures are percentage of people whose income during the past 12 months was below the poverty level; (1) Figures cover the Peoria, IL Metropolitan Statistical Area—see Appendix B for areas included
Source: U.S. Census Bureau, 2014-2018 American Community Survey 5-Year Estimates

EMPLOYMENT

Labor Force and Employment

Area	Civilian Labor Force			Workers Employed		
	Dec. 2018	Dec. 2019	% Chg.	Dec. 2018	Dec. 2019	% Chg.
City	51,731	50,615	-2.2	48,571	47,924	-1.3
MSA[1]	177,109	173,154	-2.2	167,247	165,096	-1.3
U.S.	162,510,000	164,007,000	0.9	156,481,000	158,504,000	1.3

Note: Data is not seasonally adjusted and covers workers 16 years of age and older; (1) Figures cover the Peoria, IL Metropolitan Statistical Area—see Appendix B for areas included
Source: Bureau of Labor Statistics, Local Area Unemployment Statistics

Unemployment Rate

Area	2019											
	Jan.	Feb.	Mar.	Apr.	May	Jun.	Jul.	Aug.	Sep.	Oct.	Nov.	Dec.
City	6.8	6.0	5.8	4.6	4.6	5.1	5.4	5.5	5.0	4.9	5.0	5.3
MSA[1]	6.5	5.8	5.5	4.1	3.8	4.3	4.6	4.6	4.2	4.2	4.2	4.7
U.S.	4.4	4.1	3.9	3.3	3.4	3.8	4.0	3.8	3.3	3.3	3.3	3.4

Note: Data is not seasonally adjusted and covers workers 16 years of age and older; (1) Figures cover the
Peoria, IL Metropolitan Statistical Area—see Appendix B for areas included
Source: Bureau of Labor Statistics, Local Area Unemployment Statistics

Average Wages

Occupation	$/Hr.	Occupation	$/Hr.
Accountants and Auditors	38.50	Maintenance and Repair Workers	20.70
Automotive Mechanics	18.70	Marketing Managers	72.70
Bookkeepers	18.30	Network and Computer Systems Admin.	35.60
Carpenters	30.00	Nurses, Licensed Practical	22.20
Cashiers	11.10	Nurses, Registered	32.40
Computer Programmers	36.70	Nursing Assistants	13.60
Computer Systems Analysts	45.80	Office Clerks, General	17.20
Computer User Support Specialists	24.50	Physical Therapists	41.00
Construction Laborers	22.10	Physicians	111.80
Cooks, Restaurant	13.00	Plumbers, Pipefitters and Steamfitters	36.20
Customer Service Representatives	15.30	Police and Sheriff's Patrol Officers	24.00
Dentists	102.90	Postal Service Mail Carriers	25.00
Electricians	31.60	Real Estate Sales Agents	20.80
Engineers, Electrical	n/a	Retail Salespersons	13.10
Fast Food and Counter Workers	10.40	Sales Representatives, Technical/Scientific	40.60
Financial Managers	60.20	Secretaries, Exc. Legal/Medical/Executive	16.10
First-Line Supervisors of Office Workers	27.10	Security Guards	17.50
General and Operations Managers	52.70	Surgeons	n/a
Hairdressers/Cosmetologists	15.30	Teacher Assistants, Exc. Postsecondary*	12.20
Home Health and Personal Care Aides	12.10	Teachers, Secondary School, Exc. Sp. Ed.*	25.50
Janitors and Cleaners	12.10	Telemarketers	15.50
Landscaping/Groundskeeping Workers	13.90	Truck Drivers, Heavy/Tractor-Trailer	21.40
Lawyers	63.10	Truck Drivers, Light/Delivery Services	17.90
Maids and Housekeeping Cleaners	12.10	Waiters and Waitresses	10.40

Note: Wage data covers the Peoria, IL Metropolitan Statistical Area—see Appendix B for areas included; (*)
Hourly wages were calculated from annual wage data based on a 40 hour work week; n/a not available.
Source: Bureau of Labor Statistics, Metro Area Occupational Employment & Wage Estimates, May 2019

Employment by Occupation

Occupation Classification	City (%)	MSA[1] (%)	U.S. (%)
Management, Business, Science, and Arts	41.5	37.0	37.9
Natural Resources, Construction, and Maintenance	4.9	8.3	8.9
Production, Transportation, and Material Moving	11.9	14.1	13.3
Sales and Office	22.1	23.0	22.1
Service	19.6	17.6	17.9

Note: Figures cover employed civilians 16 years of age and older; (1) Figures cover the Peoria, IL
Metropolitan Statistical Area—see Appendix B for areas included
Source: U.S. Census Bureau, 2014-2018 American Community Survey 5-Year Estimates

Employment by Industry

Sector	MSA[1]		U.S.
	Number of Employees	Percent of Total	Percent of Total
Construction, Mining, and Logging	7,200	4.3	5.4
Education and Health Services	31,400	18.6	16.1
Financial Activities	7,000	4.1	5.8
Government	20,900	12.4	15.0
Information	1,900	1.1	1.9
Leisure and Hospitality	16,400	9.7	10.8
Manufacturing	22,600	13.4	8.4
Other Services	7,700	4.6	3.9
Professional and Business Services	22,200	13.1	14.1
Retail Trade	18,200	10.8	10.6
Transportation, Warehousing, and Utilities	7,100	4.2	4.2
Wholesale Trade	6,500	3.8	3.9

Note: Figures are non-farm employment as of December 2019. Figures are not seasonally adjusted and include workers 16 years of age and older; (1) Figures cover the Peoria, IL Metropolitan Statistical Area—see Appendix B for areas included
Source: Bureau of Labor Statistics, Current Employment Statistics, Employment, Hours, and Earnings

Occupations with Greatest Projected Employment Growth: 2019 – 2021

Occupation[1]	2019 Employment	2021 Projected Employment	Numeric Employment Change	Percent Employment Change
Combined Food Preparation and Serving Workers, Including Fast Food	140,460	145,280	4,820	3.4
Registered Nurses	133,320	137,300	3,980	3.0
Personal Care Aides	56,160	59,830	3,670	6.5
Laborers and Freight, Stock, and Material Movers, Hand	158,620	162,170	3,550	2.2
Insurance Sales Agents	49,730	52,420	2,690	5.4
Heavy and Tractor-Trailer Truck Drivers	73,100	75,610	2,510	3.4
General and Operations Managers	120,880	123,200	2,320	1.9
Cooks, Restaurant	47,520	49,620	2,100	4.4
Janitors and Cleaners, Except Maids and Housekeeping Cleaners	85,160	86,710	1,550	1.8
Financial Managers	40,420	41,900	1,480	3.7

Note: Projections cover Illinois; (1) Sorted by numeric employment change
Source: www.projectionscentral.com, State Occupational Projections, 2019–2021 Short-Term Projections

Fastest Growing Occupations: 2019 – 2021

Occupation[1]	2019 Employment	2021 Projected Employment	Numeric Employment Change	Percent Employment Change
Actuaries	1,940	2,070	130	6.7
Personal Care Aides	56,160	59,830	3,670	6.5
Statisticians	1,910	2,030	120	6.3
Nurse Practitioners	8,130	8,610	480	5.9
Physician Assistants	3,800	4,020	220	5.8
Insurance Sales Agents	49,730	52,420	2,690	5.4
Operations Research Analysts	5,080	5,350	270	5.3
Computer Numerically Controlled Machine Tool Programmers, Metal and Plastic	1,150	1,210	60	5.2
Veterinary Technologists and Technicians	4,010	4,210	200	5.0
Massage Therapists	6,720	7,050	330	4.9

Note: Projections cover Illinois; (1) Sorted by percent employment change and excludes occupations with numeric employment change less than 50
Source: www.projectionscentral.com, State Occupational Projections, 2019–2021 Short-Term Projections

TAXES

State Corporate Income Tax Rates

State	Tax Rate (%)	Income Brackets ($)	Num. of Brackets	Financial Institution Tax Rate (%)[a]	Federal Income Tax Ded.
Illinois	9.5 (h)	Flat rate	1	9.5 (h)	No

Note: Tax rates as of January 1, 2020; (a) Rates listed are the corporate income tax rate applied to financial institutions or excise taxes based on income; (h) The Illinois rate of 9.5% is the sum of a corporate income tax rate of 7.0% plus a replacement tax of 2.5%.
Source: Federation of Tax Administrators, State Corporate Income Tax Rates, January 1, 2020

State Individual Income Tax Rates

State	Tax Rate (%)	Income Brackets ($)	Personal Exemptions ($)			Standard Ded. ($)	
			Single	Married	Depend.	Single	Married
Illinois (a)	4.95	Flat rate	2,275	4,550	2,275	–	–

Note: Tax rates as of January 1, 2020; Local- and county-level taxes are not included; Federal income tax is not deductible on state income tax returns; (a) 19 states have statutory provision for automatically adjusting to the rate of inflation the dollar values of the income tax brackets, standard deductions, and/or personal exemptions. Michigan indexes the personal exemption only. Oregon does not index the income brackets for $125,000 and over.
Source: Federation of Tax Administrators, State Individual Income Tax Rates, January 1, 2020

Various State Sales and Excise Tax Rates

State	State Sales Tax (%)	Gasoline[1] (¢/gal.)	Cigarette[2] ($/pack)	Spirits[3] ($/gal.)	Wine[4] ($/gal.)	Beer[5] ($/gal.)	Recreational Marijuana (%)
Illinois	6.25	53.65	2.98	8.55	1.39	0.23	(d)

Note: All tax rates as of January 1, 2020; (1) The American Petroleum Institute has developed a methodology for determining the average tax rate on a gallon of fuel. Rates may include any of the following: excise taxes, environmental fees, storage tank fees, other fees or taxes, general sales tax, and local taxes; (2) The federal excise tax of $1.0066 per pack and local taxes are not included; (3) Rates are those applicable to off-premise sales of 40% alcohol by volume (a.b.v.) distilled spirits in 750ml containers. Local excise taxes are excluded; (4) Rates are those applicable to off-premise sales of 11% a.b.v. non-carbonated wine in 750ml containers; (5) Rates are those applicable to off-premise sales of 4.7% a.b.v. beer in 12 ounce containers; (d) 7% excise tax of value at wholesale level, 10% tax on cannabis flower or products with less than 35% THC, 20% tax on products infused with cannabis, such as edible products, 25% tax on any product with a THC concentration higher than 35%
Source: Tax Foundation, 2020 Facts & Figures: How Does Your State Compare?

State Business Tax Climate Index Rankings

State	Overall Rank	Corporate Tax Rank	Individual Income Tax Rank	Sales Tax Rank	Property Tax Rank	Unemployment Insurance Tax Rank
Illinois	35	36	13	33	40	40

Note: The index is a measure of how each state's tax laws affect economic performance. The lower the rank, the more favorable a state's tax system is for business. States without a given tax are given a ranking of 1. The scores/rankings for the District of Columbia do not affect other states. The 2020 index represents the tax climate as of July 1, 2019.
Source: Tax Foundation, State Business Tax Climate Index 2020

COMMERCIAL UTILITIES

Typical Monthly Electric Bills

Area	Commercial Service ($/month)		Industrial Service ($/month)	
	1,500 kWh	40 kW demand 14,000 kWh	1,000 kW demand 200,000 kWh	50,000 kW demand 32,500,000 kWh
City	n/a	n/a	n/a	n/a
Average[1]	203	1,612	25,706	2,520,671

Note: Figures are based on annualized rates; (1) Average based on 187 utilities surveyed; n/a not available
Source: Edison Electric Institute, Typical Bills and Average Rates Report, Summer 2019

TRANSPORTATION

Means of Transportation to Work

Area	Car/Truck/Van		Public Transportation			Bicycle	Walked	Other Means	Worked at Home
	Drove Alone	Car-pooled	Bus	Subway	Railroad				
City	79.7	9.6	3.1	0.0	0.0	0.5	2.8	1.2	3.1
MSA[1]	84.6	7.6	1.2	0.0	0.0	0.4	2.0	0.9	3.3
U.S.	76.4	9.1	2.5	1.9	0.6	0.6	2.7	1.3	4.9

Note: Figures are percentages and cover workers 16 years of age and older; (1) Figures cover the Peoria, IL Metropolitan Statistical Area—see Appendix B for areas included
Source: U.S. Census Bureau, 2014-2018 American Community Survey 5-Year Estimates

Travel Time to Work

Area	Less Than 10 Minutes	10 to 19 Minutes	20 to 29 Minutes	30 to 44 Minutes	45 to 59 Minutes	60 to 89 Minutes	90 Minutes or More
City	18.4	49.4	19.8	7.7	2.0	1.8	0.8
MSA[1]	17.4	35.5	24.9	15.2	3.8	1.8	1.4
U.S.	12.5	28.7	20.9	20.7	8.2	6.3	2.8

Note: Note: Figures are percentages and include workers 16 years old and over; (1) Figures cover the Peoria, IL Metropolitan Statistical Area—see Appendix B for areas included
Source: U.S. Census Bureau, 2014-2018 American Community Survey 5-Year Estimates

Key Congestion Measures

Area	1982	1992	2002	2012	2017
Annual Hours of Delay, Total (000)	n/a	n/a	n/a	n/a	3,556
Annual Hours of Delay, Per Auto Commuter	n/a	n/a	n/a	n/a	13
Annual Congestion Cost, Total (million $)	n/a	n/a	n/a	n/a	73
Annual Congestion Cost, Per Auto Commuter ($)	n/a	n/a	n/a	n/a	258

Note: n/a not available
Source: Texas A&M Transportation Institute, 2019 Urban Mobility Report

Freeway Travel Time Index

Area	1982	1987	1992	1997	2002	2007	2012	2017
Urban Area Index[1]	n/a	n/a	n/a	n/a	n/a	n/a	n/a	1.05
Urban Area Rank[1,2]	n/a	n/a	n/a	n/a	n/a	n/a	n/a	n/a

Note: Freeway Travel Time Index—the ratio of travel time in the peak period to the travel time at free-flow conditions. For example, a value of 1.30 indicates a 20-minute free-flow trip takes 26 minutes in the peak (20 minutes x 1.30 = 26 minutes); (1) Covers the Peoria IL urban area; (2) Rank is based on 101 larger urban areas (#1 = highest travel time index); n/a not available
Source: Texas A&M Transportation Institute, 2019 Urban Mobility Report

Public Transportation

Agency Name / Mode of Transportation	Vehicles Operated in Maximum Service[1]	Annual Unlinked Passenger Trips[2] (in thous.)	Annual Passenger Miles[3] (in thous.)
Greater Peoria Mass Transit District			
Bus (directly operated)	45	2,685.7	16,383.0
Demand Response (purchased transportation)	37	140.9	927.2

Note: (1) Number of revenue vehicles operated by the given mode and type of service to meet the annual maximum service requirement. This is the revenue vehicle count during the peak season of the year; on the week and day that maximum service is provided. Vehicles operated in maximum service (VOMS) exclude atypical days and one-time special events; (2) Number of passengers who boarded public transportation vehicles. Passengers are counted each time they board a vehicle no matter how many vehicles they use to travel from their origin to their destination. (3) Sum of the distances ridden by all passengers during the entire fiscal year.
Source: Federal Transit Administration, National Transit Database, 2018

Air Transportation

Airport Name and Code / Type of Service	Passenger Airlines[1]	Passenger Enplanements	Freight Carriers[2]	Freight (lbs)
General Wayne A. Downing Peoria International Airport (PIA)				
Domestic service (U.S. carriers - 2019)	12	340,605	4	17,112,493
International service (U.S. carriers - 2018)	0	0	0	0

Note: (1) Includes all U.S.-based major, minor and commuter airlines that carried at least one passenger during the year; (2) Includes all U.S.-based airlines and freight carriers that transported at least one pound of freight during the year.
Source: Bureau of Transportation Statistics, The Intermodal Transportation Database, Air Carriers: T-100 Domestic Market (U.S. Carriers), 2019; Bureau of Transportation Statistics, The Intermodal Transportation Database, Air Carriers: T-100 International Market (U.S. Carriers), 2018

Other Transportation Statistics

Major Highways: I-74; I-474
Amtrak Service: Yes
Major Waterways/Ports: Illinois River
Source: Amtrak.com; Google Maps

BUSINESSES

Major Business Headquarters

Company Name	Industry	Rankings Fortune[1]	Forbes[2]
Caterpillar	Construction and Farm Machinery	58	-

Note: (1) Companies that produce a 10-K are ranked 1 to 500 based on 2018 revenue; (2) All private companies with at least $2 billion in annual revenue through the end of their most current fiscal year are ranked 1 to 228; companies listed are headquartered in the city; dashes indicate no ranking
Source: Fortune, "Fortune 500," June 2019; Forbes, "America's Largest Private Companies," 2019 Rankings

Minority- and Women-Owned Businesses

Group	All Firms		Firms with Paid Employees			
	Firms	Sales ($000)	Firms	Sales ($000)	Employees	Payroll ($000)
AIAN[1]	75	(s)	22	(s)	100 - 249	(s)
Asian	292	165,321	134	161,366	1,421	37,138
Black	1,295	44,510	37	21,608	228	5,459
Hispanic	186	(s)	44	(s)	250 - 499	(s)
NHOPI[2]	n/a	n/a	n/a	n/a	n/a	n/a
Women	2,741	527,889	393	461,825	3,548	105,789
All Firms	8,053	17,242,461	2,812	17,046,888	93,399	5,965,582

Note: Figures cover firms located in the city; minority- and women-owned business are defined as firms in which the corresponding group own 51% or more of the stock or equity of the company; (1) American Indian and Alaska Native; (2) Native Hawaiian and Other Pacific Islander; (s) estimates are suppressed when publication standards are not met; n/a not available
Source: U.S. Census Bureau, 2012 Economic Census, Survey of Business Owners

HOTELS & CONVENTION CENTERS

Hotels, Motels and Vacation Rentals

Area	5 Star		4 Star		3 Star		2 Star		1 Star		Not Rated	
	Num.	Pct.[3]	Num.	Pct.[3]	Num.	Pct.[3]	Num.	Pct.[3]	Num.	Pct.[3]	Num.	Pct.[3]
City[1]	0	0.0	1	2.2	11	23.9	15	32.6	0	0.0	19	41.3
Total[2]	266	1.3	1,517	7.2	4,627	21.8	3,210	15.1	3,974	18.7	7,601	35.9

Note: (1) Figures cover Peoria and vicinity; (2) Figures cover all 100 cities in this book; (3) Percentage of hotels which have a given star rating; Star ratings are determined by priceline.com and offer an indication of the general quality of a particular hotel.
Source: priceline.com, April 27, 2020

Major Convention Centers

Name	Overall Space (sq. ft.)	Exhibit Space (sq. ft.)	Meeting Space (sq. ft.)	Meeting Rooms
Peoria Civic Center	900,000	110,000	n/a	16

Note: Table includes convention centers located in the Peoria, IL metro area; n/a not available
Source: Original research

Living Environment

COST OF LIVING

Cost of Living Index

Composite Index	Groceries	Housing	Utilities	Trans-portation	Health Care	Misc. Goods/ Services
92.9	89.7	76.5	93.7	106.3	96.8	102.7

Note: The Cost of Living Index measures regional differences in the cost of consumer goods and services, excluding taxes and non-consumer expenditures, for professional and managerial households in the top income quintile. It is based on more than 50,000 prices covering almost 60 different items for which prices are collected three times a year by chambers of commerce, economic development organizations or university applied economic centers in each participating urban area. The numbers shown should be read as a percentage above or below the national average of 100. For example, a value of 115.4 in the groceries column indicates that grocery prices are 15.4% higher than the national average. Small differences in the index numbers should not be interpreted as significant; Figures cover the Peoria IL urban area.
Source: The Council for Community and Economic Research, ACCRA Cost of Living Index, 2019

Grocery Prices

Area[1]	T-Bone Steak ($/pound)	Frying Chicken ($/pound)	Whole Milk ($/half gal.)	Eggs ($/dozen)	Orange Juice ($/64 oz.)	Coffee ($/11.5 oz.)
City[2]	10.48	1.03	0.88	1.02	3.36	4.41
Avg.	11.40	1.41	1.93	1.54	3.51	4.30
Min.	7.40	0.92	0.85	0.58	2.67	2.90
Max.	15.58	2.68	4.09	4.18	5.57	8.10

Note: (1) Values for the local area are compared with the average, minimum and maximum values for all 290 areas in the Cost of Living Index; (2) Figures cover the Peoria IL urban area; T-Bone Steak (price per pound); Frying Chicken (price per pound, whole fryer); Whole Milk (half gallon carton); Eggs (price per dozen, Grade A, large); Orange Juice (64 oz. Tropicana or Florida Natural); Coffee (11.5 oz. can, vacuum-packed, Maxwell House, Hills Bros, or Folgers).
Source: The Council for Community and Economic Research, ACCRA Cost of Living Index, 2019

Housing and Utility Costs

Area[1]	New Home Price ($)	Apartment Rent ($/month)	All Electric ($/month)	Part Electric ($/month)	Other Energy ($/month)	Telephone ($/month)
City[2]	294,117	765	-	75.48	69.26	187.00
Avg.	362,090	1,142	174.35	100.00	67.76	179.60
Min.	198,329	501	91.58	31.44	28.51	165.30
Max.	2,074,561	5,050	388.18	239.41	306.15	207.90

Note: (1) Values for the local area are compared with the average, minimum and maximum values for all 290 areas in the Cost of Living Index; (2) Figures cover the Peoria IL urban area; New Home Price (2,400 sf living area, 8,000 sf lot, in urban area with full utilities); Apartment Rent (950 sf 2 bedroom/1.5 or 2 bath, unfurnished, excluding all utilities except water); All Electric (average monthly cost for an all-electric home); Part Electric (average monthly cost for a part-electric home); Other Energy (average monthly cost for natural gas, fuel oil, coal, wood, and any other forms of energy except electricity); Telephone (price includes the base monthly rate plus taxes and fees for three lines of mobile phone service).
Source: The Council for Community and Economic Research, ACCRA Cost of Living Index, 2019

Health Care, Transportation, and Other Costs

Area[1]	Doctor ($/visit)	Dentist ($/visit)	Optometrist ($/visit)	Gasoline ($/gallon)	Beauty Salon ($/visit)	Men's Shirt ($)
City[2]	109.58	93.39	119.04	2.76	24.64	37.50
Avg.	114.85	97.58	106.10	2.50	38.15	32.15
Min.	39.00	62.22	52.22	1.53	16.88	10.27
Max.	206.67	151.53	258.67	3.79	79.29	59.30

Note: (1) Values for the local area are compared with the average, minimum and maximum values for all 290 areas in the Cost of Living Index; (2) Figures cover the Peoria IL urban area; Doctor (general practitioners routine exam of an established patient); Dentist (adult teeth cleaning and periodic oral examination); Optometrist (full vision eye exam for established adult patient); Gasoline (one gallon regular unleaded, national brand, including all taxes, cash price at self-service pump if available); Beauty Salon (woman's shampoo, trim, and blow-dry); Men's Shirt (cotton/polyester dress shirt, pinpoint weave, long sleeves).
Source: The Council for Community and Economic Research, ACCRA Cost of Living Index, 2019

HOUSING

House Price Index (HPI)

Area	National Ranking[2]	Quarterly Change (%)	One-Year Change (%)	Five-Year Change (%)
MSA[1]	227	0.59	1.77	3.09
U.S.[3]	–	1.26	5.09	32.88

Note: The HPI is a weighted repeat sales index. It measures average price changes in repeat sales or refinancings on the same properties. This information is obtained by reviewing repeat mortgage transactions on single-family properties whose mortgages have been purchased or securitized by Fannie Mae or Freddie Mac in January 1975; (1) Figures cover the Peoria, IL Metropolitan Statistical Area—see Appendix B for areas included; (2) Rankings are based on annual percentage change for all metro areas containing at least 15,000 transactions over the last 10 years and ranges from 1 to 232; (3) figures based on a weighted average of Census Division estimates using a seasonally adjusted, purchase-only index; all figures are for the period ending December 31, 2019
Source: Federal Housing Finance Agency, House Price Index, February 25, 2020

Median Single-Family Home Prices

Area	2017	2018	2019p	Percent Change 2018 to 2019
MSA[1]	122.6	124.3	120.7	-2.9
U.S. Average	248.8	261.6	274.6	5.0

Note: Figures are median sales prices of existing single-family homes in thousands of dollars; (p) preliminary; (1) Figures cover the Peoria, IL Metropolitan Statistical Area—see Appendix B for areas included
Source: National Association of Realtors, Median Sales Price of Existing Single-Family Homes for Metropolitan Areas, 4th Quarter 2019

Qualifying Income Based on Median Sales Price of Existing Single-Family Homes

Area	With 5% Down ($)	With 10% Down ($)	With 20% Down ($)
MSA[1]	25,906	24,543	21,816
U.S. Average	58,663	55,575	49,400

Note: Figures are preliminary; Qualifying income is based on a mortgage rate of 3.76%. Monthly principal and interest payment is limited to 25% of income; (1) Figures cover the Peoria, IL Metropolitan Statistical Area—see Appendix B for areas included
Source: National Association of Realtors, Qualifying Income Based on Median Sales Price of Existing Single-Family Homes for Metropolitan Areas, 4th Quarter 2019

Median Apartment Condo-Coop Home Prices

Area	2017	2018	2019p	Percent Change 2018 to 2019
MSA[1]	n/a	n/a	n/a	n/a
U.S. Average	234.3	241.0	249.5	3.5

Note: Figures are median sales prices of existing apartment condo-coop homes in thousands of dollars; (p) preliminary; n/a not available; (1) Figures cover the Peoria, IL Metropolitan Statistical Area—see Appendix B for areas included
Source: National Association of Realtors, Median Sales Price of Existing Apartment Condo-Coop Homes for Metropolitan Areas, 4th Quarter 2019

Home Value Distribution

Area	Under $50,000	$50,000 -$99,999	$100,000 -$149,999	$150,000 -$199,999	$200,000 -$299,999	$300,000 -$499,999	$500,000 -$999,999	$1,000,000 or more
City	12.6	25.4	22.4	15.5	14.2	7.2	2.4	0.4
MSA[1]	7.7	24.7	24.0	18.3	15.6	7.5	1.7	0.4
U.S.	7.6	13.0	14.0	14.3	19.2	18.3	10.5	3.1

Note: Figures are percentages and cover owner-occupied housing units; (1) Figures cover the Peoria, IL Metropolitan Statistical Area—see Appendix B for areas included
Source: U.S. Census Bureau, 2014-2018 American Community Survey 5-Year Estimates

Homeownership Rate

Area	2011 (%)	2012 (%)	2013 (%)	2014 (%)	2015 (%)	2016 (%)	2017 (%)	2018 (%)	2019 (%)
MSA[1]	n/a	n/a	n/a	n/a	n/a	n/a	n/a	n/a	n/a
U.S.	66.1	65.4	65.1	64.5	63.7	63.4	63.9	64.4	64.6

Note: (1) Figures cover the Peoria, IL Metropolitan Statistical Area—see Appendix B for areas included; n/a not available
Source: U.S. Census Bureau, Housing Vacancies and Homeownership Annual Statistics: 2011-2019

Year Housing Structure Built

Area	2010 or Later	2000 -2009	1990 -1999	1980 -1989	1970 -1979	1960 -1969	1950 -1959	1940 -1949	Before 1940	Median Year
City	3.1	8.6	7.3	7.3	14.1	13.0	14.6	8.5	23.4	1963
MSA[1]	2.8	9.1	8.9	6.3	16.9	13.1	14.9	8.1	20.0	1965
U.S.	4.1	14.3	13.9	13.5	15.3	10.7	10.4	5.0	12.8	1977

Note: Figures are percentages except for Median Year; Note: (1) Figures cover the Peoria, IL Metropolitan Statistical Area—see Appendix B for areas included
Source: U.S. Census Bureau, 2014-2018 American Community Survey 5-Year Estimates

Gross Monthly Rent

Area	Under $500	$500 -$999	$1,000 -$1,499	$1,500 -$1,999	$2,000 -$2,499	$2,500 -$2,999	$3,000 and up	Median ($)
City	16.4	59.4	18.2	3.7	1.2	0.6	0.5	784
MSA[1]	15.7	62.0	17.1	2.6	1.2	0.5	0.9	758
U.S.	9.8	38.5	29.6	12.9	5.1	2.1	2.0	1,023

Note: Figures are percentages except for Median; Gross rent is the contract rent plus the estimated average monthly cost of utilities (electricity, gas, and water and sewer) and fuels (oil, coal, kerosene, wood, etc.) if these are paid by the renter (or paid for the renter by someone else); (1) Figures cover the Peoria, IL Metropolitan Statistical Area—see Appendix B for areas included
Source: U.S. Census Bureau, 2014-2018 American Community Survey 5-Year Estimates

HEALTH

Health Risk Factors

Category	MSA[1] (%)	U.S. (%)
Adults aged 18–64 who have any kind of health care coverage	n/a	87.3
Adults who reported being in good or better health	n/a	82.4
Adults who have been told they have high blood cholesterol	n/a	33.0
Adults who have been told they have high blood pressure	n/a	32.3
Adults who are current smokers	n/a	17.1
Adults who currently use E-cigarettes	n/a	4.6
Adults who currently use chewing tobacco, snuff, or snus	n/a	4.0
Adults who are heavy drinkers[2]	n/a	6.3
Adults who are binge drinkers[3]	n/a	17.4
Adults who are overweight (BMI 25.0 - 29.9)	n/a	35.3
Adults who are obese (BMI 30.0 - 99.8)	n/a	31.3
Adults who participated in any physical activities in the past month	n/a	74.4
Adults who always or nearly always wears a seat belt	n/a	94.3

Note: n/a not available; (1) Figures cover the Peoria, IL Metropolitan Statistical Area—see Appendix B for areas included; (2) Heavy drinkers are classified as adult men having more than 14 drinks per week and adult women having more than 7 drinks per week; (3) Binge drinkers are classified as males having five or more drinks on one occasion or females having four or more drinks on one occasion
Source: Centers for Disease Control and Prevention, Behaviorial Risk Factor Surveillance System, SMART: Selected Metropolitan Area Risk Trends, 2017

Acute and Chronic Health Conditions

Category	MSA[1] (%)	U.S. (%)
Adults who have ever been told they had a heart attack	n/a	4.2
Adults who have ever been told they have angina or coronary heart disease	n/a	3.9
Adults who have ever been told they had a stroke	n/a	3.0
Adults who have ever been told they have asthma	n/a	14.2
Adults who have ever been told they have arthritis	n/a	24.9
Adults who have ever been told they have diabetes[2]	n/a	10.5
Adults who have ever been told they had skin cancer	n/a	6.2
Adults who have ever been told they had any other types of cancer	n/a	7.1
Adults who have ever been told they have COPD	n/a	6.5
Adults who have ever been told they have kidney disease	n/a	3.0
Adults who have ever been told they have a form of depression	n/a	20.5

Note: n/a not available; (1) Figures cover the Peoria, IL Metropolitan Statistical Area—see Appendix B for areas included; (2) Figures do not include pregnancy-related, borderline, or pre-diabetes
Source: Centers for Disease Control and Prevention, Behaviorial Risk Factor Surveillance System, SMART: Selected Metropolitan Area Risk Trends, 2017

Health Screening and Vaccination Rates

Category	MSA[1] (%)	U.S. (%)
Adults aged 65+ who have had flu shot within the past year	n/a	60.7
Adults aged 65+ who have ever had a pneumonia vaccination	n/a	75.4
Adults who have ever been tested for HIV	n/a	36.1
Adults who have ever had the shingles or zoster vaccine?	n/a	28.9
Adults who have had their blood cholesterol checked within the last five years	n/a	85.9

Note: n/a not available; (1) Figures cover the Peoria, IL Metropolitan Statistical Area—see Appendix B for areas included.
Source: Centers for Disease Control and Prevention, Behaviorial Risk Factor Surveillance System, SMART: Selected Metropolitan Area Risk Trends, 2017

Disability Status

Category	MSA[1] (%)	U.S. (%)
Adults who reported being deaf	n/a	6.7
Are you blind or have serious difficulty seeing, even when wearing glasses?	n/a	4.5
Are you limited in any way in any of your usual activities due of arthritis?	n/a	12.9
Do you have difficulty doing errands alone?	n/a	6.8
Do you have difficulty dressing or bathing?	n/a	3.6
Do you have serious difficulty concentrating/remembering/making decisions?	n/a	10.7
Do you have serious difficulty walking or climbing stairs?	n/a	13.6

Note: n/a not available; (1) Figures cover the Peoria, IL Metropolitan Statistical Area—see Appendix B for areas included.
Source: Centers for Disease Control and Prevention, Behaviorial Risk Factor Surveillance System, SMART: Selected Metropolitan Area Risk Trends, 2017

Mortality Rates for the Top 10 Causes of Death in the U.S.

ICD-10[a] Sub-Chapter	ICD-10[a] Code	Age-Adjusted Mortality Rate[1] per 100,000 population	
		County[2]	U.S.
Malignant neoplasms	C00-C97	164.9	152.4
Ischaemic heart diseases	I20-I25	88.4	92.7
Other forms of heart disease	I30-I51	57.8	52.5
Chronic lower respiratory diseases	J40-J47	45.9	40.4
Cerebrovascular diseases	I60-I69	40.8	37.3
Other degenerative diseases of the nervous system	G30-G31	26.2	36.4
Other external causes of accidental injury	W00-X59	43.4	35.3
Organic, including symptomatic, mental disorders	F01-F09	50.7	30.0
Hypertensive diseases	I10-I15	19.8	22.9
Diabetes mellitus	E10-E14	20.8	21.3

Note: (a) ICD-10 = International Classification of Diseases 10th Revision; (1) Mortality rates are a three year average covering 2016-2018; (2) Figures cover Peoria County.
Source: Centers for Disease Control and Prevention, National Center for Health Statistics. Underlying Cause of Death 1999-2018 on CDC WONDER Online Database

Mortality Rates for Selected Causes of Death

ICD-10[a] Sub-Chapter	ICD-10[a] Code	Age-Adjusted Mortality Rate[1] per 100,000 population	
		County[2]	U.S.
Assault	X85-Y09	9.7	6.0
Diseases of the liver	K70-K76	13.6	14.2
Human immunodeficiency virus (HIV) disease	B20-B24	Unreliable	1.6
Influenza and pneumonia	J09-J18	23.2	14.2
Intentional self-harm	X60-X84	16.0	13.9
Malnutrition	E40-E46	Suppressed	1.9
Obesity and other hyperalimentation	E65-E68	Suppressed	2.1
Renal failure	N17-N19	13.5	12.8
Transport accidents	V01-V99	10.2	12.5
Viral hepatitis	B15-B19	Suppressed	1.4

Note: (a) ICD-10 = International Classification of Diseases 10th Revision; (1) Mortality rates are a three year average covering 2016-2018; (2) Figures cover Peoria County; Data are suppressed when the data meet the criteria for confidentiality constraints; Mortality rates are flagged as unreliable when the rate would be calculated with a numerator of 20 or less.
Source: Centers for Disease Control and Prevention, National Center for Health Statistics. Underlying Cause of Death 1999-2018 on CDC WONDER Online Database

Health Insurance Coverage

Area	With Health Insurance	With Private Health Insurance	With Public Health Insurance	Without Health Insurance	Population Under Age 19 Without Health Insurance
City	93.7	65.0	41.2	6.3	2.3
MSA[1]	95.2	74.1	36.1	4.8	2.4
U.S.	90.6	67.7	34.7	9.4	5.2

Note: Figures are percentages that cover the civilian noninstitutionalized population; (1) Figures cover the Peoria, IL Metropolitan Statistical Area—see Appendix B for areas included
Source: U.S. Census Bureau, 2014-2018 American Community Survey 5-Year Estimates

Number of Medical Professionals

Area	MDs[3]	DOs[3,4]	Dentists	Podiatrists	Chiropractors	Optometrists
County[1] (number)	1,020	72	151	15	87	38
County[1] (rate[2])	557.3	39.3	83.6	8.3	48.2	21.0
U.S. (rate[2])	281.9	23.4	69.1	6.0	27.5	16.4

Note: Data as of 2018 unless noted; (1) Data covers Peoria County; (2) Rate per 100,000 population; (3) Data as of 2017 and includes all active, non-federal physicians; (4) Doctor of Osteopathic Medicine
Source: U.S. Department of Health and Human Services, Health Resources and Services Administration, Bureau of Health Professions, Area Resource File (ARF) 2018-2019

Best Hospitals

According to *U.S. News,* the Peoria, IL metro area is home to one of the best hospitals in the U.S.: **OSF Healthcare St. Francis Medical Center** (1 adult specialty). The hospital listed was nationally ranked in at least one of 16 adult or 10 pediatric specialties. Only 206 hospitals nationwide were nationally ranked in one or more adult or pediatric specialty. Twenty hospitals in the U.S. made the Honor Roll. The Best Hospitals Honor Roll takes both the national rankings and the procedure and condition ratings into account. Hospitals received points if they were nationally ranked in one of the 16 adult specialties—the higher they ranked, the more points they got—and how many ratings of "high performing" they earned in the nine procedures and conditions. *U.S. News Online, "America's Best Hospitals 2019-20"*

EDUCATION

Public School District Statistics

District Name	Schls	Pupils	Pupil/ Teacher Ratio	Minority Pupils[1] (%)	Free Lunch Eligible[2] (%)	IEP[3] (%)
Dunlap CUSD 323	8	4,492	17.2	37.4	13.3	12.5
Peoria SD 150	29	12,846	14.1	79.8	70.3	17.8

Note: Table includes school districts with 2,000 or more students; (1) Percentage of students that are not non-Hispanic white; (2) Percentage of students that are eligible for the free lunch program; (3) Percentage of students that have an Individualized Education Program.
Source: U.S. Department of Education, National Center for Education Statistics, Common Core of Data, Local Education Agency (School District) Universe Survey: School Year 2018-2019; U.S. Department of Education, National Center for Education Statistics, Common Core of Data, Public Elementary/Secondary School Universe Survey: School Year 2018-2019

Highest Level of Education

Area	Less than H.S.	H.S. Diploma	Some College, No Deg.	Associate Degree	Bachelor's Degree	Master's Degree	Prof. School Degree	Doctorate Degree
City	11.2	23.9	21.6	8.6	20.8	10.0	2.7	1.2
MSA[1]	8.3	30.0	23.1	10.3	18.6	7.4	1.5	0.9
U.S.	12.3	27.1	20.6	8.4	19.4	8.6	2.1	1.4

Note: Figures cover persons age 25 and over; (1) Figures cover the Peoria, IL Metropolitan Statistical Area—see Appendix B for areas included
Source: U.S. Census Bureau, 2014-2018 American Community Survey 5-Year Estimates

Educational Attainment by Race

Area	High School Graduate or Higher (%)					Bachelor's Degree or Higher (%)				
	Total	White	Black	Asian	Hisp.[2]	Total	White	Black	Asian	Hisp.[2]
City	88.8	92.5	79.8	94.3	67.8	34.7	39.3	13.1	76.2	21.3
MSA[1]	91.7	93.0	79.9	92.2	74.5	28.4	28.8	13.1	69.9	21.0
U.S.	87.7	89.6	85.4	86.8	67.7	31.5	32.9	21.1	53.5	15.8

Note: Figures shown cover persons 25 years old and over; (1) Figures cover the Peoria, IL Metropolitan Statistical Area—see Appendix B for areas included; (2) People of Hispanic origin can be of any race
Source: U.S. Census Bureau, 2014-2018 American Community Survey 5-Year Estimates

School Enrollment by Grade and Control

Area	Preschool (%)		Kindergarten (%)		Grades 1 - 4 (%)		Grades 5 - 8 (%)		Grades 9 - 12 (%)	
	Public	Private	Public	Private	Public	Private	Public	Private	Public	Private
City	65.2	34.8	75.9	24.1	83.3	16.7	82.2	17.8	87.2	12.8
MSA[1]	60.7	39.3	83.5	16.5	88.3	11.7	86.9	13.1	89.2	10.8
U.S.	59.0	41.0	87.7	12.3	89.6	10.4	89.5	10.5	90.2	9.8

Note: Figures shown cover persons 3 years old and over; (1) Figures cover the Peoria, IL Metropolitan Statistical Area—see Appendix B for areas included
Source: U.S. Census Bureau, 2014-2018 American Community Survey 5-Year Estimates

Average Salaries of Public School Teachers

Area	2016-17		2017-18		Change from 2016-17 to 2017-18	
	Dollars	Rank[1]	Dollars	Rank[1]	Percent	Rank[2]
Illinois	64,516	11	65,721	11	1.87	20
U.S. Average	59,539	–	60,477	–	1.58	–

Note: (1) Rank ranges from 1 to 51 where 1 indicates highest salary; (2) Rank ranges from 1 to 51 where 1 indicates highest percent change.
Source: National Education Association, Rankings & Estimates: Rankings of the States 2018 and Estimates of School Statistics 2019

Higher Education

Four-Year Colleges			Two-Year Colleges			Medical Schools[1]	Law Schools[2]	Voc/ Tech[3]
Public	Private Non-profit	Private For-profit	Public	Private Non-profit	Private For-profit			
0	3	1	0	0	0	0	0	1

Note: Figures cover institutions located within the city limits and include main campuses only; (1) includes schools accredited by the Liaison Committee on Medical Education and the American Osteopathic Association's Commission on Osteopathic College Accreditation; (2) includes ABA-accredited schools, schools with provisional ABA accreditation, and state accredited schools; (3) includes all schools with programs that are less than 2 years.
Source: National Center for Education Statistics, Integrated Postsecondary Education System (IPEDS), 2018-19; Wikipedia, List of Medical Schools in the United States, accessed May 1, 2020; Wikipedia, List of Law Schools in the United States, accessed May 1, 2020

PRESIDENTIAL ELECTION

2016 Presidential Election Results

Area	Clinton	Trump	Johnson	Stein	Other
Peoria County	48.1	45.0	4.7	1.4	0.8
U.S.	48.0	45.9	3.3	1.1	1.7

Note: Results are percentages and may not add to 100% due to rounding
Source: Dave Leip's Atlas of U.S. Presidential Elections

EMPLOYERS

Major Employers

Company Name	Industry
Advanced Technology Services	Technical job training
Ameren Illinois	Utility
Bradley University	Education
CEFCU	Banking and financial services
City of Peoria	Government
G&D Integrated	Transportation, distribution
Health Professionals Ltd.	Healthcare
HGS USA	Customer support
Hostess Brands	Food manufacturing
Illinois Central College	Education
Keystone Steel and Wire Co	Steel & wire production
Kmart Corp.	Retail
Komatsu Mining Systems	Coal business
Kroger Company	Supermarkets
Matcor Metal Fabrication	Manufacturer
Methodist Medical Center	Healthcare
OSF Saint Francis Medical Center	Healthcare
Par-A-Dice Hotel/Casino	Gambling
Pekin Hospital	Education
Pekin Insurance & Farmers Auto Insurance	Insurance
Peoria County	Government
Peoria Journal Star	Newspapers, publishing & printing
Peoria School District	Education
Proctor Hospital	Healthcare
Wal-Mart Stores	Retail

Note: Companies shown are located within the Peoria, IL Metropolitan Statistical Area.
Source: Hoovers.com; Wikipedia

PUBLIC SAFETY

Crime Rate

Area	All Crimes	Violent Crimes				Property Crimes		
		Murder	Rape[3]	Robbery	Aggrav. Assault	Burglary	Larceny-Theft	Motor Vehicle Theft
City	4,768.4	19.5	60.4	178.5	505.4	790.4	2,839.4	374.8
Suburbs[1]	n/a	1.7	51.7	18.5	141.8	291.5	n/a	75.7
Metro[2]	n/a	6.7	54.1	63.0	243.0	430.3	n/a	158.9
U.S.	2,580.1	5.0	42.6	86.2	246.8	376.0	1,594.6	228.9

Note: Figures are crimes per 100,000 population; (1) All areas within the metro area that are located outside the city limits; (2) Figures cover the Peoria, IL Metropolitan Statistical Area—see Appendix B for areas included; (3) The city and U.S. figures shown were reported using the revised Uniform Crime Reporting (UCR) definition of rape. The suburban and metro area figures shown are an aggregate total of the data submitted using both the revised and legacy UCR definitions.
Source: FBI Uniform Crime Reports, 2018

Hate Crimes

Area	Number of Quarters Reported	Number of Incidents per Bias Motivation					
		Race/Ethnicity/Ancestry	Religion	Sexual Orientation	Disability	Gender	Gender Identity
City	4	1	0	0	0	0	1
U.S.	4	4,047	1,419	1,196	159	47	168

Source: Federal Bureau of Investigation, Hate Crime Statistics 2018

Identity Theft Consumer Reports

Area	Reports	Reports per 100,000 Population	Rank[2]
MSA[1]	306	83	237
U.S.	650,572	198	-

Note: (1) Figures cover the Peoria, IL Metropolitan Statistical Area—see Appendix B for areas included;
(2) Rank ranges from 1 to 386 where 1 indicates greatest number of identity theft reports per 100,000
population
Source: Federal Trade Commission, Consumer Sentinel Network Data Book for January–December 2019

Fraud and Other Consumer Reports

Area	Reports	Reports per 100,000 Population	Rank[2]
MSA[1]	1,676	455	318
U.S.	2,590,177	789	-

Note: (1) Figures cover the Peoria, IL Metropolitan Statistical Area—see Appendix B for areas included;
(2) Rank ranges from 1 to 386 where 1 indicates greatest number of fraud and other consumer reports per
100,000 population
Source: Federal Trade Commission, Consumer Sentinel Network Data Book for January–December 2019

SPORTS

Professional Sports Teams

Team Name	League	Year Established
No teams are located in the metro area		

Source: Wikipedia, Major Professional Sports Teams of the United States and Canada, May 4, 2020

CLIMATE

Average and Extreme Temperatures

Temperature	Jan	Feb	Mar	Apr	May	Jun	Jul	Aug	Sep	Oct	Nov	Dec	Yr.
Extreme High (°F)	71	74	87	92	104	105	113	106	102	92	81	71	113
Average High (°F)	32	36	48	62	73	82	86	84	77	65	49	36	61
Average Temp. (°F)	24	28	39	51	62	72	76	74	66	55	41	29	51
Average Low (°F)	16	19	29	41	51	60	65	63	55	43	32	21	41
Extreme Low (°F)	-25	-26	-11	14	25	39	46	41	24	13	-2	-24	-26

Note: Figures cover the years 1948-1995
Source: National Climatic Data Center, International Station Meteorological Climate Summary, 9/96

Average Precipitation/Snowfall/Humidity

Precip./Humidity	Jan	Feb	Mar	Apr	May	Jun	Jul	Aug	Sep	Oct	Nov	Dec	Yr.
Avg. Precip. (in.)	1.8	1.6	2.8	3.8	4.0	3.9	3.8	3.1	3.6	2.6	2.5	2.0	35.4
Avg. Snowfall (in.)	6	5	4	1	Tr	0	0	0	Tr	Tr	2	5	23
Avg. Rel. Hum. 6am (%)	80	81	81	78	80	82	86	89	87	84	83	83	83
Avg. Rel. Hum. 3pm (%)	67	64	58	52	52	52	55	56	52	52	61	69	57

Note: Figures cover the years 1948-1995; Tr = Trace amounts (<0.05 in. of rain; <0.5 in. of snow)
Source: National Climatic Data Center, International Station Meteorological Climate Summary, 9/96

Weather Conditions

Temperature			Daytime Sky			Precipitation		
5°F & below	32°F & below	90°F & above	Clear	Partly cloudy	Cloudy	0.01 inch or more precip.	0.1 inch or more snow/ice	Thunder-storms
16	127	27	89	127	149	115	22	49

Note: Figures are average number of days per year and cover the years 1948-1995
Source: National Climatic Data Center, International Station Meteorological Climate Summary, 9/96

HAZARDOUS WASTE

Superfund Sites

The Peoria, IL metro area has no sites on the EPA's Superfund Final National Priorities List. There
are a total of 1,387 Superfund sites with a status of proposed or final on the list in the U.S. *U.S.
Environmental Protection Agency, National Priorities List, May 5, 2020*

**AIR & WATER
QUALITY**

Air Quality Trends: Ozone

	1990	1995	2000	2005	2010	2012	2014	2016	2017	2018
MSA[1]	0.071	0.082	0.072	0.075	0.064	0.072	0.064	0.067	0.066	0.070
U.S.	0.088	0.089	0.082	0.080	0.073	0.075	0.067	0.069	0.068	0.069

Note: (1) Data covers the Peoria, IL Metropolitan Statistical Area—see Appendix B for areas included. The values shown are the composite ozone concentration averages among trend sites based on the highest fourth daily maximum 8-hour concentration in parts per million. These trends are based on sites having an adequate record of monitoring data during the trend period. Data from exceptional events are included.
Source: U.S. Environmental Protection Agency, Air Quality Monitoring Information, "Air Quality Trends by City, 1990-2018"

Air Quality Index

Area	Percent of Days when Air Quality was...[2]					AQI Statistics[2]	
	Good	Moderate	Unhealthy for Sensitive Groups	Unhealthy	Very Unhealthy	Maximum	Median
MSA[1]	69.9	29.3	0.8	0.0	0.0	101	43

Note: (1) Data covers the Peoria, IL Metropolitan Statistical Area—see Appendix B for areas included; (2) Based on 365 days with AQI data in 2018. Air Quality Index (AQI) is an index for reporting daily air quality. EPA calculates the AQI for five major air pollutants regulated by the Clean Air Act: ground-level ozone, particle pollution (aka particulate matter), carbon monoxide, sulfur dioxide, and nitrogen dioxide. The AQI runs from 0 to 500. The higher the AQI value, the greater the level of air pollution and the greater the health concern. There are six AQI categories: "Good" AQI is between 0 and 50. Air quality is considered satisfactory; "Moderate" AQI is between 51 and 100. Air quality is acceptable; "Unhealthy for Sensitive Groups" When AQI values are between 101 and 150, members of sensitive groups may experience health effects; "Unhealthy" When AQI values are between 151 and 200 everyone may begin to experience health effects; "Very Unhealthy" AQI values between 201 and 300 trigger a health alert; "Hazardous" AQI values over 300 trigger warnings of emergency conditions (not shown).
Source: U.S. Environmental Protection Agency, Air Quality Index Report, 2018

Air Quality Index Pollutants

Area	Percent of Days when AQI Pollutant was...[2]					
	Carbon Monoxide	Nitrogen Dioxide	Ozone	Sulfur Dioxide	Particulate Matter 2.5	Particulate Matter 10
MSA[1]	0.0	0.0	52.6	0.0	47.4	0.0

Note: (1) Data covers the Peoria, IL Metropolitan Statistical Area—see Appendix B for areas included; (2) Based on 365 days with AQI data in 2018. The Air Quality Index (AQI) is an index for reporting daily air quality. EPA calculates the AQI for five major air pollutants regulated by the Clean Air Act: ground-level ozone, particle pollution (also known as particulate matter), carbon monoxide, sulfur dioxide, and nitrogen dioxide. The AQI runs from 0 to 500. The higher the AQI value, the greater the level of air pollution and the greater the health concern.
Source: U.S. Environmental Protection Agency, Air Quality Index Report, 2018

Maximum Air Pollutant Concentrations: Particulate Matter, Ozone, CO and Lead

	Particulate Matter 10 (ug/m^3)	Particulate Matter 2.5 Wtd AM (ug/m^3)	Particulate Matter 2.5 24-Hr (ug/m^3)	Ozone (ppm)	Carbon Monoxide (ppm)	Lead (ug/m^3)
MSA[1] Level	n/a	9.4	20	0.07	n/a	n/a
NAAQS[2]	150	15	35	0.075	9	0.15
Met NAAQS[2]	n/a	Yes	Yes	Yes	n/a	n/a

Note: (1) Data covers the Peoria, IL Metropolitan Statistical Area—see Appendix B for areas included; Data from exceptional events are included; (2) National Ambient Air Quality Standards; ppm = parts per million; ug/m^3 = micrograms per cubic meter; n/a not available.
Concentrations: Particulate Matter 10 (coarse particulate)—highest second maximum 24-hour concentration; Particulate Matter 2.5 Wtd AM (fine particulate)—highest weighted annual mean concentration; Particulate Matter 2.5 24-Hour (fine particulate)—highest 98th percentile 24-hour concentration; Ozone—highest fourth daily maximum 8-hour concentration; Carbon Monoxide—highest second maximum non-overlapping 8-hour concentration; Lead—maximum running 3-month average
Source: U.S. Environmental Protection Agency, Air Quality Monitoring Information, "Air Quality Statistics by City, 2018"

Maximum Air Pollutant Concentrations: Nitrogen Dioxide and Sulfur Dioxide

	Nitrogen Dioxide AM (ppb)	Nitrogen Dioxide 1-Hr (ppb)	Sulfur Dioxide AM (ppb)	Sulfur Dioxide 1-Hr (ppb)	Sulfur Dioxide 24-Hr (ppb)
MSA[1] Level	n/a	n/a	n/a	n/a	n/a
NAAQS[2]	53	100	30	75	140
Met NAAQS[2]	n/a	n/a	n/a	n/a	n/a

Note: (1) Data covers the Peoria, IL Metropolitan Statistical Area—see Appendix B for areas included; Data from exceptional events are included; (2) National Ambient Air Quality Standards; ppm = parts per million; ug/m³ = micrograms per cubic meter; n/a not available.
Concentrations: Nitrogen Dioxide AM—highest arithmetic mean concentration; Nitrogen Dioxide 1-Hr—highest 98th percentile 1-hour daily maximum concentration; Sulfur Dioxide AM—highest annual mean concentration; Sulfur Dioxide 1-Hr—highest 99th percentile 1-hour daily maximum concentration; Sulfur Dioxide 24-Hr—highest second maximum 24-hour concentration
Source: U.S. Environmental Protection Agency, Air Quality Monitoring Information, "Air Quality Statistics by City, 2018"

Drinking Water

Water System Name	Pop. Served	Primary Water Source Type	Violations[1]
Illinois American-Peoria	121,478	Surface	7

Note: (1) Total number of violations (both active and inactive) in the EPA database
Source: U.S. Environmental Protection Agency, Office of Ground Water and Drinking Water, Safe Drinking Water Information System (based on data extracted May 5, 2020)

Rochester, Minnesota

Background

Rochester, Minnesota is often characterized as a medical Mecca, based on the city's history of major breakthroughs in modern medicine. Before Dr. William Mayo arrived in 1864, as an examining physician for Civil War draftees, Rochester was basically a transportation hub for the wheat markets of southeastern Minnesota. However, Rochester's destiny was set when a pioneer of medicine, a determined sister of the Order of St. Francis, and a devastating tornado converged on the evening of August 21, 1883.

Dr. William Worrall (W.W.) Mayo had been schooled in Manchester England, migrated to the U.S. and worked as many things before finishing his medical training in Indiana. In 1864, he and his young family settled in Rochester and, following the Civil War, set up a medical practice.

A deadly tornado hit Rochester on August 21, 1883, killing dozens and injuring hundreds. The Mayos (father and two sons, Will and Charlie) and other Rochester physicians called upon the Sisters of St. Francis who worked tirelessly with the Drs. Mayo, and further, established St. Mary's Hospital in 1889, in spite of the Mayos' insistence that Rochester was too small for such a hospital. In 1914, St. Mary's Hospital would become the Mayo Clinic which today is a medical model of integrated medicine consisting of teamwork, pooled knowledge, and resources among physicians, used throughout the world. Dr. Mayo personally trained his students, assuming that the best way to learn medicine is by studying large numbers of cases, and by hands-on experience, known today as residency training, a standard in medical education.

The Mayo Clinic is still a world pioneer, making Rochester a medical destination, and employing over 30,000 in Rochester alone. Additional Mayo facilities have been established in Arizona and Florida. The Mayo Clinic is the largest not-for-profit medical practice in the world. In 1973, Mayo opened its medical school, the most selective in the country.

IBM is also important to Rochester's economy, employing over 4,400 employees. IBM's nickname "Big Blue" was based on the Rochester facility, which is constructed of blue panels designed to reflect the Minnesota sky. The building is the largest IBM facility under one roof in the world. In 1990, the National Building Museum acknowledged the facility for its historic significance and innovation.

The Mayo Clinic offers history and art tours, and The History Center of Olmsted County offers an impressive variety of programs, including research facilities and rare collections. Venues include tours of the historic 38-room, Mayowood Mansion and gardens—once the home of the Mayo family. Much of the architecture was the handiwork of W. W. Mayo himself.

The oldest cultural arts institution in the community, Rochester Symphony Orchestra & Chorale was founded in 1919 as a professional performing arts organization. Its earliest ensemble—the Lawler-Dodge Orchestra—was founded in 1912 as a volunteer orchestra, driven by Daisy Plummer, wife of world-famous Mayo Clinic physician, Dr. Henry Plummer, and directed by Harold Cooke. The Orchestra performed in the former Chateau Theatre where they played background music for silent movies.

The Rochester Downtown Alliance created the Summer Market and Music Festival, and STYLE, the Runway Experience. StyleICE is a unique celebration in which local downtown bars produce an all-ice experience. Everything from glasses to couches is created out of ice, and features special lighting effects and live music.

Minnesota has one of the most extensive state park systems in the nation. Likewise, Rochester's city park system is large, with more than 100 sites covering five square miles. The city also maintains 85 miles of paved trails in addition to state trails such as the Douglas State Trail. The nearest state park is Whitewater State Park.

Rochester features a humid continental climate with four distinct seasons. Summers are very warm and winters are very cold. Rochester sees an annual average of 30 inches of rainfall and 48 inches of snowfall. Significant snow accumulation is common during the winter months. Spring and fall are transitional, with a warming trend during the spring and a cooling trend during the fall. It is not uncommon to see snowfall during early spring and late fall.

Rankings

General Rankings

- Rochester was selected as one of the best places to live in the United States by *Money* magazine. The city ranked #15 out of 100. This year's list focused on cities with populations of 50,000 or greater. Beginning with a pool of 1,796 candidates, editors looked at 80 separate types of data, from local economy and housing market to education, diversity and ease of living—and then sent reporters to interview residents, search neighborhoods and look for other intangibles. *Money, "Best Places to Live, 2019" September 16, 2019*

- In their sixth annual survey, Livability.com looked at data for more than 1,000 U.S. cities to determine the rankings for Livability's "Top 100 Best Places to Live" in 2019. Rochester ranked #5. Criteria: median home value capped at $250,000; affordable living; vibrant economy; education, demographics, health care options. transportation & infrastructure; abundant lifestyle amenities. *Livability.com, "Top 100 Best Places to Live 2019" March 2019*

Business/Finance Rankings

- Experian's latest annual report on consumer credit ranked cities by the average credit score of its residents. Rochester was ranked #2 among the ten cities with the highest average credit score, meaning that its residents showed strong credit management. *www.usatoday.com, "Minneapolis Tops List of Cities With Best Average Credit Score; Greenwood Miss., at the Bottom," January 11, 2018*

- The Rochester metro area appeared on the Milken Institute "2020 Best Performing Cities" list. Rank: #58 out of 201 small metro areas. Criteria: job growth; wage and salary growth; high-tech output growth. *Milken Institute, "Best-Performing Cities 2020," February 26, 2020*

- *Forbes* ranked 203 smaller metro areas (population under 268,000) to determine the nation's "Best Small Places for Business and Careers." The Rochester metro area was ranked #37. Criteria: costs (business and living); job growth (past and projected); income growth; quality of life; educational attainment (college and high school); projected economic growth; cultural and leisure opportunities; workplace tolerance laws; net migration patterns. *Forbes, "The Best Small Places for Business and Careers 2019," October 30, 2019*

Environmental Rankings

- Rochester was highlighted as one of the cleanest metro areas for ozone air pollution in the U.S. during 2015 through 2017. The list represents cities with no monitored ozone air pollution in unhealthful ranges. *American Lung Association, "State of the Air 2019," April 24, 2019*

Safety Rankings

- To identify the safest cities in America, 24/7 Wall Street focused on violent crime categories—murder, non-negligent manslaughter, rape, robbery, and aggravated assault—and property crime as reported in the FBI's 2018 annual Uniform Crime Report. Criteria also included median income from American Community Survey and unemployment figures from Bureau of Labor Statistics. For cities with populations over 100,000, Rochester was ranked #47. *247wallst.com, "America's Safest Cities" January 15, 2020*

- The National Insurance Crime Bureau ranked 382 metro areas in the U.S. in terms of per capita rates of vehicle theft. The Rochester metro area ranked #325 (#1 = highest rate). Criteria: number of vehicle theft offenses per 100,000 inhabitants in 2018. *National Insurance Crime Bureau, "Hot Spots 2018," June 25, 2019*

Seniors/Retirement Rankings

- From its Best Cities for Successful Aging indexes, the Milken Institute generated rankings for metropolitan areas, weighing data in nine categories—health care, wellness, living arrangements, transportation and convenience, financial characteristics, education, employment, community engagement, and overall livability. The Rochester metro area was ranked #24 overall in the small metro area category. *Milken Institute, "Best Cities for Successful Aging, 2017" March 14, 2017*

- Rochester made the 2019 *Forbes* list of "25 Best Places to Retire." Criteria focused on high-quality retirement living at an affordable price, include: housing/living costs compared to the national average and state taxes; air quality; crime rates; good economic outlook; home price appreciation; college presence; doctor availability; bikeability; walkability; healthy living. *Forbes.com, "The Best Places to Retire in 2019," April 23, 2019*

Women/Minorities Rankings

- NerdWallet examined data for 529 U.S. cities and ranked them based on the environment for working women. Rochester ranked #1. Criteria: women's earnings; labor force participation rate; cost of living; unemployment rate. *www.nerdwallet.com, "Best Cities for Women in the Workforce 2016," April 4, 2016*

Business Environment

CITY FINANCES

City Government Finances

Component	2017 ($000)	2017 ($ per capita)
Total Revenues	457,950	4,081
Total Expenditures	505,289	4,502
Debt Outstanding	2,610,195	23,259
Cash and Securities[1]	2,497,662	22,256

Note: (1) Cash and security holdings of a government at the close of its fiscal year, including those of its dependent agencies, utilities, and liquor stores.
Source: U.S. Census Bureau, State & Local Government Finances 2017

City Government Revenue by Source

Source	2017 ($000)	2017 ($ per capita)	2017 (%)
General Revenue			
From Federal Government	7,670	68	1.7
From State Government	42,610	380	9.3
From Local Governments	5,760	51	1.3
Taxes			
Property	56,808	506	12.4
Sales and Gross Receipts	27,777	248	6.1
Personal Income	0	0	0.0
Corporate Income	0	0	0.0
Motor Vehicle License	0	0	0.0
Other Taxes	3,909	35	0.9
Current Charges	56,616	504	12.4
Liquor Store	0	0	0.0
Utility	168,736	1,504	36.8
Employee Retirement	0	0	0.0

Source: U.S. Census Bureau, State & Local Government Finances 2017

City Government Expenditures by Function

Function	2017 ($000)	2017 ($ per capita)	2017 (%)
General Direct Expenditures			
Air Transportation	6,597	58	1.3
Corrections	0	0	0.0
Education	0	0	0.0
Employment Security Administration	0	0	0.0
Financial Administration	2,596	23	0.5
Fire Protection	15,609	139	3.1
General Public Buildings	557	5	0.1
Governmental Administration, Other	3,918	34	0.8
Health	324	2	0.1
Highways	43,686	389	8.6
Hospitals	0	0	0.0
Housing and Community Development	1,397	12	0.3
Interest on General Debt	89,305	795	17.7
Judicial and Legal	1,966	17	0.4
Libraries	8,146	72	1.6
Parking	4,714	42	0.9
Parks and Recreation	72,335	644	14.3
Police Protection	28,341	252	5.6
Public Welfare	0	0	0.0
Sewerage	13,947	124	2.8
Solid Waste Management	0	0	0.0
Veterans' Services	0	0	0.0
Liquor Store	0	0	0.0
Utility	178,973	1,594	35.4
Employee Retirement	0	0	0.0

Source: U.S. Census Bureau, State & Local Government Finances 2017

DEMOGRAPHICS

Population Growth

Area	1990 Census	2000 Census	2010 Census	2018* Estimate	Population Growth (%)	
					1990-2018	2010-2018
City	74,151	85,806	106,769	113,913	53.6	6.7
MSA[1]	141,945	163,618	186,011	216,035	52.2	16.1
U.S.	248,709,873	281,421,906	308,745,538	322,903,030	29.8	4.6

Note: (1) Figures cover the Rochester, MN Metropolitan Statistical Area—see Appendix B for areas included; (*) 2014-2018 5-year estimated population
Source: U.S. Census Bureau, 1990 Census, Census 2000, Census 2010, 2014-2018 American Community Survey 5-Year Estimates

Household Size

Area	Persons in Household (%)							Average Household Size
	One	Two	Three	Four	Five	Six	Seven or More	
City	29.8	33.9	14.6	13.8	4.8	1.8	1.3	2.40
MSA[1]	26.2	36.8	14.3	14.0	5.4	2.3	1.1	2.50
U.S.	27.7	33.9	15.7	13.0	6.0	2.3	1.4	2.60

Note: (1) Figures cover the Rochester, MN Metropolitan Statistical Area—see Appendix B for areas included
Source: U.S. Census Bureau, 2014-2018 American Community Survey 5-Year Estimates

Race

Area	White Alone[2] (%)	Black Alone[2] (%)	Asian Alone[2] (%)	AIAN[3] Alone[2] (%)	NHOPI[4] Alone[2] (%)	Other Race Alone[2] (%)	Two or More Races (%)
City	80.3	7.8	7.2	0.4	0.1	1.1	3.1
MSA[1]	87.8	4.3	4.3	0.3	0.0	1.0	2.2
U.S.	72.7	12.7	5.4	0.8	0.2	4.9	3.2

Note: (1) Figures cover the Rochester, MN Metropolitan Statistical Area—see Appendix B for areas included; (2) Alone is defined as not being in combination with one or more other races; (3) American Indian and Alaska Native; (4) Native Hawaiian and Other Pacific Islander
Source: U.S. Census Bureau, 2014-2018 American Community Survey 5-Year Estimates

Hispanic or Latino Origin

Area	Total (%)	Mexican (%)	Puerto Rican (%)	Cuban (%)	Other (%)
City	5.9	3.8	0.4	0.3	1.3
MSA[1]	4.3	2.9	0.3	0.1	1.1
U.S.	17.8	11.2	1.7	0.7	4.2

Note: Persons of Hispanic or Latino origin can be of any race; (1) Figures cover the Rochester, MN Metropolitan Statistical Area—see Appendix B for areas included
Source: U.S. Census Bureau, 2014-2018 American Community Survey 5-Year Estimates

Segregation

Type	Segregation Indices[1]				Percent Change		
	1990	2000	2010	2010 Rank[2]	1990-2000	1990-2010	2000-2010
Black/White	n/a	n/a	n/a	n/a	n/a	n/a	n/a
Asian/White	n/a	n/a	n/a	n/a	n/a	n/a	n/a
Hispanic/White	n/a	n/a	n/a	n/a	n/a	n/a	n/a

Note: All figures cover the Metropolitan Statistical Area—see Appendix B for areas included; Figures are based on an analysis of 1990, 2000, and 2010 Census Decennial Census tract data by William H. Frey, Brookings Institution and the University of Michigan Social Science Data Analysis Network. In this analysis all racial groups (whites, blacks, and asians) are non-Hispanic members of those races. Hispanics are shown as a separate category; (1) Segregation Indices are Dissimilarity Indices that measure the degree to which the minority group is distributed differently than whites across census tracts. They range from 0 (complete integration) to 100 (complete segregation) where the value indicates the percentage of the minority group that needs to move to be distributed exactly like whites; (2) Ranges from 1 (most segregated) to 102 (least segregated); n/a not available.
Source: www.CensusScope.org

Ancestry

Area	German	Irish	English	American	Italian	Polish	French[2]	Scottish	Dutch
City	29.6	11.3	6.4	3.0	2.3	3.7	2.2	1.2	1.4
MSA[1]	36.1	11.8	6.3	3.4	1.8	3.3	2.4	1.2	1.8
U.S.	13.7	9.9	7.3	6.4	5.2	2.8	2.4	1.7	1.2

Note: Figures are the percentage of the total population reporting a particular ancestry. The nine most commonly reported ancestries in the U.S. are shown. Figures include multiple ancestries (e.g. if a person reported being Irish and Italian, they were included in both columns); (1) Figures cover the Rochester, MN Metropolitan Statistical Area—see Appendix B for areas included; (2) Excludes Basque
Source: U.S. Census Bureau, 2014-2018 American Community Survey 5-Year Estimates

Foreign-born Population

Area	Percent of Population Born in								
	Any Foreign Country	Asia	Mexico	Europe	Caribbean	Central America[2]	South America	Africa	Canada
City	13.8	5.7	1.5	1.8	0.2	0.2	0.3	3.5	0.3
MSA[1]	8.3	3.3	1.0	1.2	0.1	0.2	0.2	1.9	0.2
U.S.	13.5	4.1	3.5	1.5	1.3	1.1	0.9	0.7	0.3

Note: (1) Figures cover the Rochester, MN Metropolitan Statistical Area—see Appendix B for areas included; (2) Excludes Mexico.
Source: U.S. Census Bureau, 2014-2018 American Community Survey 5-Year Estimates

Marital Status

Area	Never Married	Now Married[2]	Separated	Widowed	Divorced
City	31.3	52.9	0.8	4.9	10.0
MSA[1]	27.3	57.5	0.8	5.0	9.5
U.S.	33.3	48.1	2.0	5.8	10.8

Note: Figures are percentages and cover the population 15 years of age and older; (1) Figures cover the Rochester, MN Metropolitan Statistical Area—see Appendix B for areas included; (2) Excludes separated
Source: U.S. Census Bureau, 2014-2018 American Community Survey 5-Year Estimates

Disability by Age

Area	All Ages	Under 18 Years Old	18 to 64 Years Old	65 Years and Over
City	10.7	4.7	8.5	30.3
MSA[1]	10.3	4.1	7.9	29.9
U.S.	12.6	4.2	10.3	35.0

Note: Figures show percent of the civilian noninstitutionalized population that reported having a disability. Disability status is determined from six types of difficulty: vision, hearing, cognitive, ambulatory, self-care, and independent living. For children under 5 years old, hearing and vision difficulty are used to determine disability status. For children between the ages of 5 and 14, disability status is determined from hearing, vision, cognitive, ambulatory, and self-care difficulties. For people aged 15 years and older, they are considered to have a disability if they have difficulty with any one of the six difficulty types; Note: (1) Figures cover the Rochester, MN Metropolitan Statistical Area—see Appendix B for areas included
Source: U.S. Census Bureau, 2014-2018 American Community Survey 5-Year Estimates

Age

Area	Percent of Population									Median Age
	Under Age 5	Age 5–19	Age 20–34	Age 35–44	Age 45–54	Age 55–64	Age 65–74	Age 75–84	Age 85+	
City	7.2	18.8	22.6	13.0	12.1	11.8	7.6	4.5	2.4	35.8
MSA[1]	6.8	19.8	19.0	12.6	12.8	13.4	8.5	4.9	2.3	38.5
U.S.	6.1	19.3	20.7	12.6	13.2	12.8	8.8	4.5	1.9	37.9

Note: (1) Figures cover the Rochester, MN Metropolitan Statistical Area—see Appendix B for areas included
Source: U.S. Census Bureau, 2014-2018 American Community Survey 5-Year Estimates

Gender

Area	Males	Females	Males per 100 Females
City	55,482	58,431	95.0
MSA[1]	106,440	109,595	97.1
U.S.	158,984,190	163,918,840	97.0

Note: (1) Figures cover the Rochester, MN Metropolitan Statistical Area—see Appendix B for areas included
Source: U.S. Census Bureau, 2014-2018 American Community Survey 5-Year Estimates

Religious Groups by Family

Area	Catholic	Baptist	Non-Den.	Methodist[2]	Lutheran	LDS[3]	Pente-costal	Presby-terian[4]	Muslim[5]	Judaism
MSA[1]	23.4	1.7	4.7	4.9	21.1	1.1	1.3	2.9	0.3	0.2
U.S.	19.1	9.3	4.0	4.0	2.3	2.0	1.9	1.6	0.8	0.7

Note: Figures are the number of adherents as a percentage of the total population; (1) Figures cover the Rochester, MN Metropolitan Statistical Area—see Appendix B for areas included; (2) Methodist/Pietist; (3) Latter Day Saints; (4) Reformed; (5) Figures are estimates
Source: Association of Statisticians of American Religious Bodies, 2010 U.S. Religion Census: Religious Congregations & Membership Study

Religious Groups by Tradition

Area	Catholic	Evangelical Protestant	Mainline Protestant	Other Tradition	Black Protestant	Orthodox
MSA[1]	23.4	19.0	21.1	2.1	<0.1	0.1
U.S.	19.1	16.2	7.3	4.3	1.6	0.3

Note: Figures are the number of adherents as a percentage of the total population; (1) Figures cover the Rochester, MN Metropolitan Statistical Area—see Appendix B for areas included
Source: Association of Statisticians of American Religious Bodies, 2010 U.S. Religion Census: Religious Congregations & Membership Study

ECONOMY

Gross Metropolitan Product

Area	2017	2018	2019	2020	Rank[2]
MSA[1]	12.6	13.2	13.9	14.4	182

Note: Figures are in billions of dollars; (1) Figures cover the Rochester, MN Metropolitan Statistical Area—see Appendix B for areas included; (2) Rank is based on 2018 data and ranges from 1 to 381
Source: U.S. Conference of Mayors, U.S. Metro Economies: GMP & Employment 2018-2020, September 2019

Economic Growth

Area	2015-17 (%)	2018 (%)	2019 (%)	2020 (%)	Rank[2]
MSA[1]	3.6	2.9	3.1	1.1	48
U.S.	1.9	2.9	2.3	2.1	–

Note: Figures are real gross metropolitan product (GMP) growth rates and represent average annual percent change; (1) Figures cover the Rochester, MN Metropolitan Statistical Area—see Appendix B for areas included; (2) Rank is based on 2017 2-year average annual percent change and ranges from 1 to 381
Source: U.S. Conference of Mayors, U.S. Metro Economies: GMP & Employment 2018-2020, September 2019

Metropolitan Area Exports

Area	2013	2014	2015	2016	2017	2018	Rank[2]
MSA[1]	1,061.0	720.5	530.2	398.0	495.3	537.6	210

Note: Figures are in millions of dollars; (1) Figures cover the Rochester, MN Metropolitan Statistical Area—see Appendix B for areas included; (2) Rank is based on 2018 data and ranges from 1 to 387
Source: U.S. Department of Commerce, International Trade Administration, Office of Trade and Economic Analysis, Industry and Analysis, Exports by Metropolitan Area, data extracted April 15, 2020

Building Permits

Area	Single-Family			Multi-Family			Total		
	2017	2018	Pct. Chg.	2017	2018	Pct. Chg.	2017	2018	Pct. Chg.
City	437	347	-20.6	617	1,068	73.1	1,054	1,415	34.3
MSA[1]	818	690	-15.6	631	1,126	78.4	1,449	1,816	25.3
U.S.	820,000	855,300	4.3	462,000	473,500	2.5	1,282,000	1,328,800	3.7

Note: (1) Figures cover the Rochester, MN Metropolitan Statistical Area—see Appendix B for areas included; Figures represent new, privately-owned housing units authorized (unadjusted data); All permit data are based on estimates with imputation
Source: U.S. Census Bureau, Manufacturing, Mining, and Construction Statistics, Building Permits, 2017, 2018

Bankruptcy Filings

Area	Business Filings			Nonbusiness Filings		
	2018	2019	% Chg.	2018	2019	% Chg.
Olmsted County	5	9	80.0	169	151	-10.7
U.S.	22,232	22,780	2.5	751,186	752,160	0.1

Note: Business filings include Chapter 7, Chapter 9, Chapter 11, Chapter 12, Chapter 13, Chapter 15, and Section 304; Nonbusiness filings include Chapter 7, Chapter 11, and Chapter 13
Source: Administrative Office of the U.S. Courts, Business and Nonbusiness Bankruptcy, County Cases Commenced by Chapter of the Bankruptcy Code, During the 12-Month Period Ending December 31, 2018 and Business and Nonbusiness Bankruptcy, County Cases Commenced by Chapter of the Bankruptcy Code, During the 12-Month Period Ending December 31, 2019

Housing Vacancy Rates

Area	Gross Vacancy Rate[2] (%)			Year-Round Vacancy Rate[3] (%)			Rental Vacancy Rate[4] (%)			Homeowner Vacancy Rate[5] (%)		
	2017	2018	2019	2017	2018	2019	2017	2018	2019	2017	2018	2019
MSA[1]	n/a	n/a	n/a	n/a	n/a	n/a	n/a	n/a	n/a	n/a	n/a	n/a
U.S.	12.7	12.3	12.0	9.9	9.7	9.5	7.2	6.9	6.7	1.6	1.5	1.4

Note: (1) Figures cover the Rochester, MN Metropolitan Statistical Area—see Appendix B for areas included; (2) The percentage of the total housing inventory that is vacant; (3) The percentage of the housing inventory (excluding seasonal units) that is year-round vacant; (4) The percentage of rental inventory that is vacant for rent; (5) The percentage of homeowner inventory that is vacant for sale; n/a not available
Source: U.S. Census Bureau, Housing Vacancies and Homeownership Annual Statistics: 2017, 2018, 2019

INCOME

Income

Area	Per Capita ($)	Median Household ($)	Average Household ($)
City	38,647	70,749	94,495
MSA[1]	37,426	71,501	93,118
U.S.	32,621	60,293	84,938

Note: (1) Figures cover the Rochester, MN Metropolitan Statistical Area—see Appendix B for areas included
Source: U.S. Census Bureau, 2014-2018 American Community Survey 5-Year Estimates

Household Income Distribution

Area	Percent of Households Earning							
	Under $15,000	$15,000 -$24,999	$25,000 -$34,999	$35,000 -$49,999	$50,000 -$74,999	$75,000 -$99,999	$100,000 -$149,999	$150,000 and up
City	8.4	7.2	7.5	11.8	17.7	14.2	17.5	15.6
MSA[1]	7.4	7.0	7.8	11.7	18.5	14.4	18.7	14.4
U.S.	10.9	9.3	9.3	12.6	17.5	12.5	14.6	13.3

Note: (1) Figures cover the Rochester, MN Metropolitan Statistical Area—see Appendix B for areas included
Source: U.S. Census Bureau, 2014-2018 American Community Survey 5-Year Estimates

Poverty Rate

Area	All Ages	Under 18 Years Old	18 to 64 Years Old	65 Years and Over
City	10.3	13.3	10.4	4.9
MSA[1]	8.5	10.8	8.3	5.6
U.S.	14.1	19.5	13.2	9.3

Note: Figures are percentage of people whose income during the past 12 months was below the poverty level; (1) Figures cover the Rochester, MN Metropolitan Statistical Area—see Appendix B for areas included
Source: U.S. Census Bureau, 2014-2018 American Community Survey 5-Year Estimates

EMPLOYMENT

Labor Force and Employment

Area	Civilian Labor Force			Workers Employed		
	Dec. 2018	Dec. 2019	% Chg.	Dec. 2018	Dec. 2019	% Chg.
City	65,150	65,938	1.2	63,521	64,352	1.3
MSA[1]	123,488	125,263	1.4	120,020	121,567	1.3
U.S.	162,510,000	164,007,000	0.9	156,481,000	158,504,000	1.3

Note: Data is not seasonally adjusted and covers workers 16 years of age and older; (1) Figures cover the Rochester, MN Metropolitan Statistical Area—see Appendix B for areas included
Source: Bureau of Labor Statistics, Local Area Unemployment Statistics

Unemployment Rate

Area	2019											
	Jan.	Feb.	Mar.	Apr.	May	Jun.	Jul.	Aug.	Sep.	Oct.	Nov.	Dec.
City	3.0	2.8	3.0	2.4	2.3	2.9	2.7	2.6	2.1	2.1	2.1	2.4
MSA[1]	3.7	3.4	3.5	2.6	2.4	2.9	2.7	2.6	2.2	2.2	2.3	3.0
U.S.	4.4	4.1	3.9	3.3	3.4	3.8	4.0	3.8	3.3	3.3	3.3	3.4

Note: Data is not seasonally adjusted and covers workers 16 years of age and older; (1) Figures cover the Rochester, MN Metropolitan Statistical Area—see Appendix B for areas included
Source: Bureau of Labor Statistics, Local Area Unemployment Statistics

Average Wages

Occupation	$/Hr.	Occupation	$/Hr.
Accountants and Auditors	30.80	Maintenance and Repair Workers	20.20
Automotive Mechanics	21.40	Marketing Managers	55.40
Bookkeepers	20.00	Network and Computer Systems Admin.	34.80
Carpenters	25.80	Nurses, Licensed Practical	23.70
Cashiers	12.40	Nurses, Registered	37.30
Computer Programmers	32.90	Nursing Assistants	16.80
Computer Systems Analysts	41.20	Office Clerks, General	18.00
Computer User Support Specialists	26.20	Physical Therapists	41.00
Construction Laborers	21.60	Physicians	114.50
Cooks, Restaurant	13.70	Plumbers, Pipefitters and Steamfitters	32.50
Customer Service Representatives	17.50	Police and Sheriff's Patrol Officers	32.40
Dentists	92.30	Postal Service Mail Carriers	25.00
Electricians	28.30	Real Estate Sales Agents	25.00
Engineers, Electrical	45.90	Retail Salespersons	14.40
Fast Food and Counter Workers	12.60	Sales Representatives, Technical/Scientific	41.50
Financial Managers	54.00	Secretaries, Exc. Legal/Medical/Executive	17.20
First-Line Supervisors of Office Workers	26.80	Security Guards	15.10
General and Operations Managers	45.20	Surgeons	n/a
Hairdressers/Cosmetologists	14.60	Teacher Assistants, Exc. Postsecondary*	15.40
Home Health and Personal Care Aides	13.50	Teachers, Secondary School, Exc. Sp. Ed.*	32.40
Janitors and Cleaners	16.00	Telemarketers	n/a
Landscaping/Groundskeeping Workers	16.20	Truck Drivers, Heavy/Tractor-Trailer	22.50
Lawyers	54.90	Truck Drivers, Light/Delivery Services	16.60
Maids and Housekeeping Cleaners	12.60	Waiters and Waitresses	13.60

Note: Wage data covers the Rochester, MN Metropolitan Statistical Area—see Appendix B for areas included; (*) Hourly wages were calculated from annual wage data based on a 40 hour work week; n/a not available.
Source: Bureau of Labor Statistics, Metro Area Occupational Employment & Wage Estimates, May 2019

Employment by Occupation

Occupation Classification	City (%)	MSA[1] (%)	U.S. (%)
Management, Business, Science, and Arts	51.8	45.9	37.9
Natural Resources, Construction, and Maintenance	5.2	8.2	8.9
Production, Transportation, and Material Moving	9.8	11.6	13.3
Sales and Office	16.7	18.2	22.1
Service	16.4	16.0	17.9

Note: Figures cover employed civilians 16 years of age and older; (1) Figures cover the Rochester, MN Metropolitan Statistical Area—see Appendix B for areas included
Source: U.S. Census Bureau, 2014-2018 American Community Survey 5-Year Estimates

Employment by Industry

Sector	MSA[1]		U.S.
	Number of Employees	Percent of Total	Percent of Total
Construction, Mining, and Logging	5,100	4.1	5.4
Education and Health Services	51,400	41.8	16.1
Financial Activities	2,700	2.2	5.8
Government	13,400	10.9	15.0
Information	1,400	1.1	1.9
Leisure and Hospitality	11,100	9.0	10.8
Manufacturing	10,800	8.8	8.4
Other Services	3,900	3.2	3.9
Professional and Business Services	5,600	4.5	14.1
Retail Trade	12,000	9.7	10.6
Transportation, Warehousing, and Utilities	2,800	2.3	4.2
Wholesale Trade	2,900	2.4	3.9

Note: Figures are non-farm employment as of December 2019. Figures are not seasonally adjusted and include workers 16 years of age and older; (1) Figures cover the Rochester, MN Metropolitan Statistical Area—see Appendix B for areas included
Source: Bureau of Labor Statistics, Current Employment Statistics, Employment, Hours, and Earnings

Occupations with Greatest Projected Employment Growth: 2019 – 2021

Occupation[1]	2019 Employment	2021 Projected Employment	Numeric Employment Change	Percent Employment Change
Personal Care Aides	77,670	81,800	4,130	5.3
Registered Nurses	69,170	71,020	1,850	2.7
Combined Food Preparation and Serving Workers, Including Fast Food	65,670	66,730	1,060	1.6
Light Truck or Delivery Services Drivers	17,520	18,560	1,040	5.9
Janitors and Cleaners, Except Maids and Housekeeping Cleaners	47,900	48,820	920	1.9
Cooks, Restaurant	28,290	28,980	690	2.4
Teacher Assistants	36,820	37,490	670	1.8
Home Health Aides	22,450	22,980	530	2.4
Carpenters	18,170	18,660	490	2.7
Financial Managers	16,170	16,630	460	2.8

Note: Projections cover Minnesota; (1) Sorted by numeric employment change
Source: www.projectionscentral.com, State Occupational Projections, 2019–2021 Short-Term Projections

Fastest Growing Occupations: 2019 – 2021

Occupation[1]	2019 Employment	2021 Projected Employment	Numeric Employment Change	Percent Employment Change
Couriers and Messengers	950	1,010	60	6.3
Physician Assistants	2,020	2,140	120	5.9
Light Truck or Delivery Services Drivers	17,520	18,560	1,040	5.9
Respiratory Therapists	1,900	2,000	100	5.3
Personal Care Aides	77,670	81,800	4,130	5.3
Massage Therapists	2,290	2,410	120	5.2
Operations Research Analysts	3,480	3,640	160	4.6
Nurse Practitioners	3,900	4,080	180	4.6
Information Security Analysts	2,890	3,020	130	4.5
Medical Assistants	10,230	10,660	430	4.2

Note: Projections cover Minnesota; (1) Sorted by percent employment change and excludes occupations with numeric employment change less than 50
Source: www.projectionscentral.com, State Occupational Projections, 2019–2021 Short-Term Projections

TAXES

State Corporate Income Tax Rates

State	Tax Rate (%)	Income Brackets ($)	Num. of Brackets	Financial Institution Tax Rate (%)[a]	Federal Income Tax Ded.
Minnesota	9.8 (n)	Flat rate	1	9.8 (n)	No

Note: Tax rates as of January 1, 2020; (a) Rates listed are the corporate income tax rate applied to financial institutions or excise taxes based on income; (n) In addition, Minnesota levies a 5.8% tentative minimum tax on Alternative Minimum Taxable Income. Minnesota also imposes a surtax ranging up to $10,380.
Source: Federation of Tax Administrators, State Corporate Income Tax Rates, January 1, 2020

State Individual Income Tax Rates

State	Tax Rate (%)	Income Brackets ($)	Personal Exemptions ($)			Standard Ded. ($)	
			Single	Married	Depend.	Single	Married
Minnesota (a)	5.35 - 9.85	26,960 - 164,401 (n)	(d)	(d)	4,250	12,400	24,800 (d)

Note: Tax rates as of January 1, 2020; Local- and county-level taxes are not included; Federal income tax is not deductible on state income tax returns; (a) 19 states have statutory provision for automatically adjusting to the rate of inflation the dollar values of the income tax brackets, standard deductions, and/or personal exemptions. Michigan indexes the personal exemption only. Oregon does not index the income brackets for $125,000 and over; (d) These states use the personal exemption/standard deduction amounts provided in the federal Internal Revenue Code; (n) The income brackets reported for Minnesota are for single individuals. For married couples filing jointly, the same tax rates apply to income brackets ranging from $39,410 to $273,470.
Source: Federation of Tax Administrators, State Individual Income Tax Rates, January 1, 2020

Various State Sales and Excise Tax Rates

State	State Sales Tax (%)	Gasoline[1] (¢/gal.)	Cigarette[2] ($/pack)	Spirits[3] ($/gal.)	Wine[4] ($/gal.)	Beer[5] ($/gal.)	Recreational Marijuana (%)
Minnesota	6.875	28.6	3.04	9.01	1.22	0.51	Not legal

Note: All tax rates as of January 1, 2020; (1) The American Petroleum Institute has developed a methodology for determining the average tax rate on a gallon of fuel. Rates may include any of the following: excise taxes, environmental fees, storage tank fees, other fees or taxes, general sales tax, and local taxes; (2) The federal excise tax of $1.0066 per pack and local taxes are not included; (3) Rates are those applicable to off-premise sales of 40% alcohol by volume (a.b.v.) distilled spirits in 750ml containers. Local excise taxes are excluded; (4) Rates are those applicable to off-premise sales of 11% a.b.v. non-carbonated wine in 750ml containers; (5) Rates are those applicable to off-premise sales of 4.7% a.b.v. beer in 12 ounce containers.
Source: Tax Foundation, 2020 Facts & Figures: How Does Your State Compare?

State Business Tax Climate Index Rankings

State	Overall Rank	Corporate Tax Rank	Individual Income Tax Rank	Sales Tax Rank	Property Tax Rank	Unemployment Insurance Tax Rank
Minnesota	45	44	46	28	26	34

Note: The index is a measure of how each state's tax laws affect economic performance. The lower the rank, the more favorable a state's tax system is for business. States without a given tax are given a ranking of 1. The scores/rankings for the District of Columbia do not affect other states. The 2020 index represents the tax climate as of July 1, 2019.
Source: Tax Foundation, State Business Tax Climate Index 2020

COMMERCIAL UTILITIES

Typical Monthly Electric Bills

Area	Commercial Service ($/month)		Industrial Service ($/month)	
	1,500 kWh	40 kW demand 14,000 kWh	1,000 kW demand 200,000 kWh	50,000 kW demand 32,500,000 kWh
City	n/a	n/a	n/a	n/a
Average[1]	203	1,612	25,706	2,520,671

Note: Figures are based on annualized rates; (1) Average based on 187 utilities surveyed; n/a not available
Source: Edison Electric Institute, Typical Bills and Average Rates Report, Summer 2019

TRANSPORTATION

Means of Transportation to Work

| Area | Car/Truck/Van | | Public Transportation | | | Bicycle | Walked | Other Means | Worked at Home |
	Drove Alone	Car-pooled	Bus	Subway	Railroad				
City	71.0	12.2	6.6	0.0	0.0	1.1	4.2	0.8	4.0
MSA[1]	74.3	11.3	4.3	0.0	0.0	0.7	3.6	0.8	5.0
U.S.	76.4	9.1	2.5	1.9	0.6	0.6	2.7	1.3	4.9

Note: Figures are percentages and cover workers 16 years of age and older; (1) Figures cover the Rochester, MN Metropolitan Statistical Area—see Appendix B for areas included
Source: U.S. Census Bureau, 2014-2018 American Community Survey 5-Year Estimates

Travel Time to Work

Area	Less Than 10 Minutes	10 to 19 Minutes	20 to 29 Minutes	30 to 44 Minutes	45 to 59 Minutes	60 to 89 Minutes	90 Minutes or More
City	19.0	56.5	13.1	6.4	2.2	1.6	1.3
MSA[1]	18.6	42.3	18.3	12.8	3.8	2.5	1.7
U.S.	12.5	28.7	20.9	20.7	8.2	6.3	2.8

Note: Note: Figures are percentages and include workers 16 years old and over; (1) Figures cover the Rochester, MN Metropolitan Statistical Area—see Appendix B for areas included
Source: U.S. Census Bureau, 2014-2018 American Community Survey 5-Year Estimates

Key Congestion Measures

Area	1982	1992	2002	2012	2017
Annual Hours of Delay, Total (000)	n/a	n/a	n/a	n/a	2,304
Annual Hours of Delay, Per Auto Commuter	n/a	n/a	n/a	n/a	19
Annual Congestion Cost, Total (million $)	n/a	n/a	n/a	n/a	47
Annual Congestion Cost, Per Auto Commuter ($)	n/a	n/a	n/a	n/a	390

Note: n/a not available
Source: Texas A&M Transportation Institute, 2019 Urban Mobility Report

Freeway Travel Time Index

Area	1982	1987	1992	1997	2002	2007	2012	2017
Urban Area Index[1]	n/a	n/a	n/a	n/a	n/a	n/a	n/a	1.10
Urban Area Rank[1,2]	n/a	n/a	n/a	n/a	n/a	n/a	n/a	n/a

Note: Freeway Travel Time Index—the ratio of travel time in the peak period to the travel time at free-flow conditions. For example, a value of 1.30 indicates a 20-minute free-flow trip takes 26 minutes in the peak (20 minutes x 1.30 = 26 minutes); (1) Covers the Rochester MN urban area; (2) Rank is based on 101 larger urban areas (#1 = highest travel time index); n/a not available
Source: Texas A&M Transportation Institute, 2019 Urban Mobility Report

Public Transportation

Agency Name / Mode of Transportation	Vehicles Operated in Maximum Service[1]	Annual Unlinked Passenger Trips[2] (in thous.)	Annual Passenger Miles[3] (in thous.)
City of Rochester Public Transportation			
Bus (purchased transportation)	52	2,010.1	7,367.4
Demand Response (purchased transportation)	5	25.9	177.8
Demand Response Taxi (purchased transportation)	1	20.2	89.0

Note: (1) Number of revenue vehicles operated by the given mode and type of service to meet the annual maximum service requirement. This is the revenue vehicle count during the peak season of the year; on the week and day that maximum service is provided. Vehicles operated in maximum service (VOMS) exclude atypical days and one-time special events; (2) Number of passengers who boarded public transportation vehicles. Passengers are counted each time they board a vehicle no matter how many vehicles they use to travel from their origin to their destination. (3) Sum of the distances ridden by all passengers during the entire fiscal year.
Source: Federal Transit Administration, National Transit Database, 2018

Air Transportation

Airport Name and Code / Type of Service	Passenger Airlines[1]	Passenger Enplanements	Freight Carriers[2]	Freight (lbs)
Rochester International Airport (RST)				
Domestic service (U.S. carriers - 2019)	11	182,968	3	10,972,900
International service (U.S. carriers - 2018)	0	0	0	0

Note: (1) Includes all U.S.-based major, minor and commuter airlines that carried at least one passenger during the year; (2) Includes all U.S.-based airlines and freight carriers that transported at least one pound of freight during the year.
Source: Bureau of Transportation Statistics, The Intermodal Transportation Database, Air Carriers: T-100 Domestic Market (U.S. Carriers), 2019; Bureau of Transportation Statistics, The Intermodal Transportation Database, Air Carriers: T-100 International Market (U.S. Carriers), 2018

Other Transportation Statistics

Major Highways:	I-90
Amtrak Service:	No
Major Waterways/Ports:	None

Source: Amtrak.com; Google Maps

BUSINESSES

Major Business Headquarters

Company Name	Industry	Rankings	
		Fortune[1]	Forbes[2]
No companies listed	-	-	-

Note: (1) Companies that produce a 10-K are ranked 1 to 500 based on 2018 revenue; (2) All private companies with at least $2 billion in annual revenue through the end of their most current fiscal year are ranked 1 to 228; companies listed are headquartered in the city; dashes indicate no ranking
Source: Fortune, "Fortune 500," June 2019; Forbes, "America's Largest Private Companies," 2019 Rankings

Minority- and Women-Owned Businesses

Group	All Firms		Firms with Paid Employees			
	Firms	Sales ($000)	Firms	Sales ($000)	Employees	Payroll ($000)
AIAN[1]	39	(s)	0	(s)	0 - 19	(s)
Asian	478	45,980	72	36,275	451	7,310
Black	431	(s)	35	(s)	1,000 - 2,499	(s)
Hispanic	219	(s)	9	(s)	20 - 99	(s)
NHOPI[2]	n/a	n/a	n/a	n/a	n/a	n/a
Women	2,801	488,834	291	422,196	2,461	59,817
All Firms	8,900	12,577,132	2,349	12,256,680	73,568	3,032,558

Note: Figures cover firms located in the city; minority- and women-owned business are defined as firms in which the corresponding group own 51% or more of the stock or equity of the company; (1) American Indian and Alaska Native; (2) Native Hawaiian and Other Pacific Islander; (s) estimates are suppressed when publication standards are not met; n/a not available
Source: U.S. Census Bureau, 2012 Economic Census, Survey of Business Owners

HOTELS & CONVENTION CENTERS

Hotels, Motels and Vacation Rentals

Area	5 Star		4 Star		3 Star		2 Star		1 Star		Not Rated	
	Num.	Pct.[3]	Num.	Pct.[3]	Num.	Pct.[3]	Num.	Pct.[3]	Num.	Pct.[3]	Num.	Pct.[3]
City[1]	1	1.8	2	3.6	17	30.9	9	16.4	4	7.3	22	40.0
Total[2]	266	1.3	1,517	7.2	4,627	21.8	3,210	15.1	3,974	18.7	7,601	35.9

Note: (1) Figures cover Rochester and vicinity; (2) Figures cover all 100 cities in this book; (3) Percentage of hotels which have a given star rating; Star ratings are determined by priceline.com and offer an indication of the general quality of a particular hotel.
Source: priceline.com, April 27, 2020

Major Convention Centers

Name	Overall Space (sq. ft.)	Exhibit Space (sq. ft.)	Meeting Space (sq. ft.)	Meeting Rooms
Mayo Civic Center	n/a	25,200	n/a	4

Note: Table includes convention centers located in the Rochester, MN metro area; n/a not available
Source: Original research

Living Environment

COST OF LIVING

Cost of Living Index

Composite Index	Groceries	Housing	Utilities	Trans-portation	Health Care	Misc. Goods/ Services
n/a	n/a	n/a	n/a	n/a	n/a	n/a

Note: The Cost of Living Index measures regional differences in the cost of consumer goods and services, excluding taxes and non-consumer expenditures, for professional and managerial households in the top income quintile. It is based on more than 50,000 prices covering almost 60 different items for which prices are collected three times a year by chambers of commerce, economic development organizations or university applied economic centers in each participating urban area. The numbers shown should be read as a percentage above or below the national average of 100. For example, a value of 115.4 in the groceries column indicates that grocery prices are 15.4% higher than the national average. Small differences in the index numbers should not be interpreted as significant; n/a not available.
Source: The Council for Community and Economic Research, ACCRA Cost of Living Index, 2019

Grocery Prices

Area[1]	T-Bone Steak ($/pound)	Frying Chicken ($/pound)	Whole Milk ($/half gal.)	Eggs ($/dozen)	Orange Juice ($/64 oz.)	Coffee ($/11.5 oz.)
City[2]	n/a	n/a	n/a	n/a	n/a	n/a
Avg.	11.40	1.41	1.93	1.54	3.51	4.30
Min.	7.40	0.92	0.85	0.58	2.67	2.90
Max.	15.58	2.68	4.09	4.18	5.57	8.10

*Note: (1) Values for the local area are compared with the average, minimum and maximum values for all 290 areas in the Cost of Living Index; (2) Figures cover the Rochester MN urban area; n/a not available; **T-Bone Steak** (price per pound); **Frying Chicken** (price per pound, whole fryer); **Whole Milk** (half gallon carton); **Eggs** (price per dozen, Grade A, large); **Orange Juice** (64 oz. Tropicana or Florida Natural); **Coffee** (11.5 oz. can, vacuum-packed, Maxwell House, Hills Bros, or Folgers).*
Source: The Council for Community and Economic Research, ACCRA Cost of Living Index, 2019

Housing and Utility Costs

Area[1]	New Home Price ($)	Apartment Rent ($/month)	All Electric ($/month)	Part Electric ($/month)	Other Energy ($/month)	Telephone ($/month)
City[2]	n/a	n/a	n/a	n/a	n/a	n/a
Avg.	362,090	1,142	174.35	100.00	67.76	179.60
Min.	198,329	501	91.58	31.44	28.51	165.30
Max.	2,074,561	5,050	388.18	239.41	306.15	207.90

*Note: (1) Values for the local area are compared with the average, minimum and maximum values for all 290 areas in the Cost of Living Index; (2) Figures cover the Rochester MN urban area; n/a not available; **New Home Price** (2,400 sf living area, 8,000 sf lot, in urban area with full utilities); **Apartment Rent** (950 sf 2 bedroom/1.5 or 2 bath, unfurnished, excluding all utilities except water); **All Electric** (average monthly cost for an all-electric home); **Part Electric** (average monthly cost for a part-electric home); **Other Energy** (average monthly cost for natural gas, fuel oil, coal, wood, and any other forms of energy except electricity); **Telephone** (price includes the base monthly rate plus taxes and fees for three lines of mobile phone service).*
Source: The Council for Community and Economic Research, ACCRA Cost of Living Index, 2019

Health Care, Transportation, and Other Costs

Area[1]	Doctor ($/visit)	Dentist ($/visit)	Optometrist ($/visit)	Gasoline ($/gallon)	Beauty Salon ($/visit)	Men's Shirt ($)
City[2]	n/a	n/a	n/a	n/a	n/a	n/a
Avg.	114.85	97.58	106.10	2.50	38.15	32.15
Min.	39.00	62.22	52.22	1.53	16.88	10.27
Max.	206.67	151.53	258.67	3.79	79.29	59.30

*Note: (1) Values for the local area are compared with the average, minimum and maximum values for all 290 areas in the Cost of Living Index; (2) Figures cover the Rochester MN urban area; n/a not available; **Doctor** (general practitioners routine exam of an established patient); **Dentist** (adult teeth cleaning and periodic oral examination); **Optometrist** (full vision eye exam for established adult patient); **Gasoline** (one gallon regular unleaded, national brand, including all taxes, cash price at self-service pump if available); **Beauty Salon** (woman's shampoo, trim, and blow-dry); **Men's Shirt** (cotton/polyester dress shirt, pinpoint weave, long sleeves).*
Source: The Council for Community and Economic Research, ACCRA Cost of Living Index, 2019

HOUSING

House Price Index (HPI)

Area	National Ranking[2]	Quarterly Change (%)	One-Year Change (%)	Five-Year Change (%)
MSA[1]	198	0.13	3.31	33.01
U.S.[3]	–	1.26	5.09	32.88

Note: The HPI is a weighted repeat sales index. It measures average price changes in repeat sales or refinancings on the same properties. This information is obtained by reviewing repeat mortgage transactions on single-family properties whose mortgages have been purchased or securitized by Fannie Mae or Freddie Mac in January 1975; (1) Figures cover the Rochester, MN Metropolitan Statistical Area—see Appendix B for areas included; (2) Rankings are based on annual percentage change for all metro areas containing at least 15,000 transactions over the last 10 years and ranges from 1 to 232; (3) figures based on a weighted average of Census Division estimates using a seasonally adjusted, purchase-only index; all figures are for the period ending December 31, 2019
Source: Federal Housing Finance Agency, House Price Index, February 25, 2020

Median Single-Family Home Prices

Area	2017	2018	2019p	Percent Change 2018 to 2019
MSA[1]	n/a	n/a	n/a	n/a
U.S. Average	248.8	261.6	274.6	5.0

Note: Figures are median sales prices of existing single-family homes in thousands of dollars; (p) preliminary; n/a not available; (1) Figures cover the Rochester, MN Metropolitan Statistical Area—see Appendix B for areas included
Source: National Association of Realtors, Median Sales Price of Existing Single-Family Homes for Metropolitan Areas, 4th Quarter 2019

Qualifying Income Based on Median Sales Price of Existing Single-Family Homes

Area	With 5% Down ($)	With 10% Down ($)	With 20% Down ($)
MSA[1]	n/a	n/a	n/a
U.S. Average	58,663	55,575	49,400

Note: Figures are preliminary; Qualifying income is based on a mortgage rate of 3.76%. Monthly principal and interest payment is limited to 25% of income; n/a not available; (1) Figures cover the Rochester, MN Metropolitan Statistical Area—see Appendix B for areas included
Source: National Association of Realtors, Qualifying Income Based on Median Sales Price of Existing Single-Family Homes for Metropolitan Areas, 4th Quarter 2019

Median Apartment Condo-Coop Home Prices

Area	2017	2018	2019p	Percent Change 2018 to 2019
MSA[1]	n/a	n/a	n/a	n/a
U.S. Average	234.3	241.0	249.5	3.5

Note: Figures are median sales prices of existing apartment condo-coop homes in thousands of dollars; (p) preliminary; n/a not available; (1) Figures cover the Rochester, MN Metropolitan Statistical Area—see Appendix B for areas included
Source: National Association of Realtors, Median Sales Price of Existing Apartment Condo-Coop Homes for Metropolitan Areas, 4th Quarter 2019

Home Value Distribution

Area	Under $50,000	$50,000 -$99,999	$100,000 -$149,999	$150,000 -$199,999	$200,000 -$299,999	$300,000 -$499,999	$500,000 -$999,999	$1,000,000 or more
City	3.9	6.0	19.4	26.0	25.0	15.8	3.4	0.4
MSA[1]	5.2	7.9	18.0	22.5	23.1	17.4	4.8	1.0
U.S.	7.6	13.0	14.0	14.3	19.2	18.3	10.5	3.1

Note: Figures are percentages and cover owner-occupied housing units; (1) Figures cover the Rochester, MN Metropolitan Statistical Area—see Appendix B for areas included
Source: U.S. Census Bureau, 2014-2018 American Community Survey 5-Year Estimates

Homeownership Rate

Area	2011 (%)	2012 (%)	2013 (%)	2014 (%)	2015 (%)	2016 (%)	2017 (%)	2018 (%)	2019 (%)
MSA[1]	n/a	n/a	n/a	n/a	n/a	n/a	n/a	n/a	n/a
U.S.	66.1	65.4	65.1	64.5	63.7	63.4	63.9	64.4	64.6

Note: (1) Figures cover the Rochester, MN Metropolitan Statistical Area—see Appendix B for areas included; n/a not available
Source: U.S. Census Bureau, Housing Vacancies and Homeownership Annual Statistics: 2011-2019

Year Housing Structure Built

Area	2010 or Later	2000 -2009	1990 -1999	1980 -1989	1970 -1979	1960 -1969	1950 -1959	1940 -1949	Before 1940	Median Year
City	6.7	19.7	14.5	14.9	13.0	10.3	9.4	3.3	8.4	1984
MSA[1]	5.5	18.6	14.7	12.2	13.4	9.1	8.0	3.5	14.9	1981
U.S.	4.1	14.3	13.9	13.5	15.3	10.7	10.4	5.0	12.8	1977

Note: Figures are percentages except for Median Year; Note: (1) Figures cover the Rochester, MN Metropolitan Statistical Area—see Appendix B for areas included
Source: U.S. Census Bureau, 2014-2018 American Community Survey 5-Year Estimates

Gross Monthly Rent

Area	Under $500	$500 -$999	$1,000 -$1,499	$1,500 -$1,999	$2,000 -$2,499	$2,500 -$2,999	$3,000 and up	Median ($)
City	9.1	46.2	27.7	12.3	2.0	1.1	1.6	942
MSA[1]	12.2	49.0	25.4	9.7	1.8	0.8	1.1	876
U.S.	9.8	38.5	29.6	12.9	5.1	2.1	2.0	1,023

Note: Figures are percentages except for Median; Gross rent is the contract rent plus the estimated average monthly cost of utilities (electricity, gas, and water and sewer) and fuels (oil, coal, kerosene, wood, etc.) if these are paid by the renter (or paid for the renter by someone else); (1) Figures cover the Rochester, MN Metropolitan Statistical Area—see Appendix B for areas included
Source: U.S. Census Bureau, 2014-2018 American Community Survey 5-Year Estimates

HEALTH

Health Risk Factors

Category	MSA[1] (%)	U.S. (%)
Adults aged 18–64 who have any kind of health care coverage	90.6	87.3
Adults who reported being in good or better health	90.8	82.4
Adults who have been told they have high blood cholesterol	30.6	33.0
Adults who have been told they have high blood pressure	26.2	32.3
Adults who are current smokers	12.4	17.1
Adults who currently use E-cigarettes	n/a	4.6
Adults who currently use chewing tobacco, snuff, or snus	3.3	4.0
Adults who are heavy drinkers[2]	5.9	6.3
Adults who are binge drinkers[3]	15.7	17.4
Adults who are overweight (BMI 25.0 - 29.9)	37.2	35.3
Adults who are obese (BMI 30.0 - 99.8)	30.5	31.3
Adults who participated in any physical activities in the past month	74.9	74.4
Adults who always or nearly always wears a seat belt	97.5	94.3

Note: n/a not available; (1) Figures cover the Rochester, MN Metropolitan Statistical Area—see Appendix B for areas included; (2) Heavy drinkers are classified as adult men having more than 14 drinks per week and adult women having more than 7 drinks per week; (3) Binge drinkers are classified as males having five or more drinks on one occasion or females having four or more drinks on one occasion
Source: Centers for Disease Control and Prevention, Behaviorial Risk Factor Surveillance System, SMART: Selected Metropolitan Area Risk Trends, 2017

Acute and Chronic Health Conditions

Category	MSA[1] (%)	U.S. (%)
Adults who have ever been told they had a heart attack	3.3	4.2
Adults who have ever been told they have angina or coronary heart disease	3.8	3.9
Adults who have ever been told they had a stroke	2.2	3.0
Adults who have ever been told they have asthma	12.8	14.2
Adults who have ever been told they have arthritis	21.7	24.9
Adults who have ever been told they have diabetes[2]	9.2	10.5
Adults who have ever been told they had skin cancer	7.0	6.2
Adults who have ever been told they had any other types of cancer	5.8	7.1
Adults who have ever been told they have COPD	5.4	6.5
Adults who have ever been told they have kidney disease	2.6	3.0
Adults who have ever been told they have a form of depression	19.2	20.5

Note: (1) Figures cover the Rochester, MN Metropolitan Statistical Area—see Appendix B for areas included; (2) Figures do not include pregnancy-related, borderline, or pre-diabetes
Source: Centers for Disease Control and Prevention, Behaviorial Risk Factor Surveillance System, SMART: Selected Metropolitan Area Risk Trends, 2017

Health Screening and Vaccination Rates

Category	MSA[1] (%)	U.S. (%)
Adults aged 65+ who have had flu shot within the past year	73.6	60.7
Adults aged 65+ who have ever had a pneumonia vaccination	85.4	75.4
Adults who have ever been tested for HIV	23.8	36.1
Adults who have ever had the shingles or zoster vaccine?	40.5	28.9
Adults who have had their blood cholesterol checked within the last five years	86.1	85.9

Note: n/a not available; (1) Figures cover the Rochester, MN Metropolitan Statistical Area—see Appendix B for areas included.
Source: Centers for Disease Control and Prevention, Behaviorial Risk Factor Surveillance System, SMART: Selected Metropolitan Area Risk Trends, 2017

Disability Status

Category	MSA[1] (%)	U.S. (%)
Adults who reported being deaf	7.9	6.7
Are you blind or have serious difficulty seeing, even when wearing glasses?	3.2	4.5
Are you limited in any way in any of your usual activities due of arthritis?	10.6	12.9
Do you have difficulty doing errands alone?	3.6	6.8
Do you have difficulty dressing or bathing?	2.3	3.6
Do you have serious difficulty concentrating/remembering/making decisions?	8.5	10.7
Do you have serious difficulty walking or climbing stairs?	10.0	13.6

Note: (1) Figures cover the Rochester, MN Metropolitan Statistical Area—see Appendix B for areas included.
Source: Centers for Disease Control and Prevention, Behaviorial Risk Factor Surveillance System, SMART: Selected Metropolitan Area Risk Trends, 2017

Mortality Rates for the Top 10 Causes of Death in the U.S.

ICD-10[a] Sub-Chapter	ICD-10[a] Code	Age-Adjusted Mortality Rate[1] per 100,000 population	
		County[2]	U.S.
Malignant neoplasms	C00-C97	130.4	152.4
Ischaemic heart diseases	I20-I25	75.8	92.7
Other forms of heart disease	I30-I51	32.1	52.5
Chronic lower respiratory diseases	J40-J47	29.3	40.4
Cerebrovascular diseases	I60-I69	27.9	37.3
Other degenerative diseases of the nervous system	G30-G31	51.1	36.4
Other external causes of accidental injury	W00-X59	29.5	35.3
Organic, including symptomatic, mental disorders	F01-F09	40.7	30.0
Hypertensive diseases	I10-I15	15.1	22.9
Diabetes mellitus	E10-E14	10.4	21.3

Note: (a) ICD-10 = International Classification of Diseases 10th Revision; (1) Mortality rates are a three year average covering 2016-2018; (2) Figures cover Olmsted County.
Source: Centers for Disease Control and Prevention, National Center for Health Statistics. Underlying Cause of Death 1999-2018 on CDC WONDER Online Database

Mortality Rates for Selected Causes of Death

ICD-10[a] Sub-Chapter	ICD-10[a] Code	Age-Adjusted Mortality Rate[1] per 100,000 population	
		County[2]	U.S.
Assault	X85-Y09	Suppressed	6.0
Diseases of the liver	K70-K76	7.9	14.2
Human immunodeficiency virus (HIV) disease	B20-B24	Suppressed	1.6
Influenza and pneumonia	J09-J18	4.7	14.2
Intentional self-harm	X60-X84	11.5	13.9
Malnutrition	E40-E46	Suppressed	1.9
Obesity and other hyperalimentation	E65-E68	Suppressed	2.1
Renal failure	N17-N19	Unreliable	12.8
Transport accidents	V01-V99	7.5	12.5
Viral hepatitis	B15-B19	Suppressed	1.4

Note: (a) ICD-10 = International Classification of Diseases 10th Revision; (1) Mortality rates are a three year average covering 2016-2018; (2) Figures cover Olmsted County; Data are suppressed when the data meet the criteria for confidentiality constraints; Mortality rates are flagged as unreliable when the rate would be calculated with a numerator of 20 or less.
Source: Centers for Disease Control and Prevention, National Center for Health Statistics. Underlying Cause of Death 1999-2018 on CDC WONDER Online Database

Health Insurance Coverage

Area	With Health Insurance	With Private Health Insurance	With Public Health Insurance	Without Health Insurance	Population Under Age 19 Without Health Insurance
City	95.7	79.2	30.2	4.3	2.6
MSA[1]	95.4	79.9	30.1	4.6	3.5
U.S.	90.6	67.7	34.7	9.4	5.2

Note: Figures are percentages that cover the civilian noninstitutionalized population; (1) Figures cover the Rochester, MN Metropolitan Statistical Area—see Appendix B for areas included
Source: U.S. Census Bureau, 2014-2018 American Community Survey 5-Year Estimates

Number of Medical Professionals

Area	MDs[3]	DOs[3,4]	Dentists	Podiatrists	Chiropractors	Optometrists
County[1] (number)	3,815	88	172	10	66	37
County[1] (rate[2])	2,462.4	56.8	110.1	6.4	42.2	23.7
U.S. (rate[2])	281.9	23.4	69.1	6.0	27.5	16.4

Note: Data as of 2018 unless noted; (1) Data covers Olmsted County; (2) Rate per 100,000 population; (3) Data as of 2017 and includes all active, non-federal physicians; (4) Doctor of Osteopathic Medicine
Source: U.S. Department of Health and Human Services, Health Resources and Services Administration, Bureau of Health Professions, Area Resource File (ARF) 2018-2019

Best Hospitals

According to *U.S. News,* the Rochester, MN metro area is home to one of the best hospitals in the U.S.: **Mayo Clinic** (Honor Roll/15 adult specialties and 6 pediatric specialties). The hospital listed was nationally ranked in at least one of 16 adult or 10 pediatric specialties. Only 206 hospitals nationwide were nationally ranked in one or more adult or pediatric specialty. Twenty hospitals in the U.S. made the Honor Roll. The Best Hospitals Honor Roll takes both the national rankings and the procedure and condition ratings into account. Hospitals received points if they were nationally ranked in one of the 16 adult specialties—the higher they ranked, the more points they got—and how many ratings of "high performing" they earned in the nine procedures and conditions. *U.S. News Online, "America's Best Hospitals 2019-20"*

According to *U.S. News,* the Rochester, MN metro area is home to one of the best children's hospitals in the U.S.: **Mayo Clinic Children's Center** (6 pediatric specialties). The hospital listed was highly ranked in at least one of 10 pediatric specialties. Ninety-one children's hospitals in the U.S. were nationally ranked in at least one specialty. Hospitals received points for being ranked in a specialty, and the 10 hospitals with the most points across the 10 specialties make up the Honor Roll. *U.S. News Online, "America's Best Children's Hospitals 2019-20"*

EDUCATION

Public School District Statistics

District Name	Schls	Pupils	Pupil/ Teacher Ratio	Minority Pupils[1] (%)	Free Lunch Eligible[2] (%)	IEP[3] (%)
Rochester Public School District	45	18,015	16.1	40.8	29.9	17.6

Note: Table includes school districts with 2,000 or more students; (1) Percentage of students that are not non-Hispanic white; (2) Percentage of students that are eligible for the free lunch program; (3) Percentage of students that have an Individualized Education Program.
Source: U.S. Department of Education, National Center for Education Statistics, Common Core of Data, Local Education Agency (School District) Universe Survey: School Year 2018-2019; U.S. Department of Education, National Center for Education Statistics, Common Core of Data, Public Elementary/Secondary School Universe Survey: School Year 2018-2019

Highest Level of Education

Area	Less than H.S.	H.S. Diploma	Some College, No Deg.	Associate Degree	Bachelor's Degree	Master's Degree	Prof. School Degree	Doctorate Degree
City	6.3	18.6	18.2	11.3	25.3	11.2	5.1	4.0
MSA[1]	6.1	24.1	20.0	12.1	22.1	9.2	3.7	2.6
U.S.	12.3	27.1	20.6	8.4	19.4	8.6	2.1	1.4

Note: Figures cover persons age 25 and over; (1) Figures cover the Rochester, MN Metropolitan Statistical Area—see Appendix B for areas included
Source: U.S. Census Bureau, 2014-2018 American Community Survey 5-Year Estimates

Educational Attainment by Race

Area	High School Graduate or Higher (%)					Bachelor's Degree or Higher (%)				
	Total	White	Black	Asian	Hisp.[2]	Total	White	Black	Asian	Hisp.[2]
City	93.7	96.1	78.2	81.8	71.7	45.7	46.9	17.6	55.8	24.0
MSA[1]	93.9	95.3	79.1	82.4	70.1	37.6	37.7	17.6	54.3	21.5
U.S.	87.7	89.6	85.4	86.8	67.7	31.5	32.9	21.1	53.5	15.8

Note: Figures shown cover persons 25 years old and over; (1) Figures cover the Rochester, MN Metropolitan Statistical Area—see Appendix B for areas included; (2) People of Hispanic origin can be of any race
Source: U.S. Census Bureau, 2014-2018 American Community Survey 5-Year Estimates

School Enrollment by Grade and Control

Area	Preschool (%)		Kindergarten (%)		Grades 1 - 4 (%)		Grades 5 - 8 (%)		Grades 9 - 12 (%)	
	Public	Private	Public	Private	Public	Private	Public	Private	Public	Private
City	53.8	46.2	78.2	21.8	87.2	12.8	85.5	14.5	92.9	7.1
MSA[1]	63.3	36.7	84.0	16.0	88.0	12.0	88.3	11.7	92.9	7.1
U.S.	59.0	41.0	87.7	12.3	89.6	10.4	89.5	10.5	90.2	9.8

Note: Figures shown cover persons 3 years old and over; (1) Figures cover the Rochester, MN Metropolitan Statistical Area—see Appendix B for areas included
Source: U.S. Census Bureau, 2014-2018 American Community Survey 5-Year Estimates

Average Salaries of Public School Teachers

Area	2016-17		2017-18		Change from 2016-17 to 2017-18	
	Dollars	Rank[1]	Dollars	Rank[1]	Percent	Rank[2]
Minnesota	57,346	19	57,782	20	0.76	35
U.S. Average	59,539	–	60,477	–	1.58	–

Note: (1) Rank ranges from 1 to 51 where 1 indicates highest salary; (2) Rank ranges from 1 to 51 where 1 indicates highest percent change.
Source: National Education Association, Rankings & Estimates: Rankings of the States 2018 and Estimates of School Statistics 2019

Higher Education

Four-Year Colleges			Two-Year Colleges			Medical Schools[1]	Law Schools[2]	Voc/ Tech[3]
Public	Private Non-profit	Private For-profit	Public	Private Non-profit	Private For-profit			
1	3	1	1	0	0	1	0	2

Note: Figures cover institutions located within the city limits and include main campuses only; (1) includes schools accredited by the Liaison Committee on Medical Education and the American Osteopathic Association's Commission on Osteopathic College Accreditation; (2) includes ABA-accredited schools, schools with provisional ABA accreditation, and state accredited schools; (3) includes all schools with programs that are less than 2 years.
Source: National Center for Education Statistics, Integrated Postsecondary Education System (IPEDS), 2018-19; Wikipedia, List of Medical Schools in the United States, accessed May 1, 2020; Wikipedia, List of Law Schools in the United States, accessed May 1, 2020

According to *U.S. News & World Report*, the Rochester, MN metro area is home to one of the top 75 medical schools for research in the U.S.: **Mayo Clinic School of Medicine (Alix)** (#6 tie). The rankings are based on a weighted average of 11 measures of quality: quality assessment; peer assessment score; assessment score by residency directors; research activity; total research activity; average research activity per faculty member; student selectivity; median MCAT total score; median undergraduate GPA; acceptance rate; and faculty resources. *U.S. News & World Report, "America's Best Graduate Schools, Medical, 2021"*

PRESIDENTIAL ELECTION

2016 Presidential Election Results

Area	Clinton	Trump	Johnson	Stein	Other
Olmsted County	45.3	44.5	4.4	1.4	4.4
U.S.	48.0	45.9	3.3	1.1	1.7

Note: Results are percentages and may not add to 100% due to rounding
Source: Dave Leip's Atlas of U.S. Presidential Elections

EMPLOYERS

Major Employers

Company Name	Industry
Benchmark Electronics	Contract mfg/design/engineering
Cardinal of Minnesota	Res. services/dev. disabilities
Charter Communications	Cable & other pay television services
City of Rochester	Municipal government
Crenlo	Fabricated metal
Federal Medical Center	Corrections/medical
Halcon	Furniture manufacturer
Hiawatha Homes	Res. services/dev. disabilities
IBM	Electronics
Interstate Hotels & Resorts	Hotel/restaurant services
Kemps	Food processing
Mayo Clinic	Healthcare
McNeilus Steel	Steel fabrication
McNeilus Truck	Mobile concrete mixers, garbage trucks
Olmstead County	Government
Olmstead Medical Center	Healthcare
Pace Dairy	Food processing
RCTC	Post-secondary education
Reichel Foods	Refrigerated lunch & snacks
Rochester Meat Company	Meat processor
Rochester Medical Corp	Medical device manufacturer
Rochester Public Schools	Education
Samaritan Bethany	Health care of the aging
Seneca Food	Food processing
Think Bank	Banking and financial services

Note: Companies shown are located within the Rochester, MN Metropolitan Statistical Area.
Source: Hoovers.com; Wikipedia

PUBLIC SAFETY

Crime Rate

Area	All Crimes	Violent Crimes				Property Crimes		
		Murder	Rape[3]	Robbery	Aggrav. Assault	Burglary	Larceny -Theft	Motor Vehicle Theft
City	2,274.5	4.3	49.6	35.0	105.1	301.6	1,667.8	111.1
Suburbs[1]	731.3	1.0	24.3	6.8	50.6	147.0	459.6	41.9
Metro[2]	1,553.3	2.7	37.8	21.8	79.6	229.4	1,103.2	78.7
U.S.	2,580.1	5.0	42.6	86.2	246.8	376.0	1,594.6	228.9

Note: Figures are crimes per 100,000 population; (1) All areas within the metro area that are located outside the city limits; (2) Figures cover the Rochester, MN Metropolitan Statistical Area—see Appendix B for areas included; (3) The city and U.S. figures shown were reported using the revised Uniform Crime Reporting (UCR) definition of rape. The suburban and metro area figures shown are an aggregate total of the data submitted using both the revised and legacy UCR definitions.
Source: FBI Uniform Crime Reports, 2018

Hate Crimes

Area	Number of Quarters Reported	Number of Incidents per Bias Motivation					
		Race/Ethnicity/ Ancestry	Religion	Sexual Orientation	Disability	Gender	Gender Identity
City	4	2	3	0	0	0	0
U.S.	4	4,047	1,419	1,196	159	47	168

Source: Federal Bureau of Investigation, Hate Crime Statistics 2018

Identity Theft Consumer Reports

Area	Reports	Reports per 100,000 Population	Rank[2]
MSA[1]	141	64	318
U.S.	650,572	198	-

Note: (1) Figures cover the Rochester, MN Metropolitan Statistical Area—see Appendix B for areas included; (2) Rank ranges from 1 to 386 where 1 indicates greatest number of identity theft reports per 100,000 population
Source: Federal Trade Commission, Consumer Sentinel Network Data Book for January–December 2019

Fraud and Other Consumer Reports

Area	Reports	Reports per 100,000 Population	Rank[2]
MSA[1]	933	424	345
U.S.	2,590,177	789	-

Note: (1) Figures cover the Rochester, MN Metropolitan Statistical Area—see Appendix B for areas included; (2) Rank ranges from 1 to 386 where 1 indicates greatest number of fraud and other consumer reports per 100,000 population
Source: Federal Trade Commission, Consumer Sentinel Network Data Book for January–December 2019

SPORTS

Professional Sports Teams

Team Name	League	Year Established

No teams are located in the metro area
Source: Wikipedia, Major Professional Sports Teams of the United States and Canada, May 4, 2020

CLIMATE

Average and Extreme Temperatures

Temperature	Jan	Feb	Mar	Apr	May	Jun	Jul	Aug	Sep	Oct	Nov	Dec	Yr.
Extreme High (°F)	55	63	79	91	92	101	102	100	97	90	74	62	102
Average High (°F)	21	26	38	55	68	78	82	79	70	59	40	26	54
Average Temp. (°F)	12	18	29	45	57	67	71	69	60	48	32	19	44
Average Low (°F)	3	8	20	34	46	56	60	58	48	38	24	10	34
Extreme Low (°F)	-40	-29	-31	5	21	35	42	35	23	11	-20	-33	-40

Note: Figures cover the years 1948-1995
Source: National Climatic Data Center, International Station Meteorological Climate Summary, 9/96

Average Precipitation/Snowfall/Humidity

Precip./Humidity	Jan	Feb	Mar	Apr	May	Jun	Jul	Aug	Sep	Oct	Nov	Dec	Yr.
Avg. Precip. (in.)	0.8	0.8	1.8	2.8	3.4	4.0	4.2	3.9	3.1	2.0	1.7	1.0	29.4
Avg. Snowfall (in.)	9	8	10	4	Tr	0	0	0	Tr	1	6	10	47
Avg. Rel. Hum. 6am (%)	80	81	82	80	80	82	86	88	87	82	83	83	83
Avg. Rel. Hum. 3pm (%)	72	68	65	54	52	53	56	57	56	54	66	74	61

Note: Figures cover the years 1948-1995; Tr = Trace amounts (<0.05 in. of rain; <0.5 in. of snow)
Source: National Climatic Data Center, International Station Meteorological Climate Summary, 9/96

Weather Conditions

Temperature			Daytime Sky			Precipitation		
5°F & below	32°F & below	90°F & above	Clear	Partly cloudy	Cloudy	0.01 inch or more precip.	0.1 inch or more snow/ice	Thunder-storms
46	165	9	87	126	152	114	40	41

Note: Figures are average number of days per year and cover the years 1948-1995
Source: National Climatic Data Center, International Station Meteorological Climate Summary, 9/96

HAZARDOUS WASTE

Superfund Sites

The Rochester, MN metro area has no sites on the EPA's Superfund Final National Priorities List. There are a total of 1,387 Superfund sites with a status of proposed or final on the list in the U.S.
U.S. Environmental Protection Agency, National Priorities List, May 5, 2020

**AIR & WATER
QUALITY**

Air Quality Trends: Ozone

	1990	1995	2000	2005	2010	2012	2014	2016	2017	2018
MSA[1]	n/a	n/a	n/a	n/a	n/a	n/a	n/a	n/a	n/a	n/a
U.S.	0.088	0.089	0.082	0.080	0.073	0.075	0.067	0.069	0.068	0.069

Note: (1) Data covers the Rochester, MN Metropolitan Statistical Area—see Appendix B for areas included; n/a not available. The values shown are the composite ozone concentration averages among trend sites based on the highest fourth daily maximum 8-hour concentration in parts per million. These trends are based on sites having an adequate record of monitoring data during the trend period. Data from exceptional events are included.
Source: U.S. Environmental Protection Agency, Air Quality Monitoring Information, "Air Quality Trends by City, 1990-2018"

Air Quality Index

Area	Percent of Days when Air Quality was...[2]					AQI Statistics[2]	
	Good	Moderate	Unhealthy for Sensitive Groups	Unhealthy	Very Unhealthy	Maximum	Median
MSA[1]	80.9	19.1	0.0	0.0	0.0	98	38

Note: (1) Data covers the Rochester, MN Metropolitan Statistical Area—see Appendix B for areas included; (2) Based on 361 days with AQI data in 2018. Air Quality Index (AQI) is an index for reporting daily air quality. EPA calculates the AQI for five major air pollutants regulated by the Clean Air Act: ground-level ozone, particle pollution (aka particulate matter), carbon monoxide, sulfur dioxide, and nitrogen dioxide. The AQI runs from 0 to 500. The higher the AQI value, the greater the level of air pollution and the greater the health concern. There are six AQI categories: "Good" AQI is between 0 and 50. Air quality is considered satisfactory; "Moderate" AQI is between 51 and 100. Air quality is acceptable; "Unhealthy for Sensitive Groups" When AQI values are between 101 and 150, members of sensitive groups may experience health effects; "Unhealthy" When AQI values are between 151 and 200 everyone may begin to experience health effects; "Very Unhealthy" AQI values between 201 and 300 trigger a health alert; "Hazardous" AQI values over 300 trigger warnings of emergency conditions (not shown).
Source: U.S. Environmental Protection Agency, Air Quality Index Report, 2018

Air Quality Index Pollutants

Area	Percent of Days when AQI Pollutant was...[2]					
	Carbon Monoxide	Nitrogen Dioxide	Ozone	Sulfur Dioxide	Particulate Matter 2.5	Particulate Matter 10
MSA[1]	0.0	0.0	41.0	0.0	59.0	0.0

Note: (1) Data covers the Rochester, MN Metropolitan Statistical Area—see Appendix B for areas included; (2) Based on 361 days with AQI data in 2018. The Air Quality Index (AQI) is an index for reporting daily air quality. EPA calculates the AQI for five major air pollutants regulated by the Clean Air Act: ground-level ozone, particle pollution (also known as particulate matter), carbon monoxide, sulfur dioxide, and nitrogen dioxide. The AQI runs from 0 to 500. The higher the AQI value, the greater the level of air pollution and the greater the health concern.
Source: U.S. Environmental Protection Agency, Air Quality Index Report, 2018

Maximum Air Pollutant Concentrations: Particulate Matter, Ozone, CO and Lead

	Particulate Matter 10 (ug/m³)	Particulate Matter 2.5 Wtd AM (ug/m³)	Particulate Matter 2.5 24-Hr (ug/m³)	Ozone (ppm)	Carbon Monoxide (ppm)	Lead (ug/m³)
MSA[1] Level	n/a	8.3	20	0.056	n/a	n/a
NAAQS[2]	150	15	35	0.075	9	0.15
Met NAAQS[2]	n/a	Yes	Yes	Yes	n/a	n/a

Note: (1) Data covers the Rochester, MN Metropolitan Statistical Area—see Appendix B for areas included; Data from exceptional events are included; (2) National Ambient Air Quality Standards; ppm = parts per million; ug/m³ = micrograms per cubic meter; n/a not available.
Concentrations: Particulate Matter 10 (coarse particulate)—highest second maximum 24-hour concentration; Particulate Matter 2.5 Wtd AM (fine particulate)—highest weighted annual mean concentration; Particulate Matter 2.5 24-Hour (fine particulate)—highest 98th percentile 24-hour concentration; Ozone—highest fourth daily maximum 8-hour concentration; Carbon Monoxide—highest second maximum non-overlapping 8-hour concentration; Lead—maximum running 3-month average
Source: U.S. Environmental Protection Agency, Air Quality Monitoring Information, "Air Quality Statistics by City, 2018"

Maximum Air Pollutant Concentrations: Nitrogen Dioxide and Sulfur Dioxide

	Nitrogen Dioxide AM (ppb)	Nitrogen Dioxide 1-Hr (ppb)	Sulfur Dioxide AM (ppb)	Sulfur Dioxide 1-Hr (ppb)	Sulfur Dioxide 24-Hr (ppb)
MSA[1] Level	n/a	n/a	n/a	n/a	n/a
NAAQS[2]	53	100	30	75	140
Met NAAQS[2]	n/a	n/a	n/a	n/a	n/a

Note: (1) Data covers the Rochester, MN Metropolitan Statistical Area—see Appendix B for areas included; Data from exceptional events are included; (2) National Ambient Air Quality Standards; ppm = parts per million; ug/m³ = micrograms per cubic meter; n/a not available.
Concentrations: Nitrogen Dioxide AM—highest arithmetic mean concentration; Nitrogen Dioxide 1-Hr—highest 98th percentile 1-hour daily maximum concentration; Sulfur Dioxide AM—highest annual mean concentration; Sulfur Dioxide 1-Hr—highest 99th percentile 1-hour daily maximum concentration; Sulfur Dioxide 24-Hr—highest second maximum 24-hour concentration
Source: U.S. Environmental Protection Agency, Air Quality Monitoring Information, "Air Quality Statistics by City, 2018"

Drinking Water

Water System Name	Pop. Served	Primary Water Source Type	Violations[1]
Rochester	114,011	Ground	0

Note: (1) Total number of violations (both active and inactive) in the EPA database
Source: U.S. Environmental Protection Agency, Office of Ground Water and Drinking Water, Safe Drinking Water Information System (based on data extracted May 5, 2020)

Maximum Air Pollutant Concentrations: Nitrogen Dioxide and Sulfur Dioxide

	Nitrogen Dioxide AM (ppb)	Sulfur Dioxide AM (ppb)	Sulfur Dioxide 1h (ppb)	Sulfur Dioxide 24h (ppb)
MSA Level	n/a	n/a	n/a	n/a
NAAQS	53	100	30	140
MofN AQS	n/a	n/a	n/a	n/a

Drinking Water

Water System Name	Primary Water Source	Population Served	Violation
Rochester	Ground	114,011	0

Sioux Falls, South Dakota

Background

Sioux Falls, in southeastern South Dakota, is named for the falls on the Big Sioux River where it is located. It is the seat of Minnehaha County and overlaps Lincoln County. Sioux Falls is a Great Plains city, rich in history and scenic attractions, a dynamic economic center, and a splendid family town, offering an extensive range of outdoor activities.

The city was founded prior to the Civil War by settlers who were attracted by the nearby stone quarries and the possibility of harnessing the river for water power. Many Scottish, English, and Norwegian immigrants came to the area and used their skills as stonecutters. The community was incorporated as a village in 1877 and as a city in 1883.

At the city's popular Falls Park, the remains of a water-driven mill testify to the importance of the river. The city has preserved much of its early architectural charm, with five separate historical districts preserving buildings of considerable interest. Of particular interest are the R.F. Pettigrew home, residence of the state's first U.S. senator, and the Minnehaha County Courthouse.

Sioux Falls's restoration "Phillips to the Falls" program joined the park to the rest of downtown by extending Phillips Avenue north to Falls Park and expands the park to the south.

Sioux Falls offers one of the Midwest's most dynamic business environments, partly due to the lack of a state corporate income tax, and is home to industry leaders in agri-business, distribution and trade, financial services, high-tech manufacturing, health care, retail and tourism. City infrastructure work continues on 23,000 acres, an area larger than half the present size of the city, in eastern Sioux Falls, to prepare the area for growth. Two of this city's largest companies are Wells Fargo and Citigroup.

The city is at the heart of a large agricultural and stock-raising area, producing corn and soybeans, and serving as a regional center for stockyards and meat-packing plants. Industries in Sioux Falls also produce computer components, electronics, and artificial flowers. Some of the nation's leading credit card operations are based in the city, employment opportunities are varied and abundant, and the city's unemployment rate is generally half that of the state as a whole. Air travel is available through the Sioux Falls Regional Airport, which connects conveniently to major air hubs.

Sioux Falls is an important center of higher education, home to the University of South Dakota, Dakota State University, South Dakota State University, Northern State University, Augustana College, National American University, Colorado Technical University at Sioux Falls, and Southeast Technical Institute. The Federal Earth Resource Observation System operates a major data collection and analysis site nearby.

The city and its environs are home to a variety of recreation, such as the Catfish Bay Water Ski & Stage Show, Empire Golf Sport Dome, Great Bear Recreation Park, Huset's Speedway, and Wild Water West, the state's largest water and amusement park. The Downtown River Greenway Project includes significant greenway reconstruction on the east bank of the Big Sioux River.

The modern Washington Pavilion of Arts and Science in the Sioux Falls historic downtown district features a performing arts space, a domed Omni theater, a science museum, and display areas for the city's Fine Arts Center. The Sioux Falls Jazz and Blues Festival will celebrate its 30the anniversary in 2021.

The climate is continental with frequent daily or weekly weather changes, a result of differing, usually cold, air masses, which move in very rapidly. During the late fall and winter, cold fronts accompanied by strong, gusty winds can cause temperatures to drop significantly during a 24-hour period. Rainfall is heavier during the spring and summer, and thunderstorms are frequent. Summer daytime temperatures can be high, but the nights are usually comfortable.

Rankings

General Rankings

- Sioux Falls was selected as one of the best places to live in the United States by *Money* magazine. The city ranked #50 out of 100. This year's list focused on cities with populations of 50,000 or greater. Beginning with a pool of 1,796 candidates, editors looked at 80 separate types of data, from local economy and housing market to education, diversity and ease of living—and then sent reporters to interview residents, search neighborhoods and look for other intangibles. *Money, "Best Places to Live, 2019" September 16, 2019*

- In their sixth annual survey, Livability.com looked at data for more than 1,000 U.S. cities to determine the rankings for Livability's "Top 100 Best Places to Live" in 2019. Sioux Falls ranked #7. Criteria: median home value capped at $250,000; affordable living; vibrant economy; education, demographics, health care options. transportation & infrastructure; abundant lifestyle amenities. *Livability.com, "Top 100 Best Places to Live 2019" March 2019*

Business/Finance Rankings

- Experian's latest annual report on consumer credit ranked cities by the average credit score of its residents. Sioux Falls was ranked #7 among the ten cities with the highest average credit score, meaning that its residents showed strong credit management. *www.usatoday.com, "Minneapolis Tops List of Cities With Best Average Credit Score; Greenwood Miss., at the Bottom," January 11, 2018*

- The Sioux Falls metro area appeared on the Milken Institute "2020 Best Performing Cities" list. Rank: #24 out of 201 small metro areas. Criteria: job growth; wage and salary growth; high-tech output growth. *Milken Institute, "Best-Performing Cities 2020," February 26, 2020*

- *Forbes* ranked 203 smaller metro areas (population under 268,000) to determine the nation's "Best Small Places for Business and Careers." The Sioux Falls metro area was ranked #1. Criteria: costs (business and living); job growth (past and projected); income growth; quality of life; educational attainment (college and high school); projected economic growth; cultural and leisure opportunities; workplace tolerance laws; net migration patterns. *Forbes, "The Best Small Places for Business and Careers 2019," October 30, 2019*

Dating/Romance Rankings

- Sioux Falls was selected as one of the most romantic cities in the U.S. by video-rental kiosk company Redbox. The city ranked #7 out of 20. Criteria: number of romance-related rentals in 2016. *Redbox, "20 Most Romantic Cities," February 6, 2017*

Health/Fitness Rankings

- *Men's Health* ranked 100 major U.S. cities in terms of the best cities for men. Sioux Falls ranked #50. Criteria: health; fitness; quality of life. *Men's Health, "The Best & Worst Cities for Men Who Want to Be Fit and Happy," January 1, 2016*

Real Estate Rankings

- *WalletHub* compared the most populated U.S. cities, as well as at least two of the most populated cities in each state, for a total of 179, to determine which had the best markets for real estate agents. Sioux Falls ranked #14 where demand was high and pay was the best. Criteria: sales per agent; annual median wage for real-estate agents; monthly average starting salary for real estate agents; real estate job density and competition; unemployment rate; home turnover rate; housing-market health index; and other relevant metrics. *www.WalletHub.com, "2019's Best Places to Be a Real Estate Agent," April 24, 2019*

- The Sioux Falls metro area was identified as one of the 20 best housing markets in the U.S. in 2019. The area ranked #15 out of 180 markets. Criteria: year-over-year change of median sales price of existing single-family homes between the 4th quarter of 2018 and the 4th quarter of 2019. *National Association of Realtors®, Median Sales Price of Existing Single-Family Homes for Metropolitan Areas, 4th Quarter 2019*

Safety Rankings

- Allstate ranked the 200 largest cities in America in terms of driver safety. Sioux Falls ranked #72. Criteria: internal property damage claims over a two-year period from January 2016 to December 2017. The report helps increase the importance of safety and awareness behind the wheel. *Allstate, "Allstate America's Best Drivers Report, 2019" June 24, 2019*

- The National Insurance Crime Bureau ranked 382 metro areas in the U.S. in terms of per capita rates of vehicle theft. The Sioux Falls metro area ranked #159 (#1 = highest rate). Criteria: number of vehicle theft offenses per 100,000 inhabitants in 2018. *National Insurance Crime Bureau, "Hot Spots 2018," June 25, 2019*

Seniors/Retirement Rankings

- From its Best Cities for Successful Aging indexes, the Milken Institute generated rankings for metropolitan areas, weighing data in nine categories—health care, wellness, living arrangements, transportation and convenience, financial characteristics, education, employment, community engagement, and overall livability. The Sioux Falls metro area was ranked #5 overall in the small metro area category. *Milken Institute, "Best Cities for Successful Aging, 2017" March 14, 2017*

Women/Minorities Rankings

- *Women's Health*, together with the site Yelp, identified the 15 "Wellthiest" spots in the U.S. Sioux Falls appeared among the top for happiest, healthiest, outdoorsiest and Zen-iest. *Women's Health, "The 15 Wellthiest Cities in the U.S." July 5, 2017*

- Personal finance website *WalletHub* compared more than 180 U.S. cities—including the 150 most populated U.S. cities, plus at least two of the most populated cities in each state—across two key dimensions, "Hispanic Business-Friendliness" and "Hispanic Purchasing Power", to arrive at the most favorable conditions for Hispanic entrepreneurs. Sioux Falls was ranked #19 out of 182. Criteria includes: share of Hispanic-Owned Businesses; Hispanic entrepreneurship rate to median annual income of Hispanics; Small Business-Friendliness score; cost of living; and number of Hispanics with at least a bachelor's degree. *WalletHub.com, "2019's Best Cities for Hispanic Entrepreneurs," May 1, 2019*

Miscellaneous Rankings

- *WalletHub* compared the 150 most populated U.S. cities to determine their operating efficiency. A "Quality of Services" score was constructed for each city and then divided by the total budget per capita to reveal which were managed the best. Sioux Falls ranked #11. Criteria: financial stability; economy; education; safety; health; infrastructure and pollution. *www.WalletHub.com, "2019's Best- & Worst-Run Cities in America," July 1, 2019*

Business Environment

CITY FINANCES

City Government Finances

Component	2017 ($000)	2017 ($ per capita)
Total Revenues	384,713	2,243
Total Expenditures	342,239	1,995
Debt Outstanding	380,916	2,221
Cash and Securities[1]	772,340	4,502

Note: (1) Cash and security holdings of a government at the close of its fiscal year, including those of its dependent agencies, utilities, and liquor stores.
Source: U.S. Census Bureau, State & Local Government Finances 2017

City Government Revenue by Source

Source	2017 ($000)	2017 ($ per capita)	2017 (%)
General Revenue			
From Federal Government	8,943	52	2.3
From State Government	9,183	54	2.4
From Local Governments	0	0	0.0
Taxes			
Property	57,499	335	14.9
Sales and Gross Receipts	141,541	825	36.8
Personal Income	0	0	0.0
Corporate Income	0	0	0.0
Motor Vehicle License	0	0	0.0
Other Taxes	5,597	33	1.5
Current Charges	52,498	306	13.6
Liquor Store	0	0	0.0
Utility	44,208	258	11.5
Employee Retirement	47,974	280	12.5

Source: U.S. Census Bureau, State & Local Government Finances 2017

City Government Expenditures by Function

Function	2017 ($000)	2017 ($ per capita)	2017 (%)
General Direct Expenditures			
Air Transportation	0	0	0.0
Corrections	0	0	0.0
Education	0	0	0.0
Employment Security Administration	0	0	0.0
Financial Administration	2,378	13	0.7
Fire Protection	23,353	136	6.8
General Public Buildings	2,394	14	0.7
Governmental Administration, Other	7,714	45	2.3
Health	10,924	63	3.2
Highways	67,927	396	19.8
Hospitals	0	0	0.0
Housing and Community Development	5,606	32	1.6
Interest on General Debt	6,455	37	1.9
Judicial and Legal	1,483	8	0.4
Libraries	7,884	46	2.3
Parking	2,118	12	0.6
Parks and Recreation	40,454	235	11.8
Police Protection	29,637	172	8.7
Public Welfare	0	0	0.0
Sewerage	35,115	204	10.3
Solid Waste Management	7,497	43	2.2
Veterans' Services	0	0	0.0
Liquor Store	0	0	0.0
Utility	41,286	240	12.1
Employee Retirement	30,344	176	8.9

Source: U.S. Census Bureau, State & Local Government Finances 2017

DEMOGRAPHICS

Population Growth

Area	1990 Census	2000 Census	2010 Census	2018* Estimate	Population Growth (%) 1990-2018	Population Growth (%) 2010-2018
City	102,262	123,975	153,888	174,151	70.3	13.2
MSA[1]	153,500	187,093	228,261	255,438	66.4	11.9
U.S.	248,709,873	281,421,906	308,745,538	322,903,030	29.8	4.6

Note: (1) Figures cover the Sioux Falls, SD Metropolitan Statistical Area—see Appendix B for areas included; (*) 2014-2018 5-year estimated population
Source: U.S. Census Bureau, 1990 Census, Census 2000, Census 2010, 2014-2018 American Community Survey 5-Year Estimates

Household Size

Area	Persons in Household (%) One	Two	Three	Four	Five	Six	Seven or More	Average Household Size
City	32.3	33.8	13.1	12.3	5.3	2.0	1.2	2.40
MSA[1]	28.8	35.1	13.5	13.3	6.1	2.2	1.1	2.50
U.S.	27.7	33.9	15.7	13.0	6.0	2.3	1.4	2.60

Note: (1) Figures cover the Sioux Falls, SD Metropolitan Statistical Area—see Appendix B for areas included
Source: U.S. Census Bureau, 2014-2018 American Community Survey 5-Year Estimates

Race

Area	White Alone[2] (%)	Black Alone[2] (%)	Asian Alone[2] (%)	AIAN[3] Alone[2] (%)	NHOPI[4] Alone[2] (%)	Other Race Alone[2] (%)	Two or More Races (%)
City	84.5	6.0	2.5	2.4	0.0	1.5	3.0
MSA[1]	88.3	4.2	1.8	1.9	0.0	1.2	2.5
U.S.	72.7	12.7	5.4	0.8	0.2	4.9	3.2

Note: (1) Figures cover the Sioux Falls, SD Metropolitan Statistical Area—see Appendix B for areas included; (2) Alone is defined as not being in combination with one or more other races; (3) American Indian and Alaska Native; (4) Native Hawaiian and Other Pacific Islander
Source: U.S. Census Bureau, 2014-2018 American Community Survey 5-Year Estimates

Hispanic or Latino Origin

Area	Total (%)	Mexican (%)	Puerto Rican (%)	Cuban (%)	Other (%)
City	5.3	3.3	0.3	0.0	1.7
MSA[1]	4.1	2.5	0.2	0.0	1.3
U.S.	17.8	11.2	1.7	0.7	4.2

Note: Persons of Hispanic or Latino origin can be of any race; (1) Figures cover the Sioux Falls, SD Metropolitan Statistical Area—see Appendix B for areas included
Source: U.S. Census Bureau, 2014-2018 American Community Survey 5-Year Estimates

Segregation

Type	Segregation Indices[1] 1990	2000	2010	2010 Rank[2]	Percent Change 1990-2000	1990-2010	2000-2010
Black/White	n/a	n/a	n/a	n/a	n/a	n/a	n/a
Asian/White	n/a	n/a	n/a	n/a	n/a	n/a	n/a
Hispanic/White	n/a	n/a	n/a	n/a	n/a	n/a	n/a

Note: All figures cover the Metropolitan Statistical Area—see Appendix B for areas included; Figures are based on an analysis of 1990, 2000, and 2010 Census Decennial Census tract data by William H. Frey, Brookings Institution and the University of Michigan Social Science Data Analysis Network. In this analysis all racial groups (whites, blacks, and asians) are non-Hispanic members of those races. Hispanics are shown as a separate category; (1) Segregation Indices are Dissimilarity Indices that measure the degree to which the minority group is distributed differently than whites across census tracts. They range from 0 (complete integration) to 100 (complete segregation) where the value indicates the percentage of the minority group that needs to move to be distributed exactly like whites; (2) Ranges from 1 (most segregated) to 102 (least segregated); n/a not available.
Source: www.CensusScope.org

Ancestry

Area	German	Irish	English	American	Italian	Polish	French[2]	Scottish	Dutch
City	35.6	10.8	5.1	3.5	1.6	1.7	2.3	1.3	5.7
MSA[1]	38.0	10.5	5.1	3.9	1.4	1.6	2.2	1.1	6.5
U.S.	13.7	9.9	7.3	6.4	5.2	2.8	2.4	1.7	1.2

Note: Figures are the percentage of the total population reporting a particular ancestry. The nine most commonly reported ancestries in the U.S. are shown. Figures include multiple ancestries (e.g. if a person reported being Irish and Italian, they were included in both columns); (1) Figures cover the Sioux Falls, SD Metropolitan Statistical Area—see Appendix B for areas included; (2) Excludes Basque
Source: U.S. Census Bureau, 2014-2018 American Community Survey 5-Year Estimates

Foreign-born Population

Area	Any Foreign Country	Asia	Mexico	Europe	Caribbean	Central America[2]	South America	Africa	Canada
City	8.1	2.3	0.5	0.9	0.1	0.9	0.1	3.2	0.1
MSA[1]	5.9	1.6	0.4	0.7	0.1	0.6	0.1	2.2	0.1
U.S.	13.5	4.1	3.5	1.5	1.3	1.1	0.9	0.7	0.3

Note: (1) Figures cover the Sioux Falls, SD Metropolitan Statistical Area—see Appendix B for areas included; (2) Excludes Mexico.
Source: U.S. Census Bureau, 2014-2018 American Community Survey 5-Year Estimates

Marital Status

Area	Never Married	Now Married[2]	Separated	Widowed	Divorced
City	34.1	48.3	1.5	5.2	11.0
MSA[1]	30.5	52.9	1.3	5.1	10.2
U.S.	33.3	48.1	2.0	5.8	10.8

Note: Figures are percentages and cover the population 15 years of age and older; (1) Figures cover the Sioux Falls, SD Metropolitan Statistical Area—see Appendix B for areas included; (2) Excludes separated
Source: U.S. Census Bureau, 2014-2018 American Community Survey 5-Year Estimates

Disability by Age

Area	All Ages	Under 18 Years Old	18 to 64 Years Old	65 Years and Over
City	10.3	3.7	9.0	30.5
MSA[1]	9.8	3.5	8.5	29.6
U.S.	12.6	4.2	10.3	35.0

Note: Figures show percent of the civilian noninstitutionalized population that reported having a disability. Disability status is determined from six types of difficulty: vision, hearing, cognitive, ambulatory, self-care, and independent living. For children under 5 years old, hearing and vision difficulty are used to determine disability status. For children between the ages of 5 and 14, disability status is determined from hearing, vision, cognitive, ambulatory, and self-care difficulties. For people aged 15 years and older, they are considered to have a disability if they have difficulty with any one of the six difficulty types; Note: (1) Figures cover the Sioux Falls, SD Metropolitan Statistical Area—see Appendix B for areas included
Source: U.S. Census Bureau, 2014-2018 American Community Survey 5-Year Estimates

Age

Area	Under Age 5	Age 5–19	Age 20–34	Age 35–44	Age 45–54	Age 55–64	Age 65–74	Age 75–84	Age 85+	Median Age
City	7.6	19.8	23.8	13.1	11.6	11.9	7.2	3.2	1.8	34.2
MSA[1]	7.7	20.6	21.7	13.2	12.1	12.0	7.5	3.4	1.8	35.0
U.S.	6.1	19.3	20.7	12.6	13.2	12.8	8.8	4.5	1.9	37.9

Note: (1) Figures cover the Sioux Falls, SD Metropolitan Statistical Area—see Appendix B for areas included
Source: U.S. Census Bureau, 2014-2018 American Community Survey 5-Year Estimates

Gender

Area	Males	Females	Males per 100 Females
City	86,757	87,394	99.3
MSA[1]	128,146	127,292	100.7
U.S.	158,984,190	163,918,840	97.0

Note: (1) Figures cover the Sioux Falls, SD Metropolitan Statistical Area—see Appendix B for areas included
Source: U.S. Census Bureau, 2014-2018 American Community Survey 5-Year Estimates

Religious Groups by Family

Area	Catholic	Baptist	Non-Den.	Methodist[2]	Lutheran	LDS[3]	Pente-costal	Presby-terian[4]	Muslim[5]	Judaism
MSA[1]	14.9	3.0	1.5	3.9	21.4	0.7	1.1	6.2	0.3	0.1
U.S.	19.1	9.3	4.0	4.0	2.3	2.0	1.9	1.6	0.8	0.7

Note: Figures are the number of adherents as a percentage of the total population; (1) Figures cover the Sioux Falls, SD Metropolitan Statistical Area—see Appendix B for areas included; (2) Methodist/Pietist; (3) Latter Day Saints; (4) Reformed; (5) Figures are estimates
Source: Association of Statisticians of American Religious Bodies, 2010 U.S. Religion Census: Religious Congregations & Membership Study

Religious Groups by Tradition

Area	Catholic	Evangelical Protestant	Mainline Protestant	Other Tradition	Black Protestant	Orthodox
MSA[1]	14.9	12.9	28.1	1.2	0.1	0.1
U.S.	19.1	16.2	7.3	4.3	1.6	0.3

Note: Figures are the number of adherents as a percentage of the total population; (1) Figures cover the Sioux Falls, SD Metropolitan Statistical Area—see Appendix B for areas included
Source: Association of Statisticians of American Religious Bodies, 2010 U.S. Religion Census: Religious Congregations & Membership Study

ECONOMY

Gross Metropolitan Product

Area	2017	2018	2019	2020	Rank[2]
MSA[1]	19.6	20.5	21.5	22.4	127

Note: Figures are in billions of dollars; (1) Figures cover the Sioux Falls, SD Metropolitan Statistical Area—see Appendix B for areas included; (2) Rank is based on 2018 data and ranges from 1 to 381
Source: U.S. Conference of Mayors, U.S. Metro Economies: GMP & Employment 2018-2020, September 2019

Economic Growth

Area	2015-17 (%)	2018 (%)	2019 (%)	2020 (%)	Rank[2]
MSA[1]	1.2	1.6	3.2	2.2	206
U.S.	1.9	2.9	2.3	2.1	–

Note: Figures are real gross metropolitan product (GMP) growth rates and represent average annual percent change; (1) Figures cover the Sioux Falls, SD Metropolitan Statistical Area—see Appendix B for areas included; (2) Rank is based on 2017 2-year average annual percent change and ranges from 1 to 381
Source: U.S. Conference of Mayors, U.S. Metro Economies: GMP & Employment 2018-2020, September 2019

Metropolitan Area Exports

Area	2013	2014	2015	2016	2017	2018	Rank[2]
MSA[1]	433.0	455.3	375.0	334.3	386.8	400.0	234

Note: Figures are in millions of dollars; (1) Figures cover the Sioux Falls, SD Metropolitan Statistical Area—see Appendix B for areas included; (2) Rank is based on 2018 data and ranges from 1 to 387
Source: U.S. Department of Commerce, International Trade Administration, Office of Trade and Economic Analysis, Industry and Analysis, Exports by Metropolitan Area, data extracted April 15, 2020

Building Permits

Area	Single-Family			Multi-Family			Total		
	2017	2018	Pct. Chg.	2017	2018	Pct. Chg.	2017	2018	Pct. Chg.
City	1,192	1,083	-9.1	1,202	898	-25.3	2,394	1,981	-17.3
MSA[1]	1,533	1,380	-10.0	1,381	1,008	-27.0	2,914	2,388	-18.1
U.S.	820,000	855,300	4.3	462,000	473,500	2.5	1,282,000	1,328,800	3.7

Note: (1) Figures cover the Sioux Falls, SD Metropolitan Statistical Area—see Appendix B for areas included; Figures represent new, privately-owned housing units authorized (unadjusted data); All permit data are based on estimates with imputation
Source: U.S. Census Bureau, Manufacturing, Mining, and Construction Statistics, Building Permits, 2017, 2018

Bankruptcy Filings

Area	Business Filings			Nonbusiness Filings		
	2018	2019	% Chg.	2018	2019	% Chg.
Minnehaha County	10	18	80.0	343	349	1.7
U.S.	22,232	22,780	2.5	751,186	752,160	0.1

Note: Business filings include Chapter 7, Chapter 9, Chapter 11, Chapter 12, Chapter 13, Chapter 15, and Section 304; Nonbusiness filings include Chapter 7, Chapter 11, and Chapter 13
Source: Administrative Office of the U.S. Courts, Business and Nonbusiness Bankruptcy, County Cases Commenced by Chapter of the Bankruptcy Code, During the 12-Month Period Ending December 31, 2018 and Business and Nonbusiness Bankruptcy, County Cases Commenced by Chapter of the Bankruptcy Code, During the 12-Month Period Ending December 31, 2019

Housing Vacancy Rates

Area	Gross Vacancy Rate[2] (%)			Year-Round Vacancy Rate[3] (%)			Rental Vacancy Rate[4] (%)			Homeowner Vacancy Rate[5] (%)		
	2017	2018	2019	2017	2018	2019	2017	2018	2019	2017	2018	2019
MSA[1]	n/a	n/a	n/a	n/a	n/a	n/a	n/a	n/a	n/a	n/a	n/a	n/a
U.S.	12.7	12.3	12.0	9.9	9.7	9.5	7.2	6.9	6.7	1.6	1.5	1.4

Note: (1) Figures cover the Sioux Falls, SD Metropolitan Statistical Area—see Appendix B for areas included; (2) The percentage of the total housing inventory that is vacant; (3) The percentage of the housing inventory (excluding seasonal units) that is year-round vacant; (4) The percentage of rental inventory that is vacant for rent; (5) The percentage of homeowner inventory that is vacant for sale; n/a not available
Source: U.S. Census Bureau, Housing Vacancies and Homeownership Annual Statistics: 2017, 2018, 2019

INCOME

Income

Area	Per Capita ($)	Median Household ($)	Average Household ($)
City	31,802	59,017	77,185
MSA[1]	32,390	63,940	81,022
U.S.	32,621	60,293	84,938

Note: (1) Figures cover the Sioux Falls, SD Metropolitan Statistical Area—see Appendix B for areas included
Source: U.S. Census Bureau, 2014-2018 American Community Survey 5-Year Estimates

Household Income Distribution

Area	Percent of Households Earning							
	Under $15,000	$15,000 -$24,999	$25,000 -$34,999	$35,000 -$49,999	$50,000 -$74,999	$75,000 -$99,999	$100,000 -$149,999	$150,000 and up
City	9.8	8.4	10.7	13.9	18.6	14.3	14.6	9.7
MSA[1]	8.3	7.7	10.0	13.0	18.9	15.6	16.3	10.1
U.S.	10.9	9.3	9.3	12.6	17.5	12.5	14.6	13.3

Note: (1) Figures cover the Sioux Falls, SD Metropolitan Statistical Area—see Appendix B for areas included
Source: U.S. Census Bureau, 2014-2018 American Community Survey 5-Year Estimates

Poverty Rate

Area	All Ages	Under 18 Years Old	18 to 64 Years Old	65 Years and Over
City	11.3	14.3	10.6	8.7
MSA[1]	9.2	11.2	8.7	7.6
U.S.	14.1	19.5	13.2	9.3

Note: Figures are percentage of people whose income during the past 12 months was below the poverty level; (1) Figures cover the Sioux Falls, SD Metropolitan Statistical Area—see Appendix B for areas included
Source: U.S. Census Bureau, 2014-2018 American Community Survey 5-Year Estimates

EMPLOYMENT

Labor Force and Employment

Area	Civilian Labor Force			Workers Employed		
	Dec. 2018	Dec. 2019	% Chg.	Dec. 2018	Dec. 2019	% Chg.
City	104,940	106,508	1.5	102,038	103,166	1.1
MSA[1]	153,233	155,466	1.5	149,175	150,743	1.1
U.S.	162,510,000	164,007,000	0.9	156,481,000	158,504,000	1.3

Note: Data is not seasonally adjusted and covers workers 16 years of age and older; (1) Figures cover the Sioux Falls, SD Metropolitan Statistical Area—see Appendix B for areas included
Source: Bureau of Labor Statistics, Local Area Unemployment Statistics

Unemployment Rate

Area	2019											
	Jan.	Feb.	Mar.	Apr.	May	Jun.	Jul.	Aug.	Sep.	Oct.	Nov.	Dec.
City	3.2	3.2	3.2	2.9	2.7	2.7	2.4	2.8	2.7	2.6	2.8	3.1
MSA[1]	3.1	3.2	3.1	2.8	2.6	2.7	2.4	2.7	2.6	2.6	2.8	3.0
U.S.	4.4	4.1	3.9	3.3	3.4	3.8	4.0	3.8	3.3	3.3	3.3	3.4

Note: Data is not seasonally adjusted and covers workers 16 years of age and older; (1) Figures cover the Sioux Falls, SD Metropolitan Statistical Area—see Appendix B for areas included
Source: Bureau of Labor Statistics, Local Area Unemployment Statistics

Average Wages

Occupation	$/Hr.	Occupation	$/Hr.
Accountants and Auditors	34.00	Maintenance and Repair Workers	18.40
Automotive Mechanics	20.00	Marketing Managers	66.90
Bookkeepers	17.10	Network and Computer Systems Admin.	31.60
Carpenters	18.50	Nurses, Licensed Practical	18.90
Cashiers	11.60	Nurses, Registered	28.90
Computer Programmers	29.00	Nursing Assistants	13.60
Computer Systems Analysts	35.30	Office Clerks, General	12.90
Computer User Support Specialists	19.70	Physical Therapists	35.00
Construction Laborers	15.30	Physicians	110.40
Cooks, Restaurant	12.90	Plumbers, Pipefitters and Steamfitters	21.50
Customer Service Representatives	16.00	Police and Sheriff's Patrol Officers	29.90
Dentists	89.30	Postal Service Mail Carriers	25.30
Electricians	23.20	Real Estate Sales Agents	44.20
Engineers, Electrical	39.90	Retail Salespersons	15.30
Fast Food and Counter Workers	10.90	Sales Representatives, Technical/Scientific	50.30
Financial Managers	70.80	Secretaries, Exc. Legal/Medical/Executive	14.60
First-Line Supervisors of Office Workers	25.00	Security Guards	14.10
General and Operations Managers	68.80	Surgeons	135.40
Hairdressers/Cosmetologists	14.10	Teacher Assistants, Exc. Postsecondary*	12.10
Home Health and Personal Care Aides	13.30	Teachers, Secondary School, Exc. Sp. Ed.*	22.90
Janitors and Cleaners	13.00	Telemarketers	n/a
Landscaping/Groundskeeping Workers	14.70	Truck Drivers, Heavy/Tractor-Trailer	21.10
Lawyers	72.90	Truck Drivers, Light/Delivery Services	18.00
Maids and Housekeeping Cleaners	11.30	Waiters and Waitresses	10.60

Note: Wage data covers the Sioux Falls, SD Metropolitan Statistical Area—see Appendix B for areas included; (*) Hourly wages were calculated from annual wage data based on a 40 hour work week; n/a not available.
Source: Bureau of Labor Statistics, Metro Area Occupational Employment & Wage Estimates, May 2019

Employment by Occupation

Occupation Classification	City (%)	MSA[1] (%)	U.S. (%)
Management, Business, Science, and Arts	36.8	37.3	37.9
Natural Resources, Construction, and Maintenance	7.7	8.9	8.9
Production, Transportation, and Material Moving	15.0	14.1	13.3
Sales and Office	24.4	24.1	22.1
Service	16.1	15.6	17.9

Note: Figures cover employed civilians 16 years of age and older; (1) Figures cover the Sioux Falls, SD Metropolitan Statistical Area—see Appendix B for areas included
Source: U.S. Census Bureau, 2014-2018 American Community Survey 5-Year Estimates

Employment by Industry

Sector	MSA[1]		U.S.
	Number of Employees	Percent of Total	Percent of Total
Construction, Mining, and Logging	9,000	5.6	5.4
Education and Health Services	33,800	21.2	16.1
Financial Activities	15,900	9.9	5.8
Government	14,600	9.1	15.0
Information	2,600	1.6	1.9
Leisure and Hospitality	15,300	9.6	10.8
Manufacturing	14,100	8.8	8.4
Other Services	5,900	3.7	3.9
Professional and Business Services	15,500	9.7	14.1
Retail Trade	18,400	11.5	10.6
Transportation, Warehousing, and Utilities	6,100	3.8	4.2
Wholesale Trade	8,600	5.4	3.9

Note: Figures are non-farm employment as of December 2019. Figures are not seasonally adjusted and include workers 16 years of age and older; (1) Figures cover the Sioux Falls, SD Metropolitan Statistical Area—see Appendix B for areas included
Source: Bureau of Labor Statistics, Current Employment Statistics, Employment, Hours, and Earnings

Occupations with Greatest Projected Employment Growth: 2019 – 2021

Occupation[1]	2019 Employment	2021 Projected Employment	Numeric Employment Change	Percent Employment Change
Registered Nurses	13,070	13,550	480	3.7
Combined Food Preparation and Serving Workers, Including Fast Food	8,900	9,230	330	3.7
Janitors and Cleaners, Except Maids and Housekeeping Cleaners	9,990	10,290	300	3.0
Sales Representatives, Wholesale and Manufacturing, Except Technical and Scientific Products	5,550	5,780	230	4.1
Heavy and Tractor-Trailer Truck Drivers	8,900	9,090	190	2.1
Laborers and Freight, Stock, and Material Movers, Hand	6,580	6,770	190	2.9
Accountants and Auditors	5,150	5,330	180	3.5
Welders, Cutters, Solderers, and Brazers	3,490	3,660	170	4.9
Personal Care Aides	3,030	3,190	160	5.3
Management Analysts	3,500	3,650	150	4.3

Note: Projections cover South Dakota; (1) Sorted by numeric employment change
Source: www.projectionscentral.com, State Occupational Projections, 2019–2021 Short-Term Projections

Fastest Growing Occupations: 2019 – 2021

Occupation[1]	2019 Employment	2021 Projected Employment	Numeric Employment Change	Percent Employment Change
Software Developers, Systems Software	700	760	60	8.6
Software Developers, Applications	1,070	1,150	80	7.5
Market Research Analysts and Marketing Specialists	1,010	1,070	60	5.9
Industrial Machinery Mechanics	1,280	1,350	70	5.5
Home Health Aides	1,110	1,170	60	5.4
Emergency Medical Technicians and Paramedics	1,140	1,200	60	5.3
Personal Care Aides	3,030	3,190	160	5.3
Heating, Air Conditioning, and Refrigeration Mechanics and Installers	1,210	1,270	60	5.0
Welders, Cutters, Solderers, and Brazers	3,490	3,660	170	4.9
Cooks, Restaurant	2,020	2,110	90	4.5

Note: Projections cover South Dakota; (1) Sorted by percent employment change and excludes occupations with numeric employment change less than 50
Source: www.projectionscentral.com, State Occupational Projections, 2019–2021 Short-Term Projections

TAXES

State Corporate Income Tax Rates

State	Tax Rate (%)	Income Brackets ($)	Num. of Brackets	Financial Institution Tax Rate (%)[a]	Federal Income Tax Ded.
South Dakota	None	–	–	6.0-0.25 (b)	No

Note: Tax rates as of January 1, 2020; (a) Rates listed are the corporate income tax rate applied to financial institutions or excise taxes based on income; (b) Minimum tax is $800 in California, $250 in District of Columbia, $50 in Arizona and North Dakota (banks), $400 ($100 banks) in Rhode Island, $200 per location in South Dakota (banks), $100 in Utah, $300 in Vermont.
Source: Federation of Tax Administrators, State Corporate Income Tax Rates, January 1, 2020

State Individual Income Tax Rates

State	Tax Rate (%)	Income Brackets ($)	Personal Exemptions ($)			Standard Ded. ($)	
			Single	Married	Depend.	Single	Married
South Dakota			– No state income tax –				

Note: Tax rates as of January 1, 2020; Local- and county-level taxes are not included
Source: Federation of Tax Administrators, State Individual Income Tax Rates, January 1, 2020

Various State Sales and Excise Tax Rates

State	State Sales Tax (%)	Gasoline[1] (¢/gal.)	Cigarette[2] ($/pack)	Spirits[3] ($/gal.)	Wine[4] ($/gal.)	Beer[5] ($/gal.)	Recreational Marijuana (%)
South Dakota	4.5	30	1.53	4.67	1.31	0.27	Not legal

Note: All tax rates as of January 1, 2020; (1) The American Petroleum Institute has developed a methodology for determining the average tax rate on a gallon of fuel. Rates may include any of the following: excise taxes, environmental fees, storage tank fees, other fees or taxes, general sales tax, and local taxes; (2) The federal excise tax of $1.0066 per pack and local taxes are not included; (3) Rates are those applicable to off-premise sales of 40% alcohol by volume (a.b.v.) distilled spirits in 750ml containers. Local excise taxes are excluded; (4) Rates are those applicable to off-premise sales of 11% a.b.v. non-carbonated wine in 750ml containers; (5) Rates are those applicable to off-premise sales of 4.7% a.b.v. beer in 12 ounce containers.
Source: Tax Foundation, 2020 Facts & Figures: How Does Your State Compare?

State Business Tax Climate Index Rankings

State	Overall Rank	Corporate Tax Rank	Individual Income Tax Rank	Sales Tax Rank	Property Tax Rank	Unemployment Insurance Tax Rank
South Dakota	2	1	1	35	22	44

Note: The index is a measure of how each state's tax laws affect economic performance. The lower the rank, the more favorable a state's tax system is for business. States without a given tax are given a ranking of 1. The scores/rankings for the District of Columbia do not affect other states. The 2020 index represents the tax climate as of July 1, 2019.
Source: Tax Foundation, State Business Tax Climate Index 2020

COMMERCIAL UTILITIES

Typical Monthly Electric Bills

Area	Commercial Service ($/month)		Industrial Service ($/month)	
	1,500 kWh	40 kW demand 14,000 kWh	1,000 kW demand 200,000 kWh	50,000 kW demand 32,500,000 kWh
City	203	1,548	23,650	1,887,119
Average[1]	203	1,612	25,706	2,520,671

Note: Figures are based on annualized rates; (1) Average based on 187 utilities surveyed
Source: Edison Electric Institute, Typical Bills and Average Rates Report, Summer 2019

TRANSPORTATION

Means of Transportation to Work

Area	Car/Truck/Van		Public Transportation			Bicycle	Walked	Other Means	Worked at Home
	Drove Alone	Car-pooled	Bus	Subway	Railroad				
City	84.4	8.4	0.9	0.0	0.0	0.5	2.0	0.8	3.2
MSA[1]	84.4	7.9	0.6	0.0	0.0	0.4	1.9	0.7	4.0
U.S.	76.4	9.1	2.5	1.9	0.6	0.6	2.7	1.3	4.9

Note: Figures are percentages and cover workers 16 years of age and older; (1) Figures cover the Sioux Falls, SD Metropolitan Statistical Area—see Appendix B for areas included
Source: U.S. Census Bureau, 2014-2018 American Community Survey 5-Year Estimates

Travel Time to Work

Area	Less Than 10 Minutes	10 to 19 Minutes	20 to 29 Minutes	30 to 44 Minutes	45 to 59 Minutes	60 to 89 Minutes	90 Minutes or More
City	16.7	52.3	21.9	5.5	1.4	1.4	0.9
MSA[1]	16.6	44.0	24.5	10.1	2.3	1.4	1.0
U.S.	12.5	28.7	20.9	20.7	8.2	6.3	2.8

Note: Note: Figures are percentages and include workers 16 years old and over; (1) Figures cover the Sioux Falls, SD Metropolitan Statistical Area—see Appendix B for areas included
Source: U.S. Census Bureau, 2014-2018 American Community Survey 5-Year Estimates

Key Congestion Measures

Area	1982	1992	2002	2012	2017
Annual Hours of Delay, Total (000)	n/a	n/a	n/a	n/a	3,274
Annual Hours of Delay, Per Auto Commuter	n/a	n/a	n/a	n/a	18
Annual Congestion Cost, Total (million $)	n/a	n/a	n/a	n/a	68
Annual Congestion Cost, Per Auto Commuter ($)	n/a	n/a	n/a	n/a	376

Note: n/a not available
Source: Texas A&M Transportation Institute, 2019 Urban Mobility Report

Freeway Travel Time Index

Area	1982	1987	1992	1997	2002	2007	2012	2017
Urban Area Index[1]	n/a	n/a	n/a	n/a	n/a	n/a	n/a	1.06
Urban Area Rank[1,2]	n/a	n/a	n/a	n/a	n/a	n/a	n/a	n/a

Note: Freeway Travel Time Index—the ratio of travel time in the peak period to the travel time at free-flow conditions. For example, a value of 1.30 indicates a 20-minute free-flow trip takes 26 minutes in the peak (20 minutes x 1.30 = 26 minutes); (1) Covers the Sioux Falls SD urban area; (2) Rank is based on 101 larger urban areas (#1 = highest travel time index); n/a not available
Source: Texas A&M Transportation Institute, 2019 Urban Mobility Report

Public Transportation

Agency Name / Mode of Transportation	Vehicles Operated in Maximum Service[1]	Annual Unlinked Passenger Trips[2] (in thous.)	Annual Passenger Miles[3] (in thous.)
Sioux Falls Transit			
Bus (directly operated)	19	782.1	3,270.4
Demand Response (directly operated)	20	91.4	664.5

Note: (1) Number of revenue vehicles operated by the given mode and type of service to meet the annual maximum service requirement. This is the revenue vehicle count during the peak season of the year; on the week and day that maximum service is provided. Vehicles operated in maximum service (VOMS) exclude atypical days and one-time special events; (2) Number of passengers who boarded public transportation vehicles. Passengers are counted each time they board a vehicle no matter how many vehicles they use to travel from their origin to their destination. (3) Sum of the distances ridden by all passengers during the entire fiscal year.
Source: Federal Transit Administration, National Transit Database, 2018

Air Transportation

Airport Name and Code / Type of Service	Passenger Airlines[1]	Passenger Enplanements	Freight Carriers[2]	Freight (lbs)
Joe Foss Field (FSD)				
Domestic service (U.S. carriers - 2019)	19	575,797	7	37,208,443
International service (U.S. carriers - 2018)	2	112	1	13,158,856

Note: (1) Includes all U.S.-based major, minor and commuter airlines that carried at least one passenger during the year; (2) Includes all U.S.-based airlines and freight carriers that transported at least one pound of freight during the year.
Source: Bureau of Transportation Statistics, The Intermodal Transportation Database, Air Carriers: T-100 Domestic Market (U.S. Carriers), 2019; Bureau of Transportation Statistics, The Intermodal Transportation Database, Air Carriers: T-100 International Market (U.S. Carriers), 2018

Other Transportation Statistics

Major Highways:	I-29; I-90
Amtrak Service:	No
Major Waterways/Ports:	None

Source: Amtrak.com; Google Maps

BUSINESSES

Major Business Headquarters

Company Name	Industry	Rankings	
		Fortune[1]	Forbes[2]
No companies listed	-	-	-

Note: (1) Companies that produce a 10-K are ranked 1 to 500 based on 2018 revenue; (2) All private companies with at least $2 billion in annual revenue through the end of their most current fiscal year are ranked 1 to 228; companies listed are headquartered in the city; dashes indicate no ranking
Source: Fortune, "Fortune 500," June 2019; Forbes, "America's Largest Private Companies," 2019 Rankings

Minority- and Women-Owned Businesses

Group	All Firms		Firms with Paid Employees			
	Firms	Sales ($000)	Firms	Sales ($000)	Employees	Payroll ($000)
AIAN[1]	79	19,348	11	16,165	39	1,411
Asian	289	42,962	59	34,299	185	6,123
Black	274	12,216	7	4,501	99	1,298
Hispanic	241	(s)	11	(s)	500 - 999	(s)
NHOPI[2]	n/a	n/a	n/a	n/a	n/a	n/a
Women	4,164	736,156	459	644,347	4,910	135,921
All Firms	15,083	26,509,536	4,125	25,969,295	106,961	4,173,394

Note: Figures cover firms located in the city; minority- and women-owned business are defined as firms in which the corresponding group own 51% or more of the stock or equity of the company; (1) American Indian and Alaska Native; (2) Native Hawaiian and Other Pacific Islander; (s) estimates are suppressed when publication standards are not met; n/a not available
Source: U.S. Census Bureau, 2012 Economic Census, Survey of Business Owners

HOTELS & CONVENTION CENTERS

Hotels, Motels and Vacation Rentals

Area	5 Star		4 Star		3 Star		2 Star		1 Star		Not Rated	
	Num.	Pct.[3]	Num.	Pct.[3]	Num.	Pct.[3]	Num.	Pct.[3]	Num.	Pct.[3]	Num.	Pct.[3]
City[1]	0	0.0	0	0.0	15	26.8	13	23.2	4	7.1	24	42.9
Total[2]	266	1.3	1,517	7.2	4,627	21.8	3,210	15.1	3,974	18.7	7,601	35.9

Note: (1) Figures cover Sioux Falls and vicinity; (2) Figures cover all 100 cities in this book; (3) Percentage of hotels which have a given star rating; Star ratings are determined by priceline.com and offer an indication of the general quality of a particular hotel.
Source: priceline.com, April 27, 2020

Major Convention Centers

Name	Overall Space (sq. ft.)	Exhibit Space (sq. ft.)	Meeting Space (sq. ft.)	Meeting Rooms
Sioux Falls Convention Center	100,000	50,000	n/a	12

Note: Table includes convention centers located in the Sioux Falls, SD metro area; n/a not available
Source: Original research

Living Environment

COST OF LIVING

Cost of Living Index

Composite Index	Groceries	Housing	Utilities	Trans-portation	Health Care	Misc. Goods/ Services
92.5	96.3	86.3	84.7	91.9	107.7	96.3

Note: The Cost of Living Index measures regional differences in the cost of consumer goods and services, excluding taxes and non-consumer expenditures, for professional and managerial households in the top income quintile. It is based on more than 50,000 prices covering almost 60 different items for which prices are collected three times a year by chambers of commerce, economic development organizations or university applied economic centers in each participating urban area. The numbers shown should be read as a percentage above or below the national average of 100. For example, a value of 115.4 in the groceries column indicates that grocery prices are 15.4% higher than the national average. Small differences in the index numbers should not be interpreted as significant; Figures cover the Sioux Falls SD urban area.
Source: The Council for Community and Economic Research, ACCRA Cost of Living Index, 2019

Grocery Prices

Area[1]	T-Bone Steak ($/pound)	Frying Chicken ($/pound)	Whole Milk ($/half gal.)	Eggs ($/dozen)	Orange Juice ($/64 oz.)	Coffee ($/11.5 oz.)
City[2]	7.66	1.91	2.11	0.99	2.99	4.51
Avg.	11.40	1.41	1.93	1.54	3.51	4.30
Min.	7.40	0.92	0.85	0.58	2.67	2.90
Max.	15.58	2.68	4.09	4.18	5.57	8.10

*Note: (1) Values for the local area are compared with the average, minimum and maximum values for all 290 areas in the Cost of Living Index; (2) Figures cover the Sioux Falls SD urban area; **T-Bone Steak** (price per pound); **Frying Chicken** (price per pound, whole fryer); **Whole Milk** (half gallon carton); **Eggs** (price per dozen, Grade A, large); **Orange Juice** (64 oz. Tropicana or Florida Natural); **Coffee** (11.5 oz. can, vacuum-packed, Maxwell House, Hills Bros, or Folgers).*
Source: The Council for Community and Economic Research, ACCRA Cost of Living Index, 2019

Housing and Utility Costs

Area[1]	New Home Price ($)	Apartment Rent ($/month)	All Electric ($/month)	Part Electric ($/month)	Other Energy ($/month)	Telephone ($/month)
City[2]	334,668	845	-	81.96	43.38	177.00
Avg.	362,090	1,142	174.35	100.00	67.76	179.60
Min.	198,329	501	91.58	31.44	28.51	165.30
Max.	2,074,561	5,050	388.18	239.41	306.15	207.90

*Note: (1) Values for the local area are compared with the average, minimum and maximum values for all 290 areas in the Cost of Living Index; (2) Figures cover the Sioux Falls SD urban area; **New Home Price** (2,400 sf living area, 8,000 sf lot, in urban area with full utilities); **Apartment Rent** (950 sf 2 bedroom/1.5 or 2 bath, unfurnished, excluding all utilities except water); **All Electric** (average monthly cost for an all-electric home); **Part Electric** (average monthly cost for a part-electric home); **Other Energy** (average monthly cost for natural gas, fuel oil, coal, wood, and any other forms of energy except electricity); **Telephone** (price includes the base monthly rate plus taxes and fees for three lines of mobile phone service).*
Source: The Council for Community and Economic Research, ACCRA Cost of Living Index, 2019

Health Care, Transportation, and Other Costs

Area[1]	Doctor ($/visit)	Dentist ($/visit)	Optometrist ($/visit)	Gasoline ($/gallon)	Beauty Salon ($/visit)	Men's Shirt ($)
City[2]	141.52	98.97	123.05	2.45	30.08	23.84
Avg.	114.85	97.58	106.10	2.50	38.15	32.15
Min.	39.00	62.22	52.22	1.53	16.88	10.27
Max.	206.67	151.53	258.67	3.79	79.29	59.30

*Note: (1) Values for the local area are compared with the average, minimum and maximum values for all 290 areas in the Cost of Living Index; (2) Figures cover the Sioux Falls SD urban area; **Doctor** (general practitioners routine exam of an established patient); **Dentist** (adult teeth cleaning and periodic oral examination); **Optometrist** (full vision eye exam for established adult patient); **Gasoline** (one gallon regular unleaded, national brand, including all taxes, cash price at self-service pump if available); **Beauty Salon** (woman's shampoo, trim, and blow-dry); **Men's Shirt** (cotton/polyester dress shirt, pinpoint weave, long sleeves).*
Source: The Council for Community and Economic Research, ACCRA Cost of Living Index, 2019

HOUSING

House Price Index (HPI)

Area	National Ranking[2]	Quarterly Change (%)	One-Year Change (%)	Five-Year Change (%)
MSA[1]	121	1.04	4.83	31.38
U.S.[3]	–	1.26	5.09	32.88

Note: The HPI is a weighted repeat sales index. It measures average price changes in repeat sales or refinancings on the same properties. This information is obtained by reviewing repeat mortgage transactions on single-family properties whose mortgages have been purchased or securitized by Fannie Mae or Freddie Mac in January 1975; (1) Figures cover the Sioux Falls, SD Metropolitan Statistical Area—see Appendix B for areas included; (2) Rankings are based on annual percentage change for all metro areas containing at least 15,000 transactions over the last 10 years and ranges from 1 to 232; (3) figures based on a weighted average of Census Division estimates using a seasonally adjusted, purchase-only index; all figures are for the period ending December 31, 2019
Source: Federal Housing Finance Agency, House Price Index, February 25, 2020

Median Single-Family Home Prices

Area	2017	2018	2019p	Percent Change 2018 to 2019
MSA[1]	194.4	209.3	221.4	5.8
U.S. Average	248.8	261.6	274.6	5.0

Note: Figures are median sales prices of existing single-family homes in thousands of dollars; (p) preliminary; (1) Figures cover the Sioux Falls, SD Metropolitan Statistical Area—see Appendix B for areas included
Source: National Association of Realtors, Median Sales Price of Existing Single-Family Homes for Metropolitan Areas, 4th Quarter 2019

Qualifying Income Based on Median Sales Price of Existing Single-Family Homes

Area	With 5% Down ($)	With 10% Down ($)	With 20% Down ($)
MSA[1]	47,694	45,184	40,163
U.S. Average	58,663	55,575	49,400

Note: Figures are preliminary; Qualifying income is based on a mortgage rate of 3.76%. Monthly principal and interest payment is limited to 25% of income; (1) Figures cover the Sioux Falls, SD Metropolitan Statistical Area—see Appendix B for areas included
Source: National Association of Realtors, Qualifying Income Based on Median Sales Price of Existing Single-Family Homes for Metropolitan Areas, 4th Quarter 2019

Median Apartment Condo-Coop Home Prices

Area	2017	2018	2019p	Percent Change 2018 to 2019
MSA[1]	n/a	n/a	n/a	n/a
U.S. Average	234.3	241.0	249.5	3.5

Note: Figures are median sales prices of existing apartment condo-coop homes in thousands of dollars; (p) preliminary; n/a not available; (1) Figures cover the Sioux Falls, SD Metropolitan Statistical Area—see Appendix B for areas included
Source: National Association of Realtors, Median Sales Price of Existing Apartment Condo-Coop Homes for Metropolitan Areas, 4th Quarter 2019

Home Value Distribution

Area	Under $50,000	$50,000 -$99,999	$100,000 -$149,999	$150,000 -$199,999	$200,000 -$299,999	$300,000 -$499,999	$500,000 -$999,999	$1,000,000 or more
City	6.0	8.1	20.1	25.7	23.7	12.4	3.3	0.7
MSA[1]	5.9	9.0	19.0	23.8	24.1	13.8	3.6	0.8
U.S.	7.6	13.0	14.0	14.3	19.2	18.3	10.5	3.1

Note: Figures are percentages and cover owner-occupied housing units; (1) Figures cover the Sioux Falls, SD Metropolitan Statistical Area—see Appendix B for areas included
Source: U.S. Census Bureau, 2014-2018 American Community Survey 5-Year Estimates

Homeownership Rate

Area	2011 (%)	2012 (%)	2013 (%)	2014 (%)	2015 (%)	2016 (%)	2017 (%)	2018 (%)	2019 (%)
MSA[1]	n/a	n/a	n/a	n/a	n/a	n/a	n/a	n/a	n/a
U.S.	66.1	65.4	65.1	64.5	63.7	63.4	63.9	64.4	64.6

Note: (1) Figures cover the Sioux Falls, SD Metropolitan Statistical Area—see Appendix B for areas included; n/a not available
Source: U.S. Census Bureau, Housing Vacancies and Homeownership Annual Statistics: 2011-2019

Year Housing Structure Built

Area	2010 or Later	2000 -2009	1990 -1999	1980 -1989	1970 -1979	1960 -1969	1950 -1959	1940 -1949	Before 1940	Median Year
City	10.4	18.8	15.6	10.8	15.0	7.3	8.8	4.4	8.8	1985
MSA[1]	9.4	19.3	15.5	9.8	14.8	6.8	7.9	4.1	12.4	1984
U.S.	4.1	14.3	13.9	13.5	15.3	10.7	10.4	5.0	12.8	1977

Note: Figures are percentages except for Median Year; Note: (1) Figures cover the Sioux Falls, SD Metropolitan Statistical Area—see Appendix B for areas included
Source: U.S. Census Bureau, 2014-2018 American Community Survey 5-Year Estimates

Gross Monthly Rent

Area	Under $500	$500 -$999	$1,000 -$1,499	$1,500 -$1,999	$2,000 -$2,499	$2,500 -$2,999	$3,000 and up	Median ($)
City	9.8	67.5	17.7	3.3	0.3	0.8	0.7	791
MSA[1]	10.8	66.2	17.7	3.5	0.4	0.7	0.7	792
U.S.	9.8	38.5	29.6	12.9	5.1	2.1	2.0	1,023

Note: Figures are percentages except for Median; Gross rent is the contract rent plus the estimated average monthly cost of utilities (electricity, gas, and water and sewer) and fuels (oil, coal, kerosene, wood, etc.) if these are paid by the renter (or paid for the renter by someone else); (1) Figures cover the Sioux Falls, SD Metropolitan Statistical Area—see Appendix B for areas included
Source: U.S. Census Bureau, 2014-2018 American Community Survey 5-Year Estimates

HEALTH

Health Risk Factors

Category	MSA[1] (%)	U.S. (%)
Adults aged 18–64 who have any kind of health care coverage	83.5	87.3
Adults who reported being in good or better health	88.4	82.4
Adults who have been told they have high blood cholesterol	28.8	33.0
Adults who have been told they have high blood pressure	27.8	32.3
Adults who are current smokers	20.3	17.1
Adults who currently use E-cigarettes	n/a	4.6
Adults who currently use chewing tobacco, snuff, or snus	4.0	4.0
Adults who are heavy drinkers[2]	7.8	6.3
Adults who are binge drinkers[3]	19.4	17.4
Adults who are overweight (BMI 25.0 - 29.9)	35.5	35.3
Adults who are obese (BMI 30.0 - 99.8)	29.1	31.3
Adults who participated in any physical activities in the past month	75.1	74.4
Adults who always or nearly always wears a seat belt	88.1	94.3

Note: n/a not available; (1) Figures cover the Sioux Falls, SD Metropolitan Statistical Area—see Appendix B for areas included; (2) Heavy drinkers are classified as adult men having more than 14 drinks per week and adult women having more than 7 drinks per week; (3) Binge drinkers are classified as males having five or more drinks on one occasion or females having four or more drinks on one occasion
Source: Centers for Disease Control and Prevention, Behavioral Risk Factor Surveillance System, SMART: Selected Metropolitan Area Risk Trends, 2017

Acute and Chronic Health Conditions

Category	MSA[1] (%)	U.S. (%)
Adults who have ever been told they had a heart attack	5.0	4.2
Adults who have ever been told they have angina or coronary heart disease	4.7	3.9
Adults who have ever been told they had a stroke	2.0	3.0
Adults who have ever been told they have asthma	9.5	14.2
Adults who have ever been told they have arthritis	19.7	24.9
Adults who have ever been told they have diabetes[2]	8.8	10.5
Adults who have ever been told they had skin cancer	3.2	6.2
Adults who have ever been told they had any other types of cancer	6.4	7.1
Adults who have ever been told they have COPD	4.4	6.5
Adults who have ever been told they have kidney disease	1.6	3.0
Adults who have ever been told they have a form of depression	18.0	20.5

Note: (1) Figures cover the Sioux Falls, SD Metropolitan Statistical Area—see Appendix B for areas included; (2) Figures do not include pregnancy-related, borderline, or pre-diabetes
Source: Centers for Disease Control and Prevention, Behavioral Risk Factor Surveillance System, SMART: Selected Metropolitan Area Risk Trends, 2017

Health Screening and Vaccination Rates

Category	MSA[1] (%)	U.S. (%)
Adults aged 65+ who have had flu shot within the past year	69.1	60.7
Adults aged 65+ who have ever had a pneumonia vaccination	77.7	75.4
Adults who have ever been tested for HIV	29.3	36.1
Adults who have ever had the shingles or zoster vaccine?	41.7	28.9
Adults who have had their blood cholesterol checked within the last five years	79.3	85.9

Note: n/a not available; (1) Figures cover the Sioux Falls, SD Metropolitan Statistical Area—see Appendix B for areas included.
Source: Centers for Disease Control and Prevention, Behaviorial Risk Factor Surveillance System, SMART: Selected Metropolitan Area Risk Trends, 2017

Disability Status

Category	MSA[1] (%)	U.S. (%)
Adults who reported being deaf	6.9	6.7
Are you blind or have serious difficulty seeing, even when wearing glasses?	n/a	4.5
Are you limited in any way in any of your usual activities due of arthritis?	8.8	12.9
Do you have difficulty doing errands alone?	6.0	6.8
Do you have difficulty dressing or bathing?	3.1	3.6
Do you have serious difficulty concentrating/remembering/making decisions?	8.5	10.7
Do you have serious difficulty walking or climbing stairs?	8.4	13.6

Note: n/a not available; (1) Figures cover the Sioux Falls, SD Metropolitan Statistical Area—see Appendix B for areas included.
Source: Centers for Disease Control and Prevention, Behaviorial Risk Factor Surveillance System, SMART: Selected Metropolitan Area Risk Trends, 2017

Mortality Rates for the Top 10 Causes of Death in the U.S.

ICD-10[a] Sub-Chapter	ICD-10[a] Code	Age-Adjusted Mortality Rate[1] per 100,000 population	
		County[2]	U.S.
Malignant neoplasms	C00-C97	165.8	152.4
Ischaemic heart diseases	I20-I25	90.4	92.7
Other forms of heart disease	I30-I51	34.4	52.5
Chronic lower respiratory diseases	J40-J47	43.8	40.4
Cerebrovascular diseases	I60-I69	35.3	37.3
Other degenerative diseases of the nervous system	G30-G31	51.2	36.4
Other external causes of accidental injury	W00-X59	34.3	35.3
Organic, including symptomatic, mental disorders	F01-F09	19.2	30.0
Hypertensive diseases	I10-I15	37.0	22.9
Diabetes mellitus	E10-E14	16.3	21.3

Note: (a) ICD-10 = International Classification of Diseases 10th Revision; (1) Mortality rates are a three year average covering 2016-2018; (2) Figures cover Minnehaha County.
Source: Centers for Disease Control and Prevention, National Center for Health Statistics. Underlying Cause of Death 1999-2018 on CDC WONDER Online Database

Mortality Rates for Selected Causes of Death

ICD-10[a] Sub-Chapter	ICD-10[a] Code	Age-Adjusted Mortality Rate[1] per 100,000 population	
		County[2]	U.S.
Assault	X85-Y09	4.2	6.0
Diseases of the liver	K70-K76	15.8	14.2
Human immunodeficiency virus (HIV) disease	B20-B24	Suppressed	1.6
Influenza and pneumonia	J09-J18	15.4	14.2
Intentional self-harm	X60-X84	20.2	13.9
Malnutrition	E40-E46	5.1	1.9
Obesity and other hyperalimentation	E65-E68	Suppressed	2.1
Renal failure	N17-N19	4.9	12.8
Transport accidents	V01-V99	8.8	12.5
Viral hepatitis	B15-B19	Suppressed	1.4

Note: (a) ICD-10 = International Classification of Diseases 10th Revision; (1) Mortality rates are a three year average covering 2016-2018; (2) Figures cover Minnehaha County; Data are suppressed when the data meet the criteria for confidentiality constraints; Mortality rates are flagged as unreliable when the rate would be calculated with a numerator of 20 or less.
Source: Centers for Disease Control and Prevention, National Center for Health Statistics. Underlying Cause of Death 1999-2018 on CDC WONDER Online Database

Health Insurance Coverage

Area	With Health Insurance	With Private Health Insurance	With Public Health Insurance	Without Health Insurance	Population Under Age 19 Without Health Insurance
City	92.6	77.4	26.5	7.4	3.7
MSA[1]	93.2	79.5	25.0	6.8	3.8
U.S.	90.6	67.7	34.7	9.4	5.2

Note: Figures are percentages that cover the civilian noninstitutionalized population; (1) Figures cover the Sioux Falls, SD Metropolitan Statistical Area—see Appendix B for areas included
Source: U.S. Census Bureau, 2014-2018 American Community Survey 5-Year Estimates

Number of Medical Professionals

Area	MDs[3]	DOs[3,4]	Dentists	Podiatrists	Chiropractors	Optometrists
County[1] (number)	677	59	103	10	106	37
County[1] (rate[2])	358.9	31.3	53.4	5.2	55.0	19.2
U.S. (rate[2])	281.9	23.4	69.1	6.0	27.5	16.4

Note: Data as of 2018 unless noted; (1) Data covers Minnehaha County; (2) Rate per 100,000 population; (3) Data as of 2017 and includes all active, non-federal physicians; (4) Doctor of Osteopathic Medicine
Source: U.S. Department of Health and Human Services, Health Resources and Services Administration, Bureau of Health Professions, Area Resource File (ARF) 2018-2019

Best Hospitals

According to *U.S. News*, the Sioux Falls, SD metro area is home to one of the best hospitals in the U.S.: **Avera McKennan Hospital and University Health Center** (3 adult specialties). The hospital listed was nationally ranked in at least one of 16 adult or 10 pediatric specialties. Only 206 hospitals nationwide were nationally ranked in one or more adult or pediatric specialty. Twenty hospitals in the U.S. made the Honor Roll. The Best Hospitals Honor Roll takes both the national rankings and the procedure and condition ratings into account. Hospitals received points if they were nationally ranked in one of the 16 adult specialties—the higher they ranked, the more points they got—and how many ratings of "high performing" they earned in the nine procedures and conditions. *U.S. News Online, "America's Best Hospitals 2019-20"*

EDUCATION

Public School District Statistics

District Name	Schls	Pupils	Pupil/ Teacher Ratio	Minority Pupils[1] (%)	Free Lunch Eligible[2] (%)	IEP[3] (%)
Sioux Falls School District 49-5	43	25,018	15.8	38.5	36.9	15.9

Note: Table includes school districts with 2,000 or more students; (1) Percentage of students that are not non-Hispanic white; (2) Percentage of students that are eligible for the free lunch program; (3) Percentage of students that have an Individualized Education Program.
Source: U.S. Department of Education, National Center for Education Statistics, Common Core of Data, Local Education Agency (School District) Universe Survey: School Year 2018-2019; U.S. Department of Education, National Center for Education Statistics, Common Core of Data, Public Elementary/Secondary School Universe Survey: School Year 2018-2019

Highest Level of Education

Area	Less than H.S.	H.S. Diploma	Some College, No Deg.	Associate Degree	Bachelor's Degree	Master's Degree	Prof. School Degree	Doctorate Degree
City	8.0	25.7	20.8	11.3	23.3	7.5	2.4	1.0
MSA[1]	7.3	26.4	20.8	12.4	23.0	6.9	2.1	1.0
U.S.	12.3	27.1	20.6	8.4	19.4	8.6	2.1	1.4

Note: Figures cover persons age 25 and over; (1) Figures cover the Sioux Falls, SD Metropolitan Statistical Area—see Appendix B for areas included
Source: U.S. Census Bureau, 2014-2018 American Community Survey 5-Year Estimates

Educational Attainment by Race

Area	High School Graduate or Higher (%)					Bachelor's Degree or Higher (%)				
	Total	White	Black	Asian	Hisp.[2]	Total	White	Black	Asian	Hisp.[2]
City	92.0	94.4	71.0	70.2	64.2	34.2	36.6	11.9	37.6	11.5
MSA[1]	92.7	94.4	71.6	71.3	65.6	33.0	34.5	12.5	38.6	13.2
U.S.	87.7	89.6	85.4	86.8	67.7	31.5	32.9	21.1	53.5	15.8

Note: Figures shown cover persons 25 years old and over; (1) Figures cover the Sioux Falls, SD Metropolitan Statistical Area—see Appendix B for areas included; (2) People of Hispanic origin can be of any race
Source: U.S. Census Bureau, 2014-2018 American Community Survey 5-Year Estimates

School Enrollment by Grade and Control

Area	Preschool (%)		Kindergarten (%)		Grades 1 - 4 (%)		Grades 5 - 8 (%)		Grades 9 - 12 (%)	
	Public	Private	Public	Private	Public	Private	Public	Private	Public	Private
City	54.6	45.4	87.5	12.5	89.3	10.7	89.2	10.8	85.6	14.4
MSA[1]	57.6	42.4	87.8	12.2	89.0	11.0	90.4	9.6	88.3	11.7
U.S.	59.0	41.0	87.7	12.3	89.6	10.4	89.5	10.5	90.2	9.8

Note: Figures shown cover persons 3 years old and over; (1) Figures cover the Sioux Falls, SD Metropolitan Statistical Area—see Appendix B for areas included
Source: U.S. Census Bureau, 2014-2018 American Community Survey 5-Year Estimates

Average Salaries of Public School Teachers

Area	2016-17		2017-18		Change from 2016-17 to 2017-18	
	Dollars	Rank[1]	Dollars	Rank[1]	Percent	Rank[2]
South Dakota	46,979	48	47,631	47	1.39	28
U.S. Average	59,539	–	60,477	–	1.58	–

Note: (1) Rank ranges from 1 to 51 where 1 indicates highest salary; (2) Rank ranges from 1 to 51 where 1 indicates highest percent change.
Source: National Education Association, Rankings & Estimates: Rankings of the States 2018 and Estimates of School Statistics 2019

Higher Education

Four-Year Colleges			Two-Year Colleges			Medical Schools[1]	Law Schools[2]	Voc/ Tech[3]
Public	Private Non-profit	Private For-profit	Public	Private Non-profit	Private For-profit			
0	3	1	1	2	1	1	0	0

Note: Figures cover institutions located within the city limits and include main campuses only; (1) includes schools accredited by the Liaison Committee on Medical Education and the American Osteopathic Association's Commission on Osteopathic College Accreditation; (2) includes ABA-accredited schools, schools with provisional ABA accreditation, and state accredited schools; (3) includes all schools with programs that are less than 2 years.
Source: National Center for Education Statistics, Integrated Postsecondary Education System (IPEDS), 2018-19; Wikipedia, List of Medical Schools in the United States, accessed May 1, 2020; Wikipedia, List of Law Schools in the United States, accessed May 1, 2020

PRESIDENTIAL ELECTION

2016 Presidential Election Results

Area	Clinton	Trump	Johnson	Stein	Other
Minnehaha County	39.1	53.7	6.1	0.0	1.1
U.S.	48.0	45.9	3.3	1.1	1.7

Note: Results are percentages and may not add to 100% due to rounding
Source: Dave Leip's Atlas of U.S. Presidential Elections

EMPLOYERS

Major Employers

Company Name	Industry
Avera Health	Health care
Billion Automotive	Auto dealership
Capital One	Financial/credit card processing
CIGNA	Mail order pharmacy
Citi	Credit card processing
City of Sioux Falls	Government
Department of Veterans Affairs	Government medical facilities
Esurance	Insurance service center
Evangelical Lutheran Good Samaritan Society	Health care
First PREMIER Bank/PREMIER Bankcard	Financial/credit card processing
Hy-Vee Food Stores	Retail grocery
John Morrell & Co.	Meat processing
Lewis Drug	Retail pharmacy
LifeScape	Health care
Midcontinent Communications	Telecommunications/cable services
Minnehaha County	Government
Raven Industries	Manufacturing
Sammons Financial Group/Midland National	Insurance
Sanford Health	Health care
Sioux Falls School District 49-5	Education
StarMark Cabinetry	Manufacturing
United States Postal Service	U.S. postal service
USGS EROS Data Center/SGT	Satellite info processing
Wal-Mart and Sam's Club	Retail & wholesale
Wells Fargo	Financial/credit card/student loans

Note: Companies shown are located within the Sioux Falls, SD Metropolitan Statistical Area.
Source: Hoovers.com; Wikipedia

PUBLIC SAFETY

Crime Rate

Area	All Crimes	Violent Crimes				Property Crimes		
		Murder	Rape[3]	Robbery	Aggrav. Assault	Burglary	Larceny -Theft	Motor Vehicle Theft
City	3,369.3	2.8	67.1	59.3	307.8	361.5	2,269.1	301.7
Suburbs[1]	1,237.9	0.0	37.8	2.4	105.0	328.1	682.1	82.6
Metro[2]	2,687.9	1.9	57.7	41.1	243.0	350.8	1,761.8	231.6
U.S.	2,580.1	5.0	42.6	86.2	246.8	376.0	1,594.6	228.9

Note: Figures are crimes per 100,000 population; (1) All areas within the metro area that are located outside the city limits; (2) Figures cover the Sioux Falls, SD Metropolitan Statistical Area—see Appendix B for areas included; (3) The city and U.S. figures shown were reported using the revised Uniform Crime Reporting (UCR) definition of rape. The suburban and metro area figures shown are an aggregate total of the data submitted using both the revised and legacy UCR definitions.
Source: FBI Uniform Crime Reports, 2018

Hate Crimes

Area	Number of Quarters Reported	Number of Incidents per Bias Motivation					
		Race/Ethnicity/ Ancestry	Religion	Sexual Orientation	Disability	Gender	Gender Identity
City	4	5	0	1	0	0	0
U.S.	4	4,047	1,419	1,196	159	47	168

Source: Federal Bureau of Investigation, Hate Crime Statistics 2018

Identity Theft Consumer Reports

Area	Reports	Reports per 100,000 Population	Rank[2]
MSA[1]	162	61	327
U.S.	650,572	198	-

Note: (1) Figures cover the Sioux Falls, SD Metropolitan Statistical Area—see Appendix B for areas included; (2) Rank ranges from 1 to 386 where 1 indicates greatest number of identity theft reports per 100,000 population
Source: Federal Trade Commission, Consumer Sentinel Network Data Book for January–December 2019

Fraud and Other Consumer Reports

Area	Reports	Reports per 100,000 Population	Rank[2]
MSA[1]	1,143	430	339
U.S.	2,590,177	789	-

Note: (1) Figures cover the Sioux Falls, SD Metropolitan Statistical Area—see Appendix B for areas included; (2) Rank ranges from 1 to 386 where 1 indicates greatest number of fraud and other consumer reports per 100,000 population
Source: Federal Trade Commission, Consumer Sentinel Network Data Book for January–December 2019

SPORTS

Professional Sports Teams

Team Name	League	Year Established

No teams are located in the metro area
Source: Wikipedia, Major Professional Sports Teams of the United States and Canada, May 4, 2020

CLIMATE

Average and Extreme Temperatures

Temperature	Jan	Feb	Mar	Apr	May	Jun	Jul	Aug	Sep	Oct	Nov	Dec	Yr.
Extreme High (°F)	66	70	88	94	104	110	110	109	104	94	76	62	110
Average High (°F)	25	30	41	59	71	80	86	84	74	62	43	29	57
Average Temp. (°F)	15	20	32	47	59	69	75	72	62	50	33	20	46
Average Low (°F)	5	10	22	35	47	57	62	60	49	38	23	10	35
Extreme Low (°F)	-36	-31	-23	4	17	33	38	34	22	9	-17	-28	-36

Note: Figures cover the years 1932-1990
Source: National Climatic Data Center, International Station Meteorological Climate Summary, 9/96

Average Precipitation/Snowfall/Humidity

Precip./Humidity	Jan	Feb	Mar	Apr	May	Jun	Jul	Aug	Sep	Oct	Nov	Dec	Yr.
Avg. Precip. (in.)	0.6	0.8	1.6	2.4	3.3	3.9	2.8	3.2	2.8	1.5	1.0	0.7	24.6
Avg. Snowfall (in.)	7	8	9	2	Tr	0	0	0	Tr	Tr	5	7	38
Avg. Rel. Hum. 6am (%)	n/a	n/a	n/a	n/a	n/a	n/a	n/a	n/a	n/a	n/a	n/a	n/a	n/a
Avg. Rel. Hum. 3pm (%)	n/a	n/a	n/a	n/a	n/a	n/a	n/a	n/a	n/a	n/a	n/a	n/a	n/a

Note: Figures cover the years 1932-1990; Tr = Trace amounts (<0.05 in. of rain; <0.5 in. of snow)
Source: National Climatic Data Center, International Station Meteorological Climate Summary, 9/96

Weather Conditions

Temperature			Daytime Sky			Precipitation		
5°F & below	32°F & below	90°F & above	Clear	Partly cloudy	Cloudy	0.01 inch or more precip.	0.1 inch or more snow/ice	Thunder-storms
n/a	n/a	n/a	95	136	134	n/a	n/a	n/a

Note: Figures are average number of days per year and cover the years 1932-1990
Source: National Climatic Data Center, International Station Meteorological Climate Summary, 9/96

HAZARDOUS WASTE

Superfund Sites

The Sioux Falls, SD metro area has no sites on the EPA's Superfund Final National Priorities List. There are a total of 1,387 Superfund sites with a status of proposed or final on the list in the U.S.
U.S. Environmental Protection Agency, National Priorities List, May 5, 2020

**AIR & WATER
QUALITY**

Air Quality Trends: Ozone

	1990	1995	2000	2005	2010	2012	2014	2016	2017	2018
MSA[1]	n/a	n/a	n/a	n/a	n/a	n/a	n/a	n/a	n/a	n/a
U.S.	0.088	0.089	0.082	0.080	0.073	0.075	0.067	0.069	0.068	0.069

Note: (1) Data covers the Sioux Falls, SD Metropolitan Statistical Area—see Appendix B for areas included; n/a not available. The values shown are the composite ozone concentration averages among trend sites based on the highest fourth daily maximum 8-hour concentration in parts per million. These trends are based on sites having an adequate record of monitoring data during the trend period. Data from exceptional events are included.
Source: U.S. Environmental Protection Agency, Air Quality Monitoring Information, "Air Quality Trends by City, 1990-2018"

Air Quality Index

Area	Percent of Days when Air Quality was...[2]					AQI Statistics[2]	
	Good	Moderate	Unhealthy for Sensitive Groups	Unhealthy	Very Unhealthy	Maximum	Median
MSA[1]	84.7	14.5	0.8	0.0	0.0	115	37

Note: (1) Data covers the Sioux Falls, SD Metropolitan Statistical Area—see Appendix B for areas included; (2) Based on 365 days with AQI data in 2018. Air Quality Index (AQI) is an index for reporting daily air quality. EPA calculates the AQI for five major air pollutants regulated by the Clean Air Act: ground-level ozone, particle pollution (aka particulate matter), carbon monoxide, sulfur dioxide, and nitrogen dioxide. The AQI runs from 0 to 500. The higher the AQI value, the greater the level of air pollution and the greater the health concern. There are six AQI categories: "Good" AQI is between 0 and 50. Air quality is considered satisfactory; "Moderate" AQI is between 51 and 100. Air quality is acceptable; "Unhealthy for Sensitive Groups" When AQI values are between 101 and 150, members of sensitive groups may experience health effects; "Unhealthy" When AQI values are between 151 and 200 everyone may begin to experience health effects; "Very Unhealthy" AQI values between 201 and 300 trigger a health alert; "Hazardous" AQI values over 300 trigger warnings of emergency conditions (not shown).
Source: U.S. Environmental Protection Agency, Air Quality Index Report, 2018

Air Quality Index Pollutants

Area	Percent of Days when AQI Pollutant was...[2]					
	Carbon Monoxide	Nitrogen Dioxide	Ozone	Sulfur Dioxide	Particulate Matter 2.5	Particulate Matter 10
MSA[1]	0.0	3.0	73.7	0.0	22.5	0.8

Note: (1) Data covers the Sioux Falls, SD Metropolitan Statistical Area—see Appendix B for areas included; (2) Based on 365 days with AQI data in 2018. The Air Quality Index (AQI) is an index for reporting daily air quality. EPA calculates the AQI for five major air pollutants regulated by the Clean Air Act: ground-level ozone, particle pollution (also known as particulate matter), carbon monoxide, sulfur dioxide, and nitrogen dioxide. The AQI runs from 0 to 500. The higher the AQI value, the greater the level of air pollution and the greater the health concern.
Source: U.S. Environmental Protection Agency, Air Quality Index Report, 2018

Maximum Air Pollutant Concentrations: Particulate Matter, Ozone, CO and Lead

	Particulate Matter 10 (ug/m^3)	Particulate Matter 2.5 Wtd AM (ug/m^3)	Particulate Matter 2.5 24-Hr (ug/m^3)	Ozone (ppm)	Carbon Monoxide (ppm)	Lead (ug/m^3)
MSA[1] Level	58	5.5	16	0.069	1	n/a
NAAQS[2]	150	15	35	0.075	9	0.15
Met NAAQS[2]	Yes	Yes	Yes	Yes	Yes	n/a

Note: (1) Data covers the Sioux Falls, SD Metropolitan Statistical Area—see Appendix B for areas included; Data from exceptional events are included; (2) National Ambient Air Quality Standards; ppm = parts per million; ug/m^3 = micrograms per cubic meter; n/a not available.
Concentrations: Particulate Matter 10 (coarse particulate)—highest second maximum 24-hour concentration; Particulate Matter 2.5 Wtd AM (fine particulate)—highest weighted annual mean concentration; Particulate Matter 2.5 24-Hour (fine particulate)—highest 98th percentile 24-hour concentration; Ozone—highest fourth daily maximum 8-hour concentration; Carbon Monoxide—highest second maximum non-overlapping 8-hour concentration; Lead—maximum running 3-month average
Source: U.S. Environmental Protection Agency, Air Quality Monitoring Information, "Air Quality Statistics by City, 2018"

Maximum Air Pollutant Concentrations: Nitrogen Dioxide and Sulfur Dioxide

	Nitrogen Dioxide AM (ppb)	Nitrogen Dioxide 1-Hr (ppb)	Sulfur Dioxide AM (ppb)	Sulfur Dioxide 1-Hr (ppb)	Sulfur Dioxide 24-Hr (ppb)
MSA[1] Level	5	34	n/a	3	n/a
NAAQS[2]	53	100	30	75	140
Met NAAQS[2]	Yes	Yes	n/a	Yes	n/a

Note: (1) Data covers the Sioux Falls, SD Metropolitan Statistical Area—see Appendix B for areas included; Data from exceptional events are included; (2) National Ambient Air Quality Standards; ppm = parts per million; ug/m³ = micrograms per cubic meter; n/a not available.
Concentrations: Nitrogen Dioxide AM—highest arithmetic mean concentration; Nitrogen Dioxide 1-Hr—highest 98th percentile 1-hour daily maximum concentration; Sulfur Dioxide AM—highest annual mean concentration; Sulfur Dioxide 1-Hr—highest 99th percentile 1-hour daily maximum concentration; Sulfur Dioxide 24-Hr—highest second maximum 24-hour concentration
Source: U.S. Environmental Protection Agency, Air Quality Monitoring Information, "Air Quality Statistics by City, 2018"

Drinking Water

Water System Name	Pop. Served	Primary Water Source Type	Violations[1]
Sioux Falls	190,326	Surface	4

Note: (1) Total number of violations (both active and inactive) in the EPA database
Source: U.S. Environmental Protection Agency, Office of Ground Water and Drinking Water, Safe Drinking Water Information System (based on data extracted May 5, 2020)

Springfield, Illinois

Background

Springfield, Illinois is located the Midwest region of the United States. In the early 1800s, hunter and sugar maker Robert Pullman traveled with a small team to unexplored areas north of his home and discovered Sugar Creek, with an abundance of sugar maple trees and rich soil. He built a cabin in the area in October 1817 and became its first European settler, returning to his home in southern Illinois the following spring with the maple sugar and furs he had harvested. After Illinois entered the Union in 1818, Elisha Kelly from North Carolina discovered the Sugar Creek area and relocated his family and some friends there. They named the area Calhoun in honor of Senator John C. Calhoun of South Carolina. Another influential settler was businessman Elijah Iles who, in 1821, relocated his family there from Missouri. Iles opened the first general store. Calhoun was renamed Springfield in 1832 after Springfield, Massachusetts, a thriving town that Iles aspired to.

Abraham Lincoln, although known as Springfield, Illinois's most prominent citizen, was actually born in Hodgenville, Kentucky in 1809. He moved to the Springfield area in 1831, and into the city itself in 1837 where he practiced law and politics. Lincoln's famous farewell speech, and one of his earliest published speeches, his Lyceum address, was delivered in Springfield in January of 1838. In 1839, Springfield became the capital of Illinois due to Lincoln's efforts. In 1852, Springfield connected with the railroad system which led to its economic expansion. After Lincoln became President of the United States in 1861, Springfield became a solider training area for the Civil War, and Confederate prisoner camp. By 1900 Springfield emerged as a major player in the coal and farming industries, and a hub for the Illinois railroad.

Another celebrity resident of Springfield is architect Frank Lloyd Wright, who built the Dana Thomas House for the silver mine heiress Susan Lawrence Dana in 1902. Actually a "remodel" of Dana's Victorian mansion, this 12,000 square foot, 35-room house is the best preserved example of Lloyd's "Prairie" houses. The Dana Thomas House has the largest known collection of Wright's site-specific furniture and glass art throughout its 16 levels. It has been thoroughly renovated and is currently a museum. Other famous Springfield residents include Olympian swimmers Michael Phelps and Ryan Held, and professional athletes and authors, including Vachel Lindsay, Edgar Lee Masters, John Hay, Virginia Eiffert and Robert Fitzgerald.

Springfield is an American history buff's dream for all things Lincoln. The city houses Lincoln's home and law office, which are open to the public and listed as National Historic sites. The Abraham Lincoln Presidential Library and Museum, built in 2005, houses the original Gettysburg Address and the largest collection of Lincoln biographical works. The nearby Capitol Building is not only where Lincoln served in the House of Representatives, but also where mourners passed his body as it laid in state in 1865. Just a short walk from the Capitol is Oak Ridge Cemetery where Lincoln and his immediate family are buried at Lincoln's Tomb. More recently, former President Obama announced both his candidacy for the presidency and his choice for running mate Joe Biden at the State Capitol building in Springfield.

Two popular annual events hosted by the city are the Old Capitol Art Fair and the Route 66 Film Festival. Springfield is home to the Hoogland Center for the Arts, Springfield Theatre Center, Springfield Ballet Company, Illinois Symphony Orchestra and the Springfield Municipal Opera. And, the Illinois state legislature adopted a resolution proclaiming Springfield the "Chili Capital of the Civilized World."

Springfield has a humid, continental climate and was hit by two tornadoes in 2006.

Rankings

Business/Finance Rankings

- The Springfield metro area appeared on the Milken Institute "2020 Best Performing Cities" list. Rank: #159 out of 201 small metro areas. Criteria: job growth; wage and salary growth; high-tech output growth. *Milken Institute, "Best-Performing Cities 2020," February 26, 2020*

- *Forbes* ranked 203 smaller metro areas (population under 268,000) to determine the nation's "Best Small Places for Business and Careers." The Springfield metro area was ranked #34. Criteria: costs (business and living); job growth (past and projected); income growth; quality of life; educational attainment (college and high school); projected economic growth; cultural and leisure opportunities; workplace tolerance laws; net migration patterns. *Forbes, "The Best Small Places for Business and Careers 2019," October 30, 2019*

Environmental Rankings

- Springfield was highlighted as one of the top 104 cleanest metro areas for short-term particle pollution (24-hour PM 2.5) in the U.S. during 2015 through 2017. Monitors in these cities reported no days with unhealthful PM 2.5 levels. *American Lung Association, "State of the Air 2019," April 24, 2019*

Real Estate Rankings

- The Springfield metro area was identified as one of the 20 most affordable housing markets in the U.S. in 2019. The area ranked #16 out of 180 markets. Criteria: qualification for a mortgage loan with a 10% down payment on a typical home. *National Association of Realtors®, Qualifying Income Based on Sales Price of Existing Single-Family Homes for Metropolitan Areas, 2019*

- Springfield was ranked #19 out of 238 metro areas in terms of housing affordability in 2019 by the National Association of Home Builders (#1 = most affordable). Criteria: the share of homes sold in that area affordable to a family earning the local median income, based on standard mortgage underwriting criteria. *National Association of Home Builders®, NAHB-Wells Fargo Housing Opportunity Index, 4th Quarter 2019*

Safety Rankings

- To identify the most dangerous cities in America, 24/7 Wall Street focused on violent crime categories—murder, non-negligent manslaughter, rape, robbery, and aggravated assault—and property crime as reported in the FBI's 2018 annual Uniform Crime Report. Criteria also included median income from American Community Survey and unemployment figures from Bureau of Labor Statistics. For cities with populations over 100,000, Springfield was ranked #49. *247wallst.com, "America's Most Dangerous Cities" January 10, 2020*

- The National Insurance Crime Bureau ranked 382 metro areas in the U.S. in terms of per capita rates of vehicle theft. The Springfield metro area ranked #92 (#1 = highest rate). Criteria: number of vehicle theft offenses per 100,000 inhabitants in 2018. *National Insurance Crime Bureau, "Hot Spots 2018," June 25, 2019*

Seniors/Retirement Rankings

- From its Best Cities for Successful Aging indexes, the Milken Institute generated rankings for metropolitan areas, weighing data in nine categories—health care, wellness, living arrangements, transportation and convenience, financial characteristics, education, employment, community engagement, and overall livability. The Springfield metro area was ranked #92 overall in the small metro area category. *Milken Institute, "Best Cities for Successful Aging, 2017" March 14, 2017*

Business Environment

CITY FINANCES

City Government Finances

Component	2017 ($000)	2017 ($ per capita)
Total Revenues	467,952	4,015
Total Expenditures	503,359	4,318
Debt Outstanding	1,436,900	12,327
Cash and Securities[1]	495,748	4,253

Note: (1) Cash and security holdings of a government at the close of its fiscal year, including those of its dependent agencies, utilities, and liquor stores.
Source: U.S. Census Bureau, State & Local Government Finances 2017

City Government Revenue by Source

Source	2017 ($000)	2017 ($ per capita)	2017 (%)
General Revenue			
From Federal Government	6,789	58	1.5
From State Government	47,400	407	10.1
From Local Governments	363	3	0.1
Taxes			
Property	28,114	241	6.0
Sales and Gross Receipts	54,282	466	11.6
Personal Income	0	0	0.0
Corporate Income	0	0	0.0
Motor Vehicle License	0	0	0.0
Other Taxes	1,265	11	0.3
Current Charges	17,890	153	3.8
Liquor Store	0	0	0.0
Utility	268,121	2,300	57.3
Employee Retirement	39,276	337	8.4

Source: U.S. Census Bureau, State & Local Government Finances 2017

City Government Expenditures by Function

Function	2017 ($000)	2017 ($ per capita)	2017 (%)
General Direct Expenditures			
Air Transportation	0	0	0.0
Corrections	0	0	0.0
Education	0	0	0.0
Employment Security Administration	0	0	0.0
Financial Administration	1,981	17	0.4
Fire Protection	37,587	322	7.5
General Public Buildings	2,170	18	0.4
Governmental Administration, Other	7,583	65	1.5
Health	0	0	0.0
Highways	50,877	436	10.1
Hospitals	0	0	0.0
Housing and Community Development	7,181	61	1.4
Interest on General Debt	5,283	45	1.0
Judicial and Legal	0	0	0.0
Libraries	4,426	38	0.9
Parking	1,032	8	0.2
Parks and Recreation	2,476	21	0.5
Police Protection	45,460	390	9.0
Public Welfare	0	0	0.0
Sewerage	9,482	81	1.9
Solid Waste Management	0	0	0.0
Veterans' Services	0	0	0.0
Liquor Store	0	0	0.0
Utility	272,591	2,338	54.2
Employee Retirement	26,711	229	5.3

Source: U.S. Census Bureau, State & Local Government Finances 2017

DEMOGRAPHICS

Population Growth

Area	1990 Census	2000 Census	2010 Census	2018* Estimate	Population Growth (%)	
					1990-2018	2010-2018
City	108,997	111,454	116,250	116,459	6.8	0.2
MSA[1]	189,550	201,437	210,170	210,028	10.8	-0.1
U.S.	248,709,873	281,421,906	308,745,538	322,903,030	29.8	4.6

Note: (1) Figures cover the Springfield, IL Metropolitan Statistical Area—see Appendix B for areas included;
(*) 2014-2018 5-year estimated population
Source: U.S. Census Bureau, 1990 Census, Census 2000, Census 2010, 2014-2018 American Community
Survey 5-Year Estimates

Household Size

Area	Persons in Household (%)							Average Household Size
	One	Two	Three	Four	Five	Six	Seven or More	
City	37.4	34.3	13.5	9.1	3.1	1.5	1.1	2.20
MSA[1]	32.4	36.1	14.1	10.6	4.3	1.8	0.8	2.30
U.S.	27.7	33.9	15.7	13.0	6.0	2.3	1.4	2.60

Note: (1) Figures cover the Springfield, IL Metropolitan Statistical Area—see Appendix B for areas included
Source: U.S. Census Bureau, 2014-2018 American Community Survey 5-Year Estimates

Race

Area	White Alone[2] (%)	Black Alone[2] (%)	Asian Alone[2] (%)	AIAN[3] Alone[2] (%)	NHOPI[4] Alone[2] (%)	Other Race Alone[2] (%)	Two or More Races (%)
City	72.9	19.9	2.9	0.1	0.0	0.8	3.3
MSA[1]	82.8	12.1	1.9	0.1	0.1	0.6	2.5
U.S.	72.7	12.7	5.4	0.8	0.2	4.9	3.2

Note: (1) Figures cover the Springfield, IL Metropolitan Statistical Area—see Appendix B for areas included;
(2) Alone is defined as not being in combination with one or more other races; (3) American Indian and Alaska
Native; (4) Native Hawaiian and Other Pacific Islander
Source: U.S. Census Bureau, 2014-2018 American Community Survey 5-Year Estimates

Hispanic or Latino Origin

Area	Total (%)	Mexican (%)	Puerto Rican (%)	Cuban (%)	Other (%)
City	2.7	1.4	0.6	0.1	0.5
MSA[1]	2.2	1.2	0.4	0.1	0.5
U.S.	17.8	11.2	1.7	0.7	4.2

Note: Persons of Hispanic or Latino origin can be of any race; (1) Figures cover the Springfield, IL
Metropolitan Statistical Area—see Appendix B for areas included
Source: U.S. Census Bureau, 2014-2018 American Community Survey 5-Year Estimates

Segregation

Type	Segregation Indices[1]				Percent Change		
	1990	2000	2010	2010 Rank[2]	1990-2000	1990-2010	2000-2010
Black/White	n/a	n/a	n/a	n/a	n/a	n/a	n/a
Asian/White	n/a	n/a	n/a	n/a	n/a	n/a	n/a
Hispanic/White	n/a	n/a	n/a	n/a	n/a	n/a	n/a

Note: All figures cover the Metropolitan Statistical Area—see Appendix B for areas included; Figures are based
on an analysis of 1990, 2000, and 2010 Census Decennial Census tract data by William H. Frey, Brookings
Institution and the University of Michigan Social Science Data Analysis Network. In this analysis all racial
groups (whites, blacks, and asians) are non-Hispanic members of those races. Hispanics are shown as a
separate category; (1) Segregation Indices are Dissimilarity Indices that measure the degree to which the
minority group is distributed differently than whites across census tracts. They range from 0 (complete
integration) to 100 (complete segregation) where the value indicates the percentage of the minority group that
needs to move to be distributed exactly like whites; (2) Ranges from 1 (most segregated) to 102 (least
segregated); n/a not available.
Source: www.CensusScope.org

Ancestry

Area	German	Irish	English	American	Italian	Polish	French[2]	Scottish	Dutch
City	20.8	13.1	9.8	5.1	4.8	2.0	2.2	1.6	1.3
MSA[1]	24.4	14.0	10.6	6.2	5.0	1.9	2.5	1.8	1.4
U.S.	13.7	9.9	7.3	6.4	5.2	2.8	2.4	1.7	1.2

Note: Figures are the percentage of the total population reporting a particular ancestry. The nine most commonly reported ancestries in the U.S. are shown. Figures include multiple ancestries (e.g. if a person reported being Irish and Italian, they were included in both columns); (1) Figures cover the Springfield, IL Metropolitan Statistical Area—see Appendix B for areas included; (2) Excludes Basque
Source: U.S. Census Bureau, 2014-2018 American Community Survey 5-Year Estimates

Foreign-born Population

Area	Percent of Population Born in								
	Any Foreign Country	Asia	Mexico	Europe	Caribbean	Central America[2]	South America	Africa	Canada
City	4.2	2.5	0.3	0.5	0.2	0.1	0.1	0.4	0.1
MSA[1]	2.9	1.6	0.2	0.4	0.1	0.1	0.1	0.3	0.1
U.S.	13.5	4.1	3.5	1.5	1.3	1.1	0.9	0.7	0.3

Note: (1) Figures cover the Springfield, IL Metropolitan Statistical Area—see Appendix B for areas included; (2) Excludes Mexico.
Source: U.S. Census Bureau, 2014-2018 American Community Survey 5-Year Estimates

Marital Status

Area	Never Married	Now Married[2]	Separated	Widowed	Divorced
City	36.7	40.9	1.6	6.5	14.3
MSA[1]	31.4	47.6	1.3	6.1	13.5
U.S.	33.3	48.1	2.0	5.8	10.8

Note: Figures are percentages and cover the population 15 years of age and older; (1) Figures cover the Springfield, IL Metropolitan Statistical Area—see Appendix B for areas included; (2) Excludes separated
Source: U.S. Census Bureau, 2014-2018 American Community Survey 5-Year Estimates

Disability by Age

Area	All Ages	Under 18 Years Old	18 to 64 Years Old	65 Years and Over
City	15.2	6.1	13.2	35.2
MSA[1]	13.9	5.8	11.5	33.9
U.S.	12.6	4.2	10.3	35.0

Note: Figures show percent of the civilian noninstitutionalized population that reported having a disability. Disability status is determined from six types of difficulty: vision, hearing, cognitive, ambulatory, self-care, and independent living. For children under 5 years old, hearing and vision difficulty are used to determine disability status. For children between the ages of 5 and 14, disability status is determined from hearing, vision, cognitive, ambulatory, and self-care difficulties. For people aged 15 years and older, they are considered to have a disability if they have difficulty with any one of the six difficulty types; Note: (1) Figures cover the Springfield, IL Metropolitan Statistical Area—see Appendix B for areas included
Source: U.S. Census Bureau, 2014-2018 American Community Survey 5-Year Estimates

Age

Area	Percent of Population									Median Age
	Under Age 5	Age 5–19	Age 20–34	Age 35–44	Age 45–54	Age 55–64	Age 65–74	Age 75–84	Age 85+	
City	6.2	18.3	20.7	11.7	12.2	14.1	9.6	4.9	2.4	39.0
MSA[1]	5.8	19.0	18.6	12.2	13.4	14.2	9.7	4.9	2.2	40.2
U.S.	6.1	19.3	20.7	12.6	13.2	12.8	8.8	4.5	1.9	37.9

Note: (1) Figures cover the Springfield, IL Metropolitan Statistical Area—see Appendix B for areas included
Source: U.S. Census Bureau, 2014-2018 American Community Survey 5-Year Estimates

Gender

Area	Males	Females	Males per 100 Females
City	55,176	61,283	90.0
MSA[1]	100,919	109,109	92.5
U.S.	158,984,190	163,918,840	97.0

Note: (1) Figures cover the Springfield, IL Metropolitan Statistical Area—see Appendix B for areas included
Source: U.S. Census Bureau, 2014-2018 American Community Survey 5-Year Estimates

Religious Groups by Family

Area	Catholic	Baptist	Non-Den.	Methodist[2]	Lutheran	LDS[3]	Pente-costal	Presby-terian[4]	Muslim[5]	Judaism
MSA[1]	15.6	11.7	2.7	6.8	5.6	0.8	5.0	2.0	1.6	0.2
U.S.	19.1	9.3	4.0	4.0	2.3	2.0	1.9	1.6	0.8	0.7

Note: Figures are the number of adherents as a percentage of the total population; (1) Figures cover the Springfield, IL Metropolitan Statistical Area—see Appendix B for areas included; (2) Methodist/Pietist; (3) Latter Day Saints; (4) Reformed; (5) Figures are estimates
Source: Association of Statisticians of American Religious Bodies, 2010 U.S. Religion Census: Religious Congregations & Membership Study

Religious Groups by Tradition

Area	Catholic	Evangelical Protestant	Mainline Protestant	Other Tradition	Black Protestant	Orthodox
MSA[1]	15.6	21.5	11.7	3.2	2.1	0.1
U.S.	19.1	16.2	7.3	4.3	1.6	0.3

Note: Figures are the number of adherents as a percentage of the total population; (1) Figures cover the Springfield, IL Metropolitan Statistical Area—see Appendix B for areas included
Source: Association of Statisticians of American Religious Bodies, 2010 U.S. Religion Census: Religious Congregations & Membership Study

ECONOMY

Gross Metropolitan Product

Area	2017	2018	2019	2020	Rank[2]
MSA[1]	10.3	10.7	11.0	11.4	202

Note: Figures are in billions of dollars; (1) Figures cover the Springfield, IL Metropolitan Statistical Area—see Appendix B for areas included; (2) Rank is based on 2018 data and ranges from 1 to 381
Source: U.S. Conference of Mayors, U.S. Metro Economies: GMP & Employment 2018-2020, September 2019

Economic Growth

Area	2015-17 (%)	2018 (%)	2019 (%)	2020 (%)	Rank[2]
MSA[1]	-0.8	0.8	1.4	0.9	337
U.S.	1.9	2.9	2.3	2.1	–

Note: Figures are real gross metropolitan product (GMP) growth rates and represent average annual percent change; (1) Figures cover the Springfield, IL Metropolitan Statistical Area—see Appendix B for areas included; (2) Rank is based on 2017 2-year average annual percent change and ranges from 1 to 381
Source: U.S. Conference of Mayors, U.S. Metro Economies: GMP & Employment 2018-2020, September 2019

Metropolitan Area Exports

Area	2013	2014	2015	2016	2017	2018	Rank[2]
MSA[1]	97.5	94.4	111.7	88.3	107.5	91.2	343

Note: Figures are in millions of dollars; (1) Figures cover the Springfield, IL Metropolitan Statistical Area—see Appendix B for areas included; (2) Rank is based on 2018 data and ranges from 1 to 387
Source: U.S. Department of Commerce, International Trade Administration, Office of Trade and Economic Analysis, Industry and Analysis, Exports by Metropolitan Area, data extracted April 15, 2020

Building Permits

Area	Single-Family			Multi-Family			Total		
	2017	2018	Pct. Chg.	2017	2018	Pct. Chg.	2017	2018	Pct. Chg.
City	57	74	29.8	94	219	133.0	151	293	94.0
MSA[1]	210	193	-8.1	112	313	179.5	322	506	57.1
U.S.	820,000	855,300	4.3	462,000	473,500	2.5	1,282,000	1,328,800	3.7

Note: (1) Figures cover the Springfield, IL Metropolitan Statistical Area—see Appendix B for areas included; Figures represent new, privately-owned housing units authorized (unadjusted data); All permit data are based on estimates with imputation
Source: U.S. Census Bureau, Manufacturing, Mining, and Construction Statistics, Building Permits, 2017, 2018

Bankruptcy Filings

Area	Business Filings			Nonbusiness Filings		
	2018	2019	% Chg.	2018	2019	% Chg.
Sangamon County	8	8	0.0	472	436	-7.6
U.S.	22,232	22,780	2.5	751,186	752,160	0.1

Note: Business filings include Chapter 7, Chapter 9, Chapter 11, Chapter 12, Chapter 13, Chapter 15, and Section 304; Nonbusiness filings include Chapter 7, Chapter 11, and Chapter 13
Source: Administrative Office of the U.S. Courts, Business and Nonbusiness Bankruptcy, County Cases Commenced by Chapter of the Bankruptcy Code, During the 12-Month Period Ending December 31, 2018 and Business and Nonbusiness Bankruptcy, County Cases Commenced by Chapter of the Bankruptcy Code, During the 12-Month Period Ending December 31, 2019

Housing Vacancy Rates

Area	Gross Vacancy Rate[2] (%)			Year-Round Vacancy Rate[3] (%)			Rental Vacancy Rate[4] (%)			Homeowner Vacancy Rate[5] (%)		
	2017	2018	2019	2017	2018	2019	2017	2018	2019	2017	2018	2019
MSA[1]	n/a	n/a	n/a	n/a	n/a	n/a	n/a	n/a	n/a	n/a	n/a	n/a
U.S.	12.7	12.3	12.0	9.9	9.7	9.5	7.2	6.9	6.7	1.6	1.5	1.4

Note: (1) Figures cover the Springfield, IL Metropolitan Statistical Area—see Appendix B for areas included; (2) The percentage of the total housing inventory that is vacant; (3) The percentage of the housing inventory (excluding seasonal units) that is year-round vacant; (4) The percentage of rental inventory that is vacant for rent; (5) The percentage of homeowner inventory that is vacant for sale; n/a not available
Source: U.S. Census Bureau, Housing Vacancies and Homeownership Annual Statistics: 2017, 2018, 2019

INCOME

Income

Area	Per Capita ($)	Median Household ($)	Average Household ($)
City	33,651	53,405	75,852
MSA[1]	34,545	60,961	80,629
U.S.	32,621	60,293	84,938

Note: (1) Figures cover the Springfield, IL Metropolitan Statistical Area—see Appendix B for areas included
Source: U.S. Census Bureau, 2014-2018 American Community Survey 5-Year Estimates

Household Income Distribution

Area	Percent of Households Earning							
	Under $15,000	$15,000 -$24,999	$25,000 -$34,999	$35,000 -$49,999	$50,000 -$74,999	$75,000 -$99,999	$100,000 -$149,999	$150,000 and up
City	14.4	11.7	9.2	12.1	17.6	12.4	12.2	10.4
MSA[1]	11.1	9.8	8.7	11.8	18.0	14.0	15.0	11.7
U.S.	10.9	9.3	9.3	12.6	17.5	12.5	14.6	13.3

Note: (1) Figures cover the Springfield, IL Metropolitan Statistical Area—see Appendix B for areas included
Source: U.S. Census Bureau, 2014-2018 American Community Survey 5-Year Estimates

Poverty Rate

Area	All Ages	Under 18 Years Old	18 to 64 Years Old	65 Years and Over
City	19.6	32.2	18.4	7.7
MSA[1]	14.9	24.0	13.8	6.4
U.S.	14.1	19.5	13.2	9.3

Note: Figures are percentage of people whose income during the past 12 months was below the poverty level; (1) Figures cover the Springfield, IL Metropolitan Statistical Area—see Appendix B for areas included
Source: U.S. Census Bureau, 2014-2018 American Community Survey 5-Year Estimates

EMPLOYMENT

Labor Force and Employment

Area	Civilian Labor Force			Workers Employed		
	Dec. 2018	Dec. 2019	% Chg.	Dec. 2018	Dec. 2019	% Chg.
City	57,450	56,539	-1.6	54,565	54,362	-0.4
MSA[1]	107,834	106,114	-1.6	102,505	102,129	-0.4
U.S.	162,510,000	164,007,000	0.9	156,481,000	158,504,000	1.3

Note: Data is not seasonally adjusted and covers workers 16 years of age and older; (1) Figures cover the Springfield, IL Metropolitan Statistical Area—see Appendix B for areas included
Source: Bureau of Labor Statistics, Local Area Unemployment Statistics

Unemployment Rate

Area	2019											
	Jan.	Feb.	Mar.	Apr.	May	Jun.	Jul.	Aug.	Sep.	Oct.	Nov.	Dec.
City	5.5	4.9	4.7	3.7	3.5	4.3	4.6	4.3	3.8	3.8	3.6	3.9
MSA[1]	5.5	4.9	4.7	3.5	3.3	3.8	4.0	4.0	3.5	3.5	3.5	3.8
U.S.	4.4	4.1	3.9	3.3	3.4	3.8	4.0	3.8	3.3	3.3	3.3	3.4

Note: Data is not seasonally adjusted and covers workers 16 years of age and older; (1) Figures cover the Springfield, IL Metropolitan Statistical Area—see Appendix B for areas included
Source: Bureau of Labor Statistics, Local Area Unemployment Statistics

Average Wages

Occupation	$/Hr.	Occupation	$/Hr.
Accountants and Auditors	37.00	Maintenance and Repair Workers	19.60
Automotive Mechanics	21.50	Marketing Managers	52.90
Bookkeepers	19.30	Network and Computer Systems Admin.	36.80
Carpenters	27.10	Nurses, Licensed Practical	21.60
Cashiers	10.80	Nurses, Registered	33.70
Computer Programmers	45.80	Nursing Assistants	14.00
Computer Systems Analysts	43.40	Office Clerks, General	18.30
Computer User Support Specialists	25.00	Physical Therapists	40.00
Construction Laborers	25.30	Physicians	127.30
Cooks, Restaurant	11.80	Plumbers, Pipefitters and Steamfitters	39.60
Customer Service Representatives	16.90	Police and Sheriff's Patrol Officers	34.40
Dentists	81.70	Postal Service Mail Carriers	25.20
Electricians	32.50	Real Estate Sales Agents	n/a
Engineers, Electrical	45.80	Retail Salespersons	13.70
Fast Food and Counter Workers	10.10	Sales Representatives, Technical/Scientific	39.30
Financial Managers	58.80	Secretaries, Exc. Legal/Medical/Executive	17.30
First-Line Supervisors of Office Workers	27.50	Security Guards	22.20
General and Operations Managers	45.30	Surgeons	n/a
Hairdressers/Cosmetologists	20.30	Teacher Assistants, Exc. Postsecondary*	11.60
Home Health and Personal Care Aides	12.00	Teachers, Secondary School, Exc. Sp. Ed.*	26.40
Janitors and Cleaners	14.90	Telemarketers	n/a
Landscaping/Groundskeeping Workers	15.00	Truck Drivers, Heavy/Tractor-Trailer	20.70
Lawyers	51.10	Truck Drivers, Light/Delivery Services	16.30
Maids and Housekeeping Cleaners	12.20	Waiters and Waitresses	10.00

Note: Wage data covers the Springfield, IL Metropolitan Statistical Area—see Appendix B for areas included; (*) Hourly wages were calculated from annual wage data based on a 40 hour work week; n/a not available.
Source: Bureau of Labor Statistics, Metro Area Occupational Employment & Wage Estimates, May 2019

Employment by Occupation

Occupation Classification	City (%)	MSA[1] (%)	U.S. (%)
Management, Business, Science, and Arts	43.2	41.7	37.9
Natural Resources, Construction, and Maintenance	4.7	6.5	8.9
Production, Transportation, and Material Moving	9.6	10.2	13.3
Sales and Office	22.9	23.7	22.1
Service	19.6	17.8	17.9

Note: Figures cover employed civilians 16 years of age and older; (1) Figures cover the Springfield, IL Metropolitan Statistical Area—see Appendix B for areas included
Source: U.S. Census Bureau, 2014-2018 American Community Survey 5-Year Estimates

Employment by Industry

Sector	MSA[1]		U.S.
	Number of Employees	Percent of Total	Percent of Total
Construction, Mining, and Logging	3,000	2.7	5.4
Education and Health Services	21,800	20.0	16.1
Financial Activities	6,400	5.9	5.8
Government	27,200	24.9	15.0
Information	2,700	2.5	1.9
Leisure and Hospitality	9,800	9.0	10.8
Manufacturing	3,300	3.0	8.4
Other Services	6,100	5.6	3.9
Professional and Business Services	12,400	11.4	14.1
Retail Trade	11,600	10.6	10.6
Transportation, Warehousing, and Utilities	2,000	1.8	4.2
Wholesale Trade	2,900	2.7	3.9

Note: Figures are non-farm employment as of December 2019. Figures are not seasonally adjusted and include workers 16 years of age and older; (1) Figures cover the Springfield, IL Metropolitan Statistical Area—see Appendix B for areas included
Source: Bureau of Labor Statistics, Current Employment Statistics, Employment, Hours, and Earnings

Occupations with Greatest Projected Employment Growth: 2019 – 2021

Occupation[1]	2019 Employment	2021 Projected Employment	Numeric Employment Change	Percent Employment Change
Combined Food Preparation and Serving Workers, Including Fast Food	140,460	145,280	4,820	3.4
Registered Nurses	133,320	137,300	3,980	3.0
Personal Care Aides	56,160	59,830	3,670	6.5
Laborers and Freight, Stock, and Material Movers, Hand	158,620	162,170	3,550	2.2
Insurance Sales Agents	49,730	52,420	2,690	5.4
Heavy and Tractor-Trailer Truck Drivers	73,100	75,610	2,510	3.4
General and Operations Managers	120,880	123,200	2,320	1.9
Cooks, Restaurant	47,520	49,620	2,100	4.4
Janitors and Cleaners, Except Maids and Housekeeping Cleaners	85,160	86,710	1,550	1.8
Financial Managers	40,420	41,900	1,480	3.7

Note: Projections cover Illinois; (1) Sorted by numeric employment change
Source: www.projectionscentral.com, State Occupational Projections, 2019–2021 Short-Term Projections

Fastest Growing Occupations: 2019 – 2021

Occupation[1]	2019 Employment	2021 Projected Employment	Numeric Employment Change	Percent Employment Change
Actuaries	1,940	2,070	130	6.7
Personal Care Aides	56,160	59,830	3,670	6.5
Statisticians	1,910	2,030	120	6.3
Nurse Practitioners	8,130	8,610	480	5.9
Physician Assistants	3,800	4,020	220	5.8
Insurance Sales Agents	49,730	52,420	2,690	5.4
Operations Research Analysts	5,080	5,350	270	5.3
Computer Numerically Controlled Machine Tool Programmers, Metal and Plastic	1,150	1,210	60	5.2
Veterinary Technologists and Technicians	4,010	4,210	200	5.0
Massage Therapists	6,720	7,050	330	4.9

Note: Projections cover Illinois; (1) Sorted by percent employment change and excludes occupations with numeric employment change less than 50
Source: www.projectionscentral.com, State Occupational Projections, 2019–2021 Short-Term Projections

TAXES

State Corporate Income Tax Rates

State	Tax Rate (%)	Income Brackets ($)	Num. of Brackets	Financial Institution Tax Rate (%)[a]	Federal Income Tax Ded.
Illinois	9.5 (h)	Flat rate	1	9.5 (h)	No

Note: Tax rates as of January 1, 2020; (a) Rates listed are the corporate income tax rate applied to financial institutions or excise taxes based on income; (h) The Illinois rate of 9.5% is the sum of a corporate income tax rate of 7.0% plus a replacement tax of 2.5%.
Source: Federation of Tax Administrators, State Corporate Income Tax Rates, January 1, 2020

State Individual Income Tax Rates

State	Tax Rate (%)	Income Brackets ($)	Personal Exemptions ($)			Standard Ded. ($)	
			Single	Married	Depend.	Single	Married
Illinois (a)	4.95	Flat rate	2,275	4,550	2,275	–	–

Note: Tax rates as of January 1, 2020; Local- and county-level taxes are not included; Federal income tax is not deductible on state income tax returns; (a) 19 states have statutory provision for automatically adjusting to the rate of inflation the dollar values of the income tax brackets, standard deductions, and/or personal exemptions. Michigan indexes the personal exemption only. Oregon does not index the income brackets for $125,000 and over.
Source: Federation of Tax Administrators, State Individual Income Tax Rates, January 1, 2020

Various State Sales and Excise Tax Rates

State	State Sales Tax (%)	Gasoline[1] (¢/gal.)	Cigarette[2] ($/pack)	Spirits[3] ($/gal.)	Wine[4] ($/gal.)	Beer[5] ($/gal.)	Recreational Marijuana (%)
Illinois	6.25	53.65	2.98	8.55	1.39	0.23	(d)

Note: All tax rates as of January 1, 2020; (1) The American Petroleum Institute has developed a methodology for determining the average tax rate on a gallon of fuel. Rates may include any of the following: excise taxes, environmental fees, storage tank fees, other fees or taxes, general sales tax, and local taxes; (2) The federal excise tax of $1.0066 per pack and local taxes are not included; (3) Rates are those applicable to off-premise sales of 40% alcohol by volume (a.b.v.) distilled spirits in 750ml containers. Local excise taxes are excluded; (4) Rates are those applicable to off-premise sales of 11% a.b.v. non-carbonated wine in 750ml containers; (5) Rates are those applicable to off-premise sales of 4.7% a.b.v. beer in 12 ounce containers; (d) 7% excise tax of value at wholesale level, 10% tax on cannabis flower or products with less than 35% THC, 20% tax on products infused with cannabis, such as edible products, 25% tax on any product with a THC concentration higher than 35%
Source: Tax Foundation, 2020 Facts & Figures: How Does Your State Compare?

State Business Tax Climate Index Rankings

State	Overall Rank	Corporate Tax Rank	Individual Income Tax Rank	Sales Tax Rank	Property Tax Rank	Unemployment Insurance Tax Rank
Illinois	35	36	13	33	40	40

Note: The index is a measure of how each state's tax laws affect economic performance. The lower the rank, the more favorable a state's tax system is for business. States without a given tax are given a ranking of 1. The scores/rankings for the District of Columbia do not affect other states. The 2020 index represents the tax climate as of July 1, 2019.
Source: Tax Foundation, State Business Tax Climate Index 2020

COMMERCIAL UTILITIES

Typical Monthly Electric Bills

Area	General Service, Light ($/month)		General Service, Heavy ($/month)	
	40 kW demand 5,000 kWh	100 kW demand 10,000 kWh	500 kW demand 100,000 kWh	1,500 kW demand 500,000 kWh
City	n/a	n/a	n/a	n/a

Note: Figures are based on rates in effect January 1, 2018
Source: Memphis Light, Gas and Water, 2019 Utility Bill Comparisons for Selected U.S. Cities

TRANSPORTATION

Means of Transportation to Work

Area	Car/Truck/Van		Public Transportation			Bicycle	Walked	Other Means	Worked at Home
	Drove Alone	Car-pooled	Bus	Subway	Railroad				
City	82.1	7.7	2.2	0.1	0.0	0.7	2.4	1.4	3.5
MSA[1]	83.5	7.7	1.4	0.1	0.0	0.4	1.9	1.1	3.9
U.S.	76.4	9.1	2.5	1.9	0.6	0.6	2.7	1.3	4.9

Note: Figures are percentages and cover workers 16 years of age and older; (1) Figures cover the Springfield, IL Metropolitan Statistical Area—see Appendix B for areas included
Source: U.S. Census Bureau, 2014-2018 American Community Survey 5-Year Estimates

Travel Time to Work

Area	Less Than 10 Minutes	10 to 19 Minutes	20 to 29 Minutes	30 to 44 Minutes	45 to 59 Minutes	60 to 89 Minutes	90 Minutes or More
City	18.2	51.0	18.7	5.9	2.0	2.5	1.6
MSA[1]	16.0	41.7	23.5	11.7	3.0	2.5	1.7
U.S.	12.5	28.7	20.9	20.7	8.2	6.3	2.8

Note: Note: Figures are percentages and include workers 16 years old and over; (1) Figures cover the Springfield, IL Metropolitan Statistical Area—see Appendix B for areas included
Source: U.S. Census Bureau, 2014-2018 American Community Survey 5-Year Estimates

Key Congestion Measures

Area	1982	1992	2002	2012	2017
Annual Hours of Delay, Total (000)	n/a	n/a	n/a	n/a	2,504
Annual Hours of Delay, Per Auto Commuter	n/a	n/a	n/a	n/a	14
Annual Congestion Cost, Total (million $)	n/a	n/a	n/a	n/a	53
Annual Congestion Cost, Per Auto Commuter ($)	n/a	n/a	n/a	n/a	297

Note: n/a not available
Source: Texas A&M Transportation Institute, 2019 Urban Mobility Report

Freeway Travel Time Index

Area	1982	1987	1992	1997	2002	2007	2012	2017
Urban Area Index[1]	n/a	n/a	n/a	n/a	n/a	n/a	n/a	1.06
Urban Area Rank[1,2]	n/a	n/a	n/a	n/a	n/a	n/a	n/a	n/a

Note: Freeway Travel Time Index—the ratio of travel time in the peak period to the travel time at free-flow conditions. For example, a value of 1.30 indicates a 20-minute free-flow trip takes 26 minutes in the peak (20 minutes x 1.30 = 26 minutes); (1) Covers the Springfield IL urban area; (2) Rank is based on 101 larger urban areas (#1 = highest travel time index); n/a not available
Source: Texas A&M Transportation Institute, 2019 Urban Mobility Report

Public Transportation

Agency Name / Mode of Transportation	Vehicles Operated in Maximum Service[1]	Annual Unlinked Passenger Trips[2] (in thous.)	Annual Passenger Miles[3] (in thous.)
Springfield Mass Transit District (SMTD)			
Bus (directly operated)	48	1,544.7	5,677.8
Demand Response (directly operated)	12	78.1	493.2

Note: (1) Number of revenue vehicles operated by the given mode and type of service to meet the annual maximum service requirement. This is the revenue vehicle count during the peak season of the year; on the week and day that maximum service is provided. Vehicles operated in maximum service (VOMS) exclude atypical days and one-time special events; (2) Number of passengers who boarded public transportation vehicles. Passengers are counted each time they board a vehicle no matter how many vehicles they use to travel from their origin to their destination. (3) Sum of the distances ridden by all passengers during the entire fiscal year.
Source: Federal Transit Administration, National Transit Database, 2018

Air Transportation

Airport Name and Code / Type of Service	Passenger Airlines[1]	Passenger Enplanements	Freight Carriers[2]	Freight (lbs)
Capital Airport (SPI)				
Domestic service (U.S. carriers - 2019)	5	75,070	1	695
International service (U.S. carriers - 2018)	1	144	0	0

Note: (1) Includes all U.S.-based major, minor and commuter airlines that carried at least one passenger during the year; (2) Includes all U.S.-based airlines and freight carriers that transported at least one pound of freight during the year.
Source: Bureau of Transportation Statistics, The Intermodal Transportation Database, Air Carriers: T-100 Domestic Market (U.S. Carriers), 2019; Bureau of Transportation Statistics, The Intermodal Transportation Database, Air Carriers: T-100 International Market (U.S. Carriers), 2018

Other Transportation Statistics

Major Highways:	I-55; I-72
Amtrak Service:	Yes
Major Waterways/Ports:	None

Source: Amtrak.com; Google Maps

BUSINESSES

Major Business Headquarters

Company Name	Industry	Rankings Fortune[1]	Rankings Forbes[2]
No companies listed	-	-	-

Note: (1) Companies that produce a 10-K are ranked 1 to 500 based on 2018 revenue; (2) All private companies with at least $2 billion in annual revenue through the end of their most current fiscal year are ranked 1 to 228; companies listed are headquartered in the city; dashes indicate no ranking
Source: Fortune, "Fortune 500," June 2019; Forbes, "America's Largest Private Companies," 2019 Rankings

Minority- and Women-Owned Businesses

Group	All Firms Firms	All Firms Sales ($000)	Firms with Paid Employees Firms	Firms with Paid Employees Sales ($000)	Firms with Paid Employees Employees	Firms with Paid Employees Payroll ($000)
AIAN[1]	25	177	0	0	0	0
Asian	291	81,769	68	75,121	658	18,643
Black	1,329	21,480	37	7,705	225	2,490
Hispanic	181	(s)	36	(s)	500 - 999	(s)
NHOPI[2]	n/a	n/a	n/a	n/a	n/a	n/a
Women	3,787	601,391	437	556,184	4,192	155,176
All Firms	9,006	14,243,891	2,655	14,048,329	66,577	2,516,800

Note: Figures cover firms located in the city; minority- and women-owned business are defined as firms in which the corresponding group own 51% or more of the stock or equity of the company; (1) American Indian and Alaska Native; (2) Native Hawaiian and Other Pacific Islander; (s) estimates are suppressed when publication standards are not met; n/a not available
Source: U.S. Census Bureau, 2012 Economic Census, Survey of Business Owners

HOTELS & CONVENTION CENTERS

Hotels, Motels and Vacation Rentals

Area	5 Star Num.	5 Star Pct.[3]	4 Star Num.	4 Star Pct.[3]	3 Star Num.	3 Star Pct.[3]	2 Star Num.	2 Star Pct.[3]	1 Star Num.	1 Star Pct.[3]	Not Rated Num.	Not Rated Pct.[3]
City[1]	0	0.0	0	0.0	7	19.4	7	19.4	1	2.8	21	58.3
Total[2]	266	1.3	1,517	7.2	4,627	21.8	3,210	15.1	3,974	18.7	7,601	35.9

Note: (1) Figures cover Springfield and vicinity; (2) Figures cover all 100 cities in this book; (3) Percentage of hotels which have a given star rating; Star ratings are determined by priceline.com and offer an indication of the general quality of a particular hotel.
Source: priceline.com, April 27, 2020

Major Convention Centers

Name	Overall Space (sq. ft.)	Exhibit Space (sq. ft.)	Meeting Space (sq. ft.)	Meeting Rooms
Prairie Capital Convention Center	n/a	44,000	21,000	n/a

Note: Table includes convention centers located in the Springfield, IL metro area; n/a not available
Source: Original research

Living Environment

COST OF LIVING

Cost of Living Index

Composite Index	Groceries	Housing	Utilities	Trans- portation	Health Care	Misc. Goods/ Services
n/a	n/a	n/a	n/a	n/a	n/a	n/a

Note: The Cost of Living Index measures regional differences in the cost of consumer goods and services, excluding taxes and non-consumer expenditures, for professional and managerial households in the top income quintile. It is based on more than 50,000 prices covering almost 60 different items for which prices are collected three times a year by chambers of commerce, economic development organizations or university applied economic centers in each participating urban area. The numbers shown should be read as a percentage above or below the national average of 100. For example, a value of 115.4 in the groceries column indicates that grocery prices are 15.4% higher than the national average. Small differences in the index numbers should not be interpreted as significant; n/a not available.
Source: The Council for Community and Economic Research, ACCRA Cost of Living Index, 2019

Grocery Prices

Area[1]	T-Bone Steak ($/pound)	Frying Chicken ($/pound)	Whole Milk ($/half gal.)	Eggs ($/dozen)	Orange Juice ($/64 oz.)	Coffee ($/11.5 oz.)
City[2]	n/a	n/a	n/a	n/a	n/a	n/a
Avg.	11.40	1.41	1.93	1.54	3.51	4.30
Min.	7.40	0.92	0.85	0.58	2.67	2.90
Max.	15.58	2.68	4.09	4.18	5.57	8.10

Note: (1) Values for the local area are compared with the average, minimum and maximum values for all 290 areas in the Cost of Living Index; (2) Figures cover the Springfield IL urban area; n/a not available; T-Bone Steak (price per pound); Frying Chicken (price per pound, whole fryer); Whole Milk (half gallon carton); Eggs (price per dozen, Grade A, large); Orange Juice (64 oz. Tropicana or Florida Natural); Coffee (11.5 oz. can, vacuum-packed, Maxwell House, Hills Bros, or Folgers).
Source: The Council for Community and Economic Research, ACCRA Cost of Living Index, 2019

Housing and Utility Costs

Area[1]	New Home Price ($)	Apartment Rent ($/month)	All Electric ($/month)	Part Electric ($/month)	Other Energy ($/month)	Telephone ($/month)
City[2]	n/a	n/a	n/a	n/a	n/a	n/a
Avg.	362,090	1,142	174.35	100.00	67.76	179.60
Min.	198,329	501	91.58	31.44	28.51	165.30
Max.	2,074,561	5,050	388.18	239.41	306.15	207.90

Note: (1) Values for the local area are compared with the average, minimum and maximum values for all 290 areas in the Cost of Living Index; (2) Figures cover the Springfield IL urban area; n/a not available; New Home Price (2,400 sf living area, 8,000 sf lot, in urban area with full utilities); Apartment Rent (950 sf 2 bedroom/1.5 or 2 bath, unfurnished, excluding all utilities except water); All Electric (average monthly cost for an all-electric home); Part Electric (average monthly cost for a part-electric home); Other Energy (average monthly cost for natural gas, fuel oil, coal, wood, and any other forms of energy except electricity); Telephone (price includes the base monthly rate plus taxes and fees for three lines of mobile phone service).
Source: The Council for Community and Economic Research, ACCRA Cost of Living Index, 2019

Health Care, Transportation, and Other Costs

Area[1]	Doctor ($/visit)	Dentist ($/visit)	Optometrist ($/visit)	Gasoline ($/gallon)	Beauty Salon ($/visit)	Men's Shirt ($)
City[2]	n/a	n/a	n/a	n/a	n/a	n/a
Avg.	114.85	97.58	106.10	2.50	38.15	32.15
Min.	39.00	62.22	52.22	1.53	16.88	10.27
Max.	206.67	151.53	258.67	3.79	79.29	59.30

Note: (1) Values for the local area are compared with the average, minimum and maximum values for all 290 areas in the Cost of Living Index; (2) Figures cover the Springfield IL urban area; n/a not available; Doctor (general practitioners routine exam of an established patient); Dentist (adult teeth cleaning and periodic oral examination); Optometrist (full vision eye exam for established adult patient); Gasoline (one gallon regular unleaded, national brand, including all taxes, cash price at self-service pump if available); Beauty Salon (woman's shampoo, trim, and blow-dry); Men's Shirt (cotton/polyester dress shirt, pinpoint weave, long sleeves).
Source: The Council for Community and Economic Research, ACCRA Cost of Living Index, 2019

HOUSING

House Price Index (HPI)

Area	National Ranking[2]	Quarterly Change (%)	One-Year Change (%)	Five-Year Change (%)
MSA[1]	214	1.64	2.74	10.02
U.S.[3]	–	1.26	5.09	32.88

Note: The HPI is a weighted repeat sales index. It measures average price changes in repeat sales or refinancings on the same properties. This information is obtained by reviewing repeat mortgage transactions on single-family properties whose mortgages have been purchased or securitized by Fannie Mae or Freddie Mac in January 1975; (1) Figures cover the Springfield, IL Metropolitan Statistical Area—see Appendix B for areas included; (2) Rankings are based on annual percentage change for all metro areas containing at least 15,000 transactions over the last 10 years and ranges from 1 to 232; (3) figures based on a weighted average of Census Division estimates using a seasonally adjusted, purchase-only index; all figures are for the period ending December 31, 2019
Source: Federal Housing Finance Agency, House Price Index, February 25, 2020

Median Single-Family Home Prices

Area	2017	2018	2019p	Percent Change 2018 to 2019
MSA[1]	132.4	133.5	141.8	6.2
U.S. Average	248.8	261.6	274.6	5.0

Note: Figures are median sales prices of existing single-family homes in thousands of dollars; (p) preliminary; (1) Figures cover the Springfield, IL Metropolitan Statistical Area—see Appendix B for areas included
Source: National Association of Realtors, Median Sales Price of Existing Single-Family Homes for Metropolitan Areas, 4th Quarter 2019

Qualifying Income Based on Median Sales Price of Existing Single-Family Homes

Area	With 5% Down ($)	With 10% Down ($)	With 20% Down ($)
MSA[1]	29,619	28,060	24,943
U.S. Average	58,663	55,575	49,400

Note: Figures are preliminary; Qualifying income is based on a mortgage rate of 3.76%. Monthly principal and interest payment is limited to 25% of income; (1) Figures cover the Springfield, IL Metropolitan Statistical Area—see Appendix B for areas included
Source: National Association of Realtors, Qualifying Income Based on Median Sales Price of Existing Single-Family Homes for Metropolitan Areas, 4th Quarter 2019

Median Apartment Condo-Coop Home Prices

Area	2017	2018	2019p	Percent Change 2018 to 2019
MSA[1]	n/a	n/a	n/a	n/a
U.S. Average	234.3	241.0	249.5	3.5

Note: Figures are median sales prices of existing apartment condo-coop homes in thousands of dollars; (p) preliminary; n/a not available; (1) Figures cover the Springfield, IL Metropolitan Statistical Area—see Appendix B for areas included
Source: National Association of Realtors, Median Sales Price of Existing Apartment Condo-Coop Homes for Metropolitan Areas, 4th Quarter 2019

Home Value Distribution

Area	Under $50,000	$50,000 -$99,999	$100,000 -$149,999	$150,000 -$199,999	$200,000 -$299,999	$300,000 -$499,999	$500,000 -$999,999	$1,000,000 or more
City	11.5	26.1	22.9	14.9	14.8	6.9	2.7	0.2
MSA[1]	9.4	23.4	22.4	17.6	17.6	7.3	2.1	0.3
U.S.	7.6	13.0	14.0	14.3	19.2	18.3	10.5	3.1

Note: Figures are percentages and cover owner-occupied housing units; (1) Figures cover the Springfield, IL Metropolitan Statistical Area—see Appendix B for areas included
Source: U.S. Census Bureau, 2014-2018 American Community Survey 5-Year Estimates

Homeownership Rate

Area	2011 (%)	2012 (%)	2013 (%)	2014 (%)	2015 (%)	2016 (%)	2017 (%)	2018 (%)	2019 (%)
MSA[1]	n/a	n/a	n/a	n/a	n/a	n/a	n/a	n/a	n/a
U.S.	66.1	65.4	65.1	64.5	63.7	63.4	63.9	64.4	64.6

Note: (1) Figures cover the Springfield, IL Metropolitan Statistical Area—see Appendix B for areas included; n/a not available
Source: U.S. Census Bureau, Housing Vacancies and Homeownership Annual Statistics: 2011-2019

Year Housing Structure Built

Area	2010 or Later	2000 -2009	1990 -1999	1980 -1989	1970 -1979	1960 -1969	1950 -1959	1940 -1949	Before 1940	Median Year
City	1.8	9.2	12.8	9.6	15.5	12.8	11.8	7.0	19.4	1969
MSA[1]	2.6	10.3	13.5	9.2	16.3	12.1	12.0	6.7	17.4	1971
U.S.	4.1	14.3	13.9	13.5	15.3	10.7	10.4	5.0	12.8	1977

Note: Figures are percentages except for Median Year; Note: (1) Figures cover the Springfield, IL Metropolitan Statistical Area—see Appendix B for areas included
Source: U.S. Census Bureau, 2014-2018 American Community Survey 5-Year Estimates

Gross Monthly Rent

Area	Under $500	$500 -$999	$1,000 -$1,499	$1,500 -$1,999	$2,000 -$2,499	$2,500 -$2,999	$3,000 and up	Median ($)
City	12.6	64.1	18.9	2.4	1.0	0.7	0.2	789
MSA[1]	11.8	63.8	20.0	2.7	0.8	0.7	0.2	797
U.S.	9.8	38.5	29.6	12.9	5.1	2.1	2.0	1,023

Note: Figures are percentages except for Median; Gross rent is the contract rent plus the estimated average monthly cost of utilities (electricity, gas, and water and sewer) and fuels (oil, coal, kerosene, wood, etc.) if these are paid by the renter (or paid for the renter by someone else); (1) Figures cover the Springfield, IL Metropolitan Statistical Area—see Appendix B for areas included
Source: U.S. Census Bureau, 2014-2018 American Community Survey 5-Year Estimates

HEALTH

Health Risk Factors

Category	MSA[1] (%)	U.S. (%)
Adults aged 18–64 who have any kind of health care coverage	n/a	87.3
Adults who reported being in good or better health	n/a	82.4
Adults who have been told they have high blood cholesterol	n/a	33.0
Adults who have been told they have high blood pressure	n/a	32.3
Adults who are current smokers	n/a	17.1
Adults who currently use E-cigarettes	n/a	4.6
Adults who currently use chewing tobacco, snuff, or snus	n/a	4.0
Adults who are heavy drinkers[2]	n/a	6.3
Adults who are binge drinkers[3]	n/a	17.4
Adults who are overweight (BMI 25.0 - 29.9)	n/a	35.3
Adults who are obese (BMI 30.0 - 99.8)	n/a	31.3
Adults who participated in any physical activities in the past month	n/a	74.4
Adults who always or nearly always wears a seat belt	n/a	94.3

Note: n/a not available; (1) Figures cover the Springfield, IL Metropolitan Statistical Area—see Appendix B for areas included; (2) Heavy drinkers are classified as adult men having more than 14 drinks per week and adult women having more than 7 drinks per week; (3) Binge drinkers are classified as males having five or more drinks on one occasion or females having four or more drinks on one occasion
Source: Centers for Disease Control and Prevention, Behaviorial Risk Factor Surveillance System, SMART: Selected Metropolitan Area Risk Trends, 2017

Acute and Chronic Health Conditions

Category	MSA[1] (%)	U.S. (%)
Adults who have ever been told they had a heart attack	n/a	4.2
Adults who have ever been told they have angina or coronary heart disease	n/a	3.9
Adults who have ever been told they had a stroke	n/a	3.0
Adults who have ever been told they have asthma	n/a	14.2
Adults who have ever been told they have arthritis	n/a	24.9
Adults who have ever been told they have diabetes[2]	n/a	10.5
Adults who have ever been told they had skin cancer	n/a	6.2
Adults who have ever been told they had any other types of cancer	n/a	7.1
Adults who have ever been told they have COPD	n/a	6.5
Adults who have ever been told they have kidney disease	n/a	3.0
Adults who have ever been told they have a form of depression	n/a	20.5

Note: n/a not available; (1) Figures cover the Springfield, IL Metropolitan Statistical Area—see Appendix B for areas included; (2) Figures do not include pregnancy-related, borderline, or pre-diabetes
Source: Centers for Disease Control and Prevention, Behaviorial Risk Factor Surveillance System, SMART: Selected Metropolitan Area Risk Trends, 2017

Health Screening and Vaccination Rates

Category	MSA[1] (%)	U.S. (%)
Adults aged 65+ who have had flu shot within the past year	n/a	60.7
Adults aged 65+ who have ever had a pneumonia vaccination	n/a	75.4
Adults who have ever been tested for HIV	n/a	36.1
Adults who have ever had the shingles or zoster vaccine?	n/a	28.9
Adults who have had their blood cholesterol checked within the last five years	n/a	85.9

Note: n/a not available; (1) Figures cover the Springfield, IL Metropolitan Statistical Area—see Appendix B for areas included.
Source: Centers for Disease Control and Prevention, Behaviorial Risk Factor Surveillance System, SMART: Selected Metropolitan Area Risk Trends, 2017

Disability Status

Category	MSA[1] (%)	U.S. (%)
Adults who reported being deaf	n/a	6.7
Are you blind or have serious difficulty seeing, even when wearing glasses?	n/a	4.5
Are you limited in any way in any of your usual activities due of arthritis?	n/a	12.9
Do you have difficulty doing errands alone?	n/a	6.8
Do you have difficulty dressing or bathing?	n/a	3.6
Do you have serious difficulty concentrating/remembering/making decisions?	n/a	10.7
Do you have serious difficulty walking or climbing stairs?	n/a	13.6

Note: n/a not available; (1) Figures cover the Springfield, IL Metropolitan Statistical Area—see Appendix B for areas included.
Source: Centers for Disease Control and Prevention, Behaviorial Risk Factor Surveillance System, SMART: Selected Metropolitan Area Risk Trends, 2017

Mortality Rates for the Top 10 Causes of Death in the U.S.

ICD-10[a] Sub-Chapter	ICD-10[a] Code	Age-Adjusted Mortality Rate[1] per 100,000 population	
		County[2]	U.S.
Malignant neoplasms	C00-C97	162.2	152.4
Ischaemic heart diseases	I20-I25	89.1	92.7
Other forms of heart disease	I30-I51	62.8	52.5
Chronic lower respiratory diseases	J40-J47	35.6	40.4
Cerebrovascular diseases	I60-I69	37.7	37.3
Other degenerative diseases of the nervous system	G30-G31	23.6	36.4
Other external causes of accidental injury	W00-X59	39.4	35.3
Organic, including symptomatic, mental disorders	F01-F09	40.4	30.0
Hypertensive diseases	I10-I15	18.0	22.9
Diabetes mellitus	E10-E14	19.7	21.3

Note: (a) ICD-10 = International Classification of Diseases 10th Revision; (1) Mortality rates are a three year average covering 2016-2018; (2) Figures cover Sangamon County.
Source: Centers for Disease Control and Prevention, National Center for Health Statistics. Underlying Cause of Death 1999-2018 on CDC WONDER Online Database

Mortality Rates for Selected Causes of Death

ICD-10[a] Sub-Chapter	ICD-10[a] Code	Age-Adjusted Mortality Rate[1] per 100,000 population	
		County[2]	U.S.
Assault	X85-Y09	6.4	6.0
Diseases of the liver	K70-K76	16.8	14.2
Human immunodeficiency virus (HIV) disease	B20-B24	Suppressed	1.6
Influenza and pneumonia	J09-J18	17.5	14.2
Intentional self-harm	X60-X84	15.3	13.9
Malnutrition	E40-E46	Unreliable	1.9
Obesity and other hyperalimentation	E65-E68	Unreliable	2.1
Renal failure	N17-N19	12.8	12.8
Transport accidents	V01-V99	9.4	12.5
Viral hepatitis	B15-B19	Suppressed	1.4

Note: (a) ICD-10 = International Classification of Diseases 10th Revision; (1) Mortality rates are a three year average covering 2016-2018; (2) Figures cover Sangamon County; Data are suppressed when the data meet the criteria for confidentiality constraints; Mortality rates are flagged as unreliable when the rate would be calculated with a numerator of 20 or less.
Source: Centers for Disease Control and Prevention, National Center for Health Statistics. Underlying Cause of Death 1999-2018 on CDC WONDER Online Database

Health Insurance Coverage

Area	With Health Insurance	With Private Health Insurance	With Public Health Insurance	Without Health Insurance	Population Under Age 19 Without Health Insurance
City	95.4	67.9	42.8	4.6	1.7
MSA[1]	95.9	73.8	37.6	4.1	1.6
U.S.	90.6	67.7	34.7	9.4	5.2

Note: Figures are percentages that cover the civilian noninstitutionalized population; (1) Figures cover the Springfield, IL Metropolitan Statistical Area—see Appendix B for areas included
Source: U.S. Census Bureau, 2014-2018 American Community Survey 5-Year Estimates

Number of Medical Professionals

Area	MDs[3]	DOs[3,4]	Dentists	Podiatrists	Chiropractors	Optometrists
County[1] (number)	1,213	51	171	11	77	42
County[1] (rate[2])	617.5	26.0	87.5	5.6	39.4	21.5
U.S. (rate[2])	281.9	23.4	69.1	6.0	27.5	16.4

Note: Data as of 2018 unless noted; (1) Data covers Sangamon County; (2) Rate per 100,000 population; (3) Data as of 2017 and includes all active, non-federal physicians; (4) Doctor of Osteopathic Medicine
Source: U.S. Department of Health and Human Services, Health Resources and Services Administration, Bureau of Health Professions, Area Resource File (ARF) 2018-2019

EDUCATION

Public School District Statistics

District Name	Schls	Pupils	Pupil/ Teacher Ratio	Minority Pupils[1] (%)	Free Lunch Eligible[2] (%)	IEP[3] (%)
Springfield SD 186	35	14,084	13.9	58.1	55.7	22.0

Note: Table includes school districts with 2,000 or more students; (1) Percentage of students that are not non-Hispanic white; (2) Percentage of students that are eligible for the free lunch program; (3) Percentage of students that have an Individualized Education Program.
Source: U.S. Department of Education, National Center for Education Statistics, Common Core of Data, Local Education Agency (School District) Universe Survey: School Year 2018-2019; U.S. Department of Education, National Center for Education Statistics, Common Core of Data, Public Elementary/Secondary School Universe Survey: School Year 2018-2019

Highest Level of Education

Area	Less than H.S.	H.S. Diploma	Some College, No Deg.	Associate Degree	Bachelor's Degree	Master's Degree	Prof. School Degree	Doctorate Degree
City	9.0	26.4	21.5	7.3	21.7	9.7	3.3	1.1
MSA[1]	7.6	28.4	22.4	8.1	21.2	8.8	2.5	1.0
U.S.	12.3	27.1	20.6	8.4	19.4	8.6	2.1	1.4

Note: Figures cover persons age 25 and over; (1) Figures cover the Springfield, IL Metropolitan Statistical Area—see Appendix B for areas included
Source: U.S. Census Bureau, 2014-2018 American Community Survey 5-Year Estimates

Educational Attainment by Race

Area	High School Graduate or Higher (%)					Bachelor's Degree or Higher (%)				
	Total	White	Black	Asian	Hisp.[2]	Total	White	Black	Asian	Hisp.[2]
City	91.0	93.1	80.8	93.9	87.5	35.8	38.5	17.4	69.0	34.7
MSA[1]	92.4	93.7	81.3	94.3	87.0	33.5	34.8	17.3	65.9	32.4
U.S.	87.7	89.6	85.4	86.8	67.7	31.5	32.9	21.1	53.5	15.8

Note: Figures shown cover persons 25 years old and over; (1) Figures cover the Springfield, IL Metropolitan Statistical Area—see Appendix B for areas included; (2) People of Hispanic origin can be of any race
Source: U.S. Census Bureau, 2014-2018 American Community Survey 5-Year Estimates

School Enrollment by Grade and Control

Area	Preschool (%)		Kindergarten (%)		Grades 1 - 4 (%)		Grades 5 - 8 (%)		Grades 9 - 12 (%)	
	Public	Private	Public	Private	Public	Private	Public	Private	Public	Private
City	66.5	33.5	83.2	16.8	83.9	16.1	84.1	15.9	84.6	15.4
MSA[1]	66.5	33.5	86.3	13.7	88.4	11.6	88.4	11.6	89.7	10.3
U.S.	59.0	41.0	87.7	12.3	89.6	10.4	89.5	10.5	90.2	9.8

Note: Figures shown cover persons 3 years old and over; (1) Figures cover the Springfield, IL Metropolitan Statistical Area—see Appendix B for areas included
Source: U.S. Census Bureau, 2014-2018 American Community Survey 5-Year Estimates

Average Salaries of Public School Teachers

Area	2016-17		2017-18		Change from 2016-17 to 2017-18	
	Dollars	Rank[1]	Dollars	Rank[1]	Percent	Rank[2]
Illinois	64,516	11	65,721	11	1.87	20
U.S. Average	59,539	–	60,477	–	1.58	–

Note: (1) Rank ranges from 1 to 51 where 1 indicates highest salary; (2) Rank ranges from 1 to 51 where 1 indicates highest percent change.
Source: National Education Association, Rankings & Estimates: Rankings of the States 2018 and Estimates of School Statistics 2019

Higher Education

Four-Year Colleges			Two-Year Colleges			Medical Schools[1]	Law Schools[2]	Voc/ Tech[3]
Public	Private Non-profit	Private For-profit	Public	Private Non-profit	Private For-profit			
1	1	0	1	0	0	1	0	4

Note: Figures cover institutions located within the city limits and include main campuses only; (1) includes schools accredited by the Liaison Committee on Medical Education and the American Osteopathic Association's Commission on Osteopathic College Accreditation; (2) includes ABA-accredited schools, schools with provisional ABA accreditation, and state accredited schools; (3) includes all schools with programs that are less than 2 years.
Source: National Center for Education Statistics, Integrated Postsecondary Education System (IPEDS), 2018-19; Wikipedia, List of Medical Schools in the United States, accessed May 1, 2020; Wikipedia, List of Law Schools in the United States, accessed May 1, 2020

PRESIDENTIAL ELECTION

2016 Presidential Election Results

Area	Clinton	Trump	Johnson	Stein	Other
Sangamon County	41.6	50.8	4.6	1.5	1.6
U.S.	48.0	45.9	3.3	1.1	1.7

Note: Results are percentages and may not add to 100% due to rounding
Source: Dave Leip's Atlas of U.S. Presidential Elections

EMPLOYERS

Major Employers

Company Name	Industry
BlueCross BlueShield of Illinois	Insurance
Horace Mann Insurance Company	Insurance
Illinois National Guard	U.S. military
Memorial Health System	Healthcare
Southern Illinois University School of Med	Education
Springfield Clinic	Healthcare
Springfield School District #186	Education
St. John's Medical	Healthcare
State of Illinois	State government
U.S. Postal Service	Government/postal service
University of Illinois at Springfield	Education

Note: Companies shown are located within the Springfield, IL Metropolitan Statistical Area.
Source: Hoovers.com; Wikipedia

PUBLIC SAFETY

Crime Rate

Area	All Crimes	Violent Crimes				Property Crimes		
		Murder	Rape[3]	Robbery	Aggrav. Assault	Burglary	Larceny -Theft	Motor Vehicle Theft
City	5,620.2	7.9	81.1	188.4	555.7	1,042.5	3,528.1	216.4
Suburbs[1]	1,555.2	1.1	37.7	19.4	245.4	337.9	791.1	122.7
Metro[2]	3,800.3	4.8	61.7	112.8	416.8	727.1	2,302.7	174.4
U.S.	2,580.1	5.0	42.6	86.2	246.8	376.0	1,594.6	228.9

Note: Figures are crimes per 100,000 population; (1) All areas within the metro area that are located outside the city limits; (2) Figures cover the Springfield, IL Metropolitan Statistical Area—see Appendix B for areas included; (3) The city and U.S. figures shown were reported using the revised Uniform Crime Reporting (UCR) definition of rape. The suburban and metro area figures shown are an aggregate total of the data submitted using both the revised and legacy UCR definitions.
Source: FBI Uniform Crime Reports, 2018

Hate Crimes

Area	Number of Quarters Reported	Number of Incidents per Bias Motivation					
		Race/Ethnicity/ Ancestry	Religion	Sexual Orientation	Disability	Gender	Gender Identity
City	4	0	0	0	0	0	0
U.S.	4	4,047	1,419	1,196	159	47	168

Source: Federal Bureau of Investigation, Hate Crime Statistics 2018

Identity Theft Consumer Reports

Area	Reports	Reports per 100,000 Population	Rank[2]
MSA[1]	191	92	211
U.S.	650,572	198	-

Note: (1) Figures cover the Springfield, IL Metropolitan Statistical Area—see Appendix B for areas included; (2) Rank ranges from 1 to 386 where 1 indicates greatest number of identity theft reports per 100,000 population
Source: Federal Trade Commission, Consumer Sentinel Network Data Book for January–December 2019

Fraud and Other Consumer Reports

Area	Reports	Reports per 100,000 Population	Rank[2]
MSA[1]	1,025	494	256
U.S.	2,590,177	789	-

Note: (1) Figures cover the Springfield, IL Metropolitan Statistical Area—see Appendix B for areas included; (2) Rank ranges from 1 to 386 where 1 indicates greatest number of fraud and other consumer reports per 100,000 population
Source: Federal Trade Commission, Consumer Sentinel Network Data Book for January–December 2019

SPORTS

Professional Sports Teams

Team Name	League	Year Established
No teams are located in the metro area		

Source: Wikipedia, Major Professional Sports Teams of the United States and Canada, May 4, 2020

CLIMATE

Average and Extreme Temperatures

Temperature	Jan	Feb	Mar	Apr	May	Jun	Jul	Aug	Sep	Oct	Nov	Dec	Yr.
Extreme High (°F)	73	78	91	90	101	104	112	108	101	93	83	74	112
Average High (°F)	35	38	50	63	74	84	88	85	79	67	51	38	63
Average Temp. (°F)	27	30	41	53	64	73	78	75	68	57	43	31	54
Average Low (°F)	19	22	32	43	53	63	67	65	57	46	34	24	44
Extreme Low (°F)	-21	-24	-12	17	28	40	48	43	32	13	-3	-21	-24

Note: Figures cover the years 1948-1995
Source: National Climatic Data Center, International Station Meteorological Climate Summary, 9/96

Average Precipitation/Snowfall/Humidity

Precip./Humidity	Jan	Feb	Mar	Apr	May	Jun	Jul	Aug	Sep	Oct	Nov	Dec	Yr.
Avg. Precip. (in.)	1.8	1.7	3.1	3.6	3.8	3.9	3.3	3.1	3.3	2.6	2.4	2.1	34.9
Avg. Snowfall (in.)	6	6	4	1	Tr	0	0	0	0	Tr	1	5	21
Avg. Rel. Hum. 6am (%)	80	81	81	79	81	82	85	89	87	83	82	82	83
Avg. Rel. Hum. 3pm (%)	67	65	59	52	51	51	54	56	50	50	60	69	57

Note: Figures cover the years 1948-1995; Tr = Trace amounts (<0.05 in. of rain; <0.5 in. of snow)
Source: National Climatic Data Center, International Station Meteorological Climate Summary, 9/96

Weather Conditions

Temperature			Daytime Sky			Precipitation		
10°F & below	32°F & below	90°F & above	Clear	Partly cloudy	Cloudy	0.01 inch or more precip.	0.1 inch or more snow/ice	Thunder-storms
19	111	34	96	126	143	111	18	49

Note: Figures are average number of days per year and cover the years 1948-1995
Source: National Climatic Data Center, International Station Meteorological Climate Summary, 9/96

HAZARDOUS WASTE

Superfund Sites

The Springfield, IL metro area has no sites on the EPA's Superfund Final National Priorities List. There are a total of 1,387 Superfund sites with a status of proposed or final on the list in the U.S.
U.S. Environmental Protection Agency, National Priorities List, May 5, 2020

AIR & WATER QUALITY

Air Quality Trends: Ozone

	1990	1995	2000	2005	2010	2012	2014	2016	2017	2018
MSA[1]	n/a	n/a	n/a	n/a	n/a	n/a	n/a	n/a	n/a	n/a
U.S.	0.088	0.089	0.082	0.080	0.073	0.075	0.067	0.069	0.068	0.069

Note: (1) Data covers the Springfield, IL Metropolitan Statistical Area—see Appendix B for areas included; n/a not available. The values shown are the composite ozone concentration averages among trend sites based on the highest fourth daily maximum 8-hour concentration in parts per million. These trends are based on sites having an adequate record of monitoring data during the trend period. Data from exceptional events are included.
Source: U.S. Environmental Protection Agency, Air Quality Monitoring Information, "Air Quality Trends by City, 1990-2018"

Air Quality Index

Area	Percent of Days when Air Quality was...[2]					AQI Statistics[2]	
	Good	Moderate	Unhealthy for Sensitive Groups	Unhealthy	Very Unhealthy	Maximum	Median
MSA[1]	69.7	30.0	0.3	0.0	0.0	122	43

Note: (1) Data covers the Springfield, IL Metropolitan Statistical Area—see Appendix B for areas included; (2) Based on 363 days with AQI data in 2018. Air Quality Index (AQI) is an index for reporting daily air quality. EPA calculates the AQI for five major air pollutants regulated by the Clean Air Act: ground-level ozone, particle pollution (aka particulate matter), carbon monoxide, sulfur dioxide, and nitrogen dioxide. The AQI runs from 0 to 500. The higher the AQI value, the greater the level of air pollution and the greater the health concern. There are six AQI categories: "Good" AQI is between 0 and 50. Air quality is considered satisfactory; "Moderate" AQI is between 51 and 100. Air quality is acceptable; "Unhealthy for Sensitive Groups" When AQI values are between 101 and 150, members of sensitive groups may experience health effects; "Unhealthy" When AQI values are between 151 and 200 everyone may begin to experience health effects; "Very Unhealthy" AQI values between 201 and 300 trigger a health alert; "Hazardous" AQI values over 300 trigger warnings of emergency conditions (not shown).
Source: U.S. Environmental Protection Agency, Air Quality Index Report, 2018

Air Quality Index Pollutants

Area	Percent of Days when AQI Pollutant was...[2]					
	Carbon Monoxide	Nitrogen Dioxide	Ozone	Sulfur Dioxide	Particulate Matter 2.5	Particulate Matter 10
MSA[1]	0.0	0.0	54.3	0.0	45.7	0.0

Note: (1) Data covers the Springfield, IL Metropolitan Statistical Area—see Appendix B for areas included; (2) Based on 363 days with AQI data in 2018. The Air Quality Index (AQI) is an index for reporting daily air quality. EPA calculates the AQI for five major air pollutants regulated by the Clean Air Act: ground-level ozone, particle pollution (also known as particulate matter), carbon monoxide, sulfur dioxide, and nitrogen dioxide. The AQI runs from 0 to 500. The higher the AQI value, the greater the level of air pollution and the greater the health concern.
Source: U.S. Environmental Protection Agency, Air Quality Index Report, 2018

Maximum Air Pollutant Concentrations: Particulate Matter, Ozone, CO and Lead

	Particulate Matter 10 (ug/m³)	Particulate Matter 2.5 Wtd AM (ug/m³)	Particulate Matter 2.5 24-Hr (ug/m³)	Ozone (ppm)	Carbon Monoxide (ppm)	Lead (ug/m³)
MSA[1] Level	n/a	9.5	20	0.069	n/a	n/a
NAAQS[2]	150	15	35	0.075	9	0.15
Met NAAQS[2]	n/a	Yes	Yes	Yes	n/a	n/a

Note: (1) Data covers the Springfield, IL Metropolitan Statistical Area—see Appendix B for areas included; Data from exceptional events are included; (2) National Ambient Air Quality Standards; ppm = parts per million; ug/m³ = micrograms per cubic meter; n/a not available.
Concentrations: Particulate Matter 10 (coarse particulate)—highest second maximum 24-hour concentration; Particulate Matter 2.5 Wtd AM (fine particulate)—highest weighted annual mean concentration; Particulate Matter 2.5 24-Hour (fine particulate)—highest 98th percentile 24-hour concentration; Ozone—highest fourth daily maximum 8-hour concentration; Carbon Monoxide—highest second maximum non-overlapping 8-hour concentration; Lead—maximum running 3-month average
Source: U.S. Environmental Protection Agency, Air Quality Monitoring Information, "Air Quality Statistics by City, 2018"

Maximum Air Pollutant Concentrations: Nitrogen Dioxide and Sulfur Dioxide

	Nitrogen Dioxide AM (ppb)	Nitrogen Dioxide 1-Hr (ppb)	Sulfur Dioxide AM (ppb)	Sulfur Dioxide 1-Hr (ppb)	Sulfur Dioxide 24-Hr (ppb)
MSA[1] Level	n/a	n/a	n/a	n/a	n/a
NAAQS[2]	53	100	30	75	140
Met NAAQS[2]	n/a	n/a	n/a	n/a	n/a

Note: (1) Data covers the Springfield, IL Metropolitan Statistical Area—see Appendix B for areas included; Data from exceptional events are included; (2) National Ambient Air Quality Standards; ppm = parts per million; ug/m³ = micrograms per cubic meter; n/a not available.
Concentrations: Nitrogen Dioxide AM—highest arithmetic mean concentration; Nitrogen Dioxide 1-Hr—highest 98th percentile 1-hour daily maximum concentration; Sulfur Dioxide AM—highest annual mean concentration; Sulfur Dioxide 1-Hr—highest 99th percentile 1-hour daily maximum concentration; Sulfur Dioxide 24-Hr—highest second maximum 24-hour concentration
Source: U.S. Environmental Protection Agency, Air Quality Monitoring Information, "Air Quality Statistics by City, 2018"

Drinking Water

Water System Name	Pop. Served	Primary Water Source Type	Violations[1]
Springfield	119,395	Surface	3

Note: (1) Total number of violations (both active and inactive) in the EPA database
Source: U.S. Environmental Protection Agency, Office of Ground Water and Drinking Water, Safe Drinking Water Information System (based on data extracted May 5, 2020)

Topeka, Kansas

Background

Water might not be the first thing that comes to mind when one thinks of Topeka, the capital of Kansas, but "Kansa" is the language of the Native American tribe known as the "people of water." Topeka sits atop rich, river-bottom soil deposited along the Kansas River. Rich soil makes great farm land and "Topeka" means "a good place to dig." First used by the Native American Kaw as a natural ford over the Kansas River, the city would become a key element in the westward expansion super highway known today as the Oregon Trail—an opportunity seized by three French-Canadian brothers and their Kaw brides, who made a life for themselves ferrying westbound pioneers across the Kansas River. In fact, transportation remains a defining industry for Topeka.

Just as Topeka originated as a natural ford for Native American wanderers, it became a natural draw for railroads, and the industry that followed. The Atchison, Topeka and Santa Fe Railroad was only one in a series of rail enterprises in Topeka. Today, Burlington Northern Railroad still maintains one of the largest rail shops in the world in Topeka.

Topeka has been the site of race relations conflict since its inception. Anti-slavery and pro-slavery factions across the Kansas territory clashed in the 1800s, foreshadowing the civil war that soon followed. Nearly one hundred years later, a black elementary-school girl from Topeka, Linda Brown, put Topeka at the center of the Supreme Court case *Brown v. Board of Education.* This landmark case forever changed the tenor of race relations in America, instituting school desegregation across the country.

The city was home to other civil rights milestones, including the Women's Suffrage Movement in Kansas; Topeka native Charles Curtis being the only Vice President of Native American descent; and Topeka native Georgia Neese Clark Gray being the first woman to be appointed U.S. Treasurer.

GoTopeka and the Topeka Chamber of Commerce have been instrumental in attracting a variety of industries. Topeka is home to the Goodyear Tire and Rubber, Collective Brands (a.k.a. Payless ShoeSource), PTs Coffee Roasting Co., Frito-Lay, and a division of Mars Chocolate North America.

Redevelopment continues along areas of the Kansas River. Downtown Topeka has seen improvements to its streetscape, facades, and development of apartments and condominium lofts. Historic North Topeka is home to the renovated Great Overland Station, considered the greatest representation of classic railroad architecture in the state, and located across the river from the renovated State Capitol.

Topeka is home to Washburn University, a public institution with over 6,900 students and more than 200 academic programs. Washburn participates in an academic common market, meaning students in neighboring states (Colorado, Texas, Oklahoma, Missouri and Nebraska) are offered the same tuition discounts as Kansas residents. Washburn is often ranked as a top midwestern college.

Topeka climate is between continental and subtropical. It has hot, somewhat humid summers and cool to cold, fairly dry winters. Daily average temperature ranges from 29.7 °F in January to 79.0 °F in July. The city receives nearly 36.5 inches of precipitation during an average year, with the largest share in May and June. Thunderstorms can be severe, producing frequent lightning, large hail, and sometimes tornadoes. Kansas sits in the heart of tornado alley, and in 1966 a tornado ripped through downtown Topeka, narrowly missing the Capitol building. Topeka has also seen its share of floods, including a fatal event in 1905, and another devastating flood in 1951. Topeka has since built a series of flood control damns to help reign in the powerful Kansas River.

Rankings

Business/Finance Rankings

- The Topeka metro area appeared on the Milken Institute "2020 Best Performing Cities" list. Rank: #137 out of 201 small metro areas. Criteria: job growth; wage and salary growth; high-tech output growth. *Milken Institute, "Best-Performing Cities 2020," February 26, 2020*

- *Forbes* ranked 203 smaller metro areas (population under 268,000) to determine the nation's "Best Small Places for Business and Careers." The Topeka metro area was ranked #115. Criteria: costs (business and living); job growth (past and projected); income growth; quality of life; educational attainment (college and high school); projected economic growth; cultural and leisure opportunities; workplace tolerance laws; net migration patterns. *Forbes, "The Best Small Places for Business and Careers 2019," October 30, 2019*

Environmental Rankings

- Topeka was highlighted as one of the top 104 cleanest metro areas for short-term particle pollution (24-hour PM 2.5) in the U.S. during 2015 through 2017. Monitors in these cities reported no days with unhealthful PM 2.5 levels. *American Lung Association, "State of the Air 2019," April 24, 2019*

Real Estate Rankings

- The Topeka metro area was identified as one of the nations's 20 hottest housing markets in 2020. Criteria: listing views as an indicator of demand and median days on the market as an indicator of supply. The area ranked #19. *Realtor.com, "January Top 20 Hottest Housing Markets," February 13, 2020*

- The Topeka metro area was identified as one of the 20 most affordable housing markets in the U.S. in 2019. The area ranked #13 out of 180 markets. Criteria: qualification for a mortgage loan with a 10% down payment on a typical home. *National Association of Realtors®, Qualifying Income Based on Sales Price of Existing Single-Family Homes for Metropolitan Areas, 2019*

Safety Rankings

- The National Insurance Crime Bureau ranked 382 metro areas in the U.S. in terms of per capita rates of vehicle theft. The Topeka metro area ranked #20 (#1 = highest rate). Criteria: number of vehicle theft offenses per 100,000 inhabitants in 2018. *National Insurance Crime Bureau, "Hot Spots 2018," June 25, 2019*

Seniors/Retirement Rankings

- From its Best Cities for Successful Aging indexes, the Milken Institute generated rankings for metropolitan areas, weighing data in nine categories—health care, wellness, living arrangements, transportation and convenience, financial characteristics, education, employment, community engagement, and overall livability. The Topeka metro area was ranked #134 overall in the small metro area category. *Milken Institute, "Best Cities for Successful Aging, 2017" March 14, 2017*

Miscellaneous Rankings

- *WalletHub* compared the 150 most populated U.S. cities to determine their operating efficiency. A "Quality of Services" score was constructed for each city and then divided by the total budget per capita to reveal which were managed the best. Topeka ranked #41. Criteria: financial stability; economy; education; safety; health; infrastructure and pollution. *www.WalletHub.com, "2019's Best- & Worst-Run Cities in America," July 1, 2019*

Business Environment

CITY FINANCES

City Government Finances

Component	2017 ($000)	2017 ($ per capita)
Total Revenues	226,248	1,778
Total Expenditures	240,871	1,893
Debt Outstanding	392,099	3,081
Cash and Securities[1]	205,195	1,612

*Note: (1) Cash and security holdings of a government at the close of its fiscal year,
including those of its dependent agencies, utilities, and liquor stores.*
Source: U.S. Census Bureau, State & Local Government Finances 2017

City Government Revenue by Source

Source	2017 ($000)	2017 ($ per capita)	2017 (%)
General Revenue			
From Federal Government	6,364	50	2.8
From State Government	19,470	153	8.6
From Local Governments	17	0	0.0
Taxes			
Property	49,581	390	21.9
Sales and Gross Receipts	72,156	567	31.9
Personal Income	0	0	0.0
Corporate Income	0	0	0.0
Motor Vehicle License	0	0	0.0
Other Taxes	1,717	13	0.8
Current Charges	39,575	311	17.5
Liquor Store	0	0	0.0
Utility	29,848	235	13.2
Employee Retirement	0	0	0.0

Source: U.S. Census Bureau, State & Local Government Finances 2017

City Government Expenditures by Function

Function	2017 ($000)	2017 ($ per capita)	2017 (%)
General Direct Expenditures			
Air Transportation	0	0	0.0
Corrections	728	5	0.3
Education	0	0	0.0
Employment Security Administration	0	0	0.0
Financial Administration	2,291	18	1.0
Fire Protection	26,214	206	10.9
General Public Buildings	1,557	12	0.6
Governmental Administration, Other	2,737	21	1.1
Health	0	0	0.0
Highways	30,871	242	12.8
Hospitals	0	0	0.0
Housing and Community Development	4,055	31	1.7
Interest on General Debt	6,231	49	2.6
Judicial and Legal	3,351	26	1.4
Libraries	0	0	0.0
Parking	2,500	19	1.0
Parks and Recreation	2,980	23	1.2
Police Protection	37,329	293	15.5
Public Welfare	604	4	0.3
Sewerage	38,222	300	15.9
Solid Waste Management	0	0	0.0
Veterans' Services	0	0	0.0
Liquor Store	0	0	0.0
Utility	47,078	369	19.5
Employee Retirement	0	0	0.0

Source: U.S. Census Bureau, State & Local Government Finances 2017

DEMOGRAPHICS

Population Growth

Area	1990 Census	2000 Census	2010 Census	2018* Estimate	Population Growth (%)	
					1990-2018	2010-2018
City	121,197	122,377	127,473	126,877	4.7	-0.5
MSA[1]	210,257	224,551	233,870	233,260	10.9	-0.3
U.S.	248,709,873	281,421,906	308,745,538	322,903,030	29.8	4.6

Note: (1) Figures cover the Topeka, KS Metropolitan Statistical Area—see Appendix B for areas included; (*) 2014-2018 5-year estimated population
Source: U.S. Census Bureau, 1990 Census, Census 2000, Census 2010, 2014-2018 American Community Survey 5-Year Estimates

Household Size

Area	Persons in Household (%)							Average Household Size
	One	Two	Three	Four	Five	Six	Seven or More	
City	38.0	31.6	12.8	10.6	4.6	1.7	0.8	2.30
MSA[1]	31.1	35.9	13.4	11.5	5.2	2.0	1.0	2.40
U.S.	27.7	33.9	15.7	13.0	6.0	2.3	1.4	2.60

Note: (1) Figures cover the Topeka, KS Metropolitan Statistical Area—see Appendix B for areas included
Source: U.S. Census Bureau, 2014-2018 American Community Survey 5-Year Estimates

Race

Area	White Alone[2] (%)	Black Alone[2] (%)	Asian Alone[2] (%)	AIAN[3] Alone[2] (%)	NHOPI[4] Alone[2] (%)	Other Race Alone[2] (%)	Two or More Races (%)
City	78.5	10.6	1.7	1.0	0.1	3.2	4.9
MSA[1]	85.1	6.5	1.2	1.2	0.1	1.9	4.1
U.S.	72.7	12.7	5.4	0.8	0.2	4.9	3.2

Note: (1) Figures cover the Topeka, KS Metropolitan Statistical Area—see Appendix B for areas included; (2) Alone is defined as not being in combination with one or more other races; (3) American Indian and Alaska Native; (4) Native Hawaiian and Other Pacific Islander
Source: U.S. Census Bureau, 2014-2018 American Community Survey 5-Year Estimates

Hispanic or Latino Origin

Area	Total (%)	Mexican (%)	Puerto Rican (%)	Cuban (%)	Other (%)
City	15.0	13.1	0.7	0.1	1.1
MSA[1]	10.1	8.7	0.5	0.1	0.8
U.S.	17.8	11.2	1.7	0.7	4.2

Note: Persons of Hispanic or Latino origin can be of any race; (1) Figures cover the Topeka, KS Metropolitan Statistical Area—see Appendix B for areas included
Source: U.S. Census Bureau, 2014-2018 American Community Survey 5-Year Estimates

Segregation

Type	Segregation Indices[1]				Percent Change		
	1990	2000	2010	2010 Rank[2]	1990-2000	1990-2010	2000-2010
Black/White	n/a	n/a	n/a	n/a	n/a	n/a	n/a
Asian/White	n/a	n/a	n/a	n/a	n/a	n/a	n/a
Hispanic/White	n/a	n/a	n/a	n/a	n/a	n/a	n/a

Note: All figures cover the Metropolitan Statistical Area—see Appendix B for areas included; Figures are based on an analysis of 1990, 2000, and 2010 Census Decennial Census tract data by William H. Frey, Brookings Institution and the University of Michigan Social Science Data Analysis Network. In this analysis all racial groups (whites, blacks, and asians) are non-Hispanic members of those races. Hispanics are shown as a separate category; (1) Segregation Indices are Dissimilarity Indices that measure the degree to which the minority group is distributed differently than whites across census tracts. They range from 0 (complete integration) to 100 (complete segregation) where the value indicates the percentage of the minority group that needs to move to be distributed exactly like whites; (2) Ranges from 1 (most segregated) to 102 (least segregated); n/a not available.
Source: www.CensusScope.org

Ancestry

Area	German	Irish	English	American	Italian	Polish	French[2]	Scottish	Dutch
City	21.1	9.6	14.1	5.2	1.7	1.0	2.0	1.6	1.1
MSA[1]	26.2	11.2	13.1	6.0	1.5	1.0	2.7	1.9	1.6
U.S.	13.7	9.9	7.3	6.4	5.2	2.8	2.4	1.7	1.2

Note: Figures are the percentage of the total population reporting a particular ancestry. The nine most commonly reported ancestries in the U.S. are shown. Figures include multiple ancestries (e.g. if a person reported being Irish and Italian, they were included in both columns); (1) Figures cover the Topeka, KS Metropolitan Statistical Area—see Appendix B for areas included; (2) Excludes Basque
Source: U.S. Census Bureau, 2014-2018 American Community Survey 5-Year Estimates

Foreign-born Population

Area	Any Foreign Country	Asia	Mexico	Europe	Caribbean	Central America[2]	South America	Africa	Canada
City	5.1	1.3	2.8	0.4	0.1	0.1	0.2	0.1	0.1
MSA[1]	3.3	0.9	1.6	0.3	0.1	0.1	0.1	0.1	0.1
U.S.	13.5	4.1	3.5	1.5	1.3	1.1	0.9	0.7	0.3

Note: (1) Figures cover the Topeka, KS Metropolitan Statistical Area—see Appendix B for areas included; (2) Excludes Mexico.
Source: U.S. Census Bureau, 2014-2018 American Community Survey 5-Year Estimates

Marital Status

Area	Never Married	Now Married[2]	Separated	Widowed	Divorced
City	32.5	44.4	1.3	7.2	14.7
MSA[1]	27.1	52.6	1.0	6.7	12.6
U.S.	33.3	48.1	2.0	5.8	10.8

Note: Figures are percentages and cover the population 15 years of age and older; (1) Figures cover the Topeka, KS Metropolitan Statistical Area—see Appendix B for areas included; (2) Excludes separated
Source: U.S. Census Bureau, 2014-2018 American Community Survey 5-Year Estimates

Disability by Age

Area	All Ages	Under 18 Years Old	18 to 64 Years Old	65 Years and Over
City	15.4	3.7	13.7	38.5
MSA[1]	14.4	4.2	12.5	35.6
U.S.	12.6	4.2	10.3	35.0

Note: Figures show percent of the civilian noninstitutionalized population that reported having a disability. Disability status is determined from six types of difficulty: vision, hearing, cognitive, ambulatory, self-care, and independent living. For children under 5 years old, hearing and vision difficulty are used to determine disability status. For children between the ages of 5 and 14, disability status is determined from hearing, vision, cognitive, ambulatory, and self-care difficulties. For people aged 15 years and older, they are considered to have a disability if they have difficulty with any one of the six difficulty types; Note: (1) Figures cover the Topeka, KS Metropolitan Statistical Area—see Appendix B for areas included
Source: U.S. Census Bureau, 2014-2018 American Community Survey 5-Year Estimates

Age

Area	Under Age 5	Age 5–19	Age 20–34	Age 35–44	Age 45–54	Age 55–64	Age 65–74	Age 75–84	Age 85+	Median Age
City	6.9	19.1	21.0	11.7	11.9	12.7	9.2	5.0	2.6	36.9
MSA[1]	6.3	20.1	17.7	11.5	12.8	14.2	9.9	5.2	2.4	39.9
U.S.	6.1	19.3	20.7	12.6	13.2	12.8	8.8	4.5	1.9	37.9

Note: (1) Figures cover the Topeka, KS Metropolitan Statistical Area—see Appendix B for areas included
Source: U.S. Census Bureau, 2014-2018 American Community Survey 5-Year Estimates

Gender

Area	Males	Females	Males per 100 Females
City	60,956	65,921	92.5
MSA[1]	114,015	119,245	95.6
U.S.	158,984,190	163,918,840	97.0

Note: (1) Figures cover the Topeka, KS Metropolitan Statistical Area—see Appendix B for areas included
Source: U.S. Census Bureau, 2014-2018 American Community Survey 5-Year Estimates

Religious Groups by Family

Area	Catholic	Baptist	Non-Den.	Methodist[2]	Lutheran	LDS[3]	Pente-costal	Presby-terian[4]	Muslim[5]	Judaism
MSA[1]	12.8	9.1	4.1	7.3	3.6	1.5	2.0	1.7	0.1	0.1
U.S.	19.1	9.3	4.0	4.0	2.3	2.0	1.9	1.6	0.8	0.7

Note: Figures are the number of adherents as a percentage of the total population; (1) Figures cover the Topeka, KS Metropolitan Statistical Area—see Appendix B for areas included; (2) Methodist/Pietist; (3) Latter Day Saints; (4) Reformed; (5) Figures are estimates
Source: Association of Statisticians of American Religious Bodies, 2010 U.S. Religion Census: Religious Congregations & Membership Study

Religious Groups by Tradition

Area	Catholic	Evangelical Protestant	Mainline Protestant	Other Tradition	Black Protestant	Orthodox
MSA[1]	12.8	15.5	12.9	1.8	2.8	<0.1
U.S.	19.1	16.2	7.3	4.3	1.6	0.3

Note: Figures are the number of adherents as a percentage of the total population; (1) Figures cover the Topeka, KS Metropolitan Statistical Area—see Appendix B for areas included
Source: Association of Statisticians of American Religious Bodies, 2010 U.S. Religion Census: Religious Congregations & Membership Study

ECONOMY

Gross Metropolitan Product

Area	2017	2018	2019	2020	Rank[2]
MSA[1]	10.8	11.3	11.6	11.9	197

Note: Figures are in billions of dollars; (1) Figures cover the Topeka, KS Metropolitan Statistical Area—see Appendix B for areas included; (2) Rank is based on 2018 data and ranges from 1 to 381
Source: U.S. Conference of Mayors, U.S. Metro Economies: GMP & Employment 2018-2020, September 2019

Economic Growth

Area	2015-17 (%)	2018 (%)	2019 (%)	2020 (%)	Rank[2]
MSA[1]	1.9	1.8	1.1	-0.1	143
U.S.	1.9	2.9	2.3	2.1	–

Note: Figures are real gross metropolitan product (GMP) growth rates and represent average annual percent change; (1) Figures cover the Topeka, KS Metropolitan Statistical Area—see Appendix B for areas included; (2) Rank is based on 2017 2-year average annual percent change and ranges from 1 to 381
Source: U.S. Conference of Mayors, U.S. Metro Economies: GMP & Employment 2018-2020, September 2019

Metropolitan Area Exports

Area	2013	2014	2015	2016	2017	2018	Rank[2]
MSA[1]	303.3	365.0	363.5	305.2	300.7	285.9	262

Note: Figures are in millions of dollars; (1) Figures cover the Topeka, KS Metropolitan Statistical Area—see Appendix B for areas included; (2) Rank is based on 2018 data and ranges from 1 to 387
Source: U.S. Department of Commerce, International Trade Administration, Office of Trade and Economic Analysis, Industry and Analysis, Exports by Metropolitan Area, data extracted April 15, 2020

Building Permits

Area	Single-Family			Multi-Family			Total		
	2017	2018	Pct. Chg.	2017	2018	Pct. Chg.	2017	2018	Pct. Chg.
City	85	82	-3.5	0	0	0.0	85	82	-3.5
MSA[1]	327	330	0.9	8	26	225.0	335	356	6.3
U.S.	820,000	855,300	4.3	462,000	473,500	2.5	1,282,000	1,328,800	3.7

Note: (1) Figures cover the Topeka, KS Metropolitan Statistical Area—see Appendix B for areas included; Figures represent new, privately-owned housing units authorized (unadjusted data); All permit data are based on estimates with imputation
Source: U.S. Census Bureau, Manufacturing, Mining, and Construction Statistics, Building Permits, 2017, 2018

Bankruptcy Filings

Area	Business Filings			Nonbusiness Filings		
	2018	2019	% Chg.	2018	2019	% Chg.
Shawnee County	6	34	466.7	923	877	-5.0
U.S.	22,232	22,780	2.5	751,186	752,160	0.1

Note: Business filings include Chapter 7, Chapter 9, Chapter 11, Chapter 12, Chapter 13, Chapter 15, and Section 304; Nonbusiness filings include Chapter 7, Chapter 11, and Chapter 13
Source: Administrative Office of the U.S. Courts, Business and Nonbusiness Bankruptcy, County Cases Commenced by Chapter of the Bankruptcy Code, During the 12-Month Period Ending December 31, 2018 and Business and Nonbusiness Bankruptcy, County Cases Commenced by Chapter of the Bankruptcy Code, During the 12-Month Period Ending December 31, 2019

Housing Vacancy Rates

Area	Gross Vacancy Rate[2] (%)			Year-Round Vacancy Rate[3] (%)			Rental Vacancy Rate[4] (%)			Homeowner Vacancy Rate[5] (%)		
	2017	2018	2019	2017	2018	2019	2017	2018	2019	2017	2018	2019
MSA[1]	n/a	n/a	n/a	n/a	n/a	n/a	n/a	n/a	n/a	n/a	n/a	n/a
U.S.	12.7	12.3	12.0	9.9	9.7	9.5	7.2	6.9	6.7	1.6	1.5	1.4

Note: (1) Figures cover the Topeka, KS Metropolitan Statistical Area—see Appendix B for areas included; (2) The percentage of the total housing inventory that is vacant; (3) The percentage of the housing inventory (excluding seasonal units) that is year-round vacant; (4) The percentage of rental inventory that is vacant for rent; (5) The percentage of homeowner inventory that is vacant for sale; n/a not available
Source: U.S. Census Bureau, Housing Vacancies and Homeownership Annual Statistics: 2017, 2018, 2019

INCOME

Income

Area	Per Capita ($)	Median Household ($)	Average Household ($)
City	27,145	46,890	62,597
MSA[1]	29,548	56,125	71,553
U.S.	32,621	60,293	84,938

Note: (1) Figures cover the Topeka, KS Metropolitan Statistical Area—see Appendix B for areas included
Source: U.S. Census Bureau, 2014-2018 American Community Survey 5-Year Estimates

Household Income Distribution

Area	Percent of Households Earning							
	Under $15,000	$15,000 -$24,999	$25,000 -$34,999	$35,000 -$49,999	$50,000 -$74,999	$75,000 -$99,999	$100,000 -$149,999	$150,000 and up
City	12.8	12.0	12.2	16.1	18.5	12.4	10.9	5.0
MSA[1]	9.8	10.0	10.4	14.6	19.4	14.5	14.3	7.0
U.S.	10.9	9.3	9.3	12.6	17.5	12.5	14.6	13.3

Note: (1) Figures cover the Topeka, KS Metropolitan Statistical Area—see Appendix B for areas included
Source: U.S. Census Bureau, 2014-2018 American Community Survey 5-Year Estimates

Poverty Rate

Area	All Ages	Under 18 Years Old	18 to 64 Years Old	65 Years and Over
City	15.9	19.7	16.4	8.8
MSA[1]	12.0	15.0	12.2	7.1
U.S.	14.1	19.5	13.2	9.3

Note: Figures are percentage of people whose income during the past 12 months was below the poverty level; (1) Figures cover the Topeka, KS Metropolitan Statistical Area—see Appendix B for areas included
Source: U.S. Census Bureau, 2014-2018 American Community Survey 5-Year Estimates

EMPLOYMENT

Labor Force and Employment

Area	Civilian Labor Force			Workers Employed		
	Dec. 2018	Dec. 2019	% Chg.	Dec. 2018	Dec. 2019	% Chg.
City	61,568	61,966	0.6	59,393	59,884	0.8
MSA[1]	117,567	118,319	0.6	113,746	114,586	0.7
U.S.	162,510,000	164,007,000	0.9	156,481,000	158,504,000	1.3

Note: Data is not seasonally adjusted and covers workers 16 years of age and older; (1) Figures cover the Topeka, KS Metropolitan Statistical Area—see Appendix B for areas included
Source: Bureau of Labor Statistics, Local Area Unemployment Statistics

Unemployment Rate

Area	2019											
	Jan.	Feb.	Mar.	Apr.	May	Jun.	Jul.	Aug.	Sep.	Oct.	Nov.	Dec.
City	4.2	4.0	3.8	3.1	3.3	3.5	4.0	3.7	3.1	3.2	3.3	3.4
MSA[1]	4.0	3.8	3.7	2.8	3.0	3.2	3.7	3.4	2.8	2.9	3.0	3.2
U.S.	4.4	4.1	3.9	3.3	3.4	3.8	4.0	3.8	3.3	3.3	3.3	3.4

Note: Data is not seasonally adjusted and covers workers 16 years of age and older; (1) Figures cover the Topeka, KS Metropolitan Statistical Area—see Appendix B for areas included
Source: Bureau of Labor Statistics, Local Area Unemployment Statistics

Average Wages

Occupation	$/Hr.	Occupation	$/Hr.
Accountants and Auditors	29.90	Maintenance and Repair Workers	18.60
Automotive Mechanics	18.50	Marketing Managers	59.20
Bookkeepers	17.20	Network and Computer Systems Admin.	41.50
Carpenters	20.50	Nurses, Licensed Practical	21.50
Cashiers	10.40	Nurses, Registered	31.90
Computer Programmers	38.70	Nursing Assistants	13.60
Computer Systems Analysts	35.10	Office Clerks, General	14.30
Computer User Support Specialists	22.70	Physical Therapists	44.00
Construction Laborers	16.60	Physicians	99.60
Cooks, Restaurant	11.80	Plumbers, Pipefitters and Steamfitters	26.30
Customer Service Representatives	16.70	Police and Sheriff's Patrol Officers	24.20
Dentists	n/a	Postal Service Mail Carriers	24.70
Electricians	25.20	Real Estate Sales Agents	n/a
Engineers, Electrical	44.80	Retail Salespersons	13.10
Fast Food and Counter Workers	9.70	Sales Representatives, Technical/Scientific	40.80
Financial Managers	59.60	Secretaries, Exc. Legal/Medical/Executive	16.00
First-Line Supervisors of Office Workers	24.80	Security Guards	14.20
General and Operations Managers	39.10	Surgeons	n/a
Hairdressers/Cosmetologists	11.40	Teacher Assistants, Exc. Postsecondary*	12.80
Home Health and Personal Care Aides	11.30	Teachers, Secondary School, Exc. Sp. Ed.*	24.30
Janitors and Cleaners	13.40	Telemarketers	n/a
Landscaping/Groundskeeping Workers	16.30	Truck Drivers, Heavy/Tractor-Trailer	19.40
Lawyers	49.90	Truck Drivers, Light/Delivery Services	18.30
Maids and Housekeeping Cleaners	10.50	Waiters and Waitresses	9.70

Note: Wage data covers the Topeka, KS Metropolitan Statistical Area—see Appendix B for areas included;
(*) Hourly wages were calculated from annual wage data based on a 40 hour work week; n/a not available.
Source: Bureau of Labor Statistics, Metro Area Occupational Employment & Wage Estimates, May 2019

Employment by Occupation

Occupation Classification	City (%)	MSA[1] (%)	U.S. (%)
Management, Business, Science, and Arts	35.9	37.2	37.9
Natural Resources, Construction, and Maintenance	8.6	10.2	8.9
Production, Transportation, and Material Moving	15.2	14.6	13.3
Sales and Office	21.6	21.5	22.1
Service	18.6	16.5	17.9

Note: Figures cover employed civilians 16 years of age and older; (1) Figures cover the Topeka, KS Metropolitan Statistical Area—see Appendix B for areas included
Source: U.S. Census Bureau, 2014-2018 American Community Survey 5-Year Estimates

Employment by Industry

Sector	MSA[1]		U.S.
	Number of Employees	Percent of Total	Percent of Total
Construction, Mining, and Logging	5,200	4.7	5.4
Education and Health Services	19,200	17.2	16.1
Financial Activities	7,700	6.9	5.8
Government	26,300	23.6	15.0
Information	1,300	1.2	1.9
Leisure and Hospitality	8,700	7.8	10.8
Manufacturing	8,000	7.2	8.4
Other Services	4,700	4.2	3.9
Professional and Business Services	13,200	11.8	14.1
Retail Trade	10,700	9.6	10.6
Transportation, Warehousing, and Utilities	3,900	3.5	4.2
Wholesale Trade	2,700	2.4	3.9

Note: Figures are non-farm employment as of December 2019. Figures are not seasonally adjusted and include workers 16 years of age and older; (1) Figures cover the Topeka, KS Metropolitan Statistical Area—see Appendix B for areas included
Source: Bureau of Labor Statistics, Current Employment Statistics, Employment, Hours, and Earnings

Occupations with Greatest Projected Employment Growth: 2019 – 2021

Occupation[1]	2019 Employment	2021 Projected Employment	Numeric Employment Change	Percent Employment Change
Personal Care Aides	22,540	23,920	1,380	6.1
Combined Food Preparation and Serving Workers, Including Fast Food	33,970	35,010	1,040	3.1
Registered Nurses	31,190	32,010	820	2.6
Cooks, Restaurant	10,850	11,300	450	4.1
Construction Laborers	13,740	14,190	450	3.3
Nursing Assistants	23,970	24,410	440	1.8
Laborers and Freight, Stock, and Material Movers, Hand	21,250	21,650	400	1.9
Heavy and Tractor-Trailer Truck Drivers	21,440	21,820	380	1.8
Light Truck or Delivery Services Drivers	9,090	9,390	300	3.3
Waiters and Waitresses	20,960	21,240	280	1.3

Note: Projections cover Kansas; (1) Sorted by numeric employment change
Source: www.projectionscentral.com, State Occupational Projections, 2019–2021 Short-Term Projections

Fastest Growing Occupations: 2019 – 2021

Occupation[1]	2019 Employment	2021 Projected Employment	Numeric Employment Change	Percent Employment Change
Cargo and Freight Agents	690	740	50	7.2
Home Health Aides	2,410	2,570	160	6.6
Personal Care Aides	22,540	23,920	1,380	6.1
Physician Assistants	1,130	1,190	60	5.3
Respiratory Therapists	1,320	1,390	70	5.3
Nurse Practitioners	2,490	2,620	130	5.2
Substance Abuse, Behavioral Disorder, and Mental Health Counselors	1,810	1,890	80	4.4
Software Developers, Applications	5,790	6,040	250	4.3
Phlebotomists	1,400	1,460	60	4.3
Speech-Language Pathologists	1,470	1,530	60	4.1

Note: Projections cover Kansas; (1) Sorted by percent employment change and excludes occupations with numeric employment change less than 50
Source: www.projectionscentral.com, State Occupational Projections, 2019–2021 Short-Term Projections

TAXES

State Corporate Income Tax Rates

State	Tax Rate (%)	Income Brackets ($)	Num. of Brackets	Financial Institution Tax Rate (%)[a]	Federal Income Tax Ded.
Kansas	4.0 (k)	Flat rate	1	2.25 (k)	No

Note: Tax rates as of January 1, 2020; (a) Rates listed are the corporate income tax rate applied to financial institutions or excise taxes based on income; (k) In addition to the flat 4% corporate income tax, Kansas levies a 3.0% surtax on taxable income over $50,000. Banks pay a privilege tax of 2.25% of net income, plus a surtax of 2.125% (2.25% for savings and loans, trust companies, and federally chartered savings banks) on net income in excess of $25,000.
Source: Federation of Tax Administrators, State Corporate Income Tax Rates, January 1, 2020

State Individual Income Tax Rates

State	Tax Rate (%)	Income Brackets ($)	Personal Exemptions ($)			Standard Ded. ($)	
			Single	Married	Depend.	Single	Married
Kansas	3.1 - 5.7	15,000 - 30,000 (b)	2,250	4,500	2,250	3,000	7,500

Note: Tax rates as of January 1, 2020; Local- and county-level taxes are not included; Federal income tax is not deductible on state income tax returns; (b) For joint returns, taxes are twice the tax on half the couple's income.
Source: Federation of Tax Administrators, State Individual Income Tax Rates, January 1, 2020

Various State Sales and Excise Tax Rates

State	State Sales Tax (%)	Gasoline[1] (¢/gal.)	Cigarette[2] ($/pack)	Spirits[3] ($/gal.)	Wine[4] ($/gal.)	Beer[5] ($/gal.)	Recreational Marijuana (%)
Kansas	6.5	24.025	1.29	2.50	0.30	0.18	Not legal

Note: All tax rates as of January 1, 2020; (1) The American Petroleum Institute has developed a methodology for determining the average tax rate on a gallon of fuel. Rates may include any of the following: excise taxes, environmental fees, storage tank fees, other fees or taxes, general sales tax, and local taxes; (2) The federal excise tax of $1.0066 per pack and local taxes are not included; (3) Rates are those applicable to off-premise sales of 40% alcohol by volume (a.b.v.) distilled spirits in 750ml containers. Local excise taxes are excluded; (4) Rates are those applicable to off-premise sales of 11% a.b.v. non-carbonated wine in 750ml containers; (5) Rates are those applicable to off-premise sales of 4.7% a.b.v. beer in 12 ounce containers.
Source: Tax Foundation, 2020 Facts & Figures: How Does Your State Compare?

State Business Tax Climate Index Rankings

State	Overall Rank	Corporate Tax Rank	Individual Income Tax Rank	Sales Tax Rank	Property Tax Rank	Unemployment Insurance Tax Rank
Kansas	34	35	23	38	20	14

Note: The index is a measure of how each state's tax laws affect economic performance. The lower the rank, the more favorable a state's tax system is for business. States without a given tax are given a ranking of 1. The scores/rankings for the District of Columbia do not affect other states. The 2020 index represents the tax climate as of July 1, 2019.
Source: Tax Foundation, State Business Tax Climate Index 2020

COMMERCIAL UTILITIES

Typical Monthly Electric Bills

Area	Commercial Service ($/month)		Industrial Service ($/month)	
	1,500 kWh	40 kW demand 14,000 kWh	1,000 kW demand 200,000 kWh	50,000 kW demand 32,500,000 kWh
City	174	1,459	26,366	2,225,401
Average[1]	203	1,612	25,706	2,520,671

Note: Figures are based on annualized rates; (1) Average based on 187 utilities surveyed
Source: Edison Electric Institute, Typical Bills and Average Rates Report, Summer 2019

TRANSPORTATION

Means of Transportation to Work

Area	Car/Truck/Van		Public Transportation			Bicycle	Walked	Other Means	Worked at Home
	Drove Alone	Car-pooled	Bus	Subway	Railroad				
City	81.3	11.1	1.3	0.0	0.0	0.4	2.2	1.1	2.8
MSA[1]	82.8	10.2	0.8	0.0	0.0	0.2	1.7	0.8	3.5
U.S.	76.4	9.1	2.5	1.9	0.6	0.6	2.7	1.3	4.9

Note: Figures are percentages and cover workers 16 years of age and older; (1) Figures cover the Topeka, KS Metropolitan Statistical Area—see Appendix B for areas included
Source: U.S. Census Bureau, 2014-2018 American Community Survey 5-Year Estimates

Travel Time to Work

Area	Less Than 10 Minutes	10 to 19 Minutes	20 to 29 Minutes	30 to 44 Minutes	45 to 59 Minutes	60 to 89 Minutes	90 Minutes or More
City	17.5	54.5	15.4	7.7	1.9	2.3	0.6
MSA[1]	16.2	42.4	19.6	13.4	4.1	3.0	1.2
U.S.	12.5	28.7	20.9	20.7	8.2	6.3	2.8

Note: Note: Figures are percentages and include workers 16 years old and over; (1) Figures cover the Topeka, KS Metropolitan Statistical Area—see Appendix B for areas included
Source: U.S. Census Bureau, 2014-2018 American Community Survey 5-Year Estimates

Key Congestion Measures

Area	1982	1992	2002	2012	2017
Annual Hours of Delay, Total (000)	n/a	n/a	n/a	n/a	3,310
Annual Hours of Delay, Per Auto Commuter	n/a	n/a	n/a	n/a	21
Annual Congestion Cost, Total (million $)	n/a	n/a	n/a	n/a	71
Annual Congestion Cost, Per Auto Commuter ($)	n/a	n/a	n/a	n/a	439

Note: n/a not available
Source: Texas A&M Transportation Institute, 2019 Urban Mobility Report

Freeway Travel Time Index

Area	1982	1987	1992	1997	2002	2007	2012	2017
Urban Area Index[1]	n/a	n/a	n/a	n/a	n/a	n/a	n/a	1.08
Urban Area Rank[1,2]	n/a	n/a	n/a	n/a	n/a	n/a	n/a	n/a

Note: Freeway Travel Time Index—the ratio of travel time in the peak period to the travel time at free-flow conditions. For example, a value of 1.30 indicates a 20-minute free-flow trip takes 26 minutes in the peak (20 minutes x 1.30 = 26 minutes); (1) Covers the Topeka KS urban area; (2) Rank is based on 101 larger urban areas (#1 = highest travel time index); n/a not available
Source: Texas A&M Transportation Institute, 2019 Urban Mobility Report

Public Transportation

Agency Name / Mode of Transportation	Vehicles Operated in Maximum Service[1]	Annual Unlinked Passenger Trips[2] (in thous.)	Annual Passenger Miles[3] (in thous.)
Topeka Metropolitan Transit Authority			
Bus (directly operated)	20	1,221.1	5,079.7
Demand Response (directly operated)	7	23.8	90.4
Demand Response Taxi (purchased transportation)	8	25.3	112.3

Note: (1) Number of revenue vehicles operated by the given mode and type of service to meet the annual maximum service requirement. This is the revenue vehicle count during the peak season of the year; on the week and day that maximum service is provided. Vehicles operated in maximum service (VOMS) exclude atypical days and one-time special events; (2) Number of passengers who boarded public transportation vehicles. Passengers are counted each time they board a vehicle no matter how many vehicles they use to travel from their origin to their destination. (3) Sum of the distances ridden by all passengers during the entire fiscal year.
Source: Federal Transit Administration, National Transit Database, 2018

Air Transportation

Airport Name and Code / Type of Service	Passenger Airlines[1]	Passenger Enplanements	Freight Carriers[2]	Freight (lbs)
Topeka Regional Airport (FOE)				
Domestic service (U.S. carriers - 2019)	9	2,350	1	12,630
International service (U.S. carriers - 2018)	0	0	0	0

Note: (1) Includes all U.S.-based major, minor and commuter airlines that carried at least one passenger during the year; (2) Includes all U.S.-based airlines and freight carriers that transported at least one pound of freight during the year.
Source: Bureau of Transportation Statistics, The Intermodal Transportation Database, Air Carriers: T-100 Domestic Market (U.S. Carriers), 2019; Bureau of Transportation Statistics, The Intermodal Transportation Database, Air Carriers: T-100 International Market (U.S. Carriers), 2018

Other Transportation Statistics

Major Highways:	I-70; I-335; I-470
Amtrak Service:	Yes
Major Waterways/Ports:	Kansas River

Source: Amtrak.com; Google Maps

BUSINESSES

Major Business Headquarters

Company Name	Industry	Rankings	
		Fortune[1]	Forbes[2]
No companies listed	-	-	-

Note: (1) Companies that produce a 10-K are ranked 1 to 500 based on 2018 revenue; (2) All private companies with at least $2 billion in annual revenue through the end of their most current fiscal year are ranked 1 to 228; companies listed are headquartered in the city; dashes indicate no ranking
Source: Fortune, "Fortune 500," June 2019; Forbes, "America's Largest Private Companies," 2019 Rankings

Minority- and Women-Owned Businesses

Group	All Firms		Firms with Paid Employees			
	Firms	Sales ($000)	Firms	Sales ($000)	Employees	Payroll ($000)
AIAN[1]	107	3,424	11	2,022	30	504
Asian	217	172,137	109	168,622	1,438	66,306
Black	481	19,770	11	11,199	118	2,858
Hispanic	451	23,305	58	15,060	299	5,398
NHOPI[2]	n/a	n/a	n/a	n/a	n/a	n/a
Women	2,981	442,677	373	386,506	2,843	84,644
All Firms	8,993	16,942,793	2,869	16,712,755	63,760	2,636,157

Note: Figures cover firms located in the city; minority- and women-owned business are defined as firms in which the corresponding group own 51% or more of the stock or equity of the company; (1) American Indian and Alaska Native; (2) Native Hawaiian and Other Pacific Islander; n/a not available
Source: U.S. Census Bureau, 2012 Economic Census, Survey of Business Owners

HOTELS & CONVENTION CENTERS

Hotels, Motels and Vacation Rentals

Area	5 Star		4 Star		3 Star		2 Star		1 Star		Not Rated	
	Num.	Pct.[3]	Num.	Pct.[3]	Num.	Pct.[3]	Num.	Pct.[3]	Num.	Pct.[3]	Num.	Pct.[3]
City[1]	0	0.0	1	3.3	10	33.3	9	30.0	1	3.3	9	30.0
Total[2]	266	1.3	1,517	7.2	4,627	21.8	3,210	15.1	3,974	18.7	7,601	35.9

Note: (1) Figures cover Topeka and vicinity; (2) Figures cover all 100 cities in this book; (3) Percentage of hotels which have a given star rating; Star ratings are determined by priceline.com and offer an indication of the general quality of a particular hotel.
Source: priceline.com, April 27, 2020

Major Convention Centers

Name	Overall Space (sq. ft.)	Exhibit Space (sq. ft.)	Meeting Space (sq. ft.)	Meeting Rooms
Kansas Expocentre Exhibition Hall	n/a	44,500	n/a	n/a

Note: Table includes convention centers located in the Topeka, KS metro area; n/a not available
Source: Original research

Living Environment

COST OF LIVING

Cost of Living Index

Composite Index	Groceries	Housing	Utilities	Trans- portation	Health Care	Misc. Goods/ Services
89.4	95.5	76.0	98.1	97.7	95.7	92.1

Note: The Cost of Living Index measures regional differences in the cost of consumer goods and services, excluding taxes and non-consumer expenditures, for professional and managerial households in the top income quintile. It is based on more than 50,000 prices covering almost 60 different items for which prices are collected three times a year by chambers of commerce, economic development organizations or university applied economic centers in each participating urban area. The numbers shown should be read as a percentage above or below the national average of 100. For example, a value of 115.4 in the groceries column indicates that grocery prices are 15.4% higher than the national average. Small differences in the index numbers should not be interpreted as significant; Figures cover the Topeka KS urban area.
Source: The Council for Community and Economic Research, ACCRA Cost of Living Index, 2019

Grocery Prices

Area[1]	T-Bone Steak ($/pound)	Frying Chicken ($/pound)	Whole Milk ($/half gal.)	Eggs ($/dozen)	Orange Juice ($/64 oz.)	Coffee ($/11.5 oz.)
City[2]	9.96	1.93	1.37	0.93	3.62	4.36
Avg.	11.40	1.41	1.93	1.54	3.51	4.30
Min.	7.40	0.92	0.85	0.58	2.67	2.90
Max.	15.58	2.68	4.09	4.18	5.57	8.10

Note: (1) Values for the local area are compared with the average, minimum and maximum values for all 290 areas in the Cost of Living Index; (2) Figures cover the Topeka KS urban area; T-Bone Steak (price per pound); Frying Chicken (price per pound, whole fryer); Whole Milk (half gallon carton); Eggs (price per dozen, Grade A, large); Orange Juice (64 oz. Tropicana or Florida Natural); Coffee (11.5 oz. can, vacuum-packed, Maxwell House, Hills Bros, or Folgers).
Source: The Council for Community and Economic Research, ACCRA Cost of Living Index, 2019

Housing and Utility Costs

Area[1]	New Home Price ($)	Apartment Rent ($/month)	All Electric ($/month)	Part Electric ($/month)	Other Energy ($/month)	Telephone ($/month)
City[2]	290,994	785	-	90.32	67.93	186.70
Avg.	362,090	1,142	174.35	100.00	67.76	179.60
Min.	198,329	501	91.58	31.44	28.51	165.30
Max.	2,074,561	5,050	388.18	239.41	306.15	207.90

Note: (1) Values for the local area are compared with the average, minimum and maximum values for all 290 areas in the Cost of Living Index; (2) Figures cover the Topeka KS urban area; New Home Price (2,400 sf living area, 8,000 sf lot, in urban area with full utilities); Apartment Rent (950 sf 2 bedroom/1.5 or 2 bath, unfurnished, excluding all utilities except water); All Electric (average monthly cost for an all-electric home); Part Electric (average monthly cost for a part-electric home); Other Energy (average monthly cost for natural gas, fuel oil, coal, wood, and any other forms of energy except electricity); Telephone (price includes the base monthly rate plus taxes and fees for three lines of mobile phone service).
Source: The Council for Community and Economic Research, ACCRA Cost of Living Index, 2019

Health Care, Transportation, and Other Costs

Area[1]	Doctor ($/visit)	Dentist ($/visit)	Optometrist ($/visit)	Gasoline ($/gallon)	Beauty Salon ($/visit)	Men's Shirt ($)
City[2]	99.80	94.77	123.49	2.32	28.55	42.96
Avg.	114.85	97.58	106.10	2.50	38.15	32.15
Min.	39.00	62.22	52.22	1.53	16.88	10.27
Max.	206.67	151.53	258.67	3.79	79.29	59.30

Note: (1) Values for the local area are compared with the average, minimum and maximum values for all 290 areas in the Cost of Living Index; (2) Figures cover the Topeka KS urban area; Doctor (general practitioners routine exam of an established patient); Dentist (adult teeth cleaning and periodic oral examination); Optometrist (full vision eye exam for established adult patient); Gasoline (one gallon regular unleaded, national brand, including all taxes, cash price at self-service pump if available); Beauty Salon (woman's shampoo, trim, and blow-dry); Men's Shirt (cotton/polyester dress shirt, pinpoint weave, long sleeves).
Source: The Council for Community and Economic Research, ACCRA Cost of Living Index, 2019

HOUSING

House Price Index (HPI)

Area	National Ranking[2]	Quarterly Change (%)	One-Year Change (%)	Five-Year Change (%)
MSA[1]	85	1.19	5.42	20.20
U.S.[3]	–	1.26	5.09	32.88

Note: The HPI is a weighted repeat sales index. It measures average price changes in repeat sales or refinancings on the same properties. This information is obtained by reviewing repeat mortgage transactions on single-family properties whose mortgages have been purchased or securitized by Fannie Mae or Freddie Mac in January 1975; (1) Figures cover the Topeka, KS Metropolitan Statistical Area—see Appendix B for areas included; (2) Rankings are based on annual percentage change for all metro areas containing at least 15,000 transactions over the last 10 years and ranges from 1 to 232; (3) figures based on a weighted average of Census Division estimates using a seasonally adjusted, purchase-only index; all figures are for the period ending December 31, 2019
Source: Federal Housing Finance Agency, House Price Index, February 25, 2020

Median Single-Family Home Prices

Area	2017	2018	2019p	Percent Change 2018 to 2019
MSA[1]	128.6	132.1	135.7	2.7
U.S. Average	248.8	261.6	274.6	5.0

Note: Figures are median sales prices of existing single-family homes in thousands of dollars; (p) preliminary; (1) Figures cover the Topeka, KS Metropolitan Statistical Area—see Appendix B for areas included
Source: National Association of Realtors, Median Sales Price of Existing Single-Family Homes for Metropolitan Areas, 4th Quarter 2019

Qualifying Income Based on Median Sales Price of Existing Single-Family Homes

Area	With 5% Down ($)	With 10% Down ($)	With 20% Down ($)
MSA[1]	28,190	26,706	23,739
U.S. Average	58,663	55,575	49,400

Note: Figures are preliminary; Qualifying income is based on a mortgage rate of 3.76%. Monthly principal and interest payment is limited to 25% of income; (1) Figures cover the Topeka, KS Metropolitan Statistical Area—see Appendix B for areas included
Source: National Association of Realtors, Qualifying Income Based on Median Sales Price of Existing Single-Family Homes for Metropolitan Areas, 4th Quarter 2019

Median Apartment Condo-Coop Home Prices

Area	2017	2018	2019p	Percent Change 2018 to 2019
MSA[1]	n/a	n/a	n/a	n/a
U.S. Average	234.3	241.0	249.5	3.5

Note: Figures are median sales prices of existing apartment condo-coop homes in thousands of dollars; (p) preliminary; n/a not available; (1) Figures cover the Topeka, KS Metropolitan Statistical Area—see Appendix B for areas included
Source: National Association of Realtors, Median Sales Price of Existing Apartment Condo-Coop Homes for Metropolitan Areas, 4th Quarter 2019

Home Value Distribution

Area	Under $50,000	$50,000 -$99,999	$100,000 -$149,999	$150,000 -$199,999	$200,000 -$299,999	$300,000 -$499,999	$500,000 -$999,999	$1,000,000 or more
City	13.8	34.8	24.4	13.6	9.9	2.5	0.7	0.3
MSA[1]	10.2	25.2	23.4	18.0	15.1	6.4	1.4	0.4
U.S.	7.6	13.0	14.0	14.3	19.2	18.3	10.5	3.1

Note: Figures are percentages and cover owner-occupied housing units; (1) Figures cover the Topeka, KS Metropolitan Statistical Area—see Appendix B for areas included
Source: U.S. Census Bureau, 2014-2018 American Community Survey 5-Year Estimates

Homeownership Rate

Area	2011 (%)	2012 (%)	2013 (%)	2014 (%)	2015 (%)	2016 (%)	2017 (%)	2018 (%)	2019 (%)
MSA[1]	n/a	n/a	n/a	n/a	n/a	n/a	n/a	n/a	n/a
U.S.	66.1	65.4	65.1	64.5	63.7	63.4	63.9	64.4	64.6

Note: (1) Figures cover the Topeka, KS Metropolitan Statistical Area—see Appendix B for areas included; n/a not available
Source: U.S. Census Bureau, Housing Vacancies and Homeownership Annual Statistics: 2011-2019

Year Housing Structure Built

Area	2010 or Later	2000 -2009	1990 -1999	1980 -1989	1970 -1979	1960 -1969	1950 -1959	1940 -1949	Before 1940	Median Year
City	1.3	6.9	10.0	9.8	14.7	15.9	16.4	6.5	18.4	1965
MSA[1]	1.9	9.5	12.4	10.8	16.7	13.3	12.4	5.0	18.0	1971
U.S.	4.1	14.3	13.9	13.5	15.3	10.7	10.4	5.0	12.8	1977

Note: Figures are percentages except for Median Year; Note: (1) Figures cover the Topeka, KS Metropolitan Statistical Area—see Appendix B for areas included
Source: U.S. Census Bureau, 2014-2018 American Community Survey 5-Year Estimates

Gross Monthly Rent

Area	Under $500	$500 -$999	$1,000 -$1,499	$1,500 -$1,999	$2,000 -$2,499	$2,500 -$2,999	$3,000 and up	Median ($)
City	14.6	62.2	17.7	3.2	1.6	0.3	0.4	790
MSA[1]	15.9	60.2	18.0	3.4	1.5	0.3	0.6	786
U.S.	9.8	38.5	29.6	12.9	5.1	2.1	2.0	1,023

Note: Figures are percentages except for Median; Gross rent is the contract rent plus the estimated average monthly cost of utilities (electricity, gas, and water and sewer) and fuels (oil, coal, kerosene, wood, etc.) if these are paid by the renter (or paid for the renter by someone else); (1) Figures cover the Topeka, KS Metropolitan Statistical Area—see Appendix B for areas included
Source: U.S. Census Bureau, 2014-2018 American Community Survey 5-Year Estimates

HEALTH

Health Risk Factors

Category	MSA[1] (%)	U.S. (%)
Adults aged 18–64 who have any kind of health care coverage	87.5	87.3
Adults who reported being in good or better health	81.7	82.4
Adults who have been told they have high blood cholesterol	38.8	33.0
Adults who have been told they have high blood pressure	37.8	32.3
Adults who are current smokers	20.8	17.1
Adults who currently use E-cigarettes	5.8	4.6
Adults who currently use chewing tobacco, snuff, or snus	5.0	4.0
Adults who are heavy drinkers[2]	5.8	6.3
Adults who are binge drinkers[3]	16.3	17.4
Adults who are overweight (BMI 25.0 - 29.9)	32.5	35.3
Adults who are obese (BMI 30.0 - 99.8)	37.1	31.3
Adults who participated in any physical activities in the past month	72.6	74.4
Adults who always or nearly always wears a seat belt	94.0	94.3

Note: (1) Figures cover the Topeka, KS Metropolitan Statistical Area—see Appendix B for areas included; (2) Heavy drinkers are classified as adult men having more than 14 drinks per week and adult women having more than 7 drinks per week; (3) Binge drinkers are classified as males having five or more drinks on one occasion or females having four or more drinks on one occasion
Source: Centers for Disease Control and Prevention, Behaviorial Risk Factor Surveillance System, SMART: Selected Metropolitan Area Risk Trends, 2017

Acute and Chronic Health Conditions

Category	MSA[1] (%)	U.S. (%)
Adults who have ever been told they had a heart attack	4.3	4.2
Adults who have ever been told they have angina or coronary heart disease	4.6	3.9
Adults who have ever been told they had a stroke	2.9	3.0
Adults who have ever been told they have asthma	15.9	14.2
Adults who have ever been told they have arthritis	26.5	24.9
Adults who have ever been told they have diabetes[2]	12.4	10.5
Adults who have ever been told they had skin cancer	7.9	6.2
Adults who have ever been told they had any other types of cancer	7.6	7.1
Adults who have ever been told they have COPD	7.9	6.5
Adults who have ever been told they have kidney disease	4.2	3.0
Adults who have ever been told they have a form of depression	23.7	20.5

Note: (1) Figures cover the Topeka, KS Metropolitan Statistical Area—see Appendix B for areas included; (2) Figures do not include pregnancy-related, borderline, or pre-diabetes
Source: Centers for Disease Control and Prevention, Behaviorial Risk Factor Surveillance System, SMART: Selected Metropolitan Area Risk Trends, 2017

Health Screening and Vaccination Rates

Category	MSA[1] (%)	U.S. (%)
Adults aged 65+ who have had flu shot within the past year	61.8	60.7
Adults aged 65+ who have ever had a pneumonia vaccination	81.8	75.4
Adults who have ever been tested for HIV	28.1	36.1
Adults who have ever had the shingles or zoster vaccine?	33.0	28.9
Adults who have had their blood cholesterol checked within the last five years	86.2	85.9

Note: n/a not available; (1) Figures cover the Topeka, KS Metropolitan Statistical Area—see Appendix B for areas included.
Source: Centers for Disease Control and Prevention, Behaviorial Risk Factor Surveillance System, SMART: Selected Metropolitan Area Risk Trends, 2017

Disability Status

Category	MSA[1] (%)	U.S. (%)
Adults who reported being deaf	8.3	6.7
Are you blind or have serious difficulty seeing, even when wearing glasses?	4.4	4.5
Are you limited in any way in any of your usual activities due of arthritis?	12.8	12.9
Do you have difficulty doing errands alone?	6.4	6.8
Do you have difficulty dressing or bathing?	3.7	3.6
Do you have serious difficulty concentrating/remembering/making decisions?	12.7	10.7
Do you have serious difficulty walking or climbing stairs?	15.4	13.6

Note: (1) Figures cover the Topeka, KS Metropolitan Statistical Area—see Appendix B for areas included.
Source: Centers for Disease Control and Prevention, Behaviorial Risk Factor Surveillance System, SMART: Selected Metropolitan Area Risk Trends, 2017

Mortality Rates for the Top 10 Causes of Death in the U.S.

ICD-10[a] Sub-Chapter	ICD-10[a] Code	Age-Adjusted Mortality Rate[1] per 100,000 population	
		County[2]	U.S.
Malignant neoplasms	C00-C97	172.0	152.4
Ischaemic heart diseases	I20-I25	82.7	92.7
Other forms of heart disease	I30-I51	46.2	52.5
Chronic lower respiratory diseases	J40-J47	56.4	40.4
Cerebrovascular diseases	I60-I69	38.5	37.3
Other degenerative diseases of the nervous system	G30-G31	35.7	36.4
Other external causes of accidental injury	W00-X59	39.9	35.3
Organic, including symptomatic, mental disorders	F01-F09	47.1	30.0
Hypertensive diseases	I10-I15	30.1	22.9
Diabetes mellitus	E10-E14	24.7	21.3

Note: (a) ICD-10 = International Classification of Diseases 10th Revision; (1) Mortality rates are a three year average covering 2016-2018; (2) Figures cover Shawnee County.
Source: Centers for Disease Control and Prevention, National Center for Health Statistics. Underlying Cause of Death 1999-2018 on CDC WONDER Online Database

Mortality Rates for Selected Causes of Death

ICD-10[a] Sub-Chapter	ICD-10[a] Code	Age-Adjusted Mortality Rate[1] per 100,000 population	
		County[2]	U.S.
Assault	X85-Y09	12.8	6.0
Diseases of the liver	K70-K76	16.2	14.2
Human immunodeficiency virus (HIV) disease	B20-B24	Suppressed	1.6
Influenza and pneumonia	J09-J18	14.2	14.2
Intentional self-harm	X60-X84	22.7	13.9
Malnutrition	E40-E46	Unreliable	1.9
Obesity and other hyperalimentation	E65-E68	Unreliable	2.1
Renal failure	N17-N19	12.0	12.8
Transport accidents	V01-V99	13.4	12.5
Viral hepatitis	B15-B19	Suppressed	1.4

Note: (a) ICD-10 = International Classification of Diseases 10th Revision; (1) Mortality rates are a three year average covering 2016-2018; (2) Figures cover Shawnee County; Data are suppressed when the data meet the criteria for confidentiality constraints; Mortality rates are flagged as unreliable when the rate would be calculated with a numerator of 20 or less.
Source: Centers for Disease Control and Prevention, National Center for Health Statistics. Underlying Cause of Death 1999-2018 on CDC WONDER Online Database

Health Insurance Coverage

Area	With Health Insurance	With Private Health Insurance	With Public Health Insurance	Without Health Insurance	Population Under Age 19 Without Health Insurance
City	90.4	70.4	36.2	9.6	5.5
MSA[1]	92.3	75.9	32.9	7.7	4.5
U.S.	90.6	67.7	34.7	9.4	5.2

Note: Figures are percentages that cover the civilian noninstitutionalized population; (1) Figures cover the Topeka, KS Metropolitan Statistical Area—see Appendix B for areas included
Source: U.S. Census Bureau, 2014-2018 American Community Survey 5-Year Estimates

Number of Medical Professionals

Area	MDs[3]	DOs[3,4]	Dentists	Podiatrists	Chiropractors	Optometrists
County[1] (number)	365	47	114	10	45	45
County[1] (rate[2])	204.8	26.4	64.2	5.6	25.4	25.4
U.S. (rate[2])	281.9	23.4	69.1	6.0	27.5	16.4

Note: Data as of 2018 unless noted; (1) Data covers Shawnee County; (2) Rate per 100,000 population; (3) Data as of 2017 and includes all active, non-federal physicians; (4) Doctor of Osteopathic Medicine
Source: U.S. Department of Health and Human Services, Health Resources and Services Administration, Bureau of Health Professions, Area Resource File (ARF) 2018-2019

EDUCATION

Public School District Statistics

District Name	Schls	Pupils	Pupil/ Teacher Ratio	Minority Pupils[1] (%)	Free Lunch Eligible[2] (%)	IEP[3] (%)
Auburn Washburn	9	6,318	13.2	25.4	24.2	13.9
Seaman	7	4,010	13.7	18.4	26.1	16.4
Topeka Public Schools	27	13,159	11.4	62.6	63.4	21.9

Note: Table includes school districts with 2,000 or more students; (1) Percentage of students that are not non-Hispanic white; (2) Percentage of students that are eligible for the free lunch program; (3) Percentage of students that have an Individualized Education Program.
Source: U.S. Department of Education, National Center for Education Statistics, Common Core of Data, Local Education Agency (School District) Universe Survey: School Year 2018-2019; U.S. Department of Education, National Center for Education Statistics, Common Core of Data, Public Elementary/Secondary School Universe Survey: School Year 2018-2019

Highest Level of Education

Area	Less than H.S.	H.S. Diploma	Some College, No Deg.	Associate Degree	Bachelor's Degree	Master's Degree	Prof. School Degree	Doctorate Degree
City	9.8	32.0	23.8	6.0	18.0	7.4	2.0	1.0
MSA[1]	7.7	33.1	23.9	6.9	18.4	7.4	1.7	0.9
U.S.	12.3	27.1	20.6	8.4	19.4	8.6	2.1	1.4

Note: Figures cover persons age 25 and over; (1) Figures cover the Topeka, KS Metropolitan Statistical Area—see Appendix B for areas included
Source: U.S. Census Bureau, 2014-2018 American Community Survey 5-Year Estimates

Educational Attainment by Race

Area	High School Graduate or Higher (%)					Bachelor's Degree or Higher (%)				
	Total	White	Black	Asian	Hisp.[2]	Total	White	Black	Asian	Hisp.[2]
City	90.2	91.6	87.3	93.4	73.3	28.4	30.7	11.9	63.1	10.6
MSA[1]	92.3	93.4	87.4	88.7	76.7	28.5	29.8	12.8	56.9	13.6
U.S.	87.7	89.6	85.4	86.8	67.7	31.5	32.9	21.1	53.5	15.8

Note: Figures shown cover persons 25 years old and over; (1) Figures cover the Topeka, KS Metropolitan Statistical Area—see Appendix B for areas included; (2) People of Hispanic origin can be of any race
Source: U.S. Census Bureau, 2014-2018 American Community Survey 5-Year Estimates

School Enrollment by Grade and Control

Area	Preschool (%) Public	Private	Kindergarten (%) Public	Private	Grades 1 - 4 (%) Public	Private	Grades 5 - 8 (%) Public	Private	Grades 9 - 12 (%) Public	Private
City	69.1	30.9	93.6	6.4	88.9	11.1	89.2	10.8	92.7	7.3
MSA[1]	73.7	26.3	91.7	8.3	89.3	10.7	89.4	10.6	91.9	8.1
U.S.	59.0	41.0	87.7	12.3	89.6	10.4	89.5	10.5	90.2	9.8

Note: Figures shown cover persons 3 years old and over; (1) Figures cover the Topeka, KS Metropolitan Statistical Area—see Appendix B for areas included
Source: U.S. Census Bureau, 2014-2018 American Community Survey 5-Year Estimates

Average Salaries of Public School Teachers

Area	2016-17 Dollars	Rank[1]	2017-18 Dollars	Rank[1]	Change from 2016-17 to 2017-18 Percent	Rank[2]
Kansas	49,422	40	49,754	41	0.67	36
U.S. Average	59,539	–	60,477	–	1.58	–

Note: (1) Rank ranges from 1 to 51 where 1 indicates highest salary; (2) Rank ranges from 1 to 51 where 1 indicates highest percent change.
Source: National Education Association, Rankings & Estimates: Rankings of the States 2018 and Estimates of School Statistics 2019

Higher Education

Four-Year Colleges Public	Private Non-profit	Private For-profit	Two-Year Colleges Public	Private Non-profit	Private For-profit	Medical Schools[1]	Law Schools[2]	Voc/ Tech[3]
1	0	1	0	0	1	0	1	1

Note: Figures cover institutions located within the city limits and include main campuses only; (1) includes schools accredited by the Liaison Committee on Medical Education and the American Osteopathic Association's Commission on Osteopathic College Accreditation; (2) includes ABA-accredited schools, schools with provisional ABA accreditation, and state accredited schools; (3) includes all schools with programs that are less than 2 years.
Source: National Center for Education Statistics, Integrated Postsecondary Education System (IPEDS), 2018-19; Wikipedia, List of Medical Schools in the United States, accessed May 1, 2020; Wikipedia, List of Law Schools in the United States, accessed May 1, 2020

PRESIDENTIAL ELECTION

2016 Presidential Election Results

Area	Clinton	Trump	Johnson	Stein	Other
Shawnee County	44.2	46.8	4.4	2.3	2.3
U.S.	48.0	45.9	3.3	1.1	1.7

Note: Results are percentages and may not add to 100% due to rounding
Source: Dave Leip's Atlas of U.S. Presidential Elections

EMPLOYERS

Major Employers

Company Name	Industry
Auburn Washburn USD 437	Education
BlueCross BlueShield of Kansas	Healthcare
BNSF Railway Company	Transportation
City of Topeka	Government
Dillon Stores	Retail
Frito-Lay	Manufacturing & distribution
Goodyear Tire and Rubber Company	Manufacturing & distribution
Hill's Pet Nutrition	Retail
Joint Force Hdqrtrs/KS Army Natl Guard	U.S. military
Midwest Health Management	Healthcare
Payless ShoeSource	Retail
Reser's Fine Foods	Manufacturing & distribution
Seaman USD 345	Education
Security Benefit	Insurance & financial
Shawnee County Government	Government
Shawnee Heights USD 450	Education
St. Francis Health Care	Healthcare
State of Kansas	State government
Stormont-Vail HealthCare	Healthcare
Target Distribution Center	Manufacturing & distribution
Topeka USD 501	Education
United States Government	Federal government
Wal-Mart and Sam's Club	Retail
Washburn University	Education
Westar Energy	Utility

Note: Companies shown are located within the Topeka, KS Metropolitan Statistical Area.
Source: Hoovers.com; Wikipedia

PUBLIC SAFETY

Crime Rate

Area	All Crimes	Violent Crimes				Property Crimes		
		Murder	Rape[3]	Robbery	Aggrav. Assault	Burglary	Larceny-Theft	Motor Vehicle Theft
City	5,795.9	11.1	66.5	201.0	327.5	769.8	3,837.8	582.3
Suburbs[1]	1,961.5	7.6	31.2	10.4	198.5	375.3	1,161.8	176.8
Metro[2]	4,049.0	9.5	50.4	114.1	268.8	590.1	2,618.6	397.5
U.S.	2,580.1	5.0	42.6	86.2	246.8	376.0	1,594.6	228.9

Note: Figures are crimes per 100,000 population; (1) All areas within the metro area that are located outside the city limits; (2) Figures cover the Topeka, KS Metropolitan Statistical Area—see Appendix B for areas included; (3) The city and U.S. figures shown were reported using the revised Uniform Crime Reporting (UCR) definition of rape. The suburban and metro area figures shown are an aggregate total of the data submitted using both the revised and legacy UCR definitions.
Source: FBI Uniform Crime Reports, 2018

Hate Crimes

Area	Number of Quarters Reported	Number of Incidents per Bias Motivation					
		Race/Ethnicity/Ancestry	Religion	Sexual Orientation	Disability	Gender	Gender Identity
City	4	2	1	0	0	0	0
U.S.	4	4,047	1,419	1,196	159	47	168

Source: Federal Bureau of Investigation, Hate Crime Statistics 2018

Identity Theft Consumer Reports

Area	Reports	Reports per 100,000 Population	Rank[2]
MSA[1]	180	77	263
U.S.	650,572	198	-

Note: (1) Figures cover the Topeka, KS Metropolitan Statistical Area—see Appendix B for areas included; (2) Rank ranges from 1 to 386 where 1 indicates greatest number of identity theft reports per 100,000 population
Source: Federal Trade Commission, Consumer Sentinel Network Data Book for January–December 2019

Fraud and Other Consumer Reports

Area	Reports	Reports per 100,000 Population	Rank[2]
MSA[1]	1,492	641	81
U.S.	2,590,177	789	-

Note: (1) Figures cover the Topeka, KS Metropolitan Statistical Area—see Appendix B for areas included; (2) Rank ranges from 1 to 386 where 1 indicates greatest number of fraud and other consumer reports per 100,000 population
Source: Federal Trade Commission, Consumer Sentinel Network Data Book for January–December 2019

SPORTS

Professional Sports Teams

Team Name	League	Year Established
No teams are located in the metro area		

Source: Wikipedia, Major Professional Sports Teams of the United States and Canada, May 4, 2020

CLIMATE

Average and Extreme Temperatures

Temperature	Jan	Feb	Mar	Apr	May	Jun	Jul	Aug	Sep	Oct	Nov	Dec	Yr.
Extreme High (°F)	73	80	89	95	97	107	110	110	104	96	85	73	110
Average High (°F)	37	43	54	67	76	85	89	88	81	70	54	41	66
Average Temp. (°F)	27	33	43	55	65	74	79	77	69	57	43	32	55
Average Low (°F)	17	22	31	43	53	63	67	65	56	44	32	21	43
Extreme Low (°F)	-20	-23	-7	10	26	42	43	41	29	19	2	-26	-26

Note: Figures cover the years 1948-1990
Source: National Climatic Data Center, International Station Meteorological Climate Summary, 9/96

Average Precipitation/Snowfall/Humidity

Precip./Humidity	Jan	Feb	Mar	Apr	May	Jun	Jul	Aug	Sep	Oct	Nov	Dec	Yr.
Avg. Precip. (in.)	1.0	1.1	2.4	3.0	4.3	5.3	4.1	3.9	3.4	2.9	1.7	1.3	34.4
Avg. Snowfall (in.)	6	5	4	1	0	0	0	0	0	Tr	1	5	21
Avg. Rel. Hum. 6am (%)	77	79	79	79	84	86	86	87	87	83	80	80	82
Avg. Rel. Hum. 3pm (%)	58	57	51	48	52	54	53	52	50	47	51	58	53

Note: Figures cover the years 1948-1990; Tr = Trace amounts (<0.05 in. of rain; <0.5 in. of snow)
Source: National Climatic Data Center, International Station Meteorological Climate Summary, 9/96

Weather Conditions

Temperature			Daytime Sky			Precipitation		
10°F & below	32°F & below	90°F & above	Clear	Partly cloudy	Cloudy	0.01 inch or more precip.	0.1 inch or more snow/ice	Thunder-storms
20	123	45	111	127	127	96	15	54

Note: Figures are average number of days per year and cover the years 1948-1990
Source: National Climatic Data Center, International Station Meteorological Climate Summary, 9/96

HAZARDOUS WASTE

Superfund Sites

The Topeka, KS metro area has no sites on the EPA's Superfund Final National Priorities List.
There are a total of 1,387 Superfund sites with a status of proposed or final on the list in the U.S.
U.S. Environmental Protection Agency, National Priorities List, May 5, 2020

**AIR & WATER
QUALITY**

Air Quality Trends: Ozone

	1990	1995	2000	2005	2010	2012	2014	2016	2017	2018
MSA[1]	n/a	n/a	n/a	n/a	n/a	n/a	n/a	n/a	n/a	n/a
U.S.	0.088	0.089	0.082	0.080	0.073	0.075	0.067	0.069	0.068	0.069

*Note: (1) Data covers the Topeka, KS Metropolitan Statistical Area—see Appendix B for areas included; n/a not available. The values shown are the composite ozone concentration averages among trend sites based on the highest fourth daily maximum 8-hour concentration in parts per million. These trends are based on sites having an adequate record of monitoring data during the trend period. Data from exceptional events are included.
Source: U.S. Environmental Protection Agency, Air Quality Monitoring Information, "Air Quality Trends by City, 1990-2018"*

Air Quality Index

Area	Percent of Days when Air Quality was...[2]					AQI Statistics[2]	
	Good	Moderate	Unhealthy for Sensitive Groups	Unhealthy	Very Unhealthy	Maximum	Median
MSA[1]	74.5	25.5	0.0	0.0	0.0	99	42

*Note: (1) Data covers the Topeka, KS Metropolitan Statistical Area—see Appendix B for areas included; (2) Based on 365 days with AQI data in 2018. Air Quality Index (AQI) is an index for reporting daily air quality. EPA calculates the AQI for five major air pollutants regulated by the Clean Air Act: ground-level ozone, particle pollution (aka particulate matter), carbon monoxide, sulfur dioxide, and nitrogen dioxide. The AQI runs from 0 to 500. The higher the AQI value, the greater the level of air pollution and the greater the health concern. There are six AQI categories: "Good" AQI is between 0 and 50. Air quality is considered satisfactory; "Moderate" AQI is between 51 and 100. Air quality is acceptable; "Unhealthy for Sensitive Groups" When AQI values are between 101 and 150, members of sensitive groups may experience health effects; "Unhealthy" When AQI values are between 151 and 200 everyone may begin to experience health effects; "Very Unhealthy" AQI values between 201 and 300 trigger a health alert; "Hazardous" AQI values over 300 trigger warnings of emergency conditions (not shown).
Source: U.S. Environmental Protection Agency, Air Quality Index Report, 2018*

Air Quality Index Pollutants

Area	Percent of Days when AQI Pollutant was...[2]					
	Carbon Monoxide	Nitrogen Dioxide	Ozone	Sulfur Dioxide	Particulate Matter 2.5	Particulate Matter 10
MSA[1]	0.0	0.0	49.6	0.0	50.4	0.0

*Note: (1) Data covers the Topeka, KS Metropolitan Statistical Area—see Appendix B for areas included; (2) Based on 365 days with AQI data in 2018. The Air Quality Index (AQI) is an index for reporting daily air quality. EPA calculates the AQI for five major air pollutants regulated by the Clean Air Act: ground-level ozone, particle pollution (also known as particulate matter), carbon monoxide, sulfur dioxide, and nitrogen dioxide. The AQI runs from 0 to 500. The higher the AQI value, the greater the level of air pollution and the greater the health concern.
Source: U.S. Environmental Protection Agency, Air Quality Index Report, 2018*

Maximum Air Pollutant Concentrations: Particulate Matter, Ozone, CO and Lead

	Particulate Matter 10 (ug/m^3)	Particulate Matter 2.5 Wtd AM (ug/m^3)	Particulate Matter 2.5 24-Hr (ug/m^3)	Ozone (ppm)	Carbon Monoxide (ppm)	Lead (ug/m^3)
MSA[1] Level	61	9.7	25	0.062	n/a	n/a
NAAQS[2]	150	15	35	0.075	9	0.15
Met NAAQS[2]	Yes	Yes	Yes	Yes	n/a	n/a

*Note: (1) Data covers the Topeka, KS Metropolitan Statistical Area—see Appendix B for areas included; Data from exceptional events are included; (2) National Ambient Air Quality Standards; ppm = parts per million; ug/m^3 = micrograms per cubic meter; n/a not available.
Concentrations: Particulate Matter 10 (coarse particulate)—highest second maximum 24-hour concentration; Particulate Matter 2.5 Wtd AM (fine particulate)—highest weighted annual mean concentration; Particulate Matter 2.5 24-Hour (fine particulate)—highest 98th percentile 24-hour concentration; Ozone—highest fourth daily maximum 8-hour concentration; Carbon Monoxide—highest second maximum non-overlapping 8-hour concentration; Lead—maximum running 3-month average
Source: U.S. Environmental Protection Agency, Air Quality Monitoring Information, "Air Quality Statistics by City, 2018"*

Maximum Air Pollutant Concentrations: Nitrogen Dioxide and Sulfur Dioxide

	Nitrogen Dioxide AM (ppb)	Nitrogen Dioxide 1-Hr (ppb)	Sulfur Dioxide AM (ppb)	Sulfur Dioxide 1-Hr (ppb)	Sulfur Dioxide 24-Hr (ppb)
MSA[1] Level	n/a	n/a	n/a	n/a	n/a
NAAQS[2]	53	100	30	75	140
Met NAAQS[2]	n/a	n/a	n/a	n/a	n/a

Note: (1) Data covers the Topeka, KS Metropolitan Statistical Area—see Appendix B for areas included; Data from exceptional events are included; (2) National Ambient Air Quality Standards; ppm = parts per million; ug/m^3 = micrograms per cubic meter; n/a not available.
Concentrations: Nitrogen Dioxide AM—highest arithmetic mean concentration; Nitrogen Dioxide 1-Hr—highest 98th percentile 1-hour daily maximum concentration; Sulfur Dioxide AM—highest annual mean concentration; Sulfur Dioxide 1-Hr—highest 99th percentile 1-hour daily maximum concentration; Sulfur Dioxide 24-Hr—highest second maximum 24-hour concentration
Source: U.S. Environmental Protection Agency, Air Quality Monitoring Information, "Air Quality Statistics by City, 2018"

Drinking Water

Water System Name	Pop. Served	Primary Water Source Type	Violations[1]
City of Topeka	125,904	Surface	3

Note: (1) Total number of violations (both active and inactive) in the EPA database
Source: U.S. Environmental Protection Agency, Office of Ground Water and Drinking Water, Safe Drinking Water Information System (based on data extracted May 5, 2020)

Tulsa, Oklahoma

Background

The city of Tulsa stands at the intersection of Tulsa, Osage, Rogers, and Wagoner counties, in the northeast part of Oklahoma. Located on the Arkansas River, Tulsa sits between the Osage Hills and the foothills of the Ozark Mountains.

Tulsa was first settled by Creek Indians in 1828. In 1848, Lewis Perryman established the first trading post at the new settlement, and his son George, in 1878, developed a regular mail station at the site, which then came to be called Tulsa, probably from the Talsi or Talasi branch of the Creek Tribe.

Originally a cattle and dry goods trading center drawing attention from ranchers scattered throughout the area, Tulsa was integrated into a wider trade area in 1882, when the Frisco Railroad brought a line into the town. This facilitated a movement of new settlers into the area, and allowed "Tulsey Town" to transport cattle to the stockyards of St. Louis and Chicago and, thus, throughout the nation. The importance of the rail system can still be seen in the layout of Tulsa's downtown streets, which are aligned parallel and perpendicular to the tracks. Tulsa was incorporated as a town on January 18, 1898.

Oil was first discovered in the area in 1901 at Red Fork. In 1905, a huge strike—the world's largest at the time—was made at Glenn Pool. Since then, Tulsa's fortune has been tied to the oil industry. Oklahoma achieved statehood two years after the Glenn Pool strike, and by 1920 the city was already well-known as the "Oil Capital of the World." During this boom period, many of Tulsa's historic buildings were constructed, which explains the city's extraordinary art deco flavor in its downtown architecture. The great influx of wealthy easterners and the construction they financed left parts of the city resembling places in New York and Philadelphia.

Oil naturally fueled the growth of aviation, and Tulsa was an early center for the development of this industry. By the beginning of the Second World War, many of the nation's pilots were being trained at Spartan School of Aeronautics in the city, and Douglas Aircraft in 1942 sited a major plant there. In later years, both McDonnell-Douglas and Rockwell International based aviation and space technology operations in Tulsa.

Today, Tulsa is home to American Airlines' Maintenance & Engineering Center, one of the world's largest such commercial centers. The city is also home to a division of Lufthansa, the headquarters of Omni Air International, the Spartan School of Aeronautics, BOK Financial Corporation, the Marshall Brewing Company, Laredo Petroleum, Samson Resources, WPX Energy, and Excel Energy. The city has more than 20,000 energy jobs in a wide range of companies and specialties.

The city's location in the center of the nation makes it a hub for logistics businesses, with its busy Tulsa International Airport and Tulsa Port of Catoosa. The port is a 445-mile navigation system that links Tulsa to the Mississippi, makes Tulsa a major inland ice-free port, with a designated foreign trade zone, a 2,000-acre industrial park, and vast cargo facilities. Tulsa is also part of the Oklahoma-South Kansas Unmanned Aerial Systems (drone) industry cluster, and has received federal funding to continue its progress as a hub in this emerging industry.

The city hosts a broad range of cultural and recreational activities, including the Gilcrease Museum, holder of the world's largest collection of art and artifacts of the American West, and the Philbrook Museum of Art. Many cultural activities are sponsored by the city's several universities, including a branch of Oklahoma State University.

The city is host to the Tulsa Rose Gardens, the Municipal Rose Gardens—built by the Works Progress Administration and opened in 1934—and the Tulsa Zoo. As a result of compacts between the state of Oklahoma and various Native American tribes, tribal gaming facilities offer table card games and slot machines.

The city's Cox Business Convention Center houses facilities ranging from an assembly hall to the state's largest ballroom to 34 meeting rooms. The BOK (Bank of Oklahoma) Center is a multi-purpose arena that plays host to the Tulsa Oilers ice hockey team. The minor league baseball team, the Tulsa Drillers, play in ONEOK Field, as do the Tulsa Roughnecks FC, a men's soccer team. The University of Tulsa's men's basketball team, the Golden Hurricane, are a highly competitive program as, to a lesser degree, is Oral Roberts University's men's basketball team, the Golden Eagles.

Tulsa's weather is continental and generally mild, with unpredictable amounts of precipitation. Winters for the region bordering on the Great Plains are comparatively short and mild.

Rankings

General Rankings

- In their sixth annual survey, Livability.com looked at data for more than 1,000 U.S. cities to determine the rankings for Livability's "Top 100 Best Places to Live" in 2019. Tulsa ranked #66. Criteria: median home value capped at $250,000; affordable living; vibrant economy; education, demographics, health care options. transportation & infrastructure; abundant lifestyle amenities. *Livability.com, "Top 100 Best Places to Live 2019" March 2019*

Business/Finance Rankings

- Tulsa was the #5-ranked city for savers, according to a study by the finance site GOBankingRates, which considered the prospects for people trying to save money. Criteria: average monthly cost of grocery items; median home listing price; median rent; median income; transportation costs; gas prices; and the cost of eating out for an inexpensive and mid-range meal in 100 U.S. cities. *www.gobankingrates.com, "The 20 Best (and Worst) Places to Live If You're Trying to Save Money," August 27, 2019*

- Tulsa was ranked #5 among 100 U.S. cities for most difficult conditions for savers, according to a study by the finance site GOBankingRates. Criteria: average monthly cost of grocery items; median home listing price; median rent; median income; transportation costs; gas prices; and the cost of eating out for an inexpensive and mid-range meal. *www.gobankingrates.com, "The 20 Best (and Worst) Places to Live If You're Trying to Save Money," August 27, 2019*

- Recognizing the sizeable percentage of American workers who are self-employed, NerdWallet editors assessed the country's cities according to percentage of freelancers, median rental costs, cell phone plans/taxes, and healthcare affordability and access. By these criteria, Tulsa placed #18 among the best cities for independent workers. *www.nerdwallet.com, "Best Places for Freelance Workers," August 30, 2016*

- The Brookings Institution ranked the nation's largest cities based on income inequality. Tulsa was ranked #42 (#1 = greatest inequality). Criteria: the "95/20 ratio," a figure representing the income at which a household earns more than 95 percent of all other households, divided by the income at which a household earns more than only 20 percent of all other households. *Brookings Institution, "Household Income Inequality, Largest Cities of 97 Large U.S. Metro Areas, 2014-2016," February 5, 2018*

- The Brookings Institution ranked the 100 largest metro areas in the U.S. based on income inequality. Tulsa was ranked #44 (#1 = greatest inequality). Criteria: the "95/20 ratio," a figure representing the income at which a household earns more than 95 percent of all other households, divided by the income at which a household earns more than only 20 percent of all other households. *Brookings Institution, "Household Income Inequality, 100 Largest U.S. Metro Areas, 2014-2016," February 5, 2018*

- The Tulsa metro area appeared on the Milken Institute "2020 Best Performing Cities" list. Rank: #151 out of 200 large metro areas. Criteria: job growth; wage and salary growth; high-tech output growth. *Milken Institute, "Best-Performing Cities 2020," February 26, 2020*

- *Forbes* ranked the 200 most populous metro areas to determine the nation's "Best Places for Business and Careers." The Tulsa metro area was ranked #120. Criteria: costs (business and living); job growth (past and projected); income growth; quality of life; educational attainment (college and high school); projected economic growth; cultural and leisure opportunities; workplace tolerance laws; net migration patterns. *Forbes, "The Best Places for Business and Careers 2019: Seattle Still On Top," October 30, 2019*

Dating/Romance Rankings

- Tulsa was ranked #24 out of 25 cities that stood out for inspiring romance and attracting diners on the website OpenTable.com. Criteria: percentage of people who dined out on Valentine's Day in 2018; percentage of romantic restaurants as rated by OpenTable diner reviews; and percentage of tables seated for two. *OpenTable, "25 Most Romantic Cities in America for 2019," February 7, 2019*

Education Rankings

- Personal finance website *WalletHub* analyzed the 150 largest U.S. metropolitan statistical areas to determine where the most educated Americans are choosing to settle. Criteria: education levels; percentage of workers with degrees; education quality and attainment gap; public school quality rankings; quality and size of each metro area's universities. Tulsa was ranked #109 (#1 = most educated city). *www.WalletHub.com, "2019's Most and Least Educated Cities in America, " July 22, 2019*

- Tulsa was selected as one of America's most literate cities. The city ranked #25 out of the 82 largest U.S. cities. Criteria: number of booksellers; library resources; Internet resources; educational attainment; periodical publishing resources; newspaper circulation. *Central Connecticut State University, "America's Most Literate Cities, 2016," March 31, 2017*

Food/Drink Rankings

- Tulsa was selected as one of America's 10 most vegan-friendly cities. The city was ranked #10. *People for the Ethical Treatment of Animals, "Top 10 Vegan-Friendly Cities of 2019," November 15, 2019*

Health/Fitness Rankings

- For each of the 100 largest cities in the United States, the American Fitness Index®, published by the American College of Sports Medicine and the Anthem Foundation, evaluated community infrastructure and 33 health behaviors including preventive health, levels of chronic disease conditions, pedestrian safety, air quality, and community resources that support physical activity. Tulsa ranked #98 for "community fitness." *americanfitnessindex.org, "ACSM American Fitness Index Health and Community Fitness Status of the 100 Largest U.S. Cities," May 14, 2019*

- Tulsa was identified as a "2020 Spring Allergy Capital." The area ranked #22 out of 100. Three groups of factors were used to identify the most challenging cities for people with allergies during the spring season: annual spring pollen levels; over the counter medicine use; number of board-certified allergy specialists. *Asthma and Allergy Foundation of America, "Spring Allergy Capitals 2020," March 10, 2020*

- Tulsa was identified as a "2020 Fall Allergy Capital." The area ranked #21 out of 100. Three groups of factors were used to identify the most challenging cities for people with allergies during the fall season: annual fall pollen levels; over the counter medicine use; number of board-certified allergy specialists. *Asthma and Allergy Foundation of America, "Fall Allergy Capitals 2020," March 10, 2020*

- Tulsa was identified as a "2019 Asthma Capital." The area ranked #37 out of the nation's 100 largest metropolitan areas. Criteria: estimated asthma prevalence; crude death rate from asthma; and ER visits due to asthma. Risk factors that were analyzed but not factored in the rankings: annual pollen score; annual air quality; public smoking laws; number of board-certified asthma specialists; rescue medication use; controller medication use; uninsured rate; poverty rate. *Asthma and Allergy Foundation of America, "Asthma Capitals 2019: The Most Challenging Places to Live With Asthma," May 7, 2019*

- *Men's Health* ranked 100 major U.S. cities in terms of the best cities for men. Tulsa ranked #87. Criteria: health; fitness; quality of life. *Men's Health, "The Best & Worst Cities for Men Who Want to Be Fit and Happy," January 1, 2016*

- The Tulsa metro area ranked #175 out of 189 in The Gallup-Sharecare Well-Being Index. Criteria: purpose; social well being; financial health; community and physical health. Results are based on telephone interviews with adults, aged 18 and older, living in metropolitan areas in the 50 U.S. states and the District of Columbia. *Gallup-Sharecare, "State of American Well-Being, 2017 Community Well-Being Rankings" March 2018*

Real Estate Rankings

- *WalletHub* compared the most populated U.S. cities, as well as at least two of the most populated cities in each state, for a total of 179, to determine which had the best markets for real estate agents. Tulsa ranked #158 where demand was high and pay was the best. Criteria: sales per agent; annual median wage for real-estate agents; monthly average starting salary for real estate agents; real estate job density and competition; unemployment rate; home turnover rate; housing-market health index; and other relevant metrics. *www.WalletHub.com, "2019's Best Places to Be a Real Estate Agent," April 24, 2019*

- Tulsa was ranked #79 out of 238 metro areas in terms of housing affordability in 2019 by the National Association of Home Builders (#1 = most affordable). Criteria: the share of homes sold in that area affordable to a family earning the local median income, based on standard mortgage underwriting criteria. *National Association of Home Builders®, NAHB-Wells Fargo Housing Opportunity Index, 4th Quarter 2019*

Safety Rankings

- To identify the most dangerous cities in America, 24/7 Wall Street focused on violent crime categories—murder, non-negligent manslaughter, rape, robbery, and aggravated assault—and property crime as reported in the FBI's 2018 annual Uniform Crime Report. Criteria also included median income from American Community Survey and unemployment figures from Bureau of Labor Statistics. For cities with populations over 100,000, Tulsa was ranked #23. *247wallst.com, "America's Most Dangerous Cities" January 10, 2020*

- Statistics drawn from the FBI's Uniform Crime Report were used to rank the metropolitan statistical areas in each state where violent crime rose most over the years 2012–2017. 24/7 Wall Street found that the Tulsa metro area placed #36 of those with the largest increases in violent crime. *247wallst.com, "Cities Where Crime Is Soaring In Every State," January 11, 2020*

- Allstate ranked the 200 largest cities in America in terms of driver safety. Tulsa ranked #51. Criteria: internal property damage claims over a two-year period from January 2016 to December 2017. The report helps increase the importance of safety and awareness behind the wheel. *Allstate, "Allstate America's Best Drivers Report, 2019" June 24, 2019*

- Tulsa was identified as one of the most dangerous cities in America by NeighborhoodScout. The city ranked #50 out of 100 (#1 = most dangerous). Criteria: number of violent crimes per 1,000 residents. The editors only considered cities with 25,000 or more residents. *NeighborhoodScout.com, "Top 100 Most Dangerous Cities in the U.S. 2020" January 2, 2020*

- The National Insurance Crime Bureau ranked 382 metro areas in the U.S. in terms of per capita rates of vehicle theft. The Tulsa metro area ranked #14 (#1 = highest rate). Criteria: number of vehicle theft offenses per 100,000 inhabitants in 2018. *National Insurance Crime Bureau, "Hot Spots 2018," June 25, 2019*

Seniors/Retirement Rankings

- From its Best Cities for Successful Aging indexes, the Milken Institute generated rankings for metropolitan areas, weighing data in nine categories—health care, wellness, living arrangements, transportation and convenience, financial characteristics, education, employment, community engagement, and overall livability. The Tulsa metro area was ranked #57 overall in the large metro area category. *Milken Institute, "Best Cities for Successful Aging, 2017" March 14, 2017*

Women/Minorities Rankings

- Personal finance website *WalletHub* compared more than 180 U.S. cities—including the 150 most populated U.S. cities, plus at least two of the most populated cities in each state—across two key dimensions, "Hispanic Business-Friendliness" and "Hispanic Purchasing Power", to arrive at the most favorable conditions for Hispanic entrepreneurs. Tulsa was ranked #33 out of 182. Criteria includes: share of Hispanic-Owned Businesses; Hispanic entrepreneurship rate to median annual income of Hispanics; Small Business-Friendliness score; cost of living; and number of Hispanics with at least a bachelor's degree. *WalletHub.com, "2019's Best Cities for Hispanic Entrepreneurs," May 1, 2019*

Miscellaneous Rankings

- *WalletHub* compared the 150 most populated U.S. cities to determine their operating efficiency. A "Quality of Services" score was constructed for each city and then divided by the total budget per capita to reveal which were managed the best. Tulsa ranked #45. Criteria: financial stability; economy; education; safety; health; infrastructure and pollution. *www.WalletHub.com, "2019's Best- & Worst-Run Cities in America," July 1, 2019*

Business Environment

CITY FINANCES

City Government Finances

Component	2017 ($000)	2017 ($ per capita)
Total Revenues	993,265	2,462
Total Expenditures	905,909	2,245
Debt Outstanding	1,412,149	3,500
Cash and Securities[1]	1,669,350	4,137

Note: (1) Cash and security holdings of a government at the close of its fiscal year, including those of its dependent agencies, utilities, and liquor stores.
Source: U.S. Census Bureau, State & Local Government Finances 2017

City Government Revenue by Source

Source	2017 ($000)	2017 ($ per capita)	2017 (%)
General Revenue			
From Federal Government	40,963	102	4.1
From State Government	7,495	19	0.8
From Local Governments	25,712	64	2.6
Taxes			
Property	73,800	183	7.4
Sales and Gross Receipts	306,930	761	30.9
Personal Income	0	0	0.0
Corporate Income	0	0	0.0
Motor Vehicle License	0	0	0.0
Other Taxes	8,111	20	0.8
Current Charges	278,642	691	28.1
Liquor Store	0	0	0.0
Utility	129,580	321	13.0
Employee Retirement	42,600	106	4.3

Source: U.S. Census Bureau, State & Local Government Finances 2017

City Government Expenditures by Function

Function	2017 ($000)	2017 ($ per capita)	2017 (%)
General Direct Expenditures			
Air Transportation	41,298	102	4.6
Corrections	0	0	0.0
Education	0	0	0.0
Employment Security Administration	0	0	0.0
Financial Administration	10,473	26	1.2
Fire Protection	72,064	178	8.0
General Public Buildings	0	0	0.0
Governmental Administration, Other	16,218	40	1.8
Health	76,482	189	8.4
Highways	121,060	300	13.4
Hospitals	0	0	0.0
Housing and Community Development	7,114	17	0.8
Interest on General Debt	34,077	84	3.8
Judicial and Legal	6,196	15	0.7
Libraries	20,179	50	2.2
Parking	3,811	9	0.4
Parks and Recreation	40,798	101	4.5
Police Protection	104,702	259	11.6
Public Welfare	17,689	43	2.0
Sewerage	101,124	250	11.2
Solid Waste Management	23,493	58	2.6
Veterans' Services	0	0	0.0
Liquor Store	0	0	0.0
Utility	149,817	371	16.5
Employee Retirement	35,167	87	3.9

Source: U.S. Census Bureau, State & Local Government Finances 2017

DEMOGRAPHICS

Population Growth

Area	1990 Census	2000 Census	2010 Census	2018* Estimate	Population Growth (%)	
					1990-2018	2010-2018
City	367,241	393,049	391,906	402,223	9.5	2.6
MSA[1]	761,019	859,532	937,478	985,233	29.5	5.1
U.S.	248,709,873	281,421,906	308,745,538	322,903,030	29.8	4.6

Note: (1) Figures cover the Tulsa, OK Metropolitan Statistical Area—see Appendix B for areas included; (*) 2014-2018 5-year estimated population
Source: U.S. Census Bureau, 1990 Census, Census 2000, Census 2010, 2014-2018 American Community Survey 5-Year Estimates

Household Size

Area	Persons in Household (%)							Average Household Size
	One	Two	Three	Four	Five	Six	Seven or More	
City	35.2	32.5	13.6	10.1	5.3	2.1	1.2	2.40
MSA[1]	28.2	34.6	15.2	12.2	6.1	2.4	1.3	2.60
U.S.	27.7	33.9	15.7	13.0	6.0	2.3	1.4	2.60

Note: (1) Figures cover the Tulsa, OK Metropolitan Statistical Area—see Appendix B for areas included
Source: U.S. Census Bureau, 2014-2018 American Community Survey 5-Year Estimates

Race

Area	White Alone[2] (%)	Black Alone[2] (%)	Asian Alone[2] (%)	AIAN[3] Alone[2] (%)	NHOPI[4] Alone[2] (%)	Other Race Alone[2] (%)	Two or More Races (%)
City	64.0	15.3	3.3	4.4	0.1	5.3	7.6
MSA[1]	71.3	8.0	2.4	7.2	0.1	2.8	8.2
U.S.	72.7	12.7	5.4	0.8	0.2	4.9	3.2

Note: (1) Figures cover the Tulsa, OK Metropolitan Statistical Area—see Appendix B for areas included; (2) Alone is defined as not being in combination with one or more other races; (3) American Indian and Alaska Native; (4) Native Hawaiian and Other Pacific Islander
Source: U.S. Census Bureau, 2014-2018 American Community Survey 5-Year Estimates

Hispanic or Latino Origin

Area	Total (%)	Mexican (%)	Puerto Rican (%)	Cuban (%)	Other (%)
City	16.3	13.2	0.5	0.2	2.4
MSA[1]	9.7	7.7	0.4	0.1	1.5
U.S.	17.8	11.2	1.7	0.7	4.2

Note: Persons of Hispanic or Latino origin can be of any race; (1) Figures cover the Tulsa, OK Metropolitan Statistical Area—see Appendix B for areas included
Source: U.S. Census Bureau, 2014-2018 American Community Survey 5-Year Estimates

Segregation

Type	Segregation Indices[1]				Percent Change		
	1990	2000	2010	2010 Rank[2]	1990-2000	1990-2010	2000-2010
Black/White	61.4	58.3	56.6	47	-3.1	-4.8	-1.7
Asian/White	43.6	45.6	42.6	40	2.0	-1.1	-3.1
Hispanic/White	25.2	40.0	45.3	45	14.8	20.1	5.3

Note: All figures cover the Metropolitan Statistical Area—see Appendix B for areas included; Figures are based on an analysis of 1990, 2000, and 2010 Census Decennial Census tract data by William H. Frey, Brookings Institution and the University of Michigan Social Science Data Analysis Network. In this analysis all racial groups (whites, blacks, and asians) are non-Hispanic members of those races. Hispanics are shown as a separate category; (1) Segregation Indices are Dissimilarity Indices that measure the degree to which the minority group is distributed differently than whites across census tracts. They range from 0 (complete integration) to 100 (complete segregation) where the value indicates the percentage of the minority group that needs to move to be distributed exactly like whites; (2) Ranges from 1 (most segregated) to 102 (least segregated); n/a not available.
Source: www.CensusScope.org

Ancestry

Area	German	Irish	English	American	Italian	Polish	French[2]	Scottish	Dutch
City	11.7	9.4	7.4	6.7	2.1	1.0	2.2	2.0	1.1
MSA[1]	13.7	10.9	7.9	7.4	2.0	1.0	2.3	2.0	1.4
U.S.	13.7	9.9	7.3	6.4	5.2	2.8	2.4	1.7	1.2

Note: Figures are the percentage of the total population reporting a particular ancestry. The nine most commonly reported ancestries in the U.S. are shown. Figures include multiple ancestries (e.g. if a person reported being Irish and Italian, they were included in both columns); (1) Figures cover the Tulsa, OK Metropolitan Statistical Area—see Appendix B for areas included; (2) Excludes Basque
Source: U.S. Census Bureau, 2014-2018 American Community Survey 5-Year Estimates

Foreign-born Population

Area	Percent of Population Born in								
	Any Foreign Country	Asia	Mexico	Europe	Caribbean	Central America[2]	South America	Africa	Canada
City	11.1	2.7	5.7	0.6	0.2	0.9	0.4	0.4	0.1
MSA[1]	6.5	1.8	2.9	0.5	0.1	0.5	0.3	0.3	0.1
U.S.	13.5	4.1	3.5	1.5	1.3	1.1	0.9	0.7	0.3

Note: (1) Figures cover the Tulsa, OK Metropolitan Statistical Area—see Appendix B for areas included; (2) Excludes Mexico.
Source: U.S. Census Bureau, 2014-2018 American Community Survey 5-Year Estimates

Marital Status

Area	Never Married	Now Married[2]	Separated	Widowed	Divorced
City	34.2	42.6	2.5	5.9	14.9
MSA[1]	28.1	50.5	2.0	6.1	13.3
U.S.	33.3	48.1	2.0	5.8	10.8

Note: Figures are percentages and cover the population 15 years of age and older; (1) Figures cover the Tulsa, OK Metropolitan Statistical Area—see Appendix B for areas included; (2) Excludes separated
Source: U.S. Census Bureau, 2014-2018 American Community Survey 5-Year Estimates

Disability by Age

Area	All Ages	Under 18 Years Old	18 to 64 Years Old	65 Years and Over
City	14.8	4.9	13.8	37.7
MSA[1]	14.6	4.7	13.0	38.4
U.S.	12.6	4.2	10.3	35.0

Note: Figures show percent of the civilian noninstitutionalized population that reported having a disability. Disability status is determined from six types of difficulty: vision, hearing, cognitive, ambulatory, self-care, and independent living. For children under 5 years old, hearing and vision difficulty are used to determine disability status. For children between the ages of 5 and 14, disability status is determined from hearing, vision, cognitive, ambulatory, and self-care difficulties. For people aged 15 years and older, they are considered to have a disability if they have difficulty with any one of the six difficulty types; Note: (1) Figures cover the Tulsa, OK Metropolitan Statistical Area—see Appendix B for areas included
Source: U.S. Census Bureau, 2014-2018 American Community Survey 5-Year Estimates

Age

Area	Percent of Population									Median Age
	Under Age 5	Age 5–19	Age 20–34	Age 35–44	Age 45–54	Age 55–64	Age 65–74	Age 75–84	Age 85+	
City	7.1	20.0	22.8	12.4	11.7	12.2	7.8	4.0	1.9	35.0
MSA[1]	6.8	20.5	20.2	12.6	12.6	12.6	8.6	4.4	1.7	36.9
U.S.	6.1	19.3	20.7	12.6	13.2	12.8	8.8	4.5	1.9	37.9

Note: (1) Figures cover the Tulsa, OK Metropolitan Statistical Area—see Appendix B for areas included
Source: U.S. Census Bureau, 2014-2018 American Community Survey 5-Year Estimates

Gender

Area	Males	Females	Males per 100 Females
City	195,203	207,020	94.3
MSA[1]	483,670	501,563	96.4
U.S.	158,984,190	163,918,840	97.0

Note: (1) Figures cover the Tulsa, OK Metropolitan Statistical Area—see Appendix B for areas included
Source: U.S. Census Bureau, 2014-2018 American Community Survey 5-Year Estimates

Religious Groups by Family

Area	Catholic	Baptist	Non-Den.	Methodist[2]	Lutheran	LDS[3]	Pente-costal	Presby-terian[4]	Muslim[5]	Judaism
MSA[1]	5.8	22.9	7.6	9.2	0.8	1.2	3.3	1.3	0.3	0.3
U.S.	19.1	9.3	4.0	4.0	2.3	2.0	1.9	1.6	0.8	0.7

Note: Figures are the number of adherents as a percentage of the total population; (1) Figures cover the Tulsa, OK Metropolitan Statistical Area—see Appendix B for areas included; (2) Methodist/Pietist; (3) Latter Day Saints; (4) Reformed; (5) Figures are estimates
Source: Association of Statisticians of American Religious Bodies, 2010 U.S. Religion Census: Religious Congregations & Membership Study

Religious Groups by Tradition

Area	Catholic	Evangelical Protestant	Mainline Protestant	Other Tradition	Black Protestant	Orthodox
MSA[1]	5.8	34.6	11.3	2.2	1.6	0.1
U.S.	19.1	16.2	7.3	4.3	1.6	0.3

Note: Figures are the number of adherents as a percentage of the total population; (1) Figures cover the Tulsa, OK Metropolitan Statistical Area—see Appendix B for areas included
Source: Association of Statisticians of American Religious Bodies, 2010 U.S. Religion Census: Religious Congregations & Membership Study

ECONOMY

Gross Metropolitan Product

Area	2017	2018	2019	2020	Rank[2]
MSA[1]	57.2	60.9	63.7	67.4	55

Note: Figures are in billions of dollars; (1) Figures cover the Tulsa, OK Metropolitan Statistical Area—see Appendix B for areas included; (2) Rank is based on 2018 data and ranges from 1 to 381
Source: U.S. Conference of Mayors, U.S. Metro Economies: GMP & Employment 2018-2020, September 2019

Economic Growth

Area	2015-17 (%)	2018 (%)	2019 (%)	2020 (%)	Rank[2]
MSA[1]	-3.3	1.3	3.1	1.7	373
U.S.	1.9	2.9	2.3	2.1	—

Note: Figures are real gross metropolitan product (GMP) growth rates and represent average annual percent change; (1) Figures cover the Tulsa, OK Metropolitan Statistical Area—see Appendix B for areas included; (2) Rank is based on 2017 2-year average annual percent change and ranges from 1 to 381
Source: U.S. Conference of Mayors, U.S. Metro Economies: GMP & Employment 2018-2020, September 2019

Metropolitan Area Exports

Area	2013	2014	2015	2016	2017	2018	Rank[2]
MSA[1]	3,818.0	3,798.5	2,699.7	2,363.0	2,564.7	3,351.7	75

Note: Figures are in millions of dollars; (1) Figures cover the Tulsa, OK Metropolitan Statistical Area—see Appendix B for areas included; (2) Rank is based on 2018 data and ranges from 1 to 387
Source: U.S. Department of Commerce, International Trade Administration, Office of Trade and Economic Analysis, Industry and Analysis, Exports by Metropolitan Area, data extracted April 15, 2020

Building Permits

Area	Single-Family			Multi-Family			Total		
	2017	2018	Pct. Chg.	2017	2018	Pct. Chg.	2017	2018	Pct. Chg.
City	389	471	21.1	255	343	34.5	644	814	26.4
MSA[1]	3,160	2,845	-10.0	484	567	17.1	3,644	3,412	-6.4
U.S.	820,000	855,300	4.3	462,000	473,500	2.5	1,282,000	1,328,800	3.7

Note: (1) Figures cover the Tulsa, OK Metropolitan Statistical Area—see Appendix B for areas included; Figures represent new, privately-owned housing units authorized (unadjusted data); All permit data are based on estimates with imputation
Source: U.S. Census Bureau, Manufacturing, Mining, and Construction Statistics, Building Permits, 2017, 2018

Bankruptcy Filings

Area	Business Filings			Nonbusiness Filings		
	2018	2019	% Chg.	2018	2019	% Chg.
Tulsa County	52	44	-15.4	1,469	1,555	5.9
U.S.	22,232	22,780	2.5	751,186	752,160	0.1

Note: Business filings include Chapter 7, Chapter 9, Chapter 11, Chapter 12, Chapter 13, Chapter 15, and Section 304; Nonbusiness filings include Chapter 7, Chapter 11, and Chapter 13
Source: Administrative Office of the U.S. Courts, Business and Nonbusiness Bankruptcy, County Cases Commenced by Chapter of the Bankruptcy Code, During the 12-Month Period Ending December 31, 2018 and Business and Nonbusiness Bankruptcy, County Cases Commenced by Chapter of the Bankruptcy Code, During the 12-Month Period Ending December 31, 2019

Housing Vacancy Rates

Area	Gross Vacancy Rate[2] (%)			Year-Round Vacancy Rate[3] (%)			Rental Vacancy Rate[4] (%)			Homeowner Vacancy Rate[5] (%)		
	2017	2018	2019	2017	2018	2019	2017	2018	2019	2017	2018	2019
MSA[1]	10.2	11.7	8.4	9.8	11.6	8.0	8.5	10.1	8.5	1.9	2.6	1.6
U.S.	12.7	12.3	12.0	9.9	9.7	9.5	7.2	6.9	6.7	1.6	1.5	1.4

Note: (1) Figures cover the Tulsa, OK Metropolitan Statistical Area—see Appendix B for areas included; (2) The percentage of the total housing inventory that is vacant; (3) The percentage of the housing inventory (excluding seasonal units) that is year-round vacant; (4) The percentage of rental inventory that is vacant for rent; (5) The percentage of homeowner inventory that is vacant for sale
Source: U.S. Census Bureau, Housing Vacancies and Homeownership Annual Statistics: 2017, 2018, 2019

INCOME

Income

Area	Per Capita ($)	Median Household ($)	Average Household ($)
City	29,764	46,113	70,784
MSA[1]	29,507	54,110	74,555
U.S.	32,621	60,293	84,938

Note: (1) Figures cover the Tulsa, OK Metropolitan Statistical Area—see Appendix B for areas included
Source: U.S. Census Bureau, 2014-2018 American Community Survey 5-Year Estimates

Household Income Distribution

Area	Percent of Households Earning							
	Under $15,000	$15,000 -$24,999	$25,000 -$34,999	$35,000 -$49,999	$50,000 -$74,999	$75,000 -$99,999	$100,000 -$149,999	$150,000 and up
City	14.7	11.8	11.5	15.7	17.8	9.7	9.6	9.2
MSA[1]	11.4	10.3	10.3	14.4	18.6	12.4	12.9	9.6
U.S.	10.9	9.3	9.3	12.6	17.5	12.5	14.6	13.3

Note: (1) Figures cover the Tulsa, OK Metropolitan Statistical Area—see Appendix B for areas included
Source: U.S. Census Bureau, 2014-2018 American Community Survey 5-Year Estimates

Poverty Rate

Area	All Ages	Under 18 Years Old	18 to 64 Years Old	65 Years and Over
City	19.7	30.4	17.8	8.6
MSA[1]	14.5	21.3	13.5	7.5
U.S.	14.1	19.5	13.2	9.3

Note: Figures are percentage of people whose income during the past 12 months was below the poverty level; (1) Figures cover the Tulsa, OK Metropolitan Statistical Area—see Appendix B for areas included
Source: U.S. Census Bureau, 2014-2018 American Community Survey 5-Year Estimates

EMPLOYMENT

Labor Force and Employment

Area	Civilian Labor Force			Workers Employed		
	Dec. 2018	Dec. 2019	% Chg.	Dec. 2018	Dec. 2019	% Chg.
City	196,216	196,335	0.1	189,849	190,196	0.2
MSA[1]	480,845	481,673	0.2	465,618	466,612	0.2
U.S.	162,510,000	164,007,000	0.9	156,481,000	158,504,000	1.3

Note: Data is not seasonally adjusted and covers workers 16 years of age and older; (1) Figures cover the Tulsa, OK Metropolitan Statistical Area—see Appendix B for areas included
Source: Bureau of Labor Statistics, Local Area Unemployment Statistics

Unemployment Rate

Area	2019											
	Jan.	Feb.	Mar.	Apr.	May	Jun.	Jul.	Aug.	Sep.	Oct.	Nov.	Dec.
City	3.8	3.6	3.3	2.9	3.3	3.5	3.4	3.3	3.2	3.7	3.3	3.1
MSA[1]	3.7	3.5	3.2	2.8	3.2	3.4	3.3	3.2	3.1	3.5	3.2	3.1
U.S.	4.4	4.1	3.9	3.3	3.4	3.8	4.0	3.8	3.3	3.3	3.3	3.4

Note: Data is not seasonally adjusted and covers workers 16 years of age and older; (1) Figures cover the Tulsa, OK Metropolitan Statistical Area—see Appendix B for areas included
Source: Bureau of Labor Statistics, Local Area Unemployment Statistics

Average Wages

Occupation	$/Hr.	Occupation	$/Hr.
Accountants and Auditors	35.40	Maintenance and Repair Workers	18.10
Automotive Mechanics	19.20	Marketing Managers	62.30
Bookkeepers	20.70	Network and Computer Systems Admin.	37.40
Carpenters	21.10	Nurses, Licensed Practical	20.60
Cashiers	10.50	Nurses, Registered	31.40
Computer Programmers	38.30	Nursing Assistants	12.70
Computer Systems Analysts	37.70	Office Clerks, General	15.30
Computer User Support Specialists	23.20	Physical Therapists	40.40
Construction Laborers	15.90	Physicians	123.20
Cooks, Restaurant	11.90	Plumbers, Pipefitters and Steamfitters	24.40
Customer Service Representatives	16.20	Police and Sheriff's Patrol Officers	26.30
Dentists	73.70	Postal Service Mail Carriers	24.70
Electricians	23.70	Real Estate Sales Agents	31.20
Engineers, Electrical	48.80	Retail Salespersons	13.20
Fast Food and Counter Workers	9.20	Sales Representatives, Technical/Scientific	39.40
Financial Managers	68.30	Secretaries, Exc. Legal/Medical/Executive	16.50
First-Line Supervisors of Office Workers	26.70	Security Guards	15.00
General and Operations Managers	53.30	Surgeons	135.60
Hairdressers/Cosmetologists	13.00	Teacher Assistants, Exc. Postsecondary*	11.10
Home Health and Personal Care Aides	10.20	Teachers, Secondary School, Exc. Sp. Ed.*	25.50
Janitors and Cleaners	11.50	Telemarketers	11.00
Landscaping/Groundskeeping Workers	14.30	Truck Drivers, Heavy/Tractor-Trailer	25.90
Lawyers	63.40	Truck Drivers, Light/Delivery Services	17.30
Maids and Housekeeping Cleaners	10.80	Waiters and Waitresses	9.40

Note: Wage data covers the Tulsa, OK Metropolitan Statistical Area—see Appendix B for areas included; (*) Hourly wages were calculated from annual wage data based on a 40 hour work week; n/a not available.
Source: Bureau of Labor Statistics, Metro Area Occupational Employment & Wage Estimates, May 2019

Employment by Occupation

Occupation Classification	City (%)	MSA[1] (%)	U.S. (%)
Management, Business, Science, and Arts	36.0	36.0	37.9
Natural Resources, Construction, and Maintenance	9.4	9.9	8.9
Production, Transportation, and Material Moving	13.6	14.3	13.3
Sales and Office	23.5	23.4	22.1
Service	17.6	16.4	17.9

Note: Figures cover employed civilians 16 years of age and older; (1) Figures cover the Tulsa, OK Metropolitan Statistical Area—see Appendix B for areas included
Source: U.S. Census Bureau, 2014-2018 American Community Survey 5-Year Estimates

Employment by Industry

Sector	MSA[1]		U.S.
	Number of Employees	Percent of Total	Percent of Total
Construction	25,400	5.5	4.9
Education and Health Services	73,900	15.9	16.1
Financial Activities	23,600	5.1	5.8
Government	60,700	13.0	15.0
Information	6,600	1.4	1.9
Leisure and Hospitality	47,400	10.2	10.8
Manufacturing	54,300	11.7	8.4
Mining and Logging	6,600	1.4	0.5
Other Services	20,700	4.4	3.9
Professional and Business Services	58,100	12.5	14.1
Retail Trade	49,100	10.5	10.6
Transportation, Warehousing, and Utilities	22,100	4.7	4.2
Wholesale Trade	17,200	3.7	3.9

Note: Figures are non-farm employment as of December 2019. Figures are not seasonally adjusted and include workers 16 years of age and older; (1) Figures cover the Tulsa, OK Metropolitan Statistical Area—see Appendix B for areas included
Source: Bureau of Labor Statistics, Current Employment Statistics, Employment, Hours, and Earnings

Occupations with Greatest Projected Employment Growth: 2019 – 2021

Occupation[1]	2019 Employment	2021 Projected Employment	Numeric Employment Change	Percent Employment Change
Combined Food Preparation and Serving Workers, Including Fast Food	32,200	33,740	1,540	4.8
Laborers and Freight, Stock, and Material Movers, Hand	30,640	32,090	1,450	4.7
Cooks, Restaurant	16,980	17,960	980	5.8
Waiters and Waitresses	29,590	30,450	860	2.9
Personal Care Aides	15,510	16,360	850	5.5
Registered Nurses	35,540	36,290	750	2.1
First-Line Supervisors of Food Preparation and Serving Workers	15,820	16,380	560	3.5
Heavy and Tractor-Trailer Truck Drivers	28,410	28,920	510	1.8
General and Operations Managers	27,980	28,330	350	1.3
Home Health Aides	7,370	7,720	350	4.7

Note: Projections cover Oklahoma; (1) Sorted by numeric employment change
Source: www.projectionscentral.com, State Occupational Projections, 2019–2021 Short-Term Projections

Fastest Growing Occupations: 2019 – 2021

Occupation[1]	2019 Employment	2021 Projected Employment	Numeric Employment Change	Percent Employment Change
Cooks, Restaurant	16,980	17,960	980	5.8
Personal Care Aides	15,510	16,360	850	5.5
Veterinary Technologists and Technicians	1,130	1,190	60	5.3
Slaughterers and Meat Packers	1,310	1,380	70	5.3
Veterinary Assistants and Laboratory Animal Caretakers	1,540	1,620	80	5.2
Speech-Language Pathologists	1,960	2,060	100	5.1
Combined Food Preparation and Serving Workers, Including Fast Food	32,200	33,740	1,540	4.8
Veterinarians	1,270	1,330	60	4.7
Home Health Aides	7,370	7,720	350	4.7
Laborers and Freight, Stock, and Material Movers, Hand	30,640	32,090	1,450	4.7

Note: Projections cover Oklahoma; (1) Sorted by percent employment change and excludes occupations with numeric employment change less than 50
Source: www.projectionscentral.com, State Occupational Projections, 2019–2021 Short-Term Projections

TAXES

State Corporate Income Tax Rates

State	Tax Rate (%)	Income Brackets ($)	Num. of Brackets	Financial Institution Tax Rate (%)[a]	Federal Income Tax Ded.
Oklahoma	6.0	Flat rate	1	6.0	No

Note: Tax rates as of January 1, 2020; (a) Rates listed are the corporate income tax rate applied to financial institutions or excise taxes based on income.
Source: Federation of Tax Administrators, State Corporate Income Tax Rates, January 1, 2020

State Individual Income Tax Rates

State	Tax Rate (%)	Income Brackets ($)	Personal Exemptions ($)			Standard Ded. ($)	
			Single	Married	Depend.	Single	Married
Oklahoma	0.5 - 5.0	1,000 - 7,200 (t)	1,000	2,000	1,000	6,350	12,700

Note: Tax rates as of January 1, 2020; Local- and county-level taxes are not included; Federal income tax is not deductible on state income tax returns; (t) The income brackets reported for Oklahoma are for single persons. For married persons filing jointly, the same tax rates apply to income brackets ranging from $2,000, to $12,200.
Source: Federation of Tax Administrators, State Individual Income Tax Rates, January 1, 2020

Various State Sales and Excise Tax Rates

State	State Sales Tax (%)	Gasoline[1] (¢/gal.)	Cigarette[2] ($/pack)	Spirits[3] ($/gal.)	Wine[4] ($/gal.)	Beer[5] ($/gal.)	Recreational Marijuana (%)
Oklahoma	4.5	20	2.03	5.56	0.72	0.40	Not legal

Note: All tax rates as of January 1, 2020; (1) The American Petroleum Institute has developed a methodology for determining the average tax rate on a gallon of fuel. Rates may include any of the following: excise taxes, environmental fees, storage tank fees, other fees or taxes, general sales tax, and local taxes; (2) The federal excise tax of $1.0066 per pack and local taxes are not included; (3) Rates are those applicable to off-premise sales of 40% alcohol by volume (a.b.v.) distilled spirits in 750ml containers. Local excise taxes are excluded; (4) Rates are those applicable to off-premise sales of 11% a.b.v. non-carbonated wine in 750ml containers; (5) Rates are those applicable to off-premise sales of 4.7% a.b.v. beer in 12 ounce containers.
Source: Tax Foundation, 2020 Facts & Figures: How Does Your State Compare?

State Business Tax Climate Index Rankings

State	Overall Rank	Corporate Tax Rank	Individual Income Tax Rank	Sales Tax Rank	Property Tax Rank	Unemployment Insurance Tax Rank
Oklahoma	27	8	33	39	19	1

Note: The index is a measure of how each state's tax laws affect economic performance. The lower the rank, the more favorable a state's tax system is for business. States without a given tax are given a ranking of 1. The scores/rankings for the District of Columbia do not affect other states. The 2020 index represents the tax climate as of July 1, 2019.
Source: Tax Foundation, State Business Tax Climate Index 2020

COMMERCIAL UTILITIES

Typical Monthly Electric Bills

Area	Commercial Service ($/month)		Industrial Service ($/month)	
	1,500 kWh	40 kW demand 14,000 kWh	1,000 kW demand 200,000 kWh	50,000 kW demand 32,500,000 kWh
City	143	1,199	16,087	1,518,217
Average[1]	203	1,612	25,706	2,520,671

Note: Figures are based on annualized rates; (1) Average based on 187 utilities surveyed
Source: Edison Electric Institute, Typical Bills and Average Rates Report, Summer 2019

TRANSPORTATION

Means of Transportation to Work

Area	Car/Truck/Van		Public Transportation			Bicycle	Walked	Other Means	Worked at Home
	Drove Alone	Car-pooled	Bus	Subway	Railroad				
City	80.2	10.7	1.0	0.0	0.0	0.3	1.8	2.0	3.9
MSA[1]	83.0	9.6	0.5	0.0	0.0	0.2	1.3	1.4	4.0
U.S.	76.4	9.1	2.5	1.9	0.6	0.6	2.7	1.3	4.9

Note: Figures are percentages and cover workers 16 years of age and older; (1) Figures cover the Tulsa, OK Metropolitan Statistical Area—see Appendix B for areas included
Source: U.S. Census Bureau, 2014-2018 American Community Survey 5-Year Estimates

Travel Time to Work

Area	Less Than 10 Minutes	10 to 19 Minutes	20 to 29 Minutes	30 to 44 Minutes	45 to 59 Minutes	60 to 89 Minutes	90 Minutes or More
City	14.7	44.7	25.5	10.6	1.9	1.7	1.1
MSA[1]	13.5	34.3	26.3	18.1	4.3	2.3	1.3
U.S.	12.5	28.7	20.9	20.7	8.2	6.3	2.8

Note: Note: Figures are percentages and include workers 16 years old and over; (1) Figures cover the Tulsa, OK Metropolitan Statistical Area—see Appendix B for areas included
Source: U.S. Census Bureau, 2014-2018 American Community Survey 5-Year Estimates

Key Congestion Measures

Area	1982	1992	2002	2012	2017
Annual Hours of Delay, Total (000)	3,682	9,434	14,993	21,355	25,228
Annual Hours of Delay, Per Auto Commuter	13	25	33	37	46
Annual Congestion Cost, Total (million $)	28	99	202	382	464
Annual Congestion Cost, Per Auto Commuter ($)	240	422	523	584	669

Source: Texas A&M Transportation Institute, 2019 Urban Mobility Report

Freeway Travel Time Index

Area	1982	1987	1992	1997	2002	2007	2012	2017
Urban Area Index[1]	1.05	1.07	1.10	1.12	1.14	1.17	1.16	1.15
Urban Area Rank[1,2]	51	55	59	69	69	56	60	71

Note: Freeway Travel Time Index—the ratio of travel time in the peak period to the travel time at free-flow conditions. For example, a value of 1.30 indicates a 20-minute free-flow trip takes 26 minutes in the peak (20 minutes x 1.30 = 26 minutes); (1) Covers the Tulsa OK urban area; (2) Rank is based on 101 larger urban areas (#1 = highest travel time index)
Source: Texas A&M Transportation Institute, 2019 Urban Mobility Report

Public Transportation

Agency Name / Mode of Transportation	Vehicles Operated in Maximum Service[1]	Annual Unlinked Passenger Trips[2] (in thous.)	Annual Passenger Miles[3] (in thous.)
Metropolitan Tulsa Transit Authority (MTTA)			
Bus (directly operated)	52	2,681.0	14,155.6
Bus (purchased transportation)	12	95.0	657.1
Demand Response (purchased transportation)	28	106.8	893.8

Note: (1) Number of revenue vehicles operated by the given mode and type of service to meet the annual maximum service requirement. This is the revenue vehicle count during the peak season of the year; on the week and day that maximum service is provided. Vehicles operated in maximum service (VOMS) exclude atypical days and one-time special events; (2) Number of passengers who boarded public transportation vehicles. Passengers are counted each time they board a vehicle no matter how many vehicles they use to travel from their origin to their destination. (3) Sum of the distances ridden by all passengers during the entire fiscal year.
Source: Federal Transit Administration, National Transit Database, 2018

Air Transportation

Airport Name and Code / Type of Service	Passenger Airlines[1]	Passenger Enplanements	Freight Carriers[2]	Freight (lbs)
Tulsa International (TUL)				
Domestic service (U.S. carriers - 2019)	25	1,507,396	20	65,600,800
International service (U.S. carriers - 2018)	4	331	3	28,628

Note: (1) Includes all U.S.-based major, minor and commuter airlines that carried at least one passenger during the year; (2) Includes all U.S.-based airlines and freight carriers that transported at least one pound of freight during the year.
Source: Bureau of Transportation Statistics, The Intermodal Transportation Database, Air Carriers: T-100 Domestic Market (U.S. Carriers), 2019; Bureau of Transportation Statistics, The Intermodal Transportation Database, Air Carriers: T-100 International Market (U.S. Carriers), 2018

Other Transportation Statistics

Major Highways:	I-44
Amtrak Service:	Bus connection
Major Waterways/Ports:	Arkansas River

Source: Amtrak.com; Google Maps

BUSINESSES

Major Business Headquarters

Company Name	Industry	Rankings Fortune[1]	Rankings Forbes[2]
NGL Energy Partners	Wholesalers, Diversified	179	-
Oneok	Pipelines	256	-
QuikTrip	Convenience Stores & Gas Stations	-	29
Williams	Energy	348	-

Note: (1) Companies that produce a 10-K are ranked 1 to 500 based on 2018 revenue; (2) All private companies with at least $2 billion in annual revenue through the end of their most current fiscal year are ranked 1 to 228; companies listed are headquartered in the city; dashes indicate no ranking
Source: Fortune, "Fortune 500," June 2019; Forbes, "America's Largest Private Companies," 2019 Rankings

Fast-Growing Businesses

According to *Fortune*, Tulsa is home to one of the 100 fastest-growing companies in the world: **ONEOK** (#100). Companies were ranked by their revenue growth rate; their EPS growth rate; and their three-year annualized total return to investors for the period ending June 30, 2019. Criteria for inclusion: a company, foreign or domestic, must trade on a major U.S. stock exchange; must file quarterly reports with the SEC; must have a minimum market capitalization of $250 million; must have a stock price of at least $5 on June 30, 2019; must have been trading continuously since June 30, 2016; must have revenue and net income for the four quarters ended on or before April 30, 2019, of at least $50 million and $10 million, respectively; and must have posted a compound annual growth in revenue and earnings per share of at least 15% annually over the three years ending on or before April 30, 2019. Real estate investment trusts, limited-liability companies, limited parterships, business development companies, closed-end investment firms, companies about to be acquired, and companies that lost money in the quarter ending April 30, 2019 were excluded. *Fortune, "100 Fastest-Growing Companies," 2019*

Minority- and Women-Owned Businesses

Group	All Firms Firms	All Firms Sales ($000)	Firms with Paid Employees Firms	Firms with Paid Employees Sales ($000)	Firms with Paid Employees Employees	Firms with Paid Employees Payroll ($000)
AIAN[1]	2,644	944,152	515	879,687	4,714	168,127
Asian	1,375	464,320	414	403,848	4,567	79,893
Black	3,356	112,649	152	64,762	913	18,928
Hispanic	2,169	591,429	258	493,199	2,331	83,128
NHOPI[2]	n/a	n/a	n/a	n/a	n/a	n/a
Women	13,035	3,161,539	1,753	2,883,178	17,290	599,996
All Firms	39,908	66,485,901	10,769	64,868,275	238,963	10,754,283

Note: Figures cover firms located in the city; minority- and women-owned business are defined as firms in which the corresponding group own 51% or more of the stock or equity of the company; (1) American Indian and Alaska Native; (2) Native Hawaiian and Other Pacific Islander; n/a not available
Source: U.S. Census Bureau, 2012 Economic Census, Survey of Business Owners

HOTELS & CONVENTION CENTERS

Hotels, Motels and Vacation Rentals

Area	5 Star		4 Star		3 Star		2 Star		1 Star		Not Rated	
	Num.	Pct.[3]	Num.	Pct.[3]	Num.	Pct.[3]	Num.	Pct.[3]	Num.	Pct.[3]	Num.	Pct.[3]
City[1]	1	0.7	2	1.5	32	23.5	24	17.6	6	4.4	71	52.2
Total[2]	266	1.3	1,517	7.2	4,627	21.8	3,210	15.1	3,974	18.7	7,601	35.9

Note: (1) Figures cover Tulsa and vicinity; (2) Figures cover all 100 cities in this book; (3) Percentage of hotels which have a given star rating; Star ratings are determined by priceline.com and offer an indication of the general quality of a particular hotel.
Source: priceline.com, April 27, 2020

Major Convention Centers

Name	Overall Space (sq. ft.)	Exhibit Space (sq. ft.)	Meeting Space (sq. ft.)	Meeting Rooms
Tulsa Convention Center	227,000	102,600	n/a	35

Note: Table includes convention centers located in the Tulsa, OK metro area; n/a not available
Source: Original research

Living Environment

COST OF LIVING

Cost of Living Index

Composite Index	Groceries	Housing	Utilities	Trans-portation	Health Care	Misc. Goods/ Services
86.0	96.2	62.7	99.5	84.4	91.6	96.1

Note: The Cost of Living Index measures regional differences in the cost of consumer goods and services, excluding taxes and non-consumer expenditures, for professional and managerial households in the top income quintile. It is based on more than 50,000 prices covering almost 60 different items for which prices are collected three times a year by chambers of commerce, economic development organizations or university applied economic centers in each participating urban area. The numbers shown should be read as a percentage above or below the national average of 100. For example, a value of 115.4 in the groceries column indicates that grocery prices are 15.4% higher than the national average. Small differences in the index numbers should not be interpreted as significant; Figures cover the Tulsa OK urban area.
Source: The Council for Community and Economic Research, ACCRA Cost of Living Index, 2019

Grocery Prices

Area[1]	T-Bone Steak ($/pound)	Frying Chicken ($/pound)	Whole Milk ($/half gal.)	Eggs ($/dozen)	Orange Juice ($/64 oz.)	Coffee ($/11.5 oz.)
City[2]	10.45	1.35	2.14	1.57	3.70	3.95
Avg.	11.40	1.41	1.93	1.54	3.51	4.30
Min.	7.40	0.92	0.85	0.58	2.67	2.90
Max.	15.58	2.68	4.09	4.18	5.57	8.10

Note: (1) Values for the local area are compared with the average, minimum and maximum values for all 290 areas in the Cost of Living Index; (2) Figures cover the Tulsa OK urban area; T-Bone Steak (price per pound); Frying Chicken (price per pound, whole fryer); Whole Milk (half gallon carton); Eggs (price per dozen, Grade A, large); Orange Juice (64 oz. Tropicana or Florida Natural); Coffee (11.5 oz. can, vacuum-packed, Maxwell House, Hills Bros, or Folgers).
Source: The Council for Community and Economic Research, ACCRA Cost of Living Index, 2019

Housing and Utility Costs

Area[1]	New Home Price ($)	Apartment Rent ($/month)	All Electric ($/month)	Part Electric ($/month)	Other Energy ($/month)	Telephone ($/month)
City[2]	231,194	679	-	105.15	62.58	179.20
Avg.	362,090	1,142	174.35	100.00	67.76	179.60
Min.	198,329	501	91.58	31.44	28.51	165.30
Max.	2,074,561	5,050	388.18	239.41	306.15	207.90

Note: (1) Values for the local area are compared with the average, minimum and maximum values for all 290 areas in the Cost of Living Index; (2) Figures cover the Tulsa OK urban area; New Home Price (2,400 sf living area, 8,000 sf lot, in urban area with full utilities); Apartment Rent (950 sf 2 bedroom/1.5 or 2 bath, unfurnished, excluding all utilities except water); All Electric (average monthly cost for an all-electric home); Part Electric (average monthly cost for a part-electric home); Other Energy (average monthly cost for natural gas, fuel oil, coal, wood, and any other forms of energy except electricity); Telephone (price includes the base monthly rate plus taxes and fees for three lines of mobile phone service).
Source: The Council for Community and Economic Research, ACCRA Cost of Living Index, 2019

Health Care, Transportation, and Other Costs

Area[1]	Doctor ($/visit)	Dentist ($/visit)	Optometrist ($/visit)	Gasoline ($/gallon)	Beauty Salon ($/visit)	Men's Shirt ($)
City[2]	107.93	81.56	91.94	2.09	36.56	29.72
Avg.	114.85	97.58	106.10	2.50	38.15	32.15
Min.	39.00	62.22	52.22	1.53	16.88	10.27
Max.	206.67	151.53	258.67	3.79	79.29	59.30

Note: (1) Values for the local area are compared with the average, minimum and maximum values for all 290 areas in the Cost of Living Index; (2) Figures cover the Tulsa OK urban area; Doctor (general practitioners routine exam of an established patient); Dentist (adult teeth cleaning and periodic oral examination); Optometrist (full vision eye exam for established adult patient); Gasoline (one gallon regular unleaded, national brand, including all taxes, cash price at self-service pump if available); Beauty Salon (woman's shampoo, trim, and blow-dry); Men's Shirt (cotton/polyester dress shirt, pinpoint weave, long sleeves).
Source: The Council for Community and Economic Research, ACCRA Cost of Living Index, 2019

HOUSING

House Price Index (HPI)

Area	National Ranking[2]	Quarterly Change (%)	One-Year Change (%)	Five-Year Change (%)
MSA[1]	74	1.26	5.59	23.89
U.S.[3]	–	1.26	5.09	32.88

Note: The HPI is a weighted repeat sales index. It measures average price changes in repeat sales or refinancings on the same properties. This information is obtained by reviewing repeat mortgage transactions on single-family properties whose mortgages have been purchased or securitized by Fannie Mae or Freddie Mac in January 1975; (1) Figures cover the Tulsa, OK Metropolitan Statistical Area—see Appendix B for areas included; (2) Rankings are based on annual percentage change for all metro areas containing at least 15,000 transactions over the last 10 years and ranges from 1 to 232; (3) figures based on a weighted average of Census Division estimates using a seasonally adjusted, purchase-only index; all figures are for the period ending December 31, 2019
Source: Federal Housing Finance Agency, House Price Index, February 25, 2020

Median Single-Family Home Prices

Area	2017	2018	2019p	Percent Change 2018 to 2019
MSA[1]	160.2	165.3	173.2	4.8
U.S. Average	248.8	261.6	274.6	5.0

Note: Figures are median sales prices of existing single-family homes in thousands of dollars; (p) preliminary; (1) Figures cover the Tulsa, OK Metropolitan Statistical Area—see Appendix B for areas included
Source: National Association of Realtors, Median Sales Price of Existing Single-Family Homes for Metropolitan Areas, 4th Quarter 2019

Qualifying Income Based on Median Sales Price of Existing Single-Family Homes

Area	With 5% Down ($)	With 10% Down ($)	With 20% Down ($)
MSA[1]	37,195	35,237	31,322
U.S. Average	58,663	55,575	49,400

Note: Figures are preliminary; Qualifying income is based on a mortgage rate of 3.76%. Monthly principal and interest payment is limited to 25% of income; (1) Figures cover the Tulsa, OK Metropolitan Statistical Area—see Appendix B for areas included
Source: National Association of Realtors, Qualifying Income Based on Median Sales Price of Existing Single-Family Homes for Metropolitan Areas, 4th Quarter 2019

Median Apartment Condo-Coop Home Prices

Area	2017	2018	2019p	Percent Change 2018 to 2019
MSA[1]	n/a	n/a	n/a	n/a
U.S. Average	234.3	241.0	249.5	3.5

Note: Figures are median sales prices of existing apartment condo-coop homes in thousands of dollars; (p) preliminary; n/a not available; (1) Figures cover the Tulsa, OK Metropolitan Statistical Area—see Appendix B for areas included
Source: National Association of Realtors, Median Sales Price of Existing Apartment Condo-Coop Homes for Metropolitan Areas, 4th Quarter 2019

Home Value Distribution

Area	Under $50,000	$50,000 -$99,999	$100,000 -$149,999	$150,000 -$199,999	$200,000 -$299,999	$300,000 -$499,999	$500,000 -$999,999	$1,000,000 or more
City	9.5	24.0	23.2	15.1	13.0	9.7	4.5	1.0
MSA[1]	10.2	19.7	22.6	18.8	16.3	8.6	3.1	0.8
U.S.	7.6	13.0	14.0	14.3	19.2	18.3	10.5	3.1

Note: Figures are percentages and cover owner-occupied housing units; (1) Figures cover the Tulsa, OK Metropolitan Statistical Area—see Appendix B for areas included
Source: U.S. Census Bureau, 2014-2018 American Community Survey 5-Year Estimates

Homeownership Rate

Area	2011 (%)	2012 (%)	2013 (%)	2014 (%)	2015 (%)	2016 (%)	2017 (%)	2018 (%)	2019 (%)
MSA[1]	64.4	66.5	64.1	65.3	65.2	65.4	66.8	68.3	70.5
U.S.	66.1	65.4	65.1	64.5	63.7	63.4	63.9	64.4	64.6

Note: (1) Figures cover the Tulsa, OK Metropolitan Statistical Area—see Appendix B for areas included
Source: U.S. Census Bureau, Housing Vacancies and Homeownership Annual Statistics: 2011-2019

Year Housing Structure Built

Area	2010 or Later	2000 -2009	1990 -1999	1980 -1989	1970 -1979	1960 -1969	1950 -1959	1940 -1949	Before 1940	Median Year
City	2.8	6.1	9.1	13.6	21.1	14.6	16.9	6.4	9.3	1971
MSA[1]	5.4	14.6	12.6	14.5	19.5	10.7	10.9	4.6	7.3	1978
U.S.	4.1	14.3	13.9	13.5	15.3	10.7	10.4	5.0	12.8	1977

Note: Figures are percentages except for Median Year; Note: (1) Figures cover the Tulsa, OK Metropolitan Statistical Area—see Appendix B for areas included
Source: U.S. Census Bureau, 2014-2018 American Community Survey 5-Year Estimates

Gross Monthly Rent

Area	Under $500	$500 -$999	$1,000 -$1,499	$1,500 -$1,999	$2,000 -$2,499	$2,500 -$2,999	$3,000 and up	Median ($)
City	11.5	61.0	22.3	3.2	0.9	0.5	0.6	810
MSA[1]	11.5	58.5	24.1	4.1	0.9	0.4	0.5	831
U.S.	9.8	38.5	29.6	12.9	5.1	2.1	2.0	1,023

Note: Figures are percentages except for Median; Gross rent is the contract rent plus the estimated average monthly cost of utilities (electricity, gas, and water and sewer) and fuels (oil, coal, kerosene, wood, etc.) if these are paid by the renter (or paid for the renter by someone else); (1) Figures cover the Tulsa, OK Metropolitan Statistical Area—see Appendix B for areas included
Source: U.S. Census Bureau, 2014-2018 American Community Survey 5-Year Estimates

HEALTH

Health Risk Factors

Category	MSA[1] (%)	U.S. (%)
Adults aged 18–64 who have any kind of health care coverage	80.4	87.3
Adults who reported being in good or better health	80.2	82.4
Adults who have been told they have high blood cholesterol	34.9	33.0
Adults who have been told they have high blood pressure	37.4	32.3
Adults who are current smokers	20.0	17.1
Adults who currently use E-cigarettes	6.9	4.6
Adults who currently use chewing tobacco, snuff, or snus	6.4	4.0
Adults who are heavy drinkers[2]	4.5	6.3
Adults who are binge drinkers[3]	14.7	17.4
Adults who are overweight (BMI 25.0 - 29.9)	34.7	35.3
Adults who are obese (BMI 30.0 - 99.8)	36.0	31.3
Adults who participated in any physical activities in the past month	68.2	74.4
Adults who always or nearly always wears a seat belt	94.4	94.3

Note: (1) Figures cover the Tulsa, OK Metropolitan Statistical Area—see Appendix B for areas included; (2) Heavy drinkers are classified as adult men having more than 14 drinks per week and adult women having more than 7 drinks per week; (3) Binge drinkers are classified as males having five or more drinks on one occasion or females having four or more drinks on one occasion
Source: Centers for Disease Control and Prevention, Behaviorial Risk Factor Surveillance System, SMART: Selected Metropolitan Area Risk Trends, 2017

Acute and Chronic Health Conditions

Category	MSA[1] (%)	U.S. (%)
Adults who have ever been told they had a heart attack	5.1	4.2
Adults who have ever been told they have angina or coronary heart disease	4.1	3.9
Adults who have ever been told they had a stroke	4.8	3.0
Adults who have ever been told they have asthma	14.2	14.2
Adults who have ever been told they have arthritis	27.0	24.9
Adults who have ever been told they have diabetes[2]	11.7	10.5
Adults who have ever been told they had skin cancer	6.7	6.2
Adults who have ever been told they had any other types of cancer	6.8	7.1
Adults who have ever been told they have COPD	8.1	6.5
Adults who have ever been told they have kidney disease	3.5	3.0
Adults who have ever been told they have a form of depression	24.6	20.5

Note: (1) Figures cover the Tulsa, OK Metropolitan Statistical Area—see Appendix B for areas included; (2) Figures do not include pregnancy-related, borderline, or pre-diabetes
Source: Centers for Disease Control and Prevention, Behaviorial Risk Factor Surveillance System, SMART: Selected Metropolitan Area Risk Trends, 2017

Health Screening and Vaccination Rates

Category	MSA[1] (%)	U.S. (%)
Adults aged 65+ who have had flu shot within the past year	68.8	60.7
Adults aged 65+ who have ever had a pneumonia vaccination	81.3	75.4
Adults who have ever been tested for HIV	34.2	36.1
Adults who have ever had the shingles or zoster vaccine?	27.9	28.9
Adults who have had their blood cholesterol checked within the last five years	79.0	85.9

Note: n/a not available; (1) Figures cover the Tulsa, OK Metropolitan Statistical Area—see Appendix B for areas included.
Source: Centers for Disease Control and Prevention, Behaviorial Risk Factor Surveillance System, SMART: Selected Metropolitan Area Risk Trends, 2017

Disability Status

Category	MSA[1] (%)	U.S. (%)
Adults who reported being deaf	9.4	6.7
Are you blind or have serious difficulty seeing, even when wearing glasses?	6.2	4.5
Are you limited in any way in any of your usual activities due of arthritis?	14.2	12.9
Do you have difficulty doing errands alone?	7.7	6.8
Do you have difficulty dressing or bathing?	3.4	3.6
Do you have serious difficulty concentrating/remembering/making decisions?	13.5	10.7
Do you have serious difficulty walking or climbing stairs?	17.6	13.6

Note: (1) Figures cover the Tulsa, OK Metropolitan Statistical Area—see Appendix B for areas included.
Source: Centers for Disease Control and Prevention, Behaviorial Risk Factor Surveillance System, SMART: Selected Metropolitan Area Risk Trends, 2017

Mortality Rates for the Top 10 Causes of Death in the U.S.

ICD-10[a] Sub-Chapter	ICD-10[a] Code	Age-Adjusted Mortality Rate[1] per 100,000 population	
		County[2]	U.S.
Malignant neoplasms	C00-C97	171.1	152.4
Ischaemic heart diseases	I20-I25	114.2	92.7
Other forms of heart disease	I30-I51	32.2	52.5
Chronic lower respiratory diseases	J40-J47	52.9	40.4
Cerebrovascular diseases	I60-I69	42.1	37.3
Other degenerative diseases of the nervous system	G30-G31	40.0	36.4
Other external causes of accidental injury	W00-X59	38.9	35.3
Organic, including symptomatic, mental disorders	F01-F09	30.4	30.0
Hypertensive diseases	I10-I15	99.2	22.9
Diabetes mellitus	E10-E14	20.7	21.3

Note: (a) ICD-10 = International Classification of Diseases 10th Revision; (1) Mortality rates are a three year average covering 2016-2018; (2) Figures cover Tulsa County.
Source: Centers for Disease Control and Prevention, National Center for Health Statistics. Underlying Cause of Death 1999-2018 on CDC WONDER Online Database

Mortality Rates for Selected Causes of Death

ICD-10[a] Sub-Chapter	ICD-10[a] Code	Age-Adjusted Mortality Rate[1] per 100,000 population	
		County[2]	U.S.
Assault	X85-Y09	11.7	6.0
Diseases of the liver	K70-K76	16.5	14.2
Human immunodeficiency virus (HIV) disease	B20-B24	1.8	1.6
Influenza and pneumonia	J09-J18	14.9	14.2
Intentional self-harm	X60-X84	19.1	13.9
Malnutrition	E40-E46	1.9	1.9
Obesity and other hyperalimentation	E65-E68	Unreliable	2.1
Renal failure	N17-N19	7.6	12.8
Transport accidents	V01-V99	13.4	12.5
Viral hepatitis	B15-B19	2.6	1.4

Note: (a) ICD-10 = International Classification of Diseases 10th Revision; (1) Mortality rates are a three year average covering 2016-2018; (2) Figures cover Tulsa County; Data are suppressed when the data meet the criteria for confidentiality constraints; Mortality rates are flagged as unreliable when the rate would be calculated with a numerator of 20 or less.
Source: Centers for Disease Control and Prevention, National Center for Health Statistics. Underlying Cause of Death 1999-2018 on CDC WONDER Online Database

Health Insurance Coverage

Area	With Health Insurance	With Private Health Insurance	With Public Health Insurance	Without Health Insurance	Population Under Age 19 Without Health Insurance
City	83.4	58.9	34.9	16.6	8.0
MSA[1]	86.5	65.8	32.4	13.5	7.5
U.S.	90.6	67.7	34.7	9.4	5.2

Note: Figures are percentages that cover the civilian noninstitutionalized population; (1) Figures cover the Tulsa, OK Metropolitan Statistical Area—see Appendix B for areas included
Source: U.S. Census Bureau, 2014-2018 American Community Survey 5-Year Estimates

Number of Medical Professionals

Area	MDs[3]	DOs[3,4]	Dentists	Podiatrists	Chiropractors	Optometrists
County[1] (number)	1,742	841	450	26	247	145
County[1] (rate[2])	269.5	130.1	69.4	4.0	38.1	22.4
U.S. (rate[2])	281.9	23.4	69.1	6.0	27.5	16.4

Note: Data as of 2018 unless noted; (1) Data covers Tulsa County; (2) Rate per 100,000 population; (3) Data as of 2017 and includes all active, non-federal physicians; (4) Doctor of Osteopathic Medicine
Source: U.S. Department of Health and Human Services, Health Resources and Services Administration, Bureau of Health Professions, Area Resource File (ARF) 2018-2019

EDUCATION

Public School District Statistics

District Name	Schls	Pupils	Pupil/ Teacher Ratio	Minority Pupils[1] (%)	Free Lunch Eligible[2] (%)	IEP[3] (%)
Tulsa	77	36,512	16.2	76.4	n/a	17.2
Union	17	15,773	18.4	70.6	n/a	12.2

Note: Table includes school districts with 2,000 or more students; (1) Percentage of students that are not non-Hispanic white; (2) Percentage of students that are eligible for the free lunch program; (3) Percentage of students that have an Individualized Education Program.
Source: U.S. Department of Education, National Center for Education Statistics, Common Core of Data, Local Education Agency (School District) Universe Survey: School Year 2018-2019; U.S. Department of Education, National Center for Education Statistics, Common Core of Data, Public Elementary/Secondary School Universe Survey: School Year 2018-2019

Best High Schools

According to *U.S. News,* Tulsa is home to one of the top 500 high schools in the U.S.: **Booker T. Washington High School** (#198). Nearly 18,000 public, magnet and charter schools were ranked based on their performance on state assessments and how well they prepare students for college. *U.S. News & World Report, "Best High Schools 2020"*

Highest Level of Education

Area	Less than H.S.	H.S. Diploma	Some College, No Deg.	Associate Degree	Bachelor's Degree	Master's Degree	Prof. School Degree	Doctorate Degree
City	13.0	25.2	23.1	7.9	20.3	7.0	2.4	1.0
MSA[1]	10.8	29.2	24.0	8.7	18.7	6.0	1.7	0.8
U.S.	12.3	27.1	20.6	8.4	19.4	8.6	2.1	1.4

Note: Figures cover persons age 25 and over; (1) Figures cover the Tulsa, OK Metropolitan Statistical Area—see Appendix B for areas included
Source: U.S. Census Bureau, 2014-2018 American Community Survey 5-Year Estimates

Educational Attainment by Race

Area	High School Graduate or Higher (%)					Bachelor's Degree or Higher (%)				
	Total	White	Black	Asian	Hisp.[2]	Total	White	Black	Asian	Hisp.[2]
City	87.0	89.6	89.0	75.8	54.6	30.8	35.5	18.0	37.4	10.1
MSA[1]	89.2	90.7	89.2	78.9	61.1	27.2	29.2	19.3	37.4	12.0
U.S.	87.7	89.6	85.4	86.8	67.7	31.5	32.9	21.1	53.5	15.8

Note: Figures shown cover persons 25 years old and over; (1) Figures cover the Tulsa, OK Metropolitan Statistical Area—see Appendix B for areas included; (2) People of Hispanic origin can be of any race
Source: U.S. Census Bureau, 2014-2018 American Community Survey 5-Year Estimates

School Enrollment by Grade and Control

Area	Preschool (%)		Kindergarten (%)		Grades 1 - 4 (%)		Grades 5 - 8 (%)		Grades 9 - 12 (%)	
	Public	Private	Public	Private	Public	Private	Public	Private	Public	Private
City	70.3	29.7	89.0	11.0	88.2	11.8	86.1	13.9	84.8	15.2
MSA[1]	70.1	29.9	89.8	10.2	89.2	10.8	88.5	11.5	87.9	12.1
U.S.	59.0	41.0	87.7	12.3	89.6	10.4	89.5	10.5	90.2	9.8

Note: Figures shown cover persons 3 years old and over; (1) Figures cover the Tulsa, OK Metropolitan
Statistical Area—see Appendix B for areas included
Source: U.S. Census Bureau, 2014-2018 American Community Survey 5-Year Estimates

Average Salaries of Public School Teachers

Area	2016-17		2017-18		Change from 2016-17 to 2017-18	
	Dollars	Rank[1]	Dollars	Rank[1]	Percent	Rank[2]
Oklahoma	45,292	50	46,300	49	2.23	10
U.S. Average	59,539	–	60,477	–	1.58	–

Note: (1) Rank ranges from 1 to 51 where 1 indicates highest salary; (2) Rank ranges from 1 to 51 where 1
indicates highest percent change.
Source: National Education Association, Rankings & Estimates: Rankings of the States 2018 and Estimates of
School Statistics 2019

Higher Education

Four-Year Colleges			Two-Year Colleges			Medical Schools[1]	Law Schools[2]	Voc/ Tech[3]
Public	Private Non-profit	Private For-profit	Public	Private Non-profit	Private For-profit			
1	3	3	2	1	4	2	1	5

Note: Figures cover institutions located within the city limits and include main campuses only; (1) includes
schools accredited by the Liaison Committee on Medical Education and the American Osteopathic
Association's Commission on Osteopathic College Accreditation; (2) includes ABA-accredited schools, schools
with provisional ABA accreditation, and state accredited schools; (3) includes all schools with programs that
are less than 2 years.
Source: National Center for Education Statistics, Integrated Postsecondary Education System (IPEDS),
2018-19; Wikipedia, List of Medical Schools in the United States, accessed May 1, 2020; Wikipedia, List of Law
Schools in the United States, accessed May 1, 2020

According to *U.S. News & World Report,* the Tulsa, OK metro area is home to one of the top 200
national universities in the U.S.: **University of Tulsa** (#121 tie). The indicators used to capture
academic quality fall into a number of categories: assessment by administrators at peer institutions;
retention of students; faculty resources; student selectivity; financial resources; alumni giving; high
school counselor ratings of colleges; and graduation rate. *U.S. News & World Report, "America's
Best Colleges 2020"*

PRESIDENTIAL ELECTION

2016 Presidential Election Results

Area	Clinton	Trump	Johnson	Stein	Other
Tulsa County	35.6	58.4	6.1	0.0	0.0
U.S.	48.0	45.9	3.3	1.1	1.7

Note: Results are percentages and may not add to 100% due to rounding
Source: Dave Leip's Atlas of U.S. Presidential Elections

EMPLOYERS

Major Employers

Company Name	Industry
AHS Hillcrest Medical Center	General medical & surgical hospitals
American Airlines	Airports, flying fields, & services
BlueCross BlueShield of Oklahoma	Hospital & medical services plans
Caprock Pipeline Company	Pipelines, natural gas
County of Tulsa	Personnel management consultant
Dollar Thrifty Automotive Group	Passenger car rental
GHS Health Maintenance Organization	Health insurance carriers
IBM	Computer related consulting services
IC of Oklahoma	Truck & bus bodies
Matrix Service	Oil & gas pipeline construction
ONEOK	Natural gas transmission
Saint Francis Health System	General medical & surgical hospitals
St. John Medical Center	General medical & surgical hospitals
State Farm Fire and Casualty Company	Fire, marine, & casualty insurance
The Bama Companies	Bread, cake & related products
The Boeing Company	Missile guidance systems & equipment
The NORDAM Group	Aircraft parts & equipment, nec
The Williams Companies	Natural gas transmission

Note: Companies shown are located within the Tulsa, OK Metropolitan Statistical Area.
Source: Hoovers.com; Wikipedia

PUBLIC SAFETY

Crime Rate

Area	All Crimes	Violent Crimes				Property Crimes		
		Murder	Rape[3]	Robbery	Aggrav. Assault	Burglary	Larceny -Theft	Motor Vehicle Theft
City	6,495.6	14.9	104.7	205.9	739.7	1,190.6	3,431.5	808.4
Suburbs[1]	2,105.2	3.2	45.1	21.1	154.3	412.4	1,252.2	216.9
Metro[2]	3,884.5	7.9	69.3	96.0	391.6	727.8	2,135.4	456.6
U.S.	2,580.1	5.0	42.6	86.2	246.8	376.0	1,594.6	228.9

Note: Figures are crimes per 100,000 population; (1) All areas within the metro area that are located outside the city limits; (2) Figures cover the Tulsa, OK Metropolitan Statistical Area—see Appendix B for areas included; (3) The city and U.S. figures shown were reported using the revised Uniform Crime Reporting (UCR) definition of rape. The suburban and metro area figures shown are an aggregate total of the data submitted using both the revised and legacy UCR definitions.
Source: FBI Uniform Crime Reports, 2018

Hate Crimes

Area	Number of Quarters Reported	Number of Incidents per Bias Motivation					
		Race/Ethnicity/ Ancestry	Religion	Sexual Orientation	Disability	Gender	Gender Identity
City	4	1	0	0	0	0	0
U.S.	4	4,047	1,419	1,196	159	47	168

Source: Federal Bureau of Investigation, Hate Crime Statistics 2018

Identity Theft Consumer Reports

Area	Reports	Reports per 100,000 Population	Rank[2]
MSA[1]	1,119	113	154
U.S.	650,572	198	-

Note: (1) Figures cover the Tulsa, OK Metropolitan Statistical Area—see Appendix B for areas included; (2) Rank ranges from 1 to 386 where 1 indicates greatest number of identity theft reports per 100,000 population
Source: Federal Trade Commission, Consumer Sentinel Network Data Book for January–December 2019

Fraud and Other Consumer Reports

Area	Reports	Reports per 100,000 Population	Rank[2]
MSA[1]	4,953	498	250
U.S.	2,590,177	789	-

Note: (1) Figures cover the Tulsa, OK Metropolitan Statistical Area—see Appendix B for areas included; (2) Rank ranges from 1 to 386 where 1 indicates greatest number of fraud and other consumer reports per 100,000 population
Source: Federal Trade Commission, Consumer Sentinel Network Data Book for January–December 2019

SPORTS

Professional Sports Teams

Team Name	League	Year Established
No teams are located in the metro area		

Source: Wikipedia, Major Professional Sports Teams of the United States and Canada, May 4, 2020

CLIMATE

Average and Extreme Temperatures

Temperature	Jan	Feb	Mar	Apr	May	Jun	Jul	Aug	Sep	Oct	Nov	Dec	Yr.
Extreme High (°F)	79	86	96	102	96	103	112	110	105	98	85	80	112
Average High (°F)	46	52	61	72	80	88	93	93	85	74	61	50	71
Average Temp. (°F)	36	41	50	61	69	78	83	82	74	63	50	40	61
Average Low (°F)	25	30	38	50	59	68	72	70	63	51	39	29	50
Extreme Low (°F)	-6	-7	-3	22	35	49	51	52	35	26	10	-8	-8

Note: Figures cover the years 1948-1990
Source: National Climatic Data Center, International Station Meteorological Climate Summary, 9/96

Average Precipitation/Snowfall/Humidity

Precip./Humidity	Jan	Feb	Mar	Apr	May	Jun	Jul	Aug	Sep	Oct	Nov	Dec	Yr.
Avg. Precip. (in.)	1.6	1.9	3.2	3.7	5.6	4.3	3.4	3.0	4.1	3.5	2.6	1.9	38.9
Avg. Snowfall (in.)	3	2	2	Tr	0	0	0	0	0	Tr	1	2	10
Avg. Rel. Hum. 6am (%)	78	78	76	77	85	85	82	84	85	82	78	78	81
Avg. Rel. Hum. 3pm (%)	53	51	47	46	54	53	48	46	49	46	48	52	49

Note: Figures cover the years 1948-1990; Tr = Trace amounts (<0.05 in. of rain; <0.5 in. of snow)
Source: National Climatic Data Center, International Station Meteorological Climate Summary, 9/96

Weather Conditions

Temperature			Daytime Sky			Precipitation		
10°F & below	32°F & below	90°F & above	Clear	Partly cloudy	Cloudy	0.01 inch or more precip.	0.1 inch or more snow/ice	Thunder-storms
6	78	74	117	141	107	88	8	50

Note: Figures are average number of days per year and cover the years 1948-1990
Source: National Climatic Data Center, International Station Meteorological Climate Summary, 9/96

HAZARDOUS WASTE

Superfund Sites

The Tulsa, OK metro area is home to three sites on the EPA's Superfund National Priorities List: **Henryetta Iron and Metal** (proposed); **Tulsa Fuel and Manufacturing** (final); **Wilcox Oil Company** (final). There are a total of 1,387 Superfund sites with a status of proposed or final on the list in the U.S. *U.S. Environmental Protection Agency, National Priorities List, May 5, 2020*

AIR & WATER QUALITY

Air Quality Trends: Ozone

	1990	1995	2000	2005	2010	2012	2014	2016	2017	2018
MSA[1]	0.086	0.091	0.081	0.072	0.069	0.083	0.062	0.064	0.065	0.067
U.S.	0.088	0.089	0.082	0.080	0.073	0.075	0.067	0.069	0.068	0.069

Note: (1) Data covers the Tulsa, OK Metropolitan Statistical Area—see Appendix B for areas included. The values shown are the composite ozone concentration averages among trend sites based on the highest fourth daily maximum 8-hour concentration in parts per million. These trends are based on sites having an adequate record of monitoring data during the trend period. Data from exceptional events are included.
Source: U.S. Environmental Protection Agency, Air Quality Monitoring Information, "Air Quality Trends by City, 1990-2018"

Air Quality Index

Area	Percent of Days when Air Quality was...[2]					AQI Statistics[2]	
	Good	Moderate	Unhealthy for Sensitive Groups	Unhealthy	Very Unhealthy	Maximum	Median
MSA[1]	50.4	46.6	2.7	0.3	0.0	192	50

Note: (1) Data covers the Tulsa, OK Metropolitan Statistical Area—see Appendix B for areas included; (2) Based on 365 days with AQI data in 2018. Air Quality Index (AQI) is an index for reporting daily air quality. EPA calculates the AQI for five major air pollutants regulated by the Clean Air Act: ground-level ozone, particle pollution (aka particulate matter), carbon monoxide, sulfur dioxide, and nitrogen dioxide. The AQI runs from 0 to 500. The higher the AQI value, the greater the level of air pollution and the greater the health concern. There are six AQI categories: "Good" AQI is between 0 and 50. Air quality is considered satisfactory; "Moderate" AQI is between 51 and 100. Air quality is acceptable; "Unhealthy for Sensitive Groups" When AQI values are between 101 and 150, members of sensitive groups may experience health effects; "Unhealthy" When AQI values are between 151 and 200 everyone may begin to experience health effects; "Very Unhealthy" AQI values between 201 and 300 trigger a health alert; "Hazardous" AQI values over 300 trigger warnings of emergency conditions (not shown).
Source: U.S. Environmental Protection Agency, Air Quality Index Report, 2018

Air Quality Index Pollutants

Area	Percent of Days when AQI Pollutant was...[2]					
	Carbon Monoxide	Nitrogen Dioxide	Ozone	Sulfur Dioxide	Particulate Matter 2.5	Particulate Matter 10
MSA[1]	0.0	0.0	42.7	0.0	57.0	0.3

Note: (1) Data covers the Tulsa, OK Metropolitan Statistical Area—see Appendix B for areas included; (2) Based on 365 days with AQI data in 2018. The Air Quality Index (AQI) is an index for reporting daily air quality. EPA calculates the AQI for five major air pollutants regulated by the Clean Air Act: ground-level ozone, particle pollution (also known as particulate matter), carbon monoxide, sulfur dioxide, and nitrogen dioxide. The AQI runs from 0 to 500. The higher the AQI value, the greater the level of air pollution and the greater the health concern.
Source: U.S. Environmental Protection Agency, Air Quality Index Report, 2018

Maximum Air Pollutant Concentrations: Particulate Matter, Ozone, CO and Lead

	Particulate Matter 10 (ug/m³)	Particulate Matter 2.5 Wtd AM (ug/m³)	Particulate Matter 2.5 24-Hr (ug/m³)	Ozone (ppm)	Carbon Monoxide (ppm)	Lead (ug/m³)
MSA[1] Level	59	10.5	27	0.073	1	0.01
NAAQS[2]	150	15	35	0.075	9	0.15
Met NAAQS[2]	Yes	Yes	Yes	Yes	Yes	Yes

Note: (1) Data covers the Tulsa, OK Metropolitan Statistical Area—see Appendix B for areas included; Data from exceptional events are included; (2) National Ambient Air Quality Standards; ppm = parts per million; ug/m³ = micrograms per cubic meter; n/a not available.
Concentrations: Particulate Matter 10 (coarse particulate)—highest second maximum 24-hour concentration; Particulate Matter 2.5 Wtd AM (fine particulate)—highest weighted annual mean concentration; Particulate Matter 2.5 24-Hour (fine particulate)—highest 98th percentile 24-hour concentration; Ozone—highest fourth daily maximum 8-hour concentration; Carbon Monoxide—highest second maximum non-overlapping 8-hour concentration; Lead—maximum running 3-month average
Source: U.S. Environmental Protection Agency, Air Quality Monitoring Information, "Air Quality Statistics by City, 2018"

Maximum Air Pollutant Concentrations: Nitrogen Dioxide and Sulfur Dioxide

	Nitrogen Dioxide AM (ppb)	Nitrogen Dioxide 1-Hr (ppb)	Sulfur Dioxide AM (ppb)	Sulfur Dioxide 1-Hr (ppb)	Sulfur Dioxide 24-Hr (ppb)
MSA[1] Level	7	39	n/a	8	n/a
NAAQS[2]	53	100	30	75	140
Met NAAQS[2]	Yes	Yes	n/a	Yes	n/a

Note: (1) Data covers the Tulsa, OK Metropolitan Statistical Area—see Appendix B for areas included; Data from exceptional events are included; (2) National Ambient Air Quality Standards; ppm = parts per million; ug/m³ = micrograms per cubic meter; n/a not available.
Concentrations: Nitrogen Dioxide AM—highest arithmetic mean concentration; Nitrogen Dioxide 1-Hr—highest 98th percentile 1-hour daily maximum concentration; Sulfur Dioxide AM—highest annual mean concentration; Sulfur Dioxide 1-Hr—highest 99th percentile 1-hour daily maximum concentration; Sulfur Dioxide 24-Hr—highest second maximum 24-hour concentration
Source: U.S. Environmental Protection Agency, Air Quality Monitoring Information, "Air Quality Statistics by City, 2018"

Drinking Water

Water System Name	Pop. Served	Primary Water Source Type	Violations[1]
Tulsa	471,000	Surface	28

Note: (1) Total number of violations (both active and inactive) in the EPA database
Source: U.S. Environmental Protection Agency, Office of Ground Water and Drinking Water, Safe Drinking Water Information System (based on data extracted May 5, 2020)

Wichita, Kansas

Background

Lying in the southeastern plains of Kansas, Wichita took its name from a local Indian tribe. Starting in 1864, two white entrepreneurs, Jesse Chisholm and James R. Mead, struck up a lively trade in the area with the native people. Shortly after the tribe was relocated to Indian Territory in Oklahoma in 1867, white settlers planted roots around Chisholm's and Mead's trading post. Chisholm laid out a trail from the post to Texas, from which cowboys drove Longhorn cattle to the railhead of the Wichita and Southwestern Railroad, feeding the cows along the way.

In the 1880s, like many Plains-area cattle-shipping points, Wichita became a wide-open town, with dance halls, gambling, and saloons. Wyatt Earp served there as a lawman for a time. In 1886, the town officially became a city, having grown to over 20,000 in population, much of it due to eager speculation in prairie lands.

Other industries grew in the city. After the turn of the century, oil was discovered in the area, luring more people. The city swelled to over 100,000 by 1930. Shortly after World War I, which saw great advancements in aviation, Wichita's first airplane factory was built. The city soon became the country's leading manufacturer of aircraft. Walter H. Beech, Clyde V. Cessna, and Lloyd C. Stearman were to become famous members of the community for their early leadership in the industry.

Wichita, the largest city in the state, has long been Kansas's dominant industrial city. The oil rigs and aircraft factories kept the dire times of the Great Depression from Wichita, while much of the rest of the state was consumed by the Dust Bowl. During World War II, more airplanes rolled off the city's three assembly lines than in any other city in America. Steady aircraft industry growth continued until the 1980s, when a slump in sales occurred. By the late 1990s, however, a revival of the industry was in full swing until the early 2000s when again, major layoffs occurred. In 2012, Boeing announced it was closing its Wichita plant, but the void was filled by the creation of Spirit Aerosystems. Wichita is by now accustomed to the cyclical nature of the aircraft industry and it remains a major manufacturer of private and military aircraft, with, in addition to Spirit, Airbus Americas Engineering, Cessna, Bombardier Learjet, and Hawker Beechcraft all in operation there.

Another important Wichita company is Koch Industries, which deals in chemicals, energy, and gas liquids, among other products. The city is also heavily involved in the food industry, with large companies such as Cargill Beef headquartered here. In fact, Koch and Cargill are the two largest privately held companies in the U.S. Healthcare is also a major industry in Wichita.

Transportation to and from Wichita is easy. The Wichita Dwight D. Eisenhower Airport is the largest in the state, while the city is also serviced by the Colonel James Jabara Airport. Although Wichita does not feature passenger rail service, two railroad lines run freight service through the city.

Wichita State University, a public research institution, is the largest of the city's three universities and the third-largest in the state. The other two universities are Friends University, a private non-denominational Christian institution, and Newman University, a private Catholic school. All three schools feature sports teams, although Wichita State University is the only to compete at the Division I level. Wichita is also home to several minor league teams, including the Wind Surge (baseball), the Thunder (ice hockey), and the Force (indoor football).

Wichita has many acclaimed cultural institutions, including the Wichita Museum of Art, whose permanent collection features 7,000 objects, the Ulrich Museum of Art, located at Wichita State, and the Wichita Symphony Orchestra, the oldest professional symphony orchestra in Kansas. Since 1972, Wichita has hosted the River Festival, which features a host of events, and attracts nearly 400,000 people each year. The annual Wichita Black Arts Festival celebrates the cultural achievements of the city's African American community.

The climate in Wichita is continental but generally mild, punctuated occasionally by more intemperate weather conditions. Summers are usually warm and humid, but can be hot and dry. Winters are usually mild, with only brief periods of cold weather. Snowfall is light to moderate, with the ground rarely being covered for more than three days. Thunderstorms, occasionally severe, occur through the spring and summer months.

Rankings

General Rankings

- Wichita was selected as an "All-America City" by the National Civic League. The All-America City Award recognizes civic excellence and in 2019 honored 10 communities that best exemplify the spirit of grassroots citizen involvement and cross-sector collaborative problem solving to collectively tackle pressing and complex issues. This year's focus was on creating healthy communities. *National Civic League, 2019 All-America City Awards,* June 23, 2019

- In their sixth annual survey, Livability.com looked at data for more than 1,000 U.S. cities to determine the rankings for Livability's "Top 100 Best Places to Live" in 2019. Wichita ranked #87. Criteria: median home value capped at $250,000; affordable living; vibrant economy; education, demographics, health care options. transportation & infrastructure; abundant lifestyle amenities. *Livability.com, "Top 100 Best Places to Live 2019" March 2019*

Business/Finance Rankings

- Wichita was the #4-ranked city for savers, according to a study by the finance site GOBankingRates, which considered the prospects for people trying to save money. Criteria: average monthly cost of grocery items; median home listing price; median rent; median income; transportation costs; gas prices; and the cost of eating out for an inexpensive and mid-range meal in 100 U.S. cities. *www.gobankingrates.com, "The 20 Best (and Worst) Places to Live If You're Trying to Save Money," August 27, 2019*

- Wichita was ranked #4 among 100 U.S. cities for most difficult conditions for savers, according to a study by the finance site GOBankingRates. Criteria: average monthly cost of grocery items; median home listing price; median rent; median income; transportation costs; gas prices; and the cost of eating out for an inexpensive and mid-range meal. *www.gobankingrates.com, "The 20 Best (and Worst) Places to Live If You're Trying to Save Money," August 27, 2019*

- The Brookings Institution ranked the nation's largest cities based on income inequality. Wichita was ranked #76 (#1 = greatest inequality). Criteria: the "95/20 ratio," a figure representing the income at which a household earns more than 95 percent of all other households, divided by the income at which a household earns more than only 20 percent of all other households. *Brookings Institution, "Household Income Inequality, Largest Cities of 97 Large U.S. Metro Areas, 2014-2016," February 5, 2018*

- The Brookings Institution ranked the 100 largest metro areas in the U.S. based on income inequality. Wichita was ranked #84 (#1 = greatest inequality). Criteria: the "95/20 ratio," a figure representing the income at which a household earns more than 95 percent of all other households, divided by the income at which a household earns more than only 20 percent of all other households. *Brookings Institution, "Household Income Inequality, 100 Largest U.S. Metro Areas, 2014-2016," February 5, 2018*

- The Wichita metro area appeared on the Milken Institute "2020 Best Performing Cities" list. Rank: #150 out of 200 large metro areas. Criteria: job growth; wage and salary growth; high-tech output growth. *Milken Institute, "Best-Performing Cities 2020," February 26, 2020*

- *Forbes* ranked the 200 most populous metro areas to determine the nation's "Best Places for Business and Careers." The Wichita metro area was ranked #119. Criteria: costs (business and living); job growth (past and projected); income growth; quality of life; educational attainment (college and high school); projected economic growth; cultural and leisure opportunities; workplace tolerance laws; net migration patterns. *Forbes, "The Best Places for Business and Careers 2019: Seattle Still On Top," October 30, 2019*

Education Rankings

- Personal finance website *WalletHub* analyzed the 150 largest U.S. metropolitan statistical areas to determine where the most educated Americans are choosing to settle. Criteria: education levels; percentage of workers with degrees; education quality and attainment gap; public school quality rankings; quality and size of each metro area's universities. Wichita was ranked #86 (#1 = most educated city). *www.WalletHub.com, "2019's Most and Least Educated Cities in America," July 22, 2019*

- Wichita was selected as one of America's most literate cities. The city ranked #60 out of the 82 largest U.S. cities. Criteria: number of booksellers; library resources; Internet resources; educational attainment; periodical publishing resources; newspaper circulation. *Central Connecticut State University, "America's Most Literate Cities, 2016," March 31, 2017*

Environmental Rankings

- Wichita was highlighted as one of the top 104 cleanest metro areas for short-term particle pollution (24-hour PM 2.5) in the U.S. during 2015 through 2017. Monitors in these cities reported no days with unhealthful PM 2.5 levels. *American Lung Association, "State of the Air 2019," April 24, 2019*

Health/Fitness Rankings

- For each of the 100 largest cities in the United States, the American Fitness Index®, published by the American College of Sports Medicine and the Anthem Foundation, evaluated community infrastructure and 33 health behaviors including preventive health, levels of chronic disease conditions, pedestrian safety, air quality, and community resources that support physical activity. Wichita ranked #90 for "community fitness." *americanfitnessindex.org, "ACSM American Fitness Index Health and Community Fitness Status of the 100 Largest U.S. Cities," May 14, 2019*

- Wichita was identified as a "2020 Spring Allergy Capital." The area ranked #90 out of 100. Three groups of factors were used to identify the most challenging cities for people with allergies during the spring season: annual spring pollen levels; over the counter medicine use; number of board-certified allergy specialists. *Asthma and Allergy Foundation of America, "Spring Allergy Capitals 2020," March 10, 2020*

- Wichita was identified as a "2020 Fall Allergy Capital." The area ranked #72 out of 100. Three groups of factors were used to identify the most challenging cities for people with allergies during the fall season: annual fall pollen levels; over the counter medicine use; number of board-certified allergy specialists. *Asthma and Allergy Foundation of America, "Fall Allergy Capitals 2020," March 10, 2020*

- Wichita was identified as a "2019 Asthma Capital." The area ranked #31 out of the nation's 100 largest metropolitan areas. Criteria: estimated asthma prevalence; crude death rate from asthma; and ER visits due to asthma. Risk factors that were analyzed but not factored in the rankings: annual pollen score; annual air quality; public smoking laws; number of board-certified asthma specialists; rescue medication use; controller medication use; uninsured rate; poverty rate. *Asthma and Allergy Foundation of America, "Asthma Capitals 2019: The Most Challenging Places to Live With Asthma," May 7, 2019*

- *Men's Health* ranked 100 major U.S. cities in terms of the best cities for men. Wichita ranked #65. Criteria: health; fitness; quality of life. *Men's Health, "The Best & Worst Cities for Men Who Want to Be Fit and Happy," January 1, 2016*

- The Wichita metro area ranked #157 out of 189 in The Gallup-Sharecare Well-Being Index. Criteria: purpose; social well being; financial health; community and physical health. Results are based on telephone interviews with adults, aged 18 and older, living in metropolitan areas in the 50 U.S. states and the District of Columbia. *Gallup-Sharecare, "State of American Well-Being, 2017 Community Well-Being Rankings" March 2018*

Real Estate Rankings

■ *WalletHub* compared the most populated U.S. cities, as well as at least two of the most populated cities in each state, for a total of 179, to determine which had the best markets for real estate agents. Wichita ranked #124 where demand was high and pay was the best. Criteria: sales per agent; annual median wage for real-estate agents; monthly average starting salary for real estate agents; real estate job density and competition; unemployment rate; home turnover rate; housing-market health index; and other relevant metrics. *www.WalletHub.com, "2019's Best Places to Be a Real Estate Agent," April 24, 2019*

■ Wichita was ranked #58 out of 238 metro areas in terms of housing affordability in 2019 by the National Association of Home Builders (#1 = most affordable). Criteria: the share of homes sold in that area affordable to a family earning the local median income, based on standard mortgage underwriting criteria. *National Association of Home Builders®, NAHB-Wells Fargo Housing Opportunity Index, 4th Quarter 2019*

Safety Rankings

■ To identify the most dangerous cities in America, 24/7 Wall Street focused on violent crime categories—murder, non-negligent manslaughter, rape, robbery, and aggravated assault—and property crime as reported in the FBI's 2018 annual Uniform Crime Report. Criteria also included median income from American Community Survey and unemployment figures from Bureau of Labor Statistics. For cities with populations over 100,000, Wichita was ranked #18. *247wallst.com, "America's Most Dangerous Cities" January 10, 2020*

■ Statistics drawn from the FBI's Uniform Crime Report were used to rank the metropolitan statistical areas in each state where violent crime rose most over the years 2012–2017. 24/7 Wall Street found that the Wichita metro area placed #16 of those with the largest increases in violent crime. *247wallst.com, "Cities Where Crime Is Soaring In Every State," January 11, 2020*

■ Allstate ranked the 200 largest cities in America in terms of driver safety. Wichita ranked #24. Criteria: internal property damage claims over a two-year period from January 2016 to December 2017. The report helps increase the importance of safety and awareness behind the wheel. *Allstate, "Allstate America's Best Drivers Report, 2019" June 24, 2019*

■ Wichita was identified as one of the most dangerous cities in America by NeighborhoodScout. The city ranked #40 out of 100 (#1 = most dangerous). Criteria: number of violent crimes per 1,000 residents. The editors only considered cities with 25,000 or more residents. *NeighborhoodScout.com, "Top 100 Most Dangerous Cities in the U.S. 2020" January 2, 2020*

■ The National Insurance Crime Bureau ranked 382 metro areas in the U.S. in terms of per capita rates of vehicle theft. The Wichita metro area ranked #8 (#1 = highest rate). Criteria: number of vehicle theft offenses per 100,000 inhabitants in 2018. *National Insurance Crime Bureau, "Hot Spots 2018," June 25, 2019*

Seniors/Retirement Rankings

■ From its Best Cities for Successful Aging indexes, the Milken Institute generated rankings for metropolitan areas, weighing data in nine categories—health care, wellness, living arrangements, transportation and convenience, financial characteristics, education, employment, community engagement, and overall livability. The Wichita metro area was ranked #41 overall in the large metro area category. *Milken Institute, "Best Cities for Successful Aging, 2017" March 14, 2017*

Women/Minorities Rankings

- Personal finance website *WalletHub* compared more than 180 U.S. cities—including the 150 most populated U.S. cities, plus at least two of the most populated cities in each state—across two key dimensions, "Hispanic Business-Friendliness" and "Hispanic Purchasing Power", to arrive at the most favorable conditions for Hispanic entrepreneurs. Wichita was ranked #119 out of 182. Criteria includes: share of Hispanic-Owned Businesses; Hispanic entrepreneurship rate to median annual income of Hispanics; Small Business-Friendliness score; cost of living; and number of Hispanics with at least a bachelor's degree. *WalletHub.com, "2019's Best Cities for Hispanic Entrepreneurs," May 1, 2019*

Miscellaneous Rankings

- Wichita was selected as a 2019 Digital Cities Survey winner. The city ranked #4 in the large city (250,000 to 499,999 population) category. The survey examined and assessed how city governments are utilizing technology to improve transparency, enhance cybersecurity, and solve social challenges. Survey questions focused on ten characteristics: data governance, citizen-focused, leadership alignment, secure, staffed/supported, efficient, connected, resilient, best practices, and use of innovation. *Center for Digital Government, "2019 Digital Cities Survey," November 14, 2019*

- *WalletHub* compared the 150 most populated U.S. cities to determine their operating efficiency. A "Quality of Services" score was constructed for each city and then divided by the total budget per capita to reveal which were managed the best. Wichita ranked #47. Criteria: financial stability; economy; education; safety; health; infrastructure and pollution. *www.WalletHub.com, "2019's Best- & Worst-Run Cities in America," July 1, 2019*

Business Environment

CITY FINANCES

City Government Finances

Component	2017 ($000)	2017 ($ per capita)
Total Revenues	807,298	2,070
Total Expenditures	737,913	1,892
Debt Outstanding	2,489,801	6,385
Cash and Securities[1]	2,966,314	7,607

Note: (1) Cash and security holdings of a government at the close of its fiscal year, including those of its dependent agencies, utilities, and liquor stores.
Source: U.S. Census Bureau, State & Local Government Finances 2017

City Government Revenue by Source

Source	2017 ($000)	2017 ($ per capita)	2017 (%)
General Revenue			
From Federal Government	29,227	75	3.6
From State Government	87,257	224	10.8
From Local Governments	58,660	150	7.3
Taxes			
Property	123,970	318	15.4
Sales and Gross Receipts	51,944	133	6.4
Personal Income	0	0	0.0
Corporate Income	0	0	0.0
Motor Vehicle License	0	0	0.0
Other Taxes	8,096	21	1.0
Current Charges	120,973	310	15.0
Liquor Store	0	0	0.0
Utility	79,510	204	9.8
Employee Retirement	89,816	230	11.1

Source: U.S. Census Bureau, State & Local Government Finances 2017

City Government Expenditures by Function

Function	2017 ($000)	2017 ($ per capita)	2017 (%)
General Direct Expenditures			
Air Transportation	41,863	107	5.7
Corrections	0	0	0.0
Education	0	0	0.0
Employment Security Administration	0	0	0.0
Financial Administration	4,741	12	0.6
Fire Protection	44,161	113	6.0
General Public Buildings	16,620	42	2.3
Governmental Administration, Other	7,636	19	1.0
Health	2,084	5	0.3
Highways	85,252	218	11.6
Hospitals	0	0	0.0
Housing and Community Development	562	1	0.1
Interest on General Debt	105,537	270	14.3
Judicial and Legal	9,229	23	1.3
Libraries	8,354	21	1.1
Parking	1,017	2	0.1
Parks and Recreation	33,991	87	4.6
Police Protection	82,873	212	11.2
Public Welfare	0	0	0.0
Sewerage	64,022	164	8.7
Solid Waste Management	1,863	4	0.3
Veterans' Services	0	0	0.0
Liquor Store	0	0	0.0
Utility	93,671	240	12.7
Employee Retirement	68,537	175	9.3

Source: U.S. Census Bureau, State & Local Government Finances 2017

DEMOGRAPHICS

Population Growth

Area	1990 Census	2000 Census	2010 Census	2018* Estimate	Population Growth (%) 1990-2018	Population Growth (%) 2010-2018
City	313,693	344,284	382,368	389,563	24.2	1.9
MSA[1]	511,111	571,166	623,061	643,765	26.0	3.3
U.S.	248,709,873	281,421,906	308,745,538	322,903,030	29.8	4.6

Note: (1) Figures cover the Wichita, KS Metropolitan Statistical Area—see Appendix B for areas included; (*) 2014-2018 5-year estimated population
Source: U.S. Census Bureau, 1990 Census, Census 2000, Census 2010, 2014-2018 American Community Survey 5-Year Estimates

Household Size

Area	Persons in Household (%) One	Two	Three	Four	Five	Six	Seven or More	Average Household Size
City	33.0	31.9	13.6	11.4	6.2	2.6	1.3	2.50
MSA[1]	29.8	33.3	14.1	11.9	6.6	2.9	1.4	2.60
U.S.	27.7	33.9	15.7	13.0	6.0	2.3	1.4	2.60

Note: (1) Figures cover the Wichita, KS Metropolitan Statistical Area—see Appendix B for areas included
Source: U.S. Census Bureau, 2014-2018 American Community Survey 5-Year Estimates

Race

Area	White Alone[2] (%)	Black Alone[2] (%)	Asian Alone[2] (%)	AIAN[3] Alone[2] (%)	NHOPI[4] Alone[2] (%)	Other Race Alone[2] (%)	Two or More Races (%)
City	74.6	11.1	5.0	1.0	0.1	4.0	4.3
MSA[1]	81.4	7.5	3.6	1.0	0.1	2.6	3.8
U.S.	72.7	12.7	5.4	0.8	0.2	4.9	3.2

Note: (1) Figures cover the Wichita, KS Metropolitan Statistical Area—see Appendix B for areas included; (2) Alone is defined as not being in combination with one or more other races; (3) American Indian and Alaska Native; (4) Native Hawaiian and Other Pacific Islander
Source: U.S. Census Bureau, 2014-2018 American Community Survey 5-Year Estimates

Hispanic or Latino Origin

Area	Total (%)	Mexican (%)	Puerto Rican (%)	Cuban (%)	Other (%)
City	17.0	14.6	0.5	0.2	1.8
MSA[1]	12.8	10.7	0.4	0.2	1.5
U.S.	17.8	11.2	1.7	0.7	4.2

Note: Persons of Hispanic or Latino origin can be of any race; (1) Figures cover the Wichita, KS Metropolitan Statistical Area—see Appendix B for areas included
Source: U.S. Census Bureau, 2014-2018 American Community Survey 5-Year Estimates

Segregation

Type	Segregation Indices[1] 1990	2000	2010	2010 Rank[2]	Percent Change 1990-2000	Percent Change 1990-2010	Percent Change 2000-2010
Black/White	64.2	60.5	58.0	44	-3.7	-6.2	-2.5
Asian/White	44.9	46.2	46.5	20	1.3	1.6	0.3
Hispanic/White	34.3	42.5	42.3	56	8.1	8.0	-0.1

Note: All figures cover the Metropolitan Statistical Area—see Appendix B for areas included; Figures are based on an analysis of 1990, 2000, and 2010 Census Decennial Census tract data by William H. Frey, Brookings Institution and the University of Michigan Social Science Data Analysis Network. In this analysis all racial groups (whites, blacks, and asians) are non-Hispanic members of those races. Hispanics are shown as a separate category; (1) Segregation Indices are Dissimilarity Indices that measure the degree to which the minority group is distributed differently than whites across census tracts. They range from 0 (complete integration) to 100 (complete segregation) where the value indicates the percentage of the minority group that needs to move to be distributed exactly like whites; (2) Ranges from 1 (most segregated) to 102 (least segregated); n/a not available.
Source: www.CensusScope.org

Ancestry

Area	German	Irish	English	American	Italian	Polish	French[2]	Scottish	Dutch
City	20.0	9.5	7.5	5.2	1.8	1.1	2.2	1.8	1.6
MSA[1]	22.7	10.0	8.0	7.3	1.7	1.1	2.3	2.1	1.7
U.S.	13.7	9.9	7.3	6.4	5.2	2.8	2.4	1.7	1.2

Note: Figures are the percentage of the total population reporting a particular ancestry. The nine most commonly reported ancestries in the U.S. are shown. Figures include multiple ancestries (e.g. if a person reported being Irish and Italian, they were included in both columns); (1) Figures cover the Wichita, KS Metropolitan Statistical Area—see Appendix B for areas included; (2) Excludes Basque
Source: U.S. Census Bureau, 2014-2018 American Community Survey 5-Year Estimates

Foreign-born Population

Area	Percent of Population Born in								
	Any Foreign Country	Asia	Mexico	Europe	Caribbean	Central America[2]	South America	Africa	Canada
City	10.1	3.8	4.5	0.4	0.1	0.5	0.1	0.6	0.1
MSA[1]	7.3	2.7	3.0	0.4	0.1	0.3	0.1	0.4	0.1
U.S.	13.5	4.1	3.5	1.5	1.3	1.1	0.9	0.7	0.3

Note: (1) Figures cover the Wichita, KS Metropolitan Statistical Area—see Appendix B for areas included; (2) Excludes Mexico.
Source: U.S. Census Bureau, 2014-2018 American Community Survey 5-Year Estimates

Marital Status

Area	Never Married	Now Married[2]	Separated	Widowed	Divorced
City	32.9	46.4	1.9	5.5	13.4
MSA[1]	29.6	50.8	1.5	5.8	12.2
U.S.	33.3	48.1	2.0	5.8	10.8

Note: Figures are percentages and cover the population 15 years of age and older; (1) Figures cover the Wichita, KS Metropolitan Statistical Area—see Appendix B for areas included; (2) Excludes separated
Source: U.S. Census Bureau, 2014-2018 American Community Survey 5-Year Estimates

Disability by Age

Area	All Ages	Under 18 Years Old	18 to 64 Years Old	65 Years and Over
City	13.2	4.3	11.9	36.2
MSA[1]	12.9	4.5	11.3	35.8
U.S.	12.6	4.2	10.3	35.0

Note: Figures show percent of the civilian noninstitutionalized population that reported having a disability. Disability status is determined from six types of difficulty: vision, hearing, cognitive, ambulatory, self-care, and independent living. For children under 5 years old, hearing and vision difficulty are used to determine disability status. For children between the ages of 5 and 14, disability status is determined from hearing, vision, cognitive, ambulatory, and self-care difficulties. For people aged 15 years and older, they are considered to have a disability if they have difficulty with any one of the six difficulty types; Note: (1) Figures cover the Wichita, KS Metropolitan Statistical Area—see Appendix B for areas included
Source: U.S. Census Bureau, 2014-2018 American Community Survey 5-Year Estimates

Age

Area	Percent of Population									Median Age
	Under Age 5	Age 5–19	Age 20–34	Age 35–44	Age 45–54	Age 55–64	Age 65–74	Age 75–84	Age 85+	
City	7.4	20.4	22.5	11.8	11.9	12.4	7.9	3.9	1.8	34.8
MSA[1]	7.0	21.4	20.5	12.0	12.1	12.8	8.0	4.3	1.9	35.9
U.S.	6.1	19.3	20.7	12.6	13.2	12.8	8.8	4.5	1.9	37.9

Note: (1) Figures cover the Wichita, KS Metropolitan Statistical Area—see Appendix B for areas included
Source: U.S. Census Bureau, 2014-2018 American Community Survey 5-Year Estimates

Gender

Area	Males	Females	Males per 100 Females
City	192,025	197,538	97.2
MSA[1]	319,270	324,495	98.4
U.S.	158,984,190	163,918,840	97.0

Note: (1) Figures cover the Wichita, KS Metropolitan Statistical Area—see Appendix B for areas included
Source: U.S. Census Bureau, 2014-2018 American Community Survey 5-Year Estimates

Religious Groups by Family

Area	Catholic	Baptist	Non-Den.	Methodist[2]	Lutheran	LDS[3]	Pentecostal	Presbyterian[4]	Muslim[5]	Judaism
MSA[1]	14.5	13.5	3.2	7.2	1.8	1.4	2.0	1.7	0.2	<0.1
U.S.	19.1	9.3	4.0	4.0	2.3	2.0	1.9	1.6	0.8	0.7

Note: Figures are the number of adherents as a percentage of the total population; (1) Figures cover the Wichita, KS Metropolitan Statistical Area—see Appendix B for areas included; (2) Methodist/Pietist; (3) Latter Day Saints; (4) Reformed; (5) Figures are estimates
Source: Association of Statisticians of American Religious Bodies, 2010 U.S. Religion Census: Religious Congregations & Membership Study

Religious Groups by Tradition

Area	Catholic	Evangelical Protestant	Mainline Protestant	Other Tradition	Black Protestant	Orthodox
MSA[1]	14.5	20.7	11.1	2.4	1.9	0.2
U.S.	19.1	16.2	7.3	4.3	1.6	0.3

Note: Figures are the number of adherents as a percentage of the total population; (1) Figures cover the Wichita, KS Metropolitan Statistical Area—see Appendix B for areas included
Source: Association of Statisticians of American Religious Bodies, 2010 U.S. Religion Census: Religious Congregations & Membership Study

ECONOMY

Gross Metropolitan Product

Area	2017	2018	2019	2020	Rank[2]
MSA[1]	34.3	35.7	37.0	38.0	81

Note: Figures are in billions of dollars; (1) Figures cover the Wichita, KS Metropolitan Statistical Area—see Appendix B for areas included; (2) Rank is based on 2018 data and ranges from 1 to 381
Source: U.S. Conference of Mayors, U.S. Metro Economies: GMP & Employment 2018-2020, September 2019

Economic Growth

Area	2015-17 (%)	2018 (%)	2019 (%)	2020 (%)	Rank[2]
MSA[1]	1.9	1.5	1.8	0.5	141
U.S.	1.9	2.9	2.3	2.1	–

Note: Figures are real gross metropolitan product (GMP) growth rates and represent average annual percent change; (1) Figures cover the Wichita, KS Metropolitan Statistical Area—see Appendix B for areas included; (2) Rank is based on 2017 2-year average annual percent change and ranges from 1 to 381
Source: U.S. Conference of Mayors, U.S. Metro Economies: GMP & Employment 2018-2020, September 2019

Metropolitan Area Exports

Area	2013	2014	2015	2016	2017	2018	Rank[2]
MSA[1]	3,785.5	4,011.7	3,717.6	3,054.9	3,299.2	3,817.0	68

Note: Figures are in millions of dollars; (1) Figures cover the Wichita, KS Metropolitan Statistical Area—see Appendix B for areas included; (2) Rank is based on 2018 data and ranges from 1 to 387
Source: U.S. Department of Commerce, International Trade Administration, Office of Trade and Economic Analysis, Industry and Analysis, Exports by Metropolitan Area, data extracted April 15, 2020

Building Permits

Area	Single-Family			Multi-Family			Total		
	2017	2018	Pct. Chg.	2017	2018	Pct. Chg.	2017	2018	Pct. Chg.
City	843	532	-36.9	463	326	-29.6	1,306	858	-34.3
MSA[1]	1,634	1,223	-25.2	1,097	735	-33.0	2,731	1,958	-28.3
U.S.	820,000	855,300	4.3	462,000	473,500	2.5	1,282,000	1,328,800	3.7

Note: (1) Figures cover the Wichita, KS Metropolitan Statistical Area—see Appendix B for areas included; Figures represent new, privately-owned housing units authorized (unadjusted data); All permit data are based on estimates with imputation
Source: U.S. Census Bureau, Manufacturing, Mining, and Construction Statistics, Building Permits, 2017, 2018

Bankruptcy Filings

Area	Business Filings			Nonbusiness Filings		
	2018	2019	% Chg.	2018	2019	% Chg.
Sedgwick County	34	30	-11.8	1,399	1,381	-1.3
U.S.	22,232	22,780	2.5	751,186	752,160	0.1

Note: Business filings include Chapter 7, Chapter 9, Chapter 11, Chapter 12, Chapter 13, Chapter 15, and
Section 304; Nonbusiness filings include Chapter 7, Chapter 11, and Chapter 13
Source: Administrative Office of the U.S. Courts, Business and Nonbusiness Bankruptcy, County Cases
Commenced by Chapter of the Bankruptcy Code, During the 12-Month Period Ending December 31, 2018 and
Business and Nonbusiness Bankruptcy, County Cases Commenced by Chapter of the Bankruptcy Code, During
the 12-Month Period Ending December 31, 2019

Housing Vacancy Rates

Area	Gross Vacancy Rate[2] (%)			Year-Round Vacancy Rate[3] (%)			Rental Vacancy Rate[4] (%)			Homeowner Vacancy Rate[5] (%)		
	2017	2018	2019	2017	2018	2019	2017	2018	2019	2017	2018	2019
MSA[1]	n/a	n/a	n/a	n/a	n/a	n/a	n/a	n/a	n/a	n/a	n/a	n/a
U.S.	12.7	12.3	12.0	9.9	9.7	9.5	7.2	6.9	6.7	1.6	1.5	1.4

Note: (1) Figures cover the Wichita, KS Metropolitan Statistical Area—see Appendix B for areas included; (2)
The percentage of the total housing inventory that is vacant; (3) The percentage of the housing inventory
(excluding seasonal units) that is year-round vacant; (4) The percentage of rental inventory that is vacant for
rent; (5) The percentage of homeowner inventory that is vacant for sale; n/a not available
Source: U.S. Census Bureau, Housing Vacancies and Homeownership Annual Statistics: 2017, 2018, 2019

INCOME

Income

Area	Per Capita ($)	Median Household ($)	Average Household ($)
City	27,723	50,867	68,821
MSA[1]	28,577	55,818	72,950
U.S.	32,621	60,293	84,938

Note: (1) Figures cover the Wichita, KS Metropolitan Statistical Area—see Appendix B for areas included
Source: U.S. Census Bureau, 2014-2018 American Community Survey 5-Year Estimates

Household Income Distribution

Area	Percent of Households Earning							
	Under $15,000	$15,000 -$24,999	$25,000 -$34,999	$35,000 -$49,999	$50,000 -$74,999	$75,000 -$99,999	$100,000 -$149,999	$150,000 and up
City	13.0	10.6	11.0	14.7	19.0	11.5	12.1	8.1
MSA[1]	11.0	9.7	10.1	14.3	19.4	12.7	14.0	8.7
U.S.	10.9	9.3	9.3	12.6	17.5	12.5	14.6	13.3

Note: (1) Figures cover the Wichita, KS Metropolitan Statistical Area—see Appendix B for areas included
Source: U.S. Census Bureau, 2014-2018 American Community Survey 5-Year Estimates

Poverty Rate

Area	All Ages	Under 18 Years Old	18 to 64 Years Old	65 Years and Over
City	16.2	22.1	15.3	9.1
MSA[1]	13.3	17.9	12.5	8.3
U.S.	14.1	19.5	13.2	9.3

Note: Figures are percentage of people whose income during the past 12 months was below the poverty level;
(1) Figures cover the Wichita, KS Metropolitan Statistical Area—see Appendix B for areas included
Source: U.S. Census Bureau, 2014-2018 American Community Survey 5-Year Estimates

EMPLOYMENT

Labor Force and Employment

Area	Civilian Labor Force			Workers Employed		
	Dec. 2018	Dec. 2019	% Chg.	Dec. 2018	Dec. 2019	% Chg.
City	186,160	189,743	1.9	179,744	183,423	2.0
MSA[1]	309,641	315,547	1.9	299,636	305,590	2.0
U.S.	162,510,000	164,007,000	0.9	156,481,000	158,504,000	1.3

Note: Data is not seasonally adjusted and covers workers 16 years of age and older; (1) Figures cover the
Wichita, KS Metropolitan Statistical Area—see Appendix B for areas included
Source: Bureau of Labor Statistics, Local Area Unemployment Statistics

Unemployment Rate

Area	2019											
	Jan.	Feb.	Mar.	Apr.	May	Jun.	Jul.	Aug.	Sep.	Oct.	Nov.	Dec.
City	4.2	3.8	3.7	3.1	3.4	3.7	4.1	3.8	3.1	3.3	3.3	3.3
MSA[1]	3.9	3.6	3.6	3.0	3.2	3.5	3.9	3.6	3.0	3.1	3.1	3.2
U.S.	4.4	4.1	3.9	3.3	3.4	3.8	4.0	3.8	3.3	3.3	3.3	3.4

Note: Data is not seasonally adjusted and covers workers 16 years of age and older; (1) Figures cover the Wichita, KS Metropolitan Statistical Area—see Appendix B for areas included
Source: Bureau of Labor Statistics, Local Area Unemployment Statistics

Average Wages

Occupation	$/Hr.	Occupation	$/Hr.
Accountants and Auditors	32.40	Maintenance and Repair Workers	18.20
Automotive Mechanics	19.30	Marketing Managers	65.50
Bookkeepers	17.90	Network and Computer Systems Admin.	32.90
Carpenters	18.20	Nurses, Licensed Practical	21.40
Cashiers	10.50	Nurses, Registered	27.60
Computer Programmers	37.60	Nursing Assistants	12.50
Computer Systems Analysts	35.80	Office Clerks, General	14.20
Computer User Support Specialists	21.30	Physical Therapists	44.30
Construction Laborers	16.10	Physicians	71.00
Cooks, Restaurant	12.50	Plumbers, Pipefitters and Steamfitters	21.70
Customer Service Representatives	16.30	Police and Sheriff's Patrol Officers	23.90
Dentists	101.20	Postal Service Mail Carriers	24.70
Electricians	25.40	Real Estate Sales Agents	30.00
Engineers, Electrical	44.90	Retail Salespersons	14.10
Fast Food and Counter Workers	9.50	Sales Representatives, Technical/Scientific	42.10
Financial Managers	61.50	Secretaries, Exc. Legal/Medical/Executive	16.40
First-Line Supervisors of Office Workers	26.50	Security Guards	14.30
General and Operations Managers	48.00	Surgeons	115.60
Hairdressers/Cosmetologists	12.60	Teacher Assistants, Exc. Postsecondary*	12.60
Home Health and Personal Care Aides	11.10	Teachers, Secondary School, Exc. Sp. Ed.*	25.50
Janitors and Cleaners	12.50	Telemarketers	12.80
Landscaping/Groundskeeping Workers	15.00	Truck Drivers, Heavy/Tractor-Trailer	21.10
Lawyers	42.00	Truck Drivers, Light/Delivery Services	17.10
Maids and Housekeeping Cleaners	11.00	Waiters and Waitresses	9.90

Note: Wage data covers the Wichita, KS Metropolitan Statistical Area—see Appendix B for areas included;
(*) Hourly wages were calculated from annual wage data based on a 40 hour work week; n/a not available.
Source: Bureau of Labor Statistics, Metro Area Occupational Employment & Wage Estimates, May 2019

Employment by Occupation

Occupation Classification	City (%)	MSA[1] (%)	U.S. (%)
Management, Business, Science, and Arts	34.2	36.2	37.9
Natural Resources, Construction, and Maintenance	9.7	10.1	8.9
Production, Transportation, and Material Moving	15.8	15.4	13.3
Sales and Office	21.9	21.2	22.1
Service	18.4	17.1	17.9

Note: Figures cover employed civilians 16 years of age and older; (1) Figures cover the Wichita, KS Metropolitan Statistical Area—see Appendix B for areas included
Source: U.S. Census Bureau, 2014-2018 American Community Survey 5-Year Estimates

Employment by Industry

Sector	MSA[1]		U.S.
	Number of Employees	Percent of Total	Percent of Total
Construction, Mining, and Logging	16,300	5.3	5.4
Education and Health Services	47,300	15.3	16.1
Financial Activities	11,900	3.9	5.8
Government	43,200	14.0	15.0
Information	4,000	1.3	1.9
Leisure and Hospitality	33,100	10.7	10.8
Manufacturing	55,200	17.9	8.4
Other Services	11,200	3.6	3.9
Professional and Business Services	35,400	11.5	14.1
Retail Trade	31,900	10.3	10.6
Transportation, Warehousing, and Utilities	10,500	3.4	4.2
Wholesale Trade	8,800	2.8	3.9

Note: Figures are non-farm employment as of December 2019. Figures are not seasonally adjusted and include workers 16 years of age and older; (1) Figures cover the Wichita, KS Metropolitan Statistical Area—see Appendix B for areas included
Source: Bureau of Labor Statistics, Current Employment Statistics, Employment, Hours, and Earnings

Occupations with Greatest Projected Employment Growth: 2019 – 2021

Occupation[1]	2019 Employment	2021 Projected Employment	Numeric Employment Change	Percent Employment Change
Personal Care Aides	22,540	23,920	1,380	6.1
Combined Food Preparation and Serving Workers, Including Fast Food	33,970	35,010	1,040	3.1
Registered Nurses	31,190	32,010	820	2.6
Cooks, Restaurant	10,850	11,300	450	4.1
Construction Laborers	13,740	14,190	450	3.3
Nursing Assistants	23,970	24,410	440	1.8
Laborers and Freight, Stock, and Material Movers, Hand	21,250	21,650	400	1.9
Heavy and Tractor-Trailer Truck Drivers	21,440	21,820	380	1.8
Light Truck or Delivery Services Drivers	9,090	9,390	300	3.3
Waiters and Waitresses	20,960	21,240	280	1.3

Note: Projections cover Kansas; (1) Sorted by numeric employment change
Source: www.projectionscentral.com, State Occupational Projections, 2019–2021 Short-Term Projections

Fastest Growing Occupations: 2019 – 2021

Occupation[1]	2019 Employment	2021 Projected Employment	Numeric Employment Change	Percent Employment Change
Cargo and Freight Agents	690	740	50	7.2
Home Health Aides	2,410	2,570	160	6.6
Personal Care Aides	22,540	23,920	1,380	6.1
Physician Assistants	1,130	1,190	60	5.3
Respiratory Therapists	1,320	1,390	70	5.3
Nurse Practitioners	2,490	2,620	130	5.2
Substance Abuse, Behavioral Disorder, and Mental Health Counselors	1,810	1,890	80	4.4
Software Developers, Applications	5,790	6,040	250	4.3
Phlebotomists	1,400	1,460	60	4.3
Speech-Language Pathologists	1,470	1,530	60	4.1

Note: Projections cover Kansas; (1) Sorted by percent employment change and excludes occupations with numeric employment change less than 50
Source: www.projectionscentral.com, State Occupational Projections, 2019–2021 Short-Term Projections

TAXES

State Corporate Income Tax Rates

State	Tax Rate (%)	Income Brackets ($)	Num. of Brackets	Financial Institution Tax Rate (%)[a]	Federal Income Tax Ded.
Kansas	4.0 (k)	Flat rate	1	2.25 (k)	No

Note: Tax rates as of January 1, 2020; (a) Rates listed are the corporate income tax rate applied to financial institutions or excise taxes based on income; (k) In addition to the flat 4% corporate income tax, Kansas levies a 3.0% surtax on taxable income over $50,000. Banks pay a privilege tax of 2.25% of net income, plus a surtax of 2.125% (2.25% for savings and loans, trust companies, and federally chartered savings banks) on net income in excess of $25,000.
Source: Federation of Tax Administrators, State Corporate Income Tax Rates, January 1, 2020

State Individual Income Tax Rates

State	Tax Rate (%)	Income Brackets ($)	Personal Exemptions ($)			Standard Ded. ($)	
			Single	Married	Depend.	Single	Married
Kansas	3.1 - 5.7	15,000 - 30,000 (b)	2,250	4,500	2,250	3,000	7,500

Note: Tax rates as of January 1, 2020; Local- and county-level taxes are not included; Federal income tax is not deductible on state income tax returns; (b) For joint returns, taxes are twice the tax on half the couple's income.
Source: Federation of Tax Administrators, State Individual Income Tax Rates, January 1, 2020

Various State Sales and Excise Tax Rates

State	State Sales Tax (%)	Gasoline[1] (¢/gal.)	Cigarette[2] ($/pack)	Spirits[3] ($/gal.)	Wine[4] ($/gal.)	Beer[5] ($/gal.)	Recreational Marijuana (%)
Kansas	6.5	24.025	1.29	2.50	0.30	0.18	Not legal

Note: All tax rates as of January 1, 2020; (1) The American Petroleum Institute has developed a methodology for determining the average tax rate on a gallon of fuel. Rates may include any of the following: excise taxes, environmental fees, storage tank fees, other fees or taxes, general sales tax, and local taxes; (2) The federal excise tax of $1.0066 per pack and local taxes are not included; (3) Rates are those applicable to off-premise sales of 40% alcohol by volume (a.b.v.) distilled spirits in 750ml containers. Local excise taxes are excluded; (4) Rates are those applicable to off-premise sales of 11% a.b.v. non-carbonated wine in 750ml containers; (5) Rates are those applicable to off-premise sales of 4.7% a.b.v. beer in 12 ounce containers.
Source: Tax Foundation, 2020 Facts & Figures: How Does Your State Compare?

State Business Tax Climate Index Rankings

State	Overall Rank	Corporate Tax Rank	Individual Income Tax Rank	Sales Tax Rank	Property Tax Rank	Unemployment Insurance Tax Rank
Kansas	34	35	23	38	20	14

Note: The index is a measure of how each state's tax laws affect economic performance. The lower the rank, the more favorable a state's tax system is for business. States without a given tax are given a ranking of 1. The scores/rankings for the District of Columbia do not affect other states. The 2020 index represents the tax climate as of July 1, 2019.
Source: Tax Foundation, State Business Tax Climate Index 2020

COMMERCIAL UTILITIES

Typical Monthly Electric Bills

Area	Commercial Service ($/month)		Industrial Service ($/month)	
	1,500 kWh	40 kW demand 14,000 kWh	1,000 kW demand 200,000 kWh	50,000 kW demand 32,500,000 kWh
City	174	1,459	26,366	2,225,401
Average[1]	203	1,612	25,706	2,520,671

Note: Figures are based on annualized rates; (1) Average based on 187 utilities surveyed
Source: Edison Electric Institute, Typical Bills and Average Rates Report, Summer 2019

TRANSPORTATION

Means of Transportation to Work

Area	Car/Truck/Van		Public Transportation			Bicycle	Walked	Other Means	Worked at Home
	Drove Alone	Car-pooled	Bus	Subway	Railroad				
City	83.4	9.5	0.6	0.0	0.0	0.3	1.5	1.5	3.1
MSA[1]	83.8	9.0	0.4	0.0	0.0	0.4	1.6	1.3	3.5
U.S.	76.4	9.1	2.5	1.9	0.6	0.6	2.7	1.3	4.9

Note: Figures are percentages and cover workers 16 years of age and older; (1) Figures cover the Wichita, KS Metropolitan Statistical Area—see Appendix B for areas included
Source: U.S. Census Bureau, 2014-2018 American Community Survey 5-Year Estimates

Travel Time to Work

Area	Less Than 10 Minutes	10 to 19 Minutes	20 to 29 Minutes	30 to 44 Minutes	45 to 59 Minutes	60 to 89 Minutes	90 Minutes or More
City	13.6	45.2	27.3	9.9	1.5	1.4	1.0
MSA[1]	16.3	37.8	26.4	14.1	2.8	1.4	1.2
U.S.	12.5	28.7	20.9	20.7	8.2	6.3	2.8

Note: Note: Figures are percentages and include workers 16 years old and over; (1) Figures cover the Wichita, KS Metropolitan Statistical Area—see Appendix B for areas included
Source: U.S. Census Bureau, 2014-2018 American Community Survey 5-Year Estimates

Key Congestion Measures

Area	1982	1992	2002	2012	2017
Annual Hours of Delay, Total (000)	1,912	4,651	6,974	10,495	12,081
Annual Hours of Delay, Per Auto Commuter	13	25	29	31	36
Annual Congestion Cost, Total (million $)	15	49	94	190	224
Annual Congestion Cost, Per Auto Commuter ($)	178	298	349	412	460

Source: Texas A&M Transportation Institute, 2019 Urban Mobility Report

Freeway Travel Time Index

Area	1982	1987	1992	1997	2002	2007	2012	2017
Urban Area Index[1]	1.06	1.08	1.12	1.14	1.15	1.15	1.15	1.14
Urban Area Rank[1,2]	43	44	40	47	61	72	71	80

Note: Freeway Travel Time Index—the ratio of travel time in the peak period to the travel time at free-flow conditions. For example, a value of 1.30 indicates a 20-minute free-flow trip takes 26 minutes in the peak (20 minutes x 1.30 = 26 minutes); (1) Covers the Wichita KS urban area; (2) Rank is based on 101 larger urban areas (#1 = highest travel time index)
Source: Texas A&M Transportation Institute, 2019 Urban Mobility Report

Public Transportation

Agency Name / Mode of Transportation	Vehicles Operated in Maximum Service[1]	Annual Unlinked Passenger Trips[2] (in thous.)	Annual Passenger Miles[3] (in thous.)
Wichita Transit (WT)			
Bus (directly operated)	43	1,181.8	7,413.2
Demand Response (directly operated)	23	81.0	783.6

Note: (1) Number of revenue vehicles operated by the given mode and type of service to meet the annual maximum service requirement. This is the revenue vehicle count during the peak season of the year; on the week and day that maximum service is provided. Vehicles operated in maximum service (VOMS) exclude atypical days and one-time special events; (2) Number of passengers who boarded public transportation vehicles. Passengers are counted each time they board a vehicle no matter how many vehicles they use to travel from their origin to their destination. (3) Sum of the distances ridden by all passengers during the entire fiscal year.
Source: Federal Transit Administration, National Transit Database, 2018

Air Transportation

Airport Name and Code / Type of Service	Passenger Airlines[1]	Passenger Enplanements	Freight Carriers[2]	Freight (lbs)
Wichita Mid-Continent Airport (ICT)				
Domestic service (U.S. carriers - 2019)	22	855,971	13	21,358,926
International service (U.S. carriers - 2018)	0	0	1	60,600

Note: (1) Includes all U.S.-based major, minor and commuter airlines that carried at least one passenger during the year; (2) Includes all U.S.-based airlines and freight carriers that transported at least one pound of freight during the year.
Source: Bureau of Transportation Statistics, The Intermodal Transportation Database, Air Carriers: T-100 Domestic Market (U.S. Carriers), 2019; Bureau of Transportation Statistics, The Intermodal Transportation Database, Air Carriers: T-100 International Market (U.S. Carriers), 2018

Other Transportation Statistics

Major Highways:	I-135; I-35
Amtrak Service:	No
Major Waterways/Ports:	None

Source: Amtrak.com; Google Maps

BUSINESSES

Major Business Headquarters

Company Name	Industry	Fortune[1]	Forbes[2]
Koch Industries	Multicompany	-	2
Spirit AeroSystems Holdings	Aerospace and Defense	420	-

Note: (1) Companies that produce a 10-K are ranked 1 to 500 based on 2018 revenue; (2) All private companies with at least $2 billion in annual revenue through the end of their most current fiscal year are ranked 1 to 228; companies listed are headquartered in the city; dashes indicate no ranking
Source: Fortune, "Fortune 500," June 2019; Forbes, "America's Largest Private Companies," 2019 Rankings

Minority Business Opportunity

Wichita is home to one company which is on the *Hispanic Business* 500 list (500 largest U.S. Hispanic-owned companies based on revenue): **La Raza Pizza** (#86). Companies included must show at least 51 percent ownership by Hispanic U.S. citizens, and must maintain headquarters in one of the 50 states or Washington, D.C. *Hispanic Business, "Hispanic Business 500," June 20, 2013*

Minority- and Women-Owned Businesses

Group	Firms	Sales ($000)	Firms	Sales ($000)	Employees	Payroll ($000)
AIAN[1]	455	315,714	59	302,857	1,232	45,213
Asian	1,637	382,503	362	295,207	2,749	69,153
Black	1,871	116,159	135	80,835	1,344	32,204
Hispanic	1,779	224,116	224	176,381	1,934	53,456
NHOPI[2]	n/a	n/a	n/a	n/a	n/a	n/a
Women	10,507	1,952,465	1,223	1,689,128	11,700	342,443
All Firms	31,140	54,981,552	7,753	53,344,005	178,111	7,424,983

Note: Figures cover firms located in the city; minority- and women-owned business are defined as firms in which the corresponding group own 51% or more of the stock or equity of the company; (1) American Indian and Alaska Native; (2) Native Hawaiian and Other Pacific Islander; n/a not available
Source: U.S. Census Bureau, 2012 Economic Census, Survey of Business Owners

HOTELS & CONVENTION CENTERS

Hotels, Motels and Vacation Rentals

Area	5 Star Num.	5 Star Pct.[3]	4 Star Num.	4 Star Pct.[3]	3 Star Num.	3 Star Pct.[3]	2 Star Num.	2 Star Pct.[3]	1 Star Num.	1 Star Pct.[3]	Not Rated Num.	Not Rated Pct.[3]
City[1]	0	0.0	1	1.0	21	20.6	16	15.7	19	18.6	45	44.1
Total[2]	266	1.3	1,517	7.2	4,627	21.8	3,210	15.1	3,974	18.7	7,601	35.9

Note: (1) Figures cover Wichita and vicinity; (2) Figures cover all 100 cities in this book; (3) Percentage of hotels which have a given star rating; Star ratings are determined by priceline.com and offer an indication of the general quality of a particular hotel.
Source: priceline.com, April 27, 2020

Major Convention Centers

Name	Overall Space (sq. ft.)	Exhibit Space (sq. ft.)	Meeting Space (sq. ft.)	Meeting Rooms
Century II Performing Arts & Convention Center	n/a	200,000	n/a	20

Note: Table includes convention centers located in the Wichita, KS metro area; n/a not available
Source: Original research

Living Environment

COST OF LIVING

Cost of Living Index

Composite Index	Groceries	Housing	Utilities	Trans-portation	Health Care	Misc. Goods/ Services
91.1	94.3	69.6	99.3	95.3	96.1	102.5

Note: The Cost of Living Index measures regional differences in the cost of consumer goods and services, excluding taxes and non-consumer expenditures, for professional and managerial households in the top income quintile. It is based on more than 50,000 prices covering almost 60 different items for which prices are collected three times a year by chambers of commerce, economic development organizations or university applied economic centers in each participating urban area. The numbers shown should be read as a percentage above or below the national average of 100. For example, a value of 115.4 in the groceries column indicates that grocery prices are 15.4% higher than the national average. Small differences in the index numbers should not be interpreted as significant; Figures cover the Wichita KS urban area.
Source: The Council for Community and Economic Research, ACCRA Cost of Living Index, 2019

Grocery Prices

Area[1]	T-Bone Steak ($/pound)	Frying Chicken ($/pound)	Whole Milk ($/half gal.)	Eggs ($/dozen)	Orange Juice ($/64 oz.)	Coffee ($/11.5 oz.)
City[2]	12.06	1.34	1.49	0.82	3.56	3.86
Avg.	11.40	1.41	1.93	1.54	3.51	4.30
Min.	7.40	0.92	0.85	0.58	2.67	2.90
Max.	15.58	2.68	4.09	4.18	5.57	8.10

*Note: (1) Values for the local area are compared with the average, minimum and maximum values for all 290 areas in the Cost of Living Index; (2) Figures cover the Wichita KS urban area; **T-Bone Steak** (price per pound); **Frying Chicken** (price per pound, whole fryer); **Whole Milk** (half gallon carton); **Eggs** (price per dozen, Grade A, large); **Orange Juice** (64 oz. Tropicana or Florida Natural); **Coffee** (11.5 oz. can, vacuum-packed, Maxwell House, Hills Bros, or Folgers).*
Source: The Council for Community and Economic Research, ACCRA Cost of Living Index, 2019

Housing and Utility Costs

Area[1]	New Home Price ($)	Apartment Rent ($/month)	All Electric ($/month)	Part Electric ($/month)	Other Energy ($/month)	Telephone ($/month)
City[2]	257,033	754	-	99.98	63.24	184.30
Avg.	362,090	1,142	174.35	100.00	67.76	179.60
Min.	198,329	501	91.58	31.44	28.51	165.30
Max.	2,074,561	5,050	388.18	239.41	306.15	207.90

*Note: (1) Values for the local area are compared with the average, minimum and maximum values for all 290 areas in the Cost of Living Index; (2) Figures cover the Wichita KS urban area; **New Home Price** (2,400 sf living area, 8,000 sf lot, in urban area with full utilities); **Apartment Rent** (950 sf 2 bedroom/1.5 or 2 bath, unfurnished, excluding all utilities except water); **All Electric** (average monthly cost for an all-electric home); **Part Electric** (average monthly cost for a part-electric home); **Other Energy** (average monthly cost for natural gas, fuel oil, coal, wood, and any other forms of energy except electricity); **Telephone** (price includes the base monthly rate plus taxes and fees for three lines of mobile phone service).*
Source: The Council for Community and Economic Research, ACCRA Cost of Living Index, 2019

Health Care, Transportation, and Other Costs

Area[1]	Doctor ($/visit)	Dentist ($/visit)	Optometrist ($/visit)	Gasoline ($/gallon)	Beauty Salon ($/visit)	Men's Shirt ($)
City[2]	104.74	86.14	157.23	2.31	40.16	43.64
Avg.	114.85	97.58	106.10	2.50	38.15	32.15
Min.	39.00	62.22	52.22	1.53	16.88	10.27
Max.	206.67	151.53	258.67	3.79	79.29	59.30

*Note: (1) Values for the local area are compared with the average, minimum and maximum values for all 290 areas in the Cost of Living Index; (2) Figures cover the Wichita KS urban area; **Doctor** (general practitioners routine exam of an established patient); **Dentist** (adult teeth cleaning and periodic oral examination); **Optometrist** (full vision eye exam for established adult patient); **Gasoline** (one gallon regular unleaded, national brand, including all taxes, cash price at self-service pump if available); **Beauty Salon** (woman's shampoo, trim, and blow-dry); **Men's Shirt** (cotton/polyester dress shirt, pinpoint weave, long sleeves).*
Source: The Council for Community and Economic Research, ACCRA Cost of Living Index, 2019

HOUSING

House Price Index (HPI)

Area	National Ranking[2]	Quarterly Change (%)	One-Year Change (%)	Five-Year Change (%)
MSA[1]	53	0.56	6.19	22.18
U.S.[3]	–	1.26	5.09	32.88

Note: The HPI is a weighted repeat sales index. It measures average price changes in repeat sales or refinancings on the same properties. This information is obtained by reviewing repeat mortgage transactions on single-family properties whose mortgages have been purchased or securitized by Fannie Mae or Freddie Mac in January 1975; (1) Figures cover the Wichita, KS Metropolitan Statistical Area—see Appendix B for areas included; (2) Rankings are based on annual percentage change for all metro areas containing at least 15,000 transactions over the last 10 years and ranges from 1 to 232; (3) figures based on a weighted average of Census Division estimates using a seasonally adjusted, purchase-only index; all figures are for the period ending December 31, 2019
Source: Federal Housing Finance Agency, House Price Index, February 25, 2020

Median Single-Family Home Prices

Area	2017	2018	2019[p]	Percent Change 2018 to 2019
MSA[1]	132.9	142.0	158.2	11.4
U.S. Average	248.8	261.6	274.6	5.0

Note: Figures are median sales prices of existing single-family homes in thousands of dollars; (p) preliminary; (1) Figures cover the Wichita, KS Metropolitan Statistical Area—see Appendix B for areas included
Source: National Association of Realtors, Median Sales Price of Existing Single-Family Homes for Metropolitan Areas, 4th Quarter 2019

Qualifying Income Based on Median Sales Price of Existing Single-Family Homes

Area	With 5% Down ($)	With 10% Down ($)	With 20% Down ($)
MSA[1]	33,460	31,699	28,177
U.S. Average	58,663	55,575	49,400

Note: Figures are preliminary; Qualifying income is based on a mortgage rate of 3.76%. Monthly principal and interest payment is limited to 25% of income; (1) Figures cover the Wichita, KS Metropolitan Statistical Area—see Appendix B for areas included
Source: National Association of Realtors, Qualifying Income Based on Median Sales Price of Existing Single-Family Homes for Metropolitan Areas, 4th Quarter 2019

Median Apartment Condo-Coop Home Prices

Area	2017	2018	2019[p]	Percent Change 2018 to 2019
MSA[1]	n/a	n/a	n/a	n/a
U.S. Average	234.3	241.0	249.5	3.5

Note: Figures are median sales prices of existing apartment condo-coop homes in thousands of dollars; (p) preliminary; n/a not available; (1) Figures cover the Wichita, KS Metropolitan Statistical Area—see Appendix B for areas included
Source: National Association of Realtors, Median Sales Price of Existing Apartment Condo-Coop Homes for Metropolitan Areas, 4th Quarter 2019

Home Value Distribution

Area	Under $50,000	$50,000 -$99,999	$100,000 -$149,999	$150,000 -$199,999	$200,000 -$299,999	$300,000 -$499,999	$500,000 -$999,999	$1,000,000 or more
City	9.2	27.7	23.7	16.9	13.6	6.5	2.0	0.4
MSA[1]	9.1	25.4	23.3	18.4	14.7	7.0	1.8	0.4
U.S.	7.6	13.0	14.0	14.3	19.2	18.3	10.5	3.1

Note: Figures are percentages and cover owner-occupied housing units; (1) Figures cover the Wichita, KS Metropolitan Statistical Area—see Appendix B for areas included
Source: U.S. Census Bureau, 2014-2018 American Community Survey 5-Year Estimates

Homeownership Rate

Area	2011 (%)	2012 (%)	2013 (%)	2014 (%)	2015 (%)	2016 (%)	2017 (%)	2018 (%)	2019 (%)
MSA[1]	n/a	n/a	n/a	n/a	n/a	n/a	n/a	n/a	n/a
U.S.	66.1	65.4	65.1	64.5	63.7	63.4	63.9	64.4	64.6

Note: (1) Figures cover the Wichita, KS Metropolitan Statistical Area—see Appendix B for areas included; n/a not available
Source: U.S. Census Bureau, Housing Vacancies and Homeownership Annual Statistics: 2011-2019

Year Housing Structure Built

Area	2010 or Later	2000 -2009	1990 -1999	1980 -1989	1970 -1979	1960 -1969	1950 -1959	1940 -1949	Before 1940	Median Year
City	3.1	10.3	12.7	12.5	13.0	9.9	20.0	7.7	10.8	1971
MSA[1]	3.6	12.0	13.9	12.2	13.6	8.9	17.7	6.3	11.8	1974
U.S.	4.1	14.3	13.9	13.5	15.3	10.7	10.4	5.0	12.8	1977

Note: Figures are percentages except for Median Year; Note: (1) Figures cover the Wichita, KS Metropolitan Statistical Area—see Appendix B for areas included
Source: U.S. Census Bureau, 2014-2018 American Community Survey 5-Year Estimates

Gross Monthly Rent

Area	Under $500	$500 -$999	$1,000 -$1,499	$1,500 -$1,999	$2,000 -$2,499	$2,500 -$2,999	$3,000 and up	Median ($)
City	11.8	63.4	20.7	2.7	0.6	0.2	0.6	789
MSA[1]	11.8	61.9	21.0	3.6	0.8	0.2	0.6	796
U.S.	9.8	38.5	29.6	12.9	5.1	2.1	2.0	1,023

Note: Figures are percentages except for Median; Gross rent is the contract rent plus the estimated average monthly cost of utilities (electricity, gas, and water and sewer) and fuels (oil, coal, kerosene, wood, etc.) if these are paid by the renter (or paid for the renter by someone else); (1) Figures cover the Wichita, KS Metropolitan Statistical Area—see Appendix B for areas included
Source: U.S. Census Bureau, 2014-2018 American Community Survey 5-Year Estimates

HEALTH

Health Risk Factors

Category	MSA[1] (%)	U.S. (%)
Adults aged 18–64 who have any kind of health care coverage	83.9	87.3
Adults who reported being in good or better health	81.3	82.4
Adults who have been told they have high blood cholesterol	35.0	33.0
Adults who have been told they have high blood pressure	35.0	32.3
Adults who are current smokers	18.7	17.1
Adults who currently use E-cigarettes	6.0	4.6
Adults who currently use chewing tobacco, snuff, or snus	5.2	4.0
Adults who are heavy drinkers[2]	5.5	6.3
Adults who are binge drinkers[3]	15.6	17.4
Adults who are overweight (BMI 25.0 - 29.9)	35.2	35.3
Adults who are obese (BMI 30.0 - 99.8)	33.9	31.3
Adults who participated in any physical activities in the past month	71.6	74.4
Adults who always or nearly always wears a seat belt	94.6	94.3

Note: (1) Figures cover the Wichita, KS Metropolitan Statistical Area—see Appendix B for areas included; (2) Heavy drinkers are classified as adult men having more than 14 drinks per week and adult women having more than 7 drinks per week; (3) Binge drinkers are classified as males having five or more drinks on one occasion or females having four or more drinks on one occasion
Source: Centers for Disease Control and Prevention, Behaviorial Risk Factor Surveillance System, SMART: Selected Metropolitan Area Risk Trends, 2017

Acute and Chronic Health Conditions

Category	MSA[1] (%)	U.S. (%)
Adults who have ever been told they had a heart attack	4.2	4.2
Adults who have ever been told they have angina or coronary heart disease	4.3	3.9
Adults who have ever been told they had a stroke	2.8	3.0
Adults who have ever been told they have asthma	13.3	14.2
Adults who have ever been told they have arthritis	23.7	24.9
Adults who have ever been told they have diabetes[2]	11.3	10.5
Adults who have ever been told they had skin cancer	4.9	6.2
Adults who have ever been told they had any other types of cancer	7.4	7.1
Adults who have ever been told they have COPD	6.2	6.5
Adults who have ever been told they have kidney disease	3.0	3.0
Adults who have ever been told they have a form of depression	22.6	20.5

Note: (1) Figures cover the Wichita, KS Metropolitan Statistical Area—see Appendix B for areas included; (2) Figures do not include pregnancy-related, borderline, or pre-diabetes
Source: Centers for Disease Control and Prevention, Behaviorial Risk Factor Surveillance System, SMART: Selected Metropolitan Area Risk Trends, 2017

Health Screening and Vaccination Rates

Category	MSA[1] (%)	U.S. (%)
Adults aged 65+ who have had flu shot within the past year	55.3	60.7
Adults aged 65+ who have ever had a pneumonia vaccination	73.7	75.4
Adults who have ever been tested for HIV	31.3	36.1
Adults who have ever had the shingles or zoster vaccine?	27.9	28.9
Adults who have had their blood cholesterol checked within the last five years	84.1	85.9

Note: n/a not available; (1) Figures cover the Wichita, KS Metropolitan Statistical Area—see Appendix B for areas included.
Source: Centers for Disease Control and Prevention, Behaviorial Risk Factor Surveillance System, SMART: Selected Metropolitan Area Risk Trends, 2017

Disability Status

Category	MSA[1] (%)	U.S. (%)
Adults who reported being deaf	7.4	6.7
Are you blind or have serious difficulty seeing, even when wearing glasses?	3.8	4.5
Are you limited in any way in any of your usual activities due of arthritis?	11.4	12.9
Do you have difficulty doing errands alone?	6.7	6.8
Do you have difficulty dressing or bathing?	3.8	3.6
Do you have serious difficulty concentrating/remembering/making decisions?	12.0	10.7
Do you have serious difficulty walking or climbing stairs?	13.9	13.6

Note: (1) Figures cover the Wichita, KS Metropolitan Statistical Area—see Appendix B for areas included.
Source: Centers for Disease Control and Prevention, Behaviorial Risk Factor Surveillance System, SMART: Selected Metropolitan Area Risk Trends, 2017

Mortality Rates for the Top 10 Causes of Death in the U.S.

ICD-10[a] Sub-Chapter	ICD-10[a] Code	Age-Adjusted Mortality Rate[1] per 100,000 population	
		County[2]	U.S.
Malignant neoplasms	C00-C97	160.3	152.4
Ischaemic heart diseases	I20-I25	97.9	92.7
Other forms of heart disease	I30-I51	49.4	52.5
Chronic lower respiratory diseases	J40-J47	53.3	40.4
Cerebrovascular diseases	I60-I69	38.5	37.3
Other degenerative diseases of the nervous system	G30-G31	36.2	36.4
Other external causes of accidental injury	W00-X59	38.4	35.3
Organic, including symptomatic, mental disorders	F01-F09	45.8	30.0
Hypertensive diseases	I10-I15	16.3	22.9
Diabetes mellitus	E10-E14	24.7	21.3

Note: (a) ICD-10 = International Classification of Diseases 10th Revision; (1) Mortality rates are a three year average covering 2016-2018; (2) Figures cover Sedgwick County.
Source: Centers for Disease Control and Prevention, National Center for Health Statistics. Underlying Cause of Death 1999-2018 on CDC WONDER Online Database

Mortality Rates for Selected Causes of Death

ICD-10[a] Sub-Chapter	ICD-10[a] Code	Age-Adjusted Mortality Rate[1] per 100,000 population	
		County[2]	U.S.
Assault	X85-Y09	8.1	6.0
Diseases of the liver	K70-K76	18.1	14.2
Human immunodeficiency virus (HIV) disease	B20-B24	1.3	1.6
Influenza and pneumonia	J09-J18	15.4	14.2
Intentional self-harm	X60-X84	20.2	13.9
Malnutrition	E40-E46	1.9	1.9
Obesity and other hyperalimentation	E65-E68	1.8	2.1
Renal failure	N17-N19	16.7	12.8
Transport accidents	V01-V99	14.8	12.5
Viral hepatitis	B15-B19	1.3	1.4

Note: (a) ICD-10 = International Classification of Diseases 10th Revision; (1) Mortality rates are a three year average covering 2016-2018; (2) Figures cover Sedgwick County; Data are suppressed when the data meet the criteria for confidentiality constraints; Mortality rates are flagged as unreliable when the rate would be calculated with a numerator of 20 or less.
Source: Centers for Disease Control and Prevention, National Center for Health Statistics. Underlying Cause of Death 1999-2018 on CDC WONDER Online Database

Health Insurance Coverage

Area	With Health Insurance	With Private Health Insurance	With Public Health Insurance	Without Health Insurance	Population Under Age 19 Without Health Insurance
City	87.4	67.0	31.6	12.6	6.7
MSA[1]	89.6	71.7	29.6	10.4	5.8
U.S.	90.6	67.7	34.7	9.4	5.2

Note: Figures are percentages that cover the civilian noninstitutionalized population; (1) Figures cover the Wichita, KS Metropolitan Statistical Area—see Appendix B for areas included
Source: U.S. Census Bureau, 2014-2018 American Community Survey 5-Year Estimates

Number of Medical Professionals

Area	MDs[3]	DOs[3,4]	Dentists	Podiatrists	Chiropractors	Optometrists
County[1] (number)	1,317	189	323	12	211	136
County[1] (rate[2])	256.4	36.8	62.9	2.3	41.1	26.5
U.S. (rate[2])	281.9	23.4	69.1	6.0	27.5	16.4

Note: Data as of 2018 unless noted; (1) Data covers Sedgwick County; (2) Rate per 100,000 population; (3) Data as of 2017 and includes all active, non-federal physicians; (4) Doctor of Osteopathic Medicine
Source: U.S. Department of Health and Human Services, Health Resources and Services Administration, Bureau of Health Professions, Area Resource File (ARF) 2018-2019

EDUCATION

Public School District Statistics

District Name	Schls	Pupils	Pupil/ Teacher Ratio	Minority Pupils[1] (%)	Free Lunch Eligible[2] (%)	IEP[3] (%)
Wichita	89	49,885	13.9	67.9	67.9	15.1

Note: Table includes school districts with 2,000 or more students; (1) Percentage of students that are not non-Hispanic white; (2) Percentage of students that are eligible for the free lunch program; (3) Percentage of students that have an Individualized Education Program.
Source: U.S. Department of Education, National Center for Education Statistics, Common Core of Data, Local Education Agency (School District) Universe Survey: School Year 2018-2019; U.S. Department of Education, National Center for Education Statistics, Common Core of Data, Public Elementary/Secondary School Universe Survey: School Year 2018-2019

Highest Level of Education

Area	Less than H.S.	H.S. Diploma	Some College, No Deg.	Associate Degree	Bachelor's Degree	Master's Degree	Prof. School Degree	Doctorate Degree
City	12.1	26.2	23.9	7.7	19.1	8.0	1.8	1.1
MSA[1]	10.1	26.6	24.6	8.4	19.6	8.2	1.5	1.0
U.S.	12.3	27.1	20.6	8.4	19.4	8.6	2.1	1.4

Note: Figures cover persons age 25 and over; (1) Figures cover the Wichita, KS Metropolitan Statistical Area—see Appendix B for areas included
Source: U.S. Census Bureau, 2014-2018 American Community Survey 5-Year Estimates

Educational Attainment by Race

Area	High School Graduate or Higher (%)					Bachelor's Degree or Higher (%)				
	Total	White	Black	Asian	Hisp.[2]	Total	White	Black	Asian	Hisp.[2]
City	87.9	90.0	85.8	80.8	61.3	30.0	32.7	14.8	36.8	12.1
MSA[1]	89.9	91.5	85.4	81.8	65.1	30.3	31.9	16.9	37.4	14.5
U.S.	87.7	89.6	85.4	86.8	67.7	31.5	32.9	21.1	53.5	15.8

Note: Figures shown cover persons 25 years old and over; (1) Figures cover the Wichita, KS Metropolitan Statistical Area—see Appendix B for areas included; (2) People of Hispanic origin can be of any race
Source: U.S. Census Bureau, 2014-2018 American Community Survey 5-Year Estimates

School Enrollment by Grade and Control

Area	Preschool (%)		Kindergarten (%)		Grades 1 - 4 (%)		Grades 5 - 8 (%)		Grades 9 - 12 (%)	
	Public	Private	Public	Private	Public	Private	Public	Private	Public	Private
City	62.7	37.3	85.4	14.6	86.0	14.0	85.5	14.5	83.9	16.1
MSA[1]	62.0	38.0	84.3	15.7	86.3	13.7	87.0	13.0	86.5	13.5
U.S.	59.0	41.0	87.7	12.3	89.6	10.4	89.5	10.5	90.2	9.8

Note: Figures shown cover persons 3 years old and over; (1) Figures cover the Wichita, KS Metropolitan Statistical Area—see Appendix B for areas included
Source: U.S. Census Bureau, 2014-2018 American Community Survey 5-Year Estimates

Average Salaries of Public School Teachers

Area	2016-17		2017-18		Change from 2016-17 to 2017-18	
	Dollars	Rank[1]	Dollars	Rank[1]	Percent	Rank[2]
Kansas	49,422	40	49,754	41	0.67	36
U.S. Average	59,539	–	60,477	–	1.58	–

Note: (1) Rank ranges from 1 to 51 where 1 indicates highest salary; (2) Rank ranges from 1 to 51 where 1 indicates highest percent change.
Source: National Education Association, Rankings & Estimates: Rankings of the States 2018 and Estimates of School Statistics 2019

Higher Education

Four-Year Colleges			Two-Year Colleges			Medical Schools[1]	Law Schools[2]	Voc/ Tech[3]
Public	Private Non-profit	Private For-profit	Public	Private Non-profit	Private For-profit			
1	2	2	1	0	2	1	0	4

Note: Figures cover institutions located within the city limits and include main campuses only; (1) includes schools accredited by the Liaison Committee on Medical Education and the American Osteopathic Association's Commission on Osteopathic College Accreditation; (2) includes ABA-accredited schools, schools with provisional ABA accreditation, and state accredited schools; (3) includes all schools with programs that are less than 2 years.
Source: National Center for Education Statistics, Integrated Postsecondary Education System (IPEDS), 2018-19; Wikipedia, List of Medical Schools in the United States, accessed May 1, 2020; Wikipedia, List of Law Schools in the United States, accessed May 1, 2020

PRESIDENTIAL ELECTION

2016 Presidential Election Results

Area	Clinton	Trump	Johnson	Stein	Other
Sedgwick County	36.3	54.4	4.8	2.1	2.4
U.S.	48.0	45.9	3.3	1.1	1.7

Note: Results are percentages and may not add to 100% due to rounding
Source: Dave Leip's Atlas of U.S. Presidential Elections

EMPLOYERS

Major Employers

Company Name	Industry
AGCO Corporation	Agricultural equipment
Beechcraft Corp.	Aircraft
Boeing Defense, Space & Security	Aircraft modification
Bombardier Learjet	Aircraft
Cargill Meat Solutions	Meat products
Cessna Aircraft Company	Manufacturing
City of Wichita	Municipal government
Cox Communications	Broadband communications & entertainment company
Dillons Food Stores	Grocery stores
Koch Industries	Manufacturing, energy & commodities
McConnell Air Force Base	U.S. military
Robert J. Dole VA Medical Center	Veterans medical center
Sedgwick County	County government
Spirit AeroSystems	Manufacturing
State of Kansas	State government
U.S. Postal Service	Federal mail delivery service
Unified School District 260 Derby	Public elementary & secondary schools
Unified School District 261 Haysville	Public elementary & secondary schools
Unified School District 265 Goddard	Public elementary & secondary schools
Unified School District 490 El Dorado	Public elementary & secondary schools
United States Government	Federal government
USD 259 Wichita	Education
Via Christi Health	Healthcare
Wesley Medical Center	Health care
Wichita State University	Public higher education

Note: Companies shown are located within the Wichita, KS Metropolitan Statistical Area.
Source: Hoovers.com; Wikipedia

PUBLIC SAFETY

Crime Rate

Area	All Crimes	Violent Crimes				Property Crimes		
		Murder	Rape[3]	Robbery	Aggrav. Assault	Burglary	Larceny -Theft	Motor Vehicle Theft
City	6,798.9	9.7	96.5	146.0	927.7	871.0	4,040.1	707.9
Suburbs[1]	2,290.5	4.5	43.0	23.9	192.0	404.6	1,443.5	179.0
Metro[2]	5,058.0	7.7	75.8	98.9	643.6	690.9	3,037.4	503.7
U.S.	2,580.1	5.0	42.6	86.2	246.8	376.0	1,594.6	228.9

Note: Figures are crimes per 100,000 population; (1) All areas within the metro area that are located outside the city limits; (2) Figures cover the Wichita, KS Metropolitan Statistical Area—see Appendix B for areas included; (3) The city and U.S. figures shown were reported using the revised Uniform Crime Reporting (UCR) definition of rape. The suburban and metro area figures shown are an aggregate total of the data submitted using both the revised and legacy UCR definitions.
Source: FBI Uniform Crime Reports, 2018

Hate Crimes

Area	Number of Quarters Reported	Number of Incidents per Bias Motivation					
		Race/Ethnicity/ Ancestry	Religion	Sexual Orientation	Disability	Gender	Gender Identity
City	4	1	2	0	0	0	0
U.S.	4	4,047	1,419	1,196	159	47	168

Source: Federal Bureau of Investigation, Hate Crime Statistics 2018

Identity Theft Consumer Reports

Area	Reports	Reports per 100,000 Population	Rank[2]
MSA[1]	586	91	215
U.S.	650,572	198	-

Note: (1) Figures cover the Wichita, KS Metropolitan Statistical Area—see Appendix B for areas included; (2) Rank ranges from 1 to 386 where 1 indicates greatest number of identity theft reports per 100,000 population
Source: Federal Trade Commission, Consumer Sentinel Network Data Book for January–December 2019

Fraud and Other Consumer Reports

Area	Reports	Reports per 100,000 Population	Rank[2]
MSA[1]	3,574	554	180
U.S.	2,590,177	789	-

Note: (1) Figures cover the Wichita, KS Metropolitan Statistical Area—see Appendix B for areas included; (2) Rank ranges from 1 to 386 where 1 indicates greatest number of fraud and other consumer reports per 100,000 population
Source: Federal Trade Commission, Consumer Sentinel Network Data Book for January–December 2019

SPORTS

Professional Sports Teams

Team Name	League	Year Established
No teams are located in the metro area		

Source: Wikipedia, Major Professional Sports Teams of the United States and Canada, May 4, 2020

CLIMATE

Average and Extreme Temperatures

Temperature	Jan	Feb	Mar	Apr	May	Jun	Jul	Aug	Sep	Oct	Nov	Dec	Yr.
Extreme High (°F)	75	84	89	96	100	110	113	110	107	95	87	83	113
Average High (°F)	40	46	56	68	77	87	92	91	82	71	55	44	68
Average Temp. (°F)	30	35	45	57	66	76	81	80	71	59	45	34	57
Average Low (°F)	20	24	33	45	55	65	70	68	59	47	34	24	45
Extreme Low (°F)	-12	-21	-3	15	31	43	51	47	31	21	1	-16	-21

Note: Figures cover the years 1948-1990
Source: National Climatic Data Center, International Station Meteorological Climate Summary, 9/96

Average Precipitation/Snowfall/Humidity

Precip./Humidity	Jan	Feb	Mar	Apr	May	Jun	Jul	Aug	Sep	Oct	Nov	Dec	Yr.
Avg. Precip. (in.)	0.9	1.0	2.3	2.3	3.9	4.3	3.7	3.0	3.2	2.3	1.4	1.0	29.3
Avg. Snowfall (in.)	5	4	3	Tr	0	0	0	0	0	Tr	2	3	17
Avg. Rel. Hum. 6am (%)	78	79	77	78	83	83	78	79	82	80	79	79	80
Avg. Rel. Hum. 3pm (%)	56	54	48	46	51	47	42	43	47	47	51	56	49

Note: Figures cover the years 1948-1990; Tr = Trace amounts (<0.05 in. of rain; <0.5 in. of snow)
Source: National Climatic Data Center, International Station Meteorological Climate Summary, 9/96

Weather Conditions

Temperature			Daytime Sky			Precipitation		
10°F & below	32°F & below	90°F & above	Clear	Partly cloudy	Cloudy	0.01 inch or more precip.	0.1 inch or more snow/ice	Thunder-storms
13	110	63	117	132	116	87	13	54

Note: Figures are average number of days per year and cover the years 1948-1990
Source: National Climatic Data Center, International Station Meteorological Climate Summary, 9/96

HAZARDOUS WASTE

Superfund Sites

The Wichita, KS metro area is home to two sites on the EPA's Superfund National Priorities List: **57th and North Broadway Streets Site** (final); **Pester Refinery Co.** (final). There are a total of 1,387 Superfund sites with a status of proposed or final on the list in the U.S. *U.S. Environmental Protection Agency, National Priorities List, May 5, 2020*

AIR & WATER QUALITY

Air Quality Trends: Ozone

	1990	1995	2000	2005	2010	2012	2014	2016	2017	2018
MSA[1]	0.077	0.069	0.080	0.074	0.075	0.080	0.069	0.062	0.063	0.064
U.S.	0.088	0.089	0.082	0.080	0.073	0.075	0.067	0.069	0.068	0.069

Note: (1) Data covers the Wichita, KS Metropolitan Statistical Area—see Appendix B for areas included. The values shown are the composite ozone concentration averages among trend sites based on the highest fourth daily maximum 8-hour concentration in parts per million. These trends are based on sites having an adequate record of monitoring data during the trend period. Data from exceptional events are included.
Source: U.S. Environmental Protection Agency, Air Quality Monitoring Information, "Air Quality Trends by City, 1990-2018"

Air Quality Index

Area	Percent of Days when Air Quality was...[2]					AQI Statistics[2]	
	Good	Moderate	Unhealthy for Sensitive Groups	Unhealthy	Very Unhealthy	Maximum	Median
MSA[1]	71.5	28.5	0.0	0.0	0.0	100	41

Note: (1) Data covers the Wichita, KS Metropolitan Statistical Area—see Appendix B for areas included; (2) Based on 365 days with AQI data in 2018. Air Quality Index (AQI) is an index for reporting daily air quality. EPA calculates the AQI for five major air pollutants regulated by the Clean Air Act: ground-level ozone, particle pollution (aka particulate matter), carbon monoxide, sulfur dioxide, and nitrogen dioxide. The AQI runs from 0 to 500. The higher the AQI value, the greater the level of air pollution and the greater the health concern. There are six AQI categories: "Good" AQI is between 0 and 50. Air quality is considered satisfactory; "Moderate" AQI is between 51 and 100. Air quality is acceptable; "Unhealthy for Sensitive Groups" When AQI values are between 101 and 150, members of sensitive groups may experience health effects; "Unhealthy" When AQI values are between 151 and 200 everyone may begin to experience health effects; "Very Unhealthy" AQI values between 201 and 300 trigger a health alert; "Hazardous" AQI values over 300 trigger warnings of emergency conditions (not shown).
Source: U.S. Environmental Protection Agency, Air Quality Index Report, 2018

Air Quality Index Pollutants

Area	Percent of Days when AQI Pollutant was...[2]					
	Carbon Monoxide	Nitrogen Dioxide	Ozone	Sulfur Dioxide	Particulate Matter 2.5	Particulate Matter 10
MSA[1]	0.0	4.7	62.2	0.0	16.2	17.0

Note: (1) Data covers the Wichita, KS Metropolitan Statistical Area—see Appendix B for areas included; (2) Based on 365 days with AQI data in 2018. The Air Quality Index (AQI) is an index for reporting daily air quality. EPA calculates the AQI for five major air pollutants regulated by the Clean Air Act: ground-level ozone, particle pollution (also known as particulate matter), carbon monoxide, sulfur dioxide, and nitrogen dioxide. The AQI runs from 0 to 500. The higher the AQI value, the greater the level of air pollution and the greater the health concern.
Source: U.S. Environmental Protection Agency, Air Quality Index Report, 2018

Maximum Air Pollutant Concentrations: Particulate Matter, Ozone, CO and Lead

	Particulate Matter 10 (ug/m³)	Particulate Matter 2.5 Wtd AM (ug/m³)	Particulate Matter 2.5 24-Hr (ug/m³)	Ozone (ppm)	Carbon Monoxide (ppm)	Lead (ug/m³)
MSA[1] Level	86	8.2	20	0.067	n/a	n/a
NAAQS[2]	150	15	35	0.075	9	0.15
Met NAAQS[2]	Yes	Yes	Yes	Yes	n/a	n/a

Note: (1) Data covers the Wichita, KS Metropolitan Statistical Area—see Appendix B for areas included; Data from exceptional events are included; (2) National Ambient Air Quality Standards; ppm = parts per million; ug/m³ = micrograms per cubic meter; n/a not available.
Concentrations: Particulate Matter 10 (coarse particulate)—highest second maximum 24-hour concentration; Particulate Matter 2.5 Wtd AM (fine particulate)—highest weighted annual mean concentration; Particulate Matter 2.5 24-Hour (fine particulate)—highest 98th percentile 24-hour concentration; Ozone—highest fourth daily maximum 8-hour concentration; Carbon Monoxide—highest second maximum non-overlapping 8-hour concentration; Lead—maximum running 3-month average
Source: U.S. Environmental Protection Agency, Air Quality Monitoring Information, "Air Quality Statistics by City, 2018"

Maximum Air Pollutant Concentrations: Nitrogen Dioxide and Sulfur Dioxide

	Nitrogen Dioxide AM (ppb)	Nitrogen Dioxide 1-Hr (ppb)	Sulfur Dioxide AM (ppb)	Sulfur Dioxide 1-Hr (ppb)	Sulfur Dioxide 24-Hr (ppb)
MSA[1] Level	8	40	n/a	4	n/a
NAAQS[2]	53	100	30	75	140
Met NAAQS[2]	Yes	Yes	n/a	Yes	n/a

Note: (1) Data covers the Wichita, KS Metropolitan Statistical Area—see Appendix B for areas included; Data from exceptional events are included; (2) National Ambient Air Quality Standards; ppm = parts per million; ug/m³ = micrograms per cubic meter; n/a not available.
Concentrations: Nitrogen Dioxide AM—highest arithmetic mean concentration; Nitrogen Dioxide 1-Hr—highest 98th percentile 1-hour daily maximum concentration; Sulfur Dioxide AM—highest annual mean concentration; Sulfur Dioxide 1-Hr—highest 99th percentile 1-hour daily maximum concentration; Sulfur Dioxide 24-Hr—highest second maximum 24-hour concentration
Source: U.S. Environmental Protection Agency, Air Quality Monitoring Information, "Air Quality Statistics by City, 2018"

Drinking Water

Water System Name	Pop. Served	Primary Water Source Type	Violations[1]
City of Wichita	389,225	Surface	4

Note: (1) Total number of violations (both active and inactive) in the EPA database
Source: U.S. Environmental Protection Agency, Office of Ground Water and Drinking Water, Safe Drinking Water Information System (based on data extracted May 5, 2020)

Appendixes

Appendix A: Comparative Statistics

Table of Contents

Population Growth: City

Area	1990 Census	2000 Census	2010 Census	2018* Estimate	Population Growth (%) 1990-2018	2010-2018
Albany, NY	100,756	95,658	97,856	97,889	-2.8	0.0
Albuquerque, NM	388,375	448,607	545,852	559,202	44.0	2.4
Allentown, PA	105,066	106,632	118,032	120,410	14.6	2.0
Anchorage, AK	226,338	260,283	291,826	296,112	30.8	1.5
Ann Arbor, MI	111,018	114,024	113,934	120,641	8.7	5.9
Athens, GA	86,561	100,266	115,452	123,310	42.5	6.8
Atlanta, GA	394,092	416,474	420,003	479,655	21.7	14.2
Austin, TX	499,053	656,562	790,390	935,755	87.5	18.4
Baton Rouge, LA	223,299	227,818	229,493	225,362	0.9	-1.8
Boise City, ID	144,317	185,787	205,671	224,300	55.4	9.1
Boston, MA	574,283	589,141	617,594	679,413	18.3	10.0
Boulder, CO	87,737	94,673	97,385	107,360	22.4	10.2
Cape Coral, FL	75,507	102,286	154,305	178,593	136.5	15.7
Cedar Rapids, IA	110,829	120,758	126,326	131,360	18.5	4.0
Charleston, SC	96,102	96,650	120,083	133,762	39.2	11.4
Charlotte, NC	428,283	540,828	731,424	841,611	96.5	15.1
Chicago, IL	2,783,726	2,896,016	2,695,598	2,718,555	-2.3	0.9
Clarksville, TN	78,569	103,455	132,929	150,602	91.7	13.3
Cleveland, OH	505,333	478,403	396,815	387,398	-23.3	-2.4
College Station, TX	53,318	67,890	93,857	110,782	107.8	18.0
Colorado Springs, CO	283,798	360,890	416,427	457,502	61.2	9.9
Columbia, MO	71,069	84,531	108,500	120,248	69.2	10.8
Columbia, SC	115,475	116,278	129,272	133,352	15.5	3.2
Columbus, OH	648,656	711,470	787,033	867,628	33.8	10.2
Dallas, TX	1,006,971	1,188,580	1,197,816	1,318,806	31.0	10.1
Davenport, IA	95,705	98,359	99,685	102,318	6.9	2.6
Denver, CO	467,153	554,636	600,158	693,417	48.4	15.5
Des Moines, IA	193,569	198,682	203,433	215,932	11.6	6.1
Durham, NC	151,737	187,035	228,330	264,310	74.2	15.8
Edison, NJ	88,680	97,687	99,967	100,809	13.7	0.8
El Paso, TX	515,541	563,662	649,121	680,354	32.0	4.8
Fargo, ND	74,372	90,599	105,549	120,209	61.6	13.9
Fayetteville, NC	118,247	121,015	200,564	209,867	77.5	4.6
Fort Collins, CO	89,555	118,652	143,986	162,511	81.5	12.9
Fort Wayne, IN	205,671	205,727	253,691	264,052	28.4	4.1
Fort Worth, TX	448,311	534,694	741,206	855,786	90.9	15.5
Grand Rapids, MI	189,145	197,800	188,040	197,081	4.2	4.8
Greeley, CO	60,887	76,930	92,889	103,773	70.4	11.7
Green Bay, WI	96,466	102,313	104,057	104,818	8.7	0.7
Greensboro, NC	193,389	223,891	269,666	288,719	49.3	7.1
Honolulu, HI	376,465	371,657	337,256	350,003	-7.0	3.8
Houston, TX	1,697,610	1,953,631	2,099,451	2,295,982	35.2	9.4
Huntsville, AL	161,842	158,216	180,105	193,663	19.7	7.5
Indianapolis, IN	730,993	781,870	820,445	857,637	17.3	4.5
Jackson, MS	196,469	184,256	173,514	168,862	-14.1	-2.7
Jacksonville, FL	635,221	735,617	821,784	878,907	38.4	7.0
Kansas City, MO	434,967	441,545	459,787	481,417	10.7	4.7
Lafayette, LA	104,735	110,257	120,623	126,515	20.8	4.9
Lakeland, FL	73,375	78,452	97,422	105,958	44.4	8.8
Las Vegas, NV	261,374	478,434	583,756	626,637	139.7	7.3
Lexington, KY	225,366	260,512	295,803	318,734	41.4	7.8
Lincoln, NE	193,629	225,581	258,379	280,849	45.0	8.7
Little Rock, AR	177,519	183,133	193,524	198,135	11.6	2.4
Los Angeles, CA	3,487,671	3,694,820	3,792,621	3,959,657	13.5	4.4
Louisville, KY	269,160	256,231	597,337	617,032	129.2	3.3

Table continued on next page.

Area	1990 Census	2000 Census	2010 Census	2018* Estimate	Population Growth (%) 1990-2018	2010-2018
Madison, WI	193,451	208,054	233,209	252,086	30.3	8.1
Manchester, NH	99,567	107,006	109,565	111,657	12.1	1.9
Miami, FL	358,843	362,470	399,457	451,214	25.7	13.0
Midland, TX	89,358	94,996	111,147	135,134	51.2	21.6
Milwaukee, WI	628,095	596,974	594,833	596,886	-5.0	0.3
Minneapolis, MN	368,383	382,618	382,578	416,021	12.9	8.7
Nashville, TN	488,364	545,524	601,222	660,062	35.2	9.8
New Haven, CT	130,474	123,626	129,779	130,529	0.0	0.6
New Orleans, LA	496,938	484,674	343,829	389,648	-21.6	13.3
New York, NY	7,322,552	8,008,278	8,175,133	8,443,713	15.3	3.3
Oklahoma City, OK	445,065	506,132	579,999	637,284	43.2	9.9
Omaha, NE	371,972	390,007	408,958	465,112	25.0	13.7
Orlando, FL	161,172	185,951	238,300	275,690	71.1	15.7
Peoria, IL	114,341	112,936	115,007	114,512	0.1	-0.4
Philadelphia, PA	1,585,577	1,517,550	1,526,006	1,575,522	-0.6	3.2
Phoenix, AZ	989,873	1,321,045	1,445,632	1,610,071	62.7	11.4
Pittsburgh, PA	369,785	334,563	305,704	303,587	-17.9	-0.7
Portland, OR	485,833	529,121	583,776	639,387	31.6	9.5
Providence, RI	160,734	173,618	178,042	179,435	11.6	0.8
Provo, UT	87,148	105,166	112,488	116,146	33.3	3.3
Raleigh, NC	226,841	276,093	403,892	457,159	101.5	13.2
Reno, NV	139,950	180,480	225,221	242,633	73.4	7.7
Richmond, VA	202,783	197,790	204,214	223,787	10.4	9.6
Rochester, MN	74,151	85,806	106,769	113,913	53.6	6.7
Sacramento, CA	368,923	407,018	466,488	495,011	34.2	6.1
Salt Lake City, UT	159,796	181,743	186,440	195,701	22.5	5.0
San Antonio, TX	997,258	1,144,646	1,327,407	1,486,521	49.1	12.0
San Diego, CA	1,111,048	1,223,400	1,307,402	1,401,932	26.2	7.2
San Francisco, CA	723,959	776,733	805,235	870,044	20.2	8.0
San Jose, CA	784,324	894,943	945,942	1,026,658	30.9	8.5
Santa Rosa, CA	123,297	147,595	167,815	181,038	46.8	7.9
Savannah, GA	138,038	131,510	136,286	145,342	5.3	6.6
Seattle, WA	516,262	563,374	608,660	708,823	37.3	16.5
Sioux Falls, SD	102,262	123,975	153,888	174,151	70.3	13.2
Springfield, IL	108,997	111,454	116,250	116,459	6.8	0.2
Tallahassee, FL	128,014	150,624	181,376	190,180	48.6	4.9
Tampa, FL	279,960	303,447	335,709	376,345	34.4	12.1
Topeka, KS	121,197	122,377	127,473	126,877	4.7	-0.5
Tucson, AZ	417,942	486,699	520,116	539,216	29.0	3.7
Tulsa, OK	367,241	393,049	391,906	402,223	9.5	2.6
Tuscaloosa, AL	81,075	77,906	90,468	98,881	22.0	9.3
Virginia Beach, VA	393,069	425,257	437,994	450,135	14.5	2.8
Washington, DC	606,900	572,059	601,723	684,498	12.8	13.8
Wichita, KS	313,693	344,284	382,368	389,563	24.2	1.9
Winston-Salem, NC	168,139	185,776	229,617	242,125	44.0	5.4
U.S.	248,709,873	281,421,906	308,745,538	322,903,030	29.8	4.6

Note: (*) 2014-2018 5-year estimated population
Source: U.S. Census Bureau, 1990 Census, Census 2000, Census 2010, 2014-2018 American Community Survey 5-Year Estimates

Population Growth: Metro Area

Area	1990 Census	2000 Census	2010 Census	2018* Estimate	Population Growth (%) 1990-2018	Population Growth (%) 2010-2018
Albany, NY	809,443	825,875	870,716	880,481	8.8	1.1
Albuquerque, NM	599,416	729,649	887,077	910,012	51.8	2.6
Allentown, PA	686,666	740,395	821,173	834,615	21.5	1.6
Anchorage, AK	266,021	319,605	380,821	399,576	50.2	4.9
Ann Arbor, MI	282,937	322,895	344,791	365,961	29.3	6.1
Athens, GA	136,025	166,079	192,541	205,303	50.9	6.6
Atlanta, GA	3,069,411	4,247,981	5,268,860	5,779,463	88.3	9.7
Austin, TX	846,217	1,249,763	1,716,289	2,058,351	143.2	19.9
Baton Rouge, LA	623,853	705,973	802,484	829,642	33.0	3.4
Boise City, ID	319,596	464,840	616,561	693,952	117.1	12.6
Boston, MA	4,133,895	4,391,344	4,552,402	4,811,732	16.4	5.7
Boulder, CO	208,898	269,758	294,567	321,030	53.7	9.0
Cape Coral, FL	335,113	440,888	618,754	718,679	114.5	16.1
Cedar Rapids, IA	210,640	237,230	257,940	268,315	27.4	4.0
Charleston, SC	506,875	549,033	664,607	759,247	49.8	14.2
Charlotte, NC	1,024,331	1,330,448	1,758,038	2,473,125	141.4	40.7
Chicago, IL	8,182,076	9,098,316	9,461,105	9,536,428	16.6	0.8
Clarksville, TN	189,277	232,000	273,949	282,994	49.5	3.3
Cleveland, OH	2,102,219	2,148,143	2,077,240	2,061,766	-1.9	-0.7
College Station, TX	150,998	184,885	228,660	253,946	68.2	11.1
Colorado Springs, CO	409,482	537,484	645,613	712,266	73.9	10.3
Columbia, MO	122,010	145,666	172,786	176,515	44.7	2.2
Columbia, SC	548,325	647,158	767,598	816,664	48.9	6.4
Columbus, OH	1,405,176	1,612,694	1,836,536	2,054,062	46.2	11.8
Dallas, TX	3,989,294	5,161,544	6,371,773	7,255,028	81.9	13.9
Davenport, IA	368,151	376,019	379,690	382,720	4.0	0.8
Denver, CO	1,666,935	2,179,296	2,543,482	2,850,221	71.0	12.1
Des Moines, IA	416,346	481,394	569,633	634,201	52.3	11.3
Durham, NC	344,646	426,493	504,357	558,491	62.0	10.7
Edison, NJ	16,845,992	18,323,002	18,897,109	19,990,592	18.7	5.8
El Paso, TX	591,610	679,622	800,647	841,752	42.3	5.1
Fargo, ND	153,296	174,367	208,777	237,003	54.6	13.5
Fayetteville, NC	297,422	336,609	366,383	385,345	29.6	5.2
Fort Collins, CO	186,136	251,494	299,630	338,161	81.7	12.9
Fort Wayne, IN	354,435	390,156	416,257	431,612	21.8	3.7
Fort Worth, TX	3,989,294	5,161,544	6,371,773	7,255,028	81.9	13.9
Grand Rapids, MI	645,914	740,482	774,160	1,050,440	62.6	35.7
Greeley, CO	131,816	180,926	252,825	295,123	123.9	16.7
Green Bay, WI	243,698	282,599	306,241	317,702	30.4	3.7
Greensboro, NC	540,257	643,430	723,801	757,810	40.3	4.7
Honolulu, HI	836,231	876,156	953,207	987,638	18.1	3.6
Houston, TX	3,767,335	4,715,407	5,946,800	6,779,104	79.9	14.0
Huntsville, AL	293,047	342,376	417,593	450,612	53.8	7.9
Indianapolis, IN	1,294,217	1,525,104	1,756,241	2,007,497	55.1	14.3
Jackson, MS	446,941	497,197	539,057	580,280	29.8	7.6
Jacksonville, FL	925,213	1,122,750	1,345,596	1,475,386	59.5	9.6
Kansas City, MO	1,636,528	1,836,038	2,035,334	2,106,632	28.7	3.5
Lafayette, LA	208,740	239,086	273,738	488,969	134.2	78.6
Lakeland, FL	405,382	483,924	602,095	668,671	64.9	11.1
Las Vegas, NV	741,459	1,375,765	1,951,269	2,141,574	188.8	9.8
Lexington, KY	348,428	408,326	472,099	506,786	45.4	7.3
Lincoln, NE	229,091	266,787	302,157	327,221	42.8	8.3
Little Rock, AR	535,034	610,518	699,757	734,502	37.3	5.0
Los Angeles, CA	11,273,720	12,365,627	12,828,837	13,262,234	17.6	3.4
Louisville, KY	1,055,973	1,161,975	1,283,566	1,285,270	21.7	0.1

Table continued on next page.

Area	1990 Census	2000 Census	2010 Census	2018* Estimate	Population Growth (%)	
					1990-2018	2010-2018
Madison, WI	432,323	501,774	568,593	647,281	49.7	13.8
Manchester, NH	336,073	380,841	400,721	411,087	22.3	2.6
Miami, FL	4,056,100	5,007,564	5,564,635	6,070,944	49.7	9.1
Midland, TX	106,611	116,009	136,872	169,808	59.3	24.1
Milwaukee, WI	1,432,149	1,500,741	1,555,908	1,575,907	10.0	1.3
Minneapolis, MN	2,538,834	2,968,806	3,279,833	3,557,528	40.1	8.5
Nashville, TN	1,048,218	1,311,789	1,589,934	1,864,138	77.8	17.2
New Haven, CT	804,219	824,008	862,477	859,339	6.9	-0.4
New Orleans, LA	1,264,391	1,316,510	1,167,764	1,263,635	-0.1	8.2
New York, NY	16,845,992	18,323,002	18,897,109	19,990,592	18.7	5.8
Oklahoma City, OK	971,042	1,095,421	1,252,987	1,369,759	41.1	9.3
Omaha, NE	685,797	767,041	865,350	922,891	34.6	6.6
Orlando, FL	1,224,852	1,644,561	2,134,411	2,450,261	100.0	14.8
Peoria, IL	358,552	366,899	379,186	374,426	4.4	-1.3
Philadelphia, PA	5,435,470	5,687,147	5,965,343	6,069,448	11.7	1.7
Phoenix, AZ	2,238,480	3,251,876	4,192,887	4,673,634	108.8	11.5
Pittsburgh, PA	2,468,289	2,431,087	2,356,285	2,339,941	-5.2	-0.7
Portland, OR	1,523,741	1,927,881	2,226,009	2,417,931	58.7	8.6
Providence, RI	1,509,789	1,582,997	1,600,852	1,615,516	7.0	0.9
Provo, UT	269,407	376,774	526,810	601,388	123.2	14.2
Raleigh, NC	541,081	797,071	1,130,490	1,302,632	140.7	15.2
Reno, NV	257,193	342,885	425,417	454,427	76.7	6.8
Richmond, VA	949,244	1,096,957	1,258,251	1,281,530	35.0	1.9
Rochester, MN	141,945	163,618	186,011	216,035	52.2	16.1
Sacramento, CA	1,481,126	1,796,857	2,149,127	2,291,738	54.7	6.6
Salt Lake City, UT	768,075	968,858	1,124,197	1,185,990	54.4	5.5
San Antonio, TX	1,407,745	1,711,703	2,142,508	2,426,204	72.3	13.2
San Diego, CA	2,498,016	2,813,833	3,095,313	3,302,833	32.2	6.7
San Francisco, CA	3,686,592	4,123,740	4,335,391	4,673,221	26.8	7.8
San Jose, CA	1,534,280	1,735,819	1,836,911	1,981,616	29.2	7.9
Santa Rosa, CA	388,222	458,614	483,878	501,317	29.1	3.6
Savannah, GA	258,060	293,000	347,611	381,623	47.9	9.8
Seattle, WA	2,559,164	3,043,878	3,439,809	3,809,717	48.9	10.8
Sioux Falls, SD	153,500	187,093	228,261	255,438	66.4	11.9
Springfield, IL	189,550	201,437	210,170	210,028	10.8	-0.1
Tallahassee, FL	259,096	320,304	367,413	380,101	46.7	3.5
Tampa, FL	2,067,959	2,395,997	2,783,243	3,030,047	46.5	8.9
Topeka, KS	210,257	224,551	233,870	233,260	10.9	-0.3
Tucson, AZ	666,880	843,746	980,263	1,019,722	52.9	4.0
Tulsa, OK	761,019	859,532	937,478	985,233	29.5	5.1
Tuscaloosa, AL	176,123	192,034	219,461	241,398	37.1	10.0
Virginia Beach, VA	1,449,389	1,576,370	1,671,683	1,722,001	18.8	3.0
Washington, DC	4,122,914	4,796,183	5,582,170	6,138,382	48.9	10.0
Wichita, KS	511,111	571,166	623,061	643,765	26.0	3.3
Winston-Salem, NC	361,091	421,961	477,717	661,798	83.3	38.5
U.S.	248,709,873	281,421,906	308,745,538	322,903,030	29.8	4.6

Note: (*) 2014-2018 5-year estimated population; Figures cover the Metropolitan Statistical Area (MSA)—see Appendix B for areas included
Source: U.S. Census Bureau, 1990 Census, Census 2000, Census 2010, 2014-2018 American Community Survey 5-Year Estimates

Household Size: City

City	Persons in Household (%)							Average Household Size
	One	Two	Three	Four	Five	Six	Seven or More	
Albany, NY	44.2	31.4	12.5	6.6	3.3	1.4	0.4	2.12
Albuquerque, NM	34.1	33.5	14.1	10.9	4.8	1.4	0.9	2.48
Allentown, PA	27.9	28.8	16.0	13.0	7.8	3.6	2.6	2.73
Anchorage, AK	25.3	32.9	17.9	12.8	6.3	2.3	2.1	2.71
Ann Arbor, MI	34.7	36.8	12.0	11.0	2.9	1.4	0.7	2.27
Athens, GA	33.3	35.3	14.3	11.0	3.6	1.4	0.7	2.41
Atlanta, GA	46.8	30.2	10.7	7.2	3.1	1.1	0.7	2.22
Austin, TX	34.4	32.6	14.3	11.3	4.6	1.5	1.0	2.47
Baton Rouge, LA	36.7	32.3	15.2	8.6	4.3	1.7	0.9	2.54
Boise City, ID	34.4	34.4	14.0	10.2	4.5	1.3	0.9	2.46
Boston, MA	36.2	31.9	15.2	9.8	4.0	1.6	0.8	2.37
Boulder, CO	33.6	37.1	14.6	10.5	3.0	0.7	0.2	2.26
Cape Coral, FL	24.2	42.7	14.9	11.6	4.6	1.4	0.3	2.74
Cedar Rapids, IA	33.5	33.8	14.3	11.4	4.0	2.1	0.6	2.35
Charleston, SC	35.2	37.4	14.4	9.0	2.8	0.6	0.2	2.32
Charlotte, NC	32.0	32.4	15.6	12.1	5.1	1.5	0.9	2.56
Chicago, IL	36.8	29.4	13.9	10.3	5.3	2.2	1.7	2.52
Clarksville, TN	23.9	31.2	19.8	15.2	6.2	2.1	1.3	2.69
Cleveland, OH	44.2	27.2	12.9	8.4	4.2	1.6	1.1	2.21
College Station, TX	29.7	33.2	16.2	14.6	3.8	1.7	0.4	2.49
Colorado Springs, CO	28.9	34.8	14.4	12.6	5.9	2.0	1.1	2.52
Columbia, MO	33.0	33.7	14.5	12.4	4.4	1.2	0.5	2.32
Columbia, SC	40.4	33.1	12.2	9.1	3.6	0.8	0.5	2.23
Columbus, OH	35.3	32.2	14.6	10.1	4.7	1.7	1.1	2.39
Dallas, TX	34.8	29.1	14.1	11.3	6.2	2.5	1.7	2.57
Davenport, IA	34.5	34.1	13.6	9.8	5.0	1.8	0.8	2.46
Denver, CO	38.4	32.3	12.2	9.7	4.4	1.5	1.1	2.31
Des Moines, IA	33.3	30.2	15.2	11.6	5.6	2.4	1.4	2.50
Durham, NC	34.3	33.1	15.2	10.2	4.4	1.5	1.0	2.35
Edison, NJ	19.2	28.6	21.5	20.4	6.3	2.4	1.2	2.85
El Paso, TX	25.0	28.6	18.1	15.8	7.7	3.2	1.3	2.99
Fargo, ND	36.6	33.2	15.1	8.4	4.4	1.4	0.6	2.16
Fayetteville, NC	34.9	32.0	15.5	10.5	4.2	1.7	0.8	2.43
Fort Collins, CO	24.7	37.7	18.2	13.4	4.0	1.0	0.5	2.46
Fort Wayne, IN	31.9	32.5	14.8	11.2	5.9	2.1	1.2	2.47
Fort Worth, TX	26.3	28.7	16.3	15.0	7.9	3.3	2.1	2.88
Grand Rapids, MI	32.5	31.7	13.7	11.0	6.1	2.5	2.0	2.55
Greeley, CO	25.7	31.7	16.3	13.3	8.1	2.9	1.5	2.71
Green Bay, WI	34.0	32.4	12.3	11.1	7.0	1.4	1.6	2.39
Greensboro, NC	34.4	32.7	15.3	10.5	4.9	1.2	0.6	2.38
Honolulu, HI	33.0	31.0	14.7	10.8	5.1	2.4	2.7	2.61
Houston, TX	32.1	29.0	15.3	12.1	6.6	2.8	1.8	2.67
Huntsville, AL	35.9	33.4	14.4	10.2	4.0	1.2	0.5	2.24
Indianapolis, IN	36.8	31.4	13.6	10.2	4.7	1.9	1.1	2.51
Jackson, MS	34.2	28.6	16.1	11.0	5.6	2.0	2.1	2.60
Jacksonville, FL	30.2	33.7	16.5	11.5	5.2	1.7	0.9	2.57
Kansas City, MO	37.0	31.5	13.6	9.9	4.7	1.7	1.1	2.36
Lafayette, LA	35.0	34.5	14.5	9.3	3.9	1.7	0.8	2.42
Lakeland, FL	33.9	36.9	13.9	8.7	3.8	1.6	0.9	2.47
Las Vegas, NV	30.0	31.6	15.2	11.8	6.5	2.9	1.6	2.73
Lexington, KY	31.3	35.2	15.4	11.1	4.7	1.3	0.6	2.38
Lincoln, NE	31.6	34.9	13.8	11.5	5.1	1.9	0.9	2.39
Little Rock, AR	36.8	32.4	13.6	10.1	4.4	1.7	0.6	2.39
Los Angeles, CA	30.2	28.6	15.3	13.1	6.9	3.0	2.5	2.82

Table continued on next page.

City	Persons in Household (%)							Average Household Size
	One	Two	Three	Four	Five	Six	Seven or More	
Louisville, KY	33.2	33.1	15.2	10.8	4.8	1.6	1.0	2.44
Madison, WI	34.7	36.3	13.5	9.9	3.8	1.0	0.4	2.21
Manchester, NH	30.9	34.2	16.5	10.9	4.4	1.6	1.1	2.39
Miami, FL	38.1	29.9	15.7	9.3	4.0	1.5	1.1	2.58
Midland, TX	25.5	30.8	16.8	15.1	7.1	2.9	1.4	2.87
Milwaukee, WI	35.9	29.1	14.2	10.5	5.9	2.4	1.7	2.53
Minneapolis, MN	40.2	30.8	12.1	9.4	3.6	1.7	1.8	2.29
Nashville, TN	33.7	33.7	15.2	9.8	4.6	1.7	1.0	2.38
New Haven, CT	41.2	26.8	13.6	9.6	5.1	2.5	0.9	2.43
New Orleans, LA	45.0	29.6	12.7	7.9	2.9	1.0	0.6	2.44
New York, NY	32.2	28.4	16.1	12.4	6.0	2.5	2.1	2.62
Oklahoma City, OK	30.9	32.2	14.7	12.3	5.9	2.5	1.2	2.59
Omaha, NE	32.6	31.8	14.0	11.3	5.8	2.6	1.5	2.48
Orlando, FL	34.4	33.2	16.2	10.0	3.6	1.7	0.6	2.45
Peoria, IL	37.5	31.4	13.8	9.6	4.6	1.9	0.9	2.39
Philadelphia, PA	37.9	29.0	14.7	10.3	4.7	1.9	1.2	2.57
Phoenix, AZ	28.1	30.0	15.1	12.7	7.2	3.8	2.6	2.87
Pittsburgh, PA	43.2	32.1	13.0	7.4	2.4	1.0	0.5	2.06
Portland, OR	33.8	34.4	14.2	10.9	4.0	1.4	0.9	2.36
Providence, RI	32.7	27.9	16.2	12.2	7.3	1.9	1.5	2.68
Provo, UT	13.8	32.9	17.7	16.2	8.2	7.0	3.9	3.20
Raleigh, NC	33.2	32.0	15.4	12.4	4.6	1.3	0.7	2.43
Reno, NV	34.0	32.2	14.9	10.1	5.2	1.9	1.4	2.40
Richmond, VA	43.2	31.5	12.5	7.3	3.3	1.2	0.7	2.37
Rochester, MN	29.7	33.9	14.5	13.7	4.8	1.8	1.2	2.43
Sacramento, CA	31.2	30.5	14.7	11.8	6.1	2.9	2.4	2.66
Salt Lake City, UT	35.5	32.1	13.8	10.3	4.4	1.9	1.6	2.43
San Antonio, TX	29.3	29.5	16.2	13.1	6.9	2.8	1.8	2.94
San Diego, CA	27.4	33.4	16.4	12.8	5.8	2.5	1.5	2.71
San Francisco, CA	35.9	33.5	14.1	9.7	3.6	1.4	1.4	2.36
San Jose, CA	19.5	28.3	18.5	18.0	8.3	3.5	3.5	3.14
Santa Rosa, CA	29.2	31.9	14.8	13.5	5.8	2.2	2.2	2.67
Savannah, GA	33.5	33.6	15.6	9.4	4.8	1.7	1.0	2.53
Seattle, WA	38.7	35.2	12.4	9.1	2.8	0.7	0.6	2.12
Sioux Falls, SD	32.3	33.8	13.0	12.2	5.3	1.9	1.1	2.40
Springfield, IL	37.3	34.2	13.4	9.1	3.1	1.5	1.0	2.22
Tallahassee, FL	34.4	32.9	17.3	10.4	3.6	0.9	0.2	2.34
Tampa, FL	35.6	31.7	15.3	10.5	4.3	1.5	0.8	2.44
Topeka, KS	37.9	31.6	12.7	10.5	4.5	1.7	0.7	2.29
Tucson, AZ	34.3	31.4	14.8	10.7	5.2	2.0	1.2	2.43
Tulsa, OK	35.1	32.4	13.5	10.1	5.3	2.0	1.2	2.41
Tuscaloosa, AL	34.6	33.2	15.9	11.0	3.0	1.2	0.7	2.54
Virginia Beach, VA	24.2	33.7	18.1	15.0	5.9	1.9	0.9	2.60
Washington, DC	44.1	30.6	11.9	7.8	3.2	1.2	0.7	2.29
Wichita, KS	32.9	31.9	13.5	11.4	6.1	2.5	1.3	2.52
Winston-Salem, NC	35.1	31.4	15.1	10.0	5.5	1.8	0.9	2.44
U.S.	27.7	33.8	15.6	12.9	6.0	2.3	1.4	2.63

U.S. Census Bureau, 2014-2018 American Community Survey 5-Year Estimates

Household Size: Metro Area

Metro Area	Persons in Household (%)							Average Household Size
	One	Two	Three	Four	Five	Six	Seven or More	
Albany, NY	32.1	35.3	15.1	11.0	4.2	1.4	0.5	2.42
Albuquerque, NM	30.9	35.0	14.4	11.0	5.3	1.8	1.2	2.57
Allentown, PA	26.1	35.2	15.9	13.3	5.9	2.2	1.1	2.54
Anchorage, AK	24.8	33.3	17.3	12.9	6.6	2.4	2.3	2.84
Ann Arbor, MI	29.6	36.3	13.9	12.5	4.6	1.8	1.0	2.47
Athens, GA	28.5	35.6	15.1	13.0	4.9	1.6	0.9	2.53
Atlanta, GA	26.4	31.6	17.1	14.4	6.4	2.4	1.4	2.76
Austin, TX	27.9	33.0	15.5	13.8	6.1	2.1	1.3	2.72
Baton Rouge, LA	28.3	33.9	16.6	12.0	5.8	1.9	1.0	2.67
Boise City, ID	28.3	34.4	14.0	12.2	6.9	2.4	1.6	2.69
Boston, MA	27.8	32.8	16.7	14.4	5.5	1.7	0.8	2.55
Boulder, CO	28.1	36.7	15.8	12.7	4.7	1.3	0.4	2.46
Cape Coral, FL	28.2	44.4	11.8	8.6	4.2	1.5	0.9	2.61
Cedar Rapids, IA	29.0	36.8	13.9	12.5	4.8	2.0	0.7	2.42
Charleston, SC	28.9	35.6	16.5	11.7	4.7	1.5	0.7	2.59
Charlotte, NC	26.7	33.9	16.8	13.9	5.6	1.8	0.9	2.64
Chicago, IL	28.6	30.9	15.6	13.9	6.7	2.5	1.5	2.68
Clarksville, TN	23.8	32.3	18.6	14.8	6.6	2.4	1.1	2.67
Cleveland, OH	33.7	33.7	14.3	11.0	4.5	1.6	0.8	2.35
College Station, TX	28.0	34.0	16.0	12.8	5.1	2.6	1.1	2.58
Colorado Springs, CO	25.2	35.0	15.8	13.6	6.5	2.3	1.3	2.63
Columbia, MO	30.1	34.8	15.0	13.1	4.7	1.3	0.7	2.39
Columbia, SC	29.5	34.5	15.7	12.3	5.2	1.6	0.9	2.53
Columbus, OH	28.5	33.8	15.8	12.9	5.8	1.9	1.0	2.55
Dallas, TX	24.8	30.7	16.8	15.2	7.6	2.9	1.7	2.83
Davenport, IA	30.9	35.7	13.6	11.9	5.1	1.8	0.7	2.43
Denver, CO	28.2	33.9	15.0	13.3	5.8	2.1	1.3	2.57
Des Moines, IA	27.7	33.9	15.0	13.7	6.4	2.1	0.8	2.53
Durham, NC	30.7	35.9	15.2	11.1	4.5	1.4	0.9	2.41
Edison, NJ	27.8	29.4	16.9	14.6	6.6	2.4	1.9	2.72
El Paso, TX	23.2	28.2	18.1	16.4	8.5	3.5	1.7	3.10
Fargo, ND	30.8	34.8	15.0	11.7	5.0	1.5	0.8	2.33
Fayetteville, NC	31.4	31.5	16.4	11.9	5.5	2.0	0.9	2.59
Fort Collins, CO	24.2	40.1	16.0	12.3	5.0	1.5	0.6	2.46
Fort Wayne, IN	28.5	34.3	14.6	12.4	6.2	2.3	1.3	2.53
Fort Worth, TX	24.8	30.7	16.8	15.2	7.6	2.9	1.7	2.83
Grand Rapids, MI	24.4	35.0	14.8	14.4	6.8	2.6	1.5	2.64
Greeley, CO	20.4	33.4	17.1	15.5	8.4	3.1	1.8	2.83
Green Bay, WI	28.1	36.9	13.7	12.3	6.2	1.5	1.0	2.42
Greensboro, NC	29.6	34.7	16.0	11.5	5.3	1.7	0.9	2.49
Honolulu, HI	23.5	30.3	16.9	13.7	7.4	3.7	4.2	3.05
Houston, TX	24.1	29.6	17.2	15.5	8.1	3.2	2.0	2.90
Huntsville, AL	29.6	34.4	15.7	12.6	5.1	1.6	0.6	2.47
Indianapolis, IN	29.5	33.5	15.2	12.9	5.7	2.0	0.9	2.57
Jackson, MS	27.7	32.3	17.2	13.1	5.9	2.2	1.1	2.64
Jacksonville, FL	27.1	35.5	16.5	12.5	5.4	1.8	0.9	2.61
Kansas City, MO	29.0	33.8	15.1	12.9	5.8	2.0	1.1	2.53
Lafayette, LA	27.4	33.6	16.9	12.7	6.1	2.0	0.8	2.67
Lakeland, FL	25.0	38.1	14.9	11.5	6.0	2.5	1.6	2.84
Las Vegas, NV	28.4	32.7	15.2	12.4	6.5	2.7	1.7	2.76
Lexington, KY	28.0	35.8	16.4	12.3	5.0	1.5	0.7	2.44
Lincoln, NE	30.0	35.8	13.7	12.0	5.2	2.0	0.9	2.42
Little Rock, AR	29.6	34.5	16.3	11.7	5.0	1.8	0.8	2.55
Los Angeles, CA	24.5	28.5	17.0	15.4	7.9	3.5	2.8	3.01

Table continued on next page.

Metro Area	Persons in Household (%)							Average Household Size
	One	Two	Three	Four	Five	Six	Seven or More	
Louisville, KY	30.1	34.4	15.7	11.8	5.1	1.7	0.9	2.51
Madison, WI	29.5	37.0	14.2	12.3	4.6	1.4	0.7	2.35
Manchester, NH	25.4	36.0	16.8	13.4	5.3	1.9	1.0	2.53
Miami, FL	28.3	32.4	16.7	13.4	5.7	2.1	1.1	2.85
Midland, TX	25.1	30.5	16.2	15.8	7.4	2.8	1.9	2.91
Milwaukee, WI	31.2	34.1	14.3	12.0	5.3	1.7	1.0	2.46
Minneapolis, MN	27.8	34.1	14.8	13.8	5.8	2.1	1.3	2.56
Nashville, TN	26.1	34.7	16.7	13.4	5.8	1.9	1.0	2.60
New Haven, CT	31.7	33.1	15.6	12.2	4.7	1.7	0.7	2.52
New Orleans, LA	32.9	32.6	15.5	11.5	4.6	1.7	0.9	2.58
New York, NY	27.8	29.4	16.9	14.6	6.6	2.4	1.9	2.72
Oklahoma City, OK	28.0	34.2	15.5	12.7	5.8	2.3	1.1	2.61
Omaha, NE	28.3	33.5	14.6	13.0	6.3	2.6	1.4	2.54
Orlando, FL	25.3	34.3	17.1	13.7	5.8	2.3	1.1	2.82
Peoria, IL	30.6	35.7	14.2	11.4	4.8	2.1	0.9	2.43
Philadelphia, PA	29.1	32.1	16.2	13.6	5.7	2.0	1.0	2.61
Phoenix, AZ	26.6	34.3	14.4	12.5	6.6	3.0	2.1	2.77
Pittsburgh, PA	32.8	35.5	14.6	10.9	4.0	1.3	0.5	2.27
Portland, OR	26.8	35.1	15.5	13.5	5.5	2.1	1.3	2.57
Providence, RI	29.7	33.2	16.5	12.9	5.1	1.5	0.7	2.48
Provo, UT	11.9	28.2	15.5	15.7	12.5	9.2	6.6	3.57
Raleigh, NC	25.1	32.8	17.5	15.6	6.0	1.9	0.9	2.65
Reno, NV	29.0	34.6	15.4	11.2	5.6	2.2	1.5	2.50
Richmond, VA	29.0	34.3	16.1	12.4	5.3	1.8	0.8	2.57
Rochester, MN	26.2	36.7	14.2	14.0	5.3	2.2	1.0	2.47
Sacramento, CA	25.4	33.2	15.8	14.2	6.6	2.8	1.8	2.75
Salt Lake City, UT	22.4	30.2	15.9	14.4	8.7	4.9	3.2	3.01
San Antonio, TX	26.1	31.3	16.5	13.9	7.2	3.0	1.7	2.97
San Diego, CA	23.7	32.7	17.0	14.5	7.0	2.9	1.8	2.87
San Francisco, CA	26.3	31.8	16.9	14.6	6.1	2.3	1.6	2.71
San Jose, CA	20.4	30.2	18.8	17.7	7.2	2.9	2.5	2.98
Santa Rosa, CA	27.7	34.5	15.4	12.9	5.6	2.0	1.4	2.60
Savannah, GA	27.9	34.6	16.7	12.3	5.5	1.8	0.9	2.61
Seattle, WA	27.4	34.3	15.9	13.6	5.2	2.0	1.2	2.54
Sioux Falls, SD	28.7	35.0	13.5	13.2	6.0	2.1	1.1	2.48
Springfield, IL	32.3	36.0	14.1	10.6	4.2	1.7	0.8	2.32
Tallahassee, FL	30.0	34.8	17.3	11.5	4.2	1.2	0.7	2.43
Tampa, FL	31.0	36.7	14.5	10.7	4.5	1.5	0.8	2.49
Topeka, KS	31.0	35.9	13.4	11.5	5.1	1.9	0.9	2.41
Tucson, AZ	30.3	35.9	13.9	11.0	5.3	2.0	1.2	2.47
Tulsa, OK	28.1	34.5	15.2	12.2	6.1	2.3	1.3	2.56
Tuscaloosa, AL	28.7	34.8	16.1	13.0	4.9	1.3	0.8	2.68
Virginia Beach, VA	27.0	34.0	17.6	13.2	5.2	1.8	0.9	2.57
Washington, DC	27.1	30.6	16.6	14.7	6.4	2.6	1.6	2.75
Wichita, KS	29.7	33.3	14.0	11.8	6.6	2.8	1.4	2.57
Winston-Salem, NC	29.2	35.7	15.5	11.7	5.1	1.6	0.8	2.46
U.S.	27.7	33.8	15.6	12.9	6.0	2.3	1.4	2.63

Note: Figures cover the Metropolitan Statistical Area (MSA)—see Appendix B for areas included
Source: U.S. Census Bureau, 2014-2018 American Community Survey 5-Year Estimates

Race: City

City	White Alone[1] (%)	Black Alone[1] (%)	Asian Alone[1] (%)	AIAN[2] Alone[1] (%)	NHOPI[3] Alone[1] (%)	Other Race Alone[1] (%)	Two or More Races (%)
Albany, NY	54.2	29.9	7.0	0.3	0.0	3.3	5.4
Albuquerque, NM	73.5	3.2	2.8	4.6	0.1	11.3	4.5
Allentown, PA	59.1	14.2	2.5	0.8	0.1	18.6	4.8
Anchorage, AK	63.0	5.6	9.6	7.4	2.3	2.3	9.8
Ann Arbor, MI	71.0	6.5	17.3	0.3	0.0	0.7	4.1
Athens, GA	62.7	27.7	4.1	0.1	0.1	2.7	2.6
Atlanta, GA	40.3	51.8	4.2	0.2	0.0	1.0	2.4
Austin, TX	73.5	7.8	7.3	0.6	0.0	7.5	3.3
Baton Rouge, LA	38.7	55.0	3.2	0.2	0.0	1.4	1.4
Boise City, ID	89.1	2.1	3.1	0.6	0.2	1.7	3.3
Boston, MA	52.6	25.3	9.6	0.3	0.0	7.1	5.1
Boulder, CO	87.2	1.2	5.6	0.3	0.1	1.8	3.9
Cape Coral, FL	90.2	5.0	1.7	0.2	0.0	1.5	1.4
Cedar Rapids, IA	84.7	7.1	3.4	0.3	0.2	1.0	3.4
Charleston, SC	73.8	22.4	1.9	0.1	0.0	0.3	1.5
Charlotte, NC	49.5	35.1	6.5	0.4	0.1	5.6	2.8
Chicago, IL	49.4	30.1	6.4	0.3	0.0	10.9	2.7
Clarksville, TN	65.8	24.1	2.5	0.7	0.5	1.8	4.6
Cleveland, OH	39.8	49.6	2.4	0.5	0.0	3.4	4.3
College Station, TX	77.4	7.7	10.5	0.3	0.0	1.8	2.3
Colorado Springs, CO	78.3	6.2	3.0	0.7	0.3	5.6	6.0
Columbia, MO	76.9	10.9	6.2	0.3	0.2	1.0	4.6
Columbia, SC	52.8	40.4	2.7	0.1	0.2	1.0	2.8
Columbus, OH	59.5	28.5	5.7	0.2	0.1	1.8	4.3
Dallas, TX	62.5	24.3	3.4	0.3	0.0	7.0	2.5
Davenport, IA	81.9	11.0	2.6	0.4	0.0	0.9	3.2
Denver, CO	76.5	9.4	3.8	1.0	0.1	5.7	3.6
Des Moines, IA	75.4	11.3	6.5	0.4	0.1	2.3	4.0
Durham, NC	48.4	39.3	5.3	0.3	0.0	3.7	2.9
Edison, NJ	36.8	7.7	48.3	0.3	0.0	4.0	2.8
El Paso, TX	80.8	3.8	1.4	0.5	0.2	10.7	2.7
Fargo, ND	85.3	6.1	3.8	1.2	0.0	0.6	3.0
Fayetteville, NC	45.1	42.3	2.9	1.0	0.3	2.7	5.7
Fort Collins, CO	88.9	1.6	3.4	0.9	0.1	1.6	3.5
Fort Wayne, IN	73.8	14.9	4.6	0.2	0.0	1.9	4.5
Fort Worth, TX	64.1	19.0	4.2	0.5	0.1	8.9	3.3
Grand Rapids, MI	67.5	19.2	2.3	0.4	0.1	5.5	5.0
Greeley, CO	88.6	2.3	1.3	1.0	0.1	3.9	2.9
Green Bay, WI	76.7	4.0	4.2	3.6	0.0	6.3	5.2
Greensboro, NC	47.8	41.6	4.7	0.5	0.1	2.7	2.6
Honolulu, HI	17.5	1.9	53.3	0.1	8.2	0.9	18.2
Houston, TX	57.6	22.5	6.9	0.3	0.1	10.5	2.1
Huntsville, AL	61.6	30.6	2.7	0.4	0.1	1.7	2.9
Indianapolis, IN	61.4	28.3	3.2	0.3	0.1	3.5	3.2
Jackson, MS	16.6	82.0	0.4	0.1	0.0	0.3	0.6
Jacksonville, FL	58.7	31.0	4.8	0.2	0.1	1.8	3.4
Kansas City, MO	60.1	29.0	2.7	0.4	0.1	4.1	3.5
Lafayette, LA	64.5	30.8	1.8	0.2	0.0	0.6	2.0
Lakeland, FL	72.5	20.6	2.4	0.3	0.1	1.9	2.1
Las Vegas, NV	62.2	12.2	6.6	0.9	0.8	12.5	4.9
Lexington, KY	75.4	14.4	3.6	0.3	0.1	2.7	3.6
Lincoln, NE	85.2	4.4	4.7	0.6	0.1	1.4	3.6
Little Rock, AR	50.6	41.7	3.1	0.2	0.1	1.8	2.4
Los Angeles, CA	52.4	8.9	11.6	0.7	0.2	22.5	3.6

Table continued on next page.

City	White Alone[1] (%)	Black Alone[1] (%)	Asian Alone[1] (%)	AIAN[2] Alone[1] (%)	NHOPI[3] Alone[1] (%)	Other Race Alone[1] (%)	Two or More Races (%)
Louisville, KY	69.9	23.5	2.7	0.2	0.1	0.9	2.7
Madison, WI	78.4	6.8	9.0	0.4	0.0	1.8	3.6
Manchester, NH	84.8	5.8	5.3	0.2	0.0	1.0	3.0
Miami, FL	75.2	17.7	1.1	0.2	0.0	3.9	1.8
Midland, TX	82.3	7.8	2.3	0.7	0.0	4.7	2.1
Milwaukee, WI	44.6	38.8	4.3	0.6	0.0	7.7	4.0
Minneapolis, MN	63.8	19.4	6.1	1.4	0.0	4.7	4.6
Nashville, TN	63.2	27.9	3.6	0.2	0.1	2.5	2.6
New Haven, CT	44.1	33.0	4.7	0.4	0.0	13.5	4.3
New Orleans, LA	34.0	59.7	2.9	0.2	0.0	1.4	1.8
New York, NY	42.7	24.3	13.9	0.4	0.1	15.1	3.5
Oklahoma City, OK	67.5	14.6	4.6	2.8	0.1	4.0	6.4
Omaha, NE	77.8	12.3	3.7	0.7	0.1	2.2	3.2
Orlando, FL	60.7	25.4	4.3	0.2	0.0	6.2	3.2
Peoria, IL	59.9	27.0	5.9	0.4	0.0	2.4	4.5
Philadelphia, PA	41.2	42.3	7.2	0.4	0.0	5.9	3.0
Phoenix, AZ	72.3	6.9	3.7	2.1	0.2	10.9	3.8
Pittsburgh, PA	66.9	23.2	5.7	0.2	0.0	0.6	3.5
Portland, OR	77.1	5.8	8.1	0.7	0.7	2.1	5.5
Providence, RI	54.2	16.0	6.1	1.2	0.2	18.0	4.4
Provo, UT	88.5	0.8	2.4	0.6	1.4	2.7	3.6
Raleigh, NC	58.5	29.0	4.5	0.4	0.1	4.7	3.0
Reno, NV	76.4	2.7	6.5	1.1	0.8	7.7	4.8
Richmond, VA	45.4	47.8	2.1	0.4	0.0	1.0	3.3
Rochester, MN	80.3	7.8	7.2	0.4	0.1	1.1	3.1
Sacramento, CA	47.2	13.4	18.9	0.8	1.7	11.0	7.0
Salt Lake City, UT	73.1	2.3	5.4	1.4	1.5	13.1	3.4
San Antonio, TX	80.5	6.9	2.8	0.8	0.1	6.0	2.8
San Diego, CA	64.8	6.5	16.7	0.4	0.4	6.0	5.2
San Francisco, CA	46.7	5.2	34.2	0.3	0.3	7.7	5.4
San Jose, CA	40.0	3.0	35.4	0.5	0.5	15.3	5.2
Santa Rosa, CA	67.8	2.2	5.5	1.6	0.5	15.8	6.5
Savannah, GA	38.7	54.4	2.4	0.2	0.1	1.2	3.0
Seattle, WA	68.0	7.0	15.1	0.6	0.3	2.3	6.8
Sioux Falls, SD	84.5	6.0	2.5	2.4	0.0	1.5	3.0
Springfield, IL	72.9	19.9	2.9	0.1	0.0	0.8	3.3
Tallahassee, FL	56.9	34.8	4.4	0.2	0.0	1.0	2.6
Tampa, FL	64.9	24.2	4.2	0.3	0.1	2.6	3.8
Topeka, KS	78.5	10.6	1.7	1.0	0.1	3.2	4.9
Tucson, AZ	72.4	5.1	3.2	3.5	0.2	10.4	5.1
Tulsa, OK	64.0	15.3	3.3	4.4	0.1	5.3	7.6
Tuscaloosa, AL	51.1	44.1	2.4	0.3	0.1	1.0	1.1
Virginia Beach, VA	66.7	19.0	6.6	0.3	0.1	2.0	5.3
Washington, DC	41.0	46.9	3.9	0.3	0.0	4.9	2.9
Wichita, KS	74.6	11.1	5.0	1.0	0.1	4.0	4.3
Winston-Salem, NC	56.3	34.8	2.4	0.2	0.1	3.5	2.8
U.S.	72.7	12.7	5.4	0.8	0.2	4.9	3.2

Note: (1) Alone is defined as not being in combination with one or more other races; (2) American Indian and Alaska Native; (3) Native Hawaiian and Other Pacific Islander
Source: U.S. Census Bureau, 2014-2018 American Community Survey 5-Year Estimates

Race: Metro Area

Metro Area	White Alone[1] (%)	Black Alone[1] (%)	Asian Alone[1] (%)	AIAN[2] Alone[1] (%)	NHOPI[3] Alone[1] (%)	Other Race Alone[1] (%)	Two or More Races (%)
Albany, NY	83.0	7.8	4.3	0.2	0.0	1.4	3.2
Albuquerque, NM	74.5	2.6	2.2	5.9	0.1	10.7	4.1
Allentown, PA	83.9	5.7	2.8	0.3	0.0	4.1	3.1
Anchorage, AK	68.2	4.4	7.5	6.9	1.8	1.8	9.4
Ann Arbor, MI	73.7	11.8	9.1	0.3	0.1	0.7	4.3
Athens, GA	71.7	20.2	3.4	0.1	0.0	2.2	2.3
Atlanta, GA	54.0	33.9	5.7	0.4	0.0	3.3	2.6
Austin, TX	76.7	7.3	5.7	0.5	0.1	6.4	3.4
Baton Rouge, LA	59.4	35.4	2.0	0.2	0.0	1.2	1.9
Boise City, ID	88.9	1.0	2.0	0.8	0.2	3.9	3.2
Boston, MA	76.5	8.2	7.8	0.2	0.0	4.1	3.2
Boulder, CO	88.7	0.9	4.7	0.5	0.1	2.1	3.1
Cape Coral, FL	84.8	8.6	1.6	0.2	0.1	3.0	1.8
Cedar Rapids, IA	89.8	4.7	2.1	0.2	0.1	0.7	2.5
Charleston, SC	67.8	26.0	1.8	0.3	0.1	1.5	2.6
Charlotte, NC	67.5	22.4	3.6	0.4	0.1	3.5	2.5
Chicago, IL	65.8	16.6	6.5	0.3	0.0	8.1	2.6
Clarksville, TN	72.0	19.7	2.0	0.6	0.4	1.3	4.0
Cleveland, OH	73.5	19.9	2.2	0.3	0.0	1.3	2.8
College Station, TX	76.1	11.2	5.5	0.4	0.0	3.9	2.9
Colorado Springs, CO	80.1	6.1	2.7	0.7	0.4	4.3	5.8
Columbia, MO	81.1	8.8	4.5	0.3	0.1	1.0	4.2
Columbia, SC	59.9	33.3	2.1	0.2	0.1	1.8	2.7
Columbus, OH	75.9	15.3	4.1	0.2	0.0	1.2	3.3
Dallas, TX	69.1	15.5	6.6	0.5	0.1	5.2	3.0
Davenport, IA	85.5	7.4	2.3	0.3	0.0	1.5	3.0
Denver, CO	81.4	5.7	4.2	0.8	0.1	4.3	3.6
Des Moines, IA	86.7	5.2	4.0	0.2	0.1	1.1	2.6
Durham, NC	62.1	26.6	4.9	0.3	0.0	3.2	2.8
Edison, NJ	58.2	17.1	10.8	0.3	0.0	10.5	3.0
El Paso, TX	80.2	3.4	1.2	0.6	0.1	11.9	2.5
Fargo, ND	88.4	4.6	2.5	1.1	0.0	0.6	2.7
Fayetteville, NC	49.8	36.4	2.4	2.4	0.3	3.1	5.7
Fort Collins, CO	91.5	1.0	2.2	0.7	0.1	1.5	3.1
Fort Wayne, IN	81.7	9.9	3.2	0.2	0.0	1.5	3.5
Fort Worth, TX	69.1	15.5	6.6	0.5	0.1	5.2	3.0
Grand Rapids, MI	84.2	6.5	2.6	0.4	0.0	3.0	3.3
Greeley, CO	90.6	1.2	1.5	0.7	0.1	3.1	2.8
Green Bay, WI	87.2	2.0	2.7	2.1	0.0	3.1	2.9
Greensboro, NC	63.6	26.7	3.7	0.5	0.1	3.2	2.3
Honolulu, HI	21.0	2.4	42.5	0.2	9.5	0.9	23.5
Houston, TX	65.3	17.3	7.7	0.4	0.1	7.0	2.4
Huntsville, AL	70.8	21.9	2.3	0.6	0.1	1.4	3.0
Indianapolis, IN	77.1	15.1	3.1	0.2	0.0	2.0	2.6
Jackson, MS	47.7	49.3	1.1	0.1	0.0	0.9	0.9
Jacksonville, FL	69.7	21.5	3.8	0.2	0.1	1.5	3.2
Kansas City, MO	78.4	12.4	2.8	0.4	0.2	2.6	3.2
Lafayette, LA	70.7	24.7	1.7	0.2	0.0	0.8	1.9
Lakeland, FL	77.8	15.2	1.7	0.3	0.0	2.4	2.5
Las Vegas, NV	60.7	11.5	9.6	0.8	0.7	11.5	5.2
Lexington, KY	81.0	10.8	2.6	0.2	0.0	2.3	3.1
Lincoln, NE	86.9	3.8	4.1	0.6	0.1	1.3	3.3
Little Rock, AR	70.7	23.3	1.7	0.3	0.1	1.5	2.5
Los Angeles, CA	53.8	6.6	15.9	0.6	0.3	18.8	4.0

Table continued on next page.

Metro Area	White Alone[1] (%)	Black Alone[1] (%)	Asian Alone[1] (%)	AIAN[2] Alone[1] (%)	NHOPI[3] Alone[1] (%)	Other Race Alone[1] (%)	Two or More Races (%)
Louisville, KY	80.0	14.3	2.0	0.2	0.0	0.9	2.5
Madison, WI	85.9	4.4	4.9	0.3	0.0	1.6	2.9
Manchester, NH	89.7	2.8	4.1	0.1	0.0	0.8	2.5
Miami, FL	70.5	21.3	2.5	0.2	0.0	3.2	2.2
Midland, TX	84.1	6.4	2.1	0.7	0.0	4.5	2.1
Milwaukee, WI	72.9	16.6	3.7	0.4	0.0	3.6	2.7
Minneapolis, MN	79.2	8.3	6.5	0.6	0.0	2.1	3.3
Nashville, TN	77.9	15.2	2.6	0.3	0.1	1.6	2.4
New Haven, CT	73.8	13.2	4.0	0.2	0.0	5.6	3.2
New Orleans, LA	57.5	35.1	2.9	0.4	0.0	2.1	2.0
New York, NY	58.2	17.1	10.8	0.3	0.0	10.5	3.0
Oklahoma City, OK	73.7	10.3	3.2	3.4	0.1	2.8	6.6
Omaha, NE	84.3	7.6	2.8	0.5	0.1	1.8	2.9
Orlando, FL	70.2	16.5	4.2	0.3	0.1	5.4	3.3
Peoria, IL	84.7	9.2	2.4	0.2	0.0	0.9	2.5
Philadelphia, PA	67.0	21.0	5.8	0.2	0.0	3.3	2.7
Phoenix, AZ	77.9	5.4	3.9	2.2	0.2	6.7	3.6
Pittsburgh, PA	86.7	8.1	2.3	0.1	0.0	0.4	2.3
Portland, OR	81.2	2.8	6.5	0.8	0.5	3.2	5.0
Providence, RI	82.1	5.7	3.0	0.4	0.1	5.7	3.1
Provo, UT	91.9	0.6	1.5	0.5	0.8	1.8	2.9
Raleigh, NC	67.6	19.9	5.5	0.4	0.0	3.6	3.0
Reno, NV	78.9	2.3	5.2	1.6	0.6	7.0	4.4
Richmond, VA	61.7	29.7	3.7	0.3	0.1	1.5	3.0
Rochester, MN	87.8	4.3	4.3	0.3	0.0	1.0	2.2
Sacramento, CA	65.4	7.1	13.1	0.6	0.8	6.5	6.4
Salt Lake City, UT	79.8	1.8	3.8	0.8	1.4	9.2	3.3
San Antonio, TX	80.9	6.8	2.5	0.6	0.1	6.0	3.2
San Diego, CA	70.7	5.0	11.8	0.6	0.4	6.2	5.2
San Francisco, CA	49.9	7.3	25.7	0.5	0.7	9.8	6.1
San Jose, CA	46.1	2.4	34.9	0.5	0.4	10.6	5.0
Santa Rosa, CA	74.9	1.6	4.0	1.0	0.3	12.7	5.6
Savannah, GA	59.5	33.4	2.2	0.3	0.1	1.6	3.0
Seattle, WA	69.2	5.7	13.3	0.8	0.9	3.5	6.7
Sioux Falls, SD	88.3	4.2	1.8	1.9	0.0	1.2	2.5
Springfield, IL	82.8	12.1	1.9	0.1	0.1	0.6	2.5
Tallahassee, FL	61.0	32.8	2.8	0.2	0.0	0.9	2.2
Tampa, FL	78.0	12.1	3.4	0.3	0.1	3.0	3.2
Topeka, KS	85.1	6.5	1.2	1.2	0.1	1.9	4.1
Tucson, AZ	76.2	3.5	2.9	3.7	0.2	8.7	4.7
Tulsa, OK	71.3	8.0	2.4	7.2	0.1	2.8	8.2
Tuscaloosa, AL	62.2	34.1	1.4	0.2	0.0	1.0	1.1
Virginia Beach, VA	59.2	30.6	3.9	0.3	0.1	1.8	4.2
Washington, DC	54.1	25.3	10.0	0.3	0.1	6.1	4.2
Wichita, KS	81.4	7.5	3.6	1.0	0.1	2.6	3.8
Winston-Salem, NC	75.8	17.8	1.7	0.3	0.1	2.2	2.1
U.S.	72.7	12.7	5.4	0.8	0.2	4.9	3.2

Note: (1) Figures cover the Metropolitan Statistical Area (MSA)—see Appendix B for areas included; (1) Alone is defined as not being in combination with one or more other races; (2) American Indian and Alaska Native; (3) Native Hawaiian & Other Pacific Islander
Source: U.S. Census Bureau, 2014-2018 American Community Survey 5-Year Estimates

Hispanic Origin: City

City	Hispanic or Latino (%)	Mexican (%)	Puerto Rican (%)	Cuban (%)	Other Hispanic or Latino (%)
Albany, NY	10.2	0.8	5.3	0.4	3.8
Albuquerque, NM	49.0	28.5	0.7	0.4	19.4
Allentown, PA	52.2	2.1	28.3	0.9	20.9
Anchorage, AK	9.1	5.1	1.2	0.1	2.7
Ann Arbor, MI	4.7	2.2	0.3	0.3	2.0
Athens, GA	10.7	6.6	1.0	0.3	2.9
Atlanta, GA	4.3	2.2	0.6	0.3	1.2
Austin, TX	34.3	27.7	0.9	0.7	5.0
Baton Rouge, LA	3.7	1.2	0.2	0.2	2.1
Boise City, ID	9.0	7.2	0.3	0.1	1.5
Boston, MA	19.7	1.1	5.4	0.4	12.8
Boulder, CO	9.8	6.2	0.4	0.3	2.9
Cape Coral, FL	19.5	1.6	4.8	6.6	6.5
Cedar Rapids, IA	3.7	2.7	0.1	0.0	0.8
Charleston, SC	3.0	1.4	0.5	0.2	0.9
Charlotte, NC	14.0	5.3	1.2	0.5	7.0
Chicago, IL	29.0	21.6	3.8	0.3	3.3
Clarksville, TN	11.5	5.0	3.8	0.4	2.3
Cleveland, OH	11.6	1.2	8.4	0.2	1.8
College Station, TX	15.6	10.8	0.4	0.4	4.0
Colorado Springs, CO	17.7	11.4	1.4	0.5	4.4
Columbia, MO	3.4	2.0	0.2	0.1	1.2
Columbia, SC	5.4	2.4	1.3	0.4	1.3
Columbus, OH	5.9	3.3	0.8	0.1	1.8
Dallas, TX	41.7	35.7	0.5	0.3	5.2
Davenport, IA	8.5	7.5	0.4	0.0	0.5
Denver, CO	30.3	24.0	0.6	0.2	5.4
Des Moines, IA	13.3	10.6	0.3	0.1	2.2
Durham, NC	14.1	6.9	1.0	0.2	6.0
Edison, NJ	10.4	1.6	2.9	0.9	5.1
El Paso, TX	80.9	76.5	1.1	0.1	3.1
Fargo, ND	2.8	1.8	0.3	0.0	0.7
Fayetteville, NC	12.0	4.0	4.0	0.4	3.7
Fort Collins, CO	12.1	8.7	0.4	0.1	3.0
Fort Wayne, IN	8.9	6.5	0.6	0.1	1.7
Fort Worth, TX	35.0	30.7	1.1	0.3	2.9
Grand Rapids, MI	15.9	9.4	1.4	0.3	4.8
Greeley, CO	39.1	32.0	0.6	0.3	6.2
Green Bay, WI	15.2	11.6	1.2	0.1	2.3
Greensboro, NC	7.5	4.9	0.6	0.2	1.8
Honolulu, HI	7.3	1.9	1.9	0.2	3.2
Houston, TX	44.8	32.2	0.6	0.8	11.2
Huntsville, AL	6.0	3.7	0.8	0.2	1.3
Indianapolis, IN	10.2	7.2	0.6	0.1	2.4
Jackson, MS	1.2	0.4	0.3	0.1	0.4
Jacksonville, FL	9.6	1.9	2.9	1.2	3.5
Kansas City, MO	10.2	7.7	0.3	0.3	1.9
Lafayette, LA	4.1	1.9	0.4	0.2	1.6
Lakeland, FL	15.6	3.2	6.1	2.4	3.9
Las Vegas, NV	32.9	24.7	1.2	1.3	5.7
Lexington, KY	7.2	4.9	0.7	0.2	1.4
Lincoln, NE	7.4	5.5	0.2	0.2	1.5
Little Rock, AR	7.3	4.7	0.3	0.2	2.0
Los Angeles, CA	48.6	32.3	0.5	0.4	15.4
Louisville, KY	5.4	2.0	0.5	1.7	1.2

Table continued on next page.

City	Hispanic or Latino (%)	Mexican (%)	Puerto Rican (%)	Cuban (%)	Other Hispanic or Latino (%)
Madison, WI	6.9	4.3	0.6	0.2	1.8
Manchester, NH	9.9	1.8	4.1	0.1	4.0
Miami, FL	72.5	1.8	3.5	35.6	31.6
Midland, TX	43.6	40.7	0.5	0.3	2.1
Milwaukee, WI	18.8	13.0	4.5	0.2	1.1
Minneapolis, MN	9.6	5.9	0.5	0.2	3.1
Nashville, TN	10.4	6.2	0.6	0.3	3.4
New Haven, CT	30.3	5.6	17.8	0.3	6.5
New Orleans, LA	5.5	1.3	0.3	0.4	3.5
New York, NY	29.1	4.0	8.3	0.5	16.4
Oklahoma City, OK	19.2	16.1	0.3	0.1	2.7
Omaha, NE	13.9	10.8	0.3	0.2	2.7
Orlando, FL	31.1	1.9	15.1	2.9	11.3
Peoria, IL	6.0	4.4	0.4	0.1	1.1
Philadelphia, PA	14.5	1.2	8.7	0.3	4.2
Phoenix, AZ	42.6	38.5	0.6	0.3	3.1
Pittsburgh, PA	3.1	1.0	0.7	0.2	1.1
Portland, OR	9.7	6.8	0.4	0.4	2.1
Providence, RI	43.0	1.9	8.5	0.3	32.3
Provo, UT	16.6	11.5	0.5	0.1	4.5
Raleigh, NC	11.0	5.6	1.1	0.3	4.0
Reno, NV	24.7	19.1	0.5	0.3	4.8
Richmond, VA	6.7	1.8	0.7	0.2	4.0
Rochester, MN	5.9	3.8	0.4	0.3	1.3
Sacramento, CA	28.7	24.6	0.6	0.3	3.1
Salt Lake City, UT	21.6	17.1	0.4	0.3	3.9
San Antonio, TX	64.2	57.6	1.2	0.3	5.1
San Diego, CA	30.1	26.4	0.7	0.2	2.7
San Francisco, CA	15.2	7.8	0.6	0.3	6.6
San Jose, CA	32.0	27.7	0.6	0.1	3.6
Santa Rosa, CA	32.8	29.3	0.4	0.1	3.0
Savannah, GA	5.1	2.0	1.3	0.2	1.6
Seattle, WA	6.6	3.8	0.4	0.2	2.1
Sioux Falls, SD	5.3	3.3	0.3	0.0	1.7
Springfield, IL	2.7	1.4	0.6	0.1	0.5
Tallahassee, FL	6.9	1.1	1.5	1.4	2.8
Tampa, FL	25.7	3.2	7.7	7.6	7.2
Topeka, KS	15.0	13.1	0.7	0.1	1.1
Tucson, AZ	43.2	39.4	0.8	0.2	2.9
Tulsa, OK	16.3	13.2	0.5	0.2	2.4
Tuscaloosa, AL	3.1	1.4	0.1	0.1	1.4
Virginia Beach, VA	8.0	2.4	2.4	0.4	2.9
Washington, DC	10.9	2.1	0.8	0.5	7.6
Wichita, KS	17.0	14.6	0.5	0.2	1.8
Winston-Salem, NC	14.6	9.6	1.3	0.2	3.5
U.S.	17.8	11.2	1.7	0.7	4.2

Note: Persons of Hispanic or Latino origin can be of any race
Source: U.S. Census Bureau, 2014-2018 American Community Survey 5-Year Estimates

Hispanic Origin: Metro Area

Metro Area	Hispanic or Latino (%)	Mexican (%)	Puerto Rican (%)	Cuban (%)	Other Hispanic or Latino (%)
Albany, NY	5.0	0.7	2.4	0.2	1.7
Albuquerque, NM	48.8	28.5	0.6	0.3	19.5
Allentown, PA	16.3	1.3	8.8	0.4	5.9
Anchorage, AK	8.0	4.4	1.1	0.1	2.3
Ann Arbor, MI	4.6	2.5	0.3	0.2	1.7
Athens, GA	8.4	5.0	0.8	0.2	2.4
Atlanta, GA	10.6	5.7	1.0	0.4	3.5
Austin, TX	32.3	26.8	0.9	0.5	4.2
Baton Rouge, LA	3.9	1.7	0.2	0.1	1.8
Boise City, ID	13.5	11.6	0.4	0.1	1.5
Boston, MA	10.9	0.7	2.9	0.2	7.1
Boulder, CO	13.8	10.4	0.3	0.2	2.8
Cape Coral, FL	20.7	6.1	4.3	4.4	6.0
Cedar Rapids, IA	2.9	2.1	0.1	0.0	0.7
Charleston, SC	5.5	2.8	0.8	0.1	1.7
Charlotte, NC	10.0	4.7	1.0	0.4	3.9
Chicago, IL	21.9	17.3	2.2	0.2	2.2
Clarksville, TN	9.0	4.2	2.7	0.3	1.8
Cleveland, OH	5.7	1.2	3.4	0.1	1.0
College Station, TX	24.7	21.0	0.2	0.2	3.2
Colorado Springs, CO	16.5	10.2	1.5	0.4	4.3
Columbia, MO	3.4	2.1	0.1	0.1	1.0
Columbia, SC	5.5	2.7	1.2	0.2	1.4
Columbus, OH	4.1	2.2	0.6	0.1	1.3
Dallas, TX	28.6	23.8	0.7	0.2	3.8
Davenport, IA	8.6	7.4	0.5	0.1	0.7
Denver, CO	23.0	17.5	0.5	0.2	4.8
Des Moines, IA	7.3	5.7	0.2	0.1	1.3
Durham, NC	11.4	6.1	0.8	0.2	4.2
Edison, NJ	24.2	3.0	6.2	0.7	14.2
El Paso, TX	82.4	78.1	1.1	0.1	3.1
Fargo, ND	3.1	2.1	0.3	0.0	0.6
Fayetteville, NC	11.6	4.5	3.8	0.3	3.1
Fort Collins, CO	11.3	8.5	0.3	0.1	2.4
Fort Wayne, IN	6.6	4.9	0.4	0.1	1.3
Fort Worth, TX	28.6	23.8	0.7	0.2	3.8
Grand Rapids, MI	9.4	6.6	0.8	0.3	1.7
Greeley, CO	29.2	24.3	0.4	0.3	4.2
Green Bay, WI	7.3	5.6	0.6	0.1	0.9
Greensboro, NC	8.2	5.7	0.6	0.2	1.7
Honolulu, HI	9.8	2.8	3.1	0.2	3.8
Houston, TX	37.0	27.7	0.6	0.5	8.0
Huntsville, AL	5.1	3.2	0.7	0.2	1.0
Indianapolis, IN	6.6	4.5	0.4	0.1	1.6
Jackson, MS	2.4	1.3	0.3	0.1	0.7
Jacksonville, FL	8.5	1.7	2.8	1.1	3.0
Kansas City, MO	8.9	6.9	0.3	0.2	1.5
Lafayette, LA	3.9	2.3	0.2	0.1	1.3
Lakeland, FL	21.5	7.8	8.5	1.6	3.6
Las Vegas, NV	30.9	23.0	1.1	1.4	5.4
Lexington, KY	6.1	4.2	0.5	0.1	1.2
Lincoln, NE	6.6	4.8	0.3	0.1	1.4
Little Rock, AR	5.2	3.7	0.3	0.1	1.2
Los Angeles, CA	45.0	35.0	0.4	0.4	9.2
Louisville, KY	4.7	2.3	0.4	0.9	1.0

Table continued on next page.

Metro Area	Hispanic or Latino (%)	Mexican (%)	Puerto Rican (%)	Cuban (%)	Other Hispanic or Latino (%)
Madison, WI	5.7	3.7	0.5	0.2	1.4
Manchester, NH	6.5	1.1	2.3	0.2	2.9
Miami, FL	44.7	2.5	3.9	19.0	19.4
Midland, TX	44.1	41.5	0.5	0.3	1.9
Milwaukee, WI	10.5	7.1	2.3	0.1	0.9
Minneapolis, MN	5.8	3.9	0.3	0.1	1.5
Nashville, TN	7.1	4.4	0.5	0.2	2.0
New Haven, CT	17.6	1.8	10.5	0.3	5.0
New Orleans, LA	8.7	1.8	0.5	0.5	5.8
New York, NY	24.2	3.0	6.2	0.7	14.2
Oklahoma City, OK	13.1	10.7	0.3	0.1	2.0
Omaha, NE	10.2	7.8	0.4	0.1	1.9
Orlando, FL	29.9	2.8	15.1	2.3	9.6
Peoria, IL	3.4	2.5	0.2	0.1	0.6
Philadelphia, PA	9.2	1.8	4.5	0.3	2.6
Phoenix, AZ	30.7	27.1	0.7	0.2	2.7
Pittsburgh, PA	1.7	0.5	0.5	0.1	0.6
Portland, OR	11.8	9.2	0.3	0.2	2.0
Providence, RI	12.5	0.9	4.1	0.2	7.3
Provo, UT	11.4	7.7	0.2	0.1	3.5
Raleigh, NC	10.5	5.8	1.2	0.4	3.1
Reno, NV	24.0	18.7	0.6	0.3	4.4
Richmond, VA	6.0	1.5	1.0	0.2	3.4
Rochester, MN	4.3	2.9	0.3	0.1	1.1
Sacramento, CA	21.4	17.7	0.6	0.2	3.0
Salt Lake City, UT	17.8	13.1	0.5	0.1	4.1
San Antonio, TX	55.2	49.2	1.2	0.2	4.6
San Diego, CA	33.5	29.9	0.7	0.2	2.7
San Francisco, CA	21.8	14.3	0.7	0.2	6.6
San Jose, CA	26.8	22.6	0.5	0.1	3.5
Santa Rosa, CA	26.5	22.7	0.4	0.1	3.3
Savannah, GA	6.0	2.7	1.3	0.3	1.7
Seattle, WA	9.9	7.0	0.6	0.2	2.2
Sioux Falls, SD	4.1	2.5	0.2	0.0	1.3
Springfield, IL	2.2	1.2	0.4	0.1	0.5
Tallahassee, FL	6.4	1.9	1.3	1.0	2.2
Tampa, FL	19.0	3.7	6.2	3.9	5.1
Topeka, KS	10.1	8.7	0.5	0.1	0.8
Tucson, AZ	37.0	33.4	0.7	0.2	2.7
Tulsa, OK	9.7	7.7	0.4	0.1	1.5
Tuscaloosa, AL	3.5	2.3	0.1	0.1	1.0
Virginia Beach, VA	6.6	2.1	2.0	0.3	2.2
Washington, DC	15.5	2.2	1.1	0.3	11.9
Wichita, KS	12.8	10.7	0.4	0.2	1.5
Winston-Salem, NC	10.1	6.7	0.8	0.2	2.4
U.S.	17.8	11.2	1.7	0.7	4.2

Note: Persons of Hispanic or Latino origin can be of any race; Figures cover the Metropolitan Statistical Area (MSA)—see Appendix B for areas included
Source: U.S. Census Bureau, 2014-2018 American Community Survey 5-Year Estimates

Age: City

City	Percent of Population									Median Age
	Under Age 5	Age 5–19	Age 20–34	Age 35–44	Age 45–54	Age 55–64	Age 65–74	Age 75–84	Age 85+	
Albany, NY	5.6	18.3	31.6	10.6	10.7	10.3	6.8	3.6	2.4	31.2
Albuquerque, NM	6.1	19.2	22.8	12.9	12.2	12.3	8.5	4.4	1.7	36.3
Allentown, PA	7.5	22.9	24.4	12.3	11.2	9.9	6.4	3.4	2.1	31.8
Anchorage, AK	7.4	19.6	25.6	12.8	12.6	12.0	6.6	2.5	0.9	33.2
Ann Arbor, MI	3.8	18.5	39.7	9.6	8.4	8.4	6.6	3.3	1.6	27.5
Athens, GA	5.5	20.9	34.8	11.2	8.8	8.8	6.1	2.9	1.2	27.6
Atlanta, GA	5.7	17.0	30.4	13.8	11.8	9.9	6.8	3.3	1.4	33.2
Austin, TX	6.7	16.9	30.3	16.0	11.8	9.6	5.5	2.2	1.0	33.0
Baton Rouge, LA	6.8	19.4	28.9	10.4	10.1	10.8	7.7	3.9	1.8	31.2
Boise City, ID	5.8	19.1	23.4	13.8	12.4	11.9	8.2	3.5	1.9	36.2
Boston, MA	5.1	15.5	34.8	12.4	10.9	10.0	6.4	3.3	1.5	32.0
Boulder, CO	3.4	18.7	37.3	10.9	10.1	9.0	6.2	2.8	1.7	28.7
Cape Coral, FL	4.5	16.2	15.1	11.4	14.7	15.4	13.3	6.5	3.0	46.9
Cedar Rapids, IA	6.9	18.8	23.1	12.7	11.8	11.9	8.0	4.4	2.4	35.8
Charleston, SC	5.8	14.7	29.9	12.7	10.8	11.9	8.8	3.5	1.9	34.7
Charlotte, NC	6.8	19.5	25.0	15.0	13.1	10.5	6.2	2.7	1.1	34.1
Chicago, IL	6.5	17.3	27.4	14.0	12.0	10.9	7.0	3.6	1.4	34.3
Clarksville, TN	9.0	20.6	30.9	12.9	10.3	8.3	5.1	2.3	0.8	29.5
Cleveland, OH	6.5	18.9	23.4	11.5	12.6	13.6	7.6	4.1	1.8	36.0
College Station, TX	5.3	22.9	43.1	9.3	6.9	5.9	4.0	1.9	0.6	22.8
Colorado Springs, CO	6.6	19.5	24.5	12.4	12.1	11.6	7.9	3.7	1.5	34.6
Columbia, MO	5.8	18.6	35.5	10.9	9.7	9.2	5.9	3.0	1.3	28.2
Columbia, SC	4.9	22.7	32.9	10.3	10.1	9.4	5.9	2.6	1.1	28.3
Columbus, OH	7.3	18.3	29.4	13.0	11.6	10.4	6.1	2.7	1.2	32.2
Dallas, TX	7.7	20.1	26.2	13.8	11.9	10.2	6.0	2.9	1.2	32.7
Davenport, IA	6.6	19.2	22.6	12.1	12.4	12.6	8.0	4.1	2.4	36.1
Denver, CO	6.3	16.0	28.9	15.8	11.6	10.2	6.8	3.1	1.5	34.4
Des Moines, IA	6.9	20.5	24.2	13.1	12.0	11.7	6.7	3.3	1.6	33.9
Durham, NC	6.9	18.4	26.7	14.1	11.9	10.7	6.9	3.1	1.4	33.8
Edison, NJ	6.2	18.0	18.8	15.4	14.0	13.4	7.9	4.1	2.2	39.3
El Paso, TX	7.5	22.2	22.9	12.5	11.8	10.5	6.9	4.0	1.6	32.9
Fargo, ND	6.6	17.8	32.7	11.7	9.7	10.1	6.2	3.3	1.9	30.4
Fayetteville, NC	7.6	19.1	30.8	11.0	9.9	10.2	6.6	3.5	1.3	30.0
Fort Collins, CO	5.2	19.7	34.2	11.9	9.5	9.3	6.1	2.9	1.4	29.1
Fort Wayne, IN	7.2	21.0	22.0	12.2	11.9	12.0	8.2	3.6	1.9	34.8
Fort Worth, TX	7.9	22.9	23.3	14.0	12.4	10.0	5.8	2.6	1.2	32.5
Grand Rapids, MI	7.1	19.3	30.2	11.1	10.1	10.5	6.1	3.3	2.3	31.0
Greeley, CO	7.0	23.6	24.7	11.6	10.7	10.5	6.7	3.5	1.6	31.0
Green Bay, WI	7.8	20.0	23.6	12.1	12.5	11.6	6.9	3.6	1.9	34.1
Greensboro, NC	6.1	19.8	23.9	12.6	12.6	11.5	7.9	3.8	1.8	35.2
Honolulu, HI	5.2	13.8	22.5	12.8	13.0	12.9	10.2	5.5	4.0	41.5
Houston, TX	7.7	19.7	26.1	14.0	11.9	10.3	6.1	2.9	1.2	32.9
Huntsville, AL	6.4	17.7	23.6	11.5	12.6	12.6	8.5	5.2	1.9	36.9
Indianapolis, IN	7.3	19.6	24.1	12.9	12.3	11.9	6.9	3.4	1.5	34.2
Jackson, MS	7.3	21.8	24.7	11.8	11.0	11.6	6.9	3.0	1.7	32.4
Jacksonville, FL	6.9	18.5	23.3	12.7	13.0	12.5	8.0	3.6	1.5	35.8
Kansas City, MO	6.9	18.4	24.5	13.2	12.4	12.0	7.4	3.6	1.7	35.1
Lafayette, LA	5.7	18.5	25.5	10.9	12.2	13.2	8.2	4.0	1.7	35.1
Lakeland, FL	5.5	17.6	19.9	11.6	11.9	11.7	11.2	7.6	3.0	41.1
Las Vegas, NV	6.5	19.9	20.3	13.5	13.6	11.9	8.9	4.2	1.4	37.7
Lexington, KY	6.2	18.4	26.3	13.1	12.0	11.5	7.5	3.5	1.6	34.4
Lincoln, NE	6.6	19.8	26.9	12.2	10.7	10.9	7.5	3.6	1.7	32.6
Little Rock, AR	6.5	19.3	22.2	13.3	11.9	13.1	8.0	3.6	2.0	36.3
Los Angeles, CA	6.0	17.7	25.7	14.4	13.2	11.0	6.8	3.6	1.7	35.4

Table continued on next page.

City	Percent of Population									Median Age
	Under Age 5	Age 5–19	Age 20–34	Age 35–44	Age 45–54	Age 55–64	Age 65–74	Age 75–84	Age 85+	
Louisville, KY	6.5	18.7	21.6	12.5	13.0	13.3	8.4	4.1	1.9	37.3
Madison, WI	5.2	16.4	35.4	12.0	9.9	9.7	6.6	3.1	1.6	30.8
Manchester, NH	5.9	16.2	26.4	12.3	13.8	12.3	7.3	3.4	2.5	36.0
Miami, FL	5.8	13.2	23.0	15.0	14.7	11.6	8.6	5.4	2.7	40.2
Midland, TX	8.6	21.2	25.1	12.7	11.1	10.8	5.8	3.3	1.6	31.9
Milwaukee, WI	7.6	21.9	25.7	12.6	11.4	10.6	6.0	2.7	1.5	31.4
Minneapolis, MN	6.7	16.9	32.1	13.6	11.1	9.9	6.0	2.4	1.2	32.1
Nashville, TN	6.8	17.0	27.4	13.8	12.0	11.4	6.9	3.3	1.3	34.2
New Haven, CT	6.3	21.2	30.4	12.2	11.0	8.9	6.2	2.7	1.2	30.6
New Orleans, LA	6.0	16.7	25.3	13.1	12.3	13.3	8.2	3.6	1.6	36.3
New York, NY	6.5	16.5	24.6	13.7	12.9	11.7	7.9	4.3	1.9	36.5
Oklahoma City, OK	7.7	20.6	23.1	13.4	11.7	11.5	7.2	3.4	1.5	34.1
Omaha, NE	7.3	20.3	23.1	12.6	12.1	11.9	7.4	3.4	1.8	34.5
Orlando, FL	6.9	15.8	30.1	14.8	12.5	9.8	6.2	2.7	1.3	33.5
Peoria, IL	7.7	19.6	22.8	12.0	11.3	11.7	8.2	4.3	2.3	34.9
Philadelphia, PA	6.8	18.1	26.2	12.3	11.9	11.5	7.4	3.9	1.8	34.3
Phoenix, AZ	7.4	21.8	23.1	13.8	12.9	10.6	6.3	2.8	1.2	33.5
Pittsburgh, PA	4.9	15.3	33.2	10.3	9.8	11.9	7.8	4.3	2.4	32.9
Portland, OR	5.4	14.6	25.9	17.0	13.1	11.5	7.7	3.1	1.5	36.9
Providence, RI	6.6	21.9	29.0	12.2	11.0	9.1	5.5	3.0	1.6	30.0
Provo, UT	7.6	20.5	47.0	8.1	5.8	5.2	3.1	2.0	0.9	23.6
Raleigh, NC	6.1	19.0	27.6	14.5	12.7	9.8	6.1	2.8	1.3	33.2
Reno, NV	6.2	18.1	24.7	12.4	12.2	11.9	8.9	4.1	1.4	35.6
Richmond, VA	6.0	15.9	30.2	11.6	11.5	12.3	7.3	3.2	1.9	33.8
Rochester, MN	7.2	18.8	22.6	13.0	12.1	11.8	7.6	4.5	2.4	35.8
Sacramento, CA	6.7	19.1	25.2	13.3	11.8	11.2	7.5	3.5	1.7	34.4
Salt Lake City, UT	6.4	17.1	32.1	13.6	10.1	9.9	6.5	3.0	1.3	32.0
San Antonio, TX	7.1	21.2	24.2	13.1	12.0	10.6	6.9	3.4	1.5	33.3
San Diego, CA	6.1	16.8	27.7	13.7	12.4	11.1	7.1	3.5	1.7	34.7
San Francisco, CA	4.5	10.5	29.0	15.8	13.3	11.7	8.2	4.5	2.4	38.2
San Jose, CA	6.3	18.6	22.7	14.6	14.0	11.6	7.1	3.6	1.5	36.5
Santa Rosa, CA	5.9	18.4	21.3	13.1	12.4	12.9	9.2	4.5	2.4	38.3
Savannah, GA	6.6	18.5	28.8	11.5	10.7	10.9	7.3	3.7	1.8	32.4
Seattle, WA	4.9	12.7	31.3	15.7	12.3	10.7	7.4	3.1	1.9	35.5
Sioux Falls, SD	7.6	19.8	23.8	13.1	11.6	11.9	7.2	3.2	1.8	34.2
Springfield, IL	6.2	18.3	20.7	11.7	12.2	14.1	9.6	4.9	2.4	39.0
Tallahassee, FL	5.0	19.3	38.3	10.0	8.6	8.7	6.1	2.6	1.2	26.8
Tampa, FL	6.4	19.0	24.0	13.5	13.3	11.4	7.3	3.5	1.5	35.4
Topeka, KS	6.9	19.1	21.0	11.7	11.9	12.7	9.2	5.0	2.6	36.9
Tucson, AZ	6.2	19.1	26.6	11.6	11.1	11.4	7.9	4.1	1.9	33.4
Tulsa, OK	7.1	20.0	22.8	12.4	11.7	12.2	7.8	4.0	1.9	35.0
Tuscaloosa, AL	5.9	23.0	29.7	10.1	9.5	10.1	6.7	3.7	1.3	28.7
Virginia Beach, VA	6.4	18.3	24.0	12.9	13.0	12.0	7.8	3.8	1.6	35.9
Washington, DC	6.5	14.4	31.2	14.5	11.2	10.2	6.9	3.5	1.6	33.9
Wichita, KS	7.4	20.4	22.5	11.8	11.9	12.4	7.9	3.9	1.8	34.8
Winston-Salem, NC	6.5	20.9	22.2	12.4	12.3	11.9	7.9	4.2	1.8	35.4
U.S.	6.1	19.3	20.7	12.6	13.2	12.8	8.8	4.5	1.9	37.9

Source: U.S. Census Bureau, 2014-2018 American Community Survey 5-Year Estimates

Age: Metro Area

Metro Area	Under Age 5	Age 5–19	Age 20–34	Age 35–44	Age 45–54	Age 55–64	Age 65–74	Age 75–84	Age 85+	Median Age
Albany, NY	5.2	18.0	20.6	11.8	13.9	13.9	9.5	4.7	2.3	40.0
Albuquerque, NM	5.8	19.4	20.9	12.6	12.6	13.2	9.4	4.6	1.7	37.9
Allentown, PA	5.3	18.8	18.6	11.9	14.1	14.0	9.6	5.0	2.7	41.3
Anchorage, AK	7.3	20.3	24.3	12.9	12.7	12.4	6.8	2.5	0.9	33.7
Ann Arbor, MI	5.0	19.6	27.5	11.4	12.0	11.4	7.9	3.5	1.6	33.4
Athens, GA	5.5	20.9	27.3	12.0	11.1	10.7	7.5	3.5	1.3	32.1
Atlanta, GA	6.4	21.1	20.7	14.2	14.4	11.6	7.3	3.1	1.1	36.2
Austin, TX	6.6	19.9	24.5	15.5	12.8	10.5	6.5	2.6	1.1	34.4
Baton Rouge, LA	6.6	20.0	23.0	12.6	12.4	12.2	8.1	3.8	1.3	35.2
Boise City, ID	6.5	22.0	20.0	13.4	12.6	11.7	8.5	3.8	1.5	36.1
Boston, MA	5.4	17.7	22.1	12.5	14.1	13.1	8.5	4.4	2.1	38.7
Boulder, CO	4.7	19.5	24.2	12.7	13.2	12.7	8.1	3.4	1.6	36.2
Cape Coral, FL	4.7	15.4	15.9	10.4	12.1	14.0	15.3	8.9	3.3	48.1
Cedar Rapids, IA	6.2	19.7	19.6	12.6	13.3	12.8	8.7	4.8	2.3	38.2
Charleston, SC	6.2	18.4	22.4	13.0	12.9	12.7	9.1	3.7	1.5	37.0
Charlotte, NC	6.3	20.3	20.1	14.1	14.3	11.9	8.0	3.7	1.3	37.3
Chicago, IL	6.2	19.7	21.1	13.3	13.5	12.6	7.9	4.0	1.8	37.2
Clarksville, TN	8.6	20.7	27.9	12.4	10.7	9.4	6.2	3.1	1.1	30.5
Cleveland, OH	5.6	18.2	18.8	11.7	13.6	14.5	9.8	5.2	2.5	41.3
College Station, TX	6.1	21.0	33.4	10.8	9.6	9.0	6.0	3.0	1.2	27.6
Colorado Springs, CO	6.7	20.4	23.6	12.4	12.4	11.9	7.7	3.4	1.3	34.5
Columbia, MO	5.9	19.3	30.3	11.5	10.8	10.7	6.8	3.4	1.3	30.8
Columbia, SC	5.8	20.2	21.9	12.5	12.9	12.6	8.7	3.9	1.4	36.5
Columbus, OH	6.7	19.7	22.3	13.4	13.2	12.0	7.6	3.6	1.5	35.9
Dallas, TX	7.0	21.9	21.4	14.2	13.5	11.1	6.7	3.0	1.1	34.7
Davenport, IA	6.2	19.3	18.4	12.2	12.7	13.7	9.7	5.2	2.3	39.7
Denver, CO	6.2	19.2	22.3	14.6	13.4	12.1	7.6	3.3	1.4	36.4
Des Moines, IA	7.1	20.7	21.0	13.7	13.0	11.6	7.5	3.7	1.6	35.8
Durham, NC	5.8	18.6	22.8	13.2	12.9	12.4	8.6	3.8	1.7	37.0
Edison, NJ	6.1	18.0	21.1	13.1	13.9	12.7	8.4	4.5	2.2	38.5
El Paso, TX	7.8	23.0	23.2	12.5	11.6	10.3	6.5	3.7	1.5	32.0
Fargo, ND	7.1	19.4	27.8	12.4	10.8	10.8	6.4	3.4	1.9	32.3
Fayetteville, NC	7.8	20.4	27.1	12.0	11.3	10.5	6.6	3.2	1.1	31.4
Fort Collins, CO	5.2	18.4	25.3	12.2	11.5	12.8	9.0	4.0	1.7	35.9
Fort Wayne, IN	7.0	21.1	19.9	12.3	12.6	12.7	8.4	4.0	2.0	36.5
Fort Worth, TX	7.0	21.9	21.4	14.2	13.5	11.1	6.7	3.0	1.1	34.7
Grand Rapids, MI	6.6	20.9	21.6	12.1	12.7	12.5	7.9	3.9	1.9	35.8
Greeley, CO	7.3	22.4	21.3	13.5	12.4	11.5	7.3	3.2	1.2	34.3
Green Bay, WI	6.3	19.7	19.3	12.4	13.8	13.6	8.6	4.5	1.8	38.7
Greensboro, NC	5.8	19.7	19.7	12.4	13.9	13.0	9.1	4.6	1.9	38.7
Honolulu, HI	6.5	17.1	22.8	12.6	12.3	11.9	9.1	4.8	2.9	37.6
Houston, TX	7.4	21.9	21.9	14.2	12.9	11.2	6.6	2.9	1.0	34.2
Huntsville, AL	5.8	19.2	20.3	12.4	14.6	13.3	8.4	4.5	1.6	38.7
Indianapolis, IN	6.7	20.6	20.7	13.3	13.4	12.3	7.7	3.8	1.6	36.4
Jackson, MS	6.4	20.9	21.0	13.0	12.6	12.5	8.1	3.8	1.7	36.1
Jacksonville, FL	6.2	18.7	20.7	12.7	13.5	13.1	9.2	4.1	1.6	38.2
Kansas City, MO	6.6	20.1	20.1	13.2	13.2	12.8	8.2	4.1	1.8	37.3
Lafayette, LA	7.0	20.3	21.7	12.5	12.7	12.7	7.8	3.9	1.6	35.7
Lakeland, FL	5.9	19.0	18.8	11.8	12.3	12.3	11.3	6.5	2.2	40.3
Las Vegas, NV	6.4	19.4	21.2	13.9	13.4	11.7	8.8	4.1	1.3	37.1
Lexington, KY	6.2	19.1	23.3	13.1	12.7	12.0	8.1	3.8	1.6	35.9
Lincoln, NE	6.5	20.3	25.2	12.2	11.1	11.5	7.8	3.7	1.7	33.5
Little Rock, AR	6.5	19.7	21.4	13.0	12.6	12.4	8.7	4.1	1.7	36.7
Los Angeles, CA	6.1	18.8	22.8	13.6	13.7	11.9	7.4	3.9	1.8	36.6

Table continued on next page.

Metro Area	Percent of Population									Median Age
	Under Age 5	Age 5–19	Age 20–34	Age 35–44	Age 45–54	Age 55–64	Age 65–74	Age 75–84	Age 85+	
Louisville, KY	6.1	19.0	19.8	12.8	13.6	13.6	9.0	4.2	1.9	38.9
Madison, WI	5.7	18.3	24.4	12.8	12.7	12.4	8.2	3.7	1.7	36.0
Manchester, NH	5.3	18.1	19.7	12.4	15.4	14.4	8.7	4.1	2.0	40.5
Miami, FL	5.7	17.0	19.6	13.2	14.4	12.6	9.2	5.6	2.7	40.8
Midland, TX	8.7	22.0	24.4	12.7	11.0	10.9	5.7	3.2	1.4	31.7
Milwaukee, WI	6.3	19.7	20.4	12.4	13.2	13.3	8.3	4.2	2.2	37.7
Minneapolis, MN	6.5	19.8	20.9	13.2	13.7	12.8	7.7	3.7	1.7	36.9
Nashville, TN	6.4	19.6	22.0	13.7	13.5	12.2	7.8	3.6	1.3	36.4
New Haven, CT	5.2	18.5	20.2	11.8	14.1	13.7	9.2	4.7	2.6	40.1
New Orleans, LA	6.3	18.4	21.3	12.7	13.1	13.6	8.9	4.1	1.7	38.0
New York, NY	6.1	18.0	21.1	13.1	13.9	12.7	8.4	4.5	2.2	38.5
Oklahoma City, OK	7.0	20.5	22.4	12.9	12.0	11.9	7.9	3.8	1.5	35.0
Omaha, NE	7.3	20.9	21.0	13.0	12.6	12.1	7.7	3.6	1.7	35.5
Orlando, FL	5.9	18.9	22.2	13.6	13.4	11.6	8.3	4.2	1.7	37.0
Peoria, IL	6.5	19.4	18.8	12.3	12.7	13.5	9.4	5.1	2.5	39.2
Philadelphia, PA	5.9	18.7	20.7	12.3	13.8	13.4	8.6	4.5	2.1	38.7
Phoenix, AZ	6.5	20.5	21.1	13.1	12.6	11.4	8.7	4.5	1.7	36.4
Pittsburgh, PA	5.1	16.5	19.3	11.4	13.5	15.2	10.4	5.8	3.0	43.1
Portland, OR	5.9	18.3	21.2	14.6	13.4	12.6	8.6	3.7	1.7	37.9
Providence, RI	5.2	18.1	20.4	11.9	14.2	13.8	9.2	4.7	2.5	40.3
Provo, UT	9.8	28.4	26.8	12.5	8.3	6.7	4.4	2.3	0.7	24.7
Raleigh, NC	6.3	21.0	20.4	14.9	14.5	11.4	7.1	3.1	1.2	36.5
Reno, NV	6.0	18.3	21.4	12.2	13.1	13.3	10.0	4.2	1.5	38.3
Richmond, VA	5.9	18.8	20.6	12.7	13.9	13.3	8.9	4.0	1.8	38.7
Rochester, MN	6.8	19.8	19.0	12.6	12.8	13.4	8.5	4.9	2.3	38.5
Sacramento, CA	6.1	19.7	21.2	12.7	13.0	12.6	8.5	4.2	1.9	37.2
Salt Lake City, UT	7.8	22.8	23.4	14.5	11.3	10.0	6.2	2.9	1.1	32.5
San Antonio, TX	7.0	21.5	22.2	13.2	12.5	11.1	7.5	3.6	1.4	34.5
San Diego, CA	6.4	18.3	24.3	13.2	12.7	11.7	7.6	3.9	1.8	35.6
San Francisco, CA	5.6	16.6	22.0	14.5	14.0	12.6	8.5	4.2	2.0	38.8
San Jose, CA	6.2	18.7	22.1	14.6	14.0	11.6	7.2	3.9	1.7	37.0
Santa Rosa, CA	5.1	17.5	19.0	12.3	13.3	14.6	11.1	4.8	2.3	41.7
Savannah, GA	6.6	19.6	23.5	12.8	12.2	11.7	8.2	3.7	1.6	35.2
Seattle, WA	6.2	17.7	22.9	14.2	13.6	12.5	7.7	3.4	1.6	37.0
Sioux Falls, SD	7.7	20.6	21.7	13.2	12.1	12.0	7.5	3.4	1.8	35.0
Springfield, IL	5.8	19.0	18.6	12.2	13.4	14.2	9.7	4.9	2.2	40.2
Tallahassee, FL	5.2	18.9	27.8	11.5	11.5	11.9	8.3	3.6	1.5	33.5
Tampa, FL	5.4	17.0	18.9	12.3	13.7	13.4	10.8	5.9	2.6	42.1
Topeka, KS	6.3	20.1	17.7	11.5	12.8	14.2	9.9	5.2	2.4	39.9
Tucson, AZ	5.8	18.8	21.5	11.4	11.4	12.5	10.6	5.8	2.2	38.3
Tulsa, OK	6.8	20.5	20.2	12.6	12.6	12.6	8.6	4.4	1.7	36.9
Tuscaloosa, AL	5.9	20.5	24.8	11.8	11.6	11.9	7.9	3.8	1.6	33.9
Virginia Beach, VA	6.3	18.6	23.7	12.2	12.8	12.5	8.1	4.0	1.7	35.9
Washington, DC	6.6	19.1	21.6	14.4	14.2	12.0	7.4	3.4	1.4	36.8
Wichita, KS	7.0	21.4	20.5	12.0	12.1	12.8	8.0	4.3	1.9	35.9
Winston-Salem, NC	5.7	19.6	18.1	12.1	14.3	13.5	9.7	5.1	1.8	40.6
U.S.	6.1	19.3	20.7	12.6	13.2	12.8	8.8	4.5	1.9	37.9

Note: Figures cover the Metropolitan Statistical Area (MSA)—see Appendix B for areas included
Source: U.S. Census Bureau, 2014-2018 American Community Survey 5-Year Estimates

Segregation

Metro Area	Black/White		Asian/White		Hispanic/White	
	Index[1]	Rank[2]	Index[1]	Rank[2]	Index[1]	Rank[2]
Albany, NY	61.3	37	43.1	38	38.9	70
Albuquerque, NM	30.9	99	28.5	93	36.4	79
Allentown, PA	47.2	78	38.0	67	55.4	11
Anchorage, AK	n/a	n/a	n/a	n/a	n/a	n/a
Ann Arbor, MI	n/a	n/a	n/a	n/a	n/a	n/a
Athens, GA	n/a	n/a	n/a	n/a	n/a	n/a
Atlanta, GA	59.0	41	48.5	10	49.5	27
Austin, TX	50.1	70	41.2	49	43.2	51
Baton Rouge, LA	57.5	45	50.8	5	32.7	88
Boise City, ID	30.2	101	27.6	95	36.2	80
Boston, MA	64.0	27	45.4	23	59.6	5
Boulder, CO	n/a	n/a	n/a	n/a	n/a	n/a
Cape Coral, FL	61.6	35	25.3	96	40.2	63
Cedar Rapids, IA	n/a	n/a	n/a	n/a	n/a	n/a
Charleston, SC	41.5	88	33.4	84	39.8	66
Charlotte, NC	53.8	56	43.6	34	47.6	35
Chicago, IL	76.4	3	44.9	26	56.3	10
Clarksville, TN	n/a	n/a	n/a	n/a	n/a	n/a
Cleveland, OH	74.1	5	41.3	48	52.3	20
College Station, TX	n/a	n/a	n/a	n/a	n/a	n/a
Colorado Springs, CO	39.3	92	24.1	98	30.3	95
Columbia, MO	n/a	n/a	n/a	n/a	n/a	n/a
Columbia, SC	48.8	74	41.9	46	34.9	82
Columbus, OH	62.2	33	43.3	35	41.5	59
Dallas, TX	56.6	48	46.6	19	50.3	24
Davenport, IA	n/a	n/a	n/a	n/a	n/a	n/a
Denver, CO	62.6	31	33.4	83	48.8	31
Des Moines, IA	51.6	66	35.5	76	46.7	40
Durham, NC	48.1	75	44.0	30	48.0	33
Edison, NJ	78.0	2	51.9	3	62.0	3
El Paso, TX	30.7	100	22.2	100	43.3	50
Fargo, ND	n/a	n/a	n/a	n/a	n/a	n/a
Fayetteville, NC	n/a	n/a	n/a	n/a	n/a	n/a
Fort Collins, CO	n/a	n/a	n/a	n/a	n/a	n/a
Fort Wayne, IN	n/a	n/a	n/a	n/a	n/a	n/a
Fort Worth, TX	56.6	48	46.6	19	50.3	24
Grand Rapids, MI	64.3	26	43.2	37	50.4	23
Greeley, CO	n/a	n/a	n/a	n/a	n/a	n/a
Green Bay, WI	n/a	n/a	n/a	n/a	n/a	n/a
Greensboro, NC	54.7	53	47.7	14	41.1	61
Honolulu, HI	36.9	95	42.1	44	31.9	91
Houston, TX	61.4	36	50.4	7	52.5	18
Huntsville, AL	n/a	n/a	n/a	n/a	n/a	n/a
Indianapolis, IN	66.4	15	41.6	47	47.3	37
Jackson, MS	56.0	51	38.9	63	42.9	52
Jacksonville, FL	53.1	59	37.5	71	27.6	98
Kansas City, MO	61.2	39	38.4	65	44.4	48
Lafayette, LA	n/a	n/a	n/a	n/a	n/a	n/a
Lakeland, FL	43.9	84	28.9	91	32.3	89
Las Vegas, NV	37.6	94	28.8	92	42.0	58
Lexington, KY	n/a	n/a	n/a	n/a	n/a	n/a
Lincoln, NE	n/a	n/a	n/a	n/a	n/a	n/a
Little Rock, AR	58.8	42	39.7	59	39.7	68
Los Angeles, CA	67.8	10	48.4	12	62.2	2
Louisville, KY	58.1	43	42.2	43	38.7	73

Table continued on next page.

Metro Area	Black/White Index[1]	Black/White Rank[2]	Asian/White Index[1]	Asian/White Rank[2]	Hispanic/White Index[1]	Hispanic/White Rank[2]
Madison, WI	49.6	71	44.2	29	40.1	65
Manchester, NH	n/a	n/a	n/a	n/a	n/a	n/a
Miami, FL	64.8	23	34.2	80	57.4	8
Midland, TX	n/a	n/a	n/a	n/a	n/a	n/a
Milwaukee, WI	81.5	1	40.7	52	57.0	9
Minneapolis, MN	52.9	60	42.8	39	42.5	54
Nashville, TN	56.2	49	41.0	51	47.9	34
New Haven, CT	63.7	29	29.7	90	54.4	14
New Orleans, LA	63.9	28	48.6	9	38.3	74
New York, NY	78.0	2	51.9	3	62.0	3
Oklahoma City, OK	51.4	67	39.2	60	47.0	38
Omaha, NE	61.3	38	36.3	74	48.8	30
Orlando, FL	50.7	69	33.9	81	40.2	64
Peoria, IL	n/a	n/a	n/a	n/a	n/a	n/a
Philadelphia, PA	68.4	9	42.3	42	55.1	12
Phoenix, AZ	43.6	86	32.7	85	49.3	28
Pittsburgh, PA	65.8	17	52.4	2	28.6	97
Portland, OR	46.0	81	35.8	75	34.3	83
Providence, RI	53.5	57	40.1	55	60.1	4
Provo, UT	21.9	102	28.2	94	30.9	93
Raleigh, NC	42.1	87	46.7	16	37.1	76
Reno, NV	n/a	n/a	n/a	n/a	n/a	n/a
Richmond, VA	52.4	63	43.9	32	44.9	46
Rochester, MN	n/a	n/a	n/a	n/a	n/a	n/a
Sacramento, CA	56.9	46	49.9	8	38.9	71
Salt Lake City, UT	39.3	93	31.0	88	42.9	53
San Antonio, TX	49.0	73	38.3	66	46.1	43
San Diego, CA	51.2	68	48.2	13	49.6	25
San Francisco, CA	62.0	34	46.6	18	49.6	26
San Jose, CA	40.9	89	45.0	25	47.6	36
Santa Rosa, CA	n/a	n/a	n/a	n/a	n/a	n/a
Savannah, GA	n/a	n/a	n/a	n/a	n/a	n/a
Seattle, WA	49.1	72	37.6	69	32.8	87
Sioux Falls, SD	n/a	n/a	n/a	n/a	n/a	n/a
Springfield, IL	n/a	n/a	n/a	n/a	n/a	n/a
Tallahassee, FL	n/a	n/a	n/a	n/a	n/a	n/a
Tampa, FL	56.2	50	35.3	78	40.7	62
Topeka, KS	n/a	n/a	n/a	n/a	n/a	n/a
Tucson, AZ	36.9	96	24.8	97	46.2	42
Tulsa, OK	56.6	47	42.6	40	45.3	45
Tuscaloosa, AL	n/a	n/a	n/a	n/a	n/a	n/a
Virginia Beach, VA	47.8	76	34.3	79	32.2	90
Washington, DC	62.3	32	38.9	64	48.3	32
Wichita, KS	58.0	44	46.5	20	42.3	56
Winston-Salem, NC	n/a	n/a	n/a	n/a	n/a	n/a

Note: Figures are based on an analysis of 1990, 2000, and 2010 Census Decennial Census tract data by William H. Frey, Brookings Institution and the University of Michigan Social Science Data Analysis Network. In this analysis all racial groups (whites, blacks, and asians) are non-Hispanic members of those races. Hispanics are shown as a separate category; All figures cover the Metropolitan Statistical Area (see Appendix B for areas included); (1) Segregation Indices are Dissimilarity Indices that measure the degree to which the minority group is distributed differently than whites across census tracts. They range from 0 (complete integration) to 100 (complete [segregation) where the value indicates the percentage of the minority group that needs to move to be distributed exactly like whites; (2) Ranges from 1 (most segregated) to 102 (least segregated); n/a not available.
Source: www.CensusScope.org

Religious Groups by Family

Area[1]	Catholic	Baptist	Non-Den.	Methodist[2]	Lutheran	LDS[3]	Pente-costal	Presby-terian[4]	Muslim[5]	Judaism
Albany, NY	26.8	1.2	2.2	2.9	1.5	0.3	0.5	2.1	1.2	1.0
Albuquerque, NM	27.1	3.7	4.2	1.4	0.9	2.3	1.4	1.0	0.2	0.2
Allentown, PA	23.1	0.4	1.9	3.9	7.9	0.3	0.4	6.2	0.6	0.6
Anchorage, AK	6.9	5.0	6.4	1.3	1.9	5.1	1.8	0.6	0.2	0.1
Ann Arbor, MI	12.3	2.2	1.5	3.0	2.8	0.8	1.9	2.9	1.2	0.9
Athens, GA	4.4	16.2	2.2	8.3	0.3	0.8	2.8	2.0	0.3	0.2
Atlanta, GA	7.4	17.4	6.8	7.8	0.5	0.7	2.6	1.8	0.7	0.5
Austin, TX	16.0	10.3	4.5	3.6	1.9	1.1	0.8	1.0	1.2	0.2
Baton Rouge, LA	22.5	18.2	9.6	4.6	0.2	0.7	1.1	0.6	0.2	0.1
Boise City, ID	8.0	2.9	4.1	2.1	1.1	15.8	2.3	0.6	0.1	0.1
Boston, MA	44.3	1.1	1.0	0.9	0.3	0.4	0.6	1.6	0.4	1.4
Boulder, CO	20.1	2.3	4.7	1.7	3.0	2.9	0.4	2.0	0.1	0.7
Cape Coral, FL	16.2	4.9	3.0	2.5	1.1	0.5	4.3	1.4	0.9	0.2
Cedar Rapids, IA	18.8	2.3	3.0	7.3	11.3	0.8	1.8	3.2	0.5	0.1
Charleston, SC	6.1	12.4	7.0	10.0	1.1	0.9	2.0	2.3	0.1	0.3
Charlotte, NC	5.9	17.2	6.7	8.6	1.3	0.7	3.2	4.5	0.2	0.3
Chicago, IL	34.2	3.2	4.4	1.9	3.0	0.3	1.2	1.9	3.2	0.8
Clarksville, TN	4.0	30.9	2.2	6.1	0.5	1.5	1.8	1.0	0.1	<0.1
Cleveland, OH	28.8	4.3	3.3	2.8	2.5	0.3	1.1	2.0	0.1	1.4
College Station, TX	11.7	15.6	3.9	4.7	1.5	1.2	0.6	0.9	1.1	<0.1
Colorado Springs, CO	8.3	4.3	7.4	2.4	1.9	3.0	1.0	2.0	<0.1	0.1
Columbia, MO	6.6	14.6	5.4	4.3	1.7	1.3	1.0	2.3	0.3	0.2
Columbia, SC	3.1	18.0	5.2	9.3	3.4	1.0	2.6	3.3	0.1	0.2
Columbus, OH	11.7	5.3	3.5	4.7	2.4	0.7	1.9	2.0	0.8	0.5
Dallas, TX	13.3	18.7	7.7	5.2	0.7	1.1	2.1	0.9	2.4	0.3
Davenport, IA	14.9	4.9	2.7	5.3	8.6	0.8	1.4	2.9	0.9	0.1
Denver, CO	16.0	2.9	4.6	1.7	2.1	2.4	1.2	1.5	0.5	0.6
Des Moines, IA	13.6	4.7	3.3	6.9	8.2	0.9	2.3	2.9	0.3	0.3
Durham, NC	5.0	13.8	5.6	8.1	0.4	0.7	1.3	2.5	0.4	0.5
Edison, NJ	36.9	1.8	1.7	1.3	0.7	0.3	0.8	1.0	2.3	4.7
El Paso, TX	43.2	3.7	4.9	0.8	0.3	1.5	1.4	0.2	<0.1	0.2
Fargo, ND	17.4	0.4	0.4	3.3	32.5	0.6	1.5	1.8	0.1	<0.1
Fayetteville, NC	2.6	14.1	10.4	6.2	0.1	1.4	4.8	2.1	0.1	<0.1
Fort Collins, CO	11.8	2.2	6.3	4.3	3.4	2.9	4.7	1.9	0.1	<0.1
Fort Wayne, IN	14.2	6.0	6.8	5.1	8.5	0.4	1.4	1.6	0.2	0.1
Fort Worth, TX	13.3	18.7	7.7	5.2	0.7	1.1	2.1	0.9	2.4	0.3
Grand Rapids, MI	17.1	1.7	8.3	3.0	2.1	0.5	1.1	9.9	1.0	0.1
Greeley, CO	13.5	1.8	1.5	2.6	2.0	1.9	1.8	1.4	0.1	<0.1
Green Bay, WI	42.0	0.7	3.4	2.2	12.7	0.3	0.6	1.0	0.1	<0.1
Greensboro, NC	2.6	12.8	7.4	9.8	0.6	0.8	2.4	3.1	0.6	0.4
Honolulu, HI	18.2	1.9	2.2	0.8	0.3	5.1	4.1	1.4	<0.1	<0.1
Houston, TX	17.0	16.0	7.2	4.8	1.0	1.1	1.5	0.8	2.6	0.3
Huntsville, AL	3.9	27.6	3.1	7.5	0.7	1.1	1.2	1.7	0.2	0.1
Indianapolis, IN	10.5	10.2	7.1	4.9	1.6	0.7	1.6	1.6	0.2	0.3
Jackson, MS	3.1	34.4	7.6	10.5	0.2	0.7	2.1	2.0	0.2	0.1
Jacksonville, FL	9.8	18.5	7.7	4.5	0.6	1.1	1.9	1.6	0.6	0.4
Kansas City, MO	12.6	13.1	5.2	5.8	2.2	2.4	2.6	1.6	0.3	0.4
Lafayette, LA	47.0	14.7	3.9	2.5	0.2	0.4	2.9	0.1	0.1	<0.1
Lakeland, FL	7.5	13.6	5.0	3.9	0.9	0.7	4.0	1.6	0.4	<0.1
Las Vegas, NV	18.1	2.9	3.0	0.4	0.7	6.3	1.5	0.2	<0.1	0.3
Lexington, KY	6.7	24.9	2.3	5.9	0.4	1.0	2.1	1.3	0.1	0.3
Lincoln, NE	14.7	2.4	1.9	7.1	11.2	1.1	1.4	3.9	0.2	0.1
Little Rock, AR	4.5	25.9	6.0	7.3	0.5	0.9	2.8	0.8	0.1	0.1
Los Angeles, CA	33.8	2.7	3.6	1.0	0.6	1.7	1.7	0.9	0.7	0.9
Louisville, KY	13.6	25.0	1.7	3.7	0.6	0.8	0.9	1.1	0.5	0.4

Table continued on next page.

Area[1]	Catholic	Baptist	Non-Den.	Methodist[2]	Lutheran	LDS[3]	Pente-costal	Presby-terian[4]	Muslim[5]	Judaism
Madison, WI	21.8	1.1	1.5	3.6	12.7	0.5	0.3	2.1	0.4	0.4
Manchester, NH	31.1	1.3	2.3	1.1	0.5	0.6	0.4	2.0	0.3	0.5
Miami, FL	18.5	5.3	4.1	1.2	0.4	0.5	1.7	0.6	0.9	1.5
Midland, TX	22.4	25.2	8.8	4.2	0.6	1.2	1.6	1.8	3.7	<0.1
Milwaukee, WI	24.6	3.1	3.8	1.5	10.7	0.4	1.9	1.5	0.5	0.5
Minneapolis, MN	21.7	2.4	2.9	2.7	14.4	0.6	1.7	1.8	0.4	0.7
Nashville, TN	4.1	25.2	5.8	6.1	0.3	0.7	2.1	2.1	0.3	0.1
New Haven, CT	35.3	1.4	1.9	1.5	0.6	0.3	1.0	2.2	0.5	1.2
New Orleans, LA	31.5	8.4	3.7	2.6	0.8	0.5	2.1	0.5	0.4	0.5
New York, NY	36.9	1.8	1.7	1.3	0.7	0.3	0.8	1.0	2.3	4.7
Oklahoma City, OK	6.3	25.3	7.0	10.6	0.7	1.2	3.1	0.9	0.2	0.1
Omaha, NE	21.6	4.5	1.8	3.9	7.8	1.7	1.2	2.2	0.5	0.4
Orlando, FL	13.2	6.9	5.6	2.9	0.9	0.9	3.2	1.3	1.3	0.2
Peoria, IL	11.4	5.5	5.2	4.9	6.1	0.5	1.5	2.8	5.2	0.1
Philadelphia, PA	33.4	3.9	2.8	2.9	1.8	0.3	0.8	2.1	1.2	1.3
Phoenix, AZ	13.3	3.4	5.1	1.0	1.6	6.1	2.9	0.6	0.1	0.3
Pittsburgh, PA	32.8	2.3	2.8	5.6	3.3	0.3	1.1	4.6	0.3	0.7
Portland, OR	10.5	2.3	4.5	1.0	1.6	3.7	2.0	0.9	0.1	0.3
Providence, RI	47.0	1.4	1.2	0.8	0.5	0.3	0.5	1.0	0.1	0.7
Provo, UT	1.3	<0.1	<0.1	0.1	<0.1	88.5	0.1	<0.1	<0.1	<0.1
Raleigh, NC	9.1	12.1	5.9	6.7	0.9	0.8	2.2	2.2	0.9	0.3
Reno, NV	14.3	1.5	3.1	0.9	0.7	4.6	1.9	0.4	<0.1	0.1
Richmond, VA	5.9	19.9	5.4	6.1	0.6	0.9	1.8	2.1	2.7	0.3
Rochester, MN	23.3	1.6	4.6	4.8	21.0	1.1	1.2	2.9	0.2	0.2
Sacramento, CA	16.1	3.1	4.0	1.7	0.7	3.3	2.0	0.8	0.8	0.2
Salt Lake City, UT	8.9	0.8	0.5	0.5	0.5	58.9	0.6	0.3	0.4	0.1
San Antonio, TX	28.4	8.5	6.0	3.0	1.6	1.4	1.3	0.7	0.9	0.2
San Diego, CA	25.9	2.0	4.8	1.1	0.9	2.3	1.0	0.9	0.7	0.5
San Francisco, CA	20.7	2.5	2.4	1.9	0.5	1.5	1.2	1.1	1.2	0.8
San Jose, CA	26.0	1.3	4.2	1.0	0.5	1.4	1.1	0.7	1.0	0.6
Santa Rosa, CA	22.2	1.3	1.5	0.9	0.9	1.9	0.6	0.9	0.4	0.4
Savannah, GA	7.0	19.6	6.9	8.9	1.6	0.9	2.3	1.0	0.1	0.8
Seattle, WA	12.3	2.1	5.0	1.2	2.0	3.3	2.8	1.4	0.4	0.4
Sioux Falls, SD	14.9	3.0	1.5	3.8	21.4	0.7	1.0	6.2	0.3	<0.1
Springfield, IL	15.5	11.7	2.7	6.8	5.6	0.7	4.9	2.0	1.5	0.2
Tallahassee, FL	4.8	16.0	6.7	9.1	0.4	1.0	2.1	1.5	0.8	0.3
Tampa, FL	10.8	7.0	3.7	3.4	0.9	0.6	2.1	0.9	1.2	0.4
Topeka, KS	12.7	9.0	4.1	7.3	3.6	1.4	2.0	1.6	<0.1	0.1
Tucson, AZ	20.7	3.3	3.7	1.3	1.5	2.9	1.5	1.0	<0.1	0.5
Tulsa, OK	5.8	22.9	7.6	9.2	0.7	1.1	3.3	1.2	0.3	0.2
Tuscaloosa, AL	1.7	32.2	4.5	8.3	<0.1	0.6	1.5	1.3	0.1	<0.1
Virginia Beach, VA	6.4	11.5	6.1	5.2	0.7	0.9	1.9	2.0	2.0	0.3
Washington, DC	14.5	7.3	4.8	4.5	1.2	1.1	1.0	1.3	2.3	1.1
Wichita, KS	14.5	13.4	3.1	7.1	1.7	1.4	1.9	1.6	0.1	<0.1
Winston-Salem, NC	3.5	17.4	9.3	12.4	0.7	0.6	2.5	2.2	0.3	0.1
U.S.	19.1	9.3	4.0	4.0	2.3	2.0	1.9	1.6	0.8	0.7

Note: Figures are the number of adherents as a percentage of the total population; (1) Figures cover the Metropolitan Statistical Area—see Appendix B for areas included; (2) Methodist/Pietist; (3) Latter Day Saints; (4) Reformed; (5) Figures are estimates
Source: Association of Statisticians of American Religious Bodies, 2010 U.S. Religion Census: Religious Congregations & Membership Study

Religious Groups by Tradition

Area	Catholic	Evangelical Protestant	Mainline Protestant	Other Tradition	Black Protestant	Orthodox
Albany, NY	26.8	4.5	7.3	3.1	0.5	0.3
Albuquerque, NM	27.1	11.2	3.2	3.9	0.2	0.1
Allentown, PA	23.1	5.3	17.7	3.0	0.1	0.6
Anchorage, AK	6.9	15.6	3.5	6.8	0.3	0.6
Ann Arbor, MI	12.3	7.3	7.5	3.7	1.5	0.2
Athens, GA	4.4	21.1	9.7	1.7	2.4	0.1
Atlanta, GA	7.4	26.0	9.8	2.9	3.1	0.2
Austin, TX	16.0	16.1	6.3	3.9	1.3	0.1
Baton Rouge, LA	22.5	24.8	5.6	1.5	5.1	<0.1
Boise City, ID	8.0	12.9	4.3	16.7	<0.1	<0.1
Boston, MA	44.3	3.2	4.5	3.4	0.1	1.0
Boulder, CO	20.1	9.7	6.4	4.8	<0.1	0.2
Cape Coral, FL	16.2	14.3	4.6	2.0	0.3	0.1
Cedar Rapids, IA	18.8	13.7	17.5	1.9	0.1	0.2
Charleston, SC	6.1	19.6	11.1	1.8	7.3	0.1
Charlotte, NC	5.9	27.5	13.3	1.6	2.7	0.4
Chicago, IL	34.2	9.7	5.1	5.0	2.0	0.9
Clarksville, TN	4.0	35.3	7.2	1.6	2.4	<0.1
Cleveland, OH	28.8	9.0	7.5	2.6	2.1	0.8
College Station, TX	11.7	20.6	6.6	2.5	0.9	<0.1
Colorado Springs, CO	8.3	15.2	5.3	3.7	0.4	0.1
Columbia, MO	6.6	19.9	10.4	2.3	0.4	0.1
Columbia, SC	3.1	25.5	13.4	2.1	5.4	0.1
Columbus, OH	11.7	11.8	9.5	3.1	1.1	0.2
Dallas, TX	13.3	28.3	6.9	4.7	1.7	0.1
Davenport, IA	14.9	11.3	15.1	2.3	1.5	0.1
Denver, CO	16.0	11.0	4.5	4.6	0.3	0.3
Des Moines, IA	13.6	12.3	16.8	1.8	0.9	0.1
Durham, NC	5.0	19.3	11.7	2.9	3.1	<0.1
Edison, NJ	36.9	3.9	4.1	8.3	1.2	0.9
El Paso, TX	43.2	10.8	1.2	2.0	0.2	<0.1
Fargo, ND	17.4	10.7	30.8	0.8	<0.1	<0.1
Fayetteville, NC	2.6	26.7	7.8	1.7	4.3	0.1
Fort Collins, CO	11.8	18.8	5.9	3.9	<0.1	0.1
Fort Wayne, IN	14.2	24.6	9.1	0.9	2.4	0.2
Fort Worth, TX	13.3	28.3	6.9	4.7	1.7	0.1
Grand Rapids, MI	17.1	20.7	7.5	2.1	1.0	0.2
Greeley, CO	13.5	9.2	3.8	2.1	<0.1	<0.1
Green Bay, WI	42.0	14.1	8.1	0.6	<0.1	<0.1
Greensboro, NC	2.6	23.2	14.0	2.1	2.6	<0.1
Honolulu, HI	18.2	9.6	2.9	8.4	<0.1	<0.1
Houston, TX	17.0	24.9	6.6	4.9	1.3	0.2
Huntsville, AL	3.9	33.3	9.6	1.8	1.8	<0.1
Indianapolis, IN	10.5	18.2	9.6	1.6	1.8	0.2
Jackson, MS	3.1	41.3	9.6	1.6	8.1	0.1
Jacksonville, FL	9.8	27.1	5.6	2.9	4.2	0.2
Kansas City, MO	12.6	20.5	9.9	3.6	2.6	0.1
Lafayette, LA	47.0	12.7	3.2	0.7	9.2	<0.1
Lakeland, FL	7.5	24.6	5.2	1.4	1.7	<0.1
Las Vegas, NV	18.1	7.7	1.3	7.6	0.4	0.4
Lexington, KY	6.7	28.3	10.2	1.7	2.0	0.1
Lincoln, NE	14.7	14.8	16.2	2.0	0.1	<0.1
Little Rock, AR	4.5	33.9	8.1	1.7	3.4	<0.1
Los Angeles, CA	33.8	9.0	2.3	4.6	0.8	0.6
Louisville, KY	13.6	24.5	7.1	2.0	2.9	<0.1

Table continued on next page.

Area	Catholic	Evangelical Protestant	Mainline Protestant	Other Tradition	Black Protestant	Orthodox
Madison, WI	21.8	7.2	15.3	2.2	0.1	<0.1
Manchester, NH	31.1	5.1	4.4	1.8	<0.1	0.7
Miami, FL	18.5	11.4	2.4	3.5	1.7	0.2
Midland, TX	22.4	35.4	7.2	5.3	1.0	<0.1
Milwaukee, WI	24.6	14.6	7.1	2.3	2.4	0.6
Minneapolis, MN	21.7	12.8	14.5	2.2	0.4	0.2
Nashville, TN	4.1	32.9	8.0	1.7	3.3	0.4
New Haven, CT	35.3	3.8	6.1	2.3	0.7	0.4
New Orleans, LA	31.5	12.7	4.0	2.1	2.9	0.1
New York, NY	36.9	3.9	4.1	8.3	1.2	0.9
Oklahoma City, OK	6.3	39.0	9.8	2.7	1.9	0.1
Omaha, NE	21.6	12.1	10.7	3.2	1.4	0.1
Orlando, FL	13.2	17.8	4.7	3.2	1.2	0.3
Peoria, IL	11.4	18.9	11.1	6.1	0.9	0.1
Philadelphia, PA	33.4	6.3	8.9	3.7	1.7	0.4
Phoenix, AZ	13.3	13.2	2.6	7.8	0.1	0.3
Pittsburgh, PA	32.8	7.3	13.8	2.0	0.8	0.6
Portland, OR	10.5	11.6	3.6	5.2	0.1	0.3
Providence, RI	47.0	2.8	4.7	1.6	<0.1	0.5
Provo, UT	1.3	0.4	<0.1	88.8	<0.1	<0.1
Raleigh, NC	9.1	19.9	10.1	3.2	1.7	0.2
Reno, NV	14.3	7.6	1.9	5.1	0.2	0.1
Richmond, VA	5.9	23.6	13.3	4.5	2.4	0.1
Rochester, MN	23.3	18.9	21.0	2.0	<0.1	0.1
Sacramento, CA	16.1	11.3	2.2	5.8	0.5	0.3
Salt Lake City, UT	8.9	2.6	1.2	60.0	0.1	0.4
San Antonio, TX	28.4	16.9	5.0	3.1	0.4	<0.1
San Diego, CA	25.9	9.7	2.4	5.2	0.3	0.2
San Francisco, CA	20.7	6.1	3.8	5.2	1.0	0.6
San Jose, CA	26.0	8.2	2.4	6.8	0.1	0.4
Santa Rosa, CA	22.2	5.3	2.3	4.8	<0.1	0.2
Savannah, GA	7.0	25.0	9.4	2.6	8.5	0.1
Seattle, WA	12.3	11.9	4.6	5.9	0.3	0.4
Sioux Falls, SD	14.9	12.9	28.0	1.2	0.1	0.1
Springfield, IL	15.5	21.4	11.6	3.1	2.1	0.1
Tallahassee, FL	4.8	21.9	6.3	2.9	9.1	0.1
Tampa, FL	10.8	13.6	5.1	3.1	1.1	0.8
Topeka, KS	12.7	15.5	12.8	1.7	2.7	<0.1
Tucson, AZ	20.7	10.0	3.7	4.5	0.4	0.2
Tulsa, OK	5.8	34.6	11.2	2.1	1.5	<0.1
Tuscaloosa, AL	1.7	35.2	6.4	0.9	8.5	<0.1
Virginia Beach, VA	6.4	18.0	9.4	3.9	2.2	0.3
Washington, DC	14.5	12.4	8.7	5.9	2.3	0.6
Wichita, KS	14.5	20.7	11.0	2.4	1.8	0.2
Winston-Salem, NC	3.5	29.1	15.6	1.2	2.2	0.2
U.S.	19.1	16.2	7.3	4.3	1.6	0.3

Note: Figures are the number of adherents as a percentage of the total population; (1) Figures cover the Metropolitan Statistical Area—see Appendix B for areas included
Source: Association of Statisticians of American Religious Bodies, 2010 U.S. Religion Census: Religious Congregations & Membership Study

Ancestry: City

City	German	Irish	English	American	Italian	Polish	French[1]	Scottish	Dutch
Albany, NY	9.7	13.9	4.8	2.2	11.6	3.5	2.4	1.0	1.4
Albuquerque, NM	9.1	6.9	6.2	3.8	2.8	1.3	1.7	1.7	0.8
Allentown, PA	11.2	5.6	1.9	2.4	4.5	1.8	0.9	0.4	1.2
Anchorage, AK	15.2	9.9	7.8	4.0	2.8	2.0	2.7	2.5	1.6
Ann Arbor, MI	17.3	9.5	9.5	4.3	5.1	6.2	3.2	2.5	2.3
Athens, GA	8.9	8.4	8.6	5.1	3.3	1.5	1.6	2.7	0.9
Atlanta, GA	5.8	5.4	7.0	6.0	2.5	1.4	1.6	1.7	0.5
Austin, TX	10.6	7.4	7.3	3.3	2.8	1.7	2.3	1.9	0.7
Baton Rouge, LA	5.4	5.2	4.8	5.9	3.1	0.5	7.0	1.3	0.2
Boise City, ID	17.1	11.9	18.8	4.7	3.3	1.8	2.5	3.7	1.7
Boston, MA	4.6	13.7	4.3	2.8	7.8	2.3	1.8	1.2	0.5
Boulder, CO	18.5	13.0	10.9	2.7	6.2	3.8	2.7	3.5	1.4
Cape Coral, FL	15.0	11.9	7.8	15.4	9.8	3.6	2.2	2.2	1.5
Cedar Rapids, IA	32.6	14.4	7.8	4.3	1.7	1.5	2.2	1.5	2.3
Charleston, SC	10.2	10.5	10.4	22.1	4.2	1.7	2.1	3.0	0.6
Charlotte, NC	9.0	7.2	6.7	4.5	3.5	1.7	1.5	1.9	0.7
Chicago, IL	7.4	7.4	2.4	2.0	3.9	5.7	1.0	0.6	0.5
Clarksville, TN	11.3	8.7	5.4	9.7	3.2	1.6	1.6	1.4	0.9
Cleveland, OH	9.2	8.6	2.7	1.9	4.8	3.8	0.8	0.5	0.4
College Station, TX	17.1	8.9	8.0	3.5	3.3	2.4	3.5	2.6	0.7
Colorado Springs, CO	19.5	11.2	9.9	4.5	4.8	2.3	2.9	2.6	1.7
Columbia, MO	24.4	12.4	9.0	5.1	3.6	2.4	2.7	2.1	1.1
Columbia, SC	10.0	7.3	8.4	5.3	2.8	1.4	2.2	2.3	0.7
Columbus, OH	17.4	10.3	6.2	4.3	5.0	2.2	1.7	1.7	1.0
Dallas, TX	5.4	4.0	4.6	3.5	1.5	0.8	1.3	1.1	0.5
Davenport, IA	27.8	14.6	6.2	4.2	2.0	1.9	1.6	1.4	1.7
Denver, CO	14.0	9.7	7.8	2.9	4.4	2.6	2.4	2.1	1.4
Des Moines, IA	20.4	11.5	6.6	3.9	3.8	1.0	1.9	1.4	2.7
Durham, NC	7.3	5.9	6.9	4.2	2.8	1.8	1.5	1.7	0.7
Edison, NJ	5.1	7.0	1.6	1.8	8.4	4.9	0.7	0.5	0.3
El Paso, TX	3.6	2.3	1.6	2.7	1.1	0.4	0.7	0.5	0.2
Fargo, ND	38.0	8.7	3.9	2.1	0.9	3.0	3.7	1.1	1.1
Fayetteville, NC	8.9	7.2	7.0	4.3	3.1	1.4	1.7	1.8	0.6
Fort Collins, CO	23.3	13.0	11.4	3.7	5.7	2.9	3.6	3.0	2.0
Fort Wayne, IN	25.2	9.5	6.3	5.7	2.6	2.0	3.2	1.6	1.3
Fort Worth, TX	8.0	6.5	5.9	5.2	1.8	0.9	1.7	1.5	0.7
Grand Rapids, MI	15.5	9.1	6.8	2.7	2.9	6.8	2.5	1.7	14.1
Greeley, CO	19.0	9.3	6.8	3.5	2.5	1.5	1.6	1.9	1.1
Green Bay, WI	30.9	8.9	3.6	3.6	2.1	8.0	4.2	0.6	3.0
Greensboro, NC	7.5	5.8	7.3	4.6	2.2	1.1	1.2	1.8	0.7
Honolulu, HI	4.0	3.3	2.8	1.2	1.7	0.8	0.8	0.7	0.4
Houston, TX	4.9	3.7	3.8	4.0	1.5	0.9	1.5	0.9	0.4
Huntsville, AL	9.0	8.8	9.1	10.3	2.5	1.0	1.9	2.1	0.9
Indianapolis, IN	14.5	8.9	6.1	6.0	2.2	1.5	1.6	1.5	1.1
Jackson, MS	1.5	2.2	2.7	3.5	0.6	0.1	0.4	0.7	0.2
Jacksonville, FL	8.3	8.0	6.2	5.3	4.0	1.6	1.6	1.6	0.8
Kansas City, MO	16.0	10.7	7.2	4.1	3.6	1.4	2.1	1.6	1.2
Lafayette, LA	7.1	5.5	6.0	6.5	3.6	0.4	19.3	0.9	0.6
Lakeland, FL	10.4	7.7	9.7	7.8	4.4	1.6	2.5	1.7	1.6
Las Vegas, NV	9.4	7.9	5.6	3.7	5.7	2.3	1.7	1.4	0.8
Lexington, KY	14.3	12.0	11.1	9.8	2.8	1.6	1.9	3.0	1.1
Lincoln, NE	34.7	12.0	8.5	3.7	2.1	2.6	2.1	1.5	2.1
Little Rock, AR	7.1	7.2	7.7	6.1	1.4	1.0	1.7	1.8	0.7
Los Angeles, CA	4.1	3.5	2.9	3.2	2.6	1.4	1.1	0.7	0.4
Louisville, KY	15.4	11.5	7.7	9.9	2.4	1.0	1.8	1.6	0.9
Madison, WI	32.0	13.1	8.1	1.9	4.1	5.8	3.0	1.5	1.8

Table continued on next page.

City	German	Irish	English	American	Italian	Polish	French[1]	Scottish	Dutch
Manchester, NH	6.9	19.2	8.2	3.4	8.7	3.6	14.6	2.8	0.6
Miami, FL	1.6	1.3	0.9	3.5	2.2	0.7	0.9	0.2	0.2
Midland, TX	8.0	6.6	6.4	5.0	1.3	0.6	1.7	1.9	0.6
Milwaukee, WI	16.5	5.9	2.2	1.2	2.7	6.7	1.3	0.5	0.7
Minneapolis, MN	21.6	10.1	5.5	1.9	2.8	3.8	2.6	1.4	1.4
Nashville, TN	8.5	7.9	7.4	8.3	2.4	1.3	1.8	2.0	0.8
New Haven, CT	4.1	6.7	3.4	1.1	7.7	2.1	1.4	0.6	0.6
New Orleans, LA	6.3	5.6	4.1	2.5	4.0	0.9	5.7	1.1	0.4
New York, NY	2.9	4.3	1.6	4.5	6.4	2.4	0.8	0.5	0.3
Oklahoma City, OK	11.1	8.6	6.4	5.8	2.0	0.8	1.7	1.5	1.1
Omaha, NE	25.2	13.6	6.6	3.1	4.3	3.6	2.2	1.2	1.5
Orlando, FL	6.6	5.6	4.5	5.5	4.4	1.6	1.8	1.2	0.5
Peoria, IL	19.1	11.8	7.0	5.1	3.3	2.1	1.9	1.2	1.1
Philadelphia, PA	6.6	10.7	2.5	2.3	7.4	3.3	0.7	0.5	0.3
Phoenix, AZ	10.3	7.3	5.5	3.2	3.9	2.1	1.8	1.3	1.0
Pittsburgh, PA	19.2	15.7	5.2	4.2	12.5	7.2	1.4	1.4	0.6
Portland, OR	16.5	11.4	10.7	4.6	4.5	2.4	3.1	3.1	2.1
Providence, RI	3.2	7.8	3.9	3.0	7.6	1.9	3.0	0.9	0.3
Provo, UT	10.5	4.1	23.1	3.0	2.2	0.7	1.7	4.6	1.5
Raleigh, NC	9.0	7.7	8.9	13.2	4.1	2.0	1.6	2.4	0.6
Reno, NV	13.2	11.4	9.0	4.4	6.0	1.9	2.8	2.2	1.3
Richmond, VA	6.9	6.2	7.5	3.8	3.4	1.2	1.4	2.2	0.5
Rochester, MN	29.6	11.3	6.4	3.0	2.3	3.7	2.2	1.2	1.4
Sacramento, CA	7.1	6.3	4.6	2.0	3.5	1.0	1.6	1.3	0.8
Salt Lake City, UT	10.4	6.7	15.2	3.6	3.3	1.5	2.1	3.4	1.9
San Antonio, TX	7.2	4.3	3.6	2.9	1.7	1.1	1.4	0.9	0.4
San Diego, CA	8.8	7.1	5.7	2.5	4.1	1.7	1.9	1.5	0.8
San Francisco, CA	7.2	7.9	5.2	2.8	4.6	1.9	2.2	1.4	0.8
San Jose, CA	5.3	4.0	3.7	1.6	3.3	0.9	1.2	0.8	0.5
Santa Rosa, CA	11.1	10.2	8.8	2.9	7.4	1.4	3.1	2.1	1.1
Savannah, GA	6.1	7.0	4.7	3.6	2.6	1.2	1.5	1.5	0.7
Seattle, WA	15.3	11.2	10.3	2.5	4.2	2.8	3.1	3.1	1.6
Sioux Falls, SD	35.6	10.8	5.1	3.5	1.6	1.7	2.3	1.3	5.7
Springfield, IL	20.8	13.1	9.8	5.1	4.8	2.0	2.2	1.6	1.3
Tallahassee, FL	8.8	8.4	7.9	3.9	3.7	1.9	2.1	2.1	0.8
Tampa, FL	8.6	8.4	5.8	6.1	5.8	1.9	2.2	1.5	0.7
Topeka, KS	21.1	9.6	14.1	5.2	1.7	1.0	2.0	1.6	1.1
Tucson, AZ	11.3	8.3	6.4	3.0	3.7	2.0	2.2	1.6	1.1
Tulsa, OK	11.7	9.4	7.4	6.7	2.1	1.0	2.2	2.0	1.1
Tuscaloosa, AL	5.7	6.2	5.2	7.7	2.1	1.1	1.3	1.9	0.6
Virginia Beach, VA	11.9	11.3	9.2	9.9	5.6	2.4	2.4	2.4	1.0
Washington, DC	7.0	6.7	5.0	2.3	3.9	2.1	1.6	1.3	0.7
Wichita, KS	20.0	9.5	7.5	5.2	1.8	1.1	2.2	1.8	1.6
Winston-Salem, NC	9.8	7.0	8.2	5.7	2.6	1.1	1.4	2.1	1.1
U.S.	13.7	9.9	7.3	6.4	5.2	2.8	2.4	1.7	1.2

Note: Figures are the percentage of the total population reporting a particular ancestry. The nine most commonly reported ancestries in the U.S. are shown. Figures include multiple ancestries (e.g. if a person reported being Irish and Italian, they were included in both columns); (1) Excludes Basque
Source: U.S. Census Bureau, 2014-2018 American Community Survey 5-Year Estimates

Ancestry: Metro Area

Metro Area	German	Irish	English	American	Italian	Polish	French[1]	Scottish	Dutch
Albany, NY	15.4	21.5	9.3	4.4	16.6	6.5	6.1	1.9	3.2
Albuquerque, NM	9.0	6.8	6.3	4.1	2.9	1.3	1.7	1.7	0.8
Allentown, PA	25.0	13.5	5.9	4.5	13.0	5.4	1.6	1.1	2.4
Anchorage, AK	15.9	10.1	8.1	4.4	3.0	2.0	2.9	2.5	1.6
Ann Arbor, MI	19.3	10.5	10.0	6.8	4.9	6.6	3.3	2.6	2.2
Athens, GA	8.6	9.4	9.8	8.7	3.0	1.3	1.6	2.9	0.9
Atlanta, GA	6.8	6.9	7.2	9.5	2.5	1.3	1.4	1.7	0.7
Austin, TX	12.4	7.7	7.9	3.9	2.7	1.6	2.4	2.1	0.8
Baton Rouge, LA	7.2	7.0	5.3	7.6	4.8	0.6	12.7	1.2	0.4
Boise City, ID	16.4	9.9	17.8	5.3	3.1	1.3	2.4	3.0	2.0
Boston, MA	6.0	21.2	9.6	3.7	13.5	3.4	4.7	2.3	0.6
Boulder, CO	19.8	12.2	11.9	3.7	5.6	3.5	2.9	3.5	1.6
Cape Coral, FL	14.0	11.2	8.3	14.0	7.7	3.3	2.4	2.0	1.5
Cedar Rapids, IA	35.7	14.8	7.8	4.8	1.8	1.3	2.3	1.5	2.1
Charleston, SC	10.2	10.3	8.3	13.4	3.7	1.9	2.2	2.5	0.8
Charlotte, NC	11.5	8.7	7.9	9.0	3.9	1.7	1.7	2.3	1.0
Chicago, IL	14.6	10.9	4.2	2.7	6.7	8.9	1.5	0.9	1.2
Clarksville, TN	11.1	9.4	6.6	10.6	2.8	1.4	1.6	1.6	0.8
Cleveland, OH	19.4	13.7	7.1	3.7	9.8	7.6	1.5	1.5	1.0
College Station, TX	14.5	8.3	6.7	3.8	2.7	2.1	2.6	2.1	0.7
Colorado Springs, CO	19.9	11.3	9.7	4.6	4.9	2.5	2.9	2.8	1.7
Columbia, MO	24.7	12.0	9.9	6.2	3.7	1.9	2.6	2.2	1.2
Columbia, SC	10.5	7.7	7.6	8.7	2.3	1.2	1.7	2.0	0.8
Columbus, OH	22.8	12.8	8.6	6.4	5.5	2.4	2.0	2.2	1.3
Dallas, TX	9.0	6.9	6.8	6.4	2.1	1.1	1.7	1.6	0.8
Davenport, IA	27.8	14.3	7.6	4.4	2.4	2.1	1.9	1.5	2.1
Denver, CO	18.0	10.9	9.4	4.1	4.9	2.5	2.5	2.4	1.5
Des Moines, IA	27.7	12.9	8.5	4.4	3.3	1.4	2.0	1.8	3.3
Durham, NC	9.4	7.5	9.1	5.6	3.3	1.9	1.8	2.5	0.9
Edison, NJ	6.5	9.6	2.9	4.7	12.6	3.9	1.0	0.7	0.6
El Paso, TX	3.3	2.2	1.5	2.5	1.0	0.4	0.7	0.4	0.3
Fargo, ND	38.5	8.1	4.1	2.0	1.1	2.9	3.3	1.2	1.2
Fayetteville, NC	8.7	7.0	7.1	5.6	3.0	1.3	1.5	2.0	0.7
Fort Collins, CO	25.6	13.3	12.5	4.3	5.1	2.6	3.4	3.2	2.3
Fort Wayne, IN	27.8	9.5	6.9	7.1	2.7	1.9	3.5	1.7	1.5
Fort Worth, TX	9.0	6.9	6.8	6.4	2.1	1.1	1.7	1.6	0.8
Grand Rapids, MI	20.3	10.1	8.8	4.1	3.1	6.5	3.0	1.9	19.8
Greeley, CO	22.3	10.1	8.6	4.6	3.6	2.1	2.1	1.8	1.5
Green Bay, WI	37.1	9.7	4.0	3.9	2.2	9.6	4.4	0.8	4.6
Greensboro, NC	8.2	6.8	8.4	8.1	2.3	1.1	1.3	2.0	0.8
Honolulu, HI	5.1	3.9	3.3	1.3	2.0	0.8	1.1	0.9	0.5
Houston, TX	8.1	5.5	5.2	4.4	2.0	1.2	2.2	1.2	0.6
Huntsville, AL	9.3	9.8	9.6	11.7	2.1	1.1	1.9	2.2	0.9
Indianapolis, IN	18.6	10.4	8.0	9.5	2.6	2.0	1.9	1.8	1.5
Jackson, MS	3.9	5.9	5.7	9.9	1.5	0.3	1.4	1.4	0.4
Jacksonville, FL	10.2	9.8	8.1	7.7	4.7	1.9	2.1	2.0	0.9
Kansas City, MO	21.3	12.5	9.6	5.7	3.3	1.5	2.3	1.9	1.5
Lafayette, LA	6.4	4.6	3.8	9.8	2.6	0.4	19.3	0.7	0.3
Lakeland, FL	9.4	7.8	7.9	13.4	3.6	1.7	2.0	1.5	1.1
Las Vegas, NV	9.2	7.4	5.6	3.5	5.3	2.0	1.8	1.2	0.8
Lexington, KY	13.5	12.0	11.1	14.3	2.5	1.4	1.8	2.9	1.2
Lincoln, NE	36.6	11.9	8.4	3.8	2.0	2.7	2.1	1.5	2.4
Little Rock, AR	9.7	9.2	8.2	8.3	1.5	1.0	1.7	2.0	1.1
Los Angeles, CA	5.4	4.3	3.9	3.4	2.9	1.2	1.3	0.9	0.6
Louisville, KY	17.6	12.5	8.9	11.6	2.4	1.1	2.1	1.9	1.0
Madison, WI	37.7	13.5	8.6	2.8	3.9	5.4	2.9	1.5	2.0

Table continued on next page.

Metro Area	German	Irish	English	American	Italian	Polish	French[1]	Scottish	Dutch
Manchester, NH	8.4	20.6	12.6	3.7	10.3	4.5	13.2	3.4	0.8
Miami, FL	4.5	4.3	2.8	6.1	5.1	1.9	1.3	0.7	0.4
Midland, TX	8.1	6.6	6.2	4.8	1.3	0.6	1.8	1.7	0.6
Milwaukee, WI	33.6	9.9	4.3	2.2	4.3	10.8	2.5	0.9	1.3
Minneapolis, MN	30.1	11.0	5.6	3.0	2.7	4.4	3.4	1.3	1.5
Nashville, TN	10.2	10.0	9.2	11.8	2.8	1.4	1.9	2.2	1.0
New Haven, CT	7.9	15.1	6.8	2.8	20.8	6.3	3.6	1.3	0.6
New Orleans, LA	9.8	7.5	4.4	5.0	8.1	0.7	12.4	1.0	0.4
New York, NY	6.5	9.6	2.9	4.7	12.6	3.9	1.0	0.7	0.6
Oklahoma City, OK	12.7	9.6	7.3	7.6	2.0	0.9	1.8	1.7	1.3
Omaha, NE	29.5	14.1	7.8	3.7	4.1	3.7	2.3	1.3	1.7
Orlando, FL	8.7	7.8	6.1	7.3	5.2	1.9	2.0	1.4	0.8
Peoria, IL	28.3	12.9	8.7	6.8	4.0	2.1	2.3	1.9	1.5
Philadelphia, PA	15.1	18.4	6.9	3.3	13.2	5.1	1.4	1.3	0.8
Phoenix, AZ	12.9	8.5	7.7	4.0	4.4	2.4	2.2	1.6	1.2
Pittsburgh, PA	26.7	17.7	8.0	3.8	15.9	8.5	1.7	1.9	1.1
Portland, OR	18.1	10.8	10.6	4.9	4.0	1.8	3.0	3.0	1.9
Providence, RI	4.6	17.8	10.5	3.4	13.9	3.8	9.6	1.6	0.4
Provo, UT	10.7	4.9	27.3	4.8	2.5	0.7	2.0	5.1	1.7
Raleigh, NC	10.6	9.5	10.1	10.8	4.9	2.2	1.9	2.6	0.9
Reno, NV	14.1	11.5	9.5	4.6	6.6	2.0	2.7	2.4	1.3
Richmond, VA	9.6	8.0	10.9	6.7	3.7	1.6	1.6	2.1	0.7
Rochester, MN	36.1	11.8	6.3	3.4	1.8	3.3	2.4	1.2	1.8
Sacramento, CA	11.2	8.4	7.7	2.9	5.0	1.3	2.3	1.8	1.2
Salt Lake City, UT	10.5	5.6	20.4	4.2	3.0	0.9	1.9	3.9	2.1
San Antonio, TX	10.5	5.6	5.2	3.3	2.0	1.5	1.8	1.2	0.6
San Diego, CA	9.9	7.9	6.5	2.8	4.2	1.8	2.1	1.6	1.0
San Francisco, CA	7.8	7.5	5.8	2.4	4.9	1.5	2.0	1.5	0.8
San Jose, CA	6.3	4.8	4.6	1.8	3.8	1.2	1.5	1.1	0.7
Santa Rosa, CA	13.1	12.2	9.8	2.8	8.9	1.8	3.3	2.5	1.4
Savannah, GA	9.5	10.4	7.4	7.1	3.2	1.3	1.8	2.0	0.8
Seattle, WA	15.4	9.8	9.4	3.3	3.7	2.0	2.9	2.7	1.6
Sioux Falls, SD	38.0	10.5	5.1	3.9	1.4	1.6	2.2	1.1	6.5
Springfield, IL	24.4	14.0	10.6	6.2	5.0	1.9	2.5	1.8	1.4
Tallahassee, FL	9.0	8.5	8.2	5.5	3.2	1.6	2.1	2.3	0.9
Tampa, FL	12.4	11.0	7.8	9.3	7.5	3.1	2.7	1.8	1.1
Topeka, KS	26.2	11.2	13.1	6.0	1.5	1.0	2.7	1.9	1.6
Tucson, AZ	13.7	9.4	8.3	3.3	4.0	2.3	2.4	1.9	1.2
Tulsa, OK	13.7	10.9	7.9	7.4	2.0	1.0	2.3	2.0	1.4
Tuscaloosa, AL	5.2	6.6	5.1	11.8	1.6	0.7	1.1	1.6	0.6
Virginia Beach, VA	10.2	9.1	8.9	9.1	4.1	1.9	2.0	2.0	0.9
Washington, DC	9.6	8.5	6.9	4.2	4.3	2.3	1.6	1.7	0.8
Wichita, KS	22.7	10.0	8.0	7.3	1.7	1.1	2.3	2.1	1.7
Winston-Salem, NC	12.3	7.7	9.2	10.4	2.5	1.0	1.4	2.4	1.2
U.S.	13.7	9.9	7.3	6.4	5.2	2.8	2.4	1.7	1.2

Note: Figures are the percentage of the total population reporting a particular ancestry. The nine most commonly reported ancestries in the U.S. are shown. Figures include multiple ancestries (e.g. if a person reported being Irish and Italian, they were included in both columns); Figures cover the Metropolitan Statistical Area—see Appendix B for areas included; (1) Excludes Basque
Source: U.S. Census Bureau, 2014-2018 American Community Survey 5-Year Estimates

Foreign-born Population: City

City	Any Foreign Country	Percent of Population Born in							
		Asia	Mexico	Europe	Caribbean	Central America[1]	South America	Africa	Canada
Albany, NY	13.2	6.0	0.2	2.1	2.2	0.2	1.4	0.9	0.3
Albuquerque, NM	10.0	2.4	5.4	0.7	0.3	0.2	0.3	0.4	0.2
Allentown, PA	19.2	3.4	1.0	0.7	9.5	1.4	2.3	0.7	0.1
Anchorage, AK	10.7	6.1	0.9	1.1	0.6	0.2	0.4	0.6	0.4
Ann Arbor, MI	19.4	12.9	0.4	3.2	0.3	0.2	0.8	0.8	0.8
Athens, GA	9.9	3.0	3.0	0.9	0.3	1.0	0.9	0.6	0.2
Atlanta, GA	7.1	2.9	0.8	1.2	0.6	0.2	0.5	0.7	0.3
Austin, TX	18.5	5.7	7.8	1.3	0.6	1.6	0.6	0.7	0.3
Baton Rouge, LA	5.2	2.6	0.5	0.5	0.2	0.9	0.2	0.3	0.1
Boise City, ID	6.8	2.8	1.2	1.4	0.0	0.1	0.3	0.6	0.3
Boston, MA	28.5	7.6	0.3	3.5	8.3	2.7	2.4	3.2	0.4
Boulder, CO	11.4	4.5	1.5	2.8	0.1	0.3	1.1	0.3	0.5
Cape Coral, FL	15.1	1.4	0.6	2.3	6.4	1.2	2.5	0.1	0.5
Cedar Rapids, IA	5.5	2.8	0.7	0.5	0.2	0.1	0.1	0.9	0.1
Charleston, SC	4.5	1.7	0.6	1.2	0.2	0.1	0.2	0.3	0.2
Charlotte, NC	16.5	5.3	2.7	1.2	1.0	2.7	1.5	1.8	0.2
Chicago, IL	20.6	5.1	8.6	3.5	0.4	0.8	1.0	0.9	0.2
Clarksville, TN	5.2	1.6	1.1	1.0	0.4	0.3	0.5	0.2	0.1
Cleveland, OH	5.4	2.4	0.2	1.0	0.5	0.4	0.3	0.5	0.1
College Station, TX	13.6	7.9	1.7	1.0	0.1	0.5	1.2	0.9	0.3
Colorado Springs, CO	7.5	2.2	2.1	1.6	0.3	0.2	0.3	0.4	0.3
Columbia, MO	8.6	5.1	0.4	1.4	0.1	0.2	0.4	0.8	0.3
Columbia, SC	5.4	2.3	0.8	0.9	0.2	0.2	0.4	0.5	0.1
Columbus, OH	12.5	5.1	1.2	0.8	0.4	0.5	0.3	4.0	0.1
Dallas, TX	24.6	2.9	15.6	0.7	0.4	2.5	0.6	1.7	0.1
Davenport, IA	4.5	1.8	1.5	0.5	0.3	0.0	0.1	0.2	0.1
Denver, CO	15.6	3.1	7.7	1.4	0.2	0.9	0.6	1.5	0.3
Des Moines, IA	12.6	4.7	3.4	0.9	0.1	1.0	0.2	2.3	0.1
Durham, NC	14.7	4.5	3.3	1.0	0.6	2.8	0.6	1.4	0.4
Edison, NJ	46.5	37.2	0.8	2.9	1.4	0.4	1.9	1.6	0.2
El Paso, TX	23.8	1.1	21.2	0.6	0.2	0.3	0.2	0.2	0.0
Fargo, ND	8.8	3.5	0.1	1.1	0.1	0.1	0.2	3.4	0.2
Fayetteville, NC	7.1	2.4	0.6	1.0	0.9	0.9	0.5	0.6	0.1
Fort Collins, CO	6.6	2.8	1.3	1.2	0.1	0.2	0.5	0.3	0.2
Fort Wayne, IN	7.9	3.8	1.9	0.8	0.1	0.7	0.2	0.3	0.1
Fort Worth, TX	16.8	3.2	10.0	0.7	0.3	0.9	0.4	1.1	0.2
Grand Rapids, MI	10.5	2.0	3.2	1.2	0.5	1.8	0.1	1.4	0.3
Greeley, CO	11.3	1.1	7.4	0.4	0.2	0.8	0.3	1.1	0.1
Green Bay, WI	9.8	2.0	5.4	0.7	0.1	0.8	0.2	0.5	0.0
Greensboro, NC	10.8	3.9	2.2	1.1	0.5	0.5	0.5	2.0	0.2
Honolulu, HI	26.9	22.9	0.2	0.8	0.1	0.1	0.2	0.1	0.2
Houston, TX	29.5	6.1	11.8	1.1	1.0	6.1	1.2	1.8	0.2
Huntsville, AL	6.6	2.3	1.7	0.7	0.4	0.6	0.2	0.5	0.1
Indianapolis, IN	9.5	2.7	3.1	0.6	0.4	1.0	0.3	1.4	0.1
Jackson, MS	1.3	0.4	0.2	0.1	0.0	0.3	0.1	0.2	0.0
Jacksonville, FL	11.1	4.2	0.6	1.8	1.8	0.8	1.2	0.4	0.2
Kansas City, MO	7.7	2.3	2.3	0.5	0.4	0.6	0.2	1.2	0.1
Lafayette, LA	4.6	1.6	0.8	0.7	0.3	0.5	0.3	0.2	0.2
Lakeland, FL	10.4	2.0	1.1	0.9	3.4	0.7	1.1	0.3	0.9
Las Vegas, NV	20.8	5.1	9.4	1.6	1.1	2.1	0.8	0.4	0.3
Lexington, KY	9.5	3.5	2.6	1.0	0.2	0.5	0.3	1.3	0.1
Lincoln, NE	8.4	4.5	1.2	0.9	0.2	0.3	0.3	0.7	0.1
Little Rock, AR	7.8	2.8	2.1	0.7	0.1	1.1	0.4	0.4	0.1
Los Angeles, CA	37.3	11.1	12.9	2.4	0.3	8.4	1.1	0.7	0.4

Table continued on next page.

City	Percent of Population Born in								
	Any Foreign Country	Asia	Mexico	Europe	Caribbean	Central America[1]	South America	Africa	Canada
Louisville, KY	7.4	2.3	0.7	0.9	1.5	0.3	0.3	1.2	0.1
Madison, WI	12.0	6.5	1.7	1.4	0.1	0.3	0.8	0.8	0.2
Manchester, NH	13.6	5.1	0.5	2.4	1.3	0.9	0.8	1.7	0.8
Miami, FL	58.2	1.0	0.9	1.9	32.9	11.9	9.1	0.2	0.2
Midland, TX	13.3	1.8	9.2	0.3	0.7	0.2	0.3	0.5	0.4
Milwaukee, WI	9.8	2.8	4.8	0.8	0.3	0.2	0.2	0.7	0.1
Minneapolis, MN	15.7	4.1	2.6	1.2	0.3	0.4	1.3	5.6	0.3
Nashville, TN	13.1	3.9	3.1	0.8	0.4	1.8	0.4	2.6	0.2
New Haven, CT	16.6	4.3	3.1	2.1	2.5	0.9	2.2	1.0	0.5
New Orleans, LA	5.6	1.9	0.3	0.8	0.3	1.4	0.4	0.3	0.1
New York, NY	37.0	10.8	2.0	5.4	10.3	1.4	4.9	1.7	0.3
Oklahoma City, OK	12.0	3.5	6.0	0.4	0.1	1.0	0.3	0.6	0.1
Omaha, NE	10.5	3.2	4.0	0.7	0.2	1.1	0.2	1.1	0.1
Orlando, FL	21.2	3.0	0.5	1.5	6.9	1.2	7.1	0.7	0.3
Peoria, IL	7.9	4.7	1.4	0.7	0.1	0.2	0.4	0.3	0.1
Philadelphia, PA	13.9	5.4	0.5	2.3	2.6	0.6	0.9	1.4	0.1
Phoenix, AZ	19.5	3.3	12.2	1.3	0.3	0.8	0.4	0.7	0.4
Pittsburgh, PA	8.5	4.7	0.3	1.8	0.2	0.1	0.4	0.7	0.2
Portland, OR	13.9	5.8	2.2	2.8	0.3	0.4	0.4	1.1	0.5
Providence, RI	29.1	4.3	0.7	2.2	12.1	5.3	1.6	2.6	0.3
Provo, UT	10.7	1.7	4.7	0.5	0.1	0.5	2.1	0.3	0.3
Raleigh, NC	13.1	3.9	2.9	1.3	0.7	1.3	0.6	1.9	0.4
Reno, NV	16.0	5.1	6.7	1.2	0.1	1.7	0.5	0.3	0.3
Richmond, VA	6.7	1.5	0.8	0.6	0.3	2.2	0.4	0.8	0.1
Rochester, MN	13.8	5.7	1.5	1.8	0.2	0.2	0.3	3.5	0.3
Sacramento, CA	22.6	10.7	7.2	1.5	0.2	0.8	0.2	0.5	0.2
Salt Lake City, UT	16.7	4.6	6.2	1.8	0.3	0.7	1.3	1.0	0.4
San Antonio, TX	14.3	2.5	9.3	0.6	0.2	0.7	0.4	0.4	0.1
San Diego, CA	26.3	12.0	9.2	2.2	0.2	0.5	0.7	0.9	0.5
San Francisco, CA	34.4	22.3	2.5	4.4	0.2	2.5	1.0	0.5	0.6
San Jose, CA	39.5	25.0	9.3	2.1	0.1	1.0	0.6	0.7	0.4
Santa Rosa, CA	20.0	4.1	11.8	1.8	0.0	0.8	0.3	0.7	0.3
Savannah, GA	6.0	2.5	0.7	0.9	0.4	0.4	0.5	0.3	0.3
Seattle, WA	18.5	10.4	1.2	2.5	0.1	0.5	0.5	2.0	0.9
Sioux Falls, SD	8.1	2.3	0.5	0.9	0.1	0.9	0.1	3.2	0.1
Springfield, IL	4.2	2.5	0.3	0.5	0.2	0.1	0.1	0.4	0.1
Tallahassee, FL	8.1	3.6	0.2	0.9	1.1	0.5	0.6	0.8	0.3
Tampa, FL	16.5	3.6	1.2	1.4	6.3	1.2	1.9	0.5	0.4
Topeka, KS	5.1	1.3	2.8	0.4	0.1	0.1	0.2	0.1	0.1
Tucson, AZ	15.2	2.7	9.6	1.0	0.2	0.4	0.2	0.7	0.3
Tulsa, OK	11.1	2.7	5.7	0.6	0.2	0.9	0.4	0.4	0.1
Tuscaloosa, AL	4.5	2.2	0.4	0.5	0.1	0.8	0.2	0.3	0.1
Virginia Beach, VA	9.3	4.9	0.6	1.5	0.6	0.6	0.5	0.4	0.2
Washington, DC	14.0	2.9	0.6	2.6	1.1	2.7	1.4	2.2	0.3
Wichita, KS	10.1	3.8	4.5	0.4	0.1	0.5	0.1	0.6	0.1
Winston-Salem, NC	9.9	2.1	4.3	0.8	0.4	1.3	0.5	0.5	0.1
U.S.	13.5	4.1	3.5	1.5	1.3	1.1	0.9	0.7	0.3

Note: (1) Excludes Mexico
Source: U.S. Census Bureau, 2014-2018 American Community Survey 5-Year Estimates

Foreign-born Population: Metro Area

Metro Area	Any Foreign Country	Asia	Mexico	Europe	Caribbean	Central America[1]	South America	Africa	Canada
					Percent of Population Born in				
Albany, NY	7.9	3.3	0.2	1.8	0.7	0.1	1.1	0.4	0.2
Albuquerque, NM	9.2	1.8	5.5	0.7	0.2	0.2	0.3	0.3	0.2
Allentown, PA	9.1	2.7	0.4	1.6	2.2	0.6	1.1	0.4	0.1
Anchorage, AK	8.9	4.8	0.7	1.2	0.5	0.1	0.4	0.5	0.4
Ann Arbor, MI	12.4	7.3	0.4	2.2	0.2	0.3	0.5	0.8	0.6
Athens, GA	7.7	2.5	2.2	0.8	0.2	0.8	0.6	0.4	0.2
Atlanta, GA	13.7	4.4	2.7	1.2	1.4	1.1	1.0	1.6	0.2
Austin, TX	15.0	4.4	6.6	1.1	0.4	1.1	0.5	0.6	0.3
Baton Rouge, LA	3.9	1.5	0.8	0.3	0.2	0.8	0.2	0.2	0.1
Boise City, ID	6.5	1.6	2.8	1.1	0.0	0.1	0.3	0.3	0.3
Boston, MA	18.6	6.0	0.2	3.3	3.3	1.6	2.0	1.7	0.5
Boulder, CO	10.8	3.6	2.9	2.3	0.1	0.3	0.8	0.2	0.5
Cape Coral, FL	16.6	1.2	2.6	2.1	5.7	1.9	1.9	0.1	1.0
Cedar Rapids, IA	3.6	1.7	0.5	0.4	0.1	0.1	0.1	0.6	0.1
Charleston, SC	4.9	1.4	1.1	1.0	0.2	0.4	0.4	0.2	0.2
Charlotte, NC	9.9	2.8	2.2	1.0	0.6	1.3	0.9	0.8	0.2
Chicago, IL	17.7	5.2	6.6	3.7	0.3	0.6	0.6	0.6	0.2
Clarksville, TN	4.2	1.4	0.8	0.7	0.3	0.2	0.3	0.3	0.1
Cleveland, OH	5.8	2.2	0.3	2.2	0.2	0.2	0.2	0.3	0.2
College Station, TX	12.5	4.1	5.5	0.7	0.1	0.6	0.6	0.6	0.2
Colorado Springs, CO	6.8	1.9	1.8	1.6	0.3	0.3	0.3	0.3	0.3
Columbia, MO	6.6	3.7	0.4	1.2	0.1	0.1	0.3	0.6	0.2
Columbia, SC	5.0	1.6	1.1	0.7	0.2	0.5	0.2	0.4	0.1
Columbus, OH	7.9	3.4	0.7	0.8	0.3	0.3	0.2	2.1	0.1
Dallas, TX	18.3	5.1	8.5	0.8	0.3	1.5	0.6	1.4	0.2
Davenport, IA	5.2	1.7	1.7	0.5	0.1	0.1	0.1	0.8	0.1
Denver, CO	12.3	3.3	5.1	1.4	0.1	0.5	0.5	1.0	0.3
Des Moines, IA	7.9	3.1	1.6	1.2	0.1	0.5	0.2	1.2	0.1
Durham, NC	12.3	3.9	3.0	1.3	0.4	1.8	0.5	0.9	0.4
Edison, NJ	28.8	8.4	1.5	4.4	6.7	1.9	4.3	1.3	0.2
El Paso, TX	24.9	1.0	22.5	0.5	0.1	0.3	0.2	0.2	0.0
Fargo, ND	6.4	2.7	0.2	0.7	0.1	0.1	0.2	2.2	0.3
Fayetteville, NC	6.3	1.9	1.0	0.9	0.8	0.8	0.4	0.4	0.1
Fort Collins, CO	5.5	1.8	1.3	1.2	0.1	0.2	0.4	0.2	0.2
Fort Wayne, IN	5.8	2.7	1.3	0.6	0.1	0.5	0.2	0.2	0.1
Fort Worth, TX	18.3	5.1	8.5	0.8	0.3	1.5	0.6	1.4	0.2
Grand Rapids, MI	6.8	2.1	1.9	1.1	0.4	0.5	0.1	0.5	0.2
Greeley, CO	8.7	1.0	5.8	0.4	0.2	0.5	0.2	0.5	0.1
Green Bay, WI	5.1	1.4	2.4	0.5	0.0	0.3	0.1	0.2	0.1
Greensboro, NC	8.8	3.0	2.6	0.8	0.3	0.6	0.3	1.0	0.2
Honolulu, HI	19.5	16.0	0.2	0.7	0.1	0.1	0.2	0.1	0.2
Houston, TX	23.4	6.0	9.1	1.0	0.8	3.6	1.2	1.3	0.3
Huntsville, AL	5.1	1.8	1.2	0.7	0.3	0.4	0.2	0.3	0.2
Indianapolis, IN	6.8	2.5	1.8	0.6	0.2	0.6	0.2	0.8	0.1
Jackson, MS	2.5	0.9	0.6	0.3	0.1	0.3	0.1	0.1	0.1
Jacksonville, FL	9.1	3.2	0.5	1.7	1.4	0.6	1.0	0.3	0.2
Kansas City, MO	6.7	2.3	2.1	0.6	0.2	0.5	0.2	0.7	0.1
Lafayette, LA	3.3	1.2	0.8	0.3	0.1	0.5	0.1	0.2	0.1
Lakeland, FL	10.0	1.3	2.5	0.9	2.8	0.6	1.2	0.2	0.5
Las Vegas, NV	22.2	7.1	8.4	1.6	1.1	1.9	0.8	0.8	0.4
Lexington, KY	7.5	2.5	2.2	0.9	0.2	0.4	0.2	0.9	0.1
Lincoln, NE	7.4	3.9	1.1	0.9	0.2	0.3	0.3	0.7	0.1
Little Rock, AR	4.2	1.4	1.3	0.4	0.1	0.5	0.2	0.2	0.1
Los Angeles, CA	33.3	12.7	12.4	1.7	0.3	4.2	0.9	0.6	0.3

Table continued on next page.

Metro Area	Percent of Population Born in								
	Any Foreign Country	Asia	Mexico	Europe	Caribbean	Central America[1]	South America	Africa	Canada
Louisville, KY	5.4	1.7	0.8	0.7	0.8	0.3	0.2	0.7	0.1
Madison, WI	7.5	3.5	1.4	1.0	0.1	0.2	0.5	0.5	0.2
Manchester, NH	9.4	3.5	0.4	1.8	0.9	0.4	0.8	0.8	0.8
Miami, FL	40.4	2.1	1.1	2.3	21.1	4.2	8.6	0.4	0.6
Midland, TX	13.1	1.6	9.3	0.4	0.6	0.2	0.2	0.5	0.3
Milwaukee, WI	7.3	2.7	2.3	1.3	0.2	0.2	0.2	0.4	0.1
Minneapolis, MN	10.6	4.2	1.3	1.1	0.2	0.4	0.5	2.6	0.2
Nashville, TN	8.0	2.5	2.0	0.7	0.2	0.9	0.3	1.1	0.2
New Haven, CT	12.2	3.2	0.9	2.9	1.7	0.5	1.7	0.9	0.3
New Orleans, LA	7.6	2.1	0.6	0.5	0.7	2.7	0.5	0.3	0.1
New York, NY	28.8	8.4	1.5	4.4	6.7	1.9	4.3	1.3	0.2
Oklahoma City, OK	8.0	2.5	3.6	0.4	0.1	0.6	0.2	0.4	0.1
Omaha, NE	7.3	2.3	2.6	0.6	0.1	0.7	0.2	0.7	0.1
Orlando, FL	17.9	3.0	1.1	1.5	5.5	1.1	4.8	0.6	0.3
Peoria, IL	3.6	1.9	0.6	0.5	0.0	0.1	0.2	0.1	0.1
Philadelphia, PA	10.8	4.4	0.9	1.9	1.3	0.4	0.6	1.0	0.2
Phoenix, AZ	14.4	3.3	7.3	1.3	0.3	0.5	0.3	0.5	0.7
Pittsburgh, PA	3.8	1.9	0.1	1.0	0.1	0.1	0.2	0.3	0.1
Portland, OR	12.6	4.9	3.3	2.3	0.2	0.5	0.3	0.6	0.4
Providence, RI	13.4	2.3	0.3	4.3	2.2	1.4	1.1	1.5	0.2
Provo, UT	7.1	1.1	2.8	0.5	0.1	0.5	1.4	0.2	0.3
Raleigh, NC	12.0	4.3	2.8	1.3	0.5	1.0	0.6	1.1	0.4
Reno, NV	13.9	3.8	6.3	1.1	0.1	1.5	0.4	0.2	0.3
Richmond, VA	7.7	3.1	0.6	1.0	0.4	1.4	0.5	0.6	0.1
Rochester, MN	8.3	3.3	1.0	1.2	0.1	0.2	0.2	1.9	0.2
Sacramento, CA	18.5	8.6	4.8	2.7	0.1	0.6	0.3	0.4	0.3
Salt Lake City, UT	12.3	3.1	4.6	1.2	0.2	0.6	1.3	0.6	0.3
San Antonio, TX	11.8	2.1	7.5	0.6	0.2	0.7	0.4	0.3	0.1
San Diego, CA	23.4	9.0	10.3	1.8	0.2	0.5	0.6	0.5	0.4
San Francisco, CA	30.6	17.3	5.0	2.9	0.2	2.5	1.0	0.7	0.5
San Jose, CA	38.2	24.9	7.3	3.0	0.1	0.8	0.7	0.6	0.5
Santa Rosa, CA	16.5	2.9	9.4	1.9	0.1	0.8	0.4	0.4	0.4
Savannah, GA	5.6	2.0	1.1	0.8	0.4	0.4	0.4	0.3	0.2
Seattle, WA	18.2	9.6	2.4	2.7	0.1	0.5	0.5	1.4	0.7
Sioux Falls, SD	5.9	1.6	0.4	0.7	0.1	0.6	0.1	2.2	0.1
Springfield, IL	2.9	1.6	0.2	0.4	0.1	0.1	0.1	0.3	0.1
Tallahassee, FL	6.1	2.3	0.5	0.8	0.9	0.5	0.4	0.5	0.2
Tampa, FL	13.6	2.8	1.3	2.2	3.6	0.7	1.8	0.5	0.7
Topeka, KS	3.3	0.9	1.6	0.3	0.1	0.1	0.1	0.1	0.1
Tucson, AZ	13.0	2.4	7.7	1.2	0.1	0.3	0.3	0.5	0.4
Tulsa, OK	6.5	1.8	2.9	0.5	0.1	0.5	0.3	0.3	0.1
Tuscaloosa, AL	3.4	1.1	1.0	0.4	0.1	0.5	0.2	0.2	0.1
Virginia Beach, VA	6.6	2.9	0.4	1.1	0.6	0.7	0.4	0.5	0.1
Washington, DC	22.7	8.2	0.7	1.9	1.1	4.9	2.3	3.4	0.2
Wichita, KS	7.3	2.7	3.0	0.4	0.1	0.3	0.1	0.4	0.1
Winston-Salem, NC	6.9	1.4	3.0	0.6	0.2	0.9	0.3	0.3	0.1
U.S.	13.5	4.1	3.5	1.5	1.3	1.1	0.9	0.7	0.3

Note: Figures cover the Metropolitan Statistical Area—see Appendix B for areas included; (1) Excludes Mexico
Source: U.S. Census Bureau, 2014-2018 American Community Survey 5-Year Estimates

Marital Status: City

City	Never Married	Now Married[1]	Separated	Widowed	Divorced
Albany, NY	58.3	25.5	2.2	5.4	8.6
Albuquerque, NM	37.0	41.6	1.6	5.6	14.1
Allentown, PA	45.8	33.6	4.0	5.6	11.0
Anchorage, AK	34.2	49.0	1.6	3.3	11.9
Ann Arbor, MI	55.9	34.3	0.5	2.7	6.8
Athens, GA	55.0	31.8	1.7	3.5	8.1
Atlanta, GA	54.9	27.1	2.0	5.5	10.5
Austin, TX	43.5	40.6	1.7	3.1	11.0
Baton Rouge, LA	48.8	30.9	2.4	6.5	11.4
Boise City, ID	34.6	46.5	1.1	4.4	13.5
Boston, MA	55.8	30.2	2.7	3.9	7.4
Boulder, CO	55.2	32.7	0.8	2.6	8.7
Cape Coral, FL	25.0	51.3	1.9	7.7	14.1
Cedar Rapids, IA	34.3	46.3	1.1	6.0	12.3
Charleston, SC	42.3	40.8	1.6	5.3	10.0
Charlotte, NC	40.3	42.6	2.7	4.1	10.2
Chicago, IL	49.0	35.1	2.3	5.3	8.4
Clarksville, TN	29.6	51.5	2.4	4.1	12.4
Cleveland, OH	51.6	24.8	3.1	6.3	14.2
College Station, TX	60.5	31.6	0.8	2.1	5.0
Colorado Springs, CO	31.0	49.5	1.8	4.6	13.1
Columbia, MO	47.7	39.2	1.1	3.2	8.8
Columbia, SC	56.6	27.4	2.6	4.2	9.2
Columbus, OH	44.9	36.4	2.1	4.3	12.4
Dallas, TX	41.0	40.4	3.3	4.6	10.7
Davenport, IA	37.0	43.1	1.5	6.2	12.3
Denver, CO	42.5	39.3	1.9	4.0	12.4
Des Moines, IA	38.4	40.4	1.9	5.3	13.9
Durham, NC	42.9	39.8	2.6	4.4	10.3
Edison, NJ	25.6	60.6	1.2	6.3	6.3
El Paso, TX	34.6	45.1	3.4	5.9	11.0
Fargo, ND	43.4	42.2	1.0	4.6	8.7
Fayetteville, NC	38.1	41.3	3.8	5.4	11.4
Fort Collins, CO	46.4	41.0	0.8	3.2	8.6
Fort Wayne, IN	35.2	44.7	1.3	6.0	12.7
Fort Worth, TX	35.6	45.7	2.4	4.5	11.8
Grand Rapids, MI	46.6	36.4	1.4	5.3	10.3
Greeley, CO	34.9	46.1	1.7	5.1	12.2
Green Bay, WI	38.0	42.9	1.5	5.1	12.6
Greensboro, NC	41.9	39.0	2.4	5.6	11.1
Honolulu, HI	35.9	46.0	1.3	6.9	9.9
Houston, TX	41.0	41.3	3.2	4.6	9.9
Huntsville, AL	34.3	44.8	2.1	6.1	12.7
Indianapolis, IN	42.1	37.9	1.9	5.1	13.0
Jackson, MS	49.4	28.6	3.9	6.3	11.7
Jacksonville, FL	34.9	42.9	2.6	5.8	13.9
Kansas City, MO	40.1	39.5	2.1	5.4	12.9
Lafayette, LA	42.7	38.5	1.9	5.7	11.2
Lakeland, FL	34.5	42.0	2.1	8.5	12.9
Las Vegas, NV	35.1	42.9	2.4	5.4	14.2
Lexington, KY	38.8	42.7	1.8	4.6	12.1
Lincoln, NE	39.0	45.1	1.1	4.4	10.4
Little Rock, AR	37.7	40.2	2.8	6.2	13.2
Los Angeles, CA	45.9	38.6	2.6	4.6	8.2
Louisville, KY	36.2	41.9	2.1	6.1	13.7
Madison, WI	49.5	37.8	0.8	3.3	8.5

Table continued on next page.

City	Never Married	Now Married[1]	Separated	Widowed	Divorced
Manchester, NH	38.5	40.1	1.9	5.8	13.6
Miami, FL	40.7	35.1	3.7	6.6	13.9
Midland, TX	29.2	52.4	2.1	4.9	11.3
Milwaukee, WI	53.0	29.9	2.0	4.7	10.4
Minneapolis, MN	50.6	34.4	1.7	3.0	10.3
Nashville, TN	40.5	40.7	2.0	4.7	12.1
New Haven, CT	57.1	26.3	1.8	4.2	10.6
New Orleans, LA	49.2	29.3	2.9	6.1	12.5
New York, NY	43.5	40.2	3.0	5.5	7.8
Oklahoma City, OK	33.1	45.9	2.3	5.4	13.3
Omaha, NE	36.1	45.8	1.6	5.0	11.4
Orlando, FL	43.0	36.0	3.2	4.2	13.5
Peoria, IL	40.4	40.0	1.5	5.9	12.3
Philadelphia, PA	50.8	30.2	3.4	6.2	9.3
Phoenix, AZ	39.0	41.9	2.2	4.3	12.6
Pittsburgh, PA	52.0	30.9	1.9	5.9	9.2
Portland, OR	40.9	41.1	1.7	3.9	12.4
Providence, RI	53.6	31.2	2.6	4.1	8.4
Provo, UT	47.1	45.1	1.1	2.0	4.7
Raleigh, NC	42.7	40.3	2.5	3.9	10.6
Reno, NV	35.7	41.6	2.2	5.0	15.5
Richmond, VA	52.5	26.8	3.0	5.7	12.0
Rochester, MN	31.3	52.9	0.8	4.9	10.0
Sacramento, CA	40.2	41.0	2.5	5.3	11.1
Salt Lake City, UT	42.1	41.6	1.6	4.0	10.8
San Antonio, TX	38.3	41.4	3.0	5.2	12.0
San Diego, CA	40.1	43.9	1.8	4.2	10.0
San Francisco, CA	45.9	40.1	1.4	4.7	8.0
San Jose, CA	35.4	50.7	1.6	4.3	7.9
Santa Rosa, CA	34.7	44.1	1.9	5.6	13.6
Savannah, GA	47.4	31.1	2.7	6.2	12.6
Seattle, WA	44.4	41.1	1.2	3.5	9.9
Sioux Falls, SD	34.1	48.3	1.5	5.2	11.0
Springfield, IL	36.7	40.9	1.6	6.5	14.3
Tallahassee, FL	55.9	29.9	1.2	3.5	9.5
Tampa, FL	41.1	37.8	2.7	5.1	13.3
Topeka, KS	32.5	44.4	1.3	7.2	14.7
Tucson, AZ	42.4	35.9	2.2	5.4	14.0
Tulsa, OK	34.2	42.6	2.5	5.9	14.9
Tuscaloosa, AL	52.3	32.0	1.9	4.5	9.3
Virginia Beach, VA	30.6	50.7	2.5	5.1	11.1
Washington, DC	56.3	28.5	2.2	4.4	8.7
Wichita, KS	32.9	46.4	1.9	5.5	13.4
Winston-Salem, NC	39.8	40.5	2.9	5.9	10.8
U.S.	33.3	48.1	2.0	5.8	10.8

Note: Figures are percentages and cover the population 15 years of age and older; (1) Excludes separated
Source: U.S. Census Bureau, 2014-2018 American Community Survey 5-Year Estimates

Marital Status: Metro Area

Metro Area	Never Married	Now Married[1]	Separated	Widowed	Divorced
Albany, NY	36.3	45.8	1.9	6.0	10.0
Albuquerque, NM	34.5	44.7	1.5	5.7	13.6
Allentown, PA	31.6	49.7	2.2	6.6	9.9
Anchorage, AK	33.6	49.0	1.7	3.6	12.1
Ann Arbor, MI	42.8	44.1	0.8	3.8	8.6
Athens, GA	42.8	42.0	1.6	4.6	9.0
Atlanta, GA	35.2	47.4	2.0	4.6	10.8
Austin, TX	36.5	47.3	1.7	3.6	10.9
Baton Rouge, LA	36.7	43.6	2.2	6.0	11.6
Boise City, ID	29.8	52.3	1.1	4.5	12.2
Boston, MA	37.1	47.3	1.6	5.2	8.8
Boulder, CO	38.0	46.4	1.0	3.6	11.0
Cape Coral, FL	26.4	50.4	1.8	8.2	13.2
Cedar Rapids, IA	29.2	52.7	1.0	5.9	11.2
Charleston, SC	34.2	46.7	2.6	5.4	11.0
Charlotte, NC	32.2	49.7	2.5	5.3	10.3
Chicago, IL	37.0	46.9	1.7	5.5	8.9
Clarksville, TN	28.3	52.7	2.2	4.9	12.0
Cleveland, OH	34.8	45.0	1.7	6.7	11.8
College Station, TX	46.6	39.7	1.9	3.9	7.9
Colorado Springs, CO	29.4	52.9	1.7	4.1	12.0
Columbia, MO	41.0	44.5	1.3	3.7	9.5
Columbia, SC	36.5	44.1	3.0	5.7	10.8
Columbus, OH	34.5	47.2	1.7	4.9	11.6
Dallas, TX	32.4	50.4	2.2	4.4	10.6
Davenport, IA	29.8	50.4	1.3	6.7	11.8
Denver, CO	32.8	49.7	1.5	4.1	11.9
Des Moines, IA	29.9	52.2	1.2	5.0	11.7
Durham, NC	37.6	45.2	2.3	5.0	10.0
Edison, NJ	37.7	46.3	2.3	5.8	7.9
El Paso, TX	35.1	45.5	3.4	5.5	10.5
Fargo, ND	37.3	49.2	0.9	4.3	8.3
Fayetteville, NC	34.4	45.4	3.5	5.6	11.1
Fort Collins, CO	34.6	50.1	1.0	4.0	10.3
Fort Wayne, IN	30.8	50.5	1.1	5.9	11.7
Fort Worth, TX	32.4	50.4	2.2	4.4	10.6
Grand Rapids, MI	32.1	51.9	1.0	4.9	10.1
Greeley, CO	27.7	55.6	1.5	4.4	10.8
Green Bay, WI	30.2	53.0	1.0	5.1	10.7
Greensboro, NC	33.2	46.5	2.7	6.3	11.2
Honolulu, HI	33.7	50.2	1.2	6.3	8.6
Houston, TX	33.6	49.9	2.5	4.5	9.6
Huntsville, AL	29.8	50.8	1.8	5.7	11.8
Indianapolis, IN	32.9	48.2	1.5	5.3	12.2
Jackson, MS	35.9	43.9	2.6	6.3	11.3
Jacksonville, FL	31.1	48.0	2.1	5.8	13.0
Kansas City, MO	30.5	50.4	1.6	5.4	12.0
Lafayette, LA	35.1	45.7	1.9	5.9	11.4
Lakeland, FL	31.2	47.7	2.2	7.3	11.6
Las Vegas, NV	34.8	43.9	2.3	5.2	13.9
Lexington, KY	34.1	46.7	1.8	5.0	12.4
Lincoln, NE	36.8	47.8	1.1	4.4	10.0
Little Rock, AR	30.6	47.5	2.3	6.1	13.5
Los Angeles, CA	39.9	44.5	2.2	4.9	8.4
Louisville, KY	31.4	47.5	1.9	6.1	13.1
Madison, WI	36.2	49.2	0.9	4.2	9.6

Table continued on next page.

Metro Area	Never Married	Now Married[1]	Separated	Widowed	Divorced
Manchester, NH	30.2	51.2	1.3	5.4	11.9
Miami, FL	34.8	43.0	2.8	6.5	12.9
Midland, TX	28.6	53.0	2.2	4.8	11.4
Milwaukee, WI	36.8	46.3	1.2	5.5	10.1
Minneapolis, MN	33.1	51.4	1.1	4.4	10.0
Nashville, TN	31.7	50.1	1.7	5.0	11.5
New Haven, CT	37.8	43.9	1.3	6.2	10.9
New Orleans, LA	37.8	41.4	2.3	6.3	12.2
New York, NY	37.7	46.3	2.3	5.8	7.9
Oklahoma City, OK	31.0	48.7	2.0	5.5	12.7
Omaha, NE	31.0	51.8	1.3	5.0	10.9
Orlando, FL	34.9	45.9	2.3	5.2	11.7
Peoria, IL	29.8	50.9	1.1	6.6	11.5
Philadelphia, PA	37.2	45.4	2.2	6.1	9.1
Phoenix, AZ	33.9	47.1	1.7	5.1	12.2
Pittsburgh, PA	31.6	49.4	1.8	7.3	9.9
Portland, OR	31.7	50.1	1.6	4.5	12.2
Providence, RI	35.7	45.4	1.7	6.2	11.0
Provo, UT	32.1	58.5	1.1	2.6	5.7
Raleigh, NC	31.7	51.8	2.4	4.3	9.8
Reno, NV	31.0	48.2	1.8	5.0	14.0
Richmond, VA	34.5	46.2	2.5	5.8	11.1
Rochester, MN	27.3	57.5	0.8	5.0	9.5
Sacramento, CA	33.4	48.1	2.1	5.3	11.0
Salt Lake City, UT	31.7	52.2	1.8	4.0	10.3
San Antonio, TX	34.6	46.1	2.6	5.2	11.5
San Diego, CA	35.8	47.4	1.8	4.7	10.3
San Francisco, CA	36.3	48.5	1.6	4.8	8.8
San Jose, CA	33.5	53.1	1.5	4.3	7.7
Santa Rosa, CA	32.2	47.8	1.7	5.3	13.0
Savannah, GA	35.0	45.0	2.2	5.8	12.1
Seattle, WA	32.5	50.8	1.4	4.3	11.0
Sioux Falls, SD	30.5	52.9	1.3	5.1	10.2
Springfield, IL	31.4	47.6	1.3	6.1	13.5
Tallahassee, FL	43.8	39.4	1.5	4.5	10.7
Tampa, FL	31.0	46.1	2.2	7.1	13.7
Topeka, KS	27.1	52.6	1.0	6.7	12.6
Tucson, AZ	34.4	45.0	1.9	5.9	12.8
Tulsa, OK	28.1	50.5	2.0	6.1	13.3
Tuscaloosa, AL	40.2	42.3	1.9	5.6	10.1
Virginia Beach, VA	33.6	47.2	2.8	5.5	10.9
Washington, DC	36.0	48.8	2.0	4.3	8.8
Wichita, KS	29.6	50.8	1.5	5.8	12.2
Winston-Salem, NC	29.5	49.8	2.7	6.7	11.2
U.S.	33.3	48.1	2.0	5.8	10.8

Note: Figures are percentages and cover the population 15 years of age and older; Figures cover the Metropolitan Statistical Area—see Appendix B for areas included; (1) Excludes separated
Source: U.S. Census Bureau, 2014-2018 American Community Survey 5-Year Estimates

Disability by Age: City

City	All Ages	Under 18 Years Old	18 to 64 Years Old	65 Years and Over
Albany, NY	12.5	3.7	10.7	35.6
Albuquerque, NM	13.2	3.6	11.4	36.0
Allentown, PA	18.1	9.7	18.0	38.4
Anchorage, AK	11.1	3.6	10.1	36.6
Ann Arbor, MI	7.0	2.5	4.8	26.2
Athens, GA	11.1	5.8	9.2	33.9
Atlanta, GA	12.1	4.4	9.9	38.5
Austin, TX	8.3	3.8	6.9	31.5
Baton Rouge, LA	16.4	8.2	13.8	42.7
Boise City, ID	10.9	3.6	9.1	31.6
Boston, MA	12.2	4.9	9.4	41.5
Boulder, CO	6.4	2.2	4.5	26.0
Cape Coral, FL	12.6	3.0	9.0	29.8
Cedar Rapids, IA	10.3	3.5	8.2	30.4
Charleston, SC	9.3	2.9	6.9	28.4
Charlotte, NC	8.4	2.7	7.0	31.2
Chicago, IL	10.4	3.0	8.2	36.5
Clarksville, TN	14.6	4.5	15.6	41.9
Cleveland, OH	20.4	8.7	19.4	45.7
College Station, TX	6.0	3.8	4.5	29.9
Colorado Springs, CO	13.0	4.6	11.9	33.7
Columbia, MO	9.8	2.8	7.9	35.8
Columbia, SC	12.0	5.3	10.2	35.9
Columbus, OH	11.7	4.7	10.6	35.5
Dallas, TX	9.6	3.2	8.2	35.5
Davenport, IA	11.9	4.2	9.9	33.9
Denver, CO	9.7	3.1	7.6	34.4
Des Moines, IA	13.9	5.3	13.0	37.4
Durham, NC	9.6	3.1	7.8	33.5
Edison, NJ	7.9	3.0	5.1	29.3
El Paso, TX	13.7	4.8	11.4	44.3
Fargo, ND	9.9	2.8	7.7	36.7
Fayetteville, NC	17.2	7.0	15.9	44.7
Fort Collins, CO	8.3	3.2	6.2	32.2
Fort Wayne, IN	13.5	5.4	12.6	33.9
Fort Worth, TX	10.4	3.7	9.4	36.9
Grand Rapids, MI	13.3	5.6	11.8	38.8
Greeley, CO	11.4	2.9	10.1	37.1
Green Bay, WI	12.7	6.0	11.6	32.2
Greensboro, NC	10.4	4.0	8.2	31.8
Honolulu, HI	11.2	2.3	7.3	31.5
Houston, TX	9.4	3.1	7.7	36.4
Huntsville, AL	13.3	4.2	11.1	34.9
Indianapolis, IN	13.6	5.3	12.3	38.2
Jackson, MS	11.9	3.2	10.9	37.3
Jacksonville, FL	13.7	4.9	11.8	38.5
Kansas City, MO	12.6	4.0	11.2	36.3
Lafayette, LA	12.3	3.2	10.7	34.0
Lakeland, FL	16.0	4.4	12.1	37.7
Las Vegas, NV	13.1	4.0	11.0	36.9
Lexington, KY	12.2	4.6	10.3	35.0
Lincoln, NE	10.9	4.5	8.7	33.5
Little Rock, AR	13.3	5.8	11.5	35.4
Los Angeles, CA	10.1	3.1	7.3	37.8
Louisville, KY	14.8	4.9	13.3	37.5

Table continued on next page.

City	All Ages	Under 18 Years Old	18 to 64 Years Old	65 Years and Over
Madison, WI	8.1	3.5	6.2	26.8
Manchester, NH	14.6	5.9	12.4	40.6
Miami, FL	12.0	3.8	8.0	36.5
Midland, TX	9.4	2.5	7.8	37.6
Milwaukee, WI	13.3	5.9	12.1	39.7
Minneapolis, MN	11.2	4.7	10.2	33.8
Nashville, TN	11.6	3.7	10.0	35.9
New Haven, CT	10.6	5.2	9.0	33.9
New Orleans, LA	14.1	4.7	12.4	37.1
New York, NY	10.8	3.4	7.9	35.7
Oklahoma City, OK	13.4	4.6	12.2	39.1
Omaha, NE	11.0	3.5	9.6	33.5
Orlando, FL	10.0	5.0	8.1	34.4
Peoria, IL	12.3	2.8	11.0	33.7
Philadelphia, PA	16.3	5.9	14.7	42.6
Phoenix, AZ	10.5	3.9	9.2	35.2
Pittsburgh, PA	13.7	6.3	10.7	36.8
Portland, OR	12.4	4.6	10.3	36.1
Providence, RI	13.2	5.5	12.0	39.2
Provo, UT	8.3	4.1	7.2	37.1
Raleigh, NC	8.7	4.6	6.7	31.6
Reno, NV	12.5	5.3	10.5	32.7
Richmond, VA	15.0	6.8	13.4	36.5
Rochester, MN	10.7	4.7	8.5	30.3
Sacramento, CA	12.1	3.3	10.2	38.7
Salt Lake City, UT	10.5	2.9	8.8	36.7
San Antonio, TX	14.4	5.5	13.0	41.9
San Diego, CA	9.1	3.1	6.6	32.7
San Francisco, CA	10.3	2.4	6.6	35.5
San Jose, CA	8.5	2.4	6.0	33.5
Santa Rosa, CA	12.1	3.3	10.3	31.7
Savannah, GA	15.0	6.0	12.4	42.9
Seattle, WA	9.2	2.6	6.9	31.4
Sioux Falls, SD	10.3	3.7	9.0	30.5
Springfield, IL	15.2	6.1	13.2	35.2
Tallahassee, FL	10.3	5.0	8.5	32.7
Tampa, FL	12.0	3.9	9.8	38.7
Topeka, KS	15.4	3.7	13.7	38.5
Tucson, AZ	15.2	5.6	13.2	39.7
Tulsa, OK	14.8	4.9	13.8	37.7
Tuscaloosa, AL	10.8	2.6	9.2	33.4
Virginia Beach, VA	10.9	3.7	9.0	31.8
Washington, DC	11.8	4.1	9.8	35.8
Wichita, KS	13.2	4.3	11.9	36.2
Winston-Salem, NC	10.0	2.6	8.4	30.4
U.S.	12.6	4.2	10.3	35.0

Note: Figures show percent of the civilian noninstitutionalized population that reported having a disability. Disability status is determined from from six types of difficulty: vision, hearing, cognitive, ambulatory, self-care, and independent living. For children under 5 years old, hearing and vision difficulty are used to determine disability status. For children between the ages of 5 and 14, disability status is determined from hearing, vision, cognitive, ambulatory, and self-care difficulties. For people aged 15 years and older, they are considered to have a disability if they have difficulty with any one of the six difficulty types.
Source: U.S. Census Bureau, 2014-2018 American Community Survey 5-Year Estimates

Disability by Age: Metro Area

Metro Area	All Ages	Under 18 Years Old	18 to 64 Years Old	65 Years and Over
Albany, NY	12.1	4.2	9.8	31.0
Albuquerque, NM	14.0	3.7	12.0	37.0
Allentown, PA	13.4	5.7	10.8	32.8
Anchorage, AK	11.6	3.6	10.8	37.1
Ann Arbor, MI	9.1	3.2	7.0	28.6
Athens, GA	12.2	5.9	9.9	35.4
Atlanta, GA	10.0	3.4	8.5	32.9
Austin, TX	9.1	3.6	7.5	32.1
Baton Rouge, LA	14.2	5.7	12.4	38.9
Boise City, ID	11.7	4.0	10.3	32.8
Boston, MA	10.6	3.9	8.0	31.7
Boulder, CO	8.1	2.7	6.2	25.9
Cape Coral, FL	13.6	3.9	9.6	28.1
Cedar Rapids, IA	10.3	3.9	7.9	29.3
Charleston, SC	12.0	4.0	9.8	34.2
Charlotte, NC	10.8	3.6	9.0	33.1
Chicago, IL	9.9	3.0	7.6	32.6
Clarksville, TN	15.3	5.0	15.4	42.6
Cleveland, OH	14.3	5.3	11.8	34.6
College Station, TX	9.2	3.7	7.1	35.5
Colorado Springs, CO	12.5	4.2	11.6	33.2
Columbia, MO	11.2	3.7	9.4	36.3
Columbia, SC	13.9	4.4	12.2	36.9
Columbus, OH	11.9	4.6	10.3	34.0
Dallas, TX	9.5	3.4	7.9	34.2
Davenport, IA	12.0	4.1	9.3	32.3
Denver, CO	9.4	3.0	7.5	31.3
Des Moines, IA	10.5	3.8	9.1	31.4
Durham, NC	11.0	3.7	8.8	32.2
Edison, NJ	10.1	3.2	7.4	32.3
El Paso, TX	13.9	5.3	11.8	45.5
Fargo, ND	9.5	3.1	7.5	34.0
Fayetteville, NC	17.0	6.7	16.2	45.7
Fort Collins, CO	9.8	3.6	7.5	29.0
Fort Wayne, IN	12.8	4.5	11.5	33.6
Fort Worth, TX	9.5	3.4	7.9	34.2
Grand Rapids, MI	11.6	4.2	9.9	32.9
Greeley, CO	10.1	2.8	8.8	34.4
Green Bay, WI	11.2	4.7	9.2	30.1
Greensboro, NC	12.5	4.1	10.6	32.8
Honolulu, HI	10.9	2.8	7.5	33.0
Houston, TX	9.4	3.3	7.8	34.9
Huntsville, AL	13.7	4.8	11.4	38.0
Indianapolis, IN	12.4	4.6	10.8	35.8
Jackson, MS	12.7	4.0	10.9	36.8
Jacksonville, FL	13.4	4.7	11.3	35.6
Kansas City, MO	12.2	4.1	10.5	34.6
Lafayette, LA	14.4	4.8	13.0	39.8
Lakeland, FL	15.4	5.8	12.5	34.7
Las Vegas, NV	12.2	3.8	10.2	35.1
Lexington, KY	13.2	4.9	11.3	36.2
Lincoln, NE	10.7	4.2	8.4	33.1
Little Rock, AR	15.6	6.1	13.6	40.3
Los Angeles, CA	9.6	3.0	6.9	34.4
Louisville, KY	14.3	4.5	12.6	36.6

Table continued on next page.

Metro Area	All Ages	Under 18 Years Old	18 to 64 Years Old	65 Years and Over
Madison, WI	9.0	3.6	7.0	27.6
Manchester, NH	11.7	4.8	9.5	32.1
Miami, FL	10.9	3.4	7.3	32.6
Midland, TX	9.4	2.4	7.8	38.7
Milwaukee, WI	11.5	4.4	9.4	32.4
Minneapolis, MN	9.9	3.7	8.0	30.5
Nashville, TN	12.0	3.8	10.5	35.5
New Haven, CT	11.4	3.9	8.6	32.1
New Orleans, LA	13.9	4.7	12.0	36.3
New York, NY	10.1	3.2	7.4	32.3
Oklahoma City, OK	13.8	4.4	12.2	39.5
Omaha, NE	10.9	3.5	9.4	32.9
Orlando, FL	12.0	4.8	9.6	34.4
Peoria, IL	11.7	3.2	9.3	32.8
Philadelphia, PA	12.6	4.6	10.4	33.6
Phoenix, AZ	11.5	3.8	9.3	33.1
Pittsburgh, PA	14.3	5.2	11.2	34.0
Portland, OR	12.0	4.1	9.9	34.5
Providence, RI	13.8	5.1	11.5	34.3
Provo, UT	7.7	3.2	7.2	32.9
Raleigh, NC	9.7	3.8	7.9	32.9
Reno, NV	12.2	4.4	10.2	31.4
Richmond, VA	12.3	4.8	10.2	32.5
Rochester, MN	10.3	4.1	7.9	29.9
Sacramento, CA	11.7	3.5	9.3	35.1
Salt Lake City, UT	9.4	3.5	8.2	33.5
San Antonio, TX	13.9	5.1	12.4	39.8
San Diego, CA	9.8	3.0	7.2	33.6
San Francisco, CA	9.8	2.9	7.0	32.0
San Jose, CA	8.0	2.3	5.3	31.8
Santa Rosa, CA	12.1	3.4	9.8	29.7
Savannah, GA	13.6	5.3	11.5	37.6
Seattle, WA	10.8	3.4	8.9	33.9
Sioux Falls, SD	9.8	3.5	8.5	29.6
Springfield, IL	13.9	5.8	11.5	33.9
Tallahassee, FL	12.9	6.0	10.4	35.3
Tampa, FL	14.0	4.3	10.8	34.4
Topeka, KS	14.4	4.2	12.5	35.6
Tucson, AZ	15.2	5.2	12.5	35.4
Tulsa, OK	14.6	4.7	13.0	38.4
Tuscaloosa, AL	13.6	3.8	11.7	38.8
Virginia Beach, VA	12.8	4.8	10.8	34.6
Washington, DC	8.6	3.0	6.7	29.5
Wichita, KS	12.9	4.5	11.3	35.8
Winston-Salem, NC	12.8	3.8	10.4	34.2
U.S.	12.6	4.2	10.3	35.0

Note: Figures show percent of the civilian noninstitutionalized population that reported having a disability. Disability status is determined from from six types of difficulty: vision, hearing, cognitive, ambulatory, self-care, and independent living. For children under 5 years old, hearing and vision difficulty are used to determine disability status. For children between the ages of 5 and 14, disability status is determined from hearing, vision, cognitive, ambulatory, and self-care difficulties. For people aged 15 years and older, they are considered to have a disability if they have difficulty with any one of the six difficulty types; Figures cover the Metropolitan Statistical Area—see Appendix B for areas included
Source: U.S. Census Bureau, 2014-2018 American Community Survey 5-Year Estimates

Male/Female Ratio: City

City	Males	Females	Males per 100 Females
Albany, NY	46,109	51,780	89.0
Albuquerque, NM	272,840	286,362	95.3
Allentown, PA	58,619	61,791	94.9
Anchorage, AK	151,144	144,968	104.3
Ann Arbor, MI	59,813	60,828	98.3
Athens, GA	58,641	64,669	90.7
Atlanta, GA	233,442	246,213	94.8
Austin, TX	474,247	461,508	102.8
Baton Rouge, LA	107,346	118,016	91.0
Boise City, ID	111,515	112,785	98.9
Boston, MA	326,759	352,654	92.7
Boulder, CO	55,984	51,376	109.0
Cape Coral, FL	87,816	90,777	96.7
Cedar Rapids, IA	64,422	66,938	96.2
Charleston, SC	63,718	70,044	91.0
Charlotte, NC	404,373	437,238	92.5
Chicago, IL	1,320,499	1,398,056	94.5
Clarksville, TN	75,132	75,470	99.6
Cleveland, OH	186,844	200,554	93.2
College Station, TX	56,671	54,111	104.7
Colorado Springs, CO	228,586	228,916	99.9
Columbia, MO	57,805	62,443	92.6
Columbia, SC	67,812	65,540	103.5
Columbus, OH	423,547	444,081	95.4
Dallas, TX	653,609	665,197	98.3
Davenport, IA	50,140	52,178	96.1
Denver, CO	347,188	346,229	100.3
Des Moines, IA	106,266	109,666	96.9
Durham, NC	124,302	140,008	88.8
Edison, NJ	49,945	50,864	98.2
El Paso, TX	332,798	347,556	95.8
Fargo, ND	60,770	59,439	102.2
Fayetteville, NC	105,146	104,721	100.4
Fort Collins, CO	81,575	80,936	100.8
Fort Wayne, IN	127,627	136,425	93.6
Fort Worth, TX	418,897	436,889	95.9
Grand Rapids, MI	97,135	99,946	97.2
Greeley, CO	51,002	52,771	96.6
Green Bay, WI	52,255	52,563	99.4
Greensboro, NC	134,272	154,447	86.9
Honolulu, HI	174,225	175,778	99.1
Houston, TX	1,147,588	1,148,394	99.9
Huntsville, AL	93,149	100,514	92.7
Indianapolis, IN	413,806	443,831	93.2
Jackson, MS	78,428	90,434	86.7
Jacksonville, FL	425,235	453,672	93.7
Kansas City, MO	233,915	247,502	94.5
Lafayette, LA	61,753	64,762	95.4
Lakeland, FL	49,970	55,988	89.3
Las Vegas, NV	313,548	313,089	100.1
Lexington, KY	156,453	162,281	96.4
Lincoln, NE	140,897	139,952	100.7
Little Rock, AR	94,389	103,746	91.0
Los Angeles, CA	1,962,356	1,997,301	98.3
Louisville, KY	298,817	318,215	93.9

Table continued on next page.

City	Males	Females	Males per 100 Females
Madison, WI	124,658	127,428	97.8
Manchester, NH	56,950	54,707	104.1
Miami, FL	222,273	228,941	97.1
Midland, TX	68,615	66,519	103.2
Milwaukee, WI	287,646	309,240	93.0
Minneapolis, MN	211,095	204,926	103.0
Nashville, TN	318,215	341,847	93.1
New Haven, CT	61,715	68,814	89.7
New Orleans, LA	185,377	204,271	90.8
New York, NY	4,025,097	4,418,616	91.1
Oklahoma City, OK	313,370	323,914	96.7
Omaha, NE	229,987	235,125	97.8
Orlando, FL	132,885	142,805	93.1
Peoria, IL	54,734	59,778	91.6
Philadelphia, PA	745,543	829,979	89.8
Phoenix, AZ	801,937	808,134	99.2
Pittsburgh, PA	148,487	155,100	95.7
Portland, OR	316,291	323,096	97.9
Providence, RI	86,515	92,920	93.1
Provo, UT	57,755	58,391	98.9
Raleigh, NC	221,234	235,925	93.8
Reno, NV	122,467	120,166	101.9
Richmond, VA	106,222	117,565	90.4
Rochester, MN	55,482	58,431	95.0
Sacramento, CA	241,788	253,223	95.5
Salt Lake City, UT	100,612	95,089	105.8
San Antonio, TX	733,851	752,670	97.5
San Diego, CA	705,717	696,215	101.4
San Francisco, CA	443,970	426,074	104.2
San Jose, CA	517,100	509,558	101.5
Santa Rosa, CA	87,677	93,361	93.9
Savannah, GA	69,200	76,142	90.9
Seattle, WA	357,372	351,451	101.7
Sioux Falls, SD	86,757	87,394	99.3
Springfield, IL	55,176	61,283	90.0
Tallahassee, FL	89,861	100,319	89.6
Tampa, FL	182,229	194,116	93.9
Topeka, KS	60,956	65,921	92.5
Tucson, AZ	268,381	270,835	99.1
Tulsa, OK	195,203	207,020	94.3
Tuscaloosa, AL	47,103	51,778	91.0
Virginia Beach, VA	221,285	228,850	96.7
Washington, DC	324,881	359,617	90.3
Wichita, KS	192,025	197,538	97.2
Winston-Salem, NC	113,767	128,358	88.6
U.S.	158,984,190	163,918,840	97.0

Source: U.S. Census Bureau, 2014-2018 American Community Survey 5-Year Estimates

Male/Female Ratio: Metro Area

Metro Area	Males	Females	Males per 100 Females
Albany, NY	431,062	449,419	95.9
Albuquerque, NM	447,714	462,298	96.8
Allentown, PA	409,136	425,479	96.2
Anchorage, AK	205,056	194,520	105.4
Ann Arbor, MI	181,376	184,585	98.3
Athens, GA	99,316	105,987	93.7
Atlanta, GA	2,795,960	2,983,503	93.7
Austin, TX	1,031,342	1,027,009	100.4
Baton Rouge, LA	406,306	423,336	96.0
Boise City, ID	346,277	347,675	99.6
Boston, MA	2,337,339	2,474,393	94.5
Boulder, CO	161,355	159,675	101.1
Cape Coral, FL	351,918	366,761	96.0
Cedar Rapids, IA	132,908	135,407	98.2
Charleston, SC	370,815	388,432	95.5
Charlotte, NC	1,199,484	1,273,641	94.2
Chicago, IL	4,666,894	4,869,534	95.8
Clarksville, TN	143,611	139,383	103.0
Cleveland, OH	995,200	1,066,566	93.3
College Station, TX	128,347	125,599	102.2
Colorado Springs, CO	359,635	352,631	102.0
Columbia, MO	85,827	90,688	94.6
Columbia, SC	396,658	420,006	94.4
Columbus, OH	1,011,208	1,042,854	97.0
Dallas, TX	3,569,005	3,686,023	96.8
Davenport, IA	188,445	194,275	97.0
Denver, CO	1,422,916	1,427,305	99.7
Des Moines, IA	312,447	321,754	97.1
Durham, NC	267,188	291,303	91.7
Edison, NJ	9,669,632	10,320,960	93.7
El Paso, TX	413,701	428,051	96.6
Fargo, ND	119,356	117,647	101.5
Fayetteville, NC	191,472	193,873	98.8
Fort Collins, CO	168,615	169,546	99.5
Fort Wayne, IN	211,144	220,468	95.8
Fort Worth, TX	3,569,005	3,686,023	96.8
Grand Rapids, MI	519,862	530,578	98.0
Greeley, CO	148,627	146,496	101.5
Green Bay, WI	158,290	159,412	99.3
Greensboro, NC	362,436	395,374	91.7
Honolulu, HI	497,646	489,992	101.6
Houston, TX	3,366,774	3,412,330	98.7
Huntsville, AL	221,092	229,520	96.3
Indianapolis, IN	980,534	1,026,963	95.5
Jackson, MS	277,804	302,476	91.8
Jacksonville, FL	719,757	755,629	95.3
Kansas City, MO	1,033,710	1,072,922	96.3
Lafayette, LA	238,741	250,228	95.4
Lakeland, FL	327,706	340,965	96.1
Las Vegas, NV	1,069,779	1,071,795	99.8
Lexington, KY	248,255	258,531	96.0
Lincoln, NE	164,425	162,796	101.0
Little Rock, AR	356,158	378,344	94.1
Los Angeles, CA	6,539,217	6,723,017	97.3
Louisville, KY	627,671	657,599	95.4

Table continued on next page.

Metro Area	Males	Females	Males per 100 Females
Madison, WI	322,491	324,790	99.3
Manchester, NH	204,293	206,794	98.8
Miami, FL	2,949,546	3,121,398	94.5
Midland, TX	85,477	84,331	101.4
Milwaukee, WI	767,869	808,038	95.0
Minneapolis, MN	1,762,345	1,795,183	98.2
Nashville, TN	910,285	953,853	95.4
New Haven, CT	414,311	445,028	93.1
New Orleans, LA	610,613	653,022	93.5
New York, NY	9,669,632	10,320,960	93.7
Oklahoma City, OK	675,536	694,223	97.3
Omaha, NE	456,815	466,076	98.0
Orlando, FL	1,197,603	1,252,658	95.6
Peoria, IL	183,307	191,119	95.9
Philadelphia, PA	2,934,918	3,134,530	93.6
Phoenix, AZ	2,323,193	2,350,441	98.8
Pittsburgh, PA	1,138,170	1,201,771	94.7
Portland, OR	1,196,303	1,221,628	97.9
Providence, RI	783,956	831,560	94.3
Provo, UT	303,846	297,542	102.1
Raleigh, NC	635,012	667,620	95.1
Reno, NV	228,714	225,713	101.3
Richmond, VA	620,082	661,448	93.7
Rochester, MN	106,440	109,595	97.1
Sacramento, CA	1,120,668	1,171,070	95.7
Salt Lake City, UT	595,414	590,576	100.8
San Antonio, TX	1,199,266	1,226,938	97.7
San Diego, CA	1,661,931	1,640,902	101.3
San Francisco, CA	2,309,806	2,363,415	97.7
San Jose, CA	1,000,095	981,521	101.9
Santa Rosa, CA	245,196	256,121	95.7
Savannah, GA	185,404	196,219	94.5
Seattle, WA	1,905,037	1,904,680	100.0
Sioux Falls, SD	128,146	127,292	100.7
Springfield, IL	100,919	109,109	92.5
Tallahassee, FL	183,676	196,425	93.5
Tampa, FL	1,469,371	1,560,676	94.1
Topeka, KS	114,015	119,245	95.6
Tucson, AZ	501,879	517,843	96.9
Tulsa, OK	483,670	501,563	96.4
Tuscaloosa, AL	116,266	125,132	92.9
Virginia Beach, VA	847,777	874,224	97.0
Washington, DC	3,000,356	3,138,026	95.6
Wichita, KS	319,270	324,495	98.4
Winston-Salem, NC	318,368	343,430	92.7
U.S.	158,984,190	163,918,840	97.0

Note: Figures cover the Metropolitan Statistical Area (MSA)—see Appendix B for areas included
Source: U.S. Census Bureau, 2014-2018 American Community Survey 5-Year Estimates

Gross Metropolitan Product

MSA[1]	2017	2018	2019	2020	Rank[2]
Albany, NY	56.1	58.8	60.7	63.0	57
Albuquerque, NM	42.8	44.4	46.3	48.6	68
Allentown, PA	43.9	46.2	48.1	49.9	64
Anchorage, AK	27.4	28.3	29.3	30.6	102
Ann Arbor, MI	23.5	24.6	25.5	26.4	112
Athens, GA	10.1	10.5	10.8	11.2	205
Atlanta, GA	391.0	409.9	431.6	452.0	10
Austin, TX	145.1	156.6	164.6	174.0	25
Baton Rouge, LA	53.2	56.3	58.3	61.0	59
Boise City, ID	33.9	36.5	38.7	40.8	79
Boston, MA	449.5	472.7	493.6	515.0	8
Boulder, CO	25.6	27.2	28.7	29.9	107
Cape Coral, FL	28.3	30.0	31.8	33.4	93
Cedar Rapids, IA	17.8	18.4	18.8	19.4	141
Charleston, SC	42.5	44.6	46.7	49.0	67
Charlotte, NC	174.1	185.6	195.5	205.3	20
Chicago, IL	683.3	716.3	743.3	770.7	3
Clarksville, TN	11.0	11.6	12.2	12.6	194
Cleveland, OH	138.3	145.9	152.3	157.1	28
College Station, TX	9.9	10.6	11.2	11.7	204
Colorado Springs, CO	33.1	34.9	36.6	38.5	84
Columbia, MO	9.2	9.6	9.9	10.3	220
Columbia, SC	41.4	42.3	43.9	45.8	73
Columbus, OH	135.6	142.2	148.6	154.7	32
Dallas, TX	522.3	556.9	586.7	620.6	5
Davenport, IA	19.8	20.7	21.6	22.3	124
Denver, CO	211.6	225.3	235.8	246.9	18
Des Moines, IA	55.0	57.7	60.3	62.8	58
Durham, NC	43.4	45.5	48.0	50.7	65
Edison, NJ	1,765.5	1,851.9	1,932.1	2,007.4	1
El Paso, TX	28.3	29.4	30.5	31.5	97
Fargo, ND	15.3	16.1	16.8	17.5	156
Fayetteville, NC	17.2	17.6	18.1	18.8	149
Fort Collins, CO	17.4	18.4	19.7	20.7	139
Fort Wayne, IN	21.9	22.9	23.9	24.8	117
Fort Worth, TX	522.3	556.9	586.7	620.6	5
Grand Rapids, MI	60.6	63.6	66.2	68.3	54
Greeley, CO	12.8	13.8	14.7	15.6	178
Green Bay, WI	19.4	20.4	21.3	22.1	128
Greensboro, NC	41.5	43.0	44.3	45.7	71
Honolulu, HI	68.2	70.5	73.2	75.5	50
Houston, TX	478.1	513.9	546.1	583.7	7
Huntsville, AL	25.9	27.2	28.4	29.8	106
Indianapolis, IN	140.6	147.0	152.8	159.1	27
Jackson, MS	29.7	30.8	32.0	33.2	89
Jacksonville, FL	77.6	82.8	86.5	90.6	45
Kansas City, MO	131.8	138.2	144.1	149.7	33
Lafayette, LA	21.4	23.0	24.0	25.4	116
Lakeland, FL	21.4	22.6	23.6	24.6	119
Las Vegas, NV	112.8	119.1	124.1	130.3	36
Lexington, KY	29.7	30.8	31.9	33.0	90
Lincoln, NE	19.7	20.6	21.2	22.0	125
Little Rock, AR	38.5	39.8	41.1	42.7	76
Los Angeles, CA	1,067.7	1,125.5	1,164.2	1,207.3	2
Louisville, KY	75.3	78.1	81.3	83.9	48
Madison, WI	49.5	52.1	54.5	56.5	61

Table continued on next page.

MSA[1]	2017	2018	2019	2020	Rank[2]
Manchester, NH	28.7	30.0	31.2	32.5	94
Miami, FL	349.2	369.5	386.7	403.4	12
Midland, TX	27.1	35.0	38.1	44.4	83
Milwaukee, WI	104.6	109.2	112.8	116.2	37
Minneapolis, MN	260.9	273.1	284.6	296.0	14
Nashville, TN	134.3	142.5	149.8	156.5	30
New Haven, CT	46.1	47.8	49.7	51.2	62
New Orleans, LA	76.7	81.0	83.8	87.5	46
New York, NY	1,765.5	1,851.9	1,932.1	2,007.4	1
Oklahoma City, OK	74.2	79.6	83.2	88.3	47
Omaha, NE	63.3	65.9	68.5	71.0	52
Orlando, FL	134.1	142.4	150.7	158.6	31
Peoria, IL	19.2	20.1	20.9	21.6	133
Philadelphia, PA	445.1	465.5	485.8	504.6	9
Phoenix, AZ	248.0	264.9	280.3	294.0	16
Pittsburgh, PA	147.4	156.4	162.8	168.5	26
Portland, OR	165.9	175.7	183.8	191.1	21
Providence, RI	84.0	86.8	89.5	93.0	44
Provo, UT	25.7	27.9	29.5	31.2	104
Raleigh, NC	83.2	88.3	92.8	97.8	42
Reno, NV	26.8	28.8	30.8	32.3	99
Richmond, VA	83.0	87.2	91.0	94.7	43
Rochester, MN	12.6	13.2	13.9	14.4	182
Sacramento, CA	129.3	137.0	144.3	151.5	34
Salt Lake City, UT	87.9	93.6	97.8	102.5	41
San Antonio, TX	126.1	134.5	140.1	148.6	35
San Diego, CA	237.2	249.4	260.3	272.1	17
San Francisco, CA	512.2	547.3	578.7	605.5	6
San Jose, CA	281.6	303.1	321.2	334.7	13
Santa Rosa, CA	29.3	30.4	31.4	32.5	91
Savannah, GA	18.8	19.7	20.6	21.2	134
Seattle, WA	367.9	397.5	416.9	435.0	11
Sioux Falls, SD	19.6	20.5	21.5	22.4	127
Springfield, IL	10.3	10.7	11.0	11.4	202
Tallahassee, FL	16.4	17.1	17.9	18.7	152
Tampa, FL	148.2	156.6	164.0	172.0	24
Topeka, KS	10.8	11.3	11.6	11.9	197
Tucson, AZ	39.9	41.7	43.6	45.5	74
Tulsa, OK	57.2	60.9	63.7	67.4	55
Tuscaloosa, AL	11.8	12.4	13.0	13.4	190
Virginia Beach, VA	95.2	99.3	103.6	107.4	39
Washington, DC	539.6	562.6	585.8	612.1	4
Wichita, KS	34.3	35.7	37.0	38.0	81
Winston-Salem, NC	29.7	31.2	32.5	33.8	88

Note: Figures are in billions of dollars; (1) Metropolitan Statistical Area—see Appendix B for areas included; (2) Rank is based on 2018 data and ranges from 1 to 381.
Source: The U.S. Conference of Mayors, U.S. Metro Economies: GMP & Employment 2018-2020, September 2019

Economic Growth

MSA[1]	2015-17 (%)	2018 (%)	2019 (%)	2020 (%)	Rank[2]
Albany, NY	1.7	2.4	1.3	1.5	162
Albuquerque, NM	0.7	1.4	2.6	2.5	252
Allentown, PA	1.2	2.6	2.3	1.6	210
Anchorage, AK	-1.5	-0.9	2.4	0.6	353
Ann Arbor, MI	2.1	2.5	1.9	1.3	123
Athens, GA	6.8	1.5	1.3	1.4	6
Atlanta, GA	3.7	2.8	3.6	2.6	47
Austin, TX	6.3	4.4	3.5	2.6	9
Baton Rouge, LA	1.6	0.8	1.2	2.4	170
Boise City, ID	3.7	5.5	4.1	3.2	45
Boston, MA	2.0	3.0	2.8	2.1	134
Boulder, CO	2.5	4.1	3.9	2.1	98
Cape Coral, FL	2.7	3.7	3.7	3.0	83
Cedar Rapids, IA	-1.6	0.9	0.8	1.0	354
Charleston, SC	5.0	2.4	2.9	2.6	16
Charlotte, NC	3.4	4.2	3.7	2.8	51
Chicago, IL	0.8	2.3	2.0	1.6	247
Clarksville, TN	-0.6	3.0	3.0	1.6	331
Cleveland, OH	1.7	1.9	2.8	0.9	160
College Station, TX	1.0	3.4	3.3	1.4	224
Colorado Springs, CO	2.9	3.1	3.0	2.8	73
Columbia, MO	0.9	1.6	1.5	1.8	242
Columbia, SC	0.8	-0.1	1.9	2.3	245
Columbus, OH	2.0	2.1	2.6	1.9	130
Dallas, TX	2.7	2.8	3.7	2.7	87
Davenport, IA	-0.2	2.4	2.4	1.2	311
Denver, CO	2.6	3.7	3.0	1.9	89
Des Moines, IA	2.8	1.8	2.7	1.9	78
Durham, NC	-2.0	2.9	3.7	3.5	363
Edison, NJ	1.3	2.6	2.6	1.6	196
El Paso, TX	0.9	1.5	1.6	1.4	244
Fargo, ND	0.4	2.1	2.6	2.0	283
Fayetteville, NC	-1.0	0.0	1.2	1.5	343
Fort Collins, CO	5.3	3.7	4.7	3.1	14
Fort Wayne, IN	1.9	2.5	2.5	1.3	149
Fort Worth, TX	2.7	2.8	3.7	2.7	87
Grand Rapids, MI	1.9	3.4	2.3	1.2	139
Greeley, CO	4.1	5.3	4.5	3.9	33
Green Bay, WI	1.2	3.2	2.6	1.2	203
Greensboro, NC	-0.2	1.5	1.2	1.2	312
Honolulu, HI	1.6	1.0	1.9	0.9	165
Houston, TX	-1.7	2.9	4.6	3.1	360
Huntsville, AL	1.8	3.0	2.5	2.7	155
Indianapolis, IN	2.5	1.9	2.1	2.0	101
Jackson, MS	0.1	0.9	2.2	1.5	300
Jacksonville, FL	4.1	4.3	2.6	2.5	34
Kansas City, MO	0.6	2.6	2.4	1.7	263
Lafayette, LA	-4.9	2.6	3.0	2.0	380
Lakeland, FL	2.7	3.2	2.5	2.4	82
Las Vegas, NV	1.5	3.1	2.3	2.7	182
Lexington, KY	1.6	1.3	2.0	1.1	167
Lincoln, NE	0.3	2.1	1.3	1.5	287
Little Rock, AR	0.4	0.9	1.6	1.5	286
Los Angeles, CA	2.3	3.5	1.8	1.6	110
Louisville, KY	0.7	1.4	2.3	1.2	254
Madison, WI	2.4	3.2	2.8	1.7	107

Table continued on next page.

MSA[1]	2015-17 (%)	2018 (%)	2019 (%)	2020 (%)	Rank[2]
Manchester, NH	2.7	2.6	2.3	1.8	84
Miami, FL	3.2	3.5	2.9	2.1	56
Midland, TX	1.0	13.0	9.2	3.6	231
Milwaukee, WI	0.9	2.1	1.5	0.9	243
Minneapolis, MN	1.9	2.3	2.5	1.9	144
Nashville, TN	4.0	3.9	3.3	2.3	39
New Haven, CT	1.2	1.7	2.1	0.9	204
New Orleans, LA	-0.6	1.2	1.3	2.0	329
New York, NY	1.3	2.6	2.6	1.6	196
Oklahoma City, OK	0.7	2.8	2.9	2.2	259
Omaha, NE	0.6	1.7	2.2	1.5	272
Orlando, FL	2.4	3.8	4.0	3.0	109
Peoria, IL	-4.0	2.5	2.0	1.3	376
Philadelphia, PA	1.4	1.9	2.7	1.7	188
Phoenix, AZ	3.3	4.5	4.0	2.7	54
Pittsburgh, PA	2.0	2.6	2.5	1.3	137
Portland, OR	3.9	3.5	2.6	1.6	42
Providence, RI	0.7	1.0	1.3	1.7	262
Provo, UT	6.6	6.5	4.0	3.7	7
Raleigh, NC	3.1	3.9	3.4	3.3	62
Reno, NV	4.3	5.3	4.9	2.5	27
Richmond, VA	1.5	3.0	2.6	1.8	179
Rochester, MN	3.6	2.9	3.1	1.1	48
Sacramento, CA	2.6	3.6	3.4	2.7	90
Salt Lake City, UT	2.3	3.7	2.6	2.7	114
San Antonio, TX	4.2	2.0	2.7	1.7	30
San Diego, CA	3.1	3.0	2.6	2.3	64
San Francisco, CA	4.8	5.1	4.3	2.5	18
San Jose, CA	7.0	6.0	4.6	2.2	5
Santa Rosa, CA	2.5	1.2	1.7	1.1	100
Savannah, GA	2.3	2.7	2.4	1.2	115
Seattle, WA	4.3	6.3	3.4	2.4	29
Sioux Falls, SD	1.2	1.6	3.2	2.2	206
Springfield, IL	-0.8	0.8	1.4	0.9	337
Tallahassee, FL	3.1	2.6	2.8	1.9	61
Tampa, FL	2.7	3.5	2.9	2.6	85
Topeka, KS	1.9	1.8	1.1	-0.1	143
Tucson, AZ	2.0	2.7	2.8	2.0	133
Tulsa, OK	-3.3	1.3	3.1	1.7	373
Tuscaloosa, AL	1.0	2.8	3.4	1.5	227
Virginia Beach, VA	-0.4	2.2	2.5	1.4	323
Washington, DC	2.0	2.3	2.4	2.1	131
Wichita, KS	1.9	1.5	1.8	0.5	141
Winston-Salem, NC	-0.2	2.6	2.6	1.6	314
U.S.	1.9	2.9	2.3	2.1	–

Note: Figures are real gross metropolitan product (GMP) growth rates and represent annual average percent change;
(1) Metropolitan Statistical Area—see Appendix B for areas included; (2) Rank is based on 2017 2-year average annual percent change and ranges from 1 to 381
Source: The U.S. Conference of Mayors, U.S. Metro Economies: GMP & Employment 2018-2020, September 2019

Metropolitan Area Exports

Area	2013	2014	2015	2016	2017	2018	Rank[2]
Albany, NY	3,946.1	4,547.0	4,470.3	4,135.0	3,883.2	3,325.8	77
Albuquerque, NM	1,389.6	1,564.0	1,761.2	999.7	624.2	771.5	179
Allentown, PA	2,949.9	3,152.5	3,439.9	3,657.2	3,639.4	3,423.2	73
Anchorage, AK	518.0	571.8	421.9	1,215.4	1,675.9	1,510.8	125
Ann Arbor, MI	1,156.2	1,213.6	1,053.0	1,207.9	1,447.4	1,538.7	123
Athens, GA	286.0	320.8	327.4	332.1	297.7	378.2	236
Atlanta, GA	18,827.9	19,870.3	19,163.9	20,480.1	21,748.0	24,091.6	14
Austin, TX	8,870.8	9,400.0	10,094.5	10,682.7	12,451.5	12,929.9	28
Baton Rouge, LA	6,261.5	7,528.3	6,505.4	6,580.5	8,830.3	10,506.1	34
Boise City, ID	3,657.9	3,143.4	2,668.0	3,021.7	2,483.3	2,771.7	84
Boston, MA	22,212.8	23,378.5	21,329.5	21,168.0	23,116.2	24,450.1	13
Boulder, CO	1,046.0	1,016.1	1,039.1	956.3	1,012.0	1,044.1	157
Cape Coral, FL	442.6	496.6	487.3	540.3	592.3	668.0	197
Cedar Rapids, IA	930.2	879.0	873.5	945.0	1,071.6	1,025.0	160
Charleston, SC	3,464.3	5,866.7	6,457.5	9,508.1	8,845.2	10,943.2	32
Charlotte, NC	10,684.1	12,885.3	13,985.8	11,944.1	13,122.5	14,083.2	23
Chicago, IL	44,910.6	47,340.1	44,820.9	43,932.7	46,140.2	47,287.8	5
Clarksville, TN	315.9	323.7	296.5	376.1	360.2	435.5	224
Cleveland, OH	11,137.9	10,706.5	9,629.7	8,752.9	8,944.9	9,382.9	40
College Station, TX	108.7	129.7	122.5	113.2	145.4	153.0	318
Colorado Springs, CO	1,065.4	856.6	832.4	786.9	819.7	850.6	173
Columbia, MO	423.9	237.7	214.0	213.7	224.0	238.6	287
Columbia, SC	1,681.3	2,007.9	2,011.8	2,007.7	2,123.9	2,083.8	104
Columbus, OH	5,731.4	6,245.6	6,201.6	5,675.4	5,962.2	7,529.5	45
Dallas, TX	27,596.0	28,669.4	27,372.9	27,187.8	30,269.1	36,260.9	8
Davenport, IA	7,141.2	6,563.2	5,711.8	4,497.6	5,442.7	6,761.9	48
Denver, CO	3,618.4	4,958.6	3,909.5	3,649.3	3,954.7	4,544.3	62
Des Moines, IA	1,279.4	1,361.8	1,047.8	1,052.2	1,141.2	1,293.7	136
Durham, NC	2,971.7	2,934.0	2,807.2	2,937.4	3,128.4	3,945.8	67
Edison, NJ	106,922.8	105,266.6	95,645.4	89,649.5	93,693.7	97,692.4	2
El Paso, TX	14,359.7	20,079.3	24,560.9	26,452.8	25,814.1	30,052.0	10
Fargo, ND	817.9	782.8	543.2	474.5	519.5	553.5	208
Fayetteville, NC	344.0	375.8	256.3	179.8	231.6	260.5	280
Fort Collins, CO	986.1	1,037.4	990.7	993.8	1,034.1	1,021.8	163
Fort Wayne, IN	1,441.8	1,581.1	1,529.0	1,322.2	1,422.8	1,593.3	122
Fort Worth, TX	27,596.0	28,669.4	27,372.9	27,187.8	30,269.1	36,260.9	8
Grand Rapids, MI	5,314.8	5,244.5	5,143.0	5,168.5	5,385.8	5,420.9	54
Greeley, CO	1,287.5	1,343.6	1,240.1	1,539.6	1,492.8	1,366.5	133
Green Bay, WI	914.8	988.7	968.1	1,044.0	1,054.8	1,044.3	156
Greensboro, NC	4,278.3	3,505.5	3,286.1	3,730.4	3,537.9	3,053.5	80
Honolulu, HI	323.2	765.5	446.4	330.3	393.6	438.9	221
Houston, TX	114,962.6	118,966.0	97,054.3	84,105.5	95,760.3	120,714.3	1
Huntsville, AL	1,518.7	1,440.4	1,344.7	1,827.3	1,889.2	1,608.7	119
Indianapolis, IN	9,747.5	9,539.4	9,809.4	9,655.4	10,544.2	11,069.9	31
Jackson, MS	1,252.8	1,229.0	1,336.1	1,261.6	1,155.4	1,041.0	158
Jacksonville, FL	2,467.8	2,473.7	2,564.4	2,159.0	2,141.7	2,406.7	92
Kansas City, MO	8,012.1	8,262.9	6,723.2	6,709.8	7,015.0	7,316.9	47
Lafayette, LA	1,261.8	1,532.7	1,165.2	1,335.2	954.8	1,001.7	165
Lakeland, FL	1,907.2	2,151.9	1,318.6	995.5	1,147.2	1,299.8	135
Las Vegas, NV	2,008.2	2,509.7	2,916.2	2,312.3	2,710.6	2,240.6	98
Lexington, KY	2,294.0	2,191.4	2,065.7	2,069.6	2,119.8	2,148.0	101
Lincoln, NE	818.4	1,173.9	1,189.3	796.9	860.9	885.6	170
Little Rock, AR	2,497.5	2,463.5	1,777.5	1,871.0	2,146.1	1,607.4	120
Los Angeles, CA	76,305.7	75,471.2	61,758.7	61,245.7	63,752.9	64,814.6	3
Louisville, KY	8,898.0	8,877.3	8,037.9	7,793.3	8,925.9	8,987.0	41
Madison, WI	2,292.1	2,369.5	2,280.4	2,204.8	2,187.7	2,460.2	91

Table continued on next page.

Area	2013	2014	2015	2016	2017	2018	Rank[2]
Manchester, NH	1,445.8	1,575.4	1,556.6	1,465.2	1,714.7	1,651.4	115
Miami, FL	41,771.5	37,969.5	33,258.5	32,734.5	34,780.5	35,650.2	9
Midland, TX	164.1	122.7	110.1	69.6	69.4	63.6	358
Milwaukee, WI	8,874.6	8,696.0	7,953.6	7,256.2	7,279.1	7,337.6	46
Minneapolis, MN	23,747.5	21,198.2	19,608.6	18,329.2	19,070.9	20,016.2	21
Nashville, TN	8,702.8	9,620.9	9,353.0	9,460.1	10,164.3	8,723.7	42
New Haven, CT	1,903.9	1,834.5	1,756.3	1,819.8	1,876.3	2,082.3	105
New Orleans, LA	30,030.9	34,881.5	27,023.3	29,518.8	31,648.5	36,570.4	7
New York, NY	106,922.8	105,266.6	95,645.4	89,649.5	93,693.7	97,692.4	2
Oklahoma City, OK	1,581.7	1,622.0	1,353.1	1,260.0	1,278.8	1,489.4	127
Omaha, NE	4,255.9	4,528.5	3,753.4	3,509.7	3,756.2	4,371.6	64
Orlando, FL	3,227.7	3,134.8	3,082.7	3,363.9	3,196.7	3,131.7	79
Peoria, IL	12,184.5	11,234.8	9,826.9	7,260.1	9,403.6	9,683.6	39
Philadelphia, PA	24,929.2	26,321.3	24,236.1	21,359.9	21,689.7	23,663.2	15
Phoenix, AZ	11,473.5	12,764.4	13,821.5	12,838.2	13,223.1	13,614.9	24
Pittsburgh, PA	10,444.4	10,015.8	9,137.1	7,971.0	9,322.7	9,824.2	36
Portland, OR	17,606.8	18,667.2	18,847.8	20,256.8	20,788.8	21,442.9	17
Providence, RI	6,609.0	6,595.1	5,048.8	6,595.7	7,125.4	6,236.6	51
Provo, UT	2,789.2	2,533.4	2,216.4	1,894.8	2,065.3	1,788.1	110
Raleigh, NC	2,280.6	2,713.1	2,553.4	2,620.4	2,865.8	3,193.2	78
Reno, NV	2,117.4	2,138.9	1,943.3	2,382.1	2,517.3	2,631.7	87
Richmond, VA	4,337.2	3,307.0	3,325.9	3,525.7	3,663.7	3,535.0	71
Rochester, MN	1,061.0	720.5	530.2	398.0	495.3	537.6	210
Sacramento, CA	5,777.1	7,143.9	8,101.2	7,032.1	6,552.6	6,222.8	52
Salt Lake City, UT	11,867.2	8,361.5	10,380.5	8,653.7	7,916.9	9,748.6	37
San Antonio, TX	19,287.6	25,781.8	15,919.2	5,621.2	9,184.1	11,678.1	30
San Diego, CA	17,885.5	18,585.7	17,439.7	18,086.6	18,637.1	20,156.8	20
San Francisco, CA	25,305.3	26,863.7	25,061.1	24,506.3	29,103.8	27,417.0	11
San Jose, CA	23,413.1	21,128.8	19,827.2	21,716.8	21,464.7	22,224.2	16
Santa Rosa, CA	1,044.8	1,103.7	1,119.8	1,194.3	1,168.2	1,231.7	141
Savannah, GA	5,436.4	5,093.4	5,447.5	4,263.4	4,472.0	5,407.8	55
Seattle, WA	56,686.4	61,938.4	67,226.4	61,881.0	59,007.0	59,742.9	4
Sioux Falls, SD	433.0	455.3	375.0	334.3	386.8	400.0	234
Springfield, IL	97.5	94.4	111.7	88.3	107.5	91.2	343
Tallahassee, FL	122.5	174.0	191.2	223.1	241.1	270.8	274
Tampa, FL	6,673.0	5,817.3	5,660.4	5,702.9	6,256.0	4,966.7	59
Topeka, KS	303.3	365.0	363.5	305.2	300.7	285.9	262
Tucson, AZ	2,589.9	2,277.4	2,485.9	2,563.9	2,683.9	2,824.8	82
Tulsa, OK	3,818.0	3,798.5	2,699.7	2,363.0	2,564.7	3,351.7	75
Tuscaloosa, AL	n/a	n/a	n/a	n/a	n/a	n/a	n/a
Virginia Beach, VA	2,539.2	3,573.2	3,556.4	3,291.1	3,307.2	3,950.6	66
Washington, DC	16,225.0	13,053.6	13,900.4	13,582.4	12,736.1	13,602.7	25
Wichita, KS	3,785.5	4,011.7	3,717.6	3,054.9	3,299.2	3,817.0	68
Winston-Salem, NC	1,660.1	1,441.9	1,267.4	1,234.6	1,131.7	1,107.5	151

Note: Figures are in millions of dollars; (1) Metropolitan Statistical Area—see Appendix B for areas included; (2) Rank is based on 2018 data and ranges from 1 to 387
Source: U.S. Department of Commerce, International Trade Administration, Office of Trade and Economic Analysis, Industry and Analysis, Exports by Metropolitan Area, extracted April 15, 2020

Building Permits: City

City	Single-Family			Multi-Family			Total		
	2017	2018	Pct. Chg.	2017	2018	Pct. Chg.	2017	2018	Pct. Chg.
Albany, NY	9	6	-33.3	109	96	-11.9	118	102	-13.6
Albuquerque, NM	1,088	1,115	2.5	184	0	-100.0	1,272	1,115	-12.3
Allentown, PA	15	0	-100.0	0	0	0.0	15	0	-100.0
Anchorage, AK	800	869	8.6	219	214	-2.3	1,019	1,083	6.3
Ann Arbor, MI	105	126	20.0	7	0	-100.0	112	126	12.5
Athens, GA	189	345	82.5	176	261	48.3	365	606	66.0
Atlanta, GA	922	1,184	28.4	4,179	5,312	27.1	5,101	6,496	27.3
Austin, TX	4,440	4,433	-0.2	7,139	8,850	24.0	11,579	13,283	14.7
Baton Rouge, LA	253	282	11.5	0	58	–	253	340	34.4
Boise City, ID	810	844	4.2	350	296	-15.4	1,160	1,140	-1.7
Boston, MA	52	49	-5.8	5,033	3,553	-29.4	5,085	3,602	-29.2
Boulder, CO	74	80	8.1	128	667	421.1	202	747	269.8
Cape Coral, FL	1,842	2,245	21.9	708	356	-49.7	2,550	2,601	2.0
Cedar Rapids, IA	219	147	-32.9	313	325	3.8	532	472	-11.3
Charleston, SC	766	810	5.7	303	354	16.8	1,069	1,164	8.9
Charlotte, NC	n/a	n/a	n/a	n/a	n/a	n/a	n/a	n/a	n/a
Chicago, IL	525	439	-16.4	8,414	6,010	-28.6	8,939	6,449	-27.9
Clarksville, TN	806	669	-17.0	227	269	18.5	1,033	938	-9.2
Cleveland, OH	144	114	-20.8	36	34	-5.6	180	148	-17.8
College Station, TX	594	459	-22.7	1,319	572	-56.6	1,913	1,031	-46.1
Colorado Springs, CO	n/a	n/a	n/a	n/a	n/a	n/a	n/a	n/a	n/a
Columbia, MO	403	261	-35.2	861	2	-99.8	1,264	263	-79.2
Columbia, SC	341	449	31.7	8	28	250.0	349	477	36.7
Columbus, OH	650	555	-14.6	3,579	3,742	4.6	4,229	4,297	1.6
Dallas, TX	2,100	2,009	-4.3	5,151	6,038	17.2	7,251	8,047	11.0
Davenport, IA	104	68	-34.6	0	0	0.0	104	68	-34.6
Denver, CO	2,370	2,428	2.4	8,155	5,450	-33.2	10,525	7,878	-25.1
Des Moines, IA	173	180	4.0	1,124	391	-65.2	1,297	571	-56.0
Durham, NC	1,783	1,894	6.2	1,179	1,336	13.3	2,962	3,230	9.0
Edison, NJ	58	71	22.4	0	100	–	58	171	194.8
El Paso, TX	2,020	1,588	-21.4	897	621	-30.8	2,917	2,209	-24.3
Fargo, ND	444	313	-29.5	781	897	14.9	1,225	1,210	-1.2
Fayetteville, NC	257	241	-6.2	56	0	-100.0	313	241	-23.0
Fort Collins, CO	657	398	-39.4	720	673	-6.5	1,377	1,071	-22.2
Fort Wayne, IN	n/a	n/a	n/a	n/a	n/a	n/a	n/a	n/a	n/a
Fort Worth, TX	5,042	5,477	8.6	3,814	3,833	0.5	8,856	9,310	5.1
Grand Rapids, MI	101	124	22.8	777	690	-11.2	878	814	-7.3
Greeley, CO	120	348	190.0	229	190	-17.0	349	538	54.2
Green Bay, WI	98	101	3.1	0	0	0.0	98	101	3.1
Greensboro, NC	728	597	-18.0	881	249	-71.7	1,609	846	-47.4
Honolulu, HI	n/a	n/a	n/a	n/a	n/a	n/a	n/a	n/a	n/a
Houston, TX	5,326	5,417	1.7	4,346	7,820	79.9	9,672	13,237	36.9
Huntsville, AL	1,144	1,241	8.5	380	71	-81.3	1,524	1,312	-13.9
Indianapolis, IN	914	1,090	19.3	645	1,196	85.4	1,559	2,286	46.6
Jackson, MS	20	21	5.0	0	0	0.0	20	21	5.0
Jacksonville, FL	3,005	3,780	25.8	2,874	3,223	12.1	5,879	7,003	19.1
Kansas City, MO	824	813	-1.3	1,542	1,341	-13.0	2,366	2,154	-9.0
Lafayette, LA	n/a	n/a	n/a	n/a	n/a	n/a	n/a	n/a	n/a
Lakeland, FL	433	435	0.5	52	0	-100.0	485	435	-10.3
Las Vegas, NV	1,605	1,794	11.8	276	179	-35.1	1,881	1,973	4.9
Lexington, KY	743	733	-1.3	605	1,056	74.5	1,348	1,789	32.7
Lincoln, NE	994	859	-13.6	1,231	673	-45.3	2,225	1,532	-31.1
Little Rock, AR	592	325	-45.1	508	145	-71.5	1,100	470	-57.3
Los Angeles, CA	2,360	2,636	11.7	12,486	13,663	9.4	14,846	16,299	9.8

Table continued on next page.

City	Single-Family			Multi-Family			Total		
	2017	2018	Pct. Chg.	2017	2018	Pct. Chg.	2017	2018	Pct. Chg.
Louisville, KY	1,236	1,183	-4.3	2,056	2,080	1.2	3,292	3,263	-0.9
Madison, WI	379	334	-11.9	1,809	1,109	-38.7	2,188	1,443	-34.0
Manchester, NH	149	151	1.3	95	59	-37.9	244	210	-13.9
Miami, FL	90	80	-11.1	4,671	4,545	-2.7	4,761	4,625	-2.9
Midland, TX	761	1,222	60.6	0	0	0.0	761	1,222	60.6
Milwaukee, WI	7	39	457.1	708	717	1.3	715	756	5.7
Minneapolis, MN	137	162	18.2	2,117	3,463	63.6	2,254	3,625	60.8
Nashville, TN	3,827	3,560	-7.0	2,423	3,268	34.9	6,250	6,828	9.2
New Haven, CT	6	4	-33.3	18	456	2,433.3	24	460	1,816.7
New Orleans, LA	447	524	17.2	213	779	265.7	660	1,303	97.4
New York, NY	483	417	-13.7	21,618	20,493	-5.2	22,101	20,910	-5.4
Oklahoma City, OK	2,707	2,955	9.2	48	142	195.8	2,755	3,097	12.4
Omaha, NE	1,533	1,237	-19.3	1,697	1,650	-2.8	3,230	2,887	-10.6
Orlando, FL	828	790	-4.6	818	2,289	179.8	1,646	3,079	87.1
Peoria, IL	32	32	0.0	0	0	0.0	32	32	0.0
Philadelphia, PA	783	683	-12.8	2,606	2,556	-1.9	3,389	3,239	-4.4
Phoenix, AZ	2,932	3,732	27.3	3,900	3,530	-9.5	6,832	7,262	6.3
Pittsburgh, PA	66	90	36.4	410	553	34.9	476	643	35.1
Portland, OR	703	775	10.2	6,086	4,873	-19.9	6,789	5,648	-16.8
Providence, RI	2	1	-50.0	2	0	-100.0	4	1	-75.0
Provo, UT	223	171	-23.3	17	286	1,582.4	240	457	90.4
Raleigh, NC	1,365	1,304	-4.5	1,851	2,907	57.1	3,216	4,211	30.9
Reno, NV	1,124	1,351	20.2	1,210	1,883	55.6	2,334	3,234	38.6
Richmond, VA	326	273	-16.3	991	290	-70.7	1,317	563	-57.3
Rochester, MN	437	347	-20.6	617	1,068	73.1	1,054	1,415	34.3
Sacramento, CA	1,728	1,610	-6.8	1,115	714	-36.0	2,843	2,324	-18.3
Salt Lake City, UT	88	109	23.9	542	793	46.3	630	902	43.2
San Antonio, TX	2,489	3,266	31.2	3,711	2,663	-28.2	6,200	5,929	-4.4
San Diego, CA	1,138	774	-32.0	4,554	3,678	-19.2	5,692	4,452	-21.8
San Francisco, CA	43	28	-34.9	3,991	5,150	29.0	4,034	5,178	28.4
San Jose, CA	177	238	34.5	2,264	2,598	14.8	2,441	2,836	16.2
Santa Rosa, CA	232	1,632	603.4	112	69	-38.4	344	1,701	394.5
Savannah, GA	384	399	3.9	0	0	0.0	384	399	3.9
Seattle, WA	593	523	-11.8	9,294	7,395	-20.4	9,887	7,918	-19.9
Sioux Falls, SD	1,192	1,083	-9.1	1,202	898	-25.3	2,394	1,981	-17.3
Springfield, IL	57	74	29.8	94	219	133.0	151	293	94.0
Tallahassee, FL	379	396	4.5	1,156	1,128	-2.4	1,535	1,524	-0.7
Tampa, FL	1,010	1,109	9.8	2,165	679	-68.6	3,175	1,788	-43.7
Topeka, KS	85	82	-3.5	0	0	0.0	85	82	-3.5
Tucson, AZ	709	680	-4.1	1,338	860	-35.7	2,047	1,540	-24.8
Tulsa, OK	389	471	21.1	255	343	34.5	644	814	26.4
Tuscaloosa, AL	320	353	10.3	597	469	-21.4	917	822	-10.4
Virginia Beach, VA	646	534	-17.3	877	245	-72.1	1,523	779	-48.9
Washington, DC	352	112	-68.2	5,685	4,503	-20.8	6,037	4,615	-23.6
Wichita, KS	843	532	-36.9	463	326	-29.6	1,306	858	-34.3
Winston-Salem, NC	1,183	1,251	5.7	777	84	-89.2	1,960	1,335	-31.9
U.S.	820,000	855,300	4.3	462,000	473,500	2.5	1,282,000	1,328,800	3.7

Note: Figures represent new, privately-owned housing units authorized (unadjusted data); All permit data are based on estimates with imputation
Source: U.S. Census Bureau, Manufacturing, Mining, and Construction Statistics, Building Permits, 2017, 2018

Building Permits: Metro Area

Metro Area	Single-Family			Multi-Family			Total		
	2017	2018	Pct. Chg.	2017	2018	Pct. Chg.	2017	2018	Pct. Chg.
Albany, NY	1,212	1,231	1.6	1,134	1,008	-11.1	2,346	2,239	-4.6
Albuquerque, NM	1,996	2,086	4.5	260	100	-61.5	2,256	2,186	-3.1
Allentown, PA	938	1,082	15.4	180	164	-8.9	1,118	1,246	11.4
Anchorage, AK	851	938	10.2	297	321	8.1	1,148	1,259	9.7
Ann Arbor, MI	583	652	11.8	74	153	106.8	657	805	22.5
Athens, GA	581	729	25.5	190	340	78.9	771	1,069	38.7
Atlanta, GA	24,973	26,506	6.1	8,859	12,935	46.0	33,832	39,441	16.6
Austin, TX	16,119	17,030	5.7	10,581	13,005	22.9	26,700	30,035	12.5
Baton Rouge, LA	3,586	3,509	-2.1	53	413	679.2	3,639	3,922	7.8
Boise City, ID	6,275	6,923	10.3	1,634	1,994	22.0	7,909	8,917	12.7
Boston, MA	4,949	4,930	-0.4	9,808	9,253	-5.7	14,757	14,183	-3.9
Boulder, CO	808	899	11.3	859	2,055	139.2	1,667	2,954	77.2
Cape Coral, FL	4,841	5,803	19.9	2,113	3,918	85.4	6,954	9,721	39.8
Cedar Rapids, IA	537	490	-8.8	455	469	3.1	992	959	-3.3
Charleston, SC	4,726	4,787	1.3	2,541	2,215	-12.8	7,267	7,002	-3.6
Charlotte, NC	15,247	16,407	7.6	7,622	9,802	28.6	22,869	26,209	14.6
Chicago, IL	8,416	8,546	1.5	13,716	9,135	-33.4	22,132	17,681	-20.1
Clarksville, TN	1,558	1,516	-2.7	255	287	12.5	1,813	1,803	-0.6
Cleveland, OH	2,749	2,733	-0.6	478	248	-48.1	3,227	2,981	-7.6
College Station, TX	1,155	1,023	-11.4	1,928	833	-56.8	3,083	1,856	-39.8
Colorado Springs, CO	3,852	4,229	9.8	1,113	1,505	35.2	4,965	5,734	15.5
Columbia, MO	769	555	-27.8	865	2	-99.8	1,634	557	-65.9
Columbia, SC	4,072	4,478	10.0	557	474	-14.9	4,629	4,952	7.0
Columbus, OH	4,295	4,493	4.6	4,597	4,947	7.6	8,892	9,440	6.2
Dallas, TX	34,604	36,832	6.4	27,920	27,061	-3.1	62,524	63,893	2.2
Davenport, IA	443	490	10.6	307	69	-77.5	750	559	-25.5
Denver, CO	10,978	11,808	7.6	11,757	9,921	-15.6	22,735	21,729	-4.4
Des Moines, IA	3,697	3,233	-12.6	2,670	1,690	-36.7	6,367	4,923	-22.7
Durham, NC	3,268	3,289	0.6	1,656	2,127	28.4	4,924	5,416	10.0
Edison, NJ	11,289	11,077	-1.9	39,289	38,615	-1.7	50,578	49,692	-1.8
El Paso, TX	2,373	1,751	-26.2	904	665	-26.4	3,277	2,416	-26.3
Fargo, ND	1,065	1,080	1.4	826	1,233	49.3	1,891	2,313	22.3
Fayetteville, NC	874	803	-8.1	61	16	-73.8	935	819	-12.4
Fort Collins, CO	2,027	1,679	-17.2	908	1,265	39.3	2,935	2,944	0.3
Fort Wayne, IN	1,222	1,343	9.9	500	541	8.2	1,722	1,884	9.4
Fort Worth, TX	34,604	36,832	6.4	27,920	27,061	-3.1	62,524	63,893	2.2
Grand Rapids, MI	2,953	2,749	-6.9	1,886	1,105	-41.4	4,839	3,854	-20.4
Greeley, CO	2,777	3,194	15.0	869	913	5.1	3,646	4,107	12.6
Green Bay, WI	828	766	-7.5	348	435	25.0	1,176	1,201	2.1
Greensboro, NC	2,012	1,949	-3.1	1,043	275	-73.6	3,055	2,224	-27.2
Honolulu, HI	1,028	983	-4.4	940	1,427	51.8	1,968	2,410	22.5
Houston, TX	36,348	40,321	10.9	6,047	16,967	180.6	42,395	57,288	35.1
Huntsville, AL	2,577	2,870	11.4	382	71	-81.4	2,959	2,941	-0.6
Indianapolis, IN	6,755	7,291	7.9	2,324	1,603	-31.0	9,079	8,894	-2.0
Jackson, MS	1,671	1,325	-20.7	72	16	-77.8	1,743	1,341	-23.1
Jacksonville, FL	9,833	10,755	9.4	3,126	4,695	50.2	12,959	15,450	19.2
Kansas City, MO	5,951	5,608	-5.8	3,900	4,660	19.5	9,851	10,268	4.2
Lafayette, LA	1,746	1,657	-5.1	25	30	20.0	1,771	1,687	-4.7
Lakeland, FL	4,542	5,331	17.4	62	0	-100.0	4,604	5,331	15.8
Las Vegas, NV	9,812	9,721	-0.9	4,261	2,323	-45.5	14,073	12,044	-14.4
Lexington, KY	1,602	1,404	-12.4	724	1,368	89.0	2,326	2,772	19.2
Lincoln, NE	1,271	1,117	-12.1	1,237	687	-44.5	2,508	1,804	-28.1
Little Rock, AR	2,087	1,819	-12.8	1,128	355	-68.5	3,215	2,174	-32.4
Los Angeles, CA	10,587	10,042	-5.1	20,497	19,482	-5.0	31,084	29,524	-5.0

Table continued on next page.

Metro Area	Single-Family			Multi-Family			Total		
	2017	2018	Pct. Chg.	2017	2018	Pct. Chg.	2017	2018	Pct. Chg.
Louisville, KY	3,446	3,104	-9.9	2,339	2,409	3.0	5,785	5,513	-4.7
Madison, WI	1,656	1,623	-2.0	2,976	2,029	-31.8	4,632	3,652	-21.2
Manchester, NH	717	709	-1.1	316	697	120.6	1,033	1,406	36.1
Miami, FL	6,655	7,022	5.5	13,068	12,531	-4.1	19,723	19,553	-0.9
Midland, TX	766	1,227	60.2	0	0	0.0	766	1,227	60.2
Milwaukee, WI	1,559	1,712	9.8	2,085	2,057	-1.3	3,644	3,769	3.4
Minneapolis, MN	8,782	8,985	2.3	6,318	9,221	45.9	15,100	18,206	20.6
Nashville, TN	13,650	13,470	-1.3	6,981	5,689	-18.5	20,631	19,159	-7.1
New Haven, CT	469	406	-13.4	281	760	170.5	750	1,166	55.5
New Orleans, LA	2,720	3,046	12.0	246	818	232.5	2,966	3,864	30.3
New York, NY	11,289	11,077	-1.9	39,289	38,615	-1.7	50,578	49,692	-1.8
Oklahoma City, OK	5,132	5,430	5.8	287	300	4.5	5,419	5,730	5.7
Omaha, NE	3,158	2,791	-11.6	1,797	1,997	11.1	4,955	4,788	-3.4
Orlando, FL	14,431	16,455	14.0	4,634	12,427	168.2	19,065	28,882	51.5
Peoria, IL	247	228	-7.7	10	106	960.0	257	334	30.0
Philadelphia, PA	7,233	6,875	-4.9	6,311	6,281	-0.5	13,544	13,156	-2.9
Phoenix, AZ	20,471	23,526	14.9	8,841	7,817	-11.6	29,312	31,343	6.9
Pittsburgh, PA	2,988	2,977	-0.4	1,340	1,060	-20.9	4,328	4,037	-6.7
Portland, OR	6,211	6,869	10.6	9,772	7,311	-25.2	15,983	14,180	-11.3
Providence, RI	1,722	1,553	-9.8	288	410	42.4	2,010	1,963	-2.3
Provo, UT	5,090	5,516	8.4	2,155	1,325	-38.5	7,245	6,841	-5.6
Raleigh, NC	10,752	11,160	3.8	3,428	4,790	39.7	14,180	15,950	12.5
Reno, NV	2,091	2,255	7.8	2,473	2,195	-11.2	4,564	4,450	-2.5
Richmond, VA	4,614	4,498	-2.5	2,531	1,563	-38.2	7,145	6,061	-15.2
Rochester, MN	818	690	-15.6	631	1,126	78.4	1,449	1,816	25.3
Sacramento, CA	6,815	6,393	-6.2	2,688	1,480	-44.9	9,503	7,873	-17.2
Salt Lake City, UT	4,918	5,391	9.6	2,449	3,359	37.2	7,367	8,750	18.8
San Antonio, TX	7,535	8,013	6.3	4,981	3,484	-30.1	12,516	11,497	-8.1
San Diego, CA	4,056	3,489	-14.0	6,385	6,345	-0.6	10,441	9,834	-5.8
San Francisco, CA	4,777	4,048	-15.3	12,175	13,373	9.8	16,952	17,421	2.8
San Jose, CA	2,592	2,466	-4.9	5,947	6,278	5.6	8,539	8,744	2.4
Santa Rosa, CA	840	3,169	277.3	338	110	-67.5	1,178	3,279	178.4
Savannah, GA	1,898	2,080	9.6	220	1,078	390.0	2,118	3,158	49.1
Seattle, WA	9,997	9,134	-8.6	17,337	19,052	9.9	27,334	28,186	3.1
Sioux Falls, SD	1,533	1,380	-10.0	1,381	1,008	-27.0	2,914	2,388	-18.1
Springfield, IL	210	193	-8.1	112	313	179.5	322	506	57.1
Tallahassee, FL	1,897	2,073	9.3	1,156	1,128	-2.4	3,053	3,201	4.8
Tampa, FL	12,732	14,228	11.7	5,536	3,224	-41.8	18,268	17,452	-4.5
Topeka, KS	327	330	0.9	8	26	225.0	335	356	6.3
Tucson, AZ	2,888	3,240	12.2	1,607	1,164	-27.6	4,495	4,404	-2.0
Tulsa, OK	3,160	2,845	-10.0	484	567	17.1	3,644	3,412	-6.4
Tuscaloosa, AL	572	578	1.0	597	469	-21.4	1,169	1,047	-10.4
Virginia Beach, VA	4,404	4,168	-5.4	1,778	1,436	-19.2	6,182	5,604	-9.3
Washington, DC	14,225	13,588	-4.5	13,040	12,169	-6.7	27,265	25,757	-5.5
Wichita, KS	1,634	1,223	-25.2	1,097	735	-33.0	2,731	1,958	-28.3
Winston-Salem, NC	2,784	3,123	12.2	981	376	-61.7	3,765	3,499	-7.1
U.S.	820,000	855,300	4.3	462,000	473,500	2.5	1,282,000	1,328,800	3.7

Note: Figures cover the Metropolitan Statistical Area—see Appendix B for areas included; Figures represent new, privately-owned housing units authorized (unadjusted data); All permit data are based on estimates with imputation
Source: U.S. Census Bureau, Manufacturing, Mining, and Construction Statistics, Building Permits, 2017, 2018

Housing Vacancy Rates

Metro Area[1]	Gross Vacancy Rate[2] (%)			Year-Round Vacancy Rate[3] (%)			Rental Vacancy Rate[4] (%)			Homeowner Vacancy Rate[5] (%)		
	2017	2018	2019	2017	2018	2019	2017	2018	2019	2017	2018	2019
Albany, NY	10.5	11.6	17.8	8.3	10.4	16.0	8.5	10.8	12.3	2.1	1.7	3.0
Albuquerque, NM	8.9	8.3	7.9	8.6	7.9	7.4	9.0	7.8	6.5	2.1	1.8	1.9
Allentown, PA	9.5	9.3	7.7	8.5	7.1	5.8	5.3	5.7	4.0	1.7	0.9	1.4
Anchorage, AK	n/a	n/a	n/a	n/a	n/a	n/a	n/a	n/a	n/a	n/a	n/a	n/a
Ann Arbor, MI	n/a	n/a	n/a	n/a	n/a	n/a	n/a	n/a	n/a	n/a	n/a	n/a
Athens, GA	n/a	n/a	n/a	n/a	n/a	n/a	n/a	n/a	n/a	n/a	n/a	n/a
Atlanta, GA	8.9	7.8	7.6	8.4	7.4	7.3	7.0	6.6	7.0	1.0	1.1	1.3
Austin, TX	10.4	9.7	10.7	9.3	8.7	10.3	6.1	7.0	8.2	2.0	1.2	1.8
Baton Rouge, LA	13.6	13.0	13.9	13.0	11.8	13.0	8.7	7.6	10.2	1.0	1.4	1.9
Boise City, ID	n/a	n/a	n/a	n/a	n/a	n/a	n/a	n/a	n/a	n/a	n/a	n/a
Boston, MA	7.6	7.5	7.1	6.5	6.5	6.2	4.8	3.8	3.6	0.6	1.0	0.8
Boulder, CO	n/a	n/a	n/a	n/a	n/a	n/a	n/a	n/a	n/a	n/a	n/a	n/a
Cape Coral, FL	39.1	41.5	40.0	20.2	16.6	17.9	4.3	5.8	8.5	2.9	3.0	2.3
Cedar Rapids, IA	n/a	n/a	n/a	n/a	n/a	n/a	n/a	n/a	n/a	n/a	n/a	n/a
Charleston, SC	16.5	16.0	18.4	16.1	14.5	16.6	17.9	17.0	16.7	1.6	3.4	2.2
Charlotte, NC	6.9	8.5	9.3	6.8	8.1	9.0	5.4	5.6	7.6	0.8	1.7	1.8
Chicago, IL	8.4	7.5	7.6	8.3	7.4	7.6	7.0	7.0	5.7	1.8	1.6	1.5
Clarksville, TN	n/a	n/a	n/a	n/a	n/a	n/a	n/a	n/a	n/a	n/a	n/a	n/a
Cleveland, OH	9.2	10.4	10.1	9.2	10.3	9.9	8.0	6.9	3.8	1.2	0.9	1.1
College Station, TX	n/a	n/a	n/a	n/a	n/a	n/a	n/a	n/a	n/a	n/a	n/a	n/a
Colorado Springs, CO	n/a	n/a	n/a	n/a	n/a	n/a	n/a	n/a	n/a	n/a	n/a	n/a
Columbia, MO	n/a	n/a	n/a	n/a	n/a	n/a	n/a	n/a	n/a	n/a	n/a	n/a
Columbia, SC	11.0	8.9	10.6	10.7	8.8	10.4	6.3	9.4	9.3	2.4	1.9	1.5
Columbus, OH	6.6	7.4	4.5	6.0	7.4	4.2	6.3	8.6	4.3	1.1	1.5	0.8
Dallas, TX	7.8	7.8	7.6	7.6	7.6	7.3	7.1	7.4	6.9	0.8	1.4	1.5
Davenport, IA	n/a	n/a	n/a	n/a	n/a	n/a	n/a	n/a	n/a	n/a	n/a	n/a
Denver, CO	7.8	8.0	7.5	6.9	7.4	7.0	5.9	3.8	4.7	0.7	0.9	1.0
Des Moines, IA	n/a	n/a	n/a	n/a	n/a	n/a	n/a	n/a	n/a	n/a	n/a	n/a
Durham, NC	n/a	n/a	n/a	n/a	n/a	n/a	n/a	n/a	n/a	n/a	n/a	n/a
Edison, NJ	10.7	10.3	9.2	9.6	9.1	7.8	4.6	4.5	4.3	1.9	1.6	1.4
El Paso, TX	n/a	n/a	n/a	n/a	n/a	n/a	n/a	n/a	n/a	n/a	n/a	n/a
Fargo, ND	n/a	n/a	n/a	n/a	n/a	n/a	n/a	n/a	n/a	n/a	n/a	n/a
Fayetteville, NC	n/a	n/a	n/a	n/a	n/a	n/a	n/a	n/a	n/a	n/a	n/a	n/a
Fort Collins, CO	n/a	n/a	n/a	n/a	n/a	n/a	n/a	n/a	n/a	n/a	n/a	n/a
Fort Wayne, IN	n/a	n/a	n/a	n/a	n/a	n/a	n/a	n/a	n/a	n/a	n/a	n/a
Fort Worth, TX	7.8	7.8	7.6	7.6	7.6	7.3	7.1	7.4	6.9	0.8	1.4	1.5
Grand Rapids, MI	8.5	8.9	7.4	6.3	6.8	5.1	4.0	6.8	4.5	1.1	0.3	0.5
Greeley, CO	n/a	n/a	n/a	n/a	n/a	n/a	n/a	n/a	n/a	n/a	n/a	n/a
Green Bay, WI	n/a	n/a	n/a	n/a	n/a	n/a	n/a	n/a	n/a	n/a	n/a	n/a
Greensboro, NC	10.2	11.6	9.9	9.6	11.5	9.5	10.2	11.4	8.1	1.2	1.0	0.7
Honolulu, HI	13.9	14.0	11.7	12.4	12.9	10.9	8.0	6.5	5.7	0.9	1.4	1.8
Houston, TX	9.3	8.8	9.8	8.9	8.2	9.1	9.9	8.8	11.4	1.5	2.0	1.9
Huntsville, AL	n/a	n/a	n/a	n/a	n/a	n/a	n/a	n/a	n/a	n/a	n/a	n/a
Indianapolis, IN	10.9	8.7	7.2	10.8	8.6	6.7	11.9	9.9	7.0	1.5	1.5	1.5
Jackson, MS	n/a	n/a	n/a	n/a	n/a	n/a	n/a	n/a	n/a	n/a	n/a	n/a
Jacksonville, FL	12.5	10.1	10.1	12.0	9.3	9.8	8.5	5.6	5.2	1.5	1.3	1.0
Kansas City, MO	8.1	7.8	8.9	7.9	7.7	8.7	9.4	7.9	10.0	0.8	1.2	1.4
Lafayette, LA	n/a	n/a	n/a	n/a	n/a	n/a	n/a	n/a	n/a	n/a	n/a	n/a
Lakeland, FL	n/a	n/a	n/a	n/a	n/a	n/a	n/a	n/a	n/a	n/a	n/a	n/a
Las Vegas, NV	12.6	11.4	10.2	11.0	10.4	9.5	7.0	6.8	5.5	2.4	0.9	2.0
Lexington, KY	n/a	n/a	n/a	n/a	n/a	n/a	n/a	n/a	n/a	n/a	n/a	n/a
Lincoln, NE	n/a	n/a	n/a	n/a	n/a	n/a	n/a	n/a	n/a	n/a	n/a	n/a
Little Rock, AR	10.3	10.5	9.9	10.0	10.2	9.6	11.3	10.9	11.4	2.0	1.8	1.7
Los Angeles, CA	6.3	6.6	6.3	5.9	6.2	5.8	4.1	4.0	4.0	0.9	1.2	1.1

Table continued on next page.

Metro Area[1]	Gross Vacancy Rate[2] (%)			Year-Round Vacancy Rate[3] (%)			Rental Vacancy Rate[4] (%)			Homeowner Vacancy Rate[5] (%)		
	2017	2018	2019	2017	2018	2019	2017	2018	2019	2017	2018	2019
Louisville, KY	7.3	7.6	7.9	7.2	7.4	7.8	7.8	7.7	10.6	0.6	1.4	0.7
Madison, WI	n/a	n/a	n/a	n/a	n/a	n/a	n/a	n/a	n/a	n/a	n/a	n/a
Manchester, NH	n/a	n/a	n/a	n/a	n/a	n/a	n/a	n/a	n/a	n/a	n/a	n/a
Miami, FL	17.8	14.9	14.1	9.2	7.9	7.4	7.0	7.4	7.0	1.9	1.9	1.8
Midland, TX	n/a	n/a	n/a	n/a	n/a	n/a	n/a	n/a	n/a	n/a	n/a	n/a
Milwaukee, WI	7.9	8.1	8.0	7.0	7.8	7.8	6.5	5.9	6.6	0.9	1.4	0.6
Minneapolis, MN	4.5	3.9	4.4	4.1	3.3	3.8	4.2	4.1	4.1	0.9	0.4	0.5
Nashville, TN	6.2	5.9	7.8	6.1	5.8	7.5	7.6	7.5	8.6	0.6	0.8	1.2
New Haven, CT	10.0	10.9	11.9	9.8	10.0	11.1	6.9	5.6	8.3	2.1	1.4	1.5
New Orleans, LA	12.8	11.9	12.9	12.2	11.8	12.8	10.8	9.7	9.4	2.5	1.7	1.8
New York, NY	10.7	10.3	9.2	9.6	9.1	7.8	4.6	4.5	4.3	1.9	1.6	1.4
Oklahoma City, OK	11.1	11.5	10.8	10.8	11.2	10.4	9.9	11.8	8.6	1.9	2.7	2.7
Omaha, NE	5.9	7.1	5.6	5.4	6.1	4.8	4.7	7.1	6.3	0.9	0.7	0.6
Orlando, FL	14.3	19.4	16.0	10.5	16.2	12.7	6.9	5.8	8.3	1.5	2.6	2.5
Peoria, IL	n/a	n/a	n/a	n/a	n/a	n/a	n/a	n/a	n/a	n/a	n/a	n/a
Philadelphia, PA	8.6	9.0	8.3	8.3	8.9	8.1	7.3	6.4	7.1	1.6	1.2	1.3
Phoenix, AZ	13.7	12.6	10.3	8.1	7.8	6.2	6.0	6.2	5.0	1.5	1.4	1.0
Pittsburgh, PA	13.6	10.2	10.6	13.4	9.9	10.3	9.7	6.3	7.3	2.2	2.2	1.2
Portland, OR	6.4	6.8	6.6	6.1	6.0	5.6	4.8	3.8	4.4	1.1	1.4	0.9
Providence, RI	11.3	10.3	9.8	8.1	8.5	8.2	4.2	5.0	4.2	1.2	1.1	0.9
Provo, UT	n/a	n/a	n/a	n/a	n/a	n/a	n/a	n/a	n/a	n/a	n/a	n/a
Raleigh, NC	8.0	6.7	6.6	7.8	6.6	6.5	5.8	6.4	7.0	1.7	0.9	0.8
Reno, NV	n/a	n/a	n/a	n/a	n/a	n/a	n/a	n/a	n/a	n/a	n/a	n/a
Richmond, VA	9.1	8.0	8.5	9.1	8.0	8.5	7.2	5.4	9.5	1.2	2.1	1.3
Rochester, MN	n/a	n/a	n/a	n/a	n/a	n/a	n/a	n/a	n/a	n/a	n/a	n/a
Sacramento, CA	7.5	8.6	7.8	6.0	7.9	7.1	4.2	5.1	4.2	1.0	1.5	0.8
Salt Lake City, UT	5.0	5.0	4.8	4.8	4.7	4.8	6.2	6.1	5.0	0.6	0.5	0.8
San Antonio, TX	9.9	6.7	9.0	8.8	5.8	8.2	11.5	7.4	10.1	1.8	0.6	2.0
San Diego, CA	6.4	7.6	7.5	6.0	7.4	7.3	3.9	4.5	5.8	0.6	0.7	0.8
San Francisco, CA	6.0	7.5	7.1	5.9	7.4	6.9	4.2	5.4	3.8	0.7	0.9	0.9
San Jose, CA	6.0	5.8	5.6	5.9	5.8	5.6	3.2	4.6	3.7	0.7	0.5	0.5
Santa Rosa, CA	n/a	n/a	n/a	n/a	n/a	n/a	n/a	n/a	n/a	n/a	n/a	n/a
Savannah, GA	n/a	n/a	n/a	n/a	n/a	n/a	n/a	n/a	n/a	n/a	n/a	n/a
Seattle, WA	6.0	5.9	5.5	5.4	5.4	5.2	3.4	4.8	4.4	0.5	0.8	1.0
Sioux Falls, SD	n/a	n/a	n/a	n/a	n/a	n/a	n/a	n/a	n/a	n/a	n/a	n/a
Springfield, IL	n/a	n/a	n/a	n/a	n/a	n/a	n/a	n/a	n/a	n/a	n/a	n/a
Tallahassee, FL	n/a	n/a	n/a	n/a	n/a	n/a	n/a	n/a	n/a	n/a	n/a	n/a
Tampa, FL	16.2	16.1	16.2	12.5	11.9	12.7	9.6	9.9	10.7	2.4	2.1	1.6
Topeka, KS	n/a	n/a	n/a	n/a	n/a	n/a	n/a	n/a	n/a	n/a	n/a	n/a
Tucson, AZ	13.8	12.5	14.8	9.2	8.1	9.2	6.9	4.4	7.3	1.1	1.8	1.5
Tulsa, OK	10.2	11.7	8.4	9.8	11.6	8.0	8.5	10.1	8.5	1.9	2.6	1.6
Tuscaloosa, AL	n/a	n/a	n/a	n/a	n/a	n/a	n/a	n/a	n/a	n/a	n/a	n/a
Virginia Beach, VA	9.4	8.9	10.4	8.9	7.6	9.3	8.2	7.1	7.1	2.5	1.2	2.2
Washington, DC	7.4	7.0	7.1	7.1	6.7	6.7	6.2	6.2	5.6	1.2	1.1	1.1
Wichita, KS	n/a	n/a	n/a	n/a	n/a	n/a	n/a	n/a	n/a	n/a	n/a	n/a
Winston-Salem, NC	n/a	n/a	n/a	n/a	n/a	n/a	n/a	n/a	n/a	n/a	n/a	n/a
U.S.	12.7	12.3	12.0	9.9	9.7	9.5	7.2	6.9	6.7	1.6	1.5	1.4

Note: (1) Metropolitan Statistical Area—see Appendix B for areas included; (2) The percentage of the total housing inventory that is vacant; (3) The percentage of the housing inventory (excluding seasonal units) that is year-round vacant; (4) The percentage of rental inventory that is vacant for rent; (5) The percentage of homeowner inventory that is vacant for sale; n/a not available
Source: U.S. Census Bureau, Housing Vacancies and Homeownership Annual Statistics: 2017, 2018, 2019

Bankruptcy Filings

City	Area Covered	Business Filings			Nonbusiness Filings		
		2018	2019	% Chg.	2018	2019	% Chg.
Albany, NY	Albany County	10	12	20.0	518	500	-3.5
Albuquerque, NM	Bernalillo County	44	30	-31.8	1,161	1,071	-7.8
Allentown, PA	Lehigh County	33	16	-51.5	624	599	-4.0
Anchorage, AK	Anchorage Borough	18	17	-5.6	194	176	-9.3
Ann Arbor, MI	Washtenaw County	12	10	-16.7	583	654	12.2
Athens, GA	Clarke County	8	0	-100.0	345	338	-2.0
Atlanta, GA	Fulton County	165	173	4.8	4,465	4,013	-10.1
Austin, TX	Travis County	96	118	22.9	717	737	2.8
Baton Rouge, LA	East Baton Rouge Parish	18	37	105.6	756	771	2.0
Boise City, ID	Ada County	28	26	-7.1	888	878	-1.1
Boston, MA	Suffolk County	39	47	20.5	587	530	-9.7
Boulder, CO	Boulder County	17	30	76.5	315	372	18.1
Cape Coral, FL	Lee County	63	57	-9.5	1,106	1,254	13.4
Cedar Rapids, IA	Linn County	8	11	37.5	351	365	4.0
Charleston, SC	Charleston County	13	19	46.2	379	356	-6.1
Charlotte, NC	Mecklenburg County	53	64	20.8	1,244	1,020	-18.0
Chicago, IL	Cook County	441	413	-6.3	27,072	27,789	2.6
Clarksville, TN	Montgomery County	11	11	0.0	845	829	-1.9
Cleveland, OH	Cuyahoga County	70	69	-1.4	5,847	6,013	2.8
College Station, TX	Brazos County	12	7	-41.7	71	105	47.9
Colorado Springs, CO	El Paso County	32	39	21.9	1,585	1,525	-3.8
Columbia, MO	Boone County	7	6	-14.3	368	375	1.9
Columbia, SC	Richland County	9	11	22.2	751	837	11.5
Columbus, OH	Franklin County	65	72	10.8	4,433	4,342	-2.1
Dallas, TX	Dallas County	437	355	-18.8	3,520	3,572	1.5
Davenport, IA	Scott County	20	10	-50.0	309	329	6.5
Denver, CO	Denver County	63	68	7.9	1,302	1,338	2.8
Des Moines, IA	Polk County	22	28	27.3	848	962	13.4
Durham, NC	Durham County	8	16	100.0	361	395	9.4
Edison, NJ	Middlesex County	38	46	21.1	1,803	1,718	-4.7
El Paso, TX	El Paso County	56	63	12.5	2,133	2,079	-2.5
Fargo, ND	Cass County	6	4	-33.3	187	198	5.9
Fayetteville, NC	Cumberland County	9	8	-11.1	808	795	-1.6
Fort Collins, CO	Larimer County	25	29	16.0	594	558	-6.1
Fort Wayne, IN	Allen County	16	15	-6.3	1,398	1,294	-7.4
Fort Worth, TX	Tarrant County	190	242	27.4	4,009	4,040	0.8
Grand Rapids, MI	Kent County	28	35	25.0	928	935	0.8
Greeley, CO	Weld County	21	20	-4.8	773	691	-10.6
Green Bay, WI	Brown County	5	25	400.0	575	599	4.2
Greensboro, NC	Guilford County	25	25	0.0	742	758	2.2
Honolulu, HI	Honolulu County	39	35	-10.3	1,075	1,225	14.0
Houston, TX	Harris County	485	411	-15.3	4,756	4,527	-4.8
Huntsville, AL	Madison County	35	20	-42.9	1,410	1,463	3.8
Indianapolis, IN	Marion County	57	100	75.4	4,546	4,465	-1.8
Jackson, MS	Hinds County	12	19	58.3	1,547	1,420	-8.2
Jacksonville, FL	Duval County	102	75	-26.5	2,226	2,349	5.5
Kansas City, MO	Jackson County	22	36	63.6	2,192	2,080	-5.1
Lafayette, LA	Lafayette Parish	32	44	37.5	589	560	-4.9
Lakeland, FL	Polk County	29	31	6.9	1,366	1,466	7.3
Las Vegas, NV	Clark County	238	228	-4.2	7,574	8,184	8.1
Lexington, KY	Fayette County	19	56	194.7	717	749	4.5
Lincoln, NE	Lancaster County	9	16	77.8	665	653	-1.8
Little Rock, AR	Pulaski County	24	233	870.8	2,420	2,318	-4.2
Los Angeles, CA	Los Angeles County	1,038	882	-15.0	18,024	18,304	1.6
Louisville, KY	Jefferson County	48	50	4.2	2,722	2,893	6.3

Table continued on next page.

City	Area Covered	Business Filings 2018	2019	% Chg.	Nonbusiness Filings 2018	2019	% Chg.
Madison, WI	Dane County	22	34	54.5	772	773	0.1
Manchester, NH	Hillsborough County	28	25	-10.7	547	519	-5.1
Miami, FL	Miami-Dade County	243	215	-11.5	8,119	8,490	4.6
Midland, TX	Midland County	15	32	113.3	68	72	5.9
Milwaukee, WI	Milwaukee County	35	43	22.9	6,116	6,315	3.3
Minneapolis, MN	Hennepin County	61	62	1.6	2,124	2,032	-4.3
Nashville, TN	Davidson County	53	53	0.0	2,050	2,051	0.0
New Haven, CT	New Haven County	58	47	-19.0	1,836	1,884	2.6
New Orleans, LA	Orleans Parish	128	36	-71.9	634	683	7.7
New York, NY	Bronx County	47	44	-6.4	2,459	2,486	1.1
New York, NY	Kings County	231	327	41.6	2,762	2,743	-0.7
New York, NY	New York County	305	244	-20.0	1,167	1,210	3.7
New York, NY	Queens County	237	206	-13.1	3,400	3,708	9.1
New York, NY	Richmond County	29	22	-24.1	790	835	5.7
Oklahoma City, OK	Oklahoma County	63	89	41.3	2,255	2,147	-4.8
Omaha, NE	Douglas County	23	39	69.6	1,189	1,283	7.9
Orlando, FL	Orange County	110	154	40.0	2,876	2,956	2.8
Peoria, IL	Peoria County	14	16	14.3	555	548	-1.3
Philadelphia, PA	Philadelphia County	79	88	11.4	2,408	2,222	-7.7
Phoenix, AZ	Maricopa County	338	344	1.8	10,573	11,095	4.9
Pittsburgh, PA	Allegheny County	146	140	-4.1	2,304	2,280	-1.0
Portland, OR	Multnomah County	39	62	59.0	1,397	1,394	-0.2
Providence, RI	Providence County	34	38	11.8	1,352	1,246	-7.8
Provo, UT	Utah County	41	37	-9.8	1,349	1,408	4.4
Raleigh, NC	Wake County	93	91	-2.2	1,403	1,314	-6.3
Reno, NV	Washoe County	40	34	-15.0	921	960	4.2
Richmond, VA	Richmond city	32	18	-43.8	884	897	1.5
Rochester, MN	Olmsted County	5	9	80.0	169	151	-10.7
Sacramento, CA	Sacramento County	84	95	13.1	3,332	3,208	-3.7
Salt Lake City, UT	Salt Lake County	63	56	-11.1	4,140	4,109	-0.7
San Antonio, TX	Bexar County	189	191	1.1	2,318	2,173	-6.3
San Diego, CA	San Diego County	305	308	1.0	7,335	7,366	0.4
San Francisco, CA	San Francisco County	60	58	-3.3	553	564	2.0
San Jose, CA	Santa Clara County	95	94	-1.1	1,672	1,446	-13.5
Santa Rosa, CA	Sonoma County	50	32	-36.0	470	531	13.0
Savannah, GA	Chatham County	8	18	125.0	1,263	1,220	-3.4
Seattle, WA	King County	130	115	-11.5	2,313	2,174	-6.0
Sioux Falls, SD	Minnehaha County	10	18	80.0	343	349	1.7
Springfield, IL	Sangamon County	8	8	0.0	472	436	-7.6
Tallahassee, FL	Leon County	28	35	25.0	404	446	10.4
Tampa, FL	Hillsborough County	111	155	39.6	3,057	3,356	9.8
Topeka, KS	Shawnee County	6	34	466.7	923	877	-5.0
Tucson, AZ	Pima County	45	50	11.1	2,367	2,438	3.0
Tulsa, OK	Tulsa County	52	44	-15.4	1,469	1,555	5.9
Tuscaloosa, AL	Tuscaloosa County	10	9	-10.0	1,230	1,246	1.3
Virginia Beach, VA	Virginia Beach city	19	18	-5.3	1,607	1,606	-0.1
Washington, DC	District of Columbia	61	50	-18.0	759	789	4.0
Wichita, KS	Sedgwick County	34	30	-11.8	1,399	1,381	-1.3
Winston-Salem, NC	Forsyth County	12	17	41.7	539	537	-0.4
U.S.	U.S.	22,232	22,780	2.5	751,186	752,160	0.1

Note: Business filings include Chapter 7, Chapter 9, Chapter 11, Chapter 12, Chapter 13, Chapter 15, and Section 304; Nonbusiness filings include Chapter 7, Chapter 11, and Chapter 13
Source: Administrative Office of the U.S. Courts, Business and Nonbusiness Bankruptcy, County Cases Commenced by Chapter of the Bankruptcy Code, During the 12-Month Period Ending December 31, 2018 and Business and Nonbusiness Bankruptcy, County Cases Commenced by Chapter of the Bankruptcy Code, During the 12-Month Period Ending December 31, 2019

Income: City

City	Per Capita ($)	Median Household ($)	Average Household ($)
Albany, NY	28,402	45,500	64,982
Albuquerque, NM	29,210	51,128	69,996
Allentown, PA	20,235	40,490	55,097
Anchorage, AK	39,839	83,280	106,840
Ann Arbor, MI	40,868	63,956	92,977
Athens, GA	22,498	36,637	56,917
Atlanta, GA	43,468	55,279	98,575
Austin, TX	40,391	67,462	97,331
Baton Rouge, LA	27,329	41,761	67,336
Boise City, ID	33,287	56,798	79,565
Boston, MA	42,010	65,883	101,310
Boulder, CO	42,203	66,117	102,803
Cape Coral, FL	28,746	57,125	72,768
Cedar Rapids, IA	32,625	59,152	76,644
Charleston, SC	40,511	64,599	93,367
Charlotte, NC	36,426	60,886	90,983
Chicago, IL	34,775	55,198	85,837
Clarksville, TN	24,329	53,007	63,775
Cleveland, OH	20,085	29,008	43,920
College Station, TX	26,053	42,964	69,839
Colorado Springs, CO	32,539	61,324	80,755
Columbia, MO	28,962	49,277	71,311
Columbia, SC	28,972	45,663	72,483
Columbus, OH	27,967	51,612	66,077
Dallas, TX	32,804	50,100	82,630
Davenport, IA	27,328	50,001	65,638
Denver, CO	41,196	63,793	93,650
Des Moines, IA	27,325	52,251	67,235
Durham, NC	32,932	55,851	79,045
Edison, NJ	42,869	98,687	121,081
El Paso, TX	21,927	45,656	62,132
Fargo, ND	33,985	53,309	76,065
Fayetteville, NC	24,336	44,057	57,910
Fort Collins, CO	32,440	62,132	82,777
Fort Wayne, IN	26,213	48,023	63,932
Fort Worth, TX	28,330	59,255	79,480
Grand Rapids, MI	24,852	47,173	62,979
Greeley, CO	25,200	55,007	69,675
Green Bay, WI	25,398	47,797	61,597
Greensboro, NC	28,502	46,702	68,483
Honolulu, HI	36,175	68,873	93,502
Houston, TX	31,576	51,140	81,995
Huntsville, AL	34,589	53,840	79,274
Indianapolis, IN	27,119	46,442	65,566
Jackson, MS	21,261	37,563	54,744
Jacksonville, FL	28,793	52,576	71,800
Kansas City, MO	31,143	52,405	72,418
Lafayette, LA	32,224	50,182	76,540
Lakeland, FL	26,225	44,313	63,287
Las Vegas, NV	29,304	54,694	76,483
Lexington, KY	32,965	54,918	79,535
Lincoln, NE	30,013	55,224	73,422
Little Rock, AR	34,546	49,957	80,455
Los Angeles, CA	33,420	58,385	91,608
Louisville, KY	29,681	51,307	71,647
Madison, WI	36,372	62,906	83,233

Table continued on next page.

City	Per Capita ($)	Median Household ($)	Average Household ($)
Manchester, NH	30,351	58,227	72,376
Miami, FL	27,078	36,638	64,540
Midland, TX	40,048	79,744	111,202
Milwaukee, WI	22,605	40,036	55,556
Minneapolis, MN	37,071	58,993	85,887
Nashville, TN	33,139	55,873	78,593
New Haven, CT	25,818	41,142	63,189
New Orleans, LA	30,177	39,576	69,101
New York, NY	37,693	60,762	97,647
Oklahoma City, OK	29,581	54,034	75,485
Omaha, NE	31,798	56,780	78,728
Orlando, FL	29,930	48,511	69,685
Peoria, IL	30,158	50,688	72,101
Philadelphia, PA	26,557	43,744	65,090
Phoenix, AZ	27,870	54,765	76,711
Pittsburgh, PA	31,972	45,831	69,219
Portland, OR	38,674	65,740	90,382
Providence, RI	25,435	42,158	68,769
Provo, UT	19,879	46,532	66,703
Raleigh, NC	36,875	63,891	90,550
Reno, NV	31,477	54,916	75,128
Richmond, VA	31,635	45,117	71,732
Rochester, MN	38,647	70,749	94,495
Sacramento, CA	30,487	58,456	79,490
Salt Lake City, UT	34,711	56,370	83,449
San Antonio, TX	25,091	50,980	68,838
San Diego, CA	39,066	75,456	103,655
San Francisco, CA	64,157	104,552	149,265
San Jose, CA	43,278	104,234	133,334
Santa Rosa, CA	34,902	71,347	91,292
Savannah, GA	24,153	41,093	60,305
Seattle, WA	55,789	85,562	119,707
Sioux Falls, SD	31,802	59,017	77,185
Springfield, IL	33,651	53,405	75,852
Tallahassee, FL	26,787	43,799	64,922
Tampa, FL	34,570	50,909	83,832
Topeka, KS	27,145	46,890	62,597
Tucson, AZ	22,645	41,625	55,689
Tulsa, OK	29,764	46,113	70,784
Tuscaloosa, AL	25,364	44,120	66,136
Virginia Beach, VA	36,268	74,186	93,675
Washington, DC	53,321	82,604	121,698
Wichita, KS	27,723	50,867	68,821
Winston-Salem, NC	28,083	44,311	69,340
U.S.	32,621	60,293	84,938

Source: U.S. Census Bureau, 2014-2018 American Community Survey 5-Year Estimates

Income: Metro Area

Metro Area	Per Capita ($)	Median Household ($)	Average Household ($)
Albany, NY	36,255	68,651	88,186
Albuquerque, NM	28,342	51,998	70,518
Allentown, PA	33,227	64,877	85,022
Anchorage, AK	37,536	81,745	103,249
Ann Arbor, MI	39,486	69,434	97,553
Athens, GA	26,301	45,246	67,981
Atlanta, GA	33,481	64,766	90,245
Austin, TX	37,759	73,213	99,668
Baton Rouge, LA	30,015	56,913	78,677
Boise City, ID	28,991	57,105	76,455
Boston, MA	45,416	85,508	116,910
Boulder, CO	43,831	78,642	109,446
Cape Coral, FL	31,924	54,691	77,846
Cedar Rapids, IA	33,729	64,218	81,984
Charleston, SC	33,331	60,884	83,989
Charlotte, NC	33,180	60,822	85,826
Chicago, IL	36,368	68,715	96,140
Clarksville, TN	24,922	51,933	65,418
Cleveland, OH	32,548	54,273	76,663
College Station, TX	26,622	48,213	70,196
Colorado Springs, CO	32,418	65,335	84,480
Columbia, MO	29,365	54,043	73,099
Columbia, SC	28,688	54,491	72,254
Columbus, OH	33,082	62,898	84,117
Dallas, TX	33,897	66,982	93,649
Davenport, IA	30,141	55,941	72,778
Denver, CO	39,969	75,565	101,397
Des Moines, IA	35,560	68,669	89,538
Durham, NC	35,830	60,113	88,542
Edison, NJ	41,127	75,086	110,942
El Paso, TX	20,731	44,531	60,579
Fargo, ND	34,793	62,832	83,829
Fayetteville, NC	23,797	45,958	59,942
Fort Collins, CO	35,390	67,664	88,703
Fort Wayne, IN	28,314	54,158	71,180
Fort Worth, TX	33,897	66,982	93,649
Grand Rapids, MI	30,277	61,225	80,148
Greeley, CO	30,626	70,908	85,911
Green Bay, WI	30,926	59,830	75,756
Greensboro, NC	27,920	48,776	69,063
Honolulu, HI	35,202	82,906	105,071
Houston, TX	33,460	65,381	94,902
Huntsville, AL	33,909	62,293	83,840
Indianapolis, IN	31,953	59,232	81,060
Jackson, MS	27,110	52,057	71,748
Jacksonville, FL	31,884	58,957	80,975
Kansas City, MO	34,444	64,020	86,106
Lafayette, LA	27,297	50,486	70,556
Lakeland, FL	23,812	48,500	63,849
Las Vegas, NV	29,256	56,802	76,812
Lexington, KY	31,827	56,385	78,770
Lincoln, NE	30,917	58,478	76,653
Little Rock, AR	29,397	53,008	73,205
Los Angeles, CA	34,168	69,138	99,888
Louisville, KY	31,216	56,638	77,190
Madison, WI	37,679	69,372	90,098

Table continued on next page.

Metro Area	Per Capita ($)	Median Household ($)	Average Household ($)
Manchester, NH	39,478	78,655	99,653
Miami, FL	30,951	54,239	82,686
Midland, TX	38,849	78,581	109,443
Milwaukee, WI	34,141	59,751	83,215
Minneapolis, MN	39,647	76,870	101,071
Nashville, TN	33,606	62,718	86,319
New Haven, CT	36,678	67,128	91,559
New Orleans, LA	30,294	51,449	74,946
New York, NY	41,127	75,086	110,942
Oklahoma City, OK	30,159	57,072	77,916
Omaha, NE	33,453	65,227	85,142
Orlando, FL	28,418	55,095	76,628
Peoria, IL	31,998	59,047	77,892
Philadelphia, PA	37,345	69,465	96,710
Phoenix, AZ	30,975	60,996	83,455
Pittsburgh, PA	34,613	58,290	79,597
Portland, OR	36,476	70,724	92,944
Providence, RI	34,483	64,248	85,657
Provo, UT	24,491	70,179	88,085
Raleigh, NC	36,518	72,297	96,027
Reno, NV	33,566	61,180	83,036
Richmond, VA	34,942	66,258	88,633
Rochester, MN	37,426	71,501	93,118
Sacramento, CA	33,862	68,662	91,671
Salt Lake City, UT	31,287	71,221	91,879
San Antonio, TX	28,092	58,201	79,011
San Diego, CA	36,156	74,855	101,302
San Francisco, CA	51,822	99,592	138,580
San Jose, CA	51,822	114,742	152,740
Santa Rosa, CA	39,929	76,753	102,483
Savannah, GA	30,552	57,470	78,586
Seattle, WA	43,190	82,189	109,154
Sioux Falls, SD	32,390	63,940	81,022
Springfield, IL	34,545	60,961	80,629
Tallahassee, FL	27,903	50,401	70,526
Tampa, FL	30,932	52,882	74,702
Topeka, KS	29,548	56,125	71,553
Tucson, AZ	28,480	51,037	70,610
Tulsa, OK	29,507	54,110	74,555
Tuscaloosa, AL	25,400	50,110	66,839
Virginia Beach, VA	32,613	64,534	83,283
Washington, DC	48,059	100,732	129,877
Wichita, KS	28,577	55,818	72,950
Winston-Salem, NC	28,007	48,936	68,827
U.S.	32,621	60,293	84,938

Note: Figures cover the Metropolitan Statistical Area (MSA)—see Appendix B for areas included
Source: U.S. Census Bureau, 2014-2018 American Community Survey 5-Year Estimates

Household Income Distribution: City

City	Under $15,000	$15,000 -$24,999	$25,000 -$34,999	$35,000 -$49,999	$50,000 -$74,999	$75,000 -$99,999	$100,000 -$149,999	$150,000 and up

City	Under $15,000	$15,000 -$24,999	$25,000 -$34,999	$35,000 -$49,999	$50,000 -$74,999	$75,000 -$99,999	$100,000 -$149,999	$150,000 and up
Albany, NY	18.1	12.8	9.9	12.9	16.4	10.5	10.7	8.8
Albuquerque, NM	13.8	11.2	10.6	13.5	17.3	11.7	13.0	9.0
Allentown, PA	17.4	13.0	13.5	14.5	20.1	9.7	7.5	4.2
Anchorage, AK	5.5	5.4	6.1	9.9	18.1	13.9	20.4	20.6
Ann Arbor, MI	14.4	7.9	7.8	10.2	15.7	11.1	15.2	17.9
Athens, GA	22.2	14.8	11.5	13.2	13.7	8.3	9.9	6.4
Atlanta, GA	16.3	9.8	8.7	11.4	15.1	9.7	12.3	16.7
Austin, TX	9.2	7.1	8.3	12.2	18.0	12.2	15.9	17.1
Baton Rouge, LA	18.7	12.9	12.4	12.9	15.1	8.6	10.4	9.0
Boise City, ID	11.4	10.3	9.2	13.4	18.1	12.0	14.2	11.4
Boston, MA	17.3	8.5	6.6	8.8	13.4	10.0	15.5	19.9
Boulder, CO	14.5	7.6	8.2	9.8	14.5	10.3	14.4	20.9
Cape Coral, FL	9.7	8.6	9.2	14.4	21.5	14.8	13.9	7.8
Cedar Rapids, IA	9.2	9.2	9.8	13.4	20.4	13.3	15.4	9.3
Charleston, SC	11.5	8.5	7.3	11.7	16.8	12.9	16.4	14.9
Charlotte, NC	9.4	8.6	9.7	13.5	17.9	12.3	14.0	14.6
Chicago, IL	14.7	10.7	9.0	11.5	15.6	11.0	13.2	14.3
Clarksville, TN	11.0	8.7	11.5	16.0	22.4	13.6	12.0	4.9
Cleveland, OH	28.9	15.7	12.7	13.5	14.0	6.9	5.5	3.0
College Station, TX	22.3	11.8	9.5	11.0	12.7	10.8	12.4	9.4
Colorado Springs, CO	9.6	8.7	9.0	13.2	19.2	13.3	15.5	11.6
Columbia, MO	15.9	10.7	10.2	13.7	15.3	11.5	13.1	9.5
Columbia, SC	17.9	11.6	11.1	12.3	16.6	10.4	9.7	10.4
Columbus, OH	13.3	10.0	10.6	14.7	19.2	12.9	13.0	6.3
Dallas, TX	12.8	11.1	11.4	14.7	17.6	10.1	10.2	12.2
Davenport, IA	12.5	11.0	11.8	14.7	19.9	12.1	11.1	6.8
Denver, CO	10.9	7.7	8.6	12.1	17.4	12.3	14.9	16.1
Des Moines, IA	13.0	10.6	10.3	14.1	20.3	13.3	12.0	6.4
Durham, NC	11.4	9.3	10.0	13.6	17.5	12.4	14.0	11.7
Edison, NJ	5.0	4.6	4.9	8.7	13.6	13.8	21.3	28.0
El Paso, TX	15.1	12.4	11.4	15.1	18.3	10.5	10.8	6.5
Fargo, ND	11.1	10.5	10.6	14.4	18.1	13.5	12.4	9.4
Fayetteville, NC	14.6	12.1	13.2	16.2	18.9	11.0	8.9	5.1
Fort Collins, CO	10.7	9.0	8.7	12.7	16.9	12.9	15.9	13.2
Fort Wayne, IN	12.6	11.9	12.0	15.3	20.0	12.3	10.1	5.9
Fort Worth, TX	11.1	8.7	9.6	12.7	18.7	13.2	14.9	11.2
Grand Rapids, MI	13.8	12.4	10.9	15.3	19.0	11.9	11.0	5.7
Greeley, CO	12.5	9.6	8.5	14.5	20.2	13.2	14.1	7.3
Green Bay, WI	12.3	11.7	12.6	16.0	19.5	13.0	10.3	4.5
Greensboro, NC	14.2	11.2	12.0	15.5	18.0	10.6	10.3	8.2
Honolulu, HI	10.4	7.2	7.2	11.9	17.7	12.9	16.5	16.3
Houston, TX	12.9	11.5	11.1	13.6	16.7	10.1	11.3	12.8
Huntsville, AL	14.8	10.5	9.6	12.5	15.8	10.6	13.3	13.0
Indianapolis, IN	14.3	11.7	11.8	15.4	18.2	10.8	10.6	7.4
Jackson, MS	18.9	15.0	12.8	15.7	15.9	8.7	8.1	4.7
Jacksonville, FL	12.0	9.9	10.7	15.0	18.9	12.9	12.4	8.2
Kansas City, MO	13.1	10.7	10.4	13.9	18.1	11.6	12.9	9.2
Lafayette, LA	15.4	11.5	10.9	12.1	17.2	10.1	10.6	12.3
Lakeland, FL	13.3	12.8	12.4	16.4	18.4	10.7	9.4	6.5
Las Vegas, NV	11.7	9.8	10.5	14.2	17.7	12.7	13.4	9.9
Lexington, KY	12.6	9.8	10.4	13.1	17.6	12.0	13.2	11.3
Lincoln, NE	9.9	9.9	10.8	14.4	19.2	12.5	15.0	8.4
Little Rock, AR	13.0	11.4	10.8	14.8	16.2	10.2	11.2	12.3
Los Angeles, CA	13.0	10.0	9.2	11.9	15.8	11.0	13.6	15.5

Table continued on next page.

City	Percent of Households Earning							
	Under $15,000	$15,000 -$24,999	$25,000 -$34,999	$35,000 -$49,999	$50,000 -$74,999	$75,000 -$99,999	$100,000 -$149,999	$150,000 and up
Louisville, KY	13.3	11.0	10.3	14.3	17.9	11.7	12.2	9.3
Madison, WI	11.0	8.1	8.7	12.7	18.0	13.3	15.8	12.4
Manchester, NH	10.3	9.2	10.3	12.4	20.8	13.3	15.3	8.3
Miami, FL	21.8	15.0	11.6	12.8	14.1	8.2	7.8	8.7
Midland, TX	6.4	6.3	7.4	10.3	16.6	14.2	18.5	20.2
Milwaukee, WI	19.0	13.4	12.2	14.6	17.3	10.2	9.0	4.3
Minneapolis, MN	14.2	9.0	8.6	11.9	16.3	11.5	14.3	14.3
Nashville, TN	10.8	9.2	10.0	14.4	19.1	12.8	13.2	10.6
New Haven, CT	21.2	11.3	11.6	12.8	16.1	9.6	8.5	8.9
New Orleans, LA	22.7	12.7	10.7	12.0	13.8	8.7	9.4	10.1
New York, NY	15.0	9.4	8.2	10.5	14.7	11.0	14.0	17.2
Oklahoma City, OK	11.6	9.7	10.8	14.3	18.2	12.3	12.9	10.2
Omaha, NE	11.2	9.3	9.3	14.3	18.5	12.9	13.7	10.8
Orlando, FL	13.8	11.1	12.4	14.2	19.7	9.9	10.0	9.0
Peoria, IL	16.6	11.5	9.5	11.9	17.8	11.3	11.6	9.7
Philadelphia, PA	19.7	11.8	10.6	12.9	16.0	9.9	10.7	8.3
Phoenix, AZ	11.5	9.7	10.0	14.5	18.6	11.8	13.0	10.8
Pittsburgh, PA	18.5	12.1	10.5	11.7	16.3	10.6	10.9	9.3
Portland, OR	11.5	8.1	8.3	11.2	16.6	12.8	16.1	15.4
Providence, RI	21.4	11.9	9.5	12.2	17.0	9.6	9.4	9.1
Provo, UT	12.6	13.3	13.0	14.0	19.5	9.9	10.4	7.4
Raleigh, NC	8.2	7.6	9.3	13.7	18.6	13.1	15.2	14.4
Reno, NV	10.1	10.1	10.7	14.7	18.9	12.2	13.4	9.8
Richmond, VA	18.6	10.9	10.8	13.8	16.0	10.1	10.1	9.8
Rochester, MN	8.4	7.2	7.5	11.8	17.7	14.2	17.5	15.6
Sacramento, CA	12.6	9.4	8.8	12.3	17.8	12.5	14.6	12.0
Salt Lake City, UT	12.8	8.8	10.1	13.1	17.9	11.5	13.7	12.0
San Antonio, TX	13.5	10.8	10.9	14.0	18.8	11.7	12.2	8.2
San Diego, CA	8.5	7.0	7.2	10.7	16.3	12.7	17.3	20.2
San Francisco, CA	10.4	6.2	5.1	6.6	10.5	9.4	16.3	35.4
San Jose, CA	6.7	5.1	5.0	7.7	12.7	10.9	18.8	33.1
Santa Rosa, CA	8.0	7.2	7.6	11.1	18.5	14.9	17.2	15.6
Savannah, GA	18.2	13.0	11.6	15.4	16.3	10.6	9.0	5.8
Seattle, WA	9.3	5.7	6.0	9.2	14.4	11.6	17.8	26.0
Sioux Falls, SD	9.8	8.4	10.7	13.9	18.6	14.3	14.6	9.7
Springfield, IL	14.4	11.7	9.2	12.1	17.6	12.4	12.2	10.4
Tallahassee, FL	17.3	11.4	11.9	14.9	15.2	10.4	10.7	8.2
Tampa, FL	15.3	10.9	10.2	12.9	15.6	10.1	11.7	13.3
Topeka, KS	12.8	12.0	12.2	16.1	18.5	12.4	10.9	5.0
Tucson, AZ	16.9	13.8	11.9	15.7	17.5	10.5	8.9	4.8
Tulsa, OK	14.7	11.8	11.5	15.7	17.8	9.7	9.6	9.2
Tuscaloosa, AL	19.6	11.7	10.7	12.8	17.0	9.6	9.6	9.1
Virginia Beach, VA	5.7	5.9	7.2	12.3	19.5	15.7	19.5	14.2
Washington, DC	13.7	6.3	6.4	7.8	12.4	10.8	16.3	26.3
Wichita, KS	13.0	10.6	11.0	14.7	19.0	11.5	12.1	8.1
Winston-Salem, NC	16.0	12.0	11.9	14.8	16.9	10.5	9.4	8.4
U.S.	10.9	9.3	9.3	12.6	17.5	12.5	14.6	13.3

Source: U.S. Census Bureau, 2014-2018 American Community Survey 5-Year Estimates

Household Income Distribution: Metro Area

Metro Area	Percent of Households Earning							
	Under $15,000	$15,000 -$24,999	$25,000 -$34,999	$35,000 -$49,999	$50,000 -$74,999	$75,000 -$99,999	$100,000 -$149,999	$150,000 and up
Albany, NY	8.8	8.1	8.2	11.8	17.3	13.8	17.8	14.3
Albuquerque, NM	13.2	11.1	10.3	13.8	17.8	12.0	12.7	9.1
Allentown, PA	8.3	8.8	8.8	12.5	18.5	13.7	16.5	12.8
Anchorage, AK	6.2	5.9	6.3	10.1	17.6	13.9	20.5	19.6
Ann Arbor, MI	10.6	7.5	7.4	11.3	16.5	11.8	16.7	18.2
Athens, GA	17.1	12.4	10.8	13.4	15.1	10.0	12.4	8.8
Atlanta, GA	9.1	8.2	8.7	12.7	18.0	13.0	15.5	14.9
Austin, TX	7.8	6.5	7.7	11.4	17.8	13.2	17.7	17.9
Baton Rouge, LA	12.8	10.0	9.7	12.2	16.6	11.6	15.1	12.0
Boise City, ID	10.6	9.4	9.5	14.0	20.0	12.8	14.3	9.4
Boston, MA	9.2	6.6	6.2	8.7	14.1	11.8	18.5	25.0
Boulder, CO	9.2	6.2	7.4	10.3	15.1	12.2	16.8	22.9
Cape Coral, FL	10.4	9.7	10.7	14.4	19.9	12.3	12.6	9.9
Cedar Rapids, IA	8.0	8.5	9.0	13.1	19.3	14.4	16.6	11.2
Charleston, SC	10.6	8.7	9.1	12.3	18.8	13.3	14.9	12.2
Charlotte, NC	9.6	8.9	9.5	13.2	18.2	12.8	14.5	13.2
Chicago, IL	9.8	8.2	8.0	11.2	16.5	12.7	16.5	17.1
Clarksville, TN	11.8	9.8	11.1	15.8	20.8	12.9	12.0	5.9
Cleveland, OH	13.1	10.2	9.9	13.3	17.4	12.2	13.5	10.4
College Station, TX	16.9	11.1	10.4	13.2	15.7	11.6	12.2	9.0
Colorado Springs, CO	8.3	7.8	8.5	12.5	19.5	13.8	16.9	12.7
Columbia, MO	13.2	9.8	10.2	13.7	17.3	12.6	14.0	9.4
Columbia, SC	12.5	9.3	10.5	13.6	19.3	13.1	13.1	8.7
Columbus, OH	9.9	8.5	9.0	12.8	18.1	13.4	16.0	12.4
Dallas, TX	8.3	7.7	8.7	12.4	18.0	12.8	16.2	15.9
Davenport, IA	10.6	9.8	10.2	13.7	19.5	13.4	14.2	8.5
Denver, CO	7.3	6.2	7.3	11.4	17.5	13.7	18.4	18.3
Des Moines, IA	7.8	7.4	8.2	12.1	18.9	14.6	17.3	13.7
Durham, NC	10.5	9.4	9.3	12.8	17.0	12.2	14.2	14.7
Edison, NJ	10.9	7.9	7.3	9.7	14.3	11.4	16.3	22.3
El Paso, TX	15.4	12.6	11.8	15.3	18.3	10.4	10.4	5.9
Fargo, ND	9.5	8.9	8.9	12.6	18.4	15.1	15.2	11.4
Fayetteville, NC	14.3	11.5	12.6	15.9	18.5	11.8	10.4	5.3
Fort Collins, CO	8.4	8.2	8.3	12.4	17.4	14.1	17.1	14.2
Fort Wayne, IN	10.2	10.3	10.9	14.7	20.5	13.7	12.5	7.4
Fort Worth, TX	8.3	7.7	8.7	12.4	18.0	12.8	16.2	15.9
Grand Rapids, MI	8.1	9.3	9.3	13.7	20.2	14.2	15.2	10.0
Greeley, CO	8.0	6.9	7.7	11.9	18.5	16.4	18.0	12.6
Green Bay, WI	8.6	9.0	10.1	13.9	19.6	15.0	15.1	8.7
Greensboro, NC	13.0	11.2	11.7	15.1	18.1	11.4	11.5	8.0
Honolulu, HI	7.4	5.4	6.1	9.9	16.5	14.0	20.2	20.7
Houston, TX	9.2	8.5	8.9	11.9	17.1	12.1	15.5	16.8
Huntsville, AL	11.3	9.3	8.9	12.0	16.5	12.5	15.4	14.1
Indianapolis, IN	10.1	9.2	9.7	13.5	18.3	13.0	14.8	11.5
Jackson, MS	13.3	10.7	10.3	14.0	17.6	12.0	12.9	9.1
Jacksonville, FL	10.3	8.7	9.8	13.9	18.8	13.2	14.2	11.2
Kansas City, MO	8.9	8.2	9.0	13.0	18.2	13.6	16.1	12.9
Lafayette, LA	14.3	11.6	10.8	12.9	16.7	11.5	13.0	9.2
Lakeland, FL	11.8	11.4	11.6	16.7	19.7	11.9	10.8	6.1
Las Vegas, NV	10.4	9.2	10.4	14.2	19.0	13.2	13.8	9.8
Lexington, KY	11.9	9.6	10.2	13.1	18.1	12.7	13.7	10.8
Lincoln, NE	9.2	9.4	10.3	13.9	19.0	13.0	16.0	9.3
Little Rock, AR	12.2	10.2	10.7	14.4	18.0	12.0	13.5	9.1
Los Angeles, CA	10.0	8.3	8.0	11.1	15.9	12.2	15.9	18.5

Table continued on next page.

Metro Area	Percent of Households Earning							
	Under $15,000	$15,000 -$24,999	$25,000 -$34,999	$35,000 -$49,999	$50,000 -$74,999	$75,000 -$99,999	$100,000 -$149,999	$150,000 and up
Louisville, KY	10.8	9.8	9.7	14.0	18.7	12.8	13.8	10.4
Madison, WI	7.8	7.3	8.3	12.4	18.0	14.3	17.7	14.1
Manchester, NH	6.5	6.9	7.5	10.5	16.3	14.1	19.4	18.9
Miami, FL	12.5	10.5	10.1	13.3	17.3	11.3	12.7	12.3
Midland, TX	6.4	6.6	7.7	10.5	16.7	13.7	18.5	20.0
Milwaukee, WI	11.0	9.6	9.1	12.8	17.4	12.8	15.3	12.1
Minneapolis, MN	7.1	6.6	7.2	11.0	17.0	14.0	19.0	18.2
Nashville, TN	8.9	8.1	9.2	13.6	18.9	13.7	15.2	12.5
New Haven, CT	10.3	8.2	8.0	11.7	16.7	12.1	16.4	16.7
New Orleans, LA	15.1	11.0	10.1	12.6	16.4	11.3	12.7	10.8
New York, NY	10.9	7.9	7.3	9.7	14.3	11.4	16.3	22.3
Oklahoma City, OK	10.6	9.4	10.2	13.9	18.9	13.0	13.6	10.4
Omaha, NE	8.9	7.9	8.5	13.0	18.5	14.0	16.9	12.5
Orlando, FL	10.5	9.9	10.6	14.4	19.1	12.4	12.9	10.3
Peoria, IL	10.2	9.2	9.2	13.4	19.6	13.6	14.8	10.1
Philadelphia, PA	10.5	8.1	7.9	10.8	15.9	12.4	16.5	18.0
Phoenix, AZ	9.8	8.5	9.2	13.4	18.8	13.0	15.0	12.4
Pittsburgh, PA	11.1	10.2	9.7	12.5	17.7	12.8	14.9	11.2
Portland, OR	8.3	7.3	8.0	11.6	17.7	13.9	17.7	15.6
Providence, RI	11.8	9.1	8.2	11.2	16.4	12.7	16.6	14.0
Provo, UT	6.5	6.6	7.9	12.5	20.2	15.5	18.5	12.2
Raleigh, NC	7.0	6.9	8.0	12.1	17.6	13.6	17.7	17.0
Reno, NV	8.8	8.9	9.1	13.9	19.3	13.2	15.0	11.8
Richmond, VA	9.4	7.5	8.2	12.7	17.7	13.6	16.8	14.0
Rochester, MN	7.4	7.0	7.8	11.7	18.5	14.4	18.7	14.4
Sacramento, CA	10.0	8.0	8.1	11.0	16.9	12.9	16.8	16.4
Salt Lake City, UT	7.0	6.3	7.8	12.1	19.8	14.9	18.3	13.8
San Antonio, TX	11.0	9.2	9.7	13.0	18.7	12.9	14.5	11.0
San Diego, CA	8.1	7.0	7.5	11.0	16.5	13.0	17.7	19.3
San Francisco, CA	7.6	5.6	5.5	7.8	12.5	11.1	17.9	32.0
San Jose, CA	6.0	4.6	4.7	7.1	11.4	10.4	18.1	37.8
Santa Rosa, CA	7.5	6.9	7.2	10.3	17.0	14.4	17.5	19.3
Savannah, GA	11.1	9.7	9.6	13.5	17.9	13.5	14.4	10.4
Seattle, WA	7.2	5.7	6.4	10.1	16.3	13.5	19.1	21.6
Sioux Falls, SD	8.3	7.7	10.0	13.0	18.9	15.6	16.3	10.1
Springfield, IL	11.1	9.8	8.7	11.8	18.0	14.0	15.0	11.7
Tallahassee, FL	14.0	10.2	10.9	14.6	16.7	12.3	12.3	9.1
Tampa, FL	11.6	10.7	10.7	14.5	18.0	12.0	12.5	9.9
Topeka, KS	9.8	10.0	10.4	14.6	19.4	14.5	14.3	7.0
Tucson, AZ	12.7	11.2	10.6	14.6	18.4	11.8	11.8	8.9
Tulsa, OK	11.4	10.3	10.3	14.4	18.6	12.4	12.9	9.6
Tuscaloosa, AL	16.2	10.8	10.0	13.0	17.8	12.3	12.4	7.7
Virginia Beach, VA	9.2	8.0	8.4	12.7	19.1	14.2	16.7	11.8
Washington, DC	6.0	4.3	5.0	7.8	13.9	12.6	20.2	30.2
Wichita, KS	11.0	9.7	10.1	14.3	19.4	12.7	14.0	8.7
Winston-Salem, NC	12.9	11.5	11.2	15.2	18.0	12.4	11.1	7.6
U.S.	10.9	9.3	9.3	12.6	17.5	12.5	14.6	13.3

Note: Figures cover the Metropolitan Statistical Area (MSA)—see Appendix B for areas included
Source: Source: U.S. Census Bureau, 2014-2018 American Community Survey 5-Year Estimates

Poverty Rate: City

City	All Ages	Under 18 Years Old	18 to 64 Years Old	65 Years and Over
Albany, NY	23.8	32.7	24.0	10.0
Albuquerque, NM	17.6	24.7	16.8	10.0
Allentown, PA	26.2	36.7	23.5	15.8
Anchorage, AK	9.2	14.0	8.0	4.7
Ann Arbor, MI	22.6	11.3	27.4	7.7
Athens, GA	31.6	34.8	34.0	10.7
Atlanta, GA	21.6	34.3	19.0	16.1
Austin, TX	14.5	20.0	13.4	9.5
Baton Rouge, LA	25.2	34.9	24.7	11.9
Boise City, ID	13.5	15.1	13.4	11.1
Boston, MA	20.2	29.4	17.9	20.5
Boulder, CO	21.3	8.9	25.8	6.6
Cape Coral, FL	11.6	14.7	11.6	9.2
Cedar Rapids, IA	11.6	15.1	11.7	5.9
Charleston, SC	14.3	17.0	15.1	7.2
Charlotte, NC	14.0	20.4	12.4	8.6
Chicago, IL	19.5	28.9	17.2	15.6
Clarksville, TN	14.7	18.3	14.1	7.8
Cleveland, OH	34.6	50.9	31.7	20.8
College Station, TX	30.8	15.8	36.8	7.1
Colorado Springs, CO	12.6	17.5	11.9	7.3
Columbia, MO	22.2	15.6	26.7	4.3
Columbia, SC	22.5	29.2	22.2	12.5
Columbus, OH	20.4	30.3	18.3	11.6
Dallas, TX	20.5	32.1	17.0	14.2
Davenport, IA	16.6	23.7	15.7	8.6
Denver, CO	13.8	19.9	12.4	11.0
Des Moines, IA	17.2	25.4	15.3	10.4
Durham, NC	16.8	25.5	15.3	8.2
Edison, NJ	5.3	5.4	4.9	6.7
El Paso, TX	20.0	28.3	16.7	18.3
Fargo, ND	13.0	12.2	14.1	8.0
Fayetteville, NC	19.2	28.9	17.1	10.7
Fort Collins, CO	16.8	10.8	19.9	7.7
Fort Wayne, IN	17.3	26.7	15.4	7.3
Fort Worth, TX	16.0	22.3	13.9	11.5
Grand Rapids, MI	21.2	29.7	20.2	10.0
Greeley, CO	17.1	20.2	17.2	10.2
Green Bay, WI	16.0	22.7	14.6	9.6
Greensboro, NC	18.5	26.1	17.7	10.1
Honolulu, HI	11.3	13.4	10.8	10.9
Houston, TX	20.6	32.4	17.0	13.8
Huntsville, AL	17.7	27.4	16.7	8.7
Indianapolis, IN	19.1	28.7	17.1	9.8
Jackson, MS	26.9	41.7	23.2	13.8
Jacksonville, FL	15.9	24.1	14.0	10.6
Kansas City, MO	16.5	24.8	14.9	9.5
Lafayette, LA	19.4	26.5	18.9	10.6
Lakeland, FL	17.0	24.2	16.1	12.6
Las Vegas, NV	15.8	22.7	14.4	10.1
Lexington, KY	17.8	22.0	18.4	7.3
Lincoln, NE	14.2	15.8	15.4	6.1
Little Rock, AR	17.4	25.7	15.8	10.0
Los Angeles, CA	19.1	27.3	17.0	15.8
Louisville, KY	16.6	25.0	15.2	9.3

Table continued on next page.

City	All Ages	Under 18 Years Old	18 to 64 Years Old	65 Years and Over
Madison, WI	17.9	15.6	20.4	5.7
Manchester, NH	14.8	21.9	13.8	8.6
Miami, FL	24.3	33.0	20.5	30.4
Midland, TX	8.6	10.2	7.7	9.7
Milwaukee, WI	26.6	38.4	23.7	14.2
Minneapolis, MN	19.9	26.4	19.0	13.2
Nashville, TN	16.5	27.3	14.4	9.0
New Haven, CT	25.9	33.4	24.7	15.8
New Orleans, LA	24.6	36.6	22.2	17.7
New York, NY	18.9	26.8	16.5	18.3
Oklahoma City, OK	16.8	25.2	14.8	8.3
Omaha, NE	14.3	19.9	13.2	8.2
Orlando, FL	18.2	25.2	16.6	15.3
Peoria, IL	20.7	26.3	20.7	11.2
Philadelphia, PA	24.9	35.6	22.7	17.2
Phoenix, AZ	19.4	28.7	16.9	11.2
Pittsburgh, PA	21.4	29.4	21.4	12.6
Portland, OR	14.9	17.3	14.9	11.2
Providence, RI	26.0	34.3	23.9	20.1
Provo, UT	25.9	17.9	30.3	7.3
Raleigh, NC	13.7	19.4	12.9	6.9
Reno, NV	14.4	17.4	14.8	8.4
Richmond, VA	24.5	40.1	22.4	13.5
Rochester, MN	10.3	13.3	10.4	4.9
Sacramento, CA	18.3	24.6	17.1	12.6
Salt Lake City, UT	17.9	22.5	17.7	10.3
San Antonio, TX	18.6	27.2	16.2	12.6
San Diego, CA	13.8	17.6	13.5	9.6
San Francisco, CA	10.9	10.7	10.4	13.1
San Jose, CA	9.1	9.9	8.7	9.8
Santa Rosa, CA	11.5	16.0	11.0	7.6
Savannah, GA	22.9	32.8	22.0	11.4
Seattle, WA	11.8	12.3	11.8	11.0
Sioux Falls, SD	11.3	14.3	10.6	8.7
Springfield, IL	19.6	32.2	18.4	7.7
Tallahassee, FL	26.7	24.0	29.9	9.1
Tampa, FL	19.5	27.5	17.2	16.8
Topeka, KS	15.9	19.7	16.4	8.8
Tucson, AZ	23.4	31.4	23.0	13.1
Tulsa, OK	19.7	30.4	17.8	8.6
Tuscaloosa, AL	24.2	27.1	26.2	9.5
Virginia Beach, VA	7.6	10.6	7.2	4.9
Washington, DC	16.8	24.8	15.1	14.5
Wichita, KS	16.2	22.1	15.3	9.1
Winston-Salem, NC	21.7	32.5	20.0	10.2
U.S.	14.1	19.5	13.2	9.3

Note: Figures are percentage of people whose income during the past 12 months was below the poverty level;
Source: U.S. Census Bureau, 2014-2018 American Community Survey 5-Year Estimates

Poverty Rate: Metro Area

Metro Area	All Ages	Under 18 Years Old	18 to 64 Years Old	65 Years and Over
Albany, NY	10.4	14.3	10.3	6.0
Albuquerque, NM	17.2	23.8	16.5	10.6
Allentown, PA	10.7	16.5	9.8	6.8
Anchorage, AK	9.5	13.4	8.6	5.5
Ann Arbor, MI	14.2	12.2	16.3	6.4
Athens, GA	23.2	26.1	25.1	8.7
Atlanta, GA	13.1	18.8	11.5	8.8
Austin, TX	11.6	14.5	11.2	7.3
Baton Rouge, LA	16.1	21.8	15.2	9.9
Boise City, ID	12.6	14.9	12.3	9.7
Boston, MA	9.8	12.1	9.3	9.0
Boulder, CO	12.5	10.1	14.4	6.2
Cape Coral, FL	14.0	23.4	13.9	8.0
Cedar Rapids, IA	9.5	12.2	9.4	5.9
Charleston, SC	13.5	20.1	12.3	8.2
Charlotte, NC	12.7	18.1	11.5	8.2
Chicago, IL	12.5	17.6	11.3	9.2
Clarksville, TN	15.0	19.2	14.2	8.8
Cleveland, OH	14.8	21.7	14.0	8.9
College Station, TX	23.2	20.5	26.3	9.4
Colorado Springs, CO	10.8	14.4	10.3	6.7
Columbia, MO	18.3	15.8	21.2	5.8
Columbia, SC	15.2	20.5	14.7	8.9
Columbus, OH	13.7	19.2	12.7	7.8
Dallas, TX	12.6	18.2	11.0	8.4
Davenport, IA	13.1	19.3	12.0	8.1
Denver, CO	9.4	12.4	8.9	7.0
Des Moines, IA	10.0	13.1	9.4	6.6
Durham, NC	14.9	20.7	14.7	7.3
Edison, NJ	13.4	18.6	11.9	11.8
El Paso, TX	21.3	30.1	17.6	19.5
Fargo, ND	10.9	11.0	11.7	6.6
Fayetteville, NC	18.6	26.3	16.8	10.8
Fort Collins, CO	12.0	10.1	13.9	6.3
Fort Wayne, IN	13.6	20.8	12.2	6.5
Fort Worth, TX	12.6	18.2	11.0	8.4
Grand Rapids, MI	11.5	14.5	11.3	6.8
Greeley, CO	10.6	12.7	10.1	8.3
Green Bay, WI	10.1	13.6	9.3	7.7
Greensboro, NC	16.2	23.8	15.1	9.4
Honolulu, HI	8.7	10.7	8.3	7.8
Houston, TX	14.2	20.7	12.1	10.1
Huntsville, AL	13.3	19.2	12.3	8.5
Indianapolis, IN	13.2	18.9	12.2	7.0
Jackson, MS	17.1	24.7	15.5	10.9
Jacksonville, FL	13.3	19.2	12.4	8.6
Kansas City, MO	11.0	15.6	10.0	6.8
Lafayette, LA	18.5	25.3	16.8	13.3
Lakeland, FL	16.6	26.0	15.2	10.0
Las Vegas, NV	14.1	20.2	13.1	8.9
Lexington, KY	16.8	22.5	16.8	7.4
Lincoln, NE	12.8	14.0	14.0	5.5
Little Rock, AR	15.1	20.7	14.3	9.2
Los Angeles, CA	14.9	20.7	13.4	12.3
Louisville, KY	13.1	18.9	12.2	8.0

Table continued on next page.

Metro Area	All Ages	Under 18 Years Old	18 to 64 Years Old	65 Years and Over
Madison, WI	11.2	10.9	12.4	5.6
Manchester, NH	8.1	10.3	7.9	5.8
Miami, FL	15.4	21.3	13.5	14.9
Midland, TX	9.1	12.2	7.7	9.0
Milwaukee, WI	14.0	20.3	12.9	8.4
Minneapolis, MN	9.0	11.7	8.5	6.6
Nashville, TN	12.4	17.5	11.4	7.8
New Haven, CT	11.9	17.0	11.3	7.6
New Orleans, LA	17.5	25.8	15.8	12.4
New York, NY	13.4	18.6	11.9	11.8
Oklahoma City, OK	14.4	20.2	13.7	7.1
Omaha, NE	10.6	14.0	10.0	6.8
Orlando, FL	14.7	21.0	13.6	10.1
Peoria, IL	12.4	16.6	12.3	6.9
Philadelphia, PA	12.6	17.4	11.9	8.5
Phoenix, AZ	14.7	21.0	13.7	8.3
Pittsburgh, PA	11.5	15.6	11.3	7.9
Portland, OR	11.4	14.2	11.3	7.8
Providence, RI	12.5	17.6	11.6	9.9
Provo, UT	11.2	9.9	12.7	5.6
Raleigh, NC	10.5	14.4	9.7	6.6
Reno, NV	12.1	15.4	12.1	7.7
Richmond, VA	11.8	17.1	11.0	7.3
Rochester, MN	8.5	10.8	8.3	5.6
Sacramento, CA	14.3	18.2	14.1	9.2
Salt Lake City, UT	9.6	11.6	9.2	6.7
San Antonio, TX	14.9	21.1	13.2	10.5
San Diego, CA	12.5	16.1	12.0	8.9
San Francisco, CA	9.5	10.9	9.3	8.6
San Jose, CA	8.0	8.5	7.7	8.4
Santa Rosa, CA	10.3	12.5	10.5	7.0
Savannah, GA	14.5	19.9	13.8	7.9
Seattle, WA	9.6	11.8	9.2	7.8
Sioux Falls, SD	9.2	11.2	8.7	7.6
Springfield, IL	14.9	24.0	13.8	6.4
Tallahassee, FL	20.0	21.5	22.0	8.0
Tampa, FL	14.2	19.6	13.7	10.1
Topeka, KS	12.0	15.0	12.2	7.1
Tucson, AZ	17.8	25.1	17.9	9.0
Tulsa, OK	14.5	21.3	13.5	7.5
Tuscaloosa, AL	18.5	23.5	18.6	9.7
Virginia Beach, VA	11.7	17.4	10.6	7.1
Washington, DC	8.0	10.3	7.4	7.2
Wichita, KS	13.3	17.9	12.5	8.3
Winston-Salem, NC	16.4	24.9	15.3	8.9
U.S.	14.1	19.5	13.2	9.3

Note: Figures are percentage of people whose income during the past 12 months was below the poverty level;
Figures cover the Metropolitan Statistical Area—see Appendix B for areas included
Source: U.S. Census Bureau, 2014-2018 American Community Survey 5-Year Estimates

Employment by Industry

Metro Area[1]	(A)	(B)	(C)	(D)	(E)	(F)	(G)	(H)	(I)	(J)	(K)	(L)	(M)	(N)
Albany, NY	4.3	n/a	20.6	5.5	21.6	1.7	8.4	5.4	n/a	4.0	11.9	10.1	3.2	2.7
Albuquerque, NM	6.3	n/a	16.7	4.9	20.4	1.4	10.7	4.3	n/a	2.9	15.8	10.5	2.6	2.9
Allentown, PA	3.4	n/a	21.0	3.6	10.6	1.3	9.7	10.2	n/a	3.8	12.7	10.5	8.9	3.8
Anchorage, AK	6.9	5.3	18.3	4.6	19.6	2.1	11.1	1.1	1.5	3.5	10.4	11.9	7.0	2.9
Ann Arbor, MI	2.1	n/a	12.8	2.9	38.0	2.4	7.6	6.3	n/a	2.6	13.3	6.9	1.8	2.8
Athens, GA	n/a	n/a	n/a	n/a	28.0	n/a	11.4	n/a	n/a	n/a	8.6	11.2	n/a	n/a
Atlanta, GA	4.5	4.5	13.2	6.1	11.6	3.5	10.4	5.9	<0.1	3.6	19.3	10.4	5.6	5.4
Austin, TX	6.3	n/a	11.5	5.9	16.1	3.4	12.0	5.5	n/a	4.2	17.8	10.0	2.2	4.6
Baton Rouge, LA	11.9	11.6	13.0	4.6	18.2	1.2	10.4	7.2	0.2	4.1	12.0	9.9	3.9	3.3
Boise City, ID	7.6	n/a	14.8	5.7	14.4	1.3	10.1	8.3	n/a	3.6	14.4	11.4	3.4	4.6
Boston, MA[4]	3.8	n/a	22.5	8.1	10.4	3.2	9.8	4.1	n/a	3.5	20.7	7.9	2.4	3.0
Boulder, CO	2.9	n/a	13.2	3.5	20.5	4.1	10.0	9.6	n/a	3.1	19.4	8.9	0.9	3.4
Cape Coral, FL	11.6	n/a	11.1	4.9	15.6	0.9	15.8	2.2	n/a	4.1	13.7	14.9	2.1	2.6
Cedar Rapids, IA	5.3	n/a	14.5	7.8	11.7	2.3	8.1	13.9	n/a	3.5	10.2	10.2	7.9	4.0
Charleston, SC	5.8	n/a	11.3	4.2	17.9	1.4	13.2	7.9	n/a	3.9	15.4	11.5	4.4	2.7
Charlotte, NC	5.5	n/a	10.2	8.5	12.6	1.9	11.4	8.9	n/a	3.3	16.8	10.5	5.1	4.7
Chicago, IL[2]	3.3	3.3	16.1	7.3	11.1	1.8	10.0	7.3	<0.1	4.2	18.4	9.2	6.0	4.9
Clarksville, TN	3.4	n/a	13.3	3.2	19.7	1.0	12.9	13.3	n/a	3.4	9.9	13.6	2.8	n/a
Cleveland, OH	3.5	n/a	19.1	6.2	12.6	1.2	9.7	11.3	n/a	3.8	14.6	9.2	3.4	4.9
College Station, TX	6.1	n/a	10.1	3.1	35.6	1.1	14.2	4.9	n/a	2.7	8.1	9.8	1.5	2.3
Colorado Springs, CO	6.1	n/a	13.7	6.1	18.6	1.8	12.5	3.8	n/a	5.8	15.8	11.3	1.9	2.0
Columbia, MO	n/a	n/a	n/a	n/a	30.3	n/a	n/a	n/a	n/a	n/a	n/a	10.4	n/a	n/a
Columbia, SC	4.2	n/a	12.5	7.8	21.2	1.4	10.0	7.8	n/a	4.2	12.4	10.5	3.9	3.6
Columbus, OH	3.9	n/a	14.4	7.7	16.6	1.5	9.4	6.4	n/a	3.7	16.0	9.1	6.9	3.7
Dallas, TX[2]	5.6	n/a	11.9	9.2	11.3	2.6	9.9	6.8	n/a	3.1	19.0	9.7	4.9	5.5
Davenport, IA	n/a	n/a	n/a	n/a	n/a	n/a	n/a	n/a	n/a	n/a	n/a	n/a	n/a	n/a
Denver, CO	7.2	n/a	12.5	7.2	13.3	3.2	11.0	4.6	n/a	3.7	18.1	9.1	4.6	4.9
Des Moines, IA	5.4	n/a	14.3	15.0	12.3	1.7	9.5	5.6	n/a	3.7	13.3	10.7	3.3	4.7
Durham, NC	2.8	n/a	22.3	4.8	21.3	1.5	8.5	8.6	n/a	3.5	13.8	7.6	2.1	2.7
Edison, NJ[2]	3.6	n/a	21.6	8.6	12.9	3.5	9.4	2.7	n/a	4.1	16.3	9.0	4.0	3.7
El Paso, TX	5.2	n/a	14.7	4.1	22.3	1.4	11.4	5.1	n/a	2.7	11.2	12.3	5.2	3.8
Fargo, ND	5.9	n/a	19.1	7.9	13.9	2.1	9.7	6.9	n/a	3.4	9.9	10.4	4.1	6.2
Fayetteville, NC	4.3	n/a	11.6	2.9	31.2	0.8	12.9	6.6	n/a	3.5	8.1	12.5	3.5	1.6
Fort Collins, CO	6.5	n/a	10.7	3.9	24.4	1.9	12.3	8.3	n/a	3.7	11.8	11.2	1.9	2.9
Fort Wayne, IN	5.0	n/a	19.1	5.4	9.5	0.9	9.2	16.5	n/a	5.0	9.5	10.5	4.1	4.6
Fort Worth, TX[2]	7.0	n/a	13.0	6.2	12.6	0.9	11.3	9.1	n/a	3.7	11.2	11.0	8.7	4.8
Grand Rapids, MI	4.5	n/a	16.7	4.7	8.8	1.1	8.5	20.8	n/a	4.0	13.1	8.5	3.0	5.7
Greeley, CO	19.0	n/a	9.1	3.9	16.2	0.6	8.2	12.4	n/a	3.3	9.6	9.2	4.1	3.9
Green Bay, WI	4.1	n/a	15.4	6.7	11.3	0.8	9.5	17.5	n/a	4.9	10.5	9.6	4.7	4.6
Greensboro, NC	4.2	n/a	14.3	5.2	12.2	1.2	10.2	14.5	n/a	3.4	12.9	10.5	5.5	5.3
Honolulu, HI	5.7	n/a	13.9	4.8	20.7	1.5	16.0	2.2	n/a	4.5	12.1	10.1	5.2	2.9
Houston, TX	9.9	7.5	12.8	5.2	13.3	1.0	10.3	7.3	2.4	3.6	15.9	9.7	5.0	5.5
Huntsville, AL	3.6	n/a	9.0	2.8	21.2	1.0	9.3	10.4	n/a	3.4	24.2	10.4	1.6	2.5
Indianapolis, IN	4.9	4.9	15.0	6.4	12.5	1.2	9.9	8.4	<0.1	4.1	15.9	9.5	7.0	4.6
Jackson, MS	3.9	3.6	16.0	5.5	20.3	1.2	9.6	7.2	0.3	4.8	11.9	10.4	5.0	3.7
Jacksonville, FL	6.3	6.2	15.2	9.2	10.6	1.2	11.7	4.4	<0.1	3.6	15.4	11.2	6.8	3.9
Kansas City, MO	4.9	n/a	14.2	7.1	13.6	1.4	10.0	7.1	n/a	3.8	17.2	10.2	5.3	4.7
Lafayette, LA	10.8	4.4	16.2	5.4	13.6	1.1	10.6	8.1	6.4	3.5	10.1	12.7	3.0	4.3
Lakeland, FL	6.2	n/a	14.4	5.6	12.2	0.8	10.3	7.7	n/a	2.7	13.5	12.5	8.8	4.7
Las Vegas, NV	7.0	7.0	10.1	5.2	10.5	1.0	27.8	2.5	<0.1	3.0	14.3	10.7	5.0	2.3
Lexington, KY	4.9	n/a	13.4	3.6	19.0	0.9	10.9	10.7	n/a	3.5	13.9	10.6	4.2	3.9
Lincoln, NE	4.6	n/a	15.9	6.7	21.8	1.6	10.1	6.8	n/a	3.6	11.1	9.2	5.7	2.1
Little Rock, AR	4.8	n/a	16.0	5.9	19.3	1.1	9.1	5.6	n/a	5.0	13.2	10.6	4.7	4.3
Los Angeles, CA[2]	3.2	3.2	18.5	4.8	13.0	4.8	11.7	7.2	<0.1	3.4	14.0	9.4	4.8	4.7
Louisville, KY	4.3	n/a	14.7	6.9	10.9	1.3	9.8	12.1	n/a	3.7	13.6	9.3	8.7	4.4
Madison, WI	4.3	n/a	12.3	5.7	21.7	4.2	9.0	8.7	n/a	4.9	12.9	9.9	2.3	3.6

Table continued on next page.

Metro Area[1]	(A)	(B)	(C)	(D)	(E)	(F)	(G)	(H)	(I)	(J)	(K)	(L)	(M)	(N)
Manchester, NH[3]	4.6	n/a	23.6	6.7	10.2	3.0	8.3	6.6	n/a	4.2	15.0	10.9	2.4	4.0
Miami, FL[2]	4.3	4.2	15.7	6.7	11.8	1.7	12.0	3.4	<0.1	4.0	14.7	12.2	7.1	5.9
Midland, TX	34.0	n/a	6.0	4.2	8.3	0.8	9.5	3.7	n/a	3.5	9.5	8.9	5.0	6.0
Milwaukee, WI	3.6	3.5	20.2	5.7	9.9	1.5	8.9	13.4	<0.1	5.3	14.1	8.9	3.6	4.4
Minneapolis, MN	3.9	n/a	16.9	7.7	12.5	1.7	9.1	9.8	n/a	3.9	16.1	9.5	3.9	4.5
Nashville, TN	4.5	n/a	14.6	6.8	11.4	2.3	11.4	7.9	n/a	3.9	16.8	9.9	5.8	4.1
New Haven, CT[3]	3.7	n/a	28.4	4.1	12.5	1.2	8.7	8.0	n/a	3.8	10.5	9.9	5.0	3.8
New Orleans, LA	5.4	4.6	17.7	5.3	12.4	1.1	15.9	5.1	0.7	4.1	13.3	10.4	5.1	3.7
New York, NY[2]	3.6	n/a	21.6	8.6	12.9	3.5	9.4	2.7	n/a	4.1	16.3	9.0	4.0	3.7
Oklahoma City, OK	7.4	4.9	14.6	5.1	20.1	1.0	11.1	5.0	2.5	4.3	13.2	10.1	4.0	3.5
Omaha, NE	6.0	n/a	15.7	9.0	13.1	2.0	10.1	6.6	n/a	3.6	14.1	10.4	5.6	3.2
Orlando, FL	6.5	6.5	12.1	5.9	9.6	1.9	20.5	3.6	<0.1	3.3	17.6	11.5	3.5	3.5
Peoria, IL	4.2	n/a	18.5	4.1	12.3	1.1	9.7	13.3	n/a	4.5	13.1	10.7	4.2	3.8
Philadelphia, PA[2]	2.4	n/a	30.9	6.0	13.2	1.5	10.1	3.3	n/a	4.0	13.9	7.6	4.2	2.3
Phoenix, AZ	6.1	6.0	15.6	9.1	11.3	1.8	10.5	6.0	0.1	3.2	16.9	10.9	4.3	3.8
Pittsburgh, PA	6.0	5.1	21.7	6.3	9.7	1.6	10.0	7.3	0.9	4.0	15.4	10.0	4.1	3.5
Portland, OR	6.1	6.0	15.0	6.0	12.5	2.2	10.1	10.4	0.1	3.3	15.4	9.8	3.9	4.7
Providence, RI[3]	4.2	4.2	21.7	6.2	12.8	1.1	11.0	8.2	<0.1	4.4	12.4	11.0	3.2	3.3
Provo, UT	9.2	n/a	20.7	3.3	12.1	5.0	8.8	7.4	n/a	2.1	14.2	12.6	1.5	2.5
Raleigh, NC	6.3	n/a	12.3	5.3	15.2	3.4	11.3	5.5	n/a	3.9	18.9	11.1	2.3	3.9
Reno, NV	7.1	7.0	11.0	4.3	12.5	1.2	15.1	10.0	0.1	2.4	13.4	10.4	8.1	3.9
Richmond, VA	5.9	n/a	14.7	7.6	16.5	1.0	9.4	4.4	n/a	4.6	17.5	9.8	4.2	3.9
Rochester, MN	4.1	n/a	41.7	2.1	10.8	1.1	9.0	8.7	n/a	3.1	4.5	9.7	2.2	2.3
Sacramento, CA	6.5	6.4	16.4	5.2	23.5	1.1	10.5	3.5	<0.1	3.3	13.3	10.1	3.4	2.7
Salt Lake City, UT	6.3	n/a	11.3	7.8	14.8	2.9	8.8	7.7	n/a	2.9	16.7	10.2	5.7	4.3
San Antonio, TX	6.2	5.3	15.5	8.7	16.0	1.8	12.7	4.8	0.9	3.6	13.0	10.6	3.2	3.4
San Diego, CA	5.5	5.5	14.4	5.0	16.5	1.5	13.1	7.6	<0.1	3.5	17.1	9.9	2.3	2.9
San Francisco, CA[2]	3.5	3.5	12.4	7.2	11.0	8.3	12.5	3.2	<0.1	3.4	24.8	6.7	4.3	2.1
San Jose, CA	4.4	4.4	15.3	3.3	8.5	8.9	9.0	15.0	<0.1	2.5	21.0	7.5	1.5	2.7
Santa Rosa, CA	8.0	8.0	16.8	4.1	14.3	1.2	11.9	11.1	<0.1	3.3	11.3	11.7	2.0	3.5
Savannah, GA	4.4	n/a	14.5	3.4	12.8	1.4	14.5	10.3	n/a	4.1	10.8	11.6	8.1	3.5
Seattle, WA[2]	5.9	5.9	12.7	4.9	12.1	7.1	9.9	9.3	<0.1	3.5	15.1	11.4	3.4	4.0
Sioux Falls, SD	5.6	n/a	21.1	9.9	9.1	1.6	9.5	8.8	n/a	3.6	9.7	11.5	3.8	5.3
Springfield, IL	2.7	n/a	19.9	5.8	24.9	2.4	8.9	3.0	n/a	5.5	11.3	10.6	1.8	2.6
Tallahassee, FL	4.7	n/a	13.2	4.1	33.4	1.5	11.1	1.7	n/a	4.8	11.8	10.0	1.3	2.0
Tampa, FL	5.9	5.8	15.9	8.7	11.3	1.8	11.5	4.9	<0.1	3.3	17.9	11.4	3.0	3.8
Topeka, KS	4.6	n/a	17.2	6.9	23.5	1.1	7.8	7.1	n/a	4.2	11.8	9.5	3.4	2.4
Tucson, AZ	5.0	4.5	17.5	4.3	20.7	1.3	11.2	6.9	0.4	3.4	13.1	10.5	3.7	1.8
Tulsa, OK	6.8	5.4	15.8	5.0	13.0	1.4	10.1	11.6	1.4	4.4	12.4	10.5	4.7	3.6
Tuscaloosa, AL	6.1	n/a	8.4	3.5	25.7	1.6	10.0	14.9	n/a	3.7	10.6	10.1	3.1	1.8
Virginia Beach, VA	5.0	n/a	14.3	4.9	20.3	1.2	11.2	7.4	n/a	4.5	14.1	10.9	3.5	2.3
Washington, DC[2]	4.6	n/a	12.7	4.4	21.7	2.3	10.0	1.4	n/a	6.7	23.4	8.0	2.5	1.8
Wichita, KS	5.2	n/a	15.3	3.8	13.9	1.3	10.7	17.8	n/a	3.6	11.4	10.3	3.4	2.8
Winston-Salem, NC	4.2	n/a	20.6	5.1	11.8	0.6	10.7	12.2	n/a	3.3	13.1	11.5	3.4	3.1
U.S.	5.4	4.9	16.1	5.8	15.0	1.9	10.8	8.4	0.5	3.9	14.1	10.6	4.2	3.9

Note: All figures are percentages covering non-farm employment as of December 2019 and are not seasonally adjusted;
(1) Figures cover the Metropolitan Statistical Area (MSA) except where noted. See Appendix B for areas included; (2) Metropolitan Division; (3) New England City and Town Area; (4) New England City and Town Area Division; (A) Construction, Mining, and Logging (some areas report Construction separate from Mining and Logging); (B) Construction; (C) Education and Health Services; (D) Financial Activities; (E) Government; (F) Information; (G) Leisure and Hospitality; (H) Manufacturing; (I) Mining and Logging; (J) Other Services; (K) Professional and Business Services; (L) Retail Trade; (M) Transportation and Utilities; (N) Wholesale Trade; n/a not available
Source: Bureau of Labor Statistics, Current Employment Statistics, Employment, Hours, and Earnings, December 2019

Labor Force, Employment and Job Growth: City

City	Civilian Labor Force			Workers Employed		
	Dec. 2018	Dec. 2019	% Chg.	Dec. 2018	Dec. 2019	% Chg.
Albany, NY	45,919	46,619	1.5	44,144	44,623	1.0
Albuquerque, NM	279,966	284,609	1.6	268,264	273,259	1.8
Allentown, PA	55,039	56,275	2.2	51,980	52,716	1.4
Anchorage, AK	150,188	147,801	-1.5	142,735	140,718	-1.4
Ann Arbor, MI	66,203	66,802	0.9	64,754	65,636	1.3
Athens, GA	60,174	59,225	-1.5	57,919	57,596	-0.5
Atlanta, GA	259,861	264,779	1.8	249,233	256,964	3.1
Austin, TX	582,700	601,055	3.1	567,806	587,607	3.4
Baton Rouge, LA	112,299	111,969	-0.2	107,626	106,514	-1.0
Boise City, ID	130,157	134,753	3.5	126,969	131,600	3.6
Boston, MA	395,486	399,841	1.1	385,976	391,993	1.5
Boulder, CO	65,012	66,229	1.8	63,268	65,025	2.7
Cape Coral, FL	90,610	93,172	2.8	87,615	90,578	3.3
Cedar Rapids, IA	71,755	73,629	2.6	69,479	71,125	2.3
Charleston, SC	73,908	75,308	1.8	71,933	73,919	2.7
Charlotte, NC	489,599	499,499	2.0	471,607	483,932	2.6
Chicago, IL	1,337,746	1,322,199	-1.1	1,284,655	1,281,869	-0.2
Clarksville, TN	61,930	63,787	3.0	59,692	61,432	2.9
Cleveland, OH	157,743	156,471	-0.8	149,525	149,465	0.0
College Station, TX	61,184	62,425	2.0	59,517	60,916	2.3
Colorado Springs, CO	234,309	238,705	1.8	225,131	232,124	3.1
Columbia, MO	67,333	68,108	1.1	65,941	66,459	0.7
Columbia, SC	58,392	58,665	0.4	56,106	57,222	1.9
Columbus, OH	474,214	478,751	0.9	456,170	463,416	1.5
Dallas, TX	685,227	703,081	2.6	661,059	681,628	3.1
Davenport, IA	50,579	51,918	2.6	48,734	49,753	2.0
Denver, CO	413,181	423,917	2.6	400,411	414,090	3.4
Des Moines, IA	112,022	115,631	3.2	108,110	111,652	3.2
Durham, NC	148,309	150,280	1.3	143,134	145,981	1.9
Edison, NJ	54,208	55,345	2.1	52,943	54,066	2.1
El Paso, TX	302,157	305,478	1.1	290,645	295,039	1.5
Fargo, ND	69,345	69,702	0.5	67,902	68,423	0.7
Fayetteville, NC	77,018	76,883	-0.1	72,695	73,263	0.7
Fort Collins, CO	100,446	103,931	3.4	97,820	101,963	4.2
Fort Wayne, IN	128,555	128,470	0.0	124,362	124,594	0.1
Fort Worth, TX	435,372	444,954	2.2	420,596	431,424	2.5
Grand Rapids, MI	105,185	103,987	-1.1	101,346	100,701	-0.6
Greeley, CO	53,564	55,458	3.5	51,851	54,063	4.2
Green Bay, WI	53,873	53,859	0.0	52,441	52,110	-0.6
Greensboro, NC	145,856	147,165	0.9	139,776	141,957	1.5
Honolulu, HI	454,200	452,859	-0.3	443,631	443,191	-0.1
Houston, TX	1,152,315	1,168,794	1.4	1,107,543	1,128,145	1.8
Huntsville, AL	98,622	99,396	0.7	95,511	97,185	1.7
Indianapolis, IN	446,378	446,151	0.0	430,884	433,373	0.5
Jackson, MS	72,006	72,061	0.0	68,558	68,434	-0.1
Jacksonville, FL	457,066	469,934	2.8	441,488	457,089	3.5
Kansas City, MO	257,417	262,205	1.8	249,062	252,990	1.5
Lafayette, LA	59,359	59,376	0.0	57,014	56,669	-0.6
Lakeland, FL	46,497	47,582	2.3	44,692	46,092	3.1
Las Vegas, NV	310,971	316,225	1.6	297,219	305,003	2.6
Lexington, KY	173,811	175,216	0.8	168,655	170,118	0.8
Lincoln, NE	158,114	160,552	1.5	154,188	156,783	1.6
Little Rock, AR	97,191	96,600	-0.6	94,024	93,594	-0.4
Los Angeles, CA	2,073,954	2,095,690	1.0	1,980,928	2,011,531	1.5
Louisville, KY	400,093	402,027	0.4	385,544	388,284	0.7

Table continued on next page.

City	Civilian Labor Force			Workers Employed		
	Dec. 2018	Dec. 2019	% Chg.	Dec. 2018	Dec. 2019	% Chg.
Madison, WI	155,501	157,534	1.3	152,428	154,347	1.2
Manchester, NH	65,241	66,041	1.2	63,807	64,553	1.1
Miami, FL	232,596	234,913	1.0	226,301	231,476	2.2
Midland, TX	87,949	88,858	1.0	86,241	87,068	0.9
Milwaukee, WI	270,854	271,222	0.1	261,547	260,380	-0.4
Minneapolis, MN	242,642	245,206	1.0	236,426	238,869	1.0
Nashville, TN	399,891	413,927	3.5	390,269	404,589	3.6
New Haven, CT	64,771	65,459	1.0	62,196	63,121	1.4
New Orleans, LA	176,607	179,138	1.4	169,054	170,426	0.8
New York, NY	4,077,882	4,030,008	-1.1	3,910,165	3,904,018	-0.1
Oklahoma City, OK	318,621	322,420	1.1	309,247	313,116	1.2
Omaha, NE	241,394	243,405	0.8	233,531	236,406	1.2
Orlando, FL	165,567	170,544	3.0	160,678	166,541	3.6
Peoria, IL	51,731	50,615	-2.1	48,571	47,924	-1.3
Philadelphia, PA	709,453	729,738	2.8	675,713	690,247	2.1
Phoenix, AZ	847,789	885,177	4.4	812,482	853,111	5.0
Pittsburgh, PA	155,377	157,702	1.5	149,800	151,169	0.9
Portland, OR	375,572	376,061	0.1	362,953	366,666	1.0
Providence, RI	86,400	86,891	0.5	82,849	83,544	0.8
Provo, UT	65,846	68,223	3.6	64,371	66,963	4.0
Raleigh, NC	255,599	260,153	1.7	246,441	252,404	2.4
Reno, NV	136,883	139,960	2.2	132,409	136,175	2.8
Richmond, VA	118,041	119,856	1.5	114,136	116,483	2.0
Rochester, MN	65,150	65,938	1.2	63,521	64,352	1.3
Sacramento, CA	235,794	237,846	0.8	226,782	230,186	1.5
Salt Lake City, UT	114,206	117,922	3.2	111,330	115,531	3.7
San Antonio, TX	726,502	740,486	1.9	703,767	720,097	2.3
San Diego, CA	719,220	724,077	0.6	696,335	704,952	1.2
San Francisco, CA	575,703	589,286	2.3	562,751	578,146	2.7
San Jose, CA	552,549	558,215	1.0	537,927	545,337	1.3
Santa Rosa, CA	90,343	90,456	0.1	87,887	88,298	0.4
Savannah, GA	66,861	66,855	0.0	64,230	64,804	0.8
Seattle, WA	465,723	475,147	2.0	452,712	464,721	2.6
Sioux Falls, SD	104,940	106,508	1.4	102,038	103,166	1.1
Springfield, IL	57,450	56,539	-1.5	54,565	54,362	-0.3
Tallahassee, FL	101,007	102,369	1.3	97,436	99,536	2.1
Tampa, FL	200,468	205,639	2.5	193,591	200,162	3.3
Topeka, KS	61,568	61,966	0.6	59,393	59,884	0.8
Tucson, AZ	264,499	271,283	2.5	252,359	259,611	2.8
Tulsa, OK	196,216	196,335	0.0	189,849	190,196	0.1
Tuscaloosa, AL	47,972	48,708	1.5	46,269	47,449	2.5
Virginia Beach, VA	231,358	234,164	1.2	224,851	228,643	1.6
Washington, DC	403,201	411,233	1.9	381,701	390,807	2.3
Wichita, KS	186,160	189,743	1.9	179,744	183,423	2.0
Winston-Salem, NC	118,341	118,986	0.5	113,617	114,945	1.1
U.S.	162,510,000	164,007,000	0.9	156,481,000	158,504,000	1.3

Note: Data is not seasonally adjusted and covers workers 16 years of age and older
Source: Bureau of Labor Statistics, Local Area Unemployment Statistics

Labor Force, Employment and Job Growth: Metro Area

Metro Area[1]	Civilian Labor Force			Workers Employed		
	Dec. 2018	Dec. 2019	% Chg.	Dec. 2018	Dec. 2019	% Chg.
Albany, NY	444,430	449,737	1.1	428,744	433,120	1.0
Albuquerque, NM	435,064	442,230	1.6	416,136	423,884	1.8
Allentown, PA	438,377	448,501	2.3	421,465	428,188	1.6
Anchorage, AK	198,050	195,036	-1.5	187,329	184,796	-1.3
Ann Arbor, MI	198,749	200,349	0.8	193,447	196,082	1.3
Athens, GA	100,586	99,032	-1.5	97,069	96,483	-0.6
Atlanta, GA	3,064,919	3,128,881	2.0	2,954,188	3,045,413	3.0
Austin, TX	1,216,467	1,255,200	3.1	1,183,106	1,224,993	3.5
Baton Rouge, LA	419,165	417,880	-0.3	403,356	399,191	-1.0
Boise City, ID	368,713	381,230	3.3	358,536	371,231	3.5
Boston, MA[4]	1,676,049	1,694,809	1.1	1,637,022	1,662,542	1.5
Boulder, CO	193,860	197,746	2.0	188,603	193,839	2.7
Cape Coral, FL	344,220	353,248	2.6	332,820	344,074	3.3
Cedar Rapids, IA	144,931	148,694	2.6	140,627	143,975	2.3
Charleston, SC	388,830	395,683	1.7	377,427	387,938	2.7
Charlotte, NC	1,345,080	1,373,470	2.1	1,296,167	1,331,441	2.7
Chicago, IL[2]	3,715,565	3,674,796	-1.1	3,577,585	3,570,383	-0.2
Clarksville, TN	114,791	118,102	2.8	110,505	113,647	2.8
Cleveland, OH	1,032,230	1,026,107	-0.5	990,181	990,242	0.0
College Station, TX	134,276	137,059	2.0	130,574	133,696	2.3
Colorado Springs, CO	350,012	356,603	1.8	336,280	346,681	3.0
Columbia, MO	98,400	99,481	1.1	96,312	97,069	0.7
Columbia, SC	400,336	403,325	0.7	387,144	394,519	1.9
Columbus, OH	1,094,679	1,105,853	1.0	1,052,719	1,070,103	1.6
Dallas, TX[2]	2,647,696	2,719,675	2.7	2,559,839	2,640,356	3.1
Davenport, IA	192,766	194,473	0.8	183,841	185,909	1.1
Denver, CO	1,645,484	1,688,220	2.6	1,594,915	1,650,053	3.4
Des Moines, IA	354,790	366,728	3.3	345,318	356,630	3.2
Durham, NC	300,763	305,270	1.5	290,330	296,522	2.1
Edison, NJ[2]	7,003,235	7,008,087	0.0	6,739,424	6,780,009	0.6
El Paso, TX	363,506	367,648	1.1	349,219	354,536	1.5
Fargo, ND	137,308	138,402	0.8	134,173	135,435	0.9
Fayetteville, NC	148,471	148,437	0.0	140,719	141,883	0.8
Fort Collins, CO	202,206	209,156	3.4	196,672	205,003	4.2
Fort Wayne, IN	217,241	216,998	-0.1	210,566	210,942	0.1
Fort Worth, TX[2]	1,283,200	1,311,941	2.2	1,241,403	1,273,454	2.5
Grand Rapids, MI	581,693	575,885	-1.0	565,324	561,939	-0.6
Greeley, CO	166,631	172,545	3.5	161,756	168,655	4.2
Green Bay, WI	173,169	172,794	-0.2	168,711	167,575	-0.6
Greensboro, NC	368,399	371,920	0.9	353,343	359,136	1.6
Honolulu, HI	454,200	452,859	-0.3	443,631	443,191	-0.1
Houston, TX	3,409,645	3,462,635	1.5	3,274,879	3,336,616	1.8
Huntsville, AL	227,862	229,898	0.8	221,044	225,028	1.8
Indianapolis, IN	1,060,308	1,060,176	0.0	1,026,584	1,032,445	0.5
Jackson, MS	267,865	268,250	0.1	256,653	256,233	-0.1
Jacksonville, FL	773,003	794,684	2.8	747,902	774,172	3.5
Kansas City, MO	1,123,499	1,145,405	1.9	1,089,301	1,109,920	1.8
Lafayette, LA	210,771	210,923	0.0	201,920	200,667	-0.6
Lakeland, FL	301,209	308,057	2.2	289,523	298,597	3.1
Las Vegas, NV	1,116,543	1,136,500	1.7	1,068,623	1,096,609	2.6
Lexington, KY	270,852	273,326	0.9	262,565	265,044	0.9
Lincoln, NE	184,089	186,998	1.5	179,515	182,613	1.7
Little Rock, AR	356,666	354,854	-0.5	345,501	343,794	-0.4
Los Angeles, CA[2]	5,105,297	5,158,181	1.0	4,875,767	4,951,091	1.5
Louisville, KY	672,491	674,729	0.3	648,810	652,752	0.6

Table continued on next page.

Metro Area[1]	Civilian Labor Force			Workers Employed		
	Dec. 2018	Dec. 2019	% Chg.	Dec. 2018	Dec. 2019	% Chg.
Madison, WI	384,805	390,192	1.4	376,892	381,370	1.1
Manchester, NH[3]	122,177	123,691	1.2	119,684	121,082	1.1
Miami, FL[2]	1,378,850	1,392,870	1.0	1,340,188	1,370,836	2.2
Midland, TX	109,608	110,792	1.0	107,458	108,522	0.9
Milwaukee, WI	811,245	811,069	0.0	788,833	785,335	-0.4
Minneapolis, MN	2,015,207	2,037,880	1.1	1,957,633	1,976,964	0.9
Nashville, TN	1,064,194	1,102,127	3.5	1,038,158	1,076,372	3.6
New Haven, CT[3]	327,452	331,537	1.2	316,840	321,457	1.4
New Orleans, LA	588,801	596,687	1.3	565,484	570,042	0.8
New York, NY[2]	7,003,235	7,008,087	0.0	6,739,424	6,780,009	0.6
Oklahoma City, OK	679,720	687,962	1.2	660,322	668,536	1.2
Omaha, NE	490,069	496,578	1.3	475,528	483,022	1.5
Orlando, FL	1,333,319	1,372,173	2.9	1,290,744	1,337,648	3.6
Peoria, IL	177,109	173,154	-2.2	167,247	165,096	-1.2
Philadelphia, PA[2]	1,006,135	1,031,591	2.5	962,185	980,295	1.8
Phoenix, AZ	2,440,729	2,548,680	4.4	2,340,037	2,456,125	4.9
Pittsburgh, PA	1,197,515	1,217,975	1.7	1,152,168	1,162,800	0.9
Portland, OR	1,324,367	1,332,520	0.6	1,275,477	1,294,803	1.5
Providence, RI[3]	691,427	695,900	0.6	667,558	673,941	0.9
Provo, UT	308,549	319,576	3.5	301,129	313,261	4.0
Raleigh, NC	717,532	731,065	1.8	692,752	709,901	2.4
Reno, NV	255,886	261,692	2.2	247,446	254,486	2.8
Richmond, VA	681,880	692,884	1.6	661,756	675,329	2.0
Rochester, MN	123,488	125,263	1.4	120,020	121,567	1.2
Sacramento, CA	1,095,030	1,104,616	0.8	1,054,085	1,069,620	1.4
Salt Lake City, UT	658,253	679,607	3.2	641,313	665,544	3.7
San Antonio, TX	1,194,934	1,218,568	1.9	1,157,316	1,184,374	2.3
San Diego, CA	1,586,412	1,597,099	0.6	1,533,874	1,552,857	1.2
San Francisco, CA[2]	1,030,322	1,054,065	2.3	1,007,688	1,034,791	2.6
San Jose, CA	1,079,279	1,090,183	1.0	1,051,302	1,065,627	1.3
Santa Rosa, CA	259,469	259,689	0.0	252,394	253,575	0.4
Savannah, GA	187,501	187,692	0.1	180,998	182,609	0.8
Seattle, WA[2]	1,691,233	1,725,656	2.0	1,638,269	1,681,784	2.6
Sioux Falls, SD	153,233	155,466	1.4	149,175	150,743	1.0
Springfield, IL	107,834	106,114	-1.6	102,505	102,129	-0.3
Tallahassee, FL	192,488	195,372	1.5	185,973	190,212	2.2
Tampa, FL	1,525,777	1,566,692	2.6	1,474,374	1,525,133	3.4
Topeka, KS	117,567	118,319	0.6	113,746	114,586	0.7
Tucson, AZ	492,013	504,172	2.4	470,390	483,909	2.8
Tulsa, OK	480,845	481,673	0.1	465,618	466,612	0.2
Tuscaloosa, AL	118,009	120,183	1.8	114,289	117,420	2.7
Virginia Beach, VA	847,913	858,173	1.2	820,852	834,872	1.7
Washington, DC[2]	2,715,639	2,779,621	2.3	2,631,661	2,705,388	2.8
Wichita, KS	309,641	315,547	1.9	299,636	305,590	1.9
Winston-Salem, NC	327,543	329,944	0.7	315,378	319,404	1.2
U.S.	162,510,000	164,007,000	0.9	156,481,000	158,504,000	1.3

Note: Data is not seasonally adjusted and covers workers 16 years of age and older; (1) Figures cover the Metropolitan Statistical Area (MSA) except where noted. See Appendix B for areas included; (2) Metropolitan Division; (3) New England City and Town Area; (4) New England City and Town Area Division
Source: Bureau of Labor Statistics, Local Area Unemployment Statistics

Unemployment Rate: City

City	2019											
	Jan.	Feb.	Mar.	Apr.	May	Jun.	Jul.	Aug.	Sep.	Oct.	Nov.	Dec.
Albany, NY	4.7	4.4	4.2	3.8	4.1	4.7	5.0	4.9	4.5	4.4	4.3	4.3
Albuquerque, NM	4.7	4.5	4.2	4.0	4.1	5.0	5.0	4.6	4.3	4.3	4.1	4.0
Allentown, PA	6.5	6.3	6.5	5.7	6.2	6.5	7.0	7.3	6.3	6.4	6.1	6.3
Anchorage, AK	5.3	5.5	5.4	5.0	5.1	5.3	4.9	4.7	4.9	4.8	4.9	4.8
Ann Arbor, MI	2.6	2.4	2.6	2.1	2.3	2.8	3.4	2.6	2.2	1.9	1.8	1.7
Athens, GA	4.3	4.0	3.8	3.2	3.4	4.2	4.1	3.9	3.2	3.2	2.7	2.8
Atlanta, GA	4.5	4.1	3.9	3.4	3.6	4.1	4.0	3.9	3.2	3.2	2.9	3.0
Austin, TX	3.0	2.6	2.5	2.1	2.2	2.6	2.7	2.6	2.5	2.4	2.4	2.2
Baton Rouge, LA	5.1	4.1	3.9	3.6	4.3	5.7	5.6	5.6	5.2	5.2	5.0	4.9
Boise City, ID	3.2	2.9	2.8	2.4	2.3	2.4	2.3	2.2	2.1	2.1	2.4	2.3
Boston, MA	3.1	2.7	2.6	2.3	2.7	3.0	3.0	2.6	2.5	2.2	2.1	2.0
Boulder, CO	2.8	2.5	2.5	2.4	2.0	2.6	2.2	2.3	2.1	2.0	1.9	1.8
Cape Coral, FL	3.8	3.4	3.3	2.9	3.0	3.5	3.4	3.3	3.0	3.0	2.9	2.8
Cedar Rapids, IA	3.7	3.3	3.4	2.7	2.7	3.2	3.2	3.3	2.9	2.8	3.1	3.4
Charleston, SC	3.0	2.7	2.6	2.0	2.2	2.5	2.4	2.3	1.5	1.8	1.8	1.8
Charlotte, NC	4.2	4.0	3.8	3.4	3.7	3.9	4.1	3.9	3.3	3.3	3.4	3.1
Chicago, IL	4.9	4.4	4.0	3.8	3.7	4.4	4.5	4.3	3.6	3.6	3.3	3.1
Clarksville, TN	4.3	3.9	4.0	3.5	3.8	4.7	4.8	4.2	3.9	3.9	3.8	3.7
Cleveland, OH	6.0	6.1	5.6	4.8	5.0	5.9	6.0	5.2	4.7	4.4	4.3	4.5
College Station, TX	3.1	2.8	2.6	2.2	2.4	3.3	3.3	3.1	2.7	2.7	2.6	2.4
Colorado Springs, CO	4.3	3.8	3.6	3.2	3.0	3.4	3.3	3.1	2.8	2.8	2.8	2.8
Columbia, MO	2.7	2.5	2.5	2.0	2.3	2.7	3.0	2.8	1.9	1.9	2.3	2.4
Columbia, SC	4.7	3.7	3.7	2.7	3.2	3.8	3.5	3.1	2.2	2.4	2.5	2.5
Columbus, OH	4.2	3.7	3.5	3.1	3.2	3.9	4.0	3.9	3.6	3.4	3.3	3.2
Dallas, TX	4.0	3.7	3.5	3.1	3.1	3.6	3.7	3.6	3.3	3.2	3.2	3.1
Davenport, IA	4.4	3.8	4.2	3.3	3.3	4.2	3.9	4.2	3.7	3.7	3.9	4.2
Denver, CO	3.5	3.2	3.0	2.7	2.5	2.8	2.6	2.6	2.3	2.3	2.3	2.3
Des Moines, IA	4.5	4.1	4.3	3.2	3.0	3.4	3.2	3.3	2.9	2.9	3.0	3.4
Durham, NC	4.0	3.7	3.6	3.2	3.5	3.8	3.8	3.7	3.0	3.1	3.0	2.9
Edison, NJ	2.8	2.7	2.4	1.9	2.2	2.4	2.8	2.6	2.4	2.4	2.4	2.3
El Paso, TX	4.3	3.9	3.7	3.1	3.3	3.9	4.0	3.9	3.6	3.5	3.5	3.4
Fargo, ND	2.8	2.6	2.6	2.1	1.8	2.2	1.9	1.9	1.7	1.4	1.7	1.8
Fayetteville, NC	6.2	5.8	5.5	5.0	5.3	5.8	6.2	5.9	4.9	5.0	5.0	4.7
Fort Collins, CO	3.0	2.8	2.6	2.3	2.0	2.5	2.2	2.2	2.0	2.0	1.9	1.9
Fort Wayne, IN	4.0	3.7	3.4	2.6	2.9	3.3	3.5	3.3	2.8	3.5	3.3	3.0
Fort Worth, TX	4.0	3.5	3.5	2.9	3.0	3.7	3.8	3.6	3.3	3.3	3.2	3.0
Grand Rapids, MI	4.4	4.1	4.3	3.4	3.7	4.3	5.2	4.0	3.4	3.1	3.1	3.2
Greeley, CO	3.6	3.4	3.2	2.8	2.4	3.1	2.9	2.8	2.4	2.4	2.5	2.5
Green Bay, WI	3.4	3.6	3.6	3.2	3.2	3.8	3.8	3.4	3.0	2.9	3.2	3.2
Greensboro, NC	4.8	4.5	4.3	3.7	4.2	4.6	4.9	4.7	3.8	3.9	3.8	3.5
Honolulu, HI	2.7	2.5	2.6	2.5	2.5	3.2	2.6	2.6	2.7	2.5	2.5	2.1
Houston, TX	4.3	3.9	3.7	3.2	3.4	3.9	4.0	4.0	3.6	3.6	3.6	3.5
Huntsville, AL	3.8	3.4	3.2	2.4	2.2	3.1	2.9	2.6	2.2	2.3	2.1	2.2
Indianapolis, IN	4.1	3.8	3.6	2.8	3.0	3.4	3.5	3.4	2.9	3.0	3.1	2.9
Jackson, MS	5.5	5.0	5.2	4.9	5.4	6.6	6.3	5.7	5.5	5.1	5.1	5.0
Jacksonville, FL	3.9	3.5	3.4	3.1	3.2	3.7	3.8	3.5	3.1	3.0	2.9	2.7
Kansas City, MO	4.1	3.6	3.8	2.9	3.2	3.7	4.7	4.1	2.9	3.3	3.3	3.5
Lafayette, LA	4.9	4.0	3.9	3.7	4.2	5.3	5.1	5.0	4.8	4.9	4.7	4.6
Lakeland, FL	4.5	3.8	3.7	3.5	3.8	4.2	4.1	3.9	3.3	3.3	3.3	3.1
Las Vegas, NV	4.8	4.3	4.3	4.1	4.2	4.6	4.5	4.2	4.0	3.9	3.7	3.5
Lexington, KY	3.6	3.7	3.7	3.0	3.3	3.9	3.8	3.3	2.9	2.9	2.9	2.9
Lincoln, NE	2.9	2.9	3.0	2.7	2.8	3.2	3.0	2.8	2.6	2.5	2.5	2.3
Little Rock, AR	3.8	3.7	3.2	2.9	3.2	3.6	3.8	3.4	3.1	3.0	3.0	3.1
Los Angeles, CA	5.1	4.6	4.5	4.1	4.2	4.5	5.0	4.8	4.3	4.3	4.1	4.0
Louisville, KY	4.3	4.3	4.3	3.8	4.0	4.6	4.8	4.0	3.6	3.5	3.5	3.4

Table continued on next page.

City	2019											
	Jan.	Feb.	Mar.	Apr.	May	Jun.	Jul.	Aug.	Sep.	Oct.	Nov.	Dec.
Madison, WI	2.4	2.4	2.5	2.2	2.6	3.1	2.6	2.5	2.2	2.1	2.1	2.0
Manchester, NH	3.0	3.0	2.9	2.6	2.6	2.7	2.6	2.5	2.4	2.2	2.4	2.3
Miami, FL	2.8	2.6	2.8	2.4	2.4	2.4	2.5	2.5	2.2	1.9	1.7	1.5
Midland, TX	2.2	2.1	2.1	1.7	1.8	2.1	2.2	2.3	2.1	2.1	2.1	2.0
Milwaukee, WI	4.4	4.5	4.5	4.0	4.1	5.2	5.3	5.1	4.3	4.0	4.2	4.0
Minneapolis, MN	3.1	2.9	3.0	2.5	2.6	3.2	3.1	3.0	2.6	2.7	2.5	2.6
Nashville, TN	2.8	2.5	2.6	2.2	2.4	2.9	2.9	2.6	2.4	2.3	2.3	2.3
New Haven, CT	5.2	4.8	4.5	3.8	4.3	4.6	5.0	4.8	4.1	4.1	3.8	3.6
New Orleans, LA	5.2	4.2	4.1	3.8	4.3	5.7	5.7	5.5	5.0	5.1	4.9	4.9
New York, NY	4.9	4.6	4.3	3.7	3.8	3.9	4.3	4.2	3.5	3.7	3.4	3.1
Oklahoma City, OK	3.6	3.3	3.1	2.7	3.0	3.3	3.2	3.1	2.9	3.1	3.0	2.9
Omaha, NE	3.7	3.7	3.7	3.2	3.2	3.6	3.6	3.3	3.0	2.9	2.8	2.9
Orlando, FL	3.4	2.9	2.8	2.5	2.7	3.0	3.0	2.9	2.6	2.6	2.5	2.3
Peoria, IL	6.8	6.0	5.8	4.6	4.6	5.1	5.4	5.5	5.0	4.9	5.0	5.3
Philadelphia, PA	5.7	5.2	5.2	4.5	5.2	5.7	6.3	6.4	5.6	5.8	5.6	5.4
Phoenix, AZ	4.6	4.3	4.3	4.0	4.1	4.4	4.4	4.3	3.9	3.8	3.7	3.6
Pittsburgh, PA	4.2	4.1	4.1	3.5	4.2	4.5	4.9	4.8	4.3	4.4	4.3	4.1
Portland, OR	3.9	3.8	3.8	3.3	3.1	3.5	3.5	3.4	2.7	2.7	2.6	2.5
Providence, RI	5.4	5.1	4.9	4.0	4.2	4.3	4.9	4.7	4.1	3.6	4.1	3.9
Provo, UT	2.2	2.6	2.5	2.2	2.3	2.8	2.6	2.4	1.8	1.8	1.7	1.8
Raleigh, NC	4.1	3.8	3.7	3.3	3.7	3.9	4.0	3.8	3.1	3.2	3.1	3.0
Reno, NV	3.9	3.7	3.5	3.3	3.1	3.2	3.2	3.1	3.0	2.8	2.7	2.7
Richmond, VA	3.9	3.6	3.5	2.9	3.2	3.4	3.6	3.5	3.1	3.0	2.9	2.8
Rochester, MN	3.0	2.8	3.0	2.4	2.3	2.9	2.7	2.6	2.1	2.1	2.1	2.4
Sacramento, CA	4.5	4.1	4.1	3.5	3.4	3.9	4.2	3.9	3.3	3.4	3.3	3.2
Salt Lake City, UT	2.7	2.9	2.9	2.6	2.5	2.9	2.6	2.6	2.1	2.1	2.1	2.0
San Antonio, TX	3.5	3.2	3.1	2.6	2.7	3.3	3.4	3.3	3.0	2.9	2.9	2.8
San Diego, CA	3.6	3.2	3.3	2.7	2.7	3.2	3.4	3.3	2.8	2.9	2.8	2.6
San Francisco, CA	2.6	2.4	2.4	2.0	1.9	2.3	2.4	2.3	1.9	2.0	2.0	1.9
San Jose, CA	3.0	2.8	2.8	2.4	2.3	2.8	2.9	2.8	2.4	2.5	2.4	2.3
Santa Rosa, CA	3.4	3.1	3.1	2.6	2.5	2.9	3.0	2.8	2.3	2.4	2.5	2.4
Savannah, GA	4.5	4.0	3.9	3.4	3.5	4.0	3.9	4.1	3.4	3.3	3.0	3.1
Seattle, WA	3.1	2.7	2.7	2.1	2.4	2.6	2.8	2.5	2.5	2.3	2.3	2.2
Sioux Falls, SD	3.2	3.2	3.2	2.9	2.7	2.7	2.4	2.8	2.7	2.6	2.8	3.1
Springfield, IL	5.5	4.9	4.7	3.7	3.5	4.3	4.6	4.3	3.8	3.8	3.6	3.9
Tallahassee, FL	4.1	3.4	3.3	3.0	3.1	3.8	3.9	3.6	3.2	3.1	2.9	2.8
Tampa, FL	3.9	3.4	3.3	3.0	3.2	3.5	3.6	3.4	3.0	3.0	2.9	2.7
Topeka, KS	4.2	4.0	3.8	3.1	3.3	3.5	4.0	3.7	3.1	3.2	3.3	3.4
Tucson, AZ	5.1	4.7	4.7	4.4	4.5	5.0	5.0	4.8	4.5	4.5	4.3	4.3
Tulsa, OK	3.8	3.6	3.3	2.9	3.3	3.5	3.4	3.3	3.2	3.7	3.3	3.1
Tuscaloosa, AL	4.3	3.8	3.6	2.6	2.8	3.7	3.5	3.1	2.6	2.6	2.5	2.6
Virginia Beach, VA	3.3	3.0	2.9	2.4	2.6	2.8	2.8	2.9	2.5	2.5	2.4	2.4
Washington, DC	6.2	6.0	5.6	5.1	5.2	5.8	5.8	5.5	5.4	5.3	5.0	5.0
Wichita, KS	4.2	3.8	3.7	3.1	3.4	3.7	4.1	3.8	3.1	3.3	3.3	3.3
Winston-Salem, NC	4.6	4.2	4.0	3.6	4.0	4.4	4.5	4.3	3.5	3.6	3.6	3.4
U.S.	4.4	4.1	3.9	3.3	3.4	3.8	4.0	3.8	3.3	3.3	3.3	3.4

Note: Data is not seasonally adjusted and covers workers 16 years of age and older; All figures are percentages
Source: Bureau of Labor Statistics, Local Area Unemployment Statistics

Unemployment Rate: Metro Area

Metro Area[1]	2019											
	Jan.	Feb.	Mar.	Apr.	May	Jun.	Jul.	Aug.	Sep.	Oct.	Nov.	Dec.
Albany, NY	4.3	4.2	3.9	3.3	3.3	3.5	3.8	3.8	3.4	3.4	3.4	3.7
Albuquerque, NM	4.9	4.7	4.4	4.1	4.2	5.3	5.2	4.8	4.5	4.5	4.3	4.1
Allentown, PA	4.7	4.6	4.4	3.7	4.1	4.4	4.9	4.8	4.2	4.4	4.2	4.5
Anchorage, AK	5.9	6.1	6.0	5.5	5.5	5.8	5.3	5.0	5.2	5.1	5.3	5.3
Ann Arbor, MI	3.1	3.0	3.1	2.6	2.8	3.4	4.2	3.2	2.7	2.4	2.2	2.1
Athens, GA	4.0	3.7	3.5	2.9	3.1	3.8	3.7	3.5	2.9	2.9	2.5	2.6
Atlanta, GA	4.0	3.6	3.5	3.0	3.2	3.6	3.6	3.5	2.9	2.9	2.6	2.7
Austin, TX	3.2	2.8	2.7	2.3	2.4	2.8	2.9	2.8	2.6	2.6	2.5	2.4
Baton Rouge, LA	4.7	3.8	3.6	3.4	3.9	5.1	5.1	5.0	4.6	4.6	4.5	4.5
Boise City, ID	3.7	3.3	3.0	2.7	2.5	2.7	2.7	2.5	2.3	2.3	2.7	2.6
Boston, MA[4]	3.0	2.7	2.6	2.3	2.5	2.7	2.7	2.4	2.3	2.0	1.9	1.9
Boulder, CO	3.0	2.7	2.6	2.4	2.1	2.6	2.3	2.3	2.1	2.1	2.0	2.0
Cape Coral, FL	3.8	3.3	3.2	2.9	3.0	3.5	3.4	3.4	3.0	2.9	2.8	2.6
Cedar Rapids, IA	3.6	3.3	3.3	2.6	2.5	2.9	3.0	3.0	2.6	2.6	2.7	3.2
Charleston, SC	3.3	3.0	2.9	2.2	2.3	2.7	2.6	2.4	1.7	2.0	1.9	2.0
Charlotte, NC	4.2	3.9	3.7	3.3	3.5	3.8	3.9	3.7	3.1	3.2	3.2	3.1
Chicago, IL[2]	4.7	4.2	3.9	3.5	3.3	4.1	4.1	3.8	3.2	3.2	3.0	2.8
Clarksville, TN	4.5	4.2	4.3	3.7	4.0	4.9	4.9	4.3	4.0	4.2	3.8	3.8
Cleveland, OH	4.7	4.8	4.3	3.6	3.8	4.5	4.6	4.0	3.7	3.3	3.3	3.5
College Station, TX	3.2	2.8	2.7	2.2	2.5	3.2	3.2	3.1	2.7	2.6	2.6	2.5
Colorado Springs, CO	4.3	3.9	3.7	3.3	3.0	3.5	3.4	3.2	2.8	2.8	2.8	2.8
Columbia, MO	2.8	2.6	2.6	1.9	2.3	2.6	2.9	2.7	1.9	1.9	2.2	2.4
Columbia, SC	3.8	3.3	3.2	2.4	2.6	3.0	2.9	2.7	1.9	2.2	2.1	2.2
Columbus, OH	4.3	3.7	3.5	3.0	3.2	3.8	4.0	3.8	3.5	3.4	3.3	3.2
Dallas, TX[2]	3.8	3.5	3.3	2.9	3.0	3.5	3.6	3.5	3.2	3.1	3.1	2.9
Davenport, IA	5.4	4.8	4.8	3.6	3.5	3.9	3.9	4.1	3.9	3.8	4.0	4.4
Denver, CO	3.5	3.1	3.0	2.7	2.5	2.8	2.6	2.6	2.3	2.3	2.3	2.3
Des Moines, IA	3.4	3.1	3.2	2.5	2.4	2.8	2.7	2.6	2.3	2.3	2.4	2.8
Durham, NC	3.9	3.7	3.6	3.2	3.5	3.8	3.8	3.7	3.0	3.1	3.0	2.9
Edison, NJ[2]	4.6	4.3	3.9	3.3	3.5	3.6	4.0	3.9	3.4	3.5	3.3	3.3
El Paso, TX	4.4	4.0	3.8	3.3	3.4	4.1	4.1	4.0	3.7	3.7	3.7	3.6
Fargo, ND	3.2	3.0	3.0	2.4	2.0	2.4	2.1	2.0	1.9	1.6	1.8	2.1
Fayetteville, NC	5.9	5.4	5.1	4.6	5.0	5.4	5.7	5.4	4.6	4.7	4.7	4.4
Fort Collins, CO	3.2	2.9	2.7	2.4	2.1	2.5	2.2	2.3	2.0	2.0	2.0	2.0
Fort Wayne, IN	3.8	3.5	3.3	2.5	2.7	3.1	3.4	3.1	2.6	3.3	3.1	2.8
Fort Worth, TX[2]	4.0	3.4	3.3	2.8	2.9	3.5	3.6	3.4	3.2	3.2	3.1	2.9
Grand Rapids, MI	3.4	3.2	3.3	2.6	2.8	3.2	3.9	3.0	2.6	2.3	2.3	2.4
Greeley, CO	3.3	3.0	2.9	2.5	2.2	2.8	2.6	2.5	2.2	2.2	2.2	2.3
Green Bay, WI	3.4	3.5	3.5	3.0	3.0	3.6	3.5	3.2	2.7	2.6	2.8	3.0
Greensboro, NC	4.7	4.4	4.2	3.7	4.0	4.4	4.6	4.4	3.6	3.7	3.6	3.4
Honolulu, HI	2.7	2.5	2.6	2.5	2.5	3.2	2.6	2.6	2.7	2.5	2.5	2.1
Houston, TX	4.4	4.0	3.7	3.3	3.4	4.0	4.1	4.1	3.7	3.6	3.7	3.6
Huntsville, AL	3.7	3.3	3.0	2.3	2.1	2.9	2.7	2.5	2.1	2.2	2.1	2.1
Indianapolis, IN	3.8	3.5	3.3	2.6	2.8	3.1	3.2	3.1	2.6	2.7	2.8	2.6
Jackson, MS	4.8	4.5	4.6	4.3	4.8	5.8	5.6	5.0	4.8	4.5	4.5	4.5
Jacksonville, FL	3.8	3.3	3.2	2.9	3.0	3.4	3.5	3.3	2.9	2.8	2.7	2.6
Kansas City, MO	3.8	3.6	3.6	2.8	3.0	3.3	4.0	3.5	2.7	2.9	2.9	3.1
Lafayette, LA	5.1	4.2	4.1	3.7	4.3	5.4	5.3	5.2	4.9	4.9	4.9	4.9
Lakeland, FL	4.4	3.8	3.7	3.4	3.6	4.0	4.1	4.0	3.5	3.4	3.3	3.1
Las Vegas, NV	4.6	4.2	4.1	4.0	4.0	4.4	4.3	4.1	3.9	3.8	3.6	3.5
Lexington, KY	3.7	3.8	3.8	3.1	3.4	3.9	3.8	3.4	3.0	3.0	3.0	3.0
Lincoln, NE	2.9	2.9	3.0	2.7	2.8	3.2	3.0	2.8	2.6	2.5	2.5	2.3
Little Rock, AR	3.7	3.6	3.1	2.7	3.0	3.4	3.7	3.3	3.1	2.9	2.9	3.1
Los Angeles, CA[2]	5.0	4.6	4.5	4.1	4.1	4.5	5.0	4.8	4.3	4.3	4.1	4.0
Louisville, KY	4.2	4.2	4.1	3.5	3.7	4.2	4.4	3.8	3.4	3.3	3.3	3.3

Table continued on next page.

Metro Area[1]	2019											
	Jan.	Feb.	Mar.	Apr.	May	Jun.	Jul.	Aug.	Sep.	Oct.	Nov.	Dec.
Madison, WI	2.7	2.8	2.8	2.4	2.6	3.1	2.7	2.5	2.2	2.2	2.2	2.3
Manchester, NH[3]	2.8	2.8	2.7	2.3	2.3	2.4	2.4	2.4	2.2	2.1	2.2	2.1
Miami, FL[2]	3.0	2.6	2.8	2.5	2.4	2.5	2.6	2.6	2.3	2.0	1.7	1.6
Midland, TX	2.3	2.1	2.0	1.7	1.8	2.1	2.2	2.3	2.1	2.1	2.1	2.0
Milwaukee, WI	3.6	3.6	3.7	3.2	3.3	4.1	4.0	3.8	3.3	3.2	3.3	3.2
Minneapolis, MN	3.7	3.4	3.4	2.7	2.6	3.1	3.0	2.9	2.5	2.6	2.6	3.0
Nashville, TN	2.9	2.5	2.7	2.3	2.4	3.0	3.0	2.7	2.4	2.6	2.4	2.3
New Haven, CT[3]	4.4	4.1	3.8	3.2	3.5	3.8	3.9	3.7	3.4	3.4	3.2	3.0
New Orleans, LA	4.9	3.9	3.8	3.5	4.0	5.2	5.1	5.0	4.6	4.7	4.6	4.5
New York, NY[2]	4.6	4.3	3.9	3.3	3.5	3.6	4.0	3.9	3.4	3.5	3.3	3.3
Oklahoma City, OK	3.5	3.2	3.0	2.6	3.0	3.3	3.1	3.1	2.9	3.0	2.9	2.8
Omaha, NE	3.5	3.4	3.5	3.0	3.0	3.3	3.3	3.0	2.8	2.7	2.6	2.7
Orlando, FL	3.7	3.2	3.1	2.8	2.9	3.2	3.3	3.1	2.8	2.8	2.7	2.5
Peoria, IL	6.5	5.8	5.5	4.1	3.8	4.3	4.6	4.6	4.2	4.2	4.2	4.7
Philadelphia, PA[2]	5.2	4.9	4.7	4.2	4.8	5.2	5.8	5.9	5.1	5.3	5.1	5.0
Phoenix, AZ	4.6	4.2	4.2	3.9	4.0	4.4	4.4	4.2	3.9	3.9	3.7	3.6
Pittsburgh, PA	4.7	4.5	4.3	3.5	3.9	4.4	4.8	4.7	4.0	4.3	4.3	4.5
Portland, OR	4.2	4.1	4.1	3.6	3.4	3.8	3.8	3.7	3.1	3.0	2.9	2.8
Providence, RI[3]	4.7	4.4	4.0	3.3	3.3	3.4	3.9	3.7	3.1	2.9	3.1	3.2
Provo, UT	2.6	2.8	2.8	2.4	2.4	2.8	2.6	2.5	2.0	1.9	1.9	2.0
Raleigh, NC	3.9	3.7	3.6	3.1	3.5	3.7	3.8	3.7	3.0	3.1	3.0	2.9
Reno, NV	4.0	3.8	3.6	3.3	3.1	3.2	3.2	3.1	3.0	2.8	2.7	2.8
Richmond, VA	3.5	3.3	3.1	2.6	2.8	3.1	3.1	3.2	2.8	2.7	2.6	2.5
Rochester, MN	3.7	3.4	3.5	2.6	2.4	2.9	2.7	2.6	2.2	2.2	2.3	3.0
Sacramento, CA	4.4	4.0	4.0	3.4	3.2	3.7	3.9	3.7	3.1	3.3	3.2	3.2
Salt Lake City, UT	2.8	3.0	3.0	2.6	2.5	2.9	2.6	2.6	2.2	2.1	2.0	2.1
San Antonio, TX	3.6	3.3	3.1	2.6	2.8	3.3	3.4	3.3	3.0	3.0	3.0	2.8
San Diego, CA	3.8	3.4	3.5	2.9	2.8	3.3	3.6	3.4	2.9	3.0	2.9	2.8
San Francisco, CA[2]	2.6	2.3	2.4	1.9	1.9	2.3	2.4	2.2	1.9	2.0	1.9	1.8
San Jose, CA	3.0	2.8	2.8	2.3	2.2	2.7	2.8	2.7	2.3	2.4	2.4	2.3
Santa Rosa, CA	3.3	3.0	3.1	2.5	2.4	2.8	2.9	2.7	2.3	2.4	2.4	2.4
Savannah, GA	3.9	3.5	3.3	2.9	3.1	3.5	3.5	3.5	2.9	3.0	2.6	2.7
Seattle, WA[2]	3.5	3.1	3.0	2.4	2.7	2.9	3.1	2.8	2.8	2.7	2.6	2.5
Sioux Falls, SD	3.1	3.2	3.1	2.8	2.6	2.7	2.4	2.7	2.6	2.6	2.8	3.0
Springfield, IL	5.5	4.9	4.7	3.5	3.3	3.8	4.0	4.0	3.5	3.5	3.5	3.8
Tallahassee, FL	3.9	3.2	3.2	2.9	3.0	3.5	3.7	3.4	3.0	2.9	2.8	2.6
Tampa, FL	3.8	3.4	3.3	3.0	3.1	3.4	3.4	3.3	2.9	2.9	2.8	2.7
Topeka, KS	4.0	3.8	3.7	2.8	3.0	3.2	3.7	3.4	2.8	2.9	3.0	3.2
Tucson, AZ	4.9	4.5	4.5	4.2	4.3	4.8	4.8	4.6	4.3	4.2	4.1	4.0
Tulsa, OK	3.7	3.5	3.2	2.8	3.2	3.4	3.3	3.2	3.1	3.5	3.2	3.1
Tuscaloosa, AL	3.8	3.5	3.2	2.4	2.4	3.3	3.2	2.8	2.4	2.3	2.3	2.3
Virginia Beach, VA	3.8	3.5	3.3	2.7	3.0	3.2	3.2	3.3	2.9	2.8	2.7	2.7
Washington, DC[2]	3.8	3.5	3.3	2.8	3.0	3.3	3.3	3.3	3.0	2.9	2.8	2.7
Wichita, KS	3.9	3.6	3.6	3.0	3.2	3.5	3.9	3.6	3.0	3.1	3.1	3.2
Winston-Salem, NC	4.2	3.9	3.8	3.3	3.7	4.0	4.1	4.0	3.3	3.3	3.3	3.2
U.S.	4.4	4.1	3.9	3.3	3.4	3.8	4.0	3.8	3.3	3.3	3.3	3.4

Note: Data is not seasonally adjusted and covers workers 16 years of age and older; All figures are percentages; (1) Figures cover the Metropolitan Statistical Area (MSA) except where noted. See Appendix B for areas included; (2) Metropolitan Division; (3) New England City and Town Area; (4) New England City and Town Area Division
Source: Bureau of Labor Statistics, Local Area Unemployment Statistics

Average Hourly Wages: Occupations A – C

Metro Area[1]	Accountants/ Auditors	Automotive Mechanics	Book-keepers	Carpenters	Cashiers	Computer Program-mers	Computer Systems Analysts
Albany, NY	37.14	21.98	21.13	26.01	12.51	37.84	41.17
Albuquerque, NM	32.14	20.92	19.44	19.67	11.26	35.58	38.70
Allentown, PA	37.03	20.99	19.46	22.30	10.67	37.47	43.24
Anchorage, AK	38.28	23.09	23.68	32.08	13.58	42.80	37.35
Ann Arbor, MI	35.35	30.07	20.24	30.66	11.86	33.82	39.27
Athens, GA	32.89	20.66	17.93	20.88	10.26	39.14	39.38
Atlanta, GA	40.08	21.90	20.91	24.99	10.58	42.73	44.08
Austin, TX	36.78	25.64	20.81	18.96	11.80	44.21	42.06
Baton Rouge, LA	29.85	21.34	19.70	23.02	9.90	38.05	37.72
Boise City, ID	31.58	21.95	19.61	17.54	11.69	34.27	39.26
Boston, MA[2]	41.02	22.94	24.26	30.75	13.34	46.89	47.92
Boulder, CO	42.26	22.96	22.13	25.41	13.07	41.88	48.66
Cape Coral, FL	30.72	20.29	18.87	18.84	11.71	40.00	33.95
Cedar Rapids, IA	34.51	21.27	19.71	23.62	11.04	37.37	41.59
Charleston, SC	30.76	22.36	17.50	26.42	10.70	38.89	38.50
Charlotte, NC	40.79	22.27	20.17	18.99	10.43	45.66	47.17
Chicago, IL	38.16	23.08	21.89	33.74	11.96	46.37	43.60
Clarksville, TN	27.63	18.33	19.01	19.31	10.47	35.61	34.64
Cleveland, OH	36.21	21.98	20.08	25.85	11.43	34.06	40.53
College Station, TX	28.30	24.93	16.62	18.00	11.15	42.37	36.62
Colorado Springs, CO	36.53	24.03	19.46	22.26	13.21	37.07	48.44
Columbia, MO	28.38	21.40	16.91	23.44	10.60	32.06	38.88
Columbia, SC	29.67	20.86	18.25	23.03	10.20	39.92	37.92
Columbus, OH	37.18	20.52	20.86	24.94	11.35	41.63	43.68
Dallas, TX	39.65	22.62	21.28	18.84	11.03	47.47	46.75
Davenport, IA	34.05	20.11	19.12	24.10	10.92	42.33	44.57
Denver, CO	41.34	24.85	22.11	24.71	13.51	47.15	48.32
Des Moines, IA	36.17	22.67	21.26	21.29	11.34	39.09	41.21
Durham, NC	38.77	23.28	21.08	18.91	10.46	45.03	43.54
Edison, NJ	49.08	23.62	23.78	34.15	13.25	47.15	54.84
El Paso, TX	29.95	16.01	16.46	16.95	10.31	42.20	40.21
Fargo, ND	31.57	22.38	19.03	21.17	11.81	37.08	38.03
Fayetteville, NC	34.72	16.37	18.20	17.60	10.06	26.42	37.05
Fort Collins, CO	35.60	24.78	20.37	23.65	13.47	46.30	45.38
Fort Wayne, IN	32.05	17.53	18.55	21.15	10.53	31.88	36.04
Fort Worth, TX	39.65	22.62	21.28	18.84	11.03	47.47	46.75
Grand Rapids, MI	32.96	19.88	18.51	21.63	11.59	32.55	36.90
Greeley, CO	37.13	23.41	19.64	21.12	12.67	39.57	51.01
Green Bay, WI	33.28	19.70	19.43	25.22	10.89	36.57	41.50
Greensboro, NC	39.46	19.74	19.47	18.22	10.02	39.99	46.05
Honolulu, HI	31.79	23.62	20.85	37.81	13.09	38.72	38.28
Houston, TX	40.07	21.71	21.33	21.37	11.12	48.11	57.47
Huntsville, AL	36.24	22.25	20.03	19.26	11.06	46.48	46.81
Indianapolis, IN	36.98	21.07	20.57	24.37	10.91	44.65	40.57
Jackson, MS	30.51	18.96	19.69	15.44	10.13	38.80	30.23
Jacksonville, FL	31.81	19.03	20.08	19.26	10.93	41.29	38.89
Kansas City, MO	34.08	22.71	20.08	26.94	11.36	41.73	37.19
Lafayette, LA	32.89	18.01	18.24	20.13	9.57	37.61	38.75
Lakeland, FL	36.25	19.66	18.84	16.75	11.33	32.19	35.23
Las Vegas, NV	32.44	21.74	19.29	25.79	11.67	40.52	40.37
Lexington, KY	31.52	19.80	18.55	22.51	10.44	37.45	38.74
Lincoln, NE	32.51	22.16	18.43	19.95	11.30	34.07	35.89
Little Rock, AR	32.45	19.81	18.57	19.23	11.10	36.45	35.15
Los Angeles, CA	39.09	23.57	23.12	30.71	13.55	46.06	50.66
Louisville, KY	35.52	19.75	19.25	24.90	10.64	35.68	37.78

Table continued on next page.

Metro Area[1]	Accountants/ Auditors	Automotive Mechanics	Book-keepers	Carpenters	Cashiers	Computer Program-mers	Computer Systems Analysts
Madison, WI	34.05	22.75	20.26	26.58	11.64	40.03	45.12
Manchester, NH[2]	36.25	22.90	19.88	21.76	11.14	37.48	44.94
Miami, FL	37.70	21.81	20.99	20.27	11.15	41.69	43.26
Midland, TX	41.77	30.89	23.13	19.98	12.38	n/a	n/a
Milwaukee, WI	34.94	20.51	20.17	27.24	11.20	40.73	39.12
Minneapolis, MN	36.38	23.08	22.64	28.39	12.72	40.37	46.92
Nashville, TN	34.90	20.91	21.28	21.87	11.12	45.45	40.13
New Haven, CT[2]	39.30	23.37	23.10	28.21	12.08	43.62	38.51
New Orleans, LA	33.61	20.20	18.52	21.17	10.14	46.89	42.95
New York, NY	49.08	23.62	23.78	34.15	13.25	47.15	54.84
Oklahoma City, OK	37.06	22.24	19.29	20.42	10.56	38.08	36.42
Omaha, NE	35.06	21.89	19.86	19.93	11.68	38.98	39.66
Orlando, FL	34.31	18.21	19.18	20.47	11.19	39.76	42.44
Peoria, IL	38.53	18.65	18.31	29.95	11.09	36.71	45.80
Philadelphia, PA	40.67	22.29	21.58	30.42	11.17	45.46	50.37
Phoenix, AZ	35.87	22.38	21.00	22.49	12.55	50.11	43.81
Pittsburgh, PA	34.47	20.58	19.12	28.61	10.33	39.70	44.95
Portland, OR	36.26	23.17	21.90	27.86	13.76	42.89	46.05
Providence, RI[2]	40.32	20.30	21.93	25.67	12.58	49.06	47.32
Provo, UT	32.01	22.54	18.34	21.02	11.20	44.93	40.43
Raleigh, NC	35.40	22.29	20.05	20.43	10.54	50.56	46.02
Reno, NV	33.50	24.12	20.02	25.36	11.59	39.18	37.99
Richmond, VA	38.95	23.60	20.35	21.68	10.49	43.28	48.47
Rochester, MN	30.80	21.40	20.03	25.80	12.37	32.85	41.17
Sacramento, CA	38.83	24.47	22.29	27.62	14.13	38.83	47.61
Salt Lake City, UT	33.61	21.56	20.32	22.39	11.38	39.79	36.18
San Antonio, TX	36.17	21.80	19.81	19.68	11.38	45.59	48.05
San Diego, CA	41.93	24.43	22.67	26.74	13.28	50.01	47.34
San Francisco, CA	45.00	28.19	26.44	34.37	15.46	55.96	58.32
San Jose, CA	43.63	28.37	25.91	30.55	15.71	54.80	59.13
Santa Rosa, CA	40.63	26.25	25.14	33.87	14.80	44.48	41.28
Savannah, GA	34.86	24.77	19.74	20.59	9.96	37.34	39.94
Seattle, WA	41.55	24.80	23.46	32.88	15.30	n/a	51.29
Sioux Falls, SD	33.97	20.04	17.10	18.53	11.60	28.97	35.29
Springfield, IL	36.96	21.45	19.26	27.13	10.79	45.78	43.42
Tallahassee, FL	26.00	21.48	18.58	20.22	10.50	29.30	28.95
Tampa, FL	34.88	19.82	20.08	18.98	10.99	38.90	43.23
Topeka, KS	29.91	18.52	17.23	20.48	10.44	38.67	35.06
Tucson, AZ	34.55	19.87	19.07	18.15	12.55	44.62	41.51
Tulsa, OK	35.43	19.18	20.71	21.09	10.52	38.26	37.65
Tuscaloosa, AL	33.45	19.28	17.55	22.16	9.90	34.09	45.33
Virginia Beach, VA	34.90	23.77	19.78	21.14	10.53	38.82	45.19
Washington, DC	45.95	26.87	24.32	23.91	12.61	48.12	52.31
Wichita, KS	32.41	19.27	17.85	18.17	10.52	37.60	35.81
Winston-Salem, NC	35.17	20.03	18.71	19.76	9.76	42.63	44.48

Notes: (1) Figures cover the Metropolitan Statistical Area (MSA) except where noted. See Appendix B for areas included;
(2) New England City and Town Area; n/a not available
Source: Bureau of Labor Statistics, May 2019 Metro Area Occupational Employment and Wage Estimates

Average Hourly Wages: Occupations C – E

Metro Area	Comp. User Support Specialists	Construction Laborers	Cooks, Restaurant	Customer Service Reps.	Dentists	Electricians	Engineers, Electrical
Albany, NY	25.26	22.24	14.33	18.95	90.79	28.68	52.68
Albuquerque, NM	20.62	15.60	12.18	15.15	96.94	22.90	57.47
Allentown, PA	24.86	21.97	13.24	17.12	71.96	26.45	47.18
Anchorage, AK	29.26	27.14	14.19	19.18	n/a	35.46	52.97
Ann Arbor, MI	23.20	21.69	14.48	17.88	86.08	32.75	41.95
Athens, GA	22.01	16.34	12.48	16.00	n/a	24.44	n/a
Atlanta, GA	26.71	16.36	13.06	17.83	84.20	25.99	47.44
Austin, TX	25.33	15.71	13.11	16.69	79.01	25.61	50.72
Baton Rouge, LA	23.07	17.06	12.22	15.98	87.21	24.62	50.55
Boise City, ID	24.07	16.86	12.14	16.78	104.19	24.18	45.39
Boston, MA[2]	31.88	27.30	16.61	21.99	92.59	34.67	55.97
Boulder, CO	29.74	17.75	15.59	19.68	102.36	26.09	51.53
Cape Coral, FL	22.75	16.46	14.08	16.17	81.52	21.10	52.35
Cedar Rapids, IA	22.15	20.10	11.29	19.17	66.62	28.03	50.65
Charleston, SC	25.13	15.51	13.07	17.88	69.84	20.87	45.87
Charlotte, NC	25.03	15.28	12.91	18.54	87.85	22.31	50.50
Chicago, IL	26.10	31.19	14.41	19.29	88.64	39.10	47.02
Clarksville, TN	20.32	17.10	10.67	13.13	79.90	25.43	41.59
Cleveland, OH	24.20	23.98	13.15	18.59	97.76	27.10	42.18
College Station, TX	21.12	14.78	11.30	14.26	101.07	24.20	18.65
Colorado Springs, CO	26.44	17.07	13.59	16.01	60.46	24.27	51.47
Columbia, MO	22.37	19.48	11.98	15.20	97.87	23.07	41.86
Columbia, SC	23.79	15.95	11.67	16.52	88.79	23.50	44.86
Columbus, OH	26.77	23.02	13.54	17.86	92.65	23.80	39.78
Dallas, TX	24.63	16.53	13.21	17.94	99.61	24.23	52.96
Davenport, IA	23.30	20.77	11.63	16.46	92.01	27.48	42.03
Denver, CO	29.99	18.57	14.27	19.92	86.46	26.23	46.89
Des Moines, IA	25.88	18.67	13.92	20.37	105.37	26.15	37.91
Durham, NC	28.96	16.17	13.17	19.12	107.67	24.39	51.10
Edison, NJ	31.64	27.79	16.19	21.00	82.04	39.73	54.88
El Paso, TX	19.30	13.62	10.44	12.23	85.55	18.02	39.61
Fargo, ND	22.33	20.89	14.13	17.75	93.20	27.04	41.94
Fayetteville, NC	22.50	13.88	12.71	14.23	100.61	20.71	38.70
Fort Collins, CO	28.51	17.68	14.15	16.99	85.10	27.74	53.36
Fort Wayne, IN	21.67	19.72	12.27	18.80	82.65	26.65	45.20
Fort Worth, TX	24.63	16.53	13.21	17.94	99.61	24.23	52.96
Grand Rapids, MI	24.64	17.96	12.85	18.14	114.68	23.30	39.23
Greeley, CO	25.01	17.20	13.98	16.21	86.02	26.20	50.26
Green Bay, WI	24.42	20.16	12.82	18.33	115.17	27.29	40.63
Greensboro, NC	24.17	14.95	11.80	17.55	72.54	22.11	48.74
Honolulu, HI	24.40	28.79	16.08	18.91	98.86	37.27	42.56
Houston, TX	28.46	17.49	12.62	16.95	80.14	27.63	53.58
Huntsville, AL	23.24	17.22	12.44	17.71	n/a	23.54	51.24
Indianapolis, IN	23.61	18.50	12.80	18.39	75.84	28.31	45.05
Jackson, MS	21.70	13.83	12.21	14.74	71.64	21.94	47.93
Jacksonville, FL	24.64	16.85	12.90	17.27	89.67	21.54	44.66
Kansas City, MO	24.96	21.21	13.56	18.09	83.36	27.89	42.90
Lafayette, LA	24.51	16.86	11.94	15.38	68.02	22.80	42.74
Lakeland, FL	24.93	15.69	12.99	15.26	63.65	18.68	n/a
Las Vegas, NV	24.00	17.83	16.56	15.87	90.67	32.38	40.60
Lexington, KY	25.59	17.40	11.75	15.13	56.73	24.45	41.83
Lincoln, NE	22.84	16.48	14.06	15.89	58.01	24.44	44.77
Little Rock, AR	23.11	13.40	11.52	16.35	86.87	20.35	43.76
Los Angeles, CA	28.56	22.75	14.84	19.86	68.18	32.79	55.78
Louisville, KY	24.15	18.31	12.78	17.33	66.47	27.20	44.11

Table continued on next page.

Metro Area	Comp. User Support Specialists	Construction Laborers	Cooks, Restaurant	Customer Service Reps.	Dentists	Electricians	Engineers, Electrical
Madison, WI	27.73	21.06	12.66	19.53	116.74	26.53	44.99
Manchester, NH[2]	26.99	18.92	14.64	19.31	107.59	28.28	51.74
Miami, FL	25.83	15.87	14.63	17.17	83.15	22.25	46.45
Midland, TX	24.73	17.12	12.99	16.22	n/a	27.90	n/a
Milwaukee, WI	25.53	23.56	13.16	19.99	103.15	33.43	42.04
Minneapolis, MN	27.75	27.45	15.32	20.56	105.30	35.62	49.83
Nashville, TN	23.88	16.56	13.06	17.77	83.04	24.19	44.46
New Haven, CT[2]	28.04	21.77	14.55	19.13	113.63	30.62	48.37
New Orleans, LA	23.04	15.65	11.96	16.34	75.82	25.38	51.30
New York, NY	31.64	27.79	16.19	21.00	82.04	39.73	54.88
Oklahoma City, OK	23.59	15.97	12.52	16.40	83.46	24.64	45.21
Omaha, NE	26.30	18.46	13.70	17.60	86.30	27.55	43.76
Orlando, FL	24.59	15.97	13.80	16.27	91.87	23.94	48.65
Peoria, IL	24.48	22.10	13.00	15.28	102.94	31.59	n/a
Philadelphia, PA	28.44	24.19	14.50	19.31	88.27	36.84	51.43
Phoenix, AZ	26.32	18.47	14.17	17.53	94.38	23.59	49.26
Pittsburgh, PA	23.85	21.02	12.83	17.48	65.49	33.24	46.92
Portland, OR	28.28	22.32	15.38	19.56	93.45	37.22	45.14
Providence, RI[2]	30.49	25.33	14.88	18.95	122.22	28.58	50.61
Provo, UT	26.46	16.19	13.55	15.62	n/a	22.90	33.94
Raleigh, NC	26.13	16.40	15.52	17.16	106.48	20.77	44.04
Reno, NV	24.33	19.34	15.12	16.89	123.32	26.74	45.10
Richmond, VA	24.72	14.58	12.09	17.31	83.04	24.66	47.43
Rochester, MN	26.15	21.60	13.72	17.49	92.33	28.29	45.94
Sacramento, CA	n/a	23.57	13.80	20.27	82.00	28.63	48.32
Salt Lake City, UT	25.46	19.00	12.45	17.68	65.16	27.41	46.53
San Antonio, TX	23.59	15.76	12.26	15.91	78.68	23.65	46.14
San Diego, CA	29.23	24.31	15.01	19.39	67.18	29.25	51.01
San Francisco, CA	36.37	26.91	18.48	23.66	81.60	48.27	58.17
San Jose, CA	39.28	25.85	16.57	22.96	95.41	37.46	66.56
Santa Rosa, CA	26.38	24.01	16.32	19.49	86.63	32.45	52.32
Savannah, GA	23.54	15.27	12.16	15.53	98.26	23.63	50.04
Seattle, WA	31.68	25.34	17.22	21.45	81.87	36.51	57.20
Sioux Falls, SD	19.73	15.30	12.85	16.01	89.26	23.15	39.94
Springfield, IL	24.99	25.25	11.75	16.92	81.74	32.54	45.84
Tallahassee, FL	22.49	13.21	12.90	15.42	77.29	20.76	44.85
Tampa, FL	25.21	15.18	12.79	16.85	84.73	20.95	48.04
Topeka, KS	22.67	16.57	11.75	16.65	n/a	25.24	44.78
Tucson, AZ	24.77	16.62	13.23	15.05	n/a	22.76	41.92
Tulsa, OK	23.18	15.85	11.88	16.20	73.73	23.66	48.84
Tuscaloosa, AL	30.30	14.49	10.31	15.46	56.44	25.05	44.82
Virginia Beach, VA	26.77	15.98	12.52	15.20	84.96	23.50	45.63
Washington, DC	31.40	17.84	15.02	20.44	93.73	31.25	61.58
Wichita, KS	21.31	16.06	12.52	16.28	101.24	25.40	44.91
Winston-Salem, NC	24.42	15.04	10.97	16.44	72.62	22.40	41.38

*Notes: (1) Figures cover the Metropolitan Statistical Area (MSA) except where noted. See Appendix B for areas included;
(2) New England City and Town Area; n/a not available
Source: Bureau of Labor Statistics, May 2019 Metro Area Occupational Employment and Wage Estimates*

Average Hourly Wages: Occupations F – H

Metro Area	Fast Food and Counter Workers	Financial Managers	First-Line Supervisors/ of Office Workers	General and Operations Managers	Hair-dressers/ Cosme-tologists	Home Health and Personal Care Aides	Janitors/ Cleaners
Albany, NY	12.71	66.86	31.17	59.83	14.36	14.79	14.66
Albuquerque, NM	10.06	53.72	26.69	53.73	11.04	11.17	11.91
Allentown, PA	10.63	75.22	28.11	58.27	14.60	12.59	15.49
Anchorage, AK	12.04	55.16	30.95	57.10	13.88	15.86	15.72
Ann Arbor, MI	11.56	63.65	29.10	66.05	12.60	12.37	15.48
Athens, GA	9.41	55.43	26.14	44.78	11.73	11.64	12.18
Atlanta, GA	9.72	73.82	28.56	59.32	16.52	12.75	12.21
Austin, TX	11.19	68.81	30.94	60.03	16.55	10.77	13.47
Baton Rouge, LA	9.09	51.40	24.70	54.56	12.62	9.46	10.55
Boise City, ID	9.73	50.93	25.82	42.17	17.19	11.73	12.26
Boston, MA[2]	13.38	76.41	33.36	69.87	21.00	15.23	17.93
Boulder, CO	12.56	82.65	31.43	71.52	25.06	15.40	16.14
Cape Coral, FL	10.87	51.89	26.48	46.31	15.70	12.13	13.57
Cedar Rapids, IA	10.60	59.33	26.64	53.80	12.55	13.24	15.21
Charleston, SC	10.42	61.85	26.11	53.75	14.62	11.11	11.09
Charlotte, NC	9.98	79.88	28.71	63.42	15.61	10.69	12.16
Chicago, IL	11.52	73.96	31.01	63.72	14.89	12.77	14.98
Clarksville, TN	9.13	50.79	21.81	41.42	11.64	10.64	12.63
Cleveland, OH	10.73	72.38	29.02	61.01	13.60	11.24	14.13
College Station, TX	9.95	57.50	25.67	47.56	13.60	10.57	12.39
Colorado Springs, CO	11.77	65.52	27.45	58.64	17.93	13.51	14.29
Columbia, MO	12.09	62.04	26.92	40.26	14.89	11.50	13.94
Columbia, SC	8.97	59.48	25.52	52.23	17.00	11.02	11.87
Columbus, OH	10.30	68.79	28.42	59.02	14.62	11.84	13.73
Dallas, TX	10.46	76.09	29.51	64.59	12.89	10.35	13.15
Davenport, IA	10.45	54.23	25.25	46.95	12.12	12.41	13.69
Denver, CO	12.48	83.20	31.77	70.13	17.90	13.41	14.12
Des Moines, IA	11.04	63.63	30.82	53.83	15.35	13.54	13.65
Durham, NC	11.05	77.44	29.78	64.91	15.77	10.77	13.58
Edison, NJ	12.97	100.37	35.24	80.36	17.37	13.93	17.85
El Paso, TX	9.33	50.79	22.87	47.30	11.21	8.88	11.13
Fargo, ND	12.32	69.09	26.50	56.76	16.96	14.77	13.85
Fayetteville, NC	9.70	60.79	24.08	56.25	13.67	10.54	12.02
Fort Collins, CO	12.68	68.01	28.01	52.20	16.75	14.13	14.60
Fort Wayne, IN	10.40	56.43	27.74	51.54	12.99	11.41	12.01
Fort Worth, TX	10.46	76.09	29.51	64.59	12.89	10.35	13.15
Grand Rapids, MI	11.36	56.20	27.38	56.59	14.96	12.57	13.40
Greeley, CO	11.98	72.15	29.89	58.65	14.27	14.06	14.31
Green Bay, WI	9.94	57.88	28.14	59.73	13.79	12.10	13.68
Greensboro, NC	9.46	66.09	26.75	60.44	11.97	10.28	11.91
Honolulu, HI	12.65	60.86	29.31	57.78	17.48	13.77	15.88
Houston, TX	10.16	72.10	28.88	61.30	12.68	9.81	12.03
Huntsville, AL	9.05	62.73	25.70	66.53	11.13	9.45	12.45
Indianapolis, IN	10.07	64.04	29.90	58.90	14.82	11.68	13.44
Jackson, MS	9.30	47.68	24.30	45.38	n/a	10.31	10.90
Jacksonville, FL	10.10	62.05	27.29	51.77	17.87	12.10	12.13
Kansas City, MO	10.95	69.71	29.01	53.05	14.98	11.50	14.44
Lafayette, LA	9.24	49.32	23.91	58.92	9.92	9.96	10.19
Lakeland, FL	9.97	50.02	25.31	47.71	12.69	11.37	11.87
Las Vegas, NV	10.81	57.84	25.16	61.28	10.35	12.14	15.68
Lexington, KY	9.72	57.85	27.54	45.07	12.14	11.97	13.78
Lincoln, NE	11.16	57.16	26.38	47.98	12.08	12.86	13.50
Little Rock, AR	10.04	51.38	24.77	46.70	11.92	11.16	11.46
Los Angeles, CA	12.94	74.75	30.77	66.70	15.39	14.17	16.39

Table continued on next page.

Metro Area	Fast Food and Counter Workers	Financial Managers	First-Line Supervisors/ of Office Workers	General and Operations Managers	Hair- dressers/ Cosme- tologists	Home Health and Personal Care Aides	Janitors/ Cleaners
Louisville, KY	9.90	59.54	27.02	48.65	17.90	13.41	13.40
Madison, WI	10.51	66.59	29.92	62.63	14.77	13.33	14.96
Manchester, NH[2]	10.86	62.88	30.16	63.21	14.74	12.64	12.97
Miami, FL	10.46	67.63	28.38	53.70	14.41	11.74	12.55
Midland, TX	10.82	63.41	30.34	72.55	11.67	10.86	11.90
Milwaukee, WI	10.18	70.57	30.22	70.79	15.31	11.77	13.82
Minneapolis, MN	12.27	69.26	31.76	61.66	16.59	13.76	16.08
Nashville, TN	10.36	59.61	28.87	58.08	15.23	11.16	13.11
New Haven, CT[2]	12.33	65.10	33.02	68.40	15.01	13.06	17.45
New Orleans, LA	9.97	53.01	24.87	60.12	9.79	9.84	11.47
New York, NY	12.97	100.37	35.24	80.36	17.37	13.93	17.85
Oklahoma City, OK	10.15	55.43	26.06	54.35	12.88	11.92	12.23
Omaha, NE	11.19	58.04	27.45	50.02	16.46	13.14	13.74
Orlando, FL	10.14	64.28	26.15	48.71	13.74	11.60	11.77
Peoria, IL	10.35	60.15	27.12	52.70	15.31	12.11	12.12
Philadelphia, PA	11.24	80.70	32.32	73.68	15.44	12.61	15.05
Phoenix, AZ	12.26	61.64	27.81	54.09	15.71	12.57	13.74
Pittsburgh, PA	10.32	72.29	28.90	62.36	12.00	12.53	14.61
Portland, OR	13.22	62.47	29.54	58.29	15.46	14.23	15.73
Providence, RI[2]	12.44	76.47	31.89	72.09	15.44	14.51	15.05
Provo, UT	10.21	58.01	24.68	41.71	15.81	12.73	10.89
Raleigh, NC	9.62	67.68	27.04	70.09	14.97	11.08	11.60
Reno, NV	9.88	63.93	27.01	59.17	13.45	11.86	13.67
Richmond, VA	9.88	77.35	29.22	63.63	18.25	10.26	11.37
Rochester, MN	12.58	53.95	26.80	45.20	14.56	13.54	15.98
Sacramento, CA	12.90	64.18	30.43	58.64	15.26	13.04	15.82
Salt Lake City, UT	9.95	57.11	26.78	42.67	15.87	13.90	12.23
San Antonio, TX	10.69	68.43	26.03	57.19	12.71	10.33	12.75
San Diego, CA	13.30	71.77	29.63	67.78	16.16	13.94	16.89
San Francisco, CA	15.20	87.59	34.23	74.93	17.02	14.58	18.69
San Jose, CA	14.65	85.55	33.71	78.24	15.58	14.50	17.96
Santa Rosa, CA	13.26	66.14	29.94	59.73	15.72	14.36	16.52
Savannah, GA	9.37	46.77	26.32	48.85	11.76	10.89	11.78
Seattle, WA	14.99	72.43	35.12	67.14	21.81	15.30	18.67
Sioux Falls, SD	10.88	70.79	25.03	68.77	14.13	13.31	13.04
Springfield, IL	10.13	58.82	27.49	45.27	20.34	11.99	14.94
Tallahassee, FL	10.43	n/a	23.39	n/a	14.69	12.29	12.53
Tampa, FL	10.24	67.59	28.17	53.69	14.48	11.33	15.02
Topeka, KS	9.71	59.60	24.76	39.13	11.40	11.26	13.35
Tucson, AZ	12.14	49.12	24.74	46.13	17.22	12.18	13.35
Tulsa, OK	9.22	68.27	26.69	53.29	12.96	10.15	11.54
Tuscaloosa, AL	9.34	57.37	24.86	53.07	11.13	9.26	13.37
Virginia Beach, VA	10.19	66.74	27.90	55.99	13.37	10.17	11.58
Washington, DC	12.86	83.74	33.53	73.22	18.56	13.75	15.31
Wichita, KS	9.54	61.50	26.51	48.04	12.55	11.05	12.54
Winston-Salem, NC	9.78	73.82	26.29	61.91	11.56	10.94	11.07

Notes: (1) Figures cover the Metropolitan Statistical Area (MSA) except where noted. See Appendix B for areas included;
(2) New England City and Town Area; n/a not available
Source: Bureau of Labor Statistics, May 2019 Metro Area Occupational Employment and Wage Estimates

Average Hourly Wages: Occupations L – N

Metro Area	Landscapers	Lawyers	Maids/ House- keepers	Main- tenance/ Repairers	Marketing Managers	Network Admin.	Nurses, Licensed Practical
Albany, NY	16.61	55.63	12.65	19.95	69.54	40.97	21.53
Albuquerque, NM	14.13	52.03	10.65	18.32	47.06	38.13	23.83
Allentown, PA	15.13	55.66	12.05	21.77	64.30	38.07	24.41
Anchorage, AK	18.48	54.24	14.17	23.49	49.53	38.58	31.45
Ann Arbor, MI	15.81	63.20	12.61	18.05	63.74	37.40	25.62
Athens, GA	15.25	38.56	10.14	15.81	62.80	30.54	21.47
Atlanta, GA	14.72	65.79	10.49	19.38	69.89	43.27	21.57
Austin, TX	14.63	66.82	10.89	18.35	69.15	42.36	23.28
Baton Rouge, LA	14.59	52.19	10.11	19.84	46.62	33.99	19.19
Boise City, ID	15.53	52.91	11.15	18.17	61.75	34.51	22.97
Boston, MA[2]	19.08	81.69	16.47	24.78	70.15	47.31	30.10
Boulder, CO	18.67	n/a	13.95	23.16	88.20	44.04	26.21
Cape Coral, FL	14.08	66.18	11.83	17.79	52.57	35.97	21.13
Cedar Rapids, IA	15.66	54.57	11.90	22.61	64.86	38.74	20.72
Charleston, SC	14.39	48.48	11.10	18.58	58.20	41.92	22.10
Charlotte, NC	14.31	71.90	11.13	20.63	70.95	41.75	22.24
Chicago, IL	16.34	78.12	13.95	22.29	65.12	42.64	27.74
Clarksville, TN	13.94	35.64	11.18	20.34	n/a	35.25	20.46
Cleveland, OH	16.35	66.12	11.41	20.40	62.41	42.45	23.46
College Station, TX	14.04	56.29	11.99	16.48	68.78	32.56	22.47
Colorado Springs, CO	15.32	54.92	12.37	19.15	75.25	37.25	26.20
Columbia, MO	14.19	43.39	11.06	15.04	47.63	33.27	20.52
Columbia, SC	13.30	57.79	10.34	17.69	53.72	37.81	21.16
Columbus, OH	15.18	55.53	11.47	20.42	72.35	41.47	21.21
Dallas, TX	15.23	72.65	11.58	20.73	68.09	43.71	24.58
Davenport, IA	14.93	72.09	10.90	19.28	62.55	37.42	21.46
Denver, CO	16.98	75.05	12.95	20.94	83.90	44.37	26.68
Des Moines, IA	15.96	63.21	12.06	20.39	61.21	40.19	22.46
Durham, NC	14.73	61.76	12.59	21.10	72.51	46.32	23.57
Edison, NJ	17.75	84.00	18.03	23.20	90.77	50.51	27.22
El Paso, TX	11.12	60.05	9.60	14.89	48.75	33.62	22.96
Fargo, ND	17.71	52.21	12.81	19.71	58.14	35.51	21.43
Fayetteville, NC	12.66	56.99	10.17	18.69	n/a	41.44	22.13
Fort Collins, CO	15.68	67.69	13.02	20.57	81.85	37.31	25.53
Fort Wayne, IN	13.46	72.97	10.61	20.76	57.63	33.76	22.09
Fort Worth, TX	15.23	72.65	11.58	20.73	68.09	43.71	24.58
Grand Rapids, MI	15.40	48.62	12.53	18.26	61.15	33.59	22.49
Greeley, CO	17.32	53.55	11.68	21.67	64.61	34.64	26.85
Green Bay, WI	15.15	54.19	11.71	21.32	51.80	32.13	20.45
Greensboro, NC	14.48	56.40	10.00	19.59	66.25	39.79	21.26
Honolulu, HI	18.35	53.20	19.58	23.46	52.81	39.38	24.20
Houston, TX	13.93	74.77	10.97	19.55	82.00	47.94	23.24
Huntsville, AL	13.87	59.80	10.34	18.46	70.21	38.52	19.16
Indianapolis, IN	15.51	53.88	11.38	19.79	57.76	41.96	22.75
Jackson, MS	13.07	49.93	10.48	15.84	42.18	32.98	18.97
Jacksonville, FL	13.51	60.93	11.66	19.47	61.84	37.78	21.56
Kansas City, MO	18.01	57.70	11.30	20.23	70.75	40.50	22.43
Lafayette, LA	13.71	43.96	9.53	16.77	48.52	32.39	18.58
Lakeland, FL	13.21	43.35	10.77	19.55	57.87	35.19	20.64
Las Vegas, NV	15.06	64.40	15.76	23.05	69.18	41.71	27.98
Lexington, KY	15.44	52.98	10.64	19.45	48.13	30.32	21.38
Lincoln, NE	13.86	46.65	13.08	20.93	43.70	34.43	21.12
Little Rock, AR	13.31	44.27	10.43	16.03	59.58	34.37	21.16
Los Angeles, CA	17.38	85.80	15.11	21.96	75.89	44.83	28.23
Louisville, KY	15.58	56.25	11.39	21.05	61.35	35.88	21.49

Table continued on next page.

Metro Area	Landscapers	Lawyers	Maids/ House-keepers	Main-tenance/ Repairers	Marketing Managers	Network Admin.	Nurses, Licensed Practical
Madison, WI	16.89	58.03	13.08	21.17	60.00	37.93	23.54
Manchester, NH[2]	16.52	61.80	12.16	21.81	74.30	42.31	27.03
Miami, FL	14.20	72.28	11.70	18.01	62.25	41.57	22.99
Midland, TX	14.53	75.11	12.22	19.03	76.11	43.93	25.09
Milwaukee, WI	16.23	70.54	12.41	20.82	64.02	37.75	24.13
Minneapolis, MN	17.78	61.85	14.53	23.02	71.45	43.14	24.46
Nashville, TN	12.71	62.37	11.84	19.37	62.42	38.87	21.39
New Haven, CT[2]	20.17	62.60	14.06	24.41	64.28	42.56	27.31
New Orleans, LA	12.70	59.37	10.79	18.29	46.04	33.09	21.17
New York, NY	17.75	84.00	18.03	23.20	90.77	50.51	27.22
Oklahoma City, OK	13.92	56.72	10.66	17.57	61.40	36.98	20.87
Omaha, NE	16.15	59.14	12.08	20.68	52.47	40.22	22.13
Orlando, FL	13.34	56.41	11.51	17.11	54.92	40.21	21.76
Peoria, IL	13.90	63.13	12.05	20.70	72.69	35.55	22.20
Philadelphia, PA	16.60	75.42	13.32	21.46	75.14	40.94	27.29
Phoenix, AZ	14.47	67.36	12.45	19.68	60.19	41.75	26.82
Pittsburgh, PA	14.66	66.25	11.87	19.73	66.49	37.06	21.92
Portland, OR	18.15	59.50	14.53	21.39	60.77	42.47	26.32
Providence, RI[2]	16.85	57.97	14.49	22.10	76.92	44.58	27.61
Provo, UT	15.31	73.09	12.02	18.50	56.11	39.03	22.44
Raleigh, NC	15.18	68.47	11.01	20.18	72.37	43.52	22.35
Reno, NV	15.10	61.20	12.83	21.76	66.32	41.89	29.59
Richmond, VA	16.10	69.42	11.38	20.36	81.92	43.83	22.18
Rochester, MN	16.15	54.88	12.55	20.16	55.41	34.75	23.71
Sacramento, CA	18.45	67.75	16.44	21.19	71.07	45.30	28.99
Salt Lake City, UT	15.70	68.65	12.61	20.12	62.44	39.69	27.61
San Antonio, TX	14.00	61.68	11.30	17.52	74.11	39.20	22.02
San Diego, CA	16.24	69.26	14.52	21.39	71.32	47.38	29.96
San Francisco, CA	21.12	90.82	19.92	27.04	87.37	50.18	33.41
San Jose, CA	21.00	105.01	17.47	26.35	96.02	58.39	32.77
Santa Rosa, CA	18.98	73.32	15.18	23.74	69.97	43.51	31.38
Savannah, GA	13.16	55.37	10.23	17.51	55.24	36.24	20.72
Seattle, WA	19.31	66.58	15.28	23.16	79.87	47.67	29.02
Sioux Falls, SD	14.70	72.86	11.27	18.37	66.87	31.58	18.94
Springfield, IL	15.02	51.10	12.15	19.58	52.94	36.84	21.61
Tallahassee, FL	12.69	56.18	10.24	16.37	44.33	32.35	20.16
Tampa, FL	13.59	54.03	11.75	17.97	64.95	39.43	22.02
Topeka, KS	16.27	49.93	10.52	18.55	59.15	41.48	21.49
Tucson, AZ	14.17	61.92	11.99	17.05	52.26	38.34	24.53
Tulsa, OK	14.27	63.43	10.84	18.12	62.33	37.35	20.62
Tuscaloosa, AL	14.39	45.79	10.09	15.62	44.79	39.87	18.51
Virginia Beach, VA	13.30	60.58	11.11	19.04	66.58	38.30	20.81
Washington, DC	16.25	86.34	14.85	23.67	83.51	48.80	26.41
Wichita, KS	15.00	41.96	10.96	18.15	65.54	32.86	21.37
Winston-Salem, NC	13.60	61.65	10.77	19.10	64.11	38.49	21.48

Notes: (1) Figures cover the Metropolitan Statistical Area (MSA) except where noted. See Appendix B for areas included; (2) New England City and Town Area; n/a not available
Source: Bureau of Labor Statistics, May 2019 Metro Area Occupational Employment and Wage Estimates

Average Hourly Wages: Occupations N – P

Metro Area	Nurses, Registered	Nursing Assistants	Office Clerks	Physical Therapists	Physicians	Plumbers	Police Officers
Albany, NY	34.54	15.09	17.56	37.55	87.07	35.55	32.99
Albuquerque, NM	36.08	14.31	12.78	41.89	108.24	21.68	26.84
Allentown, PA	33.22	15.55	17.68	38.82	93.90	29.04	33.67
Anchorage, AK	42.72	18.47	22.22	51.38	121.44	38.71	44.53
Ann Arbor, MI	38.14	16.59	16.00	42.08	89.37	34.45	31.51
Athens, GA	32.97	12.77	15.16	38.25	102.25	n/a	20.53
Atlanta, GA	35.39	14.62	16.45	42.17	114.29	24.93	23.46
Austin, TX	34.70	14.18	19.14	42.65	108.99	24.66	35.27
Baton Rouge, LA	29.94	11.64	13.28	43.05	101.12	27.42	21.14
Boise City, ID	34.39	14.67	16.87	38.72	112.11	23.63	28.83
Boston, MA[2]	46.40	17.42	20.30	43.40	87.00	36.80	36.18
Boulder, CO	38.48	17.07	20.98	43.76	129.70	25.34	41.32
Cape Coral, FL	33.57	14.66	16.44	41.85	124.47	22.49	25.35
Cedar Rapids, IA	28.76	14.40	17.67	38.06	110.95	29.76	30.43
Charleston, SC	33.00	14.10	13.49	38.82	83.02	22.84	23.14
Charlotte, NC	31.71	13.03	16.60	41.41	89.36	21.61	25.03
Chicago, IL	37.22	14.87	18.71	45.28	87.57	43.02	39.51
Clarksville, TN	30.29	13.97	15.59	41.45	97.81	24.91	21.41
Cleveland, OH	34.45	14.23	18.60	42.01	96.52	30.85	29.51
College Station, TX	34.12	12.64	15.75	40.66	65.58	22.18	30.28
Colorado Springs, CO	35.95	15.56	19.43	39.94	94.23	23.54	33.70
Columbia, MO	33.16	12.41	16.00	38.99	57.44	25.86	23.69
Columbia, SC	30.91	12.93	13.19	42.36	69.71	21.70	21.03
Columbus, OH	32.83	13.59	18.57	41.82	105.49	25.84	37.40
Dallas, TX	36.89	14.24	17.79	44.69	95.61	24.57	34.71
Davenport, IA	26.27	13.36	15.54	35.98	117.47	30.34	29.23
Denver, CO	37.39	17.10	21.23	42.12	107.95	28.56	39.43
Des Moines, IA	30.19	15.50	17.70	41.77	103.24	28.38	31.84
Durham, NC	32.95	14.32	17.70	37.39	50.89	23.83	24.60
Edison, NJ	44.85	18.39	18.07	46.82	88.03	36.25	39.92
El Paso, TX	35.76	12.54	14.72	44.27	92.03	18.43	29.83
Fargo, ND	32.75	15.78	19.84	38.22	120.73	25.99	30.97
Fayetteville, NC	34.52	11.98	15.19	40.74	102.94	19.53	21.24
Fort Collins, CO	36.49	16.09	19.81	40.18	99.14	24.23	39.40
Fort Wayne, IN	28.82	13.79	16.37	42.33	111.10	27.80	28.26
Fort Worth, TX	36.89	14.24	17.79	44.69	95.61	24.57	34.71
Grand Rapids, MI	32.80	14.17	17.90	41.75	98.50	24.07	30.04
Greeley, CO	33.72	14.37	18.66	40.76	118.89	24.76	35.52
Green Bay, WI	32.05	14.79	17.65	43.11	127.09	33.55	33.86
Greensboro, NC	32.84	12.73	15.97	42.47	132.56	23.95	23.51
Honolulu, HI	51.23	18.05	16.97	45.22	112.83	36.23	38.25
Houston, TX	39.11	13.65	19.70	41.16	89.21	26.43	31.57
Huntsville, AL	27.81	12.71	12.54	41.51	120.55	23.82	24.96
Indianapolis, IN	34.11	14.32	17.33	42.41	118.33	26.67	29.97
Jackson, MS	30.88	11.92	14.19	43.06	48.76	21.31	17.97
Jacksonville, FL	31.78	13.10	16.92	39.41	113.96	23.15	27.56
Kansas City, MO	32.76	13.68	16.48	40.23	86.36	33.14	26.42
Lafayette, LA	29.30	10.13	12.71	40.62	79.56	25.18	20.95
Lakeland, FL	30.42	12.92	16.19	44.68	119.28	20.56	27.45
Las Vegas, NV	43.91	17.19	17.36	54.78	99.70	29.40	37.15
Lexington, KY	30.12	13.99	14.58	40.63	107.80	29.31	22.25
Lincoln, NE	31.68	14.61	14.84	40.92	101.82	25.16	30.84
Little Rock, AR	31.87	13.24	16.37	39.89	74.14	23.09	23.26
Los Angeles, CA	51.05	16.73	18.84	47.41	106.93	27.24	52.12
Louisville, KY	31.11	14.03	15.20	41.05	92.36	27.26	27.09

Table continued on next page.

Metro Area	Nurses, Registered	Nursing Assistants	Office Clerks	Physical Therapists	Physicians	Plumbers	Police Officers
Madison, WI	38.70	16.31	17.68	41.28	99.00	31.20	31.09
Manchester, NH[2]	36.01	16.28	19.65	40.52	120.44	27.01	29.65
Miami, FL	33.61	13.11	16.77	40.46	93.33	21.99	34.32
Midland, TX	32.71	15.29	19.70	47.03	131.97	21.40	30.64
Milwaukee, WI	35.56	14.88	18.18	42.19	113.60	36.31	34.98
Minneapolis, MN	40.58	17.82	19.89	40.23	111.80	38.80	37.30
Nashville, TN	31.28	13.76	17.26	37.30	103.38	28.14	24.02
New Haven, CT[2]	40.43	17.13	19.09	46.88	89.88	35.84	35.13
New Orleans, LA	33.41	11.97	12.65	42.03	87.20	25.57	22.67
New York, NY	44.85	18.39	18.07	46.82	88.03	36.25	39.92
Oklahoma City, OK	31.98	12.93	14.55	43.56	68.38	25.66	27.05
Omaha, NE	32.33	15.04	16.79	39.44	80.88	30.84	31.80
Orlando, FL	31.25	13.19	16.27	43.07	85.53	20.75	27.67
Peoria, IL	32.43	13.64	17.15	40.95	111.76	36.16	24.02
Philadelphia, PA	37.33	15.22	18.98	45.35	106.93	32.17	35.58
Phoenix, AZ	38.08	16.08	19.31	42.87	105.21	24.71	34.24
Pittsburgh, PA	32.63	14.99	17.41	39.93	65.66	30.15	32.56
Portland, OR	45.87	16.87	18.85	42.26	79.14	36.74	38.62
Providence, RI[2]	39.51	15.79	18.70	41.47	99.93	27.32	31.18
Provo, UT	31.89	13.75	16.44	43.45	98.82	25.65	25.40
Raleigh, NC	32.58	12.99	16.79	40.40	125.26	22.12	25.42
Reno, NV	37.89	15.68	18.71	44.23	124.43	30.74	33.91
Richmond, VA	35.34	13.58	17.69	47.00	86.29	26.17	27.27
Rochester, MN	37.25	16.80	18.04	40.99	114.52	32.46	32.37
Sacramento, CA	60.85	18.91	17.98	50.34	106.89	30.51	46.92
Salt Lake City, UT	33.67	14.60	16.71	39.08	100.53	25.95	28.37
San Antonio, TX	34.81	13.22	16.70	38.90	94.21	21.71	28.43
San Diego, CA	50.42	18.20	17.74	45.92	100.86	28.45	43.53
San Francisco, CA	66.35	21.68	22.56	49.26	83.65	41.94	57.33
San Jose, CA	67.67	19.13	22.45	49.27	108.06	41.36	61.10
Santa Rosa, CA	49.84	18.10	19.89	49.00	106.99	39.05	53.01
Savannah, GA	30.80	12.79	15.82	39.50	95.10	23.26	21.27
Seattle, WA	43.62	16.88	21.27	42.86	116.08	38.57	40.55
Sioux Falls, SD	28.92	13.63	12.86	34.97	110.38	21.53	29.86
Springfield, IL	33.70	13.99	18.30	40.02	127.29	39.57	34.38
Tallahassee, FL	30.29	12.16	14.96	40.75	100.58	21.39	26.70
Tampa, FL	33.39	13.83	17.10	39.66	105.00	22.20	29.88
Topeka, KS	31.86	13.61	14.25	43.96	99.56	26.31	24.18
Tucson, AZ	35.85	14.99	19.00	43.28	81.02	22.43	n/a
Tulsa, OK	31.41	12.69	15.30	40.44	123.20	24.42	26.34
Tuscaloosa, AL	28.46	12.24	12.48	46.06	99.51	22.76	n/a
Virginia Beach, VA	33.55	15.95	15.61	41.48	105.72	23.45	26.39
Washington, DC	40.08	15.58	19.91	45.02	89.51	28.23	35.68
Wichita, KS	27.63	12.47	14.17	44.34	71.03	21.71	23.87
Winston-Salem, NC	33.00	13.58	15.97	47.46	n/a	21.53	21.13

Notes: (1) Figures cover the Metropolitan Statistical Area (MSA) except where noted. See Appendix B for areas included;
(2) New England City and Town Area; n/a not available
Source: Bureau of Labor Statistics, May 2019 Metro Area Occupational Employment and Wage Estimates

Average Hourly Wages: Occupations P – S

Metro Area	Postal Mail Carriers	R.E. Sales Agents	Retail Sales-persons	Sales Reps., Technical/ Scientific	Secretaries, Exc. Leg./ Med./Exec.	Security Guards	Surgeons
Albany, NY	24.96	34.46	14.54	56.00	20.56	17.12	n/a
Albuquerque, NM	25.43	26.68	12.82	56.39	17.40	13.86	113.48
Allentown, PA	25.44	24.40	12.56	43.05	18.25	13.40	115.66
Anchorage, AK	25.47	37.94	16.23	38.89	20.83	20.05	n/a
Ann Arbor, MI	25.06	25.28	14.10	51.95	21.23	13.94	n/a
Athens, GA	23.97	25.84	11.38	21.79	16.49	15.10	130.36
Atlanta, GA	24.49	27.10	13.02	35.86	17.40	13.03	117.03
Austin, TX	25.01	34.53	13.98	49.58	18.09	15.33	112.07
Baton Rouge, LA	24.54	19.34	12.17	34.98	16.20	15.36	n/a
Boise City, ID	24.75	24.19	13.88	39.88	17.17	12.53	106.74
Boston, MA[2]	26.16	39.80	15.18	47.68	23.27	18.12	116.38
Boulder, CO	25.09	31.69	15.88	48.70	19.55	15.86	86.97
Cape Coral, FL	24.77	26.26	13.28	39.75	17.93	13.12	101.97
Cedar Rapids, IA	25.13	20.14	13.55	46.45	18.39	18.97	n/a
Charleston, SC	24.28	24.24	13.54	35.85	17.73	15.72	n/a
Charlotte, NC	24.94	24.22	13.71	47.17	18.95	14.95	111.31
Chicago, IL	25.61	20.23	13.94	42.47	20.02	16.20	119.04
Clarksville, TN	24.28	17.19	12.95	26.67	15.95	17.32	n/a
Cleveland, OH	25.17	24.05	13.28	43.00	18.30	16.42	132.63
College Station, TX	24.98	31.67	12.61	41.78	16.08	12.70	n/a
Colorado Springs, CO	24.78	33.53	14.63	52.48	17.23	16.09	134.85
Columbia, MO	24.80	25.47	15.72	35.62	17.65	14,39	n/a
Columbia, SC	24.31	21.46	13.27	40.50	17.59	16.37	n/a
Columbus, OH	24.56	21.85	13.62	36.59	18.91	16.89	125.18
Dallas, TX	25.14	38.22	13.68	40.80	18.46	14.46	114.62
Davenport, IA	24.55	37.97	14.65	37.61	16.42	15.01	133.08
Denver, CO	25.38	39.64	15.59	53.91	20.23	16.52	118.86
Des Moines, IA	24.91	23.36	13.94	43.02	19.60	16.34	109.13
Durham, NC	25.20	21.19	12.38	65.76	20.06	23.17	n/a
Edison, NJ	25.68	49.86	15.53	53.68	20.94	17.58	115.36
El Paso, TX	25.00	26.10	11.81	n/a	14.38	13.25	n/a
Fargo, ND	24.69	24.29	14.69	38.10	18.48	16.01	n/a
Fayetteville, NC	24.47	25.89	11.73	n/a	17.23	18.02	n/a
Fort Collins, CO	24.60	27.84	13.60	52.70	18.34	12.77	133.14
Fort Wayne, IN	24.94	21.73	12.59	43.05	17.28	16.98	n/a
Fort Worth, TX	25.14	38.22	13.68	40.80	18.46	14.46	114.62
Grand Rapids, MI	24.92	21.72	13.60	41.87	18.17	13.79	n/a
Greeley, CO	24.18	n/a	16.87	44.66	17.83	16.04	n/a
Green Bay, WI	24.93	27.20	14.06	42.09	17.72	13.53	n/a
Greensboro, NC	25.00	19.85	13.40	42.34	17.44	13.94	129.02
Honolulu, HI	26.41	33.35	16.03	43.47	21.07	16.43	128.37
Houston, TX	24.87	37.77	12.51	43.26	18.87	15.00	108.70
Huntsville, AL	25.17	36.64	13.56	42.33	18.00	15.53	n/a
Indianapolis, IN	25.17	24.76	14.19	50.45	17.77	14.76	81.36
Jackson, MS	24.74	n/a	13.25	47.02	16.51	12.17	128.98
Jacksonville, FL	25.76	29.63	12.48	41.14	17.56	12.68	n/a
Kansas City, MO	24.74	22.83	12.99	38.32	18.41	18.68	128.92
Lafayette, LA	24.76	19.19	12.83	28.98	14.57	11.82	n/a
Lakeland, FL	24.80	27.63	13.63	47.59	16.10	12.40	118.97
Las Vegas, NV	25.42	32.83	13.49	46.05	19.42	15.98	n/a
Lexington, KY	24.91	24.19	12.67	38.63	17.92	12.38	n/a
Lincoln, NE	24.79	23.42	13.22	43.32	17.60	17.82	n/a
Little Rock, AR	24.96	n/a	13.34	30.80	15.93	14.20	n/a
Los Angeles, CA	26.41	35.05	15.86	43.81	21.57	15.82	104.59
Louisville, KY	25.23	27.84	12.80	53.79	17.63	12.19	133.34

Table continued on next page.

Metro Area	Postal Mail Carriers	R.E. Sales Agents	Retail Sales-persons	Sales Reps., Technical/ Scientific	Secretaries, Exc. Leg./ Med./Exec.	Security Guards	Surgeons
Madison, WI	24.86	25.42	13.44	36.19	18.99	16.63	n/a
Manchester, NH[2]	24.86	22.53	13.19	44.71	18.49	16.64	n/a
Miami, FL	25.59	32.03	13.40	40.66	17.84	14.15	78.86
Midland, TX	23.77	44.39	15.83	44.80	18.56	17.28	n/a
Milwaukee, WI	25.12	25.92	13.11	43.66	18.93	14.69	n/a
Minneapolis, MN	25.35	22.33	14.62	41.14	20.71	17.40	n/a
Nashville, TN	24.92	22.18	14.46	41.71	19.03	14.17	n/a
New Haven, CT[2]	25.21	n/a	15.13	48.92	22.47	16.03	n/a
New Orleans, LA	24.67	n/a	12.51	32.02	17.12	14.97	n/a
New York, NY	25.68	49.86	15.53	53.68	20.94	17.58	115.36
Oklahoma City, OK	24.88	25.77	14.02	42.91	15.95	16.61	n/a
Omaha, NE	24.98	24.88	14.11	26.09	17.76	17.20	131.52
Orlando, FL	24.84	25.58	13.11	43.76	17.05	12.80	101.11
Peoria, IL	25.04	20.78	13.05	40.58	16.09	17.50	n/a
Philadelphia, PA	25.58	28.99	14.81	37.44	20.29	15.09	127.28
Phoenix, AZ	25.41	25.50	13.94	40.46	18.25	14.44	n/a
Pittsburgh, PA	25.05	34.59	13.75	39.90	17.72	13.70	120.27
Portland, OR	24.69	25.00	15.21	52.13	20.85	15.28	n/a
Providence, RI[2]	24.96	35.62	15.42	42.38	21.10	14.85	134.00
Provo, UT	24.06	23.64	12.84	46.12	16.36	20.44	n/a
Raleigh, NC	24.73	26.28	13.33	50.28	18.50	16.92	n/a
Reno, NV	25.45	18.37	15.03	44.19	19.70	14.60	105.15
Richmond, VA	24.39	28.17	13.79	45.62	18.91	13.40	134.71
Rochester, MN	24.97	25.03	14.35	41.54	17.16	15.13	n/a
Sacramento, CA	25.71	32.27	14.74	44.06	20.43	15.00	n/a
Salt Lake City, UT	25.57	n/a	14.15	44.64	18.41	16.82	130.86
San Antonio, TX	24.86	30.79	13.63	42.80	16.68	16.38	102.25
San Diego, CA	26.15	38.78	15.12	43.84	20.97	15.39	n/a
San Francisco, CA	27.03	34.17	16.74	50.33	24.60	18.55	123.49
San Jose, CA	27.22	45.31	18.46	52.12	23.42	19.38	129.97
Santa Rosa, CA	25.71	29.07	17.05	53.10	21.75	16.52	n/a
Savannah, GA	24.68	25.10	12.52	42.58	16.59	15.04	n/a
Seattle, WA	25.65	32.81	18.24	47.10	22.51	19.70	107.67
Sioux Falls, SD	25.34	44.17	15.28	50.25	14.58	14.09	135.43
Springfield, IL	25.24	n/a	13.71	39.28	17.25	22.23	n/a
Tallahassee, FL	24.66	27.06	13.95	37.27	17.98	14.93	123.92
Tampa, FL	25.17	32.23	13.27	42.53	17.22	15.97	50.93
Topeka, KS	24.65	n/a	13.06	40.81	16.01	14.15	n/a
Tucson, AZ	25.46	21.18	13.62	41.38	17.28	13.80	n/a
Tulsa, OK	24.70	31.21	13.22	39.42	16.48	15.01	135.61
Tuscaloosa, AL	24.04	24.16	13.63	37.42	17.19	16.64	n/a
Virginia Beach, VA	24.51	32.40	12.14	40.72	18.19	15.90	n/a
Washington, DC	24.97	30.88	14.65	48.87	23.04	21.33	127.40
Wichita, KS	24.73	29.97	14.12	42.09	16.36	14.28	115.60
Winston-Salem, NC	25.20	24.51	12.53	49.27	18.44	17.91	n/a

Notes: (1) Figures cover the Metropolitan Statistical Area (MSA) except where noted. See Appendix B for areas included; (2) New England City and Town Area; n/a not available
Source: Bureau of Labor Statistics, May 2019 Metro Area Occupational Employment and Wage Estimates

Average Hourly Wages: Occupations T – W

Metro Area	Teacher Assistants[3]	Teachers, Secondary School[3]	Telemarketers	Truck Drivers, Heavy	Truck Drivers, Light	Waiters/ Waitresses
Albany, NY	14.95	32.77	17.45	22.98	18.56	14.17
Albuquerque, NM	9.88	24.90	13.79	20.92	18.47	9.34
Allentown, PA	14.08	34.46	12.63	23.29	18.72	12.62
Anchorage, AK	18.35	39.47	n/a	29.40	23.44	12.76
Ann Arbor, MI	14.54	28.76	n/a	23.03	19.07	12.47
Athens, GA	9.46	27.13	n/a	23.92	19.34	10.84
Atlanta, GA	11.50	29.12	13.81	22.63	18.51	10.66
Austin, TX	12.32	28.22	18.28	20.35	21.07	11.67
Baton Rouge, LA	10.38	25.38	n/a	19.94	15.37	9.42
Boise City, ID	12.21	24.59	14.14	22.85	17.78	11.30
Boston, MA[2]	17.33	38.79	21.88	25.12	20.73	15.91
Boulder, CO	15.76	31.99	n/a	20.06	17.69	12.98
Cape Coral, FL	14.73	32.03	12.63	19.57	16.56	11.29
Cedar Rapids, IA	12.73	26.93	13.51	17.90	15.26	10.53
Charleston, SC	12.09	27.01	10.04	20.08	17.49	9.34
Charlotte, NC	12.29	24.41	16.19	21.92	16.72	10.96
Chicago, IL	14.18	38.20	13.76	24.54	22.31	11.50
Clarksville, TN	13.31	32.63	n/a	18.91	16.01	10.63
Cleveland, OH	14.28	33.31	12.36	23.08	18.35	10.63
College Station, TX	9.70	23.10	n/a	19.76	16.54	9.56
Colorado Springs, CO	13.73	24.42	n/a	21.89	18.03	13.44
Columbia, MO	13.13	25.81	n/a	20.10	17.91	10.16
Columbia, SC	12.37	28.06	15.35	21.16	16.84	9.87
Columbus, OH	14.54	32.82	14.69	22.51	17.63	11.76
Dallas, TX	11.56	28.50	16.18	23.37	20.10	9.99
Davenport, IA	13.02	27.94	13.60	22.23	16.00	10.84
Denver, CO	15.13	28.86	15.41	24.88	19.21	12.33
Des Moines, IA	12.68	29.07	15.33	24.30	17.56	11.01
Durham, NC	12.35	25.56	11.44	21.67	18.22	11.88
Edison, NJ	16.53	43.29	16.83	26.20	19.84	17.29
El Paso, TX	13.39	32.24	10.11	23.24	16.01	9.64
Fargo, ND	15.90	30.26	n/a	23.69	18.89	11.38
Fayetteville, NC	11.51	22.57	n/a	18.68	16.36	10.26
Fort Collins, CO	13.87	26.66	n/a	19.76	18.00	15.30
Fort Wayne, IN	12.04	25.70	n/a	20.82	16.24	12.17
Fort Worth, TX	11.56	28.50	16.18	23.37	20.10	9.99
Grand Rapids, MI	13.70	28.75	13.72	21.59	19.08	14.47
Greeley, CO	13.98	25.29	n/a	25.01	18.15	11.52
Green Bay, WI	15.54	27.87	n/a	21.23	16.77	9.49
Greensboro, NC	11.61	24.06	13.58	23.59	17.45	9.53
Honolulu, HI	14.83	30.06	12.55	24.27	18.13	26.65
Houston, TX	10.83	29.39	14.48	21.96	19.88	11.83
Huntsville, AL	12.13	25.69	11.69	18.96	15.47	9.20
Indianapolis, IN	12.76	26.62	17.27	22.03	18.35	12.24
Jackson, MS	9.63	22.01	n/a	23.86	16.99	11.05
Jacksonville, FL	12.46	30.53	11.92	22.06	18.02	12.61
Kansas City, MO	12.93	27.24	14.29	23.64	18.28	10.88
Lafayette, LA	11.20	24.81	n/a	19.52	14.15	9.61
Lakeland, FL	11.00	23.81	14.10	21.40	19.50	11.50
Las Vegas, NV	15.68	28.17	12.73	23.28	18.27	11.70
Lexington, KY	15.76	28.50	n/a	22.72	19.57	10.42
Lincoln, NE	14.61	30.14	11.74	24.92	18.18	11.97
Little Rock, AR	10.79	26.95	11.19	22.35	13.63	10.47
Los Angeles, CA	17.84	40.11	15.39	23.02	20.09	15.55
Louisville, KY	14.91	27.07	13.86	24.13	19.17	10.60

Table continued on next page.

Metro Area	Teacher Assistants[3]	Teachers, Secondary School[3]	Telemarketers	Truck Drivers, Heavy	Truck Drivers, Light	Waiters/Waitresses
Madison, WI	15.25	27.53	11.53	25.08	17.61	12.17
Manchester, NH[2]	14.34	26.86	n/a	23.54	17.20	12.34
Miami, FL	11.96	27.58	13.11	20.00	17.68	12.55
Midland, TX	11.41	27.42	n/a	23.72	20.25	9.00
Milwaukee, WI	15.40	30.13	15.31	23.74	16.74	11.12
Minneapolis, MN	16.12	32.39	16.30	25.49	20.96	14.42
Nashville, TN	12.20	25.93	15.74	23.19	17.29	9.80
New Haven, CT[2]	14.61	37.24	17.76	24.73	18.42	12.83
New Orleans, LA	11.35	25.40	15.54	21.77	18.36	9.41
New York, NY	16.53	43.29	16.83	26.20	19.84	17.29
Oklahoma City, OK	10.72	22.65	12.67	22.00	16.57	10.38
Omaha, NE	14.05	29.35	12.32	21.53	17.21	12.68
Orlando, FL	12.07	27.29	12.11	21.76	17.94	12.48
Peoria, IL	12.21	25.52	15.53	21.39	17.93	10.41
Philadelphia, PA	13.77	33.04	16.23	23.87	18.15	12.30
Phoenix, AZ	12.81	25.36	16.07	23.11	18.37	18.29
Pittsburgh, PA	13.90	34.48	12.57	24.95	17.25	12.99
Portland, OR	16.72	37.34	16.86	24.33	19.02	14.84
Providence, RI[2]	16.61	36.97	16.88	22.63	18.54	13.99
Provo, UT	12.95	34.94	16.24	18.97	18.02	13.03
Raleigh, NC	11.96	26.26	13.38	22.70	16.24	13.24
Reno, NV	10.50	24.94	14.18	24.26	19.97	10.16
Richmond, VA	12.26	28.47	13.87	21.11	19.59	11.30
Rochester, MN	15.42	32.40	n/a	22.54	16.64	13.55
Sacramento, CA	16.93	40.36	14.02	24.29	19.67	14.33
Salt Lake City, UT	12.80	28.19	15.22	23.61	20.16	11.22
San Antonio, TX	11.53	27.61	18.50	20.54	19.36	10.30
San Diego, CA	16.40	40.34	14.78	23.24	21.92	15.42
San Francisco, CA	19.10	44.88	16.07	24.73	23.46	18.18
San Jose, CA	19.21	42.74	n/a	25.70	23.37	15.20
Santa Rosa, CA	16.89	n/a	n/a	26.74	21.08	15.41
Savannah, GA	12.34	26.96	n/a	20.25	15.08	10.18
Seattle, WA	18.31	35.10	20.70	25.51	21.37	19.96
Sioux Falls, SD	12.13	22.87	n/a	21.10	18.01	10.59
Springfield, IL	11.55	26.38	n/a	20.67	16.31	10.02
Tallahassee, FL	12.69	23.85	17.00	18.11	17.19	11.39
Tampa, FL	13.72	29.07	12.88	20.97	16.88	13.02
Topeka, KS	12.79	24.27	n/a	19.42	18.33	9.70
Tucson, AZ	12.87	20.20	14.47	21.88	17.19	16.47
Tulsa, OK	11.09	25.48	10.95	25.87	17.25	9.37
Tuscaloosa, AL	9.15	24.43	n/a	21.59	17.70	9.01
Virginia Beach, VA	12.86	34.16	10.43	20.20	17.76	11.19
Washington, DC	16.33	38.83	14.94	23.42	20.25	14.84
Wichita, KS	12.57	25.45	12.80	21.06	17.14	9.92
Winston-Salem, NC	11.16	23.95	13.30	21.61	16.85	9.77

Notes: (1) Figures cover the Metropolitan Statistical Area (MSA) except where noted. See Appendix B for areas included;
(2) New England City and Town Area; (3) Hourly wages were calculated from annual wage data assuming a 40 hour work week;
n/a not available
Source: Bureau of Labor Statistics, May 2019 Metro Area Occupational Employment and Wage Estimates

Means of Transportation to Work: City

City	Car/Truck/Van		Public Transportation			Bicycle	Walked	Other Means	Worked at Home
	Drove Alone	Car-pooled	Bus	Subway	Railroad				
Albany, NY	59.1	10.3	14.4	0.1	0.0	1.1	11.3	1.4	2.2
Albuquerque, NM	80.2	9.2	1.9	0.0	0.1	1.2	1.9	1.1	4.4
Allentown, PA	66.3	18.3	4.9	0.1	0.0	0.2	5.5	0.8	4.0
Anchorage, AK	76.3	11.6	1.5	0.0	0.0	1.4	3.1	2.2	3.9
Ann Arbor, MI	53.2	6.7	10.6	0.1	0.0	4.2	16.6	0.8	7.7
Athens, GA	73.0	10.2	4.9	0.1	0.0	1.6	3.9	1.2	5.2
Atlanta, GA	67.6	6.5	6.8	3.4	0.2	1.0	4.9	1.9	7.8
Austin, TX	74.1	9.1	3.5	0.1	0.1	1.3	2.4	1.3	8.1
Baton Rouge, LA	80.0	9.8	2.6	0.0	0.0	0.5	3.3	1.0	2.8
Boise City, ID	80.4	7.5	0.6	0.0	0.0	2.8	2.0	1.0	5.7
Boston, MA	38.8	5.9	14.3	17.3	1.0	2.2	14.7	2.6	3.3
Boulder, CO	51.3	5.6	7.3	0.0	0.0	10.3	11.0	1.1	13.3
Cape Coral, FL	83.3	8.5	0.1	0.0	0.0	0.2	0.7	1.3	6.0
Cedar Rapids, IA	84.4	8.9	1.0	0.0	0.0	0.4	1.7	1.0	2.7
Charleston, SC	77.0	6.1	0.8	0.0	0.0	2.7	5.1	1.6	6.5
Charlotte, NC	76.6	9.8	2.7	0.4	0.2	0.2	2.1	1.2	6.8
Chicago, IL	49.0	7.8	13.5	12.9	1.8	1.7	6.5	2.0	4.8
Clarksville, TN	86.5	6.9	1.1	0.0	0.0	0.0	1.6	1.5	2.5
Cleveland, OH	70.0	10.2	9.2	0.4	0.1	0.7	5.3	1.2	2.9
College Station, TX	78.9	8.8	3.0	0.0	0.0	2.7	2.5	1.0	3.1
Colorado Springs, CO	78.6	11.0	1.0	0.0	0.0	0.6	1.9	0.9	6.1
Columbia, MO	76.7	10.3	1.6	0.0	0.0	1.2	5.1	1.0	4.2
Columbia, SC	64.1	6.4	1.7	0.0	0.0	0.6	21.4	2.3	3.6
Columbus, OH	79.8	8.4	3.1	0.0	0.0	0.7	3.0	1.0	4.1
Dallas, TX	76.5	11.1	3.2	0.5	0.3	0.2	1.9	1.5	4.7
Davenport, IA	84.7	7.2	1.2	0.0	0.0	0.4	2.2	0.5	3.9
Denver, CO	69.6	8.0	4.8	0.9	0.5	2.3	4.5	1.4	8.0
Des Moines, IA	79.9	10.1	2.4	0.0	0.0	0.4	2.7	1.1	3.4
Durham, NC	76.3	10.1	3.7	0.0	0.0	0.7	2.5	1.4	5.3
Edison, NJ	69.4	9.5	0.4	0.6	12.3	0.3	1.9	1.0	4.6
El Paso, TX	81.0	10.7	1.7	0.0	0.0	0.2	1.5	1.7	3.2
Fargo, ND	83.0	7.9	1.1	0.0	0.0	0.7	3.5	0.7	3.0
Fayetteville, NC	78.0	9.2	0.7	0.0	0.0	0.2	7.4	1.3	3.2
Fort Collins, CO	72.4	7.8	2.1	0.0	0.0	5.8	4.0	0.9	6.9
Fort Wayne, IN	83.7	9.2	0.8	0.0	0.0	0.3	1.4	0.8	3.8
Fort Worth, TX	81.9	11.1	0.6	0.0	0.2	0.2	1.3	1.0	3.7
Grand Rapids, MI	75.3	10.7	3.9	0.1	0.0	1.0	4.0	1.4	3.7
Greeley, CO	78.7	12.2	0.7	0.0	0.0	0.8	2.9	1.2	3.5
Green Bay, WI	79.5	10.5	1.1	0.0	0.0	0.6	2.7	2.1	3.5
Greensboro, NC	82.6	7.9	1.3	0.0	0.0	0.2	1.8	0.8	5.4
Honolulu, HI	56.6	13.3	11.8	0.0	0.0	1.7	8.7	4.1	3.8
Houston, TX	77.1	10.9	3.6	0.1	0.1	0.4	2.0	2.1	3.7
Huntsville, AL	86.2	6.9	0.4	0.0	0.0	0.2	1.2	1.4	3.7
Indianapolis, IN	82.3	9.0	1.9	0.0	0.0	0.5	1.9	1.1	3.3
Jackson, MS	84.5	10.4	0.8	0.0	0.0	0.1	1.9	0.5	1.8
Jacksonville, FL	80.0	9.7	1.9	0.0	0.0	0.5	1.8	1.5	4.6
Kansas City, MO	81.0	8.1	2.7	0.0	0.0	0.2	1.9	1.3	4.8
Lafayette, LA	82.9	8.4	1.0	0.0	0.0	1.2	2.1	1.0	3.4
Lakeland, FL	80.0	10.7	0.7	0.0	0.1	0.5	1.7	1.5	4.8
Las Vegas, NV	77.8	9.9	4.0	0.0	0.0	0.3	1.6	2.5	3.8
Lexington, KY	78.5	9.3	1.9	0.0	0.0	0.6	3.9	1.5	4.3
Lincoln, NE	81.0	9.1	1.3	0.0	0.0	1.3	3.3	0.6	3.3
Little Rock, AR	82.6	9.4	0.8	0.0	0.0	0.1	1.6	1.4	4.1
Los Angeles, CA	69.4	8.8	8.2	0.9	0.2	1.0	3.5	1.9	6.1

Table continued on next page.

City	Car/Truck/Van		Public Transportation			Bicycle	Walked	Other Means	Worked at Home
	Drove Alone	Car-pooled	Bus	Subway	Railroad				
Louisville, KY	79.8	9.0	3.0	0.0	0.0	0.4	2.1	1.6	4.1
Madison, WI	64.2	7.1	9.2	0.0	0.0	4.7	9.4	1.2	4.2
Manchester, NH	78.7	11.6	0.7	0.0	0.1	0.3	3.3	1.3	4.0
Miami, FL	69.7	8.4	8.6	1.0	0.2	1.0	3.8	2.4	4.8
Midland, TX	85.8	9.9	0.2	0.0	0.0	0.1	0.6	1.1	2.3
Milwaukee, WI	72.3	10.3	7.5	0.0	0.1	0.9	4.7	0.9	3.4
Minneapolis, MN	60.7	7.5	11.8	1.2	0.3	4.1	7.3	1.8	5.4
Nashville, TN	78.6	10.1	2.1	0.0	0.0	0.2	2.3	1.0	5.8
New Haven, CT	57.5	9.1	11.2	0.2	1.2	2.9	12.2	1.0	4.8
New Orleans, LA	68.4	8.9	6.7	0.1	0.0	3.1	5.1	2.5	5.2
New York, NY	22.3	4.5	10.2	44.0	1.5	1.2	9.9	2.2	4.2
Oklahoma City, OK	82.0	11.0	0.5	0.0	0.0	0.1	1.6	1.0	3.7
Omaha, NE	82.1	9.1	1.3	0.0	0.0	0.3	2.3	1.2	3.7
Orlando, FL	78.8	8.4	3.8	0.1	0.0	0.5	1.8	1.7	4.9
Peoria, IL	79.7	9.6	3.1	0.0	0.0	0.5	2.8	1.2	3.1
Philadelphia, PA	50.9	8.2	16.5	5.2	2.8	2.1	8.4	2.0	3.8
Phoenix, AZ	74.5	12.6	2.9	0.1	0.1	0.7	1.6	1.9	5.7
Pittsburgh, PA	55.5	8.3	17.1	0.4	0.0	1.9	10.7	1.3	4.9
Portland, OR	57.8	8.4	9.8	1.1	0.2	6.3	5.6	2.6	8.2
Providence, RI	63.5	12.5	4.9	0.1	1.3	1.0	10.0	1.1	5.6
Provo, UT	63.0	11.9	1.8	0.2	1.2	2.7	12.7	1.5	4.9
Raleigh, NC	78.5	8.6	1.9	0.1	0.0	0.4	1.6	1.2	7.7
Reno, NV	76.2	11.7	2.3	0.0	0.0	0.8	3.6	1.2	4.1
Richmond, VA	71.4	10.0	5.2	0.1	0.1	2.2	5.2	1.7	4.1
Rochester, MN	71.0	12.2	6.6	0.0	0.0	1.1	4.2	0.8	4.0
Sacramento, CA	74.7	10.6	2.3	0.2	0.5	1.9	2.8	1.8	5.2
Salt Lake City, UT	67.5	11.0	4.9	0.4	0.7	2.5	5.5	2.5	5.1
San Antonio, TX	79.0	11.1	2.9	0.0	0.0	0.2	1.8	1.3	3.7
San Diego, CA	74.8	8.7	3.5	0.0	0.1	0.9	3.0	1.8	7.1
San Francisco, CA	32.9	7.3	21.8	8.6	1.5	4.0	11.4	5.8	6.6
San Jose, CA	76.0	11.7	2.8	0.2	1.2	0.8	1.7	1.5	4.2
Santa Rosa, CA	77.9	10.7	1.7	0.0	0.0	1.4	1.9	1.2	5.2
Savannah, GA	73.0	10.4	4.3	0.2	0.0	1.9	4.4	2.1	3.6
Seattle, WA	47.6	7.3	19.9	1.3	0.1	3.6	11.0	2.0	7.2
Sioux Falls, SD	84.4	8.4	0.9	0.0	0.0	0.5	2.0	0.8	3.2
Springfield, IL	82.1	7.7	2.2	0.1	0.0	0.7	2.4	1.4	3.5
Tallahassee, FL	79.3	8.4	2.4	0.0	0.0	0.9	3.3	1.5	4.2
Tampa, FL	77.3	8.9	2.4	0.0	0.0	1.2	2.4	1.3	6.5
Topeka, KS	81.3	11.1	1.3	0.0	0.0	0.4	2.2	1.1	2.8
Tucson, AZ	74.3	10.7	3.6	0.0	0.0	2.6	3.1	1.8	4.0
Tulsa, OK	80.2	10.7	1.0	0.0	0.0	0.3	1.8	2.0	3.9
Tuscaloosa, AL	83.3	8.8	0.2	0.0	0.0	0.6	2.2	0.5	4.2
Virginia Beach, VA	82.1	8.6	0.8	0.0	0.0	0.5	2.7	1.4	3.7
Washington, DC	34.3	5.3	13.7	20.6	0.3	4.5	13.1	2.1	6.1
Wichita, KS	83.4	9.5	0.6	0.0	0.0	0.3	1.5	1.5	3.1
Winston-Salem, NC	82.6	8.1	1.6	0.0	0.0	0.2	2.0	0.9	4.6
U.S.	76.4	9.1	2.5	1.9	0.6	0.6	2.7	1.3	4.9

Note: Figures are percentages and cover workers 16 years of age and older
Source: U.S. Census Bureau, 2014-2018 American Community Survey 5-Year Estimates

Means of Transportation to Work: Metro Area

Metro Area	Car/Truck/Van		Public Transportation			Bicycle	Walked	Other Means	Worked at Home
	Drove Alone	Car-pooled	Bus	Subway	Railroad				
Albany, NY	79.8	7.8	3.5	0.1	0.1	0.3	3.5	0.9	4.1
Albuquerque, NM	80.3	9.7	1.4	0.0	0.2	0.9	1.7	1.1	4.8
Allentown, PA	81.6	8.4	1.6	0.0	0.1	0.2	2.4	1.1	4.5
Anchorage, AK	75.7	11.4	1.4	0.0	0.0	1.1	2.9	3.1	4.5
Ann Arbor, MI	71.7	7.9	5.1	0.0	0.0	1.6	7.1	0.7	5.9
Athens, GA	76.9	10.2	3.0	0.0	0.0	1.0	2.6	1.0	5.2
Atlanta, GA	77.6	9.5	2.1	0.8	0.1	0.2	1.3	1.6	6.9
Austin, TX	76.5	9.5	2.0	0.1	0.1	0.8	1.7	1.2	8.2
Baton Rouge, LA	84.6	8.9	0.9	0.0	0.0	0.3	1.5	1.1	2.8
Boise City, ID	79.8	9.0	0.3	0.0	0.0	1.3	1.6	1.0	6.9
Boston, MA	66.7	7.2	4.2	6.6	2.1	1.0	5.4	1.7	5.2
Boulder, CO	65.4	7.4	4.6	0.0	0.0	4.5	5.0	1.0	12.0
Cape Coral, FL	79.9	9.8	0.7	0.0	0.0	0.7	1.0	2.2	5.6
Cedar Rapids, IA	84.4	8.3	0.6	0.0	0.0	0.3	2.0	0.7	3.7
Charleston, SC	81.0	8.1	0.8	0.0	0.0	0.7	2.5	1.2	5.6
Charlotte, NC	80.7	9.1	1.3	0.2	0.1	0.1	1.4	1.1	6.1
Chicago, IL	70.2	7.8	4.5	4.3	3.2	0.7	3.0	1.3	5.0
Clarksville, TN	84.6	7.4	0.8	0.0	0.0	0.1	3.5	1.3	2.4
Cleveland, OH	81.9	7.4	2.7	0.2	0.0	0.3	2.3	1.1	4.2
College Station, TX	79.4	10.9	1.8	0.0	0.0	1.7	2.1	1.0	3.1
Colorado Springs, CO	77.4	10.4	0.7	0.0	0.0	0.4	3.5	1.1	6.5
Columbia, MO	78.5	10.6	1.1	0.0	0.0	0.8	3.8	0.9	4.3
Columbia, SC	80.6	8.7	0.7	0.0	0.0	0.2	4.3	2.0	3.6
Columbus, OH	82.5	7.5	1.6	0.0	0.0	0.4	2.2	0.9	4.8
Dallas, TX	80.8	9.7	0.9	0.2	0.2	0.2	1.3	1.3	5.4
Davenport, IA	85.3	7.0	0.9	0.0	0.0	0.3	1.9	0.9	3.7
Denver, CO	75.7	8.2	3.0	0.7	0.4	0.8	2.1	1.2	7.9
Des Moines, IA	83.7	8.0	1.2	0.0	0.0	0.2	1.8	0.7	4.5
Durham, NC	75.3	9.3	3.8	0.0	0.0	0.8	3.2	1.2	6.3
Edison, NJ	50.2	6.5	7.4	19.3	3.9	0.6	5.9	1.9	4.4
El Paso, TX	80.4	10.6	1.4	0.0	0.0	0.2	1.8	1.9	3.5
Fargo, ND	82.5	8.2	0.8	0.0	0.0	0.6	2.9	0.8	4.2
Fayetteville, NC	80.5	9.2	0.5	0.0	0.0	0.1	5.0	1.3	3.3
Fort Collins, CO	75.0	8.6	1.4	0.0	0.0	3.3	2.6	1.0	8.0
Fort Wayne, IN	84.6	8.5	0.6	0.0	0.0	0.2	1.3	0.7	4.0
Fort Worth, TX	80.8	9.7	0.9	0.2	0.2	0.2	1.3	1.3	5.4
Grand Rapids, MI	82.1	9.0	1.4	0.0	0.0	0.4	2.2	0.8	4.0
Greeley, CO	80.1	10.2	0.5	0.0	0.0	0.4	2.1	0.9	5.7
Green Bay, WI	83.7	8.0	0.6	0.0	0.0	0.3	2.1	1.1	4.3
Greensboro, NC	83.4	8.9	0.7	0.0	0.0	0.1	1.3	0.8	4.8
Honolulu, HI	64.0	14.4	8.3	0.0	0.0	1.0	5.4	2.8	3.9
Houston, TX	80.6	10.1	2.0	0.0	0.0	0.3	1.3	1.5	4.2
Huntsville, AL	88.0	6.3	0.2	0.0	0.0	0.1	0.8	1.1	3.5
Indianapolis, IN	83.9	8.0	0.9	0.0	0.0	0.3	1.5	0.9	4.5
Jackson, MS	86.2	9.3	0.3	0.0	0.0	0.1	1.0	0.8	2.2
Jacksonville, FL	80.8	8.7	1.2	0.0	0.0	0.6	1.6	1.6	5.5
Kansas City, MO	83.5	8.1	0.9	0.0	0.0	0.2	1.3	0.9	5.1
Lafayette, LA	83.7	9.5	0.5	0.0	0.0	0.5	1.9	1.2	2.8
Lakeland, FL	82.5	10.0	0.5	0.0	0.0	0.3	1.0	1.4	4.2
Las Vegas, NV	78.7	9.8	3.7	0.0	0.0	0.3	1.5	2.1	3.8
Lexington, KY	79.6	9.6	1.3	0.0	0.0	0.4	3.3	1.4	4.4
Lincoln, NE	81.3	8.9	1.1	0.0	0.0	1.1	3.3	0.6	3.7
Little Rock, AR	84.1	9.6	0.5	0.0	0.0	0.1	1.3	1.1	3.4
Los Angeles, CA	75.1	9.6	4.3	0.5	0.3	0.8	2.5	1.5	5.5

Table continued on next page.

Metro Area	Car/Truck/Van		Public Transportation			Bicycle	Walked	Other Means	Worked at Home
	Drove Alone	Car-pooled	Bus	Subway	Railroad				
Louisville, KY	82.1	8.7	1.8	0.0	0.0	0.2	1.6	1.2	4.3
Madison, WI	74.7	7.8	4.3	0.0	0.0	2.3	5.1	1.0	4.9
Manchester, NH	81.4	8.3	0.7	0.0	0.1	0.2	2.0	0.9	6.4
Miami, FL	78.2	9.1	3.0	0.3	0.2	0.6	1.6	1.6	5.5
Midland, TX	85.6	9.4	0.2	0.0	0.0	0.1	1.0	1.0	2.8
Milwaukee, WI	80.8	7.9	3.3	0.0	0.1	0.5	2.6	0.8	4.1
Minneapolis, MN	77.6	8.2	4.2	0.2	0.2	0.9	2.3	1.0	5.5
Nashville, TN	81.3	9.4	0.9	0.0	0.1	0.1	1.4	1.1	5.7
New Haven, CT	78.1	8.3	3.0	0.1	1.0	0.5	3.6	0.9	4.5
New Orleans, LA	78.6	9.7	2.5	0.0	0.0	1.1	2.4	1.6	4.0
New York, NY	50.2	6.5	7.4	19.3	3.9	0.6	5.9	1.9	4.4
Oklahoma City, OK	82.9	9.7	0.4	0.0	0.0	0.3	1.7	1.0	4.0
Omaha, NE	84.2	8.1	0.8	0.0	0.0	0.2	1.8	1.0	3.8
Orlando, FL	80.2	9.7	1.6	0.0	0.1	0.4	1.0	1.5	5.5
Peoria, IL	84.6	7.6	1.2	0.0	0.0	0.4	2.0	0.9	3.3
Philadelphia, PA	72.9	7.5	5.2	1.8	2.3	0.6	3.6	1.1	4.9
Phoenix, AZ	76.4	11.1	1.8	0.1	0.0	0.8	1.5	1.8	6.6
Pittsburgh, PA	77.1	8.2	5.1	0.2	0.0	0.3	3.4	1.1	4.6
Portland, OR	70.4	9.3	4.8	0.7	0.2	2.3	3.3	1.8	7.1
Providence, RI	80.5	8.7	1.5	0.2	0.9	0.3	3.3	0.8	3.8
Provo, UT	73.4	11.4	0.9	0.2	0.8	1.0	4.1	1.3	6.9
Raleigh, NC	79.8	8.6	0.9	0.0	0.0	0.2	1.1	0.9	8.3
Reno, NV	77.8	11.4	1.8	0.0	0.0	0.6	2.7	1.3	4.5
Richmond, VA	81.4	8.7	1.4	0.1	0.1	0.5	1.7	1.2	5.0
Rochester, MN	74.3	11.3	4.3	0.0	0.0	0.7	3.6	0.8	5.0
Sacramento, CA	76.8	9.5	1.7	0.2	0.3	1.5	1.9	1.4	6.7
Salt Lake City, UT	74.9	11.7	2.2	0.4	0.5	0.8	2.3	1.4	5.9
San Antonio, TX	79.8	10.6	1.9	0.0	0.0	0.2	1.7	1.2	4.6
San Diego, CA	76.3	8.7	2.5	0.0	0.2	0.7	2.9	1.8	7.0
San Francisco, CA	58.1	9.7	7.5	7.4	1.3	2.0	4.7	2.8	6.5
San Jose, CA	75.1	10.6	2.4	0.2	1.4	1.7	2.0	1.4	5.0
Santa Rosa, CA	74.7	11.2	1.7	0.1	0.1	1.0	3.1	1.1	7.1
Savannah, GA	80.3	9.4	1.8	0.1	0.0	0.9	2.3	1.6	3.7
Seattle, WA	68.0	9.9	8.7	0.4	0.5	1.1	4.0	1.3	6.1
Sioux Falls, SD	84.4	7.9	0.6	0.0	0.0	0.4	1.9	0.7	4.0
Springfield, IL	83.5	7.7	1.4	0.1	0.0	0.4	1.9	1.1	3.9
Tallahassee, FL	81.5	9.0	1.4	0.0	0.0	0.5	2.1	1.4	4.1
Tampa, FL	79.5	8.5	1.3	0.0	0.0	0.7	1.4	1.5	6.9
Topeka, KS	82.8	10.2	0.8	0.0	0.0	0.2	1.7	0.8	3.5
Tucson, AZ	76.9	9.9	2.4	0.0	0.0	1.6	2.3	1.9	5.0
Tulsa, OK	83.0	9.6	0.5	0.0	0.0	0.2	1.3	1.4	4.0
Tuscaloosa, AL	85.4	8.8	0.3	0.0	0.0	0.3	1.3	0.5	3.4
Virginia Beach, VA	81.4	8.4	1.4	0.1	0.0	0.4	3.4	1.4	3.6
Washington, DC	66.0	9.4	4.9	7.8	0.8	0.9	3.3	1.4	5.6
Wichita, KS	83.8	9.0	0.4	0.0	0.0	0.4	1.6	1.3	3.5
Winston-Salem, NC	84.1	8.5	0.7	0.0	0.0	0.1	1.3	0.9	4.4
U.S.	76.4	9.1	2.5	1.9	0.6	0.6	2.7	1.3	4.9

Note: Figures are percentages and cover workers 16 years of age and older; (1) Figures cover the Metropolitan Statistical Area—see Appendix B for areas included
Source: U.S. Census Bureau, 2014-2018 American Community Survey 5-Year Estimates

Travel Time to Work: City

City	Less Than 10 Minutes	10 to 19 Minutes	20 to 29 Minutes	30 to 44 Minutes	45 to 59 Minutes	60 to 89 Minutes	90 Minutes or More
Albany, NY	15.7	43.8	22.7	11.7	3.4	1.8	0.8
Albuquerque, NM	10.9	36.9	27.8	17.2	3.1	2.7	1.3
Allentown, PA	11.6	34.9	27.9	15.2	4.4	4.2	1.8
Anchorage, AK	16.6	45.4	22.5	10.3	2.5	1.2	1.5
Ann Arbor, MI	13.5	44.8	19.6	13.7	4.8	2.7	0.8
Athens, GA	16.6	49.5	16.4	8.6	3.7	3.1	2.0
Atlanta, GA	6.8	29.3	26.7	21.4	7.6	5.0	3.1
Austin, TX	9.6	32.4	24.4	21.4	7.0	3.8	1.4
Baton Rouge, LA	11.1	39.0	26.2	15.9	3.6	2.7	1.5
Boise City, ID	13.9	46.4	24.7	11.0	1.7	1.2	1.1
Boston, MA	6.9	19.5	20.0	29.9	11.6	9.7	2.3
Boulder, CO	18.6	46.4	16.0	9.7	5.2	3.2	1.0
Cape Coral, FL	8.1	24.2	23.9	27.2	9.2	5.4	2.0
Cedar Rapids, IA	17.7	49.8	18.2	9.5	2.1	1.5	1.1
Charleston, SC	11.2	32.4	25.9	22.2	5.4	1.6	1.3
Charlotte, NC	8.7	28.3	25.9	24.5	7.2	3.6	1.9
Chicago, IL	4.6	15.9	17.6	30.3	15.0	12.9	3.6
Clarksville, TN	11.2	35.1	24.2	15.9	5.3	6.8	1.5
Cleveland, OH	9.9	33.3	26.1	19.9	4.9	3.8	2.0
College Station, TX	17.0	55.9	18.1	5.9	0.6	1.5	1.0
Colorado Springs, CO	11.9	36.6	28.0	15.1	3.5	2.7	2.2
Columbia, MO	19.7	55.1	13.0	7.7	2.7	0.9	0.9
Columbia, SC	31.4	36.6	17.1	10.4	1.7	1.8	0.9
Columbus, OH	10.2	34.8	30.1	18.4	3.6	1.9	1.1
Dallas, TX	8.2	26.5	23.1	26.3	8.3	5.5	2.0
Davenport, IA	17.1	47.8	19.7	9.6	3.2	1.4	1.2
Denver, CO	8.3	29.1	24.4	25.2	7.5	3.9	1.5
Des Moines, IA	13.3	44.0	26.5	11.6	2.2	1.4	1.1
Durham, NC	10.1	37.6	25.6	17.7	4.1	3.2	1.7
Edison, NJ	6.8	23.9	17.5	18.2	10.6	13.6	9.4
El Paso, TX	9.6	34.8	27.7	19.9	4.3	2.1	1.7
Fargo, ND	21.0	56.6	16.3	3.2	0.9	1.3	0.7
Fayetteville, NC	19.9	39.1	22.8	11.5	3.2	1.9	1.6
Fort Collins, CO	16.9	43.2	19.7	10.6	5.0	3.4	1.3
Fort Wayne, IN	13.1	39.9	27.7	12.2	3.2	2.2	1.7
Fort Worth, TX	8.8	28.2	22.2	23.8	8.9	6.2	2.0
Grand Rapids, MI	15.7	42.5	23.8	11.8	3.1	2.1	1.0
Greeley, CO	16.8	37.8	16.2	14.3	5.4	7.3	2.2
Green Bay, WI	17.9	48.7	19.6	7.6	3.3	1.7	1.3
Greensboro, NC	12.1	41.7	24.4	14.2	3.2	2.8	1.5
Honolulu, HI	8.3	35.3	23.5	21.9	5.7	4.0	1.3
Houston, TX	7.6	25.8	22.4	27.3	8.8	6.2	1.8
Huntsville, AL	12.5	43.1	26.6	14.1	2.2	0.6	1.0
Indianapolis, IN	9.9	30.2	30.1	21.6	4.1	2.5	1.5
Jackson, MS	9.2	38.3	29.8	17.8	2.8	1.2	1.0
Jacksonville, FL	8.6	28.1	28.1	24.6	6.1	2.8	1.7
Kansas City, MO	11.4	33.5	28.3	19.5	4.7	1.7	1.0
Lafayette, LA	16.2	42.3	20.7	12.1	2.2	2.5	3.9
Lakeland, FL	10.9	42.8	20.9	15.5	5.5	3.0	1.5
Las Vegas, NV	7.4	24.4	29.5	28.2	5.8	2.7	2.0
Lexington, KY	13.1	38.0	27.0	14.7	3.4	2.4	1.3
Lincoln, NE	17.0	44.8	22.8	9.5	2.7	2.1	1.0
Little Rock, AR	13.8	43.7	27.5	10.8	1.9	1.2	1.1
Los Angeles, CA	6.2	22.3	19.3	28.1	10.6	10.0	3.6
Louisville, KY	9.1	32.5	30.5	20.3	4.1	2.3	1.2

Table continued on next page.

City	Less Than 10 Minutes	10 to 19 Minutes	20 to 29 Minutes	30 to 44 Minutes	45 to 59 Minutes	60 to 89 Minutes	90 Minutes or More
Madison, WI	15.0	40.9	23.8	15.0	2.7	1.8	0.8
Manchester, NH	15.0	38.0	19.0	14.2	5.8	4.8	3.2
Miami, FL	5.0	22.2	22.4	31.2	9.8	7.4	2.1
Midland, TX	16.1	49.5	16.9	11.3	2.6	2.0	1.6
Milwaukee, WI	10.4	36.6	25.5	19.0	4.1	2.9	1.4
Minneapolis, MN	8.3	32.2	30.8	20.3	4.2	3.0	1.2
Nashville, TN	8.8	29.0	26.9	23.8	6.7	3.4	1.4
New Haven, CT	14.2	39.5	20.4	13.2	4.3	5.2	3.3
New Orleans, LA	9.7	34.0	25.0	20.2	4.6	4.5	2.1
New York, NY	4.0	12.3	13.5	27.3	16.3	19.2	7.5
Oklahoma City, OK	11.2	35.9	29.4	17.5	3.1	1.5	1.5
Omaha, NE	14.4	41.4	27.5	12.3	2.1	1.4	0.9
Orlando, FL	7.9	27.5	26.8	25.7	6.4	3.6	2.2
Peoria, IL	18.4	49.4	19.8	7.7	2.0	1.8	0.8
Philadelphia, PA	5.9	18.9	19.8	28.2	12.5	10.4	4.2
Phoenix, AZ	9.2	27.7	25.3	24.4	7.2	4.4	1.8
Pittsburgh, PA	9.9	31.9	25.5	22.1	5.4	3.7	1.6
Portland, OR	7.7	27.1	27.3	23.8	7.5	4.8	1.9
Providence, RI	13.1	40.6	20.0	12.7	5.5	4.6	3.4
Provo, UT	21.7	45.7	16.7	9.2	2.3	2.8	1.5
Raleigh, NC	10.1	32.7	26.4	20.8	5.4	2.8	1.8
Reno, NV	14.8	45.1	21.3	11.0	3.6	2.7	1.4
Richmond, VA	10.2	38.5	27.9	16.1	3.0	2.6	1.6
Rochester, MN	19.0	56.5	13.1	6.4	2.2	1.6	1.3
Sacramento, CA	8.7	32.5	24.8	21.5	5.6	3.6	3.3
Salt Lake City, UT	12.5	45.2	23.3	12.5	3.5	2.1	1.0
San Antonio, TX	8.8	31.2	26.9	22.1	6.0	3.1	1.9
San Diego, CA	7.7	32.5	28.0	21.6	5.2	3.1	1.8
San Francisco, CA	4.0	18.4	20.8	30.2	11.9	11.2	3.5
San Jose, CA	5.3	23.1	22.8	27.3	10.5	8.2	2.7
Santa Rosa, CA	14.4	40.2	20.0	13.7	4.0	4.6	3.2
Savannah, GA	17.4	38.9	21.5	13.7	4.4	2.8	1.3
Seattle, WA	6.8	23.4	24.6	28.4	10.0	5.3	1.5
Sioux Falls, SD	16.7	52.3	21.9	5.5	1.4	1.4	0.9
Springfield, IL	18.2	51.0	18.7	5.9	2.0	2.5	1.6
Tallahassee, FL	15.1	45.0	23.5	12.2	1.8	1.4	1.0
Tampa, FL	11.5	30.6	23.5	21.6	6.8	4.2	1.8
Topeka, KS	17.5	54.5	15.4	7.7	1.9	2.3	0.6
Tucson, AZ	12.3	34.6	24.5	19.9	4.6	2.5	1.6
Tulsa, OK	14.7	44.7	25.5	10.6	1.9	1.7	1.1
Tuscaloosa, AL	14.0	42.8	28.2	7.7	3.0	3.5	0.9
Virginia Beach, VA	10.4	30.1	27.8	22.2	5.3	2.8	1.4
Washington, DC	5.3	19.0	23.0	32.0	12.0	6.8	2.0
Wichita, KS	13.6	45.2	27.3	9.9	1.5	1.4	1.0
Winston-Salem, NC	13.6	42.1	23.0	13.5	3.7	2.3	1.8
U.S.	12.5	28.7	20.9	20.7	8.2	6.3	2.8

Note: Figures are percentages and include workers 16 years old and over
Source: U.S. Census Bureau, 2014-2018 American Community Survey 5-Year Estimates

Travel Time to Work: Metro Area

Metro Area	Less Than 10 Minutes	10 to 19 Minutes	20 to 29 Minutes	30 to 44 Minutes	45 to 59 Minutes	60 to 89 Minutes	90 Minutes or More
Albany, NY	12.7	31.8	25.1	20.2	6.2	2.6	1.4
Albuquerque, NM	10.8	32.4	26.1	20.0	5.6	3.4	1.6
Allentown, PA	12.4	27.6	22.9	18.4	7.5	7.2	4.0
Anchorage, AK	15.9	41.5	20.9	10.6	4.5	4.3	2.4
Ann Arbor, MI	11.0	32.9	24.0	19.5	7.1	4.3	1.3
Athens, GA	13.6	42.1	20.9	12.8	5.0	3.5	2.2
Atlanta, GA	7.1	22.3	19.7	24.7	12.2	10.3	3.6
Austin, TX	9.6	27.3	22.3	22.9	10.1	6.0	1.9
Baton Rouge, LA	9.4	27.6	22.6	22.9	9.1	6.2	2.2
Boise City, ID	12.4	35.3	25.6	18.8	4.6	2.1	1.3
Boston, MA	9.1	22.4	18.1	24.2	11.9	10.8	3.5
Boulder, CO	14.7	35.3	21.2	16.5	6.7	4.3	1.3
Cape Coral, FL	8.5	25.9	22.7	26.1	9.8	5.0	2.0
Cedar Rapids, IA	17.6	40.7	21.9	13.1	3.6	2.0	1.2
Charleston, SC	9.0	25.6	24.7	26.3	8.5	4.2	1.6
Charlotte, NC	9.7	27.1	22.7	24.1	9.5	5.0	2.0
Chicago, IL	8.4	21.6	18.4	25.0	12.4	10.8	3.4
Clarksville, TN	15.7	32.6	21.3	17.0	5.9	5.8	1.6
Cleveland, OH	11.3	28.1	25.4	23.2	7.4	3.3	1.4
College Station, TX	17.1	47.3	19.5	10.1	2.6	2.0	1.3
Colorado Springs, CO	12.0	33.1	26.7	17.6	5.0	3.3	2.2
Columbia, MO	16.8	49.1	18.2	10.3	3.3	1.1	1.0
Columbia, SC	12.7	29.5	24.1	21.8	6.8	3.4	1.7
Columbus, OH	11.1	30.1	26.6	21.5	6.4	3.0	1.3
Dallas, TX	8.9	25.2	21.2	25.3	10.6	6.8	2.1
Davenport, IA	17.9	37.8	24.2	13.4	3.6	1.8	1.2
Denver, CO	8.3	25.1	23.0	26.0	10.0	5.7	1.8
Des Moines, IA	15.0	36.1	27.4	15.7	3.2	1.5	1.2
Durham, NC	10.2	33.2	24.5	20.3	6.1	4.1	1.6
Edison, NJ	7.1	18.7	16.3	23.7	12.4	14.9	7.0
El Paso, TX	10.5	32.6	26.8	21.0	5.0	2.3	1.8
Fargo, ND	19.0	51.2	18.5	7.1	1.8	1.5	1.0
Fayetteville, NC	15.8	33.5	25.2	16.9	4.5	2.3	1.9
Fort Collins, CO	14.9	35.1	22.0	15.0	6.1	5.1	1.8
Fort Wayne, IN	13.7	35.6	27.8	15.3	3.7	2.1	1.7
Fort Worth, TX	8.9	25.2	21.2	25.3	10.6	6.8	2.1
Grand Rapids, MI	14.9	35.1	25.0	16.3	4.7	2.5	1.5
Greeley, CO	12.1	27.9	19.2	21.8	9.0	7.6	2.5
Green Bay, WI	18.2	39.8	21.9	12.7	3.9	2.0	1.5
Greensboro, NC	12.1	35.3	25.4	18.2	4.9	2.6	1.6
Honolulu, HI	9.2	24.4	19.4	25.6	9.8	8.5	3.0
Houston, TX	7.9	23.6	19.5	26.1	11.6	8.9	2.4
Huntsville, AL	9.8	33.0	28.3	21.3	5.3	1.3	1.0
Indianapolis, IN	11.5	27.8	24.6	23.7	7.4	3.5	1.5
Jackson, MS	10.1	29.6	26.2	23.2	6.0	3.4	1.5
Jacksonville, FL	9.0	25.7	24.8	25.4	8.9	4.4	1.8
Kansas City, MO	12.3	30.9	25.3	21.4	6.7	2.5	1.0
Lafayette, LA	15.7	32.6	20.6	17.8	5.0	3.6	4.7
Lakeland, FL	8.8	31.0	22.6	20.6	9.2	5.3	2.4
Las Vegas, NV	7.6	27.9	29.4	25.5	5.1	2.6	1.9
Lexington, KY	14.6	34.6	24.8	17.7	4.5	2.4	1.3
Lincoln, NE	17.0	41.7	23.5	11.5	3.0	2.1	1.1
Little Rock, AR	12.9	32.4	24.1	19.7	6.9	2.9	1.3
Los Angeles, CA	7.2	24.7	19.7	25.4	10.1	9.5	3.5
Louisville, KY	9.9	30.1	27.1	22.5	6.3	2.7	1.4

Table continued on next page.

Metro Area	Less Than 10 Minutes	10 to 19 Minutes	20 to 29 Minutes	30 to 44 Minutes	45 to 59 Minutes	60 to 89 Minutes	90 Minutes or More
Madison, WI	16.1	32.6	24.0	18.8	5.0	2.3	1.1
Manchester, NH	11.5	29.1	19.9	19.8	8.6	7.4	3.8
Miami, FL	6.6	23.0	22.4	27.5	10.2	7.8	2.6
Midland, TX	15.9	46.1	18.3	12.7	3.0	2.6	1.6
Milwaukee, WI	12.1	31.6	25.6	21.1	5.6	2.6	1.3
Minneapolis, MN	10.4	27.4	25.1	23.5	8.1	4.3	1.4
Nashville, TN	9.4	26.5	21.9	23.4	10.5	6.4	1.9
New Haven, CT	11.7	31.7	23.0	19.7	6.5	4.6	2.9
New Orleans, LA	10.5	30.8	22.2	21.1	7.4	5.6	2.5
New York, NY	7.1	18.7	16.3	23.7	12.4	14.9	7.0
Oklahoma City, OK	12.6	32.3	25.7	20.1	5.5	2.3	1.5
Omaha, NE	14.4	36.6	27.1	15.7	3.5	1.7	1.0
Orlando, FL	7.3	23.3	23.4	27.9	10.7	5.2	2.2
Peoria, IL	17.4	35.5	24.9	15.2	3.8	1.8	1.4
Philadelphia, PA	9.4	23.9	20.3	23.9	10.9	8.4	3.2
Phoenix, AZ	10.0	26.8	23.7	23.7	8.7	5.3	1.7
Pittsburgh, PA	12.0	26.9	21.0	22.4	9.6	6.1	2.0
Portland, OR	10.3	27.2	22.6	23.0	9.1	5.7	2.1
Providence, RI	12.3	30.4	21.9	19.2	7.3	5.8	3.0
Provo, UT	18.5	35.9	19.5	15.2	5.3	3.8	1.7
Raleigh, NC	9.4	27.5	25.0	23.7	8.2	4.4	1.8
Reno, NV	12.3	39.0	24.7	15.5	4.1	2.7	1.6
Richmond, VA	9.0	29.3	27.3	22.8	6.4	3.1	2.1
Rochester, MN	18.6	42.3	18.3	12.8	3.8	2.5	1.7
Sacramento, CA	10.4	28.6	22.4	22.7	8.0	4.6	3.4
Salt Lake City, UT	10.8	33.1	27.7	19.3	5.3	2.7	1.0
San Antonio, TX	9.1	28.7	24.2	23.0	8.4	4.4	2.1
San Diego, CA	8.6	29.4	24.6	23.1	7.3	4.8	2.1
San Francisco, CA	6.6	22.4	17.7	23.8	12.3	12.5	4.7
San Jose, CA	6.9	25.4	23.4	24.6	9.3	7.4	2.9
Santa Rosa, CA	15.6	32.3	19.8	16.8	5.7	6.1	3.8
Savannah, GA	11.7	30.6	23.5	21.3	7.3	4.2	1.4
Seattle, WA	7.8	22.7	21.0	25.4	11.1	8.8	3.3
Sioux Falls, SD	16.6	44.0	24.5	10.1	2.3	1.4	1.0
Springfield, IL	16.0	41.7	23.5	11.7	3.0	2.5	1.7
Tallahassee, FL	11.2	34.0	24.2	20.9	5.7	2.5	1.5
Tampa, FL	9.7	27.2	21.7	23.1	9.8	6.4	2.1
Topeka, KS	16.2	42.4	19.6	13.4	4.1	3.0	1.2
Tucson, AZ	10.9	28.9	24.3	23.7	7.3	3.0	1.7
Tulsa, OK	13.5	34.3	26.3	18.1	4.3	2.3	1.3
Tuscaloosa, AL	10.7	32.2	28.4	16.4	5.9	4.7	1.6
Virginia Beach, VA	11.2	30.9	24.1	21.3	7.0	3.9	1.6
Washington, DC	5.9	19.0	17.8	25.7	14.0	13.0	4.5
Wichita, KS	16.3	37.8	26.4	14.1	2.8	1.4	1.2
Winston-Salem, NC	11.9	33.9	24.7	18.8	5.9	3.0	2.0
U.S.	12.5	28.7	20.9	20.7	8.2	6.3	2.8

Note: Figures are percentages and include workers 16 years old and over; Figures cover the Metropolitan Statistical Area—see Appendix B for areas included
Source: U.S. Census Bureau, 2014-2018 American Community Survey 5-Year Estimates

2016 Presidential Election Results

City	Area Covered	Clinton	Trump	Johnson	Stein	Other
Albany, NY	Albany County	59.4	34.2	3.4	1.8	1.2
Albuquerque, NM	Bernalillo County	52.2	34.5	10.8	1.3	1.2
Allentown, PA	Lehigh County	50.0	45.3	2.5	0.9	1.4
Anchorage, AK	State of Alaska	36.6	51.3	5.9	1.8	4.4
Ann Arbor, MI	Washtenaw County	67.6	26.6	3.1	1.3	1.4
Athens, GA	Clarke County	65.1	28.0	4.4	0.7	1.8
Atlanta, GA	Fulton County	67.7	26.8	3.6	0.1	1.8
Austin, TX	Travis County	65.8	27.1	4.7	1.6	0.8
Baton Rouge, LA	East Baton Rouge Parish	52.3	43.1	2.5	0.8	1.2
Boise City, ID	Ada County	38.7	47.9	5.1	1.6	6.7
Boston, MA	Suffolk County	78.4	16.1	2.6	1.4	1.5
Boulder, CO	Boulder County	70.3	22.0	4.3	2.0	1.4
Cape Coral, FL	Lee County	37.9	58.1	2.1	0.6	1.2
Cedar Rapids, IA	Linn County	50.3	41.3	4.7	0.9	2.7
Charleston, SC	Charleston County	50.6	42.8	4.1	1.0	1.5
Charlotte, NC	Mecklenburg County	62.3	32.9	3.3	0.3	1.3
Chicago, IL	Cook County	73.9	20.8	2.7	1.5	1.1
Clarksville, TN	Montgomery County	37.7	56.1	4.1	0.9	1.2
Cleveland, OH	Cuyahoga County	65.4	30.3	2.1	0.9	1.3
College Station, TX	Brazos County	34.4	57.6	5.7	0.8	1.5
Colorado Springs, CO	El Paso County	33.9	56.2	6.2	1.3	2.4
Columbia, MO	Boone County	49.0	43.2	5.1	1.5	1.2
Columbia, SC	Richland County	64.0	31.1	2.3	0.8	1.7
Columbus, OH	Franklin County	59.8	33.9	3.4	1.0	1.9
Dallas, TX	Dallas County	60.2	34.3	3.1	0.8	1.5
Davenport, IA	Scott County	46.9	45.4	4.1	0.9	2.7
Denver, CO	Denver County	73.7	18.9	4.5	1.7	1.3
Des Moines, IA	Polk County	51.7	40.4	4.3	0.8	2.8
Durham, NC	Durham County	77.7	18.2	2.6	0.3	1.3
Edison, NJ	Middlesex County	58.8	37.4	1.7	1.1	1.1
El Paso, TX	El Paso County	68.5	25.7	3.5	1.4	0.9
Fargo, ND	Cass County	38.8	49.3	7.5	1.5	2.9
Fayetteville, NC	Cumberland County	56.2	40.2	2.6	0.1	0.9
Fort Collins, CO	Larimer County	47.5	42.6	5.9	1.6	2.4
Fort Wayne, IN	Allen County	37.3	56.5	4.6	0.5	1.2
Fort Worth, TX	Tarrant County	43.1	51.7	3.6	0.8	0.7
Grand Rapids, MI	Kent County	44.6	47.7	4.6	1.3	1.9
Greeley, CO	Weld County	34.3	56.6	5.5	1.0	2.5
Green Bay, WI	Brown County	41.4	52.1	3.9	1.1	1.6
Greensboro, NC	Guilford County	58.0	38.1	2.6	0.3	1.0
Honolulu, HI	Honolulu County	61.5	31.6	3.7	2.3	1.0
Houston, TX	Harris County	54.0	41.6	3.0	0.9	0.5
Huntsville, AL	Madison County	38.4	54.8	4.1	0.8	1.9
Indianapolis, IN	Marion County	58.0	35.5	5.0	0.2	1.3
Jackson, MS	Hinds County	71.1	26.6	1.1	0.5	0.8
Jacksonville, FL	Duval County	47.1	48.5	2.6	0.7	1.1
Kansas City, MO	Jackson County	55.5	38.1	3.6	1.2	1.7
Lafayette, LA	Lafayette Parish	31.0	64.6	2.7	0.8	0.9
Lakeland, FL	Polk County	40.9	54.9	2.4	0.6	1.3
Las Vegas, NV	Clark County	52.4	41.7	2.9	0.0	2.9
Lexington, KY	Fayette County	51.2	41.7	3.8	1.2	2.1
Lincoln, NE	Lancaster County	45.4	45.2	5.2	1.4	2.7
Little Rock, AR	Pulaski County	56.1	38.3	2.7	1.0	1.9
Los Angeles, CA	Los Angeles County	71.8	22.4	2.6	2.2	1.0
Louisville, KY	Jefferson County	54.0	40.7	2.9	0.9	1.4
Madison, WI	Dane County	70.4	23.0	3.4	1.4	1.8

Table continued on next page.

City	Area Covered	Clinton	Trump	Johnson	Stein	Other
Manchester, NH	Hillsborough County	46.5	46.7	4.3	0.8	1.7
Miami, FL	Miami-Dade County	63.2	33.8	1.3	0.6	1.0
Midland, TX	Midland County	20.4	75.1	3.4	0.4	0.7
Milwaukee, WI	Milwaukee County	65.5	28.6	3.1	1.0	1.8
Minneapolis, MN	Hennepin County	63.1	28.2	3.6	1.5	3.6
Nashville, TN	Davidson County	59.8	33.9	3.9	1.0	1.4
New Haven, CT	New Haven County	54.2	42.0	2.4	1.3	0.1
New Orleans, LA	Orleans Parish	80.8	14.7	2.2	1.5	0.8
New York, NY	Bronx County	88.5	9.5	0.6	1.1	0.3
New York, NY	Kings County	79.5	17.5	0.9	1.5	0.6
New York, NY	New York County	86.6	9.7	1.4	1.4	0.9
New York, NY	Queens County	75.4	21.8	1.0	1.3	0.5
New York, NY	Richmond County	41.0	56.1	1.3	1.0	0.6
Oklahoma City, OK	Oklahoma County	41.2	51.7	7.1	0.0	0.0
Omaha, NE	Douglas County	47.3	45.0	4.3	1.2	2.2
Orlando, FL	Orange County	59.8	35.4	2.6	0.9	1.4
Peoria, IL	Peoria County	48.1	45.0	4.7	1.4	0.8
Philadelphia, PA	Philadelphia County	82.3	15.3	1.0	0.9	0.4
Phoenix, AZ	Maricopa County	44.8	47.7	4.3	1.2	2.0
Pittsburgh, PA	Allegheny County	55.9	39.5	2.5	0.8	1.4
Portland, OR	Multnomah County	73.3	17.0	3.2	3.2	3.2
Providence, RI	Providence County	57.5	36.6	2.7	1.3	1.9
Provo, UT	Utah County	14.0	50.2	3.2	0.5	32.2
Raleigh, NC	Wake County	57.4	37.2	3.7	0.3	1.4
Reno, NV	Washoe County	46.4	45.1	4.4	0.0	4.0
Richmond, VA	Richmond City	78.6	15.1	3.5	1.1	1.8
Rochester, MN	Olmsted County	45.3	44.5	4.4	1.4	4.4
Sacramento, CA	Sacramento County	58.0	33.8	4.3	1.8	2.2
Salt Lake City, UT	Salt Lake County	41.5	32.6	3.8	1.2	20.9
San Antonio, TX	Bexar County	53.7	40.4	3.4	1.1	1.3
San Diego, CA	San Diego County	56.3	36.6	4.0	1.7	1.4
San Francisco, CA	San Francisco County	84.5	9.2	2.2	2.4	1.7
San Jose, CA	Santa Clara County	72.7	20.6	3.6	1.8	1.3
Santa Rosa, CA	Sonoma County	68.8	22.0	3.9	3.1	2.2
Savannah, GA	Chatham County	55.1	40.4	3.1	0.3	1.1
Seattle, WA	King County	69.8	21.0	4.0	1.7	3.4
Sioux Falls, SD	Minnehaha County	39.1	53.7	6.1	0.0	1.1
Springfield, IL	Sangamon County	41.6	50.8	4.6	1.5	1.6
Tallahassee, FL	Leon County	59.8	35.0	2.9	0.9	1.4
Tampa, FL	Hillsborough County	51.0	44.2	2.6	0.8	1.4
Topeka, KS	Shawnee County	44.2	46.8	4.4	2.3	2.3
Tucson, AZ	Pima County	53.3	39.7	3.7	1.5	1.8
Tulsa, OK	Tulsa County	35.6	58.4	6.1	0.0	0.0
Tuscaloosa, AL	Tuscaloosa County	38.4	57.7	2.3	0.5	1.2
Virginia Beach, VA	Virginia Beach City	44.8	48.4	4.1	0.9	1.9
Washington, DC	District of Columbia	90.9	4.1	1.6	1.4	2.1
Wichita, KS	Sedgwick County	36.3	54.4	4.8	2.1	2.4
Winston-Salem, NC	Forsyth County	53.0	42.6	3.0	0.3	1.2
U.S.	U.S.	48.0	45.9	3.3	1.1	1.7

Note: Results are percentages and may not add to 100% due to rounding
Source: Dave Leip's Atlas of U.S. Presidential Elections

House Price Index (HPI)

Metro Area[1]	National Ranking[3]	Quarterly Change (%)	One-Year Change (%)	Five-Year Change (%)
Albany, NY	205	-0.28	3.19	13.87
Albuquerque, NM	51	0.37	6.20	20.62
Allentown, PA	149	0.06	4.41	18.99
Anchorage, AK	202	-0.54	3.28	9.31
Ann Arbor, MI	173	0.04	3.92	36.45
Athens, GA	n/r	n/a	9.56	42.77
Atlanta, GA	47	1.08	6.32	45.06
Austin, TX	22	0.95	7.19	44.12
Baton Rouge, LA	203	1.15	3.24	19.27
Boise City, ID	3	1.60	10.87	73.23
Boston, MA[2]	147	0.93	4.43	30.17
Boulder, CO	212	-0.13	2.99	50.91
Cape Coral, FL	114	1.34	4.96	42.78
Cedar Rapids, IA	216	0.69	2.67	14.49
Charleston, SC	92	0.86	5.35	43.79
Charlotte, NC	94	1.09	5.30	41.63
Chicago, IL[2]	169	0.81	3.97	20.01
Clarksville, TN	n/r	n/a	4.76	23.32
Cleveland, OH	64	0.83	5.89	25.32
College Station, TX	n/r	n/a	2.29	32.26
Colorado Springs, CO	16	1.38	7.57	50.12
Columbia, MO	184	1.66	3.70	19.33
Columbia, SC	125	0.33	4.81	23.60
Columbus, OH	83	0.58	5.45	37.45
Dallas, TX[2]	164	0.31	4.09	48.15
Davenport, IA	185	-1.22	3.68	13.08
Denver, CO	152	0.83	4.36	54.65
Des Moines, IA	213	0.60	2.75	23.59
Durham, NC	158	0.73	4.22	37.32
Edison, NJ[2]	161	0.56	4.17	25.88
El Paso, TX	98	0.95	5.23	14.41
Fargo, ND	219	0.15	2.46	21.32
Fayetteville, NC	n/r	n/a	2.03	13.23
Fort Collins, CO	176	0.26	3.89	50.30
Fort Wayne, IN	155	0.24	4.26	33.61
Fort Worth, TX[2]	108	0.79	5.11	49.94
Grand Rapids, MI	79	0.27	5.50	46.00
Greeley, CO	175	0.76	3.90	58.75
Green Bay, WI	118	1.11	4.88	29.23
Greensboro, NC	170	-0.12	3.97	23.24
Honolulu, HI	215	0.18	2.69	24.89
Houston, TX	193	-0.63	3.41	26.50
Huntsville, AL	13	2.10	7.91	23.22
Indianapolis, IN	59	0.98	6.06	33.98
Jackson, MS	150	1.60	4.41	14.17
Jacksonville, FL	26	2.31	7.05	46.18
Kansas City, MO	101	1.32	5.21	37.34
Lafayette, LA	209	-0.66	3.08	8.06
Lakeland, FL	18	1.25	7.47	52.32
Las Vegas, NV	187	0.76	3.57	58.25
Lexington, KY	99	1.16	5.22	27.81
Lincoln, NE	180	0.34	3.84	30.88
Little Rock, AR	186	1.04	3.58	13.81
Los Angeles, CA[2]	195	0.86	3.35	36.42
Louisville, KY	160	0.57	4.18	28.27

Table continued on next page.

Metro Area[1]	National Ranking[3]	Quarterly Change (%)	One-Year Change (%)	Five-Year Change (%)
Madison, WI	156	0.56	4.26	28.02
Manchester, NH	52	1.82	6.19	30.17
Miami, FL[2]	124	-0.11	4.81	45.61
Midland, TX	n/r	n/a	6.14	28.56
Milwaukee, WI	165	0.46	4.06	25.49
Minneapolis, MN	119	0.32	4.85	31.56
Nashville, TN	90	1.25	5.36	49.67
New Haven, CT	143	1.02	4.52	10.91
New Orleans, LA	84	1.06	5.42	23.21
New York, NY[2]	161	0.56	4.17	25.88
Oklahoma City, OK	55	0.60	6.13	22.05
Omaha, NE	75	1.03	5.58	32.31
Orlando, FL	46	0.67	6.34	51.54
Peoria, IL	227	0.59	1.77	3.09
Philadelphia, PA[2]	54	1.66	6.17	31.20
Phoenix, AZ	42	1.76	6.46	45.62
Pittsburgh, PA	65	0.66	5.86	25.10
Portland, OR	142	0.69	4.52	47.67
Providence, RI	107	1.19	5.13	30.04
Provo, UT	31	1.37	6.87	47.00
Raleigh, NC	130	0.42	4.76	35.35
Reno, NV	199	-0.35	3.31	60.61
Richmond, VA	138	0.79	4.63	28.61
Rochester, MN	198	0.13	3.31	33.01
Sacramento, CA	162	0.51	4.14	40.21
Salt Lake City, UT	28	1.39	7.00	48.82
San Antonio, TX	57	0.26	6.09	38.14
San Diego, CA	200	0.72	3.30	33.32
San Francisco, CA[2]	230	-1.30	-1.12	40.90
San Jose, CA	231	-1.32	-1.88	37.69
Santa Rosa, CA	225	0.45	1.99	37.15
Savannah, GA	106	0.06	5.17	32.62
Seattle, WA[2]	196	0.36	3.35	56.22
Sioux Falls, SD	121	1.04	4.83	31.38
Springfield, IL	214	1.64	2.74	10.02
Tallahassee, FL	n/r	n/a	9.59	31.33
Tampa, FL	15	1.05	7.64	56.22
Topeka, KS	85	1.19	5.42	20.20
Tucson, AZ	70	1.46	5.70	34.52
Tulsa, OK	74	1.26	5.59	23.89
Tuscaloosa, AL	n/r	n/a	3.84	20.29
Virginia Beach, VA	69	0.17	5.70	13.82
Washington, DC[2]	153	0.61	4.35	21.85
Wichita, KS	53	0.56	6.19	22.18
Winston-Salem, NC	103	2.39	5.20	26.46
U.S.[4]	–	1.26	5.09	32.88

Note: The HPI is a weighted repeat sales index. It measures average price changes in repeat sales or refinancings on the same properties. This information is obtained by reviewing repeat mortgage transactions on single-family properties whose mortgages have been purchased or securitized by Fannie Mae or Freddie Mac in January 1975; (1) figures cover the Metropolitan Statistical Area (MSA) unless noted otherwise—see Appendix B for areas included; (2) Metropolitan Division—see Appendix B for areas included; (3) Rankings are based on annual percentage change, for all MSAs containing at least 15,000 transactions over the last 10 years and ranges from 1 to 232; (4) figures based on a weighted division average; all figures are for the period ended December 31, 2019; n/a not available; n/r not ranked
Source: Federal Housing Finance Agency, House Price Index, February 25, 2020

Home Value Distribution: City

Area	Under $50,000	$50,000 -$99,999	$100,000 -$149,999	$150,000 -$199,999	$200,000 -$299,999	$300,000 -$499,999	$500,000 -$999,999	$1,000,000 or more
Albany, NY	4.8	11.3	19.8	28.0	27.2	6.8	1.6	0.4
Albuquerque, NM	4.8	4.9	18.3	25.1	28.4	15.1	3.0	0.5
Allentown, PA	5.5	24.6	33.6	23.0	8.4	3.5	0.8	0.6
Anchorage, AK	5.7	2.3	4.3	7.5	28.0	39.7	11.4	0.9
Ann Arbor, MI	2.0	4.2	6.5	10.0	27.6	34.4	13.5	1.7
Athens, GA	7.5	15.0	20.7	20.8	18.8	12.0	4.4	0.7
Atlanta, GA	5.8	12.1	10.1	11.0	16.8	18.2	17.9	8.1
Austin, TX	2.7	2.6	6.2	11.3	24.9	30.8	17.8	3.7
Baton Rouge, LA	6.6	18.4	16.2	18.9	20.2	12.7	5.6	1.4
Boise City, ID	4.4	2.6	11.7	20.6	30.1	23.0	6.7	0.9
Boston, MA	2.0	0.4	0.8	1.9	10.1	37.2	35.9	11.8
Boulder, CO	5.0	1.4	2.5	3.7	4.7	16.1	47.1	19.5
Cape Coral, FL	2.0	5.4	14.7	22.5	30.2	18.7	5.5	0.8
Cedar Rapids, IA	5.3	16.8	35.0	20.3	15.7	5.1	1.4	0.3
Charleston, SC	2.1	3.0	5.6	10.9	26.7	28.6	16.9	6.1
Charlotte, NC	2.6	10.0	19.7	17.6	19.5	17.6	9.9	3.1
Chicago, IL	3.2	7.8	12.0	15.3	23.4	23.0	11.5	3.8
Clarksville, TN	4.7	17.2	28.9	26.3	16.6	5.2	0.8	0.3
Cleveland, OH	29.7	45.6	13.2	5.4	3.0	1.8	0.9	0.3
College Station, TX	2.4	1.9	9.6	25.4	33.9	21.6	4.5	0.7
Colorado Springs, CO	3.6	2.7	8.2	17.5	33.3	26.0	7.4	1.2
Columbia, MO	3.3	8.5	20.1	23.2	25.2	15.8	3.7	0.1
Columbia, SC	4.6	16.1	21.3	15.1	15.6	15.5	10.3	1.5
Columbus, OH	6.6	21.8	25.3	20.4	17.1	6.6	1.8	0.3
Dallas, TX	7.6	22.1	15.6	9.7	12.3	16.8	11.6	4.2
Davenport, IA	6.6	25.3	29.5	16.1	14.9	6.3	1.0	0.4
Denver, CO	1.9	2.2	4.7	9.0	21.9	32.3	23.4	4.6
Des Moines, IA	6.5	23.7	34.7	19.4	10.0	4.2	1.4	0.1
Durham, NC	1.7	6.4	17.3	22.1	28.6	17.8	5.2	0.9
Edison, NJ	2.7	1.8	1.9	2.5	18.7	47.4	23.6	1.4
El Paso, TX	5.5	26.7	32.2	17.9	11.7	4.6	1.2	0.3
Fargo, ND	3.6	5.6	16.1	24.9	30.0	15.9	3.5	0.5
Fayetteville, NC	5.3	26.8	27.1	18.7	14.1	6.0	1.6	0.4
Fort Collins, CO	3.5	1.0	2.4	5.8	25.9	47.3	13.2	1.0
Fort Wayne, IN	11.3	32.2	28.8	14.8	8.6	3.2	1.0	0.1
Fort Worth, TX	7.2	20.6	20.3	19.0	18.9	9.8	3.4	0.8
Grand Rapids, MI	6.1	23.8	32.1	20.9	11.4	4.3	1.2	0.1
Greeley, CO	8.6	3.5	11.2	18.4	34.2	20.2	3.6	0.2
Green Bay, WI	3.3	22.5	37.0	19.4	11.4	4.8	1.3	0.3
Greensboro, NC	3.4	20.1	25.2	18.3	17.2	11.0	3.8	1.0
Honolulu, HI	1.0	1.0	0.9	1.4	8.0	22.9	43.0	21.8
Houston, TX	6.3	21.8	18.4	12.2	13.4	15.0	9.4	3.3
Huntsville, AL	5.8	19.1	15.5	16.4	22.2	15.6	4.3	1.1
Indianapolis, IN	8.2	24.6	28.5	17.4	10.5	7.3	2.7	0.6
Jackson, MS	19.5	36.6	19.3	10.5	7.0	4.6	1.9	0.5
Jacksonville, FL	8.7	17.7	18.8	18.7	20.9	10.5	3.6	1.1
Kansas City, MO	11.7	19.2	19.8	18.2	18.0	9.3	3.2	0.7
Lafayette, LA	6.1	8.7	15.0	23.8	23.6	15.1	6.0	1.7
Lakeland, FL	19.9	18.8	16.9	18.8	14.0	8.0	2.9	0.6
Las Vegas, NV	3.0	6.4	11.5	17.7	30.0	23.2	6.7	1.6
Lexington, KY	3.1	10.5	21.8	21.4	21.4	15.3	5.2	1.3
Lincoln, NE	4.1	11.1	28.4	23.7	20.7	9.6	2.0	0.4
Little Rock, AR	7.0	20.1	17.4	17.5	15.4	14.8	6.3	1.4
Los Angeles, CA	1.6	0.9	0.7	1.1	6.3	28.2	41.3	19.9
Louisville, KY	6.2	17.0	25.7	17.6	16.5	12.3	4.0	0.6

Table continued on next page.

Area	Under $50,000	$50,000 -$99,999	$100,000 -$149,999	$150,000 -$199,999	$200,000 -$299,999	$300,000 -$499,999	$500,000 -$999,999	$1,000,000 or more
Madison, WI	1.9	2.6	9.4	21.5	35.4	23.1	5.6	0.6
Manchester, NH	2.6	3.8	8.8	25.4	45.3	13.1	0.9	0.1
Miami, FL	2.7	6.3	7.7	11.1	24.0	27.0	14.5	6.6
Midland, TX	5.6	10.4	13.4	19.1	25.7	17.7	6.9	1.1
Milwaukee, WI	9.5	29.3	29.5	17.2	9.5	3.2	1.5	0.3
Minneapolis, MN	1.8	5.1	12.1	18.0	30.5	21.7	8.9	1.8
Nashville, TN	2.5	6.5	17.2	19.2	24.3	20.1	8.7	1.5
New Haven, CT	2.5	8.2	17.3	23.6	27.1	14.9	5.5	1.0
New Orleans, LA	3.2	8.7	14.8	19.1	19.4	19.9	11.5	3.4
New York, NY	3.2	1.4	2.0	2.6	7.2	26.1	39.5	17.8
Oklahoma City, OK	8.5	18.8	20.9	20.3	18.0	9.7	3.2	0.6
Omaha, NE	4.9	16.2	28.4	20.7	17.4	9.0	2.8	0.7
Orlando, FL	4.2	13.5	14.1	13.9	23.6	21.5	7.6	1.6
Peoria, IL	12.6	25.4	22.4	15.5	14.2	7.2	2.4	0.4
Philadelphia, PA	7.3	20.3	19.5	18.3	18.5	10.5	4.4	1.3
Phoenix, AZ	5.3	8.7	12.9	18.4	23.7	21.0	8.5	1.6
Pittsburgh, PA	12.8	30.5	17.4	12.0	11.5	9.6	5.4	0.8
Portland, OR	2.4	0.8	2.1	5.9	20.3	39.2	26.5	2.8
Providence, RI	2.2	6.7	18.4	26.0	20.6	15.3	9.1	1.8
Provo, UT	4.0	1.3	8.6	16.7	35.2	24.1	8.1	2.0
Raleigh, NC	2.3	3.0	13.8	20.5	25.8	22.9	10.1	1.5
Reno, NV	5.2	4.2	5.5	9.7	25.4	37.7	10.4	1.8
Richmond, VA	2.4	12.2	14.9	15.6	20.8	20.6	10.6	2.8
Rochester, MN	3.9	6.0	19.4	26.0	25.0	15.8	3.4	0.4
Sacramento, CA	3.1	2.6	5.1	9.4	26.8	36.2	15.1	1.7
Salt Lake City, UT	3.2	2.1	8.4	15.4	23.4	29.0	15.8	2.8
San Antonio, TX	7.9	26.8	20.4	17.6	16.1	8.4	2.3	0.5
San Diego, CA	2.0	1.0	0.9	1.4	6.8	29.6	45.0	13.4
San Francisco, CA	1.3	0.5	0.4	0.5	1.3	5.0	40.4	50.7
San Jose, CA	1.8	1.7	1.4	1.0	1.9	10.0	53.6	28.6
Santa Rosa, CA	3.4	2.5	1.8	1.5	6.8	36.3	42.4	5.4
Savannah, GA	6.5	21.5	21.3	19.1	17.5	9.6	3.5	1.1
Seattle, WA	0.9	0.4	0.6	1.4	6.7	27.0	48.7	14.3
Sioux Falls, SD	6.0	8.1	20.1	25.7	23.7	12.4	3.3	0.7
Springfield, IL	11.5	26.1	22.9	14.9	14.8	6.9	2.7	0.2
Tallahassee, FL	4.0	10.6	17.1	21.0	25.6	17.4	3.4	0.9
Tampa, FL	5.2	14.0	13.5	13.8	18.2	19.1	12.1	4.1
Topeka, KS	13.8	34.8	24.4	13.6	9.9	2.5	0.7	0.3
Tucson, AZ	11.1	15.9	24.7	22.9	17.4	5.9	1.9	0.3
Tulsa, OK	9.5	24.0	23.2	15.1	13.0	9.7	4.5	1.0
Tuscaloosa, AL	5.3	11.6	22.4	18.3	19.3	14.3	7.3	1.6
Virginia Beach, VA	2.7	1.4	6.3	13.3	34.3	29.3	10.7	2.0
Washington, DC	1.7	1.0	1.3	2.5	10.9	26.2	39.2	17.3
Wichita, KS	9.2	27.7	23.7	16.9	13.6	6.5	2.0	0.4
Winston-Salem, NC	7.0	20.2	25.7	19.9	12.5	9.0	4.8	0.8
U.S.	7.6	13.0	14.0	14.3	19.2	18.3	10.5	3.1

Note: Figures are percentages and cover owner-occupied housing units.
Source: U.S. Census Bureau, 2014-2018 American Community Survey 5-Year Estimates

Home Value Distribution: Metro Area

MSA[1]	Under $50,000	$50,000 -$99,999	$100,000 -$149,999	$150,000 -$199,999	$200,000 -$299,999	$300,000 -$499,999	$500,000 -$999,999	$1,000,000 or more
Albany, NY	4.6	7.8	13.6	21.2	29.3	19.0	3.8	0.6
Albuquerque, NM	6.2	8.1	18.3	22.4	24.8	14.8	4.4	0.9
Allentown, PA	4.3	7.9	15.1	20.4	27.8	20.1	3.8	0.6
Anchorage, AK	5.3	2.9	4.9	10.0	30.4	36.0	9.7	0.8
Ann Arbor, MI	6.5	6.9	9.1	15.2	24.6	26.1	9.9	1.6
Athens, GA	9.6	14.1	18.3	16.7	20.4	14.9	5.1	0.9
Atlanta, GA	4.6	11.3	16.3	18.0	21.2	18.7	8.3	1.6
Austin, TX	3.7	4.5	8.9	14.9	27.1	25.7	12.3	2.8
Baton Rouge, LA	9.2	13.2	15.9	20.7	22.6	13.3	4.1	0.9
Boise City, ID	4.8	5.4	15.2	20.1	27.4	21.0	5.4	0.7
Boston, MA	1.9	1.1	1.9	4.1	16.4	38.9	28.9	6.7
Boulder, CO	3.4	1.0	1.9	4.0	13.4	32.0	34.8	9.5
Cape Coral, FL	7.3	11.2	13.4	16.2	22.4	18.7	8.3	2.5
Cedar Rapids, IA	6.5	14.5	27.8	19.4	20.1	8.7	2.5	0.6
Charleston, SC	6.8	8.6	12.9	16.1	22.1	19.4	10.6	3.4
Charlotte, NC	5.3	12.5	18.3	17.4	20.5	16.9	7.2	1.8
Chicago, IL	3.6	8.0	13.2	16.7	24.8	21.8	9.4	2.3
Clarksville, TN	7.0	19.0	24.3	21.7	17.7	8.1	1.7	0.6
Cleveland, OH	8.2	21.0	22.1	17.8	17.6	9.9	2.7	0.6
College Station, TX	11.1	14.9	14.9	18.7	21.2	13.9	4.4	1.0
Colorado Springs, CO	3.7	2.6	7.8	17.0	31.6	27.2	9.0	1.1
Columbia, MO	4.5	9.7	20.7	21.6	23.6	15.0	4.5	0.5
Columbia, SC	9.5	17.4	23.3	18.3	16.7	10.2	3.9	0.8
Columbus, OH	5.2	14.6	19.7	19.2	21.5	14.7	4.4	0.7
Dallas, TX	5.3	13.5	16.5	16.7	21.3	18.2	6.8	1.8
Davenport, IA	7.9	24.3	25.0	17.1	15.2	8.2	1.9	0.4
Denver, CO	2.7	1.7	3.4	7.7	22.9	39.2	19.5	2.9
Des Moines, IA	4.8	12.3	20.4	20.6	23.9	13.7	3.9	0.4
Durham, NC	4.8	7.9	14.5	16.9	23.4	21.3	9.8	1.4
Edison, NJ	2.4	1.6	2.7	4.5	14.9	35.7	29.3	8.8
El Paso, TX	8.3	28.0	31.2	16.7	10.5	4.1	1.1	0.2
Fargo, ND	4.1	6.2	16.0	23.2	28.9	16.6	4.4	0.6
Fayetteville, NC	8.8	23.9	24.1	19.4	16.3	5.9	1.2	0.4
Fort Collins, CO	4.5	1.4	2.1	6.9	25.7	41.6	16.0	1.8
Fort Wayne, IN	9.3	26.4	26.7	16.2	12.9	6.4	1.8	0.4
Fort Worth, TX	5.3	13.5	16.5	16.7	21.3	18.2	6.8	1.8
Grand Rapids, MI	7.3	13.4	22.2	21.0	20.4	11.6	3.2	0.7
Greeley, CO	5.7	3.6	6.7	12.8	29.9	30.4	9.8	1.0
Green Bay, WI	4.3	13.0	24.4	22.8	23.1	9.5	2.4	0.6
Greensboro, NC	7.4	20.5	23.9	17.5	16.6	10.1	3.2	0.7
Honolulu, HI	0.9	0.8	0.8	1.1	6.1	20.7	53.5	16.0
Houston, TX	5.9	14.4	18.4	17.5	20.0	15.3	6.5	2.1
Huntsville, AL	7.0	14.7	18.1	18.4	23.0	14.7	3.5	0.6
Indianapolis, IN	6.3	17.7	23.8	18.4	17.0	12.1	4.0	0.8
Jackson, MS	12.9	20.0	19.5	17.2	16.9	9.6	3.0	0.9
Jacksonville, FL	6.8	14.0	15.5	17.0	22.9	16.2	6.0	1.7
Kansas City, MO	6.8	14.2	18.7	19.1	21.5	14.4	4.5	0.8
Lafayette, LA	15.4	17.5	16.3	19.0	18.3	9.4	3.4	0.7
Lakeland, FL	16.0	21.3	17.5	18.3	16.9	7.6	1.9	0.6
Las Vegas, NV	4.3	6.0	10.5	16.6	30.3	24.0	6.8	1.5
Lexington, KY	4.1	11.3	22.7	20.7	20.4	14.2	5.3	1.3
Lincoln, NE	3.9	10.6	26.1	22.5	21.3	12.1	3.0	0.5
Little Rock, AR	8.6	18.5	22.7	19.5	17.5	9.5	3.0	0.8
Los Angeles, CA	2.3	1.5	1.1	1.5	6.1	27.9	44.2	15.3
Louisville, KY	5.7	15.4	23.6	18.6	19.7	12.2	4.0	0.8

Table continued on next page.

MSA[1]	Under $50,000	$50,000 -$99,999	$100,000 -$149,999	$150,000 -$199,999	$200,000 -$299,999	$300,000 -$499,999	$500,000 -$999,999	$1,000,000 or more
Madison, WI	2.4	4.0	10.7	18.3	32.4	24.5	6.6	1.1
Manchester, NH	2.3	2.6	6.4	13.9	38.4	29.7	6.1	0.7
Miami, FL	4.9	8.6	10.1	12.8	22.5	25.6	11.2	4.2
Midland, TX	9.5	11.8	12.9	17.1	24.0	17.1	6.5	1.1
Milwaukee, WI	4.1	9.7	15.9	18.9	26.6	18.5	5.4	1.0
Minneapolis, MN	3.1	3.4	9.7	18.5	31.7	24.3	7.9	1.3
Nashville, TN	3.6	7.7	16.1	18.0	23.8	19.9	9.0	1.9
New Haven, CT	2.4	4.9	11.2	17.1	29.1	26.4	7.8	1.2
New Orleans, LA	4.7	9.5	17.7	21.4	24.0	15.4	5.7	1.5
New York, NY	2.4	1.6	2.7	4.5	14.9	35.7	29.3	8.8
Oklahoma City, OK	8.2	18.9	22.0	19.3	17.5	9.9	3.3	0.9
Omaha, NE	4.5	13.1	25.7	20.4	20.6	12.1	3.0	0.6
Orlando, FL	7.1	10.7	13.6	18.1	26.1	17.4	5.5	1.5
Peoria, IL	7.7	24.7	24.0	18.3	15.6	7.5	1.7	0.4
Philadelphia, PA	3.9	7.5	10.7	15.1	26.4	25.3	9.5	1.6
Phoenix, AZ	6.2	6.6	10.6	16.6	26.4	22.7	8.8	2.1
Pittsburgh, PA	9.6	21.4	19.8	17.6	16.8	10.9	3.3	0.6
Portland, OR	3.8	1.4	3.0	7.0	24.7	39.1	18.8	2.3
Providence, RI	2.5	2.3	6.8	15.6	33.1	29.2	9.0	1.6
Provo, UT	2.7	1.0	5.4	13.7	34.3	31.5	10.1	1.3
Raleigh, NC	4.0	5.5	13.7	16.9	24.8	25.3	8.7	1.2
Reno, NV	4.6	4.0	5.8	10.1	25.8	33.5	12.9	3.3
Richmond, VA	2.7	5.7	13.1	19.0	29.1	22.0	7.3	1.2
Rochester, MN	5.2	7.9	18.0	22.5	23.1	17.4	4.8	1.0
Sacramento, CA	3.5	1.9	3.0	6.0	20.0	40.6	22.5	2.6
Salt Lake City, UT	3.6	1.4	6.9	14.2	30.8	30.5	11.2	1.4
San Antonio, TX	7.8	20.0	17.4	17.9	18.8	12.7	4.3	1.1
San Diego, CA	3.0	2.0	1.5	1.6	6.5	32.2	42.4	10.8
San Francisco, CA	1.6	1.1	0.9	1.0	3.7	15.4	44.6	31.6
San Jose, CA	1.7	1.3	1.2	0.9	1.8	8.5	43.4	41.2
Santa Rosa, CA	3.5	2.8	1.7	1.3	5.0	26.7	47.2	11.8
Savannah, GA	5.9	12.8	17.7	19.3	22.3	14.0	6.5	1.6
Seattle, WA	3.1	1.4	2.6	5.5	18.2	33.8	28.3	7.0
Sioux Falls, SD	5.9	9.0	19.0	23.8	24.1	13.8	3.6	0.8
Springfield, IL	9.4	23.4	22.4	17.6	17.6	7.3	2.1	0.3
Tallahassee, FL	8.6	15.9	16.4	18.1	21.8	14.6	3.9	0.8
Tampa, FL	9.9	15.2	15.0	16.8	21.4	14.6	5.7	1.4
Topeka, KS	10.2	25.2	23.4	18.0	15.1	6.4	1.4	0.4
Tucson, AZ	9.0	12.1	18.0	19.3	20.9	14.1	5.6	0.9
Tulsa, OK	10.2	19.7	22.6	18.8	16.3	8.6	3.1	0.8
Tuscaloosa, AL	12.6	14.6	19.2	20.3	19.6	9.8	3.3	0.7
Virginia Beach, VA	3.7	3.7	10.3	17.6	31.3	24.6	7.6	1.2
Washington, DC	1.8	1.1	2.5	5.3	17.9	35.1	30.0	6.3
Wichita, KS	9.1	25.4	23.3	18.4	14.7	7.0	1.8	0.4
Winston-Salem, NC	7.9	18.0	25.2	19.8	16.0	9.2	3.2	0.7
U.S.	7.6	13.0	14.0	14.3	19.2	18.3	10.5	3.1

Note: (1) Figures cover the Metropolitan Statistical Area (MSA)—see Appendix B for areas included; Figures are percentages and cover owner-occupied housing units.
Source: U.S. Census Bureau, 2014-2018 American Community Survey 5-Year Estimates

Homeownership Rate

Metro Area	2011	2012	2013	2014	2015	2016	2017	2018	2019
Albany, NY	72.4	70.6	67.9	67.5	65.9	61.3	64.1	62.2	61.2
Albuquerque, NM	67.1	62.8	65.9	64.4	64.3	66.9	67.0	67.9	70.0
Allentown, PA	75.7	75.5	71.5	68.2	69.2	68.9	73.1	72.1	67.8
Anchorage, AK	n/a	n/a	n/a	n/a	n/a	n/a	n/a	n/a	n/a
Ann Arbor, MI	n/a	n/a	n/a	n/a	n/a	n/a	n/a	n/a	n/a
Athens, GA	n/a	n/a	n/a	n/a	n/a	n/a	n/a	n/a	n/a
Atlanta, GA	65.8	62.1	61.6	61.6	61.7	61.5	62.4	64.0	64.2
Austin, TX	58.4	60.1	59.6	61.1	57.5	56.5	55.6	56.1	59.0
Baton Rouge, LA	72.0	71.4	66.6	64.8	64.2	64.8	66.9	66.6	66.2
Boise City, ID	n/a	n/a	n/a	n/a	n/a	n/a	n/a	n/a	n/a
Boston, MA	65.5	66.0	66.3	62.8	59.3	58.9	58.8	61.0	60.9
Boulder, CO	n/a	n/a	n/a	n/a	n/a	n/a	n/a	n/a	n/a
Cape Coral, FL	n/a	n/a	n/a	n/a	62.9	66.5	65.5	75.1	72.0
Cedar Rapids, IA	n/a	n/a	n/a	n/a	n/a	n/a	n/a	n/a	n/a
Charleston, SC	n/a	n/a	n/a	n/a	65.8	62.1	67.7	68.8	70.7
Charlotte, NC	63.6	58.3	58.9	58.1	62.3	66.2	64.6	67.9	72.3
Chicago, IL	67.7	67.1	68.2	66.3	64.3	64.5	64.1	64.6	63.4
Clarksville, TN	n/a	n/a	n/a	n/a	n/a	n/a	n/a	n/a	n/a
Cleveland, OH	69.8	64.2	65.8	69.2	68.4	64.8	66.6	66.7	64.4
College Station, TX	n/a	n/a	n/a	n/a	n/a	n/a	n/a	n/a	n/a
Colorado Springs, CO	n/a	n/a	n/a	n/a	n/a	n/a	n/a	n/a	n/a
Columbia, MO	n/a	n/a	n/a	n/a	n/a	n/a	n/a	n/a	n/a
Columbia, SC	69.0	65.6	68.9	69.5	66.1	63.9	70.7	69.3	65.9
Columbus, OH	59.7	60.7	60.5	60.0	59.0	57.5	57.9	64.8	65.7
Dallas, TX	62.6	61.8	59.9	57.7	57.8	59.7	61.8	62.0	60.6
Davenport, IA	n/a	n/a	n/a	n/a	n/a	n/a	n/a	n/a	n/a
Denver, CO	63.0	61.8	61.0	61.9	61.6	61.6	59.3	60.1	63.5
Des Moines, IA	n/a	n/a	n/a	n/a	n/a	n/a	n/a	n/a	n/a
Durham, NC	n/a	n/a	n/a	n/a	n/a	n/a	n/a	n/a	n/a
Edison, NJ	50.9	51.5	50.6	50.7	49.9	50.4	49.9	49.7	50.4
El Paso, TX	n/a	n/a	n/a	n/a	n/a	n/a	n/a	n/a	n/a
Fargo, ND	n/a	n/a	n/a	n/a	n/a	n/a	n/a	n/a	n/a
Fayetteville, NC	n/a	n/a	n/a	n/a	n/a	n/a	n/a	n/a	n/a
Fort Collins, CO	n/a	n/a	n/a	n/a	n/a	n/a	n/a	n/a	n/a
Fort Wayne, IN	n/a	n/a	n/a	n/a	n/a	n/a	n/a	n/a	n/a
Fort Worth, TX	62.6	61.8	59.9	57.7	57.8	59.7	61.8	62.0	60.6
Grand Rapids, MI	76.4	76.9	73.7	71.6	75.8	76.2	71.7	73.0	75.2
Greeley, CO	n/a	n/a	n/a	n/a	n/a	n/a	n/a	n/a	n/a
Green Bay, WI	n/a	n/a	n/a	n/a	n/a	n/a	n/a	n/a	n/a
Greensboro, NC	62.7	64.9	67.9	68.1	65.4	62.9	61.9	63.2	61.7
Honolulu, HI	54.1	56.1	57.9	58.2	59.6	57.9	53.8	57.7	59.0
Houston, TX	61.3	62.1	60.5	60.4	60.3	59.0	58.9	60.1	61.3
Huntsville, AL	n/a	n/a	n/a	n/a	n/a	n/a	n/a	n/a	n/a
Indianapolis, IN	68.3	67.1	67.5	66.9	64.6	63.9	63.9	64.3	66.2
Jackson, MS	n/a	n/a	n/a	n/a	n/a	n/a	n/a	n/a	n/a
Jacksonville, FL	68.0	66.6	69.9	65.3	62.5	61.8	65.2	61.4	63.1
Kansas City, MO	68.5	65.1	65.6	66.1	65.0	62.4	62.4	64.3	65.0
Lafayette, LA	n/a	n/a	n/a	n/a	n/a	n/a	n/a	n/a	n/a
Lakeland, FL	n/a	n/a	n/a	n/a	n/a	n/a	n/a	n/a	n/a
Las Vegas, NV	52.9	52.6	52.8	53.2	52.1	51.3	54.4	58.1	56.0
Lexington, KY	n/a	n/a	n/a	n/a	n/a	n/a	n/a	n/a	n/a
Lincoln, NE	n/a	n/a	n/a	n/a	n/a	n/a	n/a	n/a	n/a
Little Rock, AR	n/a	n/a	n/a	n/a	65.8	64.9	61.0	62.2	65.0
Los Angeles, CA	50.1	49.9	48.7	49.0	49.1	47.1	49.1	49.5	48.2
Louisville, KY	61.7	63.3	64.5	68.9	67.7	67.6	71.7	67.9	64.9
Madison, WI	n/a	n/a	n/a	n/a	n/a	n/a	n/a	n/a	n/a

Table continued on next page.

Metro Area	2011	2012	2013	2014	2015	2016	2017	2018	2019
Manchester, NH	n/a	n/a	n/a	n/a	n/a	n/a	n/a	n/a	n/a
Miami, FL	64.2	61.8	60.1	58.8	58.6	58.4	57.9	59.9	60.4
Midland, TX	n/a	n/a	n/a	n/a	n/a	n/a	n/a	n/a	n/a
Milwaukee, WI	62.3	61.9	60.0	55.9	57.0	60.4	63.9	62.3	56.9
Minneapolis, MN	69.1	70.8	71.7	69.7	67.9	69.1	70.1	67.8	70.2
Nashville, TN	69.6	64.9	63.9	67.1	67.4	65.0	69.4	68.3	69.8
New Haven, CT	66.3	62.2	62.0	62.4	64.6	59.4	58.7	65.0	65.1
New Orleans, LA	63.9	62.4	61.4	60.6	62.8	59.3	61.7	62.6	61.1
New York, NY	50.9	51.5	50.6	50.7	49.9	50.4	49.9	49.7	50.4
Oklahoma City, OK	69.6	67.3	67.6	65.7	61.4	63.1	64.7	64.6	64.3
Omaha, NE	71.6	72.4	70.6	68.7	69.6	69.2	65.5	67.8	66.9
Orlando, FL	68.6	68.0	65.5	62.3	58.4	58.5	59.5	58.5	56.1
Peoria, IL	n/a	n/a	n/a	n/a	n/a	n/a	n/a	n/a	n/a
Philadelphia, PA	69.7	69.5	69.1	67.0	67.0	64.7	65.6	67.4	67.4
Phoenix, AZ	63.3	63.1	62.2	61.9	61.0	62.6	64.0	65.3	65.9
Pittsburgh, PA	70.3	67.9	68.3	69.1	71.0	72.2	72.7	71.7	71.5
Portland, OR	63.7	63.9	60.9	59.8	58.9	61.8	61.1	59.2	60.0
Providence, RI	61.3	61.7	60.1	61.6	60.0	57.5	58.6	61.3	63.5
Provo, UT	n/a	n/a	n/a	n/a	n/a	n/a	n/a	n/a	n/a
Raleigh, NC	66.7	67.7	65.5	65.5	67.4	65.9	68.2	64.9	63.0
Reno, NV	n/a	n/a	n/a	n/a	n/a	n/a	n/a	n/a	n/a
Richmond, VA	65.2	67.0	65.4	72.6	67.4	61.7	63.1	62.9	66.4
Rochester, MN	n/a	n/a	n/a	n/a	n/a	n/a	n/a	n/a	n/a
Sacramento, CA	57.2	58.6	60.4	60.1	60.8	60.5	60.1	64.1	61.6
Salt Lake City, UT	66.4	66.9	66.8	68.2	69.1	69.2	68.1	69.5	69.2
San Antonio, TX	66.5	67.5	70.1	70.2	66.0	61.6	62.5	64.4	62.6
San Diego, CA	55.2	55.4	55.0	57.4	51.8	53.3	56.0	56.1	56.7
San Francisco, CA	56.1	53.2	55.2	54.6	56.3	55.8	55.7	55.6	52.8
San Jose, CA	60.4	58.6	56.4	56.4	50.7	49.9	50.4	50.4	52.4
Santa Rosa, CA	n/a	n/a	n/a	n/a	n/a	n/a	n/a	n/a	n/a
Savannah, GA	n/a	n/a	n/a	n/a	n/a	n/a	n/a	n/a	n/a
Seattle, WA	60.7	60.4	61.0	61.3	59.5	57.7	59.5	62.5	61.5
Sioux Falls, SD	n/a	n/a	n/a	n/a	n/a	n/a	n/a	n/a	n/a
Springfield, IL	n/a	n/a	n/a	n/a	n/a	n/a	n/a	n/a	n/a
Tallahassee, FL	n/a	n/a	n/a	n/a	n/a	n/a	n/a	n/a	n/a
Tampa, FL	68.3	67.0	65.3	64.9	64.9	62.9	60.4	64.9	68.0
Topeka, KS	n/a	n/a	n/a	n/a	n/a	n/a	n/a	n/a	n/a
Tucson, AZ	67.2	64.9	66.1	66.7	61.4	56.0	60.1	63.8	60.1
Tulsa, OK	64.4	66.5	64.1	65.3	65.2	65.4	66.8	68.3	70.5
Tuscaloosa, AL	n/a	n/a	n/a	n/a	n/a	n/a	n/a	n/a	n/a
Virginia Beach, VA	62.3	62.0	63.3	64.1	59.4	59.6	65.3	62.8	63.0
Washington, DC	67.6	66.9	66.0	65.0	64.6	63.1	63.3	62.9	64.7
Wichita, KS	n/a	n/a	n/a	n/a	n/a	n/a	n/a	n/a	n/a
Winston-Salem, NC	n/a	n/a	n/a	n/a	n/a	n/a	n/a	n/a	n/a
U.S.	66.1	65.4	65.1	64.5	63.7	63.4	63.9	64.4	64.6

Note: Figures are percentages and cover the Metropolitan Statistical Area—see Appendix B for areas included
Source: U.S. Census Bureau, Housing Vacancies and Homeownership Annual Statistics: 2011-2019

Year Housing Structure Built: City

City	2010 or Later	2000 -2009	1990 -1999	1980 -1989	1970 -1979	1960 -1969	1950 -1959	1940 -1949	Before 1940	Median Year
Albany, NY	1.2	2.1	3.0	6.3	9.3	8.1	10.1	7.7	52.2	<1940
Albuquerque, NM	3.4	16.5	15.5	15.9	19.2	10.9	11.4	4.4	2.8	1981
Allentown, PA	1.8	5.0	3.8	5.0	11.7	11.9	16.5	7.8	36.5	1953
Anchorage, AK	3.2	12.2	11.4	26.3	28.7	10.6	5.8	1.3	0.4	1981
Ann Arbor, MI	3.1	6.1	11.0	10.7	16.8	18.0	13.5	5.6	15.3	1969
Athens, GA	3.1	18.0	20.1	15.9	17.2	11.6	6.7	2.4	4.9	1984
Atlanta, GA	6.5	22.9	10.7	8.0	8.5	12.8	12.0	6.1	12.5	1978
Austin, TX	10.1	18.7	15.8	20.3	16.6	7.9	5.2	2.6	2.9	1987
Baton Rouge, LA	4.9	10.2	8.9	13.0	21.9	18.1	12.0	5.7	5.4	1974
Boise City, ID	5.0	12.6	22.4	15.5	19.6	7.0	7.1	4.4	6.3	1984
Boston, MA	3.8	6.5	4.1	6.0	7.9	8.2	7.3	5.8	50.4	<1940
Boulder, CO	5.0	8.3	10.1	17.1	22.9	18.7	8.6	2.0	7.3	1976
Cape Coral, FL	2.7	39.1	17.8	22.4	12.2	4.8	0.6	0.1	0.1	1995
Cedar Rapids, IA	5.3	11.6	13.2	8.2	14.6	14.6	12.4	4.2	15.8	1972
Charleston, SC	9.3	21.0	12.6	14.8	11.2	8.6	6.0	4.3	12.2	1985
Charlotte, NC	6.8	23.6	20.1	15.3	11.9	9.7	6.9	2.8	2.9	1990
Chicago, IL	2.0	8.1	4.7	4.2	7.2	9.7	12.1	9.3	42.7	1948
Clarksville, TN	12.1	23.4	21.7	12.5	12.1	9.2	4.6	2.2	2.4	1993
Cleveland, OH	1.3	3.6	3.2	2.3	5.2	7.3	12.7	11.2	53.2	<1940
College Station, TX	14.1	23.8	20.0	16.6	17.7	3.8	2.3	0.8	0.8	1994
Colorado Springs, CO	4.7	16.3	15.9	18.9	18.5	10.3	7.5	1.8	6.0	1983
Columbia, MO	10.0	21.9	17.7	13.6	12.7	10.4	5.6	2.4	5.7	1990
Columbia, SC	5.7	16.3	10.9	9.6	10.6	11.9	13.7	10.4	11.0	1973
Columbus, OH	4.7	11.9	15.3	13.0	15.1	12.2	10.9	5.0	11.9	1977
Dallas, TX	5.5	11.1	10.3	17.5	17.6	13.5	13.7	5.3	5.5	1977
Davenport, IA	2.9	9.0	7.1	6.0	16.1	13.8	11.0	6.0	28.0	1964
Denver, CO	7.2	11.6	6.6	7.5	14.4	11.2	15.2	6.9	19.3	1968
Des Moines, IA	2.5	7.3	6.8	6.2	13.5	10.7	16.0	8.4	28.6	1958
Durham, NC	8.6	22.0	17.1	15.9	10.5	8.8	6.6	4.0	6.4	1989
Edison, NJ	1.2	4.9	9.4	23.9	14.1	20.1	17.1	4.6	4.7	1972
El Paso, TX	8.6	15.5	13.7	13.4	16.9	11.3	11.8	4.4	4.4	1981
Fargo, ND	12.6	15.7	18.4	14.3	13.9	6.6	6.9	2.7	9.0	1988
Fayetteville, NC	6.2	12.7	17.8	16.9	21.7	13.3	6.8	2.8	1.8	1982
Fort Collins, CO	7.7	18.5	20.8	16.1	19.1	7.5	3.4	1.7	5.2	1988
Fort Wayne, IN	1.1	6.5	14.3	12.1	16.9	14.7	12.5	6.7	15.3	1970
Fort Worth, TX	8.2	25.8	11.4	12.8	10.3	8.3	11.6	5.2	6.4	1986
Grand Rapids, MI	1.7	4.3	6.1	7.2	8.9	10.2	15.4	8.9	37.3	1952
Greeley, CO	4.8	19.7	15.8	10.8	20.7	10.5	6.7	2.8	8.3	1981
Green Bay, WI	1.6	7.6	9.6	12.6	18.0	13.3	14.7	6.2	16.4	1970
Greensboro, NC	3.9	15.0	18.0	17.7	15.1	11.0	10.1	3.8	5.4	1983
Honolulu, HI	3.2	7.5	8.1	9.5	25.4	22.8	12.5	5.6	5.3	1971
Houston, TX	6.9	13.9	9.9	14.3	21.6	13.8	10.6	4.5	4.4	1978
Huntsville, AL	9.5	14.0	11.0	14.9	14.0	20.9	10.2	2.8	2.8	1980
Indianapolis, IN	2.7	9.5	13.1	11.9	14.1	13.4	12.5	6.0	16.6	1971
Jackson, MS	1.7	5.7	6.7	10.5	24.4	20.1	19.5	6.9	4.4	1970
Jacksonville, FL	4.9	19.4	15.5	15.5	12.7	10.5	11.2	5.0	5.2	1983
Kansas City, MO	3.6	10.3	9.3	8.5	12.4	13.1	14.4	6.7	21.7	1965
Lafayette, LA	6.1	13.2	9.5	18.4	22.0	13.1	10.0	4.4	3.3	1979
Lakeland, FL	2.7	15.5	13.0	20.2	20.8	10.5	8.5	3.1	5.7	1981
Las Vegas, NV	3.9	23.5	32.0	17.2	9.9	7.6	4.0	1.4	0.4	1993
Lexington, KY	5.1	16.1	15.9	14.6	14.5	13.5	9.9	3.0	7.4	1981
Lincoln, NE	5.8	14.2	15.0	10.6	15.1	10.7	11.2	3.3	14.1	1977
Little Rock, AR	4.9	10.9	12.5	15.4	19.9	14.1	9.7	4.9	7.7	1977
Los Angeles, CA	2.4	5.7	5.7	10.2	13.8	14.0	17.6	10.0	20.5	1961
Louisville, KY	3.5	11.2	11.9	7.0	13.1	13.6	15.0	7.3	17.3	1968

Table continued on next page.

City	2010 or Later	2000 -2009	1990 -1999	1980 -1989	1970 -1979	1960 -1969	1950 -1959	1940 -1949	Before 1940	Median Year
Madison, WI	5.5	15.2	13.2	11.1	14.1	11.4	10.6	4.9	14.0	1976
Manchester, NH	1.7	6.6	8.1	16.3	10.2	7.8	10.3	6.3	32.8	1961
Miami, FL	5.4	19.5	6.3	8.1	12.9	10.2	15.2	12.6	9.8	1972
Midland, TX	10.6	8.6	14.5	18.9	13.0	12.1	17.8	3.1	1.4	1981
Milwaukee, WI	1.3	3.4	2.8	4.0	8.4	10.5	20.9	9.8	38.9	1951
Minneapolis, MN	4.5	6.9	3.5	6.5	9.2	7.6	10.0	6.9	44.8	1948
Nashville, TN	7.2	15.0	12.3	15.4	15.4	12.7	11.2	4.7	6.2	1980
New Haven, CT	2.9	4.2	2.7	7.2	8.4	8.8	8.8	7.1	49.9	1940
New Orleans, LA	2.8	7.6	3.7	7.4	13.2	11.2	11.9	7.8	34.4	1957
New York, NY	2.2	5.7	3.7	4.7	7.1	12.7	13.0	10.2	40.7	1949
Oklahoma City, OK	8.0	13.4	10.0	15.3	15.9	12.6	10.7	5.7	8.4	1978
Omaha, NE	2.7	6.6	12.5	11.0	15.8	14.8	11.5	4.4	20.6	1969
Orlando, FL	7.9	22.1	16.1	17.5	14.1	7.3	8.9	3.1	3.0	1988
Peoria, IL	3.1	8.6	7.3	7.3	14.1	13.0	14.6	8.5	23.4	1963
Philadelphia, PA	2.1	3.1	3.2	3.8	6.9	10.8	16.2	12.3	41.6	1947
Phoenix, AZ	3.4	17.0	16.2	17.3	19.6	11.6	10.4	2.7	1.9	1982
Pittsburgh, PA	1.9	3.0	3.4	4.5	7.0	8.3	12.4	9.2	50.4	<1940
Portland, OR	4.7	10.7	8.8	6.2	10.7	9.2	12.1	8.3	29.3	1960
Providence, RI	0.7	4.5	4.0	5.0	9.1	5.9	8.4	6.7	55.6	<1940
Provo, UT	3.6	11.8	21.5	13.4	18.5	10.2	7.8	5.4	7.8	1980
Raleigh, NC	8.5	25.8	19.5	17.3	10.7	8.2	4.8	2.1	3.1	1992
Reno, NV	4.6	20.5	19.3	14.1	17.9	9.8	7.4	3.0	3.5	1986
Richmond, VA	3.0	5.1	4.9	6.2	11.4	13.0	15.2	9.6	31.8	1956
Rochester, MN	6.7	19.7	14.5	14.9	13.0	10.3	9.4	3.3	8.4	1984
Sacramento, CA	1.5	15.9	8.9	15.6	14.8	11.6	13.0	7.8	10.9	1975
Salt Lake City, UT	3.9	6.3	7.1	7.8	12.8	9.6	13.2	9.6	29.7	1958
San Antonio, TX	6.3	16.2	13.8	16.6	15.3	10.2	10.2	5.7	5.6	1982
San Diego, CA	3.0	10.4	11.6	18.1	21.2	12.5	12.2	4.3	6.9	1977
San Francisco, CA	2.8	6.5	4.4	5.3	7.5	8.2	8.4	9.3	47.7	1942
San Jose, CA	4.2	9.5	10.7	12.7	24.4	18.9	11.4	3.1	5.2	1975
Santa Rosa, CA	2.0	12.7	12.6	19.4	22.8	11.6	8.3	5.0	5.6	1979
Savannah, GA	5.4	11.1	7.2	9.8	12.9	13.3	14.7	8.6	17.0	1967
Seattle, WA	8.1	13.3	8.4	8.0	8.3	8.9	10.4	8.5	26.0	1966
Sioux Falls, SD	10.4	18.8	15.6	10.8	15.0	7.3	8.8	4.4	8.8	1985
Springfield, IL	1.8	9.2	12.8	9.6	15.5	12.8	11.8	7.0	19.4	1969
Tallahassee, FL	3.1	18.8	21.2	17.6	17.5	9.5	7.8	3.0	1.5	1986
Tampa, FL	6.4	18.2	12.4	11.7	12.3	10.0	15.1	5.2	8.7	1979
Topeka, KS	1.3	6.9	10.0	9.8	14.7	15.9	16.4	6.5	18.4	1965
Tucson, AZ	2.3	12.8	13.5	15.7	21.6	11.5	14.9	4.0	3.7	1977
Tulsa, OK	2.8	6.1	9.1	13.6	21.1	14.6	16.9	6.4	9.3	1971
Tuscaloosa, AL	10.5	19.3	14.9	11.8	14.4	9.9	9.5	5.4	4.2	1986
Virginia Beach, VA	3.6	11.3	13.7	28.2	21.6	12.7	6.2	1.4	1.1	1982
Washington, DC	5.8	8.5	3.0	4.3	7.5	11.6	12.8	11.7	34.9	1953
Wichita, KS	3.1	10.3	12.7	12.5	13.0	9.9	20.0	7.7	10.8	1971
Winston-Salem, NC	3.8	14.6	12.1	13.9	16.3	14.1	12.0	5.4	7.8	1977
U.S.	4.1	14.3	13.9	13.5	15.3	10.7	10.4	5.0	12.8	1977

Note: Figures are percentages except for Median Year
Source: U.S. Census Bureau, 2014-2018 American Community Survey 5-Year Estimates

Year Housing Structure Built: Metro Area

Metro Area	2010 or Later	2000 -2009	1990 -1999	1980 -1989	1970 -1979	1960 -1969	1950 -1959	1940 -1949	Before 1940	Median Year
Albany, NY	3.6	8.6	9.7	11.2	12.2	9.2	10.7	5.7	29.1	1965
Albuquerque, NM	3.4	17.8	18.4	17.1	17.8	9.6	9.1	3.7	3.1	1984
Allentown, PA	2.4	11.6	10.5	10.9	12.4	9.7	11.5	5.4	25.6	1968
Anchorage, AK	3.8	17.5	12.9	25.7	24.8	8.9	4.8	1.1	0.4	1984
Ann Arbor, MI	2.9	13.4	17.2	11.5	16.2	12.2	10.6	4.4	11.6	1977
Athens, GA	3.6	18.9	21.4	17.5	16.1	9.5	5.7	2.1	5.1	1987
Atlanta, GA	4.7	25.0	21.9	17.9	13.0	7.9	4.9	2.0	3.0	1991
Austin, TX	13.2	26.3	18.5	17.0	12.1	5.2	3.5	1.9	2.4	1994
Baton Rouge, LA	7.7	21.2	14.4	14.9	17.4	10.6	7.1	2.9	3.8	1986
Boise City, ID	8.0	25.0	22.3	10.8	16.7	4.8	4.5	3.0	4.9	1992
Boston, MA	3.2	7.6	7.4	10.5	11.2	10.3	10.7	5.4	33.7	1960
Boulder, CO	5.2	12.3	19.2	17.3	20.9	12.0	4.9	1.7	6.5	1982
Cape Coral, FL	4.2	32.2	17.9	21.3	15.0	5.6	2.6	0.5	0.7	1992
Cedar Rapids, IA	5.5	14.6	14.6	7.4	13.8	12.5	10.0	3.8	17.8	1974
Charleston, SC	9.2	22.4	16.7	17.1	14.3	8.9	5.3	2.5	3.7	1989
Charlotte, NC	7.2	24.8	20.0	13.7	11.7	8.5	6.6	3.2	4.3	1991
Chicago, IL	1.9	11.6	11.1	8.9	14.1	11.7	13.1	6.2	21.4	1968
Clarksville, TN	9.6	21.1	20.7	11.4	15.2	10.0	6.0	2.7	3.3	1991
Cleveland, OH	1.8	7.1	8.8	6.6	12.4	13.4	18.2	7.8	23.9	1960
College Station, TX	11.0	20.7	18.4	16.9	16.7	5.7	5.4	2.4	2.7	1990
Colorado Springs, CO	6.0	19.4	17.0	17.7	17.2	9.0	6.8	1.5	5.4	1986
Columbia, MO	8.3	20.6	18.8	13.9	16.0	9.6	5.1	2.2	5.5	1988
Columbia, SC	6.7	20.2	18.1	14.8	16.2	9.9	7.2	3.2	3.7	1987
Columbus, OH	4.6	14.5	16.6	11.8	14.4	11.4	10.3	4.1	12.3	1978
Dallas, TX	8.0	20.9	16.4	18.4	14.4	8.8	7.5	2.7	2.8	1987
Davenport, IA	3.1	7.5	8.1	6.3	16.8	13.8	11.9	7.3	25.0	1964
Denver, CO	5.9	16.9	15.2	14.3	19.0	9.5	9.4	3.0	6.8	1982
Des Moines, IA	9.1	17.7	12.9	8.7	13.7	8.8	9.3	4.3	15.5	1979
Durham, NC	7.4	20.1	18.9	16.5	12.7	9.0	6.4	3.2	5.8	1988
Edison, NJ	2.2	6.9	6.2	7.9	9.9	13.8	15.8	8.9	28.3	1958
El Paso, TX	9.4	16.9	15.0	14.0	16.1	10.2	10.5	3.9	4.0	1984
Fargo, ND	12.1	18.7	15.4	11.5	15.1	7.4	7.7	2.8	9.4	1987
Fayetteville, NC	7.2	17.5	20.9	15.7	18.1	10.7	5.8	2.2	1.8	1987
Fort Collins, CO	7.5	19.8	20.1	14.3	19.7	7.2	3.7	1.7	5.9	1988
Fort Wayne, IN	3.0	11.0	15.2	11.1	15.0	12.7	10.8	5.4	15.9	1973
Fort Worth, TX	8.0	20.9	16.4	18.4	14.4	8.8	7.5	2.7	2.8	1987
Grand Rapids, MI	3.5	12.8	16.6	12.2	14.3	9.7	10.5	5.2	15.2	1977
Greeley, CO	8.4	30.2	16.6	7.6	15.4	6.3	4.4	2.5	8.7	1993
Green Bay, WI	4.1	15.4	16.2	12.1	15.7	9.9	9.3	4.4	12.8	1979
Greensboro, NC	3.8	16.1	18.7	15.6	15.0	10.8	9.4	4.4	6.2	1983
Honolulu, HI	4.2	10.6	11.7	12.3	24.3	18.8	10.6	4.1	3.4	1975
Houston, TX	9.7	22.2	14.7	15.7	17.4	8.7	6.4	2.7	2.5	1988
Huntsville, AL	8.9	20.7	18.0	15.8	12.0	13.4	6.7	2.1	2.3	1989
Indianapolis, IN	5.2	16.0	16.7	10.6	12.9	10.9	10.4	4.5	12.9	1979
Jackson, MS	4.4	17.3	17.3	14.2	18.7	12.0	9.2	3.4	3.4	1982
Jacksonville, FL	6.7	23.2	16.8	16.8	12.5	8.4	8.1	3.5	4.0	1988
Kansas City, MO	3.7	14.0	14.5	12.3	15.8	11.9	11.6	4.6	11.7	1976
Lafayette, LA	8.2	16.9	12.9	15.7	16.6	10.2	9.5	4.4	5.5	1982
Lakeland, FL	4.2	24.6	17.7	18.6	15.4	7.9	6.4	2.0	3.3	1988
Las Vegas, NV	5.6	31.0	29.3	15.0	10.7	5.2	2.1	0.7	0.4	1995
Lexington, KY	5.3	17.6	17.0	14.4	14.7	11.7	8.2	3.3	7.9	1983
Lincoln, NE	5.9	14.7	15.0	10.2	15.4	10.4	10.3	3.1	14.9	1977
Little Rock, AR	7.7	18.7	17.2	14.4	17.2	10.6	7.0	3.3	3.9	1986
Los Angeles, CA	2.3	6.2	7.6	12.4	16.1	16.0	18.8	8.5	12.0	1967
Louisville, KY	3.5	13.5	14.5	9.3	15.4	12.3	12.6	6.3	12.7	1974

Table continued on next page.

Metro Area	2010 or Later	2000 -2009	1990 -1999	1980 -1989	1970 -1979	1960 -1969	1950 -1959	1940 -1949	Before 1940	Median Year
Madison, WI	5.1	16.6	15.8	11.1	15.4	9.4	8.0	3.7	14.8	1979
Manchester, NH	2.5	10.3	10.6	20.9	15.2	9.6	7.0	3.7	20.2	1976
Miami, FL	3.0	13.4	15.0	19.5	21.6	12.4	9.9	2.9	2.2	1980
Midland, TX	11.4	11.0	15.5	18.6	12.4	10.9	15.7	3.0	1.5	1983
Milwaukee, WI	2.1	8.3	10.7	8.1	12.9	11.4	16.7	6.9	23.0	1963
Minneapolis, MN	4.0	14.7	14.3	14.6	14.8	9.9	9.8	3.7	14.2	1978
Nashville, TN	8.3	20.2	18.3	14.5	13.9	9.6	7.2	3.3	4.7	1988
New Haven, CT	1.5	5.6	7.4	12.4	13.0	12.3	15.0	7.1	25.8	1962
New Orleans, LA	3.0	12.3	9.8	13.3	19.1	14.0	10.0	5.0	13.5	1974
New York, NY	2.2	6.9	6.2	7.9	9.9	13.8	15.8	8.9	28.3	1958
Oklahoma City, OK	7.8	15.2	11.5	15.0	17.2	12.2	9.8	4.9	6.3	1980
Omaha, NE	5.4	14.8	12.8	10.0	14.7	12.0	8.9	3.6	17.6	1975
Orlando, FL	6.7	24.6	21.0	20.4	13.3	6.0	5.3	1.3	1.5	1991
Peoria, IL	2.8	9.1	8.9	6.3	16.9	13.1	14.9	8.1	20.0	1965
Philadelphia, PA	2.5	8.0	9.6	10.0	12.1	12.0	15.8	7.9	22.2	1963
Phoenix, AZ	5.1	26.1	20.5	17.4	16.2	7.4	5.2	1.3	0.9	1991
Pittsburgh, PA	2.3	6.5	7.7	7.4	12.0	11.4	16.9	9.0	26.7	1958
Portland, OR	5.0	14.8	18.7	11.4	17.5	8.6	7.1	4.6	12.3	1980
Providence, RI	1.6	6.3	8.1	10.9	12.2	10.7	11.7	6.5	32.1	1960
Provo, UT	10.9	26.9	19.9	9.3	14.5	5.2	5.2	3.2	5.0	1994
Raleigh, NC	10.1	27.1	23.4	15.5	9.6	6.0	3.9	1.7	2.8	1995
Reno, NV	4.2	21.8	21.1	15.2	18.7	9.0	5.4	2.1	2.5	1988
Richmond, VA	4.9	15.3	15.5	15.9	15.4	9.7	9.6	4.5	9.2	1981
Rochester, MN	5.5	18.6	14.7	12.2	13.4	9.1	8.0	3.5	14.9	1981
Sacramento, CA	2.8	17.9	15.0	16.7	18.4	11.0	10.2	3.7	4.3	1981
Salt Lake City, UT	7.1	15.7	15.8	12.9	18.7	8.9	8.9	3.8	8.2	1981
San Antonio, TX	9.5	21.1	14.7	15.7	13.7	8.5	7.8	4.3	4.7	1987
San Diego, CA	2.9	12.0	12.6	19.1	22.6	12.0	10.8	3.5	4.4	1979
San Francisco, CA	2.5	7.8	8.3	11.3	14.9	13.4	13.7	7.9	20.2	1966
San Jose, CA	4.4	9.3	10.6	12.5	21.8	18.3	14.3	3.8	5.0	1974
Santa Rosa, CA	1.9	10.7	13.4	18.7	21.3	11.4	8.8	5.1	8.7	1978
Savannah, GA	7.3	21.8	16.1	13.5	11.9	8.2	8.2	4.7	8.2	1987
Seattle, WA	6.3	15.5	15.8	14.7	14.4	11.0	7.6	4.5	10.3	1982
Sioux Falls, SD	9.4	19.3	15.5	9.8	14.8	6.8	7.9	4.1	12.4	1984
Springfield, IL	2.6	10.3	13.5	9.2	16.3	12.1	12.0	6.7	17.4	1971
Tallahassee, FL	3.3	19.1	22.8	19.2	16.1	8.5	6.6	2.4	1.8	1988
Tampa, FL	4.4	16.7	14.3	20.2	21.4	10.0	8.4	2.0	2.8	1983
Topeka, KS	1.9	9.5	12.4	10.8	16.7	13.3	12.4	5.0	18.0	1971
Tucson, AZ	3.8	18.6	17.7	17.6	19.9	8.5	9.0	2.6	2.4	1984
Tulsa, OK	5.4	14.6	12.6	14.5	19.5	10.7	10.9	4.6	7.3	1978
Tuscaloosa, AL	7.8	20.6	18.5	13.6	14.6	9.6	7.6	4.1	3.5	1988
Virginia Beach, VA	4.8	12.9	15.3	19.4	15.9	11.9	9.8	4.4	5.7	1981
Washington, DC	5.3	14.8	14.6	15.9	14.3	12.1	9.5	5.0	8.5	1980
Wichita, KS	3.6	12.0	13.9	12.2	13.6	8.9	17.7	6.3	11.8	1974
Winston-Salem, NC	3.5	15.9	17.3	15.7	16.6	11.3	9.0	4.3	6.5	1982
U.S.	4.1	14.3	13.9	13.5	15.3	10.7	10.4	5.0	12.8	1977

Note: Figures are percentages except for Median Year; Figures cover the Metropolitan Statistical Area—see Appendix B for areas included
Source: U.S. Census Bureau, 2014-2018 American Community Survey 5-Year Estimates

Gross Monthly Rent: City

City	Under $500	$500 -$999	$1,000 -$1,499	$1,500 -$1,999	$2,000 -$2,499	$2,500 -$2,999	$3,000 and up	Median ($)
Albany, NY	11.1	45.9	35.6	5.7	1.0	0.4	0.3	951
Albuquerque, NM	8.7	55.4	28.5	5.8	1.0	0.2	0.4	855
Allentown, PA	10.2	44.4	36.5	7.4	1.3	0.1	0.1	968
Anchorage, AK	3.6	20.6	39.9	19.0	12.2	3.3	1.4	1,306
Ann Arbor, MI	4.4	26.8	39.2	17.5	7.4	2.3	2.4	1,213
Athens, GA	8.4	61.0	23.5	4.9	1.9	0.2	0.1	844
Atlanta, GA	11.1	31.4	33.9	16.4	4.6	1.4	1.2	1,099
Austin, TX	3.1	22.9	44.7	20.2	6.0	1.6	1.5	1,225
Baton Rouge, LA	9.8	56.7	24.5	5.3	2.8	0.7	0.3	860
Boise City, ID	6.3	55.6	31.1	4.6	1.3	0.3	0.9	910
Boston, MA	17.7	12.0	18.6	22.9	14.3	7.0	7.6	1,539
Boulder, CO	2.9	12.8	36.8	25.4	11.6	5.0	5.4	1,466
Cape Coral, FL	1.2	28.4	48.0	16.7	3.9	0.9	0.9	1,172
Cedar Rapids, IA	18.2	62.3	16.5	2.0	0.5	0.1	0.3	751
Charleston, SC	7.1	25.3	39.3	19.4	4.9	2.1	1.9	1,208
Charlotte, NC	4.1	36.4	43.8	11.9	2.7	0.5	0.6	1,086
Chicago, IL	9.6	34.6	30.9	14.7	5.9	2.5	1.9	1,077
Clarksville, TN	6.1	49.6	35.1	7.5	1.5	0.1	0.1	946
Cleveland, OH	23.6	58.7	14.3	2.3	0.7	0.3	0.1	700
College Station, TX	2.9	50.0	27.7	12.6	5.2	1.4	0.3	972
Colorado Springs, CO	4.2	39.7	35.9	15.1	3.2	1.3	0.7	1,072
Columbia, MO	6.8	60.3	24.2	5.1	3.0	0.5	0.2	854
Columbia, SC	11.7	49.9	29.5	6.9	1.5	0.1	0.5	910
Columbus, OH	6.9	52.5	32.4	6.1	1.5	0.3	0.2	928
Dallas, TX	4.8	46.7	33.2	9.9	3.2	1.2	1.0	987
Davenport, IA	9.4	68.0	17.6	2.9	0.6	1.0	0.5	757
Denver, CO	8.8	24.2	35.4	20.1	7.8	2.4	1.4	1,217
Des Moines, IA	9.7	63.1	22.5	3.7	0.7	0.1	0.1	822
Durham, NC	7.1	42.4	38.8	9.1	1.6	0.4	0.6	1,005
Edison, NJ	2.1	7.5	41.4	35.2	10.9	2.2	0.8	1,491
El Paso, TX	17.5	53.8	23.4	4.1	0.7	0.3	0.2	814
Fargo, ND	8.4	67.0	18.6	4.1	1.7	0.1	0.1	796
Fayetteville, NC	6.1	53.8	34.7	4.7	0.5	0.0	0.1	928
Fort Collins, CO	3.3	24.8	39.7	23.8	6.4	1.4	0.6	1,278
Fort Wayne, IN	13.5	71.5	12.5	1.6	0.6	0.2	0.1	735
Fort Worth, TX	5.6	43.1	33.6	13.2	2.9	1.0	0.7	1,015
Grand Rapids, MI	10.4	53.2	26.8	6.9	2.3	0.3	0.1	895
Greeley, CO	11.6	43.6	28.7	13.3	2.0	0.5	0.3	950
Green Bay, WI	13.5	72.7	12.8	0.5	0.3	0.0	0.1	701
Greensboro, NC	7.5	65.1	22.8	2.9	0.9	0.4	0.4	846
Honolulu, HI	6.7	14.2	31.4	22.0	10.8	6.1	8.9	1,465
Houston, TX	4.1	47.1	31.8	11.5	3.0	1.2	1.3	990
Huntsville, AL	13.2	60.2	22.8	2.7	0.6	0.1	0.4	804
Indianapolis, IN	6.8	61.8	25.6	4.5	0.8	0.2	0.3	865
Jackson, MS	12.8	61.4	22.4	2.8	0.4	0.1	0.1	824
Jacksonville, FL	6.5	40.6	40.3	10.1	1.9	0.3	0.4	1,029
Kansas City, MO	9.7	51.8	30.1	6.2	1.4	0.3	0.5	899
Lafayette, LA	10.1	56.1	25.8	5.9	1.7	0.4	0.2	874
Lakeland, FL	5.9	48.4	36.5	6.9	1.4	0.6	0.4	968
Las Vegas, NV	5.2	39.4	40.1	11.6	2.5	0.7	0.5	1,057
Lexington, KY	9.6	54.9	27.8	5.0	1.8	0.4	0.4	864
Lincoln, NE	11.5	59.8	22.4	4.3	0.7	0.3	1.0	822
Little Rock, AR	9.8	58.4	25.8	3.9	1.1	0.5	0.5	850
Los Angeles, CA	5.4	18.3	34.0	21.5	11.0	5.1	4.8	1,376
Louisville, KY	14.7	57.4	22.7	3.9	0.8	0.3	0.2	812

Table continued on next page.

City	Under $500	$500 -$999	$1,000 -$1,499	$1,500 -$1,999	$2,000 -$2,499	$2,500 -$2,999	$3,000 and up	Median ($)
Madison, WI	3.8	39.7	38.4	12.4	3.8	1.4	0.6	1,068
Manchester, NH	7.4	33.4	43.6	12.4	2.1	0.6	0.3	1,086
Miami, FL	10.8	30.6	29.2	16.5	7.2	3.3	2.5	1,120
Midland, TX	2.2	26.1	42.9	19.1	6.9	2.2	0.7	1,233
Milwaukee, WI	9.9	61.2	23.3	4.1	1.1	0.3	0.2	842
Minneapolis, MN	13.8	37.8	30.0	12.4	4.0	1.2	0.8	985
Nashville, TN	8.8	38.0	36.9	11.5	3.2	0.9	0.6	1,033
New Haven, CT	12.7	21.2	41.7	17.8	4.8	1.1	0.7	1,179
New Orleans, LA	12.6	40.5	32.4	10.5	2.6	0.8	0.7	973
New York, NY	10.9	15.6	30.0	21.4	10.0	5.0	7.1	1,396
Oklahoma City, OK	8.3	59.7	24.6	5.6	1.1	0.3	0.4	849
Omaha, NE	8.3	53.5	30.1	5.8	1.2	0.5	0.6	896
Orlando, FL	3.8	30.6	46.2	15.2	3.2	0.6	0.5	1,139
Peoria, IL	16.4	59.4	18.2	3.7	1.2	0.6	0.5	784
Philadelphia, PA	11.4	38.1	33.6	10.5	3.9	1.4	1.2	1,007
Phoenix, AZ	5.2	45.0	36.7	10.1	2.1	0.6	0.4	999
Pittsburgh, PA	14.7	43.6	26.9	10.2	3.2	0.8	0.6	922
Portland, OR	7.0	27.0	36.7	18.6	6.9	2.1	1.6	1,187
Providence, RI	19.4	33.7	35.0	7.9	2.2	0.7	0.9	972
Provo, UT	13.8	52.0	22.7	8.9	2.2	0.2	0.2	844
Raleigh, NC	4.0	37.8	43.0	11.4	2.5	0.5	0.7	1,074
Reno, NV	6.7	47.0	30.7	12.5	2.3	0.6	0.3	967
Richmond, VA	12.2	40.2	34.3	10.1	2.5	0.3	0.4	979
Rochester, MN	9.1	46.2	27.7	12.3	2.0	1.1	1.6	942
Sacramento, CA	6.4	29.2	38.6	19.9	4.5	1.1	0.3	1,179
Salt Lake City, UT	9.6	47.1	29.6	10.8	2.2	0.4	0.3	938
San Antonio, TX	8.2	47.0	33.8	8.8	1.4	0.4	0.5	958
San Diego, CA	3.5	12.4	28.4	25.5	17.5	7.7	4.9	1,611
San Francisco, CA	9.5	13.6	16.8	16.5	13.8	11.3	18.5	1,805
San Jose, CA	4.6	7.4	16.3	23.1	19.6	14.1	15.0	1,970
Santa Rosa, CA	5.7	10.1	32.4	28.7	16.1	5.3	1.7	1,531
Savannah, GA	10.8	42.1	37.0	7.2	1.6	0.4	0.8	977
Seattle, WA	6.8	13.3	30.1	26.3	12.6	6.1	4.8	1,496
Sioux Falls, SD	9.8	67.5	17.7	3.3	0.3	0.8	0.7	791
Springfield, IL	12.6	64.1	18.9	2.4	1.0	0.7	0.2	789
Tallahassee, FL	5.8	44.8	37.0	8.5	3.1	0.6	0.3	995
Tampa, FL	8.3	34.1	37.0	13.7	4.3	1.5	1.1	1,082
Topeka, KS	14.6	62.2	17.7	3.2	1.6	0.3	0.4	790
Tucson, AZ	9.1	58.1	26.2	4.9	1.0	0.2	0.5	825
Tulsa, OK	11.5	61.0	22.3	3.2	0.9	0.5	0.6	810
Tuscaloosa, AL	11.9	60.5	20.6	3.9	1.8	0.4	1.0	843
Virginia Beach, VA	3.1	13.9	47.9	25.0	6.9	1.6	1.6	1,339
Washington, DC	10.6	14.6	25.4	20.0	13.0	7.8	8.6	1,487
Wichita, KS	11.8	63.4	20.7	2.7	0.6	0.2	0.6	789
Winston-Salem, NC	12.2	63.5	19.8	2.7	1.3	0.2	0.4	782
U.S.	9.8	38.5	29.6	12.9	5.1	2.1	2.0	1,023

Note: Figures are percentages except for Median; Gross rent is the contract rent plus the estimated average monthly cost of utilities (electricity, gas, and water and sewer) and fuels (oil, coal, kerosene, wood, etc.) if these are paid by the renter (or paid for the renter by someone else).
Source: U.S. Census Bureau, 2014-2018 American Community Survey 5-Year Estimates

Gross Monthly Rent: Metro Area

MSA[1]	Under $500	$500 -$999	$1,000 -$1,499	$1,500 -$1,999	$2,000 -$2,499	$2,500 -2,999	$3,000 and up	Median ($)
Albany, NY	8.9	43.2	35.4	8.7	2.4	0.8	0.7	983
Albuquerque, NM	8.5	53.9	29.5	6.5	1.0	0.2	0.4	873
Allentown, PA	10.0	37.1	37.9	11.5	2.3	0.5	0.7	1,031
Anchorage, AK	3.8	22.5	39.3	18.8	11.3	2.9	1.2	1,276
Ann Arbor, MI	5.5	37.1	36.7	13.1	4.4	1.6	1.6	1,083
Athens, GA	9.0	60.7	22.9	4.9	1.8	0.4	0.3	844
Atlanta, GA	4.9	34.0	43.4	13.5	2.8	0.8	0.7	1,106
Austin, TX	3.1	24.3	43.7	20.4	5.6	1.5	1.3	1,217
Baton Rouge, LA	9.2	52.5	27.9	7.2	2.4	0.4	0.4	904
Boise City, ID	9.1	52.1	31.6	5.2	1.2	0.3	0.5	914
Boston, MA	12.9	14.7	28.0	22.8	11.9	5.1	4.6	1,404
Boulder, CO	4.3	16.1	36.0	25.2	11.1	3.8	3.6	1,411
Cape Coral, FL	4.4	35.7	41.2	11.4	4.0	1.3	2.0	1,093
Cedar Rapids, IA	19.0	62.0	16.2	1.8	0.5	0.2	0.4	731
Charleston, SC	6.4	33.1	39.1	14.9	3.6	1.6	1.4	1,114
Charlotte, NC	6.3	45.2	35.8	9.3	2.2	0.6	0.5	986
Chicago, IL	7.7	34.6	34.0	14.9	5.3	1.9	1.5	1,092
Clarksville, TN	9.0	50.4	32.1	7.2	1.1	0.2	0.0	902
Cleveland, OH	13.8	58.6	22.0	3.7	1.0	0.3	0.4	800
College Station, TX	5.6	54.2	25.3	9.9	3.8	1.0	0.2	917
Colorado Springs, CO	4.0	36.5	35.6	18.5	3.3	1.4	0.7	1,118
Columbia, MO	7.2	60.9	24.0	4.4	2.8	0.4	0.2	849
Columbia, SC	8.2	51.8	30.8	6.8	1.6	0.4	0.4	920
Columbus, OH	8.1	51.5	31.7	6.4	1.6	0.5	0.3	925
Dallas, TX	3.7	38.2	38.1	14.0	3.8	1.2	0.9	1,085
Davenport, IA	17.0	61.3	16.2	3.6	0.7	0.6	0.7	746
Denver, CO	5.3	22.0	38.0	22.8	8.3	2.1	1.5	1,292
Des Moines, IA	7.8	56.1	28.2	5.7	1.2	0.3	0.7	880
Durham, NC	7.4	42.4	36.8	9.4	2.2	0.7	1.1	1,002
Edison, NJ	9.4	15.3	32.6	22.1	10.1	4.7	5.8	1,391
El Paso, TX	17.2	54.0	23.3	4.4	0.7	0.3	0.2	812
Fargo, ND	9.1	64.2	18.8	5.5	1.8	0.3	0.2	806
Fayetteville, NC	7.0	53.1	33.8	5.3	0.7	0.1	0.1	920
Fort Collins, CO	4.6	27.8	37.5	22.2	5.6	1.6	0.7	1,228
Fort Wayne, IN	14.4	69.0	13.7	2.0	0.7	0.2	0.1	739
Fort Worth, TX	3.7	38.2	38.1	14.0	3.8	1.2	0.9	1,085
Grand Rapids, MI	8.6	60.0	23.8	5.3	1.7	0.2	0.4	860
Greeley, CO	9.4	39.5	31.2	15.0	3.1	1.0	0.8	1,014
Green Bay, WI	10.9	71.2	16.1	1.1	0.3	0.0	0.3	760
Greensboro, NC	10.9	65.3	19.8	2.5	0.9	0.3	0.4	809
Honolulu, HI	5.5	11.1	25.0	20.6	13.7	9.7	14.4	1,703
Houston, TX	4.2	41.0	34.9	14.0	3.6	1.2	1.1	1,055
Huntsville, AL	12.9	59.8	22.8	3.3	0.7	0.1	0.3	807
Indianapolis, IN	6.8	57.6	28.1	5.6	1.2	0.4	0.4	888
Jackson, MS	11.3	55.3	27.9	4.2	0.6	0.4	0.3	870
Jacksonville, FL	5.8	38.6	39.5	12.3	2.7	0.6	0.6	1,059
Kansas City, MO	8.8	49.4	31.9	7.1	1.8	0.4	0.6	929
Lafayette, LA	16.4	57.9	19.7	4.2	1.4	0.2	0.1	792
Lakeland, FL	7.2	49.2	32.6	8.6	1.8	0.4	0.2	944
Las Vegas, NV	3.2	38.5	40.5	13.5	3.0	0.7	0.5	1,088
Lexington, KY	11.0	57.2	25.5	4.2	1.4	0.3	0.3	840
Lincoln, NE	11.8	59.7	22.4	4.1	0.7	0.3	1.0	819
Little Rock, AR	10.4	61.7	22.9	3.9	0.6	0.3	0.2	826
Los Angeles, CA	4.3	15.0	33.1	24.6	12.5	5.7	4.8	1,463
Louisville, KY	13.7	57.6	23.4	3.9	0.8	0.3	0.3	821

Table continued on next page.

MSA[1]	Under $500	$500 -$999	$1,000 -$1,499	$1,500 -$1,999	$2,000 -$2,499	$2,500 -2,999	$3,000 and up	Median ($)
Madison, WI	5.2	45.3	35.3	10.2	2.7	0.8	0.4	996
Manchester, NH	6.8	27.8	42.3	18.8	3.3	0.8	0.3	1,154
Miami, FL	5.4	20.5	38.7	22.1	8.2	2.9	2.2	1,295
Midland, TX	2.6	25.5	42.7	19.1	7.2	2.2	0.6	1,233
Milwaukee, WI	8.2	56.0	27.7	5.8	1.6	0.4	0.3	885
Minneapolis, MN	9.5	36.3	34.4	14.3	3.7	1.0	0.8	1,052
Nashville, TN	8.8	40.5	35.1	11.0	3.0	0.9	0.7	1,008
New Haven, CT	10.3	26.5	41.5	15.7	4.2	1.0	0.8	1,133
New Orleans, LA	9.5	44.4	34.6	8.6	1.9	0.5	0.5	969
New York, NY	9.4	15.3	32.6	22.1	10.1	4.7	5.8	1,391
Oklahoma City, OK	8.4	58.6	25.5	5.8	1.1	0.3	0.3	858
Omaha, NE	8.6	53.0	29.7	6.3	1.3	0.5	0.7	900
Orlando, FL	2.9	29.6	45.9	16.8	3.3	0.8	0.7	1,161
Peoria, IL	15.7	62.0	17.1	2.6	1.2	0.5	0.9	758
Philadelphia, PA	8.3	31.3	38.0	14.5	4.9	1.6	1.3	1,114
Phoenix, AZ	4.0	38.8	39.2	13.1	3.1	1.0	0.9	1,077
Pittsburgh, PA	16.7	53.5	21.5	5.3	1.7	0.6	0.7	807
Portland, OR	5.2	26.5	41.1	18.6	5.8	1.5	1.4	1,193
Providence, RI	16.2	40.0	31.3	9.0	2.2	0.6	0.6	945
Provo, UT	7.4	43.4	31.3	13.4	3.1	0.8	0.6	991
Raleigh, NC	4.8	38.2	41.2	11.5	2.7	0.7	0.8	1,066
Reno, NV	5.7	44.4	32.2	13.7	2.8	0.7	0.6	999
Richmond, VA	7.4	34.1	42.0	12.6	2.6	0.7	0.7	1,083
Rochester, MN	12.2	49.0	25.4	9.7	1.8	0.8	1.1	876
Sacramento, CA	4.7	27.5	37.0	21.0	6.7	2.0	1.1	1,219
Salt Lake City, UT	5.8	38.5	38.4	13.5	2.6	0.7	0.6	1,062
San Antonio, TX	7.6	44.0	34.5	10.6	2.1	0.6	0.7	987
San Diego, CA	3.6	12.0	30.9	25.6	15.7	7.1	5.1	1,569
San Francisco, CA	6.2	10.4	20.2	22.8	17.1	10.6	12.7	1,790
San Jose, CA	3.8	6.3	13.8	21.5	20.9	15.3	18.3	2,108
Santa Rosa, CA	5.4	11.8	30.2	26.7	16.4	6.1	3.3	1,549
Savannah, GA	8.1	37.4	41.0	10.3	2.2	0.4	0.6	1,045
Seattle, WA	5.5	17.4	33.6	25.6	10.7	4.1	3.1	1,403
Sioux Falls, SD	10.8	66.2	17.7	3.5	0.4	0.7	0.7	792
Springfield, IL	11.8	63.8	20.0	2.7	0.8	0.7	0.2	797
Tallahassee, FL	7.4	45.9	35.0	8.2	2.8	0.5	0.2	971
Tampa, FL	5.0	38.3	38.5	13.0	3.1	1.2	0.9	1,070
Topeka, KS	15.9	60.2	18.0	3.4	1.5	0.3	0.6	786
Tucson, AZ	8.1	52.6	29.7	6.7	1.5	0.7	0.7	885
Tulsa, OK	11.5	58.5	24.1	4.1	0.9	0.4	0.5	831
Tuscaloosa, AL	15.4	57.8	20.6	3.9	1.4	0.2	0.6	820
Virginia Beach, VA	7.2	28.4	40.7	17.0	4.4	1.3	1.0	1,154
Washington, DC	4.7	8.5	27.3	31.0	15.9	7.0	5.6	1,653
Wichita, KS	11.8	61.9	21.0	3.6	0.8	0.2	0.6	796
Winston-Salem, NC	14.3	64.4	17.3	2.6	0.8	0.2	0.3	752
U.S.	9.8	38.5	29.6	12.9	5.1	2.1	2.0	1,023

Note: (1) Figures cover the Metropolitan Statistical Area (MSA)—see Appendix B for areas included; Figures are percentages except for Median; Gross rent is the contract rent plus the estimated average monthly cost of utilities (electricity, gas, and water and sewer) and fuels (oil, coal, kerosene, wood, etc.) if these are paid by the renter (or paid for the renter by someone else).
Source: U.S. Census Bureau, 2014-2018 American Community Survey 5-Year Estimates

Highest Level of Education: City

City	Less than H.S.	H.S. Diploma	Some College, No Deg.	Associate Degree	Bachelors Degree	Masters Degree	Profess. School Degree	Doctorate Degree
Albany, NY	10.6	24.9	18.0	8.0	19.2	13.0	3.4	3.0
Albuquerque, NM	10.3	22.6	23.9	8.5	19.1	10.6	2.6	2.5
Allentown, PA	21.4	37.1	18.4	7.7	9.9	3.7	0.9	0.8
Anchorage, AK	6.2	23.8	26.0	8.7	21.9	9.2	2.9	1.3
Ann Arbor, MI	2.9	7.3	10.4	3.8	30.5	26.9	7.3	10.8
Athens, GA	13.0	21.0	16.8	6.5	21.0	12.8	2.9	5.9
Atlanta, GA	9.7	19.4	16.1	4.9	27.7	14.7	5.3	2.2
Austin, TX	10.9	16.0	17.4	5.3	31.5	13.2	3.2	2.6
Baton Rouge, LA	12.0	27.5	22.7	4.7	19.2	8.6	2.7	2.5
Boise City, ID	5.1	21.4	23.8	8.7	26.9	9.6	2.6	1.9
Boston, MA	13.6	20.1	13.2	4.6	26.5	14.3	4.6	3.2
Boulder, CO	3.5	6.7	12.4	3.5	35.0	24.5	6.0	8.3
Cape Coral, FL	8.3	36.0	21.2	11.1	15.8	5.5	1.2	0.8
Cedar Rapids, IA	6.3	26.1	22.9	12.2	23.2	6.7	1.5	1.1
Charleston, SC	5.4	17.6	16.9	8.2	32.9	12.8	4.3	2.1
Charlotte, NC	11.1	17.6	20.1	7.6	28.4	11.4	2.6	1.1
Chicago, IL	15.5	22.9	17.6	5.7	22.7	10.9	3.2	1.6
Clarksville, TN	7.4	28.0	28.0	10.1	18.2	6.6	0.7	1.0
Cleveland, OH	20.4	33.0	22.9	7.1	10.4	4.2	1.4	0.6
College Station, TX	5.7	11.5	17.6	7.5	28.8	15.3	3.3	10.3
Colorado Springs, CO	6.7	19.7	24.0	10.5	23.5	12.0	2.0	1.5
Columbia, MO	5.0	17.6	18.3	6.3	27.5	15.7	4.7	4.8
Columbia, SC	11.1	20.2	18.8	7.0	23.8	12.6	4.1	2.4
Columbus, OH	10.5	25.5	21.0	7.3	23.2	9.2	1.8	1.5
Dallas, TX	23.5	21.6	18.0	4.6	20.4	8.1	2.8	1.1
Davenport, IA	9.3	32.8	21.4	10.2	17.5	6.7	1.4	0.7
Denver, CO	12.9	17.0	16.9	5.3	29.2	12.6	4.1	1.9
Des Moines, IA	13.9	30.1	21.0	9.2	17.8	5.5	1.7	0.8
Durham, NC	12.1	16.2	16.6	6.4	25.7	14.2	4.2	4.6
Edison, NJ	7.9	20.4	11.7	5.4	29.3	20.2	2.8	2.3
El Paso, TX	20.4	23.4	23.7	7.9	16.4	6.2	1.3	0.7
Fargo, ND	6.1	20.1	19.9	14.5	27.8	7.6	2.2	1.9
Fayetteville, NC	8.5	23.6	30.2	10.9	17.5	7.0	1.4	0.9
Fort Collins, CO	3.5	14.9	18.9	8.2	32.1	15.7	2.7	4.0
Fort Wayne, IN	11.5	28.7	22.2	10.0	18.1	7.0	1.7	0.9
Fort Worth, TX	18.3	25.1	21.2	6.9	19.2	6.9	1.5	1.0
Grand Rapids, MI	13.4	22.4	20.8	7.8	23.4	8.9	1.9	1.4
Greeley, CO	16.0	26.4	24.1	8.8	15.6	6.8	1.2	1.1
Green Bay, WI	12.6	31.4	20.0	11.2	17.7	5.4	1.0	0.7
Greensboro, NC	10.2	22.0	22.3	8.1	23.6	9.6	2.4	1.8
Honolulu, HI	11.2	24.1	18.3	10.1	23.2	7.9	3.2	2.0
Houston, TX	21.7	22.7	18.2	5.3	19.5	8.5	2.5	1.6
Huntsville, AL	9.6	19.2	20.3	8.0	26.0	13.0	1.7	2.2
Indianapolis, IN	14.5	28.0	19.9	7.3	19.7	7.5	2.1	1.1
Jackson, MS	14.4	25.5	24.8	7.7	15.8	7.8	2.7	1.2
Jacksonville, FL	10.8	28.5	22.8	10.2	18.7	6.6	1.7	0.7
Kansas City, MO	10.4	25.5	22.5	7.3	21.4	9.3	2.4	1.2
Lafayette, LA	11.8	26.0	20.9	4.4	24.8	8.0	2.6	1.4
Lakeland, FL	11.2	34.3	19.2	9.0	17.0	6.9	1.5	0.9
Las Vegas, NV	15.6	27.8	24.9	7.7	15.7	5.7	1.8	0.7
Lexington, KY	9.1	20.0	20.3	7.6	24.3	11.8	3.8	3.0
Lincoln, NE	6.8	21.8	21.7	10.9	24.8	9.2	2.2	2.6
Little Rock, AR	8.7	22.1	21.8	6.1	24.3	10.0	4.1	2.9
Los Angeles, CA	23.0	19.4	17.8	6.1	22.1	7.5	2.7	1.4
Louisville, KY	11.1	28.7	23.0	8.0	17.2	8.6	2.2	1.2

Table continued on next page.

City	Less than H.S.	H.S. Diploma	Some College, No Deg.	Associate Degree	Bachelors Degree	Masters Degree	Profess. School Degree	Doctorate Degree
Madison, WI	4.7	14.0	15.3	8.1	32.6	15.7	4.4	5.2
Manchester, NH	12.9	30.3	19.0	9.1	19.2	7.3	1.5	0.7
Miami, FL	23.0	29.4	12.6	7.1	17.0	6.5	3.3	1.1
Midland, TX	15.7	25.0	22.6	7.8	20.6	5.7	1.7	0.7
Milwaukee, WI	16.6	29.9	22.1	7.2	15.5	6.4	1.3	0.9
Minneapolis, MN	10.3	15.7	17.3	7.2	29.9	13.2	3.9	2.4
Nashville, TN	11.7	22.9	19.2	6.5	25.1	9.8	2.8	2.0
New Haven, CT	14.8	31.4	14.1	4.4	16.0	10.7	4.2	4.5
New Orleans, LA	13.8	22.9	21.7	4.7	21.1	9.5	4.3	2.0
New York, NY	18.4	24.0	13.8	6.4	21.8	10.9	3.2	1.5
Oklahoma City, OK	13.8	25.3	23.3	7.3	19.8	7.4	2.1	1.1
Omaha, NE	11.2	22.3	22.3	7.7	23.7	8.6	2.7	1.5
Orlando, FL	9.8	23.8	18.8	10.9	24.4	8.3	2.8	1.2
Peoria, IL	11.2	23.9	21.6	8.6	20.8	10.0	2.7	1.2
Philadelphia, PA	16.1	33.0	16.6	5.7	16.7	7.9	2.5	1.5
Phoenix, AZ	18.5	23.4	22.2	7.8	18.0	7.2	1.9	1.0
Pittsburgh, PA	7.6	26.2	15.2	8.1	22.7	12.6	4.0	3.7
Portland, OR	7.8	15.4	20.8	6.9	29.4	13.4	4.0	2.2
Providence, RI	20.0	29.2	15.5	5.0	16.2	8.5	2.8	2.8
Provo, UT	7.6	14.7	26.0	9.1	28.8	9.0	1.4	3.3
Raleigh, NC	8.3	15.6	18.0	7.7	32.2	13.1	2.8	2.3
Reno, NV	12.1	22.4	24.8	7.8	20.3	8.4	2.2	2.0
Richmond, VA	15.0	22.3	18.5	5.7	22.8	10.8	3.0	1.9
Rochester, MN	6.3	18.6	18.2	11.3	25.3	11.2	5.1	4.0
Sacramento, CA	15.3	20.9	22.4	8.8	20.6	7.8	2.9	1.3
Salt Lake City, UT	11.5	17.0	18.7	7.0	25.4	12.1	4.5	3.7
San Antonio, TX	18.0	26.0	22.5	7.6	16.6	6.6	1.7	1.0
San Diego, CA	12.1	15.3	19.9	7.4	26.8	11.9	3.6	3.0
San Francisco, CA	11.5	12.3	13.8	5.3	34.3	15.1	4.9	2.8
San Jose, CA	15.8	17.0	17.0	7.5	25.4	13.3	1.9	2.2
Santa Rosa, CA	14.3	18.8	25.1	9.6	20.2	7.9	2.6	1.5
Savannah, GA	13.0	26.6	25.6	6.7	17.1	8.4	1.5	1.1
Seattle, WA	5.4	9.8	15.3	6.7	36.2	17.6	5.1	3.8
Sioux Falls, SD	8.0	25.7	20.8	11.3	23.3	7.5	2.4	1.0
Springfield, IL	9.0	26.4	21.5	7.3	21.7	9.7	3.3	1.1
Tallahassee, FL	6.5	16.8	19.0	9.8	26.4	13.5	3.9	4.1
Tampa, FL	12.7	25.5	16.4	8.0	22.7	9.4	3.6	1.6
Topeka, KS	9.8	32.0	23.8	6.0	18.0	7.4	2.0	1.0
Tucson, AZ	15.1	23.8	25.6	8.8	16.2	7.6	1.5	1.6
Tulsa, OK	13.0	25.2	23.1	7.9	20.3	7.0	2.4	1.0
Tuscaloosa, AL	10.5	27.0	20.7	5.2	21.1	9.6	2.5	3.4
Virginia Beach, VA	6.8	21.4	26.1	10.5	22.6	9.5	2.1	1.1
Washington, DC	9.4	17.2	12.9	3.0	24.4	20.7	8.3	4.3
Wichita, KS	12.1	26.2	23.9	7.7	19.1	8.0	1.8	1.1
Winston-Salem, NC	12.5	24.5	21.6	7.3	20.4	8.8	3.1	1.8
U.S.	12.3	27.1	20.6	8.4	19.4	8.6	2.1	1.4

Note: Figures cover persons age 25 and over
Source: U.S. Census Bureau, 2014-2018 American Community Survey 5-Year Estimates

Highest Level of Education: Metro Area

Metro Area	Less than H.S.	H.S. Diploma	Some College, No Deg.	Associate Degree	Bachelors Degree	Masters Degree	Profess. School Degree	Doctorate Degree
Albany, NY	7.7	26.5	16.7	12.2	20.2	12.2	2.4	2.1
Albuquerque, NM	11.6	24.5	23.9	8.4	17.7	9.7	2.1	2.1
Allentown, PA	10.3	34.4	17.3	9.3	17.9	8.0	1.5	1.2
Anchorage, AK	6.6	26.0	26.9	8.9	19.8	8.3	2.4	1.1
Ann Arbor, MI	4.8	14.9	18.0	7.1	26.2	18.8	4.6	5.6
Athens, GA	12.7	24.8	17.0	7.3	18.9	11.5	3.1	4.7
Atlanta, GA	10.8	24.1	19.9	7.4	23.6	10.2	2.4	1.5
Austin, TX	10.3	19.1	20.2	6.4	28.3	11.3	2.4	1.9
Baton Rouge, LA	12.4	32.1	21.7	6.0	18.0	6.6	1.8	1.3
Boise City, ID	8.4	26.2	25.3	9.1	21.0	7.1	1.6	1.3
Boston, MA	8.6	22.4	14.7	7.1	25.7	14.9	3.4	3.1
Boulder, CO	4.9	12.3	15.8	6.2	33.1	18.6	4.0	5.0
Cape Coral, FL	12.0	30.8	20.3	9.1	17.4	7.1	2.2	1.1
Cedar Rapids, IA	5.7	29.0	22.1	12.4	21.8	6.8	1.4	0.9
Charleston, SC	9.5	25.6	20.6	9.6	22.5	8.8	2.3	1.2
Charlotte, NC	11.2	23.8	21.3	9.0	23.2	8.7	1.8	0.9
Chicago, IL	11.7	24.1	19.7	7.2	22.7	10.7	2.6	1.4
Clarksville, TN	9.4	29.9	26.6	9.9	15.8	6.7	1.0	0.8
Cleveland, OH	9.8	29.1	22.0	8.4	18.6	8.5	2.4	1.2
College Station, TX	13.9	22.8	20.0	6.5	20.0	9.3	2.3	5.1
Colorado Springs, CO	6.2	20.4	24.4	11.2	22.8	11.8	1.8	1.4
Columbia, MO	5.8	21.2	19.7	7.2	25.8	12.5	3.7	3.9
Columbia, SC	10.5	27.1	21.6	8.9	19.7	9.0	1.8	1.4
Columbus, OH	8.7	27.8	19.8	7.5	23.0	9.5	2.2	1.4
Dallas, TX	14.8	22.4	21.4	6.9	22.5	8.9	1.8	1.1
Davenport, IA	9.0	30.8	23.0	10.4	17.1	7.3	1.6	0.8
Denver, CO	9.2	20.0	20.2	7.6	27.2	11.5	2.6	1.5
Des Moines, IA	7.6	24.9	20.3	10.4	25.5	8.0	2.4	1.0
Durham, NC	10.8	18.7	16.7	7.3	23.7	13.7	4.1	5.1
Edison, NJ	13.7	25.0	15.1	6.8	22.9	11.8	3.1	1.6
El Paso, TX	22.6	23.9	23.1	7.7	15.3	5.6	1.2	0.6
Fargo, ND	5.4	21.2	21.0	14.5	27.0	7.6	1.8	1.5
Fayetteville, NC	9.9	25.8	29.0	11.1	15.8	6.4	1.1	0.8
Fort Collins, CO	4.2	19.2	21.1	9.1	27.6	13.2	2.2	3.3
Fort Wayne, IN	10.3	30.4	21.7	10.7	17.7	6.8	1.6	0.8
Fort Worth, TX	14.8	22.4	21.4	6.9	22.5	8.9	1.8	1.1
Grand Rapids, MI	9.1	27.3	21.9	9.3	21.5	8.2	1.7	1.1
Greeley, CO	11.9	27.5	24.7	9.1	18.4	6.4	1.1	0.8
Green Bay, WI	8.2	32.6	19.6	12.4	19.1	6.0	1.4	0.6
Greensboro, NC	13.2	27.1	22.0	8.8	18.9	7.2	1.5	1.3
Honolulu, HI	8.3	26.2	20.5	10.7	22.5	7.8	2.5	1.5
Houston, TX	16.8	23.1	20.9	6.8	20.7	8.3	2.0	1.5
Huntsville, AL	10.3	22.8	20.6	8.0	23.9	11.4	1.4	1.6
Indianapolis, IN	10.6	28.0	19.7	7.8	21.9	8.7	2.1	1.2
Jackson, MS	12.7	25.2	22.5	9.4	18.2	8.3	2.4	1.3
Jacksonville, FL	9.4	27.9	22.2	10.0	20.1	7.6	1.9	1.0
Kansas City, MO	8.2	25.6	22.1	7.6	23.1	9.9	2.3	1.1
Lafayette, LA	16.8	36.2	18.9	5.3	16.1	4.7	1.2	0.7
Lakeland, FL	15.2	35.4	20.9	8.5	13.2	5.0	1.0	0.7
Las Vegas, NV	14.3	28.6	25.4	7.9	15.8	5.6	1.6	0.8
Lexington, KY	10.4	24.4	20.6	7.9	21.2	10.1	3.1	2.3
Lincoln, NE	6.5	22.2	21.6	11.5	24.5	9.1	2.2	2.5
Little Rock, AR	9.7	29.3	23.4	7.6	18.8	7.6	2.1	1.5
Los Angeles, CA	19.8	19.8	19.5	7.2	21.9	8.0	2.5	1.4
Louisville, KY	10.5	30.0	22.4	8.4	17.1	8.3	2.1	1.1

Table continued on next page.

Metro Area	Less than H.S.	H.S. Diploma	Some College, No Deg.	Associate Degree	Bachelors Degree	Masters Degree	Profess. School Degree	Doctorate Degree
Madison, WI	4.8	21.1	18.2	10.4	27.6	11.7	3.0	3.1
Manchester, NH	8.2	26.3	18.4	9.8	23.8	10.6	1.6	1.3
Miami, FL	14.6	26.8	17.7	9.4	19.8	7.6	2.8	1.2
Midland, TX	16.4	26.0	22.5	7.9	19.4	5.6	1.5	0.6
Milwaukee, WI	8.9	26.6	20.9	8.6	22.6	8.9	2.3	1.3
Minneapolis, MN	6.5	21.5	20.3	10.5	26.9	10.1	2.5	1.6
Nashville, TN	10.5	27.1	20.4	7.3	22.6	8.6	2.1	1.5
New Haven, CT	9.9	30.9	16.9	7.4	18.8	11.0	3.0	2.1
New Orleans, LA	13.4	28.5	22.6	5.8	18.9	7.0	2.7	1.3
New York, NY	13.7	25.0	15.1	6.8	22.9	11.8	3.1	1.6
Oklahoma City, OK	11.1	27.2	24.1	7.5	19.5	7.5	1.9	1.2
Omaha, NE	8.6	23.7	22.9	8.9	23.6	8.8	2.1	1.3
Orlando, FL	10.5	26.2	20.4	11.6	20.8	7.6	1.9	1.0
Peoria, IL	8.3	30.0	23.1	10.3	18.6	7.4	1.5	0.9
Philadelphia, PA	9.7	29.4	16.9	7.0	21.9	10.6	2.7	1.9
Phoenix, AZ	12.8	23.2	24.7	8.5	19.6	8.2	1.9	1.2
Pittsburgh, PA	6.4	33.2	16.3	10.1	20.8	9.5	2.2	1.6
Portland, OR	8.2	20.0	24.0	8.9	24.4	10.2	2.6	1.8
Providence, RI	13.1	28.8	18.1	8.6	19.1	8.9	1.9	1.5
Provo, UT	5.9	16.7	26.9	10.8	27.2	8.9	1.7	1.8
Raleigh, NC	8.7	18.2	18.4	8.9	29.2	12.3	2.2	2.2
Reno, NV	11.7	24.0	25.7	8.3	19.1	7.7	2.0	1.7
Richmond, VA	10.5	25.5	20.4	7.4	22.7	9.9	2.2	1.5
Rochester, MN	6.1	24.1	20.0	12.1	22.1	9.2	3.7	2.6
Sacramento, CA	11.0	21.2	24.9	9.9	21.3	7.7	2.6	1.5
Salt Lake City, UT	9.5	23.1	24.4	9.0	21.7	8.5	2.2	1.5
San Antonio, TX	15.2	26.3	22.9	8.0	17.7	7.3	1.6	1.0
San Diego, CA	12.9	18.4	22.4	8.2	23.5	9.7	2.8	2.1
San Francisco, CA	11.1	15.7	17.8	6.7	28.7	13.4	3.8	2.8
San Jose, CA	12.1	14.8	15.6	7.0	26.9	17.2	2.7	3.6
Santa Rosa, CA	12.0	18.8	24.8	9.5	22.0	8.5	2.9	1.5
Savannah, GA	10.4	26.5	24.1	7.8	19.3	8.4	2.1	1.4
Seattle, WA	7.5	19.6	21.5	9.4	26.2	11.3	2.6	1.9
Sioux Falls, SD	7.3	26.4	20.8	12.4	23.0	6.9	2.1	1.0
Springfield, IL	7.6	28.4	22.4	8.1	21.2	8.8	2.5	1.0
Tallahassee, FL	9.4	23.8	19.9	8.9	21.9	10.2	3.0	3.0
Tampa, FL	10.6	29.1	20.8	9.9	19.1	7.5	1.9	1.1
Topeka, KS	7.7	33.1	23.9	6.9	18.4	7.4	1.7	0.9
Tucson, AZ	11.7	22.5	25.1	8.8	18.4	9.2	2.3	2.0
Tulsa, OK	10.8	29.2	24.0	8.7	18.7	6.0	1.7	0.8
Tuscaloosa, AL	12.6	31.4	21.4	7.0	16.9	7.3	1.4	2.0
Virginia Beach, VA	8.9	25.0	25.1	9.6	19.2	9.2	1.8	1.2
Washington, DC	9.3	18.2	16.2	5.8	25.7	17.4	4.3	3.2
Wichita, KS	10.1	26.6	24.6	8.4	19.6	8.2	1.5	1.0
Winston-Salem, NC	13.6	29.5	21.3	9.2	17.1	6.5	1.7	1.1
U.S.	12.3	27.1	20.6	8.4	19.4	8.6	2.1	1.4

Note: Figures cover persons age 25 and over; Figures cover the Metropolitan Statistical Area—see Appendix B for areas included
Source: U.S. Census Bureau, 2014-2018 American Community Survey 5-Year Estimates

School Enrollment by Grade and Control: City

City	Preschool (%)		Kindergarten (%)		Grades 1 - 4 (%)		Grades 5 - 8 (%)		Grades 9 - 12 (%)	
	Public	Private	Public	Private	Public	Private	Public	Private	Public	Private
Albany, NY	69.8	30.2	94.1	5.9	89.2	10.8	85.0	15.0	86.4	13.6
Albuquerque, NM	61.6	38.4	86.5	13.5	90.9	9.1	89.6	10.4	91.4	8.6
Allentown, PA	75.4	24.6	83.0	17.0	88.8	11.2	87.0	13.0	90.2	9.8
Anchorage, AK	52.1	47.9	91.1	8.9	91.8	8.2	93.5	6.5	94.5	5.5
Ann Arbor, MI	25.3	74.7	92.2	7.8	91.3	8.7	84.3	15.7	94.6	5.4
Athens, GA	62.8	37.2	91.3	8.7	91.9	8.1	87.6	12.4	85.7	14.3
Atlanta, GA	55.8	44.2	85.5	14.5	87.3	12.7	80.4	19.6	79.1	20.9
Austin, TX	50.2	49.8	87.9	12.1	89.3	10.7	89.1	10.9	91.1	8.9
Baton Rouge, LA	65.3	34.7	75.1	24.9	79.7	20.3	77.2	22.8	80.3	19.7
Boise City, ID	32.3	67.7	87.8	12.2	87.8	12.2	92.0	8.0	90.4	9.6
Boston, MA	50.7	49.3	85.5	14.5	85.6	14.4	88.1	11.9	88.5	11.5
Boulder, CO	43.0	57.0	83.3	16.7	91.1	8.9	91.3	8.7	94.9	5.1
Cape Coral, FL	73.8	26.2	95.1	4.9	93.9	6.1	93.2	6.8	92.2	7.8
Cedar Rapids, IA	65.4	34.6	85.9	14.1	88.1	11.9	92.3	7.7	92.6	7.4
Charleston, SC	46.1	53.9	79.6	20.4	83.6	16.4	78.4	21.6	79.6	20.4
Charlotte, NC	48.6	51.4	90.5	9.5	90.0	10.0	88.5	11.5	88.9	11.1
Chicago, IL	60.9	39.1	80.1	19.9	86.1	13.9	86.5	13.5	87.4	12.6
Clarksville, TN	59.1	40.9	93.1	6.9	92.3	7.7	93.8	6.2	94.0	6.0
Cleveland, OH	73.8	26.2	82.3	17.7	79.9	20.1	79.3	20.7	81.7	18.3
College Station, TX	43.2	56.8	86.2	13.8	84.3	15.7	92.9	7.1	91.6	8.4
Colorado Springs, CO	56.2	43.8	89.9	10.1	92.8	7.2	92.8	7.2	91.9	8.1
Columbia, MO	38.0	62.0	72.2	27.8	82.8	17.2	85.7	14.3	85.5	14.5
Columbia, SC	54.1	45.9	71.4	28.6	88.6	11.4	87.1	12.9	86.6	13.4
Columbus, OH	58.1	41.9	87.2	12.8	88.5	11.5	87.1	12.9	88.4	11.6
Dallas, TX	69.0	31.0	89.7	10.3	91.5	8.5	91.2	8.8	91.3	8.7
Davenport, IA	68.6	31.4	86.3	13.7	88.4	11.6	85.7	14.3	94.0	6.0
Denver, CO	64.7	35.3	88.0	12.0	91.3	8.7	90.5	9.5	92.4	7.6
Des Moines, IA	76.1	23.9	92.6	7.4	90.0	10.0	90.6	9.4	91.3	8.7
Durham, NC	47.3	52.7	89.5	10.5	88.8	11.2	87.8	12.2	91.3	8.7
Edison, NJ	27.9	72.1	67.8	32.2	89.2	10.8	88.9	11.1	91.0	9.0
El Paso, TX	78.2	21.8	93.2	6.8	95.0	5.0	94.6	5.4	95.9	4.1
Fargo, ND	51.9	48.1	89.8	10.2	88.2	11.8	89.5	10.5	93.0	7.0
Fayetteville, NC	61.5	38.5	87.9	12.1	88.2	11.8	88.2	11.8	89.4	10.6
Fort Collins, CO	45.0	55.0	92.9	7.1	95.9	4.1	95.0	5.0	94.8	5.2
Fort Wayne, IN	51.7	48.3	86.0	14.0	82.2	17.8	81.0	19.0	79.4	20.6
Fort Worth, TX	63.5	36.5	88.8	11.2	93.2	6.8	90.2	9.8	92.0	8.0
Grand Rapids, MI	65.4	34.6	78.1	21.9	83.6	16.4	84.7	15.3	84.8	15.2
Greeley, CO	69.8	30.2	78.8	21.2	92.4	7.6	91.6	8.4	95.0	5.0
Green Bay, WI	70.9	29.1	88.6	11.4	92.0	8.0	88.1	11.9	91.1	8.9
Greensboro, NC	56.5	43.5	89.1	10.9	93.9	6.1	90.2	9.8	92.4	7.6
Honolulu, HI	34.2	65.8	81.4	18.6	85.2	14.8	74.5	25.5	74.5	25.5
Houston, TX	68.1	31.9	91.3	8.7	94.0	6.0	92.7	7.3	93.5	6.5
Huntsville, AL	54.7	45.3	86.0	14.0	82.8	17.2	83.6	16.4	86.1	13.9
Indianapolis, IN	57.0	43.0	84.7	15.3	88.5	11.5	86.1	13.9	88.5	11.5
Jackson, MS	69.6	30.4	85.5	14.5	91.1	8.9	91.0	9.0	87.8	12.2
Jacksonville, FL	56.6	43.4	82.7	17.3	83.5	16.5	81.6	18.4	83.9	16.1
Kansas City, MO	58.7	41.3	87.1	12.9	90.3	9.7	87.4	12.6	85.9	14.1
Lafayette, LA	58.7	41.3	71.2	28.8	74.9	25.1	71.4	28.6	79.3	20.7
Lakeland, FL	58.3	41.7	86.9	13.1	87.8	12.2	84.7	15.3	89.8	10.2
Las Vegas, NV	64.3	35.7	86.4	13.6	91.8	8.2	91.9	8.1	92.6	7.4
Lexington, KY	46.5	53.5	88.6	11.4	86.3	13.7	84.3	15.7	85.6	14.4
Lincoln, NE	51.0	49.0	76.1	23.9	85.2	14.8	86.1	13.9	85.6	14.4
Little Rock, AR	52.2	47.8	78.8	21.2	83.8	16.2	80.0	20.0	78.6	21.4
Los Angeles, CA	61.1	38.9	88.1	11.9	88.9	11.1	88.4	11.6	88.9	11.1
Louisville, KY	53.0	47.0	80.5	19.5	82.3	17.7	80.9	19.1	80.9	19.1

Table continued on next page.

City	Preschool (%)		Kindergarten (%)		Grades 1 - 4 (%)		Grades 5 - 8 (%)		Grades 9 - 12 (%)	
	Public	Private	Public	Private	Public	Private	Public	Private	Public	Private
Madison, WI	55.7	44.3	85.4	14.6	89.6	10.4	85.0	15.0	92.4	7.6
Manchester, NH	49.0	51.0	85.9	14.1	90.3	9.7	92.2	7.8	89.5	10.5
Miami, FL	56.6	43.4	87.0	13.0	86.6	13.4	86.8	13.2	89.3	10.7
Midland, TX	60.1	39.9	86.6	13.4	83.7	16.3	85.6	14.4	89.2	10.8
Milwaukee, WI	75.2	24.8	76.3	23.7	75.7	24.3	76.4	23.6	81.6	18.4
Minneapolis, MN	57.0	43.0	85.7	14.3	87.6	12.4	87.2	12.8	87.2	12.8
Nashville, TN	48.7	51.3	88.9	11.1	85.7	14.3	82.8	17.2	82.6	17.4
New Haven, CT	79.7	20.3	90.1	9.9	94.6	5.4	91.9	8.1	93.6	6.4
New Orleans, LA	51.1	48.9	80.2	19.8	81.5	18.5	80.7	19.3	78.9	21.1
New York, NY	60.1	39.9	79.6	20.4	82.9	17.1	82.5	17.5	82.9	17.1
Oklahoma City, OK	73.4	26.6	91.6	8.4	91.7	8.3	89.5	10.5	90.7	9.3
Omaha, NE	56.1	43.9	81.7	18.3	86.1	13.9	85.9	14.1	85.3	14.7
Orlando, FL	61.5	38.5	83.2	16.8	92.3	7.7	84.8	15.2	92.4	7.6
Peoria, IL	65.2	34.8	75.9	24.1	83.3	16.7	82.2	17.8	87.2	12.8
Philadelphia, PA	54.5	45.5	79.0	21.0	79.2	20.8	79.2	20.8	81.4	18.6
Phoenix, AZ	62.9	37.1	90.9	9.1	93.3	6.7	92.6	7.4	93.6	6.4
Pittsburgh, PA	55.5	44.5	79.0	21.0	74.8	25.2	74.9	25.1	81.3	18.7
Portland, OR	40.2	59.8	84.0	16.0	87.7	12.3	87.5	12.5	85.8	14.2
Providence, RI	53.9	46.1	87.0	13.0	86.5	13.5	84.7	15.3	86.8	13.2
Provo, UT	50.4	49.6	95.3	4.7	94.7	5.3	95.5	4.5	89.4	10.6
Raleigh, NC	41.4	58.6	88.9	11.1	90.4	9.6	89.3	10.7	91.2	8.8
Reno, NV	57.9	42.1	84.6	15.4	93.0	7.0	92.6	7.4	94.2	5.8
Richmond, VA	56.3	43.7	90.2	9.8	88.3	11.7	78.9	21.1	86.9	13.1
Rochester, MN	53.8	46.2	78.2	21.8	87.2	12.8	85.5	14.5	92.9	7.1
Sacramento, CA	67.2	32.8	91.9	8.1	93.0	7.0	92.8	7.2	92.1	7.9
Salt Lake City, UT	52.3	47.7	89.5	10.5	92.0	8.0	91.3	8.7	94.1	5.9
San Antonio, TX	70.0	30.0	91.1	8.9	93.0	7.0	93.0	7.0	93.3	6.7
San Diego, CA	54.0	46.0	92.5	7.5	91.5	8.5	91.0	9.0	90.9	9.1
San Francisco, CA	36.1	63.9	75.2	24.8	71.8	28.2	69.0	31.0	76.0	24.0
San Jose, CA	41.6	58.4	81.3	18.7	87.6	12.4	87.9	12.1	87.5	12.5
Santa Rosa, CA	52.8	47.2	94.9	5.1	95.0	5.0	95.2	4.8	91.8	8.2
Savannah, GA	63.0	37.0	97.6	2.4	91.3	8.7	89.1	10.9	88.8	11.2
Seattle, WA	30.7	69.3	79.8	20.2	81.2	18.8	76.8	23.2	80.7	19.3
Sioux Falls, SD	54.6	45.4	87.5	12.5	89.3	10.7	89.2	10.8	85.6	14.4
Springfield, IL	66.5	33.5	83.2	16.8	83.9	16.1	84.1	15.9	84.6	15.4
Tallahassee, FL	43.8	56.2	87.4	12.6	85.4	14.6	81.1	18.9	86.9	13.1
Tampa, FL	56.5	43.5	84.5	15.5	90.8	9.2	86.1	13.9	86.9	13.1
Topeka, KS	69.1	30.9	93.6	6.4	88.9	11.1	89.2	10.8	92.7	7.3
Tucson, AZ	71.0	29.0	86.7	13.3	90.5	9.5	91.1	8.9	93.0	7.0
Tulsa, OK	70.3	29.7	89.0	11.0	88.2	11.8	86.1	13.9	84.8	15.2
Tuscaloosa, AL	58.7	41.3	94.7	5.3	86.9	13.1	90.0	10.0	88.8	11.2
Virginia Beach, VA	37.2	62.8	80.4	19.6	90.4	9.6	89.6	10.4	92.8	7.2
Washington, DC	77.5	22.5	91.8	8.2	87.2	12.8	82.1	17.9	83.0	17.0
Wichita, KS	62.7	37.3	85.4	14.6	86.0	14.0	85.5	14.5	83.9	16.1
Winston-Salem, NC	54.5	45.5	91.6	8.4	91.5	8.5	89.9	10.1	93.3	6.7
U.S.	59.0	41.0	87.7	12.3	89.6	10.4	89.5	10.5	90.2	9.8

Note: Figures shown cover persons 3 years old and over
Source: U.S. Census Bureau, 2014-2018 American Community Survey 5-Year Estimates

School Enrollment by Grade and Control: Metro Area

Metro Area	Preschool (%)		Kindergarten (%)		Grades 1 - 4 (%)		Grades 5 - 8 (%)		Grades 9 - 12 (%)	
	Public	Private	Public	Private	Public	Private	Public	Private	Public	Private
Albany, NY	47.1	52.9	89.7	10.3	91.1	8.9	91.2	8.8	91.4	8.6
Albuquerque, NM	64.8	35.2	86.5	13.5	89.8	10.2	89.6	10.4	91.0	9.0
Allentown, PA	48.0	52.0	82.2	17.8	89.4	10.6	89.6	10.4	90.7	9.3
Anchorage, AK	55.1	44.9	89.8	10.2	90.3	9.7	90.9	9.1	92.1	7.9
Ann Arbor, MI	44.1	55.9	86.4	13.6	87.3	12.7	86.9	13.1	92.0	8.0
Athens, GA	63.9	36.1	91.2	8.8	90.0	10.0	85.3	14.7	85.1	14.9
Atlanta, GA	57.8	42.2	86.7	13.3	90.9	9.1	89.7	10.3	89.8	10.2
Austin, TX	51.7	48.3	89.2	10.8	90.8	9.2	90.6	9.4	92.4	7.6
Baton Rouge, LA	57.5	42.5	75.5	24.5	81.0	19.0	81.2	18.8	81.0	19.0
Boise City, ID	38.0	62.0	86.4	13.6	91.3	8.7	93.0	7.0	91.0	9.0
Boston, MA	45.8	54.2	87.8	12.2	91.1	8.9	90.1	9.9	86.9	13.1
Boulder, CO	50.8	49.2	85.8	14.2	90.7	9.3	90.4	9.6	94.5	5.5
Cape Coral, FL	64.6	35.4	91.9	8.1	92.1	7.9	92.1	7.9	91.8	8.2
Cedar Rapids, IA	67.2	32.8	87.2	12.8	88.4	11.6	92.1	7.9	93.9	6.1
Charleston, SC	51.9	48.1	86.4	13.6	89.9	10.1	89.4	10.6	90.4	9.6
Charlotte, NC	51.3	48.7	90.1	9.9	90.4	9.6	89.3	10.7	90.3	9.7
Chicago, IL	59.0	41.0	84.3	15.7	89.0	11.0	89.2	10.8	90.5	9.5
Clarksville, TN	62.6	37.4	91.6	8.4	88.7	11.3	90.8	9.2	90.4	9.6
Cleveland, OH	54.7	45.3	82.3	17.7	82.0	18.0	82.4	17.6	84.4	15.6
College Station, TX	57.5	42.5	85.3	14.7	88.2	11.8	91.2	8.8	93.1	6.9
Colorado Springs, CO	60.3	39.7	89.1	10.9	92.3	7.7	92.3	7.7	92.6	7.4
Columbia, MO	44.5	55.5	77.9	22.1	85.3	14.7	88.3	11.7	88.7	11.3
Columbia, SC	55.6	44.4	85.6	14.4	91.3	8.7	92.2	7.8	91.7	8.3
Columbus, OH	53.6	46.4	86.2	13.8	89.0	11.0	88.3	11.7	89.5	10.5
Dallas, TX	58.3	41.7	89.6	10.4	92.4	7.6	92.1	7.9	92.4	7.6
Davenport, IA	72.0	28.0	88.4	11.6	91.3	8.7	91.4	8.6	93.9	6.1
Denver, CO	60.2	39.8	90.4	9.6	92.7	7.3	92.1	7.9	92.3	7.7
Des Moines, IA	65.1	34.9	90.1	9.9	91.3	8.7	91.1	8.9	91.7	8.3
Durham, NC	45.2	54.8	88.1	11.9	88.9	11.1	89.3	10.7	90.0	10.0
Edison, NJ	53.9	46.1	82.2	17.8	85.8	14.2	86.0	14.0	85.5	14.5
El Paso, TX	81.8	18.2	93.9	6.1	95.5	4.5	94.7	5.3	96.2	3.8
Fargo, ND	56.9	43.1	91.6	8.4	88.8	11.2	89.2	10.8	93.0	7.0
Fayetteville, NC	63.1	36.9	87.3	12.7	88.5	11.5	88.0	12.0	89.5	10.5
Fort Collins, CO	52.5	47.5	91.4	8.6	92.2	7.8	91.9	8.1	93.6	6.4
Fort Wayne, IN	48.1	51.9	80.4	19.6	79.6	20.4	79.2	20.8	81.0	19.0
Fort Worth, TX	58.3	41.7	89.6	10.4	92.4	7.6	92.1	7.9	92.4	7.6
Grand Rapids, MI	63.0	37.0	82.8	17.2	84.9	15.1	85.5	14.5	86.2	13.8
Greeley, CO	70.7	29.3	88.1	11.9	91.5	8.5	92.5	7.5	93.2	6.8
Green Bay, WI	68.9	31.1	86.6	13.4	89.9	10.1	89.5	10.5	93.5	6.5
Greensboro, NC	50.8	49.2	88.5	11.5	90.3	9.7	89.4	10.6	91.0	9.0
Honolulu, HI	37.1	62.9	79.5	20.5	87.0	13.0	79.1	20.9	77.0	23.0
Houston, TX	59.2	40.8	90.4	9.6	93.0	7.0	93.0	7.0	93.4	6.6
Huntsville, AL	52.8	47.2	86.7	13.3	84.1	15.9	84.9	15.1	86.8	13.2
Indianapolis, IN	50.8	49.2	86.8	13.2	89.3	10.7	88.6	11.4	89.1	10.9
Jackson, MS	56.8	43.2	75.1	24.9	85.7	14.3	85.7	14.3	85.3	14.7
Jacksonville, FL	52.4	47.6	84.9	15.1	85.6	14.4	84.2	15.8	86.8	13.2
Kansas City, MO	55.9	44.1	88.9	11.1	89.2	10.8	88.8	11.2	89.7	10.3
Lafayette, LA	66.4	33.6	78.1	21.9	80.0	20.0	78.5	21.5	79.5	20.5
Lakeland, FL	67.5	32.5	88.4	11.6	90.2	9.8	86.7	13.3	91.2	8.8
Las Vegas, NV	60.6	39.4	89.2	10.8	92.4	7.6	93.0	7.0	93.3	6.7
Lexington, KY	49.5	50.5	85.8	14.2	87.6	12.4	85.6	14.4	86.7	13.3
Lincoln, NE	49.6	50.4	77.1	22.9	84.4	15.6	86.1	13.9	86.3	13.7
Little Rock, AR	60.2	39.8	86.8	13.2	89.7	10.3	88.4	11.6	87.1	12.9
Los Angeles, CA	58.8	41.2	88.5	11.5	90.8	9.2	90.9	9.1	91.5	8.5
Louisville, KY	50.8	49.2	81.7	18.3	83.2	16.8	82.1	17.9	82.0	18.0

Table continued on next page.

Metro Area	Preschool (%)		Kindergarten (%)		Grades 1 - 4 (%)		Grades 5 - 8 (%)		Grades 9 - 12 (%)	
	Public	Private	Public	Private	Public	Private	Public	Private	Public	Private
Madison, WI	64.4	35.6	88.2	11.8	90.4	9.6	89.4	10.6	94.4	5.6
Manchester, NH	41.0	59.0	82.5	17.5	88.0	12.0	89.7	10.3	88.1	11.9
Miami, FL	50.4	49.6	83.6	16.4	86.5	13.5	86.5	13.5	87.1	12.9
Midland, TX	58.9	41.1	87.4	12.6	86.0	14.0	87.5	12.5	89.9	10.1
Milwaukee, WI	56.4	43.6	78.4	21.6	79.4	20.6	80.2	19.8	85.1	14.9
Minneapolis, MN	59.6	40.4	88.3	11.7	89.2	10.8	89.7	10.3	91.3	8.7
Nashville, TN	45.4	54.6	87.5	12.5	87.6	12.4	85.5	14.5	84.6	15.4
New Haven, CT	63.7	36.3	88.2	11.8	92.4	7.6	90.6	9.4	89.8	10.2
New Orleans, LA	53.7	46.3	76.5	23.5	77.3	22.7	77.3	22.7	75.1	24.9
New York, NY	53.9	46.1	82.2	17.8	85.8	14.2	86.0	14.0	85.5	14.5
Oklahoma City, OK	72.3	27.7	90.7	9.3	91.3	8.7	90.2	9.8	91.4	8.6
Omaha, NE	57.8	42.2	85.6	14.4	87.6	12.4	87.4	12.6	87.4	12.6
Orlando, FL	56.6	43.4	81.4	18.6	87.3	12.7	86.5	13.5	89.7	10.3
Peoria, IL	60.7	39.3	83.5	16.5	88.3	11.7	86.9	13.1	89.2	10.8
Philadelphia, PA	44.5	55.5	81.3	18.7	85.0	15.0	84.1	15.9	83.6	16.4
Phoenix, AZ	60.3	39.7	90.6	9.4	92.4	7.6	92.8	7.2	93.2	6.8
Pittsburgh, PA	49.6	50.4	85.3	14.7	88.4	11.6	88.0	12.0	89.5	10.5
Portland, OR	43.4	56.6	87.0	13.0	88.7	11.3	89.9	10.1	90.9	9.1
Providence, RI	54.0	46.0	88.5	11.5	90.0	10.0	88.9	11.1	87.2	12.8
Provo, UT	51.1	48.9	93.2	6.8	93.3	6.7	94.1	5.9	94.5	5.5
Raleigh, NC	39.2	60.8	87.3	12.7	89.1	10.9	88.6	11.4	89.7	10.3
Reno, NV	58.9	41.1	85.3	14.7	93.0	7.0	92.0	8.0	93.5	6.5
Richmond, VA	43.3	56.7	88.9	11.1	90.4	9.6	88.4	11.6	90.2	9.8
Rochester, MN	63.3	36.7	84.0	16.0	88.0	12.0	88.3	11.7	92.9	7.1
Sacramento, CA	61.0	39.0	90.4	9.6	91.9	8.1	92.6	7.4	93.0	7.0
Salt Lake City, UT	55.9	44.1	90.2	9.8	92.8	7.2	92.9	7.1	93.7	6.3
San Antonio, TX	65.3	34.7	90.8	9.2	93.1	6.9	92.2	7.8	93.0	7.0
San Diego, CA	54.1	45.9	90.8	9.2	92.3	7.7	92.3	7.7	92.3	7.7
San Francisco, CA	41.1	58.9	84.4	15.6	86.1	13.9	86.0	14.0	87.5	12.5
San Jose, CA	36.5	63.5	80.2	19.8	85.8	14.2	86.2	13.8	86.7	13.3
Santa Rosa, CA	50.2	49.8	94.1	5.9	91.6	8.4	91.5	8.5	90.5	9.5
Savannah, GA	60.1	39.9	93.7	6.3	87.0	13.0	85.7	14.3	86.0	14.0
Seattle, WA	39.8	60.2	85.0	15.0	88.6	11.4	88.8	11.2	90.5	9.5
Sioux Falls, SD	57.6	42.4	87.8	12.2	89.0	11.0	90.4	9.6	88.3	11.7
Springfield, IL	66.5	33.5	86.3	13.7	88.4	11.6	88.4	11.6	89.7	10.3
Tallahassee, FL	49.1	50.9	86.0	14.0	84.9	15.1	81.6	18.4	86.5	13.5
Tampa, FL	58.9	41.1	85.9	14.1	87.9	12.1	87.5	12.5	89.2	10.8
Topeka, KS	73.7	26.3	91.7	8.3	89.3	10.7	89.4	10.6	91.9	8.1
Tucson, AZ	61.5	38.5	88.4	11.6	91.2	8.8	90.9	9.1	92.1	7.9
Tulsa, OK	70.1	29.9	89.8	10.2	89.2	10.8	88.5	11.5	87.9	12.1
Tuscaloosa, AL	66.3	33.7	89.0	11.0	86.9	13.1	89.3	10.7	88.6	11.4
Virginia Beach, VA	52.5	47.5	85.5	14.5	89.4	10.6	89.8	10.2	91.4	8.6
Washington, DC	44.9	55.1	86.7	13.3	88.7	11.3	87.6	12.4	88.3	11.7
Wichita, KS	62.0	38.0	84.3	15.7	86.3	13.7	87.0	13.0	86.5	13.5
Winston-Salem, NC	54.5	45.5	90.8	9.2	92.5	7.5	89.6	10.4	91.7	8.3
U.S.	59.0	41.0	87.7	12.3	89.6	10.4	89.5	10.5	90.2	9.8

Note: Figures shown cover persons 3 years old and over; Figures cover the Metropolitan Statistical Area—see Appendix B for areas included

Source: U.S. Census Bureau, 2014-2018 American Community Survey 5-Year Estimates

Educational Attainment by Race: City

City	High School Graduate or Higher (%)					Bachelor's Degree or Higher (%)				
	Total	White	Black	Asian	Hisp.[1]	Total	White	Black	Asian	Hisp.[1]
Albany, NY	89.4	93.5	83.0	84.2	80.0	38.6	50.4	14.3	52.0	22.3
Albuquerque, NM	89.7	91.2	93.1	84.9	82.3	34.7	37.6	30.0	48.9	21.1
Allentown, PA	78.6	81.0	82.2	79.7	68.8	15.3	18.4	8.7	35.0	6.3
Anchorage, AK	93.8	96.6	94.1	81.3	85.1	35.3	42.2	20.2	25.1	20.4
Ann Arbor, MI	97.1	98.3	87.8	96.6	91.8	75.5	78.0	36.6	84.2	69.2
Athens, GA	87.0	90.5	79.6	95.1	54.1	42.7	54.0	16.6	76.8	15.2
Atlanta, GA	90.3	97.4	83.7	96.6	80.5	49.9	77.0	24.0	84.2	42.4
Austin, TX	89.1	90.7	89.6	93.7	71.5	50.4	53.5	27.5	76.1	24.4
Baton Rouge, LA	88.0	96.1	82.1	85.1	76.1	33.1	53.8	15.6	51.7	22.5
Boise City, ID	94.9	95.7	82.6	87.3	83.3	41.1	41.4	27.5	51.7	20.4
Boston, MA	86.4	92.4	83.4	77.3	68.4	48.5	64.6	21.5	51.5	22.0
Boulder, CO	96.5	97.4	93.0	91.5	75.9	73.9	74.9	50.8	72.6	43.4
Cape Coral, FL	91.7	92.0	88.4	89.6	86.2	23.3	23.6	20.8	20.6	18.9
Cedar Rapids, IA	93.7	94.9	82.9	86.1	76.5	32.5	33.2	15.8	51.3	20.4
Charleston, SC	94.6	97.3	85.7	91.8	92.9	52.0	60.4	21.6	68.9	43.7
Charlotte, NC	88.9	92.3	89.6	81.1	60.2	43.5	54.2	28.5	57.1	17.0
Chicago, IL	84.5	88.2	84.6	87.7	67.1	38.4	49.8	20.7	60.7	15.6
Clarksville, TN	92.6	93.1	92.2	85.0	87.1	26.5	27.2	23.6	34.4	17.0
Cleveland, OH	79.6	82.0	78.6	72.5	67.2	16.6	23.6	9.3	39.4	8.3
College Station, TX	94.3	94.9	89.4	95.8	82.5	57.7	57.7	29.5	81.4	44.6
Colorado Springs, CO	93.3	95.0	93.6	85.2	77.7	39.0	42.1	23.6	44.6	20.1
Columbia, MO	95.0	96.4	88.8	92.8	88.3	52.8	56.1	19.1	69.2	39.4
Columbia, SC	88.9	94.7	81.7	94.1	78.7	42.9	61.6	19.1	71.4	31.9
Columbus, OH	89.5	91.7	86.4	84.4	72.5	35.7	41.3	18.7	57.5	21.5
Dallas, TX	76.5	74.4	86.0	83.7	49.2	32.3	38.1	17.8	64.3	9.9
Davenport, IA	90.7	92.1	81.8	82.1	73.9	26.2	27.6	12.6	36.8	14.7
Denver, CO	87.1	89.2	86.8	81.9	62.5	47.9	52.8	24.1	51.6	14.6
Des Moines, IA	86.1	89.3	81.4	61.7	56.5	25.8	28.3	13.9	19.8	8.3
Durham, NC	87.9	90.3	87.6	92.1	47.4	48.7	59.9	33.4	73.5	12.6
Edison, NJ	92.1	92.5	93.7	93.2	81.0	54.6	37.1	31.1	75.9	25.3
El Paso, TX	79.6	80.2	95.0	90.4	75.4	24.7	25.0	29.7	53.0	20.4
Fargo, ND	93.9	95.7	80.4	76.5	81.9	39.5	40.6	22.4	51.1	17.3
Fayetteville, NC	91.5	93.7	90.5	85.1	87.5	26.8	30.5	23.0	41.0	20.9
Fort Collins, CO	96.5	96.8	98.0	94.2	83.4	54.5	55.0	41.0	69.0	30.2
Fort Wayne, IN	88.5	91.7	83.2	58.9	60.0	27.6	30.5	13.7	32.5	9.6
Fort Worth, TX	81.7	83.9	87.6	81.1	57.5	28.6	32.7	20.3	40.8	10.9
Grand Rapids, MI	86.6	90.9	81.6	71.5	50.8	35.6	42.3	16.6	42.4	10.7
Greeley, CO	84.0	85.9	73.1	70.0	65.2	24.6	25.5	21.1	35.6	8.2
Green Bay, WI	87.4	90.7	85.8	70.5	49.3	24.8	27.4	11.6	17.9	6.1
Greensboro, NC	89.8	93.4	89.0	71.7	59.2	37.4	48.7	23.2	38.9	15.6
Honolulu, HI	88.8	97.5	97.1	85.2	90.6	36.4	52.3	24.1	35.9	27.4
Houston, TX	78.3	77.3	88.0	86.5	57.3	32.1	36.3	22.2	58.2	12.5
Huntsville, AL	90.4	93.3	84.4	89.8	62.2	42.9	49.0	26.3	57.9	20.4
Indianapolis, IN	85.5	87.7	84.1	75.0	55.9	30.4	35.4	17.6	46.1	11.6
Jackson, MS	85.6	92.9	83.8	92.2	57.3	27.5	53.6	20.8	66.0	22.8
Jacksonville, FL	89.2	90.8	86.7	86.4	81.5	27.8	30.7	18.0	47.3	24.3
Kansas City, MO	89.6	93.1	86.1	80.1	69.6	34.3	42.6	16.0	47.1	17.2
Lafayette, LA	88.2	92.5	77.3	94.4	49.6	36.8	45.7	14.2	50.3	20.4
Lakeland, FL	88.8	89.6	85.8	86.6	79.1	26.3	27.5	15.9	57.1	18.5
Las Vegas, NV	84.4	87.2	88.4	90.2	62.7	23.9	26.2	17.5	40.4	9.7
Lexington, KY	90.9	93.3	84.1	90.6	60.2	42.9	47.0	19.5	66.6	17.5
Lincoln, NE	93.2	94.8	87.8	78.7	70.6	38.8	39.9	23.0	45.2	20.2
Little Rock, AR	91.3	93.8	88.4	94.4	61.8	41.3	54.1	21.5	73.0	10.1
Los Angeles, CA	77.0	80.4	88.2	90.1	55.4	33.7	38.8	25.8	54.4	11.7
Louisville, KY	88.9	90.0	86.6	79.9	77.9	29.2	32.3	16.3	45.7	25.8

Table continued on next page.

City	High School Graduate or Higher (%)					Bachelor's Degree or Higher (%)				
	Total	White	Black	Asian	Hisp.[1]	Total	White	Black	Asian	Hisp.[1]
Madison, WI	95.3	96.9	87.6	90.4	76.9	57.9	60.1	20.6	70.5	34.0
Manchester, NH	87.1	87.9	86.3	77.1	69.0	28.7	28.0	24.4	45.9	12.3
Miami, FL	77.0	78.2	71.7	86.8	74.7	27.9	30.7	12.8	62.3	24.3
Midland, TX	84.3	84.8	84.3	81.4	68.5	28.8	30.2	18.1	47.7	11.0
Milwaukee, WI	83.4	88.8	82.0	70.2	60.6	24.2	34.5	12.4	28.2	8.9
Minneapolis, MN	89.7	95.9	75.0	82.2	57.5	49.4	59.9	14.2	53.0	18.4
Nashville, TN	88.3	90.3	87.1	77.0	58.7	39.7	44.7	27.4	47.1	15.2
New Haven, CT	85.2	87.8	85.3	96.4	71.6	35.4	47.8	20.1	80.1	13.0
New Orleans, LA	86.2	95.4	80.5	74.4	79.4	36.8	62.9	18.8	39.2	34.2
New York, NY	81.6	88.2	83.0	75.6	67.7	37.4	50.2	24.2	41.7	17.9
Oklahoma City, OK	86.2	87.5	89.2	81.3	54.0	30.3	32.8	20.3	42.4	9.9
Omaha, NE	88.8	90.9	86.0	67.7	52.0	36.6	39.3	19.2	47.9	11.5
Orlando, FL	90.2	92.8	84.3	91.0	85.9	36.7	41.9	21.4	58.0	27.4
Peoria, IL	88.8	92.5	79.8	94.3	67.8	34.7	39.3	13.1	76.2	21.3
Philadelphia, PA	83.9	88.2	84.0	71.3	65.8	28.6	39.7	16.6	38.7	14.0
Phoenix, AZ	81.5	84.0	87.4	84.7	60.7	28.2	30.1	21.4	56.0	9.9
Pittsburgh, PA	92.4	93.9	88.4	90.7	85.3	42.9	48.1	18.7	77.3	45.1
Portland, OR	92.2	94.5	86.4	77.9	74.7	49.0	53.0	23.1	38.7	28.9
Providence, RI	80.0	85.5	82.6	76.8	69.1	30.2	38.6	18.9	47.1	10.5
Provo, UT	92.4	93.0	97.6	92.7	73.3	42.5	43.0	24.7	57.1	18.9
Raleigh, NC	91.7	95.6	89.9	87.7	59.7	50.4	61.1	30.4	61.3	22.0
Reno, NV	87.9	89.8	90.5	89.9	61.9	32.9	34.5	19.4	45.3	12.2
Richmond, VA	85.0	91.4	78.5	83.0	51.2	38.5	60.3	14.8	64.7	12.8
Rochester, MN	93.7	96.1	78.2	81.8	71.7	45.7	46.9	17.6	55.8	24.0
Sacramento, CA	84.7	88.9	89.3	79.0	71.2	32.6	39.3	20.7	36.3	17.0
Salt Lake City, UT	88.5	94.3	82.0	82.4	60.2	45.7	51.0	25.5	59.2	14.9
San Antonio, TX	82.0	82.1	90.4	86.4	74.3	25.9	26.0	24.1	52.4	16.2
San Diego, CA	87.9	89.2	90.7	88.6	68.3	45.3	47.8	25.2	52.6	19.9
San Francisco, CA	88.5	96.4	89.0	79.3	78.7	57.1	72.6	28.6	45.7	33.7
San Jose, CA	84.2	88.1	91.7	87.0	66.1	42.7	43.0	35.6	55.5	14.6
Santa Rosa, CA	85.7	90.6	88.7	85.0	61.4	32.2	36.6	29.4	38.5	11.7
Savannah, GA	87.0	92.1	82.8	90.2	78.4	28.1	42.7	15.3	54.0	27.9
Seattle, WA	94.6	97.6	86.0	87.2	81.9	62.8	68.8	27.3	58.1	43.0
Sioux Falls, SD	92.0	94.4	71.0	70.2	64.2	34.2	36.6	11.9	37.6	11.5
Springfield, IL	91.0	93.1	80.8	93.9	87.5	35.8	38.5	17.4	69.0	34.7
Tallahassee, FL	93.5	96.6	87.7	96.9	86.2	47.9	55.8	28.5	83.2	38.2
Tampa, FL	87.3	89.5	82.0	88.4	76.4	37.3	42.7	17.6	63.0	22.3
Topeka, KS	90.2	91.6	87.3	93.4	73.3	28.4	30.7	11.9	63.1	10.6
Tucson, AZ	84.9	88.0	85.4	84.6	72.3	26.8	29.2	21.8	46.9	13.4
Tulsa, OK	87.0	89.6	89.0	75.8	54.6	30.8	35.5	18.0	37.4	10.1
Tuscaloosa, AL	89.5	94.6	84.6	89.6	74.7	36.6	52.5	17.5	72.0	12.1
Virginia Beach, VA	93.2	94.9	90.6	88.7	82.7	35.2	37.7	25.4	41.0	24.5
Washington, DC	90.6	97.7	86.4	94.3	70.5	57.6	88.9	26.6	81.4	46.1
Wichita, KS	87.9	90.0	85.8	80.8	61.3	30.0	32.7	14.8	36.8	12.1
Winston-Salem, NC	87.5	89.6	87.0	84.8	55.2	34.2	41.8	20.8	61.9	11.8
U.S.	87.7	89.6	85.4	86.8	67.7	31.5	32.9	21.1	53.5	15.8

Note: Figures shown cover persons 25 years old and over; (1) People of Hispanic origin can be of any race
Source: U.S. Census Bureau, 2014-2018 American Community Survey 5-Year Estimates

Educational Attainment by Race: Metro Area

Metro Area	High School Graduate or Higher (%)					Bachelor's Degree or Higher (%)				
	Total	White	Black	Asian	Hisp.[1]	Total	White	Black	Asian	Hisp.[1]
Albany, NY	92.3	93.7	84.3	86.1	82.3	36.8	37.6	19.2	63.6	24.8
Albuquerque, NM	88.4	90.2	92.4	87.1	80.3	31.6	34.5	28.9	49.1	18.5
Allentown, PA	89.7	90.9	86.9	86.9	74.0	28.6	29.3	19.4	55.5	12.4
Anchorage, AK	93.4	95.5	93.8	81.4	86.1	31.7	36.2	19.7	24.9	19.6
Ann Arbor, MI	95.2	96.4	88.9	95.9	84.7	55.2	57.0	27.1	82.0	41.6
Athens, GA	87.3	89.9	78.8	91.7	54.7	38.2	43.7	15.9	69.7	16.6
Atlanta, GA	89.2	90.6	90.0	87.0	64.3	37.8	41.8	29.3	56.9	20.0
Austin, TX	89.7	91.0	90.6	92.2	73.2	43.9	45.6	29.4	70.6	22.2
Baton Rouge, LA	87.6	90.9	82.3	86.4	69.7	27.7	32.4	17.8	51.5	17.2
Boise City, ID	91.6	93.0	86.5	87.2	66.4	31.0	31.7	26.9	46.4	10.5
Boston, MA	91.4	94.0	85.1	85.7	71.0	47.2	49.7	25.8	61.7	21.8
Boulder, CO	95.1	96.0	91.7	90.3	73.4	60.8	61.7	36.5	67.5	25.8
Cape Coral, FL	88.0	89.6	76.0	89.0	69.6	27.8	29.0	15.9	40.2	14.3
Cedar Rapids, IA	94.3	95.2	83.2	82.8	78.8	30.8	31.2	16.0	49.6	25.9
Charleston, SC	90.5	93.4	84.0	87.2	72.4	34.8	41.4	16.1	50.4	19.8
Charlotte, NC	88.8	90.5	88.1	84.6	63.0	34.7	37.1	25.7	57.5	17.0
Chicago, IL	88.3	91.1	87.4	90.8	66.7	37.4	40.9	22.3	64.4	14.4
Clarksville, TN	90.6	91.1	89.3	84.5	86.6	24.3	24.7	21.0	37.2	18.6
Cleveland, OH	90.2	92.1	84.1	87.6	74.1	30.7	33.9	14.8	63.0	14.9
College Station, TX	86.1	87.7	83.9	94.7	61.2	36.7	39.0	15.5	79.4	15.8
Colorado Springs, CO	93.8	95.1	94.1	86.3	80.3	37.8	40.0	26.2	42.9	20.1
Columbia, MO	94.2	95.2	87.6	92.9	80.5	46.0	47.7	18.1	67.2	35.1
Columbia, SC	89.5	91.5	87.1	89.3	64.3	31.9	36.6	22.0	53.9	19.5
Columbus, OH	91.3	92.4	87.2	88.3	75.0	36.1	37.7	21.1	63.4	25.0
Dallas, TX	85.2	85.6	90.4	88.1	58.8	34.4	35.1	26.2	60.5	13.1
Davenport, IA	91.0	92.4	79.9	83.8	72.6	26.7	27.2	16.1	48.0	15.7
Denver, CO	90.8	92.3	89.3	85.2	69.6	42.9	45.1	26.3	51.9	15.7
Des Moines, IA	92.4	94.1	84.2	75.7	61.5	36.9	38.0	19.4	40.6	13.2
Durham, NC	89.2	91.4	87.0	92.7	50.7	46.6	53.1	29.6	72.9	15.4
Edison, NJ	86.3	90.6	85.1	83.3	70.6	39.4	44.7	25.1	53.8	18.9
El Paso, TX	77.4	78.4	94.8	90.4	73.1	22.7	23.2	29.5	51.3	18.6
Fargo, ND	94.6	95.9	79.8	80.3	79.7	37.9	38.7	23.1	49.2	17.6
Fayetteville, NC	90.1	92.1	90.0	83.5	83.7	24.1	25.8	22.6	35.6	19.1
Fort Collins, CO	95.8	96.1	96.7	92.0	82.1	46.3	46.6	37.6	63.9	23.1
Fort Wayne, IN	89.7	91.7	84.0	62.4	62.2	26.9	28.3	14.9	36.1	10.0
Fort Worth, TX	85.2	85.6	90.4	88.1	58.8	34.4	35.1	26.2	60.5	13.1
Grand Rapids, MI	90.9	92.9	84.1	75.9	62.1	32.4	33.9	18.6	36.6	13.8
Greeley, CO	88.1	89.1	80.9	84.4	66.7	26.7	27.2	29.8	39.5	8.5
Green Bay, WI	91.8	93.4	86.0	81.1	55.8	27.2	28.0	13.2	39.5	8.4
Greensboro, NC	86.8	88.8	86.6	74.4	55.2	28.9	31.7	22.0	39.3	11.8
Honolulu, HI	91.7	97.2	97.0	88.6	92.7	34.3	47.7	28.7	35.4	24.5
Houston, TX	83.2	83.1	90.4	87.2	62.9	32.4	32.9	27.0	56.8	14.3
Huntsville, AL	89.7	91.0	85.9	90.5	67.3	38.3	40.3	29.2	58.5	23.0
Indianapolis, IN	89.4	91.0	85.2	82.7	61.5	33.9	36.0	19.8	55.0	16.1
Jackson, MS	87.3	92.0	82.6	86.7	59.9	30.2	38.2	20.7	59.9	20.1
Jacksonville, FL	90.6	91.9	86.9	87.3	83.9	30.5	32.8	18.5	48.2	26.9
Kansas City, MO	91.8	93.3	88.3	85.7	68.0	36.4	38.9	20.0	54.6	16.7
Lafayette, LA	83.2	86.3	74.9	69.5	64.1	22.8	26.1	11.8	31.1	12.2
Lakeland, FL	84.8	85.9	81.5	82.4	71.7	20.0	20.3	15.0	44.1	13.6
Las Vegas, NV	85.7	87.9	88.9	90.3	65.8	23.9	25.3	17.4	37.9	9.9
Lexington, KY	89.6	91.2	84.0	90.9	58.7	36.8	38.8	18.8	63.3	15.0
Lincoln, NE	93.5	95.0	87.8	78.5	70.9	38.3	39.1	23.1	45.0	20.5
Little Rock, AR	90.3	91.6	87.4	89.1	67.3	30.1	32.5	20.9	55.1	13.5
Los Angeles, CA	80.2	82.7	89.8	87.9	61.3	33.7	35.9	26.4	52.4	12.7
Louisville, KY	89.5	90.1	87.1	84.6	73.4	28.6	29.9	17.4	51.8	22.4

Table continued on next page.

Metro Area	High School Graduate or Higher (%)					Bachelor's Degree or Higher (%)				
	Total	White	Black	Asian	Hisp.[1]	Total	White	Black	Asian	Hisp.[1]
Madison, WI	95.2	96.2	88.9	90.2	75.6	45.5	45.8	21.5	67.9	25.5
Manchester, NH	91.8	92.2	88.0	88.1	72.2	37.3	36.6	24.2	63.9	18.7
Miami, FL	85.4	86.9	80.8	87.3	80.0	31.5	34.4	19.3	50.2	26.7
Midland, TX	83.6	84.0	84.1	84.0	67.4	27.2	28.2	18.5	53.8	10.2
Milwaukee, WI	91.1	94.1	82.8	83.5	67.8	35.1	39.2	14.1	51.4	14.1
Minneapolis, MN	93.5	96.1	82.4	80.8	67.2	41.2	43.4	21.4	44.6	18.7
Nashville, TN	89.5	90.5	87.5	83.1	63.2	34.8	36.0	26.9	50.1	16.1
New Haven, CT	90.1	91.7	87.4	90.0	74.6	34.9	37.0	21.1	65.3	15.8
New Orleans, LA	86.6	90.5	81.5	77.6	74.3	29.8	36.2	17.9	38.8	19.0
New York, NY	86.3	90.6	85.1	83.3	70.6	39.4	44.7	25.1	53.8	18.9
Oklahoma City, OK	88.9	89.9	90.2	84.5	60.1	30.1	31.5	21.3	46.1	12.5
Omaha, NE	91.4	92.8	87.4	75.2	59.5	35.8	37.1	22.2	49.1	14.4
Orlando, FL	89.5	91.1	85.5	88.4	83.6	31.3	32.8	21.9	51.6	22.4
Peoria, IL	91.7	93.0	79.9	92.2	74.5	28.4	28.8	13.1	69.9	21.0
Philadelphia, PA	90.3	92.8	86.9	84.2	69.4	37.0	41.1	20.6	56.1	17.5
Phoenix, AZ	87.2	89.0	89.6	88.1	67.1	30.8	31.8	24.7	57.2	12.5
Pittsburgh, PA	93.6	94.1	89.5	87.6	88.4	34.1	34.4	20.0	69.7	34.8
Portland, OR	91.8	93.3	88.2	86.7	67.8	38.9	39.5	27.0	50.4	19.0
Providence, RI	86.9	88.6	84.3	83.6	71.2	31.4	32.8	21.9	48.4	13.5
Provo, UT	94.1	94.7	94.1	94.1	73.7	39.6	39.9	32.7	59.2	20.3
Raleigh, NC	91.3	93.7	88.6	91.8	61.4	45.9	49.4	30.2	72.7	19.8
Reno, NV	88.3	90.1	90.0	90.4	62.5	30.4	31.9	20.0	44.0	11.0
Richmond, VA	89.5	92.2	84.6	87.7	66.8	36.3	42.0	21.3	61.8	21.1
Rochester, MN	93.9	95.3	79.1	82.4	70.1	37.6	37.7	17.6	54.3	21.5
Sacramento, CA	89.0	91.9	89.6	83.6	73.6	33.0	34.4	22.4	43.0	17.5
Salt Lake City, UT	90.5	93.8	85.8	85.6	67.3	33.9	36.2	25.6	48.3	13.2
San Antonio, TX	84.8	85.1	91.5	87.0	75.6	27.7	27.9	27.9	52.1	16.6
San Diego, CA	87.1	88.1	91.2	89.1	68.8	38.1	39.0	25.2	50.6	17.1
San Francisco, CA	88.9	93.1	90.3	87.2	70.6	48.7	54.8	27.7	54.5	20.5
San Jose, CA	87.9	90.1	91.9	90.7	68.4	50.4	48.4	38.1	64.9	16.5
Santa Rosa, CA	88.0	92.3	90.8	87.4	62.1	34.9	38.6	28.5	43.1	12.7
Savannah, GA	89.6	91.9	85.5	88.0	80.9	31.2	36.7	19.0	49.5	26.0
Seattle, WA	92.5	94.8	89.1	88.5	72.4	42.0	42.9	24.9	54.4	21.3
Sioux Falls, SD	92.7	94.4	71.6	71.3	65.6	33.0	34.5	12.5	38.6	13.2
Springfield, IL	92.4	93.7	81.3	94.3	87.0	33.5	34.8	17.3	65.9	32.4
Tallahassee, FL	90.6	93.8	83.5	96.2	81.2	38.0	43.3	23.0	79.7	31.8
Tampa, FL	89.4	90.5	86.4	85.6	79.2	29.6	30.0	22.2	51.0	21.3
Topeka, KS	92.3	93.4	87.4	88.7	76.7	28.5	29.8	12.8	56.9	13.6
Tucson, AZ	88.3	90.8	88.3	86.0	75.5	31.9	34.5	25.9	50.6	15.8
Tulsa, OK	89.2	90.7	89.2	78.9	61.1	27.2	29.2	19.3	37.4	12.0
Tuscaloosa, AL	87.4	89.8	83.2	85.2	71.6	27.6	32.7	16.5	67.0	11.5
Virginia Beach, VA	91.1	93.7	86.8	87.1	83.5	31.5	35.8	21.4	42.5	24.0
Washington, DC	90.7	93.6	91.2	91.2	66.9	50.6	58.5	34.3	64.9	25.4
Wichita, KS	89.9	91.5	85.4	81.8	65.1	30.3	31.9	16.9	37.4	14.5
Winston-Salem, NC	86.4	87.4	86.3	86.6	53.7	26.4	27.4	20.9	51.8	11.0
U.S.	87.7	89.6	85.4	86.8	67.7	31.5	32.9	21.1	53.5	15.8

Note: Figures shown cover persons 25 years old and over; Figures cover the Metropolitan Statistical Area—see Appendix B for areas included; (1) People of Hispanic origin can be of any race
Source: U.S. Census Bureau, 2014-2018 American Community Survey 5-Year Estimates

Cost of Living Index

Urban Area	Composite	Groceries	Housing	Utilities	Transp.	Health	Misc.
Albany, NY	108.3	116.1	113.7	100.3	101.4	102.3	105.6
Albuquerque, NM	93.8	104.8	84.5	87.7	97.2	99.8	96.6
Allentown, PA	104.4	98.4	114.0	103.4	104.8	94.6	100.6
Anchorage, AK	124.5	132.6	140.0	124.0	114.8	144.2	109.7
Ann Arbor, MI	n/a	n/a	n/a	n/a	n/a	n/a	n/a
Athens, GA	n/a	n/a	n/a	n/a	n/a	n/a	n/a
Atlanta, GA	102.8	103.4	103.5	85.1	103.6	107.1	106.0
Austin, TX	99.7	91.2	105.5	95.2	90.7	105.8	101.4
Baton Rouge	99.4	102.6	92.3	85.4	100.5	104.5	106.5
Boise City, ID	98.7	94.5	97.5	81.9	108.5	103.0	102.8
Boston, MA	151.0	109.3	228.6	120.5	112.0	118.3	129.3
Boulder, CO	n/a	n/a	n/a	n/a	n/a	n/a	n/a
Cape Coral, FL	100.6	107.8	89.6	98.8	98.7	108.5	106.3
Cedar Rapids, IA	96.2	94.8	83.0	102.1	96.6	107.0	103.9
Charleston, SC	97.2	99.7	93.2	120.4	86.6	97.5	95.9
Charlotte, NC	98.2	101.7	88.8	95.6	90.7	105.1	106.0
Chicago, IL	120.6	101.9	155.7	92.4	125.9	100.0	109.4
Clarksville, TN	n/a	n/a	n/a	n/a	n/a	n/a	n/a
Cleveland, OH	96.9	106.0	83.3	96.1	99.4	104.4	102.6
College Station, TX	n/a	n/a	n/a	n/a	n/a	n/a	n/a
Colorado Springs, CO	101.1	95.9	101.3	97.2	97.7	108.6	104.1
Columbia, MO	91.8	95.5	75.0	100.0	92.0	102.6	99.8
Columbia, SC	93.5	103.1	72.7	126.2	87.1	79.9	100.5
Columbus, OH	92.6	98.6	81.2	89.1	95.5	88.5	99.7
Dallas, TX	108.2	100.2	118.8	106.8	96.7	105.4	106.7
Davenport, IA	92.0	99.7	76.9	98.9	105.8	105.3	93.7
Denver, CO	111.3	98.3	139.3	80.5	100.9	103.6	106.6
Des Moines, IA	89.9	95.2	80.2	90.1	99.1	95.4	92.3
Durham, NC	n/a	n/a	n/a	n/a	n/a	n/a	n/a
Edison, NJ[1]	120.6	108.7	149.3	105.8	107.8	102.5	112.4
El Paso, TX	87.7	102.3	73.7	85.7	99.0	99.3	89.0
Fargo, ND	98.6	111.5	77.6	90.5	100.4	120.1	108.9
Fayetteville, NC	n/a	n/a	n/a	n/a	n/a	n/a	n/a
Fort Collins, CO	n/a	n/a	n/a	n/a	n/a	n/a	n/a
Fort Wayne, IN	86.9	86.7	62.3	95.7	99.5	101.5	98.6
Fort Worth, TX	94.9	92.4	88.4	107.2	96.9	101.5	96.2
Grand Rapids, MI	94.1	92.8	87.4	98.5	104.1	92.3	96.3
Greeley, CO	n/a	n/a	n/a	n/a	n/a	n/a	n/a
Green Bay, WI	91.1	91.0	77.9	97.4	97.7	101.8	96.6
Greensboro, NC[2]	90.8	101.4	66.7	94.6	92.0	119.5	100.5
Honolulu, HI	192.9	165.0	332.6	172.3	138.2	118.8	124.2
Houston, TX	95.8	88.4	91.2	105.8	95.2	92.0	100.3
Huntsville, AL	91.3	95.1	66.6	99.0	97.3	96.4	104.7
Indianapolis, IN	92.4	94.1	78.4	105.4	97.9	90.6	98.0
Jackson, MS	n/a	n/a	n/a	n/a	n/a	n/a	n/a
Jacksonville, FL	91.7	98.4	88.0	97.7	86.0	83.7	92.7
Kansas City, MO	95.8	102.4	82.6	100.6	92.6	105.9	101.7
Lafayette, LA	88.9	101.8	72.0	88.0	104.7	88.0	93.3
Lakeland, FL	n/a	n/a	n/a	n/a	n/a	n/a	n/a
Las Vegas, NV	103.6	95.8	118.3	98.6	114.0	100.2	94.2
Lexington, KY	92.7	89.9	83.7	95.6	96.7	78.9	100.7
Lincoln, NE	93.0	95.6	78.7	90.2	93.4	105.8	102.2
Little Rock, AR	96.0	95.1	88.1	97.4	94.7	89.6	103.2
Los Angeles, CA	146.7	116.3	230.6	106.2	134.8	110.8	112.0
Louisville, KY	94.1	91.8	79.8	94.6	98.1	105.2	103.7
Madison, WI	107.0	107.6	108.6	99.8	104.4	124.0	106.0

Table continued on next page.

Urban Area	Composite	Groceries	Housing	Utilities	Transp.	Health	Misc.
Manchester, NH	108.9	102.2	109.6	117.9	104.1	116.0	108.9
Miami, FL	115.0	110.5	144.3	102.0	101.5	100.6	102.7
Midland, TX	102.1	93.6	91.5	106.6	104.1	96.5	112.6
Milwaukee, WI	96.7	93.4	100.5	94.8	99.8	115.9	92.4
Minneapolis, MN	106.6	103.6	102.9	97.5	104.4	105.6	113.9
Nashville, TN	98.9	99.5	98.5	97.0	97.9	92.4	100.4
New Haven, CT	122.3	111.0	128.5	136.7	110.6	115.8	121.9
New Orleans, LA	105.0	102.6	125.5	81.5	101.3	115.1	96.1
New York, NY[3]	181.6	128.4	339.0	121.4	113.7	107.1	123.1
Oklahoma City, OK	86.0	93.3	69.6	95.3	86.2	95.0	92.1
Omaha, NE	92.3	96.8	83.6	99.4	98.3	96.4	93.3
Orlando, FL	92.1	100.7	85.1	97.2	89.3	88.3	94.1
Peoria, IL	92.9	89.7	76.5	93.7	106.3	96.8	102.7
Philadelphia, PA	110.9	118.7	116.5	105.6	116.1	101.8	104.8
Phoenix, AZ	99.3	99.7	103.8	109.5	107.2	90.1	91.9
Pittsburgh, PA	103.1	111.9	105.7	116.1	114.0	93.1	92.6
Portland, OR	134.7	112.4	186.4	87.1	131.0	115.6	119.4
Providence, RI	119.2	106.7	132.8	126.4	112.1	109.3	114.6
Provo, UT	98.2	93.0	96.1	84.7	100.7	94.5	105.4
Raleigh, NC	95.4	92.7	89.0	98.3	90.9	103.8	100.9
Reno, NV	114.1	118.7	125.8	85.9	126.3	113.9	107.6
Richmond, VA	94.2	89.0	86.0	97.6	86.9	106.7	102.1
Rochester, MN	n/a	n/a	n/a	n/a	n/a	n/a	n/a
Sacramento, CA	118.4	120.2	134.2	102.9	139.0	113.6	104.8
Salt Lake City, UT	103.6	108.0	106.7	87.8	103.6	105.7	103.6
San Antonio, TX	89.5	88.0	82.2	87.6	89.1	87.2	96.5
San Diego, CA	142.1	116.1	216.3	123.2	129.2	107.3	107.3
San Francisco, CA	197.9	131.3	368.9	123.0	145.3	129.6	133.4
San Jose, CA	n/a	n/a	n/a	n/a	n/a	n/a	n/a
Santa Rosa, CA	n/a	n/a	n/a	n/a	n/a	n/a	n/a
Savannah, GA	89.5	95.7	66.2	96.0	94.9	106.1	100.0
Seattle, WA	157.5	129.1	227.6	108.0	137.8	128.6	136.2
Sioux Falls, SD	92.5	96.3	86.3	84.7	91.9	107.7	96.3
Springfield, IL	n/a	n/a	n/a	n/a	n/a	n/a	n/a
Tallahassee, FL	97.5	107.4	93.3	86.5	96.2	99.6	99.9
Tampa, FL	91.2	104.8	79.2	85.9	99.4	98.3	93.7
Topeka, KS	89.4	95.5	76.0	98.1	97.7	95.7	92.1
Tucson, AZ	97.5	100.5	87.9	99.9	101.1	98.7	102.0
Tulsa, OK	86.0	96.2	62.7	99.5	84.4	91.6	96.1
Tuscaloosa, AL	n/a	n/a	n/a	n/a	n/a	n/a	n/a
Virginia Beach, VA[4]	94.1	92.7	89.1	97.4	92.2	90.4	98.7
Washington, DC	159.9	116.0	277.1	117.9	110.6	95.8	118.1
Wichita, KS	91.1	94.3	69.6	99.3	95.3	96.1	102.5
Winston-Salem, NC	90.8	101.4	66.7	94.6	92.0	119.5	100.5
U.S.	100.0	100.0	100.0	100.0	100.0	100.0	100.0

Note: The Cost of Living Index measures regional differences in the cost of consumer goods and services, excluding taxes and non-consumer expenditures, for professional and managerial households in the top income quintile. It is based on more than 50,000 prices covering almost 60 different items for which prices are collected three times a year by chambers of commerce, economic development organizations or university applied economic centers in each participating urban area. The numbers shown should be read as a percentage above or below the national average of 100. For example, a value of 115.4 in the groceries column indicates that grocery prices are 15.4% higher than the national average. Small differences in the index numbers should not be interpreted as significant. In cases where data is not available for the city, data for the metro area or for a neighboring city has been provided and noted as follows: (1) Middlesex-Monmouth NJ; (2) Winston-Salem, NC; (3) Brooklyn, NY; (4) Hampton Roads-SE Virginia
Source: The Council for Community and Economic Research (formerly ACCRA), Cost of Living Index, 2019

Grocery Prices

Urban Area	T-Bone Steak ($/pound)	Frying Chicken ($/pound)	Whole Milk ($/half gal.)	Eggs ($/dozen)	Orange Juice ($/64 oz.)	Coffee ($/11.5 oz.)
Albany, NY	11.15	1.40	2.27	2.59	3.77	4.27
Albuquerque, NM	11.41	1.70	2.10	1.77	3.62	5.42
Allentown, PA	13.11	1.39	1.94	1.42	3.35	3.68
Anchorage, AK	14.19	1.70	2.81	2.43	4.21	5.44
Ann Arbor, MI	n/a	n/a	n/a	n/a	n/a	n/a
Athens, GA	n/a	n/a	n/a	n/a	n/a	n/a
Atlanta, GA	13.63	1.35	2.09	1.15	3.48	4.77
Austin, TX	8.89	1.20	1.74	1.78	3.16	4.18
Baton Rouge	10.19	1.50	2.67	2.18	3.86	4.12
Boise City, ID	11.02	1.10	1.46	1.24	3.89	4.65
Boston, MA	13.17	1.43	2.10	1.89	3.63	4.42
Boulder, CO	n/a	n/a	n/a	n/a	n/a	n/a
Cape Coral, FL	11.26	1.72	2.59	1.60	3.86	3.87
Cedar Rapids, IA	11.88	1.75	2.14	1.55	3.04	4.52
Charleston, SC	10.17	1.23	2.00	1.60	3.55	3.89
Charlotte, NC	10.79	1.21	2.08	1.29	3.92	3.91
Chicago, IL	12.57	1.66	2.09	1.36	3.99	4.19
Clarksville, TN	n/a	n/a	n/a	n/a	n/a	n/a
Cleveland, OH	14.31	1.49	1.63	1.43	3.87	4.80
College Station, TX	n/a	n/a	n/a	n/a	n/a	n/a
Colorado Springs, CO	11.85	1.47	1.48	1.33	3.34	4.77
Columbia, MO	10.84	1.55	1.97	1.24	3.63	4.41
Columbia, SC	11.84	1.25	1.98	1.22	3.60	4.37
Columbus, OH	12.81	1.22	1.45	1.01	3.09	7.47
Dallas, TX	9.66	1.47	1.85	1.20	3.78	5.05
Davenport, IA	11.55	1.66	2.30	1.36	2.98	4.58
Denver, CO	12.90	1.45	1.71	1.58	3.42	4.64
Des Moines, IA	10.37	1.76	2.13	1.56	2.99	4.22
Durham, NC	n/a	n/a	n/a	n/a	n/a	n/a
Edison, NJ[1]	13.20	1.72	2.18	1.68	3.55	4.19
El Paso, TX	8.23	1.95	2.10	1.84	4.09	4.39
Fargo, ND	13.65	1.95	2.59	1.81	4.01	4.14
Fayetteville, NC	n/a	n/a	n/a	n/a	n/a	n/a
Fort Collins, CO	n/a	n/a	n/a	n/a	n/a	n/a
Fort Wayne, IN	12.87	0.96	1.37	0.84	3.24	3.97
Fort Worth, TX	8.96	1.39	1.51	1.18	3.24	4.21
Grand Rapids, MI	11.76	1.21	1.94	1.49	3.36	3.17
Greeley, CO	n/a	n/a	n/a	n/a	n/a	n/a
Green Bay, WI	13.00	1.71	1.35	0.79	3.49	4.19
Greensboro, NC[2]	12.05	1.42	1.56	1.36	3.88	3.90
Honolulu, HI	11.29	2.45	4.09	4.18	5.32	8.10
Houston, TX	10.51	1.23	1.35	1.24	3.32	3.45
Huntsville, AL	12.38	1.53	1.47	0.85	3.48	4.08
Indianapolis, IN	11.62	1.36	1.48	1.04	3.47	4.26
Jackson, MS	n/a	n/a	n/a	n/a	n/a	n/a
Jacksonville, FL	10.39	1.18	2.08	1.56	3.44	3.77
Kansas City, MO	12.07	1.73	2.02	1.33	3.27	4.27
Lafayette, LA	12.16	1.33	2.09	1.86	3.71	4.08
Lakeland, FL	n/a	n/a	n/a	n/a	n/a	n/a
Las Vegas, NV	7.52	1.21	2.51	2.09	4.18	4.92
Lexington, KY	10.67	1.04	1.64	1.03	3.27	3.83
Lincoln, NE	10.97	1.47	2.35	1.70	3.12	3.91
Little Rock, AR	11.27	1.22	1.81	1.33	2.91	4.01
Los Angeles, CA	11.38	1.76	2.17	2.74	3.83	5.11
Louisville, KY	13.36	1.33	1.25	0.74	3.39	4.02

Table continued on next page.

Urban Area	T-Bone Steak ($/pound)	Frying Chicken ($/pound)	Whole Milk ($/half gal.)	Eggs ($/dozen)	Orange Juice ($/64 oz.)	Coffee ($/11.5 oz.)
Madison, WI	14.20	1.67	2.11	1.18	3.32	4.81
Manchester, NH	13.04	1.43	2.87	1.51	3.27	4.03
Miami, FL	13.95	1.56	2.76	1.67	3.54	3.44
Midland, TX	10.87	1.29	1.54	1.89	3.22	4.25
Milwaukee, WI	11.95	1.31	1.70	0.94	3.05	4.27
Minneapolis, MN	13.60	2.12	2.58	1.82	3.70	4.69
Nashville, TN	12.57	1.59	1.94	1.19	3.59	4.44
New Haven, CT	13.82	1.80	2.37	2.13	3.75	4.06
New Orleans, LA	11.82	1.13	2.29	1.82	3.71	3.87
New York, NY[3]	12.83	2.20	2.62	2.40	4.30	4.96
Oklahoma City, OK	10.39	1.49	1.84	1.33	3.15	4.07
Omaha, NE	11.14	1.59	1.63	1.33	3.28	4.31
Orlando, FL	10.82	1.42	2.49	1.71	3.40	3.81
Peoria, IL	10.48	1.03	0.88	1.02	3.36	4.41
Philadelphia, PA	12.88	1.51	2.10	2.16	4.18	4.62
Phoenix, AZ	12.70	1.91	1.59	1.88	3.69	4.73
Pittsburgh, PA	12.98	1.83	2.00	1.56	3.59	4.79
Portland, OR	13.55	1.63	1.95	1.98	3.94	5.24
Providence, RI	12.12	1.59	3.09	1.82	3.30	4.16
Provo, UT	11.42	1.61	1.41	1.29	3.62	4.36
Raleigh, NC	9.37	1.03	1.82	1.56	3.65	3.58
Reno, NV	11.24	1.39	2.63	2.49	3.74	5.79
Richmond, VA	10.09	1.06	1.51	1.02	3.24	3.42
Rochester, MN	n/a	n/a	n/a	n/a	n/a	n/a
Sacramento, CA	13.01	1.48	2.40	2.91	3.53	6.48
Salt Lake City, UT	11.90	2.59	1.56	2.11	3.68	4.51
San Antonio, TX	10.01	0.98	1.39	1.77	3.11	4.04
San Diego, CA	10.60	1.76	2.17	2.74	3.83	5.15
San Francisco, CA	15.58	1.56	2.65	3.67	4.39	6.69
San Jose, CA	n/a	n/a	n/a	n/a	n/a	n/a
Santa Rosa, CA	n/a	n/a	n/a	n/a	n/a	n/a
Savannah, GA	10.73	1.60	1.86	1.40	3.37	4.01
Seattle, WA	14.68	2.04	1.99	1.97	4.18	5.69
Sioux Falls, SD	7.66	1.91	2.11	0.99	2.99	4.51
Springfield, IL	n/a	n/a	n/a	n/a	n/a	n/a
Tallahassee, FL	11.09	1.58	2.52	1.36	3.82	3.73
Tampa, FL	9.55	1.75	2.37	1.68	3.09	3.95
Topeka, KS	9.96	1.93	1.37	0.93	3.62	4.36
Tucson, AZ	12.43	1.67	1.54	1.67	3.27	4.99
Tulsa, OK	10.45	1.35	2.14	1.57	3.70	3.95
Tuscaloosa, AL	n/a	n/a	n/a	n/a	n/a	n/a
Virginia Beach, VA[4]	9.26	1.22	1.68	1.07	3.45	3.92
Washington, DC	13.31	1.74	2.36	1.74	3.83	4.90
Wichita, KS	12.06	1.34	1.49	0.82	3.56	3.86
Winston-Salem, NC	12.05	1.42	1.56	1.36	3.88	3.90
Average*	11.40	1.41	1.93	1.54	3.51	4.30
Minimum*	7.40	0.92	0.85	0.58	2.67	2.90
Maximum*	15.58	2.68	4.09	4.18	5.57	8.10

Note: T-Bone Steak (price per pound); Frying Chicken (price per pound, whole fryer); Whole Milk (half gallon carton); Eggs (price per dozen, Grade A, large); Orange Juice (64 oz. Tropicana or Florida Natural); Coffee (11.5 oz. can, vacuum-packed, Maxwell House, Hills Bros, or Folgers); (*) Values for the local area are compared with the average, minimum, and maximum values for all 290 areas in the Cost of Living Index report; n/a not available; In cases where data is not available for the city, data for the metro area or for a neighboring city has been provided and noted as follows: (1) Middlesex-Monmouth NJ; (2) Winston-Salem, NC; (3) Brooklyn, NY; (4) Hampton Roads-SE Virginia
Source: The Council for Community and Economic Research (formerly ACCRA), Cost of Living Index, 2019

Housing and Utility Costs

Urban Area	New Home Price ($)	Apartment Rent ($/month)	All Electric ($/month)	Part Electric ($/month)	Other Energy ($/month)	Telephone ($/month)
Albany, NY	433,356	1,190	-	70.13	96.46	183.90
Albuquerque, NM	311,767	941	-	91.78	39.78	180.80
Allentown, PA	394,322	1,469	-	96.51	78.76	184.70
Anchorage, AK	543,470	1,227	-	110.69	129.15	179.90
Ann Arbor, MI	n/a	n/a	n/a	n/a	n/a	n/a
Athens, GA	n/a	n/a	n/a	n/a	n/a	n/a
Atlanta, GA	370,059	1,209	-	88.48	35.32	180.70
Austin, TX	335,082	1,484	-	105.64	47.75	181.10
Baton Rouge	327,638	1,055	128.94	-	-	174.60
Boise City, ID	349,211	1,131	-	66.23	58.58	165.90
Boston, MA	716,119	3,454	-	67.96	163.66	176.80
Boulder, CO	n/a	n/a	n/a	n/a	n/a	n/a
Cape Coral, FL	319,458	1,017	163.03	-	-	182.60
Cedar Rapids, IA	323,537	791	-	122.94	54.21	176.50
Charleston, SC	295,161	1,323	227.31	-	-	182.60
Charlotte, NC	297,282	1,202	158.72	-	-	175.60
Chicago, IL	517,211	2,131	-	80.25	52.14	199.00
Clarksville, TN	n/a	n/a	n/a	n/a	n/a	n/a
Cleveland, OH	284,000	1,083	-	77.88	81.73	176.20
College Station, TX	n/a	n/a	n/a	n/a	n/a	n/a
Colorado Springs, CO	343,668	1,310	-	99.43	62.28	177.80
Columbia, MO	287,072	727	-	96.39	67.58	186.40
Columbia, SC	260,179	843	-	112.50	133.03	181.10
Columbus, OH	267,385	1,111	-	74.29	65.24	175.50
Dallas, TX	389,520	1,588	-	135.82	52.18	181.10
Davenport, IA	284,507	871	-	93.38	69.08	184.00
Denver, CO	515,298	1,500	-	54.25	54.96	182.10
Des Moines, IA	327,713	685	-	77.52	65.21	175.00
Durham, NC	n/a	n/a	n/a	n/a	n/a	n/a
Edison, NJ[1]	518,589	1,731	-	120.27	68.70	175.50
El Paso, TX	255,750	944	-	81.88	43.38	181.10
Fargo, ND	279,364	911	-	74.92	62.59	184.00
Fayetteville, NC	n/a	n/a	n/a	n/a	n/a	n/a
Fort Collins, CO	n/a	n/a	n/a	n/a	n/a	n/a
Fort Wayne, IN	211,226	780	-	96.48	59.30	179.90
Fort Worth, TX	275,038	1,303	-	137.44	52.18	180.30
Grand Rapids, MI	281,576	1,182	-	97.35	69.16	176.70
Greeley, CO	n/a	n/a	n/a	n/a	n/a	n/a
Green Bay, WI	294,559	803	-	80.66	83.63	175.30
Greensboro, NC[2]	224,859	846	160.51	-	-	168.70
Honolulu, HI	1,389,623	3,015	388.18	-	-	172.60
Houston, TX	304,837	1,247	-	144.36	41.62	179.60
Huntsville, AL	226,546	859	167.28	-	-	177.50
Indianapolis, IN	258,287	1,062	-	108.07	76.54	179.90
Jackson, MS	n/a	n/a	n/a	n/a	n/a	n/a
Jacksonville, FL	282,646	1,249	159.47	-	-	183.20
Kansas City, MO	268,109	1,141	-	100.21	66.26	185.40
Lafayette, LA	253,880	885	-	87.78	50.94	171.90
Lakeland, FL	n/a	n/a	n/a	n/a	n/a	n/a
Las Vegas, NV	447,464	1,208	-	123.79	46.71	171.40
Lexington, KY	302,594	922	-	77.04	77.84	181.00
Lincoln, NE	285,102	868	-	69.68	62.56	190.10
Little Rock, AR	350,708	763	-	91.46	64.82	186.50
Los Angeles, CA	816,438	2,800	-	110.55	72.55	185.50
Louisville, KY	272,069	1,029	-	77.08	77.84	176.50

Table continued on next page.

Urban Area	New Home Price ($)	Apartment Rent ($/month)	All Electric ($/month)	Part Electric ($/month)	Other Energy ($/month)	Telephone ($/month)
Madison, WI	417,025	1,091	-	103.44	68.68	174.30
Manchester, NH	357,972	1,550	-	114.02	110.60	175.60
Miami, FL	454,502	2,155	171.70	-	-	183.80
Midland, TX	294,809	1,308	-	154.76	33.44	180.00
Milwaukee, WI	353,731	1,250	-	100.18	56.41	175.00
Minneapolis, MN	371,899	1,192	-	94.84	68.83	176.60
Nashville, TN	342,111	1,199	-	95.11	65.63	178.50
New Haven, CT	403,793	1,934	-	172.38	109.88	173.10
New Orleans, LA	446,331	1,490	-	77.05	39.66	175.80
New York, NY[3]	1,338,023	3,397	-	89.05	138.30	186.70
Oklahoma City, OK	241,727	850	-	93.97	60.92	179.40
Omaha, NE	282,378	1,042	-	89.71	69.48	190.50
Orlando, FL	278,500	1,155	158.17	-	-	182.70
Peoria, IL	294,117	765	-	75.48	69.26	187.00
Philadelphia, PA	420,084	1,490	-	103.71	76.75	186.70
Phoenix, AZ	334,870	1,424	199.93	-	-	175.40
Pittsburgh, PA	372,146	1,257	-	111.84	99.95	186.20
Portland, OR	616,272	2,542	-	80.65	60.06	165.50
Providence, RI	432,805	1,890	-	134.26	109.07	185.10
Provo, UT	359,770	1,105	-	67.77	53.84	182.30
Raleigh, NC	284,183	1,322	-	104.27	62.24	175.60
Reno, NV	463,121	1,243	-	102.75	28.51	173.60
Richmond, VA	301,136	1,070	-	88.79	77.11	173.60
Rochester, MN	n/a	n/a	n/a	n/a	n/a	n/a
Sacramento, CA	440,447	1,904	-	140.22	35.20	182.50
Salt Lake City, UT	396,378	1,273	-	74.86	55.23	183.00
San Antonio, TX	259,713	1,211	-	94.53	37.03	180.30
San Diego, CA	800,746	2,391	-	176.98	65.93	172.00
San Francisco, CA	1,297,511	4,200	-	177.61	49.30	194.10
San Jose, CA	n/a	n/a	n/a	n/a	n/a	n/a
Santa Rosa, CA	n/a	n/a	n/a	n/a	n/a	n/a
Savannah, GA	221,165	876	158.07	-	-	177.90
Seattle, WA	813,440	2,650	185.14	-	-	189.90
Sioux Falls, SD	334,668	845	-	81.96	43.38	177.00
Springfield, IL	n/a	n/a	n/a	n/a	n/a	n/a
Tallahassee, FL	327,617	1,103	125.05	-	-	184.80
Tampa, FL	255,976	1,129	123.29	-	-	184.70
Topeka, KS	290,994	785	-	90.32	67.93	186.70
Tucson, AZ	327,417	929	-	119.11	50.92	177.60
Tulsa, OK	231,194	679	-	105.15	62.58	179.20
Tuscaloosa, AL	n/a	n/a	n/a	n/a	n/a	n/a
Virginia Beach, VA[4]	309,973	1,133	-	91.27	74.15	173.60
Washington, DC	1,041,970	3,038	-	144.17	77.49	180.20
Wichita, KS	257,033	754	-	99.98	63.24	184.30
Winston-Salem, NC	224,859	846	160.51	-	-	168.70
Average*	362,090	1,142	174.35	100.00	67.76	179.60
Minimum*	198,329	501	91.58	31.44	28.51	165.30
Maximum*	2,074,561	5,050	388.18	239.41	306.15	207.90

*Note: **New Home Price** (2,400 sf living area, 8,000 sf lot, in urban area with full utilities); **Apartment Rent** (950 sf 2 bedroom/1.5 or 2 bath, unfurnished, excluding all utilities except water); **All Electric** (average monthly cost for an all-electric home); **Part Electric** (average monthly cost for a part-electric home); **Other Energy** (average monthly cost for natural gas, fuel oil, coal, wood, and any other forms of energy except electricity); **Telephone** (price includes the base monthly rate plus taxes and fees for three lines of mobile phone service); (*) Values for the local area are compared with the average, minimum, and maximum values for all 290 areas in the Cost of Living Index report; n/a not available; In cases where data is not available for the city, data for the metro area or for a neighboring city has been provided and noted as follows: (1) Middlesex-Monmouth NJ; (2) Winston-Salem, NC; (3) Brooklyn, NY; (4) Hampton Roads-SE Virginia Source: The Council for Community and Economic Research (formerly ACCRA), Cost of Living Index, 2019*

Health Care, Transportation, and Other Costs

Urban Area	Doctor ($/visit)	Dentist ($/visit)	Optometrist ($/visit)	Gasoline ($/gallon)	Beauty Salon ($/visit)	Men's Shirt ($)
Albany, NY	109.68	101.97	142.26	2.64	43.50	33.49
Albuquerque, NM	106.82	105.73	108.02	2.30	51.55	35.31
Allentown, PA	79.67	108.36	90.88	2.72	40.85	27.20
Anchorage, AK	183.95	142.44	207.79	2.92	49.25	24.99
Ann Arbor, MI	n/a	n/a	n/a	n/a	n/a	n/a
Athens, GA	n/a	n/a	n/a	n/a	n/a	n/a
Atlanta, GA	117.77	115.47	109.20	2.53	47.47	27.40
Austin, TX	115.66	112.67	115.60	2.31	47.97	30.79
Baton Rouge	112.88	108.00	122.24	2.22	48.39	43.53
Boise City, ID	126.99	92.06	121.08	2.67	37.35	42.17
Boston, MA	174.18	107.27	97.53	2.59	62.80	53.69
Boulder, CO	n/a	n/a	n/a	n/a	n/a	n/a
Cape Coral, FL	123.50	110.33	85.74	2.27	26.00	24.95
Cedar Rapids, IA	111.14	113.18	113.67	2.44	37.05	31.85
Charleston, SC	124.44	99.47	79.60	2.22	51.67	24.38
Charlotte, NC	114.02	118.47	117.17	2.28	35.60	33.12
Chicago, IL	105.00	102.00	97.00	3.25	69.77	32.00
Clarksville, TN	n/a	n/a	n/a	n/a	n/a	n/a
Cleveland, OH	108.73	109.10	86.96	2.53	34.07	38.88
College Station, TX	n/a	n/a	n/a	n/a	n/a	n/a
Colorado Springs, CO	147.37	96.62	112.63	2.38	41.67	25.87
Columbia, MO	137.89	88.73	98.53	2.34	37.29	33.87
Columbia, SC	102.00	72.89	52.22	2.24	41.08	24.65
Columbus, OH	101.19	85.08	63.69	2.50	35.60	30.65
Dallas, TX	116.41	111.13	92.19	2.33	47.62	47.43
Davenport, IA	133.08	96.72	87.50	2.45	32.58	37.77
Denver, CO	121.48	101.92	105.86	2.44	42.92	30.35
Des Moines, IA	120.67	82.28	110.26	2.40	30.44	22.15
Durham, NC	n/a	n/a	n/a	n/a	n/a	n/a
Edison, NJ[1]	93.33	115.80	107.93	2.63	37.53	36.33
El Paso, TX	109.35	94.90	99.98	2.58	28.22	26.80
Fargo, ND	181.26	103.56	106.59	2.32	36.12	43.09
Fayetteville, NC	n/a	n/a	n/a	n/a	n/a	n/a
Fort Collins, CO	n/a	n/a	n/a	n/a	n/a	n/a
Fort Wayne, IN	129.50	95.89	76.53	2.47	30.22	35.58
Fort Worth, TX	110.37	104.58	98.67	2.28	47.26	36.62
Grand Rapids, MI	97.28	91.25	96.06	2.66	36.78	17.74
Greeley, CO	n/a	n/a	n/a	n/a	n/a	n/a
Green Bay, WI	156.95	88.29	63.24	2.26	25.17	30.64
Greensboro, NC[2]	152.38	123.94	113.53	2.41	40.00	41.73
Honolulu, HI	146.82	100.67	180.04	3.44	70.67	57.78
Houston, TX	88.45	95.53	117.79	2.17	60.87	39.28
Huntsville, AL	106.72	93.69	118.50	2.23	35.94	41.39
Indianapolis, IN	94.37	93.20	58.27	2.56	39.63	46.29
Jackson, MS	n/a	n/a	n/a	n/a	n/a	n/a
Jacksonville, FL	73.08	94.07	63.27	2.36	54.33	23.33
Kansas City, MO	130.62	101.33	107.23	2.28	33.57	41.26
Lafayette, LA	91.04	80.72	89.02	2.24	39.56	23.28
Lakeland, FL	n/a	n/a	n/a	n/a	n/a	n/a
Las Vegas, NV	112.17	101.81	114.83	2.99	45.57	31.79
Lexington, KY	82.61	70.27	74.78	2.41	39.60	31.45
Lincoln, NE	139.62	93.77	102.20	2.42	40.02	47.22
Little Rock, AR	124.17	65.61	97.00	2.19	41.80	33.55
Los Angeles, CA	126.17	109.00	120.27	3.65	67.85	40.97
Louisville, KY	156.50	86.89	76.33	2.58	37.00	39.45

Table continued on next page.

Urban Area	Doctor ($/visit)	Dentist ($/visit)	Optometrist ($/visit)	Gasoline ($/gallon)	Beauty Salon ($/visit)	Men's Shirt ($)
Madison, WI	196.00	107.89	60.55	2.49	41.89	30.94
Manchester, NH	152.49	121.64	101.89	2.59	36.32	34.01
Miami, FL	98.62	106.33	105.27	2.26	53.31	31.88
Midland, TX	82.95	103.28	99.33	2.53	35.00	30.33
Milwaukee, WI	181.19	102.34	55.33	2.54	38.81	24.53
Minneapolis, MN	150.35	87.29	90.36	2.41	35.33	37.08
Nashville, TN	105.09	95.09	91.58	2.51	41.58	33.06
New Haven, CT	131.64	122.22	118.87	2.76	48.02	39.49
New Orleans, LA	150.56	107.95	89.00	2.24	42.11	34.77
New York, NY[3]	116.89	116.47	100.16	2.78	69.82	49.68
Oklahoma City, OK	101.98	91.50	102.51	2.12	39.79	20.91
Omaha, NE	129.23	75.22	111.77	2.36	34.09	21.25
Orlando, FL	79.27	92.72	75.88	2.34	47.17	20.30
Peoria, IL	109.58	93.39	119.04	2.76	24.64	37.50
Philadelphia, PA	132.00	98.89	102.00	2.82	59.50	31.23
Phoenix, AZ	99.17	88.11	95.58	2.76	44.84	23.99
Pittsburgh, PA	91.06	98.19	79.04	2.83	29.18	20.06
Portland, OR	155.28	99.47	135.00	3.30	55.33	42.90
Providence, RI	157.76	92.69	130.63	2.68	54.00	34.44
Provo, UT	111.02	91.50	83.71	2.55	38.40	23.04
Raleigh, NC	134.00	99.00	99.33	2.56	49.50	30.66
Reno, NV	154.65	106.54	116.85	3.38	39.73	22.63
Richmond, VA	138.55	100.95	115.47	2.21	46.47	28.89
Rochester, MN	n/a	n/a	n/a	n/a	n/a	n/a
Sacramento, CA	149.63	102.97	129.67	3.62	54.68	23.23
Salt Lake City, UT	110.72	113.00	90.35	2.52	43.42	25.51
San Antonio, TX	91.67	84.16	91.69	2.18	38.93	21.98
San Diego, CA	122.92	103.33	112.00	3.43	60.42	39.07
San Francisco, CA	155.67	138.48	142.26	3.79	79.29	48.15
San Jose, CA	n/a	n/a	n/a	n/a	n/a	n/a
Santa Rosa, CA	n/a	n/a	n/a	n/a	n/a	n/a
Savannah, GA	120.19	112.56	86.55	2.25	33.81	29.19
Seattle, WA	136.67	147.50	159.86	3.49	47.00	45.00
Sioux Falls, SD	141.52	98.97	123.05	2.45	30.08	23.84
Springfield, IL	n/a	n/a	n/a	n/a	n/a	n/a
Tallahassee, FL	116.71	96.54	76.53	2.43	36.07	30.99
Tampa, FL	110.42	106.13	86.59	2.40	36.56	21.98
Topeka, KS	99.80	94.77	123.49	2.32	28.55	42.96
Tucson, AZ	121.57	89.67	88.07	2.46	50.63	51.33
Tulsa, OK	107.93	81.56	91.94	2.09	36.56	29.72
Tuscaloosa, AL	n/a	n/a	n/a	n/a	n/a	n/a
Virginia Beach, VA[4]	70.83	105.02	97.60	2.33	37.00	39.54
Washington, DC	111.27	94.38	78.00	2.78	60.89	39.50
Wichita, KS	104.74	86.14	157.23	2.31	40.16	43.64
Winston-Salem, NC	152.38	123.94	113.53	2.41	40.00	41.73
Average*	114.85	97.58	106.10	2.50	38.15	32.15
Minimum*	39.00	62.22	52.22	1.53	16.88	10.27
Maximum*	206.67	151.53	258.67	3.79	79.29	59.30

*Note: **Doctor** (general practitioners routine exam of an established patient); **Dentist** (adult teeth cleaning and periodic oral examination); **Optometrist** (full vision eye exam for established adult patient); **Gasoline** (one gallon regular unleaded, national brand, including all taxes, cash price at self-service pump if available); **Beauty Salon** (woman's shampoo, trim, and blow-dry); **Men's Shirt** (cotton/polyester dress shirt, pinpoint weave, long sleeves); (*) Values for the local area are compared with the average, minimum, and maximum values for all 290 areas in the Cost of Living Index report; n/a not available; In cases where data is not available for the city, data for the metro area or for a neighboring city has been provided and noted as follows: (1) Middlesex-Monmouth NJ; (2) Winston-Salem, NC; (3) Brooklyn, NY; (4) Hampton Roads-SE Virginia*
Source: The Council for Community and Economic Research (formerly ACCRA), Cost of Living Index, 2019

Number of Medical Professionals

City	Area Covered	MDs[1]	DOs[1,2]	Dentists	Podiatrists	Chiropractors	Optometrists
Albany, NY	Albany County	581.7	38.4	91.8	8.1	20.2	18.9
Albuquerque, NM	Bernalillo County	449.8	21.9	85.2	9.0	24.5	16.8
Allentown, PA	Lehigh County	354.4	85.7	86.1	12.8	29.9	19.3
Anchorage, AK	Anchorage (B) Borough	349.2	46.5	124.5	5.1	60.7	29.2
Ann Arbor, MI	Washtenaw County	1,230.3	41.6	176.8	7.3	25.3	16.4
Athens, GA	Clarke County	311.7	14.2	51.0	4.7	22.8	16.5
Atlanta, GA	Fulton County	499.9	11.6	70.5	4.9	54.4	15.9
Austin, TX	Travis County	315.7	20.1	69.7	4.4	33.4	15.9
Baton Rouge, LA	East Baton Rouge Parish	383.9	7.8	76.0	3.9	11.3	13.6
Boise City, ID	Ada County	288.7	33.5	80.0	3.4	55.3	18.9
Boston, MA	Suffolk County	1,453.2	15.0	207.4	9.2	13.9	32.3
Boulder, CO	Boulder County	360.9	33.5	102.7	6.4	76.1	27.0
Cape Coral, FL	Lee County	191.0	29.2	48.6	8.0	26.6	13.0
Cedar Rapids, IA	Linn County	183.4	21.9	72.2	7.5	57.1	17.3
Charleston, SC	Charleston County	790.2	32.6	106.2	4.7	47.1	21.7
Charlotte, NC	Mecklenburg County	321.9	13.5	68.1	3.4	31.2	13.3
Chicago, IL	Cook County	432.9	23.3	91.1	12.4	27.8	20.2
Clarksville, TN	Montgomery County	98.4	14.0	46.1	2.4	15.1	12.6
Cleveland, OH	Cuyahoga County	712.2	56.2	105.4	17.2	17.4	16.7
College Station, TX	Brazos County	251.8	20.6	51.6	3.1	16.8	15.4
Colorado Springs, CO	El Paso County	193.8	32.2	102.5	4.2	43.0	23.4
Columbia, MO	Boone County	801.0	62.3	66.7	5.6	32.8	27.8
Columbia, SC	Richland County	357.1	17.0	90.7	6.5	24.1	19.5
Columbus, OH	Franklin County	424.9	65.8	88.5	6.3	24.3	26.4
Dallas, TX	Dallas County	333.1	21.0	83.7	3.9	35.2	13.3
Davenport, IA	Scott County	231.9	51.6	75.6	3.5	181.2	16.2
Denver, CO	Denver County	597.3	33.9	74.4	6.8	35.0	15.9
Des Moines, IA	Polk County	212.1	107.9	70.6	10.1	53.8	21.1
Durham, NC	Durham County	1,109.6	15.4	73.2	5.1	18.9	15.2
Edison, NJ	Middlesex County	372.9	20.4	88.2	10.1	24.5	19.2
El Paso, TX	El Paso County	195.7	13.9	44.4	3.9	8.6	9.8
Fargo, ND	Cass County	392.0	19.1	77.7	3.3	65.6	29.2
Fayetteville, NC	Cumberland County	200.0	22.6	103.5	5.4	10.2	18.7
Fort Collins, CO	Larimer County	242.2	32.3	77.9	5.1	55.6	20.5
Fort Wayne, IN	Allen County	263.4	26.6	64.7	5.6	21.0	25.3
Fort Worth, TX	Tarrant County	181.7	36.6	58.3	4.2	26.1	15.6
Grand Rapids, MI	Kent County	336.9	73.2	71.9	4.6	34.9	24.3
Greeley, CO	Weld County	111.6	16.4	45.2	3.2	22.9	12.1
Green Bay, WI	Brown County	242.3	23.3	76.3	3.0	45.2	18.2
Greensboro, NC	Guilford County	254.1	13.5	56.2	4.7	14.2	10.1
Honolulu, HI	Honolulu County	347.8	18.0	97.3	3.5	18.7	23.1
Houston, TX	Harris County	328.4	11.8	68.3	4.7	21.8	19.6
Huntsville, AL	Madison County	276.1	13.3	54.3	3.8	23.5	18.6
Indianapolis, IN	Marion County	435.9	21.6	88.8	6.4	15.6	19.9
Jackson, MS	Hinds County	574.5	15.4	94.1	4.2	9.7	12.2
Jacksonville, FL	Duval County	354.0	23.7	82.1	8.2	24.2	16.1
Kansas City, MO	Jackson County	301.3	58.4	87.1	6.1	44.0	19.7
Lafayette, LA	Lafayette Parish	363.3	8.7	66.3	3.7	33.4	13.6
Lakeland, FL	Polk County	127.9	10.9	32.6	4.2	17.7	10.0
Las Vegas, NV	Clark County	176.9	27.8	61.7	4.0	19.5	12.6
Lexington, KY	Fayette County	726.5	35.7	141.8	7.4	22.2	21.6
Lincoln, NE	Lancaster County	215.7	11.8	97.7	5.4	43.2	20.8
Little Rock, AR	Pulaski County	742.5	15.2	75.1	5.1	21.6	20.9
Los Angeles, CA	Los Angeles County	296.7	13.5	86.4	6.2	29.2	17.9
Louisville, KY	Jefferson County	471.9	12.7	104.3	7.7	28.4	14.7
Madison, WI	Dane County	600.7	20.5	71.4	4.4	42.6	21.8

Table continued on next page.

City	Area Covered	MDs[1]	DOs[1,2]	Dentists	Podiatrists	Chiropractors	Optometrists
Manchester, NH	Hillsborough County	238.2	23.2	80.9	5.3	25.3	19.7
Miami, FL	Miami-Dade County	341.8	17.2	65.9	9.8	17.6	13.4
Midland, TX	Midland County	156.9	9.7	55.0	2.3	12.7	12.7
Milwaukee, WI	Milwaukee County	364.0	22.3	79.1	7.1	19.6	10.7
Minneapolis, MN	Hennepin County	513.8	20.4	95.4	4.5	71.5	20.4
Nashville, TN	Davidson County	630.9	12.0	77.2	4.2	25.7	15.7
New Haven, CT	New Haven County	556.7	11.6	76.8	9.3	26.0	16.9
New Orleans, LA	Orleans Parish	771.7	18.6	71.4	3.6	8.7	6.6
New York, NY	New York City	473.2	16.8	86.8	13.3	16.1	16.9
Oklahoma City, OK	Oklahoma County	412.5	44.2	102.3	4.9	26.9	18.5
Omaha, NE	Douglas County	536.8	28.7	94.7	5.3	40.2	19.6
Orlando, FL	Orange County	309.6	23.3	48.5	3.3	26.2	12.9
Peoria, IL	Peoria County	557.3	39.3	83.6	8.3	48.2	21.0
Philadelphia, PA	Philadelphia County	559.4	48.6	73.9	17.0	15.0	17.4
Phoenix, AZ	Maricopa County	246.8	33.9	66.8	6.3	33.2	15.1
Pittsburgh, PA	Allegheny County	637.4	44.3	96.3	9.8	44.6	20.1
Portland, OR	Multnomah County	628.8	31.2	96.6	5.3	73.0	22.0
Providence, RI	Providence County	492.8	18.4	60.5	10.4	19.8	19.8
Provo, UT	Utah County	116.9	20.3	60.4	4.0	24.9	10.4
Raleigh, NC	Wake County	277.2	11.8	70.4	3.4	25.8	15.8
Reno, NV	Washoe County	293.3	21.3	70.4	4.1	26.0	22.5
Richmond, VA	Richmond City	746.6	27.7	133.3	10.9	7.0	16.2
Rochester, MN	Olmsted County	2,462.4	56.8	110.1	6.4	42.2	23.7
Sacramento, CA	Sacramento County	310.9	15.5	76.6	4.3	21.9	17.9
Salt Lake City, UT	Salt Lake County	374.1	17.7	76.6	6.1	26.8	13.4
San Antonio, TX	Bexar County	323.2	20.4	85.5	5.3	16.4	16.9
San Diego, CA	San Diego County	321.6	18.1	88.0	4.1	33.8	18.2
San Francisco, CA	San Francisco County	796.2	12.4	153.1	10.3	38.4	27.7
San Jose, CA	Santa Clara County	413.9	10.6	115.3	6.4	41.3	26.7
Santa Rosa, CA	Sonoma County	274.7	18.0	91.4	6.8	38.8	17.4
Savannah, GA	Chatham County	347.0	18.2	66.7	6.6	19.0	13.5
Seattle, WA	King County	490.7	15.9	106.5	6.4	45.5	21.5
Sioux Falls, SD	Minnehaha County	358.9	31.3	53.4	5.2	55.0	19.2
Springfield, IL	Sangamon County	617.5	26.0	87.5	5.6	39.4	21.5
Tallahassee, FL	Leon County	300.4	12.7	44.8	3.4	23.2	18.1
Tampa, FL	Hillsborough County	349.7	28.4	56.6	5.4	26.2	13.4
Topeka, KS	Shawnee County	204.8	26.4	64.2	5.6	25.4	25.4
Tucson, AZ	Pima County	360.1	25.2	63.0	5.2	18.7	15.5
Tulsa, OK	Tulsa County	269.5	130.1	69.4	4.0	38.1	22.4
Tuscaloosa, AL	Tuscaloosa County	231.0	9.1	47.9	6.2	19.6	14.8
Virginia Beach, VA	Virginia Beach City	253.5	13.8	76.4	6.9	27.1	15.8
Washington, DC	The District	793.0	16.6	118.2	8.7	9.1	14.1
Wichita, KS	Sedgwick County	256.4	36.8	62.9	2.3	41.1	26.5
Winston-Salem, NC	Forsyth County	646.8	30.0	60.7	5.8	15.8	17.1
U.S.	U.S.	281.9	23.4	69.1	6.0	27.5	16.4

Note: All figures are rates per 100,000 population; Data as of 2018 unless noted; (1) Data as of 2017 and includes all active, non-federal physicians; (2) Doctor of Osteopathic Medicine
Source: U.S. Department of Health and Human Services, Health Resources and Services Administration, Bureau of Health Professions, Area Resource File (ARF) 2018-2019

Health Insurance Coverage: City

City	With Health Insurance	With Private Health Insurance	With Public Health Insurance	Without Health Insurance	Population Under Age 19 Without Health Insurance
Albany, NY	93.8	66.5	39.9	6.2	2.4
Albuquerque, NM	91.1	60.9	41.4	8.9	3.8
Allentown, PA	87.9	47.5	48.9	12.1	5.4
Anchorage, AK	87.8	70.2	28.7	12.2	9.2
Ann Arbor, MI	97.3	87.8	19.8	2.7	1.1
Athens, GA	85.9	68.1	26.8	14.1	8.0
Atlanta, GA	88.9	68.2	28.5	11.1	5.5
Austin, TX	85.8	72.2	20.6	14.2	9.3
Baton Rouge, LA	89.1	60.5	38.1	10.9	3.0
Boise City, ID	90.8	75.5	26.9	9.2	4.0
Boston, MA	96.2	66.5	37.2	3.8	1.5
Boulder, CO	95.5	83.7	19.9	4.5	1.3
Cape Coral, FL	87.4	65.6	36.7	12.6	8.3
Cedar Rapids, IA	95.5	75.4	33.5	4.5	3.1
Charleston, SC	91.8	77.9	25.5	8.2	2.6
Charlotte, NC	87.2	68.0	26.5	12.8	6.0
Chicago, IL	89.3	58.8	37.2	10.7	3.4
Clarksville, TN	91.6	72.4	32.3	8.4	3.4
Cleveland, OH	91.3	43.0	57.1	8.7	3.2
College Station, TX	91.3	84.5	13.6	8.7	5.4
Colorado Springs, CO	91.9	69.2	35.8	8.1	4.6
Columbia, MO	93.4	82.7	20.1	6.6	3.1
Columbia, SC	90.3	71.1	29.3	9.7	2.3
Columbus, OH	90.4	63.8	34.3	9.6	5.7
Dallas, TX	76.4	50.8	31.2	23.6	14.1
Davenport, IA	94.1	66.6	38.9	5.9	2.1
Denver, CO	89.7	64.6	33.2	10.3	4.9
Des Moines, IA	92.8	64.0	40.9	7.2	3.8
Durham, NC	87.2	68.4	28.6	12.8	6.6
Edison, NJ	93.9	81.8	21.3	6.1	2.0
El Paso, TX	80.7	54.1	33.9	19.3	8.7
Fargo, ND	93.3	80.8	24.2	6.7	4.6
Fayetteville, NC	89.7	65.9	38.8	10.3	4.0
Fort Collins, CO	93.8	78.8	23.9	6.2	5.1
Fort Wayne, IN	90.0	64.4	35.7	10.0	6.0
Fort Worth, TX	81.5	60.2	27.9	18.5	11.0
Grand Rapids, MI	90.8	61.8	39.4	9.2	4.2
Greeley, CO	91.4	64.6	37.3	8.6	4.0
Green Bay, WI	91.6	65.9	35.8	8.4	4.0
Greensboro, NC	89.0	66.2	33.1	11.0	5.0
Honolulu, HI	95.7	77.6	34.0	4.3	3.1
Houston, TX	76.8	51.6	31.1	23.2	12.8
Huntsville, AL	89.5	71.9	32.6	10.5	3.8
Indianapolis, IN	88.7	61.6	36.3	11.3	6.2
Jackson, MS	86.1	51.6	43.0	13.9	4.2
Jacksonville, FL	87.8	64.1	34.4	12.2	6.6
Kansas City, MO	87.6	68.0	29.1	12.4	7.2
Lafayette, LA	89.5	67.6	32.5	10.5	4.3
Lakeland, FL	89.7	61.9	41.3	10.3	5.7
Las Vegas, NV	86.9	61.5	35.2	13.1	7.7
Lexington, KY	92.7	71.9	31.9	7.3	4.2
Lincoln, NE	92.2	78.1	25.6	7.8	4.4
Little Rock, AR	90.6	65.8	36.2	9.4	5.8
Los Angeles, CA	87.2	54.0	39.5	12.8	4.6
Louisville, KY	94.2	67.3	39.7	5.8	2.6

Table continued on next page.

City	With Health Insurance	With Private Health Insurance	With Public Health Insurance	Without Health Insurance	Population Under Age 19 Without Health Insurance
Madison, WI	95.6	83.3	22.4	4.4	2.3
Manchester, NH	90.0	64.5	35.5	10.0	3.2
Miami, FL	78.4	44.5	37.1	21.6	8.8
Midland, TX	82.4	70.6	19.3	17.6	16.3
Milwaukee, WI	90.3	53.7	44.8	9.7	3.3
Minneapolis, MN	93.0	67.0	33.9	7.0	3.9
Nashville, TN	87.2	66.2	29.9	12.8	7.1
New Haven, CT	91.0	51.5	46.2	9.0	3.2
New Orleans, LA	89.3	55.8	41.6	10.7	3.9
New York, NY	91.6	57.5	42.8	8.4	2.7
Oklahoma City, OK	85.0	63.7	31.7	15.0	6.9
Omaha, NE	89.3	70.5	28.1	10.7	5.9
Orlando, FL	83.4	60.3	29.8	16.6	9.1
Peoria, IL	93.7	65.0	41.2	6.3	2.3
Philadelphia, PA	90.9	57.0	44.1	9.1	3.5
Phoenix, AZ	85.3	56.3	36.1	14.7	9.9
Pittsburgh, PA	94.1	73.3	33.2	5.9	3.3
Portland, OR	93.1	70.5	32.4	6.9	3.0
Providence, RI	90.9	51.8	46.3	9.1	3.4
Provo, UT	87.9	77.5	16.9	12.1	11.6
Raleigh, NC	89.1	74.0	23.8	10.9	5.6
Reno, NV	89.4	67.1	32.9	10.6	7.6
Richmond, VA	86.6	61.6	34.3	13.4	6.6
Rochester, MN	95.7	79.2	30.2	4.3	2.6
Sacramento, CA	93.1	61.9	41.2	6.9	2.7
Salt Lake City, UT	86.3	71.1	22.6	13.7	11.8
San Antonio, TX	83.5	60.4	32.6	16.5	8.3
San Diego, CA	91.2	69.5	30.7	8.8	4.3
San Francisco, CA	95.6	75.2	29.1	4.4	1.7
San Jose, CA	94.3	71.9	30.2	5.7	2.3
Santa Rosa, CA	92.0	67.5	37.4	8.0	4.1
Savannah, GA	82.1	56.9	34.0	17.9	7.7
Seattle, WA	95.4	80.1	24.1	4.6	1.6
Sioux Falls, SD	92.6	77.4	26.5	7.4	3.7
Springfield, IL	95.4	67.9	42.8	4.6	1.7
Tallahassee, FL	91.3	76.3	24.1	8.7	4.2
Tampa, FL	87.9	61.6	33.7	12.1	5.1
Topeka, KS	90.4	70.4	36.2	9.6	5.5
Tucson, AZ	88.0	56.7	41.7	12.0	8.7
Tulsa, OK	83.4	58.9	34.9	16.6	8.0
Tuscaloosa, AL	92.2	71.5	31.3	7.8	2.0
Virginia Beach, VA	91.8	80.4	24.9	8.2	4.2
Washington, DC	96.0	69.6	36.0	4.0	2.1
Wichita, KS	87.4	67.0	31.6	12.6	6.7
Winston-Salem, NC	87.3	62.4	35.6	12.7	4.8
U.S.	90.6	67.7	34.7	9.4	5.2

Note: Figures are percentages that cover the civilian noninstitutionalized population
Source: U.S. Census Bureau, 2014-2018 American Community Survey 5-Year Estimates

Health Insurance Coverage: Metro Area

Metro Area	With Health Insurance	With Private Health Insurance	With Public Health Insurance	Without Health Insurance	Population Under Age 19 Without Health Insurance
Albany, NY	95.9	77.3	33.7	4.1	2.0
Albuquerque, NM	90.8	59.9	42.9	9.2	4.3
Allentown, PA	93.8	73.4	34.5	6.2	3.3
Anchorage, AK	87.0	68.4	29.7	13.0	9.6
Ann Arbor, MI	96.1	83.5	25.1	3.9	1.9
Athens, GA	87.5	69.5	28.1	12.5	6.9
Atlanta, GA	86.7	68.9	26.7	13.3	7.6
Austin, TX	87.2	74.2	21.8	12.8	8.1
Baton Rouge, LA	90.6	66.9	33.6	9.4	3.1
Boise City, ID	89.2	71.2	30.0	10.8	5.1
Boston, MA	97.0	76.3	32.7	3.0	1.4
Boulder, CO	95.0	78.9	25.7	5.0	2.0
Cape Coral, FL	85.7	61.7	42.9	14.3	9.9
Cedar Rapids, IA	96.3	77.6	32.5	3.7	2.3
Charleston, SC	89.4	70.7	31.6	10.6	5.1
Charlotte, NC	89.4	70.5	29.1	10.6	4.9
Chicago, IL	91.8	69.7	31.5	8.2	3.2
Clarksville, TN	91.5	70.0	35.2	8.5	5.0
Cleveland, OH	94.3	69.3	37.9	5.7	3.4
College Station, TX	86.5	73.0	22.5	13.5	9.8
Colorado Springs, CO	92.5	71.5	34.4	7.5	4.3
Columbia, MO	93.0	80.9	22.2	7.0	3.5
Columbia, SC	90.1	70.1	33.3	9.9	3.8
Columbus, OH	92.9	71.4	31.5	7.1	4.2
Dallas, TX	83.4	65.6	25.2	16.6	10.7
Davenport, IA	94.9	72.8	36.9	5.1	2.1
Denver, CO	92.0	72.1	29.2	8.0	4.2
Des Moines, IA	95.4	77.4	30.5	4.6	2.4
Durham, NC	89.3	71.9	28.9	10.7	5.8
Edison, NJ	92.1	67.0	35.5	7.9	3.1
El Paso, TX	79.3	51.6	34.3	20.7	9.6
Fargo, ND	94.4	82.1	24.4	5.6	4.5
Fayetteville, NC	89.4	65.4	38.1	10.6	4.0
Fort Collins, CO	93.7	75.6	29.0	6.3	4.7
Fort Wayne, IN	91.0	69.4	32.5	9.0	6.4
Fort Worth, TX	83.4	65.6	25.2	16.6	10.7
Grand Rapids, MI	94.1	75.2	31.2	5.9	3.2
Greeley, CO	92.2	70.8	31.5	7.8	4.7
Green Bay, WI	94.3	75.2	30.3	5.7	3.6
Greensboro, NC	89.3	65.8	34.6	10.7	5.2
Honolulu, HI	96.4	80.1	31.8	3.6	2.3
Houston, TX	82.0	62.2	26.6	18.0	10.6
Huntsville, AL	90.9	75.6	29.6	9.1	3.3
Indianapolis, IN	91.2	71.1	30.6	8.8	5.6
Jackson, MS	89.3	64.2	35.7	10.7	4.5
Jacksonville, FL	88.9	68.0	33.0	11.1	6.6
Kansas City, MO	90.9	75.2	27.1	9.1	5.4
Lafayette, LA	89.0	62.9	36.6	11.0	4.0
Lakeland, FL	86.8	58.2	41.5	13.2	7.6
Las Vegas, NV	87.5	64.3	32.8	12.5	7.8
Lexington, KY	93.0	71.0	33.7	7.0	4.3
Lincoln, NE	92.8	79.3	25.1	7.2	4.1
Little Rock, AR	91.8	67.3	37.8	8.2	4.8
Los Angeles, CA	89.7	60.1	36.6	10.3	4.2
Louisville, KY	94.1	71.6	35.8	5.9	3.2

Table continued on next page.

Metro Area	With Health Insurance	With Private Health Insurance	With Public Health Insurance	Without Health Insurance	Population Under Age 19 Without Health Insurance
Madison, WI	95.7	82.9	24.7	4.3	2.3
Manchester, NH	93.6	77.3	27.8	6.4	2.4
Miami, FL	84.0	58.0	33.5	16.0	8.2
Midland, TX	82.7	70.5	19.7	17.3	14.7
Milwaukee, WI	94.0	71.5	33.9	6.0	2.6
Minneapolis, MN	95.5	78.1	29.1	4.5	3.2
Nashville, TN	90.2	71.3	28.9	9.8	5.2
New Haven, CT	94.8	68.5	37.9	5.2	2.4
New Orleans, LA	89.3	60.7	38.5	10.7	4.1
New York, NY	92.1	67.0	35.5	7.9	3.1
Oklahoma City, OK	87.2	68.4	30.6	12.8	6.3
Omaha, NE	92.0	75.9	26.8	8.0	4.3
Orlando, FL	86.5	64.4	31.5	13.5	7.9
Peoria, IL	95.2	74.1	36.1	4.8	2.4
Philadelphia, PA	93.8	73.3	33.2	6.2	3.1
Phoenix, AZ	89.1	65.0	34.7	10.9	8.2
Pittsburgh, PA	95.8	77.2	35.1	4.2	1.9
Portland, OR	93.4	72.5	32.8	6.6	3.0
Providence, RI	95.6	70.4	38.5	4.4	2.2
Provo, UT	91.4	81.4	17.0	8.6	6.3
Raleigh, NC	90.5	75.5	24.5	9.5	4.8
Reno, NV	89.8	69.0	32.3	10.2	8.0
Richmond, VA	91.3	75.2	28.6	8.7	4.8
Rochester, MN	95.4	79.9	30.1	4.6	3.5
Sacramento, CA	94.1	69.1	37.4	5.9	2.9
Salt Lake City, UT	88.9	76.5	20.4	11.1	8.5
San Antonio, TX	85.4	65.3	30.9	14.6	8.0
San Diego, CA	91.3	68.2	33.0	8.7	4.5
San Francisco, CA	95.0	75.1	30.1	5.0	2.3
San Jose, CA	95.1	76.4	27.1	4.9	2.1
Santa Rosa, CA	93.1	71.1	36.1	6.9	3.0
Savannah, GA	86.5	67.6	29.4	13.5	6.1
Seattle, WA	93.9	75.6	29.0	6.1	2.7
Sioux Falls, SD	93.2	79.5	25.0	6.8	3.8
Springfield, IL	95.9	73.8	37.6	4.1	1.6
Tallahassee, FL	91.0	73.2	29.3	9.0	4.4
Tampa, FL	87.7	62.7	36.8	12.3	6.6
Topeka, KS	92.3	75.9	32.9	7.7	4.5
Tucson, AZ	90.1	62.1	41.5	9.9	8.0
Tulsa, OK	86.5	65.8	32.4	13.5	7.5
Tuscaloosa, AL	92.3	71.7	32.7	7.7	1.9
Virginia Beach, VA	90.9	75.1	29.2	9.1	4.7
Washington, DC	92.0	78.1	24.6	8.0	4.5
Wichita, KS	89.6	71.7	29.6	10.4	5.8
Winston-Salem, NC	88.7	66.1	35.0	11.3	5.1
U.S.	90.6	67.7	34.7	9.4	5.2

Note: Figures are percentages that cover the civilian noninstitutionalized population; Figures cover the Metropolitan Statistical Area (MSA)—see Appendix B for areas included
Source: U.S. Census Bureau, 2014-2018 American Community Survey 5-Year Estimates

Crime Rate: City

City	All Crimes	Violent Crimes				Property Crimes		
		Murder	Rape	Robbery	Aggrav. Assault	Burglary	Larceny -Theft	Motor Vehicle Theft
Albany, NY	4,037.8	12.2	52.9	212.6	559.4	439.4	2,629.1	132.2
Albuquerque, NM	7,544.2	12.3	85.5	353.2	913.7	1,138.5	3,860.0	1,180.9
Allentown, PA	2,655.6	9.0	40.2	150.3	138.8	380.3	1,724.9	211.9
Anchorage, AK	6,237.5	8.9	209.9	245.6	845.2	708.2	3,252.8	966.8
Ann Arbor, MI	1,796.5	1.6	44.9	36.7	137.1	175.4	1,346.2	54.7
Athens, GA[1]	3,562.0	4.8	45.6	98.5	266.6	546.8	2,415.5	184.1
Atlanta, GA	5,423.2	17.7	49.4	221.5	480.1	621.2	3,366.4	666.8
Austin, TX	3,839.9	3.3	80.9	104.9	193.1	467.4	2,729.6	260.8
Baton Rouge, LA	6,242.3	35.1	32.9	323.4	528.0	1,194.9	3,705.2	422.6
Boise City, ID	2,295.2	0.4	75.5	22.2	178.8	278.3	1,624.8	115.2
Boston, MA	2,638.8	8.1	40.0	168.7	405.7	266.7	1,583.5	166.1
Boulder, CO	3,652.0	0.0	36.0	36.0	197.5	356.2	2,800.3	226.1
Cape Coral, FL	1,579.8	1.6	9.0	27.1	104.3	219.8	1,123.1	94.7
Cedar Rapids, IA[1]	4,035.5	4.5	25.8	91.8	158.5	704.4	2,791.2	259.3
Charleston, SC	2,380.2	7.3	41.6	64.9	188.9	262.6	1,577.8	237.1
Charlotte, NC	n/a	6.3	n/a	189.1	473.3	608.9	2,812.0	324.8
Chicago, IL	4,187.7	20.7	66.1	356.1	563.1	429.8	2,379.2	372.6
Clarksville, TN	3,554.9	9.6	51.8	83.2	521.6	382.7	2,285.9	220.1
Cleveland, OH	5,861.2	22.4	119.8	460.7	846.7	1,210.9	2,428.6	772.1
College Station, TX	2,281.1	0.9	65.2	25.7	111.5	244.5	1,705.5	127.8
Colorado Springs, CO	3,899.0	6.8	102.5	109.3	336.9	578.8	2,255.5	509.2
Columbia, MO	3,179.2	4.0	72.0	84.2	200.7	444.2	2,142.6	231.4
Columbia, SC	5,795.3	12.0	67.4	167.7	491.2	753.3	3,728.5	575.1
Columbus, OH	4,025.2	11.1	91.9	215.3	176.5	702.6	2,388.9	439.0
Dallas, TX	4,013.9	11.4	60.8	292.6	400.2	665.3	1,874.6	709.0
Davenport, IA[1]	5,820.7	12.6	87.3	197.0	430.8	1,075.1	3,479.4	538.5
Denver, CO	4,401.8	9.0	99.5	168.0	453.6	552.5	2,387.4	731.9
Des Moines, IA[1]	5,083.4	12.9	33.6	167.5	456.1	1,099.1	2,734.3	579.9
Durham, NC	n/a	12.1	n/a	264.1	410.9	817.5	2,443.0	302.8
Edison, NJ	1,250.6	2.0	7.9	43.4	65.1	163.9	887.4	80.9
El Paso, TX	1,876.6	3.3	58.8	54.6	254.2	160.8	1,226.1	118.7
Fargo, ND	3,565.1	4.0	84.1	50.4	279.4	556.4	2,343.4	247.4
Fayetteville, NC[1]	n/a	11.7	n/a	142.1	537.9	885.0	3,202.0	202.0
Fort Collins, CO	2,433.9	1.8	16.7	23.2	191.5	212.3	1,880.9	107.6
Fort Wayne, IN	3,000.7	14.9	48.9	114.7	204.0	375.9	2,037.5	204.8
Fort Worth, TX	3,347.1	6.5	53.9	124.9	316.2	503.9	2,009.2	332.5
Grand Rapids, MI	2,566.0	2.5	70.3	159.2	423.1	338.8	1,437.4	134.7
Greeley, CO	2,947.1	1.9	72.7	59.6	260.9	389.5	1,901.7	260.9
Green Bay, WI	2,166.6	0.9	74.1	53.2	330.5	237.5	1,375.4	95.0
Greensboro, NC	n/a	12.6	n/a	182.7	411.5	721.8	2,398.6	231.5
Honolulu, HI	n/a	n/a	n/a	n/a	n/a	n/a	n/a	n/a
Houston, TX	5,036.1	11.8	53.8	373.6	587.0	695.8	2,804.6	509.6
Huntsville, AL[1]	5,635.0	11.3	88.1	184.5	621.0	731.7	3,462.6	535.9
Indianapolis, IN	5,402.0	18.5	77.1	351.1	826.1	893.6	2,671.9	563.7
Jackson, MS	n/a	47.0	n/a	286.7	360.2	1,248.6	2,846.6	636.1
Jacksonville, FL	3,929.6	12.2	59.2	146.5	377.9	543.5	2,464.8	325.6
Kansas City, MO	5,896.8	27.8	81.7	332.0	1,148.8	753.8	2,698.2	854.6
Lafayette, LA	5,143.7	7.1	16.5	123.8	386.4	798.6	3,515.1	296.3
Lakeland, FL	3,446.6	7.3	42.9	96.7	182.5	435.2	2,496.9	185.2
Las Vegas, NV	3,443.3	7.3	97.9	163.6	336.2	727.8	1,627.1	483.4
Lexington, KY	3,474.1	6.8	74.6	129.6	90.6	467.8	2,381.9	322.8
Lincoln, NE	3,240.6	2.1	98.1	56.1	205.8	409.6	2,319.6	149.3
Little Rock, AR	7,994.0	20.1	109.4	186.2	1,130.5	1,043.2	4,942.6	562.0
Los Angeles, CA	3,260.6	6.4	62.7	256.3	422.2	396.8	1,686.5	429.7

Table continued on next page.

City	All Crimes	Violent Crimes				Property Crimes		
		Murder	Rape	Robbery	Aggrav. Assault	Burglary	Larceny -Theft	Motor Vehicle Theft
Louisville, KY[1]	4,769.3	15.9	25.6	193.8	411.8	821.6	2,736.0	564.6
Madison, WI	3,004.4	1.9	44.9	92.9	263.9	410.5	1,984.5	205.8
Manchester, NH	3,176.2	3.6	58.3	129.2	402.1	298.9	2,137.8	146.3
Miami, FL	4,188.8	9.7	27.7	175.0	417.1	434.8	2,776.9	347.5
Midland, TX	2,261.0	3.6	42.8	42.1	199.2	269.9	1,504.9	198.5
Milwaukee, WI	4,384.5	16.6	82.1	382.6	931.6	715.1	1,486.0	770.5
Minneapolis, MN	4,703.9	7.2	100.9	276.5	408.2	721.3	2,678.5	511.4
Nashville, TN	5,124.3	13.3	69.9	308.2	721.6	528.3	3,034.0	448.9
New Haven, CT	4,738.5	7.6	45.7	243.9	545.0	571.0	2,811.4	513.8
New Orleans, LA	5,720.4	37.1	171.8	307.5	646.9	511.4	3,290.3	755.3
New York, NY	2,043.4	3.5	33.0	152.1	352.5	127.1	1,310.3	64.9
Oklahoma City, OK	4,895.0	8.0	83.0	165.7	610.6	918.9	2,552.8	556.0
Omaha, NE	4,035.8	4.7	85.9	97.2	372.2	393.7	2,416.7	665.4
Orlando, FL	5,610.8	13.6	69.8	219.1	493.6	564.7	3,824.8	425.2
Peoria, IL	4,768.4	19.5	60.4	178.5	505.4	790.4	2,839.4	374.8
Philadelphia, PA	4,005.6	22.1	69.0	331.6	486.0	409.4	2,329.5	357.9
Phoenix, AZ	4,225.0	8.0	65.7	188.3	470.6	633.6	2,385.7	472.8
Pittsburgh, PA	3,594.8	18.8	40.0	230.0	289.9	443.2	2,331.9	241.0
Portland, OR	5,979.7	3.8	66.6	160.7	288.9	676.1	3,728.8	1,054.7
Providence, RI	3,606.6	5.6	60.5	137.6	250.9	516.7	2,328.9	306.4
Provo, UT	1,946.8	1.7	59.3	18.6	95.8	177.1	1,480.7	113.6
Raleigh, NC	n/a	n/a	n/a	n/a	n/a	n/a	n/a	n/a
Reno, NV	3,047.1	2.4	69.0	120.1	456.9	425.2	1,557.4	416.1
Richmond, VA	4,347.9	22.6	33.5	186.1	275.3	487.5	2,834.8	508.0
Rochester, MN	2,274.5	4.3	49.6	35.0	105.1	301.6	1,667.8	111.1
Sacramento, CA	3,697.2	7.1	20.1	207.5	421.9	542.6	1,929.4	568.6
Salt Lake City, UT	6,907.1	4.9	120.9	204.3	400.2	790.1	4,649.8	736.8
San Antonio, TX	4,620.5	7.0	87.4	114.8	417.5	592.3	3,005.9	395.6
San Diego, CA	2,281.7	2.4	42.1	100.2	228.4	261.2	1,286.6	360.7
San Francisco, CA	6,225.0	5.2	39.8	355.9	290.0	598.5	4,461.5	474.2
San Jose, CA	2,883.3	2.7	58.7	152.1	210.8	433.4	1,290.0	735.6
Santa Rosa, CA	2,235.1	1.7	84.5	83.4	297.2	310.2	1,235.8	222.3
Savannah, GA	2,865.5	11.6	35.1	110.2	248.5	364.9	1,824.4	270.8
Seattle, WA	5,829.3	4.3	39.3	222.0	414.5	1,075.0	3,529.9	544.2
Sioux Falls, SD	3,369.3	2.8	67.1	59.3	307.8	361.5	2,269.1	301.7
Springfield, IL	5,620.2	7.9	81.1	188.4	555.7	1,042.5	3,528.1	216.4
Tallahassee, FL	5,247.8	8.3	110.7	159.5	451.0	716.6	3,403.1	398.6
Tampa, FL	2,080.2	6.9	25.4	84.5	289.9	266.4	1,290.0	117.1
Topeka, KS	5,795.9	11.1	66.5	201.0	327.5	769.8	3,837.8	582.3
Tucson, AZ	5,690.6	8.7	93.8	227.8	406.2	606.1	3,870.2	477.9
Tulsa, OK	6,495.6	14.9	104.7	205.9	739.7	1,190.6	3,431.5	808.4
Tuscaloosa, AL	4,843.6	4.9	46.2	137.6	316.4	739.9	3,289.0	309.5
Virginia Beach, VA	1,840.4	1.6	18.0	38.6	59.0	129.5	1,465.9	127.9
Washington, DC	5,211.2	22.8	63.3	307.1	548.2	254.3	3,652.6	362.9
Wichita, KS	6,798.9	9.7	96.5	146.0	927.7	871.0	4,040.1	707.9
Winston-Salem, NC	n/a	n/a	n/a	n/a	n/a	n/a	n/a	n/a
U.S.	2,580.1	5.0	42.6	86.2	246.8	376.0	1,594.6	228.9

Note: Figures are crimes per 100,000 population in 2018 except where noted; n/a not available; (1) 2017 data
Source: FBI Uniform Crime Reports, 2017, 2018

Crime Rate: Suburbs

Suburbs[1]	All Crimes	Violent Crimes				Property Crimes		
		Murder	Rape	Robbery	Aggrav. Assault	Burglary	Larceny -Theft	Motor Vehicle Theft
Albany, NY	1,939.3	0.9	36.5	43.3	132.7	199.9	1,452.0	74.1
Albuquerque, NM	2,563.1	5.1	45.6	56.9	535.4	446.5	1,228.5	245.2
Allentown, PA	1,424.2	0.7	22.1	22.8	89.0	172.8	1,055.9	60.9
Anchorage, AK	6,979.1	0.0	39.1	66.9	407.3	624.8	4,803.3	1,037.7
Ann Arbor, MI	1,829.6	4.4	76.3	41.0	251.3	252.1	1,096.9	107.6
Athens, GA[2]	1,855.9	1.2	18.1	14.5	111.2	289.0	1,349.3	72.5
Atlanta, GA	2,666.3	4.6	24.0	82.5	168.8	373.2	1,770.4	242.7
Austin, TX	1,613.3	1.8	44.6	21.5	149.8	235.6	1,080.0	80.1
Baton Rouge, LA	3,356.9	7.6	28.2	53.2	303.6	515.5	2,321.6	127.2
Boise City, ID	1,591.8	1.6	44.1	10.4	172.9	273.3	962.3	127.3
Boston, MA	1,384.8	0.8	33.4	45.2	213.8	133.2	876.4	82.0
Boulder, CO	n/a	0.9	74.2	25.7	169.5	314.8	n/a	216.3
Cape Coral, FL	1,748.8	6.5	45.5	70.8	203.7	243.9	1,023.2	155.4
Cedar Rapids, IA[2]	1,273.6	1.5	27.0	12.4	115.9	313.5	720.3	83.1
Charleston, SC	3,116.8	7.8	33.9	77.8	281.7	409.7	2,021.7	284.2
Charlotte, NC	4,936.7	4.6	n/a	52.2	191.8	442.7	1,602.2	132.5
Chicago, IL	n/a	2.2	29.4	45.8	n/a	n/a	n/a	91.9
Clarksville, TN	2,001.9	2.7	26.8	25.4	145.4	474.1	1,169.7	157.8
Cleveland, OH	n/a	n/a	n/a	n/a	n/a	n/a	n/a	n/a
College Station, TX	2,529.4	2.8	62.0	43.4	219.8	434.8	1,618.5	148.1
Colorado Springs, CO	1,720.4	4.5	77.2	23.8	202.1	225.5	999.1	188.1
Columbia, MO	1,839.8	4.7	24.8	14.2	145.4	229.4	1,261.6	159.6
Columbia, SC	3,745.4	6.4	47.0	71.5	410.5	544.5	2,286.2	379.2
Columbus, OH	1,959.2	2.5	35.2	31.1	57.6	279.8	1,452.2	100.8
Dallas, TX	1,982.9	2.4	38.1	51.2	108.1	247.2	1,348.7	187.1
Davenport, IA[2]	2,285.2	1.8	45.4	24.0	213.6	396.8	1,486.5	117.0
Denver, CO	n/a	n/a	n/a	n/a	n/a	n/a	n/a	n/a
Des Moines, IA	n/a	n/a	n/a	n/a	n/a	n/a	n/a	n/a
Durham, NC	n/a	n/a	n/a	n/a	n/a	n/a	n/a	n/a
Edison, NJ	n/a	n/a	n/a	n/a	n/a	n/a	n/a	n/a
El Paso, TX	1,270.9	5.6	37.0	17.5	172.3	179.2	781.5	77.7
Fargo, ND	1,841.2	0.8	30.2	12.6	93.9	279.9	1,296.4	127.4
Fayetteville, NC[2]	n/a	3.9	n/a	36.0	89.9	401.7	1,011.3	42.1
Fort Collins, CO	2,027.1	1.1	50.8	11.6	146.3	239.0	1,467.5	110.9
Fort Wayne, IN	1,159.6	1.4	26.2	29.0	114.5	195.2	713.4	79.9
Fort Worth, TX	2,299.2	1.9	42.5	48.5	163.2	278.4	1,569.4	195.4
Grand Rapids, MI	1,513.3	2.4	94.3	22.1	137.9	196.6	984.6	75.4
Greeley, CO	n/a	1.9	40.1	11.6	134.4	195.3	n/a	159.5
Green Bay, WI	972.5	0.0	34.1	4.2	50.3	105.6	737.3	41.0
Greensboro, NC	4,892.2	6.1	n/a	50.3	218.8	472.1	1,500.0	150.2
Honolulu, HI	n/a	n/a	n/a	n/a	n/a	n/a	n/a	n/a
Houston, TX	n/a	3.5	39.2	78.0	n/a	317.0	1,366.3	216.7
Huntsville, AL[2]	2,220.1	4.2	32.4	31.2	227.3	432.2	1,337.1	155.6
Indianapolis, IN	1,699.1	2.5	23.1	28.7	114.1	199.2	1,200.7	130.7
Jackson, MS	n/a	n/a	n/a	n/a	n/a	n/a	n/a	n/a
Jacksonville, FL	1,835.7	2.1	32.0	32.2	179.4	275.6	1,185.7	128.8
Kansas City, MO	n/a	n/a	n/a	n/a	n/a	n/a	n/a	n/a
Lafayette, LA	3,251.6	9.6	26.5	47.4	359.5	695.0	1,903.4	210.1
Lakeland, FL	1,803.9	2.7	24.8	30.5	232.3	294.8	1,085.1	133.6
Las Vegas, NV	n/a	8.3	41.2	117.6	n/a	462.4	1,405.6	337.3
Lexington, KY	2,582.2	1.0	32.7	36.3	63.8	423.9	1,857.4	167.1
Lincoln, NE	1,240.2	0.0	84.0	4.3	47.4	155.0	859.1	90.4
Little Rock, AR	n/a	5.2	50.2	53.5	369.5	n/a	1,994.8	258.0
Los Angeles, CA	2,702.8	5.1	32.1	149.9	278.7	435.2	1,407.0	394.7

Table continued on next page.

Suburbs[1]	All Crimes	Violent Crimes				Property Crimes		
		Murder	Rape	Robbery	Aggrav. Assault	Burglary	Larceny -Theft	Motor Vehicle Theft
Louisville, KY[2]	2,096.6	2.3	20.4	43.4	93.2	326.7	1,401.4	209.2
Madison, WI	1,377.6	1.2	25.3	18.1	94.7	163.7	1,001.2	73.4
Manchester, NH	1,010.1	1.0	33.1	10.2	51.6	84.6	779.7	49.9
Miami, FL	3,491.6	6.6	33.9	122.1	302.3	307.9	2,429.5	289.4
Midland, TX	2,400.0	11.5	25.9	31.7	368.8	299.6	1,293.6	368.8
Milwaukee, WI	1,663.9	1.4	20.4	33.2	68.4	137.4	1,299.1	104.0
Minneapolis, MN	2,106.6	1.2	38.5	45.7	95.6	236.9	1,512.5	176.2
Nashville, TN	n/a	4.8	32.5	28.5	245.7	238.4	1,352.9	n/a
New Haven, CT	2,341.2	2.1	20.8	66.0	99.7	276.6	1,591.2	284.9
New Orleans, LA	n/a	5.8	22.9	56.2	208.6	310.5	n/a	143.8
New York, NY	n/a	n/a	n/a	n/a	n/a	n/a	n/a	n/a
Oklahoma City, OK	2,478.1	2.7	42.5	33.7	154.5	478.9	1,522.7	243.1
Omaha, NE	n/a	n/a	n/a	n/a	n/a	n/a	n/a	n/a
Orlando, FL	2,553.9	4.4	47.4	77.4	269.3	386.8	1,607.9	160.7
Peoria, IL	n/a	1.7	51.7	18.5	141.8	291.5	n/a	75.7
Philadelphia, PA	1,935.5	7.6	16.3	96.8	235.8	202.8	1,235.3	140.9
Phoenix, AZ	2,452.0	2.8	41.1	51.7	202.9	327.7	1,653.9	171.8
Pittsburgh, PA	1,402.7	3.5	23.7	33.2	168.7	159.1	958.5	55.9
Portland, OR	2,160.8	1.3	51.5	38.4	128.7	252.9	1,391.7	296.3
Providence, RI	1,593.3	0.9	40.8	38.9	182.2	227.2	996.6	106.7
Provo, UT	1,333.5	0.6	25.8	4.9	36.5	132.0	1,063.6	70.1
Raleigh, NC	n/a	n/a	n/a	n/a	n/a	n/a	n/a	n/a
Reno, NV	2,067.4	4.6	58.6	47.5	245.5	372.9	1,137.1	201.2
Richmond, VA	1,967.8	4.6	26.4	36.2	111.3	195.7	1,471.8	121.9
Rochester, MN	731.3	1.0	24.3	6.8	50.6	147.0	459.6	41.9
Sacramento, CA	2,214.4	2.7	31.8	76.9	185.8	338.1	1,317.3	261.8
Salt Lake City, UT	3,459.3	2.3	64.5	53.3	177.2	401.2	2,373.2	387.6
San Antonio, TX	n/a	2.9	48.3	26.0	n/a	304.0	1,233.9	132.9
San Diego, CA	1,850.1	2.6	29.2	80.5	204.7	237.7	1,064.8	230.7
San Francisco, CA	2,266.8	1.7	39.5	86.2	124.1	321.6	1,477.4	216.5
San Jose, CA	2,312.9	0.5	26.5	56.5	110.4	312.9	1,533.2	272.8
Santa Rosa, CA	1,594.5	1.8	49.9	37.0	266.8	253.4	896.5	89.0
Savannah, GA	3,497.3	5.3	37.2	67.1	245.2	497.1	2,366.1	279.1
Seattle, WA	2,986.4	2.2	36.6	69.0	113.2	425.4	1,902.3	437.6
Sioux Falls, SD	1,237.9	0.0	37.8	2.4	105.0	328.1	682.1	82.6
Springfield, IL	1,555.2	1.1	37.7	19.4	245.4	337.9	791.1	122.7
Tallahassee, FL	2,481.3	5.7	35.4	39.6	306.9	470.5	1,480.9	142.3
Tampa, FL	2,173.0	3.4	40.4	50.8	197.5	255.2	1,481.2	144.5
Topeka, KS	1,961.5	7.6	31.2	10.4	198.5	375.3	1,161.8	176.8
Tucson, AZ	2,515.9	2.0	22.4	38.6	94.7	350.1	1,840.3	167.8
Tulsa, OK	2,105.2	3.2	45.1	21.1	154.3	412.4	1,252.2	216.9
Tuscaloosa, AL	2,503.0	3.3	28.5	41.7	249.6	518.3	1,449.1	212.5
Virginia Beach, VA	3,011.1	8.8	38.5	84.8	239.9	324.2	2,115.9	199.1
Washington, DC	1,533.1	3.1	28.2	58.5	96.8	119.5	1,092.2	134.9
Wichita, KS	2,290.5	4.5	43.0	23.9	192.0	404.6	1,443.5	179.0
Winston-Salem, NC	n/a	n/a	n/a	n/a	n/a	n/a	n/a	n/a
U.S.	2,580.1	5.0	42.6	86.2	246.8	376.0	1,594.6	228.9

Note: Figures are crimes per 100,000 population in 2018 except where noted; n/a not available; (1) All areas within the metro area that are located outside the city limits; (2) 2017 data
Source: FBI Uniform Crime Reports, 2017, 2018

Crime Rate: Metro Area

Metro Area[1]	All Crimes	Violent Crimes				Property Crimes		
		Murder	Rape	Robbery	Aggrav. Assault	Burglary	Larceny -Theft	Motor Vehicle Theft
Albany, NY	2,176.0	2.2	38.3	62.4	180.8	226.9	1,584.8	80.6
Albuquerque, NM	5,611.3	9.5	70.0	238.2	766.9	869.9	2,838.9	817.8
Allentown, PA	1,602.4	1.9	24.7	41.3	96.2	202.8	1,152.7	82.8
Anchorage, AK	6,280.4	8.4	200.1	235.2	819.9	703.4	3,342.5	970.9
Ann Arbor, MI	1,818.7	3.5	65.9	39.6	213.6	226.8	1,179.1	90.1
Athens, GA[3]	2,882.3	3.4	34.7	65.0	204.7	444.1	1,990.8	139.7
Atlanta, GA	2,895.7	5.7	26.1	94.1	194.7	393.9	1,903.2	278.0
Austin, TX	2,611.0	2.4	60.9	58.9	169.2	339.4	1,819.1	161.0
Baton Rouge, LA	4,117.6	14.9	29.4	124.4	362.7	694.6	2,686.3	205.1
Boise City, ID	1,812.6	1.2	54.0	14.1	174.7	274.8	1,170.3	123.5
Boston, MA[2]	1,813.8	3.3	35.7	87.5	279.4	178.8	1,118.3	110.8
Boulder, CO	n/a	0.6	61.5	29.1	178.8	328.5	n/a	219.5
Cape Coral, FL	1,706.9	5.3	36.4	59.9	179.0	237.9	1,048.0	140.3
Cedar Rapids, IA[3]	2,627.4	3.0	26.4	51.3	136.8	505.1	1,735.4	169.5
Charleston, SC	2,989.4	7.7	35.2	75.6	265.7	384.3	1,944.9	276.0
Charlotte, NC	3,166.6	5.2	27.6	101.3	292.7	502.3	2,036.0	201.5
Chicago, IL[2]	n/a	9.2	43.3	163.5	n/a	n/a	n/a	198.4
Clarksville, TN	2,805.4	6.3	39.7	55.3	340.0	426.8	1,747.2	190.0
Cleveland, OH	n/a	n/a	n/a	n/a	n/a	n/a	n/a	n/a
College Station, TX	2,418.8	1.9	63.4	35.5	171.6	350.0	1,657.2	139.1
Colorado Springs, CO	3,116.1	6.0	93.4	78.6	288.4	451.9	1,804.0	393.8
Columbia, MO	2,635.0	4.3	52.8	55.7	178.2	356.9	1,784.7	202.2
Columbia, SC	4,073.9	7.3	50.3	86.9	423.4	578.0	2,517.4	410.6
Columbus, OH	2,834.4	6.1	59.2	109.2	108.0	458.9	1,849.0	244.1
Dallas, TX[2]	2,536.2	4.8	44.3	117.0	187.7	361.1	1,492.0	329.3
Davenport, IA[3]	3,237.8	4.7	56.7	70.6	272.1	579.6	2,023.4	230.6
Denver, CO	n/a	n/a	n/a	n/a	n/a	n/a	n/a	n/a
Des Moines, IA[3]	n/a	n/a	n/a	n/a	n/a	n/a	n/a	n/a
Durham, NC	n/a	n/a	n/a	n/a	n/a	n/a	n/a	n/a
Edison, NJ[2]	n/a	n/a	n/a	n/a	n/a	n/a	n/a	n/a
El Paso, TX	1,762.6	3.8	54.7	47.6	238.8	164.3	1,142.4	111.0
Fargo, ND	2,722.8	2.5	57.7	31.9	188.8	421.3	1,831.9	188.8
Fayetteville, NC[3]	n/a	8.1	n/a	92.8	329.9	660.6	2,185.0	127.8
Fort Collins, CO	2,222.9	1.4	34.3	17.2	168.0	226.1	1,666.5	109.3
Fort Wayne, IN	2,364.2	10.3	41.1	85.1	173.1	313.4	1,579.7	161.6
Fort Worth, TX[2]	2,680.5	3.5	46.6	76.3	218.9	360.4	1,729.4	245.3
Grand Rapids, MI	1,709.5	2.4	89.8	47.6	191.0	223.1	1,069.0	86.5
Greeley, CO	n/a	1.9	51.2	28.0	177.6	261.6	n/a	194.1
Green Bay, WI	1,362.7	0.3	47.2	20.2	141.9	148.7	945.8	58.7
Greensboro, NC	3,020.6	8.6	25.8	101.0	292.5	567.6	1,843.7	181.3
Honolulu, HI	n/a	n/a	n/a	n/a	n/a	n/a	n/a	n/a
Houston, TX	n/a	6.3	44.1	176.7	n/a	443.5	1,846.7	314.5
Huntsville, AL[3]	3,685.7	7.3	56.3	97.0	396.3	560.7	2,249.3	318.9
Indianapolis, IN	3,285.3	9.3	46.3	166.8	419.1	496.7	1,830.9	316.2
Jackson, MS	n/a	n/a	n/a	n/a	n/a	n/a	n/a	n/a
Jacksonville, FL	3,073.3	8.0	48.1	99.7	296.7	433.9	1,941.7	245.1
Kansas City, MO	n/a	n/a	n/a	n/a	n/a	n/a	n/a	n/a
Lafayette, LA	3,744.0	9.0	23.9	67.3	366.5	722.0	2,322.8	232.5
Lakeland, FL	2,061.5	3.4	27.6	40.9	224.5	316.8	1,306.6	141.7
Las Vegas, NV	n/a	7.6	82.9	151.4	n/a	657.6	1,568.5	444.7
Lexington, KY	3,142.4	4.6	59.0	94.9	80.6	451.5	2,186.9	264.9
Lincoln, NE	2,963.3	1.8	96.1	49.0	183.9	374.3	2,117.1	141.2
Little Rock, AR	n/a	9.2	66.1	89.1	573.7	n/a	2,785.7	339.5
Los Angeles, CA[2]	2,924.6	5.6	44.3	192.2	335.8	419.9	1,518.1	408.6

Table continued on next page.

Metro Area[1]	All Crimes	Violent Crimes				Property Crimes		
		Murder	Rape	Robbery	Aggrav. Assault	Burglary	Larceny -Theft	Motor Vehicle Theft
Louisville, KY[3]	3,512.3	9.5	23.1	123.1	261.9	588.9	2,108.3	397.5
Madison, WI	2,013.1	1.5	32.9	47.3	160.8	260.1	1,385.3	125.1
Manchester, NH	1,593.2	1.7	39.9	42.3	145.9	142.3	1,145.3	75.9
Miami, FL[2]	3,610.0	7.1	32.9	131.1	321.8	329.4	2,488.4	299.2
Midland, TX	2,288.6	5.1	39.5	40.1	232.9	275.8	1,463.0	232.3
Milwaukee, WI	2,689.7	7.2	43.7	165.0	393.9	355.2	1,369.6	355.3
Minneapolis, MN	2,413.9	1.9	45.9	73.0	132.6	294.2	1,650.5	215.8
Nashville, TN	n/a	7.8	45.9	128.8	416.5	342.4	1,956.1	n/a
New Haven, CT	2,731.4	3.0	24.8	94.9	172.2	324.5	1,789.9	322.1
New Orleans, LA	n/a	15.5	69.1	134.3	344.8	372.9	n/a	333.8
New York, NY[2]	n/a	n/a	n/a	n/a	n/a	n/a	n/a	n/a
Oklahoma City, OK	3,606.9	5.2	61.4	95.4	367.5	684.4	2,003.8	389.2
Omaha, NE	n/a	n/a	n/a	n/a	n/a	n/a	n/a	n/a
Orlando, FL	2,895.4	5.4	49.9	93.2	294.4	406.7	1,855.6	190.3
Peoria, IL	n/a	6.7	54.1	63.0	243.0	430.3	n/a	158.9
Philadelphia, PA[2]	3,462.1	18.3	55.2	270.0	420.3	355.2	2,042.3	300.9
Phoenix, AZ	3,054.9	4.6	49.5	98.2	294.0	431.8	1,902.7	274.2
Pittsburgh, PA	1,687.7	5.5	25.8	58.8	184.5	196.1	1,137.0	80.0
Portland, OR	3,169.1	1.9	55.5	70.7	171.0	364.6	2,008.8	496.6
Providence, RI	1,817.1	1.4	43.0	49.9	189.8	259.4	1,144.7	128.9
Provo, UT	1,447.8	0.8	32.1	7.4	47.5	140.4	1,141.3	78.2
Raleigh, NC	n/a	n/a	n/a	n/a	n/a	n/a	n/a	n/a
Reno, NV	2,594.4	3.4	64.2	86.6	359.2	401.0	1,363.2	316.8
Richmond, VA	2,395.4	7.8	27.7	63.1	140.8	248.1	1,716.6	191.3
Rochester, MN	1,553.3	2.7	37.8	21.8	79.6	229.4	1,103.2	78.7
Sacramento, CA	2,536.8	3.7	29.2	105.3	237.1	382.5	1,450.4	328.5
Salt Lake City, UT	4,030.3	2.7	73.8	78.3	214.1	465.6	2,750.3	445.5
San Antonio, TX	n/a	5.4	72.2	80.3	n/a	480.3	2,317.7	293.5
San Diego, CA	2,035.4	2.5	34.7	88.9	214.9	247.8	1,160.0	286.5
San Francisco, CA[2]	4,384.3	3.5	39.6	230.5	212.8	469.7	3,073.7	354.4
San Jose, CA	2,610.7	1.6	43.3	106.4	162.8	375.8	1,406.2	514.4
Santa Rosa, CA	1,819.0	1.8	62.0	53.3	277.5	273.3	1,015.4	135.7
Savannah, GA	3,107.5	9.2	35.9	93.7	247.2	415.6	2,032.0	274.0
Seattle, WA[2]	3,677.9	2.7	37.3	106.2	186.5	583.4	2,298.2	463.5
Sioux Falls, SD	2,687.9	1.9	57.7	41.1	243.0	350.8	1,761.8	231.6
Springfield, IL	3,800.3	4.8	61.7	112.8	416.8	727.1	2,302.7	174.4
Tallahassee, FL	3,866.5	7.0	73.1	99.6	379.1	593.7	2,443.3	270.6
Tampa, FL	2,161.4	3.8	38.5	55.0	209.1	256.6	1,457.3	141.1
Topeka, KS	4,049.0	9.5	50.4	114.1	268.8	590.1	2,618.6	397.5
Tucson, AZ	4,159.7	5.5	59.4	136.5	256.0	482.6	2,891.4	328.4
Tulsa, OK	3,884.5	7.9	69.3	96.0	391.6	727.8	2,135.4	456.6
Tuscaloosa, AL	3,445.1	4.0	35.6	80.3	276.5	607.5	2,189.7	251.6
Virginia Beach, VA	2,711.8	6.9	33.2	73.0	193.7	274.4	1,949.7	180.9
Washington, DC[2]	2,053.4	5.9	33.2	93.6	160.7	138.5	1,454.4	167.2
Wichita, KS	5,058.0	7.7	75.8	98.9	643.6	690.9	3,037.4	503.7
Winston-Salem, NC	n/a	n/a	n/a	n/a	n/a	n/a	n/a	n/a
U.S.	2,580.1	5.0	42.6	86.2	246.8	376.0	1,594.6	228.9

Note: Figures are crimes per 100,000 population in 2018 except where noted; n/a not available; (1) Figures cover the Metropolitan Statistical Area except where noted; (2) Metropolitan Division (MD); (3) 2017 data
Source: FBI Uniform Crime Reports, 2017, 2018

Temperature & Precipitation: Yearly Averages and Extremes

City	Extreme Low (°F)	Average Low (°F)	Average Temp. (°F)	Average High (°F)	Extreme High (°F)	Average Precip. (in.)	Average Snow (in.)
Albany, NY	-28	37	48	58	100	35.8	63
Albuquerque, NM	-17	43	57	70	105	8.5	11
Allentown, PA	-12	42	52	61	105	44.2	32
Anchorage, AK	-34	29	36	43	85	15.7	71
Ann Arbor, MI	-21	39	49	58	104	32.4	41
Athens, GA	-8	52	62	72	105	49.8	2
Atlanta, GA	-8	52	62	72	105	49.8	2
Austin, TX	-2	58	69	79	109	31.1	1
Baton Rouge, LA	8	57	68	78	103	58.5	Trace
Boise City, ID	-25	39	51	63	111	11.8	22
Boston, MA	-12	44	52	59	102	42.9	41
Boulder, CO	-25	37	51	64	103	15.5	63
Cape Coral, FL	26	65	75	84	103	53.9	0
Cedar Rapids, IA	-34	36	47	57	105	34.4	33
Charleston, SC	6	55	66	76	104	52.1	1
Charlotte, NC	-5	50	61	71	104	42.8	6
Chicago, IL	-27	40	49	59	104	35.4	39
Clarksville, TN	-17	49	60	70	107	47.4	11
Cleveland, OH	-19	41	50	59	104	37.1	55
College Station, TX	-2	58	69	79	109	31.1	1
Colorado Springs, CO	-24	36	49	62	99	17.0	48
Columbia, MO	-20	44	54	64	111	40.6	25
Columbia, SC	-1	51	64	75	107	48.3	2
Columbus, OH	-19	42	52	62	104	37.9	28
Dallas, TX	-2	56	67	77	112	33.9	3
Davenport, IA	-24	40	50	60	108	31.8	33
Denver, CO	-25	37	51	64	103	15.5	63
Des Moines, IA	-24	40	50	60	108	31.8	33
Durham, NC	-9	48	60	71	105	42.0	8
Edison, NJ	-8	46	55	63	105	43.5	27
El Paso, TX	-8	50	64	78	114	8.6	6
Fargo, ND	-36	31	41	52	106	19.6	40
Fayetteville, NC	-9	48	60	71	105	42.0	8
Fort Collins, CO	-25	37	51	64	103	15.5	63
Fort Wayne, IN	-22	40	50	60	106	35.9	33
Fort Worth, TX	-1	55	66	76	113	32.3	3
Grand Rapids, MI	-22	38	48	57	102	34.7	73
Greeley, CO	-25	37	51	64	103	15.5	63
Green Bay, WI	-31	34	44	54	99	28.3	46
Greensboro, NC	-8	47	58	69	103	42.5	10
Honolulu, HI	52	70	77	84	94	22.4	0
Houston, TX	7	58	69	79	107	46.9	Trace
Huntsville, AL	-11	50	61	71	104	56.8	4
Indianapolis, IN	-23	42	53	62	104	40.2	25
Jackson, MS	2	53	65	76	106	55.4	1
Jacksonville, FL	7	58	69	79	103	52.0	0
Kansas City, MO	-23	44	54	64	109	38.1	21
Lafayette, LA	8	57	68	78	103	58.5	Trace
Lakeland, FL	18	63	73	82	99	46.7	Trace
Las Vegas, NV	8	53	67	80	116	4.0	1
Lexington, KY	-21	45	55	65	103	45.1	17
Lincoln, NE	-33	39	51	62	108	29.1	27
Little Rock, AR	-5	51	62	73	112	50.7	5
Los Angeles, CA	27	55	63	70	110	11.3	Trace
Louisville, KY	-20	46	57	67	105	43.9	17

Table continued on next page.

City	Extreme Low (°F)	Average Low (°F)	Average Temp. (°F)	Average High (°F)	Extreme High (°F)	Average Precip. (in.)	Average Snow (in.)
Madison, WI	-37	35	46	57	104	31.1	42
Manchester, NH	-33	34	46	57	102	36.9	63
Miami, FL	30	69	76	83	98	57.1	0
Midland, TX	-11	50	64	77	116	14.6	4
Milwaukee, WI	-26	38	47	55	103	32.0	49
Minneapolis, MN	-34	35	45	54	105	27.1	52
Nashville, TN	-17	49	60	70	107	47.4	11
New Haven, CT	-7	44	52	60	103	41.4	25
New Orleans, LA	11	59	69	78	102	60.6	Trace
New York, NY	-2	47	55	62	104	47.0	23
Oklahoma City, OK	-8	49	60	71	110	32.8	10
Omaha, NE	-23	40	51	62	110	30.1	29
Orlando, FL	19	62	72	82	100	47.7	Trace
Peoria, IL	-26	41	51	61	113	35.4	23
Philadelphia, PA	-7	45	55	64	104	41.4	22
Phoenix, AZ	17	59	72	86	122	7.3	Trace
Pittsburgh, PA	-18	41	51	60	103	37.1	43
Portland, OR	-3	45	54	62	107	37.5	7
Providence, RI	-13	42	51	60	104	45.3	35
Provo, UT	-22	40	52	64	107	15.6	63
Raleigh, NC	-9	48	60	71	105	42.0	8
Reno, NV	-16	33	50	67	105	7.2	24
Richmond, VA	-8	48	58	69	105	43.0	13
Rochester, MN	-40	34	44	54	102	29.4	47
Sacramento, CA	18	48	61	73	115	17.3	Trace
Salt Lake City, UT	-22	40	52	64	107	15.6	63
San Antonio, TX	0	58	69	80	108	29.6	1
San Diego, CA	29	57	64	71	111	9.5	Trace
San Francisco, CA	24	49	57	65	106	19.3	Trace
San Jose, CA	21	50	59	68	105	13.5	Trace
Santa Rosa, CA	23	42	57	71	109	29.0	n/a
Savannah, GA	3	56	67	77	105	50.3	Trace
Seattle, WA	0	44	52	59	99	38.4	13
Sioux Falls, SD	-36	35	46	57	110	24.6	38
Springfield, IL	-24	44	54	63	112	34.9	21
Tallahassee, FL	6	56	68	79	103	63.3	Trace
Tampa, FL	18	63	73	82	99	46.7	Trace
Topeka, KS	-26	43	55	66	110	34.4	21
Tucson, AZ	16	55	69	82	117	11.6	2
Tulsa, OK	-8	50	61	71	112	38.9	10
Tuscaloosa, AL	-6	51	63	74	106	53.5	2
Virginia Beach, VA	-3	51	60	69	104	44.8	8
Washington, DC	-5	49	58	67	104	39.5	18
Wichita, KS	-21	45	57	68	113	29.3	17
Winston-Salem, NC	-8	47	58	69	103	42.5	10

Source: National Climatic Data Center, International Station Meteorological Climate Summary, 9/96

Weather Conditions

City	Temperature			Daytime Sky			Precipitation		
	10°F & below	32°F & below	90°F & above	Clear	Partly cloudy	Cloudy	0.01 inch or more precip.	1.0 inch or more snow/ice	Thunder-storms
Albany, NY	n/a	147	11	58	149	158	133	36	24
Albuquerque, NM	4	114	65	140	161	64	60	9	38
Allentown, PA	n/a	123	15	77	148	140	123	20	31
Anchorage, AK	n/a	194	n/a	50	115	200	113	49	2
Ann Arbor, MI	n/a	136	12	74	134	157	135	38	32
Athens, GA	1	49	38	98	147	120	116	3	48
Atlanta, GA	1	49	38	98	147	120	116	3	48
Austin, TX	< 1	20	111	105	148	112	83	1	41
Baton Rouge, LA	< 1	21	86	99	150	116	113	< 1	73
Boise City, ID	n/a	124	45	106	133	126	91	22	14
Boston, MA	n/a	97	12	88	127	150	253	48	18
Boulder, CO	24	155	33	99	177	89	90	38	39
Cape Coral, FL	n/a	n/a	115	93	220	52	110	0	92
Cedar Rapids, IA	n/a	156	16	89	132	144	109	28	42
Charleston, SC	< 1	33	53	89	162	114	114	1	59
Charlotte, NC	1	65	44	98	142	125	113	3	41
Chicago, IL	n/a	132	17	83	136	146	125	31	38
Clarksville, TN	5	76	51	98	135	132	119	8	54
Cleveland, OH	n/a	123	12	63	127	175	157	48	34
College Station, TX	< 1	20	111	105	148	112	83	1	41
Colorado Springs, CO	21	161	18	108	157	100	98	33	49
Columbia, MO	17	108	36	99	127	139	110	17	52
Columbia, SC	< 1	58	77	97	149	119	110	1	53
Columbus, OH	n/a	118	19	72	137	156	136	29	40
Dallas, TX	1	34	102	108	160	97	78	2	49
Davenport, IA	n/a	137	26	99	129	137	106	25	46
Denver, CO	24	155	33	99	177	89	90	38	39
Des Moines, IA	n/a	137	26	99	129	137	106	25	46
Durham, NC	n/a	n/a	39	98	143	124	110	3	42
Edison, NJ	n/a	90	24	80	146	139	122	16	46
El Paso, TX	1	59	106	147	164	54	49	3	35
Fargo, ND	n/a	180	15	81	145	139	100	38	31
Fayetteville, NC	n/a	n/a	39	98	143	124	110	3	42
Fort Collins, CO	24	155	33	99	177	89	90	38	39
Fort Wayne, IN	n/a	131	16	75	140	150	131	31	39
Fort Worth, TX	1	40	100	123	136	106	79	3	47
Grand Rapids, MI	n/a	146	11	67	119	179	142	57	34
Greeley, CO	24	155	33	99	177	89	90	38	39
Green Bay, WI	n/a	163	7	86	125	154	120	40	33
Greensboro, NC	3	85	32	94	143	128	113	5	43
Honolulu, HI	n/a	n/a	23	25	286	54	98	0	7
Houston, TX	n/a	n/a	96	83	168	114	101	1	62
Huntsville, AL	2	66	49	70	118	177	116	2	54
Indianapolis, IN	19	119	19	83	128	154	127	24	43
Jackson, MS	1	50	84	103	144	118	106	2	68
Jacksonville, FL	< 1	16	83	86	181	98	114	1	65
Kansas City, MO	22	110	39	112	134	119	103	17	51
Lafayette, LA	< 1	21	86	99	150	116	113	< 1	73
Lakeland, FL	n/a	n/a	85	81	204	80	107	< 1	87
Las Vegas, NV	< 1	37	134	185	132	48	27	2	13
Lexington, KY	11	96	22	86	136	143	129	17	44
Lincoln, NE	n/a	145	40	108	135	122	94	19	46
Little Rock, AR	1	57	73	110	142	113	104	4	57
Los Angeles, CA	0	< 1	5	131	125	109	34	0	1

Table continued on next page.

City	Temperature			Daytime Sky			Precipitation		
	10°F & below	32°F & below	90°F & above	Clear	Partly cloudy	Cloudy	0.01 inch or more precip.	1.0 inch or more snow/ice	Thunder-storms
Louisville, KY	8	90	35	82	143	140	125	15	45
Madison, WI	n/a	161	14	88	119	158	118	38	40
Manchester, NH	n/a	171	12	87	131	147	125	32	19
Miami, FL	n/a	n/a	55	48	263	54	128	0	74
Midland, TX	1	62	102	144	138	83	52	3	38
Milwaukee, WI	n/a	141	10	90	118	157	126	38	35
Minneapolis, MN	n/a	156	16	93	125	147	113	41	37
Nashville, TN	5	76	51	98	135	132	119	8	54
New Haven, CT	n/a	n/a	7	80	146	139	118	17	22
New Orleans, LA	0	13	70	90	169	106	114	1	69
New York, NY	n/a	n/a	18	85	166	114	120	11	20
Oklahoma City, OK	5	79	70	124	131	110	80	8	50
Omaha, NE	n/a	139	35	100	142	123	97	20	46
Orlando, FL	n/a	n/a	90	76	208	81	115	0	80
Peoria, IL	n/a	127	27	89	127	149	115	22	49
Philadelphia, PA	5	94	23	81	146	138	117	14	27
Phoenix, AZ	0	10	167	186	125	54	37	< 1	23
Pittsburgh, PA	n/a	121	8	62	137	166	154	42	35
Portland, OR	n/a	37	11	67	116	182	152	4	7
Providence, RI	n/a	117	9	85	134	146	123	21	21
Provo, UT	n/a	128	56	94	152	119	92	38	38
Raleigh, NC	n/a	n/a	39	98	143	124	110	3	42
Reno, NV	14	178	50	143	139	83	50	17	14
Richmond, VA	3	79	41	90	147	128	115	7	43
Rochester, MN	n/a	165	9	87	126	152	114	40	41
Sacramento, CA	0	21	73	175	111	79	58	< 1	2
Salt Lake City, UT	n/a	128	56	94	152	119	92	38	38
San Antonio, TX	n/a	n/a	112	97	153	115	81	1	36
San Diego, CA	0	< 1	4	115	126	124	40	0	5
San Francisco, CA	0	6	4	136	130	99	63	< 1	5
San Jose, CA	0	5	5	106	180	79	57	< 1	6
Santa Rosa, CA	n/a	43	30	n/a	365	n/a	n/a	n/a	2
Savannah, GA	< 1	29	70	97	155	113	111	< 1	63
Seattle, WA	n/a	38	3	57	121	187	157	8	8
Sioux Falls, SD	n/a	n/a	n/a	95	136	134	n/a	n/a	n/a
Springfield, IL	19	111	34	96	126	143	111	18	49
Tallahassee, FL	< 1	31	86	93	175	97	114	1	83
Tampa, FL	n/a	n/a	85	81	204	80	107	< 1	87
Topeka, KS	20	123	45	110	128	127	96	15	54
Tucson, AZ	0	18	140	177	119	69	54	2	42
Tulsa, OK	6	78	74	117	141	107	88	8	50
Tuscaloosa, AL	1	57	59	91	161	113	119	1	57
Virginia Beach, VA	< 1	53	33	89	149	127	115	5	38
Washington, DC	2	71	34	84	144	137	112	9	30
Wichita, KS	13	110	63	117	132	116	87	13	54
Winston-Salem, NC	3	85	32	94	143	128	113	5	43

Note: Figures are average number of days per year
Source: National Climatic Data Center, International Station Meteorological Climate Summary, 9/96

Air Quality Index

MSA[1] (Days[2])	Percent of Days when Air Quality was...					AQI Statistics	
	Good	Moderate	Unhealthy for Sensitive Groups	Unhealthy	Very Unhealthy	Maximum	Median
Albany, NY (365)	78.9	20.3	0.8	0.0	0.0	119	38
Albuquerque, NM (365)	41.4	52.1	6.3	0.3	0.0	165	54
Allentown, PA (365)	67.4	31.2	1.4	0.0	0.0	136	42
Anchorage, AK (365)	80.3	18.6	0.8	0.3	0.0	151	30
Ann Arbor, MI (365)	77.0	21.4	1.6	0.0	0.0	150	40
Athens, GA (332)	78.9	20.5	0.6	0.0	0.0	105	39
Atlanta, GA (365)	57.3	40.0	2.7	0.0	0.0	133	48
Austin, TX (365)	65.5	32.1	2.5	0.0	0.0	115	44
Baton Rouge, LA (365)	61.4	33.4	4.9	0.3	0.0	153	45
Boise City, ID (365)	54.8	42.2	3.0	0.0	0.0	134	49
Boston, MA (365)	61.6	37.0	1.4	0.0	0.0	126	45
Boulder, CO (362)	60.5	31.5	7.7	0.3	0.0	159	46
Cape Coral, FL (365)	86.6	13.2	0.3	0.0	0.0	106	35
Cedar Rapids, IA (365)	68.2	30.7	1.1	0.0	0.0	129	44
Charleston, SC (359)	90.8	9.2	0.0	0.0	0.0	97	36
Charlotte, NC (364)	62.9	34.3	2.7	0.0	0.0	122	45
Chicago, IL (365)	32.1	60.8	5.5	1.6	0.0	177	57
Clarksville, TN (365)	79.2	20.8	0.0	0.0	0.0	90	40
Cleveland, OH (365)	55.3	40.5	4.1	0.0	0.0	138	48
College Station, TX (332)	100.0	0.0	0.0	0.0	0.0	26	0
Colorado Springs, CO (365)	61.9	33.7	4.4	0.0	0.0	133	47
Columbia, MO (245)	84.9	14.7	0.4	0.0	0.0	105	40
Columbia, SC (365)	76.4	23.3	0.3	0.0	0.0	101	40
Columbus, OH (365)	69.6	29.6	0.8	0.0	0.0	122	44
Dallas, TX (365)	51.0	39.2	7.4	2.5	0.0	166	50
Davenport, IA (365)	47.1	51.8	1.1	0.0	0.0	108	52
Denver, CO (365)	22.7	61.6	13.4	2.2	0.0	174	64
Des Moines, IA (365)	77.8	21.6	0.5	0.0	0.0	112	40
Durham, NC (359)	74.7	25.3	0.0	0.0	0.0	100	43
Edison, NJ (365)	42.7	49.9	6.6	0.5	0.3	210	53
El Paso, TX (365)	36.4	58.9	4.1	0.5	0.0	164	55
Fargo, ND (360)	87.5	12.2	0.3	0.0	0.0	121	35
Fayetteville, NC (349)	81.4	18.6	0.0	0.0	0.0	100	38
Fort Collins, CO (365)	53.4	38.9	6.8	0.8	0.0	169	50
Fort Wayne, IN (365)	66.6	31.8	1.6	0.0	0.0	122	44
Fort Worth, TX (365)	51.0	39.2	7.4	2.5	0.0	166	50
Grand Rapids, MI (365)	79.5	19.5	1.1	0.0	0.0	115	40
Greeley, CO (365)	51.2	46.0	2.7	0.0	0.0	133	50
Green Bay, WI (365)	78.9	19.5	1.4	0.3	0.0	151	41
Greensboro, NC (357)	77.6	22.1	0.3	0.0	0.0	105	41
Honolulu, HI (365)	98.1	1.9	0.0	0.0	0.0	75	30
Houston, TX (365)	45.5	44.9	7.1	1.9	0.5	204	51
Huntsville, AL (365)	75.3	24.4	0.3	0.0	0.0	115	41
Indianapolis, IN (365)	51.2	44.4	4.1	0.3	0.0	156	50
Jackson, MS (365)	69.9	29.9	0.3	0.0	0.0	112	44
Jacksonville, FL (365)	73.2	24.9	1.6	0.3	0.0	155	41
Kansas City, MO (365)	57.8	38.6	3.3	0.3	0.0	172	47
Lafayette, LA (365)	72.9	27.1	0.0	0.0	0.0	97	41
Lakeland, FL (365)	88.8	10.7	0.5	0.0	0.0	112	35
Las Vegas, NV (365)	33.4	53.2	13.2	0.3	0.0	154	61
Lexington, KY (365)	72.9	27.1	0.0	0.0	0.0	90	40
Lincoln, NE (365)	90.4	9.6	0.0	0.0	0.0	78	31
Little Rock, AR (365)	70.4	29.0	0.5	0.0	0.0	122	43
Los Angeles, CA (365)	9.6	60.3	24.7	5.2	0.3	201	77

Table continued on next page.

MSA[1] (Days[2])	Percent of Days when Air Quality was...					AQI Statistics	
	Good	Moderate	Unhealthy for Sensitive Groups	Unhealthy	Very Unhealthy	Maximum	Median
Louisville, KY (365)	56.2	40.8	2.5	0.5	0.0	166	48
Madison, WI (365)	74.2	25.2	0.5	0.0	0.0	122	42
Manchester, NH (365)	92.6	7.4	0.0	0.0	0.0	97	36
Miami, FL (365)	72.3	26.6	1.1	0.0	0.0	126	43
Midland, TX (n/a)	n/a	n/a	n/a	n/a	n/a	n/a	n/a
Milwaukee, WI (365)	64.7	32.9	1.9	0.5	0.0	169	44
Minneapolis, MN (365)	47.4	51.2	1.4	0.0	0.0	122	51
Nashville, TN (365)	67.7	30.4	1.6	0.3	0.0	151	43
New Haven, CT (365)	75.6	20.5	3.3	0.5	0.0	156	40
New Orleans, LA (365)	60.0	38.4	1.6	0.0	0.0	112	46
New York, NY (365)	42.7	49.9	6.6	0.5	0.3	210	53
Oklahoma City, OK (365)	58.1	38.6	3.3	0.0	0.0	150	47
Omaha, NE (365)	62.7	35.9	1.4	0.0	0.0	108	46
Orlando, FL (365)	84.7	14.5	0.5	0.3	0.0	151	38
Peoria, IL (365)	69.9	29.3	0.8	0.0	0.0	101	43
Philadelphia, PA (365)	36.2	58.6	4.4	0.8	0.0	164	55
Phoenix, AZ (365)	11.5	65.2	18.1	1.9	1.1	996	77
Pittsburgh, PA (365)	37.3	55.9	6.6	0.3	0.0	154	55
Portland, OR (365)	76.4	21.1	1.9	0.5	0.0	165	38
Providence, RI (365)	72.6	23.8	3.6	0.0	0.0	147	44
Provo, UT (365)	59.7	31.5	6.8	1.9	0.0	162	46
Raleigh, NC (361)	66.5	33.5	0.0	0.0	0.0	90	45
Reno, NV (365)	58.4	36.4	5.2	0.0	0.0	146	48
Richmond, VA (365)	76.7	22.7	0.5	0.0	0.0	147	41
Rochester, MN (361)	80.9	19.1	0.0	0.0	0.0	98	38
Sacramento, CA (365)	34.0	47.1	12.3	4.4	1.9	314	61
Salt Lake City, UT (365)	37.8	50.4	11.2	0.5	0.0	169	61
San Antonio, TX (365)	68.8	28.2	2.7	0.3	0.0	162	43
San Diego, CA (365)	20.0	70.4	9.6	0.0	0.0	143	64
San Francisco, CA (365)	40.3	54.5	1.9	2.5	0.8	245	53
San Jose, CA (365)	59.2	35.9	1.9	3.0	0.0	194	47
Santa Rosa, CA (365)	89.0	7.4	0.8	2.2	0.5	226	36
Savannah, GA (365)	83.0	17.0	0.0	0.0	0.0	82	38
Seattle, WA (365)	65.5	30.1	2.5	1.9	0.0	192	44
Sioux Falls, SD (365)	84.7	14.5	0.8	0.0	0.0	115	37
Springfield, IL (363)	69.7	30.0	0.3	0.0	0.0	122	43
Tallahassee, FL (358)	76.0	24.0	0.0	0.0	0.0	98	38
Tampa, FL (365)	66.3	32.3	1.4	0.0	0.0	129	43
Topeka, KS (365)	74.5	25.5	0.0	0.0	0.0	99	42
Tucson, AZ (365)	53.7	43.3	3.0	0.0	0.0	129	49
Tulsa, OK (365)	50.4	46.6	2.7	0.3	0.0	192	50
Tuscaloosa, AL (320)	82.8	16.9	0.3	0.0	0.0	115	37
Virginia Beach, VA (365)	87.9	12.1	0.0	0.0	0.0	97	36
Washington, DC (365)	53.2	44.1	2.5	0.3	0.0	166	49
Wichita, KS (365)	71.5	28.5	0.0	0.0	0.0	100	41
Winston-Salem, NC (365)	63.8	35.6	0.5	0.0	0.0	101	44

Note: The Air Quality Index (AQI) is an index for reporting daily air quality. EPA calculates the AQI for five major air pollutants regulated by the Clean Air Act: ground-level ozone, particle pollution (also known as particulate matter), carbon monoxide, sulfur dioxide, and nitrogen dioxide. The AQI runs from 0 to 500. The higher the AQI value, the greater the level of air pollution and the greater the health concern. There are six AQI categories: "Good" The AQI is between 0 and 50. Air quality is considered satisfactory; "Moderate" The AQI is between 51 and 100. Air quality is acceptable; "Unhealthy for Sensitive Groups" When AQI values are between 101 and 150, members of sensitive groups may experience health effects; "Unhealthy" When AQI values are between 151 and 200 everyone may begin to experience health effects; "Very Unhealthy" AQI values between 201 and 300 trigger a health alert; "Hazardous" AQI values over 300 trigger health warnings of emergency conditions; Data covers the entire county unless noted otherwise; (1) Data covers the Metropolitan Statistical Area—see Appendix B for areas included; (2) Number of days with AQI data in 2018

Source: U.S. Environmental Protection Agency, Air Quality Index Report, 2018

Air Quality Index Pollutants

MSA[1] (Days[2])	Percent of Days when AQI Pollutant was...					
	Carbon Monoxide	Nitrogen Dioxide	Ozone	Sulfur Dioxide	Particulate Matter 2.5	Particulate Matter 10
Albany, NY (365)	0.0	0.0	63.8	0.0	36.2	0.0
Albuquerque, NM (365)	0.0	0.3	71.0	0.0	14.0	14.8
Allentown, PA (365)	0.0	1.6	49.3	0.0	49.0	0.0
Anchorage, AK (365)	0.3	0.0	39.7	0.0	44.7	15.3
Ann Arbor, MI (365)	0.0	0.0	64.1	0.0	35.9	0.0
Athens, GA (332)	0.0	0.0	45.5	0.0	54.5	0.0
Atlanta, GA (365)	0.0	3.0	43.0	0.0	54.0	0.0
Austin, TX (365)	0.0	4.1	42.7	0.0	52.9	0.3
Baton Rouge, LA (365)	0.0	0.8	51.0	1.6	46.6	0.0
Boise City, ID (365)	0.0	0.0	41.4	0.0	55.6	3.0
Boston, MA (365)	0.0	2.5	33.2	0.0	64.4	0.0
Boulder, CO (362)	0.0	0.0	78.7	0.0	21.3	0.0
Cape Coral, FL (365)	0.0	0.0	80.5	0.0	19.5	0.0
Cedar Rapids, IA (365)	0.0	0.0	41.1	0.8	57.8	0.3
Charleston, SC (359)	0.0	0.8	58.8	0.0	40.1	0.3
Charlotte, NC (364)	0.0	0.5	60.7	0.0	38.5	0.3
Chicago, IL (365)	0.0	7.9	30.7	1.6	56.2	3.6
Clarksville, TN (365)	0.0	0.0	62.7	0.0	37.3	0.0
Cleveland, OH (365)	0.0	1.6	48.5	2.2	45.2	2.5
College Station, TX (332)	0.0	0.0	0.0	100.0	0.0	0.0
Colorado Springs, CO (365)	0.0	0.0	91.2	0.0	8.8	0.0
Columbia, MO (245)	0.0	0.0	100.0	0.0	0.0	0.0
Columbia, SC (365)	0.0	0.0	57.5	0.0	42.5	0.0
Columbus, OH (365)	0.0	5.5	52.9	0.0	41.4	0.3
Dallas, TX (365)	0.0	2.5	51.8	0.0	45.8	0.0
Davenport, IA (365)	0.0	0.3	22.5	0.0	52.9	24.4
Denver, CO (365)	0.0	15.3	63.6	0.0	15.3	5.8
Des Moines, IA (365)	0.0	1.4	61.6	0.0	37.0	0.0
Durham, NC (359)	0.0	0.0	47.1	0.6	52.1	0.3
Edison, NJ (365)	0.0	11.8	35.6	0.3	52.3	0.0
El Paso, TX (365)	0.0	7.1	52.1	0.0	40.3	0.5
Fargo, ND (360)	0.0	2.5	66.4	0.0	28.6	2.5
Fayetteville, NC (349)	0.0	0.0	55.6	0.0	41.5	2.9
Fort Collins, CO (365)	0.0	0.0	88.2	0.0	11.8	0.0
Fort Wayne, IN (365)	0.0	0.0	52.3	0.0	47.7	0.0
Fort Worth, TX (365)	0.0	2.5	51.8	0.0	45.8	0.0
Grand Rapids, MI (365)	0.0	0.0	63.8	0.0	36.2	0.0
Greeley, CO (365)	0.0	0.0	72.3	0.0	27.4	0.3
Green Bay, WI (365)	0.0	0.0	61.1	1.9	37.0	0.0
Greensboro, NC (357)	0.0	0.0	62.7	0.0	32.8	4.5
Honolulu, HI (365)	0.0	0.5	65.8	11.2	20.3	2.2
Houston, TX (365)	0.0	7.4	41.9	0.8	49.0	0.8
Huntsville, AL (365)	0.0	0.0	35.6	0.0	64.1	0.3
Indianapolis, IN (365)	0.0	0.3	39.7	3.0	57.0	0.0
Jackson, MS (365)	0.0	0.3	40.0	0.0	59.7	0.0
Jacksonville, FL (365)	0.0	0.3	39.7	1.6	54.2	4.1
Kansas City, MO (365)	0.0	3.6	51.0	0.0	43.6	1.9
Lafayette, LA (365)	0.0	0.0	55.6	0.0	44.4	0.0
Lakeland, FL (365)	0.0	0.0	75.3	0.3	24.4	0.0
Las Vegas, NV (365)	0.0	13.7	61.9	0.0	20.8	3.6
Lexington, KY (365)	0.0	3.6	34.0	0.3	61.9	0.3
Lincoln, NE (365)	0.0	0.0	62.7	21.1	16.2	0.0
Little Rock, AR (365)	0.0	0.3	40.0	0.0	59.7	0.0
Los Angeles, CA (365)	0.0	8.5	48.8	0.0	41.9	0.8

Table continued on next page.

MSA[1] (Days[2])	Percent of Days when AQI Pollutant was...					
	Carbon Monoxide	Nitrogen Dioxide	Ozone	Sulfur Dioxide	Particulate Matter 2.5	Particulate Matter 10
Louisville, KY (365)	0.0	4.4	42.2	0.0	53.4	0.0
Madison, WI (365)	0.0	0.0	49.9	0.0	49.9	0.3
Manchester, NH (365)	0.3	0.0	95.9	0.0	3.8	0.0
Miami, FL (365)	0.0	4.1	33.4	0.0	59.7	2.7
Midland, TX (n/a)	n/a	n/a	n/a	n/a	n/a	n/a
Milwaukee, WI (365)	0.0	3.3	52.1	0.0	44.7	0.0
Minneapolis, MN (365)	1.1	1.9	28.2	0.3	40.8	27.7
Nashville, TN (365)	0.0	4.7	40.5	0.0	54.8	0.0
New Haven, CT (365)	0.0	7.9	56.2	0.0	35.9	0.0
New Orleans, LA (365)	0.0	1.1	38.6	7.9	52.3	0.0
New York, NY (365)	0.0	11.8	35.6	0.3	52.3	0.0
Oklahoma City, OK (365)	0.0	1.6	49.9	0.0	47.4	1.1
Omaha, NE (365)	0.0	0.0	39.2	3.0	54.0	3.8
Orlando, FL (365)	0.0	0.0	81.4	0.0	18.6	0.0
Peoria, IL (365)	0.0	0.0	52.6	0.0	47.4	0.0
Philadelphia, PA (365)	0.0	0.8	28.2	0.0	71.0	0.0
Phoenix, AZ (365)	0.0	2.7	39.5	0.0	15.9	41.9
Pittsburgh, PA (365)	0.0	0.0	26.8	6.8	66.3	0.0
Portland, OR (365)	0.0	4.1	50.1	0.0	45.8	0.0
Providence, RI (365)	0.0	2.7	57.8	0.0	39.2	0.3
Provo, UT (365)	0.0	9.0	69.0	0.0	20.5	1.4
Raleigh, NC (361)	0.3	0.0	41.3	0.0	58.4	0.0
Reno, NV (365)	0.0	2.2	77.0	0.0	16.2	4.7
Richmond, VA (365)	0.0	2.2	60.0	0.0	37.8	0.0
Rochester, MN (361)	0.0	0.0	41.0	0.0	59.0	0.0
Sacramento, CA (365)	0.0	0.0	67.4	0.0	32.1	0.5
Salt Lake City, UT (365)	0.0	13.2	64.7	0.0	21.4	0.8
San Antonio, TX (365)	0.0	1.6	54.5	0.5	43.0	0.3
San Diego, CA (365)	0.0	0.3	55.3	0.0	44.4	0.0
San Francisco, CA (365)	0.0	3.8	16.7	0.0	79.5	0.0
San Jose, CA (365)	0.0	0.3	52.9	0.0	46.8	0.0
Santa Rosa, CA (365)	0.0	0.5	76.7	0.0	22.5	0.3
Savannah, GA (365)	0.0	0.0	27.1	10.1	62.7	0.0
Seattle, WA (365)	0.0	9.6	52.9	0.0	37.5	0.0
Sioux Falls, SD (365)	0.0	3.0	73.7	0.0	22.5	0.8
Springfield, IL (363)	0.0	0.0	54.3	0.0	45.7	0.0
Tallahassee, FL (358)	0.3	0.0	41.6	0.0	58.1	0.0
Tampa, FL (365)	0.0	0.0	50.1	3.6	45.2	1.1
Topeka, KS (365)	0.0	0.0	49.6	0.0	50.4	0.0
Tucson, AZ (365)	0.0	0.0	69.9	0.0	8.5	21.6
Tulsa, OK (365)	0.0	0.0	42.7	0.0	57.0	0.3
Tuscaloosa, AL (320)	0.0	0.0	60.9	0.0	39.1	0.0
Virginia Beach, VA (365)	0.0	10.1	59.7	0.5	29.6	0.0
Washington, DC (365)	0.0	2.5	46.3	0.0	51.2	0.0
Wichita, KS (365)	0.0	4.7	62.2	0.0	16.2	17.0
Winston-Salem, NC (365)	0.0	1.1	47.9	0.0	51.0	0.0

Note: The Air Quality Index (AQI) is an index for reporting daily air quality. EPA calculates the AQI for five major air pollutants regulated by the Clean Air Act: ground-level ozone, particle pollution (also known as particulate matter), carbon monoxide, sulfur dioxide, and nitrogen dioxide. The AQI runs from 0 to 500. The higher the AQI value, the greater the level of air pollution and the greater the health concern; (1) Data covers the Metropolitan Statistical Area—see Appendix B for areas included; (2) Number of days with AQI data in 2018
Source: U.S. Environmental Protection Agency, Air Quality Index Report, 2018

Air Quality Trends: Ozone

MSA[1]	1990	1995	2000	2005	2010	2012	2014	2016	2017	2018
Albany, NY	0.086	0.079	0.070	0.082	0.072	0.071	0.061	0.068	0.061	0.066
Albuquerque, NM	0.072	0.070	0.072	0.073	0.066	0.070	0.062	0.065	0.069	0.073
Allentown, PA	0.093	0.091	0.091	0.086	0.080	0.075	0.068	0.071	0.067	0.067
Anchorage, AK	n/a	n/a	n/a	n/a	n/a	n/a	n/a	n/a	n/a	n/a
Ann Arbor, MI	n/a	n/a	n/a	n/a	n/a	n/a	n/a	n/a	n/a	n/a
Athens, GA	n/a	n/a	n/a	n/a	n/a	n/a	n/a	n/a	n/a	n/a
Atlanta, GA	0.104	0.103	0.101	0.087	0.076	0.079	0.072	0.073	0.068	0.068
Austin, TX	0.088	0.089	0.088	0.082	0.074	0.074	0.062	0.064	0.070	0.072
Baton Rouge, LA	0.105	0.091	0.090	0.090	0.075	0.074	0.071	0.066	0.069	0.069
Boise City, ID	n/a	n/a	n/a	n/a	n/a	n/a	n/a	n/a	n/a	n/a
Boston, MA	n/a	n/a	n/a	n/a	n/a	n/a	n/a	n/a	n/a	n/a
Boulder, CO	n/a	n/a	n/a	n/a	n/a	n/a	n/a	n/a	n/a	n/a
Cape Coral, FL	n/a	n/a	n/a	n/a	n/a	n/a	n/a	n/a	n/a	n/a
Cedar Rapids, IA	n/a	n/a	n/a	n/a	n/a	n/a	n/a	n/a	n/a	n/a
Charleston, SC	0.068	0.071	0.078	0.073	0.067	0.063	0.060	0.058	0.062	0.058
Charlotte, NC	n/a	n/a	n/a	n/a	n/a	n/a	n/a	n/a	n/a	n/a
Chicago, IL	0.074	0.094	0.073	0.084	0.070	0.082	0.068	0.074	0.071	0.073
Clarksville, TN	n/a	n/a	n/a	n/a	n/a	n/a	n/a	n/a	n/a	n/a
Cleveland, OH	0.085	0.092	0.076	0.083	0.077	0.087	0.069	0.072	0.070	0.074
College Station, TX	n/a	n/a	n/a	n/a	n/a	n/a	n/a	n/a	n/a	n/a
Colorado Springs, CO	n/a	n/a	n/a	n/a	n/a	n/a	n/a	n/a	n/a	n/a
Columbia, MO	n/a	n/a	n/a	n/a	n/a	n/a	n/a	n/a	n/a	n/a
Columbia, SC	0.093	0.079	0.096	0.082	0.070	0.065	0.056	0.065	0.059	0.060
Columbus, OH	0.090	0.091	0.085	0.084	0.073	0.077	0.067	0.069	0.065	0.062
Dallas, TX	0.095	0.105	0.096	0.097	0.080	0.080	0.076	0.070	0.073	0.078
Davenport, IA	n/a	n/a	n/a	n/a	n/a	n/a	n/a	n/a	n/a	n/a
Denver, CO	0.077	0.070	0.069	0.072	0.070	0.079	0.070	0.071	0.072	0.071
Des Moines, IA	n/a	n/a	n/a	n/a	n/a	n/a	n/a	n/a	n/a	n/a
Durham, NC	n/a	n/a	n/a	n/a	n/a	n/a	n/a	n/a	n/a	n/a
Edison, NJ	0.101	0.106	0.090	0.091	0.081	0.079	0.069	0.073	0.070	0.073
El Paso, TX	0.080	0.078	0.082	0.075	0.072	0.072	0.068	0.068	0.073	0.077
Fargo, ND	n/a	n/a	n/a	n/a	n/a	n/a	n/a	n/a	n/a	n/a
Fayetteville, NC	0.087	0.081	0.086	0.084	0.071	0.068	0.061	0.064	0.063	0.064
Fort Collins, CO	0.066	0.072	0.074	0.076	0.072	0.077	0.071	0.070	0.067	0.073
Fort Wayne, IN	0.086	0.094	0.086	0.081	0.067	0.076	0.063	0.068	0.063	0.071
Fort Worth, TX	0.095	0.105	0.096	0.097	0.080	0.080	0.076	0.070	0.073	0.078
Grand Rapids, MI	0.102	0.089	0.073	0.085	0.071	0.083	0.069	0.075	0.065	0.072
Greeley, CO	n/a	n/a	n/a	n/a	n/a	n/a	n/a	n/a	n/a	n/a
Green Bay, WI	n/a	n/a	n/a	n/a	n/a	n/a	n/a	n/a	n/a	n/a
Greensboro, NC	n/a	n/a	n/a	n/a	n/a	n/a	n/a	n/a	n/a	n/a
Honolulu, HI	0.034	0.051	0.044	0.042	0.047	0.043	0.057	0.048	0.048	0.046
Houston, TX	0.119	0.114	0.102	0.087	0.079	0.080	0.064	0.066	0.070	0.073
Huntsville, AL	0.079	0.080	0.088	0.075	0.071	0.076	0.064	0.066	0.063	0.065
Indianapolis, IN	0.084	0.094	0.081	0.080	0.069	0.078	0.066	0.070	0.067	0.073
Jackson, MS	n/a	n/a	n/a	n/a	n/a	n/a	n/a	n/a	n/a	n/a
Jacksonville, FL	0.080	0.068	0.072	0.076	0.068	0.059	0.062	0.057	0.059	0.060
Kansas City, MO	0.075	0.098	0.088	0.084	0.072	0.085	0.066	0.066	0.069	0.073
Lafayette, LA	n/a	n/a	n/a	n/a	n/a	n/a	n/a	n/a	n/a	n/a
Lakeland, FL	0.066	0.071	0.079	0.074	0.064	0.071	0.063	0.064	0.072	0.065
Las Vegas, NV	n/a	n/a	n/a	n/a	n/a	n/a	n/a	n/a	n/a	n/a
Lexington, KY	0.078	0.088	0.077	0.078	0.070	0.078	0.065	0.066	0.063	0.063
Lincoln, NE	0.057	0.060	0.057	0.056	0.050	0.058	0.061	0.058	0.062	0.062
Little Rock, AR	0.080	0.086	0.090	0.083	0.072	0.078	0.066	0.064	0.060	0.066
Los Angeles, CA	0.129	0.110	0.089	0.082	0.074	0.077	0.082	0.081	0.090	0.082
Louisville, KY	0.075	0.087	0.088	0.083	0.076	0.086	0.066	0.070	0.064	0.067
Madison, WI	0.077	0.084	0.072	0.079	0.062	0.074	0.068	0.068	0.064	0.066

Table continued on next page.

MSA[1]	1990	1995	2000	2005	2010	2012	2014	2016	2017	2018
Manchester, NH	n/a	n/a	n/a	n/a	n/a	n/a	n/a	n/a	n/a	n/a
Miami, FL	0.068	0.072	0.075	0.065	0.064	0.062	0.062	0.061	0.064	0.064
Midland, TX	n/a	n/a	n/a	n/a	n/a	n/a	n/a	n/a	n/a	n/a
Milwaukee, WI	0.095	0.106	0.082	0.092	0.079	0.092	0.072	0.074	0.072	0.073
Minneapolis, MN	0.068	0.084	0.065	0.074	0.066	0.073	0.063	0.061	0.062	0.065
Nashville, TN	0.089	0.092	0.084	0.078	0.073	0.079	0.067	0.068	0.063	0.068
New Haven, CT	n/a	n/a	n/a	n/a	n/a	n/a	n/a	n/a	n/a	n/a
New Orleans, LA	0.082	0.088	0.091	0.079	0.074	0.071	0.069	0.065	0.063	0.065
New York, NY	0.101	0.106	0.090	0.091	0.081	0.079	0.069	0.073	0.070	0.073
Oklahoma City, OK	0.078	0.086	0.082	0.077	0.071	0.080	0.068	0.066	0.069	0.072
Omaha, NE	0.054	0.075	0.063	0.069	0.058	0.066	0.059	0.063	0.061	0.063
Orlando, FL	0.081	0.075	0.080	0.083	0.069	0.071	0.062	0.063	0.067	0.062
Peoria, IL	0.071	0.082	0.072	0.075	0.064	0.072	0.064	0.067	0.066	0.070
Philadelphia, PA	0.102	0.109	0.099	0.091	0.083	0.084	0.071	0.075	0.073	0.074
Phoenix, AZ	0.080	0.087	0.082	0.077	0.076	0.080	0.075	0.071	0.075	0.074
Pittsburgh, PA	0.080	0.095	0.082	0.082	0.075	0.079	0.065	0.068	0.066	0.068
Portland, OR	0.081	0.065	0.059	0.059	0.056	0.059	0.057	0.057	0.073	0.062
Providence, RI	0.106	0.107	0.087	0.090	0.072	0.072	0.067	0.075	0.076	0.074
Provo, UT	0.070	0.068	0.083	0.078	0.070	0.077	0.068	0.072	0.073	0.073
Raleigh, NC	0.093	0.081	0.087	0.082	0.071	0.071	0.063	0.069	0.066	0.063
Reno, NV	0.074	0.070	0.067	0.069	0.068	0.072	0.069	0.070	0.068	0.077
Richmond, VA	0.083	0.089	0.080	0.082	0.079	0.076	0.063	0.065	0.063	0.062
Rochester, MN	n/a	n/a	n/a	n/a	n/a	n/a	n/a	n/a	n/a	n/a
Sacramento, CA	0.088	0.093	0.087	0.087	0.074	0.079	0.073	0.077	0.073	0.079
Salt Lake City, UT	n/a	n/a	n/a	n/a	n/a	n/a	n/a	n/a	n/a	n/a
San Antonio, TX	0.090	0.095	0.078	0.084	0.072	0.081	0.069	0.071	0.073	0.072
San Diego, CA	0.111	0.090	0.079	0.074	0.071	0.069	0.072	0.070	0.073	0.067
San Francisco, CA	0.058	0.074	0.057	0.057	0.061	0.057	0.065	0.059	0.060	0.054
San Jose, CA	0.079	0.085	0.070	0.065	0.073	0.064	0.069	0.063	0.065	0.061
Santa Rosa, CA	0.063	0.071	0.061	0.050	0.053	0.058	0.062	0.055	0.062	0.055
Savannah, GA	n/a	n/a	n/a	n/a	n/a	n/a	n/a	n/a	n/a	n/a
Seattle, WA	0.082	0.062	0.056	0.053	0.053	0.059	0.052	0.054	0.076	0.067
Sioux Falls, SD	n/a	n/a	n/a	n/a	n/a	n/a	n/a	n/a	n/a	n/a
Springfield, IL	n/a	n/a	n/a	n/a	n/a	n/a	n/a	n/a	n/a	n/a
Tallahassee, FL	n/a	n/a	n/a	n/a	n/a	n/a	n/a	n/a	n/a	n/a
Tampa, FL	0.080	0.075	0.081	0.075	0.067	0.066	0.065	0.064	0.064	0.065
Topeka, KS	n/a	n/a	n/a	n/a	n/a	n/a	n/a	n/a	n/a	n/a
Tucson, AZ	0.073	0.078	0.074	0.075	0.068	0.069	0.065	0.065	0.070	0.069
Tulsa, OK	0.086	0.091	0.081	0.072	0.069	0.083	0.062	0.064	0.065	0.067
Tuscaloosa, AL	n/a	n/a	n/a	n/a	n/a	n/a	n/a	n/a	n/a	n/a
Virginia Beach, VA	0.085	0.084	0.083	0.078	0.074	0.069	0.061	0.062	0.059	0.061
Washington, DC	0.088	0.093	0.082	0.081	0.077	0.075	0.065	0.068	0.065	0.066
Wichita, KS	0.077	0.069	0.080	0.074	0.075	0.080	0.069	0.062	0.063	0.064
Winston-Salem, NC	0.084	0.086	0.089	0.080	0.078	0.074	0.067	0.069	0.066	0.064
U.S.	0.088	0.089	0.082	0.080	0.073	0.075	0.067	0.069	0.068	0.069

Note: (1) Data covers the Metropolitan Statistical Area—see Appendix B for areas included; n/a not available. The values shown are the composite ozone concentration averages among trend sites based on the highest fourth daily maximum 8-hour concentration in parts per million. These trends are based on sites having an adequate record of monitoring data during the trend period. Data from exceptional events are included.
Source: U.S. Environmental Protection Agency, Air Quality Monitoring Information, "Air Quality Trends by City, 1990-2018"

Maximum Air Pollutant Concentrations: Particulate Matter, Ozone, CO and Lead

Metro Aea	PM 10 (ug/m³)	PM 2.5 Wtd AM (ug/m³)	PM 2.5 24-Hr (ug/m³)	Ozone (ppm)	Carbon Monoxide (ppm)	Lead (ug/m³)
Albany, NY	n/a	7.5	19	0.067	1	n/a
Albuquerque, NM	229	8.3	21	0.075	1	n/a
Allentown, PA	40	8.9	23	0.073	n/a	0.13
Anchorage, AK	155	5.4	19	0.047	3	n/a
Ann Arbor, MI	n/a	8.3	21	0.072	n/a	n/a
Athens, GA	n/a	8.1	19	0.065	n/a	n/a
Atlanta, GA	38	9.5	21	0.072	2	n/a
Austin, TX	82	10	37	0.072	1	n/a
Baton Rouge, LA	84	9.5	23	0.074	2	0.01
Boise City, ID	73	9.4	33	0.068	2	n/a
Boston, MA	31	8.9	21	0.07	1	n/a
Boulder, CO	57	7.4	29	0.077	n/a	n/a
Cape Coral, FL	45	7.4	16	0.065	n/a	n/a
Cedar Rapids, IA	54	8.4	20	0.069	1	n/a
Charleston, SC	31	6.8	14	0.06	n/a	n/a
Charlotte, NC	58	8.9	17	0.07	1	n/a
Chicago, IL	78	11.2	27	0.084	2	0.31
Clarksville, TN	n/a	8.2	16	0.062	n/a	n/a
Cleveland, OH	74	11.1	24	0.076	3	0.06
College Station, TX	n/a	n/a	n/a	n/a	n/a	n/a
Colorado Springs, CO	36	6.2	16	0.073	2	n/a
Columbia, MO	n/a	n/a	n/a	0.063	n/a	n/a
Columbia, SC	30	7.9	19	0.063	1	n/a
Columbus, OH	47	9.1	25	0.067	1	0.01
Dallas, TX	40	9.6	25	0.082	1	0.01
Davenport, IA	140	8.8	21	0.071	1	n/a
Denver, CO	146	10.2	37	0.083	3	n/a
Des Moines, IA	43	8	18	0.065	1	n/a
Durham, NC	29	8.3	17	0.063	n/a	n/a
Edison, NJ	38	11.1	27	0.079	3	n/a
El Paso, TX	114	8.8	23	0.078	2	0.01
Fargo, ND	74	7	22	0.063	n/a	n/a
Fayetteville, NC	26	7.1	15	0.064	n/a	n/a
Fort Collins, CO	51	7.7	20	0.081	2	n/a
Fort Wayne, IN	n/a	9.1	22	0.072	n/a	n/a
Fort Worth, TX	40	9.6	25	0.082	1	0.01
Grand Rapids, MI	30	8.4	19	0.073	1	0
Greeley, CO	48	9.6	24	0.073	1	n/a
Green Bay, WI	n/a	6.4	19	0.072	n/a	n/a
Greensboro, NC	32	7.3	15	0.067	n/a	n/a
Honolulu, HI	31	3.7	9	0.049	3	0
Houston, TX	102	11	30	0.088	2	n/a
Huntsville, AL	33	7.4	16	0.065	n/a	n/a
Indianapolis, IN	55	10.8	28	0.076	2	n/a
Jackson, MS	80	8.9	24	0.068	2	n/a
Jacksonville, FL	203	8.7	17	0.061	1	n/a
Kansas City, MO	61	8.2	17	0.074	1	n/a
Lafayette, LA	108	8.4	22	0.065	n/a	n/a
Lakeland, FL	35	n/a	n/a	0.066	n/a	n/a
Las Vegas, NV	133	9.6	26	0.081	3	n/a
Lexington, KY	51	n/a	n/a	0.063	n/a	n/a
Lincoln, NE	n/a	7.1	19	0.062	n/a	n/a
Little Rock, AR	51	9.7	22	0.067	1	n/a
Los Angeles, CA	90	13.3	36	0.102	3	0.06
Louisville, KY	44	10.3	26	0.077	1	n/a

Table continued on next page.

Metro Area	PM 10 (ug/m³)	PM 2.5 Wtd AM (ug/m³)	PM 2.5 24-Hr (ug/m³)	Ozone (ppm)	Carbon Monoxide (ppm)	Lead (ug/m³)
Madison, WI	42	8.6	23	0.066	n/a	n/a
Manchester, NH	n/a	3.2	12	0.066	0	n/a
Miami, FL	124	8.4	18	0.066	1	n/a
Midland, TX	n/a	n/a	n/a	n/a	n/a	n/a
Milwaukee, WI	40	9.1	22	0.073	1	n/a
Minneapolis, MN	144	8.9	25	0.069	4	0.08
Nashville, TN	41	9.2	18	0.071	2	n/a
New Haven, CT	38	8.3	22	0.077	1	n/a
New Orleans, LA	63	8.6	21	0.07	2	0.08
New York, NY	38	11.1	27	0.079	3	n/a
Oklahoma City, OK	92	10.1	24	0.076	2	n/a
Omaha, NE	62	9.1	22	0.07	1	0.08
Orlando, FL	32	6.8	16	0.067	1	n/a
Peoria, IL	n/a	9.4	20	0.07	n/a	n/a
Philadelphia, PA	45	12.1	23	0.084	1	n/a
Phoenix, AZ	829	12.1	34	0.08	3	0.05
Pittsburgh, PA	67	11.5	28	0.074	3	0
Portland, OR	27	8	32	0.07	2	n/a
Providence, RI	36	8.9	20	0.079	2	n/a
Provo, UT	85	8.6	50	0.079	1	n/a
Raleigh, NC	28	8.1	16	0.063	1	n/a
Reno, NV	126	8	35	0.078	2	n/a
Richmond, VA	28	8.2	19	0.066	1	n/a
Rochester, MN	n/a	8.3	20	0.056	n/a	n/a
Sacramento, CA	252	12.8	95	0.098	4	n/a
Salt Lake City, UT	103	9	31	0.08	3	n/a
San Antonio, TX	56	7.9	33	0.073	1	n/a
San Diego, CA	54	10	29	0.08	1	0.02
San Francisco, CA	102	14.4	82	0.069	3	n/a
San Jose, CA	115	12.8	73	0.066	2	0.08
Santa Rosa, CA	205	8.3	65	0.055	1	n/a
Savannah, GA	n/a	8.5	17	0.058	n/a	n/a
Seattle, WA	60	9.3	42	0.077	1	n/a
Sioux Falls, SD	58	5.5	16	0.069	1	n/a
Springfield, IL	n/a	9.5	20	0.069	n/a	n/a
Tallahassee, FL	n/a	7.3	17	0.06	1	n/a
Tampa, FL	52	6.8	15	0.07	1	0.11
Topeka, KS	61	9.7	25	0.062	n/a	n/a
Tucson, AZ	206	5.6	12	0.071	1	n/a
Tulsa, OK	59	10.5	27	0.073	1	0.01
Tuscaloosa, AL	n/a	7.7	17	0.063	n/a	n/a
Virginia Beach, VA	21	6.6	14	0.063	1	n/a
Washington, DC	40	9.5	21	0.073	2	n/a
Wichita, KS	86	8.2	20	0.067	n/a	n/a
Winston-Salem, NC	30	9.3	22	0.067	n/a	n/a
NAAQS[1]	150	15	35	0.075	9	0.15

Note: Data from exceptional events are included; Data covers the Metropolitan Statistical Area—see Appendix B for areas included; (1) National Ambient Air Quality Standards; ppm = parts per million; ug/m³ = micrograms per cubic meter; n/a not available Concentrations: Particulate Matter 10 (coarse particulate)—highest second maximum 24-hour concentration; Particulate Matter 2.5 Wtd AM (fine particulate)—highest weighted annual mean concentration; Particulate Matter 2.5 24-Hour (fine particulate)—highest 98th percentile 24-hour concentration; Ozone—highest fourth daily maximum 8-hour concentration; Carbon Monoxide—highest second maximum non-overlapping 8-hour concentration; Lead—maximum running 3-month average Source: U.S. Environmental Protection Agency, Air Quality Monitoring Information, "Air Quality Statistics by City, 2018"

Maximum Air Pollutant Concentrations: Nitrogen Dioxide and Sulfur Dioxide

Metro Area	Nitrogen Dioxide AM (ppb)	Nitrogen Dioxide 1-Hr (ppb)	Sulfur Dioxide AM (ppb)	Sulfur Dioxide 1-Hr (ppb)	Sulfur Dioxide 24-Hr (ppb)
Albany, NY	n/a	n/a	n/a	2	n/a
Albuquerque, NM	10	45	n/a	5	n/a
Allentown, PA	9	41	n/a	6	n/a
Anchorage, AK	n/a	n/a	n/a	n/a	n/a
Ann Arbor, MI	n/a	n/a	n/a	n/a	n/a
Athens, GA	n/a	n/a	n/a	n/a	n/a
Atlanta, GA	16	47	n/a	4	n/a
Austin, TX	12	46	n/a	2	n/a
Baton Rouge, LA	10	44	n/a	29	n/a
Boise City, ID	n/a	n/a	n/a	3	n/a
Boston, MA	13	48	n/a	14	n/a
Boulder, CO	n/a	n/a	n/a	n/a	n/a
Cape Coral, FL	n/a	n/a	n/a	n/a	n/a
Cedar Rapids, IA	n/a	n/a	n/a	28	n/a
Charleston, SC	1	n/a	n/a	13	n/a
Charlotte, NC	10	35	n/a	3	n/a
Chicago, IL	18	61	n/a	28	n/a
Clarksville, TN	n/a	n/a	n/a	n/a	n/a
Cleveland, OH	11	49	n/a	53	n/a
College Station, TX	n/a	n/a	n/a	n/a	n/a
Colorado Springs, CO	n/a	n/a	n/a	9	n/a
Columbia, MO	n/a	n/a	n/a	n/a	n/a
Columbia, SC	n/a	n/a	n/a	2	n/a
Columbus, OH	10	44	n/a	n/a	n/a
Dallas, TX	11	43	n/a	8	n/a
Davenport, IA	6	30	n/a	5	n/a
Denver, CO	27	70	n/a	8	n/a
Des Moines, IA	7	34	n/a	1	n/a
Durham, NC	n/a	n/a	n/a	25	n/a
Edison, NJ	19	68	n/a	8	n/a
El Paso, TX	11	61	n/a	n/a	n/a
Fargo, ND	4	32	n/a	3	n/a
Fayetteville, NC	n/a	n/a	n/a	n/a	n/a
Fort Collins, CO	n/a	n/a	n/a	n/a	n/a
Fort Wayne, IN	n/a	n/a	n/a	n/a	n/a
Fort Worth, TX	11	43	n/a	8	n/a
Grand Rapids, MI	n/a	n/a	n/a	13	n/a
Greeley, CO	n/a	n/a	n/a	n/a	n/a
Green Bay, WI	n/a	n/a	n/a	12	n/a
Greensboro, NC	n/a	n/a	n/a	n/a	n/a
Honolulu, HI	4	27	n/a	38	n/a
Houston, TX	12	52	n/a	24	n/a
Huntsville, AL	n/a	n/a	n/a	n/a	n/a
Indianapolis, IN	14	n/a	n/a	55	n/a
Jackson, MS	7	38	n/a	3	n/a
Jacksonville, FL	11	41	n/a	40	n/a
Kansas City, MO	12	48	n/a	6	n/a
Lafayette, LA	n/a	n/a	n/a	n/a	n/a
Lakeland, FL	n/a	n/a	n/a	16	n/a
Las Vegas, NV	27	59	n/a	n/a	n/a
Lexington, KY	3	31	n/a	5	n/a
Lincoln, NE	n/a	n/a	n/a	10	n/a
Little Rock, AR	7	42	n/a	6	n/a
Los Angeles, CA	22	79	n/a	9	n/a
Louisville, KY	15	46	n/a	16	n/a

Table continued on next page.

Metro Area	Nitrogen Dioxide AM (ppb)	Nitrogen Dioxide 1-Hr (ppb)	Sulfur Dioxide AM (ppb)	Sulfur Dioxide 1-Hr (ppb)	Sulfur Dioxide 24-Hr (ppb)
Madison, WI	n/a	n/a	n/a	3	n/a
Manchester, NH	n/a	n/a	n/a	3	n/a
Miami, FL	15	46	n/a	4	n/a
Midland, TX	n/a	n/a	n/a	n/a	n/a
Milwaukee, WI	14	47	n/a	4	n/a
Minneapolis, MN	13	45	n/a	17	n/a
Nashville, TN	14	47	n/a	n/a	n/a
New Haven, CT	12	52	n/a	3	n/a
New Orleans, LA	10	45	n/a	53	n/a
New York, NY	19	68	n/a	8	n/a
Oklahoma City, OK	13	41	n/a	3	n/a
Omaha, NE	n/a	n/a	n/a	37	n/a
Orlando, FL	5	30	n/a	4	n/a
Peoria, IL	n/a	n/a	n/a	n/a	n/a
Philadelphia, PA	11	45	n/a	14	n/a
Phoenix, AZ	28	62	n/a	8	n/a
Pittsburgh, PA	10	38	n/a	130	n/a
Portland, OR	12	38	n/a	3	n/a
Providence, RI	17	37	n/a	4	n/a
Provo, UT	9	41	n/a	n/a	n/a
Raleigh, NC	9	34	n/a	3	n/a
Reno, NV	13	46	n/a	4	n/a
Richmond, VA	12	43	n/a	18	n/a
Rochester, MN	n/a	n/a	n/a	n/a	n/a
Sacramento, CA	12	58	n/a	2	n/a
Salt Lake City, UT	15	49	n/a	n/a	n/a
San Antonio, TX	7	40	n/a	n/a	n/a
San Diego, CA	15	48	n/a	1	n/a
San Francisco, CA	17	59	n/a	20	n/a
San Jose, CA	17	59	n/a	3	n/a
Santa Rosa, CA	4	41	n/a	n/a	n/a
Savannah, GA	n/a	n/a	n/a	41	n/a
Seattle, WA	20	64	n/a	8	n/a
Sioux Falls, SD	5	34	n/a	3	n/a
Springfield, IL	n/a	n/a	n/a	n/a	n/a
Tallahassee, FL	n/a	n/a	n/a	n/a	n/a
Tampa, FL	10	31	n/a	12	n/a
Topeka, KS	n/a	n/a	n/a	n/a	n/a
Tucson, AZ	8	41	n/a	2	n/a
Tulsa, OK	7	39	n/a	8	n/a
Tuscaloosa, AL	n/a	n/a	n/a	n/a	n/a
Virginia Beach, VA	7	38	n/a	21	n/a
Washington, DC	15	49	n/a	5	n/a
Wichita, KS	8	40	n/a	4	n/a
Winston-Salem, NC	7	35	n/a	5	n/a
NAAQS[1]	53	100	30	75	140

Note: Data from exceptional events are included; Data covers the Metropolitan Statistical Area—see Appendix B for areas included;
(1) National Ambient Air Quality Standards; ppb = parts per billion; n/a not available
Concentrations: Nitrogen Dioxide AM—highest arithmetic mean concentration; Nitrogen Dioxide 1-Hr—highest 98th percentile 1-hour daily maximum concentration; Sulfur Dioxide AM—highest annual mean concentration; Sulfur Dioxide 1-Hr—highest 99th percentile 1-hour daily maximum concentration; Sulfur Dioxide 24-Hr—highest second maximum 24-hour concentration
Source: U.S. Environmental Protection Agency, Air Quality Monitoring Information, "Air Quality Statistics by City, 2018"

Appendix B: Metropolitan Area Definitions

Metropolitan Statistical Areas (MSA), Metropolitan Divisions (MD), New England City and Town Areas (NECTA), and New England City and Town Area Divisions (NECTAD)

Note: In March 2020, the Office of Management and Budget (OMB) announced changes to metropolitan and micropolitan statistical area definitions. Both current and historical definitions (December 2009) are shown below. If the change only affected the name of the metro area, the counties included were not repeated.

Albany-Schenectady-Troy, NY MSA
Albany, Rensselaer, Saratoga, Schenectady and Schoharie Counties

Albuquerque, NM MSA
Bernalillo, Sandoval, Torrance, and Valencia Counties

Allentown-Bethlehem-Easton, PA-NJ MSA
Carbon, Lehigh, and Northampton Counties, PA; Warren County, NJ

Anchorage, AK MSA
Anchorage Municipality and Matanuska-Susitna Borough

Ann Arbor, MI MSA
Washtenaw County

Athens-Clarke County, GA MSA
Clarke, Madison, Oconee, and Oglethorpe Counties

Atlanta-Sandy Springs-Roswell, GA MSA
Barrow, Bartow, Butts, Carroll, Cherokee, Clayton, Cobb, Coweta, Dawson, DeKalb, Douglas, Fayette, Forsyth, Fulton, Gwinnett, Haralson, Heard, Henry, Jasper, Lamar, Meriwether, Morgan, Newton, Paulding, Pickens, Pike, Rockdale, Spalding, and Walton Counties
Previously Atlanta-Sandy Springs-Marietta, GA MSA
Barrow, Bartow, Butts, Carroll, Cherokee, Clayton, Cobb, Coweta, Dawson, DeKalb, Douglas, Fayette, Forsyth, Fulton, Gwinnett, Haralson, Heard, Henry, Jasper, Lamar, Meriwether, Newton, Paulding, Pickens, Pike, Rockdale, Spalding, and Walton Counties

Austin-Round Rock, TX MSA
Previously Austin-Round Rock-San Marcos, TX MSA
Bastrop, Caldwell, Hays, Travis, and Williamson Counties

Baton Rouge, LA MSA
Ascension, East Baton Rouge, East Feliciana, Iberville, Livingston, Pointe Coupee, St. Helena, West Baton Rouge, and West Feliciana Parishes
Previously Baton Rouge, LA MSA
Ascension, East Baton Rouge, Livingston, and West Baton Rouge Parishes

Boise City, ID MSA
Previously Boise City-Nampa, ID MSA
Ada, Boise, Canyon, Gem, and Owyhee Counties

Boston, MA

Boston-Cambridge-Newton, MA-NH MSA
Previously Boston-Cambridge-Quincy, MA-NH MSA
Essex, Middlesex, Norfolk, Plymouth, and Suffolk Counties, MA; Rockingham and Strafford Counties, NH

Boston, MA MD
Previously Boston-Quincy, MA MD
Norfolk, Plymouth, and Suffolk Counties

Boston-Cambridge-Nashua, MA-NH NECTA
Includes 157 cities and towns in Massachusetts and 34 cities and towns in New Hampshire
Previously Boston-Cambridge-Quincy, MA-NH NECTA
Includes 155 cities and towns in Massachusetts and 38 cities and towns in New Hampshire

Boston-Cambridge-Newton, MA NECTA Division
Includes 92 cities and towns in Massachusetts
Previously Boston-Cambridge-Quincy, MA NECTA Division
Includes 97 cities and towns in Massachusetts

Boulder, CO MSA
Boulder County

Cape Coral-Fort Myers, FL MSA
Lee County

Cedar Rapids, IA, MSA
Benton, Jones, and Linn Counties

Charleston-North Charleston, SC MSA
Previously Charleston-North Charleston- Summerville, SC MSA
Berkeley, Charleston, and Dorchester Counties

Charlotte-Concord-Gastonia, NC-SC MSA
Cabarrus, Gaston, Iredell, Lincoln, Mecklenburg, Rowan, and Union Counties, NC; Chester, Lancaster, and York Counties, SC
Previously Charlotte-Gastonia-Rock Hill, NC-SC MSA
Anson, Cabarrus, Gaston, Mecklenburg, and Union Counties, NC; York County, SC

Chicago, IL

Chicago-Naperville-Elgin, IL-IN-WI MSA
Previous name: Chicago-Joliet-Naperville, IL-IN-WI MSA
Cook, DeKalb, DuPage, Grundy, Kane, Kendall, Lake, McHenry, and Will Counties, IL; Jasper, Lake, Newton, and Porter Counties, IN; Kenosha County, WI

Chicago-Naperville-Arlington Heights, IL MD
Cook, DuPage, Grundy, Kendall, McHenry, and Will Counties
Previous name: Chicago-Joliet-Naperville, IL MD
Cook, DeKalb, DuPage, Grundy, Kane, Kendall, McHenry, and Will Counties

Elgin, IL MD
DeKalb and Kane Counties
Previously part of the Chicago-Joliet-Naperville, IL MD

Gary, IN MD
Jasper, Lake, Newton, and Porter Counties

Lake County-Kenosha County, IL-WI MD
Lake County, IL; Kenosha County, WI

Clarksville, TN-KY MSA
Montgomery and Stewart Counties, TN; Christian and Trigg Counties, KY

Cleveland-Elyria-Mentor, OH MSA
Cuyahoga, Geauga, Lake, Lorain, and Medina Counties

College Station-Bryan, TX MSA
Brazos, Burleson and Robertson Counties

Colorado Springs, CO MSA
El Paso and Teller Counties

Columbia, MO MSA
Boone and Howard Counties

Columbia, SC MSA
Calhoun, Fairfield, Kershaw, Lexington, Richland and Saluda Counties

Columbus, OH MSA
Delaware, Fairfield, Franklin, Licking, Madison, Morrow, Pickaway, and Union Counties

Dallas, TX

Dallas-Fort Worth-Arlington, TX MSA
Collin, Dallas, Denton, Ellis, Hunt, Johnson, Kaufman, Parker, Rockwall, Tarrant, and Wise Counties

Dallas-Plano-Irving, TX MD
Collin, Dallas, Denton, Ellis, Hunt, Kaufman, and Rockwall Counties

Davenport-Moline-Rock Island, IA-IL MSA
Henry, Mercer, and Rock Island Counties, IA; Scott County

Denver-Aurora-Lakewood, CO MSA
Previously Denver-Aurora-Broomfield, CO MSA
Adams, Arapahoe, Broomfield, Clear Creek, Denver, Douglas, Elbert, Gilpin, Jefferson, and Park Counties

Des Moines-West Des Moines, IA MSA
Dallas, Guthrie, Madison, Polk, and Warren Counties

Durham-Chapel Hill, NC MSA
Chatham, Durham, Orange, and Person Counties

Edison, NJ
See New York, NY (New York-Jersey City-White Plains, NY-NJ MD)

El Paso, TX MSA
El Paso County

Fargo, ND-MN MSA
Cass County, ND; Clay County, MN

Fayetteville, NC MSA
Cumberland, and Hoke Counties

Fort Collins, CO MSA
Previously Fort Collins-Loveland, CO MSA
Larimer County

Fort Wayne, IN MSA
Allen, Wells, and Whitley Counties

Fort Worth, TX

Dallas-Fort Worth-Arlington, TX MSA
Collin, Dallas, Denton, Ellis, Hunt, Johnson, Kaufman, Parker, Rockwall, Tarrant, and Wise Counties

Fort Worth-Arlington, TX MD
Hood, Johnson, Parker, Somervell, Tarrant, and Wise Counties

Grand Rapids-Wyoming, MI MSA
Barry, Kent, Montcalm, and Ottawa Counties
Previously Grand Rapids-Wyoming, MI MSA
Barry, Ionia, Kent, and Newaygo Counties

Greeley, CO MSA
Weld County

Green Bay, WI MSA
Brown, Kewaunee, and Oconto Counties

Greensboro-High Point, NC MSA
Guilford, Randolph, and Rockingham Counties

Honolulu, HI MSA
Honolulu County

Houston-The Woodlands-Sugar Land-Baytown, TX MSA
Austin, Brazoria, Chambers, Fort Bend, Galveston, Harris, Liberty, Montgomery, and Waller Counties
Previously Houston-Sugar Land-Baytown, TX MSA
Austin, Brazoria, Chambers, Fort Bend, Galveston, Harris, Liberty, Montgomery, San Jacinto, and Waller Counties

Huntsville, AL MSA
Limestone and Madison Counties

Indianapolis-Carmel, IN MSA
Boone, Brown, Hamilton, Hancock, Hendricks, Johnson, Marion, Morgan, Putnam, and Shelby Counties

Jackson, MS MSA
Copiah, Hinds, Madison, Rankin and Simpson Counties

Jacksonville, FL MSA
Baker, Clay, Duval, Nassau, and St. Johns Counties

Kansas City, MO-KS MSA
Franklin, Johnson, Leavenworth, Linn, Miami, and Wyandotte Counties, KS; Bates, Caldwell, Cass, Clay, Clinton, Jackson, Lafayette, Platte, and Ray Counties, MO

Lafayette, LA MSA
Acadia, Iberia, Lafayette, St. Martin, and Vermilion Parishes

Lakeland-Winter Haven, FL MSA
Polk County

Las Vegas-Henderson-Paradise, NV MSA
Previously Las Vegas-Paradise, NV MSA
Clark County

Lexington-Fayette, KY MSA
Bourbon, Clark, Fayette, Jessamine, Scott, and Woodford Counties

Lincoln, NE MSA
Lancaster and Seward Counties

Little Rock-North Little Rock-Conway, AR MSA
Faulkner, Grant, Lonoke, Perry, Pulaski, and Saline Counties

Los Angeles, CA

Los Angeles-Long Beach-Anaheim, CA MSA
Previously Los Angeles-Long Beach-Santa Ana, CA MSA
Los Angeles and Orange Counties

Los Angeles-Long Beach-Glendale, CA MD
Los Angeles County

Anaheim-Santa Ana-Irvine, CA MD
Previously Santa Ana-Anaheim-Irvine, CA MD
Orange County

Louisville/Jefferson, KY-IN MSA
Clark, Floyd, Harrison, Scott, and Washington Counties, IN; Bullitt, Henry, Jefferson, Oldham, Shelby, Spencer, and Trimble Counties, KY

Madison, WI MSA
Columbia, Dane, and Iowa Counties

Manchester, NH

Manchester-Nashua, NH MSA
Hillsborough County

Manchester, NH NECTA
Includes 11 cities and towns in New Hampshire
Previously Manchester, NH NECTA
Includes 9 cities and towns in New Hampshire

Miami, FL

Miami-Fort Lauderdale-West Palm Beach, FL MSA
Previously Miami-Fort Lauderdale-Pompano Beach, FL MSA
Broward, Miami-Dade, and Palm Beach Counties

Miami-Miami Beach-Kendall, FL MD
Miami-Dade County

Midland, TX MSA
Martin, and Midland Counties

Milwaukee-Waukesha-West Allis, WI MSA
Milwaukee, Ozaukee, Washington, and Waukesha Counties

Minneapolis-St. Paul-Bloomington, MN-WI MSA
Anoka, Carver, Chisago, Dakota, Hennepin, Isanti, Le Sueur, Mille Lacs, Ramsey, Scott, Sherburne, Sibley, Washington, and Wright Counties, MN; Pierce and St. Croix Counties, WI

Nashville-Davidson-Murfreesboro-Franklin, TN MSA
Cannon, Cheatham, Davidson, Dickson, Hickman, Macon, Robertson, Rutherford, Smith, Sumner, Trousdale, Williamson, and Wilson Counties

New Haven-Milford, CT MSA
New Haven County

New Orleans-Metarie-Kenner, LA MSA
Jefferson, Orleans, Plaquemines, St. Bernard, St. Charles, St. James, St. John the Baptist, and St. Tammany Parish
Previously New Orleans-Metarie-Kenner, LA MSA
Jefferson, Orleans, Plaquemines, St. Bernard, St. Charles, St. John the Baptist, and St. Tammany Parish

New York, NY

New York-Newark-Jersey City, NY-NJ-PA MSA
Bergen, Essex, Hudson, Hunterdon, Middlesex, Monmouth, Morris, Ocean, Passaic, Somerset, Sussex, and Union Counties, NJ; Bronx, Dutchess, Kings, Nassau, New York, Orange, Putnam, Queens, Richmond, Rockland, Suffolk, and Westchester Counties, NY; Pike County, PA
Previous name: New York-Northern New Jersey-Long Island, NY-NJ-PA MSA
Bergen, Essex, Hudson, Hunterdon, Middlesex, Monmouth, Morris, Ocean, Passaic, Somerset, Sussex, and Union Counties, NJ; Bronx, Kings, Nassau, New York, Putnam, Queens, Richmond, Rockland, Suffolk, and Westchester Counties, NY; Pike County, PA

Dutchess County-Putnam County, NY MD
Dutchess and Putnam Counties
Dutchess County was previously part of the Poughkeepsie-Newburgh-Middletown, NY MSA. Putnam County was previously part of the New York-Wayne-White Plains, NY-NJ MD

Nassau-Suffolk, NY MD
Nassau and Suffolk Counties

New York-Jersey City-White Plains, NY-NJ MD
Bergen, Hudson, Middlesex, Monmouth, Ocean, and Passaic Counties, NJ; Bronx, Kings, New York, Orange, Queens, Richmond, Rockland, and Westchester Counties, NY
Previous name: New York-Wayne-White Plains, NY-NJ MD
Bergen, Hudson, and Passaic Counties, NJ; Bronx, Kings, New York, Putnam, Queens, Richmond, Rockland, and Westchester Counties, NY

Newark, NJ-PA MD
Essex, Hunterdon, Morris, Somerset, Sussex, and Union Counties, NJ; Pike County, PA
Previous name: Newark-Union, NJ-PA MD
Essex, Hunterdon, Morris, Sussex, and Union Counties, NJ; Pike County, PA

Oklahoma City, OK MSA
Canadian, Cleveland, Grady, Lincoln, Logan, McClain, and Oklahoma Counties

Omaha-Council Bluffs, NE-IA MSA
Harrison, Mills, and Pottawattamie Counties, IA; Cass, Douglas, Sarpy, Saunders, and Washington Counties, NE

Orlando-Kissimmee-Sanford, FL MSA
Lake, Orange, Osceola, and Seminole Counties

Peoria, IL MSA
Marshall, Peoria, Stark, Tazewell, and Woodford Counties

Philadelphia, PA

Philadelphia-Camden-Wilmington, PA-NJ-DE-MD MSA
New Castle County, DE; Cecil County, MD; Burlington, Camden, Gloucester, and Salem Counties, NJ; Bucks, Chester, Delaware, Montgomery, and Philadelphia Counties, PA

Camden, NJ MD
Burlington, Camden, and Gloucester Counties

Montgomery County-Bucks County-Chester County, PA MD
Bucks, Chester, and Montgomery Counties
Previously part of the Philadelphia, PA MD

Philadelphia, PA MD
Delaware and Philadelphia Counties
Previous name: Philadelphia, PA MD
Bucks, Chester, Delaware, Montgomery, and Philadelphia Counties

Wilmington, DE-MD-NJ MD
New Castle County, DE; Cecil County, MD; Salem County, NJ

Phoenix-Mesa-Scottsdale, AZ MSA
Previously Phoenix-Mesa-Glendale, AZ MSA
Maricopa and Pinal Counties

Pittsburgh, PA MSA
Allegheny, Armstrong, Beaver, Butler, Fayette, Washington, and Westmoreland Counties

Portland-Vancouver-Hillsboro, OR-WA MSA
Clackamas, Columbia, Multnomah, Washington, and Yamhill Counties, OR; Clark and Skamania Counties, WA

Providence, RI

Providence-New Bedford-Fall River, RI-MA MSA
Previously Providence-New Bedford-Fall River, RI-MA MSA
Bristol County, MA; Bristol, Kent, Newport, Providence, and Washington Counties, RI

Providence-Warwick, RI-MA NECTA
Includes 12 cities and towns in Massachusetts and 36 cities and towns in Rhode Island
Previously Providence-Fall River-Warwick, RI-MA NECTA
Includes 12 cities and towns in Massachusetts and 37 cities and towns in Rhode Island

Provo-Orem, UT MSA
Juab and Utah Counties

Raleigh, NC MSA
Previously Raleigh-Cary, NC MSA
Franklin, Johnston, and Wake Counties

Reno, NV MSA
Previously Reno-Sparks, NV MSA
Storey and Washoe Counties

Richmond, VA MSA
Amelia, Caroline, Charles City, Chesterfield, Dinwiddie, Goochland, Hanover, Henrico, King William, New Kent, Powhatan, Prince George, and Sussex Counties; Colonial Heights, Hopewell, Petersburg, and Richmond Cities

Rochester, MN MSA
Dodge, Fillmore, Olmsted, and Wabasha Counties

Sacramento—Roseville—Arden-Arcade, CA MSA
El Dorado, Placer, Sacramento, and Yolo Counties

Salt Lake City, UT MSA
Salt Lake and Tooele Counties

San Antonio-New Braunfels, TX MSA
Atascosa, Bandera, Bexar, Comal, Guadalupe, Kendall, Medina, and Wilson Counties

San Diego-Carlsbad, CA MSA
Previously San Diego-Carlsbad-San Marcos, CA MSA
San Diego County

San Francisco, CA

San Francisco-Oakland-Hayward, CA MSA
Previously San Francisco-Oakland- Fremont, CA MSA
Alameda, Contra Costa, Marin, San Francisco, and San Mateo Counties

San Francisco-Redwood City-South San Francisco, CA MD
San Francisco and San Mateo Counties

Previously San Francisco-San Mateo-Redwood City, CA MD
Marin, San Francisco, and San Mateo Counties

San Jose-Sunnyvale-Santa Clara, CA MSA
San Benito and Santa Clara Counties

Santa Rosa, CA MSA
Previously Santa Rosa-Petaluma, CA MSA
Sonoma County

Savannah, GA MSA
Bryan, Chatham, and Effingham Counties

Seattle, WA

Seattle-Tacoma-Bellevue, WA MSA
King, Pierce, and Snohomish Counties

Seattle-Bellevue-Everett, WA MD
King and Snohomish Counties

Sioux Falls, SD MSA
Lincoln, McCook, Minnehaha, and Turner Counties

Springfield, IL MSA
Menard and Sangamon Counties

Tallahassee, FL MSA
Gadsden, Jefferson, Leon, and Wakulla Counties

Tampa-St. Petersburg-Clearwater, FL MSA
Hernando, Hillsborough, Pasco, and Pinellas Counties

Topeka, KS MSA
Jackson, Jefferson, Osage, Shawnee, and Wabaunsee Counties

Tucson, AZ MSA
Pima County

Tulsa, OK MSA
Creek, Okmulgee, Osage, Pawnee, Rogers, Tulsa, and Wagoner Counties

Tuscaloosa, AL MSA
Hale, Pickens, and Tuscaloosa Counties

Virginia Beach-Norfolk-Newport News, VA-NC MSA
Currituck County, NC; Chesapeake, Hampton, Newport News, Norfolk, Poquoson, Portsmouth, Suffolk, Virginia Beach and Williamsburg cities, VA; Gloucester, Isle of Wight, James City, Mathews, Surry, and York Counties, VA

Washington, DC

Washington-Arlington-Alexandria, DC-VA-MD-WV MSA
District of Columbia; Calvert, Charles, Frederick, Montgomery, and Prince George's Counties, MD; Alexandria, Fairfax, Falls Church, Fredericksburg, Manassas Park, and Manassas cities, VA; Arlington, Clarke, Culpepper, Fairfax, Fauquier, Loudoun, Prince William, Rappahannock, Spotsylvania, Stafford, and Warren Counties, VA; Jefferson County, WV
Previously Washington-Arlington-Alexandria, DC-VA-MD-WV MSA
District of Columbia; Calvert, Charles, Frederick, Montgomery, and Prince George's Counties, MD; Alexandria, Fairfax, Falls Church, Fredericksburg, Manassas Park, and Manassas cities, VA; Arlington, Clarke, Fairfax, Fauquier, Loudoun, Prince William, Spotsylvania, Stafford, and Warren Counties, VA; Jefferson County, WV

Washington-Arlington-Alexandria, DC-VA-MD-WV MD
District of Columbia; Calvert, Charles, and Prince George's Counties, MD; Alexandria, Fairfax, Falls Church, Fredericksburg, Manassas Park, and Manassas cities, VA; Arlington, Clarke, Culpepper, Fairfax, Fauquier, Loudoun, Prince William, Rappahannock, Spotsylvania, Stafford, and Warren Counties, VA; Jefferson County, WV
Previously Washington-Arlington-Alexandria, DC-VA-MD-WV MD
District of Columbia; Calvert, Charles, and Prince George's Counties, MD; Alexandria, Fairfax, Falls Church, Fredericksburg, Manassas Park, and Manassas cities, VA; Arlington, Clarke, Fairfax, Fauquier, Loudoun, Prince William, Spotsylvania, Stafford, and Warren Counties, VA; Jefferson County, WV

Wichita, KS MSA
Butler, Harvey, Kingman, Sedgwick, and Sumner Counties

Winston-Salem, NC MSA
Davidson, Davie, Forsyth, Stokes, and Yadkin Counties

Appendix C: Government Type and Primary County

This appendix includes the government structure of each place included in this book. It also includes the county or county equivalent in which each place is located. If a place spans more than one county, the county in which the majority of the population resides is shown.

Albuquerque, NM
Government Type: City
County: Bernalillo

Albany, NY
Government Type: City
County: Albany

Allentown, PA
Government Type: City
County: Lehigh

Anchorage, AK
Government Type: Municipality
Borough: Anchorage

Ann Arbor, MI
Government Type: City
County: Washtenaw

Athens, GA
Government Type: Consolidated
   city-county
County: Clarke

Atlanta, GA
Government Type: City
County: Fulton

Austin, TX
Government Type: City
County: Travis

Baton Rouge, LA
Government Type: Consolidated city-parish
Parish: East Baton Rouge

Boise City, ID
Government Type: City
County: Ada

Boston, MA
Government Type: City
County: Suffolk

Boulder, CO
Government Type: City
County: Boulder

Cape Coral, FL
Government Type: City
County: Lee

Cedar Rapids, IA
Government Type: City
County: Linn

Charleston, SC
Government Type: City
County: Charleston

Charlotte, NC
Government Type: City
County: Mecklenburg

Chicago, IL
Government Type: City
County: Cook

Clarksville, TN
Government Type: City
County: Montgomery

Cleveland, OH
Government Type: City
County: Cuyahoga

College Station, TX
Government Type: City
County: Brazos

Colorado Springs, CO
Government Type: City
County: El Paso

Columbia, MO
Government Type: City
County: Boone

Columbia, SC
Government Type: City
County: Richland

Columbus, OH
Government Type: City
County: Franklin

Dallas, TX
Government Type: City
County: Dallas

Davenport, IA
Government Type: City
County: Scott

Denver, CO
Government Type: City
County: Denver

Des Moines, IA
Government Type: City
County: Polk

Durham, NC
Government Type: City
County: Durham

Edison, NJ
Government Type: Township
County: Middlesex

El Paso, TX
Government Type: City
County: El Paso

Fargo, ND
Government Type: City
County: Cass

Fayetteville, NC
Government Type: City
County: Cumberland

Fort Collins, CO
Government Type: City
County: Larimer

Fort Wayne, IN
Government Type: City
County: Allen

Fort Worth, TX
Government Type: City
County: Tarrant

Grand Rapids, MI
Government Type: City
County: Kent

Greeley, CO
Government Type: City
County: Weld

Green Bay, WI
Government Type: City
County: Brown

Greensboro, NC
Government Type: City
County: Guilford

Honolulu, HI
Government Type: Census Designated Place
   (CDP)
County: Honolulu

Houston, TX
Government Type: City
County: Harris

Huntsville, AL
Government Type: City
County: Madison

Indianapolis, IN
Government Type: City
County: Marion

Jackson, MS
Government Type: City
County: Hinds

Jacksonville, FL
Government Type: City
County: Duval

Kansas City, MO
Government Type: City
County: Jackson

Lafayette, LA
Government Type: City
Parish: Lafayette

Lakeland, FL
Government Type: City
County: Polk

Las Vegas, NV
Government Type: City
County: Clark

Lexington, KY
Government Type: Consolidated city-county
County: Fayette

Lincoln, NE
Government Type: City
County: Lancaster

Little Rock, AR
Government Type: City
County: Pulaski

Los Angeles, CA
Government Type: City
County: Los Angeles

Louisville, KY
Government Type: Consolidated city-county
County: Jefferson

Madison, WI
Government Type: City
County: Dane

Manchester, NH
Government Type: City
County: Hillsborough

Miami, FL
Government Type: City
County: Miami-Dade

Midland, TX
Government Type: City
County: Midland

Milwaukee, WI
Government Type: City
County: Milwaukee

Minneapolis, MN
Government Type: City
County: Hennepin

Nashville, TN
Government Type: Consolidated city-county
County: Davidson

New Haven, CT
Government Type: City
County: New Haven

New Orleans, LA
Government Type: City
Parish: Orleans

New York, NY
Government Type: City
Counties: Bronx; Kings; New York; Queens;
    Staten Island

Oklahoma City, OK
Government Type: City
County: Oklahoma

Omaha, NE
Government Type: City
County: Douglas

Orlando, FL
Government Type: City
County: Orange

Peoria, IL
Government Type: City
County: Peoria

Philadelphia, PA
Government Type: City
County: Philadelphia

Phoenix, AZ
Government Type: City
County: Maricopa

Pittsburgh, PA
Government Type: City
County: Allegheny

Portland, OR
Government Type: City
County: Multnomah

Providence, RI
Government Type: City
County: Providence

Provo, UT
Government Type: City
County: Utah

Raleigh, NC
Government Type: City
County: Wake

Reno, NV
Government Type: City
County: Washoe

Richmond, VA
Government Type: Independent city
County: Richmond city

Rochester, MN
Government Type: City
County: Olmsted

Sacramento, CA
Government Type: City
County: Sacramento

Salt Lake City, UT
Government Type: City
County: Salt Lake

San Antonio, TX
Government Type: City
County: Bexar

San Diego, CA
Government Type: City
County: San Diego

San Francisco, CA
Government Type: City
County: San Francisco

San Jose, CA
Government Type: City
County: Santa Clara

Santa Rosa, CA
Government Type: City
County: Sonoma

Savannah, GA
Government Type: City
County: Chatham

Seattle, WA
Government Type: City
County: King

Sioux Falls, SD
Government Type: City
County: Minnehaha

Springfield, IL
Government Type: City
County: Sangamon

Tallahassee, FL
Government Type: City
County: Leon

Tampa, FL
Government Type: City
County: Hillsborough

Topeka, KS
Government Type: City
County: Shawnee

Tucson, AZ
Government Type: City
County: Pima

Tulsa, OK
Government Type: City
County: Tulsa

Tuscaloosa, AL
Government Type: City
County: Tuscaloosa

Virginia Beach, VA
Government Type: Independent city
County: Virginia Beach city

Washington, DC
Government Type: City
County: District of Columbia

Wichita, KS
Government Type: City
County: Sedgwick

Winston-Salem, NC
Government Type: City
County: Forsyth

Appendix D: Chambers of Commerce

Albany, NY
Capital Region Chamber
Albany Office
5 Computer Drive South
Colonie, NY 12205
Phone: (518) 431-1400
Fax: (518) 431-1402
http://capitalregionchamber.com

Albuquerque, NM
Albuquerque Chamber of Commerce
P.O. Box 25100
Albuquerque, NM 87125
Phone: (505) 764-3700
Fax: (505) 764-3714
http://www.abqchamber.com

Albuquerque Economic Development Dept
851 University Blvd SE, Suite 203
Albuquerque, NM 87106
Phone: (505) 246-6200
Fax: (505) 246-6219
http://www.cabq.gov/econdev

Allentown, PA
Greater Lehigh Valley Chamber of
Commerce
Allentown Office
840 Hamilton Street, Suite 205
Allentown, PA 18101
Phone: (610) 751-4929
Fax: (610) 437-4907
http://www.lehighvalleychamber.org

Anchorage, AK
Anchorage Chamber of Commerce
1016 W Sixth Avenue
Suite 303
Anchorage, AK 99501
Phone: (907) 272-2401
Fax: (907) 272-4117
http://www.anchoragechamber.org

Anchorage Economic Development
Department
900 W 5th Avenue
Suite 300
Anchorage, AK 99501
Phone: (907) 258-3700
Fax: (907) 258-6646
http://aedcweb.com

Ann Arbor, MI
Ann Arbor Area Chamber of Commerce
115 West Huron
3rd Floor
Ann Arbor, MI 48104
Phone: (734) 665-4433
Fax: (734) 665-4191
http://www.annarborchamber.org

Ann Arbor Economic Development
Department
201 S Division
Suite 430
Ann Arbor, MI 48104
Phone: (734) 761-9317
http://www.annarborspark.org

Athens, GA
Athens Area Chamber of Commerce
246 W Hancock Avenue
Athens, GA 30601
Phone: (706) 549-6800
Fax: (706) 549-5636
http://www.aacoc.org

Athens-Clarke County Economic
Development Department
246 W. Hancock Avenue
Athens, GA 30601
Phone: (706) 613-3233
Fax: (706) 613-3812
http://www.athensbusiness.org

Atlanta, GA
Metro Atlanta Chamber of Commerce
235 Andrew Young International Blvd NW
Atlanta, GA 30303
Phone: (404) 880-9000
Fax: (404) 586-8464
http://www.metroatlantachamber.com

Austin, TX
Greater Austin Chamber of Commerce
210 Barton Springs Road
Suite 400
Austin, TX 78704
Phone: (512) 478-9383
Fax: (512) 478-6389
http://www.austin-chamber.org

Baton Rouge, LA
Baton Rouge Area Chamber
451 Florida Street
Suite 1050
Baton Rouge, LA 70801
Phone (225) 381-7125
http://www.brac.org

Boise City, ID
Boise Metro Chamber of Commerce
250 S 5th Street
Suite 800
Boise City, ID 83701
Phone: (208) 472-5200
Fax: (208) 472-5201
http://www.boisechamber.org

Boston, MA
Greater Boston Chamber of Commerce
265 Franklin Street
12th Floor
Boston, MA 02110
Phone: (617) 227-4500
Fax: (617) 227-7505
http://www.bostonchamber.com

Boulder, CO
Boulder Chamber of Commerce
2440 Pearl Street
Boulder, CO 80302
Phone: (303) 442-1044
Fax: (303) 938-8837
http://www.boulderchamber.com

City of Boulder Economic Vitality Program
P.O. Box 791
Boulder, CO 80306
Phone: (303) 441-3090
http://www.bouldercolorado.gov

Cape Coral, FL
Chamber of Commerce of Cape Coral
2051 Cape Coral Parkway East
Cape Coral, FL 33904
Phone: (239) 549-6900
Fax: (239) 549-9609
http://www.capecoralchamber.com

Cedar Rapids, IA
Cedar Rapids Chamber of Commerce
424 First Avenue NE
Cedar Rapids, IA 52401
Phone: (319) 398-5317
Fax: (319) 398-5228
http://www.cedarrapids.org

Cedar Rapids Economic Development
50 Second Avenue Bridge
Sixth Floor
Cedar Rapids, IA 52401-1256
Phone: (319) 286-5041
Fax: (319) 286-5141
http://www.cedar-rapids.org

Charleston, SC
Charleston Metro Chamber of Commerce
P.O. Box 975
Charleston, SC 29402
Phone: (843) 577-2510
http://www.charlestonchamber.net

Charlotte, NC
Charlotte Chamber of Commerce
330 S Tryon Street
P.O. Box 32785
Charlotte, NC 28232
Phone: (704) 378-1300
Fax: (704) 374-1903
http://www.charlottechamber.com

Charlotte Regional Partnership
1001 Morehead Square Drive
Suite 200
Charlotte, NC 28203
Phone: (704) 347-8942
Fax: (704) 347-8981
http://www.charlotteusa.com

Chicago, IL
Chicagoland Chamber of Commerce
200 E Randolph Street
Suite 2200
Chicago, IL 60601-6436
Phone: (312) 494-6700
Fax: (312) 861-0660
http://www.chicagolandchamber.org

City of Chicago Department of Planning
and Development
City Hall, Room 1000
121 North La Salle Street
Chicago, IL 60602
Phone: (312) 744-4190
Fax: (312) 744-2271
https://www.cityofchicago.org/city/en/
depts/dcd.html

Clarksville, TN
Clarksville Area Chamber of Commerce
25 Jefferson Street
Suite 300
Clarksville, TN 37040
Phone: (931) 647-2331
http://www.clarksvillechamber.com

Cleveland, OH
Greater Cleveland Partnership
1240 Huron Rd. E
Suite 300
Cleveland, OH 44115
Phone: (216) 621-3300
https://www.gcpartnership.com

College Station, TX
Bryan-College Station Chamber of
Commerce
4001 East 29th St, Suite 175
Bryan, TX 77802
Phone: (979) 260-5200
http://www.bcschamber.org

Colorado Springs, CO
Colorado Springs Chamber and EDC
102 South Tejon Street
Suite 430
Colorado Springs, CO 80903
Phone: (719) 471-8183
https://coloradospringschamberedc.com

Columbia, MO
Columbia Chamber of Commerce
300 South Providence Rd.
P.O. Box 1016
Columbia, MO 65205-1016
Phone: (573) 874-1132
Fax: (573) 443-3986
http://www.columbiamochamber.com

Columbia, SC
The Columbia Chamber
930 Richland Street
Columbia, SC 29201
Phone: (803) 733-1110
Fax: (803) 733-1113
http://www.columbiachamber.com

Columbus, OH
Greater Columbus Chamber
37 North High Street
Columbus, OH 43215
Phone: (614) 221-1321
Fax: (614) 221-1408
http://www.columbus.org

Dallas, TX
City of Dallas Economic Development
Department
1500 Marilla Street
5C South
Dallas, TX 75201
Phone: (214) 670-1685
Fax: (214) 670-0158
http://www.dallas-edd.org

Greater Dallas Chamber of Commerce
700 North Pearl Street
Suite1200
Dallas, TX 75201
Phone: (214) 746-6600
Fax: (214) 746-6799
http://www.dallaschamber.org

Davenport, IA
Quad Cities Chamber
331 W. 3rd Street
Suite 100
Davenport, IA 52801
Phone: (563) 322-1706
https://quadcitieschamber.com

Denver, CO
Denver Metro Chamber of Commerce
1445 Market Street
Denver, CO 80202
Phone: (303) 534-8500
Fax: (303) 534-3200
http://www.denverchamber.org

Downtown Denver Partnership
511 16th Street
Suite 200
Denver, CO 80202
Phone: (303) 534-6161
Fax: (303) 534-2803
http://www.downtowndenver.com

Des Moines, IA
Des Moines Downtown Chamber
301 Grand Ave
Des Moines, IA 50309
Phone: (515) 309-3229
http://desmoinesdowntownchamber.com

Greater Des Moines Partnership
700 Locust Street
Suite 100
Des Moines, IA 50309
Phone: (515) 286-4950
Fax: (515) 286-4974
http://www.desmoinesmetro.com

Durham, NC
Durham Chamber of Commerce
P.O. Box 3829
Durham, NC 27702
Phone: (919) 682-2133
Fax: (919) 688-8351
http://www.durhamchamber.org

North Carolina Institute of Minority
Economic Development
114 W Parish Street
Durham, NC 27701
Phone: (919) 956-8889
Fax: (919) 688-7668
http://www.ncimed.com

Edison, NJ
Edison Chamber of Commerce
939 Amboy Avenue
Edison, NJ 08837
Phone: (732) 738-9482
http://www.edisonchamber.com

El Paso, TX
City of El Paso Department of Economic
Development
2 Civic Center Plaza
El Paso, TX 79901
Phone: (915) 541-4000
Fax: (915) 541-1316
http://www.elpasotexas.gov

Greater El Paso Chamber of Commerce
10 Civic Center Plaza
El Paso, TX 79901
Phone: (915) 534-0500
Fax: (915) 534-0510
http://www.elpaso.org

Southwest Indiana Chamber
318 Main Street
Suite 401
Evansville, IN 47708
Phone: (812) 425-8147
Fax: (812) 421-5883
https://swinchamber.com

Fargo, ND
Chamber of Commerce of Fargo Moorhead
202 First Avenue North
Fargo, ND 56560
Phone: (218) 233-1100
Fax: (218) 233-1200
http://www.fmchamber.com

Greater Fargo-Moorhead Economic
Development Corporation
51 Broadway, Suite 500
Fargo, ND 58102
Phone: (701) 364-1900
Fax: (701) 293-7819
http://www.gfmedc.com

Fayetteville, NC
Fayetteville Regional Chamber
1019 Hay Street
Fayetteville, NC 28305
Phone: (910) 483-8133
Fax: (910) 483-0263
http://www.fayettevillencchamber.org

Fort Collins, CO
Fort Collins Chamber of Commerce
225 South Meldrum
Fort Collins, CO 80521
Phone: (970) 482-3746
Fax: (970) 482-3774
https://fortcollinschamber.com

Fort Wayne, IN
City of Fort Wayne Economic Development
1 Main St
1 Main Street
Fort Wayne, IN 46802
Phone: (260) 427-1111
Fax: (260) 427-1375
http://www.cityoffortwayne.org

Greater Fort Wayne Chamber of Commerce
826 Ewing Street
Fort Wayne, IN 46802
Phone: (260) 424-1435
Fax: (260) 426-7232
http://www.fwchamber.org

Fort Worth, TX
City of Fort Worth Economic Development
City Hall
900 Monroe Street
Suite 301
Fort Worth, TX 76102
Phone: (817) 392-6103
Fax: (817) 392-2431
http://www.fortworthgov.org

Fort Worth Chamber of Commerce
777 Taylor Street
Suite 900
Fort Worth, TX 76102-4997
Phone: (817) 336-2491
Fax: (817) 877-4034
http://www.fortworthchamber.com

Grand Rapids, MI
Grands Rapids Area Chamber of Commerce
111 Pearl Street N.W.
Grand Rapids, MI 49503
Phone: (616) 771-0300
Fax: (616) 771-0318
http://www.grandrapids.org

Greeley, CO
Greeley Chamber of Commerce
902 7th Avenue
Greeley, CO 80631
Phone: (970) 352-3566
https://greeleychamber.com

Green Bay, WI
Economic Development
100 N Jefferson St
Room 202
Green Bay, WI 54301
Phone: (920) 448-3397
Fax: (920) 448-3063
http://www.ci.green-bay.wi.us

Green Bay Area Chamber of Commerce
300 N. Broadway
Suite 3A
Green Bay, WI 54305-1660
Phone: (920) 437-8704
Fax: (920) 593-3468
http://www.titletown.org

Greensboro, NC
Greensboro Area Chamber of Commerce
342 N. Elm Street
Greensboro, NC 27401
Phone: (336) 387-8301
Fax: (336) 275-9299
http://www.greensboro.org

Honolulu, HI
The Chamber of Commerce of Hawaii
1132 Bishop Street
Suite 402
Honolulu, HI 96813
Phone: (808) 545-4300
Fax: (808) 545-4369
http://www.cochawaii.com

Houston, TX
Greater Houston Partnership
1200 Smith Street
Suite 700
Houston, TX 77002-4400
Phone: (713) 844-3600
Fax: (713) 844-0200
http://www.houston.org

Huntsville, AL
Chamber of Commerce of
Huntsville/Madison County
225 Church Street
Huntsville, AL 35801
Phone: (256) 535-2000
Fax: (256) 535-2015
http://www.huntsvillealabamausa.com

Indianapolis, IN
Greater Indianapolis Chamber of Commerce
111 Monument Circle
Suite 1950
Indianapolis, IN 46204
Phone: (317) 464-2222
Fax: (317) 464-2217
http://www.indychamber.com

The Indy Partnership
111 Monument Circle
Suite 1800
Indianapolis, IN 46204
Phone: (317) 236-6262
Fax: (317) 236-6275
http://indypartnership.com

Jackson, MS
Greater Jackson Chamber Partnership
P.O. Box 22548
Jackson, MS 39225
Phone: (601) 948-7575
Fax: (601) 352-5539
http://www.greaterjacksonpartnership.com

Jacksonville, FL
Jacksonville Chamber of Commerce
3 Independent Drive
Jacksonville, FL 32202
Phone: (904) 366-6600
Fax: (904) 632-0617
http://www.myjaxchamber.com

Kansas City, MO
Greater Kansas City Chamber of Commerce
2600 Commerce Tower
911 Main Street
Kansas City, MO 64105
Phone: (816) 221-2424
Fax: (816) 221-7440
http://www.kcchamber.com

Kansas City Area Development Council
2600 Commerce Tower
911 Main Street
Kansas City, MO 64105
Phone: (816) 221-2121
Fax: (816) 842-2865
http://www.thinkkc.com

Lafayette, LA
Greater Lafayette Chamber of Commerce
804 East Saint Mary Blvd.
Lafayette, LA 70503
Phone: (337) 233-2705
Fax: (337) 234-8671
http://www.lafchamber.org

Lakeland, FL
Lakeland Chamber of Commerce
35 Lake Morton Dr.
Lakeland, FL 33801
Phone: (863) 688-8551
https://www.lakelandchamber.com

Las Vegas, NV
Las Vegas Chamber of Commerce
6671 Las Vegas Blvd South
Suite 300
Las Vegas, NV 89119
Phone: (702) 735-1616
Fax: (702) 735-0406
http://www.lvchamber.org

Las Vegas Office of Business Development
400 Stewart Avenue
City Hall
Las Vegas, NV 89101
Phone: (702) 229-6011
Fax: (702) 385-3128
http://www.lasvegasnevada.gov

Lexington, KY
Greater Lexington Chamber of Commerce
330 East Main Street
Suite 100
Lexington, KY 40507
Phone: (859) 254-4447
Fax: (859) 233-3304
http://www.commercelexington.com

Lexington Downtown Development
Authority
101 East Vine Street
Suite 500
Lexington, KY 40507
Phone: (859) 425-2296
Fax: (859) 425-2292
http://www.lexingtondda.com

Lincoln, NE
Lincoln Chamber of Commerce
1135 M Street
Suite 200
Lincoln, NE 68508
Phone: (402) 436-2350
Fax: (402) 436-2360
http://www.lcoc.com

Little Rock, AR
Little Rock Regional Chamber
One Chamber Plaza
Little Rock, AR 72201
Phone: (501) 374-2001
Fax: (501) 374-6018
http://www.littlerockchamber.com

Los Angeles, CA
Los Angeles Area Chamber of Commerce
350 South Bixel Street
Los Angeles, CA 90017
Phone: (213) 580-7500
Fax: (213) 580-7511
http://www.lachamber.org

Los Angeles County Economic
Development Corporation
444 South Flower Street
34th Floor
Los Angeles, CA 90071
Phone: (213) 622-4300
Fax: (213) 622-7100
http://www.laedc.org

Louisville, KY
The Greater Louisville Chamber of
Commerce
614 West Main Street
Suite 6000
Louisville, KY 40202
Phone: (502) 625-0000
Fax: (502) 625-0010
http://www.greaterlouisville.com

Madison, WI
Greater Madison Chamber of Commerce
615 East Washington Avenue
P.O. Box 71
Madison, WI 53701-0071
Phone: (608) 256-8348
Fax: (608) 256-0333
http://www.greatermadisonchamber.com

Manchester, NH
Greater Manchester Chamber of Commerce
889 Elm Street
Manchester, NH 03101
Phone: (603) 666-6600
Fax: (603) 626-0910
http://www.manchester-chamber.org

Manchester Economic Development Office
One City Hall Plaza
Manchester, NH 03101
Phone: (603) 624-6505
Fax: (603) 624-6308
http://www.yourmanchesternh.com

Miami, FL
Greater Miami Chamber of Commerce
1601 Biscayne Boulevard
Ballroom Level
Miami, FL 33132-1260
Phone: (305) 350-7700
Fax: (305) 374-6902
http://www.miamichamber.com

The Beacon Council
80 Southwest 8th Street
Suite 2400
Miami, FL 33130
Phone: (305) 579-1300
Fax: (305) 375-0271
http://www.beaconcouncil.com

Midland, TX
Midland Chamber of Commerce
109 N. Main
Midland, TX 79701
Phone: (432) 683-3381
Fax: (432) 686-3556
http://www.midlandtxchamber.com

Milwaukee, WI
Greater Milwaukee Chamber of Commerce
6815 W. Capitol Drive
Suite 300
Milwaukee, WI 53216
Phone: (414) 465-2422
http://www.gmcofc.org

Metropolitan Milwaukee Association of
Commerce
756 N. Milwaukee Street
Suite 400
Milwaukee, WI 53202
Phone: (414) 287-4100
Fax: (414) 271-7753
https://www.mmac.org

Minneapolis, MN
Minneapolis Community Development
Agency
Crown Roller Mill
105 5th Avenue South
Suite 200
Minneapolis, MN 55401
Phone: (612) 673-5095
Fax: (612) 673-5100
http://www.ci.minneapolis.mn.us

Minneapolis Regional Chamber
81 South Ninth Street
Suite 200
Minneapolis, MN 55402
Phone: (612) 370-9100
Fax: (612) 370-9195
http://www.minneapolischamber.org

Nashville, TN
Nashville Area Chamber of Commerce
211 Commerce Street
Suite 100
Nashville, TN 37201
Phone: (615) 743-3000
Fax: (615) 256-3074
http://www.nashvillechamber.com

Tennessee Valley Authority Economic
Development
400 West Summit Hill Drive
Knoxville TN 37902
Phone: (865) 632-2101
http://www.tvaed.com

New Haven, CT
Greater New Haven Chamber of Commerce
900 Chapel Street
10th Floor
New Haven, CT 06510
Phone: (203) 787-6735
https://www.gnhcc.com

New Orleans, LA
New Orleans Chamber of Commerce
1515 Poydras Street
Suite 1010
New Orleans, LA 70112
Phone: (504) 799-4260
Fax: (504) 799-4259
http://www.neworleanschamber.org

New York, NY
New York City Economic Development
Corporation
110 William Street
New York, NY 10038
Phone: (212) 619-5000
http://www.nycedc.com

The Partnership for New York City
One Battery Park Plaza
5th Floor
New York, NY 10004
Phone: (212) 493-7400
Fax: (212) 344-3344
http://www.pfnyc.org

Oklahoma City, OK
Greater Oklahoma City Chamber of
Commerce
123 Park Avenue
Oklahoma City, OK 73102
Phone: (405) 297-8900
Fax: (405) 297-8916
http://www.okcchamber.com

Omaha, NE
Omaha Chamber of Commerce
1301 Harney Street
Omaha, NE 68102
Phone: (402) 346-5000
Fax: (402) 346-7050
http://www.omahachamber.org

Orlando, FL
Metro Orlando Economic Development
Commission of Mid-Florida
301 East Pine Street
Suite 900
Orlando, FL 32801
Phone: (407) 422-7159
Fax: (407) 425.6428
http://www.orlandoedc.com

Orlando Regional Chamber of Commerce
75 South Ivanhoe Boulevard
P.O. Box 1234
Orlando, FL 32802
Phone: (407) 425-1234
Fax: (407) 839-5020
http://www.orlando.org

Peoria, IL
Peoria Area Chamber
100 SW Water Street
Peoria, IL 61602
Phone: (309) 495-5900
http://www.peoriachamber.org

Philadelphia, PA
Greater Philadelphia Chamber of
Commerce
200 South Broad Street
Suite 700
Philadelphia, PA 19102
Phone: (215) 545-1234
Fax: (215) 790-3600
http://www.greaterphilachamber.com

Phoenix, AZ
Greater Phoenix Chamber of Commerce
201 North Central Avenue
27th Floor
Phoenix, AZ 85073
Phone: (602) 495-2195
Fax: (602) 495-8913
http://www.phoenixchamber.com

Greater Phoenix Economic Council
2 North Central Avenue
Suite 2500
Phoenix, AZ 85004
Phone: (602) 256-7700
Fax: (602) 256-7744
http://www.gpec.org

Pittsburgh, PA
Allegheny County Industrial Development
Authority
425 6th Avenue
Suite 800
Pittsburgh, PA 15219
Phone: (412) 350-1067
Fax: (412) 642-2217
http://www.alleghenycounty.us

Greater Pittsburgh Chamber of Commerce
425 6th Avenue
12th Floor
Pittsburgh, PA 15219
Phone: (412) 392-4500
Fax: (412) 392-4520
http://www.alleghenyconference.org

Portland, OR
Portland Business Alliance
200 SW Market Street
Suite 1770
Portland, OR 97201
Phone: (503) 224-8684
Fax: (503) 323-9186
http://www.portlandalliance.com

Providence, RI
Greater Providence Chamber of Commerce
30 Exchange Terrace
Fourth Floor
Providence, RI 02903
Phone: (401) 521-5000
Fax: (401) 351-2090
http://www.provchamber.com

Rhode Island Economic Development
Corporation
Providence City Hall
25 Dorrance Street
Providence, RI 02903
Phone: (401) 421-7740
Fax: (401) 751-0203
http://www.providenceri.com

Provo, UT
Provo-Orem Chamber of Commerce
51 South University Avenue
Suite 215
Provo, UT 84601
Phone: (801) 851-2555
Fax: (801) 851-2557
http://www.thechamber.org

Raleigh, NC
Greater Raleigh Chamber of Commerce
800 South Salisbury Street
Raleigh, NC 27601-2978
Phone: (919) 664-7000
Fax: (919) 664-7099
http://www.raleighchamber.org

Reno, NV
Greater Reno-Sparks Chamber of
Commerce
1 East First Street
16th Floor
Reno, NV 89505
Phone: (775) 337-3030
Fax: (775) 337-3038
http://www.reno-sparkschamber.org

The Chamber Reno-Sparks-Northern
Nevada
449 S. Virginia St.
2nd Floor
Reno, NV 89501
Phone: (775) 636-9550
http://www.thechambernv.org

Richmond, VA
Greater Richmond Chamber
600 East Main Street
Suite 700
Richmond, VA 23219
Phone: (804) 648-1234
http://www.grcc.com

Greater Richmond Partnership
901 East Byrd Street
Suite 801
Richmond, VA 23219-4070
Phone: (804) 643-3227
Fax: (804) 343-7167
http://www.grpva.com

Rochester, MN
Rochester Area Chamber of Commerce
220 South Broadway
Suite 100
Rochester, MN 55904
Phone: (507) 288-1122
Fax: (507) 282-8960
http://www.rochestermnchamber.com

Sacramento, CA
Sacramento Metro Chamber
One Capitol Mall
Suite 700
Sacramento, CA 95814
Phone: (916) 552-6800
https://metrochamber.org

Salt Lake City, UT
Department of Economic Development
451 South State Street
Room 425
Salt Lake City, UT 84111
Phone: (801) 535-7240
Fax: (801) 535-6331
http://www.slcgov.com/economic-development

Salt Lake Chamber
175 E. University Blvd. (400 S)
Suite 600
Salt Lake City, UT 84111
Phone: (801) 364-3631
http://www.slchamber.com

San Antonio, TX
The Greater San Antonio Chamber of
Commerce
602 E. Commerce Street
San Antonio, TX 78205
Phone: (210) 229-2100
Fax: (210) 229-1600
http://www.sachamber.org

San Antonio Economic Development
Department
P.O. Box 839966
San Antonio, TX 78283-3966
Phone: (210) 207-8080
Fax: (210) 207-8151
http://www.sanantonio.gov/edd

San Diego, CA
San Diego Economic Development Corp.
401 B Street
Suite 1100
San Diego, CA 92101
Phone: (619) 234-8484
Fax: (619) 234-1935
http://www.sandiegobusiness.org

San Diego Regional Chamber of Commerce
402 West Broadway
Suite 1000
San Diego, CA 92101-3585
Phone: (619) 544-1300
Fax: (619) 744-7481
http://www.sdchamber.org

San Francisco, CA
San Francisco Chamber of Commerce
235 Montgomery Street
12th Floor
San Francisco, CA 94104
Phone: (415) 392-4520
Fax: (415) 392-0485
http://www.sfchamber.com

San Jose, CA
Office of Economic Development
60 South Market Street
Suite 470
San Jose, CA 95113
Phone: (408) 277-5880
Fax: (408) 277-3615
http://www.sba.gov

The Silicon Valley Organization
101 W Santa Clara Street
San Jose, CA 95113
Phone: (408) 291-5250
https://www.thesvo.com

Santa Rosa, CA
Santa Rosa Chamber of Commerce
1260 North Dutton Avenue
Suite 272
Santa Rosa, CA 95401
Phone: (707) 545-1414
http://www.santarosachamber.com

Savannah, GA
Economic Development Authority
131 Hutchinson Island Road
4th Floor
Savannah, GA 31421
Phone: (912) 447-8450
Fax: (912) 447-8455
http://www.seda.org

Savannah Chamber of Commerce
101 E. Bay Street
Savannah, GA 31402
Phone: (912) 644-6400
Fax: (912) 644-6499
http://www.savannahchamber.com

Seattle, WA
Greater Seattle Chamber of Commerce
1301 Fifth Avenue
Suite 2500
Seattle, WA 98101
Phone: (206) 389-7200
Fax: (206) 389-7288
http://www.seattlechamber.com

Sioux Falls, SD
Sioux Falls Area Chamber of Commerce
200 N. Phillips Avenue
Suite 102
Sioux Falls, SD 57104
Phone: (605) 336-1620
Fax: (605) 336-6499
http://www.siouxfallschamber.com

Springfield, IL
The Greater Springfield Chamber of
Commerce
1011 S. Second Street
Springfield, IL 62704
Phone: (217) 525-1173
Fax: (217) 525-8768
http://www.gscc.org

Tallahassee, FL
Greater Tallahassee Chamber of Commerce
300 E. Park Avenue
P.O. Box 1638
Tallahassee, FL 32301
Phone: (850) 224-8116
Fax: (850) 561-3860
http://www.talchamber.com

Tampa, FL
Greater Tampa Chamber of Commerce
P.O. Box 420
Tampa, FL 33601-0420
Phone: (813) 276-9401
Fax: (813) 229-7855
http://www.tampachamber.com

Topeka, KS
Greater Topeka Chamber of Commerce/
GO Topeka
120 SE Sixth Avenue
Suite 110
Topeka, KS 66603
Phone: (785) 234-2644
Fax: (785) 234-8656
http://www.topekachamber.org

Tucson, AZ
Tucson Metro Chamber
212 E. Broadway Blvd
Tucson, AZ 85701
Phone: (520) 792-1212
https://tucsonchamber.org

Tulsa, OK
Tulsa Regional Chamber
One West Third Street
Suite 100
Tulsa, OK 74103
Phone: (918) 585-1201
https://www.tulsachamber.com

Tuscaloosa, AL
The Chamber of Commerce of West
Alabama
2201 Jack Warner Parkway
Building C
Tuscaloosa, AL 35401
Phone: (205) 758-7588
https://tuscaloosachamber.com

Virginia Beach, VA
Hampton Roads Chamber of Commerce
500 East Main Street
Suite 700
Virginia Beach, VA 23510
Phone: (757) 664-2531
http://www.hamptonroadschamber.com

Washington, DC
District of Columbia Chamber of
Commerce
1213 K Street NW
Washington, DC 20005
Phone: (202) 347-7201
Fax: (202) 638-6762
http://www.dcchamber.org

District of Columbia Office of Planning and
Economic Development
J.A. Wilson Building
1350 Pennsylvania Ave NW
Suite 317
Washington, DC 20004
Phone: (202) 727-6365
Fax: (202) 727-6703
http://www.dcbiz.dc.gov

Wichita, KS
Wichita Regional Chamber of Commerce
350 W Douglas Avennue
Wichita, KS 67202
Phone: (316) 265-7771
https://www.wichitachamber.org

Winston-Salem, NC
Winston-Salem Chamber of Commerce
411 West Fourth Street
Suite 211
Winston-Salem, NC 27101
Phone: (336) 728-9200
http://www.winstonsalem.com

Appendix E: State Departments of Labor

Alabama
Alabama Department of Labor
P.O. Box 303500
Montgomery, AL 36130-3500
Phone: (334) 242-3072
https://www.labor.alabama.gov

Alaska
Dept of Labor and Workforce Devel.
P.O. Box 11149
Juneau, AK 99822-2249
Phone: (907) 465-2700
http://www.labor.state.ak.us

Arizona
Industrial Commission or Arizona
800 West Washington Street
Phoenix, AZ 85007
Phone: (602) 542-4411
https://www.azica.gov

Arkansas
Department of Labor
10421 West Markham
Little Rock, AR 72205
Phone: (501) 682-4500
http://www.labor.ar.gov

California
Labor and Workforce Development
445 Golden Gate Ave., 10th Floor
San Francisco, CA 94102
Phone: (916) 263-1811
http://www.labor.ca.gov

Colorado
Dept of Labor and Employment
633 17th St., 2nd Floor
Denver, CO 80202-3660
Phone: (888) 390-7936
https://www.colorado.gov/CDLE

Connecticut
Department of Labor
200 Folly Brook Blvd.
Wethersfield, CT 06109-1114
Phone: (860) 263-6000
http://www.ctdol.state.ct.us

Delaware
Department of Labor
4425 N. Market St., 4th Floor
Wilmington, DE 19802
Phone: (302) 451-3423
http://dol.delaware.gov

District of Columbia
Department of Employment Services
614 New York Ave., NE, Suite 300
Washington, DC 20002
Phone: (202) 671-1900
http://does.dc.gov

Florida
Florida Department of Economic
Opportunity
The Caldwell Building
107 East Madison St. Suite 100
Tallahassee, FL 32399-4120
Phone: (800) 342-3450
http://www.floridajobs.org

Georgia
Department of Labor
Sussex Place, Room 600
148 Andrew Young Intl Blvd., NE
Atlanta, GA 30303
Phone: (404) 656-3011
http://dol.georgia.gov

Hawaii
Dept of Labor & Industrial Relations
830 Punchbowl Street
Honolulu, HI 96813
Phone: (808) 586-8842
http://labor.hawaii.gov

Idaho
Department of Labor
317 W. Main St.
Boise, ID 83735-0001
Phone: (208) 332-3579
http://www.labor.idaho.gov

Illinois
Department of Labor
160 N. LaSalle Street, 13th Floor
Suite C-1300
Chicago, IL 60601
Phone: (312) 793-2800
https://www.illinois.gov/idol

Indiana
Indiana Department of Labor
402 West Washington Street, Room W195
Indianapolis, IN 46204
Phone: (317) 232-2655
http://www.in.gov/dol

Iowa
Iowa Workforce Development
1000 East Grand Avenue
Des Moines, IA 50319-0209
Phone: (515) 242-5870
http://www.iowadivisionoflabor.gov

Kansas
Department of Labor
401 S.W. Topeka Blvd.
Topeka, KS 66603-3182
Phone: (785) 296-5000
http://www.dol.ks.gov

Kentucky
Department of Labor
1047 U.S. Hwy 127 South, Suite 4
Frankfort, KY 40601-4381
Phone: (502) 564-3070
http://www.labor.ky.gov

Louisiana
Louisiana Workforce Commission
1001 N. 23rd Street
Baton Rouge, LA 70804-9094
Phone: (225) 342-3111
http://www.laworks.net

Maine
Department of Labor
45 Commerce Street
Augusta, ME 04330
Phone: (207) 623-7900
http://www.state.me.us/labor

Maryland
Department of Labor, Licensing &
Regulation
500 N. Calvert Street
Suite 401
Baltimore, MD 21202
Phone: (410) 767-2357
http://www.dllr.state.md.us

Massachusetts
Dept of Labor & Workforce Development
One Ashburton Place
Room 2112
Boston, MA 02108
Phone: (617) 626-7100
http://www.mass.gov/lwd

Michigan
Department of Licensing and Regulatory
Affairs
611 W. Ottawa
P.O. Box 30004
Lansing, MI 48909
Phone: (517) 373-1820
http://www.michigan.gov/lara

Minnesota
Dept of Labor and Industry
443 Lafayette Road North
Saint Paul, MN 55155
Phone: (651) 284-5070
http://www.doli.state.mn.us

Mississippi
Dept of Employment Security
P.O. Box 1699
Jackson, MS 39215-1699
Phone: (601) 321-6000
http://www.mdes.ms.gov

Missouri
Labor and Industrial Relations
P.O. Box 599
3315 W. Truman Boulevard
Jefferson City, MO 65102-0599
Phone: (573) 751-7500
https://labor.mo.gov

Montana
Dept of Labor and Industry
P.O. Box 1728
Helena, MT 59624-1728
Phone: (406) 444-9091
http://www.dli.mt.gov

Nebraska
Department of Labor
550 S 16th Street
Lincoln, NE 68508
Phone: (402) 471-9000
https://dol.nebraska.gov

Nevada
Dept of Business and Industry
3300 W. Sahara Ave
Suite 425
Las Vegas, NV 89102
Phone: (702) 486-2750
http://business.nv.gov

New Hampshire
Department of Labor
State Office Park South
95 Pleasant Street
Concord, NH 03301
Phone: (603) 271-3176
https://www.nh.gov/labor

New Jersey
Department of Labor & Workforce
Development
John Fitch Plaza, 13th Floor
Suite D
Trenton, NJ 08625-0110
Phone: (609) 777-3200
http://lwd.dol.state.nj.us/labor

New Mexico
Department of Workforce Solutions
401 Broadway, NE
Albuquerque, NM 87103-1928
Phone: (505) 841-8450
https://www.dws.state.nm.us

New York
Department of Labor
State Office Bldg. # 12
W.A. Harriman Campus
Albany, NY 12240
Phone: (518) 457-9000
https://www.labor.ny.gov

North Carolina
Department of Labor
4 West Edenton Street
Raleigh, NC 27601-1092
Phone: (919) 733-7166
https://www.labor.nc.gov

North Dakota
North Dakota Department of Labor and
Human Rights
State Capitol Building
600 East Boulevard, Dept 406
Bismark, ND 58505-0340
Phone: (701) 328-2660
http://www.nd.gov/labor

Ohio
Department of Commerce
77 South High Street, 22nd Floor
Columbus, OH 43215
Phone: (614) 644-2239
http://www.com.state.oh.us

Oklahoma
Department of Labor
4001 N. Lincoln Blvd.
Oklahoma City, OK 73105-5212
Phone: (405) 528-1500
https://www.ok.gov/odol

Oregon
Bureau of Labor and Industries
800 NE Oregon St., #32
Portland, OR 97232
Phone: (971) 673-0761
http://www.oregon.gov/boli

Pennsylvania
Dept of Labor and Industry
1700 Labor and Industry Bldg
7th and Forster Streets
Harrisburg, PA 17120
Phone: (717) 787-5279
http://www.dli.pa.gov

Rhode Island
Department of Labor and Training
1511 Pontiac Avenue
Cranston, RI 02920
Phone: (401) 462-8000
http://www.dlt.state.ri.us

South Carolina
Dept of Labor, Licensing & Regulations
P.O. Box 11329
Columbia, SC 29211-1329
Phone: (803) 896-4300
http://www.llr.state.sc.us

South Dakota
Department of Labor & Regulation
700 Governors Drive
Pierre, SD 57501-2291
Phone: (605) 773-3682
http://dlr.sd.gov

Tennessee
Dept of Labor & Workforce Development
Andrew Johnson Tower
710 James Robertson Pkwy
Nashville, TN 37243-0655
Phone: (615) 741-6642
http://www.tn.gov/workforce

Texas
Texas Workforce Commission
101 East 15th St.
Austin, TX 78778
Phone: (512) 475-2670
http://www.twc.state.tx.us

Utah
Utah Labor Commission
160 East 300 South, 3rd Floor
Salt Lake City, UT 84114-6600
Phone: (801) 530-6800
https://laborcommission.utah.gov

Vermont
Department of Labor
5 Green Mountain Drive
P.O. Box 488
Montpelier, VT 05601-0488
Phone: (802) 828-4000
http://labor.vermont.gov

Virginia
Dept of Labor and Industry
Powers-Taylor Building
13 S. 13th Street
Richmond, VA 23219
Phone: (804) 371-2327
http://www.doli.virginia.gov

Washington
Dept of Labor and Industries
P.O. Box 44001
Olympia, WA 98504-4001
Phone: (360) 902-4200
http://www.lni.wa.gov

West Virginia
Division of Labor
749 B Building 6
Capitol Complex
Charleston, WV 25305
Phone: (304) 558-7890
https://labor.wv.gov

Wisconsin
Dept of Workforce Development
201 E. Washington Ave., #A400
P.O. Box 7946
Madison, WI 53707-7946
Phone: (608) 266-6861
http://dwd.wisconsin.gov

Wyoming
Department of Workforce Services
1510 East Pershing Blvd.
Cheyenne, WY 82002
Phone: (307) 777-7261
http://www.wyomingworkforce.org

2020 Title List

Visit www.GreyHouse.com for Product Information, Table of Contents, and Sample Pages.

Opinions Throughout History

Opinions Throughout History: Drug Use & Abuse
Opinions Throughout History: Gender: Roles & Rights
Opinions Throughout History: Globalization
Opinions Throughout History: Guns in America
Opinions Throughout History: Immigration
Opinions Throughout History: National Security vs. Civil & Privacy Rights
Opinions Throughout History: Presidential Authority
Opinions Throughout History: Robotics & Artificial Intelligence
Opinions Throughout History: Social Media Issues
Opinions Throughout History: The Death Penalty
Opinions Throughout History: The Environment
Opinions Throughout History: Voters' Rights

This is Who We Were

This is Who We Were: Colonial America (1492-1775)
This is Who We Were: 1880-1899
This is Who We Were: In the 1900s
This is Who We Were: In the 1910s
This is Who We Were: In the 1920s
This is Who We Were: A Companion to the 1940 Census
This is Who We Were: In the 1940s (1940-1949)
This is Who We Were: In the 1950s
This is Who We Were: In the 1960s
This is Who We Were: In the 1970s
This is Who We Were: In the 1980s
This is Who We Were: In the 1990s
This is Who We Were: In the 2000s
This is Who We Were: In the 2010s

Working Americans

Working Americans, 1880-2011 - Vol. 1 The Working Class
Working Americans, 1880-1999 - Vol. 2: The Middle Class
Working Americans, 1880-1999 - Vol. 3: The Upper Class
Working Americans, 1880-1999 - Vol. 4: Children
Working Americans, 1880-2015 - Vol. 5: At War
Working Americans, 1880-2015 - Vol. 6: Working Women
Working Americans, 1880-2016 - Vol. 7: Social Movements
Working Americans, 1880-2017 - Vol. 8: Immigrants
Working Americans, 1770-1869 - Vol. 9: From the Revolutionary War to the Civil War
Working Americans, 1880-2009 - Vol. 10: Sports & Recreation
Working Americans, 1880-2009 - Vol. 11: Inventors & Entrepreneurs
Working Americans, 1880-2011 - Vol. 12: Our History Through Music
Working Americans, 1880-2011 - Vol. 13: Education & Educators
Working Americans, 1880-2016 - Vol. 14: African Americans
Working Americans, 1880-2018: Vol. 15: Politics & Politicians
Working Americans, 1880-2020: Vol. 16: Farming & Ranching

Education

Complete Learning Disabilities Resource Guide
Educators Resource Guide
The Comparative Guide to Elem. & Secondary Schools
Charter School Movement
Special Education: A Reference Book for Policy & Curriculum Development

General Reference

African Biographical Dictionary
American Environmental Leaders
America's College Museums
Constitutional Amendments
Encyclopedia of African-American Writing
Encyclopedia of Historical Warrior Peoples & Modern Fighting Groups
Encyclopedia of Invasions & Conquests
Encyclopedia of Prisoners of War & Internment
Encyclopedia of Religion & the Law in America
Encyclopedia of Rural America
Encyclopedia of the Continental Congresses
Encyclopedia of the United States Cabinet
Encyclopedia of War Journalism
The Environmental Debate
The Evolution Wars: A Guide to the Debates
Financial Literacy Starter Kit
From Suffrage to the Senate
The Gun Debate: An Encyclopedia of Gun Rights & Gun Control in the US
History of Canada
Human Rights and the United States
Political Corruption in America
Privacy Rights in the Digital Age
Religious Right and American Politics
Speakers of the House of Representatives
The Value of a Dollar 1600-1865 Colonial to Civil War
The Value of a Dollar 1860-2019
US Land & Natural Resources Policy
World Cultural Leaders of the 20th Century

Business Information

Business Information Resources
The Complete Broadcasting Industry Guide: Television, Radio, Cable & Streaming
Directory of Mail Order Catalogs
Environmental Resource Handbook
Food & Beverage Market Place
The Grey House Homeland Security Resources
The Grey House Performing Arts Industry Guide
Guide to Healthcare Group Purchasing Organizations
Guide to U.S. HMOs and PPOs
Guide to Venture Capital & Private Equity Firms
Hudson's Washington News Media Contacts Guide
New York State Directory
Sports Market Place

Consumer Health

Comparative Guide to American Hospitals
Complete Mental Health Resource Guide
Complete Resource Guide for Pediatric Disorders
Complete Resource Guide for People with Chronic Illness
Complete Resource Guide for People with Disabilities
Dementia Handbook & Resource Guide
Older Americans Information Resource

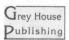

2020 Title List

Visit www.GreyHouse.com for Product Information, Table of Contents, and Sample Pages.

Statistics & Demographics

America's Top-Rated Cities
America's Top-Rated Smaller Cities
Ancestry & Ethnicity in America
The Comparative Guide to American Suburbs
The Hispanic Databook
Profiles of America
Profiles of California
Profiles of Connecticut & Rhode Island
Profiles of Florida
Profiles of Illinois
Profiles of Indiana
Profiles of Massachusetts
Profiles of Michigan
Profiles of New Jersey
Profiles of New York
Profiles of North Carolina & South Carolina
Profiles of Ohio
Profiles of Pennsylvania
Profiles of Texas
Profiles of Virginia
Profiles of Wisconsin
Weather America

Canadian Resources

Canadian Almanac & Directory
Canadian Environmental Update
Associations Canada
Financial Services Canada
Libraries Canada
Canadian Parliamentary Guide
Canadian Venture Capital & Private Equity Firms
Health Guide Canada
Major Canadian Cities: Compared & Ranked, First Edition
Canadian Who's Who
Cannabis Canada
Financial Post Directory of Directors
FP Survey: Industrials
FP Survey: Mines & Energy
FP Survey: Predecessor & Defunct
FP Bonds: Corporate
FP Bonds: Government
FP Equities: Preferreds & Derivatives
Careers & Employment Canada

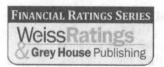

Weiss Financial Ratings

Financial Literacy Basics
Financial Literacy: How to Become an Investor
Financial Literacy: Planning for the Future
Weiss Ratings Consumer Guides
Weiss Ratings Guide to Banks
Weiss Ratings Guide to Credit Unions
Weiss Ratings Guide to Health Insurers
Weiss Ratings Guide to Life & Annuity Insurers
Weiss Ratings Guide to Property & Casualty Insurers
Weiss Ratings Investment Research Guide to Bond & Money
    Market Mutual Funds
Weiss Ratings Investment Research Guide to Exchange-Traded
    Funds
Weiss Ratings Investment Research Guide to Stock Mutual
    Funds
Weiss Ratings Investment Research Guide to Stocks

Books in Print Series

American Book Publishing Record® Annual
American Book Publishing Record® Monthly
Books In Print®
Books In Print® Supplement
Books Out Loud™
Bowker's Complete Video Directory™
Children's Books In Print®
El-Hi Textbooks & Serials In Print®
Forthcoming Books®
Law Books & Serials In Print™
Medical & Health Care Books In Print™
Publishers, Distributors & Wholesalers of the US™
Subject Guide to Books In Print®
Subject Guide to Children's Books In Print®

Grey House Publishing | Salem Press | H.W. Wilson | 4919 Route, 22 PO Box 56, Amenia NY 12501-0056

SALEM PRESS

2020 Title List

 SALEM PRESS

Visit www.SalemPress.com for Product Information, Table of Contents, and Sample Pages.

Critical Insights

Critical Insights: A Midsummer Night's Dream
Critical Insights: A Portrait of the Artist as a Young Man
Critical Insights: A Streetcar Named Desire
Critical Insights: Abraham Lincoln
Critical Insights: Absalom, Absalom!
Critical Insights: Adventures of Huckleberry Finn
Critical Insights: Aeneid
Critical Insights: Albert Camus
Critical Insights: Alice Munro
Critical Insights: Alice Walker
Critical Insights: All Quiet on the Western Front
Critical Insights: American Creative Non-Fiction
Critical Insights: American Multicultural Identity
Critical Insights: American Road Literature
Critical Insights: American Short Story
Critical Insights: American Sports Fiction
Critical Insights: American Writers in Exile
Critical Insights: Ancient Greek Literature
Critical Insights: Animal Farm
Critical Insights: Arthur Miller
Critical Insights: Barbara Kingsolver
Critical Insights: Beloved
Critical Insights: Benjamin Franklin
Critical Insights: Billy Budd, Sailor
Critical Insights: Brave New World
Critical Insights: Censored & Banned Literature
Critical Insights: Charles Dickens
Critical Insights: Civil Rights Literature, Past & Present
Critical Insights: Coming of Age
Critical Insights: Conspiracies
Critical Insights: Contemporary Canadian Fiction
Critical Insights: Contemporary Immigrant Short Fiction
Critical Insights: Contemporary Latin American Fiction
Critical Insights: Contemporary Speculative Fiction
Critical Insights: Cormac McCarthy
Critical Insights: Crime and Detective Fiction
Critical Insights: Crisis of Faith
Critical Insights: Cultural Encounters
Critical Insights: David Foster Wallace
Critical Insights: Death of a Salesman
Critical Insights: Dracula
Critical Insights: Dystopia
Critical Insights: Edith Wharton

Critical Insights: Emily Dickinson
Critical Insights: Ernest Hemingway
Critical Insights: Eugene O'Neill
Critical Insights: F. Scott Fitzgerald
Critical Insights: Fahrenheit 451
Critical Insights: Family
Critical Insights: Feminism
Critical Insights: Flannery O'Connor
Critical Insights: Flash Fiction
Critical Insights: Frederick Douglass
Critical Insights: Gabriel Garcia Marquez
Critical Insights: Gender, Sex and Sexuality
Critical Insights: Geoffrey Chaucer
Critical Insights: George Eliot
Critical Insights: George Orwell
Critical Insights: Good & Evil
Critical Insights: Great Expectations
Critical Insights: Greed
Critical Insights: Gustave Flaubert
Critical Insights: Gwendolyn Brooks
Critical Insights: Hamlet
Critical Insights: Harlan Ellison
Critical Insights: Harlem Renaissance
Critical Insights: Harry Potter Series
Critical Insights: Heart of Darkness
Critical Insights: Henry James
Critical Insights: Herman Melville
Critical Insights: Historical Fiction
Critical Insights: Holocaust Literature
Critical Insights: Horton Foote
Critical Insights: I Know Why the Caged Bird Sings
Critical Insights: In Cold Blood
Critical Insights: Inequality
Critical Insights: Invisible Man
Critical Insights: Isaac Asimov
Critical Insights: Isabel Allende
Critical Insights: Jack London
Critical Insights: James Baldwin
Critical Insights: James Joyce
Critical Insights: James McBride
Critical Insights: Jane Austen
Critical Insights: Jane Eyre
Critical Insights: John Cheever
Critical Insights: John Steinbeck
Critical Insights: John Updike
Critical Insights: Joseph Conrad
Critical Insights: King Lear
Critical Insights: Kurt Vonnegut
Critical Insights: Langston Hughes
Critical Insights: Leo Tolstoy
Critical Insights: LGBTQ Literature
Critical Insights: Life of Pi
Critical Insights: Lillian Hellman
Critical Insights: Literature of Protest
Critical Insights: Little Women
Critical Insights: Lolita
Critical Insights: Lord of the Flies
Critical Insights: Louisa May Alcott
Critical Insights: Louise Erdrich

Critical Insights: Macbeth
Critical Insights: Magical Realism
Critical Insights: Malcolm X
Critical Insights: Margaret Atwood
Critical Insights: Mario Vargas Llosa
Critical Insights: Mark Twain
Critical Insights: Martin Luther King, Jr.
Critical Insights: Mary Shelley
Critical Insights: Maya Angelou
Critical Insights: Midnight's Children
Critical Insights: Midwestern Literature
Critical Insights: Moby-Dick
Critical Insights: Modern Japanese Literature
Critical Insights: Mrs. Dalloway
Critical Insights: Nathaniel Hawthorne
Critical Insights: Nature & the Environment
Critical Insights: Neil Gaiman
Critical Insights: Nineteen Eighty-Four
Critical Insights: Of Mice and Men
Critical Insights: One Flew Over the Cuckoo's Nest
Critical Insights: One Hundred Years of Solitude
Critical Insights: Oscar Wilde
Critical Insights: Paradise Lost
Critical Insights: Paranoia, Fear & Alienation
Critical Insights: Philip Roth
Critical Insights: Political Fiction
Critical Insights: Post-Colonial Literature
Critical Insights: Pride and Prejudice
Critical Insights: Pulp Fiction of the '20s and '30s
Critical Insights: Ray Bradbury
Critical Insights: Raymond Carver
Critical Insights: Rebellion
Critical Insights: Richard Wright
Critical Insights: Robert A. Heinlein
Critical Insights: Robert Frost
Critical Insights: Roberto Bolano
Critical Insights: Romeo and Juliet
Critical Insights: Russia's Golden Age
Critical Insights: Salman Rushdie
Critical Insights: Satire
Critical Insights: Saul Bellow
Critical Insights: Sherman Alexie
Critical Insights: Short Fiction of Flannery O'Connor
Critical Insights: Slaughterhouse-Five
Critical Insights: Social Justice and American Literature
Critical Insights: Southern Gothic Literature
Critical Insights: Southwestern Literature
Critical Insights: Stephen King
Critical Insights: Survival
Critical Insights: Sylvia Plath
Critical Insights: T. S. Eliot

Grey House Publishing | Salem Press | H.W. Wilson | 4919 Route, 22 PO Box 56, Amenia NY 12501-0056

2020 Title List

Visit www.SalemPress.com for Product Information, Table of Contents, and Sample Pages.

Critical Insights (continued)

Critical Insights: Technology & Humanity
Critical Insights: Tennessee Williams
Critical Insights: The American Comic Book
Critical Insights: The American Dream
Critical Insights: The American Thriller
Critical Insights: The Awakening
Critical Insights: The Bell Jar
Critical Insights: The Canterbury Tales
Critical Insights: The Catcher in the Rye
Critical Insights: The Crucible
Critical Insights: The Diary of a Young Girl
Critical Insights: The Fantastic
Critical Insights: The Grapes of Wrath
Critical Insights: The Graphic Novel
Critical Insights: The Great Gatsby
Critical Insights: The Handmaid's Tale
Critical Insights: The Hero's Quest
Critical Insights: The Hobbit
Critical Insights: The House on Mango Street
Critical Insights: The Hunger Games Trilogy
Critical Insights: The Immigrant Experience
Critical Insights: The Inferno
Critical Insights: The Joy Luck Club
Critical Insights: The Kite Runner
Critical Insights: The Metamorphosis
Critical Insights: The Odyssey
Critical Insights: The Outsiders
Critical Insights: The Pearl
Critical Insights: The Poetry of Baudelaire
Critical Insights: The Poetry of Edgar Allan Poe
Critical Insights: The Red Badge of Courage
Critical Insights: The Scarlet Letter
Critical Insights: The Slave Narrative
Critical Insights: The Sound and the Fury
Critical Insights: The Sun Also Rises
Critical Insights: The Tales of Edgar Allan Poe
Critical Insights: The Woman Warrior
Critical Insights: Things Fall Apart
Critical Insights: Thomas Jefferson
Critical Insights: Tim O'Brien
Critical Insights: To Kill a Mockingbird
Critical Insights: Toni Morrison
Critical Insights: Violence in Literature
Critical Insights: Virginia Woolf & 20th Century Women Writers
Critical Insights: Walt Whitman
Critical Insights: War
Critical Insights: War and Peace
Critical Insights: Willa Cather
Critical Insights: William Faulkner
Critical Insights: Zora Neale Hurston
Critical Insights: Film - Alfred Hitchcock
Critical Insights: Film - Bonnie & Clyde
Critical Insights: Film - Casablanca
Critical Insights: Film - Stanley Kubrick

Literature

Critical Approaches to Literature: Feminist
Critical Approaches to Literature: Moral
Critical Approaches to Literature: Multicultural
Critical Approaches to Literature: Psychological
Critical Survey of American Literature
Critical Survey of Drama
Critical Survey of Graphic Novels: Heroes & Superheroes
Critical Survey of Graphic Novels: History, Theme, and Technique
Critical Survey of Graphic Novels: Independents and Underground Classics
Critical Survey of Graphic Novels: Manga
Critical Survey of Long Fiction
Critical Survey of Mystery and Detective Fiction
Critical Survey of Mythology & Folklore: Gods & Goddesses
Critical Survey of Mythology & Folklore: Heroes and Heroines
Critical Survey of Mythology & Folklore: Love, Sexuality, and Desire
Critical Survey of Mythology & Folklore: World Mythology
Critical Survey of Poetry
Critical Survey of Science Fiction & Fantasy Literature
Critical Survey of Shakespeare's Plays
Critical Survey of Shakespeare's Sonnets
Critical Survey of Short Fiction
Critical Survey of World Literature
Critical Survey of Young Adult Literature
Cyclopedia of Literary Characters
Cyclopedia of Literary Places
Introduction to Literary Context: American Poetry of the 20th Century
Introduction to Literary Context: American Post-Modernist Novels
Introduction to Literary Context: American Short Fiction
Introduction to Literary Context: English Literature
Introduction to Literary Context: Plays
Introduction to Literary Context: World Literature
Magill's Literary Annual
Masterplots
Masterplots, 2010-2018 Supplement
Notable African American Writers
Notable American Women Writers
Novels into Film: Adaptations & Interpretation
Recommended Reading: 600 Classics Reviewed

The Decades

The Sixties in America
The Fifties in America
The Seventies in America
The Eighties in America
The Nineties in America
The Forties in America
The Thirties in America
The Twenties in America
The 2000s in America
The 1910s in America

Grey House Publishing | Salem Press | H.W. Wilson | 4919 Route, 22 PO Box 56, Amenia NY 12501-0056

2020 Title List

Visit www.SalemPress.com for Product Information, Table of Contents, and Sample Pages.

Defining Documents in American History

Defining Documents: American West
Defining Documents: Business Ethics
Defining Documents: Capital Punishment
Defining Documents: Civil Rights
Defining Documents: Civil War
Defining Documents: Dissent & Protest
Defining Documents: Drug Policy
Defining Documents: Environment & Conservation
Defining Documents: Espionage & Intrigue
Defining Documents: Exploration and Colonial America
Defining Documents: Immigration & Immigrant Communities
Defining Documents: LGBTQ+
Defining Documents: Manifest Destiny and the New Nation
Defining Documents: Mental Health
Defining Documents: Native Americans
Defining Documents: Political Campaigns, Candidates & Discourse
Defining Documents: Postwar 1940s
Defining Documents: Prison Reform
Defining Documents: Secrets, Leaks & Scandals
Defining Documents: Slavery
Defining Documents: Supreme Court Decisions
Defining Documents: The 1900s
Defining Documents: The 1910s
Defining Documents: The 1920s
Defining Documents: The 1930s
Defining Documents: The 1950s
Defining Documents: The 1960s
Defining Documents: The 1970s
Defining Documents: The American Revolution
Defining Documents: The Cold War
Defining Documents: The Emergence of Modern America
Defining Documents: The Free Press
Defining Documents: The Gun Debate
Defining Documents: The Legacy of 9/11
Defining Documents: Reconstruction Era
Defining Documents: Vietnam War
Defining Documents: U.S. Involvement in the Middle East
Defining Documents: World War I
Defining Documents: World War II

Defining Documents in World History

Defining Documents: Asia
Defining Documents: Nationalism & Populism
Defining Documents: Renaissance & Early Modern Era
Defining Documents: The 17th Century
Defining Documents: The 18th Century
Defining Documents: The 19th Century
Defining Documents: The 20th Century (1900-1950)
Defining Documents: The Ancient World
Defining Documents: The Middle Ages
Defining Documents: The Middle East
Defining Documents: Women's Rights

Great Events from History

Great Events from History: The Ancient World
Great Events from History: The Middle Ages
Great Events from History: The Renaissance & Early Modern Era
Great Events from History: The 17th Century
Great Events from History: The 18th Century
Great Events from History: The 19th Century
Great Events from History: The 20th Century, 1901-1940
Great Events from History: The 20th Century, 1941-1970
Great Events from History: The 20th Century, 1971-2000
Great Events from History: Modern Scandals
Great Events from History: African American History
Great Events from History: The 21st Century, 2000-2016
Great Events from History: LGBTQ Events
Great Events from History: Human Rights

Great Lives from History

Computer Technology Innovators
Fashion Innovators
Great Athletes
Great Athletes of the Twenty-First Century
Great Lives from History: African Americans
Great Lives from History: American Heroes
Great Lives from History: American Women
Great Lives from History: Asian and Pacific Islander Americans
Great Lives from History: Inventors & Inventions
Great Lives from History: Jewish Americans
Great Lives from History: Latinos
Great Lives from History: Scientists and Science
Great Lives from History: The 17th Century
Great Lives from History: The 18th Century
Great Lives from History: The 19th Century
Great Lives from History: The 20th Century
Great Lives from History: The 21st Century, 2000-2017
Great Lives from History: The Ancient World
Great Lives from History: The Incredibly Wealthy
Great Lives from History: The Middle Ages
Great Lives from History: The Renaissance & Early Modern Era
Human Rights Innovators
Internet Innovators
Music Innovators
Musicians and Composers of the 20th Century
World Political Innovators

History & Government

American First Ladies
American Presidents
Civil Rights Movements: Past & Present
The 50 States
The Ancient World: Extraordinary People in Extraordinary Societies
The Bill of Rights
The Criminal Justice System
The U.S. Supreme Court

Grey House Publishing | Salem Press | H.W. Wilson | 4919 Route, 22 PO Box 56, Amenia NY 12501-0056

2020 Title List

Visit www.SalemPress.com for Product Information, Table of Contents, and Sample Pages.

Social Sciences

Countries, Peoples and Cultures
Countries: Their Wars & Conflicts: A World Survey
Education Today: Issues, Policies & Practices
Encyclopedia of American Immigration
Ethics: Questions & Morality of Human Actions
Issues in U.S. Immigration
Principles of Sociology: Group Relationships & Behavior
Principles of Sociology: Personal Relationships & Behavior
Principles of Sociology: Societal Issues & Behavior
Racial & Ethnic Relations in America
World Geography

Science

Ancient Creatures
Applied Science
Applied Science: Engineering & Mathematics
Applied Science: Science & Medicine
Applied Science: Technology
Biomes and Ecosystems
Earth Science: Earth Materials and Resources
Earth Science: Earth's Surface and History
Earth Science: Earth's Weather, Water and Atmosphere
Earth Science: Physics and Chemistry of the Earth
Encyclopedia of Climate Change
Encyclopedia of Energy
Encyclopedia of Environmental Issues
Encyclopedia of Global Resources
Encyclopedia of Mathematics and Society
Forensic Science
Notable Natural Disasters
The Solar System
USA in Space

Principles of Science

Principles of Anatomy
Principles of Astronomy
Principles of Biology
Principles of Biotechnology
Principles of Botany
Principles of Chemistry
Principles of Climatology
Principles of Communications Technology
Principles of Computer Science
Principles of Ecology
Principles of Mathematics
Principles of Modern Agriculture
Principles of Pharmacology
Principles of Physical Science
Principles of Physics
Principles of Programming & Coding
Principles of Robotics & Artificial Intelligence
Principles of Scientific Research
Principles of Sustainability
Principles of Zoology

Health

Addictions, Substance Abuse & Alcoholism
Adolescent Health & Wellness
Aging
Cancer
Community & Family Health Issues
Complementary & Alternative Medicine
Genetics and Inherited Conditions
Infectious Diseases and Conditions
Magill's Medical Guide
Nutrition
Principles of Health: Anxiety & Stress
Principles of Health: Diabetes
Principles of Health: Obesity
Principles of Health: Pain Management
Psychology & Behavioral Health
Women's Health

Careers

Careers in Building Construction
Careers in Business
Careers in Chemistry
Careers in Communications & Media
Careers in Education & Training
Careers in Environment & Conservation
Careers in Financial Services
Careers in Gaming
Careers in Green Energy
Careers in Healthcare
Careers in Hospitality & Tourism
Careers in Human Services
Careers in Information Technology
Careers in Law, Criminal Justice & Emergency Services
Careers in Manufacturing & Production
Careers in Nursing
Careers in Physics
Careers in Protective Services
Careers in Psychology & Behavioral Health
Careers in Public Administration
Careers in Sales, Insurance & Real Estate
Careers in Science & Engineering
Careers in Social Media
Careers in Sports & Fitness
Careers in Sports Medicine & Training
Careers in Technical Services & Equipment Repair
Careers in the Arts: Fine, Performing & Visual
Careers in Transportation
Careers in Writing & Editing
Careers Outdoors
Careers Overseas
Careers Working with Infants & Children

Business

Principles of Business: Accounting
Principles of Business: Economics
Principles of Business: Entrepreneurship
Principles of Business: Finance
Principles of Business: Globalization
Principles of Business: Leadership
Principles of Business: Management
Principles of Business: Marketing

Grey House Publishing | Salem Press | H.W. Wilson | 4919 Route, 22 PO Box 56, Amenia NY 12501-0056

2020 Title List

Visit www.HWWilsonInPrint.com for Product Information, Table of Contents, and Sample Pages.

The Reference Shelf

Affordable Housing
Aging in America
Alternative Facts, Post-Truth and the Information War
American Military Presence Overseas
Arab Spring
Artificial Intelligence
Business of Food, The
Campaign Trends & Election Law
Conspiracy Theories
Democracy Evolving
Dinosaurs
Embracing New Paradigms in Education
Faith & Science
Families - Traditional & New Structures
Future of U.S. Economic Relations: Mexico, Cuba, & Venezuela
Global Climate Change
Graphic Novels and Comic Books
Guns in America
Hate Crimes
Immigration
Immigration in the United States
Internet Abuses & Privacy Rights
Internet Law
Internet Safety
LGBTQ in the 21st Century
Marijuana Reform
National Debate Topic 2014/2015: The Ocean
National Debate Topic 2015/2016: Surveillance
National Debate Topic 2016/2017: US/China Relations
National Debate Topic 2017/2018: Education Reform
National Debate Topic 2018/2019: Immigration
National Debate Topic 2019/2020: Arms Sales
National Debate Topic 2020/2021: Criminal Justice Reform
New Frontiers in Space
The News and its Future
Paranormal, The
Politics of the Oceans
Pollution
Prescription Drug Abuse
Propaganda and Misinformation
Racial Tension in a Postracial Age
Reality Television
Representative American Speeches, Annual Edition
Rethinking Work
Revisiting Gender
Robotics
Russia
Social Networking
Social Services for the Poor
Space Exploration and Development
Sports in America
The American Dream
The Brain
The Digital Age
The South China Sea Conflict
The Supreme Court
The Transformation of American Cities
The Two Koreas
U.S. Infrastructure
Whistleblowers

Core Collections

Children's Core Collection
Fiction Core Collection
Graphic Novels Core Collection
Middle & Junior High School Core
Public Library Core Collection: Nonfiction
Senior High Core Collection
Young Adult Fiction Core Collection

Current Biography

Current Biography Cumulative Index 1946-2017
Current Biography Monthly Magazine
Current Biography Yearbook

Readers' Guide to Periodical Literature

Abridged Readers' Guide to Periodical Literature
Readers' Guide to Periodical Literature

Indexes

Index to Legal Periodicals & Books
Short Story Index
Book Review Digest

Sears List

Sears List of Subject Headings
Sears: Lista de Encabezamientos de Materia

History

Speeches of the American Presidents
American Reformers
American Game Changers: Invention, Innovation & Transformation

Facts About Series

Facts About American Immigration
Facts About China
Facts About the 20th Century
Facts About the Presidents
Facts About the World's Languages

Nobel Prize Winners

Nobel Prize Winners: 1901-1986
Nobel Prize Winners: 1987-1991
Nobel Prize Winners: 1992-1996
Nobel Prize Winners: 1997-2001
Nobel Prize Winners: 2002-2018

Famous First Facts

Famous First Facts
Famous First Facts About American Politics
Famous First Facts About Sports
Famous First Facts About the Environment
Famous First Facts: International Edition

American Book of Days

The American Book of Days
The International Book of Days

Grey House Publishing | Salem Press | H.W. Wilson | 4919 Route, 22 PO Box 56, Amenia NY 12501-0056